UNITED STATES CONSTITUTIONAL AND LEGAL HISTORY

A TWENTY VOLUME SERIES
REPRODUCING OVER 450 OF THE MOST
IMPORTANT ARTICLES ON THE TOPIC

Edited with Introductions by
KERMIT L. HALL

A GARLAND SERIES

UNITED STATES CONSTITUTIONAL AND LEGAL HISTORY

CONTENTS OF THE SERIES

1. Main Themes in United States Constitutional and Legal History
2. The Formation and Ratification of the Constitution
3. Federalism: A Nation of States
4. The Courts in American Life
5. The Judiciary in American Life
6. The Legal Profession
7. Judicial Review in American History
8. Race Relations and the Law in American History
9. The Law of American Slavery
10. Women, the Law, and the Constitution
11. Law, Society, and Domestic Relations
12. Civil Rights in American History
13. Crime and Criminal Law
14. Police, Prison, and Punishment
15. Civil Liberties in American History (Two Volumes)
16. The Law of Business and Commerce
17. Law, Economy, and the Power of Contract
18. Tort Law in American History
19. Land Law and Real Property in American History

CIVIL RIGHTS IN AMERICAN HISTORY

MAJOR HISTORICAL INTERPRETATIONS

Edited with an Introduction by
KERMIT L. HALL

GARLAND PUBLISHING, INC.
NEW YORK • LONDON 1987

Library of Congress Cataloging-in-Publication Data

Civil rights in American history.

(United States constitutional and legal history ; v. 12)
Bibliography: p.
1. Afro-Americans—Civil rights—History.
I. Hall, Kermit. II. Series.
KF4757.A5C5 1987   323.4'0973   86-31977
ISBN 0-8240-0140-0

The volumes in this series have been printed on acid-free, 250-year-life paper.

Printed in the United States of America.

ACKNOWLEDGMENTS

David C. Adelman, "Strangers: Civil Rights of Jews in the Colony of Rhode Island," *Rhode Island History* 13 (July 1954): 65–77. Reprinted by permission of *Rhode Island History*.

Henry M. Alexander, "The Double Primary," *Arkansas Historical Quarterly* 3 (August 1944): 217–268. Reprinted by permission of the *Arkansas Historical Quarterly*.

Raymond P. Alexander, "The Upgrading of the Negro's Status by Supreme Court Decisions," *Journal of Negro History* 30 (April 1945): 117–149. Reprinted by permission of the *Journal of Negro History*.

Chester James Antieau, "Natural Rights and the Founding Fathers—The Virginians," *Washington and Lee Law Review* 17 (Spring 1960): 43–79. Reprinted by permission of the *Washington and Lee Law Review*.

Alfred Avins, "Racial Segregation in Public Accommodations: Some Reflected Light on the Fourteenth Amendment from the Civil Rights Act of 1875," *Case Western Reserve Law Review* 18 (May 1967): 1251–1283. Reprinted by permission of *Case Western Reserve Law Review*.

Herman Belz, "The Freedmen's Bureau Act of 1865 and the Principle of No Discrimination According to Color," *Civil War History* 21 (September 1975): 197–217. Reprinted by permission of Kent State University Press.

Donald L. Burnett, Jr., "An Historical Analysis of the 1968 'Indian Civil Rights' Act," *Harvard Journal on Legislation*, 9 (1970). Reprinted by permission of the *Harvard Journal on Legislation*.

James W. Ely, Jr., "Negro Demonstrations and the Law: Danville as a Test Case," *Vanderbilt Law Review* 27 (October 1974): 927–968. Reprinted by permission of Fred B. Rothman & Company.

Ronald P. Formisano, "The Edge of Caste: Colored Suffrage in Michigan, 1827–1861," *Michigan History* 56 (Spring 1972): 19–41. Reprinted by permission of *Michigan History*.

Edward M. Gaffney, Jr., "History and Legal Interpretation: The Early Distortion of the Fourteenth Amendment by the Gilded Age Court," 25, *Catholic University Law Review*: 207 (1976).

Louis R. Harlan, "Desegregation in New Orleans Public Schools during Reconstruction," *American Historical Review* 67 (April 1962): 663–675. Reprinted by permission of the American Historical Association.

William B. Hixson, Jr., "Moorfield Storey and the Struggle for Equality," *Journal of American History* 60 (1968): 533–554. Reprinted by permission of the *Journal of American History*.

J. Woodford Howard and Cornelius Bushoven, "The *Screws* Case Revisited," *Journal of Politics* 29 (August 1967): 617–636. Reprinted by permission of the *Journal of Politics*

Donald M. Jacobs, "The Nineteenth Century Struggle over Segregated Education in the Boston Schools," *Journal of Negro Education* 39 (1970): 76–85. Reprinted by permission of the author and the *Journal of Negro Education*.

Peter J. Kellogg, "Civil Rights Consciousness in the 1940s," *The Historian* 42 (November 1979): 18–41. Reprinted by permission of *The Historian*.

Alfred H. Kelly, "The Congressional Controversy Over School Segregation, 1867–1875," *American Historical Review* 64 (April 1959): 537–563. Reprinted by permission of the American Historical Association.

J. Morgan Kousser, "Separate but *not* Equal: The Supreme Court's First Decision on Racial Discrimination in Schools," *Journal of Southern History* 46 (1980): 17–44. Reprinted by permission of the Southern Historical Association.

Irving F. Lefberg, "Chief Justice Vinson and the Politics of Desegregation," *Emory Law Journal* 24 (Spring 1975): 243–312. Reprinted by permission of the *Emory Law Journal* of the Emory University School of Law.

Leonard W. Levy and Harlan B. Phillips, "The *Roberts* Case: Source of the 'Separate but Equal' Doctrine," *American Historical Review* 56 (1951): 510–518. Reprinted by permission of the American Historical Association.

Neil R. McMillen, "Black Enfranchisement in Mississippi: Federal Enforcement and Black Protest in the 1960s," *Journal of Southern History* 43 (1977): 351–372. Reprinted by permission of the Southern Historical Association.

Note, "The Indian Bill of Rights and the Constitutional Status of Tribal Governments," *Harvard Law Review* 82 (1970). Reprinted by permission of the *Harvard Law Review*. Copyright (c) the Harvard Law Review Association.

Acknowledgments

Edgar A. Toppin, "Walter White and the Atlanta NAACP's Fight for Equal Schools, 1916–1917," *History of Education Quarterly* 7 (Spring 1967): 3–21. Reprinted by permission of the *History of Education Quarterly*.

S. Sidney Ulmer, "Earl Warren and the Brown Decision," *Journal of Politics* 33 (August 1971): 689–702. Reprinted by permission of the *Journal of Politics*.

William P. Vaughn, "Separate and Unequal: The Civil Rights Act of 1875 and Defeat of the School Integration Clause." From *Southwestern Social Science Quarterly* Vol 48, Number 2 (September 1967): 146–154. Reprinted by permission of the University of Texas Press.

Charles H. Wesley, "Negro Suffrage in the Period of Constitution-Making, 1787–1865" *Journal of Negro History* 32 (April 1947): 143–168. Reprinted by permission of the *Journal of Negro History*.

Howard C. Westwood, "Getting Justice for the Freedman," *Howard Law Journal* 16 (1971): 492–537. Reprinted by permission of the *Howard Law Journal*.

William M. Wiecek, "The Great Writ and Reconstruction: The Habeas Corpus Act of 1867," *The Journal of Southern History* 36 (November 1970): 530–548. Reprinted by permission of the Southern Historical Association.

Forrest G. Wood, "On Revising Reconstruction History: Negro Suffrage, White Disfranchisement, and Common Sense," *Journal of Negro History* 51 (April 1966): 98–113. Reprinted by permission of the *Journal of Negro History*.

CONTENTS

	Kermit L. Hall • *Introduction*	xi
1.	David C. Adelman • *Strangers: Civil Rights of Jews in the Colony of Rhode Island*	1
2.	Henry M. Alexander • *The Double Primary*	14
3.	Raymond Pace Alexander • *The Upgrading of the Negro's Status by Supreme Court Decisions*	66
4.	Chester James Antieau • *Natural Rights and the Founding Fathers—The Virginians*	99
5.	Alfred Avins • *Racial Segregation in Public Accommodations: Some Reflected Light on the Fourteenth Amendment from the Civil Rights Act of 1875*	136
6.	Herman Belz • *The Freedmen's Bureau Act of 1865 and the Principle of No Discrimination According to Color*	169
7.	Donald L. Burnett, Jr. • *An Historical Analysis of the 1968 'Indian Civil Rights' Act*	190
8.	James W. Ely, Jr. • *Negro Demonstrations and the Law: Danville as a Test Case*	260
9.	Ronald P. Formisano • *The Edge of Caste: Colored Suffrage in Michigan, 1827–1861*	302
10.	Edward M. Gaffney, Jr. • *History and Legal Interpretation: The Early Distortion of the Fourteenth Amendment by the Gilded Age Court*	325
11.	Louis R. Harlan • *Desegregation in New Orleans Public Schools during Reconstruction*	368
12.	William B. Hixson, Jr. • *Moorfield Storey and the Struggle for Equality*	381

13. J. Woodford Howard and Cornelius Bushoven • *The Screws Case Revisited* — 403

14. Donald M. Jacobs • *The Nineteenth Century Struggle over Segregated Education in the Boston Schools* — 423

15. Peter J. Kellogg • *Civil Rights Consciousness in the 1940s* — 433

16. Alfred H. Kelly • *The Congressional Controversy Over School Segregation, 1867–1875* — 457

17. J. Morgan Kousser • *Separate but not Equal: The Supreme Court's First Decision on Racial Discrimination in Schools* — 484

18. Irving F. Lefberg • *Chief Justice Vinson and the Politics of Desegregation* — 512

19. Leonard W. Levy and Harland B. Phillips • *The* Roberts *Case: Source of the "Separate but Equal" Doctrine* — 582

20. Neil R. McMillen • *Black Enfranchisement in Mississippi: Federal Enforcement and Black Protest in the 1960s* — 591

21. Note • *The Indian Bill of Rights and the Constitutional Status of Tribal Governments* — 613

22. Edgar A. Toppin • *Walter White and the Atlanta NAACP's Fight for Equal Schools, 1916–1917* — 644

23. S. Sidney Ulmer • *Earl Warren and the Brown Decision* — 663

24. William P. Vaughn • *Separate and Unequal: The Civil Rights Act of 1875 and Defeat of the School Integration Clause* — 677

25. Charles H. Wesley • *Negro Suffrage in the Period of Constitution-Making, 1787–1865* — 686

26. Howard C. Westwood • *Getting Justice for the Freedman* — 712

27. William M. Wiecek • *The Great Writ and Reconstruction: The Habeas Corpus Act of 1867* — 758

28. Forrest G. Wood • *On Revising Reconstruction History: Negro Suffrage, White Disfranchisement, and Common Sense* — 777

INTRODUCTION

The constitutional protections associated with civil liberties and civil rights have been modern developments in American constitutional history. The founding fathers, of course, were acutely aware of the need to protect and preserve liberty, but in the pre-industrial world, of which they were a part, liberty was, according to Herman Belz, "but one of several values deemed essential to a well-ordered society."[1] Liberty meant freedom from restraint; it was a manifestation of classical, liberal laissez faire thought. The idea was summed up neatly by President Thomas Jefferson when he proclaimed in his first inaugural address that "[a] wise and frugal Government, which shall restrain men from injuring one another, shall leave them otherwise free to regulate their own . . . improvement."[2] Liberty meant that government should do as little as possible.

Today, we think of liberty and rights in a different way. We have come to expect that government has a positive duty to fashion certain protections and take certain actions, either through legislative or judicial acts, that will insure access to social and economic benefits and that will remedy past social injuries and discrimination. This notion of the active state promoting conditions of liberty has found its expression in affirmative action programs that aim to compensate for past wrongs by giving preferential treatment to certain racial groups in hiring and promotion.

Two of the volumes in this collection—this one and Volume 15, *Civil Liberties in American History*—deal explicitly with the problems of liberty in American history. The decision to break the issue of liberty into two parts—civil rights and civil liberties—runs counter to much contemporary thinking that conflates them. Yet the differentiation makes sense, I believe, because it casts the social and economic groups that have been affected in sharper relief.

As Milton Konvitz has written, civil rights "refers to the constitutional and legal status and treatment of *minority groups* that are marked off from the majority by race, religion, or national origins."[3] Civil liberties, on the other hand, denotes "the rights of *individuals.*"[4] Civil liberties has a distinctly political connotation, refering to legal guarantees, mostly contained in the First Amendment to the federal Constitution, by which individuals are protected against government interference with their ability to speak, express their opinions, and associate for the purpose of political action. In this century, for example, there has never been any question that Negroes have equal freedom of religion or of the press. They have enjoyed civil liberties. But as a group they have been discriminated against on the basis of their race with respect to the schools they could attend and the public facilities they could enjoy. Their basic civil rights have been abridged.

The differentiation of individual and group rights is not clear cut. Since the late-nineteenth century, American history teaches that the enjoyment of one depends to an important extent on the other. Economic well being, something that most Negroes could not achieve because of discrimination, was crucial to full political participation and civil liberties generally. Discrimination stamped on blacks from the late-nineteenth through the mid-twentieth centuries a badge of inequality that impeded the full exercise of individual liberty.

I have chosen in this volume to concentrate on the development of black civil rights. Other minority groups have suffered as well, however. The first civil rights challenge in American history was presented by the Indians, and the government pursued a policy that withheld full civil rights unless they chose to become American citizens and left their tribes. In the twentieth century, the federal government has pursued a somewhat less dogmatic approach, seeking to balance assimilation into white society with cultural pluralism that allows the Indian to retain his or her identity. But Indians still suffer varying degrees of prejudice and discrimination, and they are neither fully incorporated into American political and social life nor wholly autonomous from it.

The Negro has presented a different set of problems, largely because of an inheritance of racial slavery. Where the Indian can make a claim to original ownership of American lands, the black was brought to America specifically for exploitation by white masters.

The evolution of black civil rights has come since the American Civil War. Only with the Fourteenth Amendment in 1868 did blacks become citizens of the United States, and only then could they make a claim on the power of the federal government to protect them against state-imposed discrimination. Yet the Supreme Court of the late-nineteenth century saw fit to read the intent of the due process and equal protection clauses of that amendment in such a way as to deny blacks complete enjoyment of their civil rights. The justices in 1896, in *Plessy* v. *Ferguson*, upheld as constitutional state laws that required racial segregation in public conveyances, on the theory that "seperate but equal" facilities were not a denial of equality.[5] The decision placed the mantle of constitutional legitimacy on other policies of racial segregation in schools, public buildings, restaurants, theaters, and public accommodations, whether publicly or privately operated.

Separate facilities were never equal; blacks suffered disproportionately. In 1951, for example, in nine states where schools were segregated by law, the average expenditure for white students was $136 and for black students $74.[6] Even where states provided separate black professional schools, the facilities were hopelessly inadequate.

This blatant discrimination put the lie to "separate but equal." It also stimulated a civil rights movement that, beginning in the early 1920s, worked through legal processes, civil disobedience, and organized political power to break down the legal and political barriers to full enjoyment of civil rights by blacks. Particularly important were the efforts of the Legal Defense Fund of the National Association for the Advancement of Colored People. Its lawyers, some black and some white, persued a litigation strategy that culminated in a series of victories that ended Jim Crow. The most famous of these was *Brown* v. *Board of Education* (1954), in which the Supreme Court held that segregated schools were inherently unequal. In subsequent cases the Court outlawed segregation in state colleges and universities, transportation, parks, municipal golf courses, public beaches, and wherever the state participated in a property's maintenance.

The civil rights movement extended its efforts beyond racial segregation. Through civil disobedience, for example, it brought sufficient political pressure to bear that Congress in the 1960s passed major civil rights and voting rights legislation. In a sense, civil rights leaders, such as Martin Luther King, Jr., shamed Americans into living up to the full meaning of terms like liberty and equality. Too, the civil rights movement by the late 1960s had begun to push for policies designed to redress in this generation the burdens imposed on blacks by prior policies of discrimination. Affirmative action programs, most of which the Supreme Court has sustained, were premised on the idea that the present generation of blacks could never reach full equality unless they were given preference in matters of hiring and promotion.

These programs have stirred a backlash from whites who have labelled them exercises in reverse discrimination. Many whites, who had been willing to accept that blacks should be given equality of opportunity, were unwilling to embrace the idea of equality of status—the notion that government should act positively to insure that blacks achieved a certain occupational or social status.

"I have a dream," proclaimed Martin Luther King from the steps of the Lincoln Memorial in August 1963, "that one day this nation will rise up and live out the true meaning of its creed: 'We hold these truths to be self-evident; that all men are created equal.'"[7] The essays in this collection treat the legal, political, and social circumstances out of which that dream emerged. They show the ways in which law and constitutionalism were structured, especially through the litigation process, to move America toward the realization of that dream. They also demonstrate, however, that historically the power of courts has cut both ways: judges have crafted doctrines that have denied and enhanced the civil rights of racial and ethnic minorities. The essays concentrate on two periods of particular importance for the developement of black civil rights: the First Reconstruction of the late 1860s and the early 1870s and the so-called Second Reconstruction of the 1950s and 1960s. At the same time, the essays clearly demonstrate the importance of the NAACP and the Supreme Court during the intervening years in making possible the wholesale revolution in civil rights that followed the *Brown* decision.

Readers will also find that Volume 8, *Race Relations and the Law in American History*, Volume 9, *The Law of American Slavery*, and Volume 10, *Women, the Law, and the Constitution*, treat different aspects of the themes raised in this volume. Taken together they suggest how far Americans have come in giving full meaning to civil rights and how far they have to go before Dr. King's dream is fully realized.

Kermit L. Hall

Notes

1. Alfred H. Kelly, Winfred A. Harbison, and Herman Belz, *The American Constitution, Its Origins and Development* 6th ed. (1983), p. 523.
2. "Jefferson's First Inaugural Address, March 4, 1801," in Henry Steele Commager, ed., *Documents of American History* (1963), p. 188.
3. Milton Konvitz, "Civil Rights," in *International Encyclopedia of the Social Sciences* (1968), 3: 312.
4. Ibid.
5. Plessy v. Ferguson, 163 U.S. 537 (1896).
6. Konvitz, "Civil Rights," p. 315.
7. As quoted in Laughlin McDonald, ed., *Racial Equality* (1977), p. 64.

ADDITIONAL READING

Herman Belz, *Emancipation and Equal Rights: Politics and Constitutionalism in the Civil War Era* (1978).
Terry Eastland and William J. Bennett, *Counting by Race: Equality from the Founding Fathers to Bakke and Webster* (1979).
Milton R. Konvitz, *Expanding Liberty: Freedom's Gains in Postwar America* (1966).
Richard Kluger, *Simple Justice: The History of Brown v. Board of Education and Black America's Struggle for Equality* (1975).
Paul L. Murphy, *The Constitution in Crisis Times* (1972).
Jack Peltason, *Fifty-Eight Lonely Men* (1961).
J. R. Pole, *The Pursuit of Equality in American History* (1978).
J. Harvie Wilkinson, III, *From Brown to Bakke: The Supreme Court and School Integration, 1954–1978* (1979).

RHODE ISLAND HISTORY

STRANGERS
Civil Rights of Jews in the Colony of Rhode Island
by DAVID C. ADELMAN*

IN 1954 Jews will celebrate the tercentenary of their settlement in the United States and the Congregation Sons of Israel and David (Temple Beth-El) in Providence, its centennial. This paper is a result of research in preparation for the celebration of both occasions.

Jews owe no greater debt of gratitude to any man in the history of the United States than to Roger Williams. In Providence he put into practice the doctrine of separation of Church and State (which others had preached before him) and was one of the most warm-hearted, generous, and liberal Christians who ever befriended the persecuted. While on a mission to England he published many statements favorable to the readmission of Jews into England and used his influence to that end. In appreciation of Williams and in memory of his father, Isaac Hahn, the first Jew to be elected to public office in Rhode Island (1884), Judge J. Jerome Hahn in 1928 conveyed to the City of Providence the Roger Williams Spring on North Main Street and the land surrounding it.

Five years after the founding of Providence Plantations the General Court of the Island towns ordered "that none bee accounted a delinquent for Doctrine, provided it be not directly repugnant to the Government or Lawes established." This provision is the distinguishing feature of the founding of Providence in the careful discrimination between liberty of conscience and contempt of law, which Williams enlarged upon in his famous parable-of-the-ship letter. Although the colony voted that "all men whatever nation soever they may be, that shall be received inhabitants of any of the towns, shall have the same privileges as Englishmen, any law to the contrary notwithstanding," they also voted that no foreigner was to be received

*Mr. Adelman, a Providence lawyer, is president of the Rhode Island Jewish Historical Society.

a freeman in any town but by consent of the legislature.[1] None but a freeman could vote or hold civil office, rights which passed to the freeman's eldest son. Although it has been stated many times that Abraham Campanall was "licensed a freeman" in 1688, the statement is incorrect. No Jew was ever admitted a freeman in the Colony of Rhode Island, and therefore no Jew had the right to vote or hold office. This disability persisted until 1843, when the state adopted its first constitution after the Dorr Rebellion.

The statute of Westminster, passed by Parliament in 1740, granted Jews the right of naturalization after seven years' residence in the colony and provided a special oath agreeable to Jews. Although it has been stated that James Lucena, a Jew, was naturalized in 1761, and Moses Lopez even earlier, original documents show that Aaron Lopez (later the most prosperous Jew in the colony) was denied naturalization in 1761 while James Lucena was naturalized as a Christian. Moses Lopez was granted a patent to make potash and was excused from civil duties because of services rendered, but he was never naturalized in the colony.

Williams wrote extensively, but nowhere does he mention the right to vote or hold office.[2] His principles, however, precluded the denial of such rights upon religious grounds. "It is the will and command of God," he wrote, "that . . . a permission of the most Paganish, Jewish, Turkish, or Antichristian consciences and worships, bee granted to all men in all Nations and Countries: and they are onely to bee fought against with that Sword which is only (in Soule matters) able to conquer, to wit, the Sword of God's Spirit, the Word of God."[3]

There were no Jews in Providence Plantations in his lifetime. The denial of naturalization to Jews and the denial of their admission to the company of freemen three-quarters of a century after his death are not a reflection upon his sincerity, but rather a lesson for our own times. And that lesson is that in a government of laws and not of men we cannot rely upon constitutional forms alone. Laws are not

[1] Samuel Greene Arnold, *History of the State of Rhode Island and Providence Plantations* (New York, 1878), I, 242.
[2] Maxwell H. Morris, "Roger Williams and the Jews," *American Jewish Archives*, III, No. 2, Jan. 1951.
[3] Roger Williams, *The Bloudy Tenent of Persecution for Cause of Conscience . . .* (London, 1644), *Publications of the Narragansett Club* (Providence, 1874), III, 3.

self-enforcing, but are interpreted and enforced by fallible human beings.

The preaching and writings of Williams and particularly his intercession with Cromwell for the readmission of Jews into England attracted the attention of Spanish and Portuguese Jews (Marranos, refugees from the Inquisition), who were continuously in search of a peaceful haven. In 1654 a small group of them landed in New Amsterdam and were promptly met with the hostility of Peter Stuyvesant, who ordered them to leave. They appealed to his superiors, the Dutch West India Company, among whose stockholders were Abraham and Isaac Pareira, wealthy refugees. Stuyvesant was ordered to allow them to remain. The tercentenary of that settlement will be celebrated the year commencing September, 1954.

Four years later another small group came to Newport, where the favorable attitude of the natives encouraged them to settle. They came in response to the news that in Newport they would find religious liberty and tolerance. Soon after the death of Roger Williams they experienced difficulties and petitioned the General Assembly, which passed the following resolution: "Voted, In answer to the petition of Simon Medus, David Brown, and associates, being Jews, presented to this Assembly, bearing date June the 24th, 1684, we declare, that they may expect as good protection here, as any stranger, being not of our nation residing amongst us in this his Majesty's Collony, ought to have, being obedient to his Majesty's laws."[4]

Sidney Rider questioned the date of the deed (1677), which conveyed land to Moses Pacheco and Mordecai Campanall for use of the "Jews and their Nation, Society or Friends" and thought the date was 1684, because that was the date of the Medus petition when Jews were first mentioned in the Records of the Colony and the name *Mordecai Campanall* did not appear in that record. However, the records of the General Treasurer show that one "Mordecai the Jew" and another "Moses the Jew" paid taxes to the colony in the years 1678 to 1680.[5] Undoubtedly these are the persons mentioned in the cemetery deed of 1677, which, being a formal document under seal, contained their surnames. The acquisition of a cemetery showed that

[4]John R. Bartlett, *Records of the Colony of Rhode Island and Providence Plantations* (Providence, 1860), III, 160.

[5]Archives of the State of Rhode Island, General Treasurer's Accounts, 1672-1711. Hereafter cited as Archives.

there was a *Minyan* (a religious quorum composed of ten males over thirteen years of age) in the community and that they had been there for a few years, as there is a lag of about ten years between the settlement of Jews in a community and their acquisition of a cemetery. A similar lag in the case of the Jews of Newport would place them there after 1654 and before 1677.

In 1685, the year after the Medus petition, Jews of Newport, including Abraham Campanall, were haled into court and their goods, wares, and merchandise attached by Surveyor General Dyre of Boston for alienage. Dyre did not appear in court for the hearing, but Governor Coddington, who presided, insisted upon hearing the defendants, for whom he gave decision, awarding them substantial costs. The Jews remained in Newport as "strangers" in the colony and were allowed to engage in trade and commerce thereafter without question.

The records of the treasurer of the colony show that Abraham Campanall paid a fine in 1686 for fornication, and the records of the Trial Court for Newport show that he was granted a retail liquor license in 1688. However, in 1897 a writer made the statement that Campanall was "licensed a freeman" in 1688, a statement which has been repeated over the years, subsequent writers relying upon prior authority rather than upon primary source. In any event, after the lapse of two hundred sixty-five years the original record proves unmistakably the contrary.[6]

John Russell Bartlett, lawyer and secretary of the state of Rhode Island, was commissioned by the General Assembly in 1860 to edit the records of the colony for publication. His work is neither accurate nor complete. From 1686 to 1689 the administration of the colony was under Sir Edmund Andros (technically in possession of the charter), who changed the names of the towns of Kingstown, East Greenwich, and Westerly to Rochester, Dedford, and Haversham. The autumn Court, held in Rochester, September, 1688, was the General Court for Portsmouth, Newport (island of Rhode Island), and King's Province (Narragansett).

On the first Tuesday in September five justices and fourteen grand jurymen were present to grant licenses and hear criminal cases. Bartlett lists fourteen names, including that of Abraham Campanall,

[6] Records of the General Court of Tryalls, 1671-1724, Superior Court, Newport, R. I.

Original in Superior Court, Newport, R. I.

MINUTES of the GENERAL COURT OF TRIALS
(Retouched negative to improve readability)

under the heading *Persons Lycenced.*

The original record contains two lists of *Persons Lycenced.* The first list contains the same names as those mentioned by Bartlett with the addition of the names of the towns in which they resided and at the foot of the list appears the word *Retailers.* The second list, not mentioned by Bartlett, contains three names under the heading *Retailers not less than a Bottle.* Each list also contains the name of a woman. Bartlett did not state the purpose for which the fourteen persons were "lycenced," but no woman was eligible to become a freeman, and the statement that Abraham Campanall was "licenced a freeman" was wishful thinking. One writer suggested that Abraham Campanall was licensed for some purpose not specified.[7] He refused to take a leap in the dark and fill in Bartlett's record.

A license, by definition, is a revocable permit of a temporary and conditional nature, not transmissible. In the colony licenses were granted by the courts. Freemen were not licensed but were "admitted to the freedom of the Colony" by the General Assembly or to "the freedom of the town" by the Town Council. No freeman was admitted during the Andros administration. As an unnaturalized "stranger" Campanall was not eligible and his record did not qualify him for admission to the select company of freemen, who were masters and landholders and who were most jealous of their prerogatives. There is no question but that Campanall and the other "Persons Lycenced" on the first list were licensed to conduct a tavern and those on the second list, "Retailers not less than a Bottle," were licensed to operate what we today call a package store. No Jew, however qualified or competent, was ever made a freeman of the Colony of Rhode Island.

The question of the naturalization of Jews did not arise in the colony until almost a century after the death of Roger Williams. They enjoyed economic freedom as traders and merchants as well as religious liberty, and although they were never more than two hundred in number, they made Newport the rival and superior in trade and commerce of New Amsterdam. No Jewish community in the colonies was held in higher esteem by its Christian neighbors.

On February 26, 1761, James Lucena applied to the General Assembly at East Greenwich for naturalization, which was granted

---

[7]Samuel Broches, *Jews in New England* (Boston, 1943), II, 7.

the following day.[8] Only one month later Aaron Lopez and Isaac Elizer, "Persons professing the Jewish Religion," applied to the Superior Court at Newport for naturalization. The Court referred

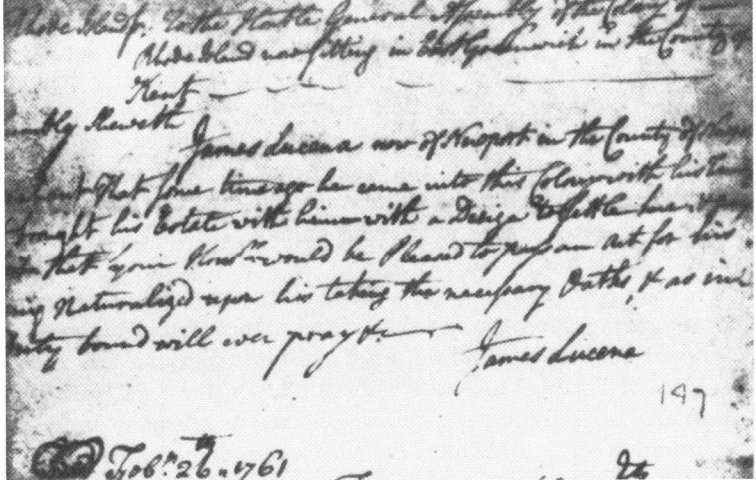

JAMES LUCENA'S OATH OF ALLEGIANCE

JAMES LUCENA'S PETITION FOR CITIZENSHIP

the applicants to the General Assembly on the grounds that the Naturalization Act of 1740 referred to in the petition, was not in Court and that only the General Assembly could act upon this petition as it had in other cases.[9] The applicants accordingly petitioned the General Assembly, which met in South Kingstown. On October 23,

[8]Archives, Petitions to the General Assembly, 1758-1761, X.
[9]Superior Court of Judicature, Newport, R. I., March Term, 1761.

1761, the Lower House granted the prayer of their petition in the following words:

> ... Shall be admitted a lawful Subject of his Majesty the King of Great Britain Shall have leave to purchase Lands within this Colony and that his Issue if he have any Shall be Inheritable.
> But Inasmuch as the Said Aaron Lopez hath declared himself to be by religion a Jew This Assembly doth not admit him nor any other of that Religion to the *full freedom of this Colony. So that the Said Aaron Lopez nor any other of said Religion is not Liable to be chosen into any Office in this Colony Nor allowed to give a Vote as a Freeman in Choosing others.* [italics mine]

The Lower House was not in doubt as to its right to grant the petition, but went out of its way to admonish the petitioners that they could not vote or hold office, even though they did not ask to be admitted freemen.

The Upper House refused to concur on the ground that the Parliamentary Act provided the manner in which foreigners should be naturalized and therefore sent them back to the Superior Court. This was only eight months after the same General Assembly had passed an Act granting naturalization to James Lucena. Lopez and Elizer appeared before the Superior Court of Newport again in March, 1762, a year after their first petition, and again the Court denied their petition in a unanimous opinion, which has been universally condemned by historians.[10]

The fact that Lucena was naturalized by the General Assembly has no bearing upon the question of the naturalization of Jews for the reason that Lucena did not appear before them as a Jew but as a subject of Portugal and took the oath "upon the true Faith of a Christian," while Lopez and Elizer appeared as "Persons professing the Jewish Religion." Moreover Lucena represented in an accompanying petition that he could and would manufacture castile soap, thereby employing many poor people as well as furnishing "a great and valuable article of commerce for export to the continent, to the West Indies etc.," an enterprise highly beneficial to the public, and he asked for the exclusive right to do so. Just as industrialists today receive various economic advantages on similar grounds, Lucena was

---

[10] *Ibid.*, March Term, 1762. Sidney S. Rider, *An Inquiry Concerning the Origin of the Clause in the Laws of Rhode Island (1719-1783) Disfranchising Roman Catholics*, Rhode Island Historical Tracts, second series, no. 1, (Providence, 1889).

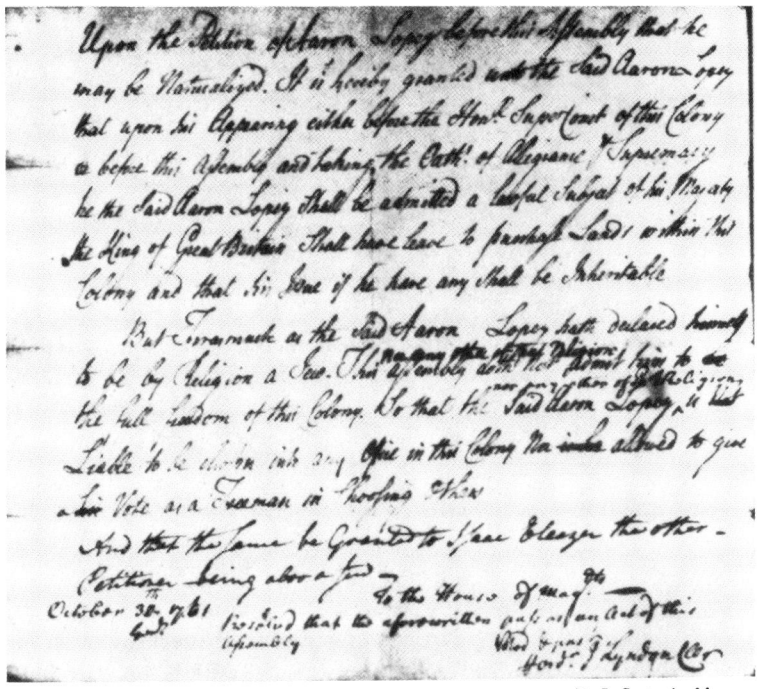

R. I. State Archives

GENERAL ASSEMBLY'S DECISION ON
LOPEZ' AND ELIZER'S PETITION FOR CITIZENSHIP

granted not only the right to exclusive manufacture of castile soap but also naturalization.

In its opinion the Court held that the Naturalization Act of 1740 was designed for increasing the inhabitants in the Plantations, but the Colony was already so full that some had removed to Nova Scotia and other places. This reason is absurd. Lopez and Elizer were already residents and intended to remain. Denial of their petition did not affect the population one way or another. The Court went on to say that by the charter granted the Colony, it appeared that the "free & quiet Enjoyment of the Christian Religion and a Desire of propagating the same were the principal views with which this Colony was settled." The Colony was not founded by King Charles in 1663 but by Williams in 1636.

Thus the Court subverted the principles of Williams and the plain language of the charter of "a lively experiment" and "full liberty in religious concernments." And finally the Court said, ". . . by a law made and passed in the year 1663, no Person who does not profess the Christian Religion can be admitted free of this Colony."

However, the petition was one for naturalization and not for admission as freemen.

The "law made and passed in 1663" was never passed as such and has been the subject of close examination by historians. It did not appear in print until 1719 in the Code of Laws, which was never enacted by the Assembly. And the phrase, "Professing Christianity," appears to be an unauthorized interpolation. The Act passed in 1684 in answer to the Medus petition seems to imply this interpretation.

Samuel G. Arnold, a lawyer and noted historian, in language that is restrained and befitting a gentleman, was nevertheless emphatic in his condemnation of the decision, when he wrote,[11]

> . . . grounds that were not only a violation of the spirit of the charter, but a direct disregard of an act of Parliament . . . The court construed the act to suit their purpose, going behind the record to pronounce upon the probable or possible intention of the act, which was an assumption of extra-judicial power . . . The decision in the case of Lopez appears to be irregular in every respect. It subverts an act of Parliament, violates the spirit of the charter, enunciates the principles never acted upon in the Colony, and finally dismisses the case on a false issue.

The questions to be answered are why the General Assembly refused to take jurisdiction and why the Court at first refused to take jurisdiction, referring the petition to the Assembly and when compelled to do so by the action of the Upper House, perverted its office unanimously. The key is supplied by Arnold, in these words,

> We know of but one cause that can explain all this, in a single word—party spirit. The strife between Ward, then chief-justice, and Hopkins, then governor, was at its height, resulting in the defeat of Hopkins at the ensuing election. Some of the details of that contest, herein recorded, exhibit as gross violations of right and of usage as does this decision, but none so utterly absurd.

Stephen Hopkins became governor in 1755 and up to 1768 was elected ten times. He was one of the most prominent and able men

[11]Arnold, op. cit., II, 494-496.

in the Colony, a charter member and trustee of Brown University, and later a delegate to the Continental Congress. His rival for the office of governorship was Samuel Ward of Westerly, who was elected three times, including 1762, the year of the Lopez decision. Judges were laymen and elected annually. Elections were held annually, the result being decided by the narrow margin created by a few pounds or shillings distributed to the right voters. The feud between these two men was bitter—personal and political—and for fourteen years kept the Colony in turmoil. Behind the feud was the struggle between Providence and Newport for dominance as well as conflict between the landholders and commercial interests.

Aaron Lopez came to Newport in 1752 and rapidly rose to become a merchant prince and ship owner, one of the wealthiest men in Newport. He carried on an extensive business with the Browns of Providence, taking the greater part of their production of iron at the Hope Furnace. Nicholas Brown and he were business partners in various ventures. At the solicitation of Nicholas Brown he contributed ten thousand board feet of lumber to the first building of Brown University and chartered a vessel to the government during the Revolution.

One of the most important industries in New England as well as one of the most competitive was that of the production of spermaceti and oil from the head matter of whales for the manufacture of candles and oil for lamps. In 1761 Lopez; Jacob Rodrigues Riviera, his father-in-law; Moses Lopez, his brother; Naphthali Hart; the Browns of Providence; and four other manufacturers formed The United Company of Spermaceti Chandlers, one of the first price fixing monopolies in America.[12] This agreement was renewed on April 13, 1763, when the Browns were allotted one-fifth of the raw material purchased and the four Jewish firms one-third. The agreement was policed by Riviera. As their leader Lopez, being of Newport, could easily have incurred the displeasure of Ward and his party.

The Browns and Lopez were closely associated in many business ventures and there can be little doubt "that the Browns supported the Hopkins political faction with all the resources at their command, including the brazen and unabashed use of money to buy the votes

[12]Broches, *op. cit.*, II, 41-44. Lee M. Friedman, *Jewish Patriots and Pioneers* (Philadelphia, 1942), 309-314.

of the electorate."[13] The buying of votes directly was a common practice.

The different decisions by the Upper and Lower Houses of the General Assembly would indicate that the control of the two Houses was divided between the governor and the chief justice. In the vernacular Lopez was *in the middle*. Political affairs follow industrial and private business.

Lopez, upon the advice of his Boston agent, took up residence in Swansea and was naturalized at Taunton, Massachusetts; and Elizer went to New York, where he was naturalized. Both of them came back to Newport to live and to carry on business until the Revolutionary War broke out.

The Declaration of Independence by Rhode Island in May, 1776, found the colony divided between Tories and Loyalists, a situation which was fertile ground for a campaign of hysteria, snooping, and smearing. In this atmosphere the Assembly passed restrictive legislation, providing for a loyalty test. Seventy-seven persons in Newport, suspected as inimical to the United Colonies of America, were summoned to appear before a committee and take the loyalty test. Among them were four Jews: Rabbi Isaac Touro, Isaac Hart, Myer Pollock, and Moses Hayes. Rabbi Touro and Pollock refused to sign on religious grounds, but Hart and Hayes refused on grounds that the test was not general. Hayes had already subscribed to a general oath in June and resenting the suspicion in which he was held, left the following written copy of his remarks to the committee:

> I have and ever shall hold the strongest principles and attachments to the just rights and privileges of this my native land, and ever have and shall conform to the rules and acts of this government and pay as I always have my proportion of its exigencies. I always have asserted my sentiments in favor of America and confess the War on its part just. I decline subscription to the Test at present from these principles first, that I deny ever being inimical to my country and call for my accusers and proof of conviction. Second, that I am an Israelite and am not allowed the liberty of a vote, or voice in common with the rest of the voters though consistent with the Constitution, and the other Colonies. Thirdly, because the Test is not general and consequently subject to many glaring inconveniences. Fourthly, Continental Congress nor the General Assembly of this nor the Legislature of the other Colonies have never in this contest taken any notice

---

[13] James B. Hedges, professor of history, Brown University, letter to the writer, August 12, 1951.

or countenance respecting the society of Israelites to which I belong. When any rule order or direction is made by Congress or General Assembly, I shall to the utmost of my power adhere to the same.[14]

Nor would Hayes let the matter rest there, but addressed a petition to the General Assembly, protesting the humiliation to which he had been subjected and requesting vindication. As a result the law was changed to apply to everyone generally.

From 1761 until 1843, when the State Constitution was adopted, there was persistent, continuous, and ever-increasing agitation on the part of the inhabitants for the removal of the political disabilities under which they lived. This agitation resulted in the repeal in 1783 of the Anti-Catholic clause and extended to Catholics the same rights as Protestants to be admitted freemen and in 1828 in the passage of an act removing all religious disqualifications. Many abortive attempts were made to pass a new State Constitution.

There is no question but that there was discrimination against Jews, but such discrimination was incidental to the fact that the Colony operated under the original charter, which placed the power of admission of freemen in the hands of landed proprietors and their successors. Control was absolute and possibly accounts for the stability of the colonial government in spite of the fact that it harbored a "motley crew of Dissenters and Non-Conformists." Even after the Revolution and statehood the colony continued to be governed under the colonial charter. In 1841 out of 14,000 persons who voted on the People's Constitution, 9,000 did not have the right to vote under the Charter. The political discrimination to which Jews were subject was also directed against Catholics and Protestants as well.

The occupation of Newport by the British during the Revolution and losses during the War of 1812 destroyed the business and commerce of that city with a resulting loss of half its population, including Jews, the last of whom left Newport in 1822. Court records show that many Jewish merchants from New York and Newport did business in Providence throughout the eighteenth century. Although the Lopez, Riviera, and Mendes families stopped in Providence for a short time in 1776,[15] Jews did not permanently settle in Providence until after the adoption of the State Constitution.

[14]Archives, Revolutionary War, Suspected Persons (1775-1783), II, 8, 9, 14, 18.
[15]*Ibid.* List of Inhabitants of the Town of Providence, July 18-23, 1776.

THE DOUBLE PRIMARY*

By

Henry M. Alexander

The double primary system is used in ten states[1] to bar plurality nominations.[2] Adopted in these states between 1902 and 1937, the system has evoked heated controversy. Claims of merit and demerit have not as yet created a public opinion definitely favorable or unfavorable. Meanwhile, the double primary continues to be a football of politics. "No where," says Louise Overacker, "has this been more true than in Arkansas."[3]

Two devices, other than the double primary, have been utilized in state government to prevent nomination by small plurality: the minimum-percentage plan and preferential voting.

Several states have required a party nominee to poll more than a specified plurality at the party primary.[4] Should no candidate's vote equal this figure, one of three alternatives is required: the nomination is made by party convention, by party committee, or at a second primary. Should no aspirant for nomination in Iowa or South Dakota poll more than thirty-five per cent of the party vote, the nomination is made by convention in the appropriate geographical area. In Michigan the state party convention has chosen the nominee when no candidate for the gubernatorial nomination polled forty per cent of votes cast in the primary.

---

*Research Paper 793, Journal Series, University of Arkansas.
[1] Ala., Ark., Fla., Ga., La., Miss., N. C., S. C., Texas, Utah. *Book of the States* (1943-44) p. 120.
[2] As used here, the terms *double, dual* and *run-off* primary system are synonymous. In deference to local usage, the first primary is termed the *preferential* and the second, the *run-off* primary. No use is made of the distinction, once current in this state, between a *preferential double primary* and a *run-off double primary*. In the former, names of all candidates for all nominations are listed on the ballot in the first primary. In the latter, this ballot contains only the names of the candidates for nominations contested by three or more aspirants.
[3] "Direct Primary Legislation, 1936-39," *American Policital Science Review*, June, 1940, pp. 499-506.
[4] Leon E. Aylsworth, "Primary Elections, Majority Nominations, and the Second Choice Ballot," *American Political Science Review*, November, 1909, pp. 563-65.

Similar provisions have been employed in Illinois and in Indiana. In Washington, should the leading candidate for nomination have less than ten per cent of the primary vote, the party committee has made the nomination. In rare instances and in units of local government, when no candidate polled a plurality equal to a minimum percentage, a second primary has been held. For example, should the leading candidate's plurality be less than twenty-five per cent in Alpena County, Michigan, this candidate and the runner-up contended for the nomination in a run-off primary.

Preferential or second-choice voting has been defined as "a device whereby a voter in a primary or general election may indicate on his ballot a first and second choice . . . with a view to combining of transferring choices when the votes are counted in such a way as to produce at least a nominal majority in favor of a particular candidate."[5] Adopted between 1907 and 1925 in eleven states,[6] systems of preferential voting differed much in the way second and subsequent choice votes were counted. Preferential voting is still used in Maryland to nominate candidates to federal, state, county, and municipal offices and to elect delegates to national party conventions. The system has been repealed in nine states and in one, Oklahoma, was declared unconstitutional by the state supreme court.[7]

Preferential voting enjoys one distinct advantage over the double primary—it gives one candidate a majority of sorts at a *single* primary. Experience with preferential voting, however, revealed serious flaws. A voter's second-choice vote might help to defeat the candidate receiving his first-choice vote. The majority given a winning candidate by preferential voting is not in all cases a true majority, since, in most states using the system, second-choice votes were rated on a par with first-choice votes. Finally, complexities inherent in the system were aggravated when two

---
[5]Quoted in W. Brooke Graves,*American State Government* (1941) p. 177.
[6]Ala., Fla., Idaho, Ind., La., Md., Minn., N. D., Okla., Wash., Wis. Merriam & Overacker, *Primary Elections* (1928) p. 83.
[7]*Dove v. Ogleby*, 244 Pacific 798 (1926).

or more candidates were to be nominated for similar offices.[8]

Established by statute or party rule, the double primary system has been in effect at different times in twelve states. Mississippi, in 1902, was first to adopt the system. Texas followed in 1903; North and South Carolina, 1915; Georgia, 1917; Louisiana, 1922; Florida and Oklahoma, 1929; Alabama, 1931; Kentucky, 1935;[9] Utah, 1937.[10] Arkansas first adopted the double primary in 1933, abandoned it in 1935, and, by compulsion of an initiated amendment in 1938, reestablished the system in 1939. Kentucky and Oklahoma, only states to cast aside the double primary permanetly, did so in 1936 and 1937.[11] Several municipalities have employed run-off primaries for local nominations —notably Lincoln, Nebraska, where Republican nominations to municipal offices, beginning in 1896, were made at a second primary in event no aspirant polled a majority at the first primary.[12] The double primary system was used in at least two Arkansas counties, Ouachita[13] and Calhoun,[14] as early as 1924. Introduced in Ouachita County by agreement of Democratic candidates for local nominations, the extra-legal run-off in this county continued in use without sanction of law or formal party rule until legal establishment of the system in 1933.

As a device to insure majority nominations, the double primary has proved more durable and lasting than preferential voting. Of the ten states abandoning preferential voting, six returned to plurality nominations, and four, Alabama, Florida, Louisiana, and Oklahoma, substituted the

---

[8] Chas. K. Lush, "Primary Elections and Majority Nominations," *American Political Science Review*, November, 1907, pp. 43-47.
[9] Louise Overacker, "Direct Primary Legislation, 1936-39," *American Political Science Review*, June, 1940, p. 503.
[10] Joe Park, "That Elusive Majority," *National Municipal Review*, October, 1940. pp. 675-78.
[11] The double primary is unique in state and local government in the United States. Double *elections*, not double primaries, have been used in other countries, notably France, Italy, and Germany. A system of double elections is extensively used in cities of the United States employing the non-partisan system of nominating and electing public officers.
[12] Ernst C. Meyer, *Nominating Systems* (1902) p. 189.
[13] F. W. Whiteside to the writer, May 2, 1944. See also *Arkansas Gazette*, March 9, 1939.
[14] *Arkansas Gazette*, March 3, 1925.

double primary system.[14a] The eleven states that have employed preferential voting in primaries did so for an average period of nine years. No state employing the double primary has discarded it permanently[15] in favor of preferential voting. Kentucky, after one year, and Oklahoma, after eight years, abandoned the double primary. In the latter state, the system was discarded because of expense to taxpayers and because, with less than three candidates filing for a nomination, two primaries in counties were frequently unnecessary.[16]

The general pattern of law and practice is substantially similar in most of the states using the double primary system. Names of all candidates for nomination to an office are listed on the ballot in the preferential primary. Any candidate polling a majority of votes cast for a particular nomination is duly nominated. Should no candidate poll a majority, the two having the largest vote contend for the nomination in a run-off primary.

The double primary established in Arkansas in 1933 was of the above general pattern. As recreated in 1939, the system in this state introduced a unique feature, one that has grown steadily in public favor. Names of candidates for a particular nomination are listed on the ballot in the first primary only if three or more aspirants file for that nomination. One polling a majority is nominated. In event no candidate polls a majority, names of the two receiving the largest number of votes are printed on the ballot in the second primary. The ballot in the second primary also contains the names of candidates whose nominations are unopposed or opposed by a single contestant. This feature of the Arkansas double primary materially reduces

---

[14a] O. Douglas Weeks, "Summary of the History and Present Status of Preferential Voting in State Direct Primary Systems," *Southwestern Social Science Quarterly*, June, 1937, pp. 64-67.

[15] Louisiana did replace a double primary system with preferntial voting, but, in 1922, reestablished the double primary. Benjamin H. Williams, "Prevention of Minority Nominations for State Officers in the Direct Primary," *Annals of the American Academy*, March, 1923, pp. 111-15.

[16] Lionel V. Murphy, "Two Trials of Oklahoma's Run-Off Primary," *Southwestern Social Science Quarterly*, September, 1933, pp. 156-74.

the number of candidates conclusively nominated in the first primary.

Double primary systems used in other states contain features which merit comment. Oklahoma's double primary law did not apply to nominations to municipal offices. The run-off primary is not held in Texas for nominations to county offices if the county executive committee of the party elects to employ plurality nominations. This decision of the executive committee may be taken either before or after the first primary and usually is determined by expressed wishes of candidates for nomination. The run-off primary in Texas counties is dispensed with at each biennial primary election in approximately fifty per cent of the counties, but more frequently in rural than urban counties. The run-off is often held one year in a particular county and omitted two years later.[17]

A second primary was unnecessary in Mississippi if all candidates for nomination to county, district, or state office agreed prior to the first primary that a plurality in this race would determine the nomination.[18] Should no candidate obtain a majority in the preferential primary in North Carolina, the runner-up may force the leading candidate into a run-off by filing a written demand within five days after results of the first primary are officially announced. Such demands for a second primary are rather frequent, particularly when the runner-up polls a sizable vote in the first race and feels that chances of defeating the leading candidate warrant the expense and effort. A run-off has been demanded in two out of the three most recent primaries to nominate a Democratic candidate for governor.[19]

Georgia employs a county-unit system in the Democratic primary for nomination of candidates for United

---

[17] O. Douglas Weeks to the writer, May 18, 1944.
[18] Ernst C. Meyer, *Nominating Systems* (1902) p. 142. This feature is not present in the current law of Mississippi, except insofar as *all candidates* for a particular nomination, in keeping with prior informal understandings, may actually withdraw in favor of the aspirant receiving a plurality in the first primary. In this event, this candidate's name would be listed on the ballot in the second primary without any opponent. The double primary systems of Arkansas and Mississippi are similar in this respect.
[19] C. B. Robson to the writer, May 18, 1944.

States senator and governor. So called "county-unit votes" are allocated to counties on a basis of two for each of their representatives in the lower house of the state legislature. A candidate winning a popular plurality in a county obtains the county-unit votes of that county. A second primary, also on a county-unit basis, is held when no candidate receives a majority of county-unit votes in the first race.[20] Should a Democratic candidate for the gubernatorial nomination in Louisiana win a clear majority in the first race, the nomination of candidates for other executive offices of the state is decided in this race even when they poll pluralities less than majorities. Utah uses an open primary. Names of the candidates of all parties are listed in party columns on a "blanket" ballot. Perforations divide the party columns and unused portions of the ballot are placed in a separate box.

Should the two leading candidates for nomination poll a tie vote in Tennessee, a second primary is held. When the leading candidate and the runner-up poll a tie vote in the second primary in South Carolina, a third primary is authorized.

Nominations were made in Arkansas at state and local conventions until 1895. An act of the General Assembly passed in that year authorized direct primaries.[21] Use of the direct primary did not become general immediately upon this authorization. Nominations to local offices continued to be made at local party conventions, though, by 1909, nominations of the dominant Democratic Party were made generally at primary elections. Candidates for county offices in Newton County, however, are chosen at Democratic conventions.[22] Democratic c o n v e n t i o n s in appropriate geographical areas are usually employed to select nominees to fill vacancies in nominations and to choose candidates to run in special elections for United States

---
[20] The system is described in Merriam & Overacker, *Primary Elections* (1928) p. 83.
[21] D. Y. Thomas, *Arkansas and Its People* (1930) pp. 254 and 284.
[22] *Arkansas Gazette*, October 6, 1940.

representative or member of either house of the General Assembly.

Nominations by the Republican Party in Arkansas to local, district, state, and federal office are made at conventions. With exception of a few counties in northwest Arkansas, the Republican Party rarely enters candidates in elections to local office. The party does not always nominate candidates for state or federal office. In a single county, Searcy, Republican nominees for county offices are chosen at a county-wide primary held on the same day as the Democratic primary but conducted at separate polling places.

All nominations for elective school offices, local school boards and county boards of education, are made by petition, as are all nominations to municipal offices in incorporated towns and a few cities of the second class.

As in five other states, direct nominations are optional in Arkansas.[23] Rules of the Democratic Party, with exceptions noted above, prescribe the primary for nominations to state and federal office and imply its use for nominations to county offices and municipal offices in cities of the first and second class. When nominees to any office are selected at a direct primary by any political party, an amendment to the constitution, ratified in 1938, demands that the nominee be chosen by majority vote. Consequently, when a party elects to employ direct nominations, it is forced by mandate of the constitution to hold double primaries.

There is no evidence of advocacy in Arkansas of preferential voting. The double primary system, however, has had influential backers and has enjoyed substantial popular favor for twenty years. The earliest evidence of dissatisfaction with plurality nominations is found in a resolution of the state Democratic committee, adopted February 22, 1898, that candidates for nomination to state office, when none obtains a majority at the party primary, be chosen at

---

[23] Ala., Del., Ga., Md., Va.

the ensuing state convention.[24] No action on this resolution was taken at the state convention.

Twenty-six years later, in 1924, the issue of plurality versus majority nominations suddenly emerged in Arkansas politics as a full-grown and burning issue in the Democratic Party. Ouachita and Calhoun Counties held their first local double primaries in 1924 and, at the state Democratic convention of that year, the double primary system won vigorous support of eminent citizens and party leaders. Tom J. Terral, then the nominee of his party for governor by virtue of a plurality of less than twenty-six per cent of votes cast in the primary off 1924, was a supporter of the double primary. Meeting in Little Rock on September 10 and 11, 1924, the convention heard former United States senator William F. Kirby in a spirited key-note address say, "The Democratic Party has always believed in majority rule, and *the time has come*,[25] in my opinion, when the nominee should be the choice of the majority of the Democrats."[26] A resolution, drafted previously by one-time Acting Governor X. O. Pindall and recommended by the committee on resolutions, headed by Brooks Hays, was formally adopted as a plank in the platform. It stated, "We believe that the nominees of the Democratic Party should always be the choice of the majority of the Democrats."[27]

Though adoption of this plank encountered no open opposition on the floor of the convention, its public announcement did not receive unanimous acclaim. In an editorial, published on the following day, the *Arkansas Gazette* characterized the plank as one of "doubtful wisdom." "Already," said the editorial, "Arkansas has too many elections and too much political turmoil."

Governor Terral, in his inaugural address to the General Assembly in 1925, urged enactment of a double primary law.[28] Bills providing for the double primary were

---
[24]D. Y. Thomas, *op. cit.*, pp. 262-63.
[25]Italics added by this writer.
[26]*Arkansas Gazette*, September 11, 1924.
[27]*Arkansas Gazette*, September 12, 1924.
[28]*Journal of the House* (1925) p. 48.

introduced in both chambers during the session: House Bill 82 by W. C. Dennison of Perry County and Senate Bill 458 by Senator John J. Dulaney of Ashdown. The former was defeated in the house on March 2 by vote of 35 to 52.[29] Senator Dulaney's bill was modeled after the double primary system in Louisiana. It provided for a second primary when no aspirant for the gubernatorial nomination polled a majority in the preferential primary. Should a candidate for governor be nominated by a majority vote in the preferential primary, however, the nominees of the party for other executive state offices would be decided by plurality vote.[30] The bill never reached the floor of the lower chamber.

Adoption in 1924 of the double primary in two counties and its successful advocacy at the state Democratic convention of the same year were a culmination of a movement to abolish plurality nominations that emerged quite as suddenly as mysteriously into a major political issue. This sudden popularity of the double primary was a strategy of anti-Klan elements in the Democratic Party who sought in this way to consolidate the anti-Klan vote in party primaries.

The Ku Klux Klan attained its greatest strength in Arkansas, as elsewhere in the South and Middle-West, during the latter part of 1924.[31] At no time however, did this organization dominate the Democratic state organization in Arkansas. In several counties units of the Klan strengthened their influence in local politics by means of so-called "Ku Klux Klan preference primaries," an informal and extra-legal means of uniting their voting strength in support of a single candidate for nomination to public office. These Klan primaries were formally condemned and the nominee so chosen was barred from the official Democratic primary ballot by a resolution added to rules of the party by the state committee in September, 1924. Drafted by anti-Klan forces, the resolution, still incorporated in published party

---
[29] *Arkansas Gazette*, March 3, 1925.
[30] *Arkansas Gazette*, February 26, 1925.
[31] Harold U. Faulkner, *American Political and Social History* (1943) p. 657.

rules,[32] states, "No one shall be eligible as a candidate in any Democratic primary in the State of Arkansas for the nomination of any United States, District, County, State, Township, or City office who shall have participated in any run-off or primary other than a run-off or primary held under the authority of the Democratic party . . . ."[33]

Candidates supported by the Klan would have a decided advantage when nominations were made by plurality vote. Local and extra-legal adoption of the double primary system during 1924 in Ouachita and Calhoun Counties was regarded as an effective counter-move to consolidate anti-Klan voting strength. The sudden emergence of the double primary as a popular issue at the state Democratic convention in 1924 is similarly explained. In his key-note address to this convention, Senator Kirby stated, "There is no room in the Democratic Party for an invisible empire." This dictum evoked prolonged applause. In the opinion of Brooks Hays, "There is a connection between the Klan practice of uniting behind one of its own members and the agitation (in 1924) for a run-off so that the anti-Klan vote would not be divided."[34]

The Klan in Arkansas vanished even more quickly than it had emerged as a factor in state politics. Published comment for and against proposed run-off legislation introduced in the legislature of 1925, running the gamut of familiar argument, contains no reference to the Klan. The Klan was not a factor in later advocacy of the double primary system in 1932 and thereafter, except as its earlier espousal introduced the system and publicized the principle of majority nominations. The run-off primary was not mentioned in the Democratic state platform of 1926 and the issue did not figure on legislative calendars during the 1927 session of the General Assembly. The double primary and the Ku Klux Klan departed from the political scene hand-in-hand.

---
[32]*Rules of the Democratic Party in Arkansas*, Democratic State Committee, January 15, 1937, Sec. 55.
[33]*Arkansas Gazette*, September 10, 1924.
[34]Brooks Hays to the writer, May 11, 1944.

An unsuccessful attempt was made at the state Democratic convention in September, 1928, to endorse the double primary in the party platform.[35] A bill providing a double primary, introduced during the 1929 session of the General Assembly, failed of enactment. Some support for the bill could have been found in the nomination of Harvey Parnell in August, 1928, by a plurality of less than forty-two per cent.[36] The bill won approval in the senate by vote of 17 to 13.[37] The *Senate Journal* records the sentiments of one member who viewed the measure as an "attempt to eliminate the poor man or woman from office . . . No Legion members has [*sic*] asked me to support it."[38] The bill was defeated in the house on March 7 by vote of 53 to 35 on motion of J. L. Shaver of Cross County to postpone indefinitely.[39]

A more vigorous attempt to enact a double primary statute was made during the legislative session of 1931. Introduced in the senate on January 28 by Senators Robert Bailey and Fletcher McElhannon, the proposal suffered cumulative emasculation by successive amendments. One amendment exempted nominations to county offices from scope of the measure. Another, proposed by Senator W. H. Abington of Beebe, was carried by vote of 21 to 10[40] to exempt nominations to state offices. As amended, the bill applied only to nomination of candidates to seats in the national Congress. In this form the measure died on the senate calendar. Senator Abington, spearhead of opposition to the bill, has continued to be a consistent and resolute opponent of the double primary system.

The next regular session of the General Assembly, that of 1933, witnessed enactment of the state's first runoff primary law. The initial step toward this objective was taken by the Pulaski County Democratic convention on August 12, 1932, in the form of unanimous approval ac-

[35] *Arkansas Gazette*, September 14 and 15, 1928.
[36] *Arkansas Gazette*, August 17, 1928.
[37] *Journal of the Senate* (1929) p. 304.
[38] *Loc. Cit.*
[39] *Journal of the House* (1929) pp. 1141-42.
[40] *Journal of the Senate* (1931) pp. 458-59.

corded a resolution proposed by Sam E. Montgomery of North Little Rock. The resolution urged the ensuing state Democratic convention to adopt a platform plank endorsing the double primary.[41] The state convention, without apparent opposition, did adopt such a plank. It stated, "This convention favors a run-off primary election law for Arkansas."[42] In light of subsequent events, it is perhaps significant that Abe Collins of DeQueen was a convention delegate.

In his inaugural to the General Assembly in January, 1933, Governor J. Marion Futrell stated, "Nominations for public office should be made by a majority of the qualified electors voting at an election. By no means should an insubstantial minority be allowed to make a nomination." Active support of the governor contributed much to enactment of a double primary statute at this session.

Introduced in the senate on the second day of the session, Senate Bill 12, by Fletcher McElhannon of Arkadelphia, was approved 28 to 0 on January 18.[43] The bill was passed in the house on February 14 by a vote of 84 to 3.[44] Governor Futrell approved the measure on February 18. Listed as Act 38 of 1933, the statute followed traditional patterns. It did not apply to nominations to either municipal or township offices. With respect to other nominations made at direct primaries, the act provided that names of all candidates for nomination be listed on the first primary ballot. Any candidate polling a majority in this primary was duly nominated. Should no one receive a majority, the two highest for each nomination were entered in a second primary held two weeks after "the general primary election," that is, on the fourth Tuesday in August. The measure also provided that "when more than one candidate is to be nominated for the same office . . . in the second primary election a clear majority is not necessary but

---
[41]*Arkansas Gazette*, August 16, 1932.
[42]*Arkansas Gazette*, September 10, 1932.
[43]*Journal of the Senate* (1933) pp. 588 89.
[44]*Journal of the House* (1933) pp. 757-58. Negative votes were cast by Edmonson of Stone, Proctor of Calhoun, and Stanfield of Garland.

that nomination will be made by plurality vote if the required number of candidates do not receive a majority." This feature of the statute, compromising the principle of majority nominations, was included to avoid the vexing problem of nominating each of two or more candidates to similar offices by a majority vote.

In view of the potent opposition in the legislature to earlier bills providing a double primary, passage of Act 38 with only three negative votes is difficult to understand.[45] The hectic Democratic primaries of 1932 may in some measure explain revival of agitation for the double primary system. The primary ballot of that year in Pulaski County, described as being "as long as your arm," contained seventy-six names exclusive of candidates for nomination to township offices and for election to party office.[46] The ballot listed seven candidates for the gubernatorial nomination, a like number for the United States senatorial nomination. Six entrants sought the nomination for lieutenant governor and twenty candidates filed for seven other contested nominations to state office. Winners in several races failed to poll a majority of the votes cast. J. M. Futrell, nominee for governor, polled less than forty-five per cent; Lee Cazort, nominee for lieutenant governor, less than thirty-one per cent.[47] Converted to the principle of majority nominations by numerous minority nominations in the primaries of this and former years, a small group of influential citizens organized a Run-Off Primary Association. This short-lived organization was formed to advocate enactment of a double primary law at the 1933 session of the General Assembly. The organization, its headquarters in Little Rock, chose J. Bruce Streett, president, and Grady Forgy, secretary. Its officers had a hand in drafting Act. 38 and its influence counted for much in obtaining passage of the statute.[47a]

The double primary was described as a "hot" issue at

---
[45] *Arkansas Gazette*, January 19, 1933.
[46] *Arkansas Gazette*, August 9 and 10, 1932.
[47] *Arkansas Gazette*, August 21, 1932.
[47a] J. Bruce Streett to the writer, August 25, 1944.

the Democratic state convention in 1934. It was successfully kept off the floor during formal proceedings.[48] During the 1935 legislative session, Act. 38 of 1933 was repealed. The repeal prompted later champions of the principle of majority nominations to embody the double primary system in a proposed constitutional amendment—beyond reach of the legislative power.

Two bills to repeal the double primary law were introduced during the 1935 session, one in the house and one in the senate. The former, sponsored by Mrs. Ella B. Hurst of Washington County, died on the house calendar. The latter, Senate Bill 7, introduced by Holloway of Lonoke County, was passed on January 30 by close vote of 18 to 16.[49] The measure, guided through the house by J. C. Childers of Lawrence County, was approved on February 5 by narrow margin of 53 to 46.[50] Signed by Governor Futrell on February 6, the bill became Act 20 of 1935.

Proponents of the double primary made strenuous attempts during the remainder of the session to obtain passage of a measure retaining the principle of majority nominations, but revised to meet objections to Act 38 of 1933. Four such bills to amend Act 38 were introduced. One, House Bill 24, by Representative O. G. Richardson, proposed to limit the run-off primary to the nomination of candidates for the United States senate and house of representatives. Three bills, one by Senator Ward of Independence and two by Senator Winfred Lake of Sevier, proposed to omit from the ballot in the first primary names of aspirants who were unopposed or opposed by a single contestant. This proposal, designed to reduce the number of races decided in the preferential primary, would have lessened likelihood that winners or losers in the preferential would influence the outcome of contests in the run-off. Senator Lake's first bill, Senate Bill 153, an amendment to Act. 38, was approved in the upper chamber by vote of 18 to 14 on January 30, the

---
[48] *Arkansas Gazette*, September 9, 1934.
[49] *Arkansas Gazette*, January 31, 1935.
[50] *Arkansas Gazette*, February 6, 1935.

same day that the senate passed the Holloway Bill repealing Act 38. Enactment of the Holloway Bill precluded a vote in the house on Senate Bill 153. Senator Lake then introduced a second measure embodying similar features but in the form of a complete measure to reestablish the double primary. His second bill, Senate Bill 295, introduced in the upper chamber on February 12, was passed by vote of 18 to 16 on February 14.[52] This measure reached the house on the following day where it was killed by a vote of 40 to 56 on February 26.[53] This extinguished hope of reestablishing the double primary during the session. Later events attach significance to the fact that Senator Lake, proponent of the double primary in the sessions of 1935 and 1937, was a resident of DeQueen.

It is difficult to explain repeal of the double primary system in 1935. The additional expense it imposed on candidates evoked complaint. For example, the county Democratic committee and convention of Lawrence County approved resolutions urging repeal.[54] The system was opposed generally by professional office-holders who, with some justification, were able to seize upon incidents occurring in 1933 and 1934 to discredit the system. A special election was called in 1933 to fill a vacancy in the United States house of representatives caused by the resignation of Heartsill Ragon. Three candidates sought the Democratic nomination in a special primary, the first to be held under terms of Act 38 of 1933. Sam Rorex one-time resident of Danville, eliminated in the first primary, was apparently instrumental in swinging the large vote of Yell County to D. D. Terry in the run-off. As a consequence, Brooks Hays, polling a plurality in the preferntial, was defeated in the second primary by Terry.

Hays, long an advocate of the double primary became interested in 1928 in the movement to require majority nominations. In that year he was runner-up in a seven-man

---
[52]*Arkansas Gazette*, February 15, 1935.
[53]*Arkansas Gazette*, February 27, 1935.
[54]*Arkansas Gazette*, February 6, 1935.

race for the gubernatorial nomination won by Harvey Parnell with a plurality of less than forty-two per cent.[55] Two years later, Hays, again an unsuccessful candidate for the gubernatorial nomination, urged adoption of the double primary system in his campaign for the nomination. Ironically, the first "victim" of the double primary in Arkansas was one of its earliest champions.

J. Oscar Humphrey, incumbent state auditor seeking renomination in the primaries of 1934, was another "victim." Humphrey led his closest competitor by 41,463 votes in the first primary.[56] In the run-off he was defeated by Charles Parker of Stephens by vote of 100,204 to 95,516.[57] It was believed that Futrell, nominated for governor in the preferential race, opposed the renomination of Humphrey and was able to bring about his defeat in the run-off. Defeat of Hays by an aspirant for nomination eliminated in the preferential and defeat of Humphrey by a nominee chosen in the preferential were pointed to by opponents of the double primary as examples of political "tampering" and "trading." These incidents explain the nature of amendments proposed in 1935 to Act 38 of 1933 and contributed to repeal of the statute. The incidents also explain unique features of the current double primary law in Arkansas.

During the 1937 session of the General Assembly, Representative Boyd Tackett of Pike County sponsored a bill to re-establish the run-off primary system. The proposal, House Bill 203, was defeated in the lower chamber on February 15 by vote of 36 to 53.[58]

In the late summer of 1937 a movement to establish the double primary system in the form of an intiated amendment to the constitution was inaugurated by Abe Collins of DeQueen, at that time president of the Arkansas Bar Association. The amendment, destined to be approved by popular vote in the general election of 1938, is far-reaching in scope. Listed as Amendment 29, it requires any

---
[55] *Arkansas Gazette*, August 17, 1928.
[56] Arkansas Gazette, September 8, 1934.
[57] *Arkansas Gazette*, September 1, 1934.
[58] *Journal of the House* (1937) pp. 712-13.

party using the direct primary to use a double primary; prohibits nominations by party committees; largely eliminates the need for special elections by giving the governor authority to fill vacancies by appointment to most elective offices; forbids such an interim appointee from succeeding himself either by appointment or election; and provides that the governor,[59] lieutenant governor, and the wives[60] and relatives of both of these officers shall be ineligible for appointment to vacancies in elective offices.

Certain events in 1937 evoked widespread and positive opposition to committee nominations and special elections. These events gave support to the view that any administration in power, aided by the influence of patronage and by extensive non-voting in special elections, could control both nominations and elections to fill vacancies. Popular support won by Amendment 29 stemmed in greater measure from this hostility to committee nominations and special elections than from opposition to plurality nominations.

Committee nominations were authorized by the state Democratic convention in 1934 in the face of strong opposition and by tactics definitely of "steam-roller" character.[61] Used, both before and after this authorization to select a nominee either to fill a vacancy in the nomination or to run in a special election, nominations by party committee caused many Democrats to support "independent" candidates nominated by petition. Supporters of independent candidates were branded as "bolters," and, under party rules and sanction of law, could be denied the privilege of voting in the party's closed primary for a period of two years. In spite of this rule and in the face of threats to bar bolters from the party primary, many candidates nominated by Democratic committees faced real opposition in special and

---

[59]While governor of Louisiana, Huey P. Long was elected to the United States senate on November 4, 1930. He continued to serve as governor, however, not taking the oath of office as United States senator until January 25, 1932. A similar situation existed during 1913 in Arkansas. Joseph T. Robinson was inaugurated governor on January 16, 1913, elected to the United States senate on January 28. Robinson continued to serve as governor until March 8, 1913. Dallas T. Herndon, *Centennial History of Arkansas* (1922) Vol. I, p. 375.
[60]Mrs. Dixie Bibb Graves served as United States senator from Alabama, by appointment of her husband, from August 20, 1937, to January 3, 1939.
[61]*Arkansas Gazette*, September 7, 1934.

general elections. More than 33,000 voters cast ballots for Carrol D. Wood, independent candidate for chief justice, against a candidate chosen by the state committee in a special election on July 18, 1933. A similar and more significant instance occurred in 1937. Chosen as the party's candidate for election to the United States senate to fill a vacancy caused by the death of Joseph T. Robinson, Carl E. Bailey, then serving as governor, was opposed by John E. Miller who resigned from the United States house of representatives to enter the race as an independent. Miller was elected on October 18, 1937, by vote of 67,283 to 43,480.[62] His majority reflected popular opposition to committee nominations.

Early drafts of Amendment 29 were completed in August, 1937, during the interval following the nomination of Bailey by the state Democratic committee and the special election. Sponsors of the proposed amendment were moved, primarily, by hostility to committee nominations and special elections and, secondarily, by hostility to plurality nominatons. The latter, however, should not be minimized. The section of Amendment 29 requiring the double primary was included in earliest drafts of the proposal. Suggestions, at one time considered, to incorporate provision for a double primary in a separate amendment were discarded. Writing on August 31, 1937, Abe Collins stated, with reference to the section of the proposed amendment requiring the double primary, "I think it is the most important part of it (draft of Amendment 29)." Opposition to minority nominations was strengthened in some quarters when, in the primary of August 11, 1936, Carl E. Bailey won the gubernatorial nomination in a five-man race by a plurality of less than thirty-two per cent of the votes cast.[63]

Amendment 29 was laboriously drafted during a period of almost a year by Abe Collins, Judge B. E. Isbell of DeQueen, and Doctor Robert A. Leflar of Fayetteville. C. T. Coleman of Little Rock and Doctor J. S. Waterman

---

[62]*Northwest Arkansas Times*, October 28, 1937.
[63]*Arkansas Gazette*, August 15, 1936 (unofficial returns).

of Fayetteville cooperated. Sponsors of the amendment represented no organization and the expense involved, approximately $700.00, was met for the most part by Mr. Collins. It was necessary to redraft and to reprint initiative petitions to prohibit a governor from appointing his wife to a vacancy in an elective office when drafts printed on earlier petitions were discovered not to accomplish this objective. This oversight arose from the little-known circumstance that a wife is not related to her spouse either by consanguinity or affinity. At least two "final" drafts were published, then revised and republished.[64]

Initiative petitions were circulated late in May, 1938. Attempts to obtain the 18,446 signatures by voluntary canvassers through cooperation of state-wide organizations of lawyers, bankers, and ministers yielded little results. Voluntary canvassers had secured about 4,000 signatures, when, two weeks before the dead line for filing, July 8, Mr. Collins felt impelled either to abandon the undertaking or to employ paid canvassers. The latter course was followed, agencies circulating petitions for other initiated measures being utilized for the purpose. Late on the last day for filing, petitions having an estimated 518 signatures in excess of the legal minimum were presented to the secretary of state.[65] As late as July 6 sponsors entertained faint hope of obtaining the required number of signers even with paid canvassers circulating petitions. Some uncertainty as to sufficiency of petitions continued until the secretary of state certified to both sufficiency of petitions and ballot title on July 13, 1938. Fortunately, perhaps, neither certification was attacked in the courts.

The press of Arkansas vigorously and almost without exception supported ratification of Amendment 29 at the general election in November, 1938. No organized opposition appeared and, on November 8, the measure was approved by narrow margin of 63,414 to 56,947. Opposition to ratification was somewhat centered in so-called "machine"

---
[64] *Arkansas Gazette*, August 22, 1937 and May 15, 1938.
[65] From files, donated by Abe Collins, in the General Library of the University of Arkansas.

counties. In eleven counties often so characterized ratification was opposed by a popular majority of 61.5 per cent of votes cast in these counties.[66]

Popular ratification of Amendment 29 apparently came as a surprise to those who later lead the agitation against the double primary. The assertion, heard repeatedly since 1938, was made immediately after the election that voters of the state were unaware, in approving the far-reaching amendment, that they were voting for the double primary system.[66a] The press gave wide publicity to this feature of the proposed amendment, but the amendment's provision for the double primary, contained in Section 5, was obscured by the text. It states, "Only the names of candidates for office nominated by an organized political party at a convention of delegates, or by a majority of all the votes cast for candidates for the office in a primary election, or by petition of electors as provided by law, shall be placed on the ballots of any election." The measure's "short title"[67] was definitely incomplete. As listed on the official election ballot, it read, "Filling Vacancies in Public Office." The measure's ballot title, too, could be described as incomprehensive and obtuse. The ballot title read, "An Amendment to the Constitution [sic] to Abolish Committee Nominations, special elections and minority rule. Providing the method for and regulating, filling of vacancies in office and the placing of the names of candidates for office on the ballots in elections, and for other purposes." In the mind of the layman the tie between an abolition of "minority rule" and a mandatory double primary is remote.

Bitter hostility to the double primary was in evidence as the General Assembly met in January for the 1939 session. A joint session of both chambers on January 13

---

[66]Official returns by counties are given in the *Arkansas Gazette*, November 29, 1938.

[66a] Inclusion of provisions dealing with two or more topics in a single proposed amendment is open to objection. The constitution of Missouri, to forbid "doubleness" in proposed amendments, provides in Art. XV, Sec. 2. that, "No proposed amendment shall contain more than one amended and revised article of this Constitution or one new article which shall not contain more than one subject and matters properly connected therewith." Construed in *State ex rel. State Highway Commission v. Thompson*, 323 Mo. 742 and *Gabbert v. Chicago . . . Ry. Co.*, 171 Mo. 84.

[67]*Arkansas Gazette*, October 15, 1938.

to hear Speaker John M. Bransford formally announce results of the preceding general election witnessed a unique and weird spectacle. The speaker was in turn announcing the popular vote on successive initiated and referred measures, when, on reaching Amendment 29, he was interrupted by Senator W. H. Abington. The Senator moved that "the Secretary of State be directed not to certify the amendment as having been adopted." Objection was made that adoption of the amendment had already been certified by the secretary of state and that, in any event, such a motion was out of order at a joint session. Observing that the motion was "unusual," Lieutenant Governor Bob Bailey, presiding, held the motion to be in order. Senator Abington, in succession, offered motions that "the joint session refuse to declare the amendment adopted" and that "the Speaker be directed not to certify it as having been adopted." "Anything to get action," he declared.

During a brief recess, called for the purpose, a formal written motion was drafted for presentation to the joint session by Senators Abington and Hendrix Powell of Pine Bluff. The motion, duly offered, read, "I move that the speaker of the House of Representatives of the Fifty-Second General Assembly declare that Amendment 32,[68] proposed, to the constitution of the state of Arkansas, submitted to and voted on at the general election on November 8, 1938, failed of adoption because of the insufficiency of the title, and the misleading contents contained therein."[69] Amused and puzzled, the joint session adjourned without action on the Abington motion, preferring to ask the opinion of the attorney general before taking such novel action. Amendment 29 was duly certified as adopted by Speaker Bransford on January 12.

On January 19, Representative Chester Holland of Fort Smith introduced a bill, House Bill 177, that went even beyond the Abington motion in its implied assumption of legislative power. Its title read, "An Act to amend

---

[68] Amendment 29 was listed on the general election ballot as proposed Amendment 32.
[69] *Arkansas Gazette,* January 13, 1939.

Amendment 29 to the constitution of the state of Arkansas, adopted at the general election, November 8, 1938, by striking out Section 5 thereof in its entirety."[70] The bill, referred to the committee on constitutional amendments, was unfavorably reported. Asked for his opinion, Attorney General Jack Holt held that a constitutional amendment could not be repealed or amended by statute. The opinion stated, "This rule has been the corner stone of all constitutional governments in all jurisdictions where there are written constitutions."[71] In spite of an adverse committee report, in the teeth of the attorney general's opinion, notwithstanding torrents of ridicule, House Bill 177 was approved by the lower chamber on March 7 by vote of 57 to 27.[72] The measure never reached the floor of the senate.

It should be noted that the obviously correct opinion of the attorney general is repugnant to a narrowly literal interpretation of initiated Amendment 7, providing for the popular initiative and referendum. By an apparent slip in draftsmanship, Amendment 7 appears to endow the General Assembly with authority, by two-thirds vote of all members, to repeal or amend constitutional law.[73] The Holland Bill and the Abington motion were proposed and supported on a basis of this interpretation of Amendment 7.

On January 27, 1939, the senate unanimously approved a resolution offered by Senator Abington, directing the president of the upper chamber to appoint a five-man committee to investigate validity of initiative petitions filed in submitting Amendment 29 to popular vote. "It is currently reported," stated the author of the resolution, "that petitions on file in the Secretary of State's office, relative to constitutional amendment 32, have the appearance of being very irregular and that many names are repeated and

---

[70] *Journal of the House* (1939) p. 171.
[71] *Arkansas Gazette*, January 25, 1939.
[72] *Journal of the House* (1939) pp. 261-62.
[73] Amendment 7, defining the term *measure* to include "any . . . constitutional amendment," states, "No measure approved by a vote of the people shall be amended or repealed by the General Assembly . . . except . . . on roll call of two-thirds of all the members elected to each house . . ." *Pope's Digest* (1937) p. 179.

that many are in the same handwriting . . . There seems to be evidence of fraud."[75] No investigation was undertaken and, it appears, no committee appointed. This line of attack upon Amendment 29 proved abortive. It is probable that popular approval of an initiated measure bars subsequent question of sufficiency of petitions.

A more substantial basis of attack upon the double primary system was contained in House Bill 158, offered by Representative John Mitchum of Independence County on January 20. The measure proposed retention of the single primary and provided, in event no candidate for nomination polled a majority, that party conventions within appropriate geographical areas be convened to designate the winner of a plurality as the nominee of the party. The substance of this measure, apparently in keeping with Amendment 29, had previously been suggested in pages of the Fort Smith *Southwest American* and the Conway *Log Cabin Democrat*. The Mitchum Bill died on the house calendar.

A final assault on Amendment 29 was launched at the session of 1939 in the form of a proposed amendment to the constitution. Foreseeing this strategy, a writer in the *Arkansas Gazette* had predicted in 1938 that, "In 1940 there probably will be an attempt made to repeal the run-off primary law by means of another amendment."[76] Submitted by the General Assembly, the proposed amendment was listed on the ballot as Amendment 30 at the general election in 1940. It was defeated. Proposed Amendment 30 repealed Amendment 29, then reenacted certain of its provisions. Like Amendment 29, it prohibited special elections, authorized the governor to fill vacancies in most elective offices by appointment, and made the governor ineligible for appointment to such vacancies. Unlike Amendment 29, it abolished the double primary, revived committee nominations, and allowed interim appointees to succeed themselves in office. It would appear that proposed

---

[75]*Arkansas Gazette*, January 28, 1939. See *Journal of the Senate* (1939) p. 326.
[76]*Arkansas Gazette*, November 13, 1938.

Amendment 30 salvaged from Amendment 29 those features favorable to the professional office-holder and sabotaged those unfavorable to interests of that craft.

The concurrent resolution to submit proposed Amendment 30 was introduced in the house on February 21, 1939, by Ernest Maner of Garland County. The resolution received approval of the lower chamber on February 24 by vote of 66 to 18[77] and of the senate on March 8 by vote of 19 to 12.[78] Approved—unnecessarily—by Governor Bailey, the amendment was defeated by popular vote of 70,131 to 96,628.[79] Of the votes cast, fifty-eight per cent were against proposed Amendment 30. It is noteworthy that Amendment 29 was ratified in 1938 by a favorable majority of fifty-three per cent. As the double primary was a lively issue during the two-year period, debated in press, forum, and on the hustings, the difference between these majorities may indicate a strengthening during the biennium of public sentiment favorable to the double primary system. In the eleven "machine" counties proposed Amendment 30 was approved by a popular majority of fifty-nine per cent of votes cast in these counties.

No evidence of organized effort to win popular approval for proposed Amendment 30 appeared during the pre-election period, though rumors of an "organized campaign" by "professional politicians" were reported in the press.[80] Contributing in no small measure to defeat of the proposed amendment was the nomination in January, 1940, of Sam Jones as candidate for governor of Louisiana in that state's second primary after Governor Earl K. Long, incumbent and brother of Huey P. Long, had won a plurality in the preferential primary.

The General Assembly of 1939 faced the constitutional necessity of enacting enabling legislation to implement Amendment 29's provision for majority nominations. Sponsors of Amendment 29, to assure passage of effective en-

[77] *Journal of the House* (1939) pp. 924-25.
[78] *Journal of the Senate* (1939) pp. 1396-97.
[79] *Arkansas Gazette*, November 22, 1940.
[80] *Arkansas Gazette*, July 21, 1940.

abling legislation, had inserted a section in the amendment to make it, in effect, self-executing. The section states, "No person holding office contrary to this amendment shall be paid any compensation for his services. Any warrant . . . issued for such services shall be void." Governor Bailey in his inaugural to the General Assembly pointed out the urgency of enabling legislation and recommended passage of a double primary law. Two bills to this end were introduced: one in the senate by James H. Pilkinton, attorney of Hope and one-time teacher of political science, and one in the house by Boyd Tackett of Glenwood and Marshall Tabler of Ben Lowood, Sevier County.

Senator Pilkinton had prepared a bill providing for the run-off primary system by October 7, 1938, prior to ratification of Amendment 29. Introduced on the first day of the session, the Pilkinton Bill, Senate Bill 6, was passed on January 17 by vote of 23 to 11.[81] The measure met defeat in the house on February 3 by vote of 37 to 55.[82]

The Tackett Bill, destined to become Act 372 of 1939, was placed in the "hopper" of the house on January 17. The measure incorporated essential features of this state's present double primary system. It differed little from the Pilkinton Bill, chiefly in its provision for a period of two weeks instead of twenty days between the two primaries. The Tacket Bill was approved in the house late in the session, on March 7, by vote of 53 to 35 and in the senate on the next to the last day of the season, March 8, by vote of 25 to 7.[83] Senator Pilkinton, guiding the Tackett Bill through the senate, was forced to obtain a certified copy of the measure when the original was found missing.[84] Governor Bailey signed the bill on March 17.

It may be noted that the senate passed both the Tackett Bill, providing for the double primary, and the Manor Resolution, repealing the constitutional requirement for the double primary, on the same day—March 8. The Tackett

---
[81] *Journal of the Senate* (1939) p. 135.
[82] *Journal of the House* (1939) p. 457.
[83] *Journal of the Senate* (1939) pp. 1394-95.
[84] *Northwest Arkansas Times*, March 8, 1939.

Bill passed by vote of 25 to 7 and the Manor Resolution by 19 to 12. The two prevailing majorities, looking in opposite directions, may reveal a conflict between constitutional compulsion and the legislative will!

Act 372 of 1939 was not to be in effect after the "primary of 1940." A temporary law was warranted, as popular approval of proposed Amendment 30 in November, 1940, would remove the constitutional mandate requiring majority nominations. The statute fixed the date for the second primary on the second Tuesday following the "general primary election," that is, on the fourth Tuesday in August. By delaying nominations until late in August this provision later gave rise to fear that insufficient time remained before general elections to allow for determination of contested nominations. Act 372, following the precedent and even the phraseology of Act 38 of 1933, provided that when "more than one candidate is to be nominated for the same office in the second primary election a clear majority is not necessary but that nomination will be made by plurality vote." This provision, clearly repugnant to the constitutional requirement of majority nominations, was included to avoid the mathematical difficulties involved when each of several candidates for similar offices must poll a majority of the ballots for nominations to such offices. The provision stems from the conviction, voiced by Senator Pilkinton, that "I do not believe the constitution requires us to do the impossible." Though in a measure sanctioned by "impossibility of performance," this authorization of plurality nominations can not be squared with Section 5 of Amendment 29. The difficulty was later solved by rule of the Democratic state committee, suggested by June P. Wooten, chairman of the committee's sub-committee on rules. The rule requires an aspirant for nomination to one of two or more similar offices to file for a particular one of such offices. The substance of this party rule is now incorporated in the double primary law of the state.

The most notable feature of Act 372 required that uncontested nominations and nominations with only two contestants be made at the second primary. This provision, favored and anticipated in 1937[85] by sponsors of Amendment 29, was designed chiefly to lessen opportunity for interference in the second race by winners or losers in the preferential race and to counteract lack of voter-interest and non-voting in the run-off primary. Passed with the emergency clause, Act 372 became effective when signed by the governor on March 17. Enactment of the measure late in the session created confusion in cities of the first class, since municipal primaries in these cities are held annually, usually in February. Faced with the constitutional requirement for majority nominations, many first class cities held their initial double primary in 1939 without sanction of enablng legislation.

Expiration of Act 372 in August, 1940, forced the 1941 session of the General Assembly to reenact enabling legislation. The legislature could give no ear to a petition praying for repeal of the double primary law contained in a resolution adopted by candidates for Democratic nominations in Baxter County in April, 1940.[86] A bill introduced in the senate on February 5 by Senator Pilkinton was approved by vote of 28 to 1[87] on February 11 and in the house by 64 to 11 on February 18. Signed by Governor Homer M. Adkins on February 25, the bill became Act 90 of 1941.

Like its predecessor, Act 90 was limited to an effectiveness of two years. This provision was added to the Pilkinton Bill by amendment approved in the upper chamber. Offered by Senator W. L. Ward of Marianna, adoption of the amendment was vigorously opposed by the bill's author.[88] Act 90 changed the dates for the primaries, providing, as does current legislation, that the preferential be held on the last Tuesday in July and the run-off two weeks later. Incorporating the substance of the current party rule, the act provides, "Where there are two or more

---
[85] From files donated by Abe Collins to the University of Arkansas.
[86] *Arkansas Gazette*, April 25, 1940.
[87] The single negative vote was cast by W. H. Abington.
[88] *Journal of the Senate* (1941) p. 358.

nominees to be selected for the same office . . . the proper committee (of the political party) shall require the candidates to designate in writing a particular position, *i. e.*, Position No. 1, 2, 3, etc., at the time a party pledge is required to be filed . . . When a candidate has once filed and designated for a certain position he shall not be permitted to thereafter change such position."

Act 90 of 1941 expired on December 31, 1942, and enactment of another enabling statute was necessary during the session of the General Assembly in 1943. This necessity was apparently overlooked until late in the session. On March 4, Representative Henry H. Pickering of Hamburg, who may claim credit for noting the legislative oversight, introduced a bill to continue the double primary system. His bill, by its terms to remain in effect indefinitely, was otherwise an almost word-for-word duplication of Act 90 of 1941. The Pickering Bill, House Bill 498, approved in the house on March 5 by vote of 75 to 0,[89] received rough treatment in the upper chamber. On the last day of the session, by vote of 10 to 15, the senate killed the measure. Senator L. L. Mitchell of Prescott immediately moved for reconsideration. This non-debatable motion was debated for almost a half hour. Senator W. L. Ward of Lee County, noting that the morning hour had expired, claimed that the bill was dead. He was duly sustained by the president of the senate. A second motion to reconsider, offered by Senator Mitchell, was ruled in order. On a second roll call the bill was duly, if somewhat irregularly, passed by vote of 21 to 9, five minutes before the senate adjourned *sine die*.[90] Signed by the governor on March 15, the statute is listed as Act 238 of 1943.

At a night session of the senate on March 9, Senate Bill 420, by W. L. Ward, to abolish the run-off primary system and restore a single primary was killed by vote of 10 to 15.[91]

---

[89] *Arkansas Gazette*, March 6, 1943.
[90] *Arkansas Gazette*, March 12, 1943.
[91] *Arkansas Gazette*, March 10, 1943.

The double primary system in Arkansas has had a checkered and stormy history. Opposition to the system is outspoken and lacks neither leadership nor strength. This writer ventures to predict, however, that this opposition will grow weaker; that the principle of majority nominations will become more secure.

Political parties in Arkansas in the state, district, county, or city may nominate candidates either by party primary or by party convention. Optional use of the primary, authorized in 1895, was retained by authors of Amendment 29 to accommodate the Republican Party. Expense of a primary is unwarranted by the limited voting strength of the minority party. Optional use of the primary was retained also to allow Democratic nominations to be made by convention to fill vacancies in nominations and to select candidates to run in special elections. Direct nominations in these circumstances would not be feasible in all cases.

Should a political party choose to nominate its candidates by primary such nominations, by provision of Amendment 29, must be made by majority vote. The wisdom of incorporating the mandate of majority nominations in the state's fundamental law, beyond reach of the General Assembly, is questionable. Objection stems from the likelihood that Arkansas may not remain a one-party state, as some authors of Amendment 29 tacitly assumed. Some profess to see national trends toward an alignment that may divide the electorate along political lines definitely liberal and conservative. Shoud this trend, or current frictions within ranks of the majority party in the southern states, usher in a two-party system in Arkansas, the constitutional requirement of majority nominations would invoke criticism. Meanwhile, the Republican Party, or any minority, is forced by Amendment 29 to select nominees either at party convention or to incur expense of two primaries.

The principle of majority rule, on the other hand, is a bed-rock ingredient of democratic political philosophy. The principle, in one-party states, is ample support for the view that constitutional law should sanction majority nominations. The General Assembly may not amend the requirement of nomination by majority vote; in enabling acts it may exercise broad discretion in giving form and effect to the constitutional mandate.

In states using the double primary system, a loser, eliminated in the preferential for a particular nomination, can be instrumental in determining the nomination made in the run-off. Nominations to different offices are made at different times. This circumstance also enables the winner, assured of nomination (and election) in the preferential primary for a particular office, to influence nominations to other offices decided in the run-off. Impact of the above criticism is lessened in Arkansas by the statutory provision that only nominations sought by three or more aspirants be contested in the preferential primary. This feature reduces the number of contests decided in the first primary and reduces the number of aspirants eliminated and the number of assured winners.

When a winner of a plurality or a runner-up in the first primary withdraws prior to the second race, the ballot in the run-off includes only the name of the single remaining aspirant. Having no opponent, this candidate polls all votes cast in the second primary. In other states, for example, in Mississippi, withdrawal of either of the two leading candidates adds the name of the candidate running third in the preferential to the run-off primary ballot. A candidate for the Democratic nomination in Mississippi is unopposed in the run-off only in event *all* of his opponents withdraw. Amendment 29 requires majority nominations in direct primaries. The current enabling statute, Act 238 of 1943, on the other hand, expressly states that "the names of *the two* candidates who received the highest number of votes for an office, or position, shall be printed upon the ballots at the general (run-off) primary election." This provision denies a place on the second primary ballot to the candidate running third in the first primary even when the winner or the runner-up or the winner and the runner-up withdraw. The unanimous vote of a single candidate without opposition in the second primary does not represent any popular choice. A valid majority may not be claimed when, by law, opponents are denied a place on the ballot. Compliance with Act 238 is repugnant to implication of Amendment 29.

A candidate polling a plurality in the preferential primary rarely withdraws.[92] A runner-up, numerical odds against him, frequently concedes defeat, assuring nomination of his opponent.[93] The expediency of withdrawal is augmented when other aspirants, eliminated in the first primary, endorse nomination of the leading candidate. A withdrawal under such circumstances may be negotiated in return for a *quid pro quo*. Were it true, as in Mississippi, that the runner-up's withdrawal placed the third-highest candidate in the run-off contest, less basis would exist for such a bargain or for suspicion and accusation, too often heard, that the runner-up's withdrawal was so predicated.

Act 238 of 1943 states that "where . . . candidates for any office . . . equal[s] twice the number of offices . . . to be filled, the names of such candidates shall be omitted from the ballot at the preferential primary . . . and placed only on the ballots of the general primary . . . ." Two candidates for a nomination, eager "to get the race over," are compelled by this provision to wait until the second primary.[94] By enlisting a "dummy" candidate, making the race a three-sided contest, the nomination may be advanced extra-legally to the first primary. A "dummy" may even withdraw after ballots are printed and before the preferential. *Bona fide* candidates, by this means, may "get the race over" at cost of a ballot fee.

A municipal preferential primary is unnecessary when no nominations to local office is sought by more than two candidates. This occurs frequently. Should a single nomination to municipal office be sought by three can-

---

[92]This did occur in 1944. A candidate for nomination as treasurer of Izard County withdrew after winning a plurality in a three-sided contest in the preferential on July 25. *Arkansas Gazette*, August 2, 1944.
[93]Newspapers in July, 1944, reported six instances.
[94]*Arkansas Gazette*, May 2, 1944.

didates, however, a preferential primary must be held at added expense to all candidates for all nominations. Under such circumstances, an accommodating city committee may list all candidates for all nominations on the preferential primary ballot and refund a large part of the ballot fees should one of the contestants in the three-sided race win a clear majority in the first primary. This procedure, followed in one known instance, does not conflict with intent of Amendment 29; it does no violence to the enabling statute.

The run-off municipal primary may be unnecessary. This may occur when all nominations are contested by three or more candidates and when, in each case, one of the three polls a majority in the preferential. Rules of the Democratic Party require election of city committeemen at the "second city general primary election."[95] Should the run-off be unnecessary, a circumstance unpredictable prior to canvass of the preferential ballots, city committeemen would be required by party rules to conduct a city-wide vote for the sole purpose of electing their successors.

State-wide primaries in Arkansas are held on the last Tuesday in July and the second Tuesday in August, after adjournment of the national Democratic convention. Unless primary dates are advanced from late-summer to late-spring, it is impractical to elect delegates to national Democratic conventions.[96] Effective use of a presidential preference primary is also impossible.[97] Spring primaries, once held in Arkansas, are objectionable for two reasons: first, incumbent federal, state, district, and county elected officers with two-year terms beginning in January are forced, if primaries are held in May, to campaign for renomination at least seven months prior to expiration of their terms; second, if not renominated, they serve as "lame ducks" during almost one-third of their terms. During this inter-

---

[95] *Rules of the Democratic Party in Arkansas* (as amended February 9, 1940), Democratic State Committee, January 15, 1937, Sec. 23.
[96] Delegates and alternates from Arkansas to national Democratic conventions are chosen now in May of presidential years by the state Democratic committee.
[97] Presidential preference primaries are now authorized by law in fourteen states. T. W. Cousens, *Politics and Political Organizations in America* (1942) p. 374. Act 103 of 1939, providing for a presidential preference primary in Arkansas, is nullified by factors that render its operation impractical.

val, particularly with respect to a "lame duck" governor, the nominee falls heir to some of the cares and duties of the office without inheriting any part of the compensation.

If no nomination is sought by more than two aspirants, the preferential primary is not held. For this reason, party officers, including delegates to national conventions, must be chosen at the second state-wide primary. The state's double primary system, if delegates to national conventions are to be popularly elected, magnifies by two weeks the objections to spring primaries.[98]

The interval between the two primaries in Arkansas is two weeks. South Carolina is the only state having a shorter intervening period. A short interval is convenient to candidates. It also hastens the official canvass and certification of returns in counties where intentional delay by officials of the local party organization is alleged. The intervening period could hardly be reduced, since, with existing facilities for communication, it would be difficult in a shorter period to canvass returns in the preferential, certify local winners to the state committee, receive the state committee's certification of names to be listed on the second primary ballot, and have these ballots printed. A brief interval has faults, intensified in Arkansas by the greater significance of the second primary. Absentee ballots are difficult to cast in the second primary.[99] A perplexing question is posed if the count in the preferential is challenged. The brief interval deprives an aspirant for nomination of opportunity to contest official returns.

Rules of the Democratic Party forbid writing-in of names on ballots used in primaries.[100] The validity of this rule was impeached by a decision of the state supreme court in 1941. The court held that Sections 4748, 4755, and

---

[98] To lessen this obstacle, spring primaries might be held in presidential years; late-summer primaries, in off-years.
[99] Absentee ballots for the second primary were available in Pulaski County on the fourth day after the first primary, held on July 25, 1944. In other counties absentee ballots can be available five days prior to the second primary if party machinery operates with maximum efficiency. About 2,000 absentee ballots are cast normally in a state-wide primary. In the primaries of 1944, about 17,000 were cast in the preferential; 10,754, in the run-off.
[100] *Rules of the Democratic Party in Arkansas* (as amended February 9, 1940), Democratic State Committee, January 15, 1937, Sec. 56.

4757 of *Pope's Digest* granted voters the privilege of adding names to primary ballots.[101] The particular question at issue in the case related to the election of an officer of the Democratic Party, but language of the opinion is broadly applicable to nominations to public office. It held that the statutes cited "give the voter the right to write on the ballot the name of one for whom he might wish to vote in a primary election, as well as in a general election." The attorney general has ruled that the decision applies to nominations to public office.[102] A sufficient number of write-in votes cast for the same or different candidates in a run-off could deprive the leading candidate of a majority. Improbable in large voting districts, this contingency is not unlikely within small areas. In this event, the constitutional requirement of majority nominations denies nomination to any candidate and creates a vacancy in the nomination. Paradoxically, the name of a candidate for nomination running third-highest in the preferential may not be *printed* on the ballot—even if the winner of a plurality and/or the runner-up in the preferential withdraw. The name could be *written-in* on the run-off ballot.

Duplicate ballots are used in both primaries. The sealed ballot box containing duplicates must be kept for a period of five months. The double primary, therefore, necessitated purchase and storage of a complete set of ballot boxes for each of the 2,087 precincts in the state, since boxes for duplicate ballots used in the first primary may not be used for the second. Statutes prior to 1941 required that duplicate boxes be kept for two years. The period was shortened in the year mentioned by the General Assembly when purchase of additional sets of boxes proved costly and the cumulative burden of storage more than taxes the cubic capacity of court houses. Appropriately, no doubt, the amending act bore the emergency clause![103]

---
[101] *Wilburn v. Moon*, 202 Ark. 899.
[102] *Arkansas Election Laws* (1944) p. 11.
[103] Act 36 of 1941.

A candidate is often nominated without opposition. Formal compliance with Amendment 29 demands that unopposed candidates be listed on ballots in the second primary. An unopposed candidate is not entitled to a certification of nomination on grounds that his candidacy is unopposed.[104] This circumstance is transferred from the area of academic interest into that of practical moment by the element of ballot fees. The unopposed candidate is assessed a *pro rata* share of the expense of both primaries.

A popular candidate seeking nomination to one of a class of similar offices is more likely to be unopposed in Arkansas than in other states. To give a required majority to one of several candidates for each nomination to a class of similar offices, it was inevitable that added advantage be bestowed upon candidates with initial advantage of strong popular support. Party rule and state statute require that positions of a class be numbered and that candidates file for nomination to a particular position. Popular candidates escape, weak candidates attract opposition. The last candidate to file may choose his opponents. Competition for this advantage, taking the convenient form of delay, has resulted in a "ticket" closed and completed almost simultaneously.

Neither party rule nor law adequately covers the area of uncertainty created by a tie vote in the first or second primary.[105] A tie is more probable in the double than in the single primary system and existing uncertainty invites awkward question and litigation.

The increased cost of the dual primary system has led to revival of interest in urban use of voting machines. A statute authorizing their use in primaries and in elections[106] is nullified by the constituional provision requiring numbered ballots and by statutes requiring duplicate ballots. No vocal advocacy exists at present in Arkansas for either the

[104]This practice, however, is followed at times by city Democratic committees. See *Arkansas Gazette*, February 18, 1942.
[105]*Arkansas Gazette*, February 27, 1939.
[106]Act 136 of 1927.

non-partisan primary or proportional representation.[107] The former would substitute a dual election for a dual primary.[108] Nominations, both in the non-partisan primary and in proportional representation are made by petition. As this means of nomination is expressly authorized in Amendment 29, the amendment places no obstacle in the way of adopting either of these electoral devices. The amendment does forbid adoption of preferential voting in primaries, since nomination by majority is not assured by this system of voting.

The order of names on primary ballots used in any one county for a particular nomination is determined by lot at a public meeting of the local Democratic committee.[109] This order would be similar on all ballots for nomination of township, municipal, and county officers, but different in different counties for nomination of district, state, and federal officers. The county or city Democratic committee conducts one or two drawings. It is customary to conduct a single drawing and retain the same order of names in the second as in the first primary, omitting names of aspirants eliminated in the preferential. Local party committees, likewise, may select one or two groups of election officials to act as judges, clerks, and guards at the two primaries.[110] It is customary for the same officials and their alternates to serve at both primaries.

Pledges, party and corrupt practice, and ballot fees must be filed or paid by a fixed date preceding the preferential primary. A single pledge and a single fee suffice for both contests. By a specified date following primaries all candidates, whether nominated or eliminated, are required

---

[107] P. R., currently in operation in seven American cities, has been used widely in cities in the British Empire and Commonwealths and, at different times, in a dozen American municipalities.
A provision of Amendment 8 in the Arkansas constitution may bar statutory adopton or authorization of P. R. in cities of this state. A brief commentary on the use, operation, and legality of P. R. may be found in Austin F. Macdonald, *American City Government and Administration* (1941) Chap. 18.

[108] Used extensively in nominations to municipal and judicial offices and, in Minnesota and Nebraska, to nominate candidates for the state legislature. A brief appraisal of non-partisan nominations is contained in T. W. Cousens, *Politics and Political Organizations in America* (1942) pp. 362-63.

[109] *Pope's Digest*, Sec. 4725.

[110] According to opinion of the attorney general. *Arkansas Gazette*, August 10, 1940.

to file a statement of campaign expenses. Informal opinions of the attorney general hold that candidates nominated or eliminated in the first primary must file this statement by the end of a thirty-day period from date of the first primary. Candidates taking part in both primaries and those listed only in the run-off may file statements of expenses thirty days after the second primary.[111]

Corrupt practice laws in Arkansas impose narrow and rigid limits upon campaign expenditures. Applying expressly to primaries and to candidates for nomination to "state, district, county, township, city, or town" office, the act makes it unlawful to "expend or cause to be expended" amounts equal, with some exceptions, to one year's salary. Candidates for nomination as governor may spend no more than $5,000. The legal maximum in this case is at most one-tenth of the necessary and legitimate cost of a statewide gubernatorial campaign. Existing limits, long obsolete and impractical, were made more obsolete and more impractical by adoption of the double primary system. The greater cost of two primaries makes compliance more improbable in case of serious candidates for nomination to higher offices. Similarly, federal statutes regulating campaign financing by candidates for nomination to the Congress impose a greater limitation in states using the dual primary than in one-party states employing the single primary.

Preceding pages relate the history of adoption of the double primary in Arkansas and describe features of the system. Following pages appraise merits and demerits.

It is difficult to make a case for the double primary outside of one-party states. Elections in Arkansas, except for presidential electors, have trivial significance. Except in a few northwestern counties, elections are saved from being mere formalities by the fact that voters then pass on initiated and referred measures. Elections in an uncertain number of rural precincts are not held. No complaint

---

[111] *Arkansas Gazette*, September 14, 1940, and August 29, 1942.

follows this economy."² The dominance of one party waters down the importance of elections; it magnifies the significance of nominations.

Operation of the dual primary in Utah, only two-party state using the system, has been unsatisfactory, "responsible for complaint from professional politicians and reformers alike." Adopted in 1937, sponsors of the system in that state "felt that nomination by a plurality after a single primary would permit the minority will of the party to prevail."¹ So unpopular is the system in Utah that the principle of direct nominations has been brought under attack.

The validity of majorities given successful candidates for nomination by the double primary system has been challenged. With the fourth, fifth, and sixth ranking candidates eliminated in the first race, may one assume that a majority prefers the leading candidate or the runner-up to the third highest? May one assume, under such circumstances, that a majority prefers to have the runner-up and not the third-highest in the run-off? Assumptions here challenged are two: that strong candidates will survive the preferential and weak candidates be eliminated. Adequately grounded upon face of the returns, these assumptions gain added support from traditional reluctance of the voter to "throw away his vote." In view of this reluctance, the voter tends to cast his ballot for one of the strong candidates, making his choice from strong rather than from all candidates. The strong candidate wins an "unearned increment"; the weak, by this erosion, loses even the votes of personal friends.

Basic support for the double primary in the South stems from the dominance of a single party. This characteristic of southern politics has been used to attack utility of the dual primary system. Substance of this attack is the view that the primary ballot offers the voter no real issue other than a personal choice from among "good Demo-

---
[112] A circumstance pertinent to a consideration of non-voting in general elections.
[113] O. Meredith Wilson to the writer, August 8, 1944.

crats." No real significance, it is contended, should be attached to the fact that one candidate in a large field polls a few more votes than another."[114] This line of attack ignores existence of factions within the dominant party, divisions which reflect real issues at least as clearly as do party alignments in some two-party states.

Non-voting in southern states, even in primaries, is greater than elsewhere when measured in terms of total population. This characteristic of southern politics is used by critics of the double primary to belittle the difference between pluralities and majorities. Neither, they charge, represents popular opinion, since the electorate is too small in proportion to population. Non-voting, however, magnifies the difference between pluralities and majorities. Where nominees are chosen by relatively few voters, it is significant that they be the choice of majorities.

Although the number of votes cast is small in states of the South, the number of candidates aspiring to public office is large. Democratic candidates, at least for higher offices, are approximately as numerous in the South as Democratic plus Republican candidates in other states. The dual primary in one-party states places the party nominee "on all-fours" with the officer-elect in two-party states.

Objection to the double primary is most vocal when an aspirant wins a plurality in the preferential and is defeated by the runner-up in the run-off. This rarely happens. Of forty-eight nominations at stake in both primaries, the winner of a plurality in the first primary in Arkansas in 1944 won the nomination in the run-off in thirty-five cases.[115] The runner-up was nominated in thirteen cases. A similar study, based on returns in other states, shows that of 170 second primary contests, the winner of a plurality in the first primary was nominated in the second primary in 129 cases and lost to the runner-up in forty-one cases.[116] In all known

---
[114]C. E. Merriam, *The American Party System* (1922) p. 268.
[115]From daily and weekly newspapers and letters, this tabulation includes nominations to all federal, state, district, and most county offices. Ignored are nominations for county coroner, county surveyor, and all township offices.
[116]Joe Park, "That Elusive Majority," *National Municipal Review*, October, 1940, pp. 675-78.

instances the ranking of the two winners in the first primary was reversed in the second primary in twenty-five per cent of the nominations. Were the runner-up never nominated in the run-off, there would be no justification whatever for the dual primary system.

The majority won in the run-off by the runner-up in the preferential, say critics, is the creation of nothing more substantial than traditional "sympathy for the under-dog." No doubt true in isolated instances, this sympathy is a valid component of public opinion. When it finds expression in election returns no more vital component is suppressed. Only in absence of any real issue will a dilute "sympathy for the under-dog" determine marks on the voter's ballot.

When nomination is made by plurality, a candidate may split his opponent's support by inducing a "dummy" candidate to enter the race. The requirement of majority nominations cuts the ground from under this campaign strategy. A "stalking horse" is of limited utility when opposition will be consolidated in the run-off contest. By entering a "dummy," an aspirant with a single *bona fide* opponent may hope to advance his nomination by two weeks. Nomination in the preferential may be sought to influence other contests carried over to the run-off, to capitalize on non-voting—greater in the first than in the second primary —or merely to minimize ill effects of uncertainty on blood pressure and digestion. Non-voting in the preferential, caused in some counties by absence of local contests from the first race, may be a significant factor in campaign strategy when an aspirant for nomination to federal, state, or district office regards these as his "weak" counties. A "stalking horse" may serve, finally, as a convenient mouthpiece; any kind of "mud" may be hurled without soiling the fingers.

Nomination by plurality gives too great advantage to the candidate with an initial bloc of support. The incumbent has such an advantage, as does the candidate with support of the "federal crowd" or of the "state crowd" or of local political leaders in "machine" counties. The requirement of a majority dilutes this advantage.

The requirement of majority nomination dissolves any advantage possessed by a candidate whose single-plank platform appeals exclusively to interests of a particular class or economic group. Support for such an aspirant for nomination may reach proportions of a plurality, if the number of candidates is large; it can rarely attain proportions of a majority. To enlist a majority, a candidate's appeal must be broad, so broad, perhaps, as to lack depth! His pledge must be to the "people"; he must represent "no particular group, no particular clan, no particular plan." The voters' choice in one-party states is restricted to the majority party; it is restricted even more by the essential similarity of appeals made by rivals who are necessarily "all things to all people." This characteristic of the double primary system will be regarded by some as a valuable bar to subversive "isms," a contribution to stability and continuity. Others will regard it as an obstacle to adoption of novel programs, a brake on progressive experimentation.[117]

The double primary system increases a candidate's legitimate campaign expenses. A short purse sometimes may purchase a plurality; only a long purse can afford a majority. The dual primary adds to the advantage of wealthy candidates with well-to-do backers. It may be, too, that less wealthy aspirants are forced to seek moneyed backers. Obligations assumed by candidates and borne by office-holders may add to influence of "money interests." This line of thought bolsters the view, set out in the preceding paragraph, that the dual primary puts a brake on progressive experimentation.

Adoption of the run-off primary system in Arkansas may have strengthened roots of the spoils system in state government—a strength evidenced by the short shrift accorded the Civil Service Act of 1937.[118] The incumbent of high office, chosen by a majority, may owe a heavier

---

[117] Radical parties in other countries using a double election system have fared badly at the polls. A. N. Holcombe, "Direct Primaries and the Second Ballot," *American Political Science Review*, November, 1911, pp. 535-52.

[118] Repealed in 1939 by vote of 64 to 28 in the lower chamber and 22 to 12 in the senate. *Arkansas Gazette*, January 19, 1939.

political debt to supporters than an officer chosen by a plurality. This obligation will be broad as well as heavy, suggesting that the double primary system may broaden the area of patronage.

It is probable that adoption of the double primary in Arkansas weakened the position of local leaders in "machine" counties, curbing their influence in state government and undermining their control in county and municipal governments. The bloc of votes so controlled in the state, estimated at approximately 24,000, usually goes to any candidate for federal, district, or state office thought most likely to win, often a candidate backed by federal or state office-holders. The advantage thus given an already favored candidate, formidable in any event, is less likely to create majorities than pluralities. A contrary opinion, that local "bosses" are benefited by the dual primary, is held in some quarters. Contending that non-voting, greater when the voter makes two trips to the polls, is more extensive in rural than in urban areas, this opinion rests on the fact that the controlled vote in "machine" counties is dominantly an urban vote. Opposition to the double primary, in the General Assembly and at the polls, is greatest in "machine" counties. Intensity and persistence of this hostility indicate strongly that the double primary system has tended in greater measure to undermine than to bolster the position of local "bosses." The writer feels that this end has been served as much by substitution of the dual for the single primary as by substitution of direct primaries for the earlier delegate-convention.

Two primaries place a burden on both candidate and voter.

Candidates complain of higher costs. Aspirants for nomination in Arkansas, in addition to expense of soliciting votes, bear the whole cost of conducting the primaries. The latter is paid in the form of ballot fees at the time of filing party pledges. The professional office-holder, in warrant of his complaint, points to small compensation paid many public officers[119] and to prevailing two-year terms. The amount of the ballot fee, fixed by party rule, is substantial: candidates for nomination to the United States senate, $225; for state office, $112.50; for congressman, $10.00 for each county in the congressional district. As above figures have remained unchanged for at least ten years,[120] it appears that the incidence of added cost to the party has fallen upon candidates for district and local offices. Their ballot fees, determined at each state-wide or municipal primary by county or city committees, vary according to the compensation of the office and the estimated number of candidates. Aspirants for district office pay a fee in each county, not over $20.00,[121] determined by county committees in the district.[122] Ballot fees paid by candidates to district and local offices appear to be substantially higher since adoption of the double primary system. The added cost may be indicated by an increase of $25.00 assessed candidates for nomination to nearly all county offices in Lonoke County in 1940.[123]

The added cost of the double primary is shared to some extent by all candidates for nomination to all offices, since a single fee is assessed all aspirants to cover costs of the two primaries whether their names are listed on the ballot in both races or in one. Amendment 29 abolished most special elections and lessened the number of special primaries. Some county committees, which prior to 1938 assessed ballot fees large enough to defray cost of special primaries, may now be able to reduce fees by amounts approaching the added cost of dual primaries.[124] In many counties prior to 1938, party committees assessed ballot

---
[119]Salaries paid in some of the twenty counties operating under locally initiated salary acts are quite small. Democratic nominations to the 124 local offices in these twenty counties were sought in 1944 by only 181 candidates.
[120]J. S. Waterman, *Reference Manual on the Public Law of Arkansas*, January 1, 1935, p. 8.
[121]This limitation, added to party rules in 1942, was adopted to curb excessive assessments, amounting at times to $75.00. *Arkansas Gazette*, January 25, 1942.
[122]Candidates for nomination to municipal offices in Little Rock in recent years have paid ballot fees of: $300.00, mayor, clerk, city attorney; and $60.00, aldermen. These fees were increased in 1944 to $400.00 and $80.00. Candidates for mayor of Fayetteville in 1939 paid $25.00; aldermen, $5.00.
[123]*Arkansas Gazette*, March 23, 1940.
[124]*Arkansas Gazette*, December 16, 1938.

fees to yield an excess. From this surplus a contribution was made to national campaign funds. In such counties it is not unlikely that smaller contributions to the national Democratic committee measure added expense imposed by the run-off primary system.[125]

The unopposed or strong candidate for the Democratic nomination needs to incur little or no campaign expense other than payment of ballot fee. Candidates facing real opposition are less fortunate. In 1940, on a basis of meager information in formal reports of campaign expenses, twenty-three candidates for nomination to eight state offices spent $44,481.[126] The eight offices in question paid an aggregate annual salary of $35,000. Five candidates for the Democratic nomination to the United States senate in 1944 reported their expenditures in sworn statements to a committee of the national senate as totaling over $302,700.[127]

The double primary increases campaign expenses and complicates the vexing problem faced by would-be candidates seeking to determine in advance the expense they incur by entering the race. Such estimate is difficult as either one or two primary contests are possible. No serious candidate is likely to file for nomination to high office until funds thought essential for a successful campaign are in sight. The dual primary may lessen the number of candidates for public office, both by reason of greater expense and by the greater uncertainty of anticipating the total of such expense.[128] This is a valid objection to the dual primary only if desirable candidates are kept from filing. Nothing is lost by elimination of perennial and "top water" contestants.

The claptrap, sham, and vituperation, characteristic of primary contests, is prolonged and intensified by the run-off primary system. H. G. Wells said, "I would as soon go

---
[125]In one instance, in a county where Republican strength lessens significance of Democratic nominations to local offices, the county Democratic committee, reluctant to assess large fees, asked unopposed candidates for nomination to state offices for contributions. The requests were granted. *Arkansas Gazette*, September 10, 1940.
[126]*Arkansas Gazette*, October 6, 1940.
[127]*Arkansas Gazette*, October 22, 1944.
[128]*Arkansas Gazette*, June 16, 1940.

live in a pen in a stockyard as into American politics." The bitterness of primary battles in southern states reduces the number of candidates for nomination and creates a nation-wide and detrimental publicity. Candidates, on the other hand, are forced to "put their cards on the table." Whispering campaigns and "roorbacks" may be launched at any time, but contestants in the preferential cannot often refrain from using political "block-busters" to hoard ammunition for battle in the run-off.

The run-off primary system adds to likelihood of corrupt practices, vote frauds, and contested returns. The weight of this objection is reduced to some extent by decisions of the United States supreme court since May, 1941, which open the way to a greater measure of federal regulation of primary contests. Candidates conduct their campaigns and election officials perform their duties under eyes of federal officials.

Adoption of the dual primary system forces the voter to make two trips to the polls. This inconvenience contributes to non-voting. However, the voter has a shorter ballot to mark. Fewer nominations are at stake in either the preferential or the run-off primary in Arkansas than there would be in a single primary. The difficulty of voting intelligently for a single nomination in the run-off is reduced to a minimum as no nomination is contested by more than two candidates.

The inconvenience of making two trips to the polls is aggravated in rural areas by distance; in cities, by separate municipal elections. Municipal elections in cities of the first class, moreover, are held annually. Texas and Tennessee, fearing removal by the Congress of the poll tax as a prerequisite for voting in national elections, have already made provision for separate state and national elections. The double primary plus separate national, state, and municipal elections add up to an intolerable inconvenience to the voter.

As nominations to different offices are at stake in Arkansas at different times, public interest in contests for nomination is spread thin. Non-voting in this state is greater in the preferential than in the run-off. In the 1942 primaries 48,704 more votes were cast in the second than in the first primary. This figure in 1944 was 16,887.[129] The small number of nominations for county offices at stake in the first primary is chiefly responsible. No nomination to county office was at stake at the first primary in 1940 in nineteen counties. In fourteen other counties nomination to a single county office was contested in the preferential.[130] In 1942 there were eight counties and in 1944 there were ten counties in which single candidates for nomination to all county offices were unopposed. In these counties there were no local races in either the preferential or the run-off. In twenty-three additional counties in 1942 and in twenty-nine in 1944 no nomination to county office was contested in the preferential. A single nomination to county office was at stake in the preferential in nineteen counties in 1942[131] and in twelve in 1944.

Non-voting in primaries throughout the state is increased when nominations to high offices in national and state governments are not contested. United States senatorial races are absent normally from primaries once in six years. Should an initiated amendment to the state constitution to be voted on in November, 1944, be approved, gubernatorial races will be at four-year instead of two-year intervals. Popular interest in state-wide primaries, in this event, will be lowest and non-voting highest in primaries with neither senatorial nor gubernatorial contests.

A review of inconvenience and expense inherent in the double primary system raises a question of "game and candle." Does compliance with the principle of majority nomination warrant the inconvenience and expense of two primaries? The dual primary system can have no effect on nominations sought by less than two aspirants. The

---

[129]In Alabama, non-voting appears greater in the second than in the first primary. Chas. W. Smith, *The Electorate in An Alabama Community*, Bureau of Public Administration, 1942.
[130]*Arkansas Gazette*, July 21 and 23, 1940. Members of the lower house of the General Assembly are regarded in this study as *state* officers.
[131]*Arkansas Gazette*, June 14, 1942.

system rarely affects nominations sought by more than two aspirants. Of a total of 594 nominations to federal, state, district, and county offices at stake in the state-wide Democratic primaries of 1944, the nominee was unopposed in 332 cases, was opposed by a single candidate in 167 cases. Nomination by plurality was nomination by majority in eighty-four per cent of the nominations at stake. Further, in nominations sought by three or more candidates, ninety-five in all, the nominee won a clear majority in the preferential in forty instances, and in thirty-five instances, the winner of a plurality in the preferential also polled a majority in the run-off. In six instances the runner-up in the preferential withdrew from the race prior to the run-off and, in a single instance, the winner of a plurality in the preferential withdrew. Thus, in 581 out of 594 nominations, the double primary system in no way affected outcome of the balloting."[12] Justification and support for the double primary system must be found in the thirteen nominations where winners polling a plurality in the preferential were losers in the run-off. Tables on the next page present a detailed analysis of the recent primaries.

The issue of negro voting in Democratic primaries will be sharpened as a larger number of Negroes qualify by payment of poll taxes. The possibility exists, too, that congressional action or constitutional amendment may remove the poll tax as a voting prerequisite.

In some of the southern states *de facto* disfranchisement of the Negro has favored counties dominated by the conservative "planter class" where negro population is usually greatest. The advantage enjoyed by these counties and by this economic class stems from their representation in state legislatures on an all-inclusive population basis. White voters in so-called "black belts" in these states, as a consequence, have been relatively over-represented in state legislatures. These voters in Georgia are given disproportionate voice in Democratic nominations by the "unit

---

[12] Nominations for county coroner, county surveyor, and all township officers are ignored.

TABLE 1. Democratic Nominations to All Federal, State, District, and to Most County Offices in the 1944 Primaries According to the Number of Candidates.[1]

	Fed.		State					County						
	Cong.		Ex. Legis.		Jud.									
	S	H	S	H	Jdgs.	P.A.'s	Jdge.	Cir. Cl.	Co. Cl.	Assr.	Treas.	Sher.	Col.	TOT'L
OFFICES	1	7	7	18	100	6	18	75	75	57	75	75	75	13 602
One Candidate		4	2	8	46	4	10	34	47	39	47	45	35	11 332
Two Candidates		1		8	33		5	23	19	13	18	17	28	2 167
Three Candidates		2	4	1	17	1	3	12	6	5	6	11	7	75
Four Candidates			1	1	2	1		3	1		2		3	14
Five Candidates	1				1			2				1	1	6
TOTALS	1	7	7	18	99	6	18	74	73	57	73	74	74	13[2]594

1. Based on official party certifications, ignoring contested returns, as reported in state newspapers and in correspondence.

2. No Democratic nominations were made at the primaries to eight offices in Newton and Searcy Counties.

TABLE 2. Democratic Nominations in the 1944 Primaries Contested by three or More Candidates and Won: by Candidates Polling a Majority in the Preferential; by Candidates Polling a Plurality in the Preferential and a Majority in the Run-Off; and by Candidates Running Second in the Preferential and Polling a Majority in the Run-off.

	Fed.		State					County						
	Cong.		Ex. Legis.		Jud.									
	S	H	S	H	Jdgs.	P.A.'s	Jdge.	Cir. Cl.	Co. Cl.	Assr.	Treas.	Sher.	Col.	TOT'L
Sought by 3 or more cands.	1	2	5	2	20	2	3	17	7	5	8	12	11	95
Nominee polls majority in 1st primary		2	4		7			7	3	1	3	5	8	40
Nominee polls plurality in 1st, majority in 2nd	1			1	9	1	1	4	4	3	4	6	1	35
Nominee polls plurality in 1st; runner-up withdraws			1		1		1	1			1	1		6
Runner-up in 1st polls majority in 2nd				1	3	1	1	5					2	13
Runner-up in 1st; leading cand. in 1st withdraws													1	1
TOTALS	1	2	5	2	20	2	3	17	7	5	8	12	11	95

system" described earlier in these pages.[133]

Other aspects of the issue of negro voting impinge directly on the double primary system. South Carolina has recently repealed all statutes regulating conduct of primaries with a view of exempting the nominating process from scope of the Fifeenth Amendment as construed in *Smith v. Allwright*—the "Texas primary case." If this avenue of escape be constitutionally valid, other states in the South no doubt will follow a similar course. This expedient, assuming its legality, is difficult in states using a double primary. Complexities inherent in the double prmary system call for a greater degree of statutory regulation. Danger of abuse, fraud, and violence, aggravated by negro voting, are potentially greater in two than in a single primary. The Brundidge Primary Election Law, initiated in 1918 by an overwhelming popular majority, reflects need felt at that time in Arkansas for state regulation of party primaries.[134]

North Carolina, with a ratio of negro to white population comparable to Arkansas, repealed its poll tax some twenty years ago. Few Negroes, however, participate in primaries or elections and no attempt has been made to use them as a balance of power.[135] Experience in North Carolina may be duplicated in Arkansas.

In the unlikely event that negro voting in Democratic primaries becomes widespread, a bidding for a united negro vote might give the Negro a balance of power among rival factions in the party. The double primary system, under such circumstances, might become a bulwark of "white supremacy" by consolidating the much larger v o t i n g strength of the white population.[136] With respect to nomina-

---

[133] Adoption of the "unit system" in Georgia grew out of rivalry between rural and urban areas. Rural areas regard the system, which capitalizes their over-representation in the lower house of the state legislature, as protecting them "against dominance by city machines and bosses." In practice, the system aids elements in larger cities, through well-placed campaign funds, to control nominations, Cullen B. Gosnell to the writer, August 14, 1944.
[134] D. Y. Thomas, *Arkansas and Its People* (1930) p. 331.
[135] North Carolina imposes a literacy test. J. M. Broughton, as quoted in *Arkansas Gazette*, May 14, 1944.
[136] White population exceeded negro population in every state in 1940. Negro population in Mississippi was 49.2 per cent of total population; in South Carolina, 42.9; in Arkansas, 24.8.

tions to all county offices and state representatives in nine Arkansas counties, on the other hand, the double primary could operate to consolidate the voting strength of negro majorities."⁷ The same would be true in many municipalities and townships. If the double primary is ever used for the purpose of consolidating white voters, existence of negro majorities in particular local units of government suggests expediency of an amendment making use of the system optional with respect to nominations to local offices.

The state's double primary system, viewed solely from the angle of municipal government, presents several aspects deserving study. Municipal officers, except in the largest cities, usually give only part of their time to official duties. Compensation is small. Burdens of cost and inconvenience placed on candidates by the double primary system are proportionately heavy. This is notably true of candidates for nomination as aldermen in those first and second class cities where nomination of council members is at large rather than by wards. Statutes require at-large nomination and election of aldermen in first class cities."⁸ As municipal elections in cities of the first class are held annually, the dual primary imposes a relatively great burden of inconvenience on voters, a circumstance favorabe to emergence and growth of machine control. The urban environment is the greenest pasture for the political "boss."

Nominations to municipal offices are rarely contested by more than two candidates. There would appear to be less warrant an cities than in larger units of government for the inconvenience and expense of two primaries. The double primary, however, consolidates anti-machine voting strength and is regarded widely as a valuable auxiliary of municipal reform.

The manner of nominating candidates, essentially a

---

¹³⁷Negro population exceeded white population in 1940 in the following counties: Chicot, Crittenden, Desha, Jefferson, Lee, Lincoln, Monroe, Phillips, St. Francis. *Population, Second Series, Arkansas*, 16th Census, Table 21.

¹³⁸Pope's Digest, Sec. 9834. Nominations and election of aldermen in cities of the second class are supposed to be by wards, according to an opinion of the attorney general to Norman McElhannon, February 8, 1944. In practice, some second class cities nominate candidates for aldermen at large. Some first class cities, moreover, nominate candidates for the city council by wards.

matter "of local concern," perhaps should be within the scope of municipal determination. Mindful of the influence local "bosses" in large cities have exercised in state and national politics, some, however, would insist that voters of the whole state have a valid concern in this aspect of municipal government. The large population and the dominant position of the state's capital city give support to this view in so far as it applies to Little Rock.

An attempt to appraise the double primary system in Arkansas is hazardous. The principle of majority nomination in one-party states warrants retention of the system. The complaint of the professional office-holder, stemming from greater expense of primary contests, would seem to merit greater consideration than it has received. Certain features of the run-off primary used in other states warrant study. The optional run-off, in opinion of this writer, is a desirable feature.[13*] The county executive committee in Texas, the runner-up in the first primary in North Carolina, may demand a second primary. Practice in North Carolina goes far to place the option within reach of minority groups. Though requiring constitutional amendment and enabling legislation, it may be desirable in Arkansas to broaden the area of county and municipal autonomy to allow voters, by ordinance of municipal council or quorum court or by local initiative, to choose between a single and a dual primary.

The double primary system allows opposing factions or interests to consolidate the whole of their voting strength when broad issues of public policy divide the electorate into pros and cons, when rival principles look in opposite directions, when forces of unrest and forces of tradition contend, when machine and reform clash. There is ample warrant for use of the dual primary to nominate candidates for public offices that guide or determine matters of policy. A list of such offices would include members of the Congress and state legislature, governor, lieutenant governor,

---

[13*]Quite similar is the choice that county committees of each party now make in Arkansas between the direct primary and the delegate-convention system for nomination of candidates for county offices. The county Republican committee in Searcy County uses the direct primary. The county Democratic committee in Newton County uses the delegate-convention. *Southwest American*, August 11, 1944.

mayor and aldermen. The narrow autonomy of county governments in Arkansas excludes county offices. Also excluded are the executive offices of the state government other than those listed, judges, prosecuting attorneys, and township offices. Officers excluded are in general those who perhaps should be selected by appointment rather than by ballot.[146]

---

[146] Views expressed relative to the proper "coverage" of the double primary system suggest the system employed in Louisiana. No run-off is held in that state for state executive offices other than governor in event a candidate for nomination as governor polls a majority in the preferential. This feature of the Louisiana double primary system could not be grafted onto the Arkansas double primary, since in this state names of all candidates for all nominations are not listed on the ballot in the first primary unless every nomination is contested by at least three candidates. The writer feels that adoption by Arkansas of the unique feature of the system in Louisiana would involve a greater loss than gain.

THE JOURNAL OF NEGRO HISTORY

Vol. XXX—April, 1945—No. 2

THE UPGRADING OF THE NEGRO'S STATUS BY SUPREME COURT DECISIONS*

The first recorded issue of color in the social order came with the emergence of Christianity, and we seem never to have been able to free ourselves from its overwhelming influence from that time until the present. In the revelation of St. Peter at Joppa, it was declared that all races were of equal standing:

"Whom God hath cleansed, call not thou common or unclean."

This is the first statement of the doctrine of equality in terms of race.

In America, as in no other country of the world, the impact of two races of different color living together in large numbers developed forces that play upon and determine the conduct, behavior, attitude and philosophy, not only of the individual, but the state and nation, and these have been vitally important influences in developing national character as a whole from a political and social point of view.

For many years, therefore, so many in fact, we of the Negro race almost despaired of a change, it became almost

---

*Delivered by Raymond Pace Alexander, member of Philadelphia Bar, former President National Bar Assn., at the Annual Meeting of the Association for the Study of Negro Life and History on Sunday, October 29, 1944, in Faneuil Hall, Boston, Massachusetts.

an established fact that if America had any general policy of race relations at all, it was one of racial segregation and discrimination. This policy had its roots and background in that soul destroying institution of slavery, a malignant growth in democracy which, like the deadly disease that it was, left its cancerous influences to spread to other parts of the national body to cast up its ugly and poisonous head in the civic, political and social life of America with increasing frequency.

Since 1865, the Negro people of America, and thousands of their liberal and courageous white friends, have insisted that a true democracy could be achieved for all people, regardless of color, and that there should be no citizens of the "second class." But all of us know, regardless of how we may try, that there are millions of people in America, many of them of considerable wealth and influence, many of whom occupy high places in our state and national government, and I deeply regret to say, in our churches, colleges, social welfare organizations and the like, who are still unwilling to believe that democracy in America should embrace in theory *and practice* the Negro. We believe that the frontiers of America consist of more than its physical geographical limits of land, from the Atlantic to the Pacific, made up of mountains and valleys, forests and plains, rivers and lakes. We believe that America has as well, a democratic frontier springing from its very national constitution and its Bill of Rights which embraces its underlying socio-political philosophy, which, by its very words and their inescapable meaning, were made to include all people regardless of race or color.

It is the assault on these democratic frontiers that has occupied the minds and attention of the leaders of Negro life and actions, the organizations and associations for their social, economic and political advancement, and, as concerns the subject of this paper particularly, the Negro lawyers of America.

That there has been a change, however, in the "conduct, behavior, attitude and philosophy" in the field of interracial relations and, in the last two decades, a pronounced advance and upgrading in the social, economic and political status of the Negro, there can be no denial. To what forces and influences may be credited this upgrading, and in what manner the field of law, the common law, federal statutes and federal directives contributed to this happy advance in race relations, may be answered in part in the following analysis.

It should be understood at the outset that what we call the great American Constitution, the body of laws adopted in 1787, does not mention civil rights at all. It was not until 1789, two years later, that what we familiarly call the Bill of Rights (the first ten Amendments to the Constitution) was adopted. The Declaration of Independence, which was preliminary to both the Constitution and the Bill of Rights, was in reality a Proclamation of Freedom; a Declaration from Englishmen in America against other Englishmen in the British Isles that they no longer could suffer the long series of abuses heaped upon them by the British Crown which acted as a tyrant, and that they therefore had the right, even the duty, to throw off such a yoke of government which was so oppressive and set up a new social order for the future of themselves and their posterity.

In 1787 when the discussion of the Bill of Rights (the first ten Amendments) was at its height, the delegates were concerned about the encroaching of the Federal Government on the power of the States. This was entirely natural because of the unhappy experiences of these men under the rule of the British Crown just recently shaken off. These ten Amendments therefore protected the *individual* against *government* or *federal* usurpation of power. Thus began, to the Negro's great loss and detriment, the theory of states' rights so frequently imbedded in the early laws and judicial decisions.

No one ever seemed to realize that the *individual* would soon need protection *against* the action of the *states* whose laws and acts were later designed to deny many millions of persons, the Negro people within their borders, the basic rights of citizenship.

For all practical purposes, because of the very small number of free Negroes in the United States at the time of the adoption of the Constitution and the Bill of Rights, it can be stated that the Negroes were not considered as a special class or any sizeable minority as such. After the War of Independence and the following period of adjustment, came the twenty years of heated sectional disputes between the North and the South on slavery and abolition, ending with the Civil War, the Emancipation Proclamation, and the three great War Amendments, the 13th, 14th and 15th, to the Federal Constitution.

The 13th Amendment, adopted in 1865, abolished slavery as well as involuntary servitude throughout the country. The 14th Amendment endowed the Negro with citizenship in the United States and the several states in which he resided. The 14th Amendment was passed in 1866. The 15th Amendment (passed in 1870 when the Ku Klux Klan was at its height) provided that it was unlawful for any state to deny the citizen the right to vote.

Now began the long struggle of a nation of people of one color, representing roughly 10 per cent of the population, within a nation of people of another color, representing the other 90 per cent of the population for social, economic and political adjustment between these two groups.

To whom did these newly created citizens look for the protection of these newly created rights, who just yesterday were held in bondage as chattels by the laws and customs of the states in which they lived? To the states? Manifestly not, but to their new creator of these rights, the Federal Government. Then suddenly, these great sons of early patriots, whose forefathers a few generations previously had fought a bloody war to free themselves from the very yokes and obstacles to freedom, the like of which these new citizens of color were seeking, used all sorts of devices, tenuous and specious arguments to deny these new freed men the privileges and immunities of citizenship which were so recently accorded them.

The path to advancement and upgrading of the American Negro was a long and arduous one fraught with the drama of hopes fulfilled to be later destroyed by one device or another by acts not alone of the legislatures of the former slave-holding states, but by the federal legislature and the courts themselves.

Without going into detail to support the last mentioned statement because of the length of the subject, there were five statutes passed by Congress after the war known as the Civil Rights Bills which were enacted to strengthen the 13th, 14th and 15th Amendments and the enforcement of the same by an elaborate program of federal supervision designed to protect the freedmen in all their basic and fundamental civil and political rights.

The first decision of the Supreme Court of the United States interpreting the 14th Amendment of the Constitution was in the famous Slaughterhouse Cases, The Butchers' Benevolent Association of New Orleans *versus* the Crescent City Livestock Company, et al, 83 U. S. 36 (1872). This decision showed how quickly the *Supreme Court* attempted, and successfully so, to whittle away the protection that was so valiantly fought for and incorporated in our Constitution and Bill of Rights after a great and bitter struggle. In this divided opinion by a none too learned justice, Mr. Justice Samuel F. Miller, the court gave the narrowest possible construction to the 14th Amendment and held that this Amendment protected rights springing from Federal citizenship, and the decision held that *Federal citizenship* was different from *state citizenship* and *rights* inherent in *State citizenship* were not subject to the protection of the 14th Amendment.

The facts of this case did not even directly or indirectly have anything to do with the Negro. It was solely and exclusively the construction of a statute of the State of Louisiana granting a monopoly to one corporation for the slaughtering of animals over a wide area. The court held that the state had enforced a valid exercise of its police power in protecting the health of the people of the state. It would seem, as professors of this branch of the law have stated time and again in trying to understand this decision, that the 14th Amendment was not even involved in this case. Mr. Justice Miller wrote the opinion for the majority of five, but a most brilliant, able and very exhaustive dissenting opinion was filed by Mr. Justice Fields, in which the Chief Justice Salmon P. Chase and Mr. Justices Bradley and Swayne joined. These Justices attacked the reasoning of the majority as "tenuous and specious." This was the era termed by the Negroes "Knocking at Closed Courtroom Doors."

Gradually, by narrow construction mostly on the opinions of a divided court, especially in the famous Civil Rights cases in which Negroes brought prosecution in their various states for discrimination on the railroads, in theaters, hotels, etc., the Supreme Court held these and like statutes unconstitutional, thereby taking from the purpose of these fine enforcement acts the very vitals and underlying reasons for which these great equalitarian laws were passed, over the hostile objections of a large minority in the Congress. (See the "Civil Rights" cases, viz. U. S. *vs.* Stanley (Kentucky), U. S. *vs.* Ryan (California), U. S. *vs.* Nichols (Missouri), U. S. *vs.* Singleton (New York), Robertson *et. ux. vs.* Memphis & Charleston Railway (Tennessee) 109 U. S. (1883). The majority opinions in the Civil Rights cases were written by Mr. Justice Bradley, who held that the Civil Rights cases were unconstitutional.

71

There was a single minority opinion by the great and learned Justice John M. Harlan. This opinion reads like the present majority opinions of the brilliant Justices of the Supreme Court as it is composed today, and would do justice to the great legal philosopher now among the departed, the late Mr. Justice Oliver Wendell Holmes, and the other two members of that brilliant triumvirate of dissenters, the late Mr. Justice Louis D. Brandeis and Mr. Justice Benjamin N. Cardozo.

Mr. Justice Harlan stated the following: "I cannot resist the conclusion that the substance and spirit of the recent Amendments to the Constitution have been sacrificed by a subtle and ingenious verbal criticism. ... Congress has power to enforce by appropriate legislation the provisions of this Article. ... Was it the purpose of the nation simply to destroy the institution of slavery and then remit the race, heretofore held in bondage, to the several states for such protection, in their civil rights, as those states, in their discretion might choose to provide? ... I insist that the National Legislature may, without transcending the limits of the Constitution, do for human liberty and the fundamental rights of American Citizenship, what it did, with the sanction of this court, for the protection of slavery and the rights of the master of fugitive slaves." (Justice Harlan was obviously referring to the case of Dred Scott (Dred Scott *vs.* Sandford, 60 U. S. 393) (1856.).

It seems to be conclusive and inescapable, therefore, that the safest and most certain guaranty of justice is the personality of the judge or judges who pass on the merits of a particular case. His intellectual and spiritual honesty and integrity and his moral courage are the tests upon which the future of the people, state or nation, may eventually depend. With the decision just mentioned and the legion of cases following, there was but a single voice in the deep wilderness, growing weaker as the strain of years bore heavily upon him, that spoke up in support of the then five million people of the darker races for whom the majority of Congress framed the 13th, 14th and 15th Amendments in order that they might achieve and enjoy the full rights of American citizenship. That was the voice of Mr. Justice John M. Harlan. It was not until a new voice ascended to the Supreme Court bench that a new philosophy of thought began to find utterance in behalf of the under-privileged and the minorities of all races, colors and creeds in this great commonwealth of states. That voice was the voice of the great judicial scholar and philosopher, the late distinguished jurist, Oliver Wendell Holmes of Massachusetts.

During the earlier years of Mr. Justice Holmes' tenure on the bench, Mr. Chief Justice White and Mr. Justice Day were often heard in brilliant decisions in support of the issues about which the subject of this paper treats. This was the era of "Cracking the Courtroom Doors."

THE RIGHT TO VOTE

It was not until about the year 1918 that the Negro began to obtain a favorable audience and a sympathetic ear in our Federal Supreme Court. The first successful case was that involving the attack on the famous Grandfather Clauses in the southern states, notably the case of Guinn *vs.* United States, 238 U. S. 347 (1915) in an opinion by Mr. Chief Justice White. The facts of the case are briefly as follows: In the year 1910 the Constitution of Oklahoma was amended, restricting the franchise or the right to vote by what is known as a "Grandfather Clause," which provided that no person could be registered unless he was able to read and write. In addition, the clause provided that should a person be denied the right to vote because he could not read or write, if he lived in some foreign country prior to January 1, 1866, or if he was eligible to register prior to that date, or if his lineal ancestor was eligible as of that date, then he was exempted and could register and vote. Of course, before 1866 Negroes were not eligible to vote at all, so the law very definitely and pointedly disfranchised the Negroes. As a result of the failure to allow Negroes to vote, certain of the election officials were indicted under the Constitution provision. Eventually the case reached the Federal Supreme Court at a time when several other states had similar cases pending covering the very same type of Grandfather Clauses. The decision in the instant case was decisive of all cases awaiting judicial interpretation. Mr. Chief Justice White, writing for the majority of the court, outlawed this statute as clearly unconstitutional with the following biting words:

". . . While this piece of legislation contains no express words of an exclusion, from the standard which it establishes, of any persons on account of race, color or previous condition of servitude prohibited by the 15th Amendment, . . . *the standard itself inherently brings that result to existence since it is based purely on a period of time before the enactment of the 15th Amendment and makes that period the controlling and dominant test of the right of suffrage.*"

This ended for quite a long while the attempts on the part of the various southern states to deny Negroes the right to register and vote at the primary and in the general election. It was not until some years later, which I shall discuss in a moment, that the famous Texas Primary Cases came before the Supreme Court with varying results until a most recent case which outlawed as unlawful and a violation of the Federal Constitution all such attempts to deny the Negro his right to vote.

CASES INVOLVING NEIGHBORHOOD SEGREGATION

The right of people of color to purchase property and freely enjoy the rights of citizenship in a city or state by building or owning property and living therein in the various sections of a city or state without discrimination or segregation has always been one in which the Negro has encountered great difficulties. A particularly important decision in the United States Supreme Court involving this very question was the case of Buchannan *vs.* Warley, 245 U. S. 16 (1917), known as the "Louisville Segregation Case." The facts briefly are as follows:

A colored man by the name of Buchannan bought a piece of property in the City of Louisville, Kentucky, and when the seller refused to settle when Buchannan tendered his money, he filed a bill for specific performance for the contract of sale. The defendant stated that Buchannan was a Negro and by virtue of an Ordinance of the City of Louisville he would be unable to occupy the land in a white block. Buchannan stated that the Ordinance was in conflict with the 14th Amendment of the Federal Constitution, but the Court of Appeals of Kentucky held that the Ordinance was valid on the ground that the Ordinance prohibited whites from living in Negro neighborhoods and Negroes from living in white neighborhoods, and any violation was punishable by criminal prosecution.

The Supreme Court of the United States in an opinion by Mr. Justice Day reversed the Court of Appeals of Kentucky and held:

"As we have seen, this court has held laws valid which separate races on the basis of equal accommodations in public conveyances, the courts of high authorities have held enactments lawful which provide for the separation in public schools of white and colored pupils where equal privileges are given. But in view of the right secured by the 14th Amendment of the Federal Constitution, such legislation must have its limitations, *and cannot be sustained where the exercise of authority exceeds the restraints of this Constitution.*

"We think these limitations are exceeded in laws and ordinances of the character now before us.

". . . It is said that such acquisitions by colored people depreciate property owned in the neighborhood by white people. But property may be acquired by undesirable white neighbors or put to disagreeable uses . . . with like results.

"We think this attempt to prevent the alienation of the property in question to a person of color was not a legitimate exercise of the police power of the state, and it is a violation of the fundamental law enacted in the 14th Amendment of the Constitution preventing state interference with property rights except by due process of law. The Ordinance cannot stand."

This was the old equal but separate theory. While the Negro was very happy to get this decision from the Supreme Court outlawing this Louisville Ordinance, nevertheless there was much danger in the phraseology of Mr. Justice Day, particularly in the first paragraph just mentioned. ". . . This court has held laws valid which separate the races on the basis of equal accommodations in public conveyances . . . and for the separation in the public schools of white and colored pupils. . . ." These statements of the learned justice came back to haunt the Negro in later appeals to the Supreme Court in cases involving the separation of races in public conveyances and the separation of white and colored pupils in public schools, and gave to a none too willing majority judicial excuse for the support of much discriminatory legislation.

RIGHT OF FAIR TRIAL

Following the decisions of our highest court, in chronological order, in order that we may more easily trace the development of sentiment in the upgrading of the Negro in his quest for the full rights of citizenship, the next important case in his long and hard fight for citizenship through judicial interpretations and judicial fiat was the famous Elaine, Arkansas, Riot Cases (Moore *vs.* Dempsey, 261 U. S. 86 (1923). The opinion of the majority was rendered by Mr. Justice Oliver Wendell Holmes. A group of Negro farmers were holding a meeting in Philips County, Arkansas, for the purpose of organizing and pooling their means as well as their thoughts to obtain a better price for their crops. They were meeting in a colored church at Elaine, Arkansas, in October, 1919. During the course of the meeting they were fired upon by a group of white men from the outside. As a result of the clash a riot took place, many of the Negroes fighting back for the protection of their own lives, and in the course of the melee some whites were killed.

Seventy-nine Negro men were arrested and tried for murder. It was only after a great deal of difficulty and the presence of United States Troops that a great mob of people who had marched to the jail for the purpose of lynching these men, were prevented from so doing under a promise by members of a local committee who called themselves the "Vigilantes" that, "if the mob would refrain from their attempts to lynch these men, they would execute those found guilty in the form of law." There were many Negro witnesses who were ready to testify in behalf of their fellowmen, but the mob had whipped them so and placed them under such fear of their lives that they agreed to testify against the men if they were given their freedom.

These seventy-nine men were brought to trial in an atmosphere completely controlled by mob violence, under the threat to lynch these defendants if the jury did not convict them. The court appointed counsel for the men, which counsel failed to ask for a change of venue and called no witnesses in defense of the Negroes, and only one of them was placed upon the stand by their counsel. The trial of the entire seventy-nine men lasted less than one hour, and the jury brought back a verdict in five minutes after it had received instructions, finding all of the men guilty of murder; twelve were sentenced to death and sixty-seven were sentenced to long prison terms.

The Supreme Court of Arkansas sustained the conviction and then an appeal to the United States Supreme Court followed.

Mr. Justice Holmes, in reversing the opinion of the Supreme Court, had this to say:

"In Frank vs. Mangum, 237 U. S. 309 (the famous Leo Frank Case) . . . it was recognized . . . that if in fact a trial is dominated by a mob so that there is an actual interference with the course of justice, there is a departure from due process of law; and that if the state supplying no corrective process, carries into execution a judgment of death or imprisonment based upon a verdict thus produced by mob domination, the state deprives the accused of his life or liberty without 'due process of law.' . . . If the case is such that the whole proceeding is a mask that counsel, jury and judge were swept to the fatal end by an irresistible wave of public passion, and that the state courts failed to correct the wrong, neither perfection in the machinery for correction nor the possibility that the trial court and counsel saw no other way of avoiding an immediate outbreak of the mob, can prevent this court from securing to the petitioners their constitutional rights."

In chronological order again, the Supreme Court, in the famous New Orleans Segregation Case (Harmon *vs.* Tyler, 273 U. S. 668 (1926), reversed in a per curiam decision the attempt on the part of the City of New Orleans to set up segregated districts for colored people in which only colored could live and white districts in which white only could live, on the authority of Buchannan *vs.* Warley, above referred to.

I have already referred to the devious methods by which the southern states attempted to deny the Negro the right to vote in their various Democratic primary elections in discussing the Oklahoma Grandfather Clause Cases. The first famous Texas primary case was that of Nixon *vs.* Herndon, 273 U. S. 536 (1927) in which Mr. Justice Holmes denied the right of the state of Texas to refuse a Negro, Doctor L. A. Nixon, the privilege of voting and participating in a Democratic party election held in the State of Texas. Of course, the Supreme Court of Texas sustained the right of the election board to refuse Dr. Nixon. He carried his case to the Supreme Court, and this is what Mr. Justice Holmes had to say:

"The Statute of Texas in the case referred to assumes to forbid Negroes to take part in the primary election, the importance of which we have indicated, discriminating against them by the distinction of color alone. States may do a good deal of classifying that is difficult to believe rational, but there are limits, and it is too clear for extended argument that color cannot be made the basis of a statutory classification affecting the rights set up in this case."

There followed in 1930 a per curiam decision sustaining the Supreme Court of Virginia in outlawing a Richmond

Segregation Case of the same type discussed heretofore in the Louisville and New Orleans Segregation Cases. This was the case of the City of Richmond *vs.* Deans, 281 U. S. 704 (1930), and it is refreshing to know that the Supreme Court of Virginia decided that the Richmond Ordinance was unconstitutional.

Not to be outdone by the first Texas primary case, the State of Texas promptly passed a new statute empowering the State Democratic Committee to set up its own limitations in primary elections, immediately after the decision of the Federal Supreme Court in the famous case of Nixon *vs.* Herndon, supra. The State of Texas Executive Committee of the Democratic Party adopted the resolution "that all white Democrats who were qualified under the Constitution and Laws of Texas . . . and *none others* shall be allowed to participate in the primary elections of the State of Texas." Dr. Nixon, also determined not to be outdone by this devious method of circumventing the decision of the highest court of the land, again presented himself to the election officials in his district to qualify to vote in the Democratic primary. Being refused this privilege, he immediately brought suit for damages in the federal courts under the Civil Rights Statute. The case was dismissed in the lower court and taken to the United States Supreme Court, and it is to be noted that four members of our Federal Supreme Court, Justices McReynolds, VanDevanter, Sutherland and Butler, dissented from the opinion of the majority, thereby making the voice of one lone person on the Supreme Bench the determining factor in deciding whether or not State Democratic Committees in the Southern States should disfranchise nine million Negroes within their borders. Mr. Justice Cardozo, speaking for the majority of the court, in the customary beautiful and brilliantly turned phrases of which he was an acknowledged master, said the following:

"Barred from voting at a primary, the petitioner has been, and this for the sole reason that his color is not white. The result for him is no different from what it was when his cause was here before. The argument for the respondent (Texas Democratic Committee) is, however, that identity of result has been attained though through essential diversity of methods. We are reminded that the 14th Amendment is the restraint upon the state and not upon private persons unconnected with a state. . . . With the problem thus laid bare and its essentials exposed to view, the cases seem to be ruled by Nixon *vs.* Herndon. . . . Delegates of the states . . . have discharged their official functions in such a way as to discriminate invidiously between white citizens and black. The 14th Amendment, adopted as it was with special solicitude for the equal protection of members of the Negro race, lays a duty upon the court to level by its judgment these barriers of color."

THE RIGHT TO BE CALLED FOR JURY SERVICE AND
THE RIGHT OF REPRESENTATION BY COUNSEL

A most important series of cases were argued in the Supreme Court on the right of the Negro to serve on both the trial jury and the grand jury in the various states in the south. Perhaps the most important of these cases was the famous "Scottsboro Case" (Powell *vs.* Alabama, 287 U. S. 45 (1932).

In this case the fundamental questions of the right of an accused to be represented by counsel was thoroughly considered by the Court. The Supreme Court held that the right to counsel meant the right of the accused to have an opportunity to confer with his counsel, the right to subpoena witnesses and compel them to appeal at trial, the right to have an adequate opportunity to prepare his case for trial and to be heard both by himself and his counsel in the latter's right to address the court and jury in his behalf.

In the second trip of this same case to the Supreme Court the questions of the continuous and systematic exclusion of Negroes from service on the grand and petit juries of the state of Alabama came up for review. This court, in 1935 (Norris *vs.* Alabama, 294 U. S. 587, 55 S. St. 579, and the companion case of Paterson *vs.* Alabama, 294 U. S. 600; 55 S. Ct. 575) declared such practice to be illegal restraint upon these constitutional rights and a denial of due process to the Negro defendant, and again reversed the conviction of the court of Alabama. (See Strauder *vs.* West Virginia (1879) 100 U. S. 339; Neal *vs.* Delaware (1880), 103 U. S. 370.)

FREEDOM OF SPEECH AND ASSEMBLY

In the case of Herndon *vs.* Lowery, 301 U. S. 242, decided in 1937, the question of the constitutionality of an old Georgia statute against insurrection was called in question. Here, a young Negro named Angelo Herndon was charged with distributing literature of the Communist Party in a rural Georgia town in which literature he urged the Negro farmer and share-cropper to organize for their protection and to attend meetings sponsored by the Communist Party. He was tried and convicted under the old Georgia insurrection statute and sentenced to life imprisonment. The United States Supreme Court held this statute unconstitutional as an unreasonable limitation to freedom of speech and assembly in violation of the due process clause of the Federal Constitution, in that the statute was too vague and failed to furnish a sufficiently ascertainable standard of guilt.

THE TEXAS PRIMARY DECISION
UPHOLDING THE WHITE PRIMARY

The State of Texas finally achieved a victory in its attempt to disfranchise the million Negroes within its borders in the case of Grovey *vs.* Townsend, 295 U. S. 45, decided in 1936. This victory, however, as disastrous as it was in the pursuit of the Negro in his march to full citizenship, was, happily for the cause of American democracy, only a temporary one. It did last, however, eight years, from 1936 to April, 1944, when the recent case of Smith *vs.* Allwright *et al* (decided April 3, 1944) was handed down by a strong majority opinion of 8 and only one dissent.

The Supreme Court in the Grovey Case, in an opinion

by Mr. Justice Owen W. Roberts, sustained the right of the Texas State Democratic Committee to set up qualifications of persons to vote in the Democratic Primary Election. It made no difference whether these persons were to vote in State or Federal elections. The Court said that the Texas Democratic Convention was not a State agency, and though the laws of the State of Texas provided how and when State Primaries would be held, yet this did not make the Texas State Democratic Convention a State agency, and that it could, similarly to a private club, regulate who should be admitted as members.

The case of Jeff Hollins (Hollins vs. Oklahoma, 295 U. S. 204 (1935)) presented another issue of the Right to be Represented by Counsel on the second trial of this case. The facts are very interesting and can be briefly stated as follows: The defendant, Hollins, was convicted December 29, 1931, at a trial which was held in the basement of the prison in Sapula, Oklahoma. He was charged with rape. There was no lawyer appointed for him and none to advise him on his rights and none to represent him at trial. He was found guilty of murder and sentenced to death. A stay of execution was had three days before his scheduled execution. The Supreme Court of Oklahoma reversed this conviction and sent it back for a new trial.

At the second trial of the case, the question was raised in the lower court and argued in the United States Supreme Court on the question of a systematic exclusion of Negroes from service on the jury panel to try this defendant. The Supreme Court in a per curiam decision on the basis of earlier decisions declared this to be a denial of due process and therefore the conviction to be void.

FORCED CONFESSION OF DEFENDANTS BY PHYSICAL VIOLENCE

The extortion of confessions by force, physical torture, threats and violence upon defendants charged in criminal cases has given rise to a long series of cases in the various southern states, many of which have been appealed to the highest federal tribunal. The most noteworthy of these cases, and the one that has given a strong admonition to the states that have been guilty of such conduct, is the case of Brown, Ellington and Shields *vs.* State of Mississippi (297 U. S. 278 (1936)). In this case the defendants were indicted for the murder of one Raymond Stewart in April of 1934. They entered pleas of not guilty. The court appointed counsel to defend them and they were found guilty and sentenced to death.

The only evidence that the state had against these defendants was an alleged confession which it was shown was obtained through force and physical torture. When these defendants were arrested and denied the crime, the sheriff hanged one of the defendants by a rope to a tree, and then when he was released just before strangulation, he was tied to the tree and severely beaten. When he refused to "confess," he was permitted to return home, but was later seized and whipped severely until he agreed to "confess." This confession was used at the trial and was the only evidence against the defendants. At the time of the trial Ellington stated he was tortured and produced evidence, showing the marks of the rope around his neck which were still visible at the time of the trial. The sheriff admitted the whipping of Ellington and very boldly stated that he "did not think he had whipped him too much for a Negro and not as much as I would have done if it were left to me." Other witnesses admitted that they had beaten the defendant into submission, but the Supreme Court of Mississippi affirmed the judgment of death.

Mr. Chief Justice Hughes, however, speaking for the United States Supreme Court, said the following in reversing the Supreme Court of Mississippi:

"The rack and torture chamber may not be substituted for the witness stand. It would be difficult to conceive of methods more revolting to the sense of justice than those taken to procure the confessions of these petitioners, and the use of the confessions thus obtained as the basis for a conviction and sentence was a clear denial of due process.

"The duty of maintaining the constitutional rights of a person on trial for his life rises above mere rules of procedure and whenever the court is clearly satisfied that such violations exist, it will refuse to sanction such and will apply the corrective."

In Hale vs. Kentncky (303 U. S. 613 (1938)), the Supreme Court, in a per curiam decision, sustained the right of a Negro on trial for his life in Kentucky to have members of his own race called for service on the jury selected to try him for a criminal offense. In this case the defendant proved that the jury commissioners had demonstrated a long continued, unvarying and wholesale exclusion of Negroes from jury service in that county on account of their race and color, and for no other reason. He was convicted of murder and sentenced to die. The Supreme Court of Kentucky affirmed the appeal, but the United States Supreme Court reversed the decision which re-established the principle that a systematic and arbitrary exclusion of Negroes from jury service, solely on account of their race and color, constituted a denial of the equal protection of the laws guaranteed by the 14th Amendment.

THE EQUAL RIGHT TO EDUCATION IN STATE SUPPORTED UNIVERSITY

Perhaps one of the most important and far-reaching cases in the history of the fight of the Negro for a full citizenship status that has ever been carried to the Supreme Court, is the famous case in the State of Missouri, in the matter of Missouri, *ex rel.* Gaines *vs.* Canada, *et al.* (Lloyd Gaines *vs.* University of Missouri) (305 U. S. 337). Lloyd Gaines was a young Negro with excellent qualifications who attempted to enter the University of Missouri Law School, but was refused solely because of his race or color. Asserting that this refusal was a denial by the state of Missouri of the equal protection of the laws in violation of the 14th

Amendment, he brought an action of mandamus to compel the University to admit him. He was urged by the University of Missouri officials to accept a scholarship that the state was willing to offer, to send him outside of the State of Missouri for study. This he refused to do. Then the University defended on the ground that the local Negro University (Lincoln University) offered a law course which was then in preparation and would be ready in the very near future. The lower court as well as the Supreme Court of Missouri dismissed the petition for mandamus. The Supreme Court, however, in a decision by Mr. Chief Justice Hughes, from which there were two dissenting opinions, reversed the Supreme Court of Missouri and held the action of the University of Missouri to be a denial of due process.[85] The dissenting Justices were Mr. Justices McReynolds and Butler. The majority opinion of Chief Justice Hughes stressed the following points:

"The basic consideration is not as to what sort of opportunities other states provide, or whether they are as good as the State of Missouri, but as to what opportunities Missouri itself furnishes to white students and denies to Negroes solely upon the ground of color. The admissibility of laws separating the races and the enjoyment of privileges afforded by the state rests wholly upon the equality of the privileges which the laws give to the separated groups within the state. The question here is not of a duty of a state to supply legal training or the equality of training which it does supply, but of its duty when it does supply such training to furnish it to the residents of the state upon the basis of an equality of right. By the operation of the laws of Missouri, a privilege has been created for white law students which is denied to Negroes by reason of their race alone. The white resident is afforded legal education within the state. The Negro resident, having the same qualification, is refused this and must go outside of the state to obtain it. That is the denial of the equality of legal right to the enjoyment of the privilege which the state has set up and the provision for the payment of tuition fees in another state does not remove the discrimination.

"Here, the petitioner's right is a personal one. It was as an individual that he was entitled to the equal protection of the laws, and the state was bound to furnish him within its borders facilities for legal education substantially equal to those which the state there afforded for persons of the white race, whether or not other Negroes sought the same opportunities."

This was one of the most brilliant, courageous and forceful statements supporting the fundamental purpose of the 14th Amendment that has ever been declared by our Supreme Court.

OPENING OF COURTROOM DOORS

Following this case the complexion of the Supreme Court radically changed. It was shortly after this case, through the death and resignation of several of these Justices of the Supreme Court, that the hand of the present Chief Executive was strongly felt in placing new, younger and liberal minds on the bench of our highest tribunal. With the elevation of Mr. Chief Justice Stone and the appointment by President Roosevelt of Justices (1) Reed, (2) Black, (3) Frankfurter, (4) Murphy, (5) Jackson, (6) Douglas and (7) Rutledge, with the sole remaining conservative being Mr. Justice Roberts from Pennsylvania, there is at present a group of Justices to whom the Negroes of America can look for the most sympathetic, broad and liberal construction of not only the Amendments to the Constitution for whose benefit they were passed, but to a favorable construction of the remaining Civil Rights Statutes and all cases affecting the political, civil, social and economic rights that the Negro and all minorities may from time to time present to this court for interpretation. The fears of the Negroes as to how Mr. Justice Black would decide cases involving their fundamental rights were immediately dispelled upon his filing the now famous opinion in the case of Chambers vs. Florida, 309 U. S. 227 (1940). In this case four Negroes were charged with murder and convicted. Their cases were appealed five times to the Supreme Court of Florida. After the fifth appeal, the case was carried to the United States Supreme Court. Mr. Justice Black, on behalf of the United States Supreme Court, reversed the conviction of these men on the ground that the confessions used to convict them were extorted by force and violence. In his opinion, Mr. Justice Black stated:

". . . Today, as in ages past, we are not without tragic proof that the exalted power of some government to punish manufactured crime dictatorially is the handmaid of tyranny. Under our constitutional system courts stand against any winds that blow as havens of refuge for those who might otherwise suffer because they are helpless, weak, outnumbered, or because they are non-conforming victims of prejudice and public excitement. Due process of law . . . commands that no such practice as that disclosed by this record shall send any accused to his death. No higher duty, no more solemn responsibility rests upon this court, than that of translating into living law and maintaining this constitutional shield deliberately planned and inscribed for the benefit of every human being subject to our constitution, of whatever race, creed or persuasion." [87]

Several cases involving the civil rights of Negroes were decided within a year or two after the elevation of the above-mentioned Justices to the Supreme Court bench, and all were decided favorably to the cause of the litigants. These cases were Canty *vs.* Alabama, 309 U. S. 629 (1940) in which the Supreme Court reversed a decision of the lower court of Alabama and its Supreme Court, ordering a new trial for the defendant charged with murder, thus voiding a death sentence of the State of Alabama because of irregularities in the trial of the lower court.

White *vs.* Texas, 309 U. S. 631 (1940). The Supreme Court granted a writ of certiorari and reversed on authority of previous cases, the conviction and sentence to death from the State of Texas.

RESTRICTIVE COVENANTS RESULTING IN RESIDENTIAL SEGREGATIONS

Earlier we have seen that the Supreme Court has outlawed residential discrimination by city ordinances (Buchannan *vs.* Warley, 245 U. S. 60 (1917).

In the case of Lee *vs.* Hansberry, U. S. 61, S. Ct. 521, 70 L. Ed. 969 (1940), the respondent, Hansberry, a Negro, bought some land in Chicago's so-called restricted area. This property was covered by a restriction against use by colored persons by a covenant or contract signed by a large majority of the adjoining property owners. The Illinois Supreme Court ruled the covenant to be valid and that the Negro purchasers could not occupy the land in question. The Federal Supreme Court reversed the Illinois Court and held that the Negro purchasers were not bound by this agreement to which they had not been a party, and to hold them so bound was a denial of due process.

(It should be stated here, however, that the flat issue of the validity of such contracts or restrictive covenants was not altogether before the court and therefore not squarely and satisfactorily settled.)

Railroad Discriminations

The case of Congressman Mitchell *vs.* Chicago, Rock Is. & Pac. Ry., U. S. 61 S. Ct. 873, 85 L. Ed. 811 (1941), deserves attention here. It will be recalled that former Chief Justice Hughes, then an Associate Justice, in the case of McCabe *vs.* Atchison, Topeka and Santa Fe R. R., 235 U. S. 151, in 1914, said in supporting the separate coach law of a state, that whenever the case came before this Court of an exclusion of the Negro travelling interstate from service on sleeping cars, parlor cars on dining cars, even where the demand for such service was too small to make profitable equal facilities, the court would grant relief.

Congressman Arthur Mitchell, Negro Democratic representative from Illinois, gave the Supreme Court the opportunity to fulfill that statement of Mr. Justice Hughes, made in 1914. And the Supreme Court did not fail to adhere to its promise. The facts in this case disclosed that the Negro Congressman was denied Pullman accommodations on a trip from Chicago to Hot Springs, Arkansas after the train entered Arkansas and was made to leave the Pullman and go into a 2nd class Jim Crow coach provided for colored passengers only. Mr. Chief Justice Hughes said for the Court:

"This was manifestly a discrimination against him in the course of his interstate journey and admittedly that discrimination 'was based solely upon the fact that he was a Negro. The question whether this was a discrimination forbidden by the Interstate Commerce Act is not a question of segregation but equality of treatment. The denial to appellant equality of accommodations because of his race would be an invasion of a fundamental right which is guaranteed against state actions by the 14th Amendment."

In Ward *vs.* Texas, 316 U. S. 547 (1942), Mr. Justice Byrnes, since retired from the bench, set aside a conviction of the lower court of Texas on the ground that the confession admitted in evidence, allegedly signed by the accused, was the result of force and violence.

JURY EXCLUSION

In Hill *vs.* Texas, 316 U. S. 400 (1942), Mr. Chief Justice Stone reaffirmed the principle that "equal protection of laws is more than an abstract right. It is a command which the state must respect for benefits of which every person may demand. Not the least merit of our constitutional system is that it safeguards and extends to all—the least deserving as well as the most virtuous." This was a case involving the systematic exclusion of Negroes from the jury panel in the county where this case was tried.

In the United States *vs.* Adams, Bordenave and Mitchell, 319 U. S. 312 (1943), Mr. Justice Black, on a question raised by the three defendants who were members of the armed forces of the country, sentenced to death under an alleged crime on a civilian woman within the camp confines of Camp Claiborne, Louisiana, reversed the conviction of these men on the ground that the federal courts of the State of Louisiana had no jurisdiction and released these three defendants from the custody of the civilian authorities to the army for further proceedings as the case warranted.

The last decision of the Supreme Court affecting the Negro's civil rights was decided on April 3, 1944, and this is the now famous case known as the Texas Primary Case, Smith *vs.* Allwright, *et al.*

Eight of the nine Justices of the Supreme Court decided in favor of the voter, Dr. Loney E. Smith, the single dissent, being by Mr. Justice Roberts, who wrote the opinion of the Supreme Court in the Grovey *vs.* Townsend case just referred to, allowing such denial of right to vote. This case began in Houston, Texas, in 1941 and was an action for damages for the refusal to permit qualified Negro voters to vote in the Democratic primary election in Texas. The case was based upon a violation of the 14th and 15th Amendments and the Federal Civil Rights Statutes. As was expected, the lower Texas court ruled against Dr. Smith. The United States Circuit Court of Appeals sustained the lower court, but the Supreme Court of the United States overruled its former decision by expressly stating so, and for all times declared the case of Grovey *vs.* Townsend, which sustained the State of Texas in its attempt to outlaw Negro voters, to be void. Mr. Justice Reed stated:

> "The United States is a constitutional democracy. Its organic law grants to all citizens a right to participate in the choice of election officials without restrictions by any state because of race. This grant to the people of the opportunity for choice is not to be nullified by a state through casting its electoral process in a form which permits a private organization to practice racial discrimination in the election. Constitutional rights would be of little value if they could be thus indirectly denied."

Civil Rights Prosecution

A new section of the Department of Justice known as the Civil Rights Section has given light to the remaining Civil Rights Statute and has actively engaged in the enforcing of the conspiracy section in these various codes, particularly all cases involving the interference of the right to vote and anti-peonage laws.

The United States *vs.* Classic, 313 U. S. 299, and United

States *vs.* Saylor, decided May 22, 1924, and Taylor *vs.* Georgia, 313 U. S. 25, and Pollock *vs.* Williams, decided April 10, 1944, are all cases in which the Civil Rights Unit in the Criminal Division of the Department of Justice actively prosecuted, as a result of which our Supreme Court decided that Labor Contract Statutes of Georgia and Florida, which lean towards peonage conditions and involuntary servitude, were declared unconstitutional. These cases placed the right to freedom from involuntary servitude on such a broad base, that the way had been opened to an attack on the "enticing labor" and "emigrant agents" statutes, and some of the vagrancy statutes and "work or fight" orders, which experience has proved to be in reality, indirect means of enforcing involuntary servitude, especially against Negro farmhands and laborers.

Economic Action at Law

I have deliberately removed from the chronological order involving the Negro a very interesting and far-reaching case that represented the first case involving the attempt by Negroes to force businesses that have many customers among Negroes, to employ Negroes among their personnel. This was the case of the New Negro Alliance *vs.* Sanitary Grocery Co., 303 U. S. 552; 58 S. Ct. 703, decided in 1938. Here, an association of individuals, organizing themselves together as a group interested in seeking to uplift themselves economically and provide jobs at the time of widespread unemployment for their members and the Negro people generally, tried to bargain with the owners of the Defendant Company, unsuccessfully, by peaceful conferences. In order to implement their demands that this Company, operating stores all over the District of Columbia, should employ Negro salesgirls and clerks at its store in the thickly populated Negro district, some of the members, by peaceful and quiet means, picketed the particular store with signs.

"Buy where you can work."

"This store refuses to hire colored clerks and salespeople."

It worked. Not a colored purchaser entered the store, and as a consequence the owners brought suit in the courts of the District of Columbia to enjoin these picketers from parading their complaint in front of their stores to the damage of their business. It would seem that the old adage "That you may hire whom you please to work" would carry the case over. The lower court and the District of Columbia Court of Appeals so held, but the Supreme Court, in a 7-2 opinion (Justices Butler and McReynolds dissenting), thought differently and upheld the right of picketing in a brilliant opinion by Mr. Justice Roberts. The whole case turned on the interpretation of the Norris-LaGuardia Statute governing labor disputes and the restraint placed upon the courts of the country by that Act to issue injunctions against labor in its right to strike, and to force employers, by peaceful means, such as picketing, to bargain with them.

The majority of the Court said that an association of individuals of a particular race, in seeking to uplift itself, may properly organize and seek out a particular business, firm or company with which this group of people does business, to do business, in turn, with them, by hiring or employing members of that particular race of people, and such falls within the definitions of labor disputes as contemplated by the Act. The dissenting Justices, Butler and McReynolds, were bitter and denunciatory of the majority opinions.

EQUALIZATION OF TEACHERS' SALARIES

This most important class of cases which has meant so much to the colored teachers throughout the South was brought on the first instance in the Federal Courts for the District of Maryland. The original case was Walter Mills vs. Board of Education of Anne Arundel County, Maryland,

30 F. Supp. 245 (D. Md. 1939). (See also Mills *vs.* Loundes, 26 F. Supp. 792, 801: (1940) 53 Harv. Law Rev. 669.) In this case, evidence disclosed a systematic practice engaged in for years by the State of Maryland and all the Southern states, allowing one scale of salaries for white teachers serving the same class of students as colored, and another scale of salaries for colored teachers, the latter, performing the same kind of services, fulfilling the same standards and requirements for employment, but receiving from 25 to 40 per cent less compensation than their white fellow workers. The lower court found race discrimination to be a fact, and that the only reason for the difference in pay was based on discrimination on account of color alone, and held that the colored teacher was unconstitutionally discriminated against in the practice of his profession by the County of Arundel, Maryland, the defendant, and issued the injunctions sought by the school teachers. Judge W. Calvin Chesnut of the U. S. District Court of Maryland wrote the opinion of the lower court in such a sweeping and able manner that the defendant school board took no appeal therefrom.

See: Alston *vs.* School Board of the City of Norfolk, Virginia, C.C.A. 4th Cir. (1940); 112 F (2nd) 992.

THE FIGHT AGAINST DISCRIMINATION BY LABOR UNIONS

Just before going to press the Supreme Court, in a far-reaching decision by a unanimous court, on December 18, 1944, declared that the Railway Labor Act (48 Stat. 1185), 45 U. S. C. sec 151 et. seq., imposes on a Labor Union which assumes to act as the exclusive bargaining agent of a class of railway employees, the duty to represent all the employees of the craft and this agent, in its bargaining with the employer, cannot make contracts, which result in discrimination against certain members of that craft because of their race or color, and when such violations of duty on the part of such bargaining agent appears, the courts will step in and enjoin such violations of duty which the statute above referred to clearly imposes on such union representative.

The facts and history of this case (Bester W. Steele *vs.* Louisville and Nashville R. R. Co., Brotherhood of Locomotive Firemen and Enginemen, *et al.,* No. 45 U. S. Sup. Ct., Oct. Term 1944) are important for a clear understanding of the significance of the issues involved.

For a quarter of a century prior to 1930 almost all the trains in the South, both passenger and freight, were "fired" by Negro locomotive firemen. With the improvement in design of locomotives and their use of automatic stokers and ash removers, and particularly with the introduction of Diesel and oil burning locomotives, there was an increasing demand for the jobs as firemen by white railway workers. Gradually Negro workers were eased out of the better runs and placed on long-hour night and holiday freight runs and shifting engine jobs about the yards—the most unsatisfactory and least-paying jobs. The brotherhood had worked out plans that would ultimately force out of the employ of the southern railroads all their Negro employees in this craft (locomotive firemen). The Brotherhood of Locomotive Firemen and Enginemen could not be appealed to by the Negro workers, who were in fact a large minority of this class of workers, because the union expressly, by their ritual, refused membership to Negro workers. Therefore, Steele, petitioner in the case, took his case to the court and asked for relief under the theory that the respondent Brotherhood, as a labor organization, was, under sec. 2 of the Act (supra) the exclusive bargaining agent of the craft of firemen, was so recognized by it, and as such, the order of the Brotherhood (respondent) of March 28, 1940, notifying some 21 Railroads that the proposed new collective bargaining agreement designed to exclude ultimately *all* Negro firemen from the 21 southern railroads service, was illegal and of no effect. No notice was served on the Negro firemen nor was any opportunity given them to be heard on the agreement submitted to the respondent railroads; and in fact the orders were put into effect before their existence was disclosed to the Negro firemen. The petitioner showed that he and his fellow workers, for whom he asked leave to sue, were performing their service satisfactory.

The Supreme Court of Alabama took jurisdiction of the case, but held that no cause of action was shown. The Supreme Court of the United States, in an opinion written by Mr. Chief Justice Stone, held that "Congress, in enacting the Railway Labor Act and authorizing a labor union chosen to represent the craft, did not intend (it) to sacrifice the rights of the minority of the craft without imposing on it any duty to protect the minority."

The Court held that since the Negro workers were barred from membership in the union, "the Act required, in fact *commands,* the bargaining agent to act for them, and, citing the order of the National Mediation Board in the case of Employees of St. Paul Union Depot (No. R. 635), once a craft or class has designated its representative, such representative is responsible under the law to act for *all* employees—members as well as those who are not members." The court therefore enjoined the Brotherhood from enforcing such a flagrant and violently discriminating order.

Mr. Justice Murphy, in a concurring opinion, felt compelled to say the following regarding the underlying issue of race prejudice which was so pregnant throughout this case.

"The economic discrimination against Negroes practiced by the Brotherhood and the railroad under color of Congressional authority raised a grave constitutional issue that should be squarely faced.

"The utter disregard for the dignity and the well-being of colored citizens shown by this record is so pronounced as to demand the invocation of constitutional condemnation. To decide the case and to analyze the statute solely upon the basis of legal niceties, while remaining mute and placid as to the obvious and oppressive deprivation of constitutional guarantees, is to make the judicial function something less than it should be.

"The constitutional problem inherent in this instance is clear. Congress, through the Railway Labor Act, has conferred upon the union selected by a majority of a craft or class of Railway workers the power to represent the entire craft or class in all collective bargaining matters. While such union is essentially a private organization, its power to represent and bind all members of a class or craft is derived solely from Congress. The act contains no language which directs the manner in which the bargaining representative shall perform its duties. But it cannot be assumed that Congress meant to authorize the representative to act so as to ignore rights guaranteed by the Constitution. Otherwise the Act would bear the stigma of unconstitutionality under the Fifth Amendment in this respect. For that reason I am willing to read the statute as not permitting or allowing any action by the bargaining representative in the exercise of its delegated powers which would in effect violate the constitutional rights of individuals.

"If the Court's construction of the statute rests upon this basis, I agree. But I am not sure that such is the basis. Suffice it to say, however, that this constitutional issue cannot be lightly dismissed. The cloak of racism surrounding the actions of the Brotherhood in refusing membership to Negroes and in entering into and enforcing agreements discriminating against them, all under the guise of Congressional authority, still remains. No statutory interpretation can erase this ugly example of economic cruelty against colored citizens of the United States. Nothing can destroy the fact that the accident of birth had been used as the basis to abuse individual rights by an organization purporting to act in conformity with its Congressional mandates. Any attempt to interpret the Act must take that fact into account and must realize that the constitutionality of the statute in this respect depends upon the answer given.

"The Constitution voices its disapproval whenever economic discrimination is applied under authority of Law against any race, creed or color. A sound democracy cannot allow such discrimination to go unchallenged. Racism is far too virulent today to permit the slightest refusal, in the light of a Constitution that abhors it, to expose and condemn it wherever it appears in the course of a statutory interpretation."

(See the remarks of the same Justice in his dissenting opinion in the case of the Removal of Japanese citizens from their Pacific Coast Homes under the war evacuation program, (*In re* Fred Toyosaburo Korsmatsu, decided Dec. 18, 1944.) The court held in a majority opinion written by Mr. Justice Hugo L. Black, to which there were three dissents, that the constitutional rights of the Japanese-American citizens were not violated. Mr. Justice Murphy again expressed grave fear over the rise of racism, saying that "such expulsion goes over the very brink of constitutional power and falls into the ugly abyss of racism."

This case closes for the present (Jan. 3, 1945) the struggle of the Negro for economic, civic and political freedom and his effort, so bravely and courageously fought over a half century, for full citizenship in the framework of American Democracy, through the most difficult of all methods, that of "citizenship through judicial fiat."

It is important to note, and emphasis should be placed on the fact, that in almost every leading case related in this article, the cases were initiated, appealed and argued exclusively by Negro attorneys. An enormous amount of credit should be given to the National Association for the Advancement of Colored People, and their staff of attorneys throughout the country, and particularly their former Chief Counsel, Charles H. Houston, Judge William H. Hastie and their present chief counsel, Thurgood Marshall, and their various associate counsel, for their monumental work and unusual success in their frequent appearances in our Federal Supreme Court.

CIVIL RIGHTS

In recent years there has been a marked change, both in the attitude of Congress and the Courts towards the strengthening and the protection of civil rights. How much may be achieved in any litigation attempting to force employment relations and to upgrade the Negro worker from unskilled positions in industry, or to force his employment in a particular industry which had heretofore failed to employ him and discriminated against him in all lines of employment, is open to great question. Undoubtedly remedial legislation from Congress would be necessary to guarantee the right of employment in industry in peace time. Some steps have been taken, and much progress has been made in this field by the passage of such Legislation as the National Labor Relations Act and the Fair Labor Standards Act. However, these Acts go but little distance in the ultimate aim of travel of the Negro worker, and this means more than six millions of peacetime employables among the Negroes of America. Whether the Negro must await the results of his present efforts to have the Congress pass a permanent Fair Employment Practice Bill to supplement the war measure, a purely temporary and, as yet, unenforceable one, (Executive Orders Nos. 8802 and 9346) or continue to resort to the tremendously slow and unsatisfactory "judicial fiat" method explored in this article depends on America's answer to the challenge of its vaunted ideals of democracy, everywhere so proudly expressed, but no where so proudly practiced. It depends on the answer to the question, "Does America in fact and in truth acknowledge the democratic belief in the dignity and rights of all men regardless of race or color?"

RAYMOND PACE ALEXANDER
Member of the Philadelphia Bar

NATURAL RIGHTS
AND THE FOUNDING FATHERS—THE VIRGINIANS

CHESTER JAMES ANTIEAU*

The philosophy of natural rights was championed by such Founding Fathers as Richard Bland, Patrick Henry, Thomas Jefferson, Richard Henry Lee, James Madison, George Mason, Robert Carter Nicholas, Peyton Randolph, George Washington, and George Wythe. Indeed, it would be amazing if any Revolutionary leader of the Commonwealth could be found who did not subscribe to the doctrines of natural law and right. Moreover, the doctrine was not limited to the select few who directed Virginia's destinies, but was widely held and continually expressed by the popular assemblages throughout the Commonwealth during Revolutionary days.

As early as February 27, 1766, a number of prominent planters adopted at Leedstown articles of association asserting their "fundamental rights ... founded on reason, law and compact."[1] Two years later the Burgesses were indicating to Parliament that they intended to secure "full enjoyment of all our natural and constitutional rights and privileges."[2] On July 18, 1774, a meeting attended by the substantial citizens of Fairfax County adopted the famous Fairfax Resolves wherein they indicated that their most precious rights belonged to them "by the laws of nature." This great resolution was the first assertion by a representative body in America that the colonists alone had the right to enact laws governing their affairs. The citizens of the County resolved "that the claim, lately assumed and exercised by the British Parliament, of making all such laws as they think fit, to govern the people of these colonies, and to extort from us our money without our consent, is not only diametrically contrary to the first principles of the Constitution, and the original compacts by which we are dependent upon the British Crown and government; but *it is totally incompatible with the privileges of a free people and the natural rights of mankind*, will render our own legislatures merely nominal and nugatory, and is calculated to reduce us from a state of freedom and happiness to slavery and misery."[3] George Washington was in the

---

*Professor of Law, Georgetown.
[1] 3 Freeman, George Washington 154 (1948) [hereinafter cited as Freeman].
[2] Id. at 198-99.
[3] The resolves are set forth in 1 Rowland, Life of Mason 418 (1892) [hereinafter cited as Rowland].

chair on this occasion, and the Resolves were almost certainly drafted by George Mason. It was on the twenty-sixth of the same month that the freeholders of Albemarle County adopted similar resolutions to defend their "natural rights" and "the common rights of mankind." Evidence is strong that these resolutions came from the pen of Thomas Jefferson.[4]

On January seventeenth of the following year the Committee of Safety of Fairfax County organized the Fairfax Independent Company, and the resolutions of that day, probably authored by George Mason, indicated the propriety of defending our "natural rights" and "those inestimable rights which we inherit from our ancestors."[5] In June, 1775, when the landing of armed forces in Virginia was threatened, the Independent Company wrote to the Williamsburg Volunteers:

> "We are determined at all events, to act on that occasion as men of spirit ought to do in defence of their natural rights and country's cause."[6]

The same month the Prince Edward County Committee adopted resolves that they were ready to defend their "inherent, legal and just rights and privileges."[7]

On June 12, 1776, the Virginia Convention adopted the Declaration of Rights, which was to become one of the most influential documents in American history. It solemnly asserted "that all men ... have certain inherent natural rights." This was the first deliberate adoption of the natural rights philosophy as the basis for political organization anywhere in the world.[8] Throughout the period immediately preceding and overlapping the Revolution the dissentient religious bodies were vigorously claiming their natural right to be free from the established church.[9]

Although the doctrine of natural rights played a most important role in severing our ties with England, the philosophy was clearly much more than a handy weapon of utility and opportunism. After the Revolution had been won, the people and such leaders as Thomas Jefferson continued to assert its primary role in defining man's rela-

---

[4] 1 The Papers of Thomas Jefferson 117 (Boyd ed. 1950) [hereinafter cited as Boyd].
[5] 1 Rowland 182.
[6] 2 Force, American Archives 872 (1843).
[7] Id. at 1023.
[8] This was the product of George Mason. See also Clark, Natural Rights, 16 Annals 212 (1900).
[9] Gewehr, The Great Awakening in Virginia 1740-1790 135 (1930).

tion to his temporal government. When the Statute for Religious Freedom was adopted in 1785, it recognized that man "has a natural right" to religious freedom. It concluded with the statement "that the rights hereby asserted are of the natural rights of mankind and that if any act shall be hereafter passed to repeal the present or to narrow its operations, such act will be an infringement of natural right."[10] Three years later there was much opposition in the Convention of June, 1788, called at Richmond to deliberate ratification of the United States Constitution, because it contained inadequate provision for the natural rights dear to Virginians.[11] That October the Assembly adopted a resolution, the work of Patrick Henry, requesting Congress to call a national convention at once to put into the Constitution a bill of rights "to secure to ourselves and our latest posterity the great and inalienable rights of mankind."[12] Just prior to the ending of the memorable century, in 1798, there was again much stress placed upon our natural rights in the Virginia Assembly by Messrs. Daniel, Mercer, Nicholas, and Taylor who argued, for the majority, that the federal alien and sedition laws were utterly invalid as violative of our natural rights of freedom and expression.[13]

The Natural Rights

In their most generalized expressions the Founding Fathers spoke of their natural rights to life and liberty, adding at times, property, and on other occasions, the pursuit of happiness. To some contemporaries the alternative use of property and the pursuit of happiness may seem strange, but to many of the Fathers property meant the right to develop one's properties, that is, his faculties. The particular natural rights on which there was the largest measure of agreement among the Virginians were (1) freedom of conscience, (2) freedom of communication, (3) the right to be free from arbitrary laws, (4) the rights of assembly and petition, (5) the property right, (6) the right of self-government, to which were frequently appended (a) the right of expatriation and (b) a right to change the form of government. Later parts of this paper will be concerned with the meaning of these rights

---

[10]Compare the different wordings in 12 Hening's Statutes 84-86 (1923) [hereinafter cited as Hening]; Morison, The American Revolution, Sources and Documents 206 (1929) [hereinafter cited as Morison]; Padover, The Complete Jefferson 946-47 (1943) [hereinafter cited as Padover].
[11]Morison 307; Morgan, The True Patrick Henry 348 (1907); Tyler, Patrick Henry 326 (1887).
[12]Id. at 349-50.
[13]2 Howison, History of Virginia 352 (1847).

to the Founding Fathers, as well as their ideas on permissible limitations. Additionally, some Virginians included in their natural rights such concepts as trial by jury, freedom from ex post facto laws, the right to an impartial judge, and a right to defend their liberties by force, although to Jefferson and others these were more properly deemed "fences" to assure the enjoyment of the more basic rights indicated earlier.

BASES OF THE NATURAL RIGHTS

The Virginia Founding Fathers were in substantial agreement that the ultimate source of our natural rights was our Creator. Men "are endowed by their Creator" with inherent and inalienable rights, said Thomas Jefferson in the memorable language of the Declaration of Independence.[14] Earlier Jefferson had written in his Summary View that "the God who gave us life gave us liberty at the same time."[15] We have natural rights of the intellect, he indicated, "because Almighty God hath created the mind free. . . ."[16] Speaking of the natural right of expatriation, Jefferson said in the Summary View: "The evidence of this natural right, like that of our right to life, liberty, the use of our faculties, the pursuit of happiness, is not left to the feeble and sophistical investigations of reason, but is impressed on the sense of every man. We do not claim these under the charters of kings or legislators, but under the King of kings."[17] In his Notes on Virginia, Jefferson wrote: "And can the liberties of a nation be thought secure when we have removed their only firm basis, a conviction in the minds of the people that these liberties are the gift of God?"[18] Speaking there of our natural rights, he concluded: "We are answerable for them to our God."[19] It was in the Summary View in which Jefferson asserted that Parliament had no power to encroach "upon those rights which God and the laws have given equally and independently to all."[20] Later in life Jefferson wrote that we must follow "those moral rules which the Author of our being has implanted in man as the law of his nature to govern him in his associated, as well as individual charac-

---

[14] The Writings of Thomas Jefferson 29 (Mem. ed. 1905) [hereinafter cited as Memorial Edition]; 1 Boyd 315.

[15] 1 Memorial Edition 209-10.

[16] The Bill for Establishing Religious Freedom in Virginia; Morison 206.

[17] 12 Works of Thomas Jefferson 66 (Ford ed. 1904-05).

[18] Answer to Query XVIII; 3 The Writings of Thomas Jefferson 266-67 (Ford ed. 1892-99) [hereinafter cited as Ford].

[19] Jefferson, Notes on the State of Virginia 159 (Peden ed. 1955) [hereinafter cited as Peden]; Wright, A Source Book of American Political Theory 158 (1929).

[20] 1 Boyd 121.

ter."[21] That the natural rights of man came from God, in Jefferson's belief, was beyond doubt.

His fellow Virginians were ready to join in asserting that our rights came from "the great Author of nature,"[22] which assertion was simply sharing in such a view held by practically all of our Revolutionary leaders. Typically, John Adams wrote in his Dissertation on the Canon and Feudal Law, "I say RIGHTS, for such they have, undoubtedly, antecedent to all earthly government,—Rights that cannot be repealed or restrained by human laws—Rights, derived from the great Legislator of the universe."[23] A later Virginian, John Randolph Tucker, outstanding authority on constitutional rights, nicely emphasized how our Founding Fathers understood that our natural rights and liberties come from God. Tucker wrote: "Liberty, which means this exclusive right of each man to self-use—that is, the exclusive use of the Divine gifts to him, under trust and responsibility to God, does not come, therefore, through any social compact of men, or as a gift from society or from government. It is the gift of God! It is a liberty of self-use, inalienable by himself, because that would be breach of duty and surrender of the trust Divinely vested; and inalienably by any and all others, because of sacrilegious robbery of that with which he is Divinely invested." And this, holds Tucker, is the philosophy adopted in the Declaration of Independence.

Thomas Jefferson and many of his contemporaries understood that the natural rights of man depended upon teleological considerations. So viewed, and accepting the premise that man's goal is being with his Creator for eternity, man has the duty to abide by His will and directions, because they are necessary to satisfy man's duties. Jefferson wrote that "the true office is to declare and enforce our natural rights and duties."[24] The existence of natural duties and the relationship of rights to duties were quite apparent to Jefferson, and anyone who has studied the man should realize that the only natural duties Jefferson acknowledged were not to temporal kings, but to the Creator.

James Madison was even more explicit that the source of rights exists in man's duty to his Creator. Writing of the unalienable right

---

[21]Letter to the North Carolina General Assembly (1808); N. Y. Times, Nov. 23, 1939, p. 32, col. 2-5.
[22]Preface to Williamsburg edition of Dickinson's Letters to a Farmer in Pennsylvania (1768); 2 Life and Writings of John Dickinson 290 (Ford ed. 1895).
[23]Published in Boston Gazette in August, 1765; Umbreit, Founding Fathers 114 (1941).
[24]Letter to Francis W. Gilmer, June 7, 1816; 10 Ford 32.

of religion in his Memorial and Remonstrance, he stated that the right is unalienable

> "because what is here a right towards men, is a duty towards the creator. It is the duty of every man to render to the Creator such homeage, and such only, as he believes to be acceptable to Him. His duty is precedent, both in order of time and in degree of obligation, to the claims of Civil Society. Before any man can be considered as a member of Civil Society, he must be considered as a subject of the Governor of the Universe: And if a member of Civil Society, who enters into any subordinate Association, must always do it with a reservation of his duty to the general authority; much more must every man who becomes a member of any particular Civil Society, do it with a saving of his allegiance to the Universal Sovereign."[25]

Another leading Virginian, George Mason, was equally clear in asserting that the obligation of man to his Maker was the source of natural rights. In 1772 he wrote:

> "Now all acts of legislature apparently contrary to natural right and justice, are, in our laws, and must be in the nature of things, considered as void. The laws of nature are the laws of God: *A legislature must not obstruct our obedience to him from whose punishments they cannot protect us.* All human constitutions which contradict His laws, we are in conscience bound to disobey. Such have been the adjudications of our courts of justice."[26]

The imperative necessity of understanding ends and duties in order to delineate natural rights was appreciated not only by Messrs. Jefferson, Madison, and Mason, but also by Virginians generally in our formative period. The members of the Virginia convention that ratified the United States Constitution saw and stated that the natural rights of conscience and religion are predicated upon an obligation to God. They contended that it was because of "the duty which we owe to our Creator," that "all men have an equal, natural and unalienable right to the free exercise of religion according to the dictates of conscience."[27]

There is ample evidence that the Founding Fathers were aware of the ontological basis of our natural rights. It is because we are rational, intellectual, social, spiritual, and political beings that we naturally have rights to develop our intellect, to hear appeals made

---

[25]Memorial and Remonstrance Against Religious Assessments; Humphrey, Nationalism and Religion in America 395 (1924).
[26]Argument in Robin v. Hardaway, 2 Va. (Jefferson) 109 (1772).
[27]3 Elliot's Debates 367, 659 (1861 ed.)

to reason that can make clearer the proper means to our ordained end, rights to assemble with our fellow men to discuss more effective socio-political groupings better suited for the development of our faculties and the protection of our basic rights, as well as freedom of conscience and religion.[28] When later in life Thomas Jefferson was explaining why he and the other Fathers believed in natural rights, he wrote: "We believed, with them, that man was a rational animal, endowed by nature with rights, and with an innate sense of justice...."[29] We have natural rights of the intellect, according to Jefferson, because "Almighty God hath created the mind free."[30] Jefferson saw with the scholastics that natural law was the participation of rational men in God's divine law; natural law and rights can be discovered, he wrote, by "the head and heart of every rational and honest man. It is there nature has written her moral laws, and where every man may read them for himself."[31] "Questions of natural right," he added, "are triable by their conformity with the moral sense and reason of man."[32]

It has been aptly noted that Jefferson considered moral sense and natural rights as necessary allies.[33] When other Founding Fathers posited our natural rights upon nature, it was in the sense that they referred to the nature of man as above defined. To George Mason the natural rights were "the sacred rights of human nature,"[34] and to Richard Henry Lee they were "the just and proper rights of human nature."[35] Patrick Henry came by his awareness of natural rights not from the record of Anglo-Saxon history or the perusal of either colonial charters or a "state of nature;" according to Jefferson, Henry "drew all natural rights from a purer source—the feelings of his own heart."[36]

---

[28] See Lucey, Natural Law and American Legal Realism, 30 Geo. L.J. 493 (1942).
[29] Letter to Judge William Johnson, June 12, 1823; 15 Memorial Edition 441.
[30] The Bill for Establishing Religious Freedom in Virginia; Morison 206.
[31] Letter of Aug. 28, 1789; 3 Memorial Edition 228.
[32] Opinion rendered, April 28, 1793, "On the Question Whether the United States have a Right to Renounce their Treaties with France;" Basic Writings of Thomas Jefferson 316.
[33] Koch, The Philosophy of Thomas Jefferson 138 (1957).
[34] Letter to his son John, May 20, 1790; Hill, George Mason, Constitutionalist 249 (1938).
[35] Letter to John Dickinson, July 25, 1768. See also Letters to Landon Carter, Feb. 24, 1766; to Samuel Adams, May 8, 1774; and to George Washington, Nov. 13, 1775. Letters of Thomas Jefferson 14, 29, 110, 156 (Ballagh ed. 1911) [hereinafter cited as Ballagh].
[36] 12 Works, op. cit. supra note 17, at 33; Miller, Origins of the American Revolution 175 (1943).

The Fathers rather frequently indicated that our rights were founded on the law of nature. Richard Henry Lee rather typically spoke of "our just and legal possession of property and freedom, founded in the law of nature."[37] Richard Bland often recurred to "the Law of Nature, and those Rights of Mankind which flow from it."[38] In his Summary View in 1774 Thomas Jefferson said that the colonists were "claiming their rights derived from the laws of nature."[39] Similarly, in the Declaration of Independence he stated that our rights were derived "from the laws of nature and of nature's God."[40] The Virginians were obviously not alone in sensing a relationship between natural rights and the law of nature. The assembled colonists at the First Continental Congress agreed to found their rights "upon the laws of nature, the principles of the English Constitution, the charters and compacts."[41] The order is highly significant, and as revolution began the last two sources virtually disappeared from American thinking.

At times the Founding Fathers spoke of natural rights as being the gift of nature, but in practically every instance it was meant the gift of God which clothed us with a distinctive nature, as aforesaid. For instance, James Madison, who clearly acknowledged the Deistic source of right, wrote: "The equal right of every citizen to the free exercise of his religion according to the dictates of conscience is held by the same tenure with all our other rights. If we recur to its origin, it is equally the gift of nature...."[42] "The laws of nature are the laws of God; whose authority can be superseded by no power on earth," wrote George Mason.[43] And George Washington admonished us that as a nation we should forever respect "the eternal rules of order and right which Heaven itself has ordained."[44] Carl Becker, outstanding scholar on Jefferson and the American Revolution, has concluded that

---

[37]Preface to Williamsburg edition of Dickinson's Letter to a Farmer in Pennsylvania (1768); 2 Life and Writings of John Dickinson, op. cit. supra note 22, at 290.
[38]Bland, An Inquiry into the Rights of the British Colonies 26 (Swem ed. 1766).
[39]1 Boyd 134.
[40]Id. at 315.
[41]Burnett, The Continental Congress 41 (1941). A few representatives from other states, particularly Duane and Galloway, were reluctant to posit colonial rights upon the law of nature, but there is not the slightest suggestion that any Virginian denied the law of nature and the doctrine of natural rights as the worthiest foundation for American rights. Indeed, the decision of the Congress to place reliance upon the laws of nature was largely the work of Richard Henry Lee. Mapp, The Virginia Experiment 371 (1957).
[42]Brant, James Madison, Virginia Revolutionary 249, 254 (1941).
[43]Argument in Robin v. Hardaway, 2 Va. (Jefferson) 109 (1772).
[44]Farewell Address; Commager, Documents of American History 169-75 (1938).

to the Founding Fathers "the natural rights philosophy was essentially at one with the Christian faith."[45]

Clearly to our ancestors the basis of right was moral and metaphysical. Occasionally Jefferson supported his arguments for natural rights with references to rights long possessed by the Anglo-Saxons, but his basis for right was solely metaphysical. Even Cornelia LeBoutillier, who cannot be accused of bias or even sympathy for such a foundation, has written: "Of all the Founding Fathers, Thomas Jefferson, perhaps, most lays himself open to suspicion of the metaphysical approach. There is no question but that he has this preoccupation, as he refers to the rights of man."[46]

The identification of natural rights to common law rights by early Americans has been greatly exaggerated,[47] and the Fathers knew that the common law hardly provided guarantees for the kind of freedom of religion and freedom of communication that they had in mind. Only rarely would one of the leaders of Revolutionary America suggest that his natural rights were those possessed by savages in an imagined "state of nature." Burlamaqui was, of course, known to many of the Fathers, but hedonism obviously was scarcely the basis for men who recognized their natural rights as concomitants to natural duties owed to the Almighty. It is impossible to conclude that the utilitarianism of Bentham or of Hume had the slightest significance as the source of right to the Founding Fathers. Nor was John Locke of any great inspiration to the Virginians. Gilbert Chinard has written that "it is very doubtful if [Jefferson] was greatly influenced by [Locke]."[48] The same is surely true of his fellow Virginians; these men had been well nurtured in the jurisprudence of Hooker, Bellarmine, Grotius, Thomas Aquinas, and Vattel, and the influence is omnipresent.[49]

ACCEPTED LIMITATIONS UPON THE EXERCISE OF NATURAL RIGHTS

With veritable unanimity the Founding Fathers from Virginia understood that ordinarily there could be socio-political limitations upon the exercise of the natural rights. The exception is generally limited to the natural right known as freedom of conscience. Here, Thomas Jefferson was quite typical of his colleagues in stating, "Our

---

[45]Becker, What is Still Living in the Political Philosophy of Thomas Jefferson?, 48 Am. Hist. Rev. 691, 695 (1943).
[46]LeBoutillier, American Democracy and Natural Law 110 (1950).
[47]Umbreit, op. cit. supra note 23, at 17-18.
[48]Chinard, The Commonplace Book of Thomas Jefferson 54 (1926).
[49]See, e.g., Brant, op. cit. supra note 42, at 249, 254, for the influence of Robert Bellarmine and Thomas Aquinas.

rulers have authority over such natural rights, only as we have submitted to them. The rights of conscience we never submitted, we could not submit. We are answerable for them to our God."[50] Moreover, at times some of the Virginians spoke as though other natural rights might be beyond restraint by the state. Thus, Richard Bland, referring to the natural right to retire from society, wrote: "This natural Right remains with every Man, and he cannot justly be deprived of it by any civil authority."[51] There are, indeed, statements by Jefferson which, taken alone, might indicate that he accepted no legislative diminution of our natural rights. He once wrote: "The true office is to declare and enforce only our natural rights and duties, and to take none of them from us...."[52] On another occasion he stated rather broadly that "our liberty depends on the freedom of the press, and that cannot be limited without being lost."[53]

Jefferson and his contemporaries generally understood that the natural rights were subject in their exercise to the limitations imposed by the natural law. "All natural rights," said Jefferson, "may be abridged or modified ... by the law," meaning, obviously, the natural law.[54] In accepting the proposition that natural rights were subject in their exercise to the limitations contained in natural law principles, the Founders of our country had before them the very clear statement of Blackstone who especially influenced the lawyers of the time. Blackstone had written in his famous *Commentaries:*

> "This natural liberty consists properly in a power of acting as one thinks fit, without any restraint or control, *unless by the law of nature....*"[55]

Natural law limitations upon the exercise of natural rights embrace in principle (1) consideration for the common good, (2) respect for the equal rights of others, and (3) realization that when the basis of the right is absent, the exercise of the claimed right can properly be denied. All these were understood by the Founding Fathers. In discussing natural rights and their exercise, Jefferson observed, "The law of the majority is the natural law of every society of men."[56] By this he gave no blessing to arbitrariness of a legislative majority, but meant

---

[50]3 Ford 263; Wright, op. cit. supra note 19, at 158.
[51]Bland, op. cit. supra note 38, at 10.
[52]Letter to Francis W. Gilmer, June 7, 1816; 10 Ford 32.
[53]Letter To Dr. James Currie, Jan. 18, 1786; 4 Ford 132.
[54]Patterson, The Constitutional Principles of Thomas Jefferson 53 (1953).
[55]1 Blackstone, Commentaries 40 (12th ed. 1793).
[56]7 Writings of Thomas Jefferson 496 (Washington ed. 1857) [hereinafter cited as Washington].

rather that respect for the good of the majority is an ever present limitation upon the exercise of individual rights. "A man has no natural right in opposition to his social duties," Jefferson added.[57] When the exercise of natural rights, other than freedom of conscience, imperiled the common good, the exercise could be restrained by the group. According to George Mason, even freedom of religion could be limited when "any man disturb the peace, the happiness, or safety of society."[58] Very similarly, James Madison indicated that no man should be "subjected to any penalties or disabilities unless under color of religion, any man disturb the peace, the happiness, or safety of society."[59]

Patrick Henry might have subscribed to the same limitations. If he drafted the sixteenth article of the Virginia Declaration of Rights, as has been suggested at times, there is reason to believe he did not deem freedom of religion an absolute right, for the article qualifies the right in these words: "unless under the color of religion any man disturb the peace."[60] However, his record as an attorney before the Revolution indicates that he was both willing and effective in defending the Baptists in their demands for freedom of religion and speech when they were charged with disturbing the peace.[61] Jefferson, too, undoubtedly accepted limits upon the natural right of religious practice. He wrote: "Whatsoever is prejudicial to the commonwealth in their ordinary uses and therefore prohibited by the laws, ought not to be permitted to churches in their sacred rights. For instance, it is unlawful in the ordinary course of things or in a private house to murder a child. It should not be permitted any sect then to sacrifice children."[62] George Washington also recognized limitations upon freedom of religion. He wrote that every man, "being accountable to God alone for his religious opinion, ought to be protected in worshipping the Deity according to the dictates of his own conscience," so long as he conducted "himself as a good citizen."[63] In writing to the Quakers, President Washington indicated that our laws should treat the conscientious scruples of all men "with great delicacy and tenderness," insofar "as a due regard to the protection and essential interests of the nation may justify and permit."[64] Washington realized

---

[57] Letter to Danbury Baptist Association; Bates, Religious Liberty 384 (1946).
[58] Brant, op. cit. supra note 42, at 241.
[59] Id. at 245.
[60] Morgan, op. cit. supra note 11, at 266-67.
[61] Id. at 125.
[62] 1 Boyd 547-48.
[63] 30 The Writings of George Washington 321 n.83 (Fitzpatrick ed. 1939).
[64] 12 The Writings of Washington 168-69 (Sparks ed. 1846).

well that the task of delimiting natural rights would not be easy. "It is at all times difficult," he said, "to draw with precision the line between those rights which must be surrendered and those which may be reserved."[65]

Not only could freedom of religion be limited according to the Fathers, but so too could freedom of expression and other natural rights when they broke out into acts injurious to others. "The legitimate powers of government," wrote Jefferson, "extend to such acts only as are not injurious to others."[66] When the equal rights of others were being violated by activity, natural rights could be restrained, at least by the democratically elected representatives of the people whose natural rights were being limited. Jefferson said: "This, like all other natural rights, may be abridged or modified in its exercise by their own consent, or by the law of those who depute them, if they meet in the right of others."[67]

It is of the utmost importance to perceive that the Founding Fathers, in consenting to limitations upon the natural rights, taught us that these rights could not be restrained by the state nor denied unless it was imperatively necessary to safeguard the common good against immediate danger. In stating that the evidence of natural law and natural rights can be seen by the mind and heart of every rational man, Jefferson observed: "It is there nature has written her moral laws, and where every man may read them for himself. He will never read there the permission to annul his obligations for a time, or forever, whenever they become dangerous, useless or disagreeable.... And though he may, under certain degrees of danger, yet *the danger must be imminent, and the degree great.*"[68] This insistence that natural rights prevailed unless there was a clear and present danger to a vital interest of society was made by others. For instance, Madison stated that "all men are entitled to the free exercise of religion, according to the dictates of conscience, unpunished, and unrestrained by the magistrate, *unless the preservation of equal liberty and the existence of the state are manifestly endangered.*"[69]

For government to deny a natural right because of some supposed tendency to harm sometime in the future was unthinkable to Jefferson. In his Bill for Establishing Religious Freedom in Virginia he wrote: "That to suffer the civil magistrate to intrude his powers into

---

[65] Monaghan, Heritage of Freedom 44 (1947).
[66] 3 Ford 263.
[67] 7 Washington 496.
[68] 3 Memorial Edition 228.
[69] Brant, op. cit. supra note 42, at 246.

the field of opinion and to restrain the profession of principles on supposition of their ill tendency is a dangerous fallacy, which at once destroys religious liberty."[70] "It is time enough," Jefferson added, "for the rightful purposes of civil government for its officers to interfere when principles break out into overt acts against peace and good order."[71] Even the influential Blackstone, whose ideas of personal freedom were inadequately developed, stated in his *Commentaries:* "Political or civil liberty, which is that of a member of society, is no other than natural liberty, so far restrained by human laws (and no further) as is necessary and expedient for the general advantage of the public."[72] If Blackstone was unwilling to condone inroads upon natural rights that were not "necessary and expedient" to protect the common weal, it can be assumed safely that the Virginia readers, more enthusiastic and understanding exponents of the doctrine, would have countenanced no greater limitations by the state.

As has been suggested, the Founding Fathers from Virginia knew well that the equal rights of others must be considered in ascertaining the permissible limits upon the exercise of natural rights. The natural law accepted by these men stood not only for the proposition that man is social by his nature, but also that his existence in society necessarily imposes limitations upon the enjoyment of his natural rights. The common good obviously is not advanced by allowing a single religious zealot to play a phonograph loudly upon the steps of a church making impossible the worship within of some five hundred others. It was Jefferson who said, "No man has a natural right to commit aggression on the equal rights of another." He added that "this is all from which the law ought to restrain him."[73] On another occasion he stated: "Rightful liberty is unobstructed action according to our will within limits drawn around us by the equal rights of others."[74] Well known to most of these early Americans was the definition of justice from Justinian, preserved and repeated by the jurists of the middle ages: "Justitia est constans et perpetua voluntas jus suum cuique tribuendi."[75] "Every denomination of Christians," said Richard Henry Lee, "has a right to pursue its own religious modes, *interfering not with others.*"[76]

---

[70] Bland, op. cit. supra note 38; Padover 946-47.
[71] Ibid.
[71]1 Blackstone, op. cit. supra note 55, at 40.
[73] Letter to Francis W. Gilmer, June 7, 1816; 10 Ford 32.
[74] Letter to Isaac H. Tiffany, April 4, 1819; Dumbauld, The Political Writings of Thomas Jefferson 55 (1955).
[75]1 Justinian, Institutes 1 (1852).
[76]2 Letters of Richard Henry Lee 401 (Ballagh ed. 1914). (Emphasis added.)

Since the natural right sometimes referred to as freedom of communication was designed to enable us to help ourselves and others to our ordained end and to make temporal society a more effective institution for accommodating our temporal needs, the peddling of untruths is never embraced within such a natural right. This was well comprehended by the Fathers. As much as Jefferson loved freedom of the press, he held it subject to these natural law limitations. It ought to be restrained, he urged, "within the legal and wholesome limits of truth."[77] In his Draught of a Fundamental Constitution for the Commonwealth of Virginia in 1783, he suggested a clause: "Printing presses shall be subject to no other restraint than liableness to legal prosecution for false facts printed and published."[78] Clearly, to Jefferson untruths had no right to enter the market place of thought. Nevertheless, although there is no natural right to utter or publish defamatory untruths, it does not follow that the criminal sanctions of the state should be used to incarcerate such individuals who pervert freedom of communication. There is much to be said for the social policy contained in the Draft for the Virginia Constitution of 1776, which read: "Printing presses shall be free, except so far as by commission of private injury cause may be given of private action."[79] One can believe that Jefferson felt much this way; when a clergyman allegedly libelled him he had the prosecution dismissed.[80]

Because of the lack of appeal to rational ends when force and violence take over, most of the Founding Fathers qualified the natural right to assemble by phrasing this as a "right of the people to assemble peaceably."[81] Perhaps the Fathers knew better than our generation that when printing is used for peddling for profit pornographies and obscenities it is no longer a natural right. As devoted a believer in natural rights and freedom of expression as Patrick Henry stated: "I acknowledge that licentiousness is dangerous, and that it ought to be provided against."[82] There is evidence to conclude that even Thomas Jefferson was willing to have the state prosecute those who degenerated in expression to licentiousness clearly endangering community morals.[83]

---

[77]Miller, Crisis in Freedom 231 (1951).
[78]Peden 220.
[79]1 Boyd 363.
[80]Letter to Wilson Cary Nicholas, June 13, 1809; 9 Ford 253.
[81]Richard Henry Lee, Draft for Declaration of Rights (Prepared Oct 2, 1787); 2 Ballagh, op. cit. supra note 76, at 442. See Monaghan, op. cit. supra note 65, at 58.
[82]Morison 323.
[83]Letter to Thomas McKean, Feb. 19, 1803; 8 Ford 218; 3 Memorial Edition 228; Mott, Jefferson and the Press 7 (1943).

The Natural Rights Enumerated

Conscience and Religion

Practically all of the Founding Fathers from Virginia who espoused the doctrine of natural rights included among their rights the freedoms of conscience and religion. When it was referred to as the right of conscience, it at times meant an absolute right to believe and, at other times, a right to practice one's faith openly. "The rights of conscience," according to Jefferson, could never be submitted to temporal legislators.[84] On another occasion he wrote: "All persons shall have a full and free liberty of religious opinion."[85] Moreover, in his Bill for Religious Freedom which eventually passed in 1785, Jefferson stated that "no man shall ... suffer on account of his religious opinions of beliefs...."[86] James Madison agreed that liberty of conscience was one of the "choicest liberties of the people." "The rights of conscience," he added, were "not included in the surrender implied by the social state."[87] This right of conscience was clearly fundamental to Patrick Henry, who so stated in the debates in the Virginia Convention on the ratification of the United States Constitution.[88] Similarly, George Washington, a great believer in the natural rights philosophy, wrote that all Americans are entitled to enjoy "the exercise of their inherent natural rights," the foremost being "liberty of conscience."[89]

To most of the Virginians the present natural right was something more than a right of belief, of conscience, and something more than the toleration of Locke. It was a natural right to worship their God openly. The Virginia Declaration of Rights, authored largely by George Mason, and adopted unanimously by the Virginia Convention, read in Article Sixteen:

> "That religion, or the duty which we owe to our Creator, and the manner of discharging it, can be directed only by reason and conviction, not by force or violence; and therefore all men are equally entitled to the free exercise of religion, according to the dictates of conscience; and that it is the mutual duty of all to practice Christian forebearance, love, and charity towards each other."

---

[84] Peden 159.
[85] Draft of a Constitution for Virginia (1776); 1 Boyd 334, 363.
[86] 12 Hening 84.
[87] 9 Works, op. cit. supra note 17, at 485.
[88] Morgan, op. cit. supra note 11, at 348; Morison 322.
[89] Letter to Hebrew Congregation of Newport, R.I., Aug. 7, 1790; Monaghan, op. cit. supra note 65, at 44.

It was here that Mason wrote: "All men have an equal, natural and unalienable right to the free exercise of religion, according to the dictates of conscience...."[90] In the later words of Jefferson: "The convention of May 1776, in their declaration of rights, declared it to be a truth, and a natural right, that the exercise of religion should be free."[91] Richard Henry Lee fully agreed that "every denomination of Christians has a right to pursue its own religious modes."[92]

The men of the Presbytery of Hanover on May 19, 1785, adopted a memorial in opposition to a pending bill providing funds for teachers of the Christian religion. The document stated: "Religion is altogether personal, and the right of exercising it unalienable; and it is not, cannot, and ought not to be, resigned to the will of the society at large; and much less to the Legislature, which derives its authority wholly from the consent of the people, and is limited by the original intention of civil associations."[93] In December of that year Jefferson's Bill for Religious Freedom was finally passed, providing that man would not only have a right to religious opinion, "but that all men shall be free to profess, and by argument to maintain, their opinion in matters of religion." This, it was added, was "of the natural right of mankind."[94]

To Jefferson freedom of religion certainly meant the right to preach what one desired. In his Notes on Virginia he wrote: "The legitimate powers of government extend to such acts only as are injurious to others. But it does me no injury for my neighbor to say there are twenty gods, or no god."[95] The Virginia Convention that ratified the Constitution accompanied its ratification with a list of proposed amendments and a bill of rights. Number twenty shows the importance of free exercise of religious liberty to that body. It reads:

"That religion, or the duty which we owe to our Creator, and the manner of discharging it can be directed only by reason and conviction, not by force or violence, and therefore all men have an equal, natural and unalienable right to the free exercise of religion according to the dictates of conscience."[96]

Even freedom to worship or to exercise publicly one's religion was considered veritably an absolute right by some of the Fathers. James

---

[90]Id. at 57-58.
[91]Peden 158.
[92]Letter to John Adams, Oct. 24, 1785; 2 Ballagh 401.
[93]Humphrey, op. cit. supra note 25, at 400-01.
[94]12 Hening 84-86; Morison 206; Padover 946-47.
[95]Peden 159.
[96]3 Elliot's Debates, op. cit. supra note 27, at 376, 659.

Madison, in his Memorial and Remonstrance against Religious Assessments wrote:

> "The Religion then of every man must be left to the conviction and conscience of every man; and it is the right of every man to exercise it as these may dictate. This right is in its nature an unalienable right. It is unalienable; because the opinions of men, depending only on evidence contemplated by their own minds, cannot follow the dictates of other men: It is unalienable also; because what is here a right towards men, is a duty towards the Creator. It is the duty of every man to render to the Creator such homeage, and such only, as he believes to be acceptable to Him. This duty is precedent, both in order of time and in degree of obligation to the claims of Civil Society. Before any man can be considered as a member of Civil Society, he must be considered as a subject of the Governor of the Universe: And if a member of Civil Society, who enters into any subordinate Association, must always do it with a reservation of his duty to the general authority; much more must every man who becomes a member of any particular Civil Society, do it with a saving of his allegiance to the Universal Sovereign. We maintain, therefore, that in matters of Religion, no man's right is abridged by the institution of Civil Society, and that religion is wholly exempt from its cognizance."[97]

Again, in a resolution of the Virginia House of Burgesses drafted in 1776 by Jefferson, it was announced that any act would be invalid "which renders criminal the maintaining any opinions in matters of religion, forbearing to repair the church, or the exercising any mode of worship whatever or as prescribes punishments for the same...."[98] And, in 1783 in his draft of a proposed Constitution for Virginia, Jefferson wrote: "The general assembly shall not have power... ot restrain [any person] from professing and supporting his religious beliefs."[99]

Primarily, to the Founding Fathers from Virginia freedom of religion as a natural right meant that a man was not to suffer civil disabilities because of his religious beliefs. This was emphasized by Jefferson in his Bill for Establishing Religious Freedom, wherein he stated that man "has a natural right" to freedom of religion in the sense that he was to be deprived of no civil right or office because of his religious convictions. He wrote:

> "Almighty God hath created the mind free... our civil rights have no dependence on our religious opinions... that therefore

---

[97] Humphrey, op. cit. supra note 25, at 395.
[98] 1 Boyd 530.
[99] Padover 113.

the proscribing any citizen as unworthy the public confidence by laying upon him an incapacity of being called to offices of trust and emolument, unless he profess or renounce this or that religious opinion, is depriving him injuriously of those privileges and advantages to which in common with his fellow-citizens he has a natural right."[100]

In his draft of a Constitution for Virginia in 1783 Jefferson added that "the general assembly shall not have power ... to abridge the civil rights of any person on account of his religious beliefs...."[101] To Jefferson the deprivation of political right and office to dissenters from the Established Church was a matter of grave injustice and a denial of natural right. "We have no right to prejudice another because he is of another church," he wrote.[102]

Similarly, this natural right meant to the Virginians that no religious denomination should be assigned to inferior status by the law. George Mason in his Virginia Declaration of Rights adopted by the Virginia Convention of June 12, 1776, stated: "All men have an equal natural and unalienable right to the free exercise of religion, according to the dictates of conscience, and ... no particular religious sect or society of Christians ought to be favored or established by law, in preference to others."[103] On October 24, 1776, the Presbytery of Hanover asserted "their natural rights" to religious liberty and indicated that this especially meant to them that they were not to be relegated to an inferior citizenship because of their faith.[104]

To Jefferson religious liberty further meant freedom from a legal requirement compelling attendance at the Established Church. In his draft of a Constitution for Virginia of June, 1776, he added to his basic freedom of religion clause: "Nor shall any person be compelled to frequent or maintain any religious service or institution."[105] Clearly, to Jefferson it was a violation of natural right to force a man to contribute to a church whose doctrines he could not accept. "No man," he wrote, "shall be compelled to frequent or support any religious worship, place, or ministry whatsover, nor shall be enforced, restrained, molested or burdened in his body or goods...." "The rights hereby asserted," he concluded, "are of the natural rights of mankind."[106]

---

[100] 12 Hening 84-86; Morison 206; Padover 946-47.
[101] Id. at 113.
[102] Notes for argument on Virginia legislation disestablishing the church (1776); 1 Boyd 546.
[103] Monaghan, op. cit. supra note 65, at 57-58.
[104] Commanger, op. cit supra note 44, at 124.
[105] 1 Boyd 344, 363.
[106] Bill for Establishing Religious Freedom; 12 Hening 84-86.

Again, in his Draught for a Fundamental Constitution in 1783 he wrote: "The general assembly shall not have power ... to restrain [one] from professing and supporting that belief, or to compel him to contributions, other than those he shall have personally stipulated."[107] James Madison was equally of the belief that freedom of religion embraced a freedom from assessments imposed by the state for a church to which the individual did not subscribe.[108]

The Founding Fathers from Virginia were not in agreement as to whether freedom of religion would permit an individual to be compelled by law to support the church of his own choice. George Washington saw no harm in a proposed bill to tax for support of teachers of the Christian Religion in Virginia. He wrote: "Although no man's sentiments are more opposed to any kind of restraint upon religious principles than mine, yet I confess, I am not among the number of those who are so alarmed at making men pay toward the support of that which they profess."[109] Richard Henry Lee was of a like mind; in a letter to James Madison he wrote: "The experience of all times shows Religion to be the guardian of morals—And he must be a very inattentive observer in our Country, who does not see that avarice is accomplishing the destruction of religion, for want of a legal obligation to contribute something to its support. The Declaration of Rights, it seems to me, rather contends against forcing modes of faith and forms of worship, than against compelling contribution for the support of religion in general."[110] Patrick Henry, Edmund Randolph, John Page, and John Marshall were in substantial agreement with this position. However, Thomas Jefferson, James Madison, George Mason, Colonel George Nicholas, and Robert Carter were opposed to the bill, and it was never passed.[111] Jefferson's views are expressed in the preamble to his Bill for Religious Freedom, wherein he stated:

> "That to compel a man to furnish contributions of money for the propagation of opinions which he disbelieves and abhors, is sinful and tyrannical; that even the forcing him to support this or that teacher of his own religious persuasion, is depriving him of the comfortable liberty of giving his contributions to the particular pastor whose morals he would make his pat-

---

[107] Padover 113.
[108] Memorial and Remonstrance again Religious Assessments (1785); Humphrey, op. cit. supra note 25, at 395.
[109] Letter to George Mason (1785); id. at 401.
[110] Nov. 26, 1784; 2 Ballagh 304.
[111] 2 Rowland 90; Nevins, The American States During and After the Revolution 434 (1927).

tern, and whose powers he feels most persuasive to righteousness...."[112]

When it came to the public exercise of religious worship, most of the Revolutionary Virginians were in general agreement that the common good might at times require some limitations upon the natural right. As James Madison indicated, no man should be subjected to penalties or disabilities unless "under color of religion," he "disturb the peace, the happiness, or safety of Society."[113] Very similarly, George Mason stated that the "fullest toleration in the exercise of religion" should be enjoyed by all men, "unpunished and unrestrained by the magistrate, unless, under color of religion, any man disturb the peace, the happiness, or the safety of society."[114] Although before the Revolution Patrick Henry enthusiastically defended the Baptists in their demands for freedom of religion, even when they were charged with disturbing the peace, there is the suggestion that he was willing to accept limitations upon the natural right when the safety of the community might be endangered.[115] Moreover, Richard Henry Lee wrote that it is "perfectly consonant... with our Revolution principles professed throughout all the states, that every denomination of Christians has a right to pursue its own religious modes, *interfering not with others*."[116] Recall, too, that Jefferson accepted that "whatsoever is prejudicial to the commonwealth in their ordinary uses and therefore prohibited by the laws, ought not to be permitted to churches in their sacred rights."[117]

Although the natural right of religion might be limited at times, it was not enough to Jefferson that there might be some "ill tendency" from the practice of one's faith. He stated that "to suffer the civil magistrate to intrude his powers into the field of opinion, and to restrain the profession or propagation of principles, on supposition of their ill tendency, is a dangerous fallacy, which at once destroys all religious liberty."[118] As indicated at greater length in the earlier paragraphs concerned with limitations upon natural rights, the natural right to worship God could be denied or limited, according to these Founding Fathers, only when it definitely and immediately imperiled the common good.

---

[112] 12 Hening 84-86.
[113] Brant, op. cit. supra note 42, at 245.
[114] Virginia Declaration of Rights, § 14; id. at 241.
[115] Morgan, op. cit. supra note 11, at 266-67.
[116] Letter to John Adams, Oct. 24, 1785; 2 Ballagh 401.
[117] Notes for argument on Virginia legislation disestablishing the church (1776); 1 Boyd 547-48.
[118] 12 Hening 84-86.

Life, Liberty, and the Pursuit of Happiness

To all of the Founding Fathers from Virginia, life and liberty were natural rights. Illustratively, Richard Henry Lee stated in the First Continental Congress: "Life and liberty, which is necessary for the security of life, cannot be given up when we enter society."[119] Additionally, a natural right to seek happiness was often recognized. As early as 1766 Richard Bland spoke of man's "natural right to promote happiness."[120] And the Virginia Declaration of Rights, drafted by George Mason and adopted at a general convention of delegates from throughout the Commonwealth on June 12, 1776, declared that "all men are by nature free and independent, and have certain inherent rights, of which, when they enter into a state of society, they cannot by any compact deprive or divest their posterity; namely, the enjoyment of life and liberty, with the means of acquiring and possessing property, and pursuing and obtaining happiness."[121]

Locke's emphasis upon the property right was disregarded, and Burlamaqui's preference for happiness was substituted by Thomas Jefferson in the Declaration of Independence of July 4th of the same year, wherein it was solemnly stated "that all men are created equal, that they are endowed by their Creator with certain unalienable rights, that among these are life, liberty, and the pursuit of happiness."[122] The "pursuit of happiness" had not been referred to in the Declarations and Resolves of the First Continental Congress on October 14, 1774, which asserted: "That the inhabitants of the English Colonies in North America, by the immutable laws of nature, the principles of the English Constitution, and the several charters or compacts, have the following rights: 1. That they are entitled to life, liberty and property, and they have never ceded to any sovereign power whatever, a right to dispose of either without their consent."[123] Both property and the pursuit of happiness were often added to life and liberty as basic natural rights. For example, George Mason, in drafting a proposed declaration of rights for the United States Constitution, suggested that "all freemen have certain essential inherent rights... among which are the enjoyment of life and liberty, with the means of acquiring, possessing, and protecting property, and pursuing and obtaining happiness and safety."[124]

---

[119] 12 English Historical Documents 805 (1953).
[120] Bland, op. cit. supra note 38, at 10.
[121] Morison 149; 12 Hening 110.
[122] 1 Boyd 429.
[123] Morison 118.
[124] 2 Rowland 445.

Although all of the Founding Fathers recognized liberty as a natural right, they have not left clear evidence of what they meant by the term. Undoubtedly, however, it meant something more than freedom from arbitrary physical restraint. Carl Becker has said that to Jefferson liberty as a natural right meant freedom of opinion, freedom of occupation and enterprise, and freedom from arbitrary political authority; and his conclusion seems sound.[125] Jefferson surely recognized freedom of religion and freedom of expression as basic natural rights, as is fully developed elsewhere in this paper. Liberty to Jefferson further included the right to labor and to enjoy the products of one's labor.[126]

The right to develop one's faculties was generally recognized as a natural right of the individual.[127] As early as 1764 Richard Bland had indicated that freedom from arbitrary laws was one of the natural rights of man.[128] Two years later he explained that if Parliament should abandon the colonies to a foreign tyrant the colonists "have a natural Right to defend their liberties by open force."[129] Bland was undoubtedly one of the first of the Fathers to assert that the colonists had a natural right of resistance against tyrannical or arbitrary rule.[130] Thomas Jefferson was in complete agreement that we have the natural right to self-defense against those who would arbitrarily deprive us of our life or liberty.[131] To Jefferson, too, the natural right to liberty was violated by slavery. Referring to the slavery wrought by the English king, Jefferson said: "He has waged cruel war against human nature itself, violating its most sacred rights of life and liberty in the persons of a distant people who never offended him."[132]

The natural right of liberty embraced man's freedom to retire from any particular political state and to emigrate elsewhere. This right of expatriation was early appreciated as a natural right. In 1766, in "An Inquiry into the Rights of the British Colonies," Richard Bland said: "This natural Right remains with every Man, and he cannot justly be deprived of it by any civil authority." When men enter society,

---

[125]Becker, op. cit. supra note 45, at 695.
[126]Letter to James Madison, Oct. 28, 1785; 8 Works, op. cit. supra note 17, at 196; Koch, op cit. supra note 33, at 136.
[127]Koch, Jefferson and Madison 79 (1950).
[128]Bland, The Colonel Dismounted 22 (1764).
[129]Bland, op. cit. supra note 38, at 26.
[130]Rossiter, Seedtime of the Republic 268 (1953).
[131]Letter to W. C. Claiborne, May 3, 1810; 12 Ford 383; Letter to George Rogers Clark, Jan. 29, 1780; 3 Boyd 276.
[132]1 Memorial Edition 34-35.

Bland observed, "they retain so much of their natural freedom as to have a right to retire from the Society, to renounce the Benefits of it, to enter into another Society, and to settle in another Country; for their Engagements to the Society, and their Submission to the publick Authority of the State, do not oblige them to continue in it longer than they find it will conduce to their Happiness, which they have a natural Right to promote." Bland concluded that all men have "a natural right to quit the society of which they are members and to retire into another country."[133] Similarly, Thomas Jefferson in his "Summary View" reminded the Crown that our people "possessed a right, which nature has given to all men, of departing from the country in which chance, not choice, has placed them...."[134] It is worth noting that in 1868 the United States Congress formally announced our national policy to be in accord with the views of these Founding Fathers from Virginia—that it is the "natural and inherent right of all people" to divest themselves of allegiance to any state.[135]

The Property Right

When Thomas Jefferson omitted from the Declaration of Independence the third in the triumvirate of Locke's natural rights—life, liberty, and property—and substituted, as would have Burlamaqui, "life, liberty and the pursuit of happiness," he rather clearly indicated that to him property was not a highly significant natural right. On another occasion Jefferson wrote to a friend, "No individual has, of natural right, a separate property in an acre of land."[136] In correspondence with Madison he indicated that specific property claims were civil and not natural rights. Jefferson wrote: "No man can by natural right oblige the lands he occupied."[137] On another occasion he stated: "Whenever there is in any country uncultivated lands and unemployed poor, it is clear that the laws of property have been so far extended as to violate natural right."[138] We may safely conclude that Jefferson believed in a natural right to occupy and work uncultivated lands and that he recognized that man would naturally have a property right in the fruits of his labors from the soil.[139]

---

[133]Bland, op. cit. supra note 38, at 10, 14.
[134]1 Boyd 121.
[135]15 Stat. 223 (1868). See Perez v. Brownell, 356 U.S. 44, 48 (1958).
[136]Letter to Isaac McPherson, Aug. 13, 1813; Dumbauld, op. cit supra note 74, at 56.
[137]Letter to James Madison, Sept. 6, 1789; 5 Ford 116.
[138]Koch, op. cit. supra note 127, at 65; 7 Ford 35-36.
[139]Koch, op. cit. supra note 127, at 78.

The term "property" as a natural right had many diverse meanings to the Founding Fathers. At times it meant that the individual had a property right in the sense that he had a natural right to develop his properties, *i.e.*, his natural faculties and talents. Probably the most acceptable definition went beyond the bundle of rights in realty and personalty and comprehended development of the individual personality. James Madison has given us much insight into the way in which the word was used by the Fathers who spoke of it as a natural right. He states that the term "embraces everything to which a man may attach a value and have a right; and which leaves to every one else the like advantage.... A man has property in his opinions and a free communication of them. He has a property of peculiar value in his religious opinions, and in the profession and practice dictated by them. He has a property very dear to him in the safety and liberty of his person. He has an equal property in the free use of his faculties and free choice of the objects on which to employ them. In a word, as a man is said to have a right to his property, he may be equally said to have a property in his rights."[140]

On other occasions some of the Founding Fathers from Virginia used the term "property" in this context as connoting more narrowly the common law rights in realty and chattels. George Mason, for example, in drafting the Virginia Declaration of Rights, adopted by the Convention of June 12, 1776, declared that among the natural rights are "the acquiring and possessing property."[141] Later he spoke of the inherent right to "the means of acquiring, possessing, and protecting property."[142] Similarly, Richard Henry Lee in his preface to the Williamsburg edition of Dickinson's Letters of a Farmer in Pennsylvania in 1768 wrote that "the great Author of nature" has given man his natural rights including "liberty, the virtuous enjoyment and free possession of property honestly gained."[143] Seemingly the term is being used here in its narrow, legalistic sense. The natural right to property included not only its acquisition and enjoyment, but also its disposition as well. Richard Henry Lee announced "that the disposal of their own Property is the inherent Right of Freemen."[144] Moreover,

---

[140] 6 The Writings of James Madison 101 (Hunt ed. 1906) [hereinafter cited as Hunt]. It was in this sense that Locke and Jefferson used the word. Koch, op. cit. supra note 127, at 79.

[141] Monaghan, op. cit. supra note 65, at 57-58.

[142] A proposed Declaration of Rights for the United States Constitution; 2 Rowland 445.

[143] 2 Life and Writings of John Dickinson, op. cit. supra note 22, at 290.

[144] Resolves for the Virginia Assembly, June, 1774; 1 Ballagh 115.

the property right embraced a natural right to defend one's property. Richard Bland, deeply devoted to the theory of natural rights, wrote: "If a man invades my property, he becomes an aggressor, and puts himself into a state of war with me; I have a right to oppose this invader."[145] Thomas Jefferson agreed and suggested that every man has a natural right to recapture his property wrongfully taken.[146]

To the Founding Fathers property as a natural right meant, for the time being, primarily that Parliament could not tax the colonists and thus indirectly take from them their property. On May 29, 1765, Patrick Henry had introduced resolutions into the Virginia House of Burgesses, four of which were adopted, by which that body indicated that it had the exclusive right to tax the property of Virginians.[147] Three years later the same body was demanding the "full enjoyment of all our natural and constitutional rights and privileges," adding: "No power on earth has a right to impose taxes upon the people or to take the smallest portion of their property without their consent, given by their representatives in Parliament."[148]

Of all the Founding Fathers from Virginia, James Madison has given us the clearest understanding of what property meant as a natural right. In his essay on "Property" that appeared in the National Gazette on March 29, 1792, Madison stated that arbitrary limitations and restrictions upon the acquisition of property were violative of right. There was no doubt in his mind that the right to possess property sprang from the law of nature.[149] Madison was equally willing to add that the natural right included protection by the government of the owner's realty and chattels. He wrote: "Government is instituted to protect property of every sort; as well as that which lies in the various rights of individuals, as that which the term particularly expresses. This being the end of government, that alone is a *just* government which *impartially* secures to every man, whatever is his *own*."[150] To Madison arbitrary limitations and controls upon the use of property were contrary to natural right, and to his fellow Virginians arbitrary controls were wrong.[151] Like all other natural rights,

---

[145]Meade, Patrick Henry, Patriot in the Making 198 (1957).
[146]Letter to W. C. Claiborne, May 3, 1810; Dumbauld, op. cit. supra note 74, at 57.
[147]Gipson, The Coming of the Revolution 87 (1954).
[148]3 Freeman 198-99.
[149]6 Hunt 102; Burns, James Madison, Philosopher of the Constitution 71, 75 (1938).
[150]6 Hunt 102.
[151]Burns, op. cit. supra note 149, at 75. See also Bland, op. cit. supra note 128, at 22.

however, the property right was subject to reasonable regulation to protect other members of the community in their legitimate rights. Governmentally condoned monopolies were to Madison a denial of the property rights of others.[152] Furthermore, the natural right to property was clearly infringed by both arbitrary taxes and unequal taxation.[153] Lastly, by indirection Madison made the point that the property right would be violated if the state took property from the individual without just compensation or for purposes not public.[154]

There is abundant evidence from the Virginians that arbitrary taxation was generally deemed violative of the natural right to property. This is developed in the following section.

The Right to Govern and Tax Themselves

Undoubtedly one of the most important natural rights to the Virginia Founding Fathers was the right of self-government. Thomas Jefferson's writings are replete with recognitions of this right. He stated:

> "Every man, and every body of men on earth, possesses the right of self-government. They receive it with their being from the hand of nature. Individuals exercise it by their single will; collections of men by that of their majority; for the law of the majority is the natural law of every society of men. When a certain description of men are to transact together a particular business, the times and places of their meeting and separating, depend on their own will; they make a part of the natural right of self-government. This, like all other natural rights, may be abridged or modified in its exercise by their own consent, or by the law of those who depute them, if they meet in the right of others; but as far as it is not abridged or modified, they retain it as a natural right, and may exercise them in what form they please, either exclusively by themselves, or in association with others, or by others altogether, as they shall agree."[155]

On the 26th of July 1774, the freeholders of Albemarle County adopted Resolutions, almost surely from the pen of Jefferson, to the effect that no legislature had power over them except their own "duly constituted and appointed with their own consent" and that they held these rights "as common rights of mankind."[156]

---

[152]6 Hunt 103.
[153]Ibid.
[154]Ibid.
[155]7 Washington 496; Caldwell, The Jurisprudence of Thomas Jefferson, 18 Ind. L.J. 193 (1943).
[156]1 Boyd 117.

Eight days earlier the freemen of Fairfax County meeting in Alexandria had passed several resolves, including what was in all probability the first assertion of the natural right to self-government by an American representative body. These men declared and resolved:

> "That the claim, lately assumed and exercised by the British Parliament, of making all such laws as they think fit, to govern the people of these colonies, and to extort from us our money without our consent, is not only diametrically contrary to the first principles of the Constitution, and the original compacts by which we are dependent upon the British Crown and government; but it is totally incompatible with the privileges of a free people and the natural rights of mankind, will render our own legislatures merely nominal and nugatory, and is calculated to reduce us from a state of freedom and happiness to slavery and misery."[157]

George Washington was in the chair on this occasion, and the resolves were undoubtedly from the pen of George Mason. Soon thereafter they were carried by Washington to Williamsburg and presented to the Burgesses.[158] All of the Virginians in the First Continental Congress were in full agreement with that conclave's Declaration of Rights, which included "a right in the people to participate in their legislative council," at least as to matters of "taxation and internal polity."[159]

Before most of the Founding Fathers considered revolution and independence, they had accepted a natural right of freedom from taxation by governmental bodies in which the taxpayers were not represented. Later, of course, this was absorbed into the natural right of self-government. As early as 1763 Richard Bland in "The Colonel Dismounted" had stated that "any tax respecting our INTERNAL polity, which may hereafter be imposed on us by Act of Parliament, is arbitrary, as depriving us of our Rights, and may be opposed."[160] Three years later Bland averred the natural right of the Virginians to be subjected to laws only when passed by a legislature in which they were represented, and the natural right to be taxed only under the same circumstances. He wrote: "I have proved irrefragably that the Colonies are not represented in Parliament, and consequently upon your own Position, that no new Law can bind them that is made without the concurrence of their Representatives; and if so, then

---

[157] 1 Rowland 418.
[158] Id. at 421.
[159] Declaration and Resolves of Oct. 14, 1774; Documents Illustrative of the Formation of the Union of the American States 1 (Tansill ed. 1927).
[160] Meade, op. cit. supra note 145, at 198.

every Act of Parliament that imposes internal Taxes upon the Colonies is an Act of Power, and not of Right."[161]

On February 27, 1766, a group of prominent planters met at Leedstown and drew up articles of association, in which they asserted that they were entitled to rights "founded on reason, law and compact" and that among them was the right that man "cannot be taxed, but by the consent of a Parliament in which he is represented by persons chosen by the people, and who themselves pay a part of the tax they impose on others." This, proclaimed these early Virginians, was "a fundamental right."[162] Two years later the Virginia House of Burgesses drafted a memorial to the House of Lords and a remonstrance to the House of Commons, in which they set forth that "no power on earth has a right to impose taxes upon the people or to take the smallest portion of their property without their consent, given by their representatives in Parliament." The Burgesses served notice that they wanted "full enjoyment of all our natural and constitutional rights and privileges."[163] The famous Fairfax Resolves, mentioned earlier, joined in the assertion that taxation by a Parliament in which the taxpayers were unrepresented was a denial of natural right.[164] George Washington is also on record as indicating that to him Parliament's imposition of taxes upon the colonists was contrary to natural law.[165] Everywhere throughout the Colonies the voice was the same, as witnessed by the Resolution of the Stamp Act Congress asserting the natural right of Americans "that no taxes be imposed on them but with their own consent, given personally or by their representatives."[166]

Suggestions that the doctrine of natural rights was enforced by the Founding Fathers solely to provide an intellectual base for revolution are unsound. As late as 1790 Thomas Jefferson was writing of the instant natural rights: "Every man, and every body of men on earth possesses the right of self-government. They receive it with their being from the hand of nature."[167] Caleb Patterson is indeed correct when he concludes that "self-government must be placed high among the blessings which Jefferson claimed as a natural right of man."[168]

Many of the Founding Fathers from Virginia recognized a natu-

---

[161] Bland, op. cit. supra note 38, at 24.
[162] 3 Freeman 154.
[163] Id. at 198-99.
[164] 1 Rowland 418.
[165] 2 Ford 421.
[166] Resolutions of the Stamp Act Congress, Oct. 9, 1765; Morison 32.
[167] Opinion on the Residence Bill, July 15, 1790; 5 Ford 205.
[168] Patterson, op. cit. supra note 54, at 52.

ral right in the people to alter or abolish their form of government. George Mason, draftsman of the Virginia Declaration of Rights adopted by the Virginia Convention of June 12, 1776, wrote: "Whenever any government shall be found inadequate, or contrary to these purposes, a majority of the community hath an indubitable, unalienable, and indefeasible right to reform, alter, and establish another, or abolish it."[169] Later, when suggesting amendments to the United States Constitution for the Virginia convention concerned with its ratification, Mason spoke of the right to "alter, or abolish it and to establish another in such manner as shall be judged most conducive to the public weal."[170] Patrick Henry also recognized "an indubitable, inalienable and indefeasible right to reform, alter or abolish" the governmental form of the moment.[171] Moreover, James Madison originally wished to amend the United States Constitution by prefixing a declaration that "the people have an indubitable, unalienable, and indefeasible right to reform or change their Government, whenever it be found adverse or inadequate to the purposes of its institution."[172]

Thomas Jefferson probably even more than his contemporaries believed that "whenever any form of government becomes destructive of these ends"—man's "inherent and inalienable rights"—"it is the right of the people to alter or abolish it."[173] Through Gilmer, Jefferson was the disciple of St. Robert Bellarmine, who had written that "if there be legitimate cause," the people may change the kind of government in which they find themselves.[174] There is additional evidence that Virginians of the time rather widely subscribed to a natural right to alter the government. John Leland, a highly respected Baptist minister, asserted in 1791 in his well-received essay on the "Rights of Conscience" that "whenever government is found inadequate to preserve the liberty and property of the people they have an indubitable right to alter it so as to answer their purposes."

Freedom of Communication

There are some indications that the Founding Fathers from Virginia considered certain aspects of what we call freedom of communication to be within the concept of natural rights. Thomas Jefferson, for instance, deemed freedom of communication between the

---
[169] Monaghan, op. cit. supra note 65, at 57-58.
[170] 2 Rowland 283.
[171] Wirt, Patrick Henry 277 (1817).
[172] Speech in Congress, June 8, 1789; 5 Hunt 376.
[173] 1 Memorial Edition 29.
[174] Bellarmine, De Laicis 27 (Murphy transl. 1928).

people and their representatives to be a natural right.[175] The members of the First Continental Congress in their Declarations and Resolves asserted on October 14, 1774, that the inhabitants of the English Colonies in North America, by the immutable laws of nature, the principles of the English Constitution, and the several charters or compacts "have a right peaceably to assemble, consider of their grievances, and petition the king; and that all prosecutions, prohibitory proclamations, and commitments for the same, are illegal."[176] George Mason similarly concluded that by nature men have "a right peaceably to assemble together to consult for their common good, or to instruct their representatives."[177] His Virginia Declaration of Rights, adopted by the General Convention on July 12, 1776, follows the assertion of man's inherent rights with the later statement that "the Freedom of the press is one of the great bulwarks of liberty, and can never be restrained but by despotick governments." There were those who not only opposed the Alien and Sedition laws, but who, like James Madison and John Taylor, believed these limitations upon the press to be inimical to natural rights.[178] Of course, Patrick Henry considered freedom of the press as a basic right.[179] And Richard Henry Lee assuredly believed that freedom of the press was to be included in declarations of right, but it cannot be said that he considered it a natural right.[180]

Thomas Jefferson did not deem free presses to be a matter of basic natural rights; rather, he considered this freedom as a "fence" to protect the people in the enjoyment of their more basic rights.[181] This is not to say that freedom of the press was unimportant to Jefferson. He clearly believed that expressions of opinion were not to be punished by the state because of some ill tendency.[182] The Sedition Act to him was patently unconstitutional.[183] Most of his contemporaries from Virginia deemed the Alien and Sedition laws, in their punishment of newspaper editors for their opinions, to be the very worst form of violating freedom of the press.[184] Once Jefferson somewhat

---

[175]Letter to James Monroe, Sept. 7, 1797; 8 Works, op. cit. supra note 17, at 339.
[176]Burnett, op. cit. supra note 41, at 58; Morison 119-20.
[177]2 Rowland 447.
[178]2 Howison, op. cit. supra note 13, at 352.
[179]Morgan, op. cit. supra note 11, at 348.
[180]2 Ballagh 442.
[181]Letter to Noah Webster, 1790; 8 Memorial Edition 112-13.
[182]See Jefferson's Bill for Establishing Religious Freedom in Virginia; Morison 206.
[183]10 Ford 141; 8 Ford 56.
[184]2 Howison, op. cit. supra note 13, at 352.

loosely remarked that "our liberty depends on the freedom of the press, and that cannot be limited without being lost."[185] There is good reason to believe that some limitations upon the press were acceptable to Jefferson. In his draft for a constitution for Virginia in 1776 he wrote: "Printing presses shall be free, except so far as by commission of private injury cause may be given of private action."[186] Libel and slander were beyond the pale to Jefferson, and their punishment he would have admitted, at least by actions brought by those individuals injured.[187] Freedom of the press, said Jefferson, ought to be restrained "within the legal and wholesome limits of the truth."[188] Nevertheless, when he was allegedly libelled by a clergyman, Jefferson was willing to order the dismissal of the prosecution.[189]

Like Jefferson, James Madison considered freedom of the press as one of the "choicest liberties of the people." He was instantly willing to join Jefferson in denouncing the Alien and Sedition Acts as unwarranted denials of freedom of communication. The Virginia Resolutions of 1798 were written by Madison, with encouragement from Jefferson, who had shortly before drafted the Kentucky Resolutions. Both stressed the theory of natural and essential rights and condemned the federal legislation as unjustified. When Madison was questioned if the federal government had the power to punish for libellous attacks against itself, he forcefully responded in the negative.[190] To Madison freedom of communication included "the right of freely examining public characters and measures" which he explained as "the only effectual guardian of every other right."[191] When speech or the press concerned matters of government and the temporary custodians of power, Madison was absolutely unwilling to attempt any distinction between freedom and "licentiousness" of the press. Throughout his life he fought those who through love of power "resorted to a distinction between the freedom and licentiousness of the press" to stifle freedom of communication when its exercise was injuring neither the equal rights of others nor the common good. By such a reckless jurisprudence of appellation Madison saw that "the judge as to what is licentious may escape through any constitutional

---

[185] Letter to Dr. James Currie, Jan. 18, 1786; 4 Ford 132.
[186] 1 Boyd 363.
[187] Mott, op. cit. supra note 83, at 7.
[188] Miller, op. cit. supra note 77, at 231.
[189] Letter to Wilson Cary Nicholas, June 13, 1809; 9 Ford 253.
[190] 6 Hunt 389-92; Koch, op. cit. supra note 127, at 58; Burns, op. cit. supra note 149, at 82.
[191] 4 Letters and Other Writings of James Madison 540 (Congress ed. 1865).

restriction." He concluded: "A supposed freedom which admits of exceptions, alleged to be licentious, is not freedom at all. Under it men of a particular religious opinion might be excluded from office, because such exclusion would not amount to an establishment of religion, and because it might be said that their opinions are licentious. And under it Congress might denominate a religion to be heretical and licentious, and proceed to its suppression."[192]

Madison's healthy antipathy to labels should not tempt the reader to conclude that he deemed the natural rights, even freedom of religion, to be absolutes. It can be stated quite categorically that he was willing for society to limit the exercise of natural rights when such overt action constituted a clear and present danger to the natural rights of others or the security of society. Recall that he wrote: "All men are entitled to the free exercise of religion, according to the dictates of conscience, unpunished, and unrestrained by the magistrate, *unless the preservation of equal liberty and the existence of the state are manifestly endangered.*"[193] James Madison seemingly would not have imposed upon the state any obligation to provide teaching posts for erratic thinkers. In passing upon professors for the contemplated University of Virginia, he advised that they had better be "orthodox" as well as "able" and that they were expected to safeguard the community against "heretical intrusions into the School of Politics."[194]

It is a great disservice to the memory of both Jefferson and Madison to cite them in defense of absolute, libertarian notions. Freedom of printing and speaking was no more an absolute right, devoid of social control, to them than it was to their contemporary Founding Fathers. Not only did the communicative right end when it deviated from the truth, but when it failed to respect the legitimate concerns of others it was equally subject to restraint. No Virginian of the time was more concerned for freedom of speech and press than Patrick Henry, and yet he stated in the debates of the Virginia Ratifying Convention of June, 1788: "I acknowledge that licentiousness is dangerous, and that it ought to be provided against."[195] Nor was the irrational rule of the mob any more acceptable than the recourse to untruths. To those who added to their rights freedom of assembly, it was uniformly "freedom to assemble peaceably."[196]

---

[192]Padover 295; Burns, op. cit. supra note 149, at 82.
[193]Brant, op. cit. supra note 42, at 246.
[194]9 Hunt 220.
[195]Morison 323.
[196]2 Ballagh, op. cit. supra note 76, at 442; 2 Rowland 447; Morison 119-20.

Some Other Occasionally Suggested Natural Rights

There are some writers, *e.g.*, Umbreit, who have remarked that the natural rights of the Founding Fathers were simply the common law rights. These writers almost uniformly urge that their thesis is proved because the Fathers termed the right of trial by jury to be a natural right.[197] The writings of the Revolutionary Americans simply do not show that they overwhelmingly or even generally asserted that the right of trial by jury was a natural right. The record is clear that Thomas Jefferson did not deem this a natural right, but only a "fence" to protect the people in their natural rights.[198] Moreover, it is suggested that most Virginians, as well as colonists generally, would have agreed. This is, of course, not to suggest that the Virginians did not treasure such a right, but it was ordinarily referred to not as a natural right but as, in the words of Madison, "one of the choicest liberties of the people,"[199] or "a fundamental right,"[200] or "the most valuable Birthright of every freeman," as Robert Carter Nicholas wrote.[201]

Claims that the Founding Fathers from Virginia alleged trial by jury to be a natural right find support almost solely in a remark of Richard Henry Lee[202] and in the arguments of Patrick Henry in the debates of the Virginia convention concerned with adopting the Constitution of the United States. Henry is reported to have said: "If you will in the language of freemen stipulate that there are rights which no man under heaven can take from you, you shall have me going along with you—not otherwise."[203] Concededly, he might well have had in mind trial by jury at the time of these remarks. Yet, as a lawyer he should have understood that there were considerable areas of litigation, such as suits in equity and even the petty offenses in criminal law, in which trial by jury was not given by Americans to themselves in either colonial governments or the contemporary state constitutions.

In procedural matters there was further insistence upon the right to an impartial judge. Thomas Jefferson, for instance, asserted that no man had "a natural right to be the judge between himself and an-

---

[197] Umbreit, op. cit. supra note 47, at 17-18.
[198] Letter to Noah Webster, 1790; 8 Memorial Edition 112-13.
[199] Koch, op. cit. supra note 127, at 58.
[200] Articles of Association of planters at Leedstown, Feb. 27, 1766; 3 Freeman 154.
[201] Considerations on the Present State of Virginia Examined 54 (Swem ed. 1919).
[202] Letters of the Federal Farmer in 1787; Ford, Pamphlets on the Constitution 315 (1888).
[203] Morgan, op. cit. supra note 11, at 348; Morison 322.

other."[204] Richard Henry Lee wanted to insert in his declaration of rights that "the right administration of justice should be secured by the freedom and independency of the Judges,"[205] but he stopped short of suggesting that there was a natural right to a free, independent, or impartial judge. Lee added: "There are other essential rights, which we have justly understood to be the rights of freemen; as freedom from hasty and unreasonable search warrants, warrants not founded on oath, and not issued with due caution, for searching and seizing men's papers, property and persons."[206] The language might possibly mean that he considered these to be natural rights, but more likely that he deemed them more akin to Jefferson's "fences" to protect the more basic natural rights. There is no considerable belief that there was a natural right to be free from ex post facto laws. Yet Thomas Jefferson once wrote: "The sentiment that ex post facto laws are against natural right is so strong in the United States that few, if any of the State constitutions have failed to proscribe them."[207]

Conclusion

There were additional natural rights suggested by some of the Founding Fathers from Virginia. Freedom from perpetual obligation, for instance, was deemed a natural right by Jefferson.[208] But the natural rights on which there was the largest agreement and the greatest significance were those discussed previously: freedom of conscience and religion, life, liberty and the pursuit of happiness, property, the right to govern and tax themselves, and freedom of communication.

Practically without exception these Founding Fathers stressed the equality of natural right. Thomas Jefferson spoke of "the equal right of every citizen, in his person and property."[209] On another occasion he wrote, "Rightful liberty is unobstructed action according to our will within limitations drawn around us by the equal rights of others."[210] "No man," he added, "has a natural right to commit aggression on the equal rights of another, and this is all and from

---

[204]Letter to Francis W. Gilmer, June 7, 1816; 10 Ford 32.
[205]Ballagh, op. cit. supra note 76, at 442.
[206]Letters of a Federal Farmer in 1787; Ford, op. cit. supra note 202, at 315.
[207]Letter to Isaac McPherson, Aug. 13, 1813; Dumbauld, op. cit. supra note 74, at 56; 13 Memorial Edition 326.
[208]Letter to Albert Gallatin, Nov. 26, 1805; 10 Works, op. cit. supra note 17, at 185.
[209]Letter to Samuel Kercheval, July 12, 1816; 15 Memorial Edition 36.
[210]Letter to Isaac H. Tiffany, April 4, 1819; Dumbauld, op. cit. supra note 74, at 55.

which the laws ought to restrain him."[211] It was in his Summary View that Jefferson stated that Parliament had no power to encroach "upon those rights which God and the laws have given equally and independently to all."[212]

Richard Bland had similarly stressed at an earlier date the equality of natural right.[213] George Mason also wrote that "all men have an equal natural and unalienable right to the free exercise of religion...."[214] Because there had been the preferred church in Virginia with discriminations against the so-called dissenters, it was equality of the natural right to religion that was most frequently asserted. Madison opposed the 1785 Bill for Religious Assessments "because, the bill violates that equality which ought to be the basis of every law, and which is more indispensable, in proportion as the validity or expediency of any law is more liable to be impeached. If 'all men are by nature equally free and independent' (the Virginia Declaration of Rights, article one) all men are to be considered as entering into Society on equal conditions; as relinquishing no more, and therefore retaining no less, one than another, of their natural rights. Above all are they to be considered as retaining an 'equal title to the free exercise of Religion according to the dictates of conscience' (the Declaration of Rights, article sixteen)."[215]

Undoubtedly a number of the Founding Fathers from Virginia knew of John Locke's ideas on natural law and natural right and were influenced by him. At a relatively early date in this period Bland was endorsing his ideas.[216] Jefferson read a good deal of Locke,[217] but it is noteworthy that he repudiated Locke's triumvirate of natural rights language in favor of Burlamaqui's in the Declaration of Independence,[218] as did George Mason.[219] Malone has noted that Jefferson did not bother to copy Locke's ideas into his notebooks,[220] and Chinard concludes that it is very doubtful if Jefferson was greatly influenced by Locke.[221] According to James Madison, the delegates read much

---

[211]Letter to Francis W. Gilmer, June 7, 1816; 10 Ford 32.
[212]1 Boyd 121.
[213]Bland, op. cit. supra note 38, at 25.
[214]Virginia Declaration of Rights; Monaghan, op. cit. supra note 65, at 58.
[215]Padover 301.
[216]Locke was cited by Bland in An Inquiry into the Rights of the British Colonies, op. cit. supra note 48. See also Rossiter, op. cit. supra note 130, at 267.
[217]Becker, Declaration of Independence 27 (1922); 1 Thorpe, Constitutional History of the United States 155 (1901).
[218]1 Boyd 315.
[219]Hill, op. cit. supra note 34, at 140.
[220]Malone, Jefferson the Virginian 175 (1948).
[221]Chinard, op. cit. supra note 48, at 54.

of Locke at the First Continental Congress,[222] and his works were undoubtedly read quite widely by the Virginians.[223] It is suggested, nevertheless, that his influence upon the Founding Fathers was much less than has been popularly supposed. A biographer of Patrick Henry asserts that Henry was "unlearned in the philosophy of Locke"[224] and that the influence upon many of the other Virginians was undoubtedly no greater.

Burlamaqui exerted a substantial influence upon some of Virginia's Founding Fathers.[225] The same may be said of Montesquieu;[226] his *Spirit of the Laws* was Jefferson's bible, according to one author.[227] Yet another biographer claims that Lord Kames was the principal source of Jefferson's ideas.[228] Vattel[229] and Grotius[230] were read by many of the Fathers, and their influence was probably considerable. The now sanctified Robert Bellarmine clearly impressed Madison, who was willing to recommend him to Jefferson.[231] His influence upon Jefferson has been noted by others,[232] and, through Filmer, who made Bellarmine's ideas widely available to English and Colonial readers, Bellarmine was persuasive not only to Madison and Jefferson, but also to George Mason and others.[233] It should be noted too that Thomas Aquinas had so much to offer James Madison that he was willing to suggest to Jefferson that Aquinas was well worth perusing.[234] The writings of the Founding Fathers from Virginia give evidence that they found ideas and inspiration also in Pufendorf,[235] Wolf,[236]

---

[222]Brant, op. cit. supra note 42, at 76.
[223]Hunt, The Virginia Declaration of Rights and Cardinal Bellarmine, 3 Catholic Hist. Rev. 276 (1917).
[224]Axelrod, Patrick Henry 98 (1947).
[225]His influence upon Bland can be detected. See also Hunt, op. cit. supra note 223, at 276; Brant, op. cit. supra note 42, at 76.
[226]Ibid.
[227]1 Thorpe, op. cit. supra note 217, at 154.
[228]Chinard, op. cit. supra note 48, at 73.
[229]For his influence on Bland see Bland's Inquiry into the Rights of the British Colonies, op. cit. supra note 38; Rossiter, op. cit. supra note 130, at 267. For his influence on Patrick Henry see Wirt, op. cit. supra note 171, at 326.
[230]1 Thorpe, op. cit. supra note 217, at 155; Le Boutillier, op. cit. supra note 46, at 118; Wirt, op. cit. supra note 171, at 326.
[231]Brant, op. cit. supra note 42, at 120.
[232]Bellarmine, op. cit. supra note 174; Hirst, Life and Letters of Thomas Jefferson 508 (1926); Ryan and Miller, The State and the Church 175 (1924).
[233]Hunt, op. cit. supra note 223, at 276.
[234]Brant, op. cit. supra note 42, at 120.
[235]LeBoutillier, op. cit. supra note 46, at 118.
[236]Ibid.

Priestly,[237] Filmer,[238] Sydney,[239] Domat,[240] and Wollaston.[241] Even such a list should not be deemed exhaustive, since many of the leaders of this day read widely over the whole range of English, Continental, and Roman jurists. They were simply the contemporary exponents of a philosophy of natural rights and natural law that had been aged over the centuries.

---

[237] 1 Thorpe, op. cit. supra note 217, at 155.
[238] Id. at 27; Bellarmine, op. cit. supra note 174; Hunt, op. cit. supra note 223, at 276.
[239] 1 Thorpe, op. cit. supra note 217, at 155; Hunt, op. cit. supra note 223, at 276.
[240] Rossiter, op. cit. supra note 139, at 267.
[241] Bland, op. cit. supra note 38; Rossiter, op. cit. supra note 130.

Racial Segregation in Public Accommodations: Some Reflected Light on the Fourteenth Amendment From the Civil Rights Act of 1875

Alfred Avins

> *In light of recent congressional and judicial reliance upon the fourteenth amendment as a constitutional justification for civil rights legislation, Dr. Avins discusses the consensus of opinion which prevailed among the amendment's framers at the time of its enactment. By recounting the matters discussed in the Thirty-Ninth through Forty-Third Congresses regarding the public accommodations legislation introduced by Senator Charles Sumner of Massachusetts and ultimately adopted as the Civil Rights Act of 1875, the author attempts to shed further light upon the scanty legislative history of the fourteenth amendment in order to ascertain its limitations. He concludes that since those who drafted, debated, and voted upon the amendment did not envision its provisions as conferring social equality upon Negro citizens, legislation prohibiting their segregation in public accommodations is an unconstitutional infringement upon individual rights.*

THE EXTENT to which the fourteenth amendment forbids racial segregation is a matter of current importance in the field of public accommodations. Section 201(d) of the Civil Rights Act of 1964[1] specifically relies on the fourteenth amendment as one of the constitutional bases for forbidding segregation in public facilities. Moreover, where the Supreme Court has found "state action" to exist, it has specifically relied on this amendment to forbid such segregation, even without a federal statute,[2] and in so doing has overruled what was long the landmark case in the field of race relations, *Plessy v. Ferguson*.[3]

THE AUTHOR (B.A., Hunter College, LL.B., Columbia University, LL.M., New York University, M.L. and J.S.D., University of Chicago, Ph.D., Cambridge University) is a Professor of Law at Memphis State University.

While direct light on the intent of the framers of the fourteenth

---

[1] 78 Stat. 243, 42 U.S.C. § 2000a (1964).
[2] See, e.g., Browder v. Gayle, 142 F. Supp. 707 (M.D. Ala.), *aff'd mem.*, 352 U.S. 903 (1956).
[3] 163 U.S. 537 (1896).

amendment respecting segregation is scanty,[4] there is abundant reflected light with respect to segregation and public accommodations from the debates on the Civil Rights Act of 1875.[5] The first section of that statute forbade discrimination in inns, public carriers, theaters, and places of amusement.

Apparently, examination of the legislative history of that act has been discouraged by the fact that it was held unconstitutional in the *Civil Rights Cases*[6] on the ground that it went beyond the "state action" limitation of the fourteenth amendment. Nevertheless, the debates in connection with that act are illuminating. This article will attempt to weave the reflected light into a pattern which will show the intent of the framers of the fourteenth amendment regarding segregation in public accommodations.

I. SUMNER AND THE AMNESTY BILL

On May 13, 1870, Senator Charles Sumner of Massachusetts, the ultra-equalitarian Radical Republican, introduced in the Senate a bill to supplement the Civil Rights Act of 1866.[7] The first section of Sumner's bill read:

> That all citizens of the United States, without distinction of race, color, or previous condition of servitude, are entitled to the equal and impartial enjoyment of any accommodation, advantage, facility, or privilege furnished by common carriers, whether on land or water; by inn-keepers; by licensed owners, managers, or lessees of theaters or other places of public amusement; by trustees, commissioners, superintendents, teachers, or other officers of common schools and other public institutions of learning, the same being supported or authorized by law; by trustees or officers of church organizations, cemetery associations, and benevolent institutions incorporated by national or State authority; and this right shall not be denied or abridged on any pretense of race, color, or previous condition of servitude.[8]

The bill died after being sent to the Judiciary Committee and re-

---

[4] *Cf.* Bickel, *The Original Understanding and the Segregation Decision*, 69 HARV. L. REV. 1, 56-59 (1955).

[5] 18 Stat. 335.

[6] 109 U.S. 3 (1883).

[7] 14 Stat. 27.

[8] CONG. GLOBE, 41st Cong., 2d Sess. 3434 (1870). See also CONG. GLOBE, 42d Cong., 1st Sess. 21 (1871); CONG. GLOBE, 42d Cong., 2d Sess. 244, 821 (1872). The bill had probably been inspired by some complaints Sumner had received from colored legislators. See CONG. GLOBE, 41st Cong., 3d Sess. 2740 (1870). There were a number of complaints by Negroes concerning railroad discrimination during this period. See, *e.g.*, CONG. GLOBE, 41st Cong., 3d Sess. 1060 (1871) (remarks of Senator Revels); *id.* at 1637 (remarks of Senator Vickers, quoting a resolution of a colored convention).

ported adversely by its chairman, Senator Lyman Trumbull of Illinois.[9] In the next session, Sumner again introduced the bill,[10] but once more it died in the Judiciary Committee.[11]

When the First Session of the Forty-Second Congress opened, Sumner introduced the bill for the third time. Having twice been rebuffed by the Judiciary Committee, he asked that the bill not be returned to that Committee again and urged its support:

> [Y]ou cannot expect repose in this country . . . until all citizens are really equal before the law. Why, sir, you know well that the Senator from Mississippi, who sat at our right only the other day, (Mr. Revels), cannot travel to his home as you can without being insulted on account of his color. And . . . has he not the same rights before the law that you have? Should you enjoy in any car a privilege which the late Senator from Mississippi should not enjoy? And yet you know his rights in the cars are not secured to him; you know that he is exposed to insult. So long as this endures, how can you expect the colored population of this country to place trust in our Government? Government insults them so long as it refrains from giving them protection in these rights of equality.[12]

However, no other Senator showed much interest, and the bill once again died of its own accord.

In the face of these repulses, Sumner moved, on December 20, 1871, to attach his proposal as a rider to the Amnesty Bill, a proposal authorized by the third section of the fourteenth amendment to lift the remaining political disabilities which that section imposed on many important Confederates.[13] This bill was supported by the President, ardently desired by southern Republicans and all Democrats, and acquiesced in, at least half-heartedly, by most northern Republicans. Its passage by the necessary two-thirds majority seemed all but assured.

When Sumner contended that his bill was designed to secure "equal rights," Senator Joshua Hill, a Georgia Republican, immediately arose to contest this. He declared that separate dining rooms in hotels and separate railway cars did not deny civil rights if the accommodations were equal. He pointed to the fact that slaves who had worshipped at the same churches as their masters before

---

[9] CONG. GLOBE, 41st Cong., 2d Sess. 5314 (1870). See also CONG. GLOBE, 42d Cong., 2d Sess. 821 (1872).
[10] CONG. GLOBE, 41st Cong., 3d Sess. 616 (1871).
[11] Id. at 1263. See also CONG. GLOBE, 42d Cong., 2d Sess. 822 (1872).
[12] CONG. GLOBE, 42d Cong., 1st Sess. 21 (1871).
[13] CONG. GLOBE, 42d Cong., 2d Sess. 237, 240-41 (1872).

the Civil War requested assistance in building separate churches after emancipation.[14] The following colloquy then occurred:

> MR. SUMNER. Mr. President, we have a vindication on this floor of inequality as a principle, as a political rule.
> MR. HILL. On which race, I would inquire, does the inequality to which the Senator refers operate?
> MR. SUMNER. On both. Why, the Senator would not allow a white man to go into the same car with a colored man.
> MR. HILL. Not unless he was invited, perhaps. (Laughter).
> MR. SUMNER. Very well, the Senator mistakes substitutes for equality. Equality is where all are alike. A substitute can never take the place of equality.[15]

The colloquy continued, with Sumner asserting that in railroads and hotels, as well as schools, Negroes should have the same rights as whites. He contended that segregation in these places was an indignity, an insult, and a wrong. Hill, however, pointed out that he himself was "subject in hotels and upon railroads to the regulations provided by the hotel proprietors for their guests, and by railroad companies for their passengers."[16] He pointed out that while both he and Negroes were entitled to "all the security and comfort that either presents to the most favored guest or passenger,"[17] physical proximity did not add to it and hence was not a denial of any right to either white or Negro. He drew on the example of segregated ladies' cars on railroads and concluded that separation was a matter of taste.

Discussion continued in the same vein. Sumner justified first, second, and third class railroad cars based on price but proclaimed that segregation was synonymous with inequality and violated the Declaration of Independence. He alluded to the large Negro voting population of Georgia and how badly Hill was representing them. Hill replied that while Sumner's views were consistent with his whole life's outlook, "he has not yet succeeded in convincing the great mass of minds, even in the far North and East,"[18] of the practicality or necessity of those views. Hill denied that race mixing in railroads added to comfort, while Sumner asserted that to select a white person as a railroad companion on a long trip was an indignity to the colored man. When Sumner decried the segregation of Frederick Douglass in a steamboat dining room because

---
[14] Id. at 241.
[15] Id. at 242.
[16] Ibid.
[17] Ibid.
[18] Id. at 243.

of his race as a violation of equal rights, Hill defended the right of companies to make regulations that constitute "no infringement of the Constitution of the country or of any existing law."[19] Sumner concluded the colloquy by asserting that Congress must annul all such regulations because they were in defiance of equality and that unless Negroes were equal before the law the promises of the Dec-

[19] *Ibid.* As to common law, at least, Hill was unquestionably correct. See Chicago & Nw. Ry. v. Williams, 55 Ill. 185 (1870); Day v. Owen, 5 Mich. 520 (1858); West Chester & Phil. R.R. v. Miles, 55 Pa. 209 (1867); Goines v. M'Candless, 4 Phil. 255 (Pa. Dist. Ct. 1861). *Day v. Owen* and *Goines v. M'Candless* suggest that the separate accommodations may be inferior; the other two cases noted above, decided after the Civil War, require equal accommodations, as does Coger v. North W. Union Packet Co., 37 Iowa 145 (1873), which did not decide the question of segregation. All of the cases, however, required carriers to take Negroes in some way. Cully v. Baltimore & O.R.R., 6 Fed. Cas. 946 (No. 3466) (D. Md. 1876), citing Field v. Baltimore City Passenger R.R. (Case No. 4763) (unreported); Pleasants v. North Beach & Mission R.R., 34 Cal. 586 (1868); Turner v. North Beach & Mission R.R., 34 Cal. 594 (1868); State v. Kimber, 3 Ohio Dec. Reprint 197 (C.P. 1859); Derry v. Lowry, 6 Phil. 30 (C.P. 1865). There are a considerable number of later federal cases holding that a carrier may offer Negroes separate accommodations only if they are equal to those accorded whites. McGuinn v. Forbes, 37 Fed. 639 (D. Md. 1889); Murphy v. Western & Atl. R.R., 23 Fed. 637 (C.C.E.D. Tenn. 1885); Logwood v. Memphis & C.R.R., 23 Fed. 318 (C.C.W.D. Tenn. 1885); The Sue, 22 Fed. 843 (D. Md. 1885); Gray v. Cincinnati So. R.R., 11 Fed. 683 (C.C.S.D. Ohio 1882); Green v. City of Bridgeton, 10 Fed. Cas. 1090 (No. 5754) (S.D. Ga. 1879); Charge to Grand Jury, 30 Fed. Cas. 1005 (No. 18260) (C.C.W.D. Tenn. 1875); Charge to Grand Jury, 30 Fed. Cas. 999 (No. 18258) (C.C.N.C. 1875). It might also be noted that at common law an innkeeper could assign whatever rooms he wanted to give to his guests. See Fell v. Knight, 8 M. & W. 269, 151 Eng. Rep. 1039 (Ex. 1841); Doyle v. Walker, 26 U.C. Rep. 502 (Q.B. 1867); ROGERS, THE LAW OF HOTEL LIFE 7 (1879); WANDELL, THE LAW OF INNS, HOTELS AND BOARDING HOUSES 75 (1888). To the same effect see *The Civil Rights Bill*, 10 WEEKLY L. BULL. 241 (1883).

It is quite likely that Sumner was aware of the common law rule permitting segregation of passengers and hotel guests. In his opening speech on the bill, he had quoted from STORY, BAILMENTS § 591 (5th ed. 1851). *Id.* at 383. The next section, § 591a, which was in every edition from the third edition published in 1832, stated that "the passengers are bound to submit to such reasonable regulations as the proprietors may adopt for the convenience and comfort of the other passengers, as well as for their own proper interests." See, in particular, *id.* § 591a. Sumner had edited the fifth edition of *Story on Bailments* and was thus unquestionably familiar with this statement of the law. See *Advertisement to the Fifth Edition* printed following Story's dedication page. However, it is probable that Sumner was reading from a later edition than that which he had edited, since the quotation from Wintermute v. Clarke, 7 N.Y. Super. 242 (1851), from which he quoted, does not appear in Story's treatise until the sixth edition, published in 1856. Commencing with the seventh edition, published in 1863, Day v. Owen, *supra,* is cited. See STORY, BAILMENTS § 591a n.6 (7th ed. 1863). And Fell v. Knight, *supra,* is noted in 2 KENT, COMMENTARIES 596 (11th ed. 1866), from which he also read. *Id.* at 383. The point that carriers could not exclude, but could segregate, Negroes, is made quite clear in the speeches of Senator Willard Saulsbury (D. Del.), John S. Carlisle (Va.) and James R. Doolittle (R. Wis.), in CONG. GLOBE., 38th Cong., 1st Sess. 1157-59 (1864), notwithstanding Mr. Justice Black's doubt on this point expressed in Bell v. Maryland, 378 U.S. 226, 336 (1964) (dissenting opinion). And the *Field* decision, cited by Mr. Justice Goldberg as a desegregation case (*id.* at 308 n.26), is more properly interpreted as a nondiscrimination case. See the *Cully* case, *supra. Cf.* Brief for the United States as Amicus Curiae, p. 51 n.91, Griffin v. Maryland, 373 U.S. 920 (1963).

laration of Independence would not be fulfilled. As the self-proclaimed defender of the Negro race, he pledged to see that they were not treated with indignity.[20] Sumner then began to read letters from Negroes complaining that hotels would not serve them. However, debate on this was concluded when Sumner's amendment was ruled out of order.[21]

The next day, Sumner moved that his amendment be adopted in the Committee of the Whole.[22] Debate centered around arguments that Sumner's amendment would kill the amnesty bill.[23] Finally, a vote was taken and the amendment lost by a vote of 30 to 29.[24] But Sumner renewed his amendment on the floor of the Senate,[25] and spoke at length in its favor on January 15, 1872. He decried the cases where Frederick Douglass was not permitted to dine with fellow commissioners and where a colored Lieutenant Governor of Louisiana "was denied the ordinary accommodations for comfort and repose" on a railway trip to Washington.[26] Sumner protested that all classes and sexes of Negroes were "shut out from the ordinary privileges of the steamboat or railcar, and driven into a vulgar sty with smokers and rude persons, where the conversation is as offensive as the scene, and then again at the road-side inn are denied that shelter and nourishment without which travel is impossible."[27] Even Massachusetts was not free from discrimination.[28]

Sumner denied that separate facilities were equal. They were equivalent, but equality demanded the same thing. He contended that "in the process of substitution, the vital elixir [of equality] exhales and escapes,"[29] even if accommodations are the same. It was an indignity to Negroes and "instinct with the spirit of slavery."[30] He concluded that the law would change adverse public opinion

---

[20] CONG. GLOBE, 42d Cong., 2d Sess. 243 (1872).
[21] Id. at 244-45.
[22] Id. at 263, 272.
[23] Id. at 272.
[24] Id. at 274.
[25] Id. at 278.
[26] Id. at 381.
[27] Id. at 382.
[28] Ibid. But Massachusetts had an antidiscrimination law. Act of May 16, 1865, MASS. STAT. 1865, ch. 277. See also Commonwealth v. Sylvester, 95 Mass. 247 (1866).
[29] CONG. GLOBE, 42d Cong., 2d Sess. 383 (1872).
[30] Ibid.

and that patronage of mixed facilities would not cease because of the requirements of his bill.[31]

Two days later Sumner was back on his feet to rebut assertions that the bill was unnecessary. He read to the Senate long excerpts from letters and resolutions by Negroes complaining of denials of equal treatment by railroads and hotels. A colored teacher traveling to Alabama from Boston could get nothing to eat for several days.[32] A hotel in Boston would not give a Negro a room during one of the worst storms of the year.[33] The colored Secretary of State of South Carolina wrote in a letter to Sumner that a federal law was needed because state courts would not enforce a similar state statute.[34] A Negro legislator from North Carolina complained that he had passed a charter through the state house of representatives for a steamboat company. On returning home, his only route was on the company's line; he was denied first-class accommodations and was placed in a colored section with very inferior facilities.[35] First-class accommodations were closed to Negroes, as were hotels, places to eat, sleeping cars, churches, and cemeteries.[36]

Senator Frederick T. Frelinghuysen, a New Jersey Republican, then rose to offer some technical amendments as to wording and to urge an amendment providing that churches, schools, cemeteries, and institutions of learning established exclusively for either colored or white people should remain segregated. To do otherwise, he contended, would allow whites to join Negro churches and wrest their valuable property from them. Since Negroes could not be given greater privileges than whites, the law would have to be modified.[37] Sumner ultimately accepted this amendment.[38]

Next, Senator Frederick A. Sawyer, a South Carolina Republican, objected that the Sumner amendment would endanger the amnesty bill. He stated that the South Carolina civil rights law[39] was enforced generally, although he conceded some lapses by courts. He favored Sumner's bill as an independent measure and spent

---

[31] *Id.* at 429-35.
[32] *Id.* at 429-30.
[33] *Id.* at 430.
[34] *Ibid.*
[35] *Id.* at 431.
[36] *Id.* at 429-35.
[37] *Id.* at 435.
[38] *Id.* at 487.

[39] South Carolina Act of Feb. 13, 1869, No. 98. Senator Sawyer had previously pointed out that under South Carolina law desegregation was enforced. CONG. GLOBE, 41st Cong., 2d Sess. 3519 (1870); CONG. GLOBE, 41st Cong., 3d Sess. 1058 (1871).

much time defending himself from Sumner's stinging attacks.[40] Hill also asserted that Negroes had ample accommodations and did not favor race-mixing.[41] Senator James W. Nye, a Radical Republican lawyer from Nevada, supported Sumner's bill. He asserted that equality before the law does not "mean that I am to be kicked from the cars because I am not blessed with a white skin."[42]

Senator Eli Saulsbury, a Delaware Democrat, made a characteristic attack on Sumner's bill as one "of social equality enforced by pains and penalties" and further declared:

> If a man chooses to ride in the same car with negroes, if he voluntarily attends the same church and sits in the same pew . . . then he chooses social equality with negroes. . . . But, if . . . he is compelled to ride in the same car . . . then it is enforced social equality, and that is what the Senator's amendment proposes.[43]

Saulsbury condemned the bill for requiring mixed railroads, theaters, hotels, churches, and cemeteries. He predicted that whites would cease to patronize places affected by the law and that they would have to close for want of business. He even asserted that churches would be closed.[44] But Nye said that since southerners were willing to ride with Negroes when they were slaves, they should not object now that they are free. He added that if they did not wish to eat with Negroes, they could leave the table.[45]

The next day, Sumner read more letters from Negroes. One complained that he could get no seat in a theater or a street car.[46] Another said that the Arkansas civil rights law[47] was a "dead letter," while a third stated that a Negro committee was refused service at a restaurant, that another colored family could not get a stateroom, and that a colored minister was refused admission to hotels, theaters, and churches.[48]

Senator Allen G. Thurman, an Ohio Democrat and a former chief justice of the state supreme court, attacked Sumner's amendment as infringing individual liberty and freedom of association, by forcing whites to associate with Negroes in places of amusement,

---

[40] CONG. GLOBE, 42d Cong., 2d Sess. 489-90 (1872).
[41] Id. at 491-92.
[42] Id. at 495.
[43] Id. app. 9.
[44] Id. app. 10-11.
[45] Id. at 706.
[46] Id. at 726.
[47] Arkansas Act of Feb. 25, 1873, No. XII, amending the act of 1868.
[48] CONG. GLOBE, 42d Cong., 2d Sess. 726-30 (1872).

clubs, and churches. He said that the bill denied "them the liberty to choose their own associates in places of public amusement, in the church, or in the school."[49] He discussed at length the right of people to form clubs, societies, and churches limited to one group.[50] After some legal arguments, Thurman returned to attack the bill for enforcing "social equality." He asked rhetorically: "[W]here have the people of the United States given up their liberty to form associations the members of which shall be exclusively black or exclusively white?"[51] He applied this concept to churches, lodges, cemeteries, and "a theater for whites alone or blacks alone."[52] Thurman concluded:

> I do not know any country in the world in which the subject or the citizen is interfered with as this bill proposes to interfere with him; to take from men the right to associate according to their own tastes when by so doing they interfere with the right of no one, and do not injure or in any way prejudice the State. I know of no country in which the liberty of free association, according to the tastes or the wishes or the interests of the persons associating, is denied to either subject or citizen. And yet, the Senator, in the name of liberty, in the name of freedom, in the name of humanity, seeks to manacle the American people and take from them liberties that they and their ancestors have enjoyed from time immemorial, and which the people in every civilized country enjoy at this day.
> I repeat again, this bill is a bill of despotism and not of liberty.[53]

Two days later, Senator Lyman Trumbull, the veteran Illinois lawyer and legislator who, as Republican Chairman of the Senate Judiciary Committee had shepherded to passage the Civil Rights Act of 1866 — the forerunner of the equal protection clause of the fourteenth amendment — and had frequently acted as spokesman and leader of the Senate Republicans in the Thirty-Ninth Congress, opposed Sumner's amendment. He confined civil rights to those enumerated in the 1866 law and said that it "did not extend . . . to social rights."[54] He added:

> The railroad corporations make regulations in regard to the manner in which their trains are to be conducted; they set aside one car for ladies, another for gentlemen; they have first and second-

---

[49] Id. app. 27.

[50] Ibid.

[51] Id. app. 29.

[52] Ibid.

[53] Ibid. See also Thurman's attack on Sumner's bill the year before. CONG. GLOBE, 42d Cong., 1st Sess. app. 216-17, 219 (1871).

[54] CONG. GLOBE, 42d Cong., 2d Sess. 901 (1872).

class passenger cars, freight cars, and saloon cars, and I suppose they have a right to make all these regulations; but whatever right the white man has the black man has also.[55]

Senator John W. Stevenson, a Kentucky Democratic lawyer, also complained that the bill was intended to "coerce social equality between the races . . . in hotels, in theaters, in railways, and other modes of public conveyance."[56]

At length, a vote was taken on Sumner's amendment to the amnesty bill. A 28 to 28 tie resulted, and the Vice-President voted in the affirmative to break it.[57] However, because a number of the amnesty bill's supporters considered Sumner's measure unconstitutional and voted against it,[58] it received less than the requisite two-thirds vote.[59]

On February 19, 1872, a bill similar to Sumner's was introduced into the House of Representatives.[60] Congressman James G. Blair, a Missouri Republican lawyer, advocated the right of business owners to provide segregated facilities. He declared that "unless the law imposes upon public carriers and hotel-keepers the duty of providing "[sic] white associates for their colored passengers and guests, there can be no question but that these officers and persons may discharge every duty enjoined upon them by law by providing separate accommodations for the colored people."[61] He said that the bill imposed unwanted social equality on whites and that hotels would be closed if it were passed.[62] He further asserted:

> Let the steam and sail vessels have their separate rooms and tables for the colored people, the railway companies separate cars, and the hotel-keepers separate rooms and tables; managers of theaters separate galleries, and public schools separate houses, rooms, and teachers, and the question of races will adjust itself quicker than by using arbitrary means . . . .
>
> Let our Republican friends come up to the work manfully, for if they have the power under the Constitution to do what they are seeking to do by this bill, they have the power to blot out all distinction on account of color. Let me insist that my Republican friends stop not here. . . . Should any white man or white child refuse to speak to a negro on the public highway, in the streets

---

[55] Ibid.
[56] Id. at 913.
[57] Id. at 919.
[58] Id. at 926-28.
[59] Id. at 928-29.
[60] Id. at 1116.
[61] Id. app. 143.
[62] Ibid.

or elsewhere, because of color, fine them and send them to the penitentiary.[63]

Congressman Henry D. McHenry, a Kentucky Democratic lawyer, also decried the bill for enforcing social equality in public accommodations.[64] He, too, concluded: "The right of a citizen to associate exclusively with those who are congenial to him, and whom he recognizes as his peers, is an individual liberty, and no Government can prostrate it to his inferiors under the specious pretext of 'equality before the law.'"[65] Congressman John M. Rice, another Kentucky Democratic lawyer, also raised the social equality argument and predicted that white patronage would be withdrawn from carriers, hotels, and theaters and that these businesses would be ruined.[66]

On May 8, the Senate again considered an amnesty bill which had been passed in the House.[67] Sumner at once attached his civil rights bill to this measure.[68] During the ensuing debate and parliamentary maneuvering, Trumbull got into a debate with Sherman of Ohio and Edmunds of Vermont. Trumbull attacked his fellow Republicans with some warmth for loading Sumner's measure on to the amnesty bill. He added:

> That is his proposition; and to pass what? A civil rights bill! Mr. President, it is a misnomer; and I now ask the Senator from Ohio, and I would be glad to give way for an answer, if he will tell me one single civil right that he has or I have that the colored people of this country have not. What is it? What civil right do I have or has he that is denied a colored man? I want to know what it is. . . .
> I know of no civil right that I have that a colored man has not, and I say it is a misnomer to talk about this being a civil rights bill. If the Senator from Ohio means social rights, if he means by legislation to force the colored people and white people to go to church together, or to be buried in the same grave-yard, that is not a civil right. I know of no right to ride in a car, no right to stop at a hotel, no right to travel possessed by the white man that the colored man has not.[69]

Edmunds then asserted that it was no more equality before the

---

[63] *Id.* app. 144.

[64] *Id.* app. 217.

[65] *Id.* app. 219. See also *id.* app. 371 (remarks of Congressman James C. Harper, D.N.C.).

[66] *Id.* app. 597. See also *id.* app. 383.

[67] *Id.* at 3179.

[68] *Id.* at 3181.

[69] *Id.* at 3189. Trumbull called Sumner's amendment a "social equality bill" the next day. *Id.* at 3254. This is precisely what the southern Democrats were calling it.

law to require "that the black man shall go to one hotel to stay and the white man shall go to another"[70] than it would be to require "that the colored man shall go into Pennsylvania Avenue or Maryland Avenue when he wants to go to the west end of the town, and the white man shall take Massachusetts or some other avenue where it is proper for white people to go."[71] When Senator Orris S. Ferry, a Connecticut Republican lawyer, asked him whether segregation by sex was any denial of equality, Edmunds replied: "Would it not be a denial of right to declare that white men, or men with red hair, or native citizens only should be entitled to travel in a particular horse-car, and that every other class of people should only be allowed to travel in another?"[72]

Trumbull then derided Edmunds' argument by saying that no one was being kept out of the cars on account of his hair color. He added that Negroes had the same legal right to be transported on a railroad or put up in a hotel as white people, and that the bill was not a civil rights bill at all.[73] Senator John Sherman, the Ohio Republican lawyer who had voted with Trumbull for the fourteenth amendment then reminded the latter that the Republicans had voted under his leadership for the Civil Rights Act of 1866 and that this bill was intended to carry out the purposes of that act by protecting "the colored people in their right to travel in the cars, [which] . . . right is denied practically in many of the States."[74] When Trumbull urged that they had this right at common law, Sherman said that a better remedy was needed.[75]

Senator Francis P. Blair, a Missouri Democratic lawyer who had switched from the Republican Party to become the losing Democratic Vice-Presidential candidate in 1868 also said that the bill was designed to give Negroes "social rights, to impose upon the whites of the community the necessity of a close association in all matters with the negroes."[76] He said that this would irritate the

---

[70] *Id.* at 3190.
[71] *Ibid.* Edmunds also said:
   I defy him to point out any distinction between the right of Congress under the Constitution in this District, for illustration, to declare that a white child shall not go to a particular public school and that he shall go to another if he goes at all, and the power to declare that a white man shall not ride in a particular horse-car that has a blue stripe across it, and that if he rides at all he shall ride on a different one. *Ibid.*
[72] *Ibid.*
[73] *Ibid.*
[74] *Id.* at 3192.
[75] *Ibid.*
[76] *Id.* at 3251.

whites, and he therefore advocated separate railway cars, hotels, and other facilities for Negroes.[77] Senator Orris S. Ferry, a Connecticut Republican lawyer, also denied the necessity for the bill on the ground that Negroes had all the common law remedies they needed to obtain service on carriers and in hotels.[78]

Trumbull, Senator Eugene Casserly, a California Democratic lawyer, and Senator James L. Alcorn, a Mississippi Republican lawyer, all declared that Negroes had the same rights under common law to travel on railways as did whites, while Edmunds and Sumner declared once again that the bill was necessary.[79] When a vote was taken on adding Sumner's civil rights bill to the amnesty bill, it resulted in a 29 to 29 tie. The Vice-President then broke the tie in Sumner's favor.[80]

Next, amendments were introduced which were obviously intended merely to make a point. Senator Henry Cooper, a Tennessee Democratic lawyer, moved to amend Sumner's bill to provide that there should be no discrimination based on pecuniary condition, so that a poor person who could not pay would have to be given accommodation. This was laughingly voted down by a vote of 35 to 7. Hill moved to require that customers be properly clothed. No roll call was even demanded on this.[81]

Ultimately, a second vote was taken on annexing Sumner's bill to the amnesty bill, and a 28 to 28 tie again resulted which the Vice-President again broke in Sumner's favor.[82] However, the 32 to 22 vote on the combined measure was less than the requisite two thirds needed for passage.[83]

Several days later, Trumbull, who was much in favor of amnesty but who had voted consistently against the amnesty bill with Sumner's amendment, moved to annex the bill as a rider to another piece of legislation.[84] When several Senators warned that Sumner would simply annex his bill to the amnesty rider, the following colloquy ensued:

---

[77] Ibid.

[78] Id. at 3257.

[79] Id. at 3264. Speaking of Trumbull, Edmunds declared: "He does not believe that it is a right belonging to a citizen of the United States to travel in a car if he is a citizen and conforms to all other conditions if his color happens to be one way rather than another." Id. at 3268.

[80] Id. at 3264-65.

[81] Id. at 3265.

[82] Id. at 3268.

[83] Id. at 3270.

[84] Id. at 3360.

> MR. TRUMBULL. . . . I want amnesty so much that I will vote for almost anything that is not unconstitutional to get it.
> MR. SCOTT. . . . Suppose . . . the civil rights bill gets on by the same process?
> MR. TRUMBULL. . . . I know of no civil rights bill.
> MR. SUMNER. . . . I know of one. (Laughter).
> MR. TRUMBULL. . . . There is a bill that has been misnamed a civil rights bill, proposing to establish social rights which is unconstitutional in its provisions, and which I shall not vote for. But the Senator from Pennsylvania and myself agreeing, and the Senator from West Virginia, I believe, agreeing, let us unite together and vote down this misnamed civil rights bill, this monstrosity that has got a name that does not belong to it, that seeks under false pretenses to impose upon the country and upon the colored people of the country by giving it a name. You cannot make a mule a horse by calling it a horse. Let us vote it down. . . . Bills misnamed civil rights — called bills to establish equal rights when they establish no equality.[85]

Sumner answered Trumbull's vehement attack with a letter from Frederick Douglass denying any desire for "social equality," and Trumbull replied by reading a newspaper clipping that Negroes wanted social equality, the accuracy of which Sumner disputed.[86] No southern Democrat arose; Trumbull was no doubt doing their work very satisfactorily.

Meanwhile, in the House a move was made to suspend the rules and pass a resolution requiring the House Judiciary Committee to report a supplemental civil rights bill, the terms of which were not set forth. Presumably they were to be at least generally similar to the Sumner Senate bill. The vote was 112 yea to 76 nay, and it lost for want of a two-thirds vote. Eleven Republicans who had voted for the fourteenth amendment voted yea; four Democrats who had voted against the amendment voted nay. Representative John A. Bingham of Ohio, who had framed the first section of the fourteenth amendment, voted in the affirmative.[87]

After sundry parliamentary maneuvers in which Trumbull and Sumner proposed to tack the amnesty bill and the civil rights bill on to various items of legislation, and which other Senators opposed because it would defeat every bill to which they were attached,[88]

---

[85] *Id.* at 3361. Trumbull also called it a "social equality bill" the next day. *Id.* at 3418, 3421.

[86] *Id.* at 3361-62.

[87] *Id.* at 3383. The Republicans voting yea were: Ames, Banks, Bingham, Dawes, Garfield, Hooper, Kelley, Ketcham, Myers, Sawyer, and Scofield. Democrats in the negative were Eldridge, Kerr, Niblack, and Randall. See also CONG. GLOBE, 42d Cong., 3d Sess. 85 (1872).

[88] CONG. GLOBE, 42d Cong., 2d Sess. 3418-27 (1872).

Senator Matthew H. Carpenter, a Wisconsin Republican, decided to break the deadlock. On May 21, at about 5 p.m., with both Sumner and Trumbull absent, and with the Senate barely having a quorum, Carpenter first called up the civil rights bill with the intention of amending it to cover only public inns, licensed places of amusement, and common carriers.[89] By passing a civil rights bill first, he could then get the amnesty bill through, he reasoned. The Senate rebuffed Democratic members' attempts to adjourn[90] and prepared to work through the night.

Democrats opposed the civil rights bill.[91] The Carpenter substitute, principally designed to eliminate the school and jury clauses, was then adopted by a vote of 22 to 20, with thirty-two senators absent,[92] and the bill then passed by a party-line vote of 28 to 14.[93]

The next morning, Sumner bitterly denounced the Carpenter substitute as "an emasculated civil rights bill"[94] and moved to add his own proposal to the pending amnesty bill.[95] This time, his entreaty that the Senate make "the Declaration of Independence in its principles and promises a living letter"[96] fell on deaf ears, and his proposal was decisively rejected, 13 to 29. The Senate then passed the amnesty bill, 38 to 2, with Sumner and one other western Radical voting in the negative.[97] That was the end of the bill for that session and that Congress.

II. Sumner's Legacy

At the opening of the First Session of the Forty-Third Congress, Sumner once again introduced his civil rights bill.[98] However, debate commenced in the House, where a copy of the bill had previously been introduced.[99] Congressman Charles A. Eldridge, a Wisconsin Democratic lawyer, immediately proposed an amendment permitting businesses to provide separate accommodations for white persons.[100] Congressman Benjamin F. Butler, Republican Chair-

---

[89] Id. at 3730.
[90] Id. at 3727-29.
[91] Id. at 3733-34. Casserly called it unconstitutional.
[92] Id. at 3735.
[93] Id. at 3736.
[94] Id. at 3737.
[95] Id. at 3238. See also id. at 3739.
[96] Ibid.
[97] Ibid.
[98] 2 Cong. Rec. 10-11 (1873).
[99] Id. at 337-38.
[100] Id. at 339.

man of the Judiciary Committee which had reported the bill, advocated its passage because Negroes who paid first-class fare were thrown into dirty cars or expelled from railroads entirely. Congressman William Lawrence, an Ohio Republican, gave an instance of this. Butler, however, added that Negroes who discriminated against whites would also be liable.[101] And Congressman Joseph H. Rainey, a South Carolina Negro Republican, complained that Negroes could not enter hotels, public conveyances, amusements, churches, and cemeteries.[102]

Congressman John T. Harris, a thoroughly unreconstructed Virginia Democrat lawyer, justified segregation on railroads by noting that white persons were also on occasion prevented from entering particular cars.[103] Another voice from the past came from Congressman Alexander H. Stephens, a Georgia Democrat and Vice-President of the Confederacy. Stephens said:

> Under our law as it stands whoever pays for a first-class car railroad ticket is entitled to a first-class car seat, whatever may be his or her condition in life, and whether white or colored. If he be a colored man who pays for such a ticket, he is entitled to a seat of equal comfort with the white man who may purchase a like ticket; but this does not entitle him of right to a seat in the same car with the white man. Railroad companies, and all public carriers, have the right by common law to assign their passengers to such seats in such coaches as they may please, provided they are of the comforts and class paid for.[104]

He was answered by Congressman Alonzo J. Ransier, a South Carolina Negro Republican, who denied that Negroes wanted social equality and asserted that they asked only for equal accommodations.[105] Representative Roger Q. Mills, a Texas Democrat, added a speech devoted to freedom of association and taste, which he asserted Congress could not control.[106]

The next day, Congressman James B. Beck, a Kentucky Democratic lawyer, offered an amendment allowing business owners to segregate their patrons.[107] Another South Carolina Negro Republican, Congressman Robert B. Elliott, also justified the bill because of "our exclusion from the public inn, from the saloon and table of

---

[101] *Id.* at 341-42.
[102] *Id.* at 344.
[103] *Id.* at 377.
[104] *Id.* at 379.
[105] *Id.* at 382-83. See also *id.* at 1311-12.
[106] *Id.* at 385.
[107] *Id.* at 405.

the steamboat, from the sleeping-coach on the railway . . . ."[108] But Congressman James H. Blount, a Georgia Democratic lawyer, replied that Negroes had their own separate facilities and were well provided for. He predicted bad feeling if the bill should pass.[109]

Next, Lawrence made the point that the bill would not change the common law but would merely give an additional means to enforce it by preventing the states from depriving Negroes of equal common law benefits, a point previously made by Butler in his opening speech.[110] Lawrence justified the bill as one to enforce the equal protection clause of the fourteenth amendment.[111] Congressman John M. Bright, a Tennessee Democratic lawyer, opposed the bill because most Negroes were laborers and could not afford first-class accommodations, and because they had their own facilities.[112] Congressman William S. Herndon, a Texas Democratic lawyer, predicted withdrawal of white patronage and closing of public places as well as danger to "our social system."[113]

The next rhetoric came from Representative William J. Purman, a Florida Republican lawyer. In the process of denying that states had "the right to enforce any condition of *inequality*,"[114] he gave examples of such laws.[115]

A Missouri Democrat followed, whose southern sympathies per-

---

[108] Id. at 408.
[109] Id. at 411.
[110] Id. at 340.
[111] Id. at 412.
[112] Id. at 416.
[113] Id. at 421.
[114] Id. at 423.
[115] Id. at 423-24.

Supposed Acts of a State-Rights Legislature.
An act to prohibit all white persons, not citizens of and not residing within the State, from being admitted and accommodated in any public inn.
An act to exclude all persons not possessed of real and personal property to the value of ten thousand dollars from all places of public amusement or entertainment for which a license from any legal authority is required.
An act to exclude all persons of the religious denomination known as Methodists from riding on any line of stagecoaches, railroads, or other means of public carriage of passengers or freight.
An act to prohibit all foreign-born citizens and their descendants from being buried in any public cemetery.
An act to exclude all persons known as the "colored race" from public inns, cemeteries, and common schools supported by public taxation, and from equal accommodations with other persons, on all public stagecoaches, steamboats, and railroads.
He lapsed into a harangue of the House, but did declare in passing that "the sixth act, which is not supposed now for illustration, but is virtually in existence in most of the States of the Union, especially in the Southern States . . . is the hostile pretended legislation that the passage of the bill under consideration will wipe out."

vaded his speech. He denied that Negroes were refused access to public facilities and declared that the objection was based on segregation, which he extolled. His position was that the equal protection clause did not abolish the right to segregate and that any such abolition would interfere with private property rights.[116]

Debate was closed the next day. An Ohio Democratic lawyer pronounced the bill to be one for social equality and hence unconstitutional.[117] Two other Democrats lauded segregation,[118] and one of them accused the Republicans of hypocrisy in attempting to abolish it.[119] The final Democratic argument, made by Congressman John D. C. Atkins of Tennessee, again accused the Republicans of hypocrisy, denounced the bill for imposing social equality, and concluded with a plea for segregation.[120] Butler then made the last speech. In sarcastic measure he rejected the social equality argument on the grounds that southerners were quite willing to associate freely with Negro slaves before the war and hence should have no objection now. He related how he had used his military authority to order a boat clerk to let a Negro sit in a dining room and occupy a stateroom against boat regulations during the war. He concluded with a general oration, and the bill was returned to the Judiciary Committee.[121]

Several days later, there was an encore to the debate. Congressman Robert B. Vance, a prominent Democrat and ex-Confederate from North Carolina, declared that the bill was a social rights bill. He said that Negroes now had the right to enter conveyances and hotels, but that they were segregated. This he supported with considerable warmth.[122] Congressman Richard H. Cain, a South Carolina Negro Republican, rose to answer Vance. Cain com-

---

[116] *Id.* at 427-30 (remarks of Congressman Aylett H. Buckner).

[117] *Id.* app. 1-3 (remarks of Congressman Milton I. Southard).

[118] *Id.* app. 3-4 (remarks of Congressman Hiram P. Bell of Georgia and John M. Glover of Missouri).

[119] *Id.* app. 5, where Glover said:
When has President Grant . . . seen fit to leave his box at the theatre and go to the pit or the gallery to get in contact with those who cannot come to him? . . . Why have we never witnessed the "civil rights" advocates setting one solitary example of the propriety, the advantage, and the excellence of a law which they propose to enforce against their remonstrating countrymen with fire and sword? Why don't we see them leaving Williard's and going to some colored hotel? Why do we not see them, by a delicious choice, going to worship in a colored church?

[120] *Id.* at 453-55.

[121] *Id.* at 457-58.

[122] *Id.* at 554-56.

plained that he and colleagues of his were not served in hotels, railroad cars, and restaurants. He saw no objection to the use of first-class accommodations by Negroes who could pay for them. He concluded that Negroes were entitled to their rights.[123] Congressman David B. Mellish, a Republican, added that in New York City, where some street car lines would not take Negro passengers and others made them wait for long periods to take exclusively colored cars, discrimination was ended when the president of the police board ordered policemen to arrest any conductor who ejected a Negro passenger from a car.[124]

On January 17, 1874, the House was treated to more oratory on the civil rights bill. Congressman Henry R. Harris, a Georgia Democrat, spent his time on a general declamation about social equality and freedom of association.[125] And Congressman Robert Hamilton, a New Jersey Democratic lawyer, urged freedom of association for white people.[126]

In the Senate, Sumner's bill was referred to the Judiciary Committee,[127] and, while the bill was under consideration there, on March 11, 1874, Sumner died. His last wish was that his civil rights bill be passed.[128] Senator Frelinghuysen reported the bill for the Judiciary Committee. He declared that it would protect white people as well as Negroes and that it was not designed to enforce social equality. He narrowed its constitutional basis to the equal protection clause of the fourteenth amendment.[129] He then said:

> As the capital invested in inns, places of amusements, and public conveyances is that of the proprietors, and as they alone can know what minute arrangements their business requires, the discretion as to the particular accommodation to be given to the guest, the traveler, and the visitor is quite wide. But as the employment these proprietors have selected touches the public, the law demands that the accommodation shall be good and suitable, and this bill adds to that requirement the condition that no person shall, in the regulation of these employments, be discriminated against merely

---

[123] *Id.* at 565-67. A few days later, Congressman Samuel S. Cox, a New York Democrat, said that Negroes did not care much for the use of expensive hotels and theaters. *Id.* at 618.

[124] *Id.* at 567.

[125] *Id.* at 726.

[126] *Id.* at 741.

[127] *Id.* at 949-51.

[128] *Id.* at 4786. See also 3 CONG. REC. 952 (1875) (remarks of Congressman Thomas Whitehead).

[129] 2 CONG. REC. 3451 (1873).

because he is an American or an Irishman, a German or a colored man.[130]

Some days later Senator Thomas M. Norwood, a Georgia Democrat, made a speech in which he accused the Republicans of passing a social equality bill which would affect only the poor whites, since the rich could afford to hire private conveyances. He sarcastically asked why the Republican congressmen chose to ride to the Capitol in their own carriages instead of public street cars filled with Negroes.[131] He caustically made suggestions as to how Congress might supervise the equality of foods served to both races at hotels.[132]

On May 20, when the Senate resumed consideration of civil rights, Senator Daniel D. Pratt, an Indiana Republican lawyer, spoke at length in support of the bill. He stated that at common law all colored people were entitled to the privileges mentioned in the bill and could maintain a suit against the proprietor who denied them. He said:

> Suppose a colored man presents himself at a public inn . . . and is either refused admittance or treated as an inferior guest — placed at the second table and consigned to the garret, or compelled to make his couch upon the floor — does any one doubt that upon an appeal to the courts, the law if justly administered would pronounce the innkeeper responsible to him in damages for the unjust discrimination? I suppose not. . . . The same is true of public carriers. . . . [A]nd all persons who behave themselves and are not afflicted with any contagious disease are entitled to equal accommodations where they pay equal fares.
>
> But it is asked, if the law be as you lay it down, where the necessity for this legislation, since the courts are open to all? My answer is, that the remedy is inadequate and too expensive, and involves too much loss of time and patience to pursue it. When a man is traveling, and far from home, it does not pay to sue every inn-keeper who, or railroad company which, insults him by unjust discrimination. Practically the remedy is worthless.
>
> Now sir, if I am right in stating the law, this bill is justified in providing a more efficient remedy, one that is so stringent in its penalties that it is likely to be obeyed, and render litigation unnecessary. Many a wrong is practiced even upon the white traveler, upon the supposition that his business will not allow him to remain and bring the wrong-doer to account, which is generally true.
>
> And let me say right here, that this measure is not confined to colored citizens; it embraces all, of whatever color.[133]

---

[130] *Id.* at 3452.
[131] *Id.* app. 236.
[132] *Id.* app. 238.
[133] *Id.* at 4081-82.

Pratt denied that the bill would promote social equality and declared that in public facilities travelers had to tolerate all types of people. He concluded with a long declamation on equality and prejudice.[134] Thurman arose to answer Pratt. He proceeded to reason that the bill must have intended mixed public facilities, but it was not until he got to the school clause that his opponents paid any attention to what he was saying, and it is probable that his observation was incorrect.[135]

The last day of Senate debate was May 22. Senator Timothy O. Howe, a Wisconsin Radical Republican, supported the bill because Negroes were being turned away from hotels and other accommodations.[136] Senator James L. Alcorn, a Mississippi Republican lawyer, then orated, adding little but generalized declamation on the "right guaranteed to [Negroes] of free transit throughout the country"[137] and Congress' right to assure colored people of equal treatment by carriers.[138] He noted the complaints of Negroes that they were not admitted to theaters in Washington and in the North, and likewise advocated the bill so they would be admitted to hotels.[139] Then, as an ex-slave holder and former Confederate elected

---

[134] *Id.* at 4082.

[135] *Id.* at 4088. He said:
That means mixed audiences, does it not? That means mixed guests at a hotel, does it not? That means mixed travelers on a railway or in a stagecoach, does it not? If not, it does not mean anything. It certainly was not intended by the committee that Mr. Saville should build another theater for the entertainment of the colored people of Washington City, or that the Baltimore and Ohio Railway or the Baltimore and Potomac Railway is to run separate cars to carry colored persons. These are the very things that are complained of. Therefore, mixture is meant in inns, in public conveyances on land or water, in theaters, in other places of public amusement....

It may be noted that the premise for the remark, that segregation was what was being complained of, is inaccurate. It was the denial of facilities, or unequal facilities, and not mere segregation, which drew Republican fire. Hence it is probable that this remark was just made to bolster his school clause argument, in opposition to Pratt, that school segregation was not permissible under the bill. Since Thurman, an opponent of the bill, was using this to rebut an argument by Pratt, a proponent, that the bill permitted segregation though not inequality, his argument can hardly be considered an accurate reflection of the intention of Congress.

[136] *Id.* at 4148.

[137] *Id.* app. 304.

[138] *Ibid.*

[139] *Id.* app. 305. He said:
Objection is made that the bill provides that the colored man shall have accommodations at public hotels. If he is denied accommodations at the public hotels, where will he get accommodations if he sees proper to travel? When upon a journey, he has no right to go to a private house. If the public houses refuse him, then an American citizen becomes a pariah in the land which guarantees to him the right of travel. The hotels are licensed institutions. When the grant of a license is made, the municipality demands of the

to the Senate by the Negro majority of Mississippi, he launched into rhetoric well calculated to endear him to his new friends.[140] Senator Henry R. Pearce, Alcorn's Republican colleague from Mississippi, urged enactment of the bill to spare Negroes from "indignities."[141]

Discussion continued into the night, as Senator Saulsbury, a Delaware Democrat, arose to protest that the bill would enforce association among the races. After observing that his colleagues were too exhausted to listen to debate, he argued that the bill was intended to enforce race-mixing in inns and theaters, a proposition he deduced from the absence of a clause specifically permitting segregation. He charged that compulsory integration was to be applied to schools, hospitals, almshouses, orphan asylums, and benevolent associations, and that whites would resent this.[142] He told the Republicans: "Do not say that you can make any separate arrangement under the provisions of this bill,"[143] thereby showing that the charge of compulsory association was made for partisan advantage and not as a true reflection of the majority's intent. His rambling discourse carried him through generalized constitutional discussion, the Negro vote, a prediction that hotels and theaters would lose their patronage, prejudice, social equality, and, finally, schools.[144] At his conclusion, the Senate had been sitting for over ten hours and it was 9:30 p.m. The Democrats wanted an adjournment, but the Republicans voted it down, and the Senate went into an all-night session.[145]

The contribution to the Democratic filibuster by Senator Merrimon of North Carolina was a self-confessed "desultory" history

---

keeper a bond for the faithful performance of his contract. The condition of the bond is that he shall provide food and lodging for the traveling public. Practically this bill requires him to comply with the conditions of his bond. He cannot be permitted to stand at his door and turn away men from the accommodations which he has in his bond agreed he would furnish on account of their complexion. He must not be permitted to look into a man's face to decide by the color of his skin whether the food and lodging shall be provided which he has obligated himself to furnish. It would be a strange government indeed that would tolerate a proceeding like this.

[140] *Id.* app. 307. One can well believe that this speech represented the views of Alcorn's Negro constituents and not his own views in light of the fact that only two years before he consistently spoke and voted against Sumner's bill. CONG. GLOBE, 42d Cong., 2d Sess. 274, 3264, 3268, 3270 (1872).

[141] 2 CONG. REC. 4154 (1873).

[142] *Id.* at 4157-58.

[143] *Id.* at 4159.

[144] *Id.* at 4159-62.

[145] *Id.* at 4162.

of the United States from the Declaration of Independence onward, replete with cases.[146] When he finally arrived at the equal protection clause of the fourteenth amendment, he said that while it forbade giving rights to some people but not to others, it permitted racial segregation. After supporting segregation by law, in schools, he indorsed the same for theaters.[147] He meandered back to a defense of segregation by law in theaters, inns, cemeteries, and schools,[148] and ultimately concluded with a protracted harangue on race-mixing, hybrids, and school destruction.[149]

At 1:30 a.m., with the Republicans still refusing to adjourn,[150] Senator William T. Hamilton, a Maryland Democratic lawyer, launched into a lengthy oration. He advocated separate churches, cemeteries, hotels, places of amusement, and other facilities, and predicted that the bill would destroy the white patronage of hotels.[151]

The early hours of the morning were taken up principally with the school clause.[152] In the course of discussing segregated schools, Senator Edmunds of Vermont, a staunch Radical Republican supporter of Sumner, contended that the fourteenth amendment forbade state segregation in carriers,[153] while Senator Aaron A. Sargent, a California Republican lawyer, denied that this was the effect

---

[146] *Id.* app. 307-12.

[147] *Id.* app. 313. He said:
Can't be denied that the States have power to regulate theaters — the manner of conducting them? Have they not always exercised power to do so? They are supreme in that respect. If they judge that it is necessary that one class of people shall go into one apartment and another class into another, with a view to good order and decency, why is it not competent to do that? . . . . By our system of government, the States are left to regulate society within their respective jurisdictions.

[148] *Id.* app. 315.

[149] *Id.* app. 316-18 (1873).

[150] *Id.* at 4166.

[151] *Id.* app. 367-70.

[152] *Id.* at 4167-75.

[153] *Id.* at 4172-73. Replying to Senator Sargent, he declared:
But the Senator's argument results in exactly this: that the fourteenth amendment does not, as it respects common schools, level a distinction which a state may have a right to make on account of race and color. If it does not level that distinction, then it does not level a distinction that a State has a right to make on the same account in respect to a railway, or a highway, or a steamboat, or any other thing; for the fourteenth amendment is general and sweeping . . . . If the State has that right, we cannot interfere with it. If the State has not that right, we cannot confer it by an act of Congress, because such an act of Congress would be in violation of the fourteenth amendment itself. *Ibid.*

of the amendment.[154] Then, after the school issue was disposed of, the Senate passed the bill by a vote of 29 to 16 and adjourned after a twenty-hour session. Voting or paired against the bill were all the Democrats and four Republicans from Nebraska, Virginia, West Virginia, and Wisconsin, with the affirmative votes all cast by Republicans.[155]

The House took no action on the bill during this session. In occasional debate, Democrats attacked it in broadside harangues for

---

[154] *Id.* at 4174. He said:
Now, sir, one single remark in reply to that only which can be considered as argument in reply to my positions, and that is, that the amendment which I propose, by providing that there may be separate schools, is a violation of the fourteenth amendment, upon the same principle that a denial of the right of a colored man to ride in the same car, or to have identical accommodations in the same hotel would be a violation of the fourteenth amendment. I do not believe either of these cases cited as illustrations would be a denial of any right guaranteed by the fourteenth amendment. The fourteenth amendment was not intended merely to say that black men should have rights, but that black and white men and women should have rights. It was a guarantee of equality of right to every person within the jurisdiction of the United States, be he black or white. It is a very common thing for me and for every Senator here, and every white man in the country, when he goes to a railroad train without his wife on his arm or some female friend, to be assigned to a car separate from some other car more privileged than the one he takes, by its female society, though not perhaps better in its fittings, which is assigned to ladies or to gentlemen who have ladies with them. Is that a violation of the fourteenth amendment? Suppose the man who is thus required to take the second car on the train instead of the first should be black instead of white, would the difference in color make a violation of the fourteenth amendment?

I do not believe these things are of enough importance for us to legislate upon them here. They regulate themselves. I doubt if any white man ever felt outraged because he was told to take one car rather than another, on account of a discrimination in the car he should take. Why, then, should the black man?

So with reference to the hotel table. In most of the hotels, in all of them I believe in New York and in the larger cities, the tables are small, circular tables where families sit, or two or three persons who happen to be friends, and the guests are assigned by the landlord to the places they take. A person entering the dining-room does not take a seat at any table he sees fit; he is put here or there, wherever the landlord pleases. And in assigning rooms at a hotel, the landlord may put him in the fourth story or the first; and if he does not like his accommodation he can go to some other hotel. He has no direction in the matter, and certainly no right to demand under the fourteenth amendment that he shall be put in the third story instead of the fourth, or the second instead of the third. These hotel illustrations fail for that very reason. The fourteenth amendment does not apply to them at all. They are simply incidents of business which have existed for years, and will exist for years whether the fourteenth amendment exists or not.

If the car to which a white man without a lady is assigned, or the black man is assigned, is just as good as any other of the train, drawn by the same engine, at an equal rate of speed, where is the harm done by that regulation? And why should we interfere with the business of railroad companies and hotel-keepers in this inquisitive way, putting our noses into the smallest details of business?

[155] *Id.* at 4176.

race-mixing.[156] A Tennessee Republican doubted the constitutionality of the law, and stated that colored people were content with segregated accommodations and only complained of inferior treatment.[157]

Congressman James T. Rapier, an Alabama Negro Republican lawyer, complained that Negroes were all denied first-class railroad accommodations and replied to a prior speaker:

> And I state without fear of being gain-said, the statement of the gentleman from Tennessee to the contrary notwithstanding, that there is not an inn between Washington and Montgomery, a distance of more than a thousand miles, that will accommodate me to a bed or meal. Now, then, is there a man upon this floor who is so heartless, whose breast is so void of the better feelings, as to say that this brutal custom needs no regulation?[158]

He went on to point out that whites had a common law right to accommodations which Negroes also should have, that exclusion from first-class accommodations was the result of prejudice, and that it humiliated him. He disclaimed any desire for social equality but decried being forced into inferior cars and the fact that on railroad trips he could not get a sleeping berth.[159]

Congressman Chester B. Darrall, a Louisiana Republican, echoed these views. After noting that the Louisiana state constitution gave Negroes equal rights in public conveyances and other licensed businesses, he reassured the House that Negroes rarely insisted on exercising them and that the state law was not rigidly enforced. He read a resolution of several leading New Orleans whites advocating nondiscrimination in public conveyances and licensed resorts; the group was headed by General G. T. Beauregard, who he had neglected to mention was a prominent Republican patronage-holder. Darrall deplored the fact that wealthy New Orleans Negroes and prominent colored officeholders could not obtain first-class accommodations in carriers and hotels, and he gave examples of this. Congressman Darrall called for an end to such discrimination by passage of the bill.[160]

---

[156] *Id.* at 341-44 (remarks of Congressman William B. Read of Kentucky); *id.* app. 417-21 (remarks of Ephraim K. Wilson of Maryland); *id.* app. 481 (remarks of John J. Davis of West Virginia).

[157] *Id.* at 4593 (remarks of Congressman Roderick R. Butler).

[158] *Id.* at 4782.

[159] *Id.* at 4783-85. See also the remarks of Congressman Ransier, a South Carolina Negro Republican. *Id.* at 4786.

[160] *Id.* app. 477-80.

III. Butler's Valedictory

The elections of 1874 were a disaster for the Republican Party. The Senate remained Republican by a much-reduced margin due to holdovers, but the House of Representatives, where all the members ran for re-election, became Democratic by a wide margin.[161] Even Butler lost his seat in normally Republican Massachusetts.[162] The depression, fraud, corruption, and sundry scandals were all helpful to the Democratic Party,[163] but it also made considerable gains based on a "white backlash" vote against the civil rights bill, especially the school clause.[164]

When the "lame-duck" Second Session of the Forty-Third Congress met in the early part of 1875, Congressman Alexander White, an Alabama Republican, moved to amend the civil rights bill by specifically permitting segregation in schools and in public accommodations.[165] Butler then spoke briefly, denying that the bill was intended to promote social equality in public places and noted that people who used the services of carriers, theaters, and inns did not do so to obtain the society of others.[166] Congressman John R. Lynch, a Mississippi Republican Negro, also rebutted the social equality argument. He complained that Negro women could not get equal treatment and that he himself, when coming to Congress, was "forced to occupy a filthy smoking-car both night and day; with drunkards, gamblers, and criminals" because of color.[167]

That evening, Congressman John B. Storm, a Pennsylvania Democrat, twitted the Republicans for inconsistency in permitting school segregation but not segregation in carriers, hotels, and theaters.[168] Congressman Thomas Whitehead, a Virginia Democrat, said that the civil rights bill was hurting the Republican Party and stated that racial discrimination could not be proved.[169] In response to questioning, he affirmed that Negroes could ride in Virginia in first-class railway and street cars, while a Negro Congressman, Rainey of South Carolina, denied it.[170] Cain, a South Carolina

---

[161] U.S. Bureau of the Census, Historical Statistics of the United States, Colonial Times to 1957, 691 (1960).

[162] Trefousse, Ben Butler 230 (1957).

[163] 22 Encyc. Britannica 775 (1963 ed.).

[164] 3 Cong. Rec. 951, 952, 978, 982, 1001 & apps. 17, 20, 113 (1875).

[165] Id. at 939.

[166] Id. at 940.

[167] Id. at 944-45.

[168] Id. at 951.

[169] Id. at 952-53.

[170] Id. at 955.

Negro, then arose to rebut Whitehead and stated that a colored lady he knew was thrown out of a first-class railroad car into a smoking car when she reached Virginia.[171] The latter interrupted him to state that Negroes could ride any Richmond street car, but Rainey said he was confined to a "colored car," while Cain added the experience of a friend in support of this.[172]

When Congressman Benjamin W. Harris, a Massachusetts Republican lawyer, arose to rebut Whitehead and support the bill, the latter asked whether proprietors of hotels could, under the bill, segregate patrons:

> MR. WHITEHEAD. I just want to know whether you are in favor of a hotel-keeper being forced by law to make white and black people sit at the same table?
>
> MR. HARRIS. . . . I will tell him what the Massachusetts doctrine is. It is that when any man, white or black, respectable and well-behaved, comes into any hotel in our Commonwealth and asks to have a comfortable apartment assigned him and proper food furnished him, he has a right to it, without regard to his color. But, sir, there is nothing proposed here that would authorize any colored man to force himself on the gentleman from Virginia. This law merely provides that white and black shall be alike entitled to a common hospitality.
>
> MR. WHITEHEAD. That does not answer my question at all. Do you wish hotel-keepers to be bound to place white and black at the same table? . . .
>
> MR. HARRIS. . . . I will tell the gentleman, however, that in Massachusetts we do not make all classes of white men sit at the same table or sleep in the same bed. But every man in Massachusetts, be he white or black, can have entertainment at one of our hotels, and a black man can get entertainment there equal to that afforded to any white man, if he is respectable and pays his bill.[173]

A little later, the following colloquy occurred:

> MR. HARRIS. . . . We do not propose to make any man eat at any other man's table uninvited, but we do not propose that a white man, a keeper of a public hotel, shall kick a black man out of doors and refuse him food and shelter simply because he is a black man. That is the difference between us.
>
> MR. WHITEHEAD. We do not either.[174]

---

[171] *Id.* at 956.

[172] *Id.* at 957.

[173] *Id.* at 958.

[174] *Ibid.* Harris was, no doubt, thinking of the Massachusetts civil rights law. Mass. Act of May 16, 1865, ch. 277. In respect to the right to segregate under such a statute, *compare* People ex rel. King v. Gallagher, 93 N.Y. 438 (1883), *with* Ferguson v. Giles, 82 Mich. 358, 46 N.W. 718 (1890). See also *id.* app. 119 for the rhetoric on this subject from Congressman Eppa Hunton, another Virginia Democrat.

Thereafter, Rainey urged passage of the bill because common law remedies were too "general" and disclaimed any desire for social equality. Congressman James T. Rapier, an Alabama Negro Republican lawyer who had tried to interrupt Harris' speech to answer Whitehead, then rose to endorse Harris' answer.[175]

The next day, February 4, 1875, was the last day of House debate, and strict time limitations were imposed. A Democrat said that southern states already had civil rights laws and asserted that few Negroes used railroads or hotels.[176] A friend of Sumner brought forth the Declaration of Independence and equality of opportunity.[177] However, a New York Republican opposed the bill because few Negroes traveled in the South and because the bill would, in his view, simply stir up bad feelings.[178]

White of Alabama made a long speech in which he rejected extremists on both sides. In his view the evils to be remedied were the denials of admission to Negroes by carriers, hotels, and theaters. To him, the Senate bill provided equal rights and a community of enjoyment, the House Judiciary bill provided equal rights, separate enjoyment in schools, and a community of enjoyment elsewhere, while his bill provided separate enjoyment in all places because he opposed race-mixing.[179] In a long oration, he said that southern Republicans did not want race-mixing and that the bill was costing them every state in the South.[180]

The last Democratic bombast came from Congressman Charles A. Eldredge, a Wisconsin lawyer, whose low opinion of Negroes had not improved since he voted against the fourteenth amendment.[181] When Congressman John Y. Brown, a Kentucky Democrat whose views on Negroes were as far from the noted abolitionist's ideals as it was possible to get, arose to pour invective on Butler, the House was diverted into a party-line censuring of him.[182]

The Republicans closed the debate. A Tennessee Republican asserted that without the civil rights bill, Negroes would be consigned to inferior accommodations in carriers.[183] A Michigan Re-

---

[175] *Id.* at 959-60.
[176] *Id.* at 977-78 (remarks of Congressman James H. Blount, Georgia).
[177] *Id.* at 979 (remarks of Congressman E. Rockwood Hoar, Massachusetts).
[178] *Id.* at 982 (remarks of Congressman Simeon B. Chittenden).
[179] *Id.* app. 15.
[180] *Id.* app. 17-24.
[181] *Id.* at 982-85. See also CONG. GLOBE, 39th Cong., 1st Sess. 2545 (1866).
[182] 3 CONG. REC. 985-92 (1875).
[183] *Id.* at 998-99 (remarks of Congressman Barbour Lewis).

publican added that the bill was designed to prohibit exclusion from carriers, inns, and theaters because of color and expressed his opposition to segregation by statute.[184] A Wisconsin Republican opposed all segregation by law in public places.[185]

For the grand finale, Butler took the helm. Ridiculing the social equality arguments, Butler proceeded to take sweet revenge for Brown's attack by having his ante-bellum secessionist sentiments read. Then, "waving the bloody shirt," he concluded in an outburst of flamboyant theatrics which was to be the final notoriety of his House career.[186]

The House first voted to strike out the whole school clause, and then voted down White's substitute which, while providing for segregation in public facilities, also restored the school clause to the bill. It then decisively rejected a school integration substitute and thereafter passed the bill by a vote of 162 to 99. The vote strictly followed party lines, except that two Democrats voted with the majority and eleven Republicans, ten of them from the South and border states, voted with the minority.[187]

Senate debate was brief. Senator Thomas F. Bayard, a Delaware Democrat, ridiculed the bill for requiring the federal courts to examine whether one seat in a hotel, theater, or railway was as good as another.[188] Senator William T. Hamilton, a Maryland Democratic lawyer, urged that a theater owner should be able to select his audience.[189] He concluded with a bombastic broadside against prejudice, racial antagonism, and race-mixing.[190]

The debate was closed by Senator George F. Edmunds, the Radical Republican lawyer from Vermont who had voted for the fourteenth amendment. After accusing the Democrats of consistently opposing any rights for Negroes, he replied to their arguments that the bill was unconstitutional for want of power in Congress to pass it by asking rhetorically:

> [W]here is the authority for saying that a State shall not have a right to pass a law which shall declare that all citizens of the German race shall go upon the right-hand side of the streets and all citizens of French descent shall go upon the left, and so on, and

---

[184] *Id.* at 999 (remarks of Congressman Julius C. Burrows).
[185] *Id.* at 1002 (remarks of Congressman Charles G. Williams).
[186] *Id.* at 1005-09.
[187] *Id.* at 1011.
[188] *Id.* app. 105.
[189] *Id.* app. 115.
[190] *Id.* app. 116-17.

that all people of a particular religion shall only occupy a particular quarter of the town, and all the people of another religion another side?[191]

The bill then passed by a vote of thirty-eight Republicans in favor to twenty Democrats and six Republicans against. Of the Republicans voting in the affirmative, eight had voted for the fourteenth amendment as Senators and seven as members of the House. The most significant negative Republican vote was cast by Senator William Sprague of Rhode Island, who had voted for the amendment.[192]

IV. Summary and Conclusions

In evaluating legislative history to determine the intent of the body enacting a law, one deals in probabilities rather than in mathematical certainties. However, propositions can range from highly improbable to those of which one is morally certain.

The legislative history of the Civil Rights Act of 1875 shows that Congress was principally concerned with complaints by Negroes that they were excluded from railways and other carriers, inns, and theaters or that if admitted they were consigned to substantially inferior accommodations. These complaints of being relegated to dirty, smoke-filled railway cars or of being unable to get hotel rooms and meals, run like a thread throughout the debates. There is a noticeable absence of complaints about mere segregation per se.

In determining whether the debates reflect an intent on the part of the framers of the fourteenth amendment to abolish racial segregation, several positions may be readily identified. The Democrats were in favor of strict racial segregation by law to avoid race-mixing. However, they had also opposed the fourteenth amendment and would be likely to give it a very narrow construction. We may therefore ignore their views.

Republican moderates, such as Trumbull, joined by several Radicals, such as Senators Lot M. Morrill of Maine and William Sprague of Rhode Island who had voted for the fourteenth amendment, were of the view that states retained power even under that amendment to segregate people by law in railways and in other public places. They consistently voted and spoke against the civil rights bill on the ground that it was an unconstitutional "social equality" bill. Their position was essentially in accord with the

---

[191] Id. at 1870.
[192] Ibid.

Democratic position on this point. Trumbull even went so far as to deny that the right to ride in a railway was a civil right protected by the fourteenth amendment. Considering the fact that in 1872 Trumbull had been a member of the bar for about forty years, in public life since 1840, a justice of the Illinois Supreme Court for five years, and a United States Senator for eighteen years, over six of which he served as Chairman of the Senate Judiciary Committee, it is patent that if he did not know what he was voting for when he voted for the fourteenth amendment, no one did.

Moreover, the votes of Trumbull and the other Republican moderates were decisive in the narrowly divided Thirty-Ninth Congress. To obtain the necessary two-thirds majority after President Andrew Johnson's veto of the Freedmen's Bureau Bill[193] it was necessary to persuade two marginal Republicans to switch to the majority and to expel or exclude on flimsy grounds Senator John P. Stockton, a New Jersey Democrat.[194] Even so, the President's opponents were unsure of their necessary majority.[195] On the key test of strength, the overriding of the veto of the Civil Rights Act of 1866, the vote was 33 to 15, with one presidential supporter absent.[196] Although the vote on the fourteenth amendment was 33 to 11, the difference is accountable to the absence of presidential supporters, with only one Senator switching his position.[197] Had

---

[193] CONG. GLOBE, 39th Cong., 1st Sess. 943 (1866).

[194] CONG. GLOBE, 40th Cong., 2d Sess. 823 (1868).

[195] See CONG. GLOBE, 39th Cong., 1st Sess. 1786 (1866).

[196] Id. at 1809.

[197] Id. at 3042. An argument has been made that it was the intent of the framers of the fourteenth amendment to ban racial segregation in carriers, based on the action of Congress in forbidding exclusion of Negroes from District of Columbia streetcars in 1864. See Frank & Munro, *The Original Understanding of "Equal Protection of the Law,"* 50 COLUM. L. REV. 131, 150-53 (1950). These commentators are not so certain about hotels. Id. at 153. It is by no means certain that Congress intended to exclude the doctrine of "separate but equal" even in the District of Columbia. See CONG. GLOBE, 38th Cong., 1st Sess. 553, 817-18, 839, 3131-35 (1864). The "railroads" affected were horse-drawn streetcars. See CONG. GLOBE, 39th Cong., 1st Sess. 205 (1866) (remarks of Congressman Farnsworth); CONG. GLOBE, 40th Cong., 3d Sess. 905 (1869) (remarks of Senator Vickers); CONG. GLOBE, 41st Cong., 3d Sess. 1055 (1871) (remarks of Senator Sumner); CONG. GLOBE, 42d Cong., 2d Sess. 272 (1872) (remarks of Senator Sumner). If a Negro was compelled to wait for a "Jim Crow" car, he might be exposed to inclement weather in the meanwhile. See text accompanying note 127 *supra*. At any rate, even if Congress did ban segregation in District of Columbia streetcars, this does not prove that this ban was made nationwide via the fourteenth amendment. Most of Sumner's bills relating to District of Columbia streetcars did not pass by a two-thirds majority. For example, one of them originally failed in committee and then passed by a vote of 17 to 16, with such moderate Republican Senators who later voted for the fourteenth amendment as Lafayette S. Foster of Connecticut, James W. Grimes of Iowa, Henry S. Lane of Indiana, John Sherman of Ohio, Lyman Trumbull of Illinois, and Waitman T. Willey of West Virginia voting against it.

Trumbull, the virtual Republican spokesman, or any other moderates, defected, the razor-thin, two-thirds majority would have evaporated and there would have been no fourteenth amendment. Indeed, Morrill, Sprague, and Trumbull alone could, by such a defection, have destroyed the anti-Johnson majority, and they no doubt would have done so had the amendment contained an anti-segregation provision. Moreover, there were other moderates who would have added to such a group of defectors. Since the Radicals in the Thirty-Ninth Congress could have done nothing without the moderate vote, it is clear that the moderate views must be decisive.

However, it may be noted that even the Radicals did not intend in the Civil Rights Act of 1875 to eliminate the rights of carriers, innkeepers, and theaters to segregate their patrons, notwithstanding some confusion on this point in the lower federal courts.[198] Frelinghuysen as much as admitted the right of business to segregate, as did other members of Congress. Moreover, all proponents of the bill concurred in the position that it was merely designed to re-enact the common law, which allowed businessmen to segregate their patrons if they were given equal accommodations. Finally, no complaint was made by Negroes about segregation but only about unequal accommodations.

It is true that the Radicals were against segregation by state law, a point on which Sumner and Edmunds were particularly vociferous. No doubt the Radical position was that this was a matter

---

CONG. GLOBE, 38th Cong., 1st Sess. 3135, 3137 (1864). A defection of a group of this size would have defeated the amendment in the Senate, and it cannot be presumed that such a provision was adopted sub silentio over such Republican hostility in the constitutional amendment, especially since Grimes was a member of the Joint Committee on Reconstruction which reported out the amendment. All during the reconstruction period, the Republican Party was badly split over the desirability of racial segregation. See the discussion regarding West Chester & Phila. R.R. v. Miles, 55 Pa. 209 (1867), in CONG. GLOBE, 40th Cong., 2d Sess. 1965 (1868), between Representatives George V. Lawrence and G. W. Scofield, both Pennsylvania Republicans who had voted for the fourteenth amendment. As the amendment was the party platform for the 1866 elections, it is unreasonable to believe that any such controversial matter was contained therein as would have split the party. See JAMES, THE FRAMING OF THE FOURTEENTH AMENDMENT 110-20 (1956). Finally, the party refrained from incorporating in the fourteenth amendment even those measures which all Republicans desired and which they were prepared to enact in the District of Columbia, such as Negro suffrage. See Avins, *Literacy Tests and the Fourteenth Amendment: The Contemporary Understanding*, 30 ALBANY L. REV. 229 (1966); Avins, *Literacy Tests, The Fourteenth Amendment, and District of Columbia Voting: The Original Intent*, 1965 WASH. U.L.Q. 429. It is hardly reasonable to believe that they incorporated an even more controversial provision in the amendment such as nationwide desegregation of carriers and other public accommodations without so much as a word of discussion from the moderate Republicans.

198 *Compare* United States v. Newcomer, 27 Fed. Cas. 127 (No. 15868) (E.D. Pa. 1876), *with* United States v. Dodge, 25 Fed. Cas. 882 (No. 14976) (W.D. Tex. 1877).

to be left to the business proprietor, and if the state should decree such segregation by statute it would be a degrading mark of inferiority. But it is equally clear that the Republican moderates and a few Radicals, as noted above,[199] were not in agreement on this point, and the Radicals would never have been able to muster a two-thirds vote to put across their position in 1866.

Viewed historically, therefore, the majority decision in *Plessy v. Ferguson*[200] by a group of Justices who were contemporaries of the fourteenth amendment's adoption[201] is an accurate reflection of the original limitations on the scope of that amendment. The dissent of Mr. Justice Harlan is a virtual model, on the other hand, of the Radical position. Indeed, his analogy to segregated sides of a street may well have been taken from one of Edmunds' speeches.[202] Harlan made clear that he was concerned with segregation by law and not voluntarily or by action of a railroad in putting separate coaches on its train, as long as no legal segregation was made necessary by state statute.[203]

While the fourteenth amendment does not prohibit states from segregating persons in public accommodations, in this author's view this is a matter which ought to be left to the discretion of the individual business proprietor, as the Radicals contemplated. Such a proprietor will undoubtedly arrange his customers so as to provide the greatest amount of individual convenience and freedom of choice and association. In public places every person should have the fullest liberty to sit with others he finds compatible and to avoid the company of those he finds distasteful. Restoration of the common law rule by which the business proprietor and not the government determines this in accordance with the wishes of the customers will effectuate this end. Accordingly, although a state has the power to segregate persons by race or otherwise in public accommodations, in a modern society it would be highly inexpedient to exercise such power.

---

[199] See text accompanying note 198 *supra*.
[200] 163 U.S. 537 (1896).
[201] See Avins, Book Review, 58 COLUM. L. REV. 428, 430 n.16 (1958).
[202] 163 U.S. at 557.
[203] *Id*. at 560-61.

THE FREEDMEN'S BUREAU ACT OF 1865 AND THE PRINCIPLE OF NO DISCRIMINATION ACCORDING TO COLOR

Herman Belz

FROM THE TIME BENJAMIN F. BUTLER issued his famous contraband order of May, 1861, that escaped slaves would be employed as military laborers, the Union government was engaged in attempts to deal with the results of emancipation. The culmination of these wartime efforts was the Freedmen's Bureau Act of March 3, 1865. Historically this measure has been best remembered for its provision assigning forty acres of land to every male freedman. Yet at the time of its passage it contained a civil rights dimension that was equally if not more important than its economic content. The result of two years of legislative deliberation on freedmen's affairs, it was intended to recognize the former slaves as freemen with ordinary civil rights.

The principle of no discrimination according to color played a conspicuous part in the formation of the Freedmen's Bureau. Ironically, however, in the shaping of the 1865 act it was not Radicals with a reputation for being the special friends of the freedmen who insisted on this principle, but rather Republicans who sought to uphold the interest of loyal white refugees in the South. These same spokesmen for southern refugees were advocates, moreover, of laissez faire legal equality as a basic approach to the freedmen's question. Regarding the proposal for a permanent department of freedmen's affairs, advocated by Radicals, as an unwholesome and unsound form of guardianship, they believed that emancipated blacks should be recognized as freemen or citizens and, as the phrase had it, left severely alone to make their own labor arrangements and provide for themselves. How the famous civil rights principle of no distinction according to color was joined with laissez faire legal equality in creating the only federal agency that represented an institutional commitment to blacks in the Reconstruction era, forms the subject of this paper.

Freedmen's bureau legislation took shape in the context of the government's wartime policy toward emancipated slaves. Though varying in detail according to military command, as antislavery pressures and

* Research for this article was supported by a grant from the American Bar Foundation.

actual liberation increased in 1862 and 1863 this policy came to comprise three possible courses of action for the former slaves. They might choose voluntary colonization; seek employment as military laborers or agricultural workers on plantations leased under government authority; or enlist as soldiers of the United States. The chief concerns of this policy were military and political: emancipated slaves coming within Union lines were to be kept from placing an excessive burden upon the army, were indeed now expected to contribute to the war effort. Through employment on the soil or in the ranks the freedmen would furthermore be kept from going North, where public opinion was uniformly fearful of large scale Negro immigration. Though not insubstantial, benefits for the freed blacks were a secondary consideration in this general approach to dealing with the results of emancipation.[1]

Although Congress helped to determine this policy, in 1863 many Republican lawmakers took a more critical view of it and began to seek alternatives that would promote more directly the interests of the freed people. In particular the idea of creating a federal agency exclusively for the purpose of assisting blacks in the transition from slavery to freedom gained in favor and was expressed in legislative proposals. The accomplishment of this end, however, involved two distinct considerations which in the opinion of many Republicans might be contradictory. On the one hand it seemed necessary to provide temporary support for the freed slaves and protect them against injury and hostile treatment, especially in the form of apprenticeship arrangements that might be merely *de facto* serfdom. On the other hand almost all Republicans desired to recognize the emancipated people as freemen with the same rights, responsibilities, and personal freedom as ordinary citizens, understanding, of course, that this did not entail political or social equality. While many Republicans had no difficulty in finding both of these purposes satisfactorily and compatibly expressed in the freedmen's bureau proposals that were introduced, others saw a contradiction between what they regarded as paternalistic supervision or guardianship and genuine civil liberty.

In 1864 the Senate and the House of Representatives passed separate freedmen's bureau bills which, though placing the proposed agency in the Treasury and War departments respectively, adopted essentially the same outlook toward the immediate post-emancipation situation. The outstanding feature of each measure was the organization of freedmen's labor on a voluntary contractual basis, on abandoned plantations that were either operated directly by the government or leased to private businessmen and planters. Intended to provide relief and support for the displaced and often destitute blacks,

---

[1] V. Jacque Voegeli, *Free But Not Equal: The Midwest and the Negro during the Civil War* (Chicago, 1967), pp. 34-38, *passim*.

the two proposals also tried to resolve uncertainty about the future status of the freedmen by guaranteeing basic rights. Thus the Senate bill declared that ". . . every such freedman shall be treated in every respect as a freeman, with all proper remedies in courts of justice; and no power or control shall be exercised with regard to him except in conformity with law."[2]

While supporters of the Senate bill thought this provision a sufficient guarantee, other Congressmen, including a substantial number of Republicans, regarded it as an inadequate recognition and safeguard of the free status and rights of the former slaves. It established in their view an undesirable system of guardianship. Democrats trying to embarrass the opposition and prevent any freedmen's bill from passing were one source of criticism from the laissez faire point of view. The leading laissez faire critics, however, were antislavery Republicans from the Middle West. "Are they free men or are they not?" asked Senator James Grimes of Iowa.[3] Questions such as this reflected political rivalry between western and eastern Republicans, as well as hostility toward Negroes.[4] But Grimes's question, and the opposition to the freedmen's bureau bills of 1864, also reflected attachment to the principle of laissez faire legal equality.

Having passed separate measures, Republicans left the differences between the two bills to be composed at the second session of the Thirty-eighth Congress in December, 1864. Two main features marked the legislative situation at this time with respect to freedmen's affairs. The first was continued conflict between the War and Treasury departments for control of post-emancipation policy. Evident in the disagreement between the House and Senate, this rivalry during the legislative proceedings that ensued took the form of a debate over civilian versus military regulation of the freedmen and reflected the tension existing between the apparent need to supervise the transition from slavery to freedom while at the same time recognizing southern blacks' new status as free men.[5] The second circumstance affect-

[2] 38 Congress, H.R. No. 51, Senate amendment, June 27, 1864, sec. 4; *Congressional Globe*, 38 Cong., 1 sess., 3299 (June 27, 1964). The House bill contained a briefer and more general reference to protecting the rights of freedmen which its supporters interpreted as a guarantee of civil rights. 38 Cong., H.R. No. 51, sec. 4, Dec. 7, 1863; *Cong. Globe*, 38 Cong., 1 sess., 572-73 (Feb. 10, 1864), remarks of Thomas D. Eliot.

[3] *Ibid.*, 2972 (June 15, 1864).

[4] Midwestern Republicans who in June, 1864 led the opposition to the freedmen's bureau bill in the Senate, where Charles Sumner was its chief advocate and manager, were in part reacting against efforts by Sumner and Henry Wilson of Massachusetts to secure a bill allowing the states to fill their draft quotas by recruiting southern freedmen. The westerners charged that such an arrangement would place their states, less wealthy than Massachusetts, at a disadvantage. *Ibid.*, 3334 (June 28, 1864); Richard H. Abbott, "Massachusetts and the Recruitment of Southern Negroes, 1863-1865," *Civil War History*, XIV (Sept. 1968), 202-03.

[5] Since 1862 both military officers and treasury agents had undertaken to supervise freedmen's affairs in the occupied South. Army involvement came as escaped slaves

ing the legislative situation was a recently inaugurated movement to aid loyal white refugees in the South. This undertaking was to have an important influence on the evolution of the freedmen's bureau bill, and so requires a brief accounting.

Assisted early in the war by the Sanitary Commission, southern refugees by 1864 were attracting more widespread attention.[6] The American Freedmen's Inquiry Commission, for example, appointed in 1863 by the War department to report on the condition of emancipated slaves, stated that the aid required by blacks was no different from that which southern whites fleeing from the Confederacy would need. Similarly, the protection given the families of Negro soldiers was compared to that required by the families of white men under the same conditions.[7] Assessing the outlook for southern reconstruction, the Boston businessman and reformer Edward Atkinson suggested that the freedmen's bureau might be needed more to organize and civilize poor whites than emancipated blacks.[8] The white refugee problem also contained obvious political significance, for southerners choosing not to remain within the contracting Confederacy formed a potential constituency for the Republican party.[9]

The American Union Commission, some of whose officers played a conspicuous part in shaping the final freedmen's bureau bill, was the principal organization for aiding loyal white refugees. Founded in 1864 by moderate antislavery reformers, the A.U.C. from its inception aimed at rebuilding southern society along northern lines.[10] Refugees were not only to be given emergency relief, their civil and social condition was to be restored "upon the basis of industry, educa-

---

entered the lines of advancing Union forces, while Treasury supervision of freedmen developed as an aspect of Congressionally authorized management of abandoned and confiscated lands, the idea being that the former slaves should remain on the plantations as a free labor force. Although by December, 1864 the army had gained a larger share of control, Treasury agents still sought to extend their influence over freedmen's policy. The most comprehensive account of freedmen's policy in occupied areas is Louis S. Gerteis, *From Contraband to Freedman: Federal Policy Toward Southern Blacks 1861-1865* (Westport, Conn., 1973).

[6] Boston *Commonwealth*, Apr. 8, 1864; John Eaton, *Grant, Lincoln and the Freedmen: Reminiscences of the Civil War* (New York, 1907), pp. 37-38; Paul S. Pierce, *The Freedmen's Bureau: A Chapter in the History of Reconstruction* (Iowa City, 1904), p. 31.

[7] 38 Congress, 1 sess., *Senate Executive Documents*, No. 53, "Final Report of the American Freedmen's Inquiry Commission to the Secretary of War," May 15, 1864, p. 109.

[8] [Edward Atkinson], "The Future Supply of Cotton," *North American Review*, XCVIII (Apr., 1864), 497.

[9] Eaton, *Grant, Lincoln and the Freedman*, p. 38.

[10] [Lyman Abbott], *The American Union Commission: Its Origin, Operations and Purposes* (New York, 1865), pp. 1-2; Lyman Abbott, "Southern Evangelization," *New Englander*, XXIII (Oct. 1864), 699-708; *Report to the Contributors to the Pennsylvania Relief Association for East Tennessee* (Philadelphia, 1864), pp. 26-27.

tion, freedom and Christian morality."[11] To promote this end the A.U.C. helped southern whites obtain seed and equipment for farming; transported refugees to their homes or relocated them in new ones; operated schools and industrial training homes; advocated temporary occupation of abandoned lands for immediate sustenance and recommended changes in land tenure; and urged emigration, new industry, and a free press in the South.[12] Adopting an argument usually applied only to blacks, the A.U.C. furthermore tried to keep poor whites in the South on the theory that they were unsuited to the climate, business, and customs of the North.[13]

The special significance of the American Union Commission for the evolution of the freedmen's bureau bill lies in its assertion of the principle of no discrimination according to color as the basis for extending aid to southern white refugees. According to Lyman Abbott, an officer of the organization, A.U.C. representatives were often asked in 1864-65 whether care of the freedmen was part of its purpose and operations. The answer to this, Abbott explained, was emphatically to affirm that "The American Union Commission recognizes no distinction of caste or color. It is organized to aid the people of the South—not the black men because they are black, nor the white men because they are white, but all men because they are *men*, upon the ground of a common humanity alone." Nevertheless, Abbott went on to say, the association was careful to avoid duplication of charities and conflict of organizations by maintaining cordial understanding and cooperation with freedmen's aid societies.[14] In other words, the A.U.C. acted as a white refugee organization, but it did so under the idea—usually associated with the protection of Negro civil rights—that distinctions should not be made according to race. As in its argument against poor-white immigration into the North, the A.U.C. exhibited an unconventional and ironic attitude of racial impartiality. Partly owing to the efforts of the Commission's leaders, this same attitude was to find expression in the drafting of the freedmen's bureau bill.

Alongside the work of the A.U.C. in assisting white refugees, freedmen's aid societies continued their endeavors and pressed their views on Congress with the hope of securing a federal agency to supervise freedmen's affairs.[15] At length, in February 1865, a committee of

---

[11] Circular of the American Union Commission (n.p., n.d.), National Archives, RG 105, M-752, roll 13.

[12] *Ibid.*; American Union Commission, *Speeches of Hon. W. Dennison, J. P. Thompson, N. G. Taylor, J. R. Doolittle, J. A. Garfield . . . Washington, February 12, 1865* (New York, 1865), pp. 19-22.

[13] Petition of the Refugee Relief Commission of Ohio, National Archives, RG 233, 38A-B1.

[14] [Abbott], *The American Union Commission*, pp. 3-4, 23.

[15] George R. Bentley, *A History of the Freedmen's Bureau* (Philadelphia, 1955),

conference formulated a measure to resolve the differences between the House and Senate freedmen's bills of 1864.[16] As a solution to the problem of choosing between the War and Treasury departments as a home for the bureau, the committee proposed to create a new department of freedmen's affairs. Furthermore, showing concern for the laissez faire criticism of the 1864 bills, it sought more clearly to recognize the freed slaves' new status of civil liberty without, however, altering the basic structure of supervision provided by the earlier measures.

The conference committee bill, which was chiefly the work of Radicals Thomas D. Eliot and Charles Sumner, committed to the new department the "general superintendence of all freedmen" in the rebel states and charged the commissioner, or head, with establishing regulations protecting former slaves in the enjoyment of their rights, promoting their welfare, and securing to them and their posterity the blessings of liberty.[17] Agents of the department, described as "advisory guardians," were instructed to aid freedmen in adjusting their wages, protect them against failure of contract, arbitrate their disputes, and assure fair trial for them if involved in litigation.[18] A provision in the Senate bill of 1864 authorizing the bureau head to find homes and employment for freedmen whom he was unable to employ was retained in modified form in a section which allowed the commissioner, in such a situation, "to make provision" for former slaves with humane and suitable persons at a just compensation for their services.[19] The conference report also stipulated that department agents should be deemed in the military and liable to trial by military commission for, among other crimes, willful oppression of any freedman.[20]

The conference committee made certain minor changes in the 1864 legislation apparently for the purpose of allaying apprehension about excessive controls being placed on the freedmen. Department agents

---

pp. 46-48; Josephine S. Griffing to Lyman Trumbull, Aug. 10, 1864, Trumbull Papers, Library of Congress.

[16] The committee consisted of Republicans Thomas D. Eliot and William D. Kelley and Democrat Warren P. Noble from the House, and Republicans Charles Sumner and Jacob Howard and Democrat Charles Buckalew from the Senate.

[17] 38 Congress, H.R. No. 51, sec. 4, Report of the Conference Committee, *Cong. Globe*, 38 Cong., 2 sess., 563 (Feb. 2, 1865).

[18] H.R. No. 51, sec. 6.

[19] *Ibid.*, sec. 9. The provision in the Senate bill was itself a watered-down version of a proposal, introduced by Waitman T. Willey of West Virginia, which authorized the bureau head to initiate correspondence with state and municipal officials for the purpose of relocating freedmen in the North. Willey's proposition occasioned a sharp struggle between western Repulicans allied with border state conservatives and Democrats, and eastern Republicans. *Cong. Globe*, 1 sess., 3329-30, 3334-35, 3337 (June 28, 1864).

[20] H.R. No. 51, sec. 12. This feature was found in the Senate bill also.

were no longer instructed to see that freedmen upheld their part of labor contracts into which they entered, nor to "organize" their labor. As though to assure laissez faire critics that power would not be abused, the bill stated that the object of the department was "the good of the freedmen."[21] And the bill retained the declaration of the Senate measure that every freedman "shall be treated in all respects as a freeman, with all proper remedies in courts of justice, and no power or control shall be exercised with regard to him except in conformity with law."[22]

Land occupation arrangements in freedmen's bills provided an opportunity to recognize the civil liberty of emancipated Negroes. In this respect the conference committee measure differed appreciably though not fundamentally from the 1864 legislation. The latter, in both Senate and House versions, primarily envisioned a system of plantation leases under which freed slaves would be employed as contract laborers. Only subordinately did it hold out the possibility of independent tenure. The conference bill reversed this order of priority by stating that abandoned lands should be rented or leased to freedmen, or permitted to be cultivated, used, or occupied by them for a one year period, on terms to be agreed upon by the department and the former slaves.[23] Lands not required for freedmen could be leased to others, in which case former slaves could be employed under voluntary contracts approved by the department.[24] Described by Thomas D. Eliot as a "material modification" of the 1864 legislation, this provision, though not offering a clear expectation of permanent land ownership because of the one year limitation on freedmen's leases or occupation, in theory pointed more directly to independent land holding than either of the previous bills.[25]

While the conference report tried to obviate the conflict between civilian and military authority evident in the passage of the 1864 bills, it failed to do so because the proposed new department, a civilian agency, was in a practical sense the equivalent of the Treasury. At one level, therefore, the issue remained the same as in 1864. But this formal jurisdictional dispute was now bound up with the controversy over how best to recognize freedmen's liberty and rights.

Discussion of these issues outside Congress throws light on the legislative debate of February, 1865 that produced the final freedmen's bureau bill. As in 1864, the argument for civilian control was in part based on the contention that the free labor policy of the military re-

[21] *Ibid.*, sec. 1.
[22] *Ibid.*, sec. 4.
[23] *Ibid.*, sec. 5.
[24] *Ibid.*
[25] *Cong. Globe*, 38 Cong., 2 sess., 564 (Feb. 2, 1865); LaWanda Cox, "The Promise of Land for the Freedmen," *Mississippi Valley Historical Review*, XLV (Dec. 1958), 417.

gime of General Banks in Louisiana imposed virtual and effective serfdom on emancipated blacks.[26] Proponents of a civilian agency also charged that army officers regarded the freed people as inferior and were indifferent to their interests and advancement.[27] Still another view was that the conference bill should be supported as an experimental measure, on the theory that any freedmen's measure was better than none at all.[28] Supporters of the conference bill believed, too, that it substantially recognized the rights of the freedmen. "Details are of less moment than principles," declared the radical *Independent*. "The point to be gained is that the rights of the freedmen and the obligations of the Government to them should be recognized and authoritatively affirmed. . . . The present bill seems to do that."[29]

Opponents of a civilian agency, who included army freedmen's officials actively lobbying against the conference bill, warned that without military protection the civil liberty of freed blacks was threatened by commercial and speculative interests seeking to control postemancipation affairs.[30] Placing the freed people under the same authority as abandoned plantations, one critic argued, gave "an unpleasant twinge, as if, after all, we still clung to the idea of slavery."[31] Not only had the Treasury leasing system seemed to fail, experience showed that blacks did better when they rented or occupied lands assigned them than when they entered labor contracts.[32] Many Negroes themselves emphatically declared that working for a share of the crop and the profit was preferable to working for mere wages.[33] Yet the conference bill, critics pointed out, proposed a scheme of controlled labor as though the former slaves were incapable of supporting themselves.[34]

Political and bureaucratic rivalries formed a large part of the conflict between civilian and military control.[35] Yet ideas about freed-

[26] New Orleans *Tribune*, Dec. 10, 1864; Worcester *Daily Spy*, Feb. 6, 24, 27, 1865; *Independent*, Mar. 2, 1865.

[27] Boston *Journal*, Feb. 1, 1865, Washington correspondence; Washington *Chronicle*, Feb. 9, 1865, letter on freedmen's affairs.

[28] *Ibid.*, editorial on freedmen; *Independent*, Feb. 9, 1865, editorial.

[29] *Ibid.*

[30] Eaton, *Grant, Lincoln and the Freedmen*, p. 224.

[31] Washington *Chronicle*, Feb. 8, 1865, letter on freedmen's affairs in Congress.

[32] *Ibid.* Gerteis, *From Contraband to Freedman*, pp. 169-71.

[33] New Orleans *Tribune*, Sept. 10, 24, 1864, Jan. 28, 1865; New York *Evening Post*, Jan. 26, 1865, report of the National Freedmen's Relief Association meeting.

[34] Washington *Chronicle*, Feb. 13, 1865, letter on freedmen's affairs; *Independent*, Jan. 26, 1865, letter on the Freedmen's Bureau.

[35] Gerteis, *From Contraband to Freedman*, pp. 147-49. Gerteis holds that the conflict was a mere struggle for power which involved no essential difference in proposals for freedmen's supervision. Both the Treasury and the War department plans were in this view paternalistic, resting on the assumption that the former slaves ought to remain on the plantations as wage laborers. *Ibid.*, pp. 150, 153.

men's rights were also involved. Opponents of a civilian agency believed that military regulation was more consistent with a laissez faire, equal rights approach to post-emancipation policy. Only the army, they reasoned, had the power to uproot the prejudicial codes and customs of slavery and protect freedmen's rights in the aftermath of abolition.[36] Once the war power had established freedmen's liberty on an equal rights basis, blacks should be left alone under the peacetime powers of the states.[37] A corollary of this laissez faire outlook was an insistence on treating the races equally. "We do not want a civil control of the black man, while there is no civil control of the white man," an opponent of the conference bill wrote.[38] The military power which protected and aided whites should do the same for blacks.[39] Thus, although many antislavery men and women supported the conference bill, others saw the War department as the proper place for the freedmen's bureau in part because they wanted to avoid the danger of overlegislating for the former slaves.[40]

In the context of this public discussion, Congressional debate on the conference bill reflected concern with the status of the freedmen and the degree of government regulation to which they should be subjected in contrast to other persons. The basic argument for the proposal, as in 1864, was that temporary care of the former slaves was a necessary corollary of the government's emancipation policy.[41] The freed people were "unused to self-reliance and dependent for a season somewhat upon our sympathy and aid," declared Thomas D. Eliot, manager of the conference report in the House.[42] Reasoning that if the measure failed, blacks would remain under a policy that made them "the mere accident of the Treasury," Charles Sumner said the new department was needed to recognize and protect the freedmen's basic rights.[43]

Elaborating on this theme, Lot M. Morrill argued that because blacks possessed no security of personal right amid the disorder existing in

[36] John Eaton, public letter of February 6, 1864, enclosed in Thomas D. Eliot to Charles Sumner, Mar. 7, 1864, Sumner Papers, Harvard University Library; Eaton, *Grant, Lincoln and the Freedmen*, p. 226; *New York Times*, Feb. 9, 1865, editorial; *Independent*, Jan. 26, 1865, letter on the Freedmen's Bureau by F.A.S.

[37] Washington *Chronicle*, Feb. 13, 1865, letter on freedmen's affairs.

[38] *Independent*, Jan. 26, 1865, letter on the Freedmen's Bureau by F.A.S.

[39] Washington *Chronicle*, Feb. 8, 1865, letter on freedmen's affairs in Congress; Eaton letter of Feb. 6, 1864, in Eliot to Sumner, Mar. 7, 1864, Sumner Papers, Harvard University Library.

[40] *Liberator*, Dec. 9, 1864, letter of "M. DuPays;" Josephine S. Griffing to Charles Sumner [Nov., 1864], Sumner Papers, Harvard University Library; Springfield *Weekly Republican*, Feb. 11, 1865, editorial.

[41] *Cong. Globe*, 38 Cong., 2 sess., 768 (Feb. 13, 1865), remarks of Charles Sumner, 988 (Feb. 22, 1865), remarks of Lot M. Morrill.

[42] *Ibid.*, 564 (Feb. 9, 1865).

[43] *Ibid.*, 768 (Feb. 13, 1865).

the South, the government must mediate between them and their former masters by providing employment, support, and protection. William D. Kelley of Pennsylvania reasoned that the former slaves had no relationship to the country and its institutions other than life and nativity. In the rebel states, he pointed out, they could not be witnesses nor bring suit in court to protect themselves. Implying that the bill would rectify this situation, Kelley asserted: "We are to guide them, as the guardian guides his ward, for a brief period, until they can acquire habits and become confident and capable of self-control." In short, the government must organize the emancipated people into society. More sanguine than most others, Eliot and Sumner, the principal framers of the conference bill, confidently announced that it gave the freedmen every legal and civil right.[44]

As in the Senate debate of 1864, the leading critics of the bill were Republicans who attacked it from a laissez faire point of view. The power of general superintendence which the bill extended over the freed people, together with the authority given the new department to "make provision" for them when unable to find employment, seemed in particular to subject blacks to undue restriction. Arguing that the fewer restraints imposed by government "the sooner we shall make men of them," Representative James Wilson of Iowa urged letting the freedmen have entire responsibility for disposing of their own labor. In the Senate fellow Iowan James Grimes objected that the proposal for Negro migration which he had supported in attenuated form in 1864, had been transformed in the present measure into a potential means of hiring out blacks for indefinite periods without their consent.[45]

Several Republicans protested that the bill rested on the assumption that the Negro race needed guardianship. According to John P. Hale of New Hampshire, it gave the lie to twenty years of abolitionist teaching that freed slaves could take care of themselves. Supporters of the bill had insisted that the regulations of the new department would affect the freed people only with their voluntary consent rather than coercively. Why then, asked John B. Henderson of Missouri, should government agents make bargains and contracts for them? Contending that the bill would destroy blacks in the same manner that government policies had destroyed Indians, William Sprague of Rhode Island recommended giving the freedmen the power to protect themselves through the suffrage. Then no special government agency would be needed.[46]

Similar criticism outside Congress suggests that to a greater ex-

---

[44] *Ibid.*, 988 (Feb. 22, 1865), 689, 693 (Feb. 9, 1865), 961 (Feb. 22, 1865).
[45] *Ibid.*, 689 (Feb. 9, 1865), 959 (Feb. 21, 1865). See note 19 above.
[46] *Ibid.*, 985 (Feb. 22, 1865), 960, 963 (Feb. 21, 1865).

tent than in 1864 these objections reflected more than mere intraparty political tensions. One Washington correspondent of antislavery outlook wrote sharply that the conference bill "contemplated a sort of serfdom as a substitute for slavery." "A majority of the antislavery men of the North," he added, "believe that if the negro must have a master, as the friends of Sumner's bill admitted by supporting it, it makes very little difference whether that master comes from South Carolina or from Massachusetts."[47]

While criticism of this sort coming from whites might be taken at a certain discount according to whether its motivation was political, racial, or ideological-humanitarian, the laissez faire point of view expressed by blacks possessed an undoubted cogency. The New Orleans *Tribune*, representing the substantial free black community in Louisiana, approached the freedmen's question from this perspective. Condemning the Treasury labor plan of 1864 as "mitigated bondage," the *Tribune* rejected the notion that blacks needed superintendence. "Give the men of color an equal chance," advised the black journal, "and this is all they ask. Give them up at once to all the dangers of the horrid competitive system of modern commerce and civilization; and . . . they will, more quickly than their fellow white man, find a happy issue out of all their sufferings." Opposing "protection and tutorship," the *Tribune* recommended the creation of a board of elected freedmen to represent the emancipated population. But what blacks were given instead, complained the *Tribune*, was the conference committee freedmen's bureau bill: "the eternal question of tutorage, presented in its most complete and comprehensive form." Urging suffrage as self-protection, the black newspaper thus assailed "this final effort to domination."[48]

The most prominent black advocate of a laissez faire post-emancipation policy was Frederick Douglass. In January, 1862, when reformers and political men first began to ask what should be done with the freed slaves, Douglass professed the view that he maintained throughout the war. ". . . do nothing with them," he wrote. "Your *doing* with them is their greatest misfortune." Three years later, adverting to the evident sympathy for Negroes among antislavery people, he offered the same advice. "I look over this country at the present time," he told the Massachusetts Anti-Slavery Society, "and I see Educational Societies, Sanitary Commissions, Freedmen's Associations, and the like,—all very good: but . . . there is always more that is benevolent, I perceive, than just, manifested toward us." Attempts to "prop up the Negro" or prepare him for freedom were misconceived. The freedmen, Douglas concluded, should be given equal civil

[47] Cincinnati *Daily Commercial*, Feb. 28, 1865, Washington letter from "Mack."
[48] New Orleans *Tribune*, Feb. 7, 1865, Sept. 10, 24, 1864, Jan. 8, Mar. 12, 1865, editorials.

and political rights and left to stand alone, and if they could not then they must fall. Although he offered no specific comment on the freedmen's bureau bill, Douglass's laissez faire arguments were implicitly critical of the articulated supervisory scheme of the conference committee.[49]

If Congressional Republicans' laissez faire critique reflected concern for the rights of blacks, their second major argument against the conference bill focused on the needs of white refugees in the South. Invoking the principle of no discrimination according to race, Republican critics insisted on equal rights for white southern war victims and attacked the conference report for its exclusive attention to blacks. In part this line of attack originated in the fear, conditioned generally by northern anti-Negro prejudice, that the freedmen might receive privileges and benefits not available to whites. The argument also reflected, however, commitment to the idea that race was not a reasonable basis on which to classify or distinguish among people.

As on the guardianship issue, representatives from the racially sensitive midwestern states led the way in demanding aid for loyal white refugees. Republican Henry S. Lane of Indiana, noting the absence of any provision for white refugees in the conference report, commented sarcastically: ". . . I have an old-fashioned way of thinking which induces me to believe that a white man is as good as a negro if he behaves himself." Pointing to the land provisions of the conference measure, Henderson of Missouri asked why a distinction was made in favor of blacks over white men. James Grimes asserted that destitute Unionist whites deserved the same advantages as emancipated slaves, while John P. Hale objected to giving all the abandoned lands to the freedmen and declared: ". . . in cases of this kind, I let the white and the black stand together." With evident pleasure the Washington correspondent of the conservative New York *Herald* reported that Republicans—to the consternation and despair of Charles Sumner—were coming to the conclusion "that the poor white refugees of the South had some rights as well as the negroes."[50]

Although intraparty criticism was more pronounced than in the previous session, the conference report passed the House on February 9, 1865, with only four Republican votes cast in opposition.[51] One of these votes,—that of Robert C. Schenck of Ohio—was particularly significant, however, for it appeared alongside an attempt already begun by Schenck to formulate an alternative freedmen's bill that would

[49] Philip S. Foner (ed.), *The Life and Writings of Frederick Douglass* (New York, 1955), III, 188-89, IV, 164.

[50] *Cong. Globe*, 38 Cong., 2 sess., 985 (Feb. 22, 1865), 962, 959 (Feb. 21, 1865), 984; New York *Herald*, Feb. 23, 1865, Washington correspondence.

[51] *Cong. Globe*, 38 Cong., 2 sess., 694 (Feb. 9, 1865). The vote was 64 to 62.

satisfy both the laissez faire critics and those who desired to assist loyal white refugees.

Indicative of the considerable bipartisan support it would receive, Schenck's alternative plan originated in a Democratic resolution of January, 1865 urging legislation to aid loyal southern refugees.[52] As chairman of the Committee on Military Affairs, to which the resolution was referred, Schenck on January 24 introduced a bill combining this purpose with aid to the freedmen. On February 9 he reported this freedmen and refugees bill back from committee with amendments.

Schenck's plan was to create in the War department a bureau of refugees and freedmen, to continue during the rebellion and to have effect in rebel states and in loyal districts within the operation of the army. Notably brief in comparison to previous freedmen's proposals, the bill contained but two substantive provisions. The first gave the bureau authority to supervise, manage, and control all subjects relating to refugees and freedmen, while the second authorized the President to provide relief assistance to freedmen and refugees and assign to the bureau for their benefit the temporary use of abandoned lands.[53]

On the same day that the House voted on the conference report, Schenck, who was regarded as an influential Radical, presented his freedmen and refugees bill as a laissez faire, equal rights alternative.[54] Assuming that a military framework was necessary for any freedmen's legislation, Schenck in presenting his plan stressed the temporary nature of the problem facing Congress. The condition of the freedmen was merely an incident of the war, he reasoned, and would end about the time the war concluded. Accordingly he believed there was no need to create a permanent department of government to deal with post-emancipation affairs.[55]

Schenck's most telling argument, however, invoked the principle of no distinction according to color within the framework of laissez faire legal equality. In contrast to the bill of the conference committee, he pointed out, the proposal of the military affairs committee

[52] Resolution introduced by John Law of Indiana, Jan. 5, 1865, National Archives, RG 233, 38A-B1.

[53] 38 Congress, H.R. No. 698, sec. 1-2, MS, National Archives, RG 233, 38A-B1; Cong. Globe, 38 Cong., 2 sess., 691 (Feb. 9, 1865).

[54] Schenck was a former Whig who served as brigadier general of volunteers in 1861-62. Injured at the second battle of Bull Run, he left the army and, partly at the request of Lincoln and Secretary of War Stanton, ran against Democrat Clement L. Vallandigham for a seat in the Thirty-eighth Congress. The correspondent of the Cincinnati *Gazette* characterized Schenck as "particularly hated of all Democrats, who make it a point sometimes not to listen to him, but after Thad Stevens and Winter Davis no Unionist is surer of attention to what he has to say." Kenneth W. Wheeler (ed.), *For the Union: Ohio Leaders in the Civil War* (Columbus, 1968), pp. 24-25; Cincinnati *Gazette*, Jan. 24, 1865, Washington correspondence.

[55] Cong. Globe, 38 Cong., 2 sess., 691 (Feb. 9, 1865).

"makes no discrimination on account of color. . . ." This was, he said, a "peculiarity" of the plan. Faithful to the laissez faire point of view, Schenck added that the principal danger for both freedmen and white refugees was that too much government assistance would encourage them to remain paupers. Thus the purpose of the bill was to put the former slaves and white refugees "in a condition to shift for themselves and become independent of this help from the authorities of the country at the earliest time. . . ."[56]

Schenck's attempt to formulate and win support for an alternative freedmen's bureau bill was abetted by the American Union Commission, the white refugee relief organization. In early January, upon learning of the House resolution directing an inquiry into the condition of loyal refugees, the president of the A.U.C., Joseph P. Thompson, wrote to Schenck describing the work of his organization and requesting a conference.[57] Representatives of the A.U.C. then went to Washington and circulated among members of Congress a memorial outlining the white refugee problem and recommending a course of action.[58] At the invitation of a bipartisan group which included a few members of Congress, the A.U.C. on February 12, 1865 held a public meeting at the capitol to publicize the loyal white refugee issue and win backing for Schenck's bill. Among several speakers in the hall of the House of Representatives, Joseph P. Thompson and the black abolitionist Henry Highland Garnet underscored the laissez faire theme in rejecting the idea of class legislation and cautioning against a long state of dependence for both black and white.[59] Army freedmen's officials John Eaton and Asa Fiske were meanwhile in Washington trying to influence opinion against the bill of the conference committee.[60]

On February 18 Schenck brought the freedmen and refugees bill to the floor of the House. Although the conference bill had already been approved and was awaiting action in the Senate, the chances of passing the new measure appeared good. On its introduction both Republicans and Democrats had expressed support. Democrat John Chanler of New York called it a "pertinent, wise, and proper" means

[56] *Ibid.*

[57] Joseph P. Thompson to Robert C. Schenck, Jan. 9, 1865, National Archives, RG 233, 38A-B1.

[58] Joseph P. Thompson to O. O. Howard, May 20, 1865, Howard Papers, Bowdoin College Library.

[59] American Union Commission, *Speeches . . . February 12, 1865*, pp. 6, 19; Henry Highland Garnet, *A Memorial Discourse . . . February 12, 1865* (Philadelphia, 1865), pp. 85-86; Washington *Chronicle*, Feb. 13, 1865; Boston *Journal*, Feb. 13, 1865, Washington correspondence. Garnet spoke earlier in the day, Sunday, February 12, independently of the American Union Commission meeting which was held in the evening.

[60] John Eaton to Alice Eaton, Feb. 3, 1865, Eaton Papers, University of Tennessee Library; Eaton, *Grant, Lincoln and the Freedmen*, p. 224.

of caring for the emancipated blacks. Indicative of moderate Republican opinion, the New York *Times* praised Schenck's bill as much more satisfactory than the "cumbersome, . . . impracticable, and ineffective" bill of the conference committee. Given this favorable response and the subsequent A.U.C. lobbying effort, a solid base of support quickly emerged which enabled the measure to pass without debate. Schenck reminded members as he brought the bill to a vote that it was "broad and general in character and makes no distinction on account of color." By voice vote that was almost unanimous, the House agreed to follow Schenck's recommendation of approving the freedmen and refugees plan and letting the Senate choose between it and the conference bill.[61]

In the upper chamber, meanwhile, Charles Sumner on February 13 had brought forward the conference committee bill, arguing that the choice was between this measure and none at all.[62] Other issues took precedence, however, and by the time Sumner got the matter to the floor again, on February 21, the Schenck bill stood as an alternative. Significantly it received immediate and bipartisan backing.

As they attacked the conference report for its paternalistic restrictions on blacks and neglect of white refugees, laissez faire critics referred approvingly to the new House bill. James Grimes stated that it accomplished all that was necessary, in language that had a definite and well understood meaning in contrast to the merely rhetorical guarantees of liberty contained in the conference proposal. Democrat Reverdy Johnson of Maryland believed the House bill met the needs of both former slaves and loyal white refugees. After two days of debate the Senate rejected the conference report, 14 to 24, with twelve Republicans joining Democrats and border state conservatives in opposition. A second committee of conference was then requested.[63]

The second conference committee, consisting entirely of members who had sat on neither the House nor Senate emancipation or freedmen's committees, reported a measure substantially in accord with the Schenck bill.[64] It proposed to establish a bureau of refugees, freedmen, and abandoned lands within the War department, to continue during the rebellion and for one year thereafter. Within rebel

---

[61] *Cong. Globe*, 38 Cong., 2 sess., 693 (Feb. 9, 1865), 908 (Feb. 18, 1865), 989 (Feb. 22, 1865), remarks of Reverdy Johnson; New York *Times*, Feb. 9, 1865, editorial. During the Senate debate on the conference bill Johnson stated that the vote in the House on Schenck's bill was almost unanimous.

[62] *Cong. Globe*, 38 Cong., 2 sess., 768 (Feb. 13, 1865).

[63] *Ibid.*, 959 (Feb. 21, 1865), 989-90 (Feb. 22, 1865). Voting against the conference report were Cowan, Dixon, Doolittle, Grimes, Hale, Harlan, Harris, Henderson, Howe, Lane of Indiana, Ten Eyck, and Trumbull.

[64] The conference committee was composed of Republicans Schenck, Boutwell, and Democrat Rollins from the House, and Republicans Wilson, Harlan and border state Unionist Willey from the Senate.

states and in districts embraced by the operations of the army, the bureau was to exercise supervision and management of abandoned lands, and to control all subjects relating to refugees and freedmen. As in Schenck's bill, provision was made for immediate relief of destitute refugees and freedmen. The section of the bill dealing with land, however, was more elaborate and extensive than the corresponding section in the Schenck measure. The commissioner of the bureau was authorized to set aside abandoned or confiscated lands, and assign forty acres to each male citizen, whether freedman or refugee. After three years use of the land at rent equal to six per cent of its value, the freedman and refugee occupants could purchase it and receive "such title as the United States can convey. . . ."[65]

The most significant feature of this bill was its abandonment of the idea that the freedmen should be contract laborers under the indefinite supervisory power of a new government department. The first conference report, it is true, theoretically gave first call on the land to the freed blacks, with secondary provision for leases to other persons. Nevertheless, defenders of the bill seemed to envision the former slaves continuing as plantation laborers under a contract labor system essentially the same as existing Treasury department arrangements.[66] The second conference bill, in contrast, envisioned the freedmen as independent farmers, perhaps even as property owners, under their own supervision. Absent were provisions instructing bureau agents to help freed slaves adjust or apply their labor, as well as the stipulation authorizing the commissioner to "make provision" for them. Similarly omitted were all references to bureau agents acting as advisory guardians, arbitrators, or next friends of the freedmen in court proceedings.

To be sure, a degree of federal intervention was necessary, as laissez faire critics conceded. Placing the bureau in the War department, however, limiting its existence to a definite period, and charging it with emergency aid and support were ways of minimizing the government's role. The conference committee headed by Schenck further expressed its anti-paternalistic attitude in giving the bureau control over "subjects relating to freedmen and refugees," rather than giving the commissioner explicit general power to superintend and regulate the freedmen themselves as in earlier bills. While in practice this emendation would not amount to a significant difference, it reflected the intention of the bill's framers to express more clearly the idea that emancipated slaves were free men with ordinary civil rights.

Although laissez faire, civil equality purposes characterized the second conference bill, the forty acre provision has usually seemed the most important feature of the legislation. In particular it has been

---

[65] H.R. No. 51, sec. 1, 3-4, *Cong. Globe*, 38 Cong., 2 sess., 1182 (Feb. 28, 1865).
[66] *Ibid.*, 689 (Feb. 9, 1865), remarks of Thomas D. Eliot, 988 (Feb. 22, 1865), remarks of Lot M. Morrill.

taken as evidence of a more radical commitment to give land to the freedmen.[67] The intention of Congress in the second conference plan, however, was to allow temporary use of rebel estates, with the rather remote possibility of subsequent ownership, rather than to extend a firm promise of a title in fee simple.

The closest Congress came to promising land to the freedmen was the approval by the House in 1864 of a southern homestead bill which proposed to give outright forty or eighty acres of public land to Union soldiers and army laborers irrespective of color. Only in a very limited and indirect sense, however, can this be viewed as a freedmen's bill.[68] The freedmen's bureau legislation of 1864 contained no promise of land to former slaves, and though the first conference report theoretically proposed to place them on the soil, this arrangement was to be only temporary. "The time has come," said Charles Sumner in February, 1865, "when they should enjoy the results of their labor at least for a few months."[69]

While friends of the freedmen urged temporary use of rebel estates, proponents of aid to white refugees broached the same idea. Joseph P. Thompson of the A.U.C. thus recommended that white southern refugees be permitted to occupy abandoned lands in order temporarily to support themselves, and Schenck's original bill expressly proposed "the temporary use of abandoned lands and tenements" for the benefit of freedmen and refugees.[70] The second conference bill called for specific assignment of forty-acre plots and omitted the word "temporary," but since Schenck was a member of the committee that drafted this proposal it seems reasonable to suppose that it comported with his original purpose. Whether the conference committee intended anything more depended on the title that Congress could convey after three years, and this was a big question mark.[71]

[67] Cox, "The Promise of Land for the Freedmen;" William S. McFeely, *Yankee Stepfather: General O. O. Howard and the Freedmen* (New York, 1968), pp. 104-05; M. L. Benedict, *The Impeachment and Trial of Andrew Johnson* (New York, 1973), p. 38.

[68] 38 Congress, H.R. No. 276, Feb. 29, 1864, introduced by George W. Julian; *Cong. Globe*, 38 Cong., 1 sess., 1187-88 (March 18, 1865), remarks of George W. Julian.

[69] *Ibid.*, 38 Cong., 2 sess. 961 (Feb. 21, 1865).

[70] American Union Commission, *Speeches . . . February 12, 1865*, p. 20; H.R. No. 698, sec. 2, Feb. 9, 1865.

[71] The grounds for concluding that Congress intended a policy of permanent confiscation and land redistribution as a corollary of the freedmen's bureau bill are slight. Abandoned lands were held under the Captured and Abandoned Property Act of 1863, which aimed neither at permanent confiscation nor the disturbing of titles to deserted lands. Rather, abandoned lands were to be held under temporary Union control and returned to loyal owners after the war. Rebel lands might also be held under the Confiscation Act of 1862, but this contained a restriction against permanent divestiture of property. The repeal of this restriction in 1864 by separate House and Senate actions is sometimes seen as an indication of a more radical confiscation purpose. (See, for

It is nevertheless true that Congress proposed to assist the freedmen in ways that conceivably could lead to land redistribution. Yet equally if not more important than this potential economic support was the recognition of the status and rights of freemanship that land occupation, in contrast to contract labor arrangements, implied. The significance of this civil recognition can be seen in the position taken by the black New Orleans *Tribune* on the question of land and the freedmen.

Condemning the Treasury department plantation leasing and contract labor policy, the *Tribune* in early 1865 proposed that black laborers join black and white managers in a system of associated farming. This would allow emancipated slaves to feed and clothe themselves, go where they pleased, and become self-reliant, the *Tribune* explained. Receiving a low basic wage to cover necessities, freed slaves would most importantly acquire a share of the crop and become partners in the enterprise.[72] A sharecropping arrangement such as this would not only offer an economic incentive, it would recognize more clearly than a contract labor system the former slaves' status as free men.[73] A recent study of southern freedmen confirms this finding by pointing out that blacks were more concerned with the form of their labor—that it be consistent with the reflect their status as free men— than with the actual level of wages.[74] Thus by providing for independent land occupation, albeit temporary, Schenck's bill and the

---

example, James M. McPherson, *The Struggle for Equality: Abolitionists and the Negro in the Civil War and Reconstruction* [Princeton, 1964], pp. 255-59.) The Senate action, however, was prompted by a desire to prevent lands temporarily occupied by freedmen from reverting to the family of a rebel owner should the owner be killed in battle. The purpose in other words was to protect freed slaves in temporary use of the land. Finally, the Direct Tax Act of 1862 provided a third means of acquiring southern lands. This statute offered the most expeditious method of transferring titles in fee simple, but where it had been applied, in the Sea Islands of South Carolina, whites had been the principal purchasers of the land. Thus there was little basis for concluding that the government would be able to convey title in fee simple after three years occupation by freedmen or refugees. Temporary occupation seems to have been the main intention and realistic expectation. James G. Randall, *Constitutional Problems under Lincoln* (revised ed., Urbana, 1951), pp. 317-28; *Cong. Globe*, 38 Cong. 1 sess., 3306-07 (June 27, 1864); Willie Lee Rose, *Rehearsal for Reconstruction: The Port Royal Experiment* (Indianapolis, 1964), pp. 214-15, 287-88.

[72] New Orleans *Tribune*, Jan. 28, 29, Feb. 2, 1865. The only difficulty the *Tribune* anticipated was getting the land, for owners might refuse to lease to associations. The *Tribune* argued, however, that precedents were available for working the land on the plea of public necessity, and cited the example of the Prussian government threatening to take over the operation of factories in 1849 if the owners did not resume production. The *Tribune* did not propose federal confiscation.

[73] August Meier, "Negroes in the First and Second Reconstruction," *Civil War History*, XIII (June, 1967), 122, argues that sharecropping began as a compromise between blacks' desire to own or rent land and plantation owners' desire to have the freedmen work for wages under contract.

[74] Gerteis, *From Contraband to Freedman*, p. 167.

second conference committee proposal contained a laissez faire and civil rights dimension not present in earlier freedmen's bureau plans.

On March 3, 1865, the final day of the session, Congress enacted the second conference bill by voice vote. Senate approval came after very brief debate, while the House, having already agreed to substantially the same measure in the form of Schenck's bill, concurred with no discussion at all.[75] Two years after the first proposal had been introduced, Republican lawmakers had finally created a freedmen's bureau.

In analyzing Congressional action it appears that clearer recognition of the status of the former slaves as free men was an important difference between the final bill and earlier versions. Yet on this issue disagreement persisted as a few members on both sides of the aisle objected to what they still regarded as undue coercion of the freedmen.[76] There can be no doubt, however, that the inclusion of white refugees in the bill was a decisive consideration in its enactment. This had not been present in any form in earlier freedmen's legislation, and its rapid acceptance in Schenck's bill after the House had already approved the first conference committee report suggests that it was equally if not more important in creating the bureau than the abandonment of the guardianship idea.

Although they were not disinterested observers, there seems to be no reason to doubt the testimony of American Union Commission representatives that the inclusion of white refugees was decisive. Writing to the commissioner of the Freedmen's Bureau, General O. O. Howard, a few months later, Joseph P. Thompson stated that the principal objections to the first conference bill of Eliot and Sumner were fear of bureaucratic abuse in the creation of a new department, and the bill's exclusive concern for blacks. However, the alternative proposal of Robert C. Schenck and the second conference bill based upon it, Thompson explained, attracted much wider support, including that of many Democrats, because it was not exclusive. "This accounts for the naming of the Refugees first; and but for this combination," Thompson averred, "*no* bill for Freedmen could have passed the last Congress."[77] Lyman Abbott, also an officer of the A.U.C., similarly wrote that prejudice against Negroes threatened to prevent any freedmen's bureau bill from passing until a broader approach that included white refugees was undertaken.[78]

[75] *Cong. Globe*, 38 Cong., 2 sess., 1307-08 (Mar. 2, 1865), 1348, 1402 (Mar. 3, 1865).

[76] Conservative Lazarus Powell of Kentucky said the bill placed "overseers and negro-drivers" over the freedmen, while Republican Jacob Howard of Michgan criticized it for imposing a military government on the former slaves. *Ibid.*, 1307-08 (Mar. 2, 1865).

[77] Joseph P. Thompson to O. C. Howard, May 20, 1865, Howard Papers, Bowdoin College Library.

[78] [Lyman Abbott], *The Results of Emancipation in the United States of America* (New York, 1867), p. 18.

The idea that government should make no distinction among people on the basis of color had in the past and in future was to become even more closely associated with the attempt by blacks to secure political and civil equality. It was highly ironic therefore that under this principle southern white refugees were brought under the protection of the freedmen's bureau. The American Union Commission, which helped shape this outcome, was involved a year later in a similar situation concerning the non-discrimination idea which throws light on its use in the formation of the bureau.

Early in 1866 the American Union Commission and several freedmen's aid societies, run mainly by abolitionists, agreed to merge their organizations. They were unable to decide on a name, however, for agreement had not been reached on the purpose of the merged association. According to Lyman Abbott, the freedmen's groups were reluctant to give up the advantage which their executive and limited purpose of assisting blacks, signified in the names of their organizations, gave them in the eyes of a large segment of the northern public. The A.U.C. on the other hand, in order to allay sectional hostility and promote reunification, believed that whites should be aided and that race should not be a consideration in the operations of the new organization. The name of the body, A.U.C. representatives held, should reflect this outlook by containing no reference whatever to race or to the freedmen.[79] The outcome of the negotiations was a compromise in which, though the name "freedmen" was retained, whites were to be included and distinctions of race and color were to be disregarded.[80] Abbott considered the result a vindication of his position. He later wrote: ". . . the radical abolitionists, who had insisted on no distinction because of race or color when that principle was of benefit to the negro, could not deny it because it was of benefit to the white man."[81]

Just this seems to have been what happened in Congress in February, 1865. Robert C. Schenck said as much when he pointedly observed that the "peculiarity" of his refugees and freedmen's bureau bill was that it made "no discrimination on account of color—a favorite phrase, as is well understood, in these days among us all."[82]

A further irony in the use of the non-discrimination principle in the formation of the Freedmen's Bureau lies in the fact that it reflected at once resentment against blacks and commitment to the ideal of

[79] Lyman Abbott, *Reminiscences* (Boston, 1915), pp. 251, 260-61.

[80] *The American Freedman*, I (May, 1866), 18, Constitution of the American Freedmen's Union Commission.

[81] Abbott, *Reminiscences*, p. 261.

[82] *Cong. Globe*, 38 Cong., 2 sess., 691 (Feb. 9, 1865). Thomas D. Eliot denied that the first conference bill discriminated in favor of blacks. It merely recognized, Eliot said, that the time had come to pass legislation on their behalf. *Ibid.*, 693 (Feb. 9, 1865).

racially impartial legal equality. That antislavery Republican as well as Democratic lawmakers could be apprehensive lest blacks receive preferential treatment says much in retrospect about the inability of Americans in the 1860's to comprehend the dimensions and depth of the race question and the circumstances in which emancipation left the freed people. Even before the abolition of slavery had been fully accomplished political representatives were sensitive to what has been described in more recent times as reverse discrimination. At the same time, however, the use of the non-discrimination principle in conjunction with the doctrine of laissez faire legal equality represented a concession to racial egalitarianism. Republicans applied the egalitarian idea in opposing the Eliot-Sumner conference bill as a coercive and paternalistic system of guardianship which denied blacks' status as free men, and then in insisting that loyal white refugees had an equal right to any assistance which the federal government might extend to relieve dislocation and suffering caused by the war.

Given the dominance of the idea of equality before the law in mid-nineteenth century America, the logic of the situation made the application and acceptance of the principle of no discrimination according to color irresistible. Yet if it was true that including white refugees was the only way to secure the passage of freedmen's bureau legislation, as Thomas D. Eliot later conceded,[83] and if the bureau protected the rights and well being of the emancipated slaves, as most historical accounts agree it did, then ironic as the use of the non-discrimination principle was in 1865, in a larger sense it was consistent with the historic purpose of the idea as an instrument for achieving black equality before the law.

[83] Eliot said in 1868 that it would have taken another year to create the Freedmen's Bureau had it not been for Schenck's suggestion that white refugees also be brought under the provisions of the bill. *Ibid.*, 40 Cong., 2 sess., 1815 (Mar. 11, 1868).

AN HISTORICAL ANALYSIS OF THE 1968 'INDIAN CIVIL RIGHTS' ACT

Donald L. Burnett, Jr.*

Introduction

In the Indian Civil Rights Act,[1] enacted as a rider to the Civil Rights Act of 1968,[2] Congress faced a number of the problems involved in the relationship between the various Indian tribes and the federal constitutional system. In order to properly understand its provisions, however, the Act must be seen in historical perspective — in terms of the development of the place of the Indian in the American legal system and of the legislation itself. Because the debate in 1968 over the Civil Rights Act centered on the sections intended primarily to benefit other minorities, so have most of the commentaries written on it since then, and the necessary historical analyses of the Indian provisions have not been undertaken.

Judicial sensitivity is especially important in the area of Indian civil rights. The United States Commission on Civil Rights recently noted: "In enforcing the act, the courts will have the serious responsibility of drawing a balance between respect for individual rights and respect for Indian custom and tradition. Many important questions . . . will not be answered until the courts have settled them."[3] In deciding cases involving these provisions, some courts have not engaged in the sort of historical discussion and analysis that should be essential.[4] An underlying thesis of this article is that a sense of history will engender greater judicial sensitivity for the need to preserve effective tribal institutions. A better understanding of the relevant history should aid judicial analysis and guide the courts and the agencies implementing the legislation.

---

*Clerk to Henry F. McQuade, Supreme Court of Idaho; Member of the Idaho Bar; B.A., 1968, Harvard University; J.D., 1971, University of Chicago.

1 25 U.S.C. §§ 1301-03, 1311-12, 1321-26, 1331, 1341 (1970).

2 82 Stat. 73 (codified in scattered sections of 18, 25, 42 U.S.C.).

3 United States Commission on Civil Rights, American Indian Civil Rights Handbook 11 (1972).

4 *See, e.g.,* United States v. Brown, 334 F. Supp. 536 (D. Neb. 1971).

This article, first briefly outlines the history of the issue of Indian tribal sovereignty and the ways in which federal law in this area has developed. It next traces the legislative process, especially the part played by Senator Sam Ervin of North Carolina, which resulted in the Indian civil rights provisions. This analysis focuses on Senator Ervin's apparent objectives, the interests of the affected parties, the areas of conflict and accommodation, and the process of enactment. It then examines the ways in which various courts have interpreted the Act and how the tribes have been affected by it.

I. Tribal Sovereignty from 1786

A. *The Early Years: Seminal Concepts*

The federal government's Indian affairs policy originated in times when it regarded the tribes as enemy nations. In 1786, Congress delegated responsibility for Indian affairs to the War Department.[5] The Bureau of Indian Affairs (BIA) was created in 1824, and President Jackson appointed a Commissioner of Indian Affairs within the War Department in 1832.[6] The responsibility for administration in the field rested with the local agent, often a cavalry officer, who was given broad powers "to manage and superintend the intercourse with the Indians" and "to carry into effect such regulations as may be prescribed by the President."[7] The President, in turn, was "authorized to prescribe such rules and regulations as he may think fit."[8]

The states took little part in the management of Indian affairs, for the Removal Act of 1830[9] transferred many eastern tribes to the plains west of the Mississippi River where no states yet existed. Moreover, in *Worcester v. Georgia*,[10] the Supreme Court held that native tribes were not subject to the jurisdiction of the states in which they were located. Chief Justice Marshall described the

---
5 H. Driver, Indians of North America 485 (2d ed. rev. 1969).
6 *Id.* at 482.
7 Act of June 30, 1834, ch. 162, § 7, 4 Stat. 736-37.
8 *Id.* at § 17, 4 Stat. 738.
9 Act of May 28, 1830, ch. 148, 4 Stat. 411-12.
10 31 U.S. (6 Pet.) 515 (1832).

Cherokee tribe as "a distinct community, occupying its own territory with boundaries accurately described in which the laws of Georgia can have no force."[11] In an earlier decision holding that the Cherokees were not a foreign nation within the meaning of the Constitution for the purpose of determining the Supreme Court's original jurisdiction, Chief Justice Marshall had described the tribe as a ."domestic dependent nation" and had likened each Indian's relationship to the federal government to that of a "ward to his guardian."[12] These analogies reflected the traditional view that Indian tribes remained sovereign bodies empowered to regulate their own affairs, limited only by acts of Congress.[13] By virtue of the federal government's conquest, Congress was viewed as enjoying plenary authority over Indian affairs.[14] The treaties enacted under congressional authority often reserved to the Indians the right to retain their traditional institutions and to continue such essential activities as hunting and fishing.[15] Their implications were commonly broad, "[giving] the Indians every warrant to believe that they could retain their lands, their governments, and their way of life as long as they wished."[16]

Thus, the place of Indians and Indian tribes in the American system was uncertain. Indians were commonly regarded as federal wards; yet tribal organizations were acknowledged as "distinct communities" of a sovereign nature.

B. *The Era of Conquest: The Rule of the BIA*

Following the Bureau's transfer from the War Department to the Department of the Interior in 1849,[17] BIA policy continued to

---

11 *Id.* at 560.

12 Cherokee Nation v. Georgia, 30 U.S. (5 Pet.) 1 (1831).

13 *See* Note, *The Indian Bill of Rights and the Constitutional Status of Tribal Governments*, 82 HARV. L. REV. 1343, 1347 (1969).

14 *See* Crosse, *Criminal and Civil Jurisdiction in Indian Country*, 4 ARIZ. L. REV. 57 (1962).

15 *See* 2 C. KAPPLER, LAWS AND TREATIES, S. DOC. No. 452, 57th Cong., 1st Sess. (1903).

16 W. BROPHY & S. ABERLE, THE INDIAN: AMERICA'S UNFINISHED BUSINESS 25 (1966) [hereinafter cited as BROPHY]. This volume expands FUND FOR THE REPUBLIC, REPORT OF THE COMMISSION ON THE RIGHTS, LIBERTIES AND RESPONSIBILITIES OF THE AMERICAN INDIAN (W. Brophy & S. Aberle eds. 1961).

17 DRIVER, *supra* note 5, at 482.

reflect these conflicting views. The field agents still exercised the broad statutory power previously noted, but they also created indigenous police forces and courts or retained them where they already existed. Of course, this policy was not simply a concession to the sovereign powers of the tribes. The Indian police, directed by the local agent, served not only to enforce law and order, but also to set examples of acculturation to the native communities and to undermine the authority of recalcitrant chieftains and councils.[18] In the 1890's the Indian police were instrumental in suppressing the Ghost Dance movement among the Sioux, the last great organized resistance to the inexorable white dominance.[19]

The law enforced by these indigenous police detachments was a mixture of tribal custom and rudimentary codes drafted by the BIA in the early 1880's. In part, these codes were intended to supplant native customs, but they were also required because the trauma of conquest had weakened traditional social controls.[20] The "successful" experiment with Indian police encouraged the BIA to establish Indian courts with native judges. Courts of Indian offenses were established by the Secretary of the Interior in 1883, and that year's Annual Report of the Commissioner of Indian Affairs set forth rules, approved by the Secretary, governing the operation of the new courts.[21] In practice, these courts operated very informally.[22]

By the mid-1880's a structure for Indian affairs management had emerged. Alert to the uncertain legal status of the tribes and the unclear extent of their sovereign powers, the BIA adopted a middle course. Certain trappings of tribal sovereignty (in the form of Indian police and courts) were encouraged, but matters of pol-

---

18 W. HAGAN, INDIAN POLICE AND JUDGES 69-79 (1966).
19 *Id.* at 103. For an examination of what underlay the Ghost Dance movement, see P. FARB, MAN'S RISE TO CIVILIZATION AS SHOWN BY THE NORTH AMERICAN INDIANS FROM PRIMEVAL TIMES TO THE COMING OF THE INDUSTRIAL STATE 280-84 (1968).
20 HAGAN, *supra* note 18, at 9.
21 SUBCOMM. ON CONSTITUTIONAL RIGHTS OF SENATE COMM. ON THE JUDICIARY, SUMMARY REPORT OF HEARINGS AND INVESTIGATIONS ON CONSTITUTIONAL RIGHTS OF THE AMERICAN INDIAN, 99th Cong., 2d Sess., 14 (Comm. Print 1964) [hereinafter cited as SUMMARY REPORT OF HEARINGS].
22 The extent to which the native judges served the will of local BIA agents varied with circumstances and personalities; but a report of the Board of Indian Commissioners in 1892 charged that agent influence remained unduly strong, partly because appeals from court decisions could be taken to BIA administrators. HAGAN, *supra* note 18, at 110.

icy, such as the drafting of codes, remained exclusively in the hands of the Bureau.

C. *The Settlement Era: The Indians and the Law*

As white America pursued its "Manifest Destiny," Indian country ceased to be remote. Law and order on the reservations gravely concerned burgeoning numbers of settlers, and the increase in crimes committed by whites on reservations troubled the Indians as well. The new courts of Indian offenses exercised jurisdiction in civil and criminal cases in which both parties were Indian and also occasionally in cases involving whites on the reservations. But the creation of states as sovereign entities and a reluctance by the settlers to entrust serious criminal cases to Indian tribunals resulted in a substantial limitation of Indian court criminal jurisdiction.

State jurisdiction over crimes committed by whites on the reservations was extended in *United States v. McBratney*[23] in which the Supreme Court held that the United States Circuit Court for Colorado did not have exclusive jurisdiction over the murder of one white man by another on the Ute Reservation in Colorado. The Court said that the United States did not have exclusive jurisdiction over a reservation unless Congress had expressly exempted it from state jurisdiction when it had admitted the state to the Union. No such exemption had been made with respect to the Ute Reservation,[24] and, as a result, Colorado had "acquired criminal jurisdiction over its own citizens and other white persons throughout the whole of its territory . . . including the Ute Reservation. . . ."[25]

As the Supreme Court extended state criminal jurisdiction over whites on the reservations, Congress limited Indian court authority over Indians committing crimes against other Indians on the reser-

---

23 104 U.S. 621 (1881).
24 The Court sought support from United States v. Ward, 28 Fed. Cas. 397 (No. 16,639) (C.C.D. Kan. 1863) and The Kansas Indians, 72 U.S. (5 Wall.) 737 (1866). But these cases held merely that where express provisions *did* exist, Indian lands were exempt from state jurisdiction. They did not hold that express provision was an absolute prerequisite. Nevertheless, pressure to extend state jurisdiction, founded partly in fear of reservations becoming "no man's lands," was so great that *McBratney* became a landmark precedent.
25 United States v. McBratney 104 U.S. 621, 624 (1881).

vations. In the celebrated *Crow Dog* case,[26] the Oglala court had convicted the defendant of murder and ordered him to make restitution in the form of services and property to the victim's family. This form of penalty was fully consistent with traditional tribal practices, but outraged whites demanded a more severe punishment. The defendant was tried again and convicted in a Dakota Territory district court sitting as a United States circuit court. The Supreme Court held that the district court did not have jurisdiction over a crime committed in Indian country by one member of a tribe upon another of the same tribe.[27] In response, Congress eliminated tribal jurisdiction over cases involving serious crimes.

The Seven Major Crimes Act[28] gave territorial courts jurisdiction over enumerated major offenses committed by Indians within a territory, whether or not on a reservation and gave federal courts jurisdiction over such offenses when committed by Indians on a reservation within a state. The validity of the Act was established in *United States v. Kagama*,[29] in which the Supreme Court upheld the exercise of federal jurisdiction over the murder of an Indian by two other Indians on the Hoopa Valley Reservation in California. The Court recalled Congress' plenary power and reiterated Marshall's wardship concept: "These Indian tribes are the wards of the nation. They are communities dependent on the United States. Dependent largely for their daily food. Dependent for their political rights."[30]

At the same time, state courts and lower federal courts began to extend the logic of the Seven Major Crimes Act to give the states

---

26 *Ex Parte* Crow Dog, 109 U.S. 556 (1883).
27 *Id.* at 562.
28 Indian Appropriations Act of 1885, 23 Stat. 385 (1885) [informally and hereinafter referred to as Seven Major Crimes Act], *as amended* 18 U.S.C. § 1153 (1970). In the original Act of 1885, federal courts and law enforcement agencies were granted jurisdiction over cases of murder, manslaughter, rape, assault with intent to kill, arson, burglary, and larceny committed by one Indian upon another on the reservation. Incest, assault with a dangerous weapon, and embezzlement were added later. Pub. L. No. 89-707, § 1, 80 Stat. 1100, and Pub. L. No. 90-284, § 501, 82 Stat. 80, *amending* 23 Stat. 385 (1885). The Act did not abrogate existing treaties. 18 U.S.C. § 1153 (1970) (as amended). The Cherokee, expressly granted jurisdiction over all crimes committed on their reservation by 1785 treaty (7 Stat. 18), were unaffected.
29 118 U.S. 375 (1886).
30 *Id.* at 383-84.

criminal jurisdiction over Indians off the reservation.[31] The resulting diminution of the jurisdiction of tribal courts to include only less serious offenses committed by Indians while on the reservation led an Oregon district court to declare that the Indian courts were merely "educational and disciplinary instrumentalities, by which the government of the United States is endeavoring to improve and elevate the condition of these dependent tribes to whom it sustains the relation of guardian."[32]

In 1896, however, the Supreme Court clearly reaffirmed its adherence to the principle of tribal sovereignty. *Talton v. Mayes*[33] presented the question whether a Cherokee practice of using a five-man jury to institute criminal proceedings violated the grand jury requirement of the fifth amendment. In a landmark opinion, the Court held that the requirement was applicable only to the federal government,[34] saying that because the sovereign powers of Cherokee governing bodies had existed prior to the white man's arrival, the Indian courts were not federal agencies subject to the fifth amendment.[35] This reaffirmation of tribal sovereignty carried into the present century as tribal governments were acknowledged to enjoy immunity to suit without prior consent. In *Turner v. United States*,[36] the Supreme Court indicated this view as dictum, and in 1940, it held flatly that "Indian Nations are exempt from suit without Congressional authorization."[37]

---

[31] *In re* Wolf, 27 F. 606 (W.D. Ark. 1886) (conspiracy of Indians to obtain money from tribe under false pretenses); Pablo v. People, 23 Colo. 134, 46 P. 636 (1896) (murder of Indian by Indian); Hunt v. State, 4 Kan. 60 (1866) (murder of Indian by Indian); State v. Williams, 13 Wash. 335, 43 P. 15 (1895) (murder of Indian by Indian).

[32] United States v. Clapox, 35 F. 575, 577 (D. Ore. 1888).

[33] 163 U.S. 376 (1896).

[34] In this respect, *Talton* paralleled Hurtado v. California, 110 U.S. 516 (1884), in which the Supreme Court had held that states were not required by the due process clause of the fourteenth amendment to prosecute only after indictment by a grand jury.

[35] Recently, one distinguished commentator has suggested that *Talton* means only that a tribal government will not be required to grant a *remedial* right under the Constitution, the question of *fundamental* rights being left open. Lazarus, *Title II of the 1968 Civil Rights Act: An Indian Bill of Rights*, 45 No. Dak. L. Rev. 337, 341 (1969).

[36] 248 U.S. 354 (1919).

[37] United States v. United States Fidelity Co., 309 U.S. 506, 512 (1940). The Court also held the tribes immune to counterclaim except as authorized by statute.

D. *1920 to 1940: Nations in a Nation*

After World War I, Congress passed the Indian Citizenship Act, which provided that "all noncitizen Indians born within the territorial limits of the United States [are] declared to be citizens of the United States."[38] Most states extended the franchise with this new citizenship although several states did not.[39]

Following this grant of citizenship, the Secretary of the Interior hired the Brookings Institute to survey Indian tribes and to recommend further steps to bring the Indians more completely into the American mainstream. In 1928, the Institute issued the Meriam Report,[40] which revealed grim economic, educational, and health conditions on the reservations and stressed the impossibility of integrating the Indians directly into white society.[41] The Report was highly critical[42] of the Indian General Allotment Act of 1887,[43] which was an earlier attempt to achieve rapid assimilation. That Act had distributed Indian land to individual natives in 40, 80, or 100 acre allotments. Through white exploitation of native ignorance of the formalities of land titles, Indian land holdings decreased from 138 million acres in 1887 to 48 million acres in 1934.[44]

Drawing heavily on the Meriam Report and work begun during the Hoover administration,[45] New Deal appointees to the Department of the Interior were instrumental in drafting and guiding through Congress the Indian Reorganization Act of 1934,[46] a major reform measure. It cancelled the general allotment policy and radically changed BIA procedures regarding economic development and community self-government. The most important self-government provision was section 16, which authorized the tribes to adopt

---

38 8 U.S.C. § 3(c) amended 8 U.S.C. § 1401(a)(2) (1970). A number of Indians, such as those who had previously enlisted in the armed forces or who had accepted land allotments were already citizens by previous legislation. Rice, *The Position of the American Indian in the Law of the United States*, 16 J. COMP. LEG. & INT'L L. 78, 86 (3d Ser. 1934).

39 *E.g.*, Porter v. Hall, 34 Ariz. 308, 271 P. 411 (1928) (holding Indians ineligible to vote under a state statute denying the franchise to "persons under guardianship").

40 L. MERIAM, THE PROBLEM OF INDIAN ADMINISTRATION (1928).

41 *Id.* at 86-90.

42 *E.g., id.* at 7.

43 Act of Feb. 8, 1887, ch. 119, 24 stat. 388.

44 BROPHY, *supra* note 16, at 20.

45 *Id.* at 181.

46 25 U.S.C. §§ 461-79 (1970).

their own constitutions and by-laws, to be ratified by a majority of the members and by the Secretary of the Interior. An elected tribal council was authorized to pass ordinances consistent with the tribal constitution.[47] The Act authorized the establishment of tribal courts, to be manned by judges elected by the tribes or appointed by the councils and to be guided by rules drafted by the tribes themselves, subject to the Secretary's approval. Wherever a tribal court was established, it superseded the court of Indian offenses if one existed.[48] Finally, the Secretary was authorized to draft a model code as a guide to the tribes and as an operative code for those tribes who did not draft their own.[49] Although the original version of the Act provided for a court of Indian affairs with appellate jurisdiction, this provision was removed before passage, leaving unchanged the old system of appeals to BIA administrators and ultimately to the Secretary.[50]

The motivation behind the Indian Reorganization Act was to encourage the establishment of Indian governing bodies to exercise the sovereign powers which the Supreme Court in *Talton* had said belonged to the tribes. This view was expressed by Felix Cohen, one of the drafters of the Act: "These powers are subject to qualification by treaties and by express legislation by Congress, but, save as thus expressly qualified, full powers of internal sovereignty are vested in the Indian tribes and their duly constituted organs of government."[51] This notion of "internal sovereignty"[52] was to become the watchword of the courts in ensuing decades.

Because many tribes, however, were ill-prepared for self-government, the BIA often simply imposed its own code and created the tribe's constitution, by-laws, council, and court.[53] "While the trappings of autonomy had been created the substance was lacking.

---

47 The Act provided no express authority for the Secretary to review council-passed ordinances, but it became customary for him to do so through his local superintendent. *See* 25 C.F.R. § 11.1(e); *see also* SUMMARY REPORT OF HEARINGS, *supra* note 21, at 3.
48 25 C.F.R. § 11.1(b) (1969).
49 25 C.F.R. § 11 (1969).
50 H.R. REP. No. 1804, 73d Cong., 2d Sess. 6 (1934).
51 U.S. SOLICITOR FOR DEPT. OF INTERIOR, FEDERAL INDIAN LAW 143 (1940).
52 "Internal sovereignty" was contrasted with "external sovereignty" — the tribes' powers vis-a-vis non-Indians. The tribes enjoyed full sovereign independence from outside forces except for the federal government.
53 Oliver, *The Legal Status of American Indian Tribes*, 38 ORE. L. REV. 193 (1959).

No major transfers of governmental functions from the Bureau of Indian Affairs to the tribes took place."[54]

In fact, the 1934 Act strengthened the role of the BIA in tribal affairs, and the Secretary's review powers ensured that the BIA would still have considerable influence even among those tribes capable of creating their own governing bodies. While the Bureau role at first seems inconsistent with the principle of tribal sovereignty which the Act was apparently designed to implement, BIA involvement conformed with the Meriam Report which had acknowledged that true Indian self-government was a long-term objective at best, and that Indians should prepare for the eventual control of their own affairs through the gradual extension of tribal power.[55]

E. *World War II to 1955: Termination and Assimilation*

Nearly 25,000 Indians served in the American armed forces during World War II, and almost twice that number worked in industry.[56] As had been the case following World War I, new efforts were made after World War II to bring the Indians into the mainstream of American society. It appeared, however, that while white America was making room for the native American, it also threatened to destroy his Indian identity.

> The cultural conquest of the recalcitrant red man, by cajoling and by assimilation was at hand. He was measured for the melting pot. It was with this hope in mind that the Hoover Commission on postwar governmental reorganization, which had been appointed by President Truman, recommended "complete integration".... Evidently it was thought that if the Indian could fight and work like everyone else then he must be like everyone else.[57]

Advance warnings of an attempt to remove the confining but protective fabric woven into the 1934 Act appeared as early as 1943, when the Senate Indian Affairs Subcommittee called for liquidation of the BIA and termination of its services.[58] In 1947,

---

54 Schifter, *Trends in Federal Indian Administration*, 15 S.D. L. REV. 1, 4 (1970).
55 MERIAM, *supra* note 40, at 86-90.
56 DRIVER, *supra* note 5, at 495.
57 S. STEINER, THE NEW INDIANS 23 (1968).
58 S. REP. No. 310, 78th Cong., 1st Sess. 17 (1943).

the Commissioner of Indian Affairs presented a plan to the subcommittee for termination of federal services to some more "advanced" tribes.[59] The Hoover Commission, in 1948, coupled its plea for integration with a proposal to terminate federal services to tribes and to transfer these functions to the states.[60] The next year, measures were introduced in Congress to abolish the BIA[61] and to amend the Constitution to eliminate the power of Congress over Indian affairs.[62]

In 1948, Congress authorized New York to assume criminal jurisdiction over all Indians residing within its borders,[63] and a year later it extended coverage to include all civil disputes.[64] Because the Indians in New York were relatively assimilated and voiced no objection to the legislation, these actions created little controversy. The movement for further extension of state jurisdiction over Indian reservations throughout the country was slowed temporarily in 1948 when a bill to that effect failed in the Senate after passing the House.[65]

However, the move to transfer tribes from BIA guardianship to state jurisdiction gained momentum as the Bureau brought discredit on the system created in 1934. In 1950, Dillon Myer, former director of the World War II Japanese-American Relocation Program, was named Commissioner of Indian Affairs. In order to implement the BIA's plan to relocate Indians into the cities, Myer used the Bureau to control or to dispose of reservation lands and individual property.[66] The BIA also allegedly meddled in tribal politics, froze tribal funds to quiet dissent on the reservations, interfered with the tribes' efforts to obtain legal counsel, and re-

---

59 STEINER, *supra* note 57, at 23.
60 Report of the Committee on Indian Affairs to the Commission on Organization of the Executive Branch of the Government (Oct. 1948), cited in BROPHY, *supra* note 16, at 36. The idea of turning Indian problems over to the states was an old one. In 1882 the Commissioner had recommended that when the Dakota and New Mexico territories became states they be given jurisdiction over reservations, but four years later the Supreme Court warned: "They [the Indians] owe no allegiance to the States and receive from them no protection. Because of the local ill feeling, the people of the States where they are found are often their deadliest enemies." United States v. Kagama, 118 U.S. 375, 383 (1886).
61 S. 2726, 81st Cong., 1st Sess. (1949).
62 95 CONG. REC. 9745 (1949).
63 25 U.S.C. § 232 (1970).
64 25 U.S.C. § 233 (1970).
65 H.R. 4725, 89th Cong., 2d Sess. (1948).
66 *See generally* STEINER, *supra* note 57, at 179.

fused to build permanent community facilities on reservations (such as a hospital in Papago country) because it would encourage the natives to remain on their land rather than to relocate.[67]

The BIA's abuse of its power to prepare Indians for self-sufficiency moved Congress to attempt "to get out of the Indian business."[68] After bills to set tribes "free" under state jurisdiction nearly passed the Eighty-second Congress, the Eighty-third Congress adopted House Concurrent Resolution 108, stating in part:

> [I]t is the policy of Congress, as rapidly as possible, to make the Indians within the territorial limits of the United States subject to the same laws and entitled to the same privileges and responsibilities as are applicable to other citizens of the United States, to end their status as wards of the United States, and to grant them all of the rights and prerogatives pertaining to American citizenship . . . .[69]

Bills to transfer jurisdiction over Indians to California, Minnesota, Nebraska, Nevada, Oregon, and Wisconsin were introduced.[70] Of these, H.R. 1063 was enacted and became known as Public Law 280.[71] Although originally drafted to affect only Indians in California, in its final form it covered Indians in Minnesota, Nebraska, Oregon, and Wisconsin. Sections 6 and 7 permitted states whose constitutions contained disclaimers of jurisdiction over Indian affairs to amend their constitutions to exercise such jurisdiction. In making this open-ended transfer of authority Congress did not even require that the Indians be consulted before a state assumed jurisdiction over them. President Eisenhower signed the bill reluctantly, terming the legislation an "unchristianlike approach" to Indian problems, and noting further:

---

67 Cohen, *The Erosion of Indian Rights, 1950-1953*, 62 YALE L.J. 348, 352-59 (1953).

68 *Hearings on H.R. Con. Res. 108 Before the Subcomm. on Indian Affairs of the House Comm. on Interior and Insular Affairs*, 83d Cong., 1st Sess., ser. 7, at 28 (1953) (remarks of Representative Saylor of Pennsylvania), *quoted in* Oliver, *The Legal Status of American Indian Tribes*, 38 ORE. L. REV. 193, 238 n. 247 (1959).

69 H.R. Con. Res. 108, 83d Cong., 1st Sess., 99 CONG. REC. 9968 (1953).

70 These states had no disclaimers of jurisdiction over Indians written into their constitutions, and their tribes had been previously "consulted" about the transfer, although no claim was made that their consent had been obtained. H.R. REP. No. 848, 83d Cong., 1st Sess. 7-8 (1953).

71 Act of August 15, 1953, 67 Stat. 588, *as amended* 18 U.S.C. § 1162 (1970) and 28 U.S.C. § 1360 (1970).

The failure to include in these provisions a requirement of full consultation in order to ascertain the wishes and desires of the Indians and of final Federal approval, was unfortunate. I recommended, therefore, that at the earliest possible time in the next session of the Congress, the act be amended to require such consultation with the tribes . . . .[72]

The administration, however, did not submit a bill to implement the President's recommendation. While several members of Congress responded in the Second Session of the Eightythird Congress and continued to introduce modifying legislation during the remainder of the decade,[73] none was successful.

In 1954, Congress proceeded with legislation to terminate federal services to selected tribes, as contemplated by House Concurrent Resolution 108.[74] Several bills proposed to terminate tribes throughout the west and midwest. The most significant legislation to emerge was the termination of the Menominee,[75] Klamath,[76]

---

[72] Hearings on S. 961-968 and S.J. Res. 40 Before Subcomm. on Constitutional Rights of the Senate Comm. on the Judiciary, 89th Cong., 1st Sess. 243 (1965) (testimony of Eagle Seelatsee, Chairman, Yakima Tribal Council) [hereinafter cited as 1965 Hearings].

[73] S. 2625 and S. 2838 were introduced by Senators Murray and Goldwater, and H.R. 7193 by Representative Metcalf, in the next session; all of these bills died in committee. Similar bills were introduced in later years by these members of Congress, joined by Representatives Rhodes, Senner, and Olsen, and Senators Burdick and Mansfield. One bill was successfully shepherded through the Senate by Senator O'Mahoney of Wyoming, despite resistance of Senator Watkins of Utah, Chairman of the Indian Affairs Subcommittee, and despite an adverse report from the Interior Department. 102 CONG. REC. 399 (1956). However, the bill failed to clear the House Interior and Insular Affairs Committee. Id. at 661.

[74] House Concurrent Resolution 108 states in part: ". . . [A]t the earliest possible time, all of the Indian tribes and the individual members thereof located within the States of California, Florida, New York, and Texas, and all of the following named Indian tribes and individual members thereof, should be freed from Federal supervision and control and from all disabilities and limitations specially applicable to Indians: The Flathead Tribe of Montana, the Klamath Tribe of Oregon, the Menominee Tribe of Wisconsin, the Potowatamie Tribe of Kansas and Nebraska, and those members of the Chippewa Tribe who are on the Turtle Mountain Reservation, North Dakota. It is further declared to be the sense of the Congress that upon the release of such tribes and individual members thereof from such disabilities and limitations, all offices of the Bureau of Indian Affairs in the States of California, Florida, New York, and Texas and all other offices of the Bureau of Indian Affairs whose primary purpose was to serve any Indian tribe or individual Indian freed from Federal supervision should be abolished." H.R. Con. Res. 108, 83d Cong., 1st Sess., 99 CONG. REC. 9968 (1953).

[75] 25 U.S.C. § 891 et seq. (1970).

[76] 25 U.S.C. § 564 et seq. (1970).

and various western Oregon[77] tribes. The Klamaths promptly lost most of their timberlands and farmlands, which a Portland bank acting as trustee sold to the government and to private users following what appeared to be little consultation with the tribe. The tribe then began to disintegrate as a political and social organization.[78] The termination of the Menominee also caused the disintegration of the tribal structure, in addition to the near insolvency of several large tribal enterprises and the depletion of its treasury reserves before an adjustment to the new situation could be made.[79]

The termination policy sent a shock through Indian country which continues to this day.[80] The termination controversy also split the Department of the Interior and the BIA.[81] To calm the storm around him, Secretary Seaton announced in a radio broadcast that henceforth no tribe would be terminated unless it fully understood the program and clearly consented to it.[82] An old lesson had been re-learned: "The Indian tolerates his present impotent and unjust status in his relations with the Federal Government because he sees the Bureau of Indian Affairs as the lesser of two evils. . . . [T]he Bureau and only the Bureau stands between the Indian and extinction as a racial cultural entity."[83] The federal burden was again accepted as part of white society's debt to the Indian:

> As to special Indian rights, since being an Indian is hereditary, the rights at first glance seem anomalous in a democracy; when we study them, however, the anomaly fades. They are part of a quid pro quo promised solemnly by us in treaties, agreements and laws, and upheld over and again by our courts, in exchange for the whole area of the United States and for the ending of rightful independence.[84]

---

77 25 U.S.C. § 691 et seq. (1970).
78 BROPHY, supra note 16, at 199.
79 Id. at 201-03.
80 "Fear of termination pervades Indian thinking. It colors the Indian's appraisal of every proposal, suggestion and criticism." E. CAHN, OUR BROTHER'S KEEPER: THE INDIAN IN WHITE AMERICA 16 (1969).
81 BROPHY, supra note 16, at 182.
82 105 CONG. REC. 3105 (1959).
83 CAHN, supra note 80, at 14.
84 LaFarge, Termination of Federal Supervision: Disintegration and the American Indians, 311 ANNALS 41-42 (1957).

F. *The Recent Years: The Indians and the Courts*

In *Tee-Hit-Ton Indians v. United States*,[85] the Supreme Court held that certain tribal property rights established by occupancy "since time immemorial" could be cancelled by Congress at its discretion and without compensation. This much-criticized decision[86] has been seen to undercut the principle of the Indian's sovereign control of tribal lands and to run counter to the spirit of a decision in 1941 upholding the notion of sovereign control and requiring compensation for cancellation of that control.[87] In *Tee-Hit-Ton* the Court declared: "Our conclusion . . . leaves with Congress, where it belongs, the policy of Indian gratuities for the termination of Indian occupancy of government-owned land rather than making compensation for its value a rigid constitutional principle."[88] As termination fever cooled, the significance of *Tee-Hit-Ton* diminished. A number of subsequent decisions by the Court of Claims recognized the tribes' sovereign control of their lands and resources and ordered compensation on statutory, not constitutional, grounds.[89]

Lacking clear direction, lower federal courts rendered divergent, uncertain opinions on issues of tribal sovereignty. The Eighth Circuit, for example, took the traditional position in *Iron Crow v. Oglala Sioux Tribe*,[90] upholding the enforcement of a tribal court's sentence for adultery. The Tenth Circuit was guided by similar principles in *Martinez v. Southern Ute Tribe*[91] as it declined to review a decision by a tribal council which allegedly denied an Indian the benefits of tribal membership. In *Oglala Sioux Tribe v. Barta*,[92] however, a district court agreed to hear a tax collection action brought by the tribe against a non-member who was leasing tribal land. Normally such a matter would be

---

85 348 U.S. 272 (1954).
86 E.g., *The Supreme Court: 1954 Term*, 69 HARV. L. REV. 119, 150 (1955).
87 United States v. Santa Fe & Pacific R.R., 314 U.S. 339 (1941).
88 348 U.S. at 290-91 (1954).
89 *See, e.g.*, United States v. Seminole Indians, 180 Ct. Cl. 315 (1967); Whitefoot v. United States, 155 Ct. Cl. 127 (1961); and Tlingit and Haida Indians v. United States, 147 Ct. Cl. 315 (1959).
90 231 F.2d 89 (8th Cir. 1956).
91 249 F.2d 915 (10th Cir. 1957), *cert. denied*, 356 U.S. 960 (1958).
92 146 F. Supp. 917 (D.S.D. 1956).

under tribal court jurisdiction. The court suggested that the 1934 Act had changed the tribe from a sovereign entity to a federal agency: "Thus the rights derived from original sovereignty have been directly channeled into a Federal statutory scheme and all tribal powers are exercised under Federal law."[93] When the lessee appealed, the Eighth Circuit upheld the tribe's right to exact a discriminatory tax on non-Indians on the reservation, despite the due process protections of the fifth amendment or the equal protection clause of the fourteenth.[94] It also held that the lower court had not acted improperly in hearing the cases.[95] Thus, the appeals court implied that federal jurisdiction rested on the tribe's operation under federal law but that provisions of the federal Constitution remained inapplicable.

A less puzzling retreat from the tribal sovereignty principle appeared when the plaintiff in *Martinez*,[96] who had failed in federal court, sought a remedy in Colorado courts. The Colorado Supreme Court,[97] noting that the plaintiff's remedy had been denied in tribal and federal courts, reasoned that to deprive her of any remedy whatever would deny her equal protection of the laws and agreed to hear the case. The court maintained that incorporation under the 1934 Act constituted an expression of consent by the tribe to be sued in state court, because as a corporation, the tribe had recourse to state courts for protection of its rights, and it should, therefore, be required to answer the claims of others in state courts as well.

Notwithstanding the Colorado Supreme Court's decision, the movement away from tribal sovereignty during the years following 1954 slowed as two widely publicized decisions in Navaho country again reaffirmed the principle of tribal sovereignty by denying constitutional guarantees of individual rights to Indians in disputes with their tribal governments. In 1959, members of the Native American Church brought a first amendment attack in federal court on a Navaho ordinance which prohibited them from using or possessing peyote, a mild hallucinogen, as a substitute for the usual

---

93 *Id.* at 918.
94 259 F.2d 553, 556-57 (8th Cir. 1958), *cert. denied*, 358 U.S. 932 (1958).
95 *Id.* at 555-57.
96 Martinez v. Southern Ute Tribe, 249 F.2d 915 (10th Cir. 1957), *cert. denied*, 356 U.S. 960 (1958).
97 Martinez v. Southern Ute Tribe, 150 Colo. 504, 374 P. 2d 691 (1962).

Christian sacraments. In an earlier first amendment action, charging infringement of religious freedom of Protestants in a Catholic pueblo, a federal district court had dismissed for lack of jurisdiction;[98] but in *Native American Church v. Navaho Tribal Council*,[99] the Tenth Circuit did not refuse jurisdiction, even though the Navaho tribe had not organized under the 1934 Act. Rather, the court held that, with respect to freedom of religion, the Constitution did not apply to the Navaho tribe. The first and fourteenth amendments were interpreted as restrictions on the state and federal but not on tribal governments. The argument that the tribe was actually a federal agency was dismissed.

In the same year, the Supreme Court clarified limitations of state jurisdiction over civil disputes on the reservation in cases where the state had not assumed full jurisdiction under Public Law 280. In *Williams v. Lee*[100] the Court held that a state court could not compel payment by Indians for goods purchased on credit at a non-Indian's store on the reservation. The Court noted that the Navaho court system could exercise broad criminal and civil jurisdiction over suits by outsiders against tribesmen. It issued a sweeping endorsement of tribal sovereignty, suggesting the following guideline for allocating disputes between state and tribal courts: "Essentially, absent governing Acts of Congress, the question has always been whether the state action infringed on the right of reservation Indians to make their own laws and be ruled by them."[101]

Students of Indian problems, deeply affected by the failure of instant assimilation, entered the 1960's with a renewed awareness of the need to retain sovereign power in tribal institutions. This theme was struck in an independent report,[102] in the report of a Department of the Interior Task Force created by the newly ap-

---

98 Toledo v. Pueblo de Jemez, 119 F. Supp. 429 (D.N.M. 1954).
99 272 F.2d 131 (10th Cir. 1959).
100 358 U.S. 217 (1959).
101 *Id.* at 220. *But cf.* Organized Village of Kake v. Egan, 369 U.S. 60, 75 (1962) (dictum). The restriction of non-Indians to tribal courts or courts of Indian offenses for certain civil remedies, by *Williams* and subsequent decisions such as United States *ex rel.* Rollingson v. Blackfeet Tribal Court, 244 F. Supp. 474 (D. Mont. 1966), is said to have caused concern among white businessmen on the reservations. Often viewed by the Indians as exploiters, they feared they could not expect impartial treatment from a native tribunal.
102 FUND FOR THE REPUBLIC, REPORT OF THE COMMISSION ON THE RIGHTS, LIBERTIES AND RESPONSIBILITIES OF THE AMERICAN INDIAN (W. Brophy & S. Aberle eds. 1961).

pointed Secretary of the Interior, Stewart Udall,[103] and in the Declaration of Indian Purpose issued from a native American convocation at the University of Chicago in 1961.[104] Unresolved was the fundamental problem of how tribal institutions should relate to the constitutional system of the surrounding society.

II. The Ervin Indian Inquiry and Proposed Legislation

A. *Senator Ervin and the Indians*

When Congress passed the Removal Act of 1830,[105] Andrew Jackson deployed troops throughout the southeastern United States to force the Indians westward. One hundred thousand Indians were resettled, and thousands more died along the "Trail of Tears" to Oklahoma. However, some tribes, including the Choctaw, the Seminole, and a band of the Cherokee, resisted. After $50 million and 1500 men had been lost pursuing the Seminole in the Everglades for two decades, further efforts to enforce the Removal Act against southern tribes were abandoned.[106]

Unlike the Seminole who remained isolated in the Everglades and the Choctaw who regrouped in sparsely settled areas of Mississippi, the surviving Cherokee continued to live in close contact with southern white society. Acquisition of a small reservation in North Carolina over which federal jurisdiction was concluded in 1868[107] established the Cherokee people as permanent residents of that state.

The co-existence between the white man and the Indian in the South, nurtured perhaps by a sense of common defeat at the hands of armies sent from Washington, has resulted in what one observer has termed the "romantic" southern affection for the Indian and his heritage.[108] Among the southerners who have publicly proclaimed this feeling for the Indian is Senator Sam Ervin of North

---

103 Task Force on Indian Affairs, A Program for Indian Citizens (1961).
104 American Indian Chicago Conference, Declaration of Indian Purpose (June 13-20, 1961).
105 Act of May 28, 1830, ch. 148, 4 Stat. 411-12.
106 Driver, *supra* note 5, at 486.
107 *Id.* at 499.
108 Letter from Arthur Lazarus, Jr., counsel to the Association on American Indian Affairs, to the author, March 3, 1970, on file at office of Harvard Legislative Research Bureau.

Carolina.[109] His professed interest in Indian affairs may also be reinforced by a large naitve-American constituency in his home state.[110] It has surely been augmented by his repeatedly demonstrated concern for the protection of constitutional rights.

When the *Williams*[111] and *Native American Church*[112] decisions reaffirmed that systems of tribal government were largely unregulated by the Constitution, Helen Scheirbeck, a Lumbee serving with Senator Ervin's Subcommittee on Constitutional Rights, initiated a preliminary inquiry to determine whether such immunity from constitutional restraint had resulted in actual deprivations of constitutional rights by the Indian tribes. As the investigation progressed, it broadened into one of Indian rights in general, as the Subcommittee staff received numerous complaints about violations of constitutional guarantees not only by tribal authorities but also by federal, state, and local officials. However, Senator Ervin appeared to find the conflict between the Constitution and tribal sovereignty more intellectually stimulating than the broader issue of white relations with the Indians.[113] Furthermore, Senator Ervin, who had opposed previous civil rights measures, was careful at this time to separate the fledgling Indian project from the volatile issues of race relations concerning other minority groups.

In order to maintain his stand on Negro civil rights while investigating those of the Indian, Senator Ervin and his staff deftly distinguished red from black. Indians came to be known as "the minority group most in need of having their rights protected by the national government."[114] Senator Ervin was later to claim, "[e]ven though the Indians are the first Americans, the national policy relating to them has been shamefully different from that relating to other minorities."[115] The Indian project in fact later

---

109 110 CONG. REC. 22081 (1964).
110 With 40,000 Indians in 1960, North Carolina trailed only Arizona, New Mexico, Oklahoma, and California in Indian population. STEINER, *supra* note 57, at 324. 1970 figures reveal approximately 45,739 Indians in the state. UNITED STATES BUREAU OF THE CENSUS GENERAL CHARACTERISTICS OF THE POPULATION.
111 See text at note 100, *supra*.
112 See text at note 99, *supra*.
113 *See, e.g.*, 107 CONG. REC. 17121-22 (1961).
114 Letter from Lawrence M. Baskir, Chief Counsel and Staff Director, Subcommittee on Constitutional Rights of the Senate Comm. on the Judiciary, to the author, March 5, 1970, on file at office of the Harvard Legislative Research Bureau.
115 114 CONG. REC. 393 (1968).

provided Senator Ervin with occasional opportunities to embarrass his northern liberal colleagues, who were allegedly less interested in the first Americans than in the politically powerful black community.

Senator Ervin could politically afford to support Indian rights largely because of the extensive assimilation of North Carolina Indians into southern life. The Cherokee and Lumbee settlements had been fully integrated into the state's governmental structure as counties and municipalities.[116] It has been said that they represent a small, unaggressive, poorly differentiated minority in the state.[117] This integration has been facilitated, especially in the case of the Cherokee, by the early evolution of legal institutions modeled after those of their white neighbors. Their codes, courts, sheriffs, and police forces, for example, have long been in existence.[118]

While this fact freed Senator Ervin to investigate Indian rights without political difficulty at home, it limited his perspective. During the hearings, he revealed his inclination to try to duplicate the North Carolina assimilation experience on a national level. He demonstrated this predilection by focusing on how the systems of tribal justice outside North Carolina failed to conform to the country's constitutional scheme. As Senator Ervin launched the investigation, he cited the preliminary inquiries of his own staff, the Fund for the Republic Report, and the Department of the Interior Task Force Report, as factors in his decision to proceed.[119] Each had advanced the conventional thesis that deviations from constitutional government in the United States were improper in themselves and required eventual correction.[120]

---

116 *Hearings on Constitutional Rights of American Indians Before the Subcomm. on Constitutional Rights of the Senate Comm. on the Judiciary*, 87th Cong., 1st Sess., pt. 1, at 4 (1961) [hereinafter cited as *1961 Hearings — Part 1*].

117 In a 1970 school desegregation dispute, the BIA declared that the Lumbees lacked a tribal culture and did not constitute a tribe. Franklin, *Indians Resist Integration Plan in Triracial County in Carolina*, N.Y. Times, Sept. 13, 1970, § 1, at 78, col. 4.

118. HAGAN, *supra* note 18, at 19-21.

119 107 CONG. REC. 17121 (1961).

120 This language from the Fund for the Republic Report, is expanded in BROPHY, *supra* note 16, at 44: "No government should possess the authority to infringe fundamental civil liberties . . . . For any tribe to be able to override any of them violates the very assumptions on which our democratic society was established."

B. The Subcommittee Field Hearings

For the Subcommittee's first official hearing on Indian rights, Senator Ervin turned to non-Indian authorities.[121] An assistant secretary of the Department of the Interior, various BIA administrators, and interested members of Congress were heard first. Then the hearings moved west to Colorado, New Mexico, Arizona, North and South Dakota, and California before returning to Washington where further sessions were held in 1963 and 1965. Native testimony mixed self-interest and tribal loyalty, bitterness about white mistreatment and cautious acceptance of Anglo-American precepts. From this mixture emerged a broad picture of constitutional neglect which Senator Ervin was determined to remedy. The focus fell first on the tribal system.

1. Constitutional Guarantees and the Tribal System

Tribal politics is politics in a closed circle; it is intense and deeply personal.[122] Traditionally, tribal government has been fully participatory, controlled mainly by the prospect of shame before the group. One commentator described nineteenth century tribal systems:

> Law in the sense of formal written codes, of course, they did not have, but there were clearly defined customary codes of behavior enforced by public opinion and religious sanctions . . . . For most Indians the prospect of scornful glances and derisive laughter from the circle around the campfire was the chief instrument of social control.[123]

In this century, group pressure remains central, but individuality is not stifled; rather, the security of tribal identity has encouraged differentiation without fear of being ostracized and isolated. Thus, the "[c]ommunality of tribalism does not diminish the Indian's individuality. On the contrary it protects him socially and thus frees him individually. . . . The more secure his tribe is, the more secure the Indian feels — and the more independent and

---

121 *1961 Hearings — Part 1*, supra note 116.
122 Note, *The Indian: The Forgotten American*, 81 HARV. L. REV. 1818, 1830 (1968).
123 HAGAN, supra note 18, at 11.

self-confident he is."[124] Because the individual's sense of well-being is based in part on the security of the tribe, an Indian will frequently react more strongly to an attack on tribal institutions than to an attack on his own individual rights or powers.[125] This tribal orientation has been reinforced by the fact that all of the rights which the United States reserved to Indians by treaty pertained to the tribes as group entities rather than to individuals and in light of the conflict with white society over control of group-owned reservation resources.[126]

The traditional lack in most tribes of established social classes further cements tribal ties since there are fewer sources of localized power and sub-group disaffection. Tribes of the plains, prairies, and the East (such as the Cheyenne, the Creek, and the Iroquois) had well-defined systems of rank, but these were primarily based on achievement and only secondarily on heredity.[127] Certain tribes of the Northwest which maintained slave systems and the Pueblo communities of the Southwest were exceptions to this general rule. The Pueblo communities have been termed theocratic, because seats on the governing council were filled by the leaders of the many religious societies.[128] The social adhesive in the tribal systems appears to have been the collective manner in which decisions were made — community consent was required before the council would act. The emphasis was on group harmony: "In council meetings, it was considered bad form to become self-assertive and vociferous, and those who did almost never gained the assent of the council to their proposals."[129] There is some evidence that the aura of harmony was protected in the past by a policy of expurgation, as deviants were occasionally expelled or put to death.[130] Thus, no decisions were made without group consent, but the group was constantly adjusted to render consent possible.

The scope of tribal governments is generally similar to that of

---

124 STEINER, *supra* note 57, at 140.
125 *1961 Hearings — Part 1, supra* note 116, at 223 (statement of Arthur Lazarus, Jr.).
126 *Id.* at 187.
127 DRIVER, *supra* note 5, at 298, 341.
128 *Id.* at 297.
129 *Id.* at 338-39.
130 *Id.* at 297.

state or municipal governments in non-Indian communities.[131] These bodies make, enforce, and interpret laws affecting the general welfare, including the control on the reservation of criminal behavior not within federal jurisdiction by the Seven Major Crimes Act. Testimony in Washington revealed that of 247 organized tribes, 117 (most of them organized under the 1934 Act) operated under constitutions protecting individual civil rights, while 130 did not.[132] What rights provisions there were in these constitutions, however, were often incomplete.[133] In addition, 188 other tribes or bands were not organized under any tribal constitution.[134] In tribal courts, the absence of guaranteed rights was illustrated in four critical areas of due process — right to counsel, right to remain silent, right to trial by jury, and right to appeal.

The testimony at the hearings made it clear that few, if any, tribal courts allowed professional attorneys to appear before them. Courts of Indian offenses had been prevented by federal regulation from hearing professional counsel until the Secretary of the Interior revoked the regulation on May 16, 1961.[135] Generally, representation by another member of the tribe was permitted, but an assistant secretary of the Interior informed the Subcommittee that he knew of only one Indian lawyer practicing with his tribe.[136] Consequently, a de facto prohibition of professionals prevailed, in keeping with the informal nature of low-budget courts, managed by a single judge, without aid of a prosecutor.[137]

Many courts failed to advise defendants of their right to remain silent. In Phoenix, a BIA area director indicated that he knew of no tribe with protection against self-incrimination written into its constitution. In practice, however, courts for tribes which were capable of devoting substantial resources to evidence-gathering

---

[131] BROPHY, *supra* note 16, at 24.
[132] *1961 Hearings — Part 1*, *supra* note 116, at 121.
[133] *Hearings on Constitutional Rights of the American Indian Before the Subcomm. on Constitutional Rights of the Senate Comm. on the Judiciary*, 88th Cong., 1st Sess., pt. 4, at 823 (1963) [hereinafter cited as *1963 Hearings*].
[134] *1961 Hearings — Part 1*, *supra* note 116, at 166.
[135] 26 Fed. Reg. 4360 (1961).
[136] *1961 Hearings — Part 1*, *supra* note 116, at 23.
[137] The Criminal Justice Act of 1964, 18 U.S.C. § 3006A later provided legal assistance for Indians charged with violations of the Seven Major Crimes Act, and tried in U.S. district courts, but the 1964 Act did not extend to violators of tribal regulations brought before tribal courts.

usually protected the right to silence.[138] Smaller tribes, with less adequate enforcement facilities and personnel, did not offer this protection. Asked if he believed silence would prejudice a defendant's case, a Pima-Maricopa judge replied, "It certainly would."[139]

Most tribes provided for jury trial in some form, following the pattern established by regulations governing the old courts of Indian offenses. Even in those cases, however, the right to jury trial was often partially abridged. Typically, the jury consisted of six persons. They received compensation of only 50 cents per day, making it very difficult to assemble a jury. Accordingly, defense challenges were limited to three members of the jury panel. To prevent hung juries and new trials, verdicts could be decided by majority vote.[140] In some areas, moreover, the right to jury trial was lacking entirely. The Southern Utes of Colorado, for example, had no provision in their code for jury trials.[141] At Fort Totten-Devil's Lake, a BIA-appointed judge, pressured by the tribal council and police to maintain a high conviction rate,[142] simply refused all pleas of not guilty.[143] Similarly, a Standing Rock Sioux judge occasionally circumvented jury trials by incarcerating defendants even if they had not pleaded or been found guilty.[144]

Appellate procedures were similarly attenuated. Among many tribes, such as the Navaho, the court of appeals was comprised of all the trial judges sitting together as a panel.[145] Tribes with only a single judge devised more ingenious procedures; for example, the Shoshone-Bannock system provided trial by jury on appeal,[146] while the Pima-Maricopa tribal council appointed two laymen

---

138 *1963 Hearings, supra* note 133, at 862.
139 *Hearings on Constitutional Rights of the American Indian Before the Subcomm. on Constitutional Rights of the Senate Comm. on the Judiciary,* 87th Cong., 1st Sess., pt. 2, at 366 (1961) [hereinafter cited as *1961 Hearings — Part 2*].
140 25 C.F.R. § 11.7(d) (1971).
141 *1961 Hearings — Part 2, supra* note 139, at 436.
142 A BIA practice of receiving efficiency reports on judges from law enforcement personnel made such pressure inevitable. *1961 Hearings — Part 1, supra* note 116, at 88 (statement of Senator Quentin Burdick).
143 *Hearings on Constitutional Rights of the American Indian Before the Subcomm. on Constitutional Rights of the Senate Comm. on the Judiciary,* 87th Cong., 2d Sess., pt. 3, at 769 (1962) [hereinafter cited as *1962 Hearings*].
144 *Id.* at 734.
145 *1963 Hearings, supra* note 133, at 862.
146 *Id.* at 826.

when the need arose to serve with the tribal judge on a three-member appeals panel.[147]

The principal reason for the denial or abridgement of these rights was apparently the paucity of resources which most tribes could allocate to law enforcement. Prohibition of trained lawyers made possible the continued functioning of the tribal court system with untrained judges and without prosecutors. Compulsory testimony of defendants eased the costly burden of police investigation. Eliminating the jury or shifting it to the appeals level relieved pressure on court budgets. Redundancy of judges at the trial and appeals levels and ad hoc appointment of laymen for appealed cases produced similar savings. Despite strivings toward professionalism and the acceptance in principle by many tribal courts of due process requirements,[148] budgetary restrictions made infringement of these rights unavoidable. Average family incomes of $1,500,[149] land held in trust by the BIA, and meager royalties received for white development of reservation resources[150] provided inadequate bases for tribal revenue. The approximately 6000-member Pima-Maricopa tribe allotted only $4,500 annually to cover all court and police operations.[151] Even larger more affluent tribes, such as the Warm Springs Confederation, which spent $50,000 annually on judicial and law enforcement activities, regarded the financial burden of putting trained personnel in tribal courts as "impossible." The Confederation's general counsel observed that without financial assistance, "imposition upon the tribal courts of all the requirements of due process as we non-Indians know them, would mean the end of our tribal courts."[152]

Infringement of constitutional rights by tribal councils, in contrast to that by the tribal courts, appeared to manifest more than

---

147 *1961 Hearings — Part 2, supra* note 139, at 366.
148 Representative E. Y. Berry later informed Congress that the tribal judges had formed their own professional society, whose purpose was "to upgrade the Tribal court system through professional advancement and continuing education." 115 CONG. REC. 938 (1969).
149 Current estimates of Indian family income are generally in the area of $1500. CAHN, *supra* note 80, at viii; Collier, *The Red Man's Burden*, RAMPARTS, Feb., 1970, at 30.
150 CAHN, *supra* note 80, at 82-92.
151 *1961 Hearings — Part 2, supra* note 139, at 367-68.
152 *1963 Hearings, supra* note 133, at 872.

simply budgetary distress. One issue which drew Subcommittee attention to the abuse of council power was freedom of religion. The refusal of the Tenth Circuit to void the Navaho ordinance prohibiting the use of peyote in *Native American Church*[153] clearly illustrated the power of tribal councils. Outlawing the use of peyote was tantamount to outlawing the Native American Church. In the hearings, members of the Church complained to the Subcommittee that they were also victims of police harassment and of employment discrimination, even at the hands of the BIA, as a result of religious affiliation.[154]

Other witnesses also charged that some tribal councils violated individuals' constitutional rights. An attorney for the Rosebud Sioux claimed that many South Dakota tribal councils had with BIA approval enacted unconstitutional ordinances prohibiting private drunkenness.[155]

2. Constitutional Guarantees and the BIA

As the discussion of the authority of tribal councils has indicated, the BIA frequently shared culpability with tribal councils for failure to observe the requirements of due process. Because the Bureau was decentralized, with little upward accountability, there was considerable potential for the abuse of authority at the local agency level.[156] One Shoshone-Bannock attorney charged the BIA with neglect of reservation law enforcement. He claimed that although the tribe was authorized to have two chief judges and three associate judges, the BIA had without cause refused to provide more than one; and that one was considered arbitrary and prejudiced. The BIA refused to remove her from office, even when petitioned by the tribal council to do so.[157] When pressed by Subcommittee counsel in the initial hearings, Interior's Assistant Solicitor for the Division of Indian Affairs testified that he knew of no systematic study undertaken by the Department to ascertain if the code contained unconstitutional provisions.[158]

The director of the BIA's law enforcement branch further ad-

---
153 See text at note 99, *supra*.
154 *1961 Hearings — Part 2, supra* note 139, at 467-78.
155 *1962 Hearings, supra* note 143, at 608.
156 CAHN, *supra* note 80, at 147-55. Reforms in 1970, especially elimination of area offices, may help to alleviate this problem.
157 *1963 Hearings, supra* note 133, at 817.
158 *1961 Hearings — Part 1, supra* note 116, at 112.

mitted that the Bureau had never attempted to supply Indian courts with adequate law libraries and had failed even to request funds for this purpose.[159] The executive director of the National Congress of American Indians subsequently charged that the Bureau's neglect also extended to inadequate facilities, personnel, and training; the BIA simply had refused to request greater appropriations for these purposes.[160]

The Subcommittee received testimony alleging that in numerous instances attorney contracts requiring BIA approval had been delayed for such extended periods as to deprive the Indians of legal counsel. The Shoshone-Bannock reported a delay of eight months,[161] and the Quechan (Yuma) testified that a delay of 13 months had caused its prospective attorney to withdraw without ever serving.[162] The Navaho reported in later hearings that the entire staff of the tribe's chief counsel had resigned because of Bureau delay of contract approval.[163]

The Bureau's refusal to act on requests for code review, pleas for adequate resources for law enforcement, and submissions of attorney contracts contrasted sharply with its conscientious screening of tribal council legislation for adherence to BIA policy. Yet the Subcommittee failed to find statutory authority for this sort of activity.[164] Subcommittee counsel noted that there was no provision for further review by the courts of such BIA decisions; appeals were confined to the Interior bureaucracy.[165]

The thrust of the testimony was that the BIA was less interested in the adequacy of law enforcement on the reservations and in the constitutional rights of the people for whom it was responsible than in maintaining control over tribal courts and councils and over the affairs of individuals. The attitude was neatly expressed, said the Shoshone-Bannock attorney, in a remark attributed to a BIA employee at Fort Hall: "We didn't have any trouble with the Indians until they found out they had constitutional rights."[166]

---

159 *Id.* at 152.
160 *Id.* at 190, 202.
161 *1963 Hearings, supra* note 133, at 824.
162 *1961 Hearings — Part 2, supra* note 139, at 410.
163 *1965 Hearings, supra* note 72, at 300.
164 SUMMARY REPORT OF HEARINGS, *supra* note 21, at 3.
165 *1961 Hearings — Part 2, supra* note 139, at 317.
166 *1963 Hearings, supra* note 133, at 819.

3. Constitutional Guarantees and State and
Local Authorities

Subcommittee counsel indicated that a principal reason for investigating Indian rights was the large number of complaints about civil liberties violations by federal, state, and local agencies.[167] The hearings, however, produced only scattered complaints about federal officials outside the BIA.[168] Rather, if the volume of complaints is any guide to the seriousness of a problem, the greatest threat to the civil liberties of Indians was presented by the enforcement of state criminal laws by local authorities in communities relatively near Indian reservations.[169] For example, the Shoshone-Bannock and Rosebud Sioux asserted that police from surrounding communities entered the reservations, where they lacked jurisdiction, to make arrests.[170] Moreover, the Cheyenne River Sioux claimed that Indians were frequently arrested for crimes for which whites would not have been prosecuted.[171]

Testimony also revealed occasional mistreatment of Indians while in custody. The South Dakota Indian Commission charged that Indian prisoners in some city jails were compelled to perform manual labor not demanded of non-Indian prisoners.[172] The Shoshone-Bannock testified that a tribesman intoxicated on cleaning fluid was jailed by Pocatello authorities who allegedly were aware that he required hospitalization. The Indian died within

---

167 *1962 Hearings, supra* note 143, at 769.
168 A tribal judge for the Hualapai claimed that the United States attorney repeatedly refused to prosecute major criminal cases that were placed under federal jurisdiction by the Seven Major Crimes Act. *1961 Hearings — Part 2, supra* note 139, at 383-4. The Crow tribe of Montana charged federal game wardens with failing to enforce hunting and fishing regulations against non-Indians on Indian reservations. Moreover, the tribe claimed, one federal official had used his airplane to drive elk herds off the Crow Reservation into Wyoming, where white hunters waited. *1963 Hearings, supra* note 125, at 887.
169 *1961 Hearings — Part 1, supra* note 116, at 224 (testimony of Arthur Lazarus, Jr.)
170 *1963 Hearings, supra* note 133, at 827; *1962 Hearings, supra* note 143, at 639.
171 *1965 Hearings, supra* note 72, at 331.
172 *1962 Hearings, supra* note 143, at 588. The deliberate nature of this discriminatory treatment was illustrated in the testimony of the Chairman of the Crow Creek Sioux who quoted a police commissioner in a small South Dakota town: "Well, I think the boys are going to have to get some more Indians in jail, because we need a lot of snow moved over there on the north side of town." *1963 Hearings, supra* note 133, at 898.

hours.[173] The Navaho charged police in Gallup, New Mexico, with "frequent" murder of Indians, citing as a typical case the blackjack bludgeoning of a tribesman jailed for drunkenness. He died in his cell the next day without having received medical treatment.[174] Spokesmen for the Crow tribe alleged that police in Billings and Hardin, Montana, customarily released intoxicated Indians at the city limits, dropping them there even in sub-zero weather.[175]

During these hearings, non-Indian courts were linked with non-Indian police as villains.[176] The Shoshone-Bannock charged that Indian defendants confronted a presumption of guilt in courts off the reservation.[177] The Hualapai claimed that these courts cooperated with police who had made unauthorized arrests on reservations by attempting to sentence the defendants even though the courts knew they lacked jurisdiction.[178] Representatives of several tribes, as well as an assistant attorney general of South Dakota, testified that these courts sentenced Indians to penitentiary terms for "escape" when the local police negligently or intentionally allowed the prisoners to "walk away" before completing jail terms served for misdemeanors.[179] One such court was accused of ordering the release of Indian prisoners from jail and causing them to be transported to another state, where they were turned over to a farmer and forced to harvest crops.[180]

Attorneys also related to the Subcommittee deprivations of due

---

173 *Id.* at 820-21.
174 *Id.* at 860-61.
175 *Id.* at 882-83.
176 Witnesses also claimed that their rights off the reservations were being violated by local and state officials other than those involved in law enforcement. Numerous instances were reported of Indians who lived off the reservation and were legal residents of the states involved being denied care at state hospitals. *E.g., 1961 Hearings — Part 2, supra* note 139, at 650. Senator Burdick of North Dakota testified that reservation Indians were denied use of state correctional schools and that they could not be accepted in state mental institutions because they were not considered residents of the states. *1961 Hearings — Part 1, supra* note 108, at 88. Indians residing off the reservations in South Dakota were said to be issued periodic certificates of non-residency, rendering them ineligible for state welfare benefits. *1961 Hearings — Part 2, supra* note 139, at 603.
177 *1963 Hearings, supra* note 133, at 828.
178 *1961 Hearings — Part 2, supra* note 139, at 373-75.
179 *E.g., 1962 Hearings, supra* note 143, at 631, 699.
180 *1963 Hearings, supra* note 133, at 860.

process in arraignment. Right to counsel allegedly was denied or was not explained to defendants.[181] Instances of local judges disallowing pleas of not guilty were recounted.[182] One attorney claimed that in a number of cases when he surprised the prosecutor by appearing for Indian defendants, the charges were dropped. In many other cases, he asserted, the presence of a lawyer resulted in lesser sentences; in general, unrepresented Indian defendants received heavier penalties than their white counterparts.[183]

Testimony received in California revealed another form of discriminatory treatment. California was charged with failing to devote adequate resources to law enforcement on its reservations after jurisdiction over them had been extended following passage of Public Law 280. The Quechan (Yuma) testified that after California had obtained jurisdiction over its reservation, the tribe was "left stranded." Its own law enforcement system was dissolved, but the California county officials claimed that because the reservation remained federal land, the county had no jurisdiction. The tribe was, therefore, required to re-hire and to pay its own law enforcement personnel.[184] Joined by the Rincon, Pala, and Puma representatives, the Soboba Band of Mission Indians reported problems of inadequate police protection of their lands and claimed that the local sheriff occasionally failed to respond to calls for assistance.[185]

Frequently, the failure of state officials to provide law enforcement services on reservations where they were empowered to do so resulted in legal "no man's lands."[186] Such a situation had been created on the Soboba reservation. The Navaho reported a similar

---

181 *1962 Hearings, supra* note 143, at 598.
182 *1961 Hearings — Part 2, supra* note 139, at 375.
183 *1962 Hearings, supra* note 143, at 634-35.
184 *1961 Hearings — Part 2, supra* note 139, at 406-12.
185 *Id.* at 330.
186 A similar problem was found occasionally in civil disputes. A merchant, for example, could not compel an Indian on the reservation to pay a debt or to relinquish property through a non-Indian court. In practice, however, this problem has been minimized by the willingness of many tribal authorities to intervene on the merchant's behalf to avoid refusal of credit to all Indians. Moreover, some tribes have provided for concurrent state and tribal court jurisdiction in such cases, but the validity of these arrangements is in doubt unless they are preceded by tribal referendum and by state authorization under Public Law 280. See text at notes 316-17, *infra.*

difficulty, claiming that when tribal police apprehended whites for crimes such as rape, murder, and assault committed on the reservation and delivered them to New Mexico authorities for trial, the state disclaimed jurisdiction and released the prisoners.[187]

Extradition posed a related problem. Many tribes were found not to enjoy reciprocal agreements with the states, or even with other tribes. The Mescalero Apache testified that an Indian might commit an offense off the reservation, then find sanctuary on the reservation if tribal officials were not inclined to arrest and deliver him.[188] The Papago claimed that such difficulties had arisen with defendants finding refuge on other California reservations.[189]

Many of the problems of extradition, "no man's lands," and the failure of law enforcement in states extending jurisdiction over the reservations under Public Law 280 had their roots in the unwillingness of the states to accept the entire burden of law enforcement on the reservations. In addition, the assumption of jurisdiction by the state created a great deal of confusion, as, virtually overnight, tribal councils were rendered powerless to legislate and members of the tribe were required to conform to a "foreign" legal system. Arrangements for a "piecemeal" transfer of jurisdiction, by negotiation between state and tribe, with careful groundwork laid prior to each transfer of a specific function, offered a better solution. One state tried this alternative. In 1963, Idaho assumed jurisdiction over some formerly Indian responsibilities including school attendance, youth rehabilitation, public assistance, and domestic relations; but it refrained from further extension until each tribe affected gave its consent.[190]

When the field hearings ended in 1963, nearly 1100 pages of testimony had been recorded and nearly 2500 questionnaires distributed in the field had been returned. Expressions of Indian

---

187 *1963 Hearings, supra* note 133, at 856-57. Authority of New Mexico courts to try persons of crimes committed on the Navaho reservation had been established in State v. Warner, 71 N.M. 418, 379 P.2d 66 (1963). However, a recent decision in the Ninth Circuit, State *ex rel.* Merrill v. Turtle, 413 F.2d 683 (1969), held that Arizona authorities could not enter the Navaho reservation to arrest an Indian. This decision is criticized in Comment, *The "Right to Tribal Self-Government" and Jurisdiction of Indian Affairs*, 1970 UTAH L. REV. 291.
188 *1961 Hearings — Part 2, supra* note 139, at 491.
189 *Id.* at 393.
190 IDAHO CODE §§ 67-5101 to 5103 (Supp. 1969).

discontent focused on the violation of constitutional rights by tribal courts and councils, the inadequate support of tribal legal systems by the BIA, and the violation of constitutional rights by non-Indian authorities off the reservation or the failure of these authorities to provide law enforcement services on the reservation when empowered to do so. As these issues emerged, the interested parties began to take sides. Indian tribes, the Department of the Interior, other federal agencies, members of Congress, various associations of non-Indians, and state governments advocated positions on issues affecting their interests. At the hub of the controversy was Senator Ervin. His self-assigned task was to sift the information and to examine the positions of the parties in order to formulate a complete and sensible response.

C. *Proposed Legislation and the Washington Hearings*

In 1965, Senator Ervin introduced bills S. 961-968 and S.J. Res. 40, to provide a frame of reference for the hearings convened in Washington in June of that year.[191] The open-ended inquiry of 1961 through 1963 had produced a broad overview of and sufficient data on the Indian rights problem; it was, therefore, time to focus the attention of the interested parties on the specific provisions of tentative legislation.

The legislation Senator Ervin initially proposed reflected his personal interests. The first four bills affirmed his conviction that tribal systems of justice should not be allowed to operate outside the Constitution. Each measure displayed Senator Ervin's intention to bring the tribes more fully into the nation's legal mainstream, establishing the uniformity he had known in North Carolina. The bills were addressed primarily to bringing the Constitution to the reservations, integrating tribal systems into the overall legal system of the country, and protecting the principle of consent of the governed. But the legislation avoided harder, less abstract questions: how to control the sometimes arbitrary and unresponsive BIA, how to more adequately fund tribal systems

221

---

191 111 CONG. REC. 1784 (1965). Senator Ervin had introduced the same bills as S. 3041-48 and S.J. Res. 188 in 1964. At that time he cautioned that the bills were "not to be interpreted as final solutions" and acknowledged that "the language .... may be revised and concepts clarified as the Senate deliberates these matters." 110 CONG. REC. 17326 (1964).

of justice, how to halt violations of Indian rights by state and local officials. The hearings had revealed that the Indians were more concerned about these questions than they were about any others. These questions did not, however, present the theoretical constitutional dimensions to capture Senator Ervin's interest; the only mundane matters to which he responded were lawyers' contracts and the availability of legal research materials.

1. S. 961

S. 961 provided that any tribe exercising its powers of self-government would be subject to the same limitations and restraints as imposed upon the federal government by the Constitution. Senator Ervin's only concession to the special nature of Indian tribes was a recognition of their ethnic character; S. 961 would not have subjected them to the "equal protection" requirement of the fourteenth amendment, which applied only to states.

Indian reaction to S. 961 varied considerably. The Hopi claimed to be unaffected, since their constitution was already "in accordance with the U.S. Constitution."[192] Most tribes, however, echoed the sentiments of the Mescalero Apaches who were sympathetic to the purposes of the bill but deemed it "premature" because the tribes were not psychologically or financially prepared for it.[193] At the other extreme were the Pueblos, who were determined to maintain their closed, traditional societies. Their position was clear and unyielding:

> We have long held to our tradition of tribal courts and we have our own codes. Naturally, we are most familiar with the special conditions existing in our various communities, and the status of sovereignty which we have always enjoyed has made us dedicated to the task of preserving it.[194]

For the Crow tribe the question remained open: "We, at the Crow Indian Reservation, cherish the opportunity of selecting our own form of government. . . . [W]e mean the action of the Crow Tribal Council shall continue to remain as it is today. . . . [W]e are confident that the people are satisfied with the present

---

192 *1965 Hearings, supra* note 72, at 325.
193 *Id.* at 340-41.
194 *Id.* at 352.

system."[195] While such statements occasionally betrayed the hint of self-interest which was to be expected of tribal leaders with a stake in the existing order, a valid point was expressed nonetheless. American Indian tribes were many and various, and each had its unique problems; they were not equally prepared or willing to accommodate themselves to the structures of the Constitution.

A number of attorneys acknowledged this point and recommended that certain enumerated rights be protected by legislation rather than by imposing constitutional government in full.[196] The Department of the Interior and BIA also agreed that the blunt insertion of all constitutional guarantees into tribal systems would produce disorder and confusion. But the Department adamantly maintained that "Indian citizenship and tribal freedom from constitutional restraint have been incompatible."[197] Accordingly, the Department of Interior offered a substitute for S. 961 which was limited to the following guarantees: the privilege of writ of habeas corpus by order of a federal court; the right to jury trial with six-member panels in certain criminal cases; first amendment rights, excluding the prohibition of establishment of religion; fourth amendment protection against illegal search and seizure; fifth amendment rights, excluding the right to grand jury indictment; sixth amendment rights to fair trial, excluding the right to jury trial except as otherwise provided but including the right to counsel at the defendant's own expense; protection against excessive bail or fines; prohibition of ex post facto laws or bills of attainder; and the right of each member of a tribe to equal protection of its laws.[198]

Among the constitutional rights not included in the Department of the Interior's substitute which would have been guaranteed by blanket provision in S. 961 were the right to a grand jury indictment and to a jury panel in all criminal prosecutions and in all civil disputes involving more than twenty dollars, and the right to the assistance of counsel.[199] In each instance the cost which

---

195 *Id.* at 234.
196 *Id.* at 222.
197 *Id.* at 317.
198 *Id.* at 318-19.
199 Other exclusions created no controversy. The rights to bear arms and to refuse housing to soldiers were omitted on the theory that Indian tribes were not

the guarantee would impose on the already impoverished tribes was a major reason for its exclusion. In addition, the rights to a grand jury indictment and to a jury panel in civil cases were considered to be of questionable contemporary merit.

The Department of the Interior's response to the issue of the right to defense counsel revealed, however, its insensitive attitude that the Indians had testified about in the earlier hearings. The Solicitor recommended that defendants have the right to counsel but only at their own expense. He claimed that the alternative was to obtain appropriations from Congress to pay lawyers appointed by the tribal courts and, in order to maintain a balance, also to provide prosecutors for the courts. If the problem was one of maintaining a balance, there was no reason to accord the wealthy defendant a special advantage. Rather, it appeared that the BIA was reluctant to assume the initiative to obtain extra appropriations from Congress,[200] as it had similarly failed to request adequate funds to maintain tribal libraries and other facilities. In view of the Bureau's past performance, it was not surprising that it presented the choice essentially as one between the right to counsel at the defendant's expense or no right to counsel at all, instead of being prepared to seek funds for a balanced, professional tribal court system.

Wisely, the Department's substitute for S. 961 deleted fifteenth amendment protection because the tribes, as ethnic units, were required to restrict voting to an ethnically determined, rather than to a geographically defined, community. For the same reason, equal protection of the laws was guaranteed only to members of the tribe, in order that non-Indians on reservations could not claim benefits of tribal membership. Finally, laws respecting the estab-

---

authorized to maintain troops. No reason was given for exclusion of thirteenth amendment protection against involuntary servitude, but it may have had something to do with the fact that, in accord with established custom, courts of Indian offenses were authorized in civil cases to require performance of assigned duties for individuals or for the tribe in lieu of monetary restitution. 25 C.F.R. § 11, 24 (1971).

200 Another example of the Bureau's delinquency in acquiring funds for Indians had become manifest when health functions were transferred in 1955 from the BIA to the Public Health Service. Appropriations instantly increased and stood in 1969 at four times their 1955 level. A sweeping change in attitude was noted by one Bureau of the Budget official: "The difference between the aggressive presentation of the PHS and the defensive supplications of the BIA is really something to see." CAHN, *supra* note 80, at 59

lishment of religion were not prohibited, because such prohibition would have dissolved the social and political fabric of the theocratic Pueblos. The Department of the Interior and the BIA did not express long-term support for theocratic forms of government, but they did acknowledge the immediate need to maintain the social cohesion of the Pueblos during a period of transition.

The Interior-BIA position on S. 961 was thus a combination of a sound historical sense and a reluctance to do more to support the reservation court systems than had been done in the past. When sensitivity to Indian problems could be expressed without a commitment, the Department and the Bureau were sensitive; but when a commitment was required, even to the relatively innocuous matter of submitting a new appropriations request, they demurred.

2. S. 962

S. 962 authorized appeals of criminal convictions from tribal courts to federal district courts, with trials de novo on appeal. Senator Ervin thus recommended a solution to the appeals problem beyond that established by the Ninth Circuit in 1965. In *Colliflower v. Garland*,[201] the court had held that courts of Indian offenses functioned in part as federal agencies since they were

---

[201] 342 F.2d 369 (9th Cir. 1965). Lauded by Senator Ervin as "forward looking," *Colliflower* was something of a surprise, following refusal of a federal district court in Montana to issue a writ of habeas corpus on grounds that the Constitution afforded protection of due process and right to counsel only as against the federal or state governments. Glover v. United States, 219 F. Supp. 19 (D. Mont. 1963). The point of distinction appeared to be that the Montana case involved a tribal court, created by the tribe and governed by a tribal code, which could not be termed a federal agency. *Colliflower* appeared to authorize the issue of writs of habeas corpus only in criminal cases tried by courts of Indian offenses, although there was little qualitative difference between the functions of such courts and those of tribal courts.

In Settler v. Yakima Tribal Court, 419 F.2d 486 (9th Cir. 1969), *cert. denied*, 398 U.S. 903 (1970), the court held that the power of federal district courts established in *Colliflower* to issue writs of habeas corpus applied to tribal courts as well as to courts of Indian offenses. The court found no functional basis for distinguishing between the two types of courts. The Ninth Circuit also held that writs of habeas corpus may issue even if the petitioner has been punished by fine rather than by detention. In a companion case, Settler v. Lameer, 419 F.2d 1311 (9th Cir. 1969), *cert. denied*, 398 U.S. 903 (1970), the court ruled that the writ may issue when the punishment is detention even when the petitioner is free on bail. In the latter case, an appeal was still pending within the Yakima system. The Ninth Circuit apparently rejected a contention that the tribes, like states, have a legitimate interest in freedom from premature federal court intervention and took a major step toward relegating tribal courts to the screening function Senator Ervin originally had envisioned.

creations of the BIA and were governed by the BIA's model code.²⁰² As federal agencies, their decisions, therefore, were subject to limited review under the federal habeas corpus statute.²⁰³ The Ervin bill made tribal court decisions similarly reviewable and expanded the scope of the review of all Indian court decisions by providing for trial de novo. S. 962 integrated criminal justice on the reservations directly into the existing federal system and reduced the Indian courts to a screening role. Senator Ervin noted that the North Carolina magistrate system operated in this way and that it had "worked very well for one hundred years."²⁰⁴

Many tribes, while not opposed to S. 962's authorization of appeals of criminal convictions from tribal courts to federal district courts, objected to the bill's provision for trial de novo in the district court because it would severely restrict the functions of the tribal courts. The Pima-Maricopa claimed that law enforcement on the reservation would suffer as a result.²⁰⁵ The United Sioux Tribes expressed opposition because Indians could not afford to pay for the legal representation needed in federal court,²⁰⁶ and the American Civil Liberties Union called for absolute right to appointed counsel not provided by the 1964 Criminal Justice Act.²⁰⁷ The Mescalero Apache suggested that cases be remanded to the tribal courts upon a finding of error.²⁰⁸ The Fort Belknap attorney concurred, urging that this procedure would serve as a training device and improve the quality of the tribal courts. The attorney warned, however, that S. 962, like S. 961, would impose an impossible financial burden; for review by federal courts almost certainly would require the tribes to keep fuller court records, use proper procedures, and hire prosecutors.²⁰⁹

The Department and the BIA were opposed to S. 962. The Department had appellate jurisdiction over courts of Indian offenses and was unwilling to surrender it. It suggested that the district courts should be empowered to review reservation court

---

202 25 C.F.R. § 11 (1969).
203 28 U.S.C. § 2241 (1970).
204 *1965 Hearings, supra* note 72, at 91.
205 *Id.* at 328.
206 *Id.* at 148.
207 *Id.* at 224. The Criminal Justice Act of 1964, 18 U.S.C. § 3006A (1970).
208 *Id.* at 341.
209 *Id.* at 337.

decisions only upon the full exhaustion of the administrative remedy.[210] But the Department's insistence on retaining a role in the tribal justice system contradicted its earlier testimony to the effect that the Solicitor's office had received no appeals from courts of Indian offenses.[211] It became clear to Subcommittee counsel that the Department was fighting for a nominal power only, and had never regarded its appellate role with commitment.

3. S. 963

S. 963 authorized the Attorney General to investigate Indian claims of violations of their civil rights. This bill served as Senator Ervin's response to the flood of testimony about the arbitrary treatment by the BIA and the occasional brutality and discrimination by state and local officials. The bill appeared to be a broad commitment to the protection of Indian rights in general, but its breadth was circumscribed by Senator Ervin's opposition to any further growth in the investigatory function of the federal government. In any event, S. 963 was diluted in significance by its partial redundancy with authority granted to the Attorney General by previous legislation,[212] by its failure to authorize funds, and by its inappropriate reliance on the Attorney General's office to challenge arbitrary practices in another federal agency, the BIA.

Although S. 963 was considered a token gesture, it nevertheless won the support of many tribes, who welcomed any additional pressure on the federal government to investigate civil rights complaints. But the leaders of some tribes, including the Pueblos, opposed the bill, explaining, "[w]e understand, better than non-Indians, the background and traditions which shape Indian conduct and thinking, and we do not want so important a matter to be tried by those who are not familiar with them."[213] Thus, while some Indian leaders welcomed the investigation of non-Indian

---

210 This position varied from that expressed by the Assistant Secretary in 1961, when he opposed any kind of institutionalized review of reservation court decisions on the ground that such a review structure might tend to make these courts permanent, while he believed that they should eventually disappear, as all other vestiges of Indian "separateness" from the rest of society should disappear. *1961 Hearings — Part 1, supra* note 116, at 12, 26.

211 *Id.* at 115.

212 18 U.S.C. § 241 (1970).

213 *1965 Hearings, supra* note 72, at 352-53.

courts, police, and officials, they protested being subjected to that scrutiny themselves.

S. 963 also met with the opposition of the Department of the Interior. The Solicitor asserted that many of the complaints of such violations were made to the Department and were already forwarded. The Department wanted to retain its power to screen complaints before they were forwarded to the Justice Department. Indeed, it suggested substitute legislation which would have channeled all complaints pertaining to the tribal councils through the Secretary.[214] The Department's concern over the disposition of Indian complaints of interference or mistreatment appeared to be largely self-interested. Testimony which revealed that of 79 complaints screened and forwarded to the Justice Department since 1962 no convictions had been obtained cast doubt on the Department's sense of follow-up responsibility to the Indian complainants.[215] Of course, it also caused skepticism that giving new investigative and prosecutorial authority to Justice would produce impressive results.

4. S. 964

S. 964 directed the Secretary of the Interior to recommend to Congress a new model code for the courts of Indian offenses, which would serve as a guide for the tribal courts. It also provided for the establishment of special training classes for all tribal judges. The purpose of this measure was unclear. In light of S. 961 and 962, a new model code appeared to be superfluous. And although the further education of tribal judges would be helpful, there seemed little likelihood that it would bring immediate results, since most of the infringements of right in tribal courts seemed to be the result of financial restraints. None of Senator Ervin's bills authorized appropriations to remedy this basic problem.[216]

S. 964's provision for the training of tribal judges won Indian

---

214 *Id.* at 318-19.
215 *Id.* at 27.
216 The subsequent creation of the Law Enforcement Assistance Administration has partially alleviated the funding problem, since some assistance grants have been channeled to tribes. *See, e.g.,* COURT REV., Oct., 1971, at 1 (a publication of the North American Judges Association).

support, but the tribes did not agree about its provisions for a model code. Some tribes, such as Pyramid Lake Paiute and Turtle Mountain Chippewa, expressed unqualified support.[217] Many others, however, shared the Department of the Interior's criticism that the bill might effectively impose the model code on the tribes. As long as the code remained a model, cautioned the Hopi and Apache, it would be useful.[218] The Pueblos predictably were opposed, and the Chairman of the All-Pueblo Council requested that the drafting of codes be left to the tribes.[219]

The Department of the Interior objected weakly to the work that proposing the new model code would require. It claimed that the necessary allowance for variations in tribal culture and conditions would render the code meaningless, or the failure to make such an allowance would destroy many tribes as surely as would S. 961 in the form Senator Ervin had proposed. Had the Department been fully convinced of its own argument, it would have resisted S. 964 as vigorously as it resisted S. 961. Instead, the Solicitor remarked, "Let me say I do not feel very strongly about this. In fact, the Department does not take a position that this is any disaster."[220] Moreover, while it was claimed that the tribes would be deprived of valuable drafting experience if they were just handed a model code, the Solicitor expressed his belief that the tribes would use the model much as states use proposed model codes, *i.e.*, as the basis for hearings and debates. In fact, he admitted, the Department had long recommended the old model code to the tribes, and the concept of a model was not unfamiliar to them.[221]

5. S. 965, S. 966, and S. 967

While the first four bills were intended to protect individual rights, Senator Ervin's next three proposals were addressed to the problems of inadequate law enforcement, especially in those states that assumed jurisdiction over Indians in accordance with Public

---

217 *1965 Hearings, supra* note 72, at 348-49.
218 *Id.* at 326, 343.
219 *Id.* at 191.
220 *Id.* at 28.
221 *Id.* at 28-29.

Law 280.²²² In order to eliminate "no man's lands," S. 965 provided for the extension of federal jurisdiction over crimes committed by non-Indians on the reservation, if a state failed to exercise its jurisdiction.²²³ Senator Ervin's provision for federal rather than tribal jurisdiction again illustrated his determination to bring the reservations within the federal system. This measure might also have mitigated the extradition problem, since such agreements exist between state and federal authorities. It would not, however, have solved extradition problems among tribes or between tribes and the states.

With S. 966, Senator Ervin went to the heart of the jurisdiction issue. While Public Law 280 had provided for the transfer of complete jurisdiction, testimony had revealed that some states were unwilling to immediately assume the total burden; hence, these states left the tribes in confusion. The result, said Senator Ervin, was "a breakdown in the administration of justice to such a degree that Indians are being denied due process and equal protection of the law."²²⁴ He also expressed the conviction that Public Law 280 violated the principle of government by consent of the governed. Accordingly, S. 966 provided for the repeal of those sections of Public Law 280 which authorized the extension of state jurisdiction without the consent of the tribes involved. It made consent a prerequisite for the extension of jurisdiction, and it authorized the United States to accept the retrocessions of jurisdiction from states who wished to be free of the burdens that they had previously assumed. These revisions of Public Law 280 left the states free to experiment with "piecemeal" extensions of jurisdiction; but they did not authorize the tribes to initiate such agreements or arrangements.²²⁵

S. 967 filled a gap in the Seven Major Crimes Act by extending

---

222 See text between notes 71 and 72, *supra*.
223 The Assimilative Crimes Act of 1948, 18 U.S.C. § 13 (1970), incorporates state law into federal law in areas under exclusive federal jurisdiction. Thus, S. 965 was redundant in all but Public Law 280 states or others in which reservations were not exclusively under federal control.
224 *1965 Hearings*, *supra* note 72, at 4.
225 Similar legislation had been introduced in both houses by the Montana delegation in the previous session, but had died in the Interior Committees. 109 CONG. REC. 192, 568 (1963).

federal jurisdiction to cover "aggravated assault." Senator Ervin's attention apparently had been attracted by the testimony of a Hualapai judge who had told of a case in which one Indian had caused permanent injury to another Indian by pouring five gallons of boiling water on him. Because the crime was not interpreted as "assault with a deadly weapon," the federal government disclaimed jurisdiction. As a result, the offender was convicted in tribal court, which was limited by code to sentences of six months or less.[226]

The bills to alleviate the jurisdictional problems of law enforcement on the reservations received the overwhelming support of the Indians. Not even the Pueblos objected to S. 965 or S. 967. The tribal attorney from Fort Belknap claimed, however, that S. 965 was "not worth the weight of its paper."[227]

S. 966 was also favorably received. Vine Deloria, Jr., then serving as Executive Director of the National Congress of American Indians, voiced the mood of the Indians in support of gradualism and consent: "Not only will we have consent of the governed if we get S. 966 passed, but we can have the opportunity then to be released from this psychological fear on the reservation of having the whole culture run over."[228] The bill's provision for "piecemeal" agreements did, however, receive some criticism. The Mescalero Apache and the Yakima, among others, argued that if difficulties arose tribes should be able to withdraw their consent to such arrangements on reasonable notice to the states. They also asked that the tribes be able to initiate retrocessions of jurisdiction from the states — in effect, to make the consent provision retroactive.[229]

The bills Senator Ervin proposed to deal with the problems of

---

[226] *1961 Hearings — Part 2, supra* note 130, at 384.

[227] *1965 Hearings* at 337.

[228] *Id.* at 198. Other testimony demonstrated that there were adequate grounds for this fear. The United Sioux claimed that South Dakota refused to require Indian consent in its 1963 act extending jurisdiction — an act later defeated by referendum after a vigorous Sioux campaign. Said one leader: "We begged the State committee to put in a consent clause. We pointed out that if State law was good, the Indians would take it. The answer was: 'State law is so good for you we are afraid to let you vote on it because you might turn it down.'" *Id.* at 149. Spokesmen for the Seminole of Florida and Nez Perce of Idaho spoke of the better approach of their respective states which extended jurisdiction only after full consultation and tribal consent. *Id.* at 347, 350.

[229] *Id.* at 342, 344.

state jurisdiction on reservations posed no troublesome issues to the Department of Interior as its interests were not involved. Accordingly, it agreed with the positions taken by the Department of Justice. The Justice Department predictably opposed the passage of S. 965, since that bill would have thrust upon federal law enforcement authorities the responsibility for monitoring the performance of the states and assuming jurisdiction on reservations whenever the states failed to perform their duties. The Interior Department favored the consent requirement of S. 966 even though it had supported Public Law 280 when it had been adopted; but it aligned itself with the Justice Department, warning that "piecemeal" arrangements might create "unnecessary confusion in the enforcement of criminal statutes and in the administration of Indian affairs."[230] The Department of Interior offered no opinion on S. 967, pending analysis by the Justice Department of a similar bill. The Interior Department's deference to the Justice Department on these measures reinforced the impression that it responded in an accommodating fashion when no commitment of its own was required.

6. S. 968 and S.J. Res. 40

Senator Ervin's last bill and his proposed resolution were intended to halt two troublesome administrative practices of the Department of the Interior. S. 968 provided that any attorney contract submitted by a tribe for BIA approval would automatically be approved at the end of 90 days, unless contrary action were taken prior to that time. Senator Ervin considered that the long delays in the approval of attorney contracts were particularly intolerable because "no group in the United States has more problems requiring expert legal assistance than the American Indians."[231]

For the same reason, Senator Ervin urged the adoption of S.J. Res. 40 which would direct the Secretary of the Interior to revise, update, and consolidate legal materials pertaining to the Indians. The disorganized manner in which treaties, laws, executive orders, regulations, Solicitor's opinions, and other relevant documents had been compiled and distributed had impeded research on In-

---

230 *Id.* at 321.
231 *Id.* at 4.

dian rights. Moreover, testimony in earlier hearings had shown that in many instances, tribal libraries had ben inadequately supplied with such materials.[232]

As expected, S. 968 and S.J. Res. 40 met little resistance from the tribes. Most favored compelling the Department of the Interior to pass on attorney contracts more rapidly,[233] and all of them favored any measure which would help them to maintain more complete law libraries for use by their courts and councils.

The Department of the Interior's reaction to S. 968 and S.J. Res. 40 illustrated its attitude whenever pressed for a concrete commitment of its own resources. The Department opposed S. 968, arguing that the problem of delays in contract review had been solved by delegating approval authority to area directors and that it would feel compelled by any automatic deadline to issue premature notices of disapproval whenever evaluation became protracted. The Department's actual objection probably was to the limiting of its discretionary authority. Questioned by Subcommittee counsel why more than 90 days should be required to review attorney contracts, the Solicitor suggested that if Congress was dissatisfied with Interior's performance it should find another agency to review tribe-attorney contracts.[234] Of course, no other agency would, in fact, have been appropriate. The Department seemed in effect to be saying that it would rather allow contracts to go unreviewed than to commit itself to a deadline requirement.

Finally, the Department had no objection to S.J. Res. 40 insofar as it required its personnel to compile treaties, laws, and executive orders.[235] It objected, however, to having to compile regulations and all the Solicitor's opinions. The Department acknowledged that many opinions were not distributed, yet were cited as authoritative and frequently guided policy throughout the country. Assuring the Subcommittee that a central file of opinions was maintained in Washington, the Department declared, "We believe

---

232 See text at note 159, *supra*.
233 A spokesman for the Crow of Montana disagreed, citing an instance in which the tribe was charged a $279,000 fee under its attorney contract, which it felt was too high. He asserted that more complete contract review might have avoided such a situation. *1965 Hearings, supra* note 72, at 236.
234 *Id.* at 45.
235 Treaties had long been compiled, so no additional effort was required in this area. See note 15, *supra*.

that the system makes the opinions readily available to persons who have a need for them."[236] In this instance, the Department appeared willing to risk sheer unbelievability in order to prevent a commitment of personnel time and, perhaps, also to avoid wide circulation of what it had come to regard as "in-house" documents.

7. Summary

In summary, then, Indian reaction to Senator Ervin's bills was of four basic types. The first was no reaction at all. While the records of the hearings indicated that the Subcommittee received some expression of opinion from 70 to 80 tribes, most of the 247 organized tribes did not participate in the hearings, probably through no fault of the Subcommittee. A second type of reaction was that of blanket endorsement of the Subcommittee's work, often accompanied by an expression of surprised delight that so much attention was being paid to Indians.

Most of the tribes testifying exhibited a third pattern of reaction: they were sympathetic to the purposes of the legislation and amenable to the eventual merger of the Indian and non-Indian systems of justice. They were cautious, however, about taking large steps beyond their psychological preparedness or financial capability. Consultation with these tribes usually produced areas of agreement. A fourth reaction was shown principally by the Pueblos, who had always considered themselves different from and in some ways superior to the other tribes.[237] The old, stable, and very traditional Pueblo communities were in no way convinced that the values which their system embodied were inferior to those of white America. They resisted measures which threatened their culture or the structure of their authority. When not threatened, the Pueblos were cooperative; when faced with the possibility of change imposed from the outside, they were obstinate.

Throughout the debate sparked by Senator Ervin's proposals, the attitude of the Department of the Interior and of the BIA remained consistent. When vital organizational interests, such as reputation and control, were not involved, and when a commitment of resources was not required, they proved to be cooperative.

---

236 *1965 Hearings, supra* note 72, at 323.
237 *Id.* at 352.

But when confronted with the limitation of their responsibilities or influence or when pressed for a commitment to additional tasks, they resisted, even if the interests of the Indian people were compromised.

III. MAKING INDIAN LAW

A. *The Drafting of S. 1843 and its Companions*

Senator Ervin was not under immediate pressure from an assertive constituency to proceed with Indian rights legislation. It had become a labor of love to which he could allocate his energies as he chose. Some time elapsed before the revised legislation made its appearance. On May 23, 1967, the Senator introduced bills S. 1843 through 1847 and S.J. Res. 87.[238] Although S. 961 through 968 and S.J. Res. 40 had been only tentative legislation, they had largely withstood the scrutiny of the interested parties, and the new bills were generally quite similar to the ones introduced in 1965. S. 1843 revised S. 961 and 962 to provide only enumerated constitutional rights[239] and appeals to the federal courts by writ of habeas corpus instead of by trial de novo.[240] S. 1844 contained the order to draft a model code and the judge training provisions. In S. 1845 Senator Ervin maintained his resolve to repeal section 7 of Public Law 280 and added the requirement that tribal consent had to be demonstrated by referendum. Because it had been felt that "aggravated assault" did not adequately describe the type of conduct Senator Ervin was trying to include, S. 1846 proposed addition of "assault resulting in serious bodily injury" to the Seven Major

---

238 113 CONG. REC. 13473-78 (1967).

239 In the main, Senator Ervin had re-drafted S. 961 according to the recommendations of the Interior Department, but on one critical point he deviated from them. Interior originally worded its "equal protection" provision in such a way as to limit its application to *members of the tribe* located within its jurisdiction. Senator Ervin's revision, however, guaranteed equal protection to *any person* within the tribe's jurisdiction. The significance of the altered wording was that it might be construed to extend equal benefits of tribal affiliation to non-Indians residing, leasing, or owning property on reservations, and subject to regulations established by the tribal councils.

240 Senator Ervin apparently was convinced by the arguments of many tribal attorneys and United States attorneys that tiral de novo under S. 962 would put an intolerable strain on the district courts, already suffering from a chronic overload of cases. As incorporated into S. 1843, S. 962 did little more than to confirm *Colliflower.* See discussion in note 201 and in text at note 201, *supra.*

Crimes Act. Apparently unmoved by the explanations of the Interior Department, Senator Ervin's S. 1847 retained the 90-day attorney contract review deadline and his S.J. Res. 87 instructed Interior to compile and update legal materials.

Senator Ervin did, however, retreat on S. 963 which had proposed authorizing the Attorney General to investigate and prosecute cases in which Indian civil rights were involved, and on S. 965, which had suggested providing concurrent federal jurisdiction over certain crimes when the states failed to perform their law enforcement duties. Since S. 963 had met with opposition both from the Department of the Interior and tribal leadership,[241] Senator Ervin let it die quietly. S. 965, which had not provoked a particularly substantial amount of debate,[242] was apparently felt to be largely superfluous. In states not covered by Public Law 280 federal jurisdiction already existed by virtue of the Assimilative Crimes Act.[243] Since S. 1845 provided authority for Public Law 280 states to retrocede jurisdiction to the federal government when convinced that the original extension of jurisdiction had been unwise, S. 965 appeared to be relevant only when a state simply refused either to exercise jurisdiction or to retrocede it. Apparently, Senator Ervin felt that it was more prudent to await such a situation than to anticipate it, and he quietly buried the bill.

Because the Indian rights project raised a broad range of complex constitutional issues and had produced a ponderous volume of information, the only member of the Senate who fully understood it was Sam Ervin. Furthermore, since senators are specialists by committee assignment and must rely upon the understanding and good will of their colleagues, Senator Ervin had virtually full control over the destiny of the bills in the Senate. Indeed as a senatorial courtesy and as a matter of legislative diplomacy, no senator, even if he had entertained an objection, would have sought to prevent Senator Ervin from enjoying the fruit of six years' labor. Objections, if any, would have to be raised in House debate. But Senator Ervin enjoyed the luxury of allowing the bills to rest in subcommittee, able to order them reported to the floor

---

[241] See part II C 3 of this article, *supra*.
[242] See part II C 5 of this article, *supra*.
[243] See note 223, *supra*.

when the occasion suited him. Meanwhile, to gauge the proper timing, Senator Ervin was closely studying the possibility of mixing red with black in another civil rights storm engulfing Congress.

B. *Tactics of Enactment*

Although it is beyond the scope of this study to examine in detail the machinations in Congress which produced the Civil Rights Act of 1968, some relevant parts of that intriguing story may be sketched. In 1967, as part of a broader civil rights package designed primarily to protect persons exercising rights guaranteed them by previous legislation, President Johnson submitted an open housing measure[244] similar to the one that had failed in 1966.[245] The House Judiciary Committee held hearings on the civil rights bill, H.R. 2516, but ignored the open housing measure. Conservatives and others seeking passage of anti-riot legislation introduced a separate measure, H.R. 421, which also was assigned to the Judiciary Committee. Chairman Emanuel Celler bottled up H.R. 421 until Representative Colmer, a bulwark of the Mississippi Old Guard and Chairman of the House Rules Committee, threatened to hold separate hearings on the anti-riot bill.[246]

Since Chairman Celler hoped to garner borderline votes for the civil rights bill by reporting it out of committee in tandem with the anti-riot legislation, he gave in to Congressman Colmer and lent his qualified support to H.R. 421. Representative Celler then added a series of provisions protecting Negroes and others from force or violence while engaged in lawful civil rights activities,[247] and persuaded Representative Colmer to cooperate in sending the rights bill to the floor.[248] On July 11, Representative Colmer's Rules Committee cleared the anti-riot bill,[249] which the House

---

244 S. 1358, 90th Cong., 1st Sess. (1967).
245 In 1966, the House had approved an Administration open housing bill, H.R. 14765, sending it to the Senate by a vote of 259 to 157. 112 CONG. REC. 18740 (1966). Although the House measure had exempted small boarding houses and had allowed home-owners to instruct realtors to discriminate in finding buyers for their dwellings, it could not generate enough support in the Senate to survive an intense filibuster. After two unsuccessful attempts at cloture, the bill died. 23 CONG. Q. ALMANAC 773 (1967).
246 23 CONG. Q. ALMANAC 782 (1967).
247 N.Y. Times, June 23, 1967, at 1, col. 2.
248 *Id.*, June 28, 1967, at 23, col. 2.
249 *Id.*, July 12, 1967, at 23, col. 2.

passed eight days later by a resounding vote of 347 to 70.[250] Keeping faith with Representative Celler, Representative Colmer dutifully forwarded the civil rights bill to the floor where it was overwhelmingly endorsed, 326 to 93.[251]

When the anti-riot bill reached the Senate, Senator Ervin charged that it would compromise rights belonging to the states.[252] Senator James Eastland, Chairman of the Senate Judiciary Committee, apparently was so alarmed at the remarks of his maverick southern colleague that he retained jurisdiction of the bill at the full committee level, fearing that Senator Ervin's subcommittee would hold hearings to delay its passage.[253] However, Senator Eastland allowed the civil rights bill to go to Senator Ervin's subcommittee, but added an open housing provision that he predicted would kill it.[254]

Senator Ervin also was troubled by the House version of the civil rights bill. Although generally in favor of protecting constitutional rights, he had his southern constituency to consider. Moreover, as a southerner, he shared the distaste of many in his region at northern hegemony and northern hypocrisy on questions of civil rights. He complained that H.R. 2516, established a new basis of federal jurisdiction — "diversity of color" — by making interference with the exercise of civil rights by members of minority groups a federal offense. He resented the implication that non-whites could not receive justice outside the North. In subcommittee he offered a substitute to H.R. 2516, grounded on the commerce clause rather than on the fourteenth amendment, eliminating "diversity of color" and making it a federal offense for any person to interfere with the exercise of civil rights.[255] The Ervin measure also extended protection for working men exercising rights under section 7 of the National Labor Relations Act[256] and provided Indians those rights which had been included in S. 1843 through 1847 and in S.J. Res. 87. In short, Senator Ervin's goal

---

250 *Id.*, July 20, 1967, at 1, col. 6.
251 *Id.*, Aug. 17, 1967, at 1, col. 8.
252 *Id.*, July 21, 1967, at 35, col. 3.
253 *Id.*, July 27, 1967, at 1, col. 7.
254 *Id.*, Aug. 26, 1967, at 23, col. 2.
255 *See, e.g.*, 114 CONG. REC. 329-34 (1968).
256 29 U.S.C. § 158 (1970).

was either to amend the Civil rights bill into defeat or to have it pass with his Indian rights provisions attached.

Senator Ervin's tactic was based on the axiom that in some circumstances clusters of bills may be more difficult to enact than the same bills considered separately. If bill "A" could pass the Senate by a 60 to 40 vote and bills "B" and "C" each by margins of 90 to 10, and if half those opposing "B" and "C" came from the ranks of those supporting "A", then "A" with "B" and "C" appended might fail to win a majority. It was not likely that many senators would oppose Senator Ervin's Indian bill openly, but influential western congressmen in the House could be expected to resist H.R. 2516 if it returned with the Indian rights rider. These congressmen were essential to Senator Ervin's strategy.

The Indian Affairs Subcommittee of the House Interior and Insular Affairs Committee had given birth to Public Law 280 in 1953; and it was this body which had declared its intention "to get out of the Indian business."[257] The Subcommittee's membership then included Representative Aspinall, a Democrat from Colorado, and it had been chaired by Representative Berry, a Republican from South Dakota. In 1967, these two legislators remained senior authorities in their respective parties on Indian affairs legislation. Moreover, by virtue of successive Democratic administrations, Representative Aspinall had ascended to chairmanship of the full committee. Both of these congressmen had deep personal and philosophical stakes in Public Law 280.

Representative Aspinall's policy had been to remain professedly neutral on Indian legislation but far from neutral on land and water resources policy.[258] He had been a strong proponent of private and state ownership of resources currently under federal jurisdiction,[259] and Indian reservations were among the vast acreages of federally controlled land in western states. Public Law 280 had provided a simple means by which to replace federal jurisdiction with state jurisdiction in those areas. Although such a transfer did

---

257 Statement by Representative Saylor, *supra* note 68.
258 *See* CAHN, *supra* note 80, at 167.
259 Representative Aspinall had used the weight of his chairmanship to oppose the Wilderness Act of 1963 "because he believed the act would 'tie up' portions of federal lands from economic development." Henning, *The Public Land Law Review Commission*, 7 IDAHO L. REV. 77, 78 (1970).

not immediately effect a change in land ownership, it did encourage non-Indians to invest in reservation businesses and to develop reservation resources under lease agreements. In Public Law 280 states, non-Indians were not subject to the regulations of tribal councils or to the decisions of tribal courts; in any disputes, they could protect their interests in the more friendly state legislatures and tribunals.

As subcommittee chairman, Representative Berry had been instrumental in passing Public Law 280. He, too, felt it would open the reservations to economic development. His approach had always been that of the assimilationist — to bring the Indian into the American cultural and economic mainstream. Representative Berry had also played an active part in the termination legislation of 1954. He even claimed to have obtained the Indians' consent to such legislation, although at least some Indians insisted that they had not been consulted.[260] As recently as 1961, when the termination movement was all but dead, Representative Berry continued to call for evaluation and categorization of tribes to ascertain which could be terminated most expeditiously.[261]

Senator Ervin had every reason to be confident a conflict would emerge on the House floor if H.R. 2516 were amended with his Indian rights measures. The Ervin legislation would repeal the section authorizing further extensions of jurisdiction by states without tribal consent and would authorize retrocession of jurisdiction already extended. Representatives Aspinall and Berry, however, regarded Public Law 280 as so essential to the development of reservation resources and to the assimilation of the tribes that they wanted it implemented as soon as the *states* were ready. In Senator Ervin's view, the law was not so needed that it should deprive Indians of due process and fail to receive their consent; rather, he believed it should be implemented when the *tribes* were ready. The split was deep. Thus, even if the civil rights bill were to clear the Senate, resistance in the House to its changed form might force the bill back to committee or into conference.

However, Senator Ervin was not simply exploiting the Indian project to deter black civil rights legislation. Even if the House

---

[260] *See, e.g.,* N.Y. Times, June 19, 1955, at 76, col. 1.
[261] 107 CONG. REC. 2622 (1961).

failed to approve H.R. 2516 with the Indian rights amendment, the Indian bills would be in no more disadvantageous a position than if they had been passed separately by the Senate and forwarded to the House in routine manner. The bills would go to Representative Aspinall's committee and receive the same opposition they would receive on the floor as part of H.R. 2516. On the other hand, the bleak future of the bills in committee made the amendment tactic especially attractive as a positive way to secure enactment of the Indian rights legislation. If the House were determined to accept the Senate bill in toto, the Indian provisions would bypass committee, becoming law despite the objections of powerful men.

It is quite plausible that Senator Ervin had planned such a move far in advance. Undoubtedly, he was aware of the House Interior Committee's hostility to sections of his legislation amending Public Law 280. Yet he had drafted those provisions at least three years before and had remained loyal to them. They formed essential parts of his legislative package and clearly were expressions of personal conviction. While it is difficult to imagine why Senator Ervin had allowed six years' work to languish, he may have been waiting for the right opportunity to push his Indian bills.

Senator Ervin's substitute for H.R. 2516 moved through his subcommittee with little difficulty.[262] But it failed in the full committee by a single vote.[263] Senator Eastland quietly allowed H.R. 2516 to reach the floor, but only when he became confident that the bill would not be put on the calendar for 1967. Defeat in the full committee forced Senator Ervin to call his substitute to the floor in competition with H.R. 2516. Success along this route seemed unlikely; thus he faced the prospect of having to introduce provisions of the substitute as amendments. Voting on the civil rights bill would almost certainly occur under restriction of cloture rule XXII.[264] If the Parliamentarian ruled that the Indian rights amendments were not germane, the amendments would not be voted — unless supporters could convince the Senate to set aside the ruling.

One argument for the Senate's approving the Indian rights

---

262 N.Y. Times, Oct. 10, 1967, at 22, col. 1.
263 *See* 114 CONG. REC. 230 (1968) (remarks of Senator Ervin).
264 SENATE MANUAL 24-25 (1971).

amendments was that Indian rights legislation would otherwise die in committee in the House. The past record of the Aspinall committee, which had buried every other bill that inserted a consent clause into Public Law 280, lent weight to this contention.[265] Senator Ervin acted to underscore the Aspinall committee's opposition and allay suspicions of his own motives; he consolidated S. 1843 through 1847 and S.J. Res. 87 into one bill, S. 1843 as amended, and had the Judiciary Committee report the bill. It passed the Senate without opposition and was directed to the Aspinall committee. Each day the committee allowed to pass without action on the bill emphasized the need to pass the Indian rights measure as an amendment to H.R. 2516.

Just prior to the close of the First Session of the Ninetieth Congress, on a sparsely populated senate floor, Majority Leader Mike Mansfield requested and obtained unanimous consent to put H.R. 2516 on the calendar for the next session starting in 1968. Senator Ervin subsequently called up his substitute bill, but Congress encountered new pressure from the President to pass the committee bill. Senate liberals attacked Senator Ervin's measure. The liberals tested their strength when the Senate tabled the Ervin substitute on February 6, 1968, by a vote of 54 to 29.[266]

Gambling that this vote was a bellwether of senate opinion on civil rights generally, Senators Brooke and Mondale introduced an open housing amendment to H.R. 2516. To mollify borderline senators, President Johnson proposed an anti-riot act, directed at those who crossed state lines to incite riots. Events of the summer of 1967 and the action taken in the House had made it clear that Congress would pass such an act, with or without Administration support. The President's statement appeared to authorize Senators Hart, Tydings, and others managing the Administration's civil rights package to use the assurance of tough anti-riot legislation to "firm up" wavering commitments to open housing. However, when Senator Mansfield delivered the first cloture petition on the civil rights bill, some senators remained wary and provided the key votes to defeat cloture by a vote of 55 to 37 on February 20.[267] The cloture vote left the Senate's stand on open housing unclear;

---

265 See note 73, *supra.*
266 N.Y. Times, Feb. 7, 1968, at 23, col. 1.
267 *Id.,* Feb. 21, 1968, at 1, col. 2.

no one knew how that issue had affected the balloting. But when Senator Mansfield moved to table the Brooke-Mondale amendment, ostensibly because it could endanger the rest of the legislation,[268] the result was a 58 to 34 straw-vote victory for civil rights and open-housing supporters.[269]

Although a second cloture vote failed soon thereafter, the straw vote appeared to move Senator Dirksen[270] to support the Brooke-Mondale amendment with "certain exceptions." A Dirksen compromise bill reached the floor on February 28. The Senate voted that same day to table the Brooke-Mondale amendment.[271] The Dirksen bill, in the form of a substitute, paralleled Brooke-Mondale in its exemption of "Mrs. Murphy;" the Dirksen bill further exempted owners of single-family dwellings selling without a broker's assistance.

After some confusion in a third unsuccessful cloture vote, the Senate finally agreed to limit debate on the civil rights package.[272] Some 80 amendments to the Dirksen substitute had been filed prior to cloture, and each now had to be read, debated, and voted on. Among the amendments rejected were several offered by Senator Ervin.[273] However, Senator Ervin's Indian rights amendment, number 430, a duplicate of the consolidated version of S. 1843 which still languished in Representative Aspinall's committee, fared better.

Amendment 430 caused considerable consternation at the White House and among senate civil rights proponents. As a friend of disadvantaged minorities, President Johnson felt compelled to support Indian rights legislation. The President included an endorse-

---

268 24 CONG. Q. ALMANAC 158 (1968).
269 N.Y. Times, Feb. 22, 1968, at 1, col. 2.
270 Undoubtedly a prime factor in Senator Dirksen's decision to support some form of open housing legislation, even though he had opposed the 1966 bill on constitutional grounds, was the erosion of Republican resistance to cloture. In 1966, two cloture votes had produced 10 and 12 Republican votes in favor, with 21 and 20 opposed. In 1968, however, the vote was split at 18 each on the first two votes. Fully half of Senator Dirksen's party had voted against him, and even more "yea" votes might have been cast had he not openly opposed cloture. 24 CONG. Q. ALMANAC 157 (1968). Senator Dirksen had taken great pride in being the voice of the party on Capitol Hill and in the party conventions. A change of position was required if he was not to lose his footing as the party shifted under him.
271 N.Y. Times, Feb. 29, 1968, at 20, col. 3.
272 114 CONG. REC. 4960 (1968).
273 *Id.* at 5813, 5822, 5825, 5834.

ment of the amendment in his message to Congress on March 6.[274] The Johnson message may have diminished resistance to the Ervin amendment, since those torn between favoring constitutional rights for Indians and protecting the President's civil rights package could support Senator Ervin without directly opposing the White House.

Issues of Indian law became embroiled in parliamentary maneuvers. Senator Mansfield suggested a quorum was lacking,[275] perhaps in order to provide time for consultation. When the resulting order for a quorum was rescinded, Senator Mansfield assured Senator Ervin that Senator Burdick had been in contact with the House Indian Affairs Subcommittee and had learned that there was no substantial opposition to S. 1843. But pressed by Senator Ervin, Senator Burdick impeached his own sources and suggested that the Subcommittee had taken no action thus far simply because it suffered an overload of proposed legislation. Senator Ervin suggested that if the Subcommittee did not have time to report legislation it favored, the Senate should perform a service by passing the amendment so that the Indian rights bill would circumvent the Subcommittee.[276] Senator Mansfield then "reluctantly" made the point of order on germaneness. Senator Spong, serving as President Pro Tem, acquiesced in the opinion of the Parliamentarian and ruled the amendment out of order. Senator Ervin succeeded, 54 to 28, in overturning the ruling of the chair.[277] Following the vote, Senator Hart rose to support the amendment, which subsequently was approved, 81 to 0. Almost anti-climactically, the Senate then approved the Dirksen substitute, as amended, 61 to 19.[278] Three days later, on March 11, the Senate voted 71 to 20 to send H.R. 2516, as amended back to the House.[279]

On March 13, House Speaker McCormack emerged from a White House conference to announce his intention to ask the House to accept the Senate's version of H.R. 2516 in toto.[280] How-

---

274 *Id.* at 5520 (1968).
275 *Id.* at 5834.
276 *Id.* at 5837-38.
277 *Id.* at 5838.
278 *Id.* at 5839.
279 *Id.* at 5992.
280 N.Y. Times, Mar. 14, 1968, at 1, col. 7.

ever, when Representative Colmer's Rules Committee convened, it voted to postpone action on the bill until April 9 and to conduct hearings in the interim. That decision provided time for Representative Aspinall to mount a last-minute campaign against the Indian rights provisions.[281] On March 19, in the absence of his subcommittee chairman, Representative Aspinall himself convened a hearing on S. 1843.[282] Eight witnesses testified in opposition to the legislation, and three in favor.

While the one-day hearing raised no new issues and few new facts, it did generate concern that H.R. 2516 should not be passed precipitously. The hearing had provided concrete testimony both on the need to retain Public Law 280 as a tool the states could use to promote urban growth in the Southwest and on the opposition of some Indians to the enumerated rights and model code sections of the legislation. With this evidence Representative Aspinall appealed to the Rules Committee to send the Indian amendment to H.R. 2516 to committee for further study. Representative Reifel of South Dakota, the only American Indian serving in Congress and one of the Indians who supported the Ervin amendment, objected and opposed further delay of the civil rights and open housing provisions of H.R. 2516. Questioned about the Pueblos' opposition, Representative Reifel said, in effect, that he considered their objections to be ill-founded and accorded them little weight.[283]

As the Rules Committee hearings continued, Minority Leader Ford and other senior House Republicans agreed to a conference, pledging to accept the Senate version of H.R. 2516 if the conferees failed to reach agreement within ten days.[284] President Johnson exerted his influence in characteristic fashion, urging Congress to quit "fiddling and piddling" with his civil rights bill.[285]

Then, on the fourth day of April, Martin Luther King was killed.

---

281 Representative Colmer's move was also interpreted as an attempt to afford the national real estate lobby time to bring effective pressure against the open housing provisions. See 24 CONG. Q. ALMANAC 165 (1968).
282 *Hearings on Rights of Members of Indian Tribes Before the Subcomm. on Indian Affairs of the House Comm. on Interior and Insular Affairs*, 90th Cong., 2d Sess. 1 (1968).
283 114 CONG. REC. 9110-12 (1968).
284 N.Y. Times, Mar. 21, 1968, at 28, col. 1.
285 24 CONG. Q. ALMANAC 165 (1968).

The President somberly reviewed the legislation with House leaders. Representative Ford hinted that he might be changing his position.[286] As April 9 approached, civil rights forces lobbied intensely for passage of H.R. 2516 as a tribute to their assassinated leader. On the critical day, the Rules Committee defeated by one vote a motion directing H.R. 2516 to conference.[287] A resolution concurring in the Senate amendments was reported to the floor as Chairman Colmer, taking note of the disorders in Washington following the King murder, accused his fellow committeemen of legislating "under the gun."[288]

The debate on the floor on April 10 generally appeared to center on whether H.R. 2516 had been so radically altered by the Senate that its passage without further delay would impugn the integrity of the House as a deliberative body. Discussion of the Indian provisions was more specific, touching on the merits and faults of particular sections of the Ervin legislation. Several congressmen participated, but Representatives Aspinall and Reifel remained the principal figures. Representative Aspinall argued that his hearing had revealed the spectre of treaty rights in jeopardy and that by passing H.R. 2516 Congress might be destroying the rights of one minority (Indians) to aid another (blacks). He charged that certain procedural requirements in title I, such as trial by jury, could destroy the tribal courts. Predictably, he attacked the amendment's alterations of Public Law 280, focusing on the possible confusion caused by states extending or withdrawing jurisdiction over reservations.[289] In rebuttal, Representative Reifel routinely explained the amendment's provisions and assured the House that the Ervin legislation would relieve the oppressiveness of tribal governments and errors of Public Law 280.[290] Representative Reifel's efforts may well have been crucial. The House voted 229 to 195 to consider the resolution to accept H.R. 2516; and by a vote of 250 to 171, the bill was approved. The President signed

---

286 N.Y. Times, Apr. 7, 1968, at 57, col. 7.
287 The key "nay" vote was cast by Representative Anderson of Illinois who may have been encouraged by the timely adoption of an open housing ordinance by a city in his home district. 24 CONG. Q. ALMANAC 158 (1968).
288 N.Y. Times, Apr. 10, 1968, at 31, col. 4.
289 114 CONG. REC. 9614-15 (1968).
290 *Id.* at 9552-53 (1968).

it the following day.[291] In the angry clash of black and white, North and South, Indian law was made.

IV. THE IMPACT OF THE 1968 ACT ON INDIAN LAW

Even after the 1968 Civil Rights Act was passed, the Pueblos sought exemption from its Indian rights provisions. In response to their political agitation, members of the New Mexico congressional delegation introduced bills to that effect,[292] and Senator Ervin returned to New Mexico to hold a special hearing of his subcommittee. In it the Pueblos reiterated a familiar theme:

> Our whole value structure is based on the concept of harmony between the individual, his fellows, and his social institutions. For this reason, we simply do not share your society's regard for the competitive individualist. In your society, an aggressive campaigner is congratulated for his drive and political ability. In Pueblo society, such behavior would be looked down upon and distrusted by his neighbors. Even the offices themselves, now so respected, would be demeaned by subjecting them to political contest. The mutual trust between governors and governed, so much a part of our social life, would be destroyed.[293]

More specifically, the witnesses voiced concern about extending equal protection to non-Indians in their communities and about the bill of attainder problems created in tribal systems where the same body often served as the tribal council and court.

Senator Ervin's response was limited. When he returned to Washington, he introduced S. 2172 and S. 2173.[294] The first of these bills restricted the meaning of "any person" in title II to "American Indians" and provided that non-Indians on the reservations were not entitled to the equal protection of tribal laws. But

---

291 On November 21, 1968, President Johnson issued Exec. Order No. 11435, authorizing the Secretary of the Interior to accept states' retrocessions of jurisdiction over Indian country, pursuant to the Act. That order appears with title IV of the Act, at 25 U.S.C.A. § 1321-26. See Appendix for the language of the Ervin legislation as it finally appeared, as Titles II-VII of the Civil Rights Act of 1968.
292 S. 3470 and H.R. 17040, 91st Cong., 1st Sess. (1969).
293 *Hearings on S. 211 Before the Subcomm. on Constitutional Rights of the Senate Comm. on the Judiciary*, 91st Cong., 1st Sess. (1969) (reproduced in part in 2 AM. INDIAN L. NEWSLETTER 94, 95 [1969]).
294 115 CONG. REC. 12532 (1969).

Senator Ervin qualified his support for the bill by remarking that he introduced it in order "to afford Congress an opportunity to consider the advisability of such an amendment."[295] After being placed under advisement in the Senate, S. 2172 quietly disappeared. The second bill, S. 2173 provided that the model code which the Department of the Interior was instructed to draft under title III would serve as no more than a model and would not be imposed by Congress. Because fear of the title III had diminished as the BIA moved slowly to draft a new code, the bill was really addressed to a less than urgent issue. It did, however, pass the Senate on July 11, 1969;[296] but after being sent to the House of Representatives, it died in the Indian Affairs Subcommittee. The new bills Senator Ervin introduced did not respond effectively to any of the Pueblo problems because no proposal was made on the equal protection controversy or on the problem of the separation of powers. Instead, Pueblo leaders learned that their communities were expected to conform to the 1968 legislation.

That lesson has not been lost on other major tribes, who have begun to make the necessary adjustments, but "to date there has been no dramatic overall change."[297] The factors prolonging the period of transition include the need for funding (which is being met in part by the Law Enforcement Assistance Administration), the high turnover and inadequate training of tribal judges, the blurred separation of executive and judicial powers in a number of tribal governments, and the continued resistance by some tribes to congressional intrusion into their internal affairs.[298] It has been further noted that "as long as the Bureau of Indian Affairs has not changed the Code of Indian Offenses as directed by Congress, the chances are slim that the tribes having their own codes will assume any new burdens."[299]

A questionnaire to which 16 of the largest tribes responded[300]

---

295 *Id.* at 12555.
296 *Id.* at 19239.
297 Letter from William F. Meredith, Project Director, National American Indian Court Judges Association, to the author, April 29, 1971, on file at the office of the Harvard Legislative Research Bureau.
298 *Id.*
299 Letter from Arthur Lazarus, Jr., general counsel to the Association on American Indian Affairs, to the author, April 5, 1971, on file at the office of the Harvard Legislative Research Bureau.

revealed that while only seven had permitted professional, non-Indian attorneys to represent criminal defendants in tribal courts prior to 1968, 11 tribes now do, while four have expressed no policy. The only tribe which stated that it continued to bar non-Indian attorneys was later compelled to admit them by a federal district court.[301] The tribes reported a difficulty, however, in funding prosecutor's offices. Ten of the 12 tribes which lacked prosecutors prior to 1968 continue to operate without them. This financial inability to formalize tribal court proceedings has led one observer to warn that a disproportionate number of habeas corpus proceedings arising from detention by tribal authorities may require new evidentiary hearings in federal district courts, thus in part creating the system of trial de novo which Senator Ervin originally had intended to establish.[302]

In other areas where reform requires money, little change has occurred. Five of the six tribes which did not protect the defendant's right to silence (apparently in order to compensate for inadequate investigative facilities) still do not do so, or at least have no standing policy of protection. Before 1968 two tribes made no provision for trial by jury, and the same number today continue to refuse as a matter of policy to express the right, although neither tribe actually denies trial by jury to all defendants. Fifteen tribes had institutionalized appellate structures[303] prior to 1968; the number does not appear to have changed.[304]

---

300 The tribes responding were the Shoshone-Bannock, Blackfeet, Cheyenne River Sioux, Colorado River tribes, Fort Belknap, Flathead, Hopi, Jicarilla Apache, Navaho, Northern Cheyenne, Pierre (Crow Creek and Lower Brule), Rosebud Sioux, Standing Rock Sioux, Warm Springs Confederation, Wind River, and Yakima. The author mailed the questionnaires in the spring of 1971 and received replies throughout that summer. The questionnaires which support the factual propositions in the text between notes 304 and 308 are on file at the office of the Harvard Legislative Research Bureau. More detailed information on particular tribes has been compiled by the National American Indian Court Judges Association, 1345 Connecticut Avenue, N.W., Washington, D.C. 20036.

301 Towersap v. Fort Hall Indian Tribal Court, Civ. No. 4-70-37 (D. Idaho, Dec. 28, 1971). See text at note 315, *infra*.

302 *See* Note, *Criminal Procedure: Habeas Corpus as an Enforcement Procedure under the Indian Civil Rights Act of 1968*, 46 WASH. L. REV. 541, 547-50 (1971).

303 The existence of a structure does not always signify an *operating* appeals system. Meredith, *supra* note 297.

304 This conclusion necessarily reflects the author's interpretation of the significance of failure in some instances to respond directly to a particular question. This evaluation is based on comments appended to the questionnaires and on earlier testimony in the Ervin hearings.

The federal judiciary may have the most important role in administering change in the tribal justice systems. These courts, especially at the district level, will determine how broadly the 1968 legislation will affect traditional practices. In construing the statute, the federal courts should look closely at the legislative history.

The legislative history of title II appears to reflect Senator Ervin's change from an approach of imposing on the tribes the constitutional limitations applicable to the federal government to an approach (suggested by the Department of the Interior and many of the tribes) of extending certain specified protections to members of the tribes as individuals. This change was the product of a philosophical compromise between Senator Ervin's apparent view that the scope of public authority should be strictly defined by the individual's need for protection and essential services, and the view, expressed in extreme form by the Pueblos, that the scope of individual liberty should be strictly limited by the community's traditional need for harmony. While S. 961 had been rooted in a theory of government with enumerated powers, title II provided members of tribes with enumerated rights.

For the federal courts, the practical meaning of this accommodation is that title II requires a limited construction which takes an informed account of its development. It does not authorize the court to apply broadly such elusive and expanding concepts as due process, equal protection, or unreasonable search and seizure without a sensitive regard for their impact on tribal structures and values. Because this point is fully revealed only by tracing seven years of legislative history, there is a danger that it may be missed and that an unlimited construction of title II will exacerbate the tribes' difficulties adjusting to its requirements.

Three federal district court decisions illustrate this danger. In 1968, an outspoken and reportedly abrasive non-Indian attorney directing the Navaho legal aid agency was ordered expelled from the reservation by the tribal council. In an action to enjoin enforcement of the order, the attorney challenged the power of the council to enter such an order after the enactment of title II. In *Dodge v. Nakai*,[305] the federal district court held that it had pendent jurisdiction to hear the case despite the failure to exhaust a

---

[305] 298 F. Supp. 17 (D. Ariz. 1968).

remedy available in the tribal system because not all of the issues or parties involved were cognizable in the tribal courts. It also based jurisdiction to hear the non-Indian's complaint against the tribal council on the language of title II, guaranteeing equal protection of tribal laws to "any person." The court subsequently enjoined enforcement of the order, finding that it not only denied due process but also constituted a bill of attainder.[306]

In 1969, a district court in Montana held that title II did not directly authorize civil actions for damages against individuals who in their official capacities violated enumerated rights. The court did rule, however, that it had pendent jurisdiction to adjudicate such a claim if it was coupled with an action against the tribe for equitable or habeas corpus relief with which it shared a "common nucleus of operative fact."[307]

A federal court in New Mexico expanded the reasoning of these cases in a civil action for personal injuries allegedly inflicted by a Zuni Pueblo police officer upon the plaintiff in his custody.[308] The Court noted that the applicable provisions of title II bore a "striking" resemblance to the fourth and fifth amendments and said:

> The similarity of language and the legislative history of the Act establish that Congress intended these provisions to limit tribal governments as the Fourth and Fifth Amendments limit the federal government. . . . The analogy of the Indian Civil Rights Act to the Amendments is appropriate and the law governing actions against individuals for damages under the Fourth and Fifth Amendments should be applied to the Act.[309]

Thus, in a series of decisions, district courts have built upon notions of pendent jurisdiction and analogies to constitutionally protected right to extend the power of the federal judiciary. The 1968 legislation has been interpreted to empower federal courts to decide cases not previously heard by the tribal courts or brought

---

306 Dodge v. Nakai, 298 F. Supp. 26 (D. Ariz. 1969).
307 Spotted Eagle v. Blackfeet Tribe, 301 F. Supp. 85 (D. Mont. 1969). The court relied heavily on an analogous Supreme Court case, United Mine Workers v. Gibbs, 383 U.S. 715 (1966), holding that federal courts exercised pendent jurisdiction in damage claims arising under state law coupled with federal claims sharing a "common nucleus of operative fact."
308 Loncassion v. Leekity, 334 F. Supp. 370 (D.N.M. 1971).
309 Id. at 374.

to federal courts by habeas corpus, to apply developing fourth and fifth amendment concepts, and to allow damage actions not authorized by the statute. The "legislative history" to which the *Loncassion* court referred and on which the decision was said to have rested, has really received no consideration.

In a recent decision, the Tenth Circuit declined to follow the examples set by these three district courts and affirmed the action of the District Court for Wyoming. The lower court had held that title II did not extend federal jurisdiction to hear complaints of discriminatory practices in admission to tribal membership.[310] On appeal, the court assumed that the application of standards for tribal membership might raise equal protection or due process problems, but held that the pleadings disclosed no such issues.[311] Moreover, it recalled its holding in a previous case[312] that title II did not impose broad due process requirements which conflicted with a statutory system of appointing rather than electing a tribal chief. The Tenth Circuit stressed that "the Indian Bill of Rights was concerned primarily with tribal administration of justice and the imposition of tribal penalties and forfeitures and not with the specifics of tribal structure or office-holding."[313] Had the court fully examined the legislative history of title II, its analysis (more persuasive than that of the three interventionist lower courts) would have found additional support.

This tension between restraint and intervention should not arise, however, when the courts apply the various specific commands and prohibitions of the Act. The express provision for representation by defense attorneys, for example, has been strictly applied by district courts in Montana[314] and Idaho,[315] which have ordered tribal courts to permit non-Indian lawyers to represent

---

310 Pinnow v. Shoshone Tribal Council, 314 F. Supp. 1157 (D. Wyo. 1970).
311 Slattery v. Arapahoe Tribal Council, 453 F.2d 278 (10th Cir. 1971).
312 Groundhog v. Keeler, 442 F.2d 674 (10th Cir. 1971).
313 Slattery, 453 F.2d at 282. *Accord* Lefthand v. Crow Tribal Council, 329 F. Supp. 728 (D. Mont. 1971); *but cf.* Solomon v. LaRose, 335 F. Supp. 715 (D. Neb. 1971).
314 Spotted Eagle v. Blackfeet Tribe, Civ. No. 2780; Rafalsky v. Blackfeet Tribe, Civ. No. 2849; Regan v. Blackfeet Tribal Court, Civ. No. 2850 (D. Mont., July 7, 1969).
315 Towersap v. Fort Hall Indian Tribal Court, Civ. No. 4-70-37 (D. Id., December 28, 1971).

Indian defendants. In the Idaho case, the court rejected the contention of the Shoshone-Bannock that the phrase "assistance of counsel" in title II should be construed to mean only the aid of a friend within the tribe, a practice traditionally permitted by the tribal court. While the policy of allowing professional counsel in tribal courts at the defendant's expense may be subject to criticism, there is little doubt that in adhering to the plain language of the statute the court implemented the intent of the drafter of the provision.

The meaning of title IV language is generally clear and may usually be applied strictly. In *Kennerly v. District Court of the Ninth Judicial District of Montana*,[316] the United States Supreme Court invalidated a Blackfeet tribal ordinance granting Montana courts concurrent jurisdiction over civil actions against members of the tribe on the ground of its failure to conform to express title IV requirements. In so doing, the Court pointed out that Montana had not taken legislative action to extend jurisdiction under Public Law 280 and that the tribe had failed to evidence the consent of its members through referendum.[317] While this decision apparently was in accord with Senator Ervin's strong feelings about the need for consent of the governed through a vote of the members of the tribe, the Court's opinion did not fully examine the legislative history of title IV but relied mainly on surface statutory construction.

Construing merely the words of the statute is proper when they are unambiguous. The necessity for using legislative history, however, was demonstrated by the Nebraska District Court's effort to decide whether title IV required the federal government to accept all jurisdiction retroceded by Nebraska or whether the state could retain part of the jurisdiction assumed under Public Law 280.[318] The extent of the court's historical analysis was to conclude from statutory language itself that title IV was enacted to benefit the

---

316 400 U.S. 423 (1971).
317 *Compare* Annis v. Dewey County Bank, 335 F. Supp. 133 (D.S.D. 1971); Martin v. Denver Juvenile Court, 493 P.2d 1093 (Colo. 1972); Crow Tribe of Indians v. Deernose, 487 P.2d 1133 (Mont. 1971) *with* Makah Indian Tribe v. State, 76 Wash. 2d 485, 457 P.2d 590 (1969), *appeal dismissed sub nom.* Makah Indian Tribe v. Washington, 397 U.S. 316 (1970) (the cause of action had arisen prior to 1968).
318 United States v. Brown, 334 F. Supp. 536 (D. Neb. 1971).

Indians.[319] Since the tribe in question had expressed a preference to remain under state jurisdiction after title IV had been enacted, the court held that the federal government could accept a partial retrocession. The legislative history treated in this article reveals that the hearings highlighted the need for piecemeal transfers of jurisdiction by negotiation between state and tribe in order to avoid problems of extradition, "no man's lands," and inadequate law enforcement caused by "lump sum" transfers of jurisdiction.[320] In response, Senator Ervin had introduced S. 966 and maintained its provisions intact until enactment as title IV. S. 966 had authorized piecemeal transfers, but had provided that such transfers could be initiated only by the states. Although the latter provision was criticized by several tribal spokesmen, Senator Ervin retained it, apparently to assure the states that they would be affected by this repeal of section 7 of Public Law 280 only at their own option. Consequently, the language authorizing piecemeal transfers of jurisdiction was not intended solely to benefit the Indians. The partial retrocession approved in *Brown* could have been grounded more firmly in a power reserved to the states, had the legislative history been fully examined.

V. Conclusion

Each of the decisions discussed reveals a need for a closer analysis of legislative history of the Indian rights provisions. In the future the federal courts will again be asked to construe the 1968 Act in manners inconsistent with its plain language or its history. Advocates of further federal intervention into tribal criminal justice systems may seek to broaden the meaning of the due process, equal protection, or search and seizure provisions in title II, converting the enumerated rights section into what Senator Ervin had originally suggested but later rejected in S. 961. Opponents of the philosophical foundations of the legislation may argue for the special construction of particular protections or prohibitions in order to bring them into closer correspondence with tribal practices before 1968. The federal judge should refrain from exer-

---

[319] *Id.* at 541-42.
[320] See part II C 1 of this article, *supra*.

cising a broad power to establish policy when plenary power over Indian affairs rests with Congress. The judge may believe that he perceives what is best for the tribes within the court's jurisdiction; but the Indians have suffered from a surfeit of patrons in all branches of government. Given adequate resources, the tribes may best adjust to the new legislation in a judicial milieu of sensitive, restrained construction. In this difficult period of transition, the judge who seizes opportunities to demand more of the tribes than required by the letter and history of the Act might become a contemporary analogue to the BIA agent of an earlier period, who imposed tenets of personal conviction through the power of the white conqueror.

255

Appendix

Civil Rights Act

Public Law 90-284
90th Congress, H.R. 2516
April 11, 1968
An Act

To prescribe penalties for certain acts of violence or intimidation, and for other purposes.

 •   •   •   •   •   •

Title II — *Rights of Indians*

Definitions

Sec. 201. For purposes of this title, the term —
 (1) "Indian tribe" means any tribe, band, or other group of Indians subject to the jurisdiction of the United States and recognized as possessing powers of self-government;
 (2) "powers of self-government" means and includes all governmental powers possessed by an Indian tribe, executive, legislative, and judicial, and all offices, tribes, and tribunals by and through which they are executed, including courts of Indian offenses; and
 (3) "Indian court" means any Indian tribal court or court of Indian offense.

Indian Rights

Sec. 202. No Indian tribe in exercising powers of self-government shall —
 (1) make or enforce any law prohibiting the free exercise of religion, or abridging the freedom of speech, or of the press, or the right of the people peaceably to assemble and to petition for a redress of grievances;
 (2) violate the right of the people to be secure in their persons, houses, papers,

and effects against unreasonable search and seizures, nor issue warrants, but upon probable cause, supported by oath or affirmation, and particularly describing the place to be searched and the person or thing to be seized;

(3) subject any person for the same offense to be twice put in jeopardy;

(4) compel any person in any criminal case to be a witness against himself;

(5) take any private property for a public use without just compensation;

(6) deny to any person in a criminal proceeding the right to a speedy and public trial, to be informed of the nature and cause of the accusation, to be confronted with the witnesses against him, to have compulsory process for obtaining witnesses in his favor, and at his own expense to have the assistance of counsel for his defense;

(7) require excessive bail, impose excessive fines, inflict cruel and unusual punishments, and in no event impose for conviction of any one offense any penalty or punishment greater than imprisonment for a term of six months or a fine of $500, or both;

(8) deny to any person within its jurisdiction the equal protection of its laws or deprive any person of liberty or property without due process of law;

(9) pass any bill of attainder or ex post facto law; or

(10) deny to any person accused of an offense punishable by imprisonment the right, upon request, to a trial by jury of not less than six persons.

Habeas Corpus

Sec. 203. The privilege of the writ of habeas corpus shall be available to any person, in a court of the United States, to test the legality of his detention by order of an Indian tribe.

TITLE III — *Model Code Governing Courts of Indian Offenses*

Sec. 301. The Secretary of the Interior is authorized and directed to recommend to the Congress, on or before July 1, 1968, a model code to govern the administration of justice by courts of Indian offenses on Indian reservations. Such code shall include provisions which will

(1) assure that any individual being tried for an offense by a court of Indian offenses shall have the same rights, privileges, and immunities under the United States Constitution as would be guaranteed any citizen of the United States being tried in a Federal court for any similar offense,

(2) assure that any individual being tried for an offense by a court of Indian offenses will be advised and made aware of his rights under the United States Constitution, and under any tribal constitution applicable to such individual,

(3) establish proper qualifications for the office of judge of the court of Indian offenses, and

(4) provide for the establishing of educational classes for the training of judges of courts of Indian offenses. In carrying out the provisions of this title, the Secretary of the Interior shall consult with the Indians, Indian tribes, and interested agencies of the United States.

Sec. 302. There is hereby authorized to be appropriated such sum as may be necessary to carry out the provisions of this title.

TITLE IV — *Jurisdiction Over Criminal and Civil Actions*

Assumption by State

Sec. 401. (a) The consent of the United States is hereby given to any State not having jurisdiction over criminal offenses committed by or against Indians in the areas of Indian country situated within such State to assume, with the consent of the Indian tribe occupying the particular Indian country or part thereof which could be affected by such assumption, such measure of jurisdiction over any or all of such offenses committed within such Indian country or any part thereof as may be determined by such State to the same extent that such State has jurisdiction over any such offense committed elsewhere within the State, and the criminal laws of such State shall have the same force and effect within such Indian country or part thereof as they have elsewhere within that State.

(b) Nothing in this section shall authorize the alienation, encumbrance, or taxation of any real or personal property, including water rights, belonging to any Indian or any Indian tribe, band, or community that is held in trust by the United States or is subject to a restriction against alienation imposed by the United States; or shall authorize regulation of the use of such property in a manner inconsistent with any Federal treaty, agreement, or statute or with any regulation made pursuant thereto; or shall deprive any Indian or any Indian tribe, band, or community of any right, privilege, or immunity afforded under Federal treaty, agreement, or statute with respect to hunting, trapping, or fishing or the control, licensing, or regulation thereof.

Assumption by State of Civil Jurisdiction

Sec. 402. (a) The consent of the United States is hereby given to any State not having jurisdiction over civil causes of action between Indians or to which Indians are parties which arise in the areas of Indian country situated within such State to assume, with the consent of the tribe occupying the particular Indian country or part thereof which would be affected by such assumption, such measure of jurisdiction over any or all such civil causes of action arising within such Indian country or any part thereof as may be determined by such State to the same extent that such State has jurisdiction over other civil causes of action, and those civil laws of such State that are of general application to private persons or private property shall have the same force and effect within such Indian country or part thereof as they have elsewhere within that State.

(b) Nothing in this section shall authorize the alienation, encumbrance, or taxation of any real or person [sic] property, including water rights, belonging to any Indian or any Indian tribe, band, or community that is held in trust by the United States or is subject to a restriction against alienation imposed by the United States; or shall authorize regulation of the use of such property in a manner inconsistent with any Federal treaty, agreement, or statute, or with any regulation made pursuant thereto; or shall confer jurisdiction upon the State to adjudicate, in probate proceeding or otherwise, the ownership or right to possession of such property or any interest therein.

(c) Any tribal ordinance or custom heretofore or hereafter adopted by an Indian tribe, band, or community in the exercise of any authority which it may possess shall, if not inconsistent with any applicable civil law of the State be given full force and effect in the determination of civil causes of action pursuant to this section.

Retrocession of Jurisdiction by State

Sec. 403. (a) The United States is authorized to accept a retrocession by any State of all or any measure of the criminal or civil jurisdiction or both, acquired by such State pursuant to the provisions of section 1162 of title 18 of the United States Code, section 1360 of title 28 of the United States Code, or section 7 of the Act of August 15, 1953 (67 Stat. 588), as it was in effect prior to its repeal by subsection (b) of this section.

(b) Section 7 of the Act of August 15, 1953 (67 Stat. 588), is hereby repealed but such repeal shall not affect any cession of jurisdiction made pursuant to such section prior to its repeal.

Consent to Amend State Laws

Sec. 404. Notwithstanding the provisions of any enabling Act for the admission of a State, the consent of the United States is hereby given to the people of any State to amend, where necessary, their State constitution or existing statutes, as the case may be, to remove any legal impediment to the assumption of civil or criminal jurisdiction in accordance with the provisions of this title. The provisions of this title shall not become effective with respect to such assumption of jurisdiction by any such State until the people thereof have appropriately amended their State constitution or statutes as the case may be.

Actions Not to Abate

Sec. 405. (a) No action or proceeding pending before any court or agency of the United States immediately prior to any cession of jurisdiction by the United States pursuant to this title shall abate by reason of that cession. For the purposes of any such action or proceeding, such cession shall take effect on the day following the date of final determination of such action or proceeding.

(b) No cession made by the United States under this title shall deprive any court of the United States of jurisdiction to hear, determine, render judgment, or impose sentence in any criminal action instituted against any person for any offense committed before the effective date of such cession, if the offense charged in such action was cognizable under any law of the United States at the time of the commission of such offense. For the purposes of any such criminal action, such cession shall take effect on the day following the date of final determination of such action.

Special Election

Sec. 406. State jurisdiction acquired pursuant to this title with respect to criminal offenses or civil causes of action or with respect to both, shall be applicable in Indian country only where the enrolled Indians within the affected area of such Indian country accept such jurisdiction by a majority vote of the adult Indians voting at a special election held for that purpose. The Secretary of the Interior shall call such special election under such rules and regulations as he may prescribe, when requested to do so by the tribal council or other governing body, or by 20 per centum of such enrolled adults.

Title V — *Offenses Within Indian Country*

Amendment

Sec. 501. Section 1153 of title 18 of the United States Code is amended by inserting immediately after "weapon," the following: "assault resulting in serious bodily injury,".

Title VI — *Employment of Legal Counsel*

Approval

Sec. 601. Notwithstanding any other provision of law, if any application made by an Indian, Indian Tribe, Indian council, or any band or group of Indians under any law requiring the approval of the Secretary of the Interior or the Commissioner of Indian Affairs of contracts or agreements relating to the employment of legal counsel (including the choice of counsel and the fixing of fees) by any such Indians, tribe, council, band, or group is neither granted nor denied within ninety days following the making of such application, such approval shall be deemed to have been granted.

Title VII — *Materials Relating to Constitutional Rights of Indians*

Secretary of Interior to Prepare

Sec. 701. (a) In order that the constitutional rights of Indians might be fully protected, the Secretary of the Interior is authorized and directed to —

(1) have the document entitled "Indian Affairs, Laws, and Treaties" (Senate Document Numbered 319, volumes 1 and 2, Fifty-eighth Congress), revised and extended

to include all treaties, laws, Executive orders, and regulations relating to Indian affairs in force on September 1, 1967, and to have such revised document printed at the Government Printing Office;

(2) have revised and republished the treatise entitled "Federal Indian Law"; and

(3) have prepared, to the extent determined by the Secretary of the Interior to be feasible, an accurate compilation of the official opinions, published and unpublished, of the Solicitor of the Department of the Interior relating to Indian affairs rendered by the Solicitor prior to September 1, 1967, and to have such compilation printed as a Government publication at the Government Printing Office.

(b) With respect to the document entitled "Indian Affairs, Laws and Treaties" as revised and extended in accordance with paragraph (1) of subsection (a), and the compilation prepared in accordance with paragraph (3) of such subsection, the Secretary of the Interior shall take such action as may be necessary to keep such document and compilation current on an annual basis.

(c) There is authorized to be appropriated for carrying out the provisions of this title, with respect to the preparation but not including printing, such sum as may be necessary.

Negro Demonstrations and the Law: Danville as a Test Case

James W. Ely, Jr.*

The hectic events of the summer of 1963 abruptly shattered the prevailing domestic calm of the United States. Widespread Negro demonstrations that summer contrasted sharply with the peaceful 1950's and heralded the advent of the major disorders and urban riots which characterized the late 1960's. Growing directly out of the civil rights movement, the 1963 demonstrations reflected the impatience of black Americans with the leisurely implementation of *Brown v. Board of Education*[1] and the other equal rights decisions. Moreover, they indicated that Negroes were no longer content to await executive and judicial action, the impact of whicn had too often proved minimal or illusory in the past. The era of direct action had begun in early 1960 with the lunch counter sit-ins. By the spring of 1963, however, racial disturbances in Birmingham raised the level of violence and spawned numerous lesser protests across the South. The protest movement presented a serious crisis in law enforcement and respect for the law.

Perhaps the most significant of these secondary demonstrations occurred in Danville, Virginia. Overshadowed by the massive national publicity accorded the Birmingham affair, the Danville disturbances have not received a careful study.[2] The Danville experience, however, is instructive in several areas. Its study raises a series of important questions. How did the law, both state and federal, respond to the outbreak of racial demonstrations? What was the role of the courts, and of the Kennedy administration, in handling the Negro protest movement? What does the Danville imbroglio suggest about the feasibility of the resort to direct action tactics? Considered in a broader context, a study of the Danville demonstrations

---

* Assistant Professor of Law, Vanderbilt University. Member, Bar of State of New York. A.B. 1959, Princeton University; LL.B. 1962, Harvard Law School; Ph.D. 1971, University of Virginia. The author wishes to express his appreciation to the National Endowment for the Humanities and the Vanderbilt University Research Council for grants assisting part of the research on which this study is based.

1. 347 U.S. 483 (1954).

2. Two attorneys and civil rights activists have described their experiences in Danville: L. Holt, An Act of Conscience (1965); W. M. Kunstler, Deep in My Heart 211-32 (1966). For other accounts of the Danville demonstrations see A Buni, The Negro in Virginia Politics, 1902-1965, at 214-16 (1967); G. Powell, Jr., Black Cloud over Danville—the Negro Movement in Danville, Virginia, in 1963, 1968 (unpublished thesis in University of Richmond Library); "Danville on Trial," New Republic Nov. 2, 1963, at 11-12.

illustrates a major, and surprisingly successful, chapter in Virginia's resistance to any change in the racial status quo.

The City and the Demonstrations

The City of Danville is located on the Dan River in Southside Virginia, just north of the boundary with North Carolina. In 1960 the city contained a population of 46,577, of which 11,558 or 24.73 per cent were Negroes.[3] Danville was governed by nine councilmen elected at large, and the council in turn named the city manager. The largest industry was Dan River Mills, which employed about 9,500 people in Danville alone.[4] In addition, there were tobacco processing and storage plants, and factories of Corning Glass Works. Two institutions of higher education, Averett College and Stratford Junior College, were located in the city. Danville's newspapers, the morning *Register* and the afternoon *Bee*, followed a staunchly conservative editorial line.

Although Danville appeared a bustling commercial center, the past weighed heavily on the city as it did upon so much of the South. Danville had been the site of prisons for Union soldiers during the Civil War. For a week in April, 1865, the city served as the last capitol of the Confederacy after Jefferson Davis fled there from Richmond.[5] Located in the heart of the Virginia black belt, Danville had long maintained a rigidly segregationist line in the area of race relations. These racial tensions were demonstrated most vividly by the serious Danville riot of November, 1883. That disturbance developed out of the exceedingly bitter political struggle between the Virginia Democrats and the Readjusters, a relatively liberal state political faction that included blacks and Republicans.[6] During the 1880's a majority of Danville's population was black, and in 1882 Negro voters elected a Readjuster majority to the city council. The Readjuster city administration appointed black policemen and named Negroes to important municipal posts. Although the mayor and chief of police were white, Danville whites became increasingly restive. As part of their campaign in the forthcoming legislative elections, the Democrats seized upon the race issue, and particularly the situation in Danville, as a stratagem to boost the fortune

---
3. U.S. Census of Population, Virginia: General Population Characteristics, 1960.
4. For the growth of Dan River Mills see R. SMITH, MILL ON THE DAN: A HISTORY OF DAN RIVER MILLS, 1882-1950 (1960).
5. L. HAIRSTON, A BRIEF HISTORY OF DANVILLE, VIRGINIA, 1728-1954 (1955).
6. The Readjusters breached Virginia political tradition by their efforts to lure black votes. *See* J. Moore, To Carry Africa into the War: the Readjuster Movement and the Negro, 1968 (unpublished thesis in University of Virginia Library); C. PEARSON, THE READJUSTER MOVEMENT IN VIRGINIA (1917).

of their party. On Saturday, November 3, 1883—just four days prior to the election—armed whites, inflamed by Democratic campaign propaganda, fired indiscriminately into a crowd of Negroes, killing four blacks and wounding ten. The governor called out the militia and the city was subsequently placed under martial law. Both in Danville and throughout Virginia, the Democrats effectively used the Danville riot and appeals for white supremacy to regain political ascendancy.[7] No one was ever arrested or punished for the shootings. Hence, a resort to violence to defend white rule was nothing novel in Danville.[8] Subsequently, in 1906 the city was the scene of a short-lived and unsuccessful Negro boycott against the introduction of segregated streetcars.[9]

Racial attitudes in the Old Dominion had not changed appreciably when the Supreme Court decided the *Brown* case in 1954. After a brief period of indecision, the state political leadership, headed by United States Senator Harry F. Byrd, adopted a policy of massive resistance to school integration. Space does not permit an exhaustive discussion of the many legal and practical problems posed by massive resistance. Briefly stated, massive resistance was a program which sought to halt school integration anywhere in Virginia by erecting a series of defensive rings: a statewide pupil assignment plan administered by a Pupil Placement Board that would try to forestall integration by elaborate criteria and cumbersome proce-

---

7. Ten days before the election a circular entitled "Coalition Rule in Danville" appeared over the signature of several Danville businessmen. The circular was addressed to the citizens of southwest Virginia and described in lurid detail the alleged conditions of Negro domination in Danville. The purpose of the Danville circular was to solidify the white voters behind the Democratic Party. See "Coalition Rule in Danville" 1883, (circular in Virginia Historical Society).

8. Concerned about the adverse publicity given Danville in the northern press, a meeting of white citizens appointed a committee to investigate the riot. The committee report blamed the riot on Negroes and the Readjuster city administration; " . . . there was engendered in the minds of the Negroes of Danville a belief that as against the white men they would receive the support and protection of the municipal government. In consequence of which belief they became rude, insolent and intolerant to the white citizens of the town, and the bad temper and ill-feeling between the races thus generated continued to increase and was of late greatly aggravated by the heated political canvass preceding the election. . . ." *Report of the Committee of Forty* (Richmond, 1883). A committee of the United States Senate also investigated the Danville riot. The majority report, adopted by a 5-4 vote, attributed the disorders to the efforts of the Democratic Party to excite the race issue. SENATE COMM. ON PRIVILEGES AND ELECTIONS. REPORT UPON DANVILLE, VIRGINIA RIOT (Washington 1884). For scholarly treatment of the subject see C. WYNES, RACE RELATIONS IN VIRGINIA, 1870-1902 (1961); Calhoun, *The Danville Riot and Its Repercussions on the Virginia Election of 1883*, in 3 EAST CAROLINA COLLEGE PUBLICATIONS IN HISTORY, at 25-51 (1966); J. Melzer, The Danville Riot, November 3, 1883, 1963 (unpublished thesis in University of Virginia Library).

9. Meier and Rudwick, *Negro Boycotts of Segregated Streetcars in Virginia, 1904-1907*, 81 VA. MAGA. HIST. AND BIOG. at 479-87 (1973).

dures, and a statutory mandate that the governor close any school confronted with a final integration order and attempt to reorganize such school on a segregated basis. If all else failed, the governor was authorized, in his discretion, to permit a closed school to reopen with racial integration, but all state appropriations were automatically cut off to any integrated schools. A program of tuition grants was established to facilitate attendance at private schools by students adversely affected by the public school closings.[10]

The Byrd organization, as the senator's political friends were known, completely dominated the agencies of state government in the 1950's and enacted the massive resistance legislation at a special session of the Virginia legislature in September of 1956. Byrd represented the interests of white, conservative, property-owning Virginians, and, although never a race-baiter, he was personally antagonistic to racial integration. Convinced that the *Brown* opinion was "illegal and a usurpation of power," Byrd admitted that the opinion "has disturbed me more than anything that has occurred in my political career."[11] Pursuant to massive resistance, white schools in three Virginia localities were closed during the fall semester of 1958. The policy expired in January of 1959 when the Virginia Supreme Court of Appeals and a three-judge federal district court declared massive resistance unconstitutional.[12]

While there was considerable unease about the school closing aspects of massive resistance, there was at the same time no white support for racial integration. Through their elected representatives in the legislature, Danville whites gave enthusiastic support to massive resistance and bitterly battled the modification of the state's policy in the spring of 1959. Delegate C. Stuart Wheatley of Danville declared: "What some of the people do not realize and will never realize until it has been [sic] too late is that an integrated school is worse than a closed school."[13] Despite the tactical retreat from

---

10. For recent scholarship on the topic see J. Ely, Jr., The Crisis of Conservative Virginia: The Decline and Fall of Massive Resistance, 1957-1965, 1971 (unpublished dissertation in University of Virginia Library); A. Grundman, Public School Desegregation in Virginia from 1954 to the Present, 1972 (unpublished dissertation in Wayne State University Library); N. BARTLEY, THE RISE OF MASSIVE RESISTANCE: RACE AND POLITICS IN THE SOUTH DURING THE 1950's (1969). *See also* B. MUSE, VIRGINIA'S MASSIVE RESISTANCE (1961); R. GATES, THE MAKING OF MASSIVE RESISTANCE: VIRGINIA'S POLITICS OF PUBLIC SCHOOL DESEGREGATION, 1954-1956 (1964).

11. Letter from Harry F. Byrd to Samuel M. Bemiss, September 24, 1956 (Samuel M. Bemiss Papers in Virginia Historical Society).

12. Harrison v. Day, 200 Va. 439, 106 S.E.2d 636 (1959); James v. Almond, 170 F. Supp. 331 (E.D. Va. 1959).

13. Letter from C. Stuart Wheatley to J. Lindsay Almond, September 22, 1958 (Almond Executive Papers in Virginia State Library).

massive resistance to a program of containment, the Old Dominion was successful in holding school integration to token levels during the early 1960's.[14]

Danville's first modern experience with racial integration took place during 1960 in the city's public libraries, and the degree of municipal opposition did not bode well for more ambitious integration plans. The city had long maintained two libraries: the main library—the Confederate Memorial Library—reserved for whites, and a small branch library for Negroes. Each library issued its own cards, which were restricted to use in the issuing library. On April 2 a group of black students attempted to use the facilities of the Confederate Memorial Library. The city manager responded by temporarily closing the main library. Two days later, the city council reopened the main library but limited access to the present holders of library cards.[15] The Negroes filed suit in federal district court alleging that they were subject to unlawful discrimination in their use of the municipal library facilities. In May, Judge Roby C. Thompson directed Danville to cease practicing racial discrimination in the operation of its libraries and to permit all persons with library cards to use the main library.[16] Responding unanimously to the decision, the city council closed both libraries on May 20, just prior to the effective date of the court order, and scheduled a June advisory referendum to consider the fate of the libraries. The referendum produced a vigorous campaign by Negroes and a small number of whites who urged voters to keep the libraries open. The June 14 balloting showed the strong segregationist convictions of Danville whites: 2,829 votes were cast for keeping the libraries shut, 1,598 votes supported reopening on an integrated basis. Armed with the referendum results, the council voted five-four the following day to keep the libraries closed. Here the matter rested until September when the council, by another five-four vote, reopened the libraries but removed all the chairs and tables.[17]

Although the battle of the library ultimately was resolved in favor of racial integration, similar movement did not take place in

---

14. By the fall of 1963 only an estimated 3,721 Virginia Negro pupils, or 1.57% of the total, were in school with white students. SOUTHERN SCHOOL NEWS, (Dec. 1963).

15. For the municipal ordinance of April 4 restricting use of public library facilities see 5 RACE REL. L. REP. 528 (1960).

16. Giles v. Library Advisory Committee, 5 RACE REL. L. REP. 1140 (W.D. Va. 1960).

17. For the library controversy see G. Powell, Black Cloud over Danville—the Negro Movement in Danville, Virginia, in 1963, (unpublished thesis in University of Richmond Library) [hereinafter cited as Powell, Black Cloud Over Danville]; SOUTHERN SCHOOL NEWS at 10-15, 75 (June-Oct. 1960); N.Y. Times, May 20, 1960, at 27, June 15, 1960, at 28, September 18, 1960, at 72.

other areas of municipal life. In the spring of 1963 the hotels, motels, motion picture theatres, hospitals, public schools, courthouses and prison farms remained rigidly segregated.[18] All agencies of municipal government and the entire seventy-man police force were white. Danville Negroes also charged that the city and private employers discriminated against blacks in employment practices. Negro petitions to city council seeking redress of their complaints were ignored. Nine years after the *Brown* ruling, the civil rights currents had somehow bypassed Danville. It appeared to be an example of effective nullification of an unpopular judicial trend, the very goal that Virginia's massive resistance had sought in vain.

The Birmingham demonstrations were the catalyst for the outbreak of similar disturbances in Danville as Negroes took to the streets in this segregationist stronghold.[19] The initial march took place on May 31; it was peaceful and no arrests were made. The local press ignored the first marches. During the hot and muggy month of June, however, the demonstrations grew more disorderly and took the form of marches, singing and chanting, mass picketing, trespass on private property, sit-ins (including one in the city manager's office), and impeding traffic and downtown business. Danville's Municipal Building became the focal point of the disturbances. These almost daily events soon exacerbated the already tense race relations in Danville. On the evening of June 5, the Negro demonstrators sat down on a main business street, blocking all traffic. At this point the police summoned Archibald M. Aiken, judge of the Corporation Court of Danville. Aiken addressed the crowd and asked the demonstrators to disperse.[20] This command

---

18. The initial desegregation of Danville public schools was not the result of litigation. On June 19, 1963, the Pupil Placement Board assigned 10 Negro students to 4 white schools. When Danville schools opened August 26 this limited integration proceeded without incident. One can only speculate whether the demonstrations were a factor in the action of the Board. It seems unlikely that the demonstrations were a prime cause of school integration in Danville because, by 1963, Virginia had abandoned massive resistance and was following a policy of token integration. The Board made similar pupil assignments in other localities which did not experience racial disorders. School integration moved slowly in Danville for the balance of the decade. For a history of school desegregation in Danville see Medley v. School Board, 350 F. Supp. 34 (W.D. Va. 1972), *Rev'd* 482 F.2d 1061 (4th Cir. 1973), *cert. denied* 414 U.S. 1172 (1974).

19. The Danville *Register* castigated the Birmingham disorders and praised the city authorities for maintaining order "in a responsible manner." Danville Register, May 14, 1963.

20. Aiken appeared pursuant to § 18.1-247 of the Code of Virginia which provided:

Suppression of riots.—All judges and justices of the peace may suppress riots, routs, and unlawful assemblies within their jurisdiction. And it shall be the duty of each of them to go among, or as near as may be with safety to, persons riotously, tumultously, or unlawfully assembled, and in the name of the law command them to disperse; and if they shall not thereupon immediately and peacefully disperse, such judge or justice of

was ignored and Aiken was jeered. The next day, upon application by the city, Aiken issued ex parte a temporary injunction limiting the scope of the demonstrations.[21] This injunction provided the principal ground for the numerous arrests made by city authorities in the course of the summer.

More than any other person, Judge Aiken symbolized the determination of Danville whites and the city administration to crush the Negro protests. A native of Danville and the son of a judge, Aiken received his undergraduate and legal education at the University of Virginia. He had served as a Circuit Court judge and as the city attorney before being named judge of the Corporation Court by the

---

the peace giving the command, and any other present, shall command the assistance of all persons present, and of the sheriff or sergeant of the county or corporation, with his posse, if need be, in arresting and securing those so assembled. If any person present, on being required to give his assistance depart or fail to obey, he shall be deemed a rioter. VA. CODE ANN. § 18.1-247 (1950) (repealed 1968). This section was repealed in 1968 as part of a general revision of the laws dealing with riots.

21. "This day came the plaintiff, by Counsel, and presented to the Court its motion for a temporary injunction and restraining order, which motion was verified and upon the presentation and consideration of said verified motion and affidavit of T. Edward Temple, City Manager of the City of Danville;

"Upon due consideration whereof it appearing to the Court that the plaintiff herein is entitled to the temporary injunction and restraining order prayed for and that under the circumstances of this case, no notice to said named defendants herein is necessary or practicable, it is ADJUDGED, ORDERED and DECREED as follows:

"1. That said named defendants, their servants, agents and employees, their attorneys and all other persons acting in concert therewith be, and they hereby are, enjoined and restrained until the further order of this Court from participating in the following actions or conduct:

(a) Unlawfully assembling in an unauthorized manner on the public streets and in the vicinity of the public buildings of the City of Danville;

(b) Unlawful interference with the lawful operation of private enterprises and business in the City of Danville;

(c) Unlawfully obstructing the freedom of movement of the general public of the City of Danville and the general traffic of the City of Danville;

(d) Unlawfully obstructing the entrances and exits to and from both private business concerns and public facilities in the City of Danville;

(e) Participating in and inciting mob violence, rioting and inciting persons to rioting;

(f) Unlawfully carrying deadly weapons, threatening to use said deadly weapons, assaulting divers citizens in this community;

(g) Unlawfully using loud and boisterous language interrupting the peace and repose of the citizens of the community, business establishments of the community and the public works of the community;

(h) Creating and maintaining a public nuisance by reason of unlawful and unauthorized gatherings and loud, boisterous and concerted demonstrations interferring with the peace and quiet and enjoyment of the citizens of the City of Danville.

"2. This temporary injunction and restraining order shall be effective immediately and shall continue from day to day until the further order of this Court until July 6, 1963, at which time it shall stand dissolved unless prior thereto it be enlarged or further temporary or permanent injunction granted herein.

"3. And that a copy of this Order be served upon the named defendants herein."
8 RACE REL. L. REP. 435 (1963).

legislature in 1950.[22] As was the case with nearly all Virginia state judges, Aiken was an ally of Senator Byrd and held conservative social and political views.[23] Moreover, Aiken was unquestionably committed to the defense of racial segregation. In early 1959 he privately proposed a plan to "keep the public schools of Virginia permanently open and segregated, and be [sic] federal court proof."[24] Aiken's plan was designed to take advantage of the superior economic position of Virginia whites. The Judge suggested these specific steps:

1. Repeal of Section 129 of the Virginia Constitution, the section which mandated public education.
2. Repeal of the compulsory school attendance law.
3. The legislature, or localities, should impose a school tax on every child, regardless of race, who attends a public school.
4. This school tax should be a credit against the payment of state income taxes or local real property taxes.

"I imagine," Aiken explained, "most of the Negroes who have been getting a free education at the expense of the White people either could not and would not pay it." He further envisioned a limited scholarship plan for the poor, and white sponsorship of black pupils so long as they attended separate schools. Aiken reasoned that his proposal should be viewed as a revenue measure, not merely a device to prevent integration. Coming in the final, emotional days of the massive resistance controversy and raising a host of new problems, Aiken's ideas never had much chance of being adopted into law. Nonetheless, Byrd evidently found Aiken's proposal sufficiently intriguing to circulate it among his Virginia colleagues in Washington.[25] Later the same year Aiken criticized Virginia's tactical retreat from massive resistance and renewed his call for an amendment to the Virginia Constitution.[26] There can be no doubt

---

22. Danville Register, November 28, 1971.

23. In October of 1964 Aiken expressed his highest regards to Byrd and promised to do anything he could to assist Byrd's re-election bid. Aiken predicted that Byrd and Senator Barry Goldwater, the Republican presidential nominee, would carry Danville handily. Letter from Archibald M. Aiken to Harry F. Byrd, October 13, 1964 (Harry F. Byrd Papers in University of Virginia Library).

24. Letter from Archibald M. Aiken to Harry F. Byrd, January 24, 1959 (Watkins M. Abbitt Papers in University of Richmond Library).

25. William M. Tuck, congressman for Virginia's Fifth District (which included Danville), wrote to Byrd: "Many thanks for letting me see Judge Aiken's letter. I think he is undoubtedly hitting at them in the right way. His plan is worthy of serious consideration." Letter from Tuck to Byrd, January 28, 1959 (Watkins M. Abbitt Papers in University of Richmond Library).

26. Letter from Archibald M. Aiken to Harry F. Byrd, March 25, 1959 (Watkins M. Abbitt Papers in University of Richmond Library).

that Aiken found the tactics and objectives of the Negro protesters very distasteful.

Despite Judge Aiken's temporary injunction, the disorders did not cease. On the night of June 10, after a full day of protest activity, a demonstration ended in violence as police attacked Negroes massed outside the city jail with nightsticks and fire hoses.[27] The quickening tempo of events in mid-June underscored the unyielding municipal resistance. First, a special seven-man grand jury summoned by Aiken indicted the demonstration leaders under a Virginia statute outlawing conspiracy "to incite the colored population of the State to acts of violence and war against the white population. . . ."[28] For those indicted Aiken set bail at 5,000 dollars apiece.[29] Secondly, on June 11 a heavily armed detachment of forty-eight state police moved into Danville to supplement the local force. Thirdly, the city council enacted an ordinance to limit the time, place, and size of picketing or demonstrations.[30] Lastly, Councilman

---

27. Len Holt makes a convincing case that the Danville police overreacted and unnecessarily beat Negro demonstrators with clubs on the evening of June 10. L. HOLT, AN ACT OF CONSCIENCE 23-25, 93-95 (1965). Burke Marshall, Assistant Attorney General, Civil Rights Division, seems to have agreed with this assessment. In a September 18, 1963 memorandum to the Attorney General Marshall declared: "However, I am trying to develop a broader kind of case against this sort of repressive and violent police action. We have one, for example, in Danville, Virginia." Memorandum, September 18, 1963 (Burke Marshall Papers in John F. Kennedy Library). The Fourth Circuit concurred in this evaluation. "On that occasion the police were guilty of excesses, as the demonstrators had been on earlier occasions." Baines v. City of Danville, 337 F.2d 579, 584 (4th Cir. 1964), cert. denied 381 U.S. 939 (1965).

28. VA. CODE ANN. § 18.1-422 (1950).

29. 60 Danville Common Law Order Book, Corporation Court at 111-12, 139-40.

30. "An Ordinance Limiting Picketing and Demonstrations; Providing Punishment for Violations Thereof.

"WHEREAS, large, noisy, lawless and rioting groups of people, there being among these armed persons with records as habitual criminals, under the pretext of picketing, have incited racial strife, caused personal injuries and destruction of property; and,

"WHEREAS, such groups have further disrupted the peace and convenience of this community, have placed the citizenry in fear of its safety and have disrupted the orderly flow of both vehicular and pedestrian traffic; and,

"WHEREAS, there are reasonable restraints which must be imposed upon freedom of speech and assembly when such freedoms are exercised in such a manner as to endanger the personal safety and property of the citizenry; and,

"WHEREAS, it is necessary to impose reasonable regulations upon assemblies and picketing.

"NOW, THEREFORE, BE IT ORDAINED, as follows:

"(1) All assemblies and picketing shall be peaceful and unattended by noise and boisterousness, and there shall be no shouting, clapping or singing of such a nature as to disturb the peace and tranquility of the community; and,

"(2) That marching shall be in single file and pickets or demonstrators shall be spaced a distance of not less than ten feet apart, and not more than six pickets shall picket or demonstrate before any given place of business or [public facility]; and,

"(3) That all picketing or demonstrating shall be during the business or work hours of

John W. Carter, a vitriolic segregationist who was determined to crush the protests, moved to the fore as the principal spokesman for the city administration. Playing to the racial attitudes of Danville whites, Carter's popular following undercut more moderate councilmen and rendered a compromise solution impossible. Carter also helped to represent the city in the voluminous litigation which emerged from the disorders.

As the demonstrations continued, so did the arrests for violation of the Aiken injunction and the newly enacted ordinance. By June 17 there were 105 persons under arrest and awaiting trial before Judge Aiken on charges of contempt. The defendants were represented by five Danville Negro lawyers affiliated with the NAACP, by Len W. Holt, a black attorney from Norfolk,[31] and by a shifting group of civil rights attorneys that included William M. Kunstler. The proceedings in the Corporation Court proved extremely controversial and figured prominently in the subsequent efforts to remove the injunction cases to the federal district court. Although a removal petition had already been filed, and although he was without jurisdiction in the matter, Aiken began to try the cases of persons charged with disobeying his injunction. A Justice Department official related the courtroom setting to his superiors:[32]

> The proceedings before Judge Aiken have been extraordinary. The judge has entered a formal written order excluding the public from the courtroom

---

the place of business or public facility being picketed, and upon such days as such facility may be open for the transaction of business; and,

"(4) That no picketing or demonstrating shall be performed within any public building; and,

"(5) That no person under the age of eighteen years shall be permitted to march, picket or demonstrate in the City; and,

"(6) That no vehicles shall be used in any picket or demonstrating line, and that all picketers or demonstrators shall be afoot; and,

"(7) That violation of the foregoing regulations shall constitute a misdemeanor, and be punished as provided in Section 1-6 of the Code of the City of Danville, 1962."
8 RACE REL. L. REP. 698 (1963).

31. Holt was in the unique position of being both an attorney for the defendants and a defendant himself. He was arrested for violating the Aiken injunction and indicted under the racial conspiracy statute. Holt was already in trouble with the courts of Virginia. In January of 1962 he was found guilty of contempt of court and fined by the Circuit Court of the City of Hopewell. The Virginia Supreme Court of Appeals affirmed the sentence, 205 Va. 332, 136 S.E.2d 809 (1964), but the Supreme Court reversed on the grounds that, on the facts presented therein, Holt could not be punished for contempt consistent with due process. Holt v. Commonwealth of Virginia, 381 U.S. 131 (1965). Holt's conviction under the Aiken injunction was reversed by the Virginia Supreme Court of Appeals. Holt v. Commonwealth, 72 Danville Common Law Order Book, Corporation Court, 29-45.

32. Memorandum, June 19, 1963 (Burke Marshall Papers in John F. Kennedy Library). For the text of the order excluding the general public from the courtroom on the grounds that "there is danger of unlawful interference with the lawful operation of this Court" see 60 Danville Common Law Order Book, Corporation Court, 131 (1963).

because of unrest and possible violence. The only ones admitted are city personnel, court attaches, the defendants, their attorneys, witnesses, and the parents of juvenile defendants.

Witnesses, and even attorneys, are frisked for weapons. All of the city personnel, however, wear sidearms. The last two days there have been approximately 30 armed police in the courtroom. Judge Aiken has been wearing a pistol while presiding on the bench.[33]

In the course of June 17 and 18 Aiken tried two cases and both defendants were found guilty of contempt. The court imposed forty-five- and sixty-day jail sentences on the convicted defendants, together with fines.[34] Aiken permitted no discussion of the legality of his injunction and denied defense requests for an adjournment to prepare its case. In passing sentence, the judge read from a written memorandum prepared in advance of the trial. Aiken refused to release the convicted defendants on bail pending appeal reasoning that "any such suspension of the judgement would render the injunctive powers of the Court ineffective . . . ."[35] Without a stay of execution, the defendants would be compelled to serve their sentences before an appeal could be heard by the Virginia Supreme Court of Appeals, effectively denying appellate review. Moreover, Aiken refused to allow out-of-state attorneys to practice in the Corporation Court unless they produced their certificates of admission to the bar. He also conducted daily roll calls of all defendants and their attorneys, forcing the latter to waste valuable time in court. "Danville's Negroes," Kunstler wrote, "were in the grip of a reign of judicial terror."[36]

On June 19, Aiken postponed further trials for the contempt defendants, apparently planning to abide the outcome of the removal proceedings. With the trials stalled, Danville pressed other tactics to disquiet the demonstrators. Up to half of the protestors were of high school age and within the purview of the juvenile laws. Parents of such young demonstrators were arrested on charges of contributing to the delinquency of a minor by failing properly to supervise their children. In late June the first administrative level of the Virginia Employment Commission cut off unemployment in-

---

33. Aiken denied that he had ever worn a gun while on the bench, but he readily admitted that, upon police advice, he traveled armed to his office. Indeed, virtually every city official began wearing pistols in June. Although avowedly for protection, this policy of going armed was likely to have a chilling effect on the Negro demonstrations. Martin Luther King recalled: "Danville, Virginia—upright white citizens, concerned that police brutality is unsufficient to intimidate Negroes, began wearing guns in their belts." M. KING, JR., WHY WE CAN'T WAIT at 126 (1964).
34. 60 Danville Common Law Order Book, Corporation Court, 131-133 (1963).
35. *Id.* at 132.
36. W. KUNSTLER, DEEP IN MY HEART 218 (1966).

surance checks for those awaiting trial. The Commission reasoned that persons under arrest and facing possible jail terms were not "available" for work within the meaning of Virginia's unemployment insurance law. With seasonal unemployment falling heavily on Danville Negroes, the action of the Commission weakened the financial basis of the protest and tended to discourage new demonstrations.[37]

Although the Danville demonstrations were of spontaneous origin, the various civil rights groups promptly formulated a series of demands for city officials. The announced objectives of the protest included:

1. The appointment of a bi-racial committee to fix a schedule for the desegregation of schools and municipal facilities.
2. Desegregation of public accommodations, such as restaurants and hotels.
3. The employment of Negroes in municipal jobs, particularly the hiring of Negro policemen.
4. The hiring or upgrading of Negro employees by Danville merchants.
5. The dropping of all charges against the demonstrators who had been arrested.[38]

The demonstration leaders further charged that Dan River Mills had a discriminatory hiring policy under which blacks were confined to menial jobs. To dramatize this complaint against the textile company, in July civil rights organizations picketed the New York City offices of Dan River Mills demanding that the concern use its influence to end segregation in Danville.[39] Local blacks picketed and conducted sit-ins before the gates of Dan River Mills.

Obviously, several of the objectives of the demonstrators did not relate to state or municipal activities, but rather to private employers and privately owned accommodations. The city, of course, had no direct control over the operations of such private facilities. With respect to alleged private discrimination, the demonstrations both highlighted the problem and impeded its solution. Merchants, for example, worried that the white public was so angry at the demonstrators that the employment of Negro store clerks might become economically hazardous. Those demands directed squarely against the city raised a similar difficulty. Token steps

---
37. Powell, Black Cloud over Danville, *supra* note 17, at 43.
38. For the demands of Negro protestors in Danville see *id.* at 33; L. HOLT, AN ACT OF CONSCIENCE 142 (1965).
39. N.Y. Times, July 18, 1963, at 10.

might have been taken, especially in the employment area, to meet some of the protest goals. Danville officials, however, rejected any moves that might be interpreted as a concession to the racial disorders. Thus, while the demonstrations continued, the city offered no hint of a compromise solution and turned instead to a determined and ingenious effort to break up the protests. Benjamin Muse described the city's viewpoint:

> The whites feel that the Negroes should be punished for the June disorders rather than rewarded with concessions. They are not irrevocably opposed to the moves desired by the Negroes, but refuse to discuss them under pressure.[40]

In keeping with this philosophy, the city authorities never considered the demand that charges pending against the demonstrators be dropped.

A fair example of this municipal attitude is the handling of the demand for the hiring of black policemen. Muse reported in October that "[t]he city has no objection in principle, but it does not want to move while 'under the gun.' I gather that the Negro policeman will be hired shortly, but it must be in a routine way . . . ."[41] As if to confirm this assessment, later that same month, and with the disorders at an end, Danville employed a Negro policeman. In this anticlimactic fashion the demonstrators gained partial satisfaction of one of their major demands.

From the outset of the demonstrations Danville Negroes hoped for a visit from Martin Luther King, fresh from his seeming triumph in Birmingham. Indeed, King had spoken before a large crowd in this troubled city in March. After several postponements, King paid a return visit to Danville on July 11, ostensibly to lead a march in defiance of the Aiken injunction. "I have so many injunctions that I don't even look at them anymore," he declared.[42] Danville, however, was not to be a success for King. His mass demonstration on the night of July 11 drew only about eighty participants and King declined to lead the march. Coming at the very time that he was receiving massive publicity and was catapulting toward the apex of his civil rights career, King found that he could not devote sustained personal attention to the demonstrations. Historian David L. Lewis regards King's Danville campaign as a failure and compares the result there with Albany, Georgia, another disappointment for

---

40. Confidential memorandum entitled "Danville, Va." from Benjamin Muse to Burke Marshall, October 8, 1963 (Burke Marshall Papers in John F. Kennedy Library) [hereinafter cited as Muse, Danville, Va.]. Muse, an author and journalist of liberal racial views, prepared a series of reports for the Justice Department on the situation in various southern cities.
41. *Id.*
42. D. LEWIS, KING: A CRITICAL BIOGRAPHY 212 (1970).

King.[43] With King's inability to furnish effective assistance, the prospect for any meaningful success resulting from the Danville disorders was greatly lessened.

White attitudes, on the other hand, remained adamant throughout the period of the demonstrations. The disorders and marches failed to arouse support from any level of the city's white population. The local newspapers poured scorn on the protest at every turn, linking the demonstrations with crime and communism. Mayor Julian R. Stinson referred to the protestors as "hoodlums."[44] "The anti-Negro feeling at the middle-class and country club level is intense . . . ," Muse reported in October.[45] At the zenith of the controversy over Judge Aiken's conduct of the contempt trials, the Danville Bar Association adopted a resolution expressing "its support and admiration of the Honorable A. M. Aiken and of the extremely able and judicious manner in which he conducts his court, thus assuring a fair and impartial trial to every defendant, regardless of race, color, or creed."[46] No resident white lawyer took any part in the defense of the demonstrators. Likewise, the white textile workers were hostile to the civil rights campaign. Holt explained:

> For the most part the Danville textile workers are complacent members of a complacement textile workers union who consider themselves well off. . . . The Negro is both their standard and their *enemy*. Realizing this, they are told by *City Hall* that Negroes are trying to force their way into the union and thus destroy the seniority rights of the white members and their right to pass on their trades to their sons, along with forcing their daughters to sit beside Negro children in the public schools.[47]

The reaction of whites elsewhere in Virginia to the Negro demonstrations paralleled that of the Danville leaders. Virginia had generally avoided mass demonstrations and civil rights violence, and the surprised state officials reacted with dismay and support for the City of Danville. Congressman William M. Tuck commended Danville authorities for "the forthright manner" in which they dealt with the protest. Tuck was confident that the disorders could "be traced directly to troublemakers in Washington and elsewhere who have been preaching enforced integration against the will of the most thoughtful people of both races."[48] He was even moved to

---
43. *Id.* at 211-14; *see* HOLT, AN ACT OF CONSCIENCE 205-07 (1965); N.Y. Times, July 12, 1963, at 8.
44. N.Y. Times, June 11, 1963, at 22.
45. Muse, Danville, Va.
46. "Resolutions of Bar Association of Danville," 109 Cong. Rec. 12211 (1963) (remarks of Senator A. Willis Robertson).
47. L. HOLT, AN ACT OF CONSCIENCE 227 (1965).
48. Powell, Black Cloud Over Danville, *supra* note 17, at 29.

introduce legislation that would bar persons from crossing a state line for the purpose of demonstrating in violation of law. "When I consider the disgraceful concerted defiance of law which has occurred in communities such as Danville, Va., in my own Congressional district," Tuck declared, "it is perfectly obvious that the participants are responding to incitation from outsiders . . . ."[49] Similarly, United States Senator A. Willis Robertson observed: ". . . the trouble you have experienced in Danville recently was the result of outside agitation . . . ."[50]

The response of the state government was largely determined by Albertis S. Harrison, Jr., the Old Dominion's cautious and quiet governor. Cognizant of the importance of maintaining the favorable national image of Virginia, Harrison characteristically followed a low-key path. He eschewed the flamboyant role and the defiant statements that became the trademarks of Governor George C. Wallace in Alabama. Harrison realized that a relaxed executive attitude would minimize the prospects for extensive national press coverage of events in Danville, and thereby give Danville officials a freer hand to deal with the demonstrations. As the prospect for sensational press coverage dimmed, so did the chance for federal intervention. While Harrison sent state police to Danville, he publicly emphasized that better education and understanding were the solution to racial harmony. He declined to encourage the formation of bi-racial committees in Virginia communities. Harrison's desire to call as little attention as possible to the Danville disorders is best illustrated by his correspondence with State Senator William F. Stone, who represented the embattled city in the legislature. Stone called upon the governor "to make very strong statements denouncing what is going on in Danville . . . ."[51] Harrison replied that "I am as deeply conscious of what is going on in Danville as you are," but he significantly added:

> There is a great deal that I would like to say publicly about this matter. However, a Governor cannot always indulge himself that luxury.[52]

He further advised the mayor of neighboring Farmville that he doubted "the wisdom of too much activity on our part when such might provoke demonstrations."[53]

---

49. 109 Cong. Rec. 13429 (1963) (remarks of Congressman Tuck).
50. Letter from A. Willis Robertson to Landon R. Wyatt, July 11, 1963 (A. Willis Robertson Papers in College of William and Mary).
51. Letter from William F. Stone to Albertis S. Harrison, Jr., June 17, 1963 (Harrison Executive Papers in Virginia State Library).
52. Letter from Albertis S. Harrison, Jr. to William F. Stone, June 19, 1963 (Harrison Executive Papers in Virginia State Library).
53. Letter from Albertis S. Harrison, Jr. to William F. Watkins, Jr., June 20, 1963 (Harrison Executive Papers in Virginia State Library).

Harrison's thinking on the racial disorders is most fully set forth in the draft of a statement prepared for delivery on television, a speech that the governor ultimately decided not to deliver.[54] In his draft remarks Harrison offered the following comments on the situation in Danville:

1. He deplored the outbreak of racial violence in Virginia.
2. He pledged to the Negro demonstrators that "Virginia will see to it that your rights of free speech and peaceable assembly are protected to the fullest extent of the law."
3. He promised to protect the owners of private property against trespass or seizure of their place of business.
4. He stressed that the fourteenth amendment applies only to state action.
5. He defined the limits of freedom of speech:

> By this I mean to say that free speech will be protected, but the cursing and abusing of law enforcement officers will not be tolerated in this State. The right to peaceable assembly will be made fully secure, but we shall not permit mob violence to be masked as peaceable assembly. A right to demonstrate will not be equated, in Virginia, with some imagined right to take effective possession of private property. The right to petition for redress of grievances will not be converted into a license to intimidate, to coerce, and to extort. The right of protesting groups to walk the streets in freedom will not be made superior to the right of all men to walk the streets in safety.

6. He alerted units of the Virginia National Guard for possible riot duty and, contrary to his earlier position, he now urged that cities and counties consider creating bi-racial committees.
7. He concluded by saying that social "changes of this magnitude cannot successfully be imposed by compulsion, by coercion, or by the suppression of any of the rights with which free men are endowed."

Harrison's undelivered remarks indicate a painstaking effort to evaluate the first amendment rights of the Danville community and the owners of private property. Orderly, but not massive or riotous, picketing and demonstrations were to be permitted and protected. Although Harrison correctly emphasized that trespass and blocking the streets were not to be confused with freedom of expression,[55]

---

54. "Draft of a statement, intended for use on television, that might possibly be delivered by Governor Harrison, dealing with the racial disorders" (Harrison Executive Papers in Virginia State Library).
55. Compare Harrison's comments with a similar analysis of the Fourth Circuit: "Those First Amendment rights incorporated into the Fourteenth Amendment, however, are not a license to trample upon the rights of others. They must be exercised responsibly and without depriving others of their rights, the enjoyment of which is equally as precious." The court

nothing in the governor's comments constituted a threat to suppress reasonable speech and protest activities. Rather, his message called for mutual accommodation for the various legitimate interests involved in the controversy. Of course, Harrison's views did not necessarily reflect those of the Danville authorities, but they tend to establish that the state government was not itself a party to any design to crush the first amendment rights of the demonstrators. The most likely explanation for Harrison's decision not to deliver the speech is the governor's belief that any television talk, regardless of its content, would serve to highlight and possibly enflame the Danville situation.

By early July it was evident that the demonstrations had utterly failed to achieve their announced objectives. Although the disorders and consequent arrests continued on a sporadic basis, they gradually diminished. With bail money nearly gone and most potential protesters already awaiting trial, it became progressively more difficult to find Negroes willing to march. The reopening of the public schools in late August deprived the protest of a major source of demonstrators. Despite the flagging level of protest activities, city policy continued to be aggressive. On July 10, the city council amended the ordinance regulating permits for parades. The amendment specified that applications for a parade permit must be filed "not less than thirty days nor more than sixty days" before the date of the proposed parade.[56] Arrests for parading without a permit supplemented the city's other tactics. A special August report in the *New York Times* described Danville "as an example of successful resistance to Negro demonstrations demanding equality." The *Times* noted that Danville had developed "a defense strategy that is among the most unyielding, ingenious, legalistic and effective of any city in the South."[57]

The Resort to the Federal Courts

Almost immediately, the attorneys for the Danville demonstrators sought to enlist federal jurisdiction as a shield for protest activities. The proceedings before Judge Aiken and the other state and municipal actions indicated that defense efforts would not meet with success at the local state court level. Moreover, the inevitable

---

pointed out that Negro demonstrators did not have any right "to coerce acceptance of their demands through violence or threats of violence." Baines v. City of Danville, 337 F.2d 579, 586 (4th Cir. 1964), *cert. denied*, 381 U.S. 939 (1965).

56. The text of the parade permit ordinance may be found in York v. City of Danville, 207 Va. 665, 152 S.E.2d 259, 261 (1967).

57. N.Y. Times, August 11, 1963, at 71, col. 1.

delays and expenses of carrying hundreds of appeals to the Virginia Supreme Court of Appeals certainly would sap the energy and resources of the protest. One commentator has concluded that "the most prominent characteristic of state courts in the South is that a Negro will not voluntarily bring them a dispute involving his civil rights."[58] This was certainly true in Virginia, where the task of implementing racial desegregation was almost exclusively a federal court responsibility. Accordingly, the protesters attempted to fashion procedures that would produce federal court intervention. They filed a petition to remove the cases of those charged with violating the Aiken injunction to federal court on the ground that a fair trial could not be obtained in the Corporation Court. They filed original federal suits attacking the constitutionality of the Danville ordinance limiting picketing, attacking the Aiken injunction, attacking the Virginia racial conspiracy statute, and attacking the administrative decision to terminate unemployment compensation for demonstrators under arrest. In July the demonstrators brought suit to restrain enforcement of the parade ordinance, contending that it was used to suppress lawful demonstrations. Holt explained the strategy of the Negroes:

> We were fighting. This action had enhanced the probability of intervention of the federal government . . . . As Danville would pass or invoke a law, the lawyers would scamper to the federal courts with a suit.[59]

Hence, one of the principal legal questions posed by the demonstrations was whether the defendants could establish some theory to secure federal court intervention in the Danville situation. This struggle was confusing and prolonged, and ultimately the Supreme Court gave a negative answer.

The various applications for federal relief were presented to Judge Thomas J. Michie of Charlottesville. A graduate of the University of Virginia, Michie had practiced law in Charlottesville since the 1920's. A member of the Democratic Party, Michie had served as mayor of Charlottesville in the late 1950's, a period in which he gained the reputation of a moderate on racial integration. Michie had earned the enmity of the Byrd organization by opposing the school closings in Charlottesville pursuant to massive resistance and by supporting John F. Kennedy for the presidency.[60] In fact, when

---

58. Meltsner, *Southern Appellate Courts: A Dead End*, in SOUTHERN JUSTICE 138 (L. Friedman ed. 1965).
59. L. HOLT, AN ACT OF CONSCIENCE 177 (1965).
60. Letter from Francis P. Miller to Ralph A. Dungan, December 21, 1960 (Miller Papers in University of Virginia).

President Kennedy nominated Michie to the federal bench in 1961 Virginia conservatives urged their senators to defeat confirmation of the appointment. One constituent informed Senator Robertson that Michie had always been opposed to conservative government.[61] The president of the Defenders of State Sovereignty and Individual Liberty, a segregationist lobby in the Old Dominion, asserted that the appointment of Michie to a federal judgeship would be extremely unfortunate.[62] Such expressions of opposition were to no avail, and Michie was duly confirmed, but they do underscore the liberal image which Michie had acquired. As Kennedy's first appointment to the federal district bench in Virginia, one could reasonably expect that he would be more sympathetic to the plight of the Negro demonstrators than any other federal judge in the Old Dominion.

Acting first on the petition to remove the criminal proceedings to federal court, Michie declined to take immediate action on the city's motion for remand and scheduled a hearing in Danville on June 24 to receive evidence on the question. During the two day hearing, the protesters' attorneys called witnesses to show that their clients could not obtain a fair trial before Judge Aiken. Michie reserved judgment on the general removal problem, but granted writs of habeas corpus for the two defendants convicted by Aiken after their cases had been removed.[63] Yet the Aiken injunction and the municipal ordinance curtailing demonstrations remained in effect, and Michie's steps did not preclude further arrests. In a move without modern precedent, the Justice Department filed a brief supporting the removal effort. The brief reviewed the courtroom proceedings before Aiken and asserted that the trials were being "conducted in a most unjudicial atmosphere."[64] Contending that the Negro demonstrators could not receive a fair trial in the Corporation Court, the brief concluded:

> The combination of the trier of the fact who has apparently prejudged the issues and was a participant in the events culminating in the very charges to be tried, considered together with the general atmosphere of the proceedings and its inevitable result, make it quite clear, it seems to us, that a fair trial cannot be had in the Corporation Court. But that is not all. It is not simply that whatever rights defendants have to demonstrate for the equal protection

---

61. Letter from John B. Boatwright, Jr. to A. Willis Robertson, February 13, 1961 (Robertson Papers in College of William and Mary).

62. Letter from Robert B. Crawford to A. Willis Robertson, February 10, 1961 (Robertson Papers in College of William and Mary).

63. L. HOLT, AN ACT OF CONSCIENCE 6-40 (1965); W. KUNSTLER, DEEP IN MY HEART 221-22 (1966).

64. The Justice Department brief is reprinted in part in W. KUNSTLER, DEEP IN MY HEART at 219-21. *See also* N.Y. Times, July 3, 1963, at 10.

of the laws will be disregarded in the contempt trials. The situation is further aggravated by the fact that racial antagonism lies at the root of this denial. The entire controversy now before this Court stems from the conflict over Negro equality, and the proceedings in the Corporation Court which are here challenged are a direct result of this conflict. We do not suggest that Judge Aiken is racially prejudiced against the defendants; but a Court would have to close its eyes to the realities not to notice that the peculiar proceedings in the Corporation Court are the direct result of this racial conflict.

The Danville Bar Association responded to the Justice Department brief by denouncing the "unwarranted, irresponsible and unjust attack" on Aiken, and proceeded to censure the representatives of the Justice Department for making such statements.[65]

Judge Michie's next action absolutely stunned the demonstrators. News that Martin Luther King would lead a march in early July prompted Danville to seek a federal court order curtailing further demonstrations. On July 2 Michie rendered a federal injunction against the Negro protest movement on the ground that the disorders denied others in Danville federally protected rights. Almost as broad as the earlier Aiken order, the Michie injunction prohibited obstructing traffic, use of public facilities or private property, "unnecessarily loud, objectionable, offensive, and insulting noises," inciting any person to riot, and meetings at which violations of the laws of Virginia or Danville or of the federal court order were advocated.[66] The Michie injunction complicated the plight of the Negro protesters.[67] The Justice Department declined to "take any legal action to suspend issuance of the restraining order," and a representative of the Department advised Len Holt that "in my judgment, the defendants would be obliged to obey any order issued by Judge Michie whether they thought it legally sound or not and

---

65. "Resolutions of Bar Association of Danville," 109 CONG. REC. 12211 (1963) (Remarks of Senator Robertson).
66. Powell, Black Cloud Over Danville, *supra* note 17, at 47.
67. Michie's course of action was perhaps influenced by a similar injunction issued by Federal District Judge J. Robert Elliott against mass racial demonstrations in Albany, Georgia. In a suit filed by the mayor of Albany, Elliott granted a sweeping temporary order on July 20, 1962 restraining demonstration leaders from continuing to incite or encourage unlawful picketing or parading, and from engaging in acts designed to produce breaches of the peace. The suit was brought under the federal civil rights act and alleged that organized breaches of the peace had prevented city authorities from carrying out governmental functions and from according equal protection of the law to all citizens. Chief Judge Elbert P. Tuttle of the Fifth Circuit set aside the restraining order on July 24 on the basis that no federal question was raised by the complaint. Evidently neither Elliott nor Tuttle prepared formal opinions to support their actions. The events in Albany, however, may be traced in Kelly v. Page, 9 RACE REL. L. REP. 1115 (M.D. Ga., 1963), *aff'd in part, remanded in part*, 335 F.2d 114 (5th Cir. 1964). *See* N.Y. Times, July 22, 1962 at 32.

would have to pursue their remedies in the court."[68] Now confronted with two injunctions against the demonstrations, the protest leaders hurriedly asked Michie to dissolve his order. When Michie refused, Kunstler carried the matter before Chief Judge Simon E. Sobeloff of the Fourth Circuit. After hearing Kunstler, Sobeloff had a private telephone conversation with Michie, the substance of which was never disclosed. Apparently as a result of this conversation, Michie dissolved his injunction on July 10.[69]

This minor gain for the demonstrators was more than offset, however, by Michie's other actions. He remanded all the removed contempt cases to the Corporation Court.[70] Reasoning that the accused should exhaust their remedies in the state courts, he denied the request for orders restraining enforcement of the Aiken injunction and the city ordinance limiting picketing and demonstrations.[71] Virginia's political leaders were delighted with Michie's performance. Senator Robertson, for example, strongly approved Michie's course and viewed the removal proceedings as a political maneuver by Attorney General Robert F. Kennedy.[72]

In addition, Michie's actions highlighted the central role of the federal district court in determining the course of racial demonstrations. Time was a crucial factor for the demonstrators: as the period without effective federal intervention grew longer, the prospect of success became more remote. Whatever the outcome of subsequent appellate review, the district court judge was in a position to withhold or extend an immediate and hence effective federal remedy. Certainly Michie's decisions furnished no encouragement to the demonstrators while giving a legal and psychological boost to the city at a key time in the history of the Danville demonstrations.

The attorneys for the demonstrators had filed their wide array of petitions and suits on the theory that the best defense was an aggressive assault on the state court proceedings. A study of the response of the federal district judges, however, suggests that the strategy of multiple litigation backfired. It perplexed the judges and

---

68. Memorandums from Justice Dept. to Len Holt, July 3, 1963 (Burke Marshall Papers in John F. Kennedy Library).
69. W. KUNSTLER, DEEP IN MY HEART 226-27 (1966).
70. For the order, dated July 11, 1963, remanding the criminal contempt cases see Baines v. City of Danville, Civil Action No. 574, Federal Records Center, Suitland, Maryland.
71. For Michie's opinion denying injunctive relief against arrests and prosecutions under the ordinance limiting demonstrations see Chase v. McCain, 220 F. Supp. 407 (W.D. Va. 1963). Michie evidently did not prepare opinions in his disposition of the other matters before him.
72. Letter from A. Willis Robertson to Walter L. Grant, July 12, 1963 (Robertson Papers in College of William and Mary).

caused them to downgrade, indeed, to desire to escape altogether, the Danville cases. Michie, for example, expressed a sense of relief that he was not required to deal with the thorny problems in "the numerous suits" growing out of the disorders: "Again, I am happy to say that I do not have to decide that issue in this case."[73] For further evidence of this skeptical judicial attitude consider the correspondence of Judge John Paul, who was named along with Michie to a three judge panel to hear the suit challenging Virginia's racial conspiracy statute.[74] Paul complained to Michie:

> The complaint is about as badly drawn as it could be. It attacks the Virginia statute forbidding the incitement of racial hostilities and then proceeds to list a lot of alleged grievances which the Negroes have, but which seem to have no connection with the statute which is attacked. It is charged that the Negroes have been prevented from registering as voters, have been subjected to police brutality and that they have been denied bail and several other things. These matters are those which are protected by various federal statutes designed to protect the civil rights of all citizens, but there is no allegation in this complaint which invokes the protection of these federal statutes or makes them applicable to the alleged wrongs. In other words, the attack made by the plaintiffs is solely on that section of the Virginia Code which is cited in the complaint and to which I have referred. As far as I can see, no federal question arises either by virtue of federal statutory provisions or by the terms of the Constitution.[75]

In August, Paul was even more explicit:

> I might say also that, with the numerous suits which have been instituted against the city of Danville and its officials, I am in quite a state of confusion as to what the real situation is there and I cannot make very much out of the complaint in the instant case, as I previously wrote you.

He revealingly added that "I know this whole Danville business has been a headache to you . . . ."[76] Since Michie and Paul conceived of the demonstrations as a legal headache, one is hardly surprised that they were disinclined to assert federal jurisdiction.

Stymied in the district court, Kunstler and the other attorneys

---

73. Chase v. McCain, 220 F. Supp. 407, 408 (W.D. Va. 1963).
74. John Paul (1883-1964) was a resident of Harrisonburg and a member of the Republican Party. Educated at the University of Virginia, Paul was named federal district judge by President Herbert Hoover in 1932. Paul had early and consistently enforced the *Brown* edict against Virginia localities. Allen v. School Bd., 144 F. Supp. 239 (W.D. Va.), *aff'd*, 240 F.2d 59 (4th Cir. 1956), *cert. denied*, 353 U.S. 910 (1957); Kilby v. County School Bd., 3 RACE REL. L. REP. 972 (W.D. Va. 1958). Although his judicial orders caused schools to be closed in two areas pursuant to the program of massive resistance, Paul remained on friendly personal terms with Senator Byrd and other leaders of the Byrd organization. Letter from Paul to Harry F. Byrd, June 20, 1958 (John Paul Papers in University of Virginia).
75. Letter from John Paul to Thomas J. Michie, July 30, 1963 (Paul Papers in University of Virginia).
76. Letter from John Paul to Thomas J. Michie, August 21, 1963 (Paul Papers in University of Virginia).

for the protest movement again applied to the Fourth Circuit for an immediate hearing on Michie's orders. Danville authorities were jubilant when on July 22 the court decided to take no action. This inability to gain federal intervention completed the paralysis of the waning protests. In early August, Aiken modified and made permanent his earlier temporary injunction and resumed the trials of the contempt and ordinance violation cases.[77] The number of contempt defendants had swollen to 346.[78]

At this point, however, the city overplayed its hand and finally provoked limited federal court intervention. Since each defendant demanded and was granted an individual trial, it was obvious that the trials would drag on interminably and clog the entire judicial calendar in the Corporation Court. The assignment of Judge Leon M. Brazile of Hanover County to assist Aiken in holding court provided only partial relief. To alleviate this problem, the prosecutor moved on August 5 for a change of venue for the trials of some defendants. He reasoned that the crowded docket would not permit the defendants to receive speedy trials and would burden the administration of justice. Over the objection of the defendants, the court granted the motion, and some 124 cases were transferred to other courts in Virginia from 80 to 200 miles from Danville.[79] The defendants, most of them poor, were now confronted with having to travel, and transport their witnesses, a considerable distance for trial. Pressure on the defense attorneys was, of course, greatly increased by the change of venue. The court's ruling was based on a misreading of Section 19.1-224 of the Code of Virginia authorizing a change of venue "for good cause" at the request of either the accused or the state.[80] It seems evident that the venue statute was intended to accord criminal defendants a fair and impartial trial free from local prejudice. The Danville court's action, then, was a grievous misapplication of the statute and hampered the accused

---

77. On August 2 Judge Aiken issued a permanent injunction against certain named defendants "and all other persons similarly situated" and "all other persons in active concert and participation with them." 38 Danville Chancery Order Book, Corporation Court 385.

78. L. HOLT, AN ACT OF CONSCIENCE 216-17 (1965).

79. Cases were transferred to courts in Lee County, the City of Bristol, Russell County, Fairfax County, Buchanan County, Hanover County, Chesterfield County, Cumberland County, the City of Hopewell, and the City of Virginia Beach. Danville Register, Aug. 6-8, 1963; 60 Danville Common Law Order Book, Corporation Court 274-83.

80. Section 19.1-224 provides in part as follows: "—A Circuit court may, on motion of the accused or of the Commonwealth, for good cause, order the venue for the trial of a criminal case in such court to be changed to some other corporation or circuit court. Such motion when made by the accused may be made in his absence upon a petition signed and sworn to by him, which petition may, in the discretion of the judge, be acted on by him in vacation . . . ."

in offering a defense. The transfer of the trials to distant points struck many observers as a naked display of judicial power designed more to intimidate the defendants rather than enhance their chance for a fair trial.[81]

Another application to the Fourth Circuit finally produced an order favorable to the demonstrators. Attorneys for the protest movement sought an order staying all arrests, trials, and other proceedings for violation of the Aiken injunction and the ordinance restricting demonstrations.[82] Reviewing the criminal prosecutions in the state court, and noting specifically the denial of bail to those convicted and the transfer of the cases, the circuit court restrained trials for violation of the Aiken injunction and the ordinance curtailing demonstrations. Temporary relief was granted "to protect the jurisdiction of this court pending disposition of the appeals before us . . . ." The court called upon "persons of good will of both races to establish communications and to seek eventually acceptable solutions to these problems out of which these cases arise."[83] It should be noted that the Fourth Circuit order, coming on August 8, was both too little and too late as far as the demonstrators were concerned.[84] The stay only halted trials for offenses against the Aiken injunction and the ordinance regulating demonstrations. Prosecutions for trespass, contributing to the delinquency of a minor, or

---

81. L. HOLT, AN ACT OF CONSCIENCE 217 (1965).
82. Chase v. Aiken, Civil Action No. 9084, Federal Records Center, Suitland, Maryland.
83. Baines v. City of Danville, 321 F.2d 643 (4th Cir. 1963).
84. The action of the Fourth Circuit was commended by an unlikely source, the *Richmond News Leader*. Under the editorship of James J. Kilpatrick, the *News Leader* had championed massive resistance and generally opposed the civil rights movement. Nonetheless, the *News Leader* was concerned about the manner in which Danville handled the protests and hailed the Circuit Court "for suspending the gold-plated, triple-bottomed, hand-tooled stupidity of these so-called Danville trials." Charging that Danville had abridged the right of free speech, the *News Leader* assailed "trumped-up ordinances, unwarranted arrests, drum-head trials, and autocratic decrees!" Richmond News Leader, Aug. 12, 1963. Reaction from Danville was swift. The *Danville Register* described the *News Leader* editorial as "half-baked comments based upon less-than-half accurate information . . . ." Danville Register, Aug. 13, 1963. Congressman Tuck told Kilpatrick that "I was sure that you had not familiarized yourself with all of the facts in respect to the situation in Danville." William M. Tuck to James J. Kilpatrick, Aug. 14, 1963, Watkins M. Abbitt Papers, University of Richmond. In turn, the *News Leader* explained that it was not defending the excesses of the demonstrators: "When racial demonstrators run in the streets, stop automobiles, swarm into public offices, block traffic, smash windshields, hurl bricks, shoot at police cars, carry concealed weapons, trespass upon private property, prevent access to stores, lie down on bridges, and engage in noisy disturbances of the peace—and they have done all of these things in Danville—the proper course of conduct is to lock 'em up on appropriate criminal charges." The newspaper insisted, however, that while the "professional troublemakers" from various civil rights groups may "have inflamed the problem," they "found a sickness to begin with." Richmond News Leader, Aug. 15, 1963.

violating the parade permit ordinance were unaffected. Furthermore, the stay did not prevent continued arrests for all offenses, and the mass arrests were more effective than the trials in destroying the protest. In addition, by August the demonstrations were already dying in the face of the city's unyielding position. The protestors had lost the energy and will to extend their campaign and at this point, more than six weeks after the first application to Judge Michie, partial federal assistance did not suffice to revive the disorders. Danville had outlasted the demonstrators and won the victory.

On August 13 Aiken continued the criminal contempt cases until the federal appeal was determined.[85] In late 1963 and early 1964, however, he proceeded to hear cases of resisting arrest, disorderly conduct, violation of the parade permit ordinance, and trespass growing out of the summer disorders. Sentences for those found guilty typically imposed two to five days in jail and a fine, and the execution of the sentences was suspended pending an appeal.[86] Moreover, as a consequence of counsel's agreement to consolidate the injunction cases for trial, in September Aiken rescinded the orders transferring the venue of the 124 cases.[87]

While the demonstrations ended, the legal struggle over the fate of those arrested for contempt of the Aiken injunction was just beginning. That the relief held out by the Fourth Circuit was temporary as well as limited in scope became manifest a year later when the court, sitting en banc, dissolved the temporary injunction by a three-two vote.[88] The court considered the merits of the appeals from the various decisions of Judge Michie and the majority opinion by Clement F. Haynsworth, Jr. reached the following conclusions:

1. As passions in Danville ebbed the court had no reason to conclude that "in the quieter atmosphere of the present" the contempt defendants could not obtain a fair trial.[89] The majority judges were particularly impressed by the fact that the order transferring cases away from Danville had been rescinded. They assumed that bail would be available pending appeal to the Supreme Court of Appeals of Virginia, "a court which merits the high reputation it enjoys."[90] Since the temporary injunction had served its purpose of protecting the justiciability of these appeals, the order was dissolved.

---

85. 60 Danville Common Law Order Book, Corporation Court 292 (1963).
86. *Id.* at 401-07; 61 *id.* at 113-15, 232-34.
87. 60 Danville Common Law Order Book, Corporation Court 399 (1963).
88. Baines v. City of Danville, 337 F.2d 579 (4th Cir. 1964).
89. *Id.* at 594.
90. *Id.*

2. The actions challenging the ordinance limiting picketing and demonstrations, the parade permit ordinance, and the Aiken injunction were remanded to the district court for a hearing to determine whether injunctive relief against future prosecutions was appropriate. The district court was instructed to restrain further arrests under the ordinances and Aiken injunction "only if he finds that in combination they have been applied so sweepingly as to leave no reasonable room for reasonable protest, speech and assemblies."[91]

3. Under the governing statute the court had no jurisdiction to review the remand of the contempt cases to the Corporation Court.[92]

4. The suit against the Virginia Employment Commission for denying unemployment compensation benefits to defendants awaiting trial was dismissed because the Commission had never been made a party to the proceedings.[93]

Chief Judge Sobeloff and Judge J. Spencer Bell dissented in part. They raised no objection to the handling of the remand and unemployment insurance questions. The dissenters, however, were concerned about the suppressive effect of the ordinances and the Aiken injunction on attempts by the Negro defendants to express their grievances:

> The plaintiffs have alleged that the official and unofficial power structure of the white community has been successfully mobilized to deny them their First Amendment rights to protest their relegation to second class citizenship. They allege that the police, by means of violence and brutality exercised during wholesale arrests upon trumped up charges; the judiciary, by means of broad and vague injunctions; and the City Council, by means of its unconstitutional ordinances against picketing and parading, have succeeded in crushing the minority's carefully organized effort to express its discontent with the status quo.[94]

The dissenters argued that the court should have considered whether the ordinances and the Aiken injunction were "unconstitutional on their face." They felt that if the district judge should conclude that "a clear and imminent danger of irretrievable injury" to the first amendment rights of the protesters existed, then he should enjoin both pending and future criminal prosecutions.[95]

The majority and minority opinions parted company largely over the extent to which Danville had curtailed the freedom of as-

---
91. *Id.* at 596.
92. *Id.* at 596-98.
93. *Id.* at 598-99.
94. *Id.* at 599-600.
95. *Id.* at 601.

sembly and protest. Judge Haynsworth ruled that the ordinances and the Aiken injunction "were far from absolute."[96] Moreover, the majority was aware of excesses committed by the demonstrators and consequently was inclined to balance the rights of the protesters against the rights of the Danville community. Lastly, the majority argued that the pending state court proceedings would provide an adequate legal remedy for the defendants. The dissenters, on the other hand, were clearly moved by the plight of the Negro demonstrators and by their fear that municipal actions had chilled all expression of racial grievances. They suggested that the present calm in Danville, on which the majority had relied, might mean that the demonstrators "have been so cowed that they no longer dare to express themselves. . . ."[97] Their opinion gave no attention to the rights of private property owners and others in Danville.

There is only a sketchy record of the action taken by the district court on the matters remanded for additional consideration at a hearing. In December of 1966, Judge Michie refused to restrain the trials for violation of the Aiken injunction on the ground that the demonstrators must first exhaust their state court remedies.[98] No federal injunction was ever issued against further arrests and trials for violation of the various municipal ordinances and the Aiken injunction. By August of 1964 the racial disorders in Danville were long since concluded, and judicial relief of this nature was unnecessary.

The removal of the contempt cases from the Corporation Court, however, was presented anew to the Fourth Circuit on a petition for rehearing. The Civil Rights Act of 1964 amended the removal statute to permit appellate review of remand orders in civil rights cases. The circuit court ruled that the Act should be applied to appeals pending on its effective date and proceeded to reconsider the removal problem. Sitting *en banc*, the Fourth Circuit again divided by a three-two margin.[99] Chief Judge Haynsworth, writing for the majority, held that the cases were properly remanded. The majority opinion primarily analyzed 28 U.S.C. section 1443(1), which provides for the removal of civil actions on criminal proceedings

[a]gainst any person who is denied or cannot enforce in the courts of such

---

96. *Id.* at 594.
97. *Id.* at 600.
98. Danville Bee, Dec. 22, 1966.
99. Baines v. City of Danville, 357 F.2d 756 (4th Cir.) *aff'd*, 384 U.S. 890 (1966) (5-4). The majority opinion briefly treated and rejected the contention that removal could be accomplished under 28 U.S.C.A. § 1443(2), holding that removal under that section only applied to federal officers performing their duties under federal law.

State a right under any law providing for the equal civil rights of citizens of the United States, or of all persons within the jurisdiction thereof....

Haynsworth determined that the clause "a right under any law providing for the equal civil rights of citizens" did not furnish a basis for removal of first amendment claims.[100] He contended that the right of removal must appear in advance of trial and could not be predicated on supposition that the defendant would be unable to enforce a protected right during trial. Haynsworth also ruled:

> It would appear that the requirement of a showing of inability to enforce protected rights in the courts would require us to view all of its courts vertically, and that even a successful showing of unfairness in the trial court would not be sufficient unless it were also shown that the appellate court was unfair, too, or that the unfairness of the trial court was not correctable on appeal or avoidable by a change of venue.[101]

Hence, the contention of the protesters that they could not obtain a fair trial before Judge Aiken in the Corporation Court was not enough to sustain removal. Haynsworth stressed that there was no allegation of unfairness on the part of the Virginia Supreme Court of Appeals, "a court which showed its courage and faithfulness to constitutional principles when . . . it struck down Virginia's massive resistance laws . . . ."[102]

Once again Judges Sobeloff and Bell dissented in a lengthy opinion which accused the majority of giving an "extremely narrow construction" to the removal statute. Sympathetic with the aims and aspirations of the Negro protest movement, the dissenters saw the problem in the light of contemporary racial problems:

> Completely ignored in the majority opinion are the broader considerations unfolded by recent events and expounded in the latest decisions of the Supreme Court. In the full century since the Civil War, Congress has enacted ten civil rights statutes, three of them within the past ten years. The national purpose, as declared by Congress and the Court, has been made manifest. It is to make freedom a reality for the Negro, to secure him against the destruction of his most precious constitutional rights, and generally to permit him to enjoy the guarantee of citizenship equally with members of the white race. Nothing compels the continuance of a narrow legalistic interpretation of the removal provision, a statute which forms an indispensable link in the congressional plan to effectuate equal rights. It is stultifying to the recently enacted section 901, permitting appellate review of remand orders, to persist in the devitalizing construction of section 1443. Legislating a right of appeal would be of little worth if Congress did not mean to give section 1443 new force.[103]

Finding that the state appellate process was inadequate to guarantee that constitutional rights would be protected, the minority de-

---
100. *Id.* at 764.
101. *Id.* at 769.
102. *Id.*
103. *Id.* at 788.

clared that the Negro protesters were entitled to removal and a "fair trial" in the federal district court.

The Supreme Court affirmed the Fourth Circuit decision by a five-four margin[104] on the strength of its opinion in *City of Greenwood v. Peacock*.[105] Justice Potter Stewart's majority opinion closely paralleled the reasoning of Judge Haynsworth. Stewart held that the first amendment rights of free expression were not rights arising under a "law providing for . . . equal civil rights" within the meaning of 28 U.S.C. section 1443(1).[106] He further ruled that

> The civil rights removal statute does not require and does not permit the judges of the federal courts to put their brethren of the state judiciary on trial. Under § 1443(1), the vindication of the defendant's federal rights is left to the state courts except in the rare situations where it can be clearly predicted by reason of the operation of a pervasive and explicit state or federal law that those rights will inevitably be denied by the very act of bringing the defendant to trial in the state court.[107]

Stewart emphasized that any denial of federal constitutional rights uncorrected by the state courts could be remedied by Supreme Court review or federal habeas corpus. His opinion concluded with a consideration of the immense practical problem that would be placed upon the federal courts if thousands of criminal removal cases were tried annually before federal judges.[108] Justices Douglas, Brennan, Fortas, and Chief Justice Warren dissented, maintaining that the Court gave a narrow reading to the removal statute.[109]

The Kennedy Administration and Danville

Victor S. Navasky has charged that the Kennedy administration came into office with a civil rights program that was considerably more limited than the President's campaign rhetoric suggested. It was willing to encourage racial integration, but not at the price of social tranquility. Contrary to the white South's image of Attorney General Robert F. Kennedy, Navasky observed, "he was cautious to the point of timidity when it came to risking any kind of confrontation with an escalation potential."[110] Although this is how the Kennedy years appear in retrospect to the civil rights activist, the white South did indeed see Kennedy's record very differently.

President Kennedy had little choice but to maintain as cordial

---

104. Baines v. City of Danville, 384 U.S. 890, *rehearing denied*, 385 U.S. 890 (1966).
105. 384 U.S. 808 (1966).
106. *Id.* at 825.
107. *Id.* at 828.
108. *Id.* at 832-34.
109. *Id.* at 835-54.
110. V. NAVASKY, KENNEDY JUSTICE 228 (1971).

relations as possible with Virginia leaders. Byrd and Robertson headed the Senate Finance and Banking Committees respectively. Congressman Howard W. Smith was chairman of the House Rules Committee, which handled all legislation cleared for action in the House of Representatives. These powerful Virginians were in positions to delay or even block much of the New Frontier legislation, and Kennedy was understandably anxious not to alienate them if it could be avoided. Efforts by the administration to compel a reopening of public schools in Prince Edward County, although not immediately successful, had already severely strained Kennedy's dealing with Byrd and other Virginia leaders.[111]

Further, the political climate in the Old Dominion necessarily inhibited any move by the Kennedy administration to enter the Danville situation. John F. Kennedy had never been especially popular in Virginia. Richard M. Nixon had carried Virginia in 1960, with the tacit assistance of the Byrd organization, and nothing in the next few years improved Kennedy's image in the state. The administration, of course, was tarnished in Virginia by the onerous task of enforcing the *Brown* edict. More to the point, the Virginia leadership was convinced that by 1963 the administration was promoting racial demonstrations across America in order to marshall national backing for the Kennedy civil rights proposals submitted in June of that year.[112] Governor Harrison charged that "these mass demonstrations and disorders" were "given encouragement by the President himself."[113] Delegate C. Harrison Mann, Jr. complained directly to the President that members of his administration were inciting riots and bloodshed.[114] Senator Robertson likened the demonstrations to extortion and asserted that many irresponsible officials of government . . . were inciting Negroes to riot.[115]

---

111. Department of Justice press release, April 26, 1961, Byrd Papers; Richmond News Leader, April 27, 1961.

112. For example, the *Danville Register* charged that the Kennedys were promoting violence in Birmingham. "The sad conclusion of the action by the Kennedys and Dr. King is that the Government of the United States, as the tool of the Kennedys, cannot stand law and order in the South. Only by shattering enforcement of law and order, or by actions lending an impression that law and order has been shattered, can the full and brutal forces at the command of the Kennedys be applied against the people in the South who defend themselves against extra-legal action to bring about immediate total and complete race-mixing in any locality chosen by Dr. King and his colleagues in riot-making." Danville Register, May 14, 1963.

113. Harrison draft statement, *supra* note 54. *See also* letter from Harrison to Sam J. Ervin, Jr., Aug. 12, 1964 (Harrison Executive Papers).

114. Letter from C. Harrison Mann, Jr. to John F. Kennedy, June 7, 1963 (Robertson Papers in College of William and Mary).

115. Letter from A. Willis Robertson to C. Harrison Mann, Jr., June 10, 1963 (Robertson Papers in College of William and Mary).

The Kennedy strategy in Danville infuriated the Byrd leaders while, ironically, furnishing support for the Navasky assessment of the administration's limited civil rights program. Already aggravated over federal enforcement of *Brown*, the Virginians were hypersensitive to any federal action in the racial area. They saw every step by the Justice Department, however modest, as a politically inspired effort to prevent local law enforcement officials from keeping order in the state. Yet, from the point of view of Danville blacks, what did the Kennedy administration really do to assist them? There was no Justice Department intervention of any sort in June, the most tense month, and no suit was ever brought to redress police violence in Danville.[116] A brief in support of the removal petition was the only tangible move undertaken on behalf of the demonstrators. To be sure, Justice Department representatives monitored events in the troubled city closely. Department officials profitlessly urged the city and the demonstrators to negotiate their differences. This was the full extent of Kennedy administration involvement in Danville. Danville blacks were distressed at this lack of interest in their problems. Negroes intermittently picketed the FBI office in Danville, and one protester carried a revealing placard reading "What has the Justice Department Done?"[117] Holt explained:

> ... the Kennedy administration responded in characteristic fashion.... First it brought about a cessation of demonstration, if possible, and then it wielded pressure on city hall or local merchants to make minor concessions. The third step consisted of convincing the persons involved in racial protest that they had gained a great victory while simultaneously persuading city hall or the merchants that they had given up nothing important.[118]

The Danville experience illustrates the central paradox of the Kennedy civil rights intervention in the South—that the rage of southern conservatives and the disappointment of Virginia Negroes was equally merited. By justifying and seeking legal protection for the demonstrators, and by incorporating their demands in his legislative program, Kennedy inevitably, but perhaps inadvertently, encouraged and dignified the disorders. In some measure, then, Kennedy must be held responsible for the wave of urban unrest and the tendency to direct physical action which appeared in the late

---

116. In September of 1963 Burke Marshall wrote: "... I am trying to develop a broader kind of case against this sort of repressive and violent police action. We have one, for example, in Danville, Virginia, but I think it would not be wise to bring it there." Memorandum for the Attorney General, Sept. 18, 1963 (Burke Marshall Papers in John F. Kennedy Library).
117. Danville Register, Aug. 6, 1963.
118. L. HOLT, AN ACT OF CONSCIENCE 177-78 (1965).

1960's.[119] On the other hand, while he aroused heightened expectations by blacks in America, Kennedy was nonetheless too deliberate to satisfy rapidly the promises fired up by his gestures and pronouncements. In short, his moralistic rhetoric vastly outstripped his performance, a gap that was bound to fuel the very disorders that he claimed to disapprove.

This interpretation accords with the highly suggestive study of Henry Fairlie, in which he argues that Kennedy relied upon the politics of expectation.[120] Fairlie contends that the Kennedy administration governed by keeping people in a constant state of expectation and by encouraging an exaggerated notion of what politics could achieve. When the aroused hopes were necessarily unrealized, the public mood turned to the frustration and disillusionment of the 1960's. Fairlie points out that Kennedy moved on civil rights only after Negroes had taken to the streets, and concludes:

> It is false to try to manufacture a "consensus" in such a situation; and it was false in the 1960's to try to do so in the cause of civil rights. It could only be a distraction, certain in the end to provoke the frustration as much of the advocates of the cause, whose expectations had been aroused, as of its opponents, who felt with some justice that the political processes of the country had been bypassed.[121]

Disposition in the State Courts

In December of 1966 Aiken resumed the long-stalled trials of the persons accused of violating his injunction. By consent of the state and the defendants, groups of cases were consolidated and tried together by the court without a jury.[122] The trials now pro-

---

119. In his January 1963 State of the Union message Kennedy did not mention new civil rights legislation. The disorders of April and May in Birmingham induced the administration to propose a sweeping civil rights bill, which eventually became the Civil Rights Act of 1964. The Kennedy recommendations fit neatly into the administration pattern of seeking to manage the civil rights movement and channel its energy into peaceful courses. "Even the proposed new civil rights legislation . . . ," Navasky contended, "was designed to cool down trouble as much as to correct injustice." V. NAVASKY, KENNEDY JUSTICE 205 (1971). Of course, it seems most likely that there would have been no Kennedy civil rights proposal in 1963 but for the Birmingham disturbances. Thus, one could surely argue that Kennedy did in fact yield to pressure generated by mob activities in the street. In other words, the Kennedy concern about halting the demonstrations took the form of granting the demands of the protestors, a certain prescription for renewed street violence.

120. H. FAIRLIE, THE KENNEDY PROMISE: THE POLITICS OF EXPECTATION 13-16 (1973). In a similar analysis of contemporary urban problems, Edward C. Banfield has stressed the major role of expectancy in our understanding of city life. "The answer," he observed, "is that the improvements in performance, great as they have been, have not kept pace with rising expectations. In other words, although things have been getting better absolutely, they have been getting worse relative to what we think they should be." E. BANFIELD, THE UNHEAVENLY CITY: THE NATURE AND THE FUTURE OF OUR URBAN CRISIS 19 (1970).

121. FAIRLIE, supra note 120, at 255.

122. 65 Danville Common Law Order Book, Corporation Court 316; Commonwealth v. Burrell, transcript, 4.

ceeded expeditiously, and on some days Aiken heard three sets of cases.[123] As many as twenty-nine defendants were tried in a group, many of them for multiple offenses.[124] It was stipulated that when a defendant failed to appear on the date of his trial, the state could present its evidence against the defendant and that such could be used at a later trial.[125] Not all the accused were convicted. The Commonwealth's Attorney announced that he was not going to prosecute certain defendants, presumably for lack of evidence, and they were ordered discharged.[126] Additionally, Aiken dismissed other cases after hearing the evidence.[127] Numerous defendants failed to appear, and Aiken declared as many as eleven 500-dollar bonds forfeit in a single day.[128]

In the course of the trials, defense counsel routinely moved to strike the evidence of the prosecution on the following grounds:

1. that there was no showing of service of the Aiken injunction, or that the defendants had actual notice thereof;
2. that even if service had been made, the defendants were not named or described in the order and hence not within its coverage;
3. that the acts committed by the defendants were not in violation of the injunction;
4. "that the injunction denied due process of speech and assembly in violation of the First and Fourteenth Amendments to the Constitution of the United States."[129]

As would be expected, Aiken consistently overruled the motions. The leaders of the demonstration received relatively severe sentences, with Rev. Lawrence Campbell drawing the stiffest punishment of 250 days and a fine of 2,500 dollars. The usual sentence for a single violation was a ten day term at the city prison farm, of which eight days were suspended, and a fine of twenty dollars.[130] Those convicted were admitted to 500- or 1,000-dollar appeal bonds. Aiken refused to release them on personal recognizance, noting the poor experience with defendants appearing for trial.[131]

---

123. 66 Danville Common Law Order Book, Corporation Court 21-27, 32-41.
124. *Id.* at 9-11.
125. *Id.*; Commonwealth v. Burrell, transcript, 3a.
126. 65 Danville Common Law Order Book, Corporation Court 304-05; 66 *id.* at 15, 53.
127. 66 *id.* at 46, 53-56.
128. 65 *id.* at 333-37.
129. *Id.* at 305-06, 317-19; Commonwealth v. Burrell, transcript, 126-27.
130. 65 Danville Common Law Order Book, Corporation Court 317-19.
131. Commonwealth v. Bethel, transcript, 217.

Judge Aiken felt that his sentences were very mild. "I realize," he declared from the bench, "that I am being rather lenient on these people. I don't know but what I am being too lenient on them."[132] Even Samuel W. Tucker, NAACP attorney and one of the defense counsel, agreed that "the court has imposed a nominal fine and a short jail sentence."[133] Aiken's analysis of the question of sentences was most fully elaborated at the end of the first group of trials:

> The Court is considerably disappointed about these defendants. As Mr. Ferguson pointed out, not a single defendant has expressed any regret for disobeying the Court's orders. Not a single lawyer representing these defendants has expressed any regret about it that I know. They are not willing to say that they were mistaken and misguided in doing what they did, and maybe they don't think so. I don't know. I am disappointed too in the attitude of some of the leaders of this movement, especially the ministers . . . . and the Court thinks that he [defendant Reverend McGhee] ought to have been advising the people that he was leading there that night to obey the Court's order rather than leading them in demonstrations . . . . The Court feels that it is its duty to uphold the dignity and self-respect of this Court, and when this Court makes an order, it's got to be obeyed and anybody who violates it has got to pay some penalty for it even though it may be small.[134]

Assuming that the evidence supported a determination of guilt, then Aiken was unquestionably correct in passing sentence on the convicted defendants. The sentences were hardly onerous, and they served to uphold the rule of law over the resort to the streets. Surely the delay between the disorders and the time of the trial—a delay caused in large part by the futile efforts at removal—could not be considered as an excuse for criminal conduct. A contrary outcome would have permitted the demonstrators to evade the consequences of their illegal activities by the mere passage of time.

Although his punishments were moderate, Aiken's handling of defense counsel and private criticism was inexcusable and again showed all too clearly his overbearing character. On December 20, 1966, he found Ruth L. Harvey, a Danville attorney representing the defendants, guilty of contempt for allegedly misleading the court with respect to her representation of defendant Leonard Holt. At a pre-trial conference she advised Aiken that she represented Holt and that he would appear for trial. Holt subsequently failed to attend, and Miss Harvey explained that she was no longer his attorney. Aiken fined her twenty-five dollars.[135] The Virginia Supreme Court of Appeals unanimously reversed this absurd judgment, hold-

---

132. Commonwealth v. Burrell, transcript, 185.
133. Commonwealth v. Bethel, transcript, 217.
134. Id.
135. Danville Bee, Dec. 21, 1966.

ing that the statements of Miss Harvey "were not sufficient to warrant the finding of contempt against her."[136]

Even more controversial was the Taylor affair. Shortly after the trials resumed, W. Leigh Taylor, the director of education and training at Dan River Mills, wrote a personal letter to Judge Aiken in which he charged that the Judge's imposition of jail sentences "served to aggravate a situation which has been improving constantly."[137] He referred to "petulance on the part of the judge" and characterized Aiken's disposition as "an inane decision." Aiken reacted swiftly, ordering the arrest of Taylor on a charge of contempt of the judge of the court. Arrested at his mill office, Taylor admitted writing the letter and apologized to Aiken. The apology was to no avail, and Aiken found Taylor in contempt, sentencing him to ten days, eight of which were suspended, in the city prison farm and a fine of fifty dollars.[138]

In a free society, judges are not immune from criticism, and there can be no doubt that Aiken's behavior toward Taylor was a serious error which curtailed constitutionally protected freedom of speech and reflected negatively on his judicial temperament.[139] Returning to an old target, the Richmond *News Leader* declared that Aiken "has grossly abused his powers. In our opinion, he ought to be impeached."[140] In the resulting furor the Danville Bar Association once more came to Aiken's defense with a resolution which described the *News Leader* editorial as "irresponsible, despicable, thoroughly unjustified and designed to hold the dignity of the Court up for public ridicule."[141] The lawyers recorded their "highest respect for and confidence in Judge Aiken." By February of 1967, Aiken evidently thought better of his hasty action and suspended Taylor's entire jail sentence.[142]

As the federal courts anticipated, the constitutional issues raised by the Negro protest movement were resolved by the state courts. Under the rationale of the federal deference policy, as expressed by the *Peacock* opinion, it was incumbent upon the state courts to decide the criminal cases in good faith and not to permit the law to become a hindrance to the expression of unpopular views.

---

136. Harvey v. Commonwealth, 209 Va. 433, 437, 164 S. E. 2d 636, 638 (1968).
137. For the text of Taylor's letter see Danville Bee, Dec. 20, 1966.
138. 65 Danville Common Law Order Book, Corporation Court 319-20.
139. Taylor's action in sending a personal letter to Aiken scarcely presented a danger to the administration of justice. Wood v. Georgia, 370 U.S. 375 (1962).
140. Richmond News Leader, Dec. 21, 1966.
141. Danville Bee, Dec. 23, 1966.
142. 66 Danville Common Law Order Book, Corporation Court 14.

The Fourth Circuit had repeatedly expressed its confidence in the judicial integrity of Virginia's highest court. Its conscientious and deliberate treatment of the varied issues posed by the disorders amply vindicated the trust of the Circuit Court.

In early 1967 the first of a long series of appeals from the Danville Corporation Court were decided by the Supreme Court of Appeals. The most important device used by the city to halt the demonstrations was the Aiken temporary injunction of June 6, later made permanent. This injunction was considered by the Supreme Court of Appeals in *Thomas v. City of Danville*.[143] On appeal from the order entering a perpetual injunction, the defendants raised no factual or procedural questions and pressed the contention that the order was contrary to the protections of the first and fourteenth amendments. The Court ruled that a court of equity had jurisdiction to enjoin acts that were a menace to the public rights or welfare.[144] Indeed, the defendants conceded that Aiken could properly restrain obstruction of traffic and the obstruction of the use of public and private facilities. They asserted, however, that the remainder of the Aiken injunction violated their freedom of speech and assembly. The Supreme Court of Appeals unanimously disagreed and upheld the permanent injunction in the main. Relying upon *Adderly v. Florida*,[145] the court pointed out that the Constitution does not guarantee that individuals can protest whenever and however they please. Concerned about the rights of the community as a whole, the court declared: "The rights guaranteed to the defendants under the Federal Constitution were not a license for them to trample upon the rights of the public, as was done in some of the incidents in the present case."[146]

Thereupon the Supreme Court of Appeals examined each item of the Aiken injunction. It had no difficulty upholding the prohibitions against assaults on persons and damaging property, against inciting persons to riot or violation of law, and against participation in mob violence or riot. Two items of the injunction were declared invalid on the ground that freedom of speech was protected unless shown likely to produce an evil greater than mere public inconveni-

---

143. 207 Va. 656, 152 S.E.2d 265 (1967).
144. The defendants also contended that certain items in the injunction enjoined violations of criminal law and thus deprived them of the right to trial by jury with respect to such violations. The court rejected this argument, pointing out that "such injunctive restraints are not criminal in character but are civil; that their purpose is not to convict and punish for violation of the law, but to prevent such violation." 207 Va. at 664, 152 S.E.2d at 270.
145. 385 U.S. 39 (1966).
146. 207 Va. at 661, 152 S.E.2d at 269.

ence.[147] The deleted portions of the order read as follows:

4. From creating unnecessarily loud, objectionable, offensive and insulting noises, which are designed to upset the peace and tranquility of the community.

6. From engaging in any act in a violent and tumultuous manner or holding unlawful assemblies such as to unreasonably disturb or alarm the public within the City of Danville.

Lastly, the court modified the provision which restrained the defendants from participating in meetings where violations of the law or the injunction "are suggested, advocated or encouraged." The court eliminated the word "suggested," fearing that it would inhibit the mere discussion of the validity of such laws and the injunction.[148] No act that could legitimately be described as an exercise of free speech was prevented under the Aiken injunction as modified.[149]

The parade permit ordinance posed the second constitutional problem for Virginia's highest court in *York v. City of Danville*.[150] The court's opinion, again unanimous, declared that the right to conduct a parade was "subject to reasonable and nondiscriminatory regulation."[151] Nonetheless, the court held that the Danville ordinance, requiring an application for a parade permit to be filed "not less than thirty days nor more than sixty days" before the date of the parade, was arbitrary and oppressive.[152] The practical effect of this ordinance, enacted while the disorders were continuing, was to prevent the defendants from demonstrating during the thirty day waiting period. Hence, the parade ordinance was held to constitute "an arbitrary and unreasonable prior restraint upon the rights of freedom of speech and assembly . . . ."[153] The *York* opinion indicates anew that the court was prepared to uphold first amendment rights to express grievances.

The Supreme Court of Appeals readily disposed of some lesser matters emanating from the disorders. Convictions for trespass on

---

147. *Id.* at 662-63, 152 S.E.2d at 269-70.
148. *Id.* at 664, 152 S.E.2d at 270.
149. In December of 1963 Burke Marshall expressed a contrary view with respect to the Aiken injunction: "In Danville . . . there has been repressive police action, and the use of state and federal injunctions against demonstrations which will eventually be held to be unconstitutional." Memorandum for the Attorney General, Dec. 2, 1963 (Burke Marshall Papers in John F. Kennedy Library).
150. 207 Va. 665, 152 S.E.2d 259 (1967).
151. *Id.* at 669, 152 S.E.2d at 263.
152. For the text of the parade permit ordinance see 207 Va. at 667-68, 152 S.E.2d at 261-62.
153. *Id.* at 671, 152 S.E.2d at 264.

private property and blocking ingress and egress to Dan River Mills were sustained.[154] In another action, the court affirmed a forfeiture of a bail bond when a defendant failed to appear for his trial, scheduled some three and one-half years after the demonstrations had occurred.[155]

An appeal dealing with arrests under the June 6 temporary injunction reached Virginia's highest court in 1970. The court regarded the constitutionality of the order as having been settled by the *Thomas* opinion, and considered the case solely in terms of notice and the sufficiency of the evidence upon which the defendant was convicted. Since the defendant was not named in the injunction, the court ruled that the state must prove "that he had actual notice or knowledge of the injunction before he committed prohibited acts."[156] Concluding that the evidence sustained a finding of actual notice on the part of the defendant, the contempt conviction was affirmed.

Finally, in January of 1973, the Supreme Court of Appeals decided the last batch of cases emanating from the Danville disorders. The high court asked the Commonwealth's Attorney for Danville to review the pending appeals in light of the *Thomas*, *York*, and *Rollins* rulings.[157] He conceded that in many of the contempt cases the state had failed to prove notice as required in *Rollins*. Violations of the parade permit ordinance had to fall as a consequence of *York*. The Commonwealth's Attorney further stipulated that there was inadequate evidence to uphold many of the convictions for resisting arrest, disorderly conduct, and trespassing.[158] Thus, without contest the Virginia Supreme Court overturned the convictions of nearly 270 persons.[159] At the same time, the court upheld the contempt convictions of the persons named in the injunction and served with a copy thereof. Sentences for illegal picketing, trespassing, and obstructing traffic were also sustained.[160]

A month later, and nearly ten years after the demonstrations, the prolonged legal proceedings reached their anti-climactic end. Aiken having died in 1971, and the new Danville judge having disqualified himself, Judge Glynn R. Phillips, Jr. of Clintwood was assigned to hear a defense motion to suspend the fines and jail

---

154. Hubbard v. Commonwealth, 207 Va. 673, 152 S.E.2d 250 (1967).
155. McGhee v. Commonwealth, 211 Va. 434, 177 S.E.2d 649 (1970).
156. Rollins v. Commonwealth, 211 Va. 438, 441, 177 S.E.2d 639, 642 (1970).
157. Letter from William H. Fuller III to author, Apr. 25, 1973.
158. 75 Danville Common Law Order Book, Corporation Court 428-39.
159. *Id.*; Richmond News Leader, Jan. 13, 1973.
160. 75 Danville Common Law Order Book, Corporation Court 439-43.

sentences of those persons whose convictions were affirmed. Over the heated objection of the Commonwealth's Attorney, Judge Phillips suspended the jail terms, conditioned on good behavior for two years, but directed payment of fines totalling more than 5,000 dollars.[161]

Conclusion

The Danville demonstrations of 1963 were a failure. Municipal authorities made only modest concessions to the demands of the protest movement and life resumed its traditional pattern. White racial attitudes were unchanged.[162] The legal aftermath of the hectic summer events was, in an important sense, irrelevant to the successful crushing of the disorders. Probably the principal reason for the collapse of the protests was the inability of Danville Negroes to enlist meaningful assistance from either the Kennedy administration or the federal courts. During the critical months of June and July, the city was able to harass and arrest the demonstrators at will under a host of state and municipal provisions. While police violence was not a conspicuous feature of the Danville plan, the police excesses on the night of June 10 were calculated to discourage protest activities.

Judge Aiken significantly contributed to the chilling of the demonstrations.[163] His injunction provided the basis for hundreds of arrests, and the arrests in turn permitted the court to require bail of the accused awaiting trial. With many blacks unemployed or holding marginal jobs, this bail policy fell upon the poorest members of the Danville community. Moreover, Aiken's abrupt and arbitrary conduct in the first contempt trials unmistakably conveyed the impression that the demonstrators could expect swift and harsh judicial treatment at his hands. Faced with the certainty of arrest and consequent bail expenses and the likelihood of a jail term, many protesters came to have second thoughts. Aiken's deportment, then, furnished an excellent example of the utilization of the state court

---

161. 76 *id.* at 11.
162. In June of 1964 the first municipal elections after the disorders produced a complete triumph for supporters of a tough policy against demonstrations. Five candidates who defended the city's handling of the demonstrators and were allied to John W. Carter easily won all the vacancies on the city council, defeating Negro and moderate candidates. Richmond News Leader, June 10, 1964; N.Y. Times, June 10, 1964.
163. Aiken was re-named judge of the Corporation Court by the legislature in February of 1968. He was elected by a margin of 99-7, with only the Republican minority in the House of Delegates opposing him because of his advanced age. There seems to have been no open discussion of Aiken's role in the demonstration cases. *Journal of the Senate of Virginia,* Regular Session, 310-15 (1968); Richmond Times-Dispatch, Feb. 10, 1968.

trial bench as an additional club to undercut racial disorders. His stern resistance to the demonstrations exacted a heavy price in terms of judicial integrity. Aiken was all too obviously part of a municipal power structure dedicated to white supremacy and the racial status quo.

Nevertheless, it is entirely possible to offer a partial justification for the city's method of handling the unrest. In at least some measure, the Negro demonstrations of the 1960's were an attempt to create tensions and intimidate the white public into taking actions favored by the black minority, or, that failing, to provoke such a savage reaction from the whites as to arouse national public opinion. Violence and threats of violence were an integral part of this strategy. It is to the credit of Virginia leaders at all levels that they recognized this overt threat and refused to yield to extra-legal tactics. One of the most unhappy legacies of the 1960's was the widespread notion that questions of public policy should be determined by mobs in the street.[164] Not infrequently it seemed that even the federal judiciary viewed the behavior of Negro demonstrators as somehow above the law. At first glance the judicial receptivity to civil rights demands would appear to remove any necessity for protest activity, but in fact the judicial climate encouraged the belief that almost any conduct by blacks in the name of "civil rights," short of personal violence, would be upheld as a form of free expression. Whatever the flaws in Danville's handling of the demonstrations, Virginians correctly insisted upon obedience to law and established procedure. Illegal practices in Danville or errors by Judge Aiken could be corrected on appeal and did not furnish an excuse for street mobs.

Failing to coerce the whites, the Negro demonstrators sought to arouse some type of national support. Here, too, Danville Negroes were disappointed. The low profile of Governor Harrison was the decisive factor in keeping Danville out of the national headlines. Holt revealed the publicity consciousness of the protestors when he lamented that the press "had forsaken Danville, finding nothing spectacular about the routine arrests and demonstrations. . . ."[165] When some provocative events in Danville threatened to generate outside attention, national developments fortuitously overshadowed

---

164. Elliot Zashin has recently argued that the civil rights movement did not rely upon litigation or upon convincing the electorate, but "hoped to force southern whites to abandon segregation both by confronting them directly and by creating publicity that would apply still more pressure." Zashin, *Civil Rights and Civil Disobedience: the Limits of Legalism*, 52 TEX. L. REV. 285, 293 (1974).

165. L. HOLT, AN ACT OF CONSCIENCE 206 (1965).

the demonstrations. For example, the March on Washington by civil rights groups on August 28 and the maneuvers over the Kennedy civil rights proposals dominated the domestic news coverage in the summer of 1963. Without the kind of federal assistance that publicity could arouse, there was never much doubt that Danville would crush the disorders.

The demonstrators were unquestionably entitled to engage in peaceful picketing and orderly marches to express their dissatisfaction with the racial conditions in Danville. Indeed, the initial demonstrations were peaceful and without incident. Not surprisingly, the protestors soon found that the white citizens of Danville paid no attention to such activities. Accordingly, they resorted to extralegal tactics for which they erroneously claimed first amendment protection, thereby blurring both the constitutional issues and their own coercive and publicity-seeking aims. When the Corporation Court and the city council sought to halt these unlawful activities, the protestors promptly alleged that the judicial and municipal responses were overly broad and forbade conduct protected under the first amendment. Conveniently overlooked was the indisputable evidence that their own unlawful conduct had caused the prohibitions of which they complained.

Finally, the Danville imbroglio calls into question the image of the federal courts and the Kennedy administration as stalwart champions of the Negro protest movement. At no point were the demonstrators able to secure meaningful judicial relief. In the last analysis, the federal courts respected the traditional deference to the adjudication of criminal cases in the state courts. The remand of the Danville contempt cases was certainly appropriate as a matter of general policy, but it nevertheless allowed the state court to maintain the pressure against the disorders. The Kennedy administration, for its part, was simply not as aggressive on the racial front as either the Danville blacks hoped or the Virginia whites feared.

By February of 1973 the sentencing of the Danville demonstrators was finished and a violent chapter in Virginia's history closed.[166] The Danville experience suggests the limitation of mass demonstra-

---

166. The defendants indicted under Virginia's racial conspiracy statute were never brought to trial. Letter from William H. Fuller III to author, Feb. 23, 1973. Although the challenge to the constitutionality of the statute was referred to a 3-judge federal court, no action was taken after the death of Judge Paul in 1964 and the suit was dismissed in 1967 for failure to prosecute. Adams v. Aiken, Civil Action No. 584, Federal Records Center, Suitland, Maryland. A similar statute was held unconstitutional in Herndon v. Lowry, 301 U.S. 242 (1937).

tion as a tactic to encourage social change. Only under unique circumstances—favorable national publicity, clumsy and obnoxious local government authorities subject to ready vilification, timely federal assistance—could they succeed. In short, the Danville disorders show the ease with which the South could maintain racial segregation absent federal intervention.

301

The Edge Of Caste:
Colored Suffrage In Michigan, 1827-1861

RONALD P. FORMISANO

Mr. Formisano is currently associated with the Department of History at the University of Rochester, New York State.

Antebellum Michigan was a caste society, by custom and by law. A minority of blacks and whites, not all of them abolitionists, worked to ameliorate or improve free blacks' legal and social status. Throughout the North they challenged a variety of political caste barriers, ranging from such a basic goal as repealing state laws prohibiting immigration of colored citizens, to the right of blacks to serve on juries. Other demands included: the right to give evidence in courts, use of public facilities, militia service, and "personal liberty laws" pertaining to fugitive slaves.[1] In Michigan as in other states

---

1. Eugene H. Berwanger, *The Frontier Against Slavery: Western Anti-Negro Prejudice and the Slavery Extension Controversy* (Urbana: University of Illinois Press, 1967), describes the changing foci of amelioration. Benjamin Quarles, *Black Abolitionists* (New York: Oxford University Press, 1969), shows the interweaving of abolition and amelioration.

a set of ameliorationist issues existed parallel to abolitionism, but one stood preeminently as the practical and symbolic focus of amelioration: colored suffrage. "Colored" was the term most used by black and white reformers, somewhat as *black* is used today: it carried dignity.

In Michigan colored suffrage acted as a lightning rod for fears and hopes tied to the whole racial question in the North. In no other state does the suffrage seem to have channeled or dominated the discussion of race as much as in Michigan[2] The various debates over some 25 years before the Civil War make clear that whenever Michigan lawmakers approached the subject with any degree of seriousness, the alien suffrage issue intruded. In short, racial politics were inseparable from the ethnic and religious politics that so profoundly shaped the partisan loyalties of the second American party system.

For some three decades before the Civil War this northwestern frontier state, where the egalitarian ethos otherwise reigned supreme, denied black citizens the right to vote. But almost continuously from 1835 to 1861 a black and white vanguard of reformers challenged this mainstay of caste, and even the very assumptions upon which it rested. This debate, indirectly bearing on attitudes related to slavery, emancipation, and abolitionists, confronted men directly with the role of non-whites in society. When men thought about slavery and abolition, the issue of free black status in their own communities was often a step or two away in their minds. Colored suffrage faced them directly with that question.

A detailed study of the issue in one state over three decades can highlight the events and conditions influencing attitudes on suffrage and race. Michigan's experience supports the propositions that the broader the political movements against slavery extension became, the more free black rights were left out of them; and periods of severe North-South sectional anger intensified racism among an already Negrophobic white majority.[3] In the 1850s, particularly, sectional conflict between North and South, and white social group antagonisms within Northern society caused a heightening of racial consciousness, white fears, and resistance to amelioration. White allies became defensive, cautiously pragmatic, or indifferent. By 1860 the colored suffrage issue in Michigan had become almost the sole property of blacks. The claims made recently for the alleged benefits resulting from "the Republicans insistence on the humanity of the Negro" must be treated cautiously.[4] Blacks may have benefited abstractly or in the long run, but the immediate effects on black status of the Michigan political realignments of the 1850s were different. Their legal position deteriorated; tests of caste sharpened boundaries; and the blacks' psychic condition and their evaluation of their status must have become grimmer.

Roots of this racist attitude can be traced back to the eighteenth century when the frontier garrison of Detroit inherited a tradition of Indian and Negro enslavement from the French and British occupations although the institution was never widespread.[5] In the territorial period indicators of white attitudes toward blacks are few, but they presage a none too sympathetic disposition to enfranchise blacks later. In 1827 the Legislative Council, elected by popular vote since 1825, gave Michigan a black code which copied Ohio's elaborate caste laws and discouraged both blacks and slave catchers from coming to Michigan—an early display of the co-existence of anti-black and anti-slaveholder sentiments that prevailed in the 1850s.[6] White fears exploded in 1833 following the "Blackburn riot." After a black crowd rescued a fugitive slave from Detroit's jail, slightly injuring the sheriff, white vigilantism, black protests and "repeated attempts to fire the town" followed. The mayor called for federal troops, while panicky townspeople rang bells and cried out: "the niggers have risen and sheriff is killed!"[7]

Colored suffrage entered the political arena soon thereafter as the Legislative Council prepared to call a constitutional convention. Little is known of the politics involved, but a very significant pattern appeared with colored suffrage's debut: it became politically intertwined with the issue of "alien suffrage," and interacted symbolically

2. James Truslow Adams, "Disfranchisement of Negroes in New England," *American Historical Review*, XXX (April, 1925), 543-47; Charles H. Wesley, "Negro Suffrage in the Period of Constitution-Making, 1787-1865," *Journal of Negro History*, XXXII (April, 1947), 143-68; Marion Wright Thompson, "Negro Suffrage in New Jersey, 1776-1875," *Journal of Negro History*, XXXIII (April, 1948), 168-224; Morton M. Rosenberg and Dennis V. McClurg, *The Politics of Pro-Slavery Sentiment in Indiana, 1816-1861* (Muncie: Ball State University Press, 1968); Berwanger, *Frontier Against Slavery*, passim. Eric Foner, *Free Soil, Free Labor, Free Men: The Ideology of the Republican Party Before the Civil War* (New York: Oxford University Press, 1970), discusses colored suffrage generally, pp. 281-95.

3. Aileen S. Kraditor, *Means and Ends in American Abolitionism: Garrison and His Critics on Strategy and Tactics, 1834-1850* (New York: Pantheon Books, 1967); Eric Foner, "Racial Attitudes of the New York Free Soilers," *New York History*, XLVI (October, 1965), 311-29. On the latter point: Berwanger, *Frontier Against Slavery*.

4. Foner, *Free Soil, Free Labor, Free Men*, p. 290.

5. This assessment is based on an unpublished paper by David M. Katzman, "Slavery in Michigan." Professor Katzman is at work on a general study of blacks in Michigan, and he has generously given me information and criticism.

6. *Laws of the Territory of Michigan*, Vol. II (Lansing, 1871), 635. The exclusionist intent of the law was made apparent by the Detroit *Gazette*, October 1 and 8, 1829.

7. "Papers Relative to the Insurrection of Negroes," *Michigan Pioneer Collections*, XII (1908), 591-93. Silas Farmer, *History of Detroit and Michigan*, I (Detroit: S. Farmer & Co., 1884), 345-46.

with the status of ethnic minorities, especially foreign immigrants. Early in 1834 the Council briefly enfranchised Indians and "persons of color" who paid taxes. This reversed the 1819 Congressional law which limited suffrage to "free white male citizens." But the very next day the Council excluded non-whites as it broadened white suffrage to allow all free, white male *inhabitants* above 21 and three months resident to vote, although only citizens could be elected delegates. A minority of three Whigs and two Democrats opposed this bill, because they wanted voting limited to citizens and extended to non-whites.[8] These patterns would reappear: supporters of alien suffrage tended to oppose non-white voting while advocates of colored suffrage tended to oppose non-citizen voting.

In the Constitutional Convention of 1835 alien suffrage was the most controversial issue. Democrats favoring alien suffrage held a strong majority, but failed to dominate proceedings completely because of an intraparty split.[9] Nor could they prevent a few delegates from raising the issue of colored suffrage. During lengthy debates over alien suffrage, Democrat Ross Wilkins of Lenawee County, a Methodist lay preacher, appealed to the natural rights philosophy underlying the Declaration of Independence to justify striking out the word white from the franchise article.[10] Some of the convention's most prominent men disputed Wilkins. John Norvell, Democratic leader and champion of alien suffrage, denied that voting was a natural right. He believed that the Negro belonged to "a degraded cast of mankind," and he raised two spectres that defenders of white suffrage would continue to raise for years: the "flood" and "amalgamation." Norvell appealed to the delegates' "sense of honor and respectability which they cherished for themselves, their wives, their sons and daughters, whether they would suffer the negro to become an equal member in their families; whether they would go to the polls with him as a voter."[11] Joining Norvell were Democrats John R. Williams, on his way to becoming one of Detroit's most popular mayors, and Issac Crary, elected congressman in 1827. Crary made a curious appeal to utilitarianism in justifying white-only suffrage, arguing that blacks must give up

---

8. Territory of Michigan, *Acts Passed at the Extra and Second Session of Sixth Legislative Council* (Detroit, 1835), 74-76.
9. Ronald P. Formisano, "A Case Study of Party Formation: Michigan, 1835," *Mid-America*, Vol. 50 (April, 1968), 91-104.
10. Harold M. Dorr, ed., *The Michigan Constitutional Conventions of 1835-36: Debates and Proceedings* (Ann Arbor: University of Michigan Press, 1940), pp. 155-56.
11. *Debates*, pp. 157-58, 165-66.

Ross Wilkins

more of their natural rights than whites "to conduce to the greatest happiness for the greatest number."[12]

Wilkins' amendment failed by a vote of 63 to 17 with the few identifiable Whigs (who opposed alien suffrage) joining the Democratic bloc in opposing it. Democratic supporters of colored suffrage joined the Democratic bloc in opposing it. Democratic supporters of colored suffrage, however, tended also to be those who opposed alien suffrage.[13] In the future colored suffrage would continue to be not only a matter of racial but also of ethnic politics.

While some white openness to blacks probably existed, impressionistic evidence demonstrating a prevailing hostility is easily found. One article unsuccessfully submitted to the 1835 convention would have barred slaves, paupers, and colored persons from entering the state.[14] The white desire to keep schools segregated is evident throughout the antebellum period and beyond.[15] Contemporary accounts of the number of blacks in Michigan in 1837 differ, but no estimate

12. *Debates*, pp. 161-62. Alpheus White, another Detroit Democrat and prominent Irish Catholic layman, defended caste as instituted "by the Great Creator himself." His countryman Michael Stubbs of Washtenaw County joined him in voting against colored suffrage and in supporting broad suffrage for aliens, *ibid.*, pp. 163-64, Appendix A. Roll Call 17.
13. *Debates*, pp. 162, 167-68; see also remarks of E. D. Ellis, editor of the *Monroe Michigan Sentinel*, *ibid.*, p. 165.
14. Arthur R. Kooker, "The Anti-Slavery Movement in Michigan, 1796-1840; A Study in Humanitarianism on the American Frontier" (unpublished Ph.D. dissertation, University of Michigan, 1941), p. 107.
15. Farmer, *History of Detroit*, I, 750-51; Laura S. Haviland, *A Woman's Life Work* (Cincinnati: Walden & Stowe 1882), pp. 34-35, 36, 37; also, *History of St. Joseph County, Michigan* (Philadelphia: L. H. Everts & Co., 1877), pp. 181-82; John T. Blois, ed., *Gazeteer of Michigan, 1838* (Detroit: S. L. Rood & Co. 1838), p. 155.

exceeds 400—this in a white sea of over 170,000.[16] Clearly the physical presence of blacks was not the major reason for the prejudice and fear.

Critics of the abolitionists have always argued that the reformers cared too much for distant slaves and too little for their own black neighbors. Michigan abolitionists do not fit the stereotype of men with displaced guilt and aggression. Perceiving racial prejudice as "the most insuperable obstacle to the progress of universal Emancipation" they fought the reinforcing ties between segregation and colored "degredation" in their own communities.[17] In 1840-41 the new Liberty party and its organ, the Ann Arbor *Signal of Liberty*, made colored suffrage the leading issue of abolition's domestic war on slavery by launching a petition campaign directed at the state legislature.[18] Local abolition societies and churches all over the state sent petitions to the legislature the next several years praying that the legislature cease, as the state Liberty convention put it in 1845, this "cringing to slavery."[19]

The legislature ignored suffrage petitions until 1843, then reacted to a petition of "sundry colored inhabitants of Detroit" in a report written by Flavius Littlejohn, Whig-Free Soil candidate for governor in 1849. In 1843 Littlejohn was a Democrat; he has been described as having "radical" and "agrarian" leanings, but clearly his radicalism did not embrace natural rights. Claiming not to be an advocate of slavery, Littlejohn said he would "sedulously avoid the modern Utopian scheme of social equality and marital amalgamation." Littlejohn assumed black inferiority and opposed black suffrage because "the votes of the ignorant will ever receive an aristocratic

---

16. George N. Fuller, *Economic and Social Beginnings of Michigan, 1807-1837* (Lansing: Wynkoop, Hallenbeck, Crawford Co., 1917), p. 537.
17. Robert Banks, *An Oration: Delivered At A Celebration In Detroit, of the Abolition of Slavery in the West Indies, Held by Colored Americans, August 1, 1839* (Detroit, 1839). Banks was a black abolitionist and the white Detroit abolition society published his oration to combat prejudice by displaying his talents. For early concern of abolitionists with civil rights: Ann Arbor *Michigan Emigrant*, September 25, 1834, on microfilm, Michigan State Library; Farmer, *History of Detroit*, I, 346; Jackson *Michigan Freeman*, September 16, 1840, Michigan Historical Collections, Ann Arbor.
18. Theodore Foster to Birney, Dec. 14, 1841, Dwight L. Dumond, ed., *Letters of James Gillespie Birney, 1831-1857*, Vol. II (New York: D. Appleton-Century Co., Inc., 1938), 644. *Signal of Liberty*, Jan. 22, 1844.
19. *Proceedings of the Young Men's Liberty Convention* (Jackson, 1845), p. 6, Michigan Historical Collections; *Signal of Liberty*, Feb. 17, 1845. Blacks also joined in the first petitioning. *House Journal, 1841* (Detroit, 1841), p. 170. In 1843 the Liberty convention divided sharply on the seating of two colored delegates, then unanimously accepted them, *Signal*, Feb. 20, 27, July 31, 1843. Colored men participated conspicuously in the Michigan Antislavery Society conventions, *Signal*, April 28, 1841, Oct. 24, 1842.

direction."[20] Guy Carpenter, an "anti-slavery Democrat" from Lenawee County, challenged Littlejohn by reaffirming the universalism of natural rights. His republicanism knew no political distinction between the "learned and the unlearned—the high and the low—the rich and the poor—the Asiatic, African, European or American." But in Michigan part of the people did not enjoy self-government: "they are compelled to be ruled by laws which they had no voice in enacting. And they are taxed, but they are not represented." Southern slavery had no connection with suffrage in Michigan: Carpenter would not truckle to the South and oppress local citizens.[21]

The white legislature's interest in colored suffrage coincided with a growing black activism and with increasing focus on colored disfranchisement throughout the North. Black agitation for full political rights in New York state had stirred in 1837. The disfranchisement of Pennsylvania's colored citizens in 1838 no doubt affected blacks elsewhere, while the politicizing of the antislavery movement, as well as schisms among abolitionists, may have moved black reformers to take amelioration more into their own hands.[22] By 1842 Detroit had a Colored Vigilant Committee, formed to wage "moral and political warfare" for equal rights. In the summer of 1843 black activists held their first national convention. In its wake Michigan's "Colored Citizens," like those of other states, held a state convention in October at Detroit. Led by clergymen and small businessmen, they protested their exclusion from educational facilities they were taxed to support. Most of all they objected

Flavius Littlejohn

20. For a misleading description of Littlejohn, Floyd B. Streeter, *Political Parties in Michigan, 1837-1860* (Lansing: Michigan Historical Commission, 1918), pp. 83, 111. State of Michigan, *Documents Accompanying the House Journal, 1843*. (Detroit, 1843), Doc. No. 3, p. 17.
21. Richard I. Bonner, ed., *Memoirs of Lenawee County, Michigan*, Vol. 1 (Madison, Wisconsin: Western Historical Association, 1909). *Documents Accompanying the House Journal, 1843*, Doc. No. 14, pp. 68, 69, 70.
22. Quarles, *Black Abolitionists*, pp. 171, 172, 174; Howard H. Bell, "National Negro Conventions of the Middle 1840's: Moral Suasion vs. Political Action," *Journal of Negro History*, XLIII (July, 1957), 248-54.

to disfranchisement which clearly symbolized their general exclusion from the community. Their resolutions combined insightful analysis of politics with disdain for colonization and for northern proslavery "doughface" politicians. The published address showed how keenly middle-class black leaders felt discrimination and how vigorously they resented the slur of inferiority.[23]

In 1844 hundreds of white voters over the entire state joined in the petition campaign. The legislators ignored them but the flow revived the next year,[24] finally triggering two more opposing reports. Senator Samuel Denton, Washtenaw County Democrat, eloquently attacked "the preposterous peurility of making *color* a qualification for suffrage." Denton said that suffrage exclusion violated the state constitution which guaranteed all citizens that their rights be protected and gave whites separate privileges. The suffrage would give the 800 to 1000 blacks in Michigan a stake in "the collective body." But if their interests are kept "small and degraded, crime and outrage are the almost certain result." Those who believed in colored inferiority ignored "the effects produced on a race by continual servitude and a denial of education, during a series of generations. Reverse the situation of the African and the European and make one the master, and the other the slave for centuries, and the white man will possess the supposed characteristics of natural inferiority."[25] Denton's opponent in 1845, Democratic Senator Abner Pratt of Marshall, saw no reason for a change in the state constitution. Nothing was more fatal to republicanism, he said, than constant alterations of fundamental law, particularly when made "merely to gratify the whim or caprice of those who are unstable in their views as religious fanaticts [sic] or ambitious politicians." Pratt of course raised the twin spectres of the flood and amalgamation. Denton's "extraordinary" constitutional arguments if carried to their logical extent would lead to a dissolution of civil government and society: "whites and blacks would have to live in common, enjoy their property, pleasures and political honors in common, and the moment a fugitive slave arrived from Kentucky . . . he would be entitled . . . to share the white man's bliss and connubial happiness.[26]

In 1846 another black and white petition campaign elicited one more round of reports from the legislature on colored suffrage. The report endorsing suffrage is of particular significance because its author was Austin Blair of Jackson, Republican governor during the Civil War. An early example of political sociology, Blair's report dwelt frankly on the interdependence of social and political status: "He who may not vote is as powerless practically as if he were dead or enslaved." Blair regarded colored people as "long oppressed" but not inherently inferior. "If by our unjust laws we have degraded the man and besotted his intellect, it is a refinement of our cruelty to make this the pretext of our continuous oppression."[27] Senator William T. Howell, Hillsdale Democrat and later a Republican, submitted the 1846 report against colored suffrage. While Howell approved of the Declaration of Independence he argued that its phraseology regarding the equality of men did not constitute "a political injunction to allow all 'nations, kindred and tongues,' to be commingled into one individual and inseparable community."[28] Rather, Howell's view of white democracy foreshadowed the ethnocentric nationalism which would intensify in the United States in the 1880s and 1890s.

Yet while legislative committees in the 1840s reported pro and con, limited evidence indicates that blacks in many localities were attempting to vote and sometimes succeeding. In 1834 in Monroe stalwart Democrats worked at election polls all day to challenge and exclude "many Negro voters." Monroe was an old settlement, but a similar proceeding disturbed the frontier township of Almont, Lapeer County. On the other hand Negroes appear to have voted in county elections in Washtenaw, and Samuel Denton claimed that blacks voted in Detroit in 1844.[29]

Some mulattoes probably voted because they passed for white. This testified, in the eyes of reformers, to the ambiguity and irrationality of "white" suffrage. "Who," asked Denton, "is to decide

---

23. *Minutes of the State Convention of the Colored Citizens of Michigan, Detroit, October 16-27, 1843* (Detroit, 1843); *Signal of Liberty*, Jan. 23, 1843; also, State of Michigan, *House Journal, 1844* (Detroit, 1844), pp. 32, 309; *House Journal, 1845* (Detroit, 1845), p. 13; Black leaders identified in James Wellings, ed., *Directory of the City of Detroit*, 1845 (Detroit: Harsha & Willcox, 1845).
24. *House Journal, 1844*, pp. 14, 42, 51, 57-58, 66, 74, 89, 95, 101, 107, 114, 142, 223, 261, 293; *House Journal, 1845*, pp. 46, 73, 130, 143, 342.
25. State of Michigan, *Documents Accompanying the Senate Journal, 1845* (Detroit, 1845), Doc. No. 15, "Report of the Committee on State Affairs," pp. 1-2, 6, 7; Farmer, *History of Detroit*, I, 346, 700-01.
26. *Documents Accompanying the Senate Journal, 1845*, Doc. No. 15, "Minority Report of the Committee on State Affairs," pp. 13-14, 15; *Michigan Biographies*, p. 534.
27. *Documents Accompanying the House Journal, 1846* (Detroit, 1846), Doc. No. 12, pp. 1, 2-3; Austin Blair MSS, Burton Historical Collection, Detroit Public Library (BHC). It has been claimed that Blair's stand cost him re-election in 1846, but no one has ever presented evidence to support or contradict this.
28. *Documents Accompanying the Senate Journal, 1846*, Doc. No. 12, pp. 1-2.
29. James Q. Adams to Lyon, Jan. 26, 1835, Lucius Lyons MSS, William L. Clements Library, Ann Arbor; *History of Lapeer County, Michigan* (Chicago: H. R. Page & Co., 1884), p. 34; *House Journal, 1841*, p. 179. Men of mixed white, black, or Indian parentage in Northern Michigan probably voted as they had in territorial days, Clarence Edwin Carter, ed., *The Territorial Papers of the United States*, Vol. XI, *The Territory of Michigan, 1820-1829* (Washington: U. S. Gov't. Printing Off., 1943), pp. 729, 730.

the fact or the quality of color?"[30] This question received an answer in a court case growing out of a mulatto's being denied the vote in Detroit in 1844. "Gordon," of one-fourth African blood, had not been allowed to vote by election inspectors. In November 1845 a circuit court jury awarded him twelve and one-half cents damage because "the Saxon blood in him greatly predominates over the African." The Supreme Court in 1847 in *Gordon v. Farrar* reversed the decision and held that only Inspectors of Election had power to decide whether a man was white or not. An individual's oath that he was white did not supercede their judgment. Defending the inspectors was Detroit lawyer and Whig leader William A. Howard, whom the Republicans elected to Congress in 1854.[31]

The court's decision, combined with the growing sectional crisis over slavery extension from 1846 to 1849, probably caused a decline in petition agitation.[32] Indeed, the submergence of the Liberty party in the Free Soil movement also may have inhibited civil rights agitation. Eric Foner has shown that in New York State, as political antislavery broadened and became a more heterogeneous coalition, concern for free black rights disappeared from public view. In Michigan the same general trend appeared. In 1848 Free Soilers and Whigs cooperated in congressional and local elections. By 1849 the two parties united on candidates for state office: their platform wholly ignored racial political equality. Their gubernatorial candidate, Flavius Littlejohn, issued no retraction of his unequivocal rejection of colored voting in 1843.[33]

Yet suffrage sentiment remained alive, especially among black leaders and white moral reformers. When a constitutional convention gathered in 1850, long petitions from all over the state arrived asking suffrage extension. A state convention of colored citizens assembled at Marshall in March to voice its grievance of taxation without representation.[34] As in 1835, the colored suffrage issue sounded as a counterpoint to alien suffrage disputes, but now a confident Democratic majority united in enfranchising large numbers of aliens.[35] The arguments familiar on both sides reappeared with the major difference being a degeneration of tone.

The black exclusionists, particularly, asserted colored inferiority more crudely and aggressively. John S. Bagg of Detroit, Democratic stalwart and *Free Press* editor, ridiculed colored suffrage by ridiculing blacks. He would not list ten thousand reasons, said Bagg, nor would he "go to the zoophyte and trace up the numerous gradations in animal life to our noble selves, and say what rank the African holds in the chain." But if they let Africans vote the whole state would be "peopled by these dark bypeds—a species not equal to ourselves." Voting would lead to being voted for and election to high office. "What man would like to see his daughter encircled by one of these sable gentlemen, breathing in her ear the soft accents of love?" The Declaration of Independence referred only to whites. Since the federal constitution was based on slavery, a vote for Negro suffrage would violate it.[36] Bagg, sensitive to popular prejudices, knew that the climate of opinion would not only permit but approve his performance. However, not just skilled demagogues showed themselves ready to play upon men's fears. Reverend John D. Pierce, graduate of Brown and Princeton, first state Superintendent of Public Instruction and "father" of Michigan's common schools, also raised the cry of "amalgamation" and carefully defined suffrage as a "conventional" and not a natural right.[37]

Only one delegate gave a major speech for colored suffrage: DeWitt C. Leach, Free Soil-Whig from Genesee County, soon to be editor of the Jackson *American Citizen* and a key organizer of Republicanism. Leach and Joseph R. Williams, later first President of the Michigan Agricultural College established by Republicans, tried to expose Democratic inconsistency. "Universal suffrage" was the "buncombe" cry, they said, until it came to colored men. Blacks were called ignorant and vicious and delegates said they did not want to take them home, yet many ignorant foreigners would be enfranchised whom the delegates certainly would not invite into their homes. Democrat Calvin Britain, elected Lieutenant Governor in 1852, responded by calling the white foreigner "our father and brother . . . even a little 'crossing of the breed' would not disgrace either party."

30. *Documents Accompanying Senate Journal, 1845*, p. 6.
31. *Gordon v. Farrar* 2 Douglass 411 (1878).
32. *House Journal 1846*, pp. 15, 20, 21, 26, 69, 74, 78, 82, 93, 113, 114, 132, 145, "William Douglas and other colored persons," p. 123, "Geo. W. Tucker and other colored persons," p. 400; *House Journal, 1847*, "and colored persons," p. 142; *House Journal, 1848*, p. 200.
33. Eric Foner, "Racial Attitudes of the New York Free Soilers," *New York History*, XLVI (October, 1965), 312, 325-26, passim.
34. State of Michigan, *Report of the Proceedings and Debates in the Convention to Revise the Constitution, 1850* (Lansing, 1850), pp. 93, 175, 257, 137, 126, 120, 102, 218, 68, Index pp. 933-34; adverse petitions, pp. 240, 881; *Journal of the Constitutional Convention of 1850* (Lansing, 1850), p. 287. One petition from Wayne had 420 signatures of men prominent in business, politics and Protestant benevolence. For address of colored convention, Detroit *Free Press*, June 10, 1850.
35. *Report of Constitutional Convention, 1850*, p. 284; Frederick W. Stevens, *Michigan Constitutional Convention of 1850*, (n.p., n.d.), p. 23.
36. *Report of Constitutional Convention, 1850*, pp. 288-89, 285, 286-87.
37. *Ibid.*, pp. 289, 290, 291; Elias S. Woodman, "Reminiscences of the Constitutional Convention of 1850," *Michigan Pioneer Collections*, XVII (Lansing, 1910), 347-49.

DeWitt C. Leach

The convention as expected retained white suffrage, though it allowed detribalized Indians to vote, and decided to submit colored suffrage to a popular referendum.[38] Michigan voters' resistance to colored suffrage can be directly measured in the 1850 referendum— the best available index of public opinion. In the state 71.3 per cent of 44,914 votes went against colored suffrage. The total vote was 24.0 per cent less than the 60,306 cast in three congressional races on the same day, indicating apathy, disinterest, lack of information, or inability to make a decision on colored suffrage. Although opposition to non-white voting cut across party lines, a scanning of township returns suggests that *"no"* votes came mostly from Democratic strongholds.[39] Similarly, county and township returns (and county-level correlations) either support or do not contradict the commonly accepted proposition that antislavery voters (Liberty and Free Soil) tended to follow abolitionist leaders on this issue and supported equal suffrage.[40]

The county-level data correlations of Democratic voting in 1850 and 1852 (percentages) with the vote against colored suffrage were insignificant. But the comparison of township antisuffrage votes and Democratic party voting for 1850 *within* eighteen counties, representing all parts of the state except the extreme north, produced a much different result.* Seventeen of the eighteen counties showed a positive correlation between Democratic loyalty and anti-suffrage voting. In twelve of the seventeen that correlation could be described as strong; in ten it was over .500.

---

*Correlations for 18 Michigan counties of vote against colored suffrage with vote for Democrats, 1850 or 1852, by townships.

East		Central		West	
Wayne	+.462	Jackson	+.653	St. Joseph	+.059
Monroe	+.682	Eaton	+.364	Kent	+.505
Macomb	+.589	Branch	+.787	Barry	+.225
Lenawee	+.775	Kalamazoo	+.276	Cass	+.667
Hillsdale	+.462	Calhoun	+.720	Berrien	+.525
Livingston	+.555	Clinton	+.121	Allegan	−.143

For five of these counties the 1850 suffrage vote by township was compared with economic and social data regarding the potential voters in each township, data tabulated from the manuscript schedules of the 1850 federal census of population. The antisuffrage vote in the townships of these five counties was compared with *ruralness* (the percent of potential voters engaged in non-urban, farm-related occupations); with the percentage of potential voters in the *rural lower classes* (defined as general unskilled laborers, farm laborers and tenants, and farmers owning real estate worth $500 or less); and with the percent *foreign born*.# The five counties represent a rough cross-section of the settled bottom half of the state.[41] Although the data are limited, certain observations can be made. Except for

---

#1850 No Vote on Equal Suffrage in 5 Michigan counties correlated with ruralness, rural lower classes (RLC), and foreign born (FB) among potential voters.

	Rural	RLC	FG
Wayne	+.726	+.553	+.191
Eaton	−.181	−.191	+.310
Kalamazoo	+.217	+.370	+.012
St. Joseph	−.017	+.116	+.392
Barry	−.215	−.035	−.155

---

38. *Report of the Constitutional Convention, 1850*, pp. 292-93, 295, 490-91; 296-97, 482, 483, 191.
39. Streeter, *Political Parties, 1837-1860*, pp. 133-34; "Statements in from county canvassers, 1850," Great Seal and Archives, Executive Papers: Election Returns, Box 7, Michigan Historical Commission, Lansing; Kalamazoo *Gazette*, October 25, November 1, 1850, microfilm, Michigan State Library. I collected election returns by county and for all counties by minor civil divisions between 1835 and 1860 for a study of parties and voting. The returns, gathered from newspapers, county archives, and the Michigan Historical Commission archives are not always complete. For example, the referendum vote on suffrage was available by township only for those 18 counties examined here.
40. John L. Stanley, "Majority Tyranny in Tocqueville's America: The Failure of Negro Suffrage in 1846," *Political Science Quarterly*, LXXXIV (September, 1969), 423. Robert R. Dykstra and Harlan Hahn, "Northern Voters and Negro Suffrage: The Case of Iowa, 1868," *The Public Opinion Quarterly*, XXXII (Summer, 1968), 202-15.
41. *U. S. Seventh Census of the United States, 1850*. Population Schedules: Michigan; on microfilm, BHC.

Wayne, there was little association between ruralness and opposition to colored suffrage. The Wayne data are based on the county's townships excluding Detroit. Yet Detroit, the only town resembling a city or urban area in Michigan, voted 87.0 per cent "no", higher than the county aggregate "no" vote of 84.2 per cent and well above the state per cent of 71.3.

Most other towns or large villages voted more strongly against colored suffrage than the rest of the state, but the returns for all population centers are not available, and of those that are, the village returns are often aggregated with those of adjacent rural townships and of little use.[42] The available data must all be treated with caution and at this point all that can be said with any confidence is that they show no strong tendency except for the positive relationship of Democratic voting to opposition to equal suffrage.

The correlations between per cent foreign born and anti-suffrage voting were of some positive significance in only two of five counties, yet other data suggests strong hostility to colored suffrage among certain ethnocultural groups, especially in concentrated enclaves, whether in town or country. The homogenous, thriving German Catholic settlement of Westphalia, Clinton County, voted 92 per cent "no". Saginaw County, inundated by Lutheran Germans in the late 1840s, voted 83.1 per cent against; in Riga, Lenawee County, and Warren, Macomb County, pockets of Germans probably helped register high "no" votes of 84 and 77 per cent. The Fourth and Seventh wards in Detroit, both heavily German Lutheran and Catholic, voted 84 and 82 per cent "no". Detroit's Eighth ward, otherwise known as "Corktown", voted 89 per cent "no". Rural Catholic Irish, constituting almost all of the farmers in Erin, Macomb County, voted 100 per cent "no". Heavily Irish Harrison nearby also voted 100 per cent "no". In Erin, while 108 voted in the congressional election, only six failed to vote against colored suffrage. In Sanilac County, a frontier area in 1850 (under the "thumb" of the lower peninsula), Irish, Scots-Irish, English and French from Canada voted 88.9 per cent "no". The oldest white settlers in Michigan, the French Catholic natives, went heavily against colored suffrage. Ecorse, a poor, rural French township in Wayne voted 100 per cent "no", while to the south in Monroe County, Frenchtown voted 94 per cent "no". Like Frenchtown, Monroe township contained many old, "respectable" French settlers; it voted 100 per cent "no". Later in the 1850s a popular Catholic priest set off an "explosion" in Frenchtown when he tried to rent a pew to "a very respectable colored man." The reaction was unprecedented. "A prominent Frenchman gathered a gang around him after Mass, and boldly denounced the action, claiming the Negro had no soul, etc. Petitions were circulated, and the priest was told he was not wanted."[42]

Towns supporting colored suffrage could be found in various sections and represented both frontier and advanced stages of development. The presence of blacks did not seem related to pro or anti suffrage voting.[44] Only the religious factor appears to have some association with "yes" voting. Quaker influence usually acted to produce sympathy for racial political integration. In Cass County, where almost 400 of Michigan's 2500 blacks lived, some 160 dwelled in Calvin township. The predominantly Quaker voters there gave the town an unusual 60 per cent majority for colored suffrage. A few townships elsewhere voted 80, 90, even 100 per cent "yes". Such towns usually cast heavy anti-Democratic votes through the years and often were places where pietism flourished, especially Yankee evangelicalism of the Congregational-Presbyterian-Baptist variety. Although many Yankee evangelical Protestants also voted against equal suffrage, one could still conclude that "religion" or evangelicalism and hostility to Democrats were associated with suffrage sentiment.[45]

Despite the high correlation between Democratic strength and opposition to black voting, party loyalty may not have acted as an independent influence on voter decisions. Rather, the same kind of social groups voting Democratic would also tend to reject colored suffrage. Whig loyalists would also include more men willing to vote for equal suffrage, although Whig opponents of broader suffrage probably equaled or exceeded its supporters. Similarly, the kind of conscience-driven voter who would leave Whiggery to testify for abolition would be the type generally willing to support colored suffrage. Thus party loyalty primarily reinforced existing voter dis-

---

42. Population from J. D. B. DeBow, ed., *Statistical View of the United States* (Washington, 1854).
43. Frank A. O'Brien, "Le Pere Juste," *Michigan Pioneer Collections*, XXX (1901), 271. Also, *Signal of Liberty*, Oct. 27, 1841.
44. In New York, anti-suffrage voting was simply an "index" to other conditions. Stanley, *Political Science Quarterly*, LXXXIV, 424. In Michigan, there were simply too few colored persons to make such a test meaningful. All over the state lily-white townships rang up impressive majorities against equal suffrage.
45. The documentation for these assertions is too extensive to reproduce, involving county histories, newspapers, manuscripts and census data used in my forthcoming study: *The Birth of Mass Political Parties: Michigan, 1827-1861* (Princeton: Princeton University Press, 1971).

positions, especially among Democrats and Liberty-Free Soil men. Opposition to equal suffrage cut across all social groups, but probably was strongest among Democratic-tending immigrant Catholics and some new British immigrants; support seemed confined to Quakers and certain evangelical Yankees.

If partisan influences had little influence on the suffrage vote, sectionalism had even less. The referendum came in the wake of intense sectional conflict in 1849-1850, which subsided after the Compromise of 1850. The latter included a new Fugitive Slave Law, the most pro-Southern of the compromise elements. Northern reaction to the law helped elect two of three Michigan congressmen who ran as Whig-Free Soil coalitionists and narrowly missed electing a third. Simultaneously, however, voters emphatically denied colored men the franchise. As sectionalism quieted and the major parties united and quelled internal dissent, antislavery and ameliorationist zeal declined.

Whereas reformers had previously asked for colored suffrage, in the early 50's they petitioned for repeal of the new Fugitive Slave Law. Some legislators in 1851 issued a reply notable for its contempt for the petitioners.[46] A voice reflecting the reformers' despair at this point came from across the Detroit River at Sandwich, Canada, where Henry Bibb, ex-slave, printed news for blacks everywhere, especially runaways, and preached morality and temperance. Bibb advised the oppressed colored persons of Michigan "to settle in Canada, where the laws made no distinction among men." He told of how in Sandwich he had the pleasure of seeing for the first time colored men walk up to the polls and vote "unmolested by a rum-sucking mob, as would have been the case just across the river, perhaps in the name of Democracy." That Michigan allowed Indians to vote made colored disfranchisement doubly hateful.[47] Some Michigan abolitionists joined Bibb in promoting "emigration" although not much seems to have come of their plan to buy 50,000 acres there. Its significance probably lies in showing their ebbing morale and ambivalent commitment to integration.[48]

Amelioration and antislavery sagged drastically until 1854; then tremendous political turmoil erupted and sectional crisis renewed.

---

46. State of Michigan, *House Journal, 1851* (Lansing, 1851), pp. 399, 113, 385. Most of the petitions came from Lenawee County and probably from Quakers. *Documents Accompanying the Senate and House Journals, 1851* (Lansing, 1851), House Doc. No. 15, "Colored Population in Michigan," *ibid.* House Doc. No. 16, "Report of the Committee on Federal Relations, relative to the Fugitive Slave Law and Slavery in the Territories"; *Senate and House Journal, Extra Session, 1851*, p. 18.
47. *Voice of the Fugitive*, Vol. 1, No. 1, January 1, January 15, February 26, March 12, 1851.
48. *Voice of the Fugitive*, May 7, June 1, July 2, 1851.

Reaction to the Kansas-Nebraska "iniquity" (by which slavery would be permitted north of the old Missouri Compromise line) and a variety of moral reform movements brought the Republican party into being. This is usually assumed by black and white historians to have had a beneficial impact on the fortunes of blacks. But the immediate impact of sectional crisis and Republican birth did not lead to gains for free colored persons. While agitation for colored suffrage revived, the measure still failed to secure passage well after Republicans won control of the state. Some Republicans made vigorous efforts, but simultaneously white prejudice and fear of "floods" and "amalgamation" intensified. In fact, racial diatribes became a more explicit and frequent part of the political scene.

The stiffening of white hostility must be examined first in the context of mid-nineteenth century party warfare. Democrats had habitually stimulated negrophobia, first as a weapon against abolitionists, later as a defense against Whig and Free Soil anti-Southernism and antislavery.[49] After 1853 the Democratic Detroit *Free Press,* under the direction of Wilbur F. Storey, became a vocal and persistent champion of white supremacy and made "nigger" baiting of "Black Republicans" an almost daily habit. Many Democratic newspapers seem to have followed Storey's lead and helped propagate the stream of vituperation flowing from Detroit. During 1860 Stephen A. Douglas campaigned in Detroit and charged that the Republicans wanted "to establish equal rights between the white men and the Negro, and universal suffrage in favor of the Negro. (Cries of 'It shall never be.')—According to the doctrines of the democratic party, this government was made for the white man, to be administered by white men, and nobody else,—(Cheers.)."[50]

In reply, Republicans generally expressed as much racism as Whigs or Free Soilers ever had. True, such durable advocates of civil liberties as Austin Blair and former abolitionist Erastus Hussey guided the "Personal Liberty Laws" through the 1855 Republican legislature. But even these laws met some opposition in Republican ranks and were designed primarily to frustrate the Fugitive Slave

---

49. *Argus,* November 1, 1838; *Free Press,* November 7, 1850; other examples: *Argus,* November 5, 1835; Detroit *Morning Post,* December 7, 1837; *Free Press,* November 5, 1847, November 4, 1850; Centreville *Western Chronicle,* November 2, 1850, November 17, 1849.
50. Justin E. Walsh, "Radically and Thoroughly Democratic: Wilbur F. Storey and the Detroit Free Press 1853 to 1861," *Michigan History,* XLVII (Sptember, 1963), 207; the Centreville *Western Chronicle,* and Pontiac *Jacksonian* were particularly virulent; *Chronicle,* April 20, 1857, July 28, 1859, microfilm Michigan State Library; *Argus,* October 29, 1858; Douglas's speech: *Chronicle,* October 25, 1860. See also, Justin E. Walsh, *To Print the News and Raise Hell: A Biography of Wilbur F. Storey* (Chapel Hill: University of North Carolina Press, 1968).

Law and defy the South. They implied no wish that blacks be politically integrated. Some brave Republicans occasionally denounced racism publicly.[51] But Republicans usually reacted to accusations of "nigger worship" by hurling the charge back at their opponents. This was usually done defensively and with less animus against blacks, emphasizing a concern with white rights. Democrats "worshipped niggers," Republicans said, because they kowtowed to a Southern power dependent on Negro slaves. Republicans would benefit whites by limiting slavery which was harmful to free labor.[52]

In an atmosphere in which any suggested benefit to blacks brought cries of "amalgamation," prospects for colored suffrage could hardly be bright. Yet in 1855 petitioning from blacks and whites renewed, perhaps stimulated by the new Republican legislature's anticipated inclination toward moral reform projects.[53] On a local level the black farmers of Calvin Township in Cass County won the right to vote at school district meetings and to hold district offices. Republicans thus approved separate but self-controlled colored schools in Calvin. Meanwhile a Republican dominated Senate committee recommended general colored suffrage, but the legislature remained immobile as before.[54]

In 1856, perhaps because of misinterpretation of the Cass County legislation Democratic newspapers declared "NEGROES CAN'T VOTE" while Republican state Attorney General Jacob M. Howard reaffirmed the 1847 Court decision, Gordon v. Farrarr, which stated that Election Inspectors could determine a voter's color.[55] Despite these handicaps the new legislature of 1857 was beseiged with petitions from whites and blacks, but a Senate committee recommended against enfranchisement, saying it believed a majority of voters did not want it.[56] In 1859 a new and larger flurry of petitions from blacks and whites greeted the legislature. The defenders of caste

---

51. *Gazette*, August 5, 1854; another rare example: *Grand Traverse Herald*, January 14, 1859.
52. Marshall *Statesman*, July 5, 1854, August 13, 1856; Jackson *American Citizen*, April 10, December 4, 1856; Grand Rapids *Daily Eagle*, June 16, 1858; Hillsdale *Standard*, October 30, 1860; Detroit *Advertiser*, November 10 and 15, 1858; Mary Karl George, *Zachariah Chandler: A Political Biography* (East Lansing: Michigan State University Press, 1969), p. 29.
53. State of Michigan, *House Journal, 1855* (Lansing, 1855), pp. 24, 453, 462; *Senate Journal, 1855* (Lansing, 1855), pp. 112, 113.
54. *Compiled Laws of Michigan*, Vol. 1, 759.
55. Kalamazoo *Gazette*, October 31, 1856.
56. State of Michigan, *House Journal, 1857* (Lansing, 1857), pp. 175-79, 226, 468-69, 531; *Documents Accompanying the House Journal, 1857*, (Lansing, 1857), Doc. No. 9, "Petition of Olney Hawkins and 300 others of Ann Arbor"; *Senate Journal, 1857*, pp. 14, 150; *Documents Accompanying the Senate Journal, 1857*, Doc. No. 24, "Petition of Curtis Emerson, Seth C. Buel, and 91 others. . . ." *Senate Journal, 1857*, p. 319.

moved to discredit colored suffrage by proposing that intermarriage between whites and blacks, forbidden by state law, be legalized. This clearly aimed at embarrassing Republicans and capitalizing on the sensational elopement in Oakland County of a white farmer's daughter with a black hired hand. The Pontiac *Jacksonian* gloated over the wrath of the wealthy father, "a red hot abolitionist, of the whole-hog-nigger-as-good-as-any-body-style." For years he had treated colored hired men as equals, now "his own daughter was clasped in the embrace of a black, greasy nigger, willing and ready, and even enthusiastically reciprocal, in the secret game of dalliance which lovers (?) delight to celebrate their union."[57] Hysteria appeared simultaneously in the state Senate. A Democrat opposed to the enfranchisement of blacks in Cass County school districts let loose a Negrophobic ranting that virulently denied the humanity of blacks. Although 24 Republicans overwhelmed 7 Democrats and 1 Republican who tried to repeal the Cass County taxpayers' school franchise, this report was easily the acme of official racism in antebellum Michigan.[58]

In this climate it was not surprising that a Republican sponsored proposal to enfranchise males of African descent who owned unencumbered real estate valued at $200 ran into rough going. The Democrats on February 14 tried to amend the bill to enfranchise all aliens owning freeholds of $250. This failed 26 to 48 along almost straight party lines. The House then decided on the colored property franchise which, in the form of a joint resolution, needed a two-thirds majority. It gained a simple majority of 40 to 37. Solid Democratic opposition, combined with some one-fifth of the Republicans, killed equal suffrage in the House, although the earlier maneuvering (for which roll calls are not available) may have concealed even greater Republican opposition. Even if this suffrage bill had passed the House, the Republican Senate seemed little disposed to let colored men vote. Democrats pointed to the Republican voting as showing their "love for Sambo and Dinah, but their hatred of foreign born residents."[59]

During the tense electoral campaign of 1860 colored suffrage dropped out of sight. Republicans carried the state comfortably, and

---

57. *Senate Journal, 1859,* (Lansing, 1859), pp. 24, 130, 105, 227, 276; *House Journal, 1859,* pp. 32, 97, 167, 197, 168, 232, 721, 201, 204; *Jacksonian,* January 6, February 3, 1859.
58. *Senate Journal, 1859,* pp. 287-91; report of committee on expiring laws, pp. 593-97; party identifications, Detroit *Advertiser,* November 9, 1858.
59. *House Journal, 1859,* pp. 108, 399, 600-01, 602, 650, 753-54, 787, 819, 930, 931-32. *Documents Accompanying the House Journal, 1859* (Lansing, 1859), Doc. No. 25. *Michigan Argus,* March 4, April 1, 1859; Pontiac *Jacksonian,* February 17, 1859.

before Lincoln called out the troops in 1861 the Republican legislature showed even less willingness than previous legislatures to consider colored suffrage seriously. A small parade of petitions straggled in, led by one from a convention of colored citizens protesting "Taxation without Representation."[60] The House wavered between indecision and indifference while a Republican Senate committee sarcastically lectured the petitioners on writing petitions.[61]

In summarizing the suffrage struggle of the fifties, it has been generally assumed that the formation of the Republican party in the 1850s immediately helped blacks, but any weighing of this proposition must first confront the complexities of sectional, racial and ethnic politics in that decade. An 1858 Michigan Supreme Court case, *Day v. Owen,* demonstrated that as colored suffrage was derailed for another decade the lines of caste hardened. A black abolitionist William Day brought suit against the owner of the steamboat *Arrow* for refusing to carry him from Detroit to Toledo. Day offered to pay cabin fare, but though there was room in the cabin he was told that colored persons could only travel on deck. Day went by land instead and sued Owen for his embarrassment and trouble. Although a Republican lawyer represented Day, a Republican court decided against him and for the acknowledged custom of Jim Crow on the Great Lakes. Justice Randolph Manning, former Democrat but in 1859 a Republican, declared that while the right to be carried was superior to any regulation, Owen had simply denied Day "certain accomodations." Negroes, he said, echoing the Dred Scot decision, were not "a component part of the community." The carrier's regulation was long-standing and therefore reasonable, but it would not be reasonable to force him to incommode the community at large." Denying Owen's right to make his own regulations would further interfere with his "control over his own property."[62]

The race issue entered politics much more forcibly in the 1850s. The Democrats increasingly exploited white prejudice, colored suffrage became even more of a political football, and lost much of its overt white support. The suffrage debates of the 1840s, while they provoked much caste rhetoric, take on an aura of almost sedate rationality in comparison to the 1850s. Liberal integrationist sentiments, however marginal, certainly found much freer expression in the previous decade.

The slavery extension controversy raised the question of where blacks could go, and whatever their feelings about the South, most Michigan whites did not want blacks coming to Michigan. "Creeping amalgamation" was a spectre haunting the 1850s, and especially those Republicans who wanted to assure free blacks minimal legal and political rights—but who also must defend their flanks against incessant Democratic "niggering" and win elections.

Just as the slavery extension fight increased racial tensions and white resistance, so did the increase of ethnic and religious hostility after 1853. The Know Nothing movement, anti-foreign and especially anti-Catholic, had great strength in Michigan during the 1850s and was a major element in the Republican or "Fusion" coalition which won the state from 1854 through 1860. Cultural and religious issues continued to excite Michigan politics after the nativist high-tide of 1854-55.[63]

Alien suffrage debates since 1835 had demonstrated that colored rights had always been linked to other minority group social and political issues. The Democrats had exploited the Negrophobia of their ethnic supporters to reinforce party loyalty. As the Democratic political hegemony disintegrated after 1853, they desperately sought to stimulate racial fears in an attempt to undercut the Republicans' use of the sectional issue and shore up their crumbling majority. As they continued to lose elections, their frustration no doubt increased their reckless verbal aggression against the most defenseless target-group in society. Thus, the origins of Republicanism, in sectionalism and in domestic social cleavages' increased racial tension and damaged the cause of colored suffrage. The concrete political and social conditions attending the birth of the new coalition led to a heightening of caste barriers.

The reasoning in *Day v. Owen* typified the major defense of caste which could square itself with American equalitarian beliefs. Caste

---

60. In November 1860 Frederick Douglass said that "Equal Suffrage" was "almost exclusively in the hands of the colored people themselves. Neither Republicans nor Abolitionists seem to care much for it." Quoted in Philip S. Foner, *The Life and Writings of Frederick Douglass*, Vol. II, *Pre-Civil War Decade* (New York: International Pub. 1950), 525.
61. *House Journal, 1861* (Lansing, 1861), p. 1029; colored citizens' address, pp. 259-60; committee action, pp. 635, 1422. *Documents Accompanying the Senate Journal, 1861*, Doc. No. 28.
62. *Day V. Owen*, 5 Michigan 520-27 (1878). William Day was a freeborn black prominent in reform circles, Quarles, *Black Abolitionists*, pp. 134, 154-65, 217, 234-35. Two other Republican judges, one an ex-Free Soiler (I. P. Christiancy), concurred. One Republican legislator angrily and futilely proposed a bill requiring all steamboats and railroads "to allow negroes a cabin passage," *House Journal, 1859*, p. 621.
63. Formisano, *Birth of Mass Political Parties*, pp. 217-88. See also, Floyd B. Streeter, *Political Parties in Michigan 1837-1860* (Lansing: Michigan Historical Commission, 1918), pp. 178-206, and Michael Fitzgibbon Holt, *Forging a Majority: The Formation of the Republican Party in Pittsburgh, 1848-1860* (New Haven: Yale University Press, 1969), pp. 123-74, 281-82.

justified caste. Of course the arguments were more complex. Conservatives through the years stressed their "impotence in the grip of custom,"[64] or their fatalism before the dictates of nature, heaven or some other determinism. Whatever had decreed it, they could plainly see that blacks were separate and inferior, a lower caste not part of the white community. So they resisted pressure for black political integration and satisfied the imperatives of equalitarian beliefs and civil libertarian values by defining blacks as not part of their community. Their rationalizations and perceptions reinforced one another. In fairness to the white majority it should be added that many of their spokesmen made no secret of their attitudes which *preceded* their defensive rationales. Many whites regarded the existence of a colored population as unfortunate, wished it would go away, and fervently hoped it would not multiply.[65]

Those atypical progressives who stood against caste and public opinion would have begun to move toward a racially open society. They usually analyzed alleged black "degredation" by trying to understand the man-created part of the environment. Progressives assumed that men bore responsibility for some of the social boundaries of their lives and that they could act upon them. Some asserted that society itself created differences among men, and that social conditions could be influenced, adjusted or even changed by law. Advocates of political integration—not all of them abolitionists— tended to regard black development and status in the United States as shaped by history and environment, not inherent colored inferiority.

Finally, the exclusion of blacks from politics in Michigan, and all the rhetoric regarding their oppression, did not necessarily mean that black social and economic mobility was frozen.[66] Blacks however separately, may have been improving their socio-economic position even as their status worsened. Class structure within the black community may have been changing. The actual degree of integration in non-political areas, while one would hardly suppose it to have been extensive, is still a problem for systematic investigation, not assump-

---

64. The phrase is from John Dollard, *Caste and Class in a Southern Town* (New Haven: Yale University Press, 1937), p. 367.
65. For an analysis of this kind of thinking in the early republic see the chapter "Toward a White Man's Country," in Winthrop T. Jordan, *White Over Black: American Attitudes Toward the Negro, 1550-1812* (Chapel Hill: University of North Carolina Press, 1968).
66. Professor Katzman's work should provide much of the needed data. Special thanks for help with this article also go to John Waters, Herbert Gutman and Nada Wunsch.

tions. The rhetoric of political controversy and hortatory declamation is not a reliable guide to objective social conditions. The task of separating perceptions and persuasion from hard social data still remains.

HISTORY AND LEGAL INTERPRETATION: THE EARLY DISTORTION OF THE FOURTEENTH AMENDMENT BY THE GILDED AGE COURT

Edward M. Gaffney, Jr.[*]

I. LAW, HISTORY, AND LEGAL HISTORY

I can only hope that the result of the book [*A History of English Law*] will be to demonstrate, firstly, the essential incompleteness of English histories in which no account is taken of the legal point of view, and secondly, the impossibility of gaining a complete grasp of the principles of English law without a study of their history.[1]

In the preface to his monumental, fifteen-volume *A History of English Law*, Sir William Holdsworth succinctly states the mutual relationship between law and history. When considered in the American context, Sir Holdsworth's observation remains viable, but emphasis should be placed on his second observation; it seems more common for historians and students of history to be familiar with the holdings of *Marbury v. Madison*,[2] *Dred Scott v. Sandford*,[3] *Miranda v. Arizona*,[4] and *Roe v. Wade*[5] than it is for lawyers and law students to place significant constitutional rulings within their historical context.

Morton Horwitz has recently suggested that lawyers rarely pay attention to the way in which the legal tradition has been shaped by "both the internal demand of professionalization and the external demand for creating an ideological buffer zone between the claims of politics and those of law."[6] As a result, the legal tradition—the "prime matter" of American legal history—has been treated as a kind of meta-historical set of eternal values

---

[*] Instructor in Law and Religion, Boston College. B.A., 1963, St. Patrick's College; S.T.L., 1967, Gregorian University (Rome); J.D., M.A. (Legal History), 1975, Catholic University of America.
1. W. HOLDSWORTH, A HISTORY OF ENGLISH LAW viii (1931).
2. 5 U.S. (1 Cranch) 137 (1803).
3. 60 U.S. (19 How.) 393 (1856).
4. 384 U.S. 436 (1966).
5. 410 U.S. 113 (1973).
6. Horwitz, *The Conservative Tradition in the Writing of American Legal History*, 17 AM. J. LEGAL HIST. 275, 278 (1973).

rather than as the contingent, changing product of specific historical struggles within which social conflict always takes place. Horwitz noted further that, for decades, American legal history remained isolated within a narrow mold of technicalities imposed by lawyers untrained in the discipline of history or of other human sciences. Shaped by the dominant influence of Dean Roscoe Pound, the basic categories of American legal history were shot through with unexamined, conservative political choices disguised in the neutral garb of "objective" history.[7] For example, Pound thought of "the received legal tradition" as a sort of anti-Marxist medicine which would immunize legal historians against the dread disease of serious economic analysis.[8] In a similar vein, lack of skill in economic interpretation led Oliver Wendell Holmes to ascribe the 19th century movement towards fault liability to the triumph of a nonhistorical "common sense" rather than to the conscious desire of railroads and other business enterprises to reduce the costs of development and expansion.[9]

Writing in 1941, Daniel Boorstin urged a change in this approach of searching the past only for distant legal principles. He urged instead an awareness "that law itself is a part of history,"[10] a viewpoint that would lead lawyers and legal historians to a concern for the relationship between legal institutions and the rest of society, and ultimately "into the materials of economic and social history."[11]

Legal history in the broader sense advocated by Boorstin has fortunately come into its own. Witness the steady flow of perceptive articles on legal history in law reviews and scholarly journals (most notably *The American Journal of Legal History*), the gradual appearance of the *Holmes Devise History of the Supreme Court* under the general editorship of Paul A. Freund,[12] the contribution of several significant studies by a nonlawyer, Leonard W. Levy,[13] and with the recent appearance of Lawrence M. Fried-

---

7. *Id.* at 275-76.
8. *See* Pound, *The Economic Interpretation and the Law of Torts*, 53 HARV. L. REV. 365, 366 (1940).
9. Holmes, *Agency, II*, 5 HARV. L. REV. 1, 16 (1891).
10. Boorstin, *Tradition and Method in Legal History*, 54 HARV. L. REV. 424, 434 (1941).
11. *Id.* at 436.
12. Three volumes of the scheduled eleven-volume work have already appeared: C. FAIRMAN, 6 THE OLIVER WENDELL HOLMES DEVISE HISTORY OF THE SUPREME COURT OF THE UNITED STATES: RECONSTRUCTION AND REUNION, 1864-88 (1971); J. GOEBEL, JR., 1 THE OLIVER WENDELL HOLMES DEVISE HISTORY OF THE SUPREME COURT OF THE UNITED STATES: ANTECEDENTS AND BEGINNINGS TO 1801 (1971); C. SWISHER, 5 THE OLIVER WENDELL HOLMES DEVISE HISTORY OF THE SUPREME COURT OF THE UNITED STATES: THE TANEY PERIOD 1836-64 (1974).
13. L. LEVY, ORIGINS OF THE FIFTH AMENDMENT: THE RIGHT AGAINST SELF-IN-

man's *A History of American Law*, a book in which the author deals with American law "not as a kingdom unto itself, not as a set of rules and concepts, not as the province of lawyers alone, but as a mirror of society."[14]

Before defining the canons of historical method and assessing Supreme Court performance in light of them, it is important to differentiate the various meanings of the term "history" as used in the context of legal opinions. First there is "internal history," or documents which are intrinsic to the legal process, and upon which courts must rely in their every decision. Such internal history would obviously include the text of the fundamental law, or constitutions, of the United States and the several states, statutes enacted by Congress and the state legislatures, and judicial decisions which serve as binding precedents. But there is also an "external history," or history which serves either to illuminate the meaning of the constitutions and statutes in their original context, or to reveal conditions in the nation since ratification or promulgation which have a bearing on subsequent interpretation.

In a sense, then, the Supreme Court is daily engaged in the task of interpreting history, for it must constantly refer to prior texts as a reference point for its decisionmaking. The way in which members of the Court perform the task of interpreting those texts, however, as well as the use they make of external history to bolster their ratio decidendi in specific instances, together constitute grounds for an interdisciplinary dialogue between law and history. In other words, as long as Justices of the Supreme Court write history in their opinions, they should know what historians generally consider essential to an honest and fruitful performance of the historical task.

Historians have roundly criticized the Supreme Court for its use of history. In order to appreciate the point of such criticism, it is necessary first to state four canons of historical method formulated by the Canadian philosopher Bernard J. F. Lonergan: be attentive to all the data; be intelligent in interpretation of the data; be reasonable in verifying the accuracy of one's

---

CRIMINATION (1968); L. LEVY, LEGACY OF SUPPRESSION: FREEDOM OF SPEECH AND PRESS IN EARLY AMERICAN HISTORY (1960); L. LEVY, THE LAW OF THE COMMONWEALTH AND CHIEF JUSTICE SHAW: THE EVOLUTION OF AMERICAN LAW, 1830-1860 (1957).

14. L. FRIEDMAN, A HISTORY OF AMERICAN LAW 10 (1973). In the conclusion of this book, Professor Friedman states well for the American context what Holdsworth said for the English context:
> If by law one means an organized system of social control, any society of any size and complexity has law. As long as the country endures, so will its system of law, coextensive with society, reflecting its wishes and needs, in all their irrationality, ambiguity, and inconsistency . . . . A full history of American law would be nothing more or less than a full history of American life.

Id. at 595.

interpretation; and be responsible.[15] These canons form a basic touchstone against which one can evaluate the methodological integrity not only of the Court but of its critics as well. Historical knowledge is simply a specific instance of knowledge; knowledge is not attained by neglecting relevant data, by failing to grasp the significance of data, or by refusing to account reasonably for one's judgments.

Under Lonergan's method, the historian is first called on to attend to all data within the scope of his inquiry. Such attention calls for objectivity, but not the 19th century view of objectivity which embraced only that which was to be seen, a notion which demanded of the historian a "pure receptivity that admitted impressions from phenomena but excluded any subjective activity."[16] The attention involved here is to be paid by the historian, acting as a conscious subject who is bound to be influenced by his own world view and philosophy.

Second, there is the duty of the historian to be intelligent in his interpretation of the data. This duty imposes a threefold exegetical task on the historian: to understand the text, to judge the accuracy of his understanding, and to state what he judges to be the correct meaning of the text. In understanding the text, the historian may not assume the worth of what Lonergan calls the "Principle of the Empty Head"—that the less one knows, the better an exegete he will be.[17] On the contrary, "the greater the exegete's resources, the greater the likelihood that he will be able to enumerate all possible interpretations and assign to each its proper measure of probability."[18] In the context of constitutional history, for example, a knowledge of both the Articles of Confederation which preceded the Constitution and of the debates accompanying the adoption of the Constitution can be of some assistance in understanding specific constitutional texts. By the same token, however, if one relies on the Federalist Papers[19] for such understanding without recognizing their political character as the propaganda of an anti-populist party which purported to represent "the education, the talents, the virtues, and the property of the country,"[20] one is bound to have difficulty

---

15. B. LONERGAN, METHOD IN THEOLOGY 20, 53, 231-32, 302 (1972).
16. *Id.* at 234.
17. *Id.* at 157, 204-23.
18. *Id.* at 156.
19. THE FEDERALIST (J. Cooke ed. 1961).
20. Letter from John Adams to Benjamin Stoddert, Mar. 31, 1801, *reprinted in* 9 THE WORKS OF JOHN ADAMS 582 (C. Adams ed. 1854). *See also* C. BEARD, AN ECONOMIC INTERPRETATION OF THE CONSTITUTION OF THE UNITED STATES (1929); ESSAYS ON THE MAKING OF THE CONSTITUTION (L. Levy ed. 1969); M. JENSEN, THE ARTICLES OF CONFEDERATION: AN INTERPRETATION OF THE SOCIAL-CONSTITUTIONAL HISTORY OF THE AMERICAN REVOLUTION 1774-1781 (1940).

in judging the correctness of one's understanding of the text. Similarly, if one states that he has discovered the intent of the framers on a specific text, he may still be far from a correct statement of that text for purposes of resolving a present dispute, as recent litigation on the establishment clause of the first amendment amply illustrates.[21] In this sense, Justice Brennan was quite right when he acknowledged in 1963 that "an awareness of history and an appreciation of the aims of the Founding Fathers do not always resolve concrete problems."[22] The context of a statement can be crucial to its content; it can be anachronistic, then, to ask an 18th century text to resolve a subsequent issue not even imagined when the text was written.

Third, the historian must be reasonable; he must attempt to verify the accuracy of his interpretation. For Lonergan, the test is

> [whether or not] insights are invulnerable, whether or not they hit the bull's eye, whether or not they meet *all* relevant questions so that there are no further questions that can lead to further insights and so complement, qualify, correct the insights already possessed.[23]

The point here is not simply that the historian searches for the right questions as well as for answers, but that in the process his questions and answers must become interlocked in such a way as to effectuate "the eventual enclosure of the interrelated multiplicity within a higher limited unity," in order that he be able "to recognize the task as completed and to pronounce [his] interpretation as probable, highly probable, in some respects, perhaps, certain."[24]

---

21. *See* Kelly, *Clio and the Court: An Illicit Love Affair*, 1965 SUP. CT. REV. 119, 137-42, and the cases cited therein, for a discussion of the Supreme Court's application of history to the controversy over the proper delineation of the line between church and state. In his conclusion, the author notes:
> The church-state matters to which Jefferson, Madison, Fisher, Ames and the others of the First Congress were addressing themselves are not resolvable by any plausible process of historical reasoning into a solution of the problem of aid for parochial schools, lunch programs, bus transportation, [and] released time. The application of precedent, legal continuity, and balanced contemporary socio-political theory is almost certain to produce a more intelligent result than is the attempt to use a few scattered historical documents as though they possessed the qualities of Holy Writ. Most inquiry into the past illustrates dramatically the discontinuity of culture and social process rather than their continuity. A more sophisticated and restrained approach to the use of history by the Court might well take this fact into account.

Id. at 156-57.

22. Abington School Dist. v. Schempp, 374 U.S. 203, 234 (1963) (Brennan, J., concurring). Justice Brennan's opinion discusses why history can and should be treated with respect but without slavish obedience to the past.

23. B. LONERGAN, *supra* note 15, at 162.

24. *Id.* at 165.

The historian, then, cannot be value-free in the sense of refraining from all value judgments, for he is bound to make some such judgments; he should be value-free, however, at least to the extent of recognizing that his own value judgments neither constitute empirical evidence nor settle matters of fact.[25] Finally, the historian is asked to remain detached from all bias which, for Lonergan, represents a distortion or a block in intellectual development.[26] Indeed, says Lonergan, the historian has a greater need of such detachment from bias than the natural scientist whose work is more adequately objectified and publicly controlled.[27] Such detachment is not to be conceived of in terms of a naive objectivism that ignores the subjectivity of the historian. On the contrary, it is only when the historian consciously makes unremitting efforts to overcome bias and to verify his interpretations and judgments that genuine detachment in the writing of history can ever be achieved.

II. THE SUPREME COURT AND ITS USE OF HISTORY: SOME PRELIMINARY CONSIDERATIONS

Since the scope of the Supreme Court's use of history is too broad for intelligent treatment within the confines of a single article, this effort will concentrate on the Supreme Court of the "Gilded Age,"[28] *i.e.*, post-Reconstruction, and the manner in which the Court during this time utilized history in its interpretation of the fourteenth amendment. As background for that analysis, an examination of critical commentary on the Court's approach to history and examples of the Court's use of "internal history" are in order.

---

25. *See id.* at 232-33. *See also* Dray, *History and Value Judgments*, in 4 ENCYCLOPEDIA OF PHILOSOPHY 26-30 (P. Edwards ed. 1967).

26. *See* B. LONERGAN, INSIGHT: A STUDY OF HUMAN UNDERSTANDING 191-205, 218-44 (1957), in which the author differentiates four domains of bias: unconscious motivation, individual egoism, group egoism, and general egoism. *See also* B. LONERGAN, *supra* note 15, at 217-20.

27. *See* B. LONERGAN, *supra* note 15, at 230-32. Lonergan states that "the only adequate positive control is to have another historian go over the same evidence." *Id.* at 231.

28. The phrase "Gilded Age" was coined by Mark Twain and Charles Dudley Warner to describe America during the 1870's. They used it as the title of a satirical novel, in the preface to which they stated with tongue in cheek:

> In a state where there is no fever of speculation, no inflamed desire for sudden wealth, where the poor are simple-minded and contented, and the rich all honest and generous, where society is in a condition of primative purity and politics the occupation of only the capable and patriotic, there are necessarily no materials for such a history as we have constructed out of an ideal commonwealth.

S. CLEMENS & C. WARNER, THE GILDED AGE v-vi (1873). When used in the context of this article, the reference is to the Court from around 1865 until the turn of the century.

A. Early Criticism of the Court's Use of History

Students of American legal history have grown accustomed to recent attacks on the Supreme Court's use of history.[29] Today's student may be unaware, however, that critics of the Supreme Court have been questioning the Justices about their use of history from the earliest days of the Court. As early as 1816, Spencer Roane of the Virginia Supreme Court criticized the Court's use of history when he rebuked his fellow Virginian John Marshall for the Federalist Chief Justice's nationalistic dicta in *Martin v. Hunter's Lessee*,[30] which Judge Roane deemed to be contrary to the intent of the Founding Fathers on the true locus of sovereignty in the new "confederation."[31] Shortly thereafter, James Madison expressed the fear that the Marshall Court was interpreting the Constitution not according to "its true meaning as understood *by the nation* at the time of its ratification,"[32] but according to the needs of commercial interests.

The Taney Court had its historical critics as well. Indeed, two of the

---

29. *See, e.g.*, Levy, *The Right Against Self-Incrimination: History and Judicial History*, 85 POL. SCI. Q. 1 (1969). Levy claims that in their interpretations of the fifth amendment,

> [t]he justices stand censured for abusing historical evidence in a way that reflects adversely on their intellectual rectitude as well as on their historical competence . . . . The Court artfully selects historical facts from one side only, ignoring contrary data, in order to support, rationalize, or give the appearance of respectability to judgments resting on other grounds.

Id.

Others who have criticized the Court's use of history include Alfred Kelly, who charged the Court with writing "very bad history indeed," with using "evidence wrenched from its contemporary historical context," and with "carefully select[ing] those materials designed to prove the thesis at hand, suppressing all data that might impeach the desired historical conclusions," Kelly, *supra* note 21, at 126; Paul L. Murphy, who expressed chagrin at the Court's reliance on "a shockingly inaccurate use of historical data," Murphy, *Time to Reclaim: The Current Challenge of American Constitutional History*, 69 AM. HIST. REV. 64, 65 (1963); Alexander M. Bickel, who chastised the Court for its reading of the history of the fourteenth amendment with regard to racial segregation, Bickel, *The Original Understanding and the Segregation Decision*, 69 HARV. L. REV. 1 (1955); and John Wofford, who took issue with the Court's assertion that the free speech clause of the first amendment was intended to supersede the English common law of seditious libel and who, in support of his claim, gathered considerable historical evidence which the Court either overlooked or suppressed. Wofford, *The Blinding Light: The Uses of History in Constitutional Interpretation*, 31 U. CHI. L. REV. 502 (1964).

30. 14 U.S. (1 Wheat.) 304 (1816).

31. *See* 2 BRANCH HISTORICAL PAPERS 51-52, 56-57 (W. Dodd ed. 1905); C. HAINES, THE ROLE OF THE SUPREME COURT IN AMERICAN GOVERNMENT AND POLITICS—1789-1835, at 340 (1944).

32. 9 WRITINGS OF JAMES MADISON 74 (G. Hunt ed. 1901-1910), *cited in* Kelly, *supra* note 21, at 120.

critics sat on the Court.[33] Dissenting in *Dred Scott v. Sandford*,[34] Justice McLean noted that Taney's reference to the intent of the framers in regard to the citizenship for blacks overlooked a significant debate on the nature of slavery, in which James Madison opposed Pinckney's motion to extend the period of importation to 1808.[35] Another dissenter in *Dred Scott*, Justice Curtis, also challenged Taney's historical accuracy in denying the American citizenship of free persons descended from African slaves at the time the Constitution was adopted.[36] A third critic of the *Dred Scott* decision was Abraham Lincoln, who disputed the historical accuracy of Chief Justice Taney's claim that blacks were excluded from the meaning of "men" or "persons" in the Declaration of Independence.[37]

In sum, criticism of the Supreme Court's craftsmanship, although undertaken with greater zeal recently[38] than in the past, has firm antecedents in the 19th century, and, as Justice Frankfurter has acknowledged, that is as it should be:

> Judges as persons, or courts as institutions, are entitled to no greater immunity from criticism than other persons or institutions. . . . [J]udges must be kept mindful of their limitations and of their ultimate public responsibility by a vigorous stream of criticism expressed with candor however blunt.[39]

---

33. The two were Justice McLean and Justice Curtis.
34. 60 U.S. (19 How.) 393 (1857).
35. Justice McLean quoted Madison in support of his position:
    Twenty years will produce all the mischief that can be apprehended from the liberty to import slaves; so long a term will be more dishonorable to the American character than to say nothing about it in the Constitution. (Madison Papers.)
Id. at 536 (McLean, J., dissenting).
36. Justice Curtis framed the issue as follows:
    To determine whether any free persons, descended from Africans held in slavery, were citizens of the United States under the Confederation, and consequently at the time of the adoption of the Constitution of the United States, it is only necessary to know whether any such persons were citizens of either of the States under the Confederation, at the time of the adoption of the Constitution.
    Of this there can be no doubt.
Id. at 572 (Curtis, J., dissenting).
37. *See* THE LINCOLN-DOUGLAS DEBATES OF 1858, at 219, 233, 304 (R. Johannsen ed. 1965).
38. *See, e.g.*, A. BICKEL, THE LEAST DANGEROUS BRANCH: THE SUPREME COURT AT THE BAR OF POLITICS (1962); A. COX, THE WARREN COURT: CONSTITUTIONAL DECISION AS AN INSTRUMENT OF REFORM (1968); F. GRAHAM, THE DUE PROCESS REVOLUTION: THE WARREN COURT'S IMPACT ON CRIMINAL LAW (1970); P. KURLAND, POLITICS, THE CONSTITUTION, AND THE WARREN COURT (1970); C. MILLER, THE SUPREME COURT AND THE USES OF HISTORY (1969). For trenchant criticism of the Burger Court, see L. LEVY, AGAINST THE LAW: THE NIXON COURT AND CRIMINAL JUSTICE (1974).
39. Bridges v. California, 314 U.S. 252, 289 (1941) (Frankfurter, J., dissenting).

B. The Relevance of Internal History

As described above, "internal history" refers to legal documents intrinsic to the process of judicial decisionmaking. The first area of internal history subject to historical criticism is the Court's understanding of the Constitution itself. Some Justices conceive of the Constitution in a static fashion as a changeless document with invariant meaning.[40] Rather than acknowledge that significant shifts in cultural and social contexts may result in meanings never imagined in the 18th century, advocates of this "constant meaning" theory allow only for a shift in the application of the old and invariant meaning to new situations.[41]

Although few Justices have addressed themselves explicitly to the philosophical question of historical meaning, some have at least opted for a more dynamic conception of the Constitution than that espoused by the "constant meaning" proponents. Justice Brandeis, for example, expressed a strong conviction that "our Constitution is not a strait-jacket. It is a living organism. As such it is capable of growth—of expansion and adaptation to new conditions. Growth implies changes, political, economic, and social."[42]

---

40. A classic statement of this viewpoint is found in South Carolina v. United States, 199 U.S. 437 (1905), in which Justice Brewer stated: "The Constitution is a written instrument. As such its meaning does not alter. That which it meant when adopted it means now." *Id.* at 448.

41. Justice Sutherland, dissenting in Home Bldg. & Loan Ass'n v. Blaisdell, 290 U.S. 398 (1934), characterized this process by stating:

The provisions of the Federal Constitution, undoubtedly, are pliable in the sense that in appropriate cases they have the capacity of bringing within their grasp every new condition which falls within their meaning. But, their *meaning* is changeless; it is only their *application* which is extensible.

Id. at 451 (Sutherland, J., dissenting).

For a brief but perceptive essay on *Blaisdell*, see C. MILLER, *supra* note 38, at 39-51. Elsewhere in the work, Miller criticized Justice Sutherland's dichotomy between meaning and application, stating:

Many constitutional lawyers have found this distinction between meaning and application perfectly intelligible. Not only do they believe in an immortal Constitution, but they believe also in immortal constitutional essences or ideas, with a priori definitions. In this scheme the Constitution defines meanings which, when applied to various circumstances, become the judicial contribution to the Constitution. Under the influence of pragmatism in philosophy and functionalism in jurisprudence, however, most people now understand that meaning and application are at least interdependent, or that they are identical, or even that meaning depends upon application rather than the other way around.

Id. at 151.

42. Brandeis Papers, on file at Harvard Law School Library, *quoted in* A. BICKEL, THE SUPREME COURT AND THE IDEA OF PROGRESS 20 (1970). Professor Bickel noted that Justice Brandeis penned the passage for a dissent in United States v. Moreland, 258 U.S. 433 (1922), but omitted it at the behest of a colleague. *Id.*

This view of the Constitution as a developmental instrument of social meaning found adherents on the Court in numerous Justices, from Chief Justice John Marshall, who spoke of the necessity of adapting the Constitution to "various *crises* of human affairs,"[43] to Chief Justice Earl Warren, who stated: "For the Constitution to have vitality, this Court must be able to apply its principles to situations that may not have been foreseen at the time those principles were adopted."[44]

A second issue regarding "internal history" focuses on whether or not the Court should rely on legislative history in the construction of statutes presented to the Court. On the one hand, according to Chief Justice Marshall, "[w]here the mind labours to discover the design of the legislature, it seizes everything from which aid can be derived."[45] Taking a contrary position, Justice Day stated in *Standard Fashion Co. v. Magrane-Houston Co.*,[46] that there is no compulsion to resort to the "extraneous statements and often unsatisfactory aid" of legislative history when "the words of the act are plain and their meaning is apparent."[47] It should be noted that attempts to ascertain the intention of the legislature through recourse to *travaux préparatoires* are characteristic of the civil law tradition, whereas English courts generally refuse to consider such legislative material, preferring to rest their decisions on the "plain meaning" of the words used.[48] No such systematic rationale regarding the use of legislative history can be discerned from the practice of the United States Supreme Court, which seems to rely on legislative history whenever it will bolster an opinion, and to ignore it whenever it would complicate an otherwise tidy opinion. The Court has thus opened itself to charges of violation of Lonergan's first canon—be attentive—by its selectivity in the use or nonuse of material normally deemed relevant to statutory construction.

A third instance of the Court's use of internal history is its reliance on judicial precedents as controlling, at least by analogy, the case at bar. The doctrine of stare decisis is, of course, neither a facile nor an automatic determinant of the outcome of a case, since the Court must select, from among the cases offered by opposing counsel, which rules of law most nearly fit the context of the case being litigated. Historians should not fault the Justices for the mere fact that they are selective, for that is intrinsic to the judicial process. But Lonergan's first canon—be attentive—applies whenever the

---

43. McCulloch v. Maryland, 17 U.S. (4 Wheat.) 316, 415 (1819).
44. Estes v. Texas, 381 U.S. 532, 564 (1965) (Warren, C.J., concurring).
45. United States v. Fisher, 6 U.S. (2 Cranch) 358, 386 (1805).
46. 258 U.S. 346 (1922).
47. *Id.* at 356. *See generally* Edwards v. Douglas, 269 U.S. 204, 211 (1925).
48. *See* D. LLOYD, INTRODUCTION TO JURISPRUDENCE 733-43 (1972).

Justices overlook or ignore without comment precedents which are squarely on point. His second canon—be intelligent—applies whenever the Justices misstate or misunderstand the holding in a prior case. And his third canon— be reasonable—applies whenever one precedent is chosen over an equally applicable but contrary precedent because of the Justices' unexplained preferences. Value judgments, while inevitable, neither settle matters of fact nor constitute empirical evidence.

Several concrete instances suffice to illustrate this difficulty in the Court's use of internal history. First, in the 1973 abortion cases,[49] Justice Blackmun cited *State v. Murphy*[50] for the proposition that the anti-abortion legislation of the 19th century was intended solely to protect the pregnant woman, and that "[t]he few state courts called upon to interpret their laws in the late 19th and early 20th centuries did focus on the state's interest in protecting the woman's health rather than in preserving the embryo and fetus."[51] Justice Blackmun's sweeping historical generalization flew in the face of evidence presented to the Court four months earlier in the appellant's brief in *Byrn v. New York City Health & Hospitals Corp.*[52] In *Byrn*, the Court was advised of 11 state court decisions in the 19th and 20th centuries which had stated explicitly and unambiguously that protection of the life of an unborn child was at least one of the purposes of the respective state's abortion statutes;[53] the Court was also advised of nine decisions in which state courts clearly implied that one of the purposes of the relevent statute was the protection of the unborn children.[54] Most surprisingly, the one 1858 case which

---

49. Doe v. Bolton, 410 U.S. 179 (1973); Roe v. Wade, 410 U.S. 113 (1973).
50. 27 N.J.L. 112 (N.J. Sup. Ct. 1858), *cited in* Roe v. Wade, 410 U.S. 113, 151 n.48 (1973).
51. 410 U.S. at 151.
52. Brief for Appellant, Byrn v. New York City Health & Hosp. Corp., 410 U.S. 949 (1973) (appeal dismissed for want of a substantial federal question).
53. The eleven decisions cited were: Trent v. State, 15 Ala. App. 485, 73 So. 834 (1916), *cert. denied*, 198 Ala. 695, 73 So. 1002 (1917); Dougherty v. People, 1 Colo. 514 (1872); Nash v. Meyer, 54 Idaho 283, 31 P.2d 273 (1934); State v. Miller, 90 Kan. 230, 133 P. 878 (1913); State v. Gedicke, 43 N.J.L. 86 (N.J. Sup. Ct. 1881); State v. Tippie, 89 Ohio St. 35, 105 N.E. 75 (1913); Bowlan v. Lunsford, 176 Okla. 115, 54 P.2d 666 (1936); State v. Ausplund, 86 Ore. 121, 167 P. 1019 (1917), *appeal dismissed on consent*, 251 U.S. 563 (1919); State v. Howard, 32 Vt. 380 (1859); Anderson v. Commonwealth, 190 Va. 665, 58 S.E.2d 72 (1950); State v. Cox, 197 Wash. 67, 84 P.2d 357 (1938).
54. The nine decisions were: Montgomery v. State, 80 Ind. 338 (1881); State v. Moore, 25 Iowa 128 (1868); Smith v. State, 33 Me. 48 (1851); Worthington v. State, 92 Md. 222, 48 A. 355 (1901); People v. Sessions, 58 Mich. 594, 26 N.W. 291 (1886); Edwards v. State, 79 Neb. 251, 112 N.W. 611 (1907); Bennett v. Hymers, 101 N.H. 483, 147 A.2d 108 (1958); Mills v. Commonwealth, 13 Pa. 631 (1850); State v. Crook, 16 Utah 212, 51 P. 1091 (1898).

Justice Blackmun cited in support of his historical assertion had been overruled in 1881 on the very point for which Justice Blackmun cited it; in *State v. Gedicke*,[55] the New Jersey Supreme Court held that, contrary to *Murphy*, the New Jersey statute *was* designed "to protect the life of the child also, and inflict the same punishment, in case of its death, as if the mother should die."[56] Robert M. Byrn has pointed out other historical errors committed by Justice Blackmun in the abortion cases, such as the apparent acceptance of the notion that abortion was not a crime at common law.[57] Whatever one may think of the results reached in *Roe* and *Doe*, Justice Blackmun's casual use of precedents is an instance of the Court's failure in its use of internal history.

A second instance of such historical carelessness can be found in *Kastigar v. United States*,[58] in which the Court held that the grant of "use immunity"[59] rather than "transactional immunity"[60] sufficed to compel testimony of a witness before a grand jury. In a brief historical essay, Justice Powell, citing a 1562 statute,[61] extolled the virtues of the grand jury in English law, and, citing a 1612 case,[62] stated that "all subjects owed the King their 'knowledge and discovery.'"[63] Nowhere in his short historical excursus did Justice Powell note that neither the statute nor the case refer explicitly to the institution of the grand jury; further, he omits to state a highly relevant fact: that after considerable debate about the dangers which the grand jury posed for individual freedom, the English abolished this prosecutorial tool in 1925.

A third instance of slipshod historical craftsmanship is in Justice Powell's reading of the purpose of the exclusionary rule solely as a deterrent to unlawful police misconduct in violation of the fourth amendment guarantee against

---

55. 43 N.J.L. 86 (N.J. Sup. Ct. 1881).
56. *Id.* at 90.
57. Byrn, *An American Tragedy: The Supreme Court on Abortion*, 41 FORDHAM L. REV. 807 (1973). *See also* Byrn, *Wade and Bolton: Fundamental Legal Errors and Dangerous Implications*, 19 THE CATH. LAW. 243 (1973); Gaffney, *Law and Theology: A Dialogue on the Abortion Decisions*, 33 THE JURIST 134, 136-42 (1973).
58. 406 U.S. 441 (1972).
59. "Use immunity" was defined by the Court as a promise to the witness of "immunity from the use of compelled testimony and evidence derived therefrom." *Id.* at 443. The practical effect of this grant of immunity is that if the witness were subsequently prosecuted, the prosecutor would have the burden of showing that the evidence introduced was not derived from the compelled testimony but from independent sources.
60. "Transactional immunity" is a "grant [of] immunity from prosecution for offenses to which compelled testimony relates." *Id.* In other words, it is a bar to subsequent prosecution of the witness for offenses to which the compelled testimony relates.
61. 406 U.S. at 443, n.3, *citing* Statute of Elizabeth, 5 Eliz. 1, ch. 9, § 12 (1562).
62. *Id.* n.4, *citing* Countess of Shrewsbury's Case, 2 How. St. Tr. 769 (1612).
63. *Id.*

unreasonable searches and seizures. In *United States v. Calandra*,[64] the Court ruled that illegally obtained evidence and the fruits of such evidence can be used before a grand jury and held that a witness before a grand jury cannot refuse to answer questions based on evidence obtained from an unlawful search and seizure. Justice Powell asserted that the exclusionary rule was only a judicially created rule of evidence to deter unlawful police misconduct rather than a personal constitutional right of the party aggrieved by the unlawful search and seizure.[65] Once again, there is a problem of selectivity of data. To maintain his position, Justice Powell relied on an inference from Justice Frankfurter's opinion in *Wolf v. Colorado*,[66] in which the Court declined to extend the federal exclusionary rule of *Weeks v. United States*[67] to state proceedings. But Justice Powell overlooked contrary data which emerged after *Wolf*: when the Court overturned *Wolf* in the 1961 case of *Mapp v. Ohio*,[68] it rejected as erroneous Justice Frankfurter's notion that the exclusionary rule was not a constitutional requirement of the fourth amendment.[69] Dissenting in *Calandra*, Justice Brennan pointed out Justice Powell's historical oversight and noted that the exclusionary rule was adopted for at least two other purposes more significant than the deterrence of police misconduct: (1) to provide an enforcement tool giving content and meaning to the fourth amendment guarantees of personal security for one's person, papers, and effects; and (2) to insure that the judiciary avoid even the slightest appearance of sanctioning illegal government conduct.[70]

Finally, in recent years Justice Rehnquist has demonstrated that historical selectivity can lead to incongruous results which might be amusing were it not for the loss of a significant right by parties before the Supreme Court. Justice Rehnquist is apparently of the opinion that the closer in time an observer is to an event, the more probably accurate is his interpretation of the event. Specifically, as he noted in *Ham v. South Carolina*,[71] he relies on Justice Miller's dictum in the *Slaughter-House Cases*[72] that the principal purpose of the equal protection clause of the fourteenth amendment was to prohibit the states from discriminating against blacks.[73] In accordance with

---

64. 414 U.S. 338 (1974).
65. *Id.* at 347-48.
66. 338 U.S. 25 (1949).
67. 232 U.S. 383 (1914).
68. 367 U.S. 643 (1961).
69. *Id.* at 655-57.
70. 414 U.S. at 357 (Brennan, J., dissenting).
71. 409 U.S. 524, 527 (1973).
72. 83 U.S. (16 Wall.) 36 (1873).
73. *Id.* at 81. Justice Miller's characterization of the amendment's impact was as follows:
    We doubt very much whether any action of a State not directed by way of dis-

this belief, Justice Rehnquist ruled in *Ham* that the fourteenth amendment demands that a trial judge questioning prospective jurors in voir dire must probe the possibility of their racial animus against a black defendant.[74] However, even though the defendant wore a beard and was charged with possession of marijuana, Justice Rehnquist held that the trial judge need not put any question to the jurors about their possible prejudice against the long hair or beard of the defendant, or whether they had been prejudiced against the defendant by a public television broadcast against drug offenders by the State's chief witness, a police officer.[75] For Justices Douglas and Marshall, this distinction without a difference was unacceptable judicial hairsplitting. They concurred that the judge was constitutionally required to probe for racial prejudice, but dissented on the ground that the judge had abused his discretion when he precluded an inquiry into the juror's prejudice on hair length.[76] For them, the point at stake was the defendant's constitutional right to a trial by a neutral and impartial jury, which right can be infringed not only by racial bias but by subtler forms of prejudice as well. While the dissenting Justices cited cases which the opinion of the Court passed over in silence,[77] it should also be noted that Justice Rehnquist overlooked another section of the *Slaughter-House Cases*, in which Justice Miller noted: "We do not say that no one else but the negro can share in this protection."[78]

Other examples of misuses of legal history in the United States Reports are numerous, but these four should suffice to demonstrate the point of Robert Schuyler's complaint: "Unfortunately, a knowledge of American [and English] history has not yet been made a prerequisite for admission to the Supreme Court."[79]

---

crimination against the negroes as a class, or on account of their race, will ever be held to come within the purview of this provision. It is so clearly a provision for that race and that emergency, that a strong case would be necessary for its application to any other.

Id.
74. 409 U.S. at 526-27.
75. *Id.* at 527-28.
76. *Id.* at 529-30 (Douglas, J., dissenting in part); *id.* at 532-34 (Marshall, J., dissenting in part).
77. Justice Douglas cited Morford v. United States, 339 U.S. 258 (1950), and Dennis v. United States, 339 U.S. 162 (1949), as instances in which defendants were held to have the right to inquire into possible bias other than racial prejudice. 409 U.S. at 529 (Douglas, J., dissenting in part). Justice Marshall cited several cases and quoted extensively from Irvin v. Dowd, 366 U.S. 717, 722 (1961), which quoted Reynolds v. United States, 98 U.S. 145, 155 (1878): "'The theory of the law is that a juror who has formed an opinion cannot be impartial.'" 409 U.S. at 531 (Marshall, J., dissenting in part).
78. 83 U.S. (16 Wall.) at 72.
79. R. SCHUYLER, THE CONSTITUTION OF THE UNITED STATES 92 (1923). A more

III. THE GILDED AGE COURT AND THE FOURTEENTH AMENDMENT

Justice Rehnquist's opinion in *Ham* serves as an introduction to the theme explored herein: the distortion of the fourteenth amendment in the 19th century. Misuse of history becomes apparent in three areas of fourteenth amendment analysis by the Gilded Age Court: the extension of substantive due process protection to economic interests of corporate "persons," the denial of procedural due process to criminal defendants in state proceedings, and the tragic failure of the Court to safeguard the privileges and immunities of newly emancipated black citizens or to extend to them the equal protection of the laws.

The thirteenth, fourteenth and fifteenth amendments were designed to abolish slavery, to grant federal protection to the civil rights of the newly emancipated black Americans, and to secure the right to vote against racial discrimination, whether by the federal government or by the states. Nevertheless, neither the text of these amendments nor the series of civil rights statutes enacted by Congress in 1866,[80] 1870,[81] 1871,[82] and 1875[83] proved to be an effective guarantee of civil rights for blacks during the 19th century. Some of the blame for this tragic chapter in American legal history is to be laid at the doorstep of the Supreme Court for the constitutional blessings they gave to the Compromise of 1877,[84] which marked the end of Reconstruction and the abandonment of the cause of federally protected civil rights for black Americans.

Chief Justice Charles Evans Hughes once stated with more candor than discretion that "[w]e are under a Constitution, but the Constitution is what

---

trenchant comment on the same theme is found in J. O'NEILL, RELIGION AND EDUCATION UNDER THE CONSTITUTION (1949), in which the author states:
> My criticism is not that the Justices have interpreted historical facts or phrases in a way that seems to me unjustified from the standpoint of either semantics or history, but that these Justices of the Supreme Court apparently do not know the most important facts of our constitutional history which have a bearing on the questions they are deciding. The other possibility is that they do know the facts but either callously ignore them, or willfully misrepresent them.

Id. at 3. The specific focus of the author's criticism was Justice Black's opinion in Illinois *ex rel.* McCollum v. Board of Educ., 333 U.S. 203 (1948).

80. Act of April 9, 1866, ch. 31, §§ 1-10, 14 Stat. 27. The congressional debate on this Act is set forth in 1 CIVIL RIGHTS (STATUTORY HISTORY OF THE UNITED STATES) 99-150 (B. Schwartz ed. 1970).
81. Act of May 31, 1870, ch. 114, §§ 1-23, 16 Stat. 140, *as amended*, Act of Feb. 28, 1871, ch. 99, § 20, 16 Stat. 433.
82. Act of Feb. 28, 1871, ch. 99, §§ 2-19, 16 Stat. 433; Act of April 20, 1871, ch. 22, §§ 1-7, 17 Stat. 13.
83. Act of Mar. 1, 1875, ch. 114, §§ 1-5, 18 Stat. 335.
84. *See* note 192 & accompanying text *infra*.

the judges say it is."[85] Corporate interests were delighted that this was so in the decades of the Gilded Age when the Court appeared as their savior in a series of decisions that elevated laissez-faire capitalism to the stature of a constitutional imperative. But criminal defendants and black Americans who watched what they thought were solid constitutional rights evaporate into legalistic mist during the same period would have taken greater comfort had the Court followed not the gist of Chief Justice Hughes' remark, but the maxim of the sixth century Emperor Justinian: "To know the laws, one must grasp not only their words, but their force and power as well."[86] The spirit of interpretation by which the Court reversed the thrust and impact of the fourteenth amendment to favor the rich and powerful is marked by a studied focus on words rather than on their force and power.

A. Substantive Due Process: A Boon for Corporations

It is perhaps an accident of history, though a highly symbolic one, that the first test case to come before the Supreme Court on the meaning of the fourteenth amendment was presented not by poor blacks seeking judicial vindication of political and civil rights, but by white businessmen from the South who complained that a carpetbag monopoly law had deprived them of economic benefits which they deemed to be a "privilege and immunity" secured by the amendment. In the *Slaughter-House Cases*,[87] Justice Miller, writing for a 5-4 majority, ruled against the antimonopolistic plaintiffs largely because he could not accept the sweeping contention of counsel for the appellants, John A. Campbell,[88] that the Court should strike down any state law which abridged the "liberty" and "property right" of a citizen to live under a laissez-faire system. Justice Stephen Field, a pistol-packing rugged individualist from California,[89] wrote a strong dissent which cited Adam Smith's *Wealth of Nations*[90] and which urged that the fourteenth amendment was designed not only to protect blacks but to "protect the citizens of the

---

85. Hughes made the remark in an extemporaneous speech given in 1907 while he was governor of New York. M. PUSEY, CHARLES EVANS HUGHES 204 (1951). During the same period, Judge Andrew Bruce of North Dakota wrote: "We are governed by our judges and not by our legislatures . . . . It is our judges who formulate our public policies and our basic law." A. BRUCE, THE AMERICAN JUDGE 6, 8 (1924).
86. JUSTINIAN, DIGEST 1, 3:17.
87. *See* notes 72-78 & accompanying text *supra*.
88. Campbell was an Associate Justice of the Supreme Court from 1853 to 1861, when he resigned to return to his native Alabama during the Civil War. *See* H. CONNOR, JOHN ARCHIBALD CAMPBELL (1920).
89. For a description of Justice Field, see C. SWISHER, STEPHEN J. FIELD, CRAFTSMAN OF THE LAW (1930).
90. A. SMITH, INQUIRY INTO THE NATURE AND CAUSES OF THE WEALTH OF NATIONS (1776), *cited in* 83 U.S. (16 Wall.) at 110 n.1 (Field, J., dissenting).

United States against the deprivation of their common rights by state legislation."[91] Among such "inalienable rights" was the "right to pursue a lawful employment in a lawful manner, without other restraint than such as equally affects all persons,"[92] a right which Justice Field found to be violated by the Louisiana monopoly. Although Justice Field served long enough on the Court to see his broad interpretation of the due process clause utilized in a substantive sense, implying the power of the Justices to read their own economic beliefs into the Constitution, in 1873 he could not yet gather a majority. Justice Miller, anxious to refute Justice Field's thesis, engaged in judicial overkill, butchering the privileges and immunities clause so badly that it would never again serve as a useful tool for securing civil rights.[93] Further, Justice Miller intimated that the fourteenth amendment had conferred on Congress no general powers to regulate in the area of civil rights, and that the states retained most of their original powers.[94] The upshot of the case was that it laid the foundation in Justice Field's dissent for substantive due process; Judge Campbell in effect prevailed, although "not as the butchers' attorney but as a Southerner and a Democrat hostile to broad national powers."[95]

The Supreme Court during this era, as during all other periods, was composed of men who breathed in the atmosphere of their times. Several of the Justices were conservative in outlook,[96] having drawn not only their fees but their opinions from corporate wealth. Predisposed to the businessman's point of view, they were convinced that the "manifest destiny" of the nation lay in giving free rein to laissez-faire capitalism. The political and economic context of the times in large measure explains decisions of the Supreme Court during the Gilded Age,[97] but the legal historian must also focus on the legal methodology used by the Justices to bestow their constitutional blessings on corporate "persons" during a time of phenomenal economic expansion and industrialism.

One device was a new interpretation of the phrase "due process of law,"

---

91. 83 U.S. (16 Wall.) at 89 (Field, J., dissenting).
92. *Id.* at 97.
93. 83 U.S. (16 Wall.) at 75-81.
94. *See id.* at 77-78.
95. C. MAGRATH, MORRISON R. WAITE: THE TRIUMPH OF CHARACTER 117 (1963) [hereinafter cited as MAGRATH].
96. As early as 1835, Alexis de Tocqueville noted that lawyers in America, by virtue of their training, tended to end up "eminently conservative and anti-democratic." 1 A. DE TOCQUEVILLE, DEMOCRACY IN AMERICA 285 (P. Bradley ed. 1945). For a recent statement of the conservative character of the 20th century bench and bar, see J. AUERBACH, UNEQUAL JUSTICE: LAWYERS AND SOCIAL CHANGE IN MODERN AMERICA (1976).
97. *See* pp. 236-40 *infra*.

which appears in the text of the fourteenth amendment as well as in the fifth. At least since 1833, the scope of the fifth amendment had been limited to protection of the individual against attempts by the federal government to deprive him of his right to grand jury indictment, of his right against double jeopardy, of his right against the taking of life, liberty, or property without adequate notice and a fair and full hearing, and of his right to just compensation if private property were taken for a public use.[98] Edwin S. Corwin gathered considerable evidence on the meaning of due process before the Civil War, and he doubted whether the phrase was ever meant to give the courts power to restrict or overturn legislative action, even in matters of procedural fairness.[99] Whether or not Corwin is correct in his restrictive view of due process, it is clear from his research that no more than a procedural meaning was intended by the Founding Fathers. Consequently, Chief Justice Taney's use of due process in a substantive sense in *Dred Scott v. Sandford*[100] to legitimate the Court's voiding of the Missouri Compromise as an unconstitutional regulation of economic conditions, marked an unfounded departure from the original meaning of due process. And the subsequent reliance on substantive due process by Justice Field and his colleagues proves to be another species of fruit from a poisoned tree.

A second development which was incorporated into the judicial arsenal by the Gilded Age Court was the Taney Court's acceptance of the principle that a corporation was an artificial "person" for certain kinds of cases at common law.[101] This fiction, together with the Waite Court's acceptance in *Santa Clara County v. Southern Pacific Railway Co.*[102] of the proposition that corporations were intended by the framers to benefit as "persons" under the fourteenth amendment,[103] served as a solid base for the expansion of judicial protection of the rights of corporations.

---

98. Barron v. Baltimore, 32 U.S. (7 Pet.) 243 (1833), held that the Bill of Rights applied only to the federal government, not to the states.

99. Corwin, *The Doctrine of Due Process of Law Before the Civil War*, 24 HARV. L. REV. 366, 460 (1911).

100. 60 U.S. (19 How.) 393 (1857). For a detailed discussion of the *Dred Scott* decision, see V. HOPKINS, DRED SCOTT'S CASE (1971); C. SWISHER, *supra* note 12, at 592-652.

101. *See, e.g.*, Louisville, C. & C.R.R. v. Letson, 43 U.S. 497 (1844). On the origins and meaning of the doctrine of corporate personality, see Graham, *An Innocent Abroad: The Constitutional Corporate "Person"*, 2 U.C.L.A.L. REV. 155 (1955). For the history of the Taney Court's acceptance of corporate personality, see C. SWISHER, *supra* note 12, at 457-83.

102. 118 U.S. 394 (1886).

103. The Court announced this boon to corporations in two brief sentences:
The Court does not wish to hear argument on the question whether the provision in the Fourteenth Amendment to the Constitution, which forbids a State to deny to any *person* within its jurisdiction the equal protection of the laws, applies to these *corporations*. We are all of the opinion that it does.

Justice Field, then, had inherited from the Taney Court the notion of corporate personality and the tool of substantive due process. However, his attempts to combine the two in support of the position that the due process clause of the fourteenth amendment charged the Court with the duty of protecting business enterprises against unfavorable economic regulation were initially blocked by other policies with roots in the Taney Court, most notably by Chief Justice Waite's "recognition that property rights are not absolute, [his] broad view of the states' police powers, and a conscious deference to legislative policy judgments."[104] Although Justice Field's view was adopted during the 1890's (after Chief Justice Waite and Justices Miller and Bradley had been replaced by Melville Fuller, David Brewer and Henry Brown), his efforts during the Waite era were restricted to the frequent dissents in which he "waged a powerful though unsuccessful campaign for his view that the Fourteenth Amendment was the guardian angel of vested property rights."[105]

While some seeds of Justice Field's victory were sown in his dissents, others found receptive soil in casual dicta granted as doctrinal concessions by Chief Justice Waite himself and the majority for whom he wrote. One example of this pattern can be seen in the famous *Granger Cases*,[106] in which Chief Justice Waite upheld a series of statutes which were designed to protect Midwestern farmers from the Eastern-dominated railroads by subjecting the rail-

---

Id. at 396 (emphasis added).
One of the individuals principally responsible for the Court adopting this position was Roscoe Conkling. Conkling, a shrewd railroad lawyer and a former member of Congress who had served on the Joint Committee of Fifteen on Reconstruction which drafted the fourteenth amendment, had stated in an argument before the Supreme Court: "At the time the Fourteenth Amendment was ratified, individuals and joint stock companies were appealing for congressional and administrative protection against invidious and discriminating state and local taxes." STAMPP, THE ERA OF RECONSTRUCTION, 1865-1877, at 137 (1966), *quoting* Roscoe Conkling. The argument that Congress meant to protect corporations through the fourteenth amendment, coming as it did from one who had direct input into the drafting process of the amendment, has prompted some historians, most notably Charles and Mary Beard, in their RISE OF AMERICAN CIVILIZATION (1928), to suggest a "conspiracy theory" of the fourteenth amendment. Under this theory, Conkling, together with John Bingham, another member of the Joint Committee of Fifteen, subtly used their unsuspecting colleagues in Congress to promote the property interests of corporate "persons" while ostensibly protecting the civil rights of blacks. For a detailed review and rejection of the "conspiracy theory," see Boudin, *Truth and Fiction About the Fourteenth Amendment*, 16 N.Y.U.L. REV. 19 (1938), and Graham, *The "Conspiracy Theory" of the Fourteenth Amendment*, 47 YALE L.J. 371 (1938).
104. MAGRATH 185.
105. *Id.* 202.
106. Included under this title are Munn v. Illinois, 94 U.S. 113 (1877), and seven companion cases. For a discussion of the cases, see Fairman, *The So-Called Granger Cases, Lord Hale and Justice Bradley*, 5 STAN. L. REV. 587 (1953).

roads to regulation by public authorities.[107] Although the Chief Justice's views as expressed in the principal case, *Munn v. Illinois*,[108] affirmed the states' power to regulate the railroads and sparked a blistering dissent from Justice Field (who asserted that the majority opinion was "subversive of the rights of private property"[109]), there were two valuable elements buried in the *Munn* opinion that would later support the business-oriented position of Justice Field. The first was Chief Justice Waite's acknowledgement that "under certain circumstances," unspecified in *Munn*, regulatory legislation might violate due process.[110] The second point flowed from the notion that states could regulate property "affected with a public interest";[111] it implied that they could not regulate property "unaffected" with a public interest. Half a century after *Munn*, Chief Justice William Howard Taft seized on the inverse reactionary possibilities of the *Munn* doctrine and struck down regulatory statutes adverse to the economic and property interests which he and his colleagues favored.[112]

By the end of the 19th century, the Court came to occupy a position so close to the conservative views espoused by Justice Field that even he could hardly have desired a more flattering epitaph—the voice of the lone dissenter in *Slaughter-House* and *Munn* became the spokesman of the Court in *Pollock*

---

107. As described by Magrath, the contested statutes
   varied from state to state, but the main features were similar: establishment of maximum rates for railroad freight and passengers and for storing of grain by direct legislative enactment or by regulatory commissions; prohibition of discriminatory rates between places by means of the so-called "shorthaul" clause; and encouragement of competition by forbidding the consolidation of parallel lines.
MAGRATH 175.
   Depending on the railroads to get their produce to market swiftly and dependably, many midwestern farmers had mortgaged their property to buy railroad shares, and had paid high taxes to float bonds to attract railroads into their region, only to find that once established, the railroads paid scant heed to the farmers' interests, charged them exorbitant rates, and discriminated in favor of large, long-distance shippers. It should also be noted that domestic manufacturing interests had secured from Congress high protective tariffs while agricultural products were unprotected and overproduced. Farmers in the 1870's had double economic woes: prices for their basic commodities fell sharply (corn by 32 percent and wheat by 49 percent) while inflation was running at 29 percent, thereby eroding their purchasing power. *Id.* 33-37.
108. 94 U.S. 113 (1877).
109. *Id.* at 136 (Field, J., dissenting).
110. *See id.* at 125.
111. "[W]hen private property is devoted to a public use, it is subject to public regulation." *Id.* at 130.
112. *See* Williams v. Standard Oil Co., 278 U.S. 235 (1929); Ribnik v. McBride, 277 U.S. 350 (1928); Tyson & Bro. v. Banton, 273 U.S. 418 (1927); Wolff Packing Co. v. Court of Indus. Relations, 262 U.S. 522 (1923).

v. *Farmer's Loan & Trust Co.*[113] and *United States v. E.C. Knight Co.*[114] In *Pollock*, the Court struck down a proposed graduated federal income tax on corporate wealth.[115] Justice Field viewed the tax with alarm as only the beginning of an "assault on capital," which if left unchecked by the Court would result in "a war of the poor against the rich . . . constantly growing in intensity and bitterness."[116] The Court's sanction of such a tax, said Justice Field, would "mark the hour when the sure decadence of our government will commence."[117] In *Knight*, also known as the *Sugar Trust Case*, the Court gravely weakened the 5-year-old Sherman Antitrust Act[118] by relying on an "artificial and mechanical separation of 'manufacturing' from 'commerce' without regard to their economic continuity or the effects of the former on the latter."[119] And finally, three years after *Pollock* and *Knight*, the Court rejected Chief Justice Waite's philosophy of judicial restraint and deference to the legislature on matters concerning the reasonableness of rates,[120] declaring "unreasonable" rates set by the state of Nebraska on a public utility because the rates did not, in the judgment of a majority of Justices, allow a "fair return upon the value of that which it employs for the public convenience."[121]

While it is true that Justice Field could not have won over a Court to whom his economic and social views were antithetical and that he clearly appeared to the Court of the Gilded Age to speak with the voice of a prophet, it is likewise correct to suggest that he and his colleagues were either innocent of the historical data suggesting a procedural rather than a substantive meaning to due process,[122] or that they consciously rejected this data when they em-

---

113. 157 U.S. 429 (1895), *reheard*, 158 U.S. 601 (1895).
114. 156 U.S. 1 (1895).
115. Act of Aug. 27, 1894, ch. 349, §§ 27-37, 28 Stat. 553. It was not until ratification of the sixteenth amendment in 1913 that Justice Field's economics were undone.
116. 157 U.S. at 607.
117. *Id.*
118. 15 U.S.C. §§ 1-7 (1970).
119. 1 B. SCHWARTZ, THE POWERS OF GOVERNMENT 186 (1963).
120. *See, e.g.*, Chicago, B. & Q.R.R. v. Iowa, 94 U.S. 155 (1877), in which Chief Justice Waite stated:
> Our province is only to determine whether [establishment of rates] could be done at all, and under any circumstances. If it could, the legislature must decide for itself, subject to no control from us, whether the common good requires that it should be done.

Id. at 164.
121. Smyth v. Ames, 169 U.S. 466, 547 (1898).
122. *See* Corwin, *supra* note 99. For a discussion challenging Corwin's view of due process, see MAGRATH 194-97. Relying in part on Graham, *Procedure to Substance—Extra-Judicial Rise of Due Process, 1830-1860*, 40 CAL. L. REV. 483 (1952), and Graham, *The Early Antislavery Backgrounds of the Fourteenth Amendment*, 1950 WIS. L. REV. 479, 610, Magrath suggests:

ployed substantive due process as a legal instrument with which they consummated an illegitimate union between the "Gospel of Wealth" and the United States Constitution.

B. *Procedural Due Process: A Bane to Criminal Defendants*

While the Gilded Age saw a flowering of Court-protected capitalism through substantive due process, it also witnessed a diminution of procedural rights which state criminal defendants, rightly or wrongly, believed to be guaranteed to them by the fourteenth amendment. The paradoxical result was that due process of law was held to protect the private property of corporate "persons" more meaningfully than the life and liberty of natural persons accused of a crime in a state court.

Just as Justice Hugo Black argued that the fourteenth amendment was not intended to immunize corporations from state regulation,[123] he also maintained in his famous *Adamson v. California*[124] dissent that the first section of the fourteenth amendment was intended "to guarantee that thereafter no state could deprive its citizens of the privileges and protections of the Bill of Rights."[125] Justice Black maintained that the majority in *Adamson*, which included Justice Frankfurter, had erred in holding that the fifth amendment right against self-incrimination was not binding in state prosecutions because they had not taken the trouble "to appraise the relevant historical evidence of the intended scope of the first section of the [Fourteenth] Amendment."[126] Accordingly, Justice Black supplemented his historical essay with a 31-page appendix consisting mainly of extracts from debates of the Congress that framed the fourteenth amendment.

Two years after *Adamson*, two Stanford Law School professors, Charles Fairman and Stanley Morrison, published lengthy articles attacking Justice

---

[F]rom the very beginning [of the postwar Court], *all* of the justices regarded due process as furnishing protection against any purely arbitrary actions by government, irrespective of whether the arbitrary act occurred in a trial or in a regulation of property.

MAGRATH 196.
123. *See* Connecticut Gen. Life Ins. Co. v. Johnson, 303 U.S. 77 (1938), in which Justice Black asserted:
   The history of the [Fourteenth] Amendment proves that the people were told that its purpose was to protect weak and helpless human beings and were not told that it was intended to remove corporations in any fashion from control of state governments.
Id. at 87 (Black, J., dissenting).
124. 332 U.S. 46 (1947).
125. *Id.* at 74-75 (Black, J., dissenting).
126. *Id.* at 74.

Black's views.¹²⁷ Fairman maintained that contemporary evidence in the congressional debates, newspapers, campaign speeches of 1866, and gubernatorial messages, all of which called for ratification of the amendment and records of state legislatures, "overwhelmingly" refuted Justice Black's incorporation thesis.¹²⁸ Morrison corroborated Fairman's findings by conducting an examination of judicial interpretations of the fourteenth amendment, and concluded that Black's dissent amounted "simply to an effort to put into the Constitution what the framers failed to put there."¹²⁹

The chief problem with Fairman's article is the limit of its scope to the immediate background of the framing and ratification of the amendment. As Leonard Levy has shown, the entire period of debate over slavery is relevant to a proper historical understanding of the amendment.¹³⁰ Furthermore, Fairman's finding was negative: that there was not much evidence to support Justice Black's conclusion. This technique, however, is exactly what he criticizes Justice Black for doing, that is, relying heavily on negative evidence and drawing conclusions from arguments *ex silentio*.

The chief difficulty with Morrison's article is in its uncritical assumption that the judges whose decisions he examined were competent historians.¹³¹ As Levy points out, with the exception of the elder Harlan, the Justices relied upon relatively unexamined historical data.¹³² Although Levy faults both Fairman and Morrison, he goes beyond them in attacking Black not merely for writing *ex parte* law office history, but for mangling and manipulating

---

127. Fairman, *Does the Fourteenth Amendment Incorporate the Bill of Rights? The Original Understanding*, 2 STAN. L. REV. 5 (1949); Morrison, *Does the Fourteenth Amendment Incorporate the Bill of Rights? The Judicial Interpretation*, 2 STAN. L. REV. 140 (1949).
128. Fairman, *supra* note 127, at 139.
129. Morrison, *supra* note 127, at 173.
130. *See* Levy, *The Fourteenth Amendment and the Bill of Rights*, in JUDGMENTS: ESSAYS ON AMERICAN CONSTITUTIONAL HISTORY (1972). Levy supports his position by noting:
> As early as the 1830's abolitionist theories . . . were employing due process, privileges and immunities and equality to signify all fundamental rights. . . . From press, pulpit, and platform, the phrases that found their way into the Fourteenth Amendment's trilogy were invoked to support not only the abolition of slavery and equal civil rights for Negroes, but also freedom of speech, press, conscience, petition, and assembly, as well as the procedural rights of the criminally accused and such rights of property as making contracts and enjoying the fruits of one's labor.

Id. at 70.
131. This same difficulty arises with Justice Rehnquist's reliance on the *Slaughter-House Cases* for a "correct" interpretation of the equal protection clause, as discussed in notes 72-78 & accompanying text *supra*.
132. Levy, *supra* note 130, at 69.

it by his selectivity.[133] Levy concludes by asserting that the historical record is "not only complex and confusing; it is inconclusive,"[134] and by judging Fairman as the "better historian by far."[135] He concedes, however, that "even if history spoke with a loud, clear and conclusive voice, it ought not to control judgment."[136]

On the larger issue of whether the Bill of Rights *should* be incorporated into the fourteenth amendment, the Warren Court subsequently vindicated Justice Black in all respects save for the fifth amendment provision for indictment by grand jury, the seventh amendment provision for jury trial in suits at common law when the amount in controversy exceeds 20 dollars, and the eighth amendment prohibition against excessive bail, none of which have yet been made binding upon the states. After the landmark decisions of *Mapp v. Ohio,*[137] *Benton v. Maryland,*[138] *Malloy v. Hogan,*[139] *Klopfer v. North Carolina,*[140] *Duncan v. Louisiana,*[141] *Pointer v. Texas,*[142] *Washington v. Texas,*[143] *Gideon v. Wainwright,*[144] and *Robinson v. California,*[145] Justice Black wrote that while he was "not completely happy with the selective incor-

---

133. See id., in which Levy faults Justice Black for abusing history
by artfully selecting facts from one side only, by generalizing from grossly inadequate "proof," by ignoring confusion and even contradictions in the minds of some of his key historical protagonists, and by assuming that silence on the part of their opponents signified acquiescence.
Id. at 68.
134. *Id.* at 70.
135. *Id.*
136. *Id.* at 71.
137. 367 U.S. 643 (1961). The *Mapp* decision overruled Wolf v. Colorado, 338 U.S. 25 (1949), and applied the exclusionary rule of the fourth amendment to state proceedings.
138. 395 U.S. 784 (1969) (double jeopardy provision of the fifth amendment applied to the states).
139. 378 U.S. 1 (1964). In this case, the Court reversed Adamson v. California, 332 U.S. 46 (1947), and Twining v. New Jersey, 211 U.S. 78 (1908), and held that the fifth amendment right against self-incrimination applied to the states.
140. 386 U.S. 213 (1967) (sixth amendment guarantee of a speedy trial applies to state proceedings).
141. 391 U.S. 145 (1968) (sixth amendment right to trial by an impartial jury effective in state proceedings).
142. 380 U.S. 400 (1965) (sixth amendment provision for the confrontation of adverse witnesses extended to the states).
143. 388 U.S. 14 (1967) (state defendant has sixth amendment right to have compulsory process for obtaining favorable witnesses).
144. 372 U.S. 335 (1963) (sixth amendment right to assistance of counsel in noncapital felony cases extended to the states).
145. 370 U.S. 660 (1962). *Robinson* reversed O'Neil v. Vermont, 144 U.S. 323 (1892), and applied the eighth amendment prohibition against cruel and unusual punishment to the states.

poration theory," it could be supported since "it has the virtue of having worked to make most of the Bill of Rights' protections applicable to the States."[146]

In light of the evidence adduced by Howard Graham and Jacobus tenBroek on the antislavery origins of the "code words" used in the fourteenth amendment,[147] it seeems now that Justice Black's view is more accurate historically as well as jurisprudentially than either he or Fairman anticipated. In any event, it is against the background of this debate on the meaning of the fourteenth amendment that the Gilded Age Court must be assessed in its handling of procedural due process questions.

In 1884, the Court held in *Hurtado v. California*[148] that the fifth amendment requirement of a grand jury indictment before the trial of a capital case was not binding on a state despite the due process clause of the fourteenth amendment. Then in 1892, the Court ruled in *O'Neil v. Vermont*[149] that the eighth amendment prohibition against cruel and unusual punishment was not binding on a state. The Court reaffirmed its earlier *Hurtado* ruling in 1900 when it ruled in *Maxwell v. Dowd*[150] that a state may proceed to trial in a criminal case without a grand jury indictment, and added that the sixth amendment constituted no obstacle to the practice of trying defendants before an eight-member petit jury. Finally, in the 1908 case of *Twining v. New Jersey*,[151] the Court held that the due process clause of the fourteenth amendment required that states only follow the "settled usages and modes or proceedings in the common and statute law of England" as modified by judges in light of new circumstances;[152] it then added its historically unsound opinion that the fifth amendment right against self-incrimination was not among such "settled usages" and hence not "fundamental" enough to be binding on the states.[153] Thus, at regular eight-year intervals, the Court denied to state criminal defendants basic procedural safeguards found in the Bill of Rights, but which according to the Court formed no part of the fourteenth amendment's command to the states against deprivation of life, liberty or property without due process of law.

---

146. H. BLACK, A CONSTITUTIONAL FAITH 39-40 (1968). *See also* Duncan v. Louisiana, 391 U.S. 145, 164-65 (1968) (Black, J., concurring).
147. *See* J. TENBROEK, THE ANTISLAVERY ORIGINS OF THE FOURTEENTH AMENDMENT (1951); Graham, *The Early Antislavery Backgrounds of the Fourteenth Amendment*, 1950 WIS. L. REV. 479, 610.
148. 110 U.S. 516 (1884).
149. 144 U.S. 323 (1892).
150. 176 U.S. 581 (1900).
151. 211 U.S. 78 (1908).
152. *Id.* at 100.
153. *See id.* at 106-14.

Throughout this period, one voice was consistently raised in protest, that of the "great dissenter," Justice John Marshall Harlan,[154] whose career from 1877 to 1911 spanned almost the entire period of the Gilded Age. In *Hurtado*, Justice Harlan wrote in lone dissent a masterful essay on the history of the protection of fundamental human rights in the Anglo-American legal system. He argued that the similarity of language in the fifth and fourteenth amendments shows an intention to have the safeguards that had been applied to the federal government apply to the states.[155]

The *O'Neil* case raised the issue of whether the state of Vermont had inflicted cruel and unusual punishment when it sentenced the defendant to confinement at hard labor in a house of correction for 19,914 days for the crime of "selling, furnishing, and giving away intoxicating liquor without authority."[156] Even Justice Field found this penalty excessive and dissented. Justice Harlan filed a separate dissent in which he stated that he concurred fully with Justice Field that the fourteenth amendment guaranteed "immunity from cruel and unusual punishment" in state proceedings just as in federal actions.[157]

In *Maxwell*, Justice Harlan wrote another excellent historical essay, underscoring the Court's inverted values and inconsistency as reflected in its willingness to borrow from one section of the fifth amendment in order to expand substantive due process benefits for corporate "persons" while contracting procedural due process for natural persons by refusing to graft on to the fourteenth amendment another section from the fifth amendment.[158]

Finally, in *Twining*, the lone dissenter, now an old man one year from death, wrote the last of his attempts to educate his colleagues on the history of due process in Anglo-American law. In the course of this last great dissent, he stated tartly:

---

154. Although Justice Holmes is also known as the "great dissenter," the elder Harlan is at least as worthy of the title. See A. BARTH, PROPHETS WITH HONOR, GREAT DISSENTS AND GREAT DISSENTERS IN THE SUPREME COURT 22-53 (1974); Beth, *Justice Harlan and the Uses of Dissent*, 49 AM. POL. SCI. REV. 1085 (1955).
155. 110 U.S. at 541 (Harlan, J., dissenting).
156. 144 U.S. at 325.
157. *Id.* at 370 (Harlan, J., dissenting).
158. Justice Harlan framed his view by stating:
   If then the "due process of law" required by the Fourteenth Amendment does not allow a State to take private property without just compensation, but does allow the life or liberty of the citizen to be taken in a mode that is repugnant to the settled usages and the modes of proceeding authorized at the time the Constitution was adopted and which was expressly forbidden in the National Bill of Rights, it would seem that the protection of private property is of more consequence than the protection of the life and liberty of the citizen.
176 U.S. at 614 (Harlan, J., dissenting).

[A]s I read the opinion of the court, it will follow from the general principles underlying it, or from the reasoning pursued therein, that the Fourteenth Amendment would be no obstacle whatever in the way of a state law or practice under which, for instance, cruel or unusual punishments (such as the thumb screw, or the rack or burning at the stake), might be inflicted. So of a state law which infringed the right of free speech, or authorized unreasonable searches or seizures of persons, their houses, papers or effects, or a state law under which one accused of crime could be put in jeopardy twice or oftener, at the pleasure of the prosecution, for the same offense.[159]

It is appropriate to conclude this overview of the Court's interpretation of due process in the Gilded Age with the *Twining* case, for *Twining* illustrates not only the Court's failure to attend to the relevant external history of the antislavery origins of the language used in the fourteenth amendment, but also a tragic instance of the Court's reliance on inaccurate data and erroneous law office history. For example, in one sentence Justice Moody asserted in *Twining* that he resorted to "every historical test by which the meaning of the phrase [against self-incrimination in the Fifth Amendment] can be tried."[160] Earlier in the opinion, however, he had confessed that he was obliged to "pass by the meager records of early colonial times, so far as they have come to our attention, as affording light too uncertain for guidance."[161] Even earlier in his opinion, Justice Moody had cited the 1637 Massachusetts heresy trial of Anne Hutchinson, who freely and voluntarily incriminated herself. Not finding the light of this case "too uncertain for

---

159. 211 U.S. at 125 (Harlan, J., dissenting).
It is interesting to note that many of the problems Justice Harlan anticipated did indeed go unaddressed for a significant period. For example, it was 1936 before the Court, in Brown v. Mississippi, 297 U.S. 278 (1936), spoke clearly to the question of impermissible methods of obtaining a confession. Chief Justice Hughes, writing for a unanimous Court, stated:
> The rack and torture chamber may not be substituted for the witness stand.
> ... It would be difficult to conceive of methods more revolting to the sense of justice than those taken to procure the confessions of these petitioners, and the use of the confessions thus obtained as the basis for conviction and sentence was a clear denial of due process.

Id. at 285-86.
Likewise, it was 1931 before the Court clearly protected freedom of the press and of speech from invasion by state action in Near v. Minnesota, 283 U.S. 697 (1931); 1961 before the exclusionary rule which applied to the federal government in regard to evidence obtained in unlawful searches was applied to the states in Mapp v. Ohio, 367 U.S. 643 (1961); and 1969 before the double jeopardy protection of the fifth amendment was extended to state proceedings in Benton v. Maryland, 395 U.S. 784 (1969).
160. 211 U.S. at 110.
161. *Id.* at 108.

guidance," he argued that the case proved that colonial judges were "not aware of any privilege against self-incrimination or any duty to respect it."[162] Conclusions drawn from a negative pregnant are always rather dubious, but Justice Moody's is simply erroneous.

Only a few months before the Hutchinson trial, Anne Hutchinson's brother-in-law John Wheelwright had refused to answer questions about the orthodoxy of his views, grounding the refusal in his right against self-incrimination. Acting as a judge in the case, Governor Winthrop hastily explained that his court neither meant to examine the defendant by compulsory means nor sought to "draw matter from himself whereupon to proceed against him."[163] Justice Moody's resort to "every historical test" of the meaning of the fifth amendment apparently failed to disclose that the maxim *Nemo tenetur prodere seipsum* ("no one is bound to betray himself") was widely known and relied upon by the Puritans in Massachusetts.[164]

Justice Moody's historical excursus took him not only to the colonial period but also into early English legal history. He took comfort in the absence of a specific formula against self-incrimination in the Magna Charta and noted that the practice of self-incriminatory examinations continued for more than four centuries after 1215.[165] This argument, however, is, as Leonard Levy characterizes it, "mischievous over-simplification, a half-truth,"[166] for it fails to understand that the Magna Charta grew in meaning from a feudal document protecting barons from the king to an instrument of quasi-constitutional dimensions protecting the expanding liberties of all English subjects. As early as 1246, Henry III condemned self-incriminating oaths as "repugnant to the ancient Customs of the Realm" and to "his Peoples Liberties."[167] And by 1590, Robert Beale, the clerk of the Privy Council, could declare that "by the Statute of Magna Carta and the olde lawes of this realme, this othe for a man to accuse himself is utterly inhibited."[168]

---

162. *Id.* at 103-04.
163. *A Short History of the Rise, Reign, and Ruin of the Antinomians, Familists and Libertines, That Infected the Churches of New England* (1649), *reprinted in* ANTINOMIANISM IN THE COLONY OF MASSACHUSETTS BAY 194-95 (C. Adams ed. 1894).
164. *See* W. BRADFORD, BRADFORD'S HISTORY "OF PLIMOUTH PLANTATION" 465 (1898).
165. 211 U.S. at 102-08.
166. Levy, *The Right Against Self-Incrimination: History and Judicial History*, 85 POL. SCI. Q. 1 (1969).
167. *See* CLOSE ROLLS OF THE REIGN OF HENRY III, 1247-1251, at 221-22 (H.M. Lyte ed. 1922).
168. *See* Beale, *A Collection Shewinge what Jurisdication the Clergie Hath Hertofore Lawfully Used*, *quoted in* JUDGMENTS: ESSAYS ON AMERICAN CONSTITUTIONAL HISTORY 267, 280 n.21 (L. Levy ed. 1972).

Justice Moody also misspoke himself when he claimed that the Petition of Right in 1628 contained no reference to self-incrimination.[169] The Petition did in fact address this issue by censuring as "not warrantable by the laws or statutes of this realm" an oath which had operated since 1626 to coerce confessions from opponents of a tax enacted by Charles I and euphemistically described by him as a "loan."[170]

Looking at American colonial history, Justice Moody found significance in the absence of a specific enjoinder of compulsory self-incrimination by the Stamp Act Congress and the First Continental Congress, and the absence of such a prohibition in the Northwest Ordinance.[171] Failure to enumerate the principle, however, does not prove that the colonists did not count it among the fundamental rights guaranteed to them in the declaration by the First Continental Congress that they were "entitled to the common law of England,"[172] and implied in the provision in the Northwest Ordinance for "judicial proceedings according to the course of the common law."[173]

Finally, in support of the conclusion that the right against self-incrimination is not "an essential part of due process,"[174] Justice Moody mentioned that only six states provided such protection in their constitutions.[175] Yet he undermined the relevance of this statement by his acknowledgment that by 1776 the courts in all the new states protected the right, even if it was not explicitly stated in the constitution of the state.[176] Further, his tally was incorrect, since he overlooked similar provisions in the constitutions of Delaware[177] and Vermont.[178] It should also be noted that the constitutions

---

169. 211 U.S. at 107-08.
170. The incriminating oath procedure is set forth in THE CONSTITUTIONAL DOCUMENTS OF THE PURITAN REVOLUTION, 1625-1660, at 55 (S. Gardiner ed. 1906). The Petition of Right is reprinted in *id.* at 69.
171. 211 U.S. at 108. The Resolutions of the Stamp Act Congress, the Declaration and Resolves of the First Continental Congress, and the Northwest Ordinance are reprinted in SOURCES OF OUR LIBERTIES: DOCUMENTARY ORIGINS OF INDIVIDUAL LIBERTIES IN THE UNITED STATES CONSTITUTION AND BILL OF RIGHTS 270, 286, 392 (R. Perry ed. 1959).
172. Declaration and Resolves of the First Continental Congress, Fifth Resolution, *reprinted in* SOURCES OF OUR LIBERTIES, *supra* note 171, at 288.
173. Northwest Ordinance art. 2, *reprinted in* SOURCES OF OUR LIBERTIES, *supra* note 171, at 395.
174. 211 U.S. at 106.
175. *Id.* at 91. Justice Moody made reference to the constitutions of Maryland, Massachusetts, New Hampshire, North Carolina, Pennsylvania and Virginia.
176. *Id.* at 92.
177. *See* DEL. DECLARATION OF RIGHTS § 15 (1776), *reprinted in* 1 DEL. CODE ANN. at 110 (1974).
178. *See* VT. CONST. § 10 (1777), *reprinted in* SOURCES OF OUR LIBERTIES, *supra* note 171, at 366. It should be noted, however, that Vermont was not admitted to the Union

of the other states which failed to include a specific reference to the right did not contain a separate bill of rights: every state having a bill of rights guaranteed the right against compulsory self-incrimination.

In its holding that the fifth amendment right against compulsory self-incrimination was not binding on the states, *Twining* typifies the tendency of the Court during the Gilded Age to place the procedural meaning of the due process clause of the fourteenth amendment in narrow, restrictive confines. In its regrettable reliance on imprecise and inaccurate history,[179] cooked up in the New Jersey Attorney General's office to win a case rather than to relate the past truthfully, *Twining* represents a tragic instance of the principle that justice delayed is justice denied.[180]

C. *Unequal Protection of the Laws: Frustrated Hopes for Blacks*

The Court in the Gilded Age managed to butcher the privileges and immunities clause beyond recognition or usefulness in the *Slaughter-House Cases*, and it inverted the due process clause by expanding the property interests of corporate "persons" and contracting the procedural rights of criminal defendants interested in protecting their life and liberty. It remains only to survey the Court's astonishing treatment of the equal protection clause in cases involving racial discrimination to complete the picture of reversal of the historical meaning of the fourteenth amendment.

In no period of the Court's history is it more necessary to situate the Justices in the political and economic context of their time than during the Gilded Age. It is, of course, true that in no period of American history has the Court been entirely apolitical, for the Court has the solemn duty of resolving constitutional questions and national issues which often have clear political overtones or ramifications.[181] At least in this sense, then, the Supreme Court has always been and probably always will be a political institution.

---

until March 1791, when its disputes with New York over granting land titles had been settled.
179. Leonard Levy summarized the Court's understanding of history in *Twining* by stating that
> the opinion was founded on inaccurate and insufficient data. Contrary to the Court's assertion, the right against self-incrimination did evolve as an essential part of due process and as a fundamental principle of liberty and justice.

JUDGMENTS: ESSAYS ON AMERICAN CONSTITUTIONAL HISTORY 268 (L. Levy ed. 1972).
180. It was not until 1964, in Malloy v. Hogan, 378 U.S. 1 (1964), that *Twining* was overruled.
181. In 1835, Alexis de Tocqueville observed that "[s]carcely any political question arises in the United States that is not resolved, sooner or later, into a judicial question." A. DE TOQUEVILLE, DEMOCRACY IN AMERICA 137 (J. Mayer & M. Lerner ed. 1966). In

Political history is especially relevant to understanding the Court of the Gilded Age because its members participated in the political life of the country more actively than in other eras. Two Chief Justices were potential nominees to the office of the Presidency: Salmon P. Chase avidly seeking the Democratic nomination in 1868 and 1872,[182] and Morrison R. Waite unsuccessfully sought after by the Republicans in 1875 to run in the following year to succeed President Grant.[183] In response to efforts to put forward his name in 1884, Justice Harlan, like Chief Justice Waite before him, replied that for him politics and judicial duties were "utterly irreconcilable."[184] Another Associate Justice, David Davis, joined Chief Justice Chase in maneuvering for the Presidency in 1872. When Chief Justice Waite suspected Justice Davis of doing so again in 1876, the Chief Justice made one of his rare comments about a fellow judge, charging him with making "the Supreme Court the anteroom of the White House."[185]

Much more significant than such political self-seeking, however, was the direct involvement in 1877 of five members of the Court—Democrats Nathan Clifford and Stephen J. Field, and Republicans Samuel F. Miller, William Strong, and Joseph P. Bradley—in the Electoral Commission established by Congress to resolve the crisis which developed when four states filed contested returns in the closest presidential race in history.[186] These Justices not only "followed the election returns," as Finley Peter Dunne's Mr. Dooley would have said at a later date, they determined its outcome. In ruling on

---

light of this situation, de Toqueville stated that judges must know "how to understand the spirit of the age, to confront those obstacles that can be overcome, and to steer out of the current when the tide threatens to carry them away." *Id. See also* M. SHAPIRO, LAW AND POLITICS IN THE SUPREME COURT (1964).

182. *See* MAGRATH 285.

183. Chief Justice Waite refused to consent to having his name forwarded for the Presidency, declaring:

I have now no other ambition than to fill worthily the high office to which I have been called. To me it is the most desirable as well as the most honorable position in the government. . . . I would rather die with a name fit to be associated with those of my great predecessors than be 40 times a President.

Draft of an undated letter in Chief Justice Waite's Aug.-Dec. 1874 correspondence, *quoted in* Magrath 280.

184. Westin, *John Marshall Harlan and the Constitutional Rights of Negroes: The Transformation of a Southerner*, 66 YALE L.J. 637, 677 (1957).

185. Letter from Morrison R. Waite to Elihu B. Washburne, Apr. 30, 1876, *quoted in* MAGRATH 286. Two other justices so tempted were Justice Field, in both 1880 and 1884, and Justice Miller in 1884. It is the opinion of Magrath that, of the two, Justice Field was far more interested in the possibility of a presidential nomination. *See id.* at 286-87.

186. For an extended description of the contested election, see P. HAWORTH, THE HAYES-TILDEN ELECTION OF 1876 (1906); C. WOODWARD, REUNION AND REACTION 16-19, 150-165 (1951).

each of the 20 disputed electoral college votes, the Justices split along straight party lines, with the result that the office of the presidency, badly marred by the scandal and corruption rampant during the second administration of General Grant, was assigned by the Commission to Rutherford B. Hayes, the Republican Governor of Ohio, rather than to his Democratic opponent, Samuel J. Tilden, the Governor of New York, who had a popular majority of some 250,000 votes and probably a slight majority in the electoral college as well.[187]

"This outrageous display of partisanship," states historian John Garraty, "made Hayes President and left the Democrats more convinced than ever that their candidate had been deprived of office by fraud."[188] Although Garraty makes no comment as to the impact of the episode on the Court, C. Peter Magrath, biographer of Chief Justice Waite, argues that the "Court as a whole came through the Disputed Election crisis comparatively unscathed."[189] Magrath is of the opinion that "the Court was not very vulnerable to charges of having debased itself during the crisis of 1876," and suggests the contrary: that "by doing its best with an unusual and nasty chore it assisted in ending one of the Republic's few really serious political crises."[190] Magrath's rationale for absolving the highly partisan performance of the Justices on the Electoral Commission—"virtually everyone else in the country" would have behaved that way[191]—is hardly an adequate standard, even pre-Watergate, for evaluating the official acts of members of the highest tribunal in the land. Additionally, his conclusion on the impact or consequences of the episode on the Court is too facile, for in restricting the focus of judgment to only the immediate context of the Commission's work, Magrath overlooks the connection between the outcome of the Hayes-Tilden election and the infamous Compromise of 1877. According to the terms of this political horsetrading, Democrats consented to Hayes' election in

---

187. Tilden needed only one of the disputed electoral votes in order to prevail and it has been suggested that in an honest election, Tilden might have prevailed over Hayes in Florida, although not in Louisiana or South Carolina. See C. WOODWARD, *supra* note 186, at 19. It is impossible, however, to be certain of this outcome since the estimates are based largely on the fact that blacks, who at that time voted Republican as a solid bloc, were in a majority in Louisiana and South Carolina, but not in Florida. One of the few things that is certain concerning the election of 1876 is the unprecedented degree of fraud and corruption which surrounded it. In the three Southern states in question, black Republicans were kept from the polls by force and intimidation, while Republican election officials systematically threw out or invalidated thousands of Democratic ballots. See J. GARRATY, THE NEW COMMONWEALTH: 1877-1890, at 259-60 (1968).
188. J. GARRATY, *supra* note 187, at 260.
189. MAGRATH 294.
190. *Id.* at 294-95.
191. *Id.* at 294.

return for a Republican promise to end the era of radical Reconstruction in the South.[192] It is beside the point to argue that there is no evidence to demonstrate that five Justices who sat on the Electoral Commission also participated formally in negotiating the terms of the Compromise, which was more a tacit agreement among party leaders than a formal document or binding contract. The point is that all of the Justices, not merely those who served on the Commission, were fully aware of the Compromise. Breathing in the political atmosphere of the day, all of them, with the exception of Justice Harlan, deemed it their duty to act as guardians of the Compromise and to pronounce their judicial benediction on its basic terms in the civil rights cases heard from 1877 down to the close of the Gilded Age.

The remarkable shift in the Republican party's strategy toward the South by the Compromise of 1877 can be explained in terms of political opportunism calculated to keep a Republican in the White House. Louis M. Hacker notes that by 1877 the "old" radical Republicans—men like Thaddeus Stevens, Charles Sumner, and George Julian, who were abolitionists committed to political, social and economic equality for blacks—were either dead or politically impotent and had been replaced by the "new" radicals—men like Roscoe Conkling, John Logan, and James Blaine, who were opportunists eager to woo the votes of Southern blacks as long as they were necessary to maintain the thin majority of their party, but who were willing to abandon their struggle for civil rights once an alliance had been forged with Western interests sympathetic to industrial capitalism.[193]

Economic history also has general relevance to the performance of the Court during the Gilded Age,[194] and there was a direct link between economic history and the Compromise of 1877, which was not only a barometer of the political climate of the day, but a reflection of the economic mood of the country as well. Northern businessmen interested in the economic expansion of the South preferred a policy of "moderation" to the grant of real political power to Southern blacks, since the latter policy had provoked turmoil and violence, which in turn impeded the flow of capital to the area.[195]

---

192. The details of the Compromise provided that the Democrats would (1) allow Hayes to become President; (2) allow the Republicans to organize the House of Representatives; (3) protect blacks' rights in the South; and (4) help to revive the Republican party in the South. The Republicans agreed to (1) recognize the election of Democratic states in Louisiana and South Carolina; (2) end the stationing of federal troops to enforce Reconstruction in the South; (3) aid in securing internal improvements for Southern states, including an East-West railroad via a southern route; (4) include some Southern Republicans in Hayes' cabinet; and (5) give more federal jobs to Southerners. *See* C. WOODWARD, *supra* note 186.
193. *See* L. HACKER, THE TRIUMPH OF CAPITALISM 339-45 (1940).
194. *See* notes 9, 12, 13 & accompanying text *supra*.
195. Magrath characterizes the situation by noting:

It is against the background of this external political and economic history, then, that the Supreme Court's use of the internal legal history of the fourteenth amendment and the accompanying Civil Rights Acts of 1866, 1870, 1871 and 1875 must be evaluated. As Gunnar Myrdal has reminded us in his classic work on racism in America, "it must not be forgotten that the decisions of the Court had themselves a substantial share in the responsibility for the solidification of the Northern apathy."[196] In 1876, 100 years after American revolutionaries had declared as a self-evident truth that "all men are created equal," the Court handed down two voting rights cases which weakened the notion that black Americans shared in this vision of equality.[197] Taken together, these cases helped set the pattern for subsequent developments in fourteenth amendment analysis.

In *United States v. Cruikshank*,[203] the other voting rights case of the same found guilty under section 4 of the Enforcement Act of May 31, 1870[199] for refusing to receive and count the vote of a black man. Chief Justice Waite abandoned his usual philosophy of judicial deference to the legislature and found the penal sections of the 1870 Act not "appropriate legislation" for enforcing the fifteenth amendment.[200] According to the Chief Justice, "[i]t is only when the wrongful refusal at such an election is because of race, color, or previous condition of servitude, that Congress can interfere, and provide for its punishment."[201] On this narrow construction of the amendment,

---

When it became clear that the price to be paid for Negro equality included continuing military rule and a certain amount of violence—at the cost of business profits—there could be but one outcome. Capitalism was on the march and surely the Republican Party, its political prophet, would not stand in the way.

MAGRATH 115. *See also* P. BUCK, THE ROAD TO REUNION (1937), in which the author writes: "When theories of Negro equality resulted in race conflict, and conflict in higher prices of raw cotton, manufacturers were inclined to accept the view of the Southern planter rather than that of the New England zealot." *Id.* at 154.

196. G. MYRDAL, AN AMERICAN DILEMMA: THE NEGRO PROBLEM AND MODERN DEMOCRACY 516 (1944).

197. United States v. Reese, 92 U.S. 214 (1876); United States v. Cruikshank, 92 U.S. 542 (1876). The cases were brought under the Enforcement Act of May 31, 1870, ch. 114, §§ 1-23, 16 Stat. 140. This Act had been passed pursuant to the powers given Congress under section 2 of the fifteenth amendment and represented a comprehensive attempt to guarantee federal enforcement of the right to vote by blacks in the South. Section 4 of the Act, which was challenged in *Reese*, penalized the hinderance of any person from qualifying to vote, while section 6, the provision involved in *Cruikshank*, prohibited banding together or conspiring to deprive a citizen of rights secured by the Act.

198. 92 U.S. 214 (1876).
199. Act of May 31, 1870, ch. 64, 16 Stat. 140.
200. 92 U.S. at 221.
201. *Id.* at 218.

he voided key sections of the Enforcement Act as a far-reaching invasion of states' rights. He did so by a strange bit of inverted logic, construing the statute to mean more than it actually said, so that he could then conclude that by meaning that much, Congress had gone beyond the scope of the amendment.[202]

In *United States v. Cruikshank*,[203] the other voting rights case of the same year, sophistry reigned supreme when the Court reversed a conviction under section 6 of the 1870 Act. Early in 1873, a group of about 300 blacks had attended a political meeting at the Grant Parish Courthouse in the town of Colfax, Louisiana, the rally ending in a terrible riot.[204] Believing the incident to be a vicious instance of a racially motivated attack on blacks in order to inhibit the exercise of their civil rights, the Justice Department secured indictments for almost 100 white men. Nine defendants, including Cruikshank, were subsequently arrested and found guilty on charges of conspiring to interfere with the blacks' right to assemble, to bear arms, to vote, and to obtain equal protection of the laws safeguarding persons and property. Presiding over the trial jointly with Circuit Judge William Woods, Justice Bradley voiced a difference of opinion with his colleague over the sufficiency of the indictment.[205] In his circuit opinion, Justice Bradley stated that the affirmative protection of the fundamental rights of citizenship "does not devolve upon [the federal government] . . . but belongs to the state government as a part of its residuary sovereignty."[206] Under this view, the fourteenth amendment gave to Congress no affirmative power to furnish redress against hostile state laws, for "the only constitutional guaranty of . . . privileges and immunities is, that no state shall pass any law to abridge them . . . ."[207] While Justice Bradley acknowledged that the fifteenth amendment concededly empowered Congress to forbid "outrage, violence, and combinations on the part of individuals"[208] interfering with the right to vote, he believed that the indictments in the case were defective for failure to aver improper state action and for failure to allege racial animus as the basis of the mass killing of blacks at the courthouse. Chief Justice Waite expressed an incredible degree of naiveté and legal sophistry when he upheld Justice Bradley on

---

202. *See id.* at 220-21.
203. 92 U.S. 542 (1876).
204. A marker outside the town of Colfax tells the white Southerners' version of the event: "On this site occurred the Colfax Riot in which three white men and 150 Negroes were slain. This event on April 13, 1873 marked the end of carpetbag misrule in the South." *Cited in* C. FAIRMAN, *supra* note 12, at 1377.
205. United States v. Cruikshank, 25 F. Cas. 707 (No. 14,897) (C.C.D. La. 1874).
206. *Id.* at 710.
207. *Id.* at 714.
208. *Id.* at 713.

the insufficiency of the indictments, stating, "We may suspect that race was the cause of the hostility; but it is not so averred."[209] More ominous for future interpretation of the fourteenth amendment was his conclusion that the amendment did not reach the indictments in *Cruikshank*.[210]

The tragic implication of *Cruikshank* and *Reese* for black Americans was poignantly highlighted in two letters of the period written by federal attorneys working in the South. In 1875, while the cases were still pending on the Supreme Court docket, a band of whites murdered four blacks after an election in Columbus, Mississippi, and as a result of such violent intimidation the voting strength of blacks in that town dropped from 1,200 to 17.[211] Henry Whitfield, United States Attorney in the area, reported that prosecutions would be "utterly futile":

> Notorious violations of the election laws have been absolutely ignored by grand jurors who had direct and personal knowledge of the violation. It is impossible to get the witnesses, *who have personal knowledge of the facts*, to tell the truth, or what they know, even, in presence of the grand jury, for fear of their lives, or for considerations of policy, protection of personal friends, accomplishment of political and party purposes etc. . . . .
>
> The only hope now is through the officers and Court of the United States. If these fail, then a large mass of the people here are without remedy, or protection, *by reason of the practical nullification of the Constitution and laws of the Country.*[212]

Nearly three years after the Court dashed that "only hope" in *Reese* and *Cruikshank*, another federal attorney, L. C. Northrop, gave a vivid description of the situation he faced in Charleston, South Carolina:

> I have been forced by the unfortunate condition here, to give to Reese et al and Cruikshank et al my severest study. I made

---

209. 92 U.S. at 556.
210. *Id.* at 554-56. The Chief Justice reached this result by reasoning that the fourteenth amendment
> prohibits a State from denying to any person within its jurisdiction the equal protection of the laws; but this provision does not . . . add any thing to the rights which one citizen has under the Constitution against another. The equality of the rights of citizens is a principle of republicanism. . . . [But] that duty was originally assumed by the States; and it still remains there. The only obligation resting upon the United States is to see that the States do not deny the right. This the amendment guarantees, but no more. The power of the national government is limited to the enforcement of this guaranty.

Id. at 554-55.
211. MAGRATH 125.
212. Letter from Henry Whitfield to Edwards Pierrepont, Nov. 6, 1875, *quoted in* MAGRATH 125.

last spring a careful abstract with notes, of these and all kindred cases and came to the conclusion then, which is much stronger now, that with the single exception of a few sections, relating to the elections of federal officers, the federal election laws are a delusion and farce. . . . If red shirts break up meetings by violence, there is no remedy, unless it can be proved to have been done on account or race, etc., which cant [sic] be proved. . . . It is hard to sit quietly and see such things, with the powerful arm of the Government, bound in conscience to protect its citizens, tied behind its back by these decisions. With colored men crowding my office, it is hard to make them understand my utter helplessness.[213]

In 1883, in cases involving legislation enforcing the equal protection clause, the Court delivered two more severe blows to the civil rights advocates. In *United States v. Harris*,[214] the Court invalidated section 2 of the Ku Klux Klan Act of 1871,[215] which provided penalties in cases involving conspiracies to deprive individuals of the equal protection of the laws. This provision, wrote Justice William B. Woods (another Hayes appointee), exceeded the authority given to Congress in the fourteenth amendment, because the amendment did not reach acts of private persons. Congress was therefore powerless to curb the Klan's lynching and mob violence because such activity was not carried on by state officers or under color of state law. Nor could the federal government lay upon the states an affirmative duty to protect black citizens from Klan terrorism, for the Civil War Amendments reached only "state action," not state inaction or sins of omission of the grossest sort.

Magrath states that it was the *Civil Rights Cases*[216] "that pleased the South most and best signif[y] the Supreme Court's role as constitutional guardian of the Compromise of 1877."[217] In the *Civil Rights Cases*, the Court was faced squarely with a choice between Jim Crow[218] and the Civil Rights Act

---

213. Letter from L.C. Northrop to Charles Devens, Jan. 14, 1879, *quoted in* MAGRATH 132-33.
214. 106 U.S. 629 (1883).
215. Act of Apr. 20, 1871, ch. 114, § 2, 17 Stat. 13.
216. 109 U.S. 3 (1883).
217. MAGRATH 142.
218. This was the name given to a series of segregation laws which rigidly and systematically excluded blacks from contact or communication with whites. As Woodward noted, these laws
> lent the sanction of the law to a racial ostracism that extended to churches and schools, to housing and jobs, to eating and drinking. Whether by law or by custom, they extended to virtually all forms of public transportation, to sports and recreations, to hospitals, orphanages, prisons, and asylums, and ultimately to funeral homes, morgues, and cemeteries.

C. WOODWARD, THE STRANGE CAREER OF JIM CROW 7 (3d rev. ed. 1974).

of 1875.[219] The latter was the most significant piece of civil rights legislation enacted by the Congress to enforce the Civil War Amendments. Five cases, involving denial of equal service or accommodations to blacks in a theater in San Francisco, an opera house in New York, and a hotel, restaurant, and train in the South were consolidated for a decision on the constitutionality of the Act. It seems difficult today, more than a decade after the Court upheld the Civil Rights Act of 1964,[220] to imagine that the Court previously found a similar Act of Congress unconstitutional. But the Court of the Gilded Age did just that, striking down the equal accommodations provisions of the 1875 Act by a vote of eight to one. Building on the "state action" foundation laid by Chief Justice Waite in *Cruikshank*, the Court held that the fourteenth amendment only spoke to actions by state officials and did "not authorize Congress to create a code of municipal law for the regulation of private rights . . . ."[221] And, as if blacks needed a reminder that the days of Reconstruction were over and that the welcome mat for blacks on their way to the court had been removed, Justice Bradley added with cruel irony that the effects of slavery wear off over time and that there comes a time when the former slave "takes the rank of a mere citizen, and ceases to be the special favorite of the laws."[222]

It was the elder Justice Harlan, a Kentucky colonel and former slaveholder,[223] previously opposed to the ratification of all three Civil War Amend-

---

219. Act of Mar. 1, 1875, ch. 114, §§ 1-5, 18 Stat. 335. The specific section of the Act challenged provided in part:
> That all persons within the jurisdiction of the United States shall be entitled to the full and equal enjoyment of the accommodations . . . of inns, public conveyances on land or water, theaters, and other places of public amusement; subject only to the conditions and limitations established by law, and applicable alike to citizens of every race and color, regardless of any previous condition of servitude.

Id. § 1.
220. Heart of Atlanta Motel, Inc. v. United States, 379 U.S. 241 (1964). *See also* Katzenbach v. McClung, 379 U.S. 294 (1964).
221. 109 U.S. at 11.
222. *Id.* at 25.
223. Justice Harlan's nomination to the Supreme Court was opposed by a Union Army General who wrote to the Senate Judiciary Committee that, during the Civil War, Harlan had told him that he
> had no more conscientious scruples in buying and selling a horse, that the right of property in a Negro was identical with that of the property in a horse, and that the liberation of slaves by our general government was a direct violation of the Constitution of the United States.

Letter from Speed S. Fry to William Brown, Nov. 2, 1877, *quoted in* Westin, *supra* note 184, at 669-70.

ments, who, to quote Justinian, showed greater understanding of the historical "force and power" of those Amendments, "not merely of their words."[224] His dissent remains today a masterpiece of judicial wisdom.[225]

The Court during the Gilded Age also displayed considerable ability at sleight of hand in its use of the commerce clause to defend Jim Crow. In 1878, the Court struck down a Louisiana law prohibiting segregation on steamboats by employing the rule of *Cooley v. Wardens*[226] to hold that regulation of steamboats traveling up and down the Mississippi required uniform national regulation.[227] But in 1890, in *Louisville, New Orleans & Texas Railway Co. v. Mississippi*,[228] the Court upheld as only intrastate in scope a Jim Crow law *requiring* segregation on railroad cars traveling within the state of Mississippi, even though Congress had presumably exercised its plenary power and "occupied the field" by the passage of the Interstate Commerce Act[229] in 1887. Justice Harlan again dissented, pointing out the obvious inconsistency in commerce clause interpretation, and implied that the only consistency in the cases was the interest of the Court in upholding segregation.[230]

Given a green light by the Supreme Court in the *Civil Rights Cases* and the Mississippi railroad case, some legislatures proceeded to expand the reach

---

224. JUSTINIAN, DIGEST 1, 3:17.
225. The dissent reads in part:
   I cannot resist the conclusion that the substance and spirit of the recent amendments of the Constitution have been sacrificed by a subtle and ingenious verbal criticism. . . . Constitutional provisions, adopted in the interest of liberty, and for the purpose of securing, through national legislation, if need be, rights inhering in a state of freedom, and belonging to American citizenship, have been so construed as to defeat the ends the people desired to accomplish, which they attempted to accomplish, and which they supposed they had accomplished by changes in their fundamental law.
109 U.S. at 26 (Harlan, J., dissenting).
   What I affirm is that no State, nor the officers of any State, nor any corporation or individual wielding power under State authority for the public benefit or the public convenience, can, consistently either with the freedom established by the fundamental law, or with that equality of civil rights which now belongs to every citizen, discriminate against freemen or citizens, in those rights, because of their race, or because they once labored under the disabilities of slavery imposed upon them as a race.
Id. at 59.
226. 53 U.S. (12 How.) 299 (1851). In *Cooley*, Justice Curtis ruled that the congressional commerce power, although plenary, was concurrent with that of the states, at least as to those matters affecting commerce which do not of their nature require uniform national resolution.
227. Hall v. DeCuir, 95 U.S. 485 (1878).
228. 133 U.S. 587 (1890).
229. Act of Feb. 4, 1887, ch. 104, 24 Stat. 379 (codified in scattered sections of 49 U.S.C.).
230. 133 U.S. at 594 (Harlan, J., dissenting).

of Jim Crow into every nook and cranny of social life.[231] C. Vann Woodward noted that the purpose of the Jim Crow laws was to sustain the illusion of white superiority and that their effect was to promote the illusion of black inferiority.[232] In 1896, the Court had an opportunity to curb such racial aggressions in the celebrated case of *Plessy v. Ferguson*.[233] Instead, it upheld a Louisiana statute which was enacted "to promote the comfort of passengers on railway trains" by requiring "equal but separate accommodations" on trains.[234] The plaintiff, Homer Adolph Plessy, had challenged the statute in the court of state judge John Ferguson on fourteenth amendment grounds, contending that state action requiring racial segregation violated the equal protection clause. Justice Henry B. Brown, appointed to the Supreme Court in 1890 by President Harrison, upheld Judge Ferguson's rejection of this contention, reflecting the apathy to the race problem shared by the eight-man majority on the Court and probably a similar proportion of the country.[235] In framing his customary dissent, Justice Harlan penned some of his most memorable phrases, including his prediction that "the judgment this day rendered will, in time, prove to be quite as pernicious as the decision made by this tribunal in the *Dred Scott case*."[236] By way of explanation of the reasons for the stance he assumed in the dissent, he stated:

---

231. Woodward cites a host of state and local enactments mandating segregation in a variety of settings, including an Alabama law which prohibited white female nurses from attending to black male patients; an Oklahoma law which banned interracial boating or fishing; North Carolina and Virginia statutes which outlawed fraternal organizations that permitted members of different races to address each other as "brother"; New Orleans ordinances providing for separate red-light districts for segregated prostitutes; and a Birmingham ordinance which made it unlawful for blacks and whites to play dominoes or checkers "together or in each other's company." C. WOODWARD, *supra* note 218, at 99, 118, 100, & 102.

232. As Woodward characterizes it, this purposeful humiliation
> put the authority of the state or city in the voice of the street-car conductor, the railway brakeman, the bus driver, the theater usher, and also into the voice of the hoodlum of the public parks and playgrounds. They [Jim Crow laws] gave free rein and the majesty of the law to mass aggressions that might otherwise have been curbed, blunted or deflected.

Id. at 107-08.

233. 163 U.S. 537 (1896).

234. Acts of 1890, No. 111, *quoted in* A. BARTH, *supra* note 154, at 30.

235. Justice Brown wrote with remarkable smugness and insensitivity:
> We consider the underlying fallacy of the plaintiff's argument to consist in the assumption that the enforced separation of the two races stamps the colored race with a badge of inferiority. If this be so, it is not by reason of anything found in the act, but solely because the colored race chooses to put that construction upon it.

163 U.S. at 551.

236. *Id.* at 559 (Harlan, J., dissenting).

The destinies of the two races, in this country, are indissolubly linked together, and the interests of both require that the common government of all shall not permit the seeds of race hate to be planted under the sanction of law.[237]

Finally, in 1908 in *Berea College v. Kentucky*,[238] the Court sustained a Kentucky statute which, by prohibiting integration in privately incorporated educational institutions, forced the college to close its doors to black students. Seeking to avoid the obvious constitutional issue in the case, the Court based its decision on the right of the states to change the terms of corporate charters granted by the legislature. The elder Justice Harlan saw through this ploy and noted that the Kentucky statute was not really a regulation of corporate business, but was essentially an education statute requiring racial segregation and was therefore void under the equal protection clause as an "invasion of the rights of liberty and property guaranteed by the Fourteenth Amendment against hostile state action . . . ."[239] The aging gadfly left his colleagues with a poignant and penetrating question in his last dissent in a civil rights case:

Have we become so inoculated with prejudice of race that an American government, professedly based on the principles of freedom, and charged with the protection of all citizens alike, can make distinctions between such citizens in the matter of their voluntary meeting for innocent purposes simply because of their respective races?[240]

IV. CONCLUSION: HISTORY AS A NECESSITY AND A DUTY

Justice Harlan's question in *Berea College* has stinging force when it is remembered that the Supreme Court during the Gilded Age had moved, gradually at first but then with increasing momentum, to a position adverse to state regulation of corporate "persons" when their profits would thereby fall below a judicially determined "reasonable rate."[241] In *Berea College*,

---

237. *Id.* at 560 (Harlan, J., dissenting).
238. 211 U.S. 45 (1908).
239. *Id.* at 67 (Harlan, J., dissenting). Speaking to the question of incorporation, Justice Harlan noted:
   There is no magic in the fact of incorporation which will so transform the act of teaching the two races in the same school at the same time that such teaching can be deemed lawful when conducted by private individuals, but unlawful when conducted by the representatives of corporations.
Id. at 65 (Harlan, J., dissenting).
240. *Id.* at 69 (Harlan, J., dissenting).
241. *See* L. BETH, THE DEVELOPMENT OF THE AMERICAN CONSTITUTION: 1877-1917, at 191 (1971).

in which the issue concerned people rather than profits, and equal educational opportunity rather than a "fair return" on corporate investment, the Court found no difficulty in allowing the Commonwealth of Kentucky to intervene in the business of an educational "corporation" and to radically alter its policy under the guise of modifying its corporate charter.

The irony of the *Berea College* case, then, symbolizes the paradoxical result of the judicial interpretation of the fourteenth amendment in the first four decades after the amendment was adopted. In 1873, the *Slaughter-House* Court butchered the privileges and immunities clause beyond recognition or usefulness. The Court then transformed the due process clause, giving it substantive content in the area of economic regulation of corporations, an area almost certainly not intended by its framers, while limiting its sweep in the area of procedural fairness to criminal defendants, an area most clearly intended by the framers. And by the close of the Gilded Age, the Court had repeatedly instructed black Americans that Congress was powerless to reverse the blatantly unequal protection of the laws which they experienced after the Compromise of 1877, when a dubiously elected President sacrificed the cause of racial justice in the name of national conciliation and a Chief Justice led the Supreme Court in pronouncing solemn constitutional benediction on the arrangement.

Hopefully it is clear that the law does not have a life all its own and that one cannot, therefore, understand legal history without raising questions of political, economic, and social history as well. Hopefully it has also become clear from the sorts of cases reviewed that the quality of the Court's use of history should not be of interest to constitutional scholars and lawyers and other professional specialists alone. The Supreme Court in our society has been entrusted not with the business of maintaining political compromises which benefit a few or even a majority, but with the nobler task of safeguarding for all "a constitution . . . intended to endure for ages to come"[242] as a basic statement of constitutive social meaning which "We the People . . . do ordain and establish."[243] Hence, the Court's public authority in American life can only be diminished when it fails to be attentive, intelligent, and reasonable in its use of history. Conversely, the Court can only increase its stature when it shows reverence for our past heritage, especially as it is expressed in the documents which we have enshrined as fundamental or constitutive of our national self-understanding, when it displays insight not only as to the original intent of such documents, but also as to their present meaning in a rapidly changing world, and when it recognizes that "the law is not

---

242. McCulloch v. Maryland, 17 U.S. (4 Wheat.) 316, 415 (1819).
243. U.S. CONST. preamble.

majestic enough in the American system to endure for good but unexplained or unexplicable reason."[244]

Justice Holmes once wrote that "it ought always to be remembered that historic continuity with the past is not a duty, it is only a necessity."[245] In light of the above considerations, however, the Court would do better to heed Justice Frankfurter's revision of Justice Holmes' distinction without a difference, and to acknowledge that judges

> are under a special duty not to over-emphasize the episodic aspects of life and not to undervalue its organic processes—its continuities and relationships. For judges at least it is important to remember that continuity with the past is not only a necessity but even a duty.[246]

---

244. C. MILLER, *supra* note 38, at 14.
245. O.W. HOLMES, COLLECTED LEGAL PAPERS 139 (1920).
246. Frankfurter, *Some Reflections on the Reading of Statutes*, 47 COLUM. L. REV. 527, 534-35 (1947).

Desegregation in New Orleans Public Schools during Reconstruction

LOUIS R. HARLAN*

IT is a fact not generally known even to historians that the New Orleans public schools during the Reconstruction period underwent substantial racial desegregation over a period of six and a half years, an experience shared by no other southern community until after 1954 and by few northern communities at the time. This essay is limited to a summary of the evidence that there was indeed desegregation in New Orleans in the 1870's and to an effort to explain it chiefly in terms of circumstances in New Orleans at the time. It is obvious that New Orleans, as the only real urban center in the overwhelmingly rural South, could not be an example from which any general conclusions can be drawn about Reconstruction in the region or even in Louisiana as a whole. The experience of one southern urban community during Reconstruction, however, may hold interest for students of the rapidly urbanizing contemporary South.

For a generation of historians rather suddenly concerned with past struggles over civil rights, the interest of this study lies partly in the new crop that it makes in the much-plowed field of Reconstruction history. The historians both of Louisiana Reconstruction[1] and of southern education[2] have pronounced the desegregation experiment of New Orleans an almost total failure. The conclusions of historians of the Dunning school may be explained by their preoccupation with political themes or their racialistic and sectional blind spots, but perhaps a better explanation is that they read in the partisan

---

* An associate professor at the University of Cincinnati, Mr. Harlan's major field of interest is southern United States history, especially education and race relations. He is the author of *Separate and Unequal: Public School Campaigns in the Southern Seaboard States, 1901-1915* (Chapel Hill, N. C., 1958).

[1] Alcée Fortier, *Louisiana Studies* (New Orleans, 1894), 267-68; John R. Ficklen, *History of Reconstruction in Louisiana* (Baltimore, 1910), 207-208; Ella Lonn, *Reconstruction in Louisiana after 1868* (New York, 1918), 54-55, 357; John S. Kendall, *History of New Orleans* (3 vols., Chicago, 1922), I, 331, 665; Roger W. Shugg, *Origins of Class Struggle in Louisiana* (University, La., 1939), 226; Garnie W. McGinty, *Louisiana Redeemed* (New Orleans, 1941), 24. George W. Cable, *Strange True Stories of Louisiana* (New York, 1889), 221-32, is more accurate, though limited to a single public school.

[2] Horace M. Bond, *The Education of the Negro in the American Social Order* (New York, 1934), 52; Charles W. Dabney, *Universal Education in the South* (2 vols., Chapel Hill, N. C., 1936), I, 368-71; Harry S. Ashmore, *The Negro and the Schools* (Chapel Hill, N. C., 1954), 7-8; John Hope Franklin, "Jim Crow Goes to School," *South Atlantic Quarterly*, LVIII (Spring 1959), 225-35; Alfred H. Kelly, "The Congressional Controversy over School Segregation, 1867-1875," *American Historical Review*, LXIV (Apr. 1959), 537-63.

663

press the headlined stories of white walkouts and Negro evictions, but failed to note the undramatic evidence of the return of most of these pupils in the following days and months. Historians of southern education seem to have relied too heavily on a secondary source by the Louisiana educational historian Thomas H. Harris, who in turn depended vaguely on the "testimony of men who lived through the period." Harris declared in 1924: "The schools were never mixed. The law was evaded from the first, and the negroes were about as active in evading it as the whites."[3]

It is with some surprise, therefore, that we read the testimony in 1874 of Thomas W. Conway, the Radical state superintendent and prime mover of New Orleans desegregation:

I had fully concluded to put the system of mixed schools to a thorough, practical test, and I did. The white pupils all left ... and the school-house was virtually in the hands of the colored pupils. This was the picture one day. What will you think when I tell you that before I reached my office that day, the children of both races who, on the school question, seemed like deadly enemies, were, many of them, joined in a circle, playing on the green, under the shade of the widespreading live oak. In a few days I went back to see how the school was progressing, and, to my surprise, found nearly all the former pupils returned to their places; and that the school, like all the schools in the city, reported at the close of the year a larger attendance than at any time since the close of the war. The children were simply kind to each other in the school-room as in the streets and elsewhere! A year ago I visited the same school and saw therein about as many colored children as whites, with not a single indication of any ill-feeling whatever.

All that is wanted in this matter of civil rights is to let the foes of the measure simply understand that we mean it. Do this, and as in the case of the enemies of free schools in Louisiana, they will be quiet.[4]

The whole truth, of course, embraces both the historians' evidence of evasion and strident resistance and Conway's idyl of dancing on the green. Evasion lasted for three years, until the last legal recourse was exhausted, and then desegregation began. As desegregation spread slowly into more and more schools, as Conway said, there was indeed resistance, but it was fruitless, sporadic, separated by long periods of tacit acceptance, and successful in the end only because Reconstruction itself failed.

The forces of evasion were in effect even before the state constitution in 1867 prohibited the establishment of separate schools and required that no public school should deny admission on account of race or color.[5] On the eve

---

[3] Thomas H. Harris, *The Story of Public Education in Louisiana* (New Orleans, 1924), 30; an undocumented work.
[4] Conway to the editor of the Washington *National Republican*, in Washington *New National Era*, June 4, 1874.
[5] New Orleans *Tribune*, Oct. 27, 1867 [all New Orleans newspapers hereafter cited without place name].

of the constitutional convention the city hastily established its first Negro schools to give credibility to its stand for "separate but equal" rather than desegregated schools,[6] and Freedmen's Bureau officials opposed to mixed schools[7] hastily transferred their local schools to the city board.[8] State Superintendent Robert M. Lusher resigned before the end of his term to become the state agent of the Peabody Education Fund, which spent more money in Louisiana than in any other state to aid a system of private white schools.[9]

In New Orleans, where whites outnumbered Negroes nearly three to one, white Republicans in the city government cooperated with the city school board in efforts to thwart Superintendent Conway in his equally determined effort to give desegregation a thorough trial in that city. The city's newspapers meanwhile undertook to create an atmosphere of resistance and fear, advocating desertion of the schools en masse by the whites, establishment of private schools, and refusal to pay school taxes, and predicting the destruction of the public schools and race war.[10] The city school board resorted to a pupil placement system[11] and all of the legal stratagems so familiar today. The loopholes of every school law were sought out, and a bewildering succession of suits and injunctions cluttered the courts. At one time five school cases were simultaneously on the dockets. Finally the sands of delay ran out; a court decision of December 1870 was acknowledged by all parties to be decisive, and desegregation began within a month.[12]

To overcome the forces of delay and evasion, the Radicals found it necessary to centralize and strengthen the school system. The city school board was replaced by another appointed by the state board of education, which in turn was appointed by the governor. The city board was allowed by state law

[6] *Tribune*, July 24, 1867; *Times*, July 31, Sept. 19, Oct. 1, 9, 11, 15, 16, 20, 1867; *Crescent*, Sept. 15, 17, 1867; Minutes of New Orleans City Board of School Directors [hereafter cited as Sch. Bd. Min.], Sept. 16, Oct. 2, 9, 1867 (VII, 203-14, 219-26), MSS volumes in Orleans Parish School Board Office, New Orleans.
[7] L. Jolissaint, Parish of Orleans School Report, Sept. 15, 1868, Tri-Monthly Report Book of Office of Assistant Sub-Assistant Commissioner, Parish of Orleans, Louisiana, Bureau of Refugees, Freedmen, and Abandoned Lands, National Archives; *Crescent*, Sept. 17, 1867; *Picayune*, Dec. 4, 1867.
[8] Sch. Bd. Min., Nov. 6, Dec. 4, 1867 (VII, 235-37, 251-53); *Times*, Dec. 25, 1867.
[9] *Picayune*, Apr. 14, 1868; Peabody Education Fund, *Proceedings of the Trustees* (6 vols., Boston, 1867-1914), I, 91, 262-63, 408-12, 434-39 (July 1868, Feb. 1871, Oct. 1874).
[10] See, e.g., *Picayune*, Oct. 22, 1867, Aug. 13, 1868, Nov. 24, 1870; *Commercial Bulletin*, Feb. 7, 1870; *Times*, May 2, 1868, Feb. 17, Apr. 10, 1870.
[11] Sch. Bd. Min., May 21, 27, 1868 (VII, 323, 327-28). According to the *Picayune*, Jan. 12, 1871, "everything worked smoothly, attempts at mixing the schools being frustrated by the plan adopted by Mr. Van Norden, the President of the Board, who issued permits on which alone admission could be gained, to applicants, and taking good care that no negroes were admitted into white schools."
[12] *Annual Report of the State Superintendent of Public Education for the Year 1870* [hereafter cited as *Annual Report*] (New Orleans, 1871), 17-28; *Picayune* and *Times* throughout 1869-1870, esp. *Times*, Dec. 20, 1870; *Picayune*, Jan. 12, 1871; *Commercial Bulletin*, Jan. 11, 12, 1871. On earlier desegregation efforts, see *ibid.*, Apr. 27, 30, May 17, 18, June 30, 1870; Sch. Bd. Min., May 21, 27, June 3, 1868 (VII, 322-28, 336-37).

to estimate its annual needs and require the city government to levy and collect a local tax sufficient to supply the amount. The high salaries that this arrangement made possible, though often tardily paid, attracted good local teachers and created a reasonably good *esprit de corps*.

The extent of desegregation cannot be measured precisely because the official reports made no separate accounting of the races and because the population of New Orleans was so peculiarly mixed, with so many very light colored persons and swarthy white ones, that observers often found it impossible to distinguish between them.[13] Nevertheless, there is considerable evidence of desegregation in official records and in newspapers, particularly in the reports of the annual examinations or closing exercises of the schools. From such sources it is possible to identify by name twenty-one desegregated schools and some others that may have been desegregated, about one-third of the city's public schools.[14] The school authorities at no time initiated desegregation, but simply required the admission of Negro children to white or mixed schools whenever they applied. Thus by choice or social pressure a majority of the city's school children attended either the separate Negro schools or white schools.[15] A surprising number of colored children, nevertheless, entered mixed schools under this arrangement. In 1877 the number was estimated at three hundred,[16] but that was some six months after the end of Reconstruction. Other evidence indicates that between five hundred and one thousand Negroes and several thousand whites attended mixed schools at the height of desegregation.[17] Light colored children, who could move about more easily in the white world, were usually the first to enter mixed schools and the last to leave them after Reconstruction, but children "as black as ebony"

[13] *Times*, Oct. 6, 1873; *Louisianian*, Sept. 4, 1875.

[14] These were: Barracks, Bayou Bridge, Bayou Road, Beauregard, Bienville, Central Boys' High, Claiborne, Fillmore, Fisk, Franklin, Keller, Lower Girls' High, Madison, Paulding, Pontchartrain (Milneburg), Rampart, Robertson, St. Anne, St. Philip, Spain, Webster schools certainly desegregated, and Cut-off Road, Dunn, Gentilly, McDonoghville vaguely reported to be so. See *Bulletin*, Jan. 11, Feb. 1, 1871, Dec. 11, 18, 19, 1874; *Republican*, Apr. 12, 1873, Dec. 12, 1874; *Picayune*, June 23, 1871, Dec. 11, 12, 19, 1874, Feb. 19, Nov. 10, 1875, Nov. 20, 1876, Dec. 6, 1877; *Times*, Apr. 10, June 7, Oct. 6, Dec. 13, 1873, Dec. 18, 19, 1874, Feb. 19, 1875, Sept. 20, 22, 1876; *L'Abeille*, Dec 18, 1874; report on Claiborne Boys' School, Mar. 10, 1873, Special Reports of Principals, Louisiana Department of Education Miscellaneous Papers, Department of Archives and Manuscripts, Louisiana State University; *Annual Report, 1872*, 242–43. Contemporaries estimated that between one-third and one-half of the schools were desegregated. *Annual Report, 1872*, 18; *Republican*, July 18, 1873, Sept. 16, 1875; Edward Lawrence, "Color in the New Orleans Schools," *Harper's Weekly*, XIX (Feb. 13, 1875), 147–48; *Louisianian*, Feb. 13, 1875.

[15] *Annual Reports, 1869,* 13, *1871,* 308.

[16] City Superintendent William O. Rogers, in *Annual Report, 1877,* 303.

[17] The six leading desegregated schools alone were reported to have more than five hundred Negro pupils. *Picayune*, Dec. 11, 1874; *Times*, June 7, Dec. 13, 1873, Dec. 18, 1874; *Bulletin*, Dec. 19, 1874; *Republican*, Apr. 12, 1873; report on Claiborne Boys' School, Mar. 10, 1873, Education Archives, LSU.

were reported "side by side with the fairest Caucasians" in the same classrooms.[18]

All of the five mixed schools with seventy-five or more Negroes enrolled were in the Second and Third Districts, below Canal Street, where descendants of the original French and Spanish inhabitants and the Irish, German, and Italian immigrants predominated. In this downtown area there was no rigid residential separation, and the houses of prostitution as well as schoolhouses were desegregated, though without causing as much public excitement. Since nearly all of the schools in these districts were desegregated,[19] one might assume that the character of the Latin or immigrant population explained everything. But this is not so. Negro residential areas were dispersed throughout the city, and some of the largest schools in the so-called American districts, the First and Fourth, contained Negro children.[20] One of these, the Fisk School, contained "a considerable number."[21] Below New Orleans proper, in the Fifth and Seventh Districts, the scattered settlements on both sides of the river contained some desegregated primary schools.[22] Of the city's three public high schools, two were desegregated. At the Lower Girls' High School, desegregation proceeded peacefully for years, about one-fifth of the students being colored.[23] At the Central Boys' High several Negro pupils attended after 1875,[24] and a Negro was professor of mathematics there for two years, until after the end of Reconstruction.[25]

Desegregation caused only a temporary decline of enrollment in the schools as a whole and in the mixed schools themselves. Enrollment dropped from 24,892 to 19,091 in the first year of desegregation, but then rose steadily to 26,251 in 1875, which was higher than at any other time in the nineteenth century.[26] The report that 21,000 of these were white and 5,000 colored[27]

[18] *Bulletin*, Dec. 15, 1874.
[19] *Ibid.*, Oct. 22, 1874; *L'Abeille*, Apr. 16, 1876.
[20] Fisk, Franklin, Madison, Paulding, and Webster Schools in the First District and Keller School in the Fourth District.
[21] *Times*, Dec. 18, 1874.
[22] Pontchartrain, Cut-off Road, Dunn, Gentilly, and McDonoghville.
[23] Cable, *Strange True Stories of Louisiana*, 219–32; Dora R. Miller to Cable, May 31, 1889, Feb. 10, May 5, 1890, George W. Cable Papers, Howard-Tilton Memorial Library, Tulane University; *Republican*, Apr. 12, 1873; *Times*, Dec. 17, 18, 1874.
[24] *Ibid.*, Jan. 12, 13, Feb. 4, 1875; *Bulletin*, Jan. 13, 1875; *Picayune*, Feb. 19, 1875; *Republican*, Mar. 3, 1875.
[25] Harris, *Public Education in Louisiana*, 46; Sch. Bd. Min., Sept. 11, 1875, Dec. 6, 1876, Nov. 7, 1877 (VIII, 60, 200, IX, 174, 177).
[26] *Annual Reports, 1871*, 321, 326, *1875*, 12, *1877*, 289, *1879*, 13; Robert M. Lusher, MSS autobiography, June 1890, Robert M. Lusher Papers, LSU. Kendall, *History of New Orleans*, II, 531, reported 23,668 enrolled in 1899.
[27] *Picayune*, Jan. 12, 1875, as reported in *Times-Picayune*, Jan. 25, 1937, clipping in New Orleans Public Schools vertical file, Louisiana Room, LSU; *Times*, Oct. 6, 1873; *Annual Report, 1877*, 303.

indicates that there were actually more white pupils in the public schools during desegregation than either before or after.

In the desegregated schools the same trend was evident. The Fillmore Boys' School in the Third District, for example, was desegregated in 1871, when its enrollment was 377, and soon contained 100 colored pupils. In 1873 the conservative New Orleans *Times* reported 700 enrolled, "wonderful" attendance, and good discipline. Fillmore School was the largest in the city, crowded to capacity. In 1874 its enrollment reached 890, and the following year more of its graduates qualified for the high school, through competitive examinations, than those of any other boys' school.[28] Other mixed schools with large Negro enrollments had similar records of increasing enrollment and high academic standing. At the Bienville School, where attendance was cut in half in 1871 by desegregation and a river flood, both enrollment and average attendance by 1874 exceeded the levels prior to desegregation. It sent more of its graduates to high school in 1873 than any two other boys' schools.[29]

Why would desegregated schools be so crowded in a community as race conscious as New Orleans? The explanation seems to be that the quality of instruction was higher in those schools than in most of the others, because of the system of classification of elementary schools. Nearly all the mixed schools were classified as Grammar A schools, which had more teachers and a higher salary scale, and sent more graduates to the high schools than the Grammar B schools and Primary schools. Apparently this was why Negro children chose to enter them and why whites also attended them regardless of color, so that their enrollment steadily increased. Most of the Negro schools were Grammar B, and, according to report, "the mixed schools are the best in the city, and the colored schools the poorest—the poorest in quarters, furniture, text-books, and in every way."[30]

Desegregation of the public schools caused enrollment in private and parochial schools to increase, but not enough to damage the public schools. The most ambitious plan of the period, "an elaborate design for the establishment of schools by private enterprise," was presented to a mass meeting of citizens of the Second and Third Districts by former state superintendent Robert M. Lusher.[31] It temporarily evoked much enthusiasm, but Lusher

[28] *Picayune*, June 23, 1871, Dec. 12, 1874; *Times*, Dec. 13, 1873; *Annual Reports, 1874,* 183, *1875*, 208.
[29] *Commercial Bulletin*, Jan. 12, 31, 1871; *Picayune*, June 23, Dec. 11, 1871; *Republican*, June 23, 1871; *Times*, June 7, Oct. 6, Dec. 12, 1873; *Annual Reports, 1871*, 375, *1874*, 183, *1875*, 208-10.
[30] *Republican*, July 18, 1873; *Times*, June 18, 1870.
[31] *Commercial Bulletin*, May 25, June 8, 1870; *Times*, May 25, 1870; *Picayune*, June 8, 1870.

later wrote: "The failure of the Canvassers appointed to raise means for making the plan effectual, to collect a sufficient amount, unfortunately caused the plan to be abandoned."[32] No coordination of private school efforts was ever developed.

Existing Catholic parochial schools, new Presbyterian and Episcopalian parochial schools, and the old and new private schools all expanded. Enrollment in these schools rose from about ten thousand in 1869 to seventeen thousand in 1873, but then declined to fourteen thousand the next year and subsequently even further.[33] "Parochial schools on the pay system are virtually a failure," confessed Father Abram J. Ryan, editor of the local Catholic weekly; the reason he gave was economic: "poor families who have three or four, sometimes eight or ten children . . . cannot possibly send them to the parochial schools at the rate of $2 or even $1 per month, each."[34] This consideration applied with even greater force to the private schools, where tuition was normally twice as high.[35]

Predicted racial violence and tax resistance did not materialize, and after experimenting with walkouts from mixed schools and with private schools, the people of New Orleans learned to live with the change. For three years, from the fall of 1871 until the fall of 1874, the tumult and the shouting diminished.[36] At the risk of oversimplification, two explanations may be suggested. First, desegregation was administered with such skill that the opposition was disarmed, but foremost, for reasons largely political, thousands of New Orleans whites and the leading newspapers actually sought to win the Negro's vote on a basis of recognizing his civil rights.

Though statesmanlike qualities are not generally attributed to Reconstruction leaders, and the school officials were certainly not plaster saints, they administered the New Orleans schools efficiently and without major scandal. "If an irrational prejudice is exhibited on one side of this question," said Superintendent Conway, "let it not be met by an equally irrational precipitancy on the other side. This great question of education for the people

---

[32] Lusher, autobiographical MSS, May 31, 1889, Lusher Papers; Harris, *Public Education in Louisiana*, 56.

[33] *Annual Reports, 1869*, 27, 76, *1873*, 72, 284; *Morning Star and Catholic Messenger*, Jan. 31, 1869, Oct. 18, 1874. The figure for 1869 is a compromise between the state report, which estimated 1,200 in parochial schools, the Catholic press, which estimated 5,000 to 6,000, and the city superintendent, who estimated 15,000. *Reports of the United States Commissioner of Education, 1873*, 547, *1874*, 535, *1877*, 315 (Washington, D. C., 1874, 1875, 1879), estimate 13,779 enrolled in 1873, 14,235 in 1874, 12,000 in 1877.

[34] *Morning Star and Catholic Messenger*, May 22, 1870, July 4, 1875.

[35] *Picayune*, Sept. 17, 1875.

[36] There were a few exceptions, such as editorials in *Picayune*, Jan. 4, 1872; *Times*, Apr. 10, 1873. Their news columns, however, reported favorably on desegregated schools. See *Times*, Dec. 13, 1872, June 7, 1873; *Picayune*, Sept. 29, Dec. 11, 1872.

... should not be imperiled by injudicious action, even in behalf of a principle confessedly just and equitable."[37] Though rewarded with diatribes for their pains,[38] Conway, his Negro successor William G. Brown, and City Superintendent Charles W. Boothby pursued a "firm and yet moderate course" and conducted a school system good enough to win loyalty from the teachers and even occasional compliments from the opposition.[39]

The complex reasons why many New Orleans whites embraced or acquiesced in Negro civil rights between 1871 and 1874 have been treated elsewhere by T. Harry Williams[40] and can only be outlined here. The central fact was that Louisiana Negroes had a majority of the votes and were protected against intimidation by federal troops. As Reconstruction continued in Louisiana after its demise in other states, native whites realized that they had to win a substantial segment of the Negro vote if they hoped to oust the carpetbaggers. The Negroes were ably led, not so much by the white carpetbaggers as by their own well-educated New Orleans persons of color and Negro carpetbaggers. It was to these colored leaders that the white conservatives made overtures when the inevitable conflicts of interest developed between the white and colored wings of the Radical Republicans.

In 1871 and 1872 New Departure Democrats and new parties that abandoned the Democratic label partly because of its unpopularity among Negroes made bids for Negro votes by platform promises of recognition of civil rights and by parading a few Negro speakers at their rallies.[41] The vague commitments were insufficient to win the Negro vote in the election of 1872, and this failure led to the specific commitments of the unification movement of 1873. Simply stated, the unification movement proposed a fusion of the native white and Negro voters in which the Negroes would promise to assist in ousting the carpetbaggers and cutting the taxes and the whites would guarantee the Negroes full civil rights: suffrage, office holding, desegregated transportation and places of public resort, and mixed schools. Confederate General P. G. T. Beauregard, the merchant Isaac N. Marks, and a thousand other New Orleans citizens of both races signed a unification mani-

[37] *Annual Reports, 1869,* 12–13, *1871,* 47.
[38] *Times,* Nov. 24, 1870; *Bulletin,* Oct. 22, 1874; *L'Abeille,* Feb. 21, 1875.
[39] The moderation was owing partly to opposition and occasional insubordination. M. C. Cole to Thomas W. Conway, Sept. 9, 1871, William G. Brown to City Board of School Directors, June 1873, Department of Education Archives, LSU; Conway to Henry C. Warmoth, Nov. 18, 1871, Henry C. Warmoth Papers, Southern Historical Collection, University of North Carolina; *Republican,* Oct. 7, 1870; *Commercial Bulletin,* Apr. 27, 28, 1870; *Times,* May 6, 1870, July 3, 1873.
[40] T. Harry Williams, "The Louisiana Unification Movement of 1873," *Journal of Southern History,* XI (Aug. 1945), 349–69.
[41] E. John Ellis to Thomas C. W. Ellis, Feb. 29, 1872, E. John and Thomas C. W. Ellis Papers, LSU.

festo endorsing desegregated schools in unmistakable terms and presented it for endorsement to cheering crowds. In this atmosphere it is understandable that the press and pulpits ceased to thunder against desegregation. After Marks had read the school clause of the manifesto to a mass meeting and a voice interrupted to ask, "Will you send your children to the public schools?" that is, to desegregated schools, the question was greeted with "hisses and other demonstrations" and an invitation to leave the hall.[42] The unification movement failed to achieve the interracial political alliance it sought, because of the reluctance of many whites, particularly in the rural areas, to concede so much to the Negroes, and because of Negro suspicion that the white unificationists would be unwilling or unable to make good their commitments. The movement did give desegregation a breathing spell, however, and its spirit continued to animate some New Orleans whites. Marks, stating his freedom of racial bias, took a seat on the city school board and helped to administer school desegregation.[43] In 1875 George W. Cable sent carefully reasoned arguments for mixed schools to a New Orleans paper,[44] and in the same year David F. Boyd, president of the state university, tried to publish a proposal to desegregate his school.[45]

To most New Orleans whites, however, the failure of unification was the signal for a change in policy and leadership. If Negroes could not be persuaded to vote with the whites, then enough Negroes had to be kept from the polls to ensure a white majority. The White League arose in 1874, spread quickly from the rural parishes to New Orleans, staged a three-day *coup d'état* in September until the arrival of federal troops, and installed a Conservative city government in December. In the same period the position of mixed schools was weakened by the removal from the congressional civil rights bill of the school desegregation clause.[46] The stage was set for the well-known school riots of December 1874, which reflected the momentary political climate of that period as clearly as the acquiescent mood of the previous three years reflected an opposite policy.

During three days of rioting, mobs often described as high school boys or "boy regulators" rudely ejected from mixed schools colored children who had been peacefully attending for years, insulted teachers, beat and threatened

---

[42] *Times*, July 16, 1873; *Picayune*, July 16, 1873.
[43] Sch. Bd. Min., Jan. 12, 1876 (VIII, 125).
[44] These are in George W. Cable, *The Negro Question*, ed. Arlin Turner (Garden City, N. Y., 1958), 26–36.
[45] David F. Boyd, "Some Ideas on Education: The True Solution of the Question of 'Color' in Our Schools, Colleges & Universities, &c, &c," [Dec. 12 or 13] 1875, Walter L. Fleming Collection, LSU.
[46] Kelly, "Congressional Controversy over School Segregation," 558; *Picayune*, Dec. 18, 1874.

to hang the city superintendent.[47] What is not generally understood is that the White League and its newspaper supporters instigated and directed the mobs, which were composed mostly of men and adolescents not enrolled in the high schools, using a handful of high school rowdies as fronts.[48] Moreover, the riots failed to achieve their objective. Sober citizens persuaded the White League to call off "the boys," and the schools reopened after the holidays on a desegregated basis,[49] remaining so for another two and a half years, until after Reconstruction.

Even after the end of Reconstruction, it appeared at first that desegregation might survive the change. The schools remained mixed through the remainder of the term, and Negroes were appointed to the school boards.[50] But when the city school board voted to segregate the schools the following fall, the governor gave a Negro delegation neither aid nor comfort.[51] Resort to the state and federal courts proved equally futile. The Negroes lost three test cases despite the mandatory provisions of the state constitution,[52] and the constitution itself was rewritten in 1879 to permit separate schools and in 1898 to require them.

An obvious conclusion is that the southern devices of evasion and resistance broke down, largely through their own internal weaknesses. On the other hand, New Orleans whites never really surrendered their concept of the public school as a sort of private club. The chief significance of the New Orleans experiment with desegregation, however, centers around the fact, which was not merely incidental, that it occurred in a deep southern state with a large Negro population.

It was really universal suffrage—Negro suffrage protected by strong federal sanctions—that produced the mixed schools and sustained them through the years of trial. Negro votes in the constitutional convention secured the mixed school clause, and Negro votes elected school officers who would carry it out. Negro votes were the consideration for which whites were will-

[47] *Times, Picayune, Bulletin, L'Abeille, Republican, Louisianian* for Dec. 15-19, 1874; a convenient summary is *Annual Report, 1874*, liii–lxxxvi.
[48] "Notes on Mixed School Embroglio Dec. 1874," at end of Ephraim S. Stoddard diary for 1874-75, Ephraim S. Stoddard Collection, Tulane University; Dora R. Miller to Cable, Feb. 10, May 5, 1890, Cable Papers; Lawrence, "Color in the New Orleans Schools," 147-48; Cable, *Strange True Stories of Louisiana*, 223-32; *Times*, Dec. 19, 20, 1874, Jan. 3, 1875; *Republican*, Dec. 19, 1874; *Picayune*, Dec. 20, 1874; *Louisianian*, Dec. 26, 1874.
[49] *Bulletin*, Jan. 13, 1875; *Times*, Feb. 4, 19, 1875; *Republican*, Mar. 3, 1875; *L'Abeille*, Apr. 16, 1876.
[50] Lusher Diary, Mar. 31, 1877, Lusher Papers; Barnes F. Lathrop, ed., "An Autobiography of Francis T. Nicholls, 1834-1881," *Louisiana Historical Quarterly*, XVII (Apr. 1934), 257, 261.
[51] Sch. Bd. Min., June 22, July 3, 1877 (IX, 56-60, 63-64); *Picayune*, June 27, 1877; *Democrat*, June 27, 28, 1877.
[52] See *Times*, Sept. 27, 28, 30, Oct. 3, 24, 31, Nov. 29, 1877, May 22, 1878; *Picayune*, Oct. 6, 24, 1877; *Louisianian*, Sept. 29, 1877, Nov. 29, 1879.

ing to bargain acquiescence in desegregation. And when the compromise of 1877 removed the federal sanctions for Negro suffrage, the mixed schools were an early casualty. Desegregation was only part of a broader social struggle in which the ballot was the primary lever of power.

New Orleans desegregation is not entirely explained by Negro votes, however, since the Negro majority was in rural Louisiana, where schools were only rarely desegregated.[53] In the adjacent rural state of Mississippi, the Negro majority permitted separate schools to be established by a local-option school law.[54] It would seem that any rural effort at mixed schools in the lower South was foredoomed by the weak economic position of Negro sharecroppers, the lack of demand for educated labor in the cotton fields, and the desire of white planters to maintain racial segregation as a means of social control. In southern states outside of the cotton belt, of course, the Negro minority was too weak politically to win desegregation against almost unanimous white opposition.[55]

If the key to desegregation was to be found in the city, then why was the New Orleans experience so different from that of Charleston, South Carolina?[56] The South Carolina constitution of 1868 also required desegregation, and that state also had a Negro majority of voters. Yet the state officials successfully opposed desegregation, and neither the Negro legislators nor the Charleston Negro community pressed the issue.[57] Explanation of the difference between these two urban centers involves consideration of such intangible but very real influences as the singular character of New Orleans and the structure of leadership in the New Orleans Negro community.

With a population of 200,000, New Orleans was metropolitan in size and in the radiating influence of its river trade and railroad connections. Linked with continental Europe by its Creole tradition, its large and diverse immigrant population, and the cultural ties of more recent French émigrés, and linked by trade with racially complex Latin America, it was in many re-

[53] *Annual Report, 1871*, 120, 189; *Louisianian*, Mar. 13, 1875.
[54] Governor James L. Alcorn defended this policy in Washington *New Era*, June 2, 1870; *Congressional Globe*, 42 Cong., 2 sess., 3258 (May 9, 1872). Some Negro dissatisfaction is indicated in Vernon L. Wharton, *The Negro in Mississippi, 1865–1890* (Chapel Hill, N. C., 1947), 243–46; correspondence from Mississippi in Washington *New National Era*, Apr. 4, May 2, June 6, 1872, Apr. 10, 1873, July 2, 1874.
[55] See William G. Brownlow in *Congressional Record*, 43 Cong., 1 sess., 4144 (May 27, 1874). Only in Louisiana, Mississippi, and South Carolina, states with Negro majorities, did the Reconstruction constitutions contain school desegregation clauses.
[56] This was suggested by Professor August Meier, Morgan State College, in floor discussion of this paper at the Southern Historical Association meeting, Tulsa, Okla., Nov. 11, 1960.
[57] Francis B. Simkins and Robert H. Woody, *South Carolina during Reconstruction* (Chapel Hill, N. C., 1932), 434–39; Dabney, *Universal Education in the South*, I, 234–35; Richard H. Cain in *Congressional Record*, 43 Cong., 1 sess., 565 (Jan. 10, 1874); *ibid.*, 43 Cong., 2 sess., 957, 960, 981 (Feb. 3, 4, 1875). South Carolina did experiment with desegregating its state university.

spects the nation's most cosmopolitan city. Travelers, immigrants, and clients frequently reminded New Orleans citizens that southern racial attitudes and practices were not widely accepted.[58]

In many other ways New Orleans was unique among southern cities. Desegregated worship in the Catholic churches, which claimed about half of the city's population, possibly modified racial attitudes.[59] The colored population was residentially dispersed throughout the city and was only about one-fourth of the total population; it was not so large as to induce in whites the fear of being engulfed if racial barriers were lowered. The city had opposed secession and was part of the Confederacy less than two years, whereas it underwent Reconstruction for almost nine years prior to desegregation and for some fifteen years in all. The interest of many New Orleans leaders in sugar protection and in federal subsidies for river and harbor improvement and railroads made them ideologically more amenable to Whiggish Republicanism than the cotton planters of the Charleston area. The prominence of New Orleans merchants in the unification movement of 1873 suggests that many of them were more concerned with economic development than with social control. They were willing to compromise on racial issues in order to free themselves from a political regime on which they blamed the city's economic plight. Thus political polarization by race was incomplete and ephemeral.

The vigorous and ambitious leadership of the New Orleans Negro community was also a powerful stimulus to desegregation. The basis for the high quality of this leadership was laid during the slavery period, when the free Negroes of New Orleans enjoyed a status "probably unequaled in any other part of the South."[60] Whereas the Charleston free Negroes formed a truncated social pyramid in which artisans were the highest large class,[61] the New Orleans *gens de couleur* included a number of substantial merchants, cotton factors, caterers, doctors and lawyers, even newspaper editors and poets. Negroes also had much social freedom in cosmopolitan New Orleans. "The whole behavior of the Negro toward the whites," says Joseph G. Tregle, "was singularly free of that deference and circumspection which might have been expected in a slave community."[62] Though the social weather became

[58] See "A Frenchman" to the editor, *Times*, July 1, 1877.
[59] George Rose, *The Great Country* (London, 1868), 191.
[60] Joseph G. Tregle, Jr., "Early New Orleans Society: A Reappraisal," *Journal of Southern History*, XVIII (Feb. 1952), 34.
[61] E. Horace Fitchett, "The Traditions of the Free Negro in Charleston, South Carolina," *Journal of Negro History*, XXV (Apr. 1940), 142–43; George B. Tindall, *South Carolina Negroes, 1877–1900* (Columbia, S. C., 1952), 129–52; Simkins and Woody, *South Carolina*, 26, 91; E. Franklin Frazier, *Black Bourgeoisie* (Glencoe, Ill., 1957), 32.
[62] Tregle, "Early New Orleans Society," 33; Donald E. Everett, "Free Persons of Color in New Orleans, 1803–1865," unpublished doctoral dissertation, Tulane University, 1953; Annie

stormier in the last years of slavery, the colored elite regained self-confidence during the Union occupation, serving as officers in the Union army and eventually as officeholders in the state government. Soon after the war they won a crucial struggle for desegregation of streetcars against almost the same arguments and dire predictions later used to obstruct school desegregation.[63]

The light-skinned New Orleans Negroes, abandoning an early effort to be classed legally as whites, merged their lot with that of the Negro masses and forged an impressive Negro solidarity on racial questions. Since New Orleans was the state capital in this period, they were able to incorporate the darker skinned rural political leaders into their upper-class circle.[64] There is little evidence in the Reconstruction period that the colored bourgeoisie of New Orleans was as isolated from the Negro masses as E. Franklin Frazier has found the same class in the mid-twentieth century.[65] Well educated in private schools, in the North, and in France, they maintained a highly articulate newspaper press and an efficient if opportunistic political organization. They held about half of the seats on the city school board and protected the desegregation experiment against occasional desertion and failure of nerve on the part of their white colleagues. Sharing with most professional men the belief that "knowledge is power," these Negro leaders pressed their own children steadily into desegregated schools in search of equal educational opportunities.

New Orleans desegregation, then, achieved its successes in the 1870's through a unique conjunction of circumstances. A political coalition was temporarily created between the rural Negro majority, the urban Negro minority, and northern Republicans in control of federal and state governments. New Orleans was a metropolitan and cosmopolitan, not merely polyglot, center, in which the southern rural mores were challenged by other traditions, values, and interests. The prior development of a free Negro elite in New Orleans provided the leadership and steadfastness which outsiders could not furnish. Such a fortuitous convergence, however, depended too heavily on one *sine qua non*, the temporary sojourn of federal power in the South. Not until the whole region came more closely to resemble New Orleans, not until an urban South and a more strongly based Negro community emerged, could the experiment be renewed auspiciously.

L. W. Stahl, "The Free Negro in Ante-Bellum Louisiana," *Louisiana Historical Quarterly*, XXV (Apr. 1942), 301–96.
[63] *Tribune*, June 25, 1865, May 4, 7, 9, 12, 1867.
[64] Donald E. Everett, "Demands of the New Orleans Free Colored Population for Political Equality, 1862–1865," *Louisiana Historical Quarterly*, XXXVIII (Apr. 1955), 55–64; Germaine A. Memelo [Reed], "The Development of State Laws Concerning the Negro in Louisiana 1864–1900," unpublished master's thesis, Louisiana State University, 1956, 72–82; unanimous petition of Louisiana Negro legislators for passage of the civil rights bill, in *Congressional Globe*, 42 Cong., 2 sess., 815 (Feb. 5, 1872).
[65] Frazier, *Black Bourgeoisie*, 24–26.

Moorfield Storey and the Struggle for Equality

WILLIAM B. HIXSON, JR.

THE organization of the National Association for the Advancement of Colored People in 1909 and 1910 was the joint achievement of Negro militants and of white reformers. That some Negroes decided to assert their human dignity and demand their constitutional rights is not surprising. What is surprising, since anti-Negro prejudice was far more bitter and more widespread then than now, is that some white men and women joined them in their struggle for equality.

Two of the white founders of the Association—Oswald Garrison Villard and Mary White Ovington—have, in their autobiographies, indicated some of the factors that impelled them toward championing the Negro's cause.[1] Both—Villard, particularly, because of his Garrison ancestry—have some claim to be considered inheritors of the civil rights tradition of the previous century. But Ovington, as a social worker trying to alleviate the condition of the poor, and Villard, as a crusading journalist and an ardent civil-libertarian, tended to sympathize automatically with the victims and outcasts of society, a reaction more characteristic of twentieth-century liberalism than of nineteenth-century reform. It is unclear, therefore, whether their dedication to the Negro's cause came primarily from the abolitionist memories to their childhoods or from the liberal environment in which they spent their careers.

In contrast, the first president of the Association and its counsel in its first three important cases before the Supreme Court cannot be considered a twentieth-century liberal. Until he died in 1929, at the age of eighty-four, Moorfield Storey adhered to the values he had acquired as a pillar of the legal profession and as a Mugwump reformer in the late-nineteenth

---

This article received the Organization of American Historians' Pelzer Award for 1968. Mr. Hixson is a graduate student at Columbia University and instructor of History in Michigan State University. The author wishes to thank Mr. Charles M. Storey for permission to quote from his father's letters.

[1] Oswald Garrison Villard, *Fighting Years: Memoirs of a Liberal Editor* (New York, 1939); Mary White Ovington, *The Walls Came Tumbling Down* (New York, 1947).

century. Although willing to accept social legislation on the state level, he consistently opposed federal intervention and remained suspicious of the more ambitious programs of the progressive movement. Storey's outlook on racial matters was little different from that of Villard and Ovington, but because the reinforcing effect of a general liberalism is absent, the sources of his dedication to the Negro's cause is easier to follow. Specifically, his legal arguments on behalf of the National Association for the Advancement of Colored People reveal the influence of Charles Sumner, who made the most notable nineteenth-century argument that the law must make no racial distinctions.

As they found that the general statements of equality in the state constitutions failed to reach the massive discrimination against the free Negroes of the North, abolitionists tended to demand specific prohibitions on racial discrimination.[2] In 1849, Sumner introduced into American jurisprudence this new meaning of the phrase "equality before the law." In that year, he served as counsel for a Negro couple whose daughter was prohibited by the rules of the Boston School Committee from attending the neighborhood public school because it was restricted to whites. Since only Negro children were prevented from attending the schools nearest them, and were instead sent to all-Negro schools often at a considerable distance, they were made, Sumner argued, to feel inferior; and white children were made to regard them as such. The Negro schools did not have facilities equal to those attended by whites, but even if they had been equal, Sumner explained, "this compulsory segregation from the mass of the citizens is of itself an *inequality* we condemn." In view of the general principles of "equality before the law" embodied in the Massachusetts constitution, the Boston School Committee could not, in justice, make such a distinction.[3]

Sumner took this commitment to civil equality with him into the Senate two years later and, once emancipation became a certainty, devoted the remaining years of his career to securing civil equality for all the citizens of the United States. Though directly responsible for minor gains for Negroes

[2] Louis Ruchames, "Race, Marriage, and Abolition in Massachusetts," *Journal of Negro History*, XL (July 1955), 250-73; Louis Ruchames, "Jim Crow Railroads in Massachusetts," *American Quarterly*, VIII (Spring 1956), 61-75.

[3] *Roberts v. City of Boston*, 59 Mass. 158; Charles Sumner, *The Works of Charles Sumner* (15 vols., Boston, 1870-1883), II, 364. Charles Sumner's argument was rejected by the Supreme Judicial Court; but, several years later, the legislature abolished the remaining segregated schools in Massachusetts. In 1896, however, the Supreme Court cited *Roberts* to support its decision in the fundamental case upholding segregation, *Plessy v. Ferguson*, 163 U. S. 357 (1896). *Plessy*, of course, has been overturned in a number of Court decisions since 1954, and today Sumner's view has been upheld by all branches of the federal government.

during the Civil War,[4] his greater significance lies in his articulation of the emerging postwar northern sentiment that the Negro be granted the rights of citizenship.[5] Ultimately, his persistent demands for universal manhood suffrage were realized in the Fifteenth Amendment; but his other great goal, a bill prohibiting segregation in all public facilities for education, recreation, and transportation, remained unfulfilled at the time of his death.[6]

This was the man with whom Storey had spent two of the most impressionable years of his life. Through his father he had received an invitation in the fall of 1867 to become Sumner's personal secretary, and in late November of that year the twenty-two-year-old Storey, fresh from a year at Harvard law school, left for Washington.[7] Upon moving into Sumner's house the following January, Storey soon became aware of some of the senator's idiosyncracies.

> Mr. Sumner is not great at conversation, properly so called, I think. He can make himself very agreeable if he likes, and frequently does, but he either does all the talking himself and goes off into long disquisitions, or he simply draws out the other person and lets him do the talking, so it is a monologue on one side or the other.[8]

As the months passed, Storey became the daily companion of a man desperately in search of friendship beyond the calculated associations of official Washington. That Sumner himself bore much of the responsibility for his social isolation has been one of the main arguments of his detractors,[9] but he seems to have had a genuine affection for Storey, one which the younger

---

[4] Edward L. Pierce, *Memoir and Letters of Charles Sumner* (4 vols., Boston, 1877-1893), IV, 175-83, cites three such achievements during the Civil War: the inclusion of Negroes as inventors, mail carriers, and witnesses in federal courts; sponsorship of the first Negro attorney to practice before the Supreme Court (the attorney's acceptance by the Court implicitly revoked the *Dred Scott* doctrine that Negroes were not citizens); and the abolition of official segregation on Washington streetcars.

[5] W. R. Brock, *An American Crisis: Congress and Reconstruction, 1865-1867* (London, 1962), 78-79.

[6] Passed in greatly weakened form in 1875 (notably without the provisions for desegregated schools), it was this Civil Rights Act which the Supreme Court declared unconstitutional in the *Civil Rights Cases*, 109 U. S. 3 (1883).

[7] Moorfield Storey, unpublished "autobiography," Storey Collection (in the possession of Charles M. Storey, Jamaica Plain, Massachusetts).

[8] Storey to Mariana Storey, Feb. 2, 1868, *ibid*.

[9] The historiographical controversy about Sumner the man and Sumner the senator shows no sign of diminishing. In the first volume of a two-volume biography, David Donald, *Charles Sumner and the Coming of the Civil War* (New York, 1960), stresses Sumner's weaknesses in both roles. His interpretation has, however, been challenged by Louis Ruchames, "The Pulitzer Prize Treatment of Charles Sumner," *Massachusetts Review*, II (Summer 1961), 749-69; and by Paul Goodman, "David Donald's *Charles Sumner* Reconsidered," *New England Quarterly*, XXXVII (Sept. 1964), 373-87.

man returned in full. "I recall too many instances of his kindly thought for myself and others not to feel that his essential nature has been much misrepresented,"[10] Storey wrote fifty years later; and until he died, he missed few opportunities to defend Sumner against the bitter criticism that was beginning to engulf his reputation.

In a biography of Sumner, written for the *American Statesmen* series, Storey conceded that the senator had important flaws.

> He was a man of great ability but not of the highest intellectual power, nor was he a master of style. He was not incisive in thought or speech. His orations were overloaded, his rhetoric was often turgid, he was easily led into irrelevance and undue stress upon undisputed points. His untiring industry as a reader had filled his memory with associations which perhaps he valued unduly. Originally modest and not self-confident, the result of his long contest was to make him egotistical and dogmatic.[11]

He was willing to say this against Sumner, but little more; and the views of a man who lived in the same house, and saw his subject day in and day out, cannot be easily brushed aside. In the last analysis, he agreed with Emerson: "It characterizes a man for me that he hates Charles Sumner: for it shows that he cannot discriminate between a foible and a vice."[12] For Storey, Sumner's virtues clearly overshadowed his weaknesses. "Sumner," he wrote, "was by nature essentially simple, sincere, affectionate, and kindly, and in the words of a classmate he was possessed by a 'life-and-death earnestness.' "[13] He may have been dogmatic, but "as you would probably be somewhat intolerant in dealing with a man who defended forgery or murder, so he who regarded slavery as the sum of all villainies was somewhat intolerant with a man who undertook to defend that, especially if he came from the North."[14]

In the spring of 1869, Storey completed his clerkship with Sumner and returned to Boston. Apparently he had cut himself off from the influence of Sumner's ideas as well. During the last three decades of the nineteenth century, he enjoyed a prosperous legal career and devoted his remaining time to the various civic interests of his fellow Mugwumps: civil service reform, low tariffs, independent politics, and anti-imperialism. The Mugwumps began as opponents of both the corruption of the Grant administration and

---

[10] Moorfield Storey, "Charles Sumner," Edward Waldo Emerson, ed., *The Early Years of the Saturday Club, 1855-1870* (Boston, 1918), 303.
[11] Moorfield Storey, *Charles Sumner* (Boston, 1900), 431.
[12] Edward Waldo Emerson and Waldo Emerson Forbes, eds., *The Journals of Ralph Waldo Emerson* (10 vols., Boston, 1909-1914), X, 294.
[13] Storey, "Sumner," 299.
[14] Storey to Curtis Guild, Jr., Jan. 9, 1911, copy, Storey Collection.

the radicalism of the Greenbackers. Regarding themselves as the guardians of social and moral order, they began to question the unlimited application of the principle of self-government; the first victim of their growing skepticism about democracy was the recently enfranchised freedman.

Seeing only the corruption of the Radical regimes in the South, as early as 1872 many Mugwumps urged the end of Reconstruction; and they soon became among the most articulate supporters of the idea of sectional reconciliation. President Rutherford B. Hayes' withdrawal of federal troops from the South in the spring of 1877 was more symbolic than substantial; of far greater importance in the "road to reunion" were the Supreme Court decisions, between 1875 and 1883, which seriously weakened the Reconstruction legislation protecting the freedmen's civil rights. Like the other Mugwumps, Storey does not appear to have protested the Court's decisions. Indeed, when Senator George F. Hoar and Representative Henry Cabot Lodge made a final effort to restore federal protection to Negro voters in 1890, Storey condemned their bill as attacking "the root of constitutional government and . . . parent of the grossest abuses and gravest disturbances."[15]

Though it is doubtful that many Mugwumps preserved the concern for the freedmen that they had shown in the aftermath of the Civil War, it is quite possible that a minority of them (Storey, for example) acquiesced in the dismantling of federal protection of civil rights in the 1870s and 1880s on the assumption that, since southerners themselves appeared to accept Negro rights, there was no need for federal interference. Certainly, both the pledges of southern leaders such as Wade Hampton, Lucius Q. C. Lamar, and Alexander Stephens, and the investigations of the former abolitionist Thomas Wentworth Higginson confirmed this view.[16] It is easy to say that Higginson, a staunch supporter of Hayes' policy, and the southerners, still fearful of the reassertion of federal power, had vested interests in the Compromise of 1877 and that this bias may have colored their views. But, if the argument advanced by C. Vann Woodward[17] and supported by

---

[15] Moorfield Storey, *To the Voters of Massachusetts* (issued as a broadside by the Independent Cleveland Headquarters, 1892), Storey Collection. For the Mugwump role in helping defeat the Hoar-Lodge bill, see Stanley P. Hirshson, *Farewell to the Bloody Shirt: Northern Republicans & the Southern Negro, 1877-1893* (Bloomington, 1962), 123-42.

[16] "Ought the Negro to be Disfranchised? Ought He to Have Been Enfranchised?" *North American Review*, LXXVIII (March 1879), 225-84; Thomas Wentworth Higginson, "Some War Scenes Revisited," *Atlantic Monthly*, XLII (July 1878), 1-9.

[17] C. Vann Woodward, *The Strange Career of Jim Crow* (second revised edition, New York, 1966), 11-109.

a series of monographs[18] is to be accepted, integrated facilities and Negro participation in politics continued in many parts of the South until the turn of the century.

In the 1890s, to heal the wounds from the bitter fights between industry-oriented Redeemers and angry farmers, the doctrine of "white supremacy" was invoked in full force. The proscriptive devices which followed—the "legal" disfranchisement and statutory segregation of the Negro—received constitutional endorsement from the Supreme Court and widespread approval by the American public. No Mugwump had tried harder to assimilate "home rule" for the South with equal rights for the Negro than Carl Schurz. But this new proscription, beginning in the 1890s, led him to write Storey that "unless the reaction now going on be stopped, we shall have to fight the old anti-slavery battle again";[19] and before his death, Schurz publicly warned the South against finding itself "once more in a position provokingly offensive to the moral sense and the enlightened spirit of the world outside...."[20]

The trend, beginning in the 1890s, seems to have evoked within Storey the dedication to civil equality that he had received from his close association with Sumner. By the early years of the twentieth century, his concept of civil equality (like Sumner's) embraced not only the Negro but also all minorities. "The absurd prejudices of race and color" would become, for Storey, equally obnoxious and equally worthy of attack "whether they bar the Negro from his rights as a man, the foreigner from his welcome to our shores, the Filipino from his birthright of independence, or the Hebrew from social recognition...."[21] He sharply qualified the anti-immigrant aspersions he had made in his Mugwump days and began to defend immigrant citizenship;[22] and after 1899, he fought continuously on behalf of Philippine independence. But his main concern was, as Sumner's had been, with the protection of the Negro American's civil and political rights and with the expansion of his opportunity for advancement in all areas of American society.

[18] Charles E. Wynes, *Race Relations in Virginia, 1870-1902* (Charlottesville, 1961); Frenise A. Logan, *The Negro in North Carolina, 1876-1894* (Chapel Hill, 1964); George Brown Tindall, *South Carolina Negroes, 1877-1900* (Columbia, S.C., 1952); Vernon Lane Wharton, *The Negro in Mississippi, 1865-1890* (Chapel Hill, 1947).
[19] Carl Schurz to Storey, June 26, 1903, Storey Collection.
[20] Frederic Bancroft, ed., *Speeches, Correspondence, and Political Papers of Carl Schurz* (6 vols., New York, 1913), VI, 343.
[21] *Crisis*, I (Feb. 1911), 5.
[22] In particular, Storey championed the cause of the Japanese against intense discrimination. Storey to Robert L. O'Brien, April 15, 1924; Storey to Charles Evans Hughes, April 16, 1924, Storey Collection. He also urged the resettlement of the oppressed Armenians in the United States and Canada. Storey to Augustus P. Loring, Nov. 20, 1922, *ibid*.

Storey's defense of the Negro first emerged as a theme in the debate over Philippine annexation in 1899-1900. Unlike some of his associates in the anti-imperialist movement whose prejudices led them to oppose the incorporation of another colored people,[23] he was shifting his own attitudes in a different direction. The denial of self-government to the Filipinos was wrong in itself, he argued, but doubly wrong because it would be used to rationalize the denial of civil and political rights to Negroes at home. By the time of his anti-imperialist campaign for Congress in 1900, Storey had firmly linked in his own mind the suppression of Negroes in the South and the suppression of the natives in the Pacific possessions:

> No man of anti-slavery antecedents can fail to regard with horror the treatment of the colored race in the South and the attempt to disfranchise them. The whole reaction against this unhappy race, both in the northern and southern states, is deplorable. While, however, the President and the Republican Party are denying the doctrine of human equality which the party was formed to maintain, and are justifying conquest and despotic methods in the Philippines and Porto Rico by the argument that the inhabitants of these islands are unfit for freedom because of their race or color, it is only to be expected that the same doctrines will be applied at home.[24]

Four years later, as the Roosevelt administration took no action to stem the mounting tide of disfranchisement and segregation, the reasons seemed apparent. "The Philippine war has paralyzed the conscience of the Republican Party," Storey said; "it cannot denounce the suppression of the Negro vote in the South by any argument that does not return to condemn the suppression of the Philippine vote in Luzon and Samar."[25]

Significantly, it was a remark attributed to the administrator of Roosevelt's Philippine policy, Secretary of War Elihu Root, that Negro suffrage had been a failure, which elicited Storey's first major public defense of Negro citizenship. Just as no country had the right to deny national independence to another, no race within a country had the right to deny citizenship to another. The purpose of Congressional Reconstruction, he told an audience, had not been to establish good government, but to grant self-government to the emancipated slaves:

> The object was not primarily to secure well-tilled fields, well-ordered towns, an industrious laboring class, nor even a legislature, a bench, and an executive taken from the ablest men in the state. All these results had been secured by

---

[23] See Christopher Lasch, "The Anti-Imperialists, the Philippines, and the Inequality of Man," *Journal of Southern History*, XXIV (Aug. 1958), 319-31.
[24] Boston *Herald*, Sept. 19, 1900.
[25] Moorfield Storey, *The Importance to America of Philippine Independence. Address to the Harvard Democratic Club, October 28, 1904* (Boston, 1904), 9.

slavery. Had these been the object of our policy, slavery need never have been destroyed. It was because these advantages, the material prosperity of a few, had been gained by the degradation of a whole race,—because millions of human beings had been denied the rights and hopes of humanity, that slavery was abolished, and unless we carried the work through we had better never have begun it. The same reason that led us to abolish slavery forbade us to establish any legal inequality between man and man. Anything less than equality of rights was sure to be the seed of future trouble.[26]

There had been corruption under the Reconstruction regimes, "an orgy of corruption after Negro suffrage was granted . . . ."—this Storey freely admitted. "But," he asked, pointing to the current outcry against the "bosses," "can we insist that the color is the cause? While Pennsylvania bows to Quay; while Montana elects Clark; while Addicks owns Delaware; while the trials at St. Louis reveal the nature of her rulers, and Minneapolis is punishing Ames, are we sure that white suffrage is a success?" And the South, which was still fighting corruption, could hardly blame its present condition on the black man, for, in the broadest sense, "since 1876 Negro suffrage *has not been tried* and therefore has not failed."[27]

In his defense of civil rights, Storey may have begun as one of those who, as his friend Charles Francis Adams, Jr., put it, "plant themselves firmly on what Rufus Choate once referred to as the 'glittering generalities of the Declaration of Independence.' "[28] But, in an age when moral judgments were increasingly argued on the basis of empirical evidence, Storey found that his commitments led to factual disagreements. His first debate was with the historians. Although Storey was consulted by his friend James Ford Rhodes when he wrote his multivolume history, Storey, nevertheless, remained one of the more persistent critics of the completed work.[29] Rhodes, Storey felt, had drawn a one-sided picture of actual conditions during Reconstruction; discussions with prominent white southerners had given Storey the impression, at least, he wrote to Rhodes, "that we in the North have a very exaggerated notion of the trouble in the South" occasioned by the carpetbag regimes.[30]

Simultaneously, Storey carried on a somewhat more extended debate with Adams. Increasingly drawn to the South through his researches on Robert

[26] Moorfield Storey, *Negro Suffrage is not a Failure. Address before the New England Suffrage Conference, March 20, 1903* (Boston, 1903), 7.
[27] *Ibid.*, 16.
[28] Charles Francis Adams, Jr., *The "Solid South" and the Afro-American Race Problem. Address in Richmond, Virginia, October 28, 1908* (Richmond, 1908), 17.
[29] James Ford Rhodes, *History of the United States from the Compromise of 1850 to the Final Restoration of Home Rule at the South* (8 vols., New York, 1893-1906), VI, p. vii; Robert Cruden, *James Ford Rhodes: The Man, The Historian, His Work* (Cleveland, 1961), 95.
[30] Storey to James Ford Rhodes, May 12, 1906, copy, Storey Collection.

E. Lee, Adams thought that "the reconstruction policy of 1866 we forced on the helpless states of the Confederacy was worse than a crime; it was a political blunder, as ungenerous as it was gross."[31] But it was not true, Storey wrote to Adams, "that the reconstruction policy was 'conceived in passion' and devoid of statesmanship. It is the fashion to forget that white reconstruction was tried faithfully and that Johnson's white legislatures at once passed laws which in effect re-established slavery."[32] Nor was it true, Storey argued, that Reconstruction had been engineered by a small group of "vindictive" Radicals:

The reconstruction policy was largely framed and was supported by the most conservative men in the Senate like Trumbull, Grimes, Sherman and the group that voted against impeachment.... the policy was adopted in view of the exigencies of the time by the sober judgment of the men who were then in control of the Republican Party, and Thad Stevens was only one force.[33]

Against the natural and social scientists, Storey was less sure in his arguments than he had been against the historians. By the time he died, he had acquired a notable collection of books on Negro history and society, but studies in psychology and anthropology were absent. He had been isolated too long from scientific thought to be more than vaguely aware that a new wave of anthropologists was attacking long-established notions of biological and cultural "superiority."[34] Instead, he used whatever arguments he could and combined the general knowledge acquired in a liberal education, the personal experience of sixty years, and the discipline of a sharp legal mind. In 1913, for example, he exchanged views on "race purity" with Harvard's president, Charles W. Eliot. For Eliot, who is currently enjoying a reputation as an exponent of racial tolerance,[35] "the experience of the

---

[31] Adams, The "Solid South," 19.
[32] Mark A. DeWolfe Howe, Portrait of an Independent: Moorfield Storey, 1845-1929 (Boston, 1932), 307; Storey, Sumner, 287, 300, 322.
[33] Storey to Adams, Feb. 11, 1914, copy, Storey Collection. It is interesting to note, first, that Storey's library included a number of contemporary works challenging the Rhodes interpretation, such as The Facts of Reconstruction (New York, 1913), by John R. Lynch, a Negro politician from Mississippi; and, second, that Storey was one of the earliest white supporters of Carter G. Woodson's Association for the Study of Negro Life and History, whose Journal of Negro History has consistently defended the Negro against the hostile bias of earlier scholarship.
[34] Storey's first exposure to Franz Boas, for example, seems to have occurred when he was already president of the NAACP. In a letter to W. E. B. Du Bois, he wrote, "There was a course of Lowell Lectures ... on the so-called 'inferior races' in which the lecturer [probably Boas] reached conclusions most favorable to our cause." Storey to W. E. B. Du Bois, Nov. 22, 1910, copy, Storey Collection. Whether Storey ever actually read Boas, or any other "modern" anthropologist, for that matter, remains an open question.
[35] Charles W. Eliot's views of either immigrants in general or Jews in particular should not be demeaned, but his defense—like that of Theodore Roosevelt, a very different man—

world demonstrates upon an immense scale that peoples far advanced in the scale of civilization cannot profitably mix with backward peoples. The purer a race is kept, the more likely it is to maintain itself and prosper."[36] Storey disagreed and argued:

> A priori, it is hard to see why the admixture of different breeds which has produced such wonderful results in the vegetable and animal worlds should be so disastrous to the human race. Nature demands variety, and intermarriage between members of the same family or class long persisted in tends to produce degenerates. Even the fact that the results are jeered at and called hard names is not conclusive. The term 'cur' has long been a term of reproach, but no one who knows dogs can fail to admit that the most admirable qualities of canine nature are very commonly found in dogs of very mixed ancestry.[37]

Whatever the merits of the abstract issue, Storey never doubted the absurdity of "race purity" in American society, where there had been widespread sexual contact:

> You wish to keep the white blood pure [he wrote a southern correspondent] and free from contamination with an inferior strain. Let me ask you, do you? If the public opinion of the South disgraced a man who established relations with colored women, and became the parent of colored children, I should acquiesce in your contention, but it does not, and it is not the presence of a marriage ceremony which makes the contamination but the mingling of blood as a fact. From the time when the colored people were first brought into this country until now there has been no instinct which prevents the mingling of blood, and until there is I feel that it is not race pride which controls the action of the white people of the South.[38]

Whatever the causes of the trend toward racial discrimination, a sudden awareness of the need to preserve "racial purity" was not one of them. Storey had traveled in the South before the days of institutionalized Jim Crow, and he particularly remembered one incident of interracial harmony on a New Orleans streetcar:

> There was no trace of objection to this association of white and colored during the whole trip, but had we crossed the street and taken the railroad train these same people would have been given separate cars. Such discrimination is fashion, not instinct, and other illustrations in abundance could be given. It is a bad fashion, not an uncontrollable instinct, against which we contend.[39]

seems to have been confined to the white race and its "assimilable" ethnic groups. Unlike Storey, Eliot accepted both the retention of the Philippines and the enforcement of segregation in the South. Henry James, *Charles W. Eliot: President of Harvard University, 1869-1909* (2 vols., Boston, 1930), II, 53-54, 118-19, 166-68, 210-11.
[36] Springfield *Republican*, Feb. 26, 1913.
[37] *Ibid.*, Feb. 27, 1913.
[38] Storey to Alexander Lawton, June 25, 1923, copy, Storey Collection.
[39] Draft of speech, possibly that presented before the Boston branch of the NAACP,

To all those—whether historians or biologists, his friends or occasional correspondents—who justified their demands for the subjugation of the Negro by his supposed "inferiority," Storey answered that their case against the Negro remained unproven:

When the colored men have had an equal chance with the white man, and as for many years, we can then form a sound opinion as to their respective abilities, but in my own time I have seen men belonging to races which were deemed inferior establish their right to be regarded as the equal of all their fellow men. A notable instance is the case of the Jews, who are treated in Russia very much as the colored men are treated in the South, are denied social equality, herded together in quarters, and generally regarded as hopelessly inferior. We know in the United States that this opinion is unfounded.[40]

Those who wanted to subjugate the Negro were really unsure of the racial "inferiority" they tried to establish. He asked the irrefutable questions, "If the Negro is so hopelessly inferior, why do the whites fear the effect of education? Why do they struggle against his progress upward?" He could only conclude: "The attempt to prevent him from rising, by violence or by adverse legislation, is a confession that the assumption of white superiority is unsafe."[41]

Storey's contention that Negroes could not be fairly judged unless granted equal opportunities is best revealed in his continual fight against discrimination in private institutions. His correspondence is full of incidents of minor indignities suffered by Negroes: a doctor barred from the staff of a public hospital, a girl refused dormitory accommodations at Smith College, a worker barred from employment by a "lily-white" union.[42] In two notable campaigns he successfully fought against the exclusion of Negroes from the American Bar Association[43] and against the segregation of Negro students in separate dormitories at Harvard College.[44] But, in the presence of mounting racial oppression, Storey had long recognized that in-

Dec. 1, 1913, Moorfield Storey Papers (Manuscript Division, Library of Congress).
[40] Storey to N. F. Lamb, Feb. 16, 1913, copy, Storey Collection.
[41] Storey, letter to an unnamed newspaper, scrapbook 2, Storey Papers.
[42] Storey to A. Shuman, March 25, 1913; Storey to Marion Burton, Oct. 14, 1913; Storey to Du Bois, June 1, 1917, Storey Collection.
[43] Storey to Albert E. Pillsbury, March 4, 1912, copy, *ibid.*; Stephen S. Gregory to Storey, March 25, 1912; Storey, petition to the members of the American Bar Association, Storey Papers; Storey to E. Furness, April 30, 1913; Storey to Lucien H. Alexander, Nov. 3, 1914; Storey to James C. Crosby, Oct. 24, 1919, copies, Storey Collection.
[44] Storey to Julian Mack, June 6, 1922; Storey to Charles C. Jackson, June 20, 1922, copies, Storey Collection; Lewis Gannett to Storey, June 2, July 26, Aug. 2, 1922, Storey Papers; Storey to John Jay Chapman, Jan. 18, 22, 1923, copies, Storey Collection.

dividual gestures on behalf of equal opportunity would do little to turn the tide:

> The whites in the South are one party in the contest, and the interests of the other party are not safe in their hands. They had the full charge of the Negro problem for a great many years, and they made a great mess of it, so that I desire to reserve the right to bring to bear all the public opinion that we can muster in favor of the Negro in the South and elsewhere.[45]

To implement his argument that the United States "is the country of all its citizens, and black men have under our Constitution all the rights of white men,"[46] in 1910 he accepted the presidency of the National Association for the Advancement of Colored People.

Unlike W. E. B. Du Bois, Villard, Ovington, and Joel and Arthur Spingarn, Storey had little to do with the day-to-day problems of the NAACP. Any organization devoted to securing complete equality before the law, however, would be largely dependent upon litigation for the realization of its goals; and here someone with Storey's legal skill and professional prestige was invaluable. Relying on the careful investigations conducted by Association branches and the preliminary preparation of cases by local lawyers, Storey appears to have determined the constitutional basis for the Association's arguments. In several notable cases before the Supreme Court, he was thus able to halt the judicial trend of three decades toward racial proscription.

When the Association was formed, the effective expression of civil equality in public policy had been severely limited by two judicial doctrines: "state action," which appeared to exempt private discrimination and intimidation from the prohibitions of the Fourteenth Amendment;[47] and the "separate-but-equal" doctrine, which required proof of actual inequality of facilities to show a denial of "the equal protection of the laws."[48] Though opposed to segregation on principle, the NAACP was forced to work within that framework—fully aware that only those acts of government whose

---

[45] Storey to Adams, Nov. 19, 1908, copy, Storey Collection.
[46] Storey to Bolton Smith, Feb. 24, 1921, copy, *ibid*.
[47] That private discrimination could not be prohibited under the Fourteenth Amendment was the basis of the Court's decision in the *Civil Rights Cases*, 109 U. S. 3 (1883). Between 1875 and 1883 the Court also exempted the intimidation of Negro voters from the prohibitions of the Amendment not only on the basis that the Amendment covered only "state action" but also on the basis that the right to assemble preceded the Constitution and thus was protected only by state law. *U. S. v. Cruikshank et al.*, 92 U. S. 542 (1875); *U. S. v. Reese et al.*, 92 U. S. 214 (1876); *U. S. v. Harris*, 106 U. S. 629 (1883).
[48] *Plessy v. Ferguson*, 163 U. S. 537 (1896). The Court had already ruled, under the commerce clause, that although a state could not prohibit segregation in interstate transportation (*Hall v. DeCuir*, 95 U. S. 485 [1877]), a state could require it (*Louisville, New Orleans and Texas Railway Company v. Mississippi*, 133 U. S. 587 [1890]).

denial of "equal protection" were blatant would be declared unconstitutional by the Supreme Court.[49] In the years since Reconstruction, there were two main decisions to which the Association could appeal as precedents: a West Virginia case affirming the constitutional right of Negroes to sit on juries,[50] and a California case striking down those building requirements for laundries framed in such a way as to effectively prohibit Chinese establishments alone.[51]

The first Supreme Court case in which Storey appeared for the Association involved the constitutionality of the Oklahoma "grandfather clause." The "grandfather clause" was one aspect of the "legal" disfranchisement of the Negro in the southern states. States imposed restrictive suffrage requirements while at the same time passing exemptive clauses under which illiterate whites might vote.[52] In a case arising from the first of the disfranchising states, Mississippi, the Court had held that the requirements themselves, bypassing as they did "race, color, or previous condition of servitude," did not violate the prohibitions of the Fifteenth Amendment; only the discriminatory enforcement of those requirements would be unconstitutional.[53] In several other cases decided during this period, the Court dismissed voting suits on a variety of grounds: the election in question had already been

[49] The NAACP was content to work within the "separate-but-equal" framework until the beginning of its final onslaught against school segregation after *Sweatt* v. *Painter*, 339 U. S. 629 (1950). A case within that framework, which distantly involved Storey, was *McCabe* v. *Atchison, Topeka & Santa Fe Railway Company*, 235 U. S. 151 (1914). The effect of the decision, which involved the constitutionality of an Oklahoma statute limiting Pullman accommodations to whites, was weakened, however, because the Negro plaintiffs had not actually sought accommodations and could not point to any denial of their rights. The NAACP participated in the case, but Storey did not because, as he put it, "it seemed to me that the petitioners did not state a case which would justify the Court in granting the relief and deciding the question." Storey to William Monroe Trotter, Dec. 2, 1914, copy, Storey Collection. See also Charles S. Mangum, Jr., *The Legal Status of the Negro* (Chapel Hill, 1940), 203-07. The Court ruled that equal accommodations must be provided in all interstate Pullman facilities. *Mitchell* v. *United States*, 313 U. S. 80 (1941).
[50] *Strauder* v. *West Virginia*, 100 U. S. 303 (1880).
[51] *Yick Wo* v. *Hopkins*, 118 U. S. 356 (1886).
[52] The exemptive clauses typically took two forms. The "understanding clause" which permitted persons to vote who "understood" the state constitution when read to them (Alabama, Mississippi, South Carolina, and Virginia) or who "understood the duties of a citizen under a republican form of government" (Georgia). The "grandfather clause," in contrast, permitted persons to vote who were entitled to vote before 1867 and the descendants of such voters (Louisiana and North Carolina); or those who had fought in wars in which United States forces participated and the descendants of such veterans (Alabama, Georgia, and Virginia). Though the exemptive clauses expired shortly after they were passed (Arkansas, Florida, Tennessee, and Texas had no exemptive clauses), other restrictions on Negro suffrage were permanent. These included the institution of the poll tax in every southern state and of statewide party rules barring Negroes from Democratic primaries (except in Florida, North Carolina, and Tennessee). See Gilbert Thomas Stephenson, *Race Distinctions in American Law* (New York, 1910), 299-310; V. O. Key, Jr., *Southern Politics in State and Nation* (New York, 1949), 617-20.
[53] *Williams* v. *Mississippi*, 170 U. S. 213 (1898).

held, registration could not be enforced under the provisions which the plaintiff charged were invalid, and plaintiffs could not sue for damages in equity.[54]

In 1907, Oklahoma was admitted to the Union. The constitution provided for universal manhood suffrage, with only residence requirements. In 1910, however, an amendment was added which required a literacy test for all voters except those who were "on January 1, 1866, or at any time prior thereto, entitled to vote under any form of government" or anyone who was a "lineal descendant of such person." Obviously, few Negroes were entitled to vote in the United States of 1865. Acting under a Reconstruction statute, still viable as far as intimidation in congressional elections was concerned, the federal government brought indictments against certain registrars, in part for their administration of the act. They were convicted and sentenced to one year in a federal penitentiary. They appealed to the Eighth Circuit Court; the sentence was affirmed; they appealed to the Supreme Court. Action on the part of the government had been continued during the transition from the Taft to the Wilson administrations; when the case was finally argued, the government was represented by John W. Davis, a decade away from his presidential nomination. The role of the NAACP was limited to an *amicus curiae* brief, which had been filed by Storey.

In his own attitudes toward suffrage, Storey differentiated between personal principle and legal precedent. As a matter of principle, "I rather agree with Clay that no people is fit for any government except self-government, though I do not feel certain that any of us are any too competent."[55] But as a matter of law, "The denial or abridgement of the right to vote need not be illegal or unconstitutional. An educational qualification for example, is neither. . . . The same would be true of a property qualification."[56] But, even though such restrictions might be "constitutional," if they were used, the second section of the Fourteenth Amendment would automatically come into force:

when any state denies to any male person who is an inhabitant of that state and at the same time a citizen of the United States the right to vote, or in any way abridges it, except for participation in rebellion or other crime, the basis of representation shall be reduced. [Storey's paraphrase.]

But if the Court accepted his argument on this point and "reactivated" the

[54] *Mills* v. *Green*, 159 U. S. 651 (1898); *Giles* v. *Harris*, 189 U. S. 475 (1903); *Giles* v. *Teasley*, 193 U. S. 146 (1903); *Jones* v. *Montague*, 194 U. S. 147 (1904); Mangum, *Legal Status of the Negro*, 394-405.
[55] Storey to Smith, March 11, 1921, copy, Storey Collection.
[56] Storey to Trotter, Jan. 7, 1921, copy, *ibid.*

Moorfield Storey 547

second section, two consequences might occur. On the one hand, "if the South finds that it loses power because the basis of representation is reduced, it would be a constant motive to modify their laws and admit colored men to the polls. . . ." On the other hand, Storey felt, the South just might accept such conditions as the price of white supremacy. If it did, the Negroes would remain disfranchised while the North would be apt to say "that they would not disturb the situation as long as they profited by it in the increased representation [for themselves]."[57]

With this unfortunate possibility in mind, he dropped any idea of relying on the Fourteenth Amendment in his argument and decided to litigate under the Fifteenth Amendment instead.

Because he favored the latter approach, Storey was personally committed to his brief in the "grandfather clause" case. "If it is possible for an ingenious scrivener to accomplish that purpose of disfranchisement by careful phrasing, the provisions of the Constitution which establish and protect the rights of some ten million colored citizens of the United States are not worth the paper on which they are written, and all constitutional safeguards are weakened."[58] Like Davis, he argued that the *effect* of the Oklahoma amendment was discriminatory and, therefore (citing the *Yick Wo* v. *Hopkins* precedent), unconstitutional. In its decision, the Court paid homage to state control over elections: "the [Fifteenth] Amendment does not change, modify or deprive the States of their full power as to suffrage except of course as to the subject with which the Amendment deals and to the extent that obedience to its command is necessary." This case, however, was manifestly one involving the denial of suffrage for reasons of "race, color or previous condition of servitude." The Court concluded:

We are unable to discover how, unless the prohibitions of the Fifteenth Amendment were considered, the slightest reason was afforded for basing the classification upon a period of time prior to the Fifteenth Amendment. Certainly it cannot be said that there was any peculiar necromancy in the time named which engendered attributes affecting the qualification to vote which would not exist at another and different period unless the Fifteenth Amendment was in view.[59]

[57] Storey to May C. Nerney, Aug. 6, 1915, copy, *ibid.* Storey thought action to enforce the second section could be brought either by a state's "to ask the Supreme Court by mandamus to compel a statute making a new apportionment," or by a citizen's suit to ask "that the officers of a state be restrained from acting under the current apportionment." He acknowledged that the second section, if enforced, might also restrict the representation of those northern states with literacy tests. Storey to Turner M. Hackman, Sept. 20, 1916, copy, *ibid.*
[58] *Brief for the N.A.A.C.P. in Frank Guinn and J. J. Beal vs. the United States, in the Supreme Court, October Term, 1913* (Washington, 1913), 4.
[59] *Guinn and Beal* v. *United States*, 238 U. S. 362, 347, 365 (1915). The following year Oklahoma enacted a measure allowing all those who had voted under the old amendment

Though the Supreme Court struck down the "grandfather clauses," other barriers—among them, the all-white primaries of a one-party South—remained for those Negroes who were courageous enough to attempt to vote. In Texas the Democratic state committee passed a resolution in 1922 excluding Negroes from the party primaries. One Negro sued, and again the Supreme Court on appeal ruled that no issue was presented since the election had already occurred.[60] Various factions within Texas politics pushed for a more thorough exclusion, and in 1923 the legislature passed a bill which prohibited Negro participation in party primaries. Dr. L. A. Nixon, head of the El Paso NAACP chapter, brought suit for damages; the suit was dismissed by the District Court, but finally taken on appeal by the Supreme Court. Storey had regarded the statute as "absurd" and hoped "the Supreme Court will sustain the case."[61] Though the NAACP's case was finally argued by Fred Knollenberg and Arthur Spingarn, Storey helped to prepare the brief. Its main point was that the 1923 act violated the Fifteenth as well as the Fourteenth Amendments because Texas statutes considered the primary a public election; thus Negro exclusion violated the prohibition of denial of the suffrage because of "race, color or previous condition of servitude" of the one amendment, and the guarantee of "the equal protection of the laws" of the other.[62] Speaking for the Court, Oliver Wendell Holmes succinctly declared the Texas statute unconstitutional: "We find it unnecessary to consider the Fifteenth Amendment, because it seems to us hard to imagine a more direct and obvious infringement of the Fourteenth."[63]

In addition to the more blatant disfranchising procedures, another area that seemed to the Association to involve discriminatory "state action" was enforced residential segregation. The first targets were residential-

to re-register in a sixteen-day period; others—Negroes—could enroll only with the approval of registrars. This statute was finally declared unconstitutional. *Lane* v. *Wilson et al.*, 307 U. S. 268 (1939).

[60] *Love et al.* v. *Griffith et al.*, 266 U. S. 32 (1924); Mangum, *Legal Status of the Negro*, 405-16.

[61] Storey to Walter White, Jan. 10, 1925, copy, Storey Collection.

[62] *Brief for Plaintiff in Error, L. A. Nixon against C. C. Herndon and Charles Porres, in the Supreme Court, October Term, 1925* (Washington, 1925).

[63] *Nixon* v. *Herndon*, 273 U. S. 536, 540-41 (1927). Following the decision, the state legislature allowed each party to set its own qualifications. This, the Supreme Court held, was still "state action" and therefore unconstitutional. *Nixon* v. *Condon et al.*, 286 U. S. 73 (1932). Then, the state Democratic convention adopted an exclusionary policy; this, the Court ruled, could be permitted. *Grovey* v. *Townsend*, 295 U. S. 45 (1935). A decade later, using a decision that involved election frauds in Louisiana—*United States* v. *Classic*, 313 U. S. 299 (1941)—which stated that primaries were an integral part of the election process, the Court ruled unconstitutional all primaries excluding any citizen because of his race. *Smith* v. *Allwright*, 321 U. S. 649 (1944).

segregation ordinances. The original of such ordinances involved the Chinese in San Francisco and was declared unconstitutional by a United States District Court as violating both the treaty with China and the Fourteenth Amendment.[64] In the early years of the twentieth century, however, the device more often represented the conclusion of the trend toward racial proscription in the South. Beginning with Baltimore, southern cities passed ordinances freezing areas with a majority of one race into permanent "white" or "black" sections.[65] The Baltimore ordinances was declared unconstitutional by the Maryland Supreme Court on the grounds that it did not adequately protect the rights of the present owners of property and that a municipality did not have the authority to enact such an ordinance.[66] Where the rights of owners were clearly protected, however, state courts tended to uphold similar statutes.[67]

The city of Louisville passed an ordinance classifying certain blocks as "white" and "colored"; and no owner or resident of the other race on such a block would be compelled to sell his property, but, when he did so, the property would revert to the predominant race in the classified area. Drawn as it was to protect rights of ownership, the ordinance passed a test in the Kentucky State Supreme Court.[68] For the NAACP, already active in the fight against enforced segregation, the Kentucky decision presented a major challenge. The Association decided to test the ordinance. In the fall of 1914, therefore, William Warley, head of the Louisville chapter, arranged to buy a lot for $250 from a sympathetic white, Charles H. Buchanan. To provide a cause for legal action, Warley said he would pay the final $100 after he made sure the transaction did not violate the ordinance. When he found that it did, he then refused to pay; Buchanan brought suit, but the chancery court ruled for Warley. Buchanan then appealed to the state supreme court, which also ruled against him. By 1916 the case was on the docket of the United States Supreme Court, and Storey, assisted by the Louisville attorney, Clayton L. Blakey, was prepared to present the NAACP's argument. Perhaps because only seven justices were sitting at the time, Chief Justice Edward J. White ordered a rehearing the following term, and the case was finally argued early in 1917.

[64] *In re Lee Sing et al.*, 43 Fed. 359 (C.C.N.D. Cal., 1890).
[65] See Mangum, *Legal Status of the Negro*, 140-46; Roger L. Rice, "Residential Segregation by Law, 1910-1917," *Journal of Southern History*, XXIV (May 1968), 179-99.
[66] *State v. Gurry*, 121 Md. 534, 88 Atl. 228 (1913). A North Carolina court reached the same conclusion on the last point. *State v. Darnell*, 166 N. C. 300, 81 S. E. 338 (1914).
[67] *Hopkins et al.* v. *City of Richmond*, 117 Va. 692, 86 S. E. 139 (1915); *Harris* v. *City of Louisville*, 165 Ky. 559, 177 S. W. 472 (1915); *Harden* v. *City of Atlanta*, 147 Ga. 248, 93 S. E. 401 (1917).
[68] *Harris v. City of Louisville*, 165 Ky. 559.

The spectacle of the NAACP defending a white property-owner trying to collect payment from an unwilling Negro (even if it was pre-arranged) was not without its ironies. The defendant, as Storey explained, "is not complaining of discrimination against the colored race. He is not trying to enforce their rights, but to enforce his own."[69] By restricting the freedom of Louisville citizens, black and white, to buy and sell property, the ordinance had deprived them of income from the sale of property without the due process of law and thus had violated the Fourteenth Amendment. That may have been Storey's most persuasive argument as far as the Court was concerned, but for him there were more important reasons for arguing the case. Nowhere else in a court of law was Storey's passionate dedication to civil equality so apparent.

The law ostensibly was passed to curtail "ill-feeling between the races," but Storey ridiculed the idea that an alley could serve as an effective barrier between racially different blocks; and he then went on to challenge the whole presumption of "race purity." The defendant's counsel talked of "racial barriers which Providence and not human law has erected," Storey argued. "Had Providence in fact erected such a barrier it would have been impassable and no human law would have been needed. It is because no such divine barrier exists that they seek to establish one by human legislation."[70] The ordinance discriminated against "the better class of Negroes" who wished to move out of the ghetto, and this discrimination, he claimed, was the purpose of the ordinance. "No one outside a courtroom would imagine for an instant that the predominant purpose of this ordinance was not to prevent the Negro citizens of Louisville—however industrious, thrifty, and well-educated they might be—from approaching that condition vaguely described as 'social equality.' "[71] It was specious to say that the law also affected whites, for it was the Negro's advancement that was being hindered. Storey quoted Anatole France's aphorism that the law forbids the rich, as well as the poor, from sleeping under the bridges of Paris and added, "A law which forbids a Negro to rise is not made just because it forbids a white man to fall."[72]

With the intention of hindering the mobility of its Negro population, Louisville was not only denying its property rights secured by the "privileges-and-immunities" clause of the Fourteenth Amendment but was also denying it "the equal protection of the laws." Whatever the trend of de-

[69] *Brief for the Plaintiff in Error on Rehearing, in Charles H. Buchanan vs. William Warley, in the Supreme Court, October Term, 1916* (Washington, 1916), 11-12.
[70] *Ibid.*, 22.
[71] *Ibid.*, 17.
[72] *Ibid.*, 33.

cisions from *Plessy* v. *Ferguson* onward, Storey concluded, the "separate-but-equal" doctrine had no relevance in a case of such obvious statutory discrimination. Nor, as the city's representatives claimed, could the ordinance be regarded as a legitimate exercise of the police power. Such power could operate only against the "injurious consequences of individuals," not against classes. The Negro was the victim, not the instigator, of social disorder; just because white men "do not like him as a neighbor, they pass an ordinance depriving him of his right to live where he pleases, and they justify it on the ground that it is necessary to protect them from being tempted to assault him if he exercises that right."[73]

In his argument Storey compared Negroes with employers, who were also victims, as he saw it, of an organized assault upon their rights as property-owners. Such analogies reflected his own view, but no doubt also pleased a conservative Court. Indeed, some commentators have argued that it was solicitude for property rights, and not for the victims of discrimination, that motivated the Court to rule for Storey's client.[74] It is true that the decision made no mention of the aspirations of Negroes. Significantly, however, the Court did impose limitations upon the "separate-but-equal" doctrine and the sociological assumptions behind it:

That there exists a serious and difficult problem arising from a feeling of race hostility which the law is powerless to control, and to which it must give a measure of consideration, may be freely admitted. But its solution cannot be promoted by depriving citizens of their constitutional rights and privileges.[75]

There were situations in which, under the *Plessy* precedent, it would uphold segregation legislation, the Court continued and it would not permit such legislation to restrict the right to buy and sell property, secured under the "privileges and immunities" clause. By limiting real estate transactions to persons of the same race, the Louisville ordinance—and all other such ordinances—restricted that right and thus were unconstitutional.

Storey, who had been worried before he argued the case ("You know how ingenious the Court sometimes is in finding a method of avoiding a disagreeable question. . . ."[76]), was overjoyed with the decision. "I cannot help thinking," he wrote Villard, "it is the most important decision that has been made since the *Dred Scott* case, and happily this time it is the right way."[77]

[72] *Ibid.*, 45.
[73] Mangum, *Legal Status of the Negro*, 139; Jack Greenberg, *Race Relations and American Law* (New York, 1959), 277-78.
[74] *Buchanan* v. *Warley*, 245 U. S. 60, 80-81 (1917).
[75] Storey to Wells Blodgett, Sept. 15, 1916, copy, Storey Collection.
[76] Storey to Oswald Garrison Villard, Nov. 6, 1917, copy, *ibid.* Villard had written him:

As Negroes began moving in large numbers to the North during and after World War I, new devices were found to keep them segregated. The most prominent was the restrictive convenant, a contractual agreement among property-owners not to sell to Negroes for a specified number of years; the courts would enforce the agreements. California and Michigan courts declared the future restriction void, but concurred with other state courts on the validity of restrictions against current purchase or occupancy.[78] Storey denied the validity of the restrictions and cited the Buchanan ruling that the "attempt to prevent the alienation of the property in question to a person of color was not a legitimate exercise of the police power of the State."[79] He argued that "if public policy does not justify the state in making this restriction, neither does it justify the restriction when imposed by a private citizen. . . ."[80] The case the NAACP entered came from the Supreme Court of the District of Columbia. One party to a covenant, John J. Buckley, had successfully sought an injunction against another, Irene H. Corrigan, to prevent the sale of property to a Negro, Helen Curtis. Louis Marshall argued the case on appeal before the United States Supreme Court, but Storey played a major role in preparing the brief.

To a greater extent than the previous briefs the NAACP had prepared for the Supreme Court, that of Marshall and Storey in this case attempted to counter in advance any questions the Court might raise. Their first point was that enforcement of the covenant by the lower court deprived Corrigan of the right to dispose of her property without the "due process of law" guaranteed by the Fifth Amendment. Partly because both men hoped that a favorable ruling from the Court would void all such covenants throughout the United States, and partly because Storey at least believed that the Fourteenth Amendment extended to all territory under American jurisdiction,[81] their brief also contended that judicial enforcement of those covenants violated the Fourteenth Amendment as well. Yet, as far as the Court was concerned, the Fourteenth Amendment, even more than the Fifth, applied only

"That the Supreme Court has stood by us on this is the most hopeful thing that has happened for some time in this dark period of our country's history." Villard to Storey, Nov. 5, 1917, *ibid.*
[78] Mangum, *Legal Status of the Negro*, 149-51.
[79] *Buchanan* v. *Warley*, 245 U. S. 60, 82 (1917).
[80] Storey to W. Hayes McKenney, Nov. 23, 1922, copy, Storey Collection.
[81] This is an inference based upon two pieces of evidence. Marshall was hesitant about arguing that the Fourteenth Amendment applied to the District. Charles Reznikoff, ed., *Louis Marshall, Champion of Liberty: Selected Papers and Addresses* (2 vols., Philadelphia, 1957), I, 461-62. But in the final brief, nine pages were spent arguing this very point and placing heavy emphasis on the implication of the Court's decision in the Insular Cases of 1901, *DeLima* v. *Bidwell*, 182 U. S. 1 (1901), and *Downes* v. *Bidwell*, 182 U. S. 244 (1901). *Brief for Appellants, Irene Hand Corrigan and Helen Curtis vs. John J. Buckley, in the Supreme Court, October Term, 1925* (Washington, 1925), 17-26.

to cases of "state action." What if the Court dismissed the case on the ground that the covenant constituted private discrimination?

To counter this contingency, Marshall and Storey decided to argue that the covenant went against "public policy."[82] "Public policy," as Marshall had written to Storey, "is largely based upon constitutional and statutory definitions as to what the policy of a State is"[83]—in this case, the common law prohibitions on contracts in restraint of the alienation of property, statutory prohibitions on contracts in restraint of trade, and, most of all, the implications of the Court's decision in *Buchanan* v. *Warley*. There the Court had prohibited municipal governments from segregating residential areas. Since "there can be no permissible distinction between citizens based on race, creed, or color if we are to remain a harmonious nation,"[84] the Court could not now permit such segregation to be furthered through judicially enforced private agreements.

As Marshall and Storey had foreseen, the Court could find no case of "state action" presented. But it also refused to consider their "public policy" argument and, in a somewhat opaque decision, dismissed the case for want of jurisdiction.[85] Storey was "not surprised at the decision," and wrote: "I deplore it bitterly for the same rules will be tried not only against colored people but against everybody who by social position, nationality, religion, or perhaps politics is objected to by their neighbors."[86] This, the only major case lost by the NAACP in Storey's lifetime, was only a temporary defeat. Twenty years later, the Supreme Court decided that the judicial enforcement of restrictive covenants was indeed "state action" and therefore unconstitutional.[87] In a companion case, the Court extended its ruling to the District of Columbia.[88]

"Those who would hold the Negroes down, who would deprive them of

[82] Storey to Marshall, Dec. 3, 1924, copy, Storey Collection; Reznikoff, *Selected Papers and Addresses*, I, 459-61.
[83] Reznikoff, *Selected Papers and Addresses*, I, 461.
[84] *Brief for Appellants . . . Corrigan . . . vs. . . . Buckley*, 40.
[85] *Corrigan et al.* v. *Buckley*, 271 U. S. 323 (1926).
[86] Storey to James W. Johnson, May 26, 1926, copy, Storey Collection.
[87] *Shelley et ux* v. *Kraemer et ux*, 334 U. S. 1 (1948). Many commentators on this case have been misled by the Court's assertion that it was not considering the "validity" of the covenants, as supposedly it had in *Corrigan*, but only the constitutionality of their judicial enforcement. However, it was precisely the issue of their enforcement in the courts that Storey and Marshall had emphasized in their *Corrigan* brief. It would be more accurate to say that a different Court, two decades later, reinterpreted the concept of "state action" to include such judicial enforcement. Five years later, in *Barrows* v. *Jackson*, 346 U. S. 349 (1953), the Court deprived covenants of whatever "validity" they still possessed by ruling that damage suits against the sellers were also unconstitutional. Clement E. Vose, *Caucasians Only: The Supreme Court, the NAACP, and the Restrictive Covenant Cases* (Berkeley, 1959).
[88] *Hurd et ux* v. *Hodge et al.*, 334 U. S. 24 (1948).

their rights, now understand that any attempt of that sort is going to be met by proceedings in the courts backed by an adequate organization," Storey wrote prophetically in 1926, "and in the courts our rights are safer than anywhere else in this great country."[89] The NAACP's success in achieving the total destruction of the legal embodiment of "white supremacy" was launched with the victories won by Storey. It has been said that the founding of the National Association for the Advancement of Colored People represented a "new abolitionism," a second commitment of some white Americans to fight for the freedom of their black countrymen. In the case of Storey's advocacy on behalf of the NAACP, it would be more accurate to say that it represented the culmination of the original abolitionist commitment—that of Charles Sumner and his idea of "equality before the law."

[89] Storey, statement in NAACP press release, Dec. 20, 1926, copy, Storey Papers.

THE *SCREWS* CASE REVISITED*

WOODFORD HOWARD, *The Johns Hopkins University*

and

CORNELIUS BUSHOVEN, *Duke University*

FOR RACIAL JUSTICE, as well as for reapportionment, the Warren Court appears to have been operating under a vacuum theory of judicial functions in the American political system. Contrary to Robert A. Dahl's argument in 1957 that the Supreme Court can direct the course of national policy only as part of dominant lawmaking coalitions, the most aggressive uses of judicial power in the last decade have occurred precisely where political processes were stalemated or atrophied.[1] Filling power vacuums by judicial action may have been motivated less by theory than appears. The weaponry used also has ranged from the "passive virtues" to the blunderbuss.[2] Still, regardless how much southern compliance with the 1964 Civil Rights Act may shake recent theorizing about the high court's "legitimating" role, it is indisputable that a judicial oligarchy pioneered, at great risk to its power and prestige, a momentous shift in government responsiveness toward the interests of a racial minority, long inarticulate and caught in a vacuum of power.

The national political stalemate has now been broken. Federal agencies have been mandated to lead a massive reconstruction of Negro life. Federal judges predictably have fallen back into more customary patterns of developing law in statutory interstices and penumbral situations. Even state courts are falling into line.[3]

---

*The authors wish to express their thanks to the Duke University Council on Research and the Ford Grant for Research in Public Affairs for support while conducting the research for this paper.

[1] Robert A. Dahl, "Decision Making in a Democracy: The Role of the Supreme Court as a National Policy-Maker," *Journal of Public Law*, v. 6 (Fall, 1957), pp. 293-295.

[2] Cf. Alpheus T. Mason, *The Supreme Court from Taft to Warren* (Baton Rouge: Louisiana State University Press, 1958), pp. 158-213; and Walter F. Murphy, "Deeds under a Doctrine: Civil Liberties in the 1963 Term," *APSR*, v. 59 (March, 1965), pp. 72-79. See Alexander M. Bickel, "The Passive Virtues," *Harvard Law Review*, v. 75 (November, 1961), pp. 40-79.

[3] *Mulkey v. Reitman*, 413 P. 2d 825 (1966).

[617]

Nevertheless, while officials struggle to fashion remedies for three centuries of neglect, it is useful to recall that the period of judicial pioneering in race relations was not an unbroken creative march or that the present is exempt from frustrating compromises along the way. The problem of protecting Negroes and civil rights workers against private retaliation and local police brutality remains hardly less intractable than when federal protection of civil liberties began in earnest over a generation ago.

Screws v. *United States* was a landmark in the evolution of federal remedies in race relations, a decision which not only underscored the difficulties of judicial intervention but structured the options now open to federal authorities. Because of its bearing on problems that are still very much alive, this essay revisits the passage of the *Screws* case through the Supreme Court in the spring of 1945, under a frank assumption that historical reconstruction of the decision may illuminate current issues of public policy as well as the workings of the appellate process.

The *Screws* case involved the familiar problem of unpunished police brutality against Negroes in the South. Claude M. Screws was a Georgia sheriff who, with two accomplices, beat to death an "uppity" Negro prisoner named Robert Hall. Although the case was clearly "a shocking and revolting episode in law enforcement," Screws was not brought to trial in state courts because, as the prosecutor explained, the sheriff filed no complaint.[4] The Civil Rights Section of the Department of Justice, hoping to develop a modern case law in support of federal protection of civil rights in the states, then prosecuted Screws under an archaic Reconstruction statute which punished deprivation of federal rights by officials acting "under color of any law." In contrast to the usual outcome, the jury convicted Screws and the Court of Appeals affirmed, one judge dissenting.[5]

When the Supreme Court granted *certiorari* to Screws, the case was widely understood to represent a milestone in federal civil liberties law. Screws' case was more than the first test of Section 20 of the old Civil Rights Act as a weapon against police brutality. It rested on a theory of state action and of due process offenses which, if approved by the Justices, would go far toward reviving the little-used federal civil rights statutes into potent weapons against a broad

[4]*Screws* v. *United States*, 325 U.S. 91, 160 (1945).
[5]140 F. 2d 662 (1944).

variety of discriminatory acts. Though Section 20 itself defined only a misdemeanor, punishable by no more than a $1,000 fine and a year in jail, the companion conspiracy statute (Section 19) created a felony with penalties ranging up to $5,000 and ten years in jail.[6] Neither statute, of course, carried the sting of state penalties for murder; and federal prosecutions faced special obstacles in southern juries. But the implications of the *Screws* case were rich in practical significance. Acceptance of the government's contentions by the Court would enable an activist federal executive and a responsive federal judiciary to punish criminal conduct which politically captive local officials and politically stalemated Congressmen were unable to condemn. Moreover, federal authorities would be able to punish official deprivation of constitutional rights even when such conduct violated state law. Expansion of Section 20 to include due process rights also would lead inexorably to expansion of parallel statutes which outlawed conspiracies and authorized private civil suits. And because these civil rights statutes were tied to rights "secured by the Constitution" and the Fourteenth Amendment, both of which were undergoing revolutionary libertarian expansion in the courts, acceptance of the government's contentions in *Screws* would arm federal prosecutors and courts with a "sword" whose potential strength was limited only by the discretion of judges and a legisla-

---

[6]Section 20 of the Criminal Code then read: "Whoever, under color of any law, statute, ordinance, regulation, or custom, willfully subjects, or causes to be subjected, any inhabitants of any State, Territory, or District to the deprivation of any rights, privileges, or immunities secured or protected by the Constitution and the laws of the United States, or to different punishments, pains, or penalties, on account of such inhabitant being an alien, or by reason of his color, or race, than are prescribed for the punishment of citizens, shall be fined not more than $1,000, or imprisoned not more than one year, or both." (18 U.S.C. 52.) Section 19 of the Criminal Code then read: "If two or more persons conspire to injure, oppress, threaten, or intimidate any citizen in the free exercise or enjoyment of any right or privilege secured to him by the Constitution or laws of the United States, or because of his having so exercised the same, or if two or more persons go in disguise on the highway, or on the premises of another, with intent to prevent or hinder his free exercise or enjoyment of any right or privileges so secured, they shall be fined not more than $5,000 and imprisoned not more than ten years, and shall, moreover, be thereafter ineligible to any office, or place of honor, profit, or trust created by the Constitution or laws of the United States." (18 U.S.C. 51.) These sections are now numbered 242 and 241 respectively. For clarity, these sections will be referred to as 19 and 20 in this paper. For the evolution of the statutes, see the appendix to the opinion of Frankfurter, J., in *United States* v. *Williams*, 341 U.S. 58, 83-84 (1951).

tive veto which liberals, too, could checkmate. Screws' case was a libertarian's dream of by-passing a filibustered Congress.

The *Screws* case, in this sense, expressed a new philosophy of positive federal protection of civil rights which filtered into top echelons of the Department of Justice and the federal courts during the New Deal. The leaders of this movement, to be sure, were fully aware of the scant statutory authority undergirding criminal prosecution of civil rights violators. The Supreme Court not only had restricted the Fourteenth Amendment and enactments based thereon to state action, but also had nullified most of the Reconstruction statutes designed to protect Negroes.[7] And three generations of federal dormancy had left the remaining segments lifeless. Between 1880 and 1939, only a handful of prosecutions under the conspiracy statutes, most of them involving voting rights, had survived the high court. Only two prosecutions under Section 20 were on record—neither of them involving conduct that violated state law, and neither of them reviewed by the Justices.[8] The permeating result was official Jim Crowism in a federal vacuum.

Renewed federal efforts in the late 1930's, nonetheless, yielded striking results. The Criminal Division of the Department of Justice launched a three-year study of the applicability of civil rights statutes to situations of aggravated local tyranny in conjunction with the labor wars; and in 1939, the high court sustained an injunction under the civil remedies statute against the muzzling of labor organizers by the Hague machine in Jersey City.[9] Attorney General Frank Murphy, acting on a suggestion of CIO counsel Lee Pressman and after consulting American Civil Liberties Union leaders Roger Baldwin and Morris L. Ernst, then consolidated the effort by establishing a special Civil Liberties Unit within the Justice Department in February, 1939. The resources at the disposal of the unit—a dozen lawyers and three assistants—were severely limited at first.

[7] *Civil Rights Cases*, 109 U.S. 3 (1883).
[8] *United States* v. *Buntin*, 10 F. 730 (1882) and *United States* v. *Stone*, 188 F. 836 (1911). For a list of Section 19 cases, see opinion of Rutledge, J., *Screws* v. *United States*, 325 U.S. 91, 127-28.
[9] *Hague* v. *C.I.O.*, 307 U.S. 496 (1939). A grand jury refused to indict Hague, however, and a jury refused to convict in the Harlan County peonage cases, which were brought under the criminal provisions of the civil rights statutes. See memo, Brien McMahon to Frank Murphy, February 3, 1939. Box 63, Murphy Papers. The Michigan Historical Collections of the University of Michigan. All correspondence and memoranda cited in this paper come from this source.

But creation of the agency was a well-timed step in pushing the federal government over the threshold of activist commitment. A separate civil liberties organization not only would serve as a central clearing house for complaints, but also would give organizational identity to libertarian interests and obtain increased access for civil liberties groups to the executive. Agency lawyers could investigate aggravated situations involving the rights of substantial numbers, select cases and conduct defenses, and explore the potentialities of existing statutes in case law. Once planted, the germ of civil liberties organization within the government grew into a Civil Rights Section at the time of *Screws* and became a full-fledged Division in 1957; and the experience gained proved fruitful for expanded federal activity which became politically possible two decades later.[10]

Choosing their cases carefully, government attorneys won critical victories in the courts. In *United States* v. *Classic* (1941), the Supreme Court sustained prosecution of state election officers under Sections 19 and 20 for deprivation of rights to vote in a congressional primary.[11] In *Smith* v. *Allwright* (1944), the state action principle was extended to state primaries.[12] *Screws* v. *United States* turned into a crucial case because the Justices were asked to extend the criminal statutes beyond voting rights to the multiple rights protected by the due process clause of the Fourteenth Amendment.

Because they had rested on electoral rights inferred from the First Article and the Fifteenth Amendment, the White Primary Cases were not precisely apposite to *Screws*. Yet the recent flurry of civil rights litigation was important for more reasons than legal logic. For one thing, every Justice in *Screws* except Wiley Rutledge had been exposed to the problem before and thus was personally committed in one way or another. Chief Justice Stone had written the Court's sweeping definition of state action in *Classic*. Justice Reed had authored the equally sweeping majority opinion in *Smith* v. *Allwright*. Justices Douglas, Black, and Murphy had dissented in *Classic* on the ground that a crime of conspiracy to deprive a person of a nonenumerated right lacked an ascertainable standard of guilt. But none of them expressed the same misgivings in *Smith*, which

[10] *Ibid*. Memo, Brien McMahon to Frank Murphy, March 4, 1939. Box 65. See Robert K. Carr, *Federal Protection of Civil Rights: Quest for a Sword* (Ithaca: Cornell University Press, 1947).
[11] 313 U.S. 299 (1941).
[12] 321 U.S. 649 (1944).

was a civil damage suit. Justice Murphy, a board member of both the ACLU and the NAACP before entering the Court, had launched the Civil Liberties Unit largely on his own responsibility. Justice Jackson had been Solicitor General during the *Hague* case and the Attorney General responsible for prosecuting *Classic*. Justice Frankfurter, a founding member of the American Civil Liberties Union, concurred without opinion in *Smith;* but Frankfurter had supported the first White Primary decision and had even been assigned the majority opinion in the second until Stone reassigned the case to Justice Reed after Jackson suggested that the decision would be more palatable to southerners if it came from a Kentucky moderate.[13] Given his past libertarian record on the race issue, it was by no means certain that Justice Frankfurter would be unfavorably disposed to Screws' conviction.

Of the two remaining Justices, Roberts and Rutledge, only Roberts appeared unalterably opposed to expanded federal criminal authority. Though Roberts himself had supported *Hague* and *Classic*, he smarted over being the victim of Stone's tactics in the White Primary Cases, which undercut his own *Grovey v. Townsend* opinion *sub silentio*.[14] By the mid-1940's, moreover, Roberts found himself at odds with the Court over releasing criminals, regardless of guilt, as a means of reforming police. As Roberts saw it, nine men in Washington were too limited, physically and functionally, to supervise the entire criminal system with the truncated remedy of new trials for guilty criminals. He maintained in the *McNabb* case—"We must stop it."[15]

Besides providing a virtual deposition of judicial attitudes toward aggressive federal protection of citizens' rights, the prior litigation also meant that the Court faced the issues raised by *Screws* with the advantages of "incremental" decision-making.[16] That is,

[13]Alpheus T. Mason, *Harlan Fiske Stone: Pillar of the Law* (New York: Viking Press, 1956), p. 615.

[14]295 U.S. 45 (1935).

[15]Conference notes, No. 25, Box 132. *McNabb v. United States*, 318 U.S. 332 (1943).

[16]See Martin Shapiro, "Stability and Change in Judicial Decision-making: Incrementalism or Stare Decisis?" *Law in Transition Quarterly*, v. 2 (Summer, 1965), pp. 134-157; Richard M. Cyert and James G. March, *A Behavioral Theory of the Firm* (Englewood Cliffs: Prentice-Hall, Inc., 1963); David Braybrooke and Charles E. Lindblom, *A Strategy of Decision* (New York: Free Press, 1963); and Aaron Wildavsky, *The Politics of the Budgetary Process* (Boston: Little, Brown, 1964).

rather than digesting a revolutionary principle all at once, the Justices had proceeded in piecemeal fashion, focusing on a progression of questions case by case.

Classic had raised two questions—(1) whether a right to vote in a congressional primary was a right secured by the Constitution, (2) whether deprivation of such a right in violation of state law also violated Sections 19 and 20. In answering affirmatively the Court had supplied extraordinarily broad interpretations of both statutory offenses and state action. In *Smith* v. *Allwright,* which extended federal authority to state primaries, the Court had enlarged civil remedies to include equal protection rights, applied tests of fact as well as law, and advanced the principle that delegation of state functions to private parties was still state action. Even though both cases had opened up "sweeping constitutional vistas," neither decision had been reached inadvertently or haphazardly.

Smith v. *Allwright,* especially, had provoked greater internal debate and difficulty than met the eye. Justice Murphy's notes of conferences, though they should be interpreted cautiously as the perceptions of one among nine, suggest that in *Smith* the Court had broached the limits of innovation. While most Justices agreed that *Grovey* should be overruled forthrightly, for example, Justice Frankfurter thought it should be done round-about. While ultimately only Justice Roberts dissented, Murphy recorded both Black and Jackson as initially voting to affirm a demurrer against the claim. Justice Jackson expressed acute discomfort over the collision with rights of the people to form groups, and both he and Rutledge voiced concern over the implications for judicial supervision of state elections which this decision made possible. Chief Justice Stone, hesitant before entering that thicket, answered Jackson: "not all primaries but this primary." And manifesting common misgivings, Stone exclaimed: "I wait for light."[17]

Since the Justices already had gone so far in the White Primary Cases, however, the Civil Rights Section could hardly be blamed in *Screws* for asking the Court to apply the same concepts to Fourteenth Amendment rights. After all, the very purpose of the Amendment had been protection of Negroes, not property rights or labor unions. The great Holmes himself had written approvingly that Section 19 applied to "all Federal rights . . . and in the lump."[18]

---
[17]Conference notes, November 13, 1943, and undated. No. 51, Box 133.
[18]*United States* v. *Mosley,* 238 U.S. 383, 387 (1915).

Refinement of due process rights by increments was the very mode of analysis advanced in the recently embraced "fair trial" rule of *Palko v. Connecticut* and *Betts v. Brady*.[19] Developing a modern case law in lieu of a statute by the same process was also a primary objective of the Civil Rights Section itself. Hopes understandably ran high. For if the Court would now do for due process rights what *Classic* and *Smith* had done for state action and equal protection, federal authorities could protect Negroes with a potent criminal sword as well as with a constitutional shield.

Judicial action, however, raised painful dilemmas at every turn. In the first place, the next step was a leap into the unknown. The White Primary Cases, for all their boldness, had been based on fairly plain representation guarantees of the First Article and the Fifteenth Amendment. They also involved rights which were thought to arouse least southern resistance. The *Screws* case, by contrast, was the first to prosecute state officials for violating due process rights of the Fourteenth Amendment. Given the broad coverage of that Amendment, how could anyone have advance notice of the substantive offense? The vagueness problem which had led Justices Black, Douglas, and Murphy to dissent in *Classic* was now far more serious. The Court would have to incorporate a law library into the civil rights statutes, as one Justice remarked, to comprehend the rights which the Court itself could define only case by case. Surely Congress had not intended to make the statute so all-embracing; but, if it did, at least three, and possibly six, Justices believed that such a broad coverage would make the statute unconstitutionally vague.[20]

To strike down the statute as indefinite, or to escape *via* legislative history, offered a disturbing choice. "I shudder from declaring [the] statute unconstitutional," one Justice reportedly remarked. "When we go into legislative history it will go bad for us." Passage of neither the Fourteenth Amendment nor the Civil Rights Acts had impeccable history. Inquiry into legislative intent might well produce the conclusion, as another Justice put it, that the Radical Congress had intended a broad expansion of federal crimes, and "to hell with state courts." If the Court decided to nullify the measure, this would be the first major act of Congress struck down since the 1937 court-packing imbroglio. And politically, the chances of Congress' enacting another civil rights statute were nil. Moreover, how could the

[19]302 U.S. 319 (1937); 316 U.S. 455 (1942).
[20]Conference notes, No. 42, Box 133.

Court invalidate Screws' indictment without undermining the recently decided White Primary Cases? The Justices' overt change of front on the status of primaries in the electoral process already had provoked a deep fissure over the meaning of state action and an acrid denunciation of the Court by Roberts for treating prior decisions as restricted railroad tickets, "good for this day and train only."[21] The political and legal implications of those cases did not permit retreat. Some basis of distinction had to be found.

One method, favored by Justice Reed, was to trim state action by holding that the phrase, "under color of any law," applied only to abuses directed by the state, not to those which also violated state law. The trouble was that nearly all the precedents, including *Classic*, had held that any act by a state agent or under state authority constituted state action, whether commanded by the state or not. "If you don't say that," the Chief Justice remarked, "you do not have any 14th Amendment."[22]

A second alternative, close to the first and embraced by Justice Frankfurter, was to revive the theory of the *Barney* case, which withheld federal punishment from acts that violated state law for want of finality of official state action. The trouble here was that the Court had expressly scuttled *Barney* long before *Classic*, and for the obvious reason that state inaction would rob federal rights of their force.[23] A third possibility, which attracted Justices Jackson and Rutledge, was to trim the offense by holding that the second phrase of Section 20, "on account of being an alien, or by reason of his color," was a qualifying phrase, which restricted the offenses to acts motivated by racial discrimination. But the Court in *Classic* also had considered and expressly rejected that distinction when it concluded that Congress had created two separate offenses. Though the discrimination argument might have drawn new adherents were the question fresh, the Court was now past it.[24] Still another alternative mentioned in conference was to admit that the statute covered the slaying, but to accept Screws' argument of self-defense. Yet

---

[21]*Ibid.*, Conference notes, Nos. 51 and 59, Box 133. 321 U.S. 649, 669 (1944).

[22]Conference notes, No. 42, Box 133. Cf. *Barney* v. *City of New York*, 193 U.S. 430, 438 (1904); and *United States* v. *Raines*, 362 U.S. 17, 25-26 (1960).

[23]*Barney* v. *City of New York*, 193 U.S. 430 (1904). Cf. *Home Tel. & Tel. Co.* v. *Los Angeles*, 227 U.S. 278, 294 (1913).

[24]Conference notes; memorandum opinions of Reed and Jackson, JJ., No. 42, Box 133.

that suggestion, which would have cut even deeper into state law, was merely a mark of how desperately most of the Justices sought to avoid the second and underlying dilemma, the effect on the administration of law by state governments.

The *Screws* case posed a peculiarly delicate issue of federalism, because the Court was asked to approve federal indictment of a state official for conduct that violated state law and customarily was of primary state concern. If the federal government could punish every instance of police brutality in the states, as one Justice frankly stated, "every officer in the Union could be indicted' for search and seizure, and for assaults on prisoners . . . unless we define due process finer than we have. . . ." If the federal government could discipline "every petty offender" who violated due process as well as state law, then what would prevent deterioration of local responsibility for criminal justice? Contrary to popular myths, New Deal Justices were fearful of the same revolution in federalism that had led the post-Civil War Court to take a dim view of Reconstruction statutes. Contrary to state rights oratory, New Deal Justices were no less sensitive to the fact that indefinite offenses also meant indefinite federal power. The essential problem was how, in the absence of state concern, federal officials could stimulate a local responsibility without replacing it. "You can't run these things from Washington," one Justice observed:

> Problems of local justice must be left to their communities. If we sustain this every time a Negro is beaten you are going to have F.M. [Frank Murphy] and others jumping on [the] State for action. And then your local officers will lay down on the Job—So will the local judge. They will say let Washington do it.

When reminded that due process was an expansive concept in the nineteenth century, the same Justice denied that the Radical Congress had grafted all due process rights onto civil rights statutes. When reminded that Congress at least had in mind the deprivation of Negro suffrage, he replied: "I consider this period one of the most shameful of our times." "Stephens and Sumner were not giving it this interpretation." "This interpretation belongs to Frank," though he ruefully admitted, as Murphy appears to have charged, that "we are going to be misunderstood as favoring a beating."[25]

The Chief Justice at first seemed willing to affirm the conviction; but as consensus formed about the dual dangers of indefiniteness and

---

[25]Conference notes, No. 42, Box 133.

expansive federal power, the question rapidly resolved itself into how much of *Classic* could be saved. Only Murphy and Rutledge supported Stone's position, and even Rutledge confessed that he was attracted to the narrow, discrimination argument. Justice Black, while sharing Justice Douglas' aversion to the vagueness of the indictment, manifested the same resistance to federal control over local law enforcement that he exposed, much to the surprise of libertarian commentators, in the racial sit-in cases of the 1960's. Three Justices—Roberts, Frankfurter, and Jackson—appeared ready to reverse the conviction, and perhaps even *Classic*, if they could have "put it on grounds we could stomach!" Thus, Murphy's notes record the Chief Justice as giving a virtuoso performance in *Classic's* defense. Against charges of vagueness, he retorted, "it is not as vague as Sherman Act cases." Against charges that federal prosecutors would preempt state rights to punish state officials, he replied: "but here he is doing it under color of his office." "Here you have [a] command of Congress. It says take jurisdiction. It doesn't say to do it when [the] state fails to act.... We can't go back to [the] *Barney* case to emasculate the Amendment." Civil War Amendments and statutes were not aimed at rightful state action, but abuse of state power.[26]

Still, Stone himself was deeply troubled by the implications of the case. The Court had blown up badly over state action in *Smith v. Allwright*, and litigants were pressing that principle to its limits. "Whoever writes this I hope will keep us out of state action," he commented at the outset. But recognizing that such hopes were vain and that retrenchment was inevitable, Stone urged his colleagues to "leave some of the specific things under the 14th." And in a clear case of persuasion, he acknowledged the force of the indefiniteness objection. "It may be the key to this is its vagueness when applied to [the] 14th Amendment," said the Chief. "We should consider it very carefully."[27]

Eager to salvage as much of their handwork as possible, Stone and then Justice Reed swung behind a compromise solution presumably suggested by Justice Douglas. Without qualifying *Classic's* broad interpretation of offenses, the Court would narrow the effect by imposing a stricter standard of intent. Remanding the case for new trial, the Court would hold that the statutory requirement of

[26]*Ibid.* Cf. Black, J., in *Cox* v. *Louisiana*, 379 U.S. 536, 580 (1965); and in *Lance* v. *Plummer*, 384 U.S. 929 (1966).
[27]Conference notes, No. 42, Box 133.

"willful" deprivation be construed as meaning that a defendant had a "specific intent" to deny a recognized constitutional right. Given the nature of southern juries, everyone knew that this construction of the statute would "leave mighty little scope for its application." But "incrementalism," a fancy label for trial-and-error method, presupposes the assumed advantage of case law systems over codes— retreat when principles are carried beyond practical tolerances. While the Chief Justice refused to concede that the White Primary Cases had been ill-advised, compromise at least would save the statute and, as Justice Douglas argued, preserve *Classic* as a rule of law "good for more than one day only."[28]

Yet compromise produced stalemate. One majority sustained the statute and another reversed the conviction, but the membership was not the same. At first, indeed, Justice Douglas' opinion for the Court attracted only three other votes—Stone, Black, and Reed. Four Justices dissented in opposing directions, and Justice Jackson hovered in between.

Justices Frankfurter and Roberts, who regarded the statute as unconstitutional, pounded away at the flaw which also troubled Justice Reed. How could a broad definition of intent make indefinite offenses definite? "It is true also of a statute that it cannot lift itself by its bootstraps," Justice Frankfurter observed in a hard-hitting memorandum.

> I can understand a statute prohibiting specifically the deprivation of enumerated constitutional rights. But if the Act makes it a crime to deprive another of any right guaranteed by the Constitution—and §20 substantially does that—I do not see how we escape facing decision as to what constitutional rights are covered by §20 by saying that in any event whatever they are they must be taken away 'willfully.' I am unable to understand how all the considerations of unconstitutional vagueness which are marshalled in the early part of the draft opinion disappear by holding that that which is otherwise too vaguely defined must be 'willfully' committed. . . .
>
> I cannot appreciate how the intrinsic vagueness of the terms of §20 is removed by making the statute applicable only where the defendant had 'the requisite bad purpose.' Does that not amount to saying that the black heart of defendant enables him to know what are the constitutional rights deprivation of which the statute forbids, although we as judges are not able to define their classes or limits, or, at least, are not prepared to state what they are unless it is to say that §20 protects whatever rights the Constitution protects?

[28]Mason, *Stone, op. cit.*, p. 638. 325 U.S. 91, 112 (1945).

While loathe to strike down an act of Congress for fear of restricting its freedom of action, Justice Frankfurter saw no question in the case of denying adequate *power* to Congress. "There is no difficulty in passing effective legislation for the protection of civil rights against improper State action," he said. "What we are concerned with here is something very basic in a democratic society, namely, the avoidance of the injustice of prohibiting conduct in terms so vague as to make the understanding of what conduct is proscribed a guess-work too difficult for confident judgment even for the judges of the highest Court in the land."[29]

Justice Jackson, while "reluctant to add what can be no more than a confession of personal bewilderment to a subject already in a state of impeccable confusion," blamed the Court rather than Congress for the *Screws* predicament. Since *Betts* v. *Brady* in 1942, Justice Jackson had frequently voiced belief that the history of Reconstruction weakened any feeling of sanctity on his part for the Fourteenth Amendment. Though somewhat embarrassed by his responsibility for the *Classic* prosecution, which had led to his disqualification from that case, Jackson now summoned history and administrative necessity in defense of a much narrower view of the statute and state action than *Classic* had approved. "I am disturbed by no doubts as to the constitutionality of what Congress actually has done in enacting the statute under consideration," he observed in a memorandum to conference, "but I have considerable misgivings about what the Court has done to it. This legislation originated in the Reconstruction Period and its aim was a narrow one." The statute, he contended, was aimed only against acts of racial discrimination and "that class of wrongs against federal rights which state law or custom sheltered or at least ignored, and which therefore could be said to be state action under the Fourteenth Amendment." For those limited purposes, he maintained, congressional language was not inept. If construed narrowly to mean that a deprivation of federal

[29] Memorandum to conference, December 13, 1944. No. 42. Box 133. Justice Douglas called this criticism "wide of the mark. For the specific intent required by the Act," he said, "is *an intent to deprive a person of a right which has been made specific either by the express terms of the Constitution or laws of the United States or by decisions interpreting them.* . . . Of course, willful conduct cannot make definite that which is undefined. But willful violators of constitutional requirements, *which have been defined,* certainly are in no position to say that they had no adequate advance warning that they would be visited with punishment." Italics added. *Screws* v. *United States,* 325 U.S. 91, 104-105.

rights was an offense only when committed by reason of color or race, the Act would require a specific intent to discriminate on account of race, and thus its coverage would be restricted to a fairly definite class of cases. Accordingly, Justice Jackson proposed that Screws' conviction be reversed on the ground that the deprivation of rights was not state action.[30]

Alternately, if the Court held to the broader interpretations of *Classic*, Justice Jackson then offered a fallback position of restricting the statue to deprivation of voting rights.

> I would not extend the application of this statute beyond the ground already taken in the *Classic* case [he wrote]. While I cannot say that the logic of that decision cannot reasonably be made to include this one, the very indefiniteness which it introduces seems to forbid such an expansion, particularly when it is a criminal act we are construing. I agree with the opinion of the majority that if this Act means what it is contended to mean, it is dangerously indefinite and perhaps unconstitutionally so. But we must remember that a large part of all that ill-defined indecisiveness we are reading into the statute by the very decision that deplores it. The Court is first choosing the broadest among possible meanings, which makes the Act so indecisive we do not know what it may punish; then it holds the Act so vague that heroic measures must be taken to rescue it from unconstitutionality....
>
> My vote, therefore, is to hold that this deprivation of rights was not committed under color of any law or custom, was not the act of the State of Georgia, and therefore I would reverse the conviction. But if a majority of the Court overrules this ground of reversal, I cannot agree to reversal on the ground suggested. That is, if the Court is to hold this a proper case for prosecution under the Act, I find no error in the procedure which led to conviction. It impresses me as well prosecuted, vigorously and ably defended and presided over impartially.
>
> It seems to me that the Court is introducing unwarranted procedural barriers to any conviction under the Act in order to compensate for unwarranted expansion of the substance of the offense. What, in short, it seems to me to do is to make more prosecutions possible and fewer convictions probable—about the most mischievous thing I can imagine.[31]

Assurances by the Department of Justice that federal power would be used sparingly, he added, were doubtless well-intended but of uncertain duration. The argument that local law enforcement officers

---

[30]Memorandum to conference, circulated February 2, 1945. No. 42, Box 133. Conference notes, No. 837, Box 132. *Betts* v. *Brady*, 316 U.S. 455 (1942). For the anti-discrimination origins of Section 20, see Douglas, J., 325 U.S. 91, 98-99.

[31]Memorandum to conference, pp. 5-6, note 30 *supra*.

could not be trusted to do their duty was "an ominous sign indeed." "And if the whole burden of such law enforcement must be carried in the Central Government," Jackson noted, "at least the Department should be armed with something better for legal weapons than the old-fashioned scatter gun of Section 20."[32]

Ultimately, the memoranda of Justices Frankfurter and Jackson were woven into Justice Roberts' dissent, which somehow lost the brilliance of both. Posing the issue broadly, whether states should be relieved from the duty of punishing their own errant officials for murder, and expressing universal hope that "the cure is a reinvigoration of State responsibility . . . not an undue incursion of remote federal authority," the minority predicted that the statute could become a "dangerous instrument of political intimidation and coercion in the hands of those so inclined." The only way to preserve traditional federal balances, they believed, was to narrow state action under the statutes to activities directed or condoned by the states, if need be by resurrecting *Barney*. Section 20 was not coextensive with the Fourteenth Amendment. Congress, not the Court, was the proper agency to define the federal rights whose deprivation duplicated state criminal law.[33]

Posing the issue in reverse, whether local officials could violate constitutional rights with impunity, Justice Murphy protested the remand and predicted that the decision would frustrate the small federal relief available. "Knowledge of a comprehensive law library is unnecessary for officers of the law to know that the right to murder individuals in the course of their duties is unrecognized in this nation," he declared. The Constitution, the statute, and "their own consciences told them that."[34] And with "simple, but unanswerable logic," Murphy hammered both sides with "realities."[35] While not denying that severe vagueness problems would arise eventually, he reminded the brethren that the *Screws* case did not raise them. In contrast to *Classic*, the right deprived here was the right to life, a right specifically enumerated by the Fourteenth Amendment, and one abridged because of race. If elsewhere Murphy had earned criticism for discussing abstractions *in vacuo,* now the tables were

[32] *Ibid.*
[33] 325 U.S. 91, 160-161, 148-149.
[34] *Ibid.,* pp. 136-137.
[35] Julius Cohen, "The Screws Case: Federal Protection of Negro Rights," *Columbia Law Review,* v. 46 (January, 1946), p. 104.

turned. It would be time enough to consider the "vice of vagueness" when it arose.

Murphy's dissent was also a rebuke to minority contentions that the *Screws* indictment was a "needless extension of federal criminal authority into matters that normally are of State concern."³⁶ Angered by challenge to the premises behind creation of the Civil Rights Section, he asserted that the federal government had to intervene "unless constitutional guarantees are to become atrophied." The precise purpose of the enactment was to protect "the inarticulate and the friendless" from "the cruelties of bigoted and ruthless authority" in the states. Congress, not judges, had decreed that this vacuum be filled. Yet federal intervention would be "futile if courts disregard reality." While Justices could hardly say so, state responsibilities would not be met without outside pressure. Expectations of resurging local responsibility or of congressional relief, suggestions of publicity or of private civil suits as alternative remedies, which circulated through the Court, all were utopian. The real question here was a federal remedy or none.³⁷

Justice Rutledge, in a separate dissent, agreed point by point. This was an act of murder, and abuse of authority which a long course of decision from *ex parte Virginia* to *Classic* had sustained as state action. No petition, no brief had raised questions of vagueness and criminal intent. Appellate courts had injected those. Nor were these issues fresh. *Classic* had rejected a clearer vagueness claim; surely the due process right to life was as definite as the equal protection rights upheld in *Smith* v. *Allwright*. "There can be no judicial hack work cutting out some of the great rights the Amendment secures but leaving in others," Rutledge asserted. "The *Classic* decision must stand or fall by this one. There is no solid room for distinction. Only chaos of principle could result from the effort to maintain that decision while holding the statute impotent to cover these facts." For Rutledge, as for Murphy, "a deeper implication" was at work in the *Screws* case—an effort to cripple the fragile federal role only recently revived.³⁸ If the Court narrowed the meaning of state action in criminal statutes, how could it resist doing the same for the Fourteenth Amendment itself?

³⁶325 U.S. 91, 145.
³⁷*Ibid.*, pp. 134-138.
³⁸See 100 U.S. 339 (1880). Draft dissent, February 20, 1945, p. 11. No. 42, Box 133.

There was another implication to Rutledge, however—the implication of the appellate function and of the Court's reputation in stalemate. However shocking the crime, however distorted he considered the compromise solution, deadlock in a criminal proceeding was worse. Foregoing personal opinion, as he did later in the Illinois reapportionment case, *Colegrove* v. *Green,* Rutledge swung his vote to Douglas in order to achieve a firm result.[39] The statute was saved, as a result, and Screws' conviction was reversed without an "opinion of the Court."

The consequences of the Supreme Court decision conformed to predictions in uncanny ways. On the one hand, a second jury refused to convict; and Sheriff Screws, suffering no apparent loss of local popularity, was elected to the Georgia Senate in 1958. The refusal of the Court to retreat from the broad interpretation of state action, on the other hand, left *Classic* and *Smith* v. *Allwright* standing as crucial underpinnings for the modern law of equal protection pioneered by the federal judiciary. For all the lament of libertarians over the surgery performed on criminal statutes in *Screws,* a retreat along the lines proposed by Justices Roberts, Frankfurter, and Jackson would have made much more difficult the Supreme Court's subsequent plunge into desegregation of public facilities, not to mention its supervision of voting rights and legislative reapportionment.[40] By adhering to expansive concepts of state action, the *Screws* case contributed to the gradual consolidation of precedents which supported the Court's constitutional initiatives in the following decades.

Furthermore, by preserving Section 20 of the civil rights statutes, the *Screws* case thickened the judiciary's armor on the statutory front. Nevertheless, an evenly divided Court narrowed the coverage of the conspiracy section so severely in 1951 that a weakened Section 20 remained the federal government's primary legal weapon against racial violence until the Warren Court cleared the conspiracy path in the *Guest* and *Price* decisions of 1966.[41] By that time, however, the constitutional principle of state action had become so well consolidated that it came as no great surprise when the Justices

[39]Memorandum to conference, February 24, 1945. No. 42, Box 133. See 328 U.S. 549, 564 (1946).
[40]*Brown* v. *Board of Education,* 347 U.S. 483 (1954); *Baker* v. *Carr,* 369 U.S. 186 (1962).
[41]*Williams* v. *United States,* 341 U.S. 97 (1951). *United States* v. *Guest,* 383 U.S. 745 (1966); *United States* v. *Price,* 383 U.S. 787 (1966).

unanimously rejected the narrow interpretation of state action for both sections of the criminal statutes. In 1966, the Court conclusively repudiated Justice Frankfurter's prior position that due process rights were excluded from Section 19, and even absorbed into Section 20 private action that was willfully mixed with the activity of state agents.[42] If the interplay between constitutional and statutory growth were not plain enough, it should also be remembered that the specific intent standard of *Screws* was what enabled the Justices—without re-examination or the reservations of Douglas' original—to avoid the vice of vagueness problem in 1966.[43] Whatever the price in statutory effectiveness, the *Screws* case can only be viewed as a major constitutional victory for federal protection of civil rights.

Practically speaking, however, there is no denying that the mode of salvaging Section 20 in *Screws* seriously blunted the "sword" of the Civil Rights Division. Even after a sustained season of civil disobedience in the streets made it politically expedient for Congress to break the impasse of a century, the police brutality problem remains much as before—a troublesome legal void. Congress has enacted no additional criminal penalties nor a statute of enumerated rights, despite uncontroverted suggestions from the high bench that statutory enumeration of rights, the form which Section 20 took in the beginning, would free civil liberties legislation of constitutional problems.[44] And the impact of *Screws* reverberates through the resulting administration of federal law.

The Civil Rights Commission report of 1961 manifested deep frustration over the practical obstacles to convictions. While potential federal action probably spurs local initiative, experience has shown that the specific intent standard is confusing to use and difficult to satisfy, even with nonsouthern juries.[45] Of the thousands of

[42]*Ibid.* See John Silad, "A Constitutional Forecast: Demise of the 'State Action' Limit on the Equal Protection Guarantee," *Columbia Law Review*, v. 66 (May, 1966), p. 855.

[43]See note 29 *supra;* 383 U.S. 745, 753-754, 760; 383 U.S. 787, 760.

[44]"'Of course Congress can prohibit the deprivation of enumerated constitutional rights," Roberts, J., 325 U.S. 91, 153. See Note, "Discretion to Prosecute Federal Civil Rights Crimes," *Yale Law Review*, v. 74 (June, 1965), pp. 1297-1312.

[45]*Justice*, 1961 Commission on Civil Rights Report, Book 5, pp. 8-9, 46-52. See also Carr, *op. cit.*, pp. 114-115, and Harry H. Shapiro, "Limitations in Prosecuting Civil Rights Violations," *Cornell Law Quarterly*, v. 46 (Summer, 1961), pp. 532-554.

complaints received annually by the Civil Rights Division, no prosecution under the conspiracy section survived the high court after *Classic* until the Philadelphia, Mississippi trials of 1966. Results under the "color of law" section have been meager even during the quickening civil rights agitation of the 1960's. In the fiscal years 1961-1963, the Department of Justice prosecuted a yearly average of twenty-three cases under both sections; indictments were returned in sixteen cases, and convictions obtained in only three. In 1964-1965, the Department prosecuted a yearly average of forty cases, with a total yield of twenty-seven indictments and six convictions.[46] Regardless of constitutional issues and the temper of southern juries, Justice Jackson's forecast has yet to be proven wrong.

Nor has the Supreme Court itself escaped feedback from *Screws*. Despite appearances, libertarian Justices have been wary through the years about defining the threshold of state action.[47] Even Justice Murphy apparently voted against *certiorari* petitions in the *Enoch Pratt Free Library* case, a significant lower court decision expanding state action, for fear of risking defeat and "another mess like *Screws*."[48] Even as they stretch the old Civil Rights Act to cover "all rights" and private action, contemporary Justices have drawn back from the collision of state-federal judiciaries inherent in expansive interpretations of civil rights removal statutes.[49] They also have cast longing eyes to Congress for aid. How else can one explain their advisory opinion in *United States* v. *Guest* that the enabling clause of the Fourteenth Amendment would sustain a criminal statute punishing all conspiracies, with or without state action, that interfere with Fourteenth Amendment rights?[50]

A generation after the *Screws* case, it is plain that the field of federal punishment of civil rights violations does not conclusively refute Dahl's propositions about the limits of Supreme Court policy-making in a pluralist political environment. The conflict of values was simply too complex for judicial resolution without imposing restraints on innovation. For similar reasons, it is also plain that

[46] Figures from Department of Justice sources.
[47] 383 U.S. 745, 756.
[48] Cert. note, No. 113, Box 136. *Enoch Pratt Free Library of Baltimore* v. *Kerr*, 326 U.S. 721 (1945). Cf. *Shelley* v. *Kraemer*, 334 U.S. 1 (1948).
[49] *Georgia* v. *Rachel*, 384 U.S. 780 (1966); *City of Greenwood* v. *Peacock*, 384 U.S. 808 (1966).
[50] See opinion of Brennan, J., 383 U.S. 745, 782. *New York Times*, April 3, 1966, IV, 10:1.

the *Screws* case overtaxes the bi-polar models of the appellate process popular among current analysts. Whether the models are the reason versus ideology dualities of the Hart-Arnold debate, or the attitude versus precedent antimonies of behavioral scientists, there were simply too many values in collision and articulated on the Court for bi-polar categorization, or efficient quantitative analysis.[51] The decision in the *Screws* case may be interpreted most fruitfully within the framework of incrementalism theory, which permits both ratiocination and adjustment of interests, under the special stimulus of fashioning remedies for perversion of law. By the same token, however, men of good will are still hoping for resurgence of local responsibility to punish shocking episodes in law enforcement. They are also still saying "let Washington do it," and they are still frustrated over unpunished police murders by that route. Meantime, the struggle of the federal government to use the feeble remains of Section 20 as its principal weapon against local police brutality leads inescapably to the conclusion that in the *Screws* case, *all* the Justices were right. The irony is that the longer civil rights violence goes unremedied, the closer Congress may come to accepting the Court's prolonged invitation to act. And if current trends hold, the next chapter in the law of race relations may well be the clash of liberties involved as racial equality collides with rights of privacy and the dragnet of criminal conspiracy.

[51]See Henry M. Hart, Jr., "Foreward: The Time Chart of the Justices, The Supreme Court, 1958 Term," *Harvard Law Review*, v. 73 (November, 1959), pp. 84-125; Thurman Arnold, "Professor Hart's Theology," *Harvard Law Review*, v. 73 (May, 1960), pp. 1299-1317. Glendon Schubert, *The Judicial Mind* (Evanston: Northwestern University Press, 1965); Theodore L. Becker, *Political Behavioralism and Modern Jurisprudence* (Chicago: Rand McNally & Company, 1964). The authors assume that, at present levels of sophistication, the point of diminishing returns for *efficient* quantitative analysis is reached at three variables. Cf. Schubert, *loc. cit.* The *Screws* case involved at least five identifiable values—*stare decisis*, local law enforcement, appellate function, the conflicting libertarian values of minority protection, and ascertainable standards of criminal responsibility. While scaling techniques conceivably could reduce this number in conjunction with other cases, we doubt that the result would hold for *Screws* without distorting reality.

The Nineteenth Century Struggle Over Segregated Education in the Boston Schools

DONALD M. JACOBS

Department of History, Northeastern University

Most of the frustrations and degradations suffered by Afro-Americans today were similarly experienced by blacks during the 18th and 19th centuries, and the Negroes' continuing fight for equal rights, especially in the area of education, has historically been an integral part of the American democratic experience. One example is the story of the battle waged by Boston's colored to end segregation in that city's public schools.

The major events in this struggle took place during the 1840s and 1850s, but the first seeds of discontent were actually planted during the latter part of the 18th century. At that time Boston's schools were not segregated.[1] However, the blacks led by Prince Hall had already petitioned the Massachusetts Legislature requesting some type of special educational facility for their children. Well aware that most of the city's colored population had only recently been freed from slavery, and that many felt themselves to be at an educational disadvantage, Hall and his fellow petitioners expressed concern that "our children . . . now receive no benefit from the free schools in the town of Boston."[2]

Turned aside by the Legislature, by the turn of the century the city's Negroes had established their own school in a house on Beacon Hill. Then in 1806, as more and more blacks began moving from the city's North End to the Hill, the colored community completed construction of the African Baptist Church on Belknap Street (now Joy Street), and the colored school was moved into a room in the church's basement.[3] In 1812, the Boston school committee placed the school within its own jurisdiction and soon was assigning to it all blacks of grammar school age.[4] In 1815 it was named the Smith School in honor of Abiel Smith, a Boston merchant whose will provided that $4,000 be given to the city for the education of the colored population.[5]

As the years passed, enrollment in the Smith School grew until by 1834 it was apparent that larger quarters were needed. Recognizing this, Samuel Eliot of the Boston Board of Aldermen began working on plans to construct a new schoolhouse

---
[1] Charles Stimpson, *Stimpson's Boston Directory* (Boston: Charles Stimpson, 1796), p. 8.
[2] Herbert Aptheker, *A Documentary History of the Negro People in the United States* (New York: Citadel Press, 1951), p. 19; Papers of Jeremy Belknap, Massachusetts Historical Society, "Collections," in *The Liberator*, I (March 12, 1831), 41.
[3] William Minot, *Address at the Dedication of the Smith School* (Boston: 1835), p. 1.
[4] George W. Williams, *History of the Negro Race from 1619 to 1880* (New York: G. P. Putnam's Sons, 1883), II, 162.
[5] *Freedom's Journal*, I (June 1, 1827), 47; Arthur Burr Darling, "Prior to Little Rock in American Education: The Roberts Case of 1849-1850," Massachusetts Historical Society, *Proceedings*, LXXII (1963), 130.

for the city's colored children. Although meeting with continued opposition, Eliot's efforts were finally rewarded when he was able to obtain enough of an allocation from Abiel Smith's 1815 bequest to erect a school building and provide a yearly appropriation for its expenses.[6]

The school was completed early in 1835. The featured speaker at the dedication ceremonies was school committeeman William Minot who confidently expressed the hope that "this school may be one efficient means of removing the prejudices heretofore existing against the character and capacity of the colored people." However, he warned his colored audience that they "must be patient, and not expect in a few years these results which it has cost nations ages to reach."[7]

Another important participant in these ceremonies was Abner Forbes who had been named the new white master of the Smith School the previous year. His appointment was an obvious attempt to please and perhaps even appease Boston's black population since Forbes was an active and ardent abolitionist.[8] William Lloyd Garrison urged his Boston Negro readers, "Let the school be crowded with scholars without delay."[9]

The city's blacks seemed to accept Forbes in the beginning. The all-Negro Garrison Juvenile Society invited the new schoolmaster to speak at their annual celebration in 1834 and he accepted. The young leader of this organization was William Cooper Nell who would later lead the fight to close down the Smith School and end segregation in the Boston schools.[10]

The master of the Smith School seemed to be everywhere at once, working to help the city's blacks elevate themselves. By 1837 he had begun an evening school for adult Negroes.[11] He was an active supporter of the Adelphic Union Library Association, a group formed by influential blacks to stimulate education among the adults.[12]

Many of the topics discussed in the Library Association's lecture series demonstrated a growing consciousness on the part of the Negroes of the need to see their condition improved. One lecture delivered in 1841 considered the question, "Do separate churches and schools for colored people tend to foster prejudice?" Prominent abolitionists were often asked to speak at the Adelphic Union's lectures, resulting in frequent addresses by William Lloyd Garrison and Wendell Phillips.[13]

By this time William Nell and several fellow Negroes were beginning to become active in movements to end segregation in the Boston schools. According to Nell, in 1840 he, Garrison, and Phillips for the first time "signed a petition, asking the city government to grant equal school rights." Although unsuccessful here, Nell continued to support Abner Forbes's efforts as principal of the Smith School, noting just after he had observed the school's annual exhibition that year how "de-

---

[6] Minot, *op. cit.*, p. 2.
[7] *Ibid.*, pp. 5, 6.
[8] *The Liberator*, III (February 2, 1833), 17.
[9] *Ibid.*, IV (April 5, 1834), 55.
[10] *Ibid.*, IV (May 17, 1834), 79.
[11] Abner Forbes to Nathaniel Southard, in *The Liberator*, VII (November 24, 1837), 190.
[12] *The Liberator*, X (May 15, 1840), 79 and X (December 18, 1840), 203.
[13] *Ibid.*, XI (January 8, 1841), 7; XII (January 21, 1842), 11; XII (March 11, 1842), 39; and XIII (February 10, 1843), 23.

lightful" and "instructive" he had found it to be.[14]

Early in 1842 the whole question of equal school rights broke out into the open in Nantucket where school committeeman Nathaniel Barney was initially unsuccessful in his attempt to have a colored child accepted into one of Nantucket's all-white public schools.[15] Later in the year this same question came up for discussion in nearby Salem where Henry Wright, a leading abolitionist and close friend of Garrison's, argued that the Negroes were being taxed to support schools which they were not allowed to attend. The same thing, he pointed out, was true in Boston where "the high school for boys . . . is closed against the colored people. . . ."[16]

Suddenly that same year while the outbursts in Nantucket and Salem were still fresh in everyone's mind, the first real rumblings of discontent began to be heard among Boston's black population. Just as Boston's schools were about to reopen in September, a letter appeared in *The Liberator* complaining that the recent Smith School exhibition had been unsatisfactory and that the money appropriated for the school was completely wasted.[17]

Not long afterward complaints against the school and its principal, Abner Forbes, began to appear in several of the city's newspapers, prompting a member of the school committee to write a letter to the editor of *The Liberator* "to correct" some of the "erroneous views presented . . . respecting . . . the Smith School" and its principal. Against the charge that the colored children of the city were being "instructed by an unsuitable master," the committeeman answered that he knew of no other school official in the city who had done so much to elevate his pupils and his school.[18]

Boston's school controversy was quiet during 1843, but the following year a group of colored parents filed a formal complaint against schoolmaster Abner Forbes. He was charged with cruelty in discipline, excessive absence from school and neglect of duty, improper treatment of the parents of his students and, most serious of all, "entertaining opinions of the intellectual character of the colored race of people, that disqualify him to be a teacher of colored children."[19] They accused the schoolmaster of writing defamatory, racially prejudiced reports to the *Boston Courier* under a pseudonym. Forbes denied the accusation and to refute these charges he requested that the *Courier* print his personal racial creed.

Unfortunately, the last of Forbes's three statements served to inflame the controversy. In the newspaper it appeared that he had written, "I believe there is no human art, or science, the acquiring of which has been specially denied them by

---

[14] *Proceedings of the Colored Citizens of Boston Celebrating the Opening of the Public Schools to Negroes* (Boston: 1856), p. 5; *The Liberator*, XI (August 27, 1841), 139.
[15] Nathaniel Barney to Representative George Bradburn in *The Liberator*, XII (March 11, 1842), 39.
[16] *The Liberator*, XII (September 9, 1842), 142.
[17] 'Justice' to William Lloyd Garrison, August 20, 1842, in *The Liberator*, XII (September 2, 1842), 139.

[18] "One of the School Board" to William Lloyd Garrison, October 1, 1842, in *The Liberator*, XII (October 7, 1842), 158.
[19] "Controversy over Caste Schools in Boston," *Collected Newspaper Reports* (Boston: Boston Public Library, 1844-1855), p. 6.

nature, if they can enjoy the facilities suited to *their* natures.[20]

The Negroes seized upon this portion of Forbes's statement, pointing out that to emphasize the difference in the races the word "their" had been italicized. The schoolmaster explained that this had merely been a printer's error, but the colored parents refused to accept this explanation and demanded that the school board dismiss Forbes completely from the Boston schools.[21]

On June 12, 1844, the school committee handed down its decision. Speaking for the Board, Frederick Emerson noted that while Abner Forbes had undoubtedly contributed much to the Boston schools and had proved his worth as an educator, recent events had caused Forbes's reputation with the Negroes of the city to suffer badly. However the committee refused to bow to the demands that he be dismissed, recommending instead that he be transferred to another school in the city. The colored leadership attacked this decision vehemently, and distributed a report bitterly denouncing the schoolmaster.[22]

Even as the Forbes controversy continued, the Negroes of Boston were making their first concerted effort to shut down the Smith School and integrate the city's all-white schools. However, the school committee refused to close the school. Angered, the blacks of the city held a protest meeting later in the month where they again complained that "separate schools" were "contrary to the laws of the Commonwealth," and demanded that the schoolmaster be dismissed at once under threat of boycott.[23]

Soon after this incident Abner Forbes left the Boston schools, eventually moving to New Hampshire where he spent his declining years.[24] Meanwhile, petition drives were launched against the Smith School, first in 1845 and then again the following year. Both failed. The school committee majority took the view that "separate schools for colored children" were "not only legal and just, but . . . best adapted to promote the education of that class of our population."[25]

However, a minority of the school committee favored the abolition of Boston's system of separate schools. Noting that both Salem and Nantucket had recently opened their public schools to Negroes, they rightly concluded that Boston was now "the only place in this Commonwealth, where any distinction whatever exists with respect to color in the common schools." Racial prejudice, they also went on to point out, arose all too naturally from segregation in the schools.[26]

After initiating still another petition drive in 1848, the Negro leadership invited some of the more influential members of the Boston school committee to come meet with them, but the committee ignored the invitation. Frustrated, the

---

20 *Ibid.*, pp. 7-8.
21 *Ibid.*, pp. 18-22.
22 *Ibid.*, pp. 8, 22.
23 Aptheker, *op. cit.*, pp. 242-244.
24 William Lloyd Garrison to Henry C. Wright, July 13, 1869, *Anti-Slavery Papers*, Boston Public Library.
25 Gilbert T. Stephenson, *Race Distinctions in American Law* (New York: Appleton, 1910), p. 168; Leon F. Litwack, *North of Slavery, The Negro in the Free States, 1790-1860* (Chicago: University of Chicago Press, 1961), p. 144.
26 *Report of the Minority of the Committee of the Primary School Board on the Caste Schools of the City of Boston* (Boston: A. J. Wright's Steam Press, 1846), pp. 2, 4, 13, 14, 18.

blacks demonstrated their anger by sending out groups of black petitioners to surround the Smith School and prevent the colored children from entering.[27]

Under such pressure the school committee majority issued another report early in 1849. Here they took a new tack, noting that many blacks were themselves concerned over what might happen if the Negro children of the city were all at once thrown into the white schools and forced to compete with the white children. They went on to express the belief that they had no right to compel the association between black and white which would result if Boston's system of separate schools was forcibly abolished.[28]

Toning down their original stand somewhat, a minority of the committee demonstrated they at least partially agreed with a portion of the majority argument. While still strongly favoring the integration of the city's schools, they recommended "that the Smith School be continued for such of the black children as may desire to attend it."[29]

The Negro leadership was not prepared to compromise. By now they viewed the Smith School as an evil symbol of caste which eventually would either have to be closed down or integrated. Confidently they now turned their attention to the Massachusetts Supreme Court where in a test case one of their comrades, Benjamin Roberts, had initiated a suit for damages against the city of Boston in behalf of his five-year-old daughter, Sarah. Roberts based his suit on an 1845 Massachusetts statute which provided that "any child, unlawfully excluded from public instruction in the Commonwealth, shall recover damages . . . against the city or town by which such public school instruction is supported."[30]

On four separate occasions Roberts had attempted to enroll his daughter in one of the white primary schools and each time she had been refused admittance. What particularly galled Benjamin Roberts was that his daughter had to pass five different white primary schools on her way to her own colored school.[31]

Charles Sumner, a bitter and eloquent foe of slavery and an ardent supporter of equal rights for Negroes, was more than willing to take the case. He was assisted by Robert Morris, the first Negro to pass the bar in Massachusetts and the second to practice law in the state.[32]

Standing before the venerable Lemuel Shaw, himself once a member of the Boston school committee but now serving his twentieth year as Chief Justice of the Massachusetts Supreme Court, Sumner argued that based on the declaration of human rights of the Massachusetts Constitution of 1780 there could be no legal justification for discrimination in the Bos-

---

[27] "Equal Schools for All Without Regard to Color or Race," *Boston Negroes' Petition* (Boston: Boston Public Library, May 21, 1851); Charles H. Wesley, "The Negro's Struggle for Freedom in its Birthplace," *Journal of Negro History*, XXX (January, 1945), 77.
[28] Litwack, *op. cit.*, p. 145.
[29] *Report of the Minority of the Committee upon the Petitions of John T. Hilton and Others Praying for the Abolition of the Smith School* (Boston: J. H. Eastburn, 1849), pp. 12-13.

[30] Luther S. Cushing, *Reports of Cases Argued and Determined in the Supreme Judicial Court of Massachusetts* (Boston: Little, Brown and Company, 1853), V, 198.
[31] Leonard W. Levy and Harlan B. Phillips, "The Roberts Case: Source of the 'Separate but Equal' Doctrine," *American Historical Review*, LVI (April, 1951), 512.
[32] *Portland American*, in *The Liberator*, XIV (July 12, 1844), 111; XVII (February 12, 1847), 27.

ton public schools. Furthermore, he pointed out, in establishing public schools, the Massachusetts Legislature had purposely contrived to use general statements which could not possibly be construed to exclude anyone for reasons of color.

Sumner went on to attack the whole concept of caste which he felt the idea of separate schools for Negroes seemed openly to approve, and he refused to accept the view that there was nothing wrong with segregated schools if they were the equivalent of the white schools, an argument that the United States Supreme Court did later adopt in the 1896 case of *Plessy v Ferguson*. Sumner also denied categorically that the Boston school committee had any right to set qualifications for admittance to the schools based on race or color.[33]

Peleg W. Chandler, the City Solicitor, argued for the Boston school committee. He skirted Sumner's moral arguments and rebutted him directly on only one point. Chandler took issue with his legal opponent's attempt to downgrade the school committee's powers, contending that that body had by law been given "general superintendence" over the schools of the city.[34]

By now the mounting pressures were beginning to tell on the Negroes themselves, for at this point trouble began to develop between the more militant colored elements and a moderate minority wing determined to challenge their leadership. The moderates supported Negro admission to the all-white public schools, but urged at the same time that the Smith School be kept open for those who might want to continue sending their children there. Filled with apprehension, this group had genuine reservations regarding total and immediate integration and desired a choice between integrated and segregated schools.[35]

The leader of the black moderates was Thomas Paul Smith. Smith was related to Thomas Paul, Jr., son of one of the early Negro leaders of Boston, who after graduating from Dartmouth College had taken a job as principal of a school in Albany, New York, and was now teaching in a small school in Providence, Rhode Island.[36] Paul, however, was homesick for Boston and Smith wanted him back as master of the Smith School.

Smith felt that if the school committee would consent to hiring a Negro principal, the majority of the city's colored would be satisfied and the school could then be kept open. To bring this about the group that favored hiring Paul began to spread rumors attacking the abilities and the fidelity of Ambrose Wellington, the capable white principal. William Nell strongly opposed this course of action.[37]

As the pressure continued to build, a more dogmatic segment of Negro opinion, led by Nell and Benjamin Roberts, began a steady verbal attack against the Smith faction, at one point referring to this group and the whites who supported them as "the colored wire-pulled" and "their white wire-pullers." If the attempt to

---

[33] *Argument of Charles Sumner Against the Constitutionality of Separate Colored Schools* (Boston: B. F. Roberts, 1849), pp. 3, 4, 10-12, 20.
[34] Cushing, *op. cit.* p. 208.
[35] *The Liberator,* XIX (September 7, 1849), 143; XIX (October 5, 1849), 160; XX (February 15, 1850), 27.
[36] *Ibid.,* XI (November 19, 1841), 187; XIII (Mary 12. 1843), 74; XIX (November 23, 1849), 187.
[37] *Ibid.,* XIX (September 7, 1849), 143.

close down the Smith School proved unsuccessful, they felt, the divisive tactics of Thomas Paul Smith and his followers would be the major reason.[38]

In the meantime a large number of colored parents were continuing their very effective boycott of the Smith School, even after it had been made public that Thomas Paul, Jr., had become an active candidate for the principal's post.[39] Obviously the only reason the school committee was considering Paul was to break the back of the boycott, hoping the Negroes would flock back to the school if its principal were one of their own and the son of one of their most respected early leaders.

At a noisy, demonstration-filled meeting most of the Negroes present promised to continue the boycott and expressed their complete disapproval of Thomas Paul's attempt to win the principal's post. As far as Nell and his followers were concerned, anyone who even expressed neutral feelings in the controversy was an enemy: "Those colored persons who are not for us in this trying hour, must be counted in the ranks of those who would deprive us of our heaven-decreed rights."[40]

Robert Morris, the colored lawyer, joined with the majority favoring the closing down of the all-Negro Smith School, and began hurling charges that Thomas Paul Smith was being paid to lobby actively for Thomas Paul's appointment as master of the Smith School, a charge Smith vigorously denied.[41] However, it appears Smith had been more actively working in support of Paul's candidacy than he professed. Through a series of letters he had convinced Dr. James McCune Smith (no relative), one of the most respected Negro leaders in New York City, to write a letter to the Boston school committee relating his own views concerning Negro educators in Negro schools. This letter was used by the committee to show that an important black leader supported the idea of a black principal for the Smith School.

When Dr. Smith heard that he had been used by one faction of Boston's colored against the other, he attempted to set the record straight by saying that Thomas Paul Smith had not given a true picture of the controversy. He had always felt "that separate organizations of all kinds, based upon the color of the skin, keep alive prejudice against color" and that "no organizations do this more effectually than colored schools."[42]

Finally, in March, 1850, the Massachusetts Supreme Court rendered its decision in the Roberts case. Judge Lemuel Shaw delivered the opinion upholding the Boston school committee's constitutional right "to make provision for the instruction of colored children, in separate schools established exclusively for them. . . ." Justice Shaw gave full support to the view of Peleg Chandler that no one, including the court itself, could legislate or abjudicate morality.[43]

Although disheartened by recent events the blacks, led by Nell and Roberts, were still determined to carry on the fight to abolish the Smith School. In June, Rob-

---

[38] Ibid.
[39] Ibid., XIX (September 14, 1849), 147; XIX (September 21, 1849), 151.
[40] Ibid., XIX (September 21, 1849), 151; XIX (October 12, 1849), 162; XIX (October 5, 1849), 160.
[41] Ibid., XIX (October 5, 1849), 160.

[42] Boston Chronotype, in The Liberator, XX (January 4, 1850), 2.
[43] Cushing, op. cit., p. 198; Stephenson, op. cit., p. 168.

erts announced plans to travel throughout the state to gather signatures for yet another petition calling for an end to segregated education in Boston.[44]

Early in 1851 the blacks were informed that the city's charter apparently justified the anti-integration stand taken by the Boston school committee. In May a bill to abolish color distinctions as a bar to Boston's public schools was soundly defeated in the Legislature.[45] Attacked on nearly all fronts, the movement now began to lose much of its initial zeal. William Nell had begun making speeches in various towns in and about the Boston area, but for the most part the activities of those favoring integration of the city's schools slowed considerably.

In 1852 a colored citizen of East Boston petitioned to be allowed to send his children to one of the local white primary schools, largely due to the expense of the daily ferry rides to and from the all-Negro school. The primary school committee refused to grant the request and chose instead to provide his children with a free pass on the ferry.[46] Rather than send their children to the Smith School, many of Boston's Negroes continued to support two independent schools, while others transported their offspring to integrated schools in other towns.[47]

In the fall of 1853, Edward Pindall, a young fair-complexioned boy, had been accepted into one of Boston's all-white schools, but later the Boston school committee learned that the boy was actually of African descent although both he and his father, who had originally appeared at the committee's office together, had easily passed for white. After learning the truth, the school committee ruled that the boy had to be removed from the white school and transferred to one of the all-Negro schools.

About this time a Committee on Public Instruction had been formed under the jurisdiction of the Boston City council. Certain members of the committee happened to be at the City Solicitor's office when the Pindall boy and his father lodged a formal complaint against the school committee and told of their plans to bring the case to court. Those present expressed amazement that a boy of such light complexion could have been refused admittance to the city's white public schools, and they felt the Pindall case demonstrated quite clearly the grave injustice of the city's whole system of separate schools for whites and Negroes.

Stirred to action, in August, 1854, the Committee on Public Instruction issued a report on the controversy in which they noted that Boston was now the only city in the Commonwealth that still maintained segregated schools. They further reported "that *no rule or regulation* excluding colored children from our schools exists."[48] At last the Negroes of Boston had gained an effective ally. An exuberant William Nell was thankful that there was now "a disposition among the aldermen and common councilmen to award

---

[44] *The Liberator*, XX (June 14, 1850), 95.
[45] "Equal Schools for All," *Boston Negroes' Petition* (Boston: Boston Public Library, May 21, 1851).
[46] *The Liberator*, XXIV (August 18, 1854), 132.
[47] *Ibid.*, XXII (December 10, 1852), 199; XXV (March 30, 1855), 52; William Cooper Nell to William Lloyd Garrison, December 1852, in Carter G. Woodson (ed.), *The Mind of the Negro as Reflected in Letters Written During the Crisis, 1800-1860* (Washington: Association for the Study of Negro Life and History, 1926), p. 340.

[48] *The Liberator*, XXIV (August 18, 1854), 132.

justice to the long-neglected colored children."⁴⁹

However, Boston's black community suffered a temporary setback in November when the jury in the Pindall case, against the pleas of Robert Morris, the boy's lawyer, reported a verdict in favor of the school committee. Yet the City Solicitor, George Hillard, while defending the reasoning used to justify the verdict, made it public he felt the law upon which it was based to be a bad one.⁵⁰

Finally, in March, 1855, a bill was placed before the Massachusetts House of Representatives which would allow black children to enter Boston's all-white public schools. It provided that for any individual applying for admission to any public school in the state, "no distinction shall be made on account of the race, color, or religious opinions of the applicant."⁵¹

Within a few short weeks the act had passed both Massachusetts houses and the bill was signed into law on April 28, 1855, by Henry Gardner, the newly-elected "Know-Nothing" governor, to take effect the following September. However the moderate black faction had its way in the end, since it was decided that the Smith School would be kept open, at least for a trial period.⁵²

Attacks against this liberal new piece of legislation came quickly. When word of its passage reached New York City, the *Herald* cried that the North was now becoming "Africanized" and that "amalgamation has commenced . . . . God save the Commonwealth of Massachusetts."⁵³

Meanwhile the people of Boston nervously awaited the crucial day. Finally on Monday, September 3, 1855, all the city's children returned to school, and the population watched carefully for any sign of trouble. However "there was none . . . in any part of the city," the *Boston Evening Telegraph* reported, and only seven colored children attended classes at the Smith School.⁵⁴

On December 17, 1855, the colored citizens of Boston held still another meeting, but this was an occasion of celebration rather than protest. A testimonial dinner was being given to honor William Cooper Nell for his role in the struggle for equal school rights. William Lloyd Garrison and Wendell Phillips were present, and both spoke briefly. The room quieted as Nell rose to thank those who had done so much to make the movement a success — Garrison, Phillips, his fellow Negroes on the various committees. But these, he felt, were not the ones mainly responsible for the final hard-won victory. "To the *women*, and the *Children* also, is the cause especially indebted for success," Nell pointed out. They were the ones who had accompanied him from house to house and from committee to committee "to see the laws of the old Bay State applied in good faith."

Nell closed his speech by relating how on the day before the white schools were to be integrated he happened to see a

---

⁴⁹ *Ibid.*
⁵⁰ *Boston Telegraph*, in *The Liberator*, XXIV (November 10, 1854), 179.
⁵¹ *Statutes of Massachusetts*, 1855, Chapter 256, section 1, in *The Liberator*, XXV (March 30, 1855), 52.
⁵² *The Liberator*, XXV (May 11, 1855), 75; XXV (August 17, 1855), 131.

⁵³ *New York Herald*, in Leon F. Litwack, "The Abolitionist Dilemma: The Anti-Slavery Movement and the Northern Negro," *New England Quarterly*, XXXIV (March, 1961), 72.
⁵⁴ *Boston Evening Telegraph*, September 3, 1855.

little colored boy walking by the all-Negro Smith School with several of his friends. As he passed the school building the boy raised his hands, pointed to the school, and happily yelled out to his companions, "Good-bye forever, colored school! Tomorrow we are like other Boston boys!"[55]

---

[55] *The Liberator*, XXV (December 28, 1855), 207; *Proceedings of the Colored Citizens of Boston, op. cit.*, pp. 8-9.

Civil Rights Consciousness in the 1940s

By
PETER J. KELLOGG*

WHEN the twentieth century began, most white Americans, including most progressive reformers, were openly racist. A benevolent paternalism or an exploitive manifest destiny were commonly expressed attitudes. By the end of World War II, white supremacy was no longer a publicly acceptable doctrine in the North, and civil rights reform to secure legal equality for black Americans was becoming an issue in national politics. This reversal of a major component of American culture came rather rapidly, the greatest shift occurring during World War II as northern liberals reacted to Nazi racism and to a public fear of domestic violence. This change in publicly proclaimed values came therefore as a response to a specific set of historical circumstances—a response thus concentrated on the issue of white prejudice rather than the place of black people in American society. A contrast manifested itself between white racism on the one hand and abstract principles of democratic equality on the other. The concern for economic and political progress which had dominated the attention of liberals during the thirties was little noticed now in the 1940s as whites, newly aware of their own racism, sought to justify the integrity of America as a democratic nation. Racism was rejected as acceptable public policy, and at the same time it was made an abstraction remote from the specific realities of black life.

It was in the liberal community that white opposition to racism developed earliest and basic white attitudes were shaped. That community included, first, a number of self-proclaimed liberals who sought to shape opinion on public issues. These liberals wrote for or read journals of opinion such as the *Nation*, the *New Republic*, *Common Sense*, and *Survey Graphic* which were the most prominent forums of liberal discussion during the years under investigation.[1] Independent liberals

---

*The author is Associate Professor of Urban Studies at the University of Wisconsin —Green Bay.

[1] The *New Republic* and the *Nation* were the most important and widely recognized organs of liberal opinion and were generally viewed as the major vehicles of liberal thought. Their contributors and correspondents included a wide variety of prominent writers, scholars, and public figures, who helped create the position of these journals as articulators of liberal thought. *Survey Graphic* stemmed from *Survey* and tended to reflect the point of view of the professional social worker; it was attuned to the social and economic conditions of different groups throughout the country. There is a good

18

Civil Rights, 1940s

were also found in activist organizations—most prominently the Union for Democratic Action and its successor, Americans for Democratic Action.[2] Liberals associated with these journals and organizations were generally independent of government and party; they responded to public issues in terms of conscience, and they undertook political calculation almost solely as a means toward advancing liberal goals and politicians. In addition to these independent liberals, there were individual politicians who identified themselves as liberals, or were generally perceived as such, and they both shaped and reflected currents of liberal thought.[3] Among them were members of the Roosevelt and

---

history of the *Survey* available in Clark A. Chambers, *Paul U. Kellogg and the Survey: Voices for Social Welfare and Social Justice* (Minneapolis, 1971). In seeking to trace the shift in public orthodoxy from racism to acceptance of civil rights reform, I first studied the liberal journals and then other intellectually oriented publications—particularly the widely circulating *Harpers* and *Atlantic Monthly* for their indication of how a general readership was being exposed to changing ideas on race. There was very little coverage of racial questions in the latter group of publications and virtually no advocacy of reform. In order to compare the ideas of black and white thinkers, *Crisis*, organ of the NAACP, and *Opportunity*, organ of the Urban League, were also read. The clearest evidence of the change in liberal attitudes appeared in the liberal journals and in some of the manuscript collections cited below.

[2] The papers of the Union for Democratic Action (UDA) and Americans for Democratic Action (ADA) are in the Wisconsin Historical Society. The Union for Democratic Action was organized in 1941 to marshal liberal support for the war against fascism abroad and for liberal principles at home. Sponsors and national board members included the first chairman, Reinhold Niebuhr; Mrs. Eleanor Roosevelt; James B. Carey, secretary-treasurer of the CIO; Louis Fisher; Walter Reuther of the United Automobile Workers; Boris Shiskin of the AFL; Freda Kirchway, editor of the *Nation;* Bruce Bliven, editor of the *New Republic;* and A. Philip Randolph, as well as a number of other prominent liberal figures. The UDA was reorganized and expanded as the ADA in 1947. The founding of the UDA is discussed briefly in Lawrence S. Wittner, *Rebels against War: The American Peace Movement* (New York, 1969), and a history of the ADA is available in Clifton Brock, *Americans for Democratic Action* (Washington, 1962).

[3] It is virtually impossible to define what an American liberal is, but I have generally used two criteria. Essentially, reputation has been accepted. If a person, organization, or journal was considered liberal by reputation or by self-definition, it was examined. In addition, individuals and organizations supporting liberal goals were studied, though obviously a stance on one issue does not define a political orientation. Some prominent political figures have been symbols of liberalism in their age, e.g., Senator Robert Wagner (see J. Joseph Huthmacher, *Senator Robert F. Wagner and the Rise of Urban Liberalism* [New York, 1968]) and Hubert Humphrey (see his papers in the Minnesota Historical Society). The papers of the ADA, the NAACP, and the Presidential Libraries of Franklin D. Roosevelt and Harry Truman have been used and contain papers and correspondence from a wide range of political figures. Debates in the *Congressional Record* have been followed for what they show of the issues of public debate. One politician who held only state office but had national impact as a leader of liberal causes was Robert Kenny, Attorney General of California, and his papers in the Bancroft Library in Berkeley have been used.

19

The Historian

Truman administrations who either officially or unofficially concerned themselves with the race issue, but their perspective tended to be essentially political or oriented toward crisis-management, and they reflected more than shaped changes in racial attitudes.[4] Finally, there was a group of experts on race relations who produced an ongoing body of scholarship and whose writings were frequently reviewed in the liberal journals. Many of them cooperated with such organizations as the National Association for the Advancement of Colored People and the American Council on Race Relations.[5] Labor unions and religious groups were at times important supporters of civil rights, but their history has a special dynamic of its own and during the forties they worked chiefly through other organizations such as the ADA.[6]

[4] In the Roosevelt administration, Harold Ickes, Harry Hopkins, and Aubrey Williams, among others, all made efforts to protect black interests; Mrs. Roosevelt herself was perhaps the most influential advocate, serving also as a conduit to the president for Walter White and Mary McLeod Bethune. (See the Ickes Papers in the Library of Congress and the Roosevelt Papers and Mrs. Roosevelt's papers at the Franklin D. Roosevelt Library; note also Harvard Sitkoff, *A New Deal for Blacks* [New York, 1978], chap. 3.) During World War II, Jonathan Daniels secured a position as an adviser on race, though his goal was clearly more containment of crises than reform. (See OF 93, OF 93C, and OF 4245G in the Roosevelt Papers.) Under Truman, David Niles was the adviser directly charged with racial and ethnic affairs, but Philleo Nash seems to have been the best informed and the most steady advocate in racial matters. (See the following papers at the Harry S. Truman Library: Truman papers, OF 93, Philleo Nash papers, Steven J. Spingarn papers, and the oral histories by Oscar L. Chapman and Spingarn.) Clark M. Clifford, Oscar R. Ewing, and others of the so-called liberal faction also had an important influence on civil rights matters, but their starting point was political. (See the Clifford and Oscar L. Chapman papers and the Ewing oral history at the Truman Library.)

[5] This group included a growing number of academic scholars, typified by the staff assembled by the Swede, Gunnar Myrdal, for his famous Carnegie study, *An American Dilemma* (New York, 1944), which contained a compendium of existing scholarship, and such scholar-activists as Carey McWilliams and Father John LaFarge. Black scholars like Charles S. Johnson and St. Clair Drake were also widely read and influential. Note also Sitkoff, *New Deal,* chap. 8.

[6] Almost all accounts of labor during the thirties ignore racial issues nearly completely or give a limited number of illustrations to show unions organizing across racial lines. For general accounts that give some discussion of labor beliefs on race, see Irving Howe and B. J. Widrick, *The U.A.W. and Walter Reuther* (New York, 1949); and Len DeCaux, *Labor Radical* (Boston, 1970). For a recent exception to the neglect of labor's role in civil rights and an argument that labor made important changes in the thirties, see Sitkoff, *New Deal,* chap. 7. For union practices from the perspective of black workers, see Horace R. Cayton and George S. Mitchell, *Black Workers and the New Unions* (Chapel Hill, North Carolina, 1939); Herbert R. Northrup, *Organized Labor and the Negro* (New York, 1944); and Ray Marshall, *The Negro Worker* (New York, 1967). The ADA papers show the vital role of organized labor in financing the ADA and, through that organization, in supporting civil rights activities. On the increasing concern of American churches with the issue of racism, see David M. Reimers, *White Protestantism and the Negro*

Civil Rights, 1940s

This study will concentrate on the independent liberals, who were the initial source of public debate on race among whites and who defined the basic terms of that debate; the study will also follow their interaction with the political liberals and the race relations experts.

To appreciate how the postwar white consciousness of race differed from its prewar counterpart, we need only recall the two previous reform eras of the twentieth century. Most progressives and New Deal reformers, save for a small minority of civil libertarians, shared the racism of their times. Theodore Roosevelt's Progressive Party, for example, refused to seat black delegates from the south at its 1912 convention, and Woodrow Wilson told "darky stories" to his cabinet and condoned increased segregation in government offices.[7] Two decades later, Franklin Roosevelt tried to ignore racial discrimination and only reluctantly made mild protests against lynching.[8] The liberals

---

(New York, 1965); John LaFarge, S.J., *The Race Question and the Negro: A Study of Catholic Doctrine on Interracial Justice* (New York, 1937, 1943); Andrew E. Murray, *Presbyterians and the Negro—A History* (Philadelphia, 1966); and Frank S. Loescher, "The Protestant Church and the Negro: Recent Pronouncements," *Social Forces*, December 1947, 197–201.

[7] See Neil A. Wynn, *The Afro-American and the Second World War* (New York, 1975), chap. 1; Thomas F. Gossett, *Race: The History of an Idea in America* (New York, 1963, 1965); Richard Hofstadter, *Social Darwinism in American Thought*, 2nd ed. (Boston, 1955); Rayford W. Logan, *The Negro in American Life and Thought: The Nadir, 1877-1901* (New York, 1954); I. A. Newby, *Jim Crow's Defense: Anti-Negro Thought in America, 1900-1930* (Baton Rouge, 1965); C. Vann Woodward, *Origins of the New South, 1877-1913* (Baton Rouge, 1951), and *The Strange Career of Jim Crow*, 2nd ed. (New York, 1966); Howard W. Allen, Aage R. Clausen, and Jerome M. Clubb, "Political Reform and Negro Rights in the Senate, 1909-1915," *Journal of Southern History* 27 (May 1971), 191–212; John Hope Franklin, *From Slavery to Freedom*, (New York, 1974), 432–527; Morton Sosna, "The South in the Saddle: Racial Politics during the Wilson Years," *Wisconsin Magazine of History* 54 (Autumn 1970): 30–49; Nancy J. Weiss, "The Negro and the New Freedom: Fighting Wilsonian Segregation," *Political Science Quarterly* 84 (March, 1969), 61–79; Dewey W. Grantham, Jr., "The Progressive Movement and the Negro," *South Atlantic Quarterly* 54 (October 1955), 461–77; William B. Hixson, Jr., *Moorfield Storey and the Abolitionist Tradition* (New York, 1972); Charles Flint Kellogg, *NAACP: A History of the National Association for the Advancement of Colored People*, vol. 1 (Baltimore, 1967); Gilbert Osofsky, "Progressivism and the Negro: New York, 1900-1915," *American Quarterly* 16 (Summer 1964): 153–68; David W. Southern, *The Malignant Heritage: Yankee Progressives and the Negro Question, 1901-1914* (Chicago, 1968); Nancy J. Weiss, "From Black Separatism to Interracial Cooperation: The Origins of Organized Efforts for Racial Advancement, 1890-1920," in *Twentieth-Century America: Recent Interpretations*, ed. Barton J. Bernstein and Allen J. Matusow, 2nd ed. (New York, 1972); and Sitkoff, *New Deal*, 190–210.

[8] See Frank Freidel, *F.D.R. and the South* (Baton Rouge, 1965), 71–102; Raymond Wolters, *Negroes and the Great Depression: The Problem of Economic Recovery* (Westport, Conn., 1970); Leslie H. Fishel, Jr., "The Negro in the New Deal," *Wisconsin Magazine of History* 47 (Winter 1964–65): 111–21; John B. Kirby, "The Roosevelt Administration and Blacks: An Ambivalent Legacy," in *Twentieth-Century America*, ed. Bernstein and

and leftists of the thirties emphasized class unity and made significant steps forward in including black people in some government programs and in the new unions, most dramatically the CIO and the Southern Tenant Farmer's Union.[9] However, for the sake of preserving class unity and protecting economic reforms in Congress, they tended to oppose civil rights measures other than antilynching and anti-poll tax legislation, which benefited labor organizers and poor whites as well as blacks.[10] The reform tradition, at the end of the thirties, showed little sign of mounting a major assault on segregation, but it had begun to raise the crucial issue of the inclusion of black Americans among those who could benefit from greater economic and social justice and to define social justice for all Americans as the prime liberal goal.

This lack of concern for civil rights measures contrasts sharply with the passions aroused over racial questions during the Truman years. By the end of the forties, several states and municipalities had passed civil rights laws and literally hundreds of interracial committees had been formed.[11] President Truman himself endorsed a comprehensive civil rights program, ended segregation in the military, and allowed himself to be put in the position of staking his reelection on a strong civil rights plank in the party platform. These events illustrate the rapid change in white attitudes during the 1940s. It was during that decade that civil rights for black people became a national issue for the first time since the abortive efforts of the reconstruction period, and it was during that decade that white America worked out basic notions about racism that shaped public response to subsequent developments.

This sudden shift in predominant white attitudes about race can be illustrated readily by the contrast in white attitudes to two dramatic events. In the spring of 1941, A. Philip Randolph rallied a large number of black Americans behind his all-Negro March on Washington Movement to demand an executive order against discrimination in defense hiring. The president, Mrs. Roosevelt, Mayor LaGuardia, and

---

Matusow; and Peter J. Kellogg, "Northern Liberals and Black America: A History of White Attitudes, 1936–1952" (Ph.D. diss., Northwestern University, 1971).

[9]On labor unions, see the works cited in note 6 and David Conrad, *The Forgotten Farmer: The Story of Share Croppers and the New Deal* (Urbana, Ill., 1965); editorial, "A Program for Farm Tenancy," *Nation*, 6 March 1937, 257; editorial, "Three Years of Roosevelt," *Nation*, 11 March 1936, 300–301; Donald H. Grubbs, *Cry From The Cotton: The Southern Tenant Farmers' Union and The New Deal* (Chapel Hill, North Carolina, 1971); and Howard Kester, *Revolt Among the Sharecroppers* (New York, 1936).

[10]See Kellogg, *Northern Liberals*, 1–84.

[11]See the material on the American Council on Race Relations in the Philleo Nash Papers at the Harry S. Truman Library (hereafter cited as HSTL); the California Federation for Civic Unity Papers in the Bancroft Library; the Humphrey Papers in the Minnesota Historical Society (hereafter cited as MHS); Leon H. Mayhew, *Law and Equal Opportunity* (Cambridge, Mass., 1968); and Paul H. Norgren and Samuel E. Hill, *Toward Fair Employment* (New York, 1964).

Civil Rights, 1940s

other liberals urged him to call off the march.[12] Only the bold persistence of Randolph and other black leaders persuaded F.D.R. to issue his famous Executive Order 8802 in June of 1941. Most white liberals either ignored or opposed Randolph's efforts until some time after Roosevelt issued the order.[13] Seven years later, however, at the Democratic convention of 1948, liberal determination to write a strong civil rights plank into the platform split the party.[14] The convention marked the first time in the twentieth century that civil rights had been a major political issue, engaging large numbers of whites in a serious political struggle. Thus, two diametrically opposed responses to a civil rights issue came from the white liberal community within seven years.

The widespread interest of white liberals in civil rights reform during the forties was a sharp and important departure from earlier attitudes and was brought about by something more complex than a steadily growing appreciation for the moral requirements of democratic ideals. The basic question is why liberal whites, after ignoring the status of black Americans for decades, suddenly made civil rights a major issue—a virtual touchstone for assessing the moral health of the democracy. Gunnar Myrdal's challenge to face the "American dilemma," widely regarded at the time as simply stating the obvious, was certainly not the cause. Partisan political needs and public fears of racial violence clearly influenced thought about race during the forties, while it was the whites' shocked reaction to Nazi racism which gave the issue its moral force and definition.

The political motive is the first one to examine in following the growth of a liberal interest in civil rights. By the end of the war, the political situation was extremely uncertain. The New Deal had been set

---

[12]See F.D.R. to MAC (probably Marvin H. McIntyre), 7 June 1941, OF 93, Franklin D. Roosevelt Papers, Franklin D. Roosevelt Library (hereafter cited as FDRL); file summary of memorandum to Wayne Coy, Office for Emergency Management, 6 June 1941, OF 93, Franklin D. Roosevelt Papers, FDRL; file summary of memorandum from the President to General Watson, 14 June 1941, OF 93, Franklin D. Roosevelt Papers, FDRL; three drafts of letter, Eleanor Roosevelt to A. Philip Randolph, 10 June 1941, Eleanor Roosevelt Papers, FDRL; A. Philip Randolph to Mrs. Roosevelt, 23 June 1941, Eleanor Roosevelt Papers, FDRL; and Jervis Anderson, "Profiles: Early Voice: III—The March," *New Yorker*, 16 December 1972, 40–85; Herbert Garfinkel, *When Negroes March: The March on Washington Movement in the Organizational Politics for FEPC* (Glencoe, Ill., 1959); and Lee Finkle, "The Conservative Aims of Militant Rhetoric: Black Protest during World War II," *Journal of American History* 60 (December 1973): 692–713.

[13]See Kellogg, *Northern Liberals*, 126–27; and the Union for Democratic Action Papers, Wisconsin Historical Society (hereafter cited as WHS). The UDA was not organized in time to be active in supporting the March on Washington Movement's drive for the executive order, but A. Philip Randolph was a founder of the UDA, which did launch a brief campaign against discrimination in defense industries later in 1941 though the efforts had little impact and were not continued for long.

[14]See below, 36–39.

aside during the conflict, and the Republicans had gained strength steadily until their narrow defeat in 1948, which was considered the greatest political upset in our history. The election of 1946 had already produced a Republican Congress, while southern Democrats and northern Republicans had been a powerful center of opposition since the late thirties. The death of Roosevelt in the final days of the war had left the Democrats without the personage that had held them together and led them to victory in four presidential elections. By 1948, the liberals' desperation had become so acute as to lead to the fiasco of their efforts to nominate Dwight Eisenhower as a supposed liberal Democrat.[15] In the context of this intense political climate, the black vote became important for two reasons. First, wartime migrations, continuing a trend that had begun in force in 1915, had significantly increased the black vote in the North, where there was no systematic denial of the franchise. Furthermore, the new black voters were concentrated in the large urban centers of key electoral states, where the vote was often close and the outcome crucial in presidential contests. Second, the black vote had itself become unaligned. After decades of loyalty to the party of Lincoln, black voters had turned to the Democrats in 1936. Although the black vote is often assumed to have been solidly Democratic ever since, it began to return to the Republicans in the forties. In order to secure that vote, the Republicans made serious efforts, including the inclusion in their 1944 platform of a civil rights plank that was stronger than the Democrats' and also Governor Dewey's support for New York State's pioneering FEPC legislation in 1945.[16] The Democrats had come to consider black voters a significant part of the New Deal coalition, and they had reason to feel a need to reinforce the loyalty of these new coalition members. Clearly, by 1948, many Democrats were fearful that the black vote would go to the Republicans.[17] Thus, during the forties, both major parties were actively competing for the black vote.

[15]There is considerable material on the campaign, which was serious, sustained, and organized, in the ADA papers. See also Alonzo L. Hamby, *Beyond the New Deal: Harry S. Truman and American Liberalism* (New York, 1973), chap. 10.

[16]See "U.D.A. Congressional Newsletter," for 1 March, 15 April, 1 July, and 1 August 1944, UDA Papers, WHS; Henry Lee Moon, *Balance of Power: The Negro Vote* (Garden City, New York, 1948); and Sitkoff, *New Deal*, chap. 4.

[17]See Milton D. Stewart to (George M.) Elsey, 19 January 1948, George M. Elsey Papers, HSTL; William L. Batt, Jr., to Philleo Nash, 8 June 1948, Philleo Nash Papers, HSTL; unsigned, undated memorandum, "Thoughts on the Republican Platform," Philleo Nash Papers, HSTL; unsigned memorandum, "A Minimum Civil Rights Program for the Eightieth Congress," 8 January 1948, Hersel Plaine folder, Philleo Nash Papers, HSTL; memorandum for Clark Clifford, unsigned and undated, George M. Elsey Papers, HSTL; Clark M. Clifford to the President, 19 November 1947, Clark M. Clifford Papers, HSTL; Moon, *Balance of Power*; and Hamby, *Beyond the New Deal*, chap. 10.

Civil Rights, 1940s

Ironically, the left, which had long, if erratically, championed racial equality, had little direct influence in creating or shaping the new consciousness of racism. Actively involved in raising racial questions during the thirties, the left downplayed race during the war lest it should prove a divisive issue that would hamper the war effort.[18] When the left had advocated racial equality in the thirties, liberals and the rest of white America had shown little response.[19] Only the CIO had made discrimination an important element in its program, partially influenced by the left but largely for the sake of labor unity and the practical necessity of avoiding strikebreaking by nonunion racial groups.[20] At the height of the left's campaign for equality during the thirties, most liberals had virtually ignored the issue or urged that it not be allowed to interfere with other goals. In the forties, when liberals began to define racism as an issue, their conception was far different from that of the left. Instead of seeing racial oppression as one extreme instance of class oppression, they saw it simply as a test of white morality, a matter of individual conscience rather than of social structure. The nature of their understanding did not stem from the left but from their own interpretation of the racial issues that emerged in the struggle against Nazi racism.[21]

After the war, the Progressive Party through Henry Wallace's 1948 presidential campaign made a much-noted attack on segregation. The Wallace campaign drew public attention to discrimination in the South during the same year that civil rights became an issue in national politics for the first time in the twentieth century, but it was not Wallace who created the issue. Liberals worried about Wallace, but they responded to him in other ways than by trying to match him on civil rights. Instead, they tried to discredit him and his followers as Communist-dominated and attacked his foreign policy stands.[22] Liberals had developed their ideas on civil rights before Wallace raised the issue,

---

[18]See Wilson Record, *Race and Radicalism: The NAACP and the Communist Party in Conflict* (Ithaca, N.Y., 1964), 81–131; *idem*, *The Negro and the Communist Party* (Chapel Hill, North Carolina, 1951), 183–86; Irving Howe and B.J. Widick, *The U.A.W. and Walter Reuther* (New York, 1949), 233; and Thomas A. Krueger, *And Promises to Keep: The Southern Conference for Human Welfare, 1938–1948* (Nashville, 1967), 57–99.

[19]Kellogg, *Northern Liberals*, 1–123; Hamby, *Beyond the New Deal*, 232–33, 243–51. But compare Sitkoff, *New Deal*, chap. 6.

[20]See Len DeCaux, *Labor Radical* (Boston, 1970), 172–74, 240; Herbert R. Northrup, *Organized Labor and the Negro* (New York, 1944), 14–15, 233–37; Ray Marshall, *The Negro Worker* (New York, 1967), 23–27; Max D. Danish, *The World of David Dubinsky* (Cleveland, 1957), 81, 153–54; and Sitkoff, *New Deal*, chap. 7.

[21]See below, 30–36.

[22]See Chester Bowles to Leon (Henderson), 5 March 1948; "Statement on Political Policy," adopted by the ADA National Board, 11 April 1948; a series of lengthy ADA Wallace memoranda which were updated periodically throughout the campaign, all in the ADA Papers, WHS; and Hamby, *Beyond the New Deal*, chaps. 8, 9, and 10.

The Historian

and, as will be argued below, they emphasized civil rights in 1948 for reasons related to the internal politics of the Democratic Party, and to thwart Republican appeals to black voters, but not in response to Wallace.[23] Thus liberal concern for civil rights predated the left's efforts of 1948 and represented an attempt to attack the southern Democrats, not to compete with the Progressives.

President Truman and his supporters gave an unprecedented amount of attention to civil rights and black voters during 1948, but they too were concerned more with competition from the Republicans than from the Progressives. Clark Clifford had laid down the outline of campaign strategy in his now famous memorandum of November 1947. He included detailed analyses of Wallace and the third party and of the black vote. The discussion of Wallace focused on foreign policy and Communist ties and did not mention the black vote, which was discussed entirely in terms of whether it would swing to the Republicans. Warning was given of "the assiduous and continuous cultivation of the New York Negro vote by Governor Dewey."[24] Clifford concluded his treatment of the black vote with a strong plea for action to prevent that vote from going Republican, but never mentioned the Progressives. "Unless there are new and real efforts (as distinguished from mere political gestures which are today thoroughly understood and strongly resented by sophisticated Negro leaders), the Negro bloc, which, certainly in Illinois and probably in New York and Ohio, *does* hold the balance of power, will go Republican."[25] Thus neither during the war nor in the turmoil of the 1948 campaign was reaction to the left a direct cause of the liberals' new attention to race.

In addition to political concerns, many white Americans also felt a need to deal with problems of race because they both feared and abhorred racial violence. There had been terrible outbreaks during the war, including repeated incidents of white brutality to black soldiers around southern military camps and the terrifying three-day riot of 1943. These and other disturbing evidences of racial unrest—combined with the historical memory of the red summer of 1919, when race riots had swept twenty-five American cities in the period of "adjustment" following World War I—produced fears of a new postwar wave of violence.[26] Many facts suggested that the nightmare of 1919

---

[23]See below, 36–39.

[24]Clark M. Clifford, "Memorandum for the President," 19 November 1947, 11, Clark M. Clifford Papers, HSTL. See also Allen Yarnell, *Democrats and Progressives: The 1948 Presidential Campaign as a Test of Postwar Liberalism* (Berkeley, 1974), ix, 52, 71–80; and Hamby, *Beyond the New Deal*, 243–51.

[25]Clifford, "Memorandum for the President," 12–13.

[26]See OF 4245G and OF 93C, Franklin D. Roosevelt Papers, FDRL: Philleo Nash Papers, HSTL; Malcolm Cowley, "Journey in the Slave States," *New Republic*, 12 October 1942, 470–71; editorial, "Race Riot," *New Republic*, 28 June 1943, 845; Clark Foreman,

Civil Rights, 1940s

might recur: housing and recreational facilities were crowded, returning black veterans were determined to assert their newly vindicated dignity publicly, and severe competition for jobs was expected.[27] These anxieties helped stimulate a nation-wide burst of activity. Led by the Rosenwald-funded American Council on Race Relations, hundreds of interracial committees mushroomed from New York to California during the final years of the war and the immediate postwar period.[28] The committees were liberal in orientation and often sponsored progressive reforms, with occasional success at the state and municipal levels, but their main emphasis was on working with police departments and trying to avoid the kinds of incident which could provoke racial violence. Not only were there literally hundreds of these local, interracial committees but the appointment of municipal and state agencies on race relations prompted the formation of a national professional organization of their staff members, the National Association of Intergroup Relations Officials.[29] The federal government maintained a nationwide network of observers to watch for trouble spots.[30] For a period, many informed persons felt a sense of great urgency about the prospects for a serious wave of racial violence, and they advised serious measures to avert it.

Harry Truman seems to have responded both to the partisan political interest in black votes and to the fears of racial violence. The famous Clark Clifford planning memorandum for the 1948 election stressed a liberal strategy and presented the black vote as one of the keys to the election.[31] Black groups had themselves been pressing Truman steadily, especially the shrewd, active NAACP and the aggressive A. Philip Randolph. Walter White of the NAACP apparently kept up enough contacts with prominent Republicans to provide a subtle but unmistakable threat of black political independence.[32] On Septem-

---

"Race Tension in the South," *New Republic*, 21 September 1942, 340–42; and Howard W. Odum, *Race and Rumors of Race* (Chapel Hill, North Carolina, 1943).

[27] See the Philleo Nash Papers, HSTL.

[28] See material cited above, note 11.

[29] There is scattered material on the formation and work of the National Association of Intergroup Relations Officials, another project of the Rosenwald Foundation, in the Philleo Nash Papers, HSTL.

[30] See OF 4245G, Franklin D. Roosevelt Papers, FDRL; and Philleo Nash Papers, HSTL.

[31] Memorandum, Clark M. Clifford to the President, 19 November 1947, Clark M. Clifford Papers, HSTL.

[32] *Ibid.*, section 4(d). See also William L. Batt, Jr., to Gael Sullivan, 20 April 1948, and William L. Batt, Jr., to Clark Clifford, 11 August 1948, Clark M. Clifford Papers, HSTL; Steven J. Spingarn to Walter White, 11 October 1940, Stephen J. Spingarn Papers, HSTL; and Joseph Lawrence to J. Howard McGrath, 18 May 1948, J. Howard McGrath Papers, HSTL.

ber 19, 1946, White and a group of prominent black leaders met with Truman to describe some of the recent incidents of violent white brutality against black people and to plead for federal action. The next day Truman wrote Attorney General Tom Clark instructing him to begin setting up what became the President's Committee on Civil Rights. The memorandum made an emotional reference to violence and lynching, concerns Truman was to cite repeatedly in later years as his motive for establishing the committee, in contrast to the political motives frequently attributed to him.[33]

Truman's instructions to the committee, as well as the context of its establishment, stressed the specific issue of providing protection for black people against white violence.[34] The committee, however, interpreted its instructions broadly, seeing violence as the result of a national pattern of discrimination and focusing its attention on that.[35] Truman may not have foreseen this extension of the committee's investigation, though he had appointed a committee of liberals, a majority belonging to the ADA; still, he endorsed the committee's wide-ranging conclusions and urged Congress to enact virtually all its recommendations.[36] He may well have been trapped by events; having appointed the committee and needing the black vote, it would have been difficult for him to reject its well-documented recommendations. Whatever Truman's personal beliefs and motives however, his presidential endorsement of the committee's report encompassed almost every civil rights reform to be enacted in the sixties.

---

[33] See Channing H. Tobias et al. to Harry S. Truman, 19 September 1946; The President to David K. Niles, 20 September 1946; and Harry S. Truman to Tom C. Clark, 20 September 1946, all in President's Secretary's Files, HSTL; Walter White in "The University of Chicago Round Table," 23 November 1947, 1-3, Philleo Nash Papers, HSTL; Harry S. Truman, address, 11 October 1952, Philleo Nash Files, HSTL; and Transcript, Stephen J. Spingarn Oral History Interview, April 1972, 573-77, HSTL.

[34] See "Statement by the President," 5 December 1946, Philleo Nash Papers, HSTL; minutes of the President's Committee on Civil Rights, 523, President's Committee on Civil Rights Records, HSTL; memorandum, "President's Conference with ADA Leaders-May 21, 1951," 4, David D. Lloyd Papers, HSTL; and Laurence C. Eklund, "Nash, Wisconsin Man, Real Help to Truman," *Milwaukee Journal*, 5 December 1948, Philleo Nash Papers, HSTL.

[35] See the minutes of the President's Committee on Civil Rights, especially pp. 118-19, President's Committee on Civil Rights Records, HSTL.

[36] See the committee's report, *To Secure these Rights: The Report of the President's Committee on Civil Rights* (New York, 1947); the President's message, "Civil Rights Program," 80th Congress, 2nd Session, House of Representatives Document No. 516, 2 February 1948; "Memorandum for Clark Clifford," 29 January 1948, George Elsey Papers, HSTL; Transcript, Stephen J. Spingarn Oral History Interview, April 1972, 317-18, HSTL; the material in the Clifford and Spingarn papers on drafting and attempting to secure passage of civil rights bills; Channing H. Tobias, "President Truman's Message on Civil Rights," 11 February 1948, Philleo Nash Files, HSTL.

Civil Rights, 1940s

Except in parts of the South, the report and Truman's civil rights message were generally well received.[37] Although Congress was not yet ready to override a filibuster in order to enact civil rights legislation, there seemed to be a wide, if far from universal, consensus that something should be done about racism, and Truman eventually did order desegregation of the armed forces, after strong pressure from A. Philip Randolph, Grant Reynolds, and others which coincided with political developments.[38] It took almost two years of struggle to overcome the army's resistance, but Truman finally accomplished the only really significant civil rights reform between Reconstruction and the sixties.[39] Another expression of the new awareness of civil rights was the platform fight in the 1948 Democratic Convention. The fight and the strong civil rights plank prompted the Dixiecrat walkout, yet Truman won the election despite the party's divisions. Civil rights seemed a viable political issue. All these events—Truman's appointment of the committee, its presentation of a wide range of reform proposals, Truman's endorsement of the report, the Democrats' adoption of a strong civil rights plank and their victory in the election despite Dixiecrat opposition, the desegregation of the military, and the significant popular support for these measures—all show a sharp change in the public climate with respect to race.

This new receptivity to civil rights reform was not inevitable, however, and it represented more than political vote-getting or fear of violence. Political needs and the problem of violence might have been met by the more traditional responses of patronage, symbolic appointments, and economic benefits, which were the means used to deal with black voters under the New Deal and by Truman himself in Missouri.[40] Opposition to racial violence, after all, had not ever been necessarily linked with civil rights reform. The Association of Southern Women for the Prevention of Lynching, for example, had carried on a long crusade during the twenties and thirties without challenging the

---

[37]See "Public Interest in the President's Civil Rights Report," Philleo Nash Files, HSTL; and American Council on Race Relations Releases, Nos. 34, 35, 38, and 39, Philleo Nash Papers, HSTL.

[38]See the correspondence during 1948 involving Truman, A. Philip Randolph, Grant Reynolds, Clark Clifford, and David Niles in OF 93, Harry S. Truman Papers, HSTL; and Transcript, E. W. Kenworthy Oral History Interview, 26 January 1971, 15–17, HSTL.

[39]See the material cited in note 38; the Clark M. Clifford Papers, HSTL; Charles Fahy Papers, HSTL; President's Committee on Equality of Treatment and Opportunity in the Armed Services: Records, HSTL; OF 1285 O, Harry S. Truman Papers, HSTL; and Richard M. Dalfiume, *Desegregation of the U.S. Armed Forces: Fighting on Two Fronts 1939–1953* (Columbia, Mo., 1969).

[40]See Harry S. Truman, Papers as Senator and Vice President, HSTL; and Harold Emery Barto, "Clark Clifford and the Presidential Election of 1948" (Ph.D. diss., Rutgers University, 1970), 131, 134, 135, 222, 223.

South's semicaste system.[41] Even in the forties, much of the work of the American Council on Race Relations had stressed opening communications and upgrading police work as preventive measures against violence, and these actions did not in themselves imply greater rights for black people. Conceivably, even more rigid segregation could have been attempted, perhaps combined with face-saving concessions like more housing and recreational facilities, as a way of limiting racial violence. Indeed, a Justice Department report following the Detroit riot of 1943 recommended just such a course when it called for increased housing and recreational facilities for black people and a limitation on black migration.[42] The latter was clearly unconstitutional and was not attempted, but the report shows the range of possibilities considered. Perhaps Chicago under Richard J. Daley represents a strategy that might have been more widely followed: patronage and limited social service benefits were used to secure the black vote while racial fears kept the white ethnic vote in line, and Chicago remained the nation's most segregated city. Such strategy was, in fact, close to the practice if not the intent of the New Deal, which offered significant economic gains but made only occasional efforts to limit segregation; it was also consistent with the national policy of the fifties; surely it must have seemed within the realm of political possibility for the national Democratic Party in the forties.

But it was not such a course that was followed. Instead, the nation moved toward the alternative of reform, and liberal politicians and publicists advocated a broad program of civil rights measures which would hardly have been put forth seriously in the thirties. What happened was clearly more than another variation of traditional ethnic politics to gain votes and clearly more than a sophisticated effort to control racial violence. Although both these needs contributed to support for civil rights reforms, they could have been met by more modest proposals and certainly did not, in themselves, evoke the moral passion and psychological intensity that came to be associated with civil rights.

The distinguishing aspect of civil rights reform, as most whites came to perceive it, was that it focused on white racism and thus became a test of the moral integrity of white America. Older images of manifest destiny and the white man's burden, promoting a paternalistic tutoring or gross exploitation of nonwhite peoples, lost their

---

[41]Wilma Dykeman and James Stokely, *Seeds of Southern Change: The Life of Will Alexander* (Chicago, 1962).

[42]On the proposal for limiting black migration, see Francis Biddle to the President, 15 July 1943, OF 4245G, Franklin D. Roosevelt Papers, FDRL; on other proposals for a repressive response, see the unsigned, undated 28-page "Report on Negro Morale" in the Philleo Nash Papers, HSTL; and Victor N. Rotnem, "Memorandum for the Attorney General," 9 August 1943, Eleanor Bontecou Papers, HSTL.

Civil Rights, 1940s

power to convince in the light of the brutal racism of the Nazis. In the context of Hitler's horrors, notions of racial superiority lost their connotations of benevolence or biological inevitability.[43] Racism now seemed an unmitigated evil, and when white observers began to compare Nazi racism with American white supremacy, they reacted with consternation. "What good is it to defend democracy against attacks from without when we allow the basic principles of democracy to be violated right here in our own country?" Representative Samuel Dickstein of New York asked the House in 1941.[44] And Frances V. Rummell said in *Common Sense*, "The world crisis, forcing upon our country the urgency of making our democracy more vital and dynamic, has also forced upon us the realization that one of our greatest limitations to that end is our own minority problems."[45] The *New Republic* warned that by tolerating racial discrimination "we are making a mockery of the theory that we are fighting for democracy, and we are giving aid and comfort to the enemy thereby."[46] A most forceful statement of this new anxiety came in a *Nation* editorial deploring the concept of a "second-class American—a phrase which white and colored alike ought to reject as a blasphemous contradiction in terms. Until Americans do so we have no right to say complacently 'We are not as these *Herrenovolk.*' "[47] Here was a heavy burden for the conscience of white America: Did not racism make white Americans *Herrenvolk* rather than democrats? Racism was now—suddenly, for the most part—seen to call into question the basic moral values and integrity of the nation, as well as of individual whites. Arthur Schlesinger, Jr., in his postwar liberal testament, *The Vital Center*, reflected the persisting attitude: "The sin of racial pride still represents the most basic challenge to the American conscience. We cannot dodge this challenge without renouncing our highest moral principles."[48]

The many liberals who had begun to see Americans, including themselves, in a new light also began to realize that others might see the same thing and that racism made America vulnerable to enemy

---

[43]For traditional racial attitudes, see materials cited above in note 7 and George M. Fredrickson, *The Black Image in the White Mind: The Debate on Afro-American Character and Destiny, 1817–1914* (New York, 1971).

[44]*Congressional Record*, 77th Congress, 1st Session, 21 May 1941, 4319. See also editorial, "Warning—Harding Ahead," *Common Sense*, January 1943, 450–51.

[45]"Negroes in '40: Their Problems Are Democracy's Problems," *Common Sense*, November 1940, 14–15.

[46]Editorial, "Back to Jim Crow," *New Republic*, 16 Feburary 1942, 221. See also editorial, "The Unprivileged One-Tenth," *New Republic*, 19 May 1941, 681; editorial, "The Home Fires Too," *New Republic*, 17 November 1941, 636–38; and editorial, *New Republic*, 4 March 1941, 389–90.

[47]Editorial, "Defeat at Detroit," *Nation*, 3 July 1943, 4.

[48]Arthur Schlesinger, Jr., *The Vital Center* (Boston, 1949), 190.

The Historian

propaganda and to loss of support in the nonwhite world at home and abroad. In 1942, white violence aimed at blocking black people from a Detroit housing project worried the editors of the *New Republic:* "We recognize the difficulties in race relations, some of them economic, but even so, the whites who tried to prevent Negroes from occupying property to which they were legally entitled were assuredly doing Hitler's work. We don't doubt that the story of that riot was told all over Asia, with Nazi trimmings, within twenty-four hours."[49] The *Nation* carried a warning that "we must have cleaner hands if we hope to convince the people of occupied Asia that they have something to gain by a United States victory."[50] Representative Martin L. Sweeney of Ohio observed, "It will not do to try to recommend our four freedoms to the world if we do not practice democracy at home. I hesitate to say what the morale of the colored boy in the Army will be when he contemplates the fact that his brother, his father, and his sister back home cannot receive Army work in the defense industries because of their color."[51] Concerned also that "propaganda must not be a lie," the editors of *Common Sense* acknowledged, "We have made little effort to wipe out the shame of our treatment of the Negro as a step towards the defeat of those who treat the Jews the same way."[52]

In particular, violence was feared as the ultimate symbol of American racism, as well as for its direct effects on the social fabric. "Three recent lynchings in Mississippi have served the Axis cause more brilliantly than could a squad of saboteurs landed from a submarine," wrote the editors of the *New Republic* in 1942.[53] A wartime riot near a military camp in Louisiana prompted the editors of *Common Sense* to observe that blacks were not wholeheartedly behind the war effort and

---

[49]Editorial, "Race Riot," *New Republic,* 9 March 1942, 317.

[50]Selden C. Menefee, "Japan's Racial War," *Nation,* 6 February 1943, 203.

[51]*Congressional Record,* 77th Congress, 1st Session, Appendix, 9 July 1941, A3314.

[52]Editorial, "Propaganda and the War," *Common Sense,* February 1942, 55. See also editorial, "The Home Fires Too," *New Republic,* 17 November 1941, 638–39; editorial, "Negro-White Relations," *New Republic,* 7 September 1942, 268; editorial, "The Unprivileged One-Tenth," *New Republic,* 19 May 1941, 681; editorial, *Nation,* 14 August 1943, 170; E. Franklin Frazier, "Brazil Has No Race Problem," *Common Sense,* November 1942, 363–65; editorial, "Signs of Hope," *Common Sense,* November 1942; Adam Clayton Powell, Jr., "Is This a 'White Man's War'?: A Negro Leader Shows the Connection between the Battle of East Asia and Race Discrimination," *Common Sense,* April 1942, 111–13; Alfred Baker Lewis, "Racism at Home," *Common Sense,* June 1942, 194–45. Moved by conscience and an old involvement as well as other war needs, the editors of *Survey Graphic* devoted the entire issue of November 1942 to the theme "Color: Unfinished Business of Democracy." The issue, edited by Alain Locke, contained articles by a number of prominent black scholars and activists and proved very popular. See Chambers, *Paul U. Kellogg,* 179–82.

[53]Editorial, *New Republic,* 2 November 1942, 560–61.

32

Civil Rights, 1940s

to argue, "It is not Hitler's fault that they are not. It is our fault."[54] Malcolm Cowley feared "another crisis as bad in its own fashion as the Civil War."[55] The *Nation* warned of the dangers of violence and pointed to the dilemma of America's commitment to a racial caste system while racism was now considered incompatible with democracy:

> In Mobile, Los Angeles, Beaumont, and Detroit, Americans infected with the spirit of fascism have attacked our fighting forces in the rear, damaging production and, what is far worse, shattering democratic morale. A succession of Detroits could conceivably mean the loss of the war; it would certainly mean the loss of the peace.
>
> It is time for us to clear our minds and hearts of the contradictions that are rotting our moral position and undermining our purpose. We cannot fight fascism abroad while turning a blind eye to fascism at home. We cannot inscribe our banners "For democracy and a caste system."[56]

It is essential to consider carefully just what these white liberals saw and what they didn't see when they began to note the issue of race in America. First of all, advocacy of white supremacy, reminiscent of Nazism, had clearly lost intellectual and moral respectability. "We cannot fight fascism abroad while turning a blind eye to fascism at home."[57] Again and again, when white Americans looked at American rasicm they saw a Nazi image, and racism was now stigmatized. Second, they saw a problem of morality, of white expression of Nazi values and failure to live up to professed democratic ideals. Racism was abhorred because it showed the racist to be immoral. The moral state of white America was therefore at stake. The intense focus on the moral state of whites emphasizes a third quality of the emerging notions of race, namely, that concern was not with black people but with white people. Virtually no attention was given to the conditions of life or needs of black America. Save for the ongoing Myrdal study and the work of some black and white American scholars, there was little investigation of the accumulated consequences of racism for the black population and almost no public discussion of the needs of black America.[58] White attitudes were the problem, and it was to white actions that liberals looked to solve the problem. Finally, these new perceptions of race in

---

[54]Editorial, "Racism at Home," *Common Sense*, February 1942, 57.

[55]"Journey in the Slave States," *New Republic*, 12 October 1942, 470. See also Elmer Anderson Carter, "Shadows of the Slave Tradition," *Survey Graphic*, November 1942, 466; editorial, "Race Riot," *New Republic*, 28 June 1943, 845; *Congressional Record*, 77th Congress, 1st Session, 16 June 1941, 5195, and Appendix, 19 December 1941, A5658; and *Congressional Record*, 78th Congress, 1st Session, Appendix, 12 April 1943, A1793.

[56]Editorial, "Defeat at Detroit," *Nation*, 3 July 1943, 4.

[57]*Ibid.*

[58]Gunnar Myrdal, *An American Dilemma* (New York, 1944).

33

the minds of independent liberals and some politicians were not related to traditional competition for ethnic votes but transcended politics as a test of the basic morality of the nation. The declared problem at this juncture was not one of winning black voters but of vindicating the democratic principles of white America, of showing that America was not racist like Nazi Germany.

Thus, during the war years, for the first time in the twentieth century, enough white Americans were beginning to perceive racism as a contradiction of democratic principles to make it a morally compelling national issue. But there was no clear understanding of how to resolve this newly acknowledged problem, and the early forties saw a great deal of groping for an answer. The establishment of racial justice did not seem to be a practical possibility and was almost always dismissed out of hand. As one writer in the *Nation* pointed out in 1943, "It is obvious that the white majority is not yet ready to abandon the disastrous policy of segregation."[59] Accepting the essentials of the status quo as unchanging, liberals met the concrete problem of racial violence, and the powerful symbol of racial injustice it provided, by urging continued black endurance. Mrs. Roosevelt, regarded as a firm supporter of black rights, wrote in the *New Republic,* "It seems trite to say to the Negro, you must have patience, when he has had patience so long.... Nevertheless, that is what we must continue to say in the interests of our government as a whole and of the Negro people."[60] Others urged whites as well as blacks to avoid any racial conflicts for the sake of the war effort: "Southern housewives who sit around passing on riot rumors and talking against Negroes, because their own servants are showing some economic independence, are feeding the fires just as dangerously—and in infinitely greater number—as are Negro leaders who demand the impossible overnight abolition of Jim Crow."[61] One author seemed unaware of his own irony when he warned blacks of the dire results of a Nazi victory, describing a situation already existing in much of the South: "Under a system in which [blacks] could not exercise the ballot, they would lose every vestige of human rights."[62] But the dominant response was perplexity. The editors of the *New Republic* admitted their confusion by calling for a new study to determine what kinds of action should be taken: "What we should at once initiate is a National Commission of Racial Relations,

---

[59]Margaret Marshall, "Some Notes on Harlem," *Nation,* 21 August 1943, 200-202.

[60]Eleanor Roosevelt, "Race, Religion and Prejudice," *New Republic,* 11 May 1942, 630.

[61]Thomas Sancton, "Trouble in Dixie: The Returning Tragic Era," *New Republic,* 4 January 1943, 11-14.

[62]Metz T.P. Lochard, "Negroes and Defense," *Nation,* 4 January 1941, 14-16. See also *Congressional Record,* 78th Congress, 1st Session, 22 April 1943, 3690; and Hans Habe, "The Nazi Plan for Negroes," *Nation,* 1 March 1941, 232-35.

with the breadth and competence to lay the issues bare and recommend remedial action. Racial hostilities may easily turn out to be the Achilles' heel of one of the strongest nations in the world."[63]

Smarting with wounded consciences, fearing serious violence, and unable to suggest a course of action, independent liberals began to search for ways to proclaim the democratic principles that they assumed (without very active testing of the fact) they were powerless to implement. Writing in 1942, Princeton professor Hadley Cantril, an expert on propaganda, pointed to a solution for their moral problem: "We do have racial injustices, we do have slums, we do have instances of labor's exploitation, we do have a very unequal system for distributing the rewards of men's productive capacities. But—and this is the point to stress—these are not our ideals."[64] One method of reaffirming democratic principles could be symbolic gestures supporting democratic values or rejecting racism. For example, many urged relief for a black sharecropper, Odell Waller, whom an all-white Virginia jury had condemned to death for killing his white landlord in a dispute. The *New Republic* lamented that Waller was not spared as a gesture indicating support of democratic ideals: "No one act alone will ever inspire 13,000,000 people to this patriotic fervor. But a new trial or a commutation of sentence for Waller, who had become a symbol, would have given them an incalculable lift of spirit, just as his execution had left a feeling of wordless bitterness."[65] Similarly, a 1942 Senate filibuster against an anti-poll tax bill was seen as telling "13,000,000 Negro citizens, to whom the poll tax is a symbol of oppression, that the symbol will remain."[66]

With great candor, Representative George H. Bender of Ohio acknowledged that such measures as the repeal of the poll tax would be of little aid to black people: "Negroes will continue to be disfranchised in the South because of arbitrary, unconstitutional registration laws. . . . This measure will in the main give the ballot to the poor white man of the South." Yet Bender still urged repeal as a symbol to the nonwhite world of America's democratic values: "We cannot say to millions in India, in China, in South America, or in our own Nation that we fight for a free democratic world unless here at home we do the deeds of democracy."[67] But he had just admitted

---

[63] Editorial, "Race Riot," *New Republic*, 28 June 1943, 845.

[64] "Propaganda for Victory," *New Republic*, 23 February 1942, 261. See also *Congressional Record*, 77th Congress, 1st Session, Appendix.

[65] Thomas Sancton, "The Waller Case," *New Republic*, 13 July 1942, 45–47.

[66] Editorial, *New Republic*, 30 November 1942, 696. See also *Congressional Record*, 77th Congress, 2nd Session, 12 October 1942, 8068, 8070–8081, and 13 October 1942, 8171–8173; 78th Congress, 1st Session, 25 May 1943, 4849, 5 July 1943, 7167, and Appendix, A1793; and 78th Congress, 2nd Session, 11 May 1944, 4319.

[67] *Congressional Record*, 77th Congress, 2nd Session, 12 October 1942, 8095.

The Historian

that this particular deed of democracy would not actually bring more democracy to nonwhite people. Repeal would be a ritual expressing white values.

Clearly, there were strong feelings that something should be done about racism in America, some way found to show the world and the nation that America did believe in democratic principles, but there was no agreement on what could or should be done and no expectation of changing the conditions of life of black America. Thus, by the end of the war many white Americans had become aware of a new domestic problem—white racism. The war produced three different issues related to race: the problem of conscience involving democratic values violated by racism; the fear of violence; and political competition for the growing, increasingly independent black vote. The three problems had emerged independently. The anxiety over conscience had been unrelated to politics. Violence was a threat in its own right. Votes were needed regardless of other circumstances. But the new preoccupation of many liberals with the evils of racism tended to collapse all racial issues into one, the racism of white America. Thus many began to think that symbolic gestures showing white repudiation of racism woud reduce the chances of violence and win black votes. They tended to assume that black people saw the issues as they did, without consulting the black population directly.

These currents seemed to come together in 1948 to make civil rights appear to be the main issue of American domestic politics. There had been the release of the report of the President's Committee on Civil Rights in the fall of 1947, Truman's endorsement of almost all the recommended legislation in February of 1948, the struggle over civil rights at the convention, the walkout of part of the South, the formation of the Dixiecrat Party, Truman's upset victory on a strong civil rights plank, and finally his order to desegregate the armed forces. It might seem that the war had not only discredited racism but had also made civil rights reform a central issue in domestic politics. But such a conclusion significantly overstates what happened. Racism had indeed lost its intellectual respectability outside the white South; race had come to be seen as a moral issue; and civil rights had become a standard item on the liberal reform agenda; yet civil rights had by no means assumed the importance it was to have for a few years in the sixties. The forties were a transition from the thirties, with their focus on class and the indifference or even racism of the progressives, to the sixties, with their passions over strictly racial injustice.

To define the important but limited role of civil rights in the thought and politics of 1948, it is helpful to review the relation of civil rights and politics that year. Although he had delivered a strong civil rights message in February 1948, Truman had not been much involved

Civil Rights, 1940s

in civil rights since then.[68] Truman forces at the Democratic convention favored the relatively weak civil rights plank reported out by the majority of the platform committee.[69] The battle over civil rights led to the adoption of a stronger, liberal-backed civil rights plank, which prompted the southern walkout, the formation of the Dixiecrat Party, and whatever mandate the election may have given civil rights. It was the liberal forces, gaining support from key city bosses dependent on black voters, who pushed through the stronger plank and provoked the walkout.[70] The liberals' motivation is a key to understanding the convention and the ambiguities of the emerging civil rights consciousness.

The rise of the issue of civil rights to the importance it had at the convention was the result of two sets of political needs, both felt by the Americans for Democratic Action, while the power of the issue to rouse such passions rested on its moral significance as a test of white America and on historic political and sectional rivalries. Although the ADA and its predecessor, the UDA, had consistently favored civil rights measures in the past, they had not previously made civil rights a priority issue or given it the prominence it received at the convention.[71] This election year was a desperate one for the liberals as well as for President Truman. The liberals had become convinced that Truman could not be reelected and had launched an extensive campaign to win the nomination for either Dwight Eisenhower or William O. Douglas.[72] Anticipating failure in those efforts, they hoped to secure the vice-presidential nomination for a young liberal or to show

---

[68] Donald R. McCoy and Richard T. Ruetten, *Quest and Response: Minority Rights and the Truman Administration* (Lawrence, Kansas, 1973), 96–118, 120–21, 129–30; Transcript, William L. Batt, Jr., Oral History Interview, November 1966, 24, 26, HSTL; Barto, "Clark Clifford," 100, 101; and Hamby, *Beyond the New Deal*, 214–15.

[69] McCoy and Ruetten, *Quest and Response*, 123–26; but see also Transcript, Samuel C. Brightman Oral History Interview, May 1967, 25, HSTL.

[70] The ADA Papers contain extensive material on the campaign to organize support for a strong civil rights plank at the convention. See especially James Loeb, Jr., to Hubert H. Humphrey, 14 April 1948, and press release, 5 July 1948, ADA Papers, WHS. See also Transcript, James I. Loeb Oral History Interview, September 1971, 11–15, HSTL; and Clifton Brock, *Americans for Democratic Action* (Washington, 1962). For a more detailed analysis of the role of the ADA in 1948, see Peter J. Kellogg, "The Americans for Democratic Action and Civil Rights in 1948: Conscience in Politics or Politics in Conscience," *Midwest Quarterly* 20 (Autumn 1978): 49–63.

[71] There is material on UDA and ADA support of civil rights measures scattered throughout the UDA Papers and the ADA Papers in the Wisconsin Historical Society. Such activity began in 1941 and continued sporadically.

[72] There is considerable material on the effort to unseat Truman in the ADA Papers. See also Loeb to Humphrey, 7–10, ADA Papers, WHS; and Chester Bowles to Hubert Humphrey, 11 February 1948, and Humphrey to Leon Henderson, 25 March 1948, Hubert H. Humphrey Papers, MHS.

liberal influence on the platform. Success in at least one of these efforts seemed essential for proving the importance of the young ADA and for preserving liberal or New Deal dominance of the party.[73]

Once it became clear that the liberals could neither unseat Truman nor dictate the vice-presidential candidate, influence on the platform became that much more essential for showing liberal power. James Loeb, Jr., the executive secretary, wrote to the executive committee of the ADA on March 16, 1948, that it was understood that "our big test lay in the 1948 elections." As one way to meet that test, he recommended that "the ADA take up the challenge of the Southern revolt." He offered three reasons: "In the first place, it looks as if the Southerners are serious, and they will have to be fought in an organized fashion. Second, a good liberal fight at the Democratic Convention on such an issue as civil rights would make it far easier to support the President if the ADA finds it necessary to do so."[74] The third reason was that the fight would be in support of the president's position. When the effort to shape the civil rights plank, organized months ahead by the ADA national office and Minneapolis' new mayor, Hubert Humphrey, proved successful, the liberals felt they had a new lease on life. But their joy was not simply over the triumph for civil rights but for the show of liberal effectiveness and the blow to southern conservatives. Civil rights was an instrument in the struggle with conservatives as much as a cause in itself.

After the convention, H.L. Mitchell, president of the National Farm Labor Union, wrote to James Loeb, Jr., secretary of the ADA, "if for no other reason, the ADA justified its existence by putting the civil rights program in the Democratic Party platform and driving out some of the southern bourbons."[75] Mortimer Hays wrote to Loeb, "ADA has established its liberal leadership and has received an unbelievably favorable press."[76] An ADA internal document showed the pride the organization took in its convention success as well as the meaning it attached to what had happened: "The ADA record in the political field far exceeded the fondest hopes of its founding fathers. Its first great achievement was the victory of the civil rights issues at the Democratic National Convention. This victory constituted the first major blow to the reactionary South which clearly hoped to gain absolute control of the Party following the death of

---

[73]Hubert Humphrey to Chester Bowles, 2 March 1948, Hubert H. Humphrey Papers, MHS; Abridged Proceedings of ADA National Board, 20 September 1947, and Chester Bowles to Leon Henderson, 22 July 1948, ADA Papers, WHS.

[74]Memorandum to Executive Committee from James Loeb, Jr., 16 March 1948, ADA Papers, WHS.

[75]H. L. Mitchell to James Loeb, Jr., 20 July 1948, ADA Papers, WHS.

[76]Mimeographed copy, Mortimer Hays to James Loeb, Jr., no date, Hubert H. Humphrey Papers, MHS.

Civil Rights, 1940s

President Roosevelt."[77] Chester Bowles wrote Hubert Humphrey just after the convention, "I think the Civil Rights issue in which you played such a major part is perhaps the single most important victory that has been won in a Democratic Convention in many years. In the past, the Democratic Party has been more or less of a hodge-podge of big city organizations, southern reactionaries, and northern liberals, held together by the leadership of a Wilson or a Roosevelt. At Philadelphia, it seems to me, we laid the groundwork for a Democratic Party based on liberal principles." Humphrey replied in agreement, "The civil rights issue was but a means of clearly identifying certain elements in our Party for what they are. I, for one, have never been convinced that our Party could survive as a powerful force if we continuously had to compromise and make peace with elements and persons who were not interested in progressive democracy."[78]

Civil rights had been available as a morally potent issue which could both justify the existence of the otherwise ineffectual ADA and separate northern liberals from southern reactionaries in a way most advantageous to the northerners. After the war had revised the white northern perception of race, civil rights advocacy gave liberals a moral advantage over the southerners. The new power of the black vote in the North prompted the added support of city bosses. So there were clear reasons of practical politics for championing civil rights at the convention, but those considerations, important as they were in making civil rights a salient issue, were not the only ones to motivate the liberals, who also expressed a great moral concern for civil rights. Witness a public statement in 1947 by Humphrey: "Our conscience in America has become corroded and encrusted with a bitter feeling of guilt because we profess a belief in justice and equality of opportunity, but we practice injustice and discrimination in every one of these United States. *The outlawing of injustice in employment by adequate and effective legislation is a major step in lifting this burden of guilt from our American conscience.*"[79] (Italics in original.) A public statement by the ADA national board in the January after the election carried the same theme: "Paramount among the great public issues before Congress is the civil rights program as enunciated by President Truman and endorsed by both major parties.... There must be no more equivocation on this important guarantee (FEPC) of civil rights which is in reality a test of our integrity as a people."[80]

Finally, having fought the good fight and seemingly jeopardized

---

[77]"Draft for the Political Commission," 1 December 1948, ADA Papers, WHS.

[78]Chester Bowles to Hubert Humphrey, 22 July 1948, and Humphrey to Bowles, 28 July 1948, Hubert H. Humphrey Papers, MHS.

[79]Humphrey, quoted in a press release from the National Council for a Permanent F.E.P.C., 21 October 1947, Hubert H. Humphrey Papers, MHS.

[80]"Proposed Civil Rights Statement by ADA National Board," ADA Papers, WHS.

The Historian

their political lives by splitting the party, the liberals had vividly demonstrated their commitment to civil rights and racial justice. Whatever the practical results of their efforts, they could now tell themselves that surely they were not racists; they could say with conviction "we are not as these *Herrenvolk.*" Thus the great need for reaffirming democratic ideals, which had been prompted by American confrontation with Nazi racism, had largely been met for ADA and Democratic Party liberals. Furthermore, there had been no postwar riots, so the fear of violence subsided, and by 1949 the American Council on Race Relations was closing its doors. The image of race in America had been transformed, but the pressures for reform were diminishing.

Only by noting the variety of motives for the 1948 conflict over civil rights and the symbolic importance this conflict held in clearing the liberals of association with racism can we understand subsequent events. The passions generated in 1948 did not last. For a few years liberals pressed for civil rights measures in Congress, and they continued to do so in increasingly routine fashion into the early 1960s. But another crisis of conscience and politics was required for any effective civil rights legislation to be enacted, and even then the problems of poverty and economic justice, so important in the thirties, received only limited attention. The concept of race as a matter of white racism rather than as a dimension of black experience within the economic and social structure of the nation would still prevail, and far more support could be mustered for measures to end discrimination by whites than for efforts to end poverty and economic injustice for blacks. The entry of civil rights into national politics in 1948 resulted from a temporary confluence of moral and political concerns. After 1948, political and moral needs tended to diverge, as many liberals, following Adlai Stevenson, sought to conciliate the white South.[81] But the moral issue was still available; white America had acknowledged its existence and, if it was put out of sight, it could not be entirely put out of mind. The idea was there, to emerge once again in response to the black protest of the sixties. The Second World War had made white racism a national shame and had provided a powerful, though not overwhelming, motive for at least limited reform to end overt forms

---

[81]The subject of the retreat from civil rights during the fifties is a study in itself. For some examples, see Transcript, "Meet the Press," 30 March 1952, interview with Adlai Stevenson, 12-13, ADA Papers, WHS; Transcript, James I. Loeb Oral History Interview, September 1971, 52, HSTL; James E. Doyle, "Working Paper for ADA National Board Discussion of Political Program, September 26-27, 1953," ADA Papers, WHS; "Minutes of the ADA National Board Meeting, September 26-27, 1953," ADA Papers, WHS; Gary W. Reichard, "Abandoning the Southern Strategy: Democrats and Civil Rights, 1952-1960," paper delivered at the Annual Meeting of the Organization of American Historians, 8 April 1977; and John Bartlow Martin, *Adlai Stevenson of Illinois* (Garden City, New York, 1976), 30, 158-59, 588-89, 596-97, 656-57, 728.

Civil Rights, 1940s

of racial discrimination. Unfortunately, the issue of race, by the nature of white America's confrontation with its own conscience, had been removed from the realm of social, political, and economic restructuring and had called forth a movement for legal equality only. Social and economic justice were not seen as elements of the new crusade and were not to be a central concern of the new civil rights consciousness. The significance of that omission became apparent when riots of underemployed black youth swept the country just as the civil rights revolution was being completed. Despite an important advance, the dilemma of race in America remains.

though
The
AMERICAN
HISTORICAL
REVIEW

Vol. LXIV, No. 3   *April, 1959*

The Congressional Controversy over School Segregation, 1867-1875

Alfred H. Kelly

ON a certain day in March, 1867, Charles Sumner of Massachusetts arose from his seat in the United States Senate to offer an amendment to the Second Reconstruction Act, then under consideration by the Congress. His proposal would have required the states under reconstruction to establish "public schools open to all without distinction of race or color."[1] The amendment, itself of little import, was the opening move in what proved to be an eight-year campaign for federal legislation to abolish racial segregation generally and in particular to prohibit segregation in the nation's public schools. The campaign was ultimately to culminate, with frustration and substantial failure, in the enactment of the Civil Rights Act of 1875.

Controversy over the "mixed school" question, as the school segregation

[1] *Cong. Globe*, 40 Cong., 1 sess., 165 (Mar. 16, 1867).

issue then was commonly designated, was not altogether new even in 1865. Before that time, however, it had involved solely local and state policy. Most of the northern states had long provided for racial segregation in some form in their public schools, since the institution had made its appearance wherever free Negro communities of any size had developed.[2] In a number of instances, equalitarian idealists had attacked school segregation in the state courts.[3] In Massachusetts, in particular, a long and spectacular campaign against the practice had been climaxed by the celebrated "separate but equal" opinion in the Roberts case, and by the subsequent passage of a statute outlawing racial segregation in the public schools of the state.[4]

The Reconstruction era for the first time gave the school segregation question the status of a national problem, because emancipation had created millions of free Negroes whose legal status and caste position became the subject of extended congressional attention. Also, the triumphant Radical Republicans in Congress included numerous idealists who were intent upon fashioning a new casteless American society. And finally, the adoption of the Fourteenth Amendment, itself in large part the product of the Radical drive for a casteless society, provided a plausible constitutional foundation from which the opponents of racial segregation were enabled to launch their attack.[5]

Any analysis of the Radical Reconstruction drive in Congress for mixed schools must recognize at the outset that the force of the campaign was due very largely to the efforts of one man, Senator Charles Sumner of Massachusetts. Sumner had first distinguished himself as a champion of mixed schools

[2] For example, *New York Laws*, 1850, chap. 143, sec. 4; *Pennsylvania Laws*, 1854, p. 623; 36 *Ohio Laws* (1838), 21; *Indiana Revised Statutes*, 1850, p. 321; *Illinois Laws*, 1857, p. 292; *Iowa Laws*, 1846, chap. 99, par. 6; *Laws of Michigan*, 1841, p. 48; *Statutes of California*, 1855, pp. 234–35.

[3] *Van Camp vs. Board of Education*, 9 Ohio 407 (1859); *Draper vs. Cambridge*, 20 Ind. 268 (1863).

[4] *Roberts vs. City of Boston*, 59 Mass. 198 (1850). *Massachusetts Statutes*, 1855, chap. 256, sec. 1. See also Leonard W. Levy and Harlan B. Phillips, "The *Roberts* Case: Source of the 'Separate but Equal' Doctrine," *American Historical Review*, LVI (Apr., 1951), 510–18.

[5] The highly controversial question of whether the Fourteenth Amendment was itself intended to prohibit school segregation is outside the scope of this paper. The author of this essay has argued elsewhere that, while the framers of the Amendment were little concerned with school segregation as such, they deliberately struck broadly at all caste and class legislation, so that a prohibition against school segregation might reasonably be construed generally as within their intent. That is, they were adopting an amendment setting forth broad purpose, not legislating. John A. Bingham of Ohio made this distinction clear on the floor of the House. See Alfred H. Kelly, "The Fourteenth Amendment Reconsidered: The Segregation Question," *Michigan Law Review*, LIV (June, 1956), 1049–86. Howard Jay Graham, "Our 'Declaratory' Fourteenth Amendment," *Stanford Law Review*, VII (Dec., 1954), 3–39, presents the same general thesis as is found in John Frank and Robert F. Monroe, "The Original Understanding of Equal Protection of the Laws," *Columbia Law Review*, L (Feb., 1950), 131–69. For a carefully expounded argument to the contrary, see Alexander M. Bickel, "The Original Understanding and the Segregation Decision," *Harvard Law Review*, LXIX (Nov., 1955), 1–65.

in his celebrated argument in the Roberts case, where he had condemned segregation as contrary to the spirit of the Declaration of Independence and the Massachusetts Constitution of 1780.[6] He never rested thereafter from the exposition of the thesis that school segregation was inimical to the best interests of American democracy.

Sumner's leadership of the Radical crusade against segregated schools was at once its inspiration and a revelation of its political weakness. For the plain truth of the matter was that he was for the most part unable to command an effective majority of his Republican colleagues on any definitive vote. A number of the senatorial faithful, among them Henry Wilson of Massachusetts, Richard Yates of Illinois, Samuel Pomeroy of Kansas, George Edmunds of Vermont, John Sherman of Ohio, and Levi P. Morton of Indiana, showed themselves willing to support the Massachusetts idealist on most occasions, but they generally allowed Sumner to lead the way. In the House, George F. and Ebenezer R. Hoar were consistently loyal to the cause, while Ben Butler, for whatever dubious reasons of his own, also eventually became an ardent champion of mixed schools.[7] But it is significant that virtually the only occasions in which Sumner found his cause sufficiently popular to command effective support in either house occurred when it happened to coincide with the momentary tactical or strategic interests of the Republican party. This was the case both in the protracted congressional fight over southern amnesty in 1872 and during the partisan maneuvering incident to the passage of the Civil Rights Act of 1875.

Republican politicians sensed, correctly enough, that there was comparatively little popular interest in national mixed school legislation. Even in the North most communities were content to allow the issue to be settled as a local or state matter rather than by a federal law. The demand from Negro voters for mixed school legislation, to be sure, was powerful and insistent, and Republican politicians on occasion were obliged to pay some attention to it. Mixed schools also offered a potential device to confirm the loyalty of southern Negro voters and so to strengthen the Republican party in the South. But it soon became clear that virtually all southern whites were extremely hostile to school desegregation, so that advocacy of mixed school legislation promised to weaken the Republican party below the Mason and Dixon line rather than strengthen it. Sound party tactics therefore called for

---

[6] The argument is in Charles Sumner, *His Complete Works* (Boston, 1900), III, 51–100.
[7] Butler and the Hoar brothers were, of course, deadly political enemies. Cf. George F. Hoar, *Autobiography of Seventy Years* (New York, 1903), I, 329–30, 340–48.

some support of Sumner's cause and even for an occasional congressional vote, but not for any decisive attempt to enact a mandatory federal mixed school statute. With the exception of a few idealists, the Republican Radicals used the mixed school question merely as a party stalking horse.

Sumner's attempt to attach a mixed school requirement to the second Reconstruction bill was a rather shrewdly chosen opening move, for it was evident that his Radical colleagues might well be far more willing to impose mandatory desegregation on the "rebel states" than upon their own constituents. The maneuver nonetheless failed,[8] and a like attempt in July, 1867, to amend the third Reconstruction bill met a similar fate.[9]

At the same time, Sumner had succeeded in inspiring some degree of self-consciousness with respect to mixed schools both in Congress and in southern Radical Republican ranks. Two of the constitutions drafted by the Radical-controlled conventions in the states then undergoing reconstruction, those of South Carolina and Louisiana, specifically prohibited racial segregation in the public schools. The other five constitutions of 1868, those of Alabama, Arkansas, Florida, Georgia, and North Carolina,[10] carried more general provisions directed toward equality in education without specifically guaranteeing mixed schools as such. These provisions, particularly those of South Carolina and Louisiana, called forth several expressions of conservative and Democratic condemnation on the floor of Congress without evoking any Radical response.[11]

Two years later, in 1870, the mixed school faction in Congress succeeded in incorporating guarantees of racially mixed schools as "conditions-subsequent" in the acts to readmit Virginia, Mississippi, and Texas to representation. This development grew out of Radical concern for the situation in the state of Virginia, where a fight over school segregation had been under way for some time. The constitutional convention of 1867–1868, after protracted debate on the subject in which both sides failed to carry their objective in any specific provision, had adopted deliberately vague and ambiguous school district and county organization provisions which everyone recognized might

---

[8] After some discussion, the Senate voted the proposal down, 20 to 20. *Cong. Globe,* 40 Cong., 1 sess., 165–70 (Mar. 16, 1867).
[9] *Ibid.,* 580–81, (July 11, 1867).
[10] Francis N. Thorpe, *The Federal and State Constitutions, Colonial Charters and other Organic Laws of the States, Territories and Colonies now or heretofore Forming the United States of America* (7 vols., Washington, D. C., 1909), I, 149, 322; III, 716, 868, 1465; V, 2817; VI, 3301.
[11] In a bitter condemnation of the Louisiana and South Carolina constitutional mixed school provisions, for example, James Beck of Kentucky asserted indignantly, "I can scarcely conceive of a more despotic, galling, and degrading provision in the fundamental law of a state pretending to be free." *Cong. Globe,* 40 Cong., 2 sess., 2449 (May 13, 1868).

later be construed as providing either for mixed schools or school segregation.[12]

In the subsequent state election campaign, Gilbert Walker, the "Conservative" candidate for governor, had repeatedly assured the people of Virginia that if he and his party were elected to office and the prospective constitution adopted, its controversial provisions "would never be enforced in a manner detrimental to the people."[13] Apparently this was generally understood to be a pledge to maintain segregated schools. In July, 1869, Walker was elected governor, his party carried a large majority in the assembly, and the constitution was overwhelmingly ratified.

Many Virginia Radicals, now despairing of achieving mixed schools otherwise, appealed in alarm to their friends in Congress.[14] The Joint Congressional Committee on Reconstruction, which then had under consideration a bill to readmit Virginia to representation, accordingly incorporated the following provision in the bill as reported in January, 1870, to the floor of the two houses:

... The Constitution of said State shall never be so amended or changed ... to prevent any person on account of race, color, or previous condition of servitude from serving as a juror or participating equally in the school fund or school privileges provided for in said Constitution.[15]

This provision was open to a serious constitutional objection, in that it would have imposed a "condition-subsequent" upon the admission of Virginia to representation. The constitutional objection to "conditions-subsequent"—that they implied a union of unequal rather than equal states—was of long standing and had been generally recognized by all constitutional lawyers since the days of the Missouri Compromise debates.[16] When the bill came up for debate in the House, John A. Bingham of Ohio, long a Radical stalwart, vigorously attacked its constitutionality. The House thereupon voted to adopt Bingham's amendment to strike out everything in the bill

---

[12] *Journal of the Virginia Constitutional Convention of 1867–1868* (Richmond, 1868), 299, 301, 333, 339, 340. As finally written, the constitution provided merely for "compactly located school districts" and for "a uniform system of free public schools." Thorpe, *Federal and State Constitutions*, VII, 3891, 3892.

[13] Representative Hulbert Paine of Wisconsin and other indignant Radicals quoted Walker to this effect on the floor of both houses. *Cong. Globe*, 41 Cong., 2 sess., 402, 543 (Jan. 12, 1870). See also H. J. Eckenrode, *The Political History of Virginia during Reconstruction* (Baltimore, Md., 1904), 120–25.

[14] In January, 1870, a Washington convention of "loyal Republican citizens of Virginia" petitioned Congress to intervene. *Cong. Globe*, 41 Cong., 2 sess., 390, 440–41 (Jan. 13, 1870).

[15] *Ibid.*, 362 (Jan. 11, 1870).

[16] Cf. Attorney General George F. Hoar's opinion of August, 1869, on the matter. *Ibid.*, 404 (Jan. 12, 1870).

after the enacting clause and simply to readmit Virginia to representation; it then passed the amended bill in that form.[17]

The Senate Radicals were little concerned, however, with constitutional niceties of this kind. After impassioned pleas by Sumner and Morton of Indiana, the upper house a few days later adopted, on a close vote, an amendment submitted by Senator Henry Wilson of Massachusetts stipulating "that the constitution of Virginia shall never be so amended as to deprive any citizen or class of citizens of the United States of the school rights and privileges secured by the constitution of said State." The Senate then passed the bill, the House soon concurred in the Senate's changes,[18] and the measure became law with the Wilson "condition-subsequent" intact.[19] A few weeks later Congress passed bills to readmit Mississippi and Texas[20] which contained similar mixed school provisions.

In actual practice, these guarantees proved to have little meaning. Indeed, the Virginia legislature in July, 1870, adopted by a large majority a Walker-sponsored public school act containing a mandatory school segregation clause.[21] Ironically, no one in Congress, not even Sumner, thereafter bothered to challenge the law.

By 1870 Sumner's little coterie had begun agitation on three additional fronts to obtain their objective. They now sought a national subsidy for primary and secondary education which would incorporate a mixed school guarantee, a reform of the school system in the District of Columbia to bring mandatory mixed schools to the city of Washington, and, most important, the passage of a comprehensive antisegregation civil rights act which would include as a principal provision an outright prohibition against racially segregated schools in the states.

Until the late 1880's bills to establish a national subsidy for public education appeared in every session of Congress. The principal interest in these measures centered in the House.[22] Most of them, like the one introduced by Representative Waitman Willey of West Virginia in 1870, proposed to appropriate the proceeds of public land sales to the states for the support of

---

[17] *Ibid.*, 493–95, 502 (Jan. 14, 1870). The vote on Bingham's amendment was 98 to 95.
[18] *Ibid.*, 643–44, 720 (Jan. 14, 21, 24, 1870). The Senate vote on the Virginia bill was 47 to 101 and that of the House 136 to 58.
[19] 16 *United States Statutes at Large*, 63.
[20] *Cong. Globe*, 41 Cong., 2 sess., 1173–84, 1253–60, 1329, 1365–66, 1969–71, 2271 (Feb. 10, 14, 16, 17; Mar. 15, 29, 1870).
[21] *Virginia Laws*, 1869–70, p. 413. See also A. A. Taylor, *The Negro in the Reconstruction of Virginia* (Washington, D. C., 1928), 146–52.
[22] Allen J. Going, "The South and the Blair Bill," *Mississippi Valley Historical Review*, XLIV (Sept., 1957), 267–71; Gordon C. Lee, *The Struggle for Federal Aid: First Phase* (New York, 1949), 40–87.

education.[23] Others, however, such as that introduced by Congressman George F. Hoar of Massachusetts in February, 1870,[24] or that presented in January, 1872, by Representative Legrand Perce, a Mississippi Negro,[25] provided for direct federal taxation, the proceeds of which were to be distributed to the states for the support of the public schools.

These bills, at least in the 1870's, nearly always carried some sort of mixed school guarantee, and indeed both sides recognized quite generally that this was one of their objectives. As a consequence, they invariably aroused bitter controversy whenever they reached the floor.

The House debate on the Perce bill in January, 1872, was particularly notable for its vitriolic character. The measure carried a specific mixed school guarantee, and conservative Republicans and Democrats alike denounced it as an ill-disguised attempt to force mixed schools upon the states. Democrat John B. Storm of Pennsylvania warned the South that "this bill is a Trojan horse. In its interior are concealed the lurking foe—mixed schools." Michael Kerr of Indiana protested that the bill "proposes to establish . . . mixed public schools . . . all over the country." And John T. Harris of Virginia cried out in an impassioned speech that "Virginia will do justice to the colored man, but money cannot purchase her to the principles of this bill. . . . We give the colored man equal political and legal rights, but social equality, Never! Never! Never!"[26]

Thereupon Representative William D. Kelley of Pennsylvania, familiarly known as "Pig-Iron," observed sarcastically

that the terror of the gentleman from Virginia excited by his fear of mixed schools, need not be so extreme. If, as he seems to apprehend, such schools should be forced upon the people of this and other States, it will in the South be but temporary; for all men know that the sun and atmosphere of the southern states soon bleach the blackest African, both in hair and complexion, to the colors characteristic of the purest Saxon lineage.[27]

At this point an outraged Virginian, Representative Frank Hereford, asked Kelley "whether he is in favor of forcing mixed schools upon the people?" But in reply Kelley quoted the evidence of Negro-white intermixture that he had seen in the Freedman's Bureau schools in the South, and

---

[23] *Cong. Globe*, 41 Cong., 2 sess., 2979 (Apr. 26, 1870).
[24] *Ibid.*, 1568 (Feb. 25, 1870). The measure would have levied a direct tax of fifty cents on every United States inhabitant. *Ibid.*, 3 sess., 1038 (Feb. 7, 1871).
[25] *Ibid.*, 42 Cong., 2 sess., 535 (Jan. 23, 1872). Perce's bill would have created a "national education fund," invested in five per cent United States bonds, the proceeds to be distributed to the states.
[26] *Ibid.*, 569, 791, 855–56 (Jan. 24; Feb. 2, 6, 1872).
[27] *Ibid.*, 858 (Feb. 6, 1872).

then repeated his insinuation against the sex morals of southern whites.[28]

However, the southerners were now determined to force a specific settlement of the mixed school issue before the bill came to final vote. As various minor amendments came up for consideration, Hereford presented the following amendment:

> Provided that no moneys belonging to any State or Territory under this act shall be withheld from any State or Territory for the reason that the laws thereof provided for separate schools for white children and black children, or refuse to organize a system of mixed schools.[29]

There was no debate on the proposal. The original voice vote on the amendment was close, but when George F. Hoar, a champion of mixed schools, called for the yeas and nays, forty-three did not vote. Included in the negative vote were all the principal Radical figures of the House—among them Bingham and Samuel Shellabarger of Ohio, Butler of Massachusetts, Kelley of Pennsylvania, Austin Blair of Michigan, and Nathaniel P. Banks of Massachusetts. Virtually all those who refused to vote, however, were Republicans. Silent Republican defections, in short, had killed the mixed school clause. The following day the House passed the expurgated school bill,[30] but thereafter it died in Senate committee.

A few weeks after Hereford had been successful in gaining adoption of his amendment to the Perce bill, he was indiscreet enough to ask suspension of the House rules for a vote on the following:

> Be it resolved, that it would be contrary to the Constitution and a tyrannical usurpation of power for Congress to force mixed schools upon the States, and equally unconstitutional and tyrannical for Congress to pass any law interfering with churches, public carriers or inn keepers, such subjects of legislation belonging of right to the States respectively.

The motion to suspend the rules to vote on this resolution, however, promptly met defeat. All the principal Radical figures of the House, including Bingham, Butler, Blair, Hoar, and Kelley, voted against the proposal, while this time an even larger group of Republicans simply voted "present."[31] In other words, a considerable group in the House, one holding an actual balance of power, was unwilling to vote positively for mixed schools but at the same time would refuse to go on record in favor of the principle of seg-

---

[28] *Ibid.*
[29] *Ibid.*, 882 (Feb. 7, 1872). The original voice vote was 82 to 80 for the amendment; on the call for yeas and nays it was 115 to 81.
[30] *Ibid.*, 903 (Feb. 8, 1872); Lee, *Struggle for Federal Aid*, 57–60; Edward MacPherson, *A Handbook of Politics* (Washington, D. C., 1872), 122.
[31] *Cong. Globe*, 42 Cong., 2 sess., 1582 (Mar. 11, 1872). The vote was 61 to 85, with 94 not voting.

regated schools, were that at all possible. In either nineteenth- or twentieth-century terms their political ambivalence is very understandable.

The campaign for mixed schools in the District of Columbia exhibited much the same inner weakness as that for desegregation through an education subsidy. The Negro school system in the District was at this time entirely distinct from that for whites, since an act of 1862 had organized the former under a separate three-man board of trustees appointed by the Secretary of the Interior.[32] Originally private in character, the Negro schools after 1862 were supported by annual appropriations from Congress, although their public status in the late 1860's was still far from unequivocal.

Beginning in January, 1870,[33] Sumner and his friends regularly introduced mixed school bills for the District in the Senate and House at every session until his death in 1874. Most of them never reached the floor, evidently because the Republican majority simply was not interested in them. In all probability there was truth in the repeated Democratic taunt that desegregation of public schools in the District struck many Republican congressmen as "too close to home."

In 1871, however, Sumner and his friends succeeded in bringing District mixed school bills out of committee and onto the floor for debate in both houses. In the Senate James W. Patterson of New Hampshire, chairman of the Committee on the District of Columbia, reported a bill to wipe out all preexisting school organization in the District and to create in its stead a single mixed school system under a superintendent, three school districts, and a common board of education. The measure carried a specific guarantee of racial integration.[34] A report from the trustees of the Negro school system, which asserted that the termination of segregated schools was not only "in the best interests of the colored people" but also "those of all classes," supported this proposal.[35] A few days later the House Committee on the District of Columbia reported out a similar measure.[36]

This little show of strength by the mixed school faction was dispelled quickly enough. In presenting his bill on the Senate floor, Patterson explained that the committee majority had added the mixed school clause over his objections, and he now moved to strike it out on the ground that it would "tend to destroy the schools of the city or to put them back ten or fifteen years." Sumner immediately protested that if the Patterson amendment

---

[32] 12 *United States Statutes at Large*, 537-38.
[33] *Cong. Globe*, 41 Cong., 2 sess., 323 (Jan. 10, 1870).
[34] *Ibid.*, 3 sess., 1053 (Feb. 8, 1871).
[35] *Sen. Exec. Docs.*, 41 Cong., 3 sess., no. 20, p. 7.
[36] *Cong. Globe*, 41 Cong., 3 sess., 1365 (Feb. 17, 1871).

were adopted, he would "oppose this bill to the last," while Matthew Carpenter of Wisconsin, John S. Harris of Louisiana, Hiram Revels of Mississippi, Frederick Sawyer of South Carolina, and Henry Wilson of Massachusetts spoke to the same end.[37]

But Allen G. Thurman of Ohio called it "despotism" to "disregard the marked differences of race that the Almighty himself has stamped upon the people," while Joshua Hill of Georgia insisted that Negroes "as a class, always prefer" segregated schools. More significantly, the great majority of senators simply remained silent. Evidently they agreed with Thomas W. Tipton of Nebraska, who expressed astonishment at the amount of time spent on the issue, asked, "Is it a crime to be practical?" and urged the Senate to get on with its business.[38] In the end, debate closed without any action whatever.

The House bill received even shorter shrift. Here the committee in reporting the measure unanimously recommended that the mixed school clause be struck out. The Radicals offered no articulate opposition to this proposal, but all sides were now disposed to bury the entire measure, which was killed by a vote to reconsider the vote by which it had been engrossed and read.[39] The explanation was simple: the advocates of mixed schools, too weak to defend the retention of the mixed school clause successfully, were not interested in the bill without it, while the Conservatives were only too glad to let the entire question die.

Of far more political significance were Sumner's repeated attempts to obtain passage of a comprehensive desegregation statute, which would include a prohibition upon racial segregation in public schools. From 1870 on the Massachusetts idealist regularly presented bills of this kind, usually for an act supplementary to the Civil Rights Act of 1866. The text of these measures was always very much the same. They proposed to prohibit discrimination in a variety of public facilities within the states—common carriers, theaters, inns, restaurants, schools, and the like—on account of race, color, or previous condition of servititude.[40] For a time they made little progress, in part through apparent lack of general interest, in part because of the hostility of Lyman Trumbull of Illinois, who as chairman of the Senate Judiciary Committee was in a position to kill them.[41]

[37] *Ibid.*, 1054–60 (Feb. 8, 1871).
[38] *Ibid.*, 1057, 1059–60 (Feb. 8, 1871).
[39] *Ibid.*, 1367 (Feb. 17, 1871). The vote was 88 to 71, with 81 not voting.
[40] The earliest of these bills was S. 916, introduced by Sumner May 13, 1870. *Cong. Globe*, 41 Cong., 2 sess., 3434.
[41] For example, the adverse report on the 1870 bill. *Ibid.*, 5314 (July 7, 1870).

Congressional Controversy, School Segregation 547

In December, 1871, however, Sumner presented his bill as a "rider" to a general amnesty measure which had come up from the House,[42] and overnight his proposal took on an extraordinary popularity with the Senate Radicals. The explanation was evident enough: the Radicals regarded amnesty as "nothing less than an attempt to revive the Democratic party" by freeing it from the onus of treason, and they now saw in Sumner's rider a delightful weapon to deal with this menace. For the rider promised to make the amnesty bill so distasteful to conservative Republicans and Democrats that they would vote against the bill itself, thereby defeating the two-thirds majority required by the Fourteenth Amendment.[43] This could be accomplished, also, without appearing to oppose President Grant, who in his recent annual message had declared himself in favor of a general amnesty law.[44] At the same time a sop could be thrown to Negro leaders, who were beginning to insist rather strongly on a mixed school law.[45]

The Radical strategem presented one serious constitutional difficulty: it was open to question whether amnesty bills were legislation at all in any ordinary sense, and it was reasonable to argue that regular legislation had no legitimate place in them. This consideration, ably presented by Thurman, Trumbull, and other Conservatives, nearly killed the rider when Sumner first presented it to the Senate. But its obvious political advantages overrode Republican constitutional doubts, and it survived to carry over for later consideration.[46]

In late January the Senate began an extended debate on Sumner's pro-

---

[42] House Bill 380, passed by the House without debate in the previous session. The bill lifted the disabilities of the Fourteenth Amendment from all former members of Congress as well as army and navy officers who had resigned to support the rebellion, and from members of state conventions adopting ordinances of secession who had voted for such ordinances. *Cong. Globe*, 42 Cong., 1 sess., 561-62 (Apr. 10, 1871).

[43] The New York *Tribune* observed that "such men as Morton, Conkling, Edmunds, Nye, and Chandler . . . are suddenly converted to Mr. Sumner's way of thinking, because it is the only way amnesty can be defeated without appearing to oppose the President." Jan. 24, 1872. See also Paul H. Buck, *The Road to Reunion* (Boston, 1947), 125-26.

[44] James Richardson, *A Compilation of the Messages and Papers of the Presidents of the United States* (New York, 1897), VII, 153. The Washington *National Republican*, an administration paper, reported that Grant himself thought it "unfortunate that it [the rider] was attached to the amnesty bill." Jan. 11, 1872. The same paper condemned the Radicals' strategy, stating that "to our second-rate mind it is the merest drivel to defend such tactics." Jan. 15, 1872.

[45] A large Negro convention early in January, 1872, resolved that "the highest good of the people demands that both races be educated together." *Ibid.*, Jan. 6, 1872. New York *Times*, Jan. 4, 1872.

[46] When Sumner first brought up the rider in Committee of the Whole, Vice-President Schuyler Colfax ruled it in order, and the Senate sustained him, 28 to 26. Immediately thereafter, however, the Committee rejected the amendment, 29 to 30. But when the Senate reconvened in regular session a few minutes later, Sumner, over conservative protests, offered his amendment once more, and it carried over without a vote for debate in January. *Cong. Globe*, 42 Cong., 2 sess., 263-74, 278 (Dec. 21, 1871).

posal, in which both sides dealt at length with both its constitutional and social merits. The conservatives, led by Trumbull of Illinois, Thurman of Ohio, Willard Saulsbury of Delaware, Garrett Davis and John W. Stevenson of Kentucky, Hill of Georgia, and Thomas J. Robertson of South Carolina, repeatedly attacked all civil rights legislation and Sumner's bill in particular as "grossly and palpably unconstitutional." This argument rested upon an extremely restrictive interpretation of the scope and effect of the Fourteenth Amendment. Thurman of Ohio, the Democrats' most effective constitutional theorist, boldly contended that the amendment actually had conferred upon Congress no new substantive legislative power at all. Instead, he said, congressional authority was limited to providing for the appellate jurisdiction of the federal courts whenever a state had "violated any of the limitations imposed."[47]

Trumbull, himself the author of the Civil Rights Act of 1866, was perforce obliged to concede that the amendment gave Congress some substantive power in the field. But he argued strenuously that guarantees against segregation were "social rights" and not "civil rights" and therefore outside the scope of the amendment. "I say it is a misnomer," he exclaimed, "to talk about this being a civil rights bill." And when Edmunds of Vermont interposed to ask "about the right to go to school," Trumbull replied firmly, "The right to go to school is not a civil right and never was."[48]

On the other hand, the Radicals argued that the "privileges or immunities" clause of the Fourteenth Amendment had endowed Congress with an extremely broad substantive power over all civil liberties. John Sherman pronounced these rights, among which he listed travel, lodgment at inns, and use of all public facilities, to be "as innumerable as the sands of the sea." The denial that attendance at public school was a civil right particularly outraged him. "It is both a right and a privilege," he insisted. If this and similar rights "are not the privileges and immunities of citizens of the United States," he cried, "then what in the name of human rights are the privileges and immunities of citizens?"[49] Attacking along the same general line, Morton and Carpenter both denounced Thurman's insistence that the amendment had in fact given Congress no new substantive legislative power whatsoever. "The Senator overlooks the fact," Morton said, "that the remedy for the violation of the Fourteenth and Fifteenth Amendments was expressly not left to the courts. The remedy was legislative, because in fact the amend-

---

[47] Ibid., 526, 761 (Jan. 23, Feb. 1, 1872).
[48] Ibid., 3189 (May 8, 1872).
[49] Ibid., 843-44 (Feb. 6, 1872).

ment itself provided that it shall be enforced by legislation on the part of Congress."[50]

Both sides also had much to say of the social significance of desegregation and of mixed schools in particular. Summer thought segregated schools "an ill disguised violation of the principle of equality," whose evil effects fell even more greatly upon white children than upon Negroes. Through segregated schools, he argued, "Pharisaism of race becomes an element of character, when, like all other Pharisaisms it should be stamped out."[51] In reply, Hill of Georgia insisted that legalized segregation was no real violation of "substantial equality,"[52] while Thomas N. Norwood of Georgia argued that "the familiar association" of mixed schools implied that if Negro and white children "later see fit to join in matrimony there shall be no impediment to it."[53] Conservative Republican Orris Ferry of Connecticut warned that "we do not like it that representatives from distant states should assist us in the control of our school fund."[54] And Carl Schurz of Missouri contended that the best way to promote the welfare of the Negro was to pass the amnesty bill forthwith and allow the South to go its way in peace.[55]

To all this the Radicals replied repeatedly that southerners ought to be required to grant the Negro civil equality as a matter both of recompense and simple social and political justice if they expected consideration in amnesty matters. James W. Nye of Nevada put this point in a very popular way:

If I had outraged the laws and Constitution of my land, if I had attempted to tear down the very temple of liberty here, and now, professing to be its friend, have not sorrow and regret enough in my heart for my bloody deeds to ask pardon, I do not deserve to be forgiven. So I take it that these friends who want to get immediately into a position to hold office had better conclude to let a Negro ride in the cars with them. . . .[56]

After some weeks of heavy and almost continuous debate, the Sumner amendment carried the day, with the casting vote of Vice-President Schuyler Colfax deciding the matter.[57] The galleries, crowded with Negroes and other Sumner supporters, gave way to "great applause," and the colored people present were unable to "restrain their joy" when the vote was an-

[50] *Ibid.*, 524 (Jan. 23, 1872).
[51] *Ibid.*, 381 ff. (Jan. 15, 1872).
[52] *Ibid.*, 491 (Feb. 6, 1872).
[53] *Ibid.*, 819 (Feb. 5, 1872).
[54] *Ibid.*, 893 (Feb. 8, 1872).
[55] *Ibid.*, 703 (Jan. 30, 1872).
[56] *Ibid.*, 495 (Jan. 22, 1872).
[57] *Ibid.*, 919 (Feb. 9, 1872). The vote was 28 to 28.

nounced.[58] Virtually the entire Radical Republican phalanx, including Simon Cameron, Roscoe Conkling, Zachariah Chandler, Pomeroy, Sherman, James Harlan of Iowa, Justin S. Morrill of Vermont, and Wilson, voted for the rider.[59] On the other hand, Republicans Schurz, Trumbull, and Lot M. Morrill of Maine voted with the Democrats, North and South, against it.

As the Radicals well knew, adoption of the rider doomed the entire amnesty bill to defeat. A few minutes later the Senate voted in favor of the measure, but with two votes less than the required constitutional majority, so that the bill was dead.[60] Significantly, many ardent supporters of general amnesty, among them Thurman, Trumbull, Saulsbury, and Tipton, voted against the bill in its final form.

In May the Senate took up a new general amnesty bill which had come up from the House some time earlier, only to have the measure encounter the same fate as its predecessor. Again, Sumner immediately introduced his civil rights rider as an amendment; again, after protracted parliamentary maneuvering the Senate adopted the rider with the aid of Vice-President Colfax's casting vote. And once more the Senate immediately thereafter voted in favor of the bill, but again this failed to constitute the necessary two-thirds constitutional majority.[61]

Almost overnight, however, the Radical attitude toward amnesty and civil rights underwent a change. The new factor in the situation was the Liberal Republican "rebellion" then in progress. Early in May the Liberals' convention in Cincinnati adopted a party plank calling for "the immediate and absolute removal of all disabilities on account of the rebellion."[62] The subsequent nomination of Horace Greeley gave the Liberal movement an almost farcical quality; nevertheless the Republican fear was soon apparent that the Liberals' amnesty plank might win southern white Republicans over to Greeley's support.

Republican strategy now called for swift passage of an amnesty bill—as the New York *Times* put it, "to heal the party breach" and "to destroy Greeley's support in the South."[63] In the Senate, John A. Logan of Illinois stated bluntly that Sumner's rider had now become extremely untimely, a

---

[58] *New York Tribune*, Feb. 10, 1874.
[59] Carpenter of Wisconsin, a Radical, finally voted against the rider because he believed that the measure's provision requiring integration in churches violated the First Amendment.
[60] *Cong. Globe*, 42 Cong., 2 sess., 929 (Feb. 9, 1872). The vote was 33 to 19.
[61] *Ibid.*, 3268, 3270 (May 9, 1872). The vote on the rider was 28 to 28; on the bill, 32 to 22.
[62] Edward Stanwood, *A History of the Presidency* (New York, 1924), I, 343; *New York Times*, May 4, 1872.
[63] *New York Times*, May 9, 11, 22, 1872; *Chicago Tribune*, May 22, 1872.

"lion in the pathway" of an amnesty bill necessary to counteract the "Cincinnati movement."[64] President Grant was already on record as opposed to the union of amnesty and civil rights,[65] and early in May a Republican caucus found an actual majority of senators in favor of abandoning the rider.[66] Republican concern for Sumner's feeling did not count too greatly, for he had flirted openly with the Cincinnati movement and expressed personal sympathy for Greeley.[67] Of course, all this meant that the civil rights rider had to be abandoned and the amnesty bill rushed through without it, even though some nominal gesture toward civil rights might still be necessary to appease Negro leaders.[68]

In an all-night session the Senate Republicans, led by Edmunds, Carpenter, Conkling, and Logan, struck a carefully negotiated bargain with Thurman and the other Democrats. The Democrats agreed to allow an emasculated version of the Sumner bill—carefully "shorn of its most objectionable features," the school clause and the jury provision—to come to an immediate vote without further debate. In return, the Republicans promised that immediately following the civil rights vote they would call up one of the pending general amnesty bills already enacted by the House and pass it at once without amendment, so that it could become law upon Grant's signature.[69]

Once agreed upon, the bargain came off almost without incident. The civil rights bill passed with the Democrats duly voting "nay." Sumner had been absent during these proceedings; arriving just before the amnesty vote, he pleaded for a mixed school clause and in desperation once more offered his bill as a rider. But the Senate coldly voted him down and then passed the amnesty bill.[70]

The Senate civil rights bill was quite obviously nothing more than a device to save party face with Negro leaders. Not only were the school and jury clauses missing; it was also too late in the session to hope for favorable House action.[71] But Republicans were jubilant at their amnesty coup, which

[64] *Cong. Globe*, 42 Cong., 2 sess., 3260 (May 9, 1872).
[65] Washington *National Republican*, Jan. 11, 1872.
[66] New York *Tribune*, May 1, 1872; New York *Herald*, May 11, 1872.
[67] New York *Times*, May 1, 17, 22, 1872; Washington *National Republican*, May 1, 1872; New York *Tribune*, May 1, 1872.
[68] As late as mid-May, Conkling in letters to the Negro convention in Washington strongly championed mixed schools and civil rights generally. New York *Times*, May 10, 13, 1872.
[69] *Cong. Globe*, 42 Cong., 2 sess., 3730-36 (May 21, 1872).
[70] *Ibid.*, 3736-38 (May 21, 1872). The civil rights bill passed 27 to 14. The Senate defeated Sumner's rider 13 to 29 and passed the amnesty bill 39 to 2.
[71] The House killed the bill, when motions "to take up" twice failed to obtain the required two-thirds majority. *Ibid.*, 3932, 4322 (May 28; June 7, 1872).

had "knocked away one of the most important planks in the Cincinnati platform."[72]

The civil rights question remained virtually at rest for the next two years. But in December, 1873, as the Forty-Third Congress convened, the issue arose once more. In the Senate, Sumner again presented his bill as an amendment to the Civil Rights Act of 1866.[73] In the House, Butler of Massachusetts, chairman of the House Judiciary Committee and the administration's party floor leader, introduced a somewhat similar measure.[74] Both were extremely comprehensive, and both carried very strongly worded mixed school clauses.[75] Apparently the Radicals had decided that the insistent demand of Negro voters for civil rights legislation had become too strong to be ignored. Significantly, Grant in his annual message to Congress for the first time specifically recommended passage of a law "to better secure the civil rights" of the "enfranchised slave."[76]

The Butler bill came up for debate early in January, 1874, before galleries crowded with Negro spectators.[77] The conservative opponents of the measure at once seized upon the Supreme Court's recent dictum in the Slaughterhouse cases, which had all but destroyed the force of the "privileges or immunities" clause,[78] to denounce the bill as hopelessly unconstitutional. The aged and withered Alexander H. Stephens of Georgia, who delivered the principal speech for the Democrats, used Justice Samuel Miller's opinion to reinforce the oft-repeated conservative contention that the amendment had bestowed no rights whatsoever definable or enforceable by Congress. Applying this analysis to the mixed school question, he asserted that Justice Miller's opinion meant that a state still retained the right "to say who may, or may not, be admitted into her public schools."[79] Harris of Virginia, Milton J. Durham of Kentucky, John N. Bright of Tennessee, and Roger Q. Mills and William S. Herndon of Texas stressed much the same argument.[80]

---

[72] Providence *Journal*, May 27, 1872. The Boston *Daily Globe* observed that the "amnesty bill takes the point out of Mr. Greeley's letter of acceptance." May 23, 1872. The New York *Times* thought that passage of the Amnesty Act "sweeps away the strongest plank in the amnesty raft." May 23, 1872. See also James G. Blaine, *Twenty Years of Congress* (Norwich, Conn., 1886), II, 514–15.

[73] *Cong. Record*, 43 Cong., 1 sess., 2 (Dec. 2, 1873).

[74] *Ibid.*, 318 (Dec. 18, 1873).

[75] Sumner's bill would have forbidden racial segregation in "common schools and public schools of learning or benevolence supported, in whole or in part, by general taxation." *Ibid.*, 3451 (Apr. 29, 1874). Butler's bill prohibited segregation in all schools "supported in whole or in part at public expense or by endowment for public use," language that covered many private as well as all public schools. *Ibid.*, 378 (Jan. 5, 1874).

[76] Richardson, *Messages*, VII, 255.

[77] New York *Times*, Jan. 6, 1874.

[78] 16 Wallace 36 (1873).

[79] *Cong. Record*, 43 Cong., 1 sess., 380–81 (Jan. 5, 1874).

[80] *Ibid.*, 376, 383, 405, 414, 420 (Jan. 5, 6, 1874).

Congressional Controversy, School Segregation 553

William Lawrence of Ohio, a much-respected man who had participated in the 1866 debates on the passage of the Fourteenth Amendment, presented the most effective constitutional reply for the bill's supporters. Recognizing the great damage which the Court had done to the "privilege or immunities" clause, he fell back heavily upon "equal protection," hitherto little heard of in civil rights debates. "Equal protection," he said, "must not be understood in any restrictive sense, but must include every benefit to be derived from law." Citing evidence from the 1866 debates in the House, he argued with some cogency that this had been the true intent of the framers of the amendment.[81]

Even more than two years earlier the social implications of the mixed school question were uppermost in everyone's mind. One southerner, Harris, quoted a letter from the Virginia superintendent of public instruction warning that the Butler bill would "immediately wipe out or practically destroy" the public schools of his state.[82] Stephens insisted that the colored people of Georgia, who already had their own schools and state university, "have no desire or wish for mixed schools."[83] And John D. Atkins of Tennessee, after asserting that God had "stamped the fiat of his condemnation" upon mixed marriages, which brought "decay and death," asked rhetorically, "Why have not the states the power to keep the races apart in the schools and elsewhere?"[84]

Butler presently retaliated with equally heavy tactics. "Was there any objection in the South," he asked, "to consorting with the Negro as a slave? Oh no," he said, "Your children and your servants' children played together; your children suckled the same mother with your servants' children; and, unless tradition speaks falsely, sometimes had the same father."[85]

Nonetheless, Butler, after two days of debate, suddenly withdrew the bill to the Judiciary Committee once more, indicating as he did so some doubt about the efficacy of the mixed school clause.[86] In reality, Butler was under extremely heavy Republican pressure to kill the mandatory mixed school clause. Barnas Sears, the highly influential general agent of the Peabody Education Fund, had been engaged for some time in a campaign to kill the mixed school clause, which he regarded as threatening with "total destruc-

---
[81] *Ibid.*, 412 (Jan. 6, 1874).
[82] *Ibid.*, 377 (Jan. 5, 1874). The Virginia representatives were stirred in particular by a joint resolution adopted by the Virginia Assembly on January 5, 1874, by large majorities, which threatened openly that if the Butler bill became law, the state would destroy the school system of Virginia rather than submit to mixed schools.
[83] *Ibid.*, 381 (Jan. 5, 1874).
[84] *Ibid.*, 453 (Jan. 7, 1874).
[85] *Ibid.*, 457 (Jan. 7, 1874).
[86] *Ibid.*, 457–58 (Jan. 7, 1874).

tion" all the recently developed white-Negro public school systems in the southern states. Sears interviewed Butler, Ebenezer R. Hoar, and numerous other friends of the bill, seeking "to induce them to omit the clause altogether, or to require only equal *privileges* of education without mixing the two races in the schools." Sears also saw President Grant, who, significantly enough, was a member of the Peabody Board of Trustees, and also obtained from him a promise to be "reasonable" about the mixed school question.[87]

Opposition of this kind was too powerful to be ignored. Since 1868 the Peabody Fund had been spending in the neighborhood of a hundred thousand dollars annually on subsidies for public schools, both white and Negro, in the southern states. Its trustees, largely composed of Republicans, included figures of such stature as Hamilton Fish, Admiral David Farragut, and President Grant himself. Sears, a former long-time president of Brown University, had the complete confidence of his trustees. This was more pressure than Butler was prepared to resist. The bill went back to committee,[88] to remain there until the following January.

The Senate was somewhat less amenable to pressure of this kind, and late in the session it passed the Sumner bill with the mixed school clause intact. Apparently, however, it took the action in considerable part as a memorial to the Massachusetts idealist, who had died the previous March.[89] The debate, which began in late April, followed much the same lines as that in the House. Thurman dwelt forcibly upon the Slaughterhouse opinion to underline his contention that Congress could not constitutionally deal with public schools.[90] In reply, Morton, Timothy Howe of Wisconsin, and F. T. Freylinghuysen of New Jersey followed Lawrence's lead in shifting to a new emphasis of the equal protection clause.

The "separate but equal" argument also played a prominent part in Senate debate for the first time. Augustus Merriman of Ohio first admitted frankly that the Fourteenth Amendment did indeed touch the right to go to school, but contended that segregation was nonetheless constitutional if a state "shall make the same provision for the black race that it makes for the

[87] Sears to Robert C. Winthrop, Chairman of the Peabody Board, Jan. 8, 1874, reprinted in J. L. M. Curry, *A Brief Sketch of George Peabody and a History of the Peabody Education Fund through Thirty Years* (Cambridge, Mass., 1898), 64–65.
[88] *New York Tribune*, Jan. 8, 1874; *New York Times*, Jan. 8, 1874. Sears's annual reports, containing extensive observations on the implications of mixed schools, are in *Proceedings of the Trustees of the Peabody Education Fund*, I (Boston, 1875).
[89] Sumner's last words were a charge to E. R. Hoar to "take care of the civil rights bill." Moorfield Storey and Edward W. Emerson, *Ebenezer Rockwood Hoar: A Memoir* (Boston, 1911), 240.
[90] *Cong. Record*, 43 Cong., 1 sess., 4084–88 (May 20, 1874).

white race."[91] But Edmunds of Vermont called the "separate but equal" argument fraudulent, and amassed a careful array of statistics to prove that the practical effect of segregation was to "destroy equality of opportunity for the Negro child."[92]

As in the House, also, a sharp dispute developed over the social implications of mixed schools. A. A. Sargent of California warned that in certain states mixed schools "will break up and utterly destroy, certainly for a long time to come, the efficacy of the common school system"[93] while John W. Johnston of Virginia warned that if Negro voters persisted in encouraging "such unconstitutional interferences as are now sought, they will wake up one of these mornings to find the doors of every public school house in the State barred to all educational advantages for their own and white children alike."[94] George S. Boutwell of Massachusetts asserted in reply that mixed schools were imperative to the growth of American democracy; in them, he said, "Negro and white alike" would eventually "be assimilated and made one in the fundamental ideal of human equality."[95]

On May 22, 1874, the Senate, after an exhausting all-night session, passed Sumner's bill. Virtually the entire Republican membership present lined up behind the measure.[96] Although the House had ample time to pass the bill before adjournment, that chamber exhibited a decided lassitude in the matter.[97] Both the Butler and Sumner bills thus carried over without further action to the next session of the Congress.

When the second session of the Forty-Third Congress assembled in December, 1874, the political situation superficially appeared to make the passage of either of the two pending civil rights bills extremely unlikely. The congressional elections in the previous fall had resulted in a Democratic landslide, so that more than half of the Republicans in the House were now "lame ducks."[98] President Grant was reported to entertain the conviction that the Radical stand on civil rights was in part responsible for the Repub-

---

[91] Ibid., appendix, 358–61 (May 21, 1874).
[92] Ibid., 4173 (May 22, 1874).
[93] Ibid., 4172 (May 22, 1874).
[94] Ibid., 4114 (May 21, 1874).
[95] Ibid., 4116 (May 21, 1874). Boutwell also argued that "separate but equal" facilities were a financial impossibility.
[96] Ibid., 4176 (May 22, 1874). The vote was 29 to 16.
[97] Butler failed on May 25 to obtain the necessary two-thirds vote to refer the Sumner bill to the House Judiciary Committee for report and possible action. The vote, 152 to 85, showed numerous moderate Republicans refusing to support Butler, even though he promised the House to strike out the mixed school clause. There were similar failures on June 1 and June 7. Ibid., 4242, 4439, 5162 (May 25; June 1, 7, 1874).
[98] James Ford Rhodes, History of the United States (New York, 1908), VII, 62, 132.

lican defeat,[99] and, significantly, he dropped all mention of a civil rights act in his annual message.[100] Quite conceivably, Republican leaders in Congress might have quietly abandoned both the Butler and Sumner bills, and simply "marked time" until a Republican return to power.

Instead, Butler, Morton, and the other Radical leaders in Congress decided to push a comprehensive legislative program through the two houses, and for tactical reasons they pushed the Butler bill into a commanding position in the forefront of that program. The Radical program, as it took shape, consisted of two principal parts: a series of bills intended to strengthen the Republican position in the South, and a variety of subsidy bills for various railroad interests. Principal measures for the South were a new enforcement bill, which among other things granted the President sweeping powers to suspend the writ of habeas corpus in several southern states;[101] a two-year army appropriation bill;[102] and the Butler civil rights bill. The most controversial subsidy bill was one to guarantee the bonds and otherwise underwrite the construction of the Texas Pacific Railroad.[103]

Radical administration Republicans were soon openly arguing that the party's success in the elections of 1876 hung on the enactment of these measures. The proposed enforcement act, they asserted, would enable the President to suppress the "white leagues" and other illicit activity against southern Republicans, Negroes, and federal authority generally, while the army act would make it possible for the President to maintain troops in the South in the next two years without depending upon the caprice of a hostile Democratic Congress. The Washington *National Republican,* a Grant- Butler administration newspaper, thought the two bills "essential to the survival of the party and the nation" and admitted that if enacted they would "secure to the Republican Party all of the southern states" in 1876.[104] The same paper acknowledged that Tom Scott and his lieutenants were bringing "powerful but entirely legitimate influences" to bear for the passage of the Texas Pacific bill, but argued that railroad subsidies were necessary to promote eco-

---

[99] New York *Tribune,* Dec. 5, 1874.
[100] The message merely emphasized the Negro's rights "as a citizen and voter." Richardson, *Messages,* VII, 299. The *Nation* thought that Grant already had virtually given "official notice" that he would veto the bill if Congress passed it. XIX, (Dec. 3, 1874), 357. However, at least one Republican, Walter Phelps of New Jersey, had been beaten apparently because of his opposition to the civil rights bill. *Ibid.,* XIX (Nov. 12, 1874), 309.
[101] *Cong. Record,* 43 Cong., 2 sess., 1748 (Feb. 24, 1875).
[102] As introduced, the bill covered only appropriations to July 1, 1876. *Ibid.,* II, 1511-19 (Dec. 7, 1874; Feb. 19, 1875). Because of opposition in the Republican caucus, the necessary two-year amendment was never actually presented. See below.
[103] *Ibid.,* 950, 1500, 1882 (Feb. 3, 19, 27, 1875).
[104] Feb. 11, 17, 1875.

nomic recovery and to align railroad capitalists and big business with the Republican party in the forthcoming election.[105]

On the other hand, many moderate Republicans, among them such influential party figures as James A. Garfield, William Dawes of Massachusetts, Walter Phelps of New Jersey, and even Speaker James G. Blaine himself, were opposed to parts or all of the Radical program.[106] They were skeptical of continued army rule in the South, fearful that passage of the force bill or the two-year army act would mean "a third term for Grant," and suspicious that passage of the Texas Pacific bill might inaugurate a series of ruthless raids on the Treasury. Liberal Republicans and Democrats, of course, saw the entire Radical program as a frank attempt to preserve anarchy in the South[107] and to set the stage for a "gigantic steal of $29,000,000 for Tom Scott."[108]

It was obvious that this program had no chance of enactment in a short session without a change in the House rules to destroy the Democrats' power to filibuster. The House rules as then constituted permitted repeated dilatory motions during debate to adjourn and to "fix a day" for adjournment.[109] Suspension or modification of the rules would require Butler to muster a two-thirds vote of the House, but without this move the entire Radical program faced failure.

[105] *Ibid.*, Jan. 2, 1875. On Scott's lobbying activities, see New York *Tribune*, Dec. 11, 1874; Feb. 13, 1875.
[106] Blaine, Garfield, Dawes, and Phelps all opposed the force bill and the two-year army act in the Republican caucus; Blaine was reported to have argued that the enforcement bill "means a third term." New York *Tribune*, Feb. 13, 15, 18, 1875. Some accounts assert that Blaine himself suggested to L. Q. C. Lamar of Mississippi the parliamentary maneuver that delayed passage of the force bill in the House and so ultimately blocked Senate enactment. Wirt Armistead Cate, *Lucius Q. C. Lamar: Secession and Reunion* (Chapel Hill, N. C., 1935), 187; Edward Mayes, *L. Q. C. Lamar, His Life, Times, and Speeches* (Nashville, Tenn., 1896), 507. Butler soon quarreled bitterly with Blaine over the latter's opposition to the Republican program. Springfield *Republican*, Mar. 1, 1875. Garfield thought the Radical program and the intervention in Louisiana might result in "the disruption of the Republican party." *Correspondence between James A. Garfield and Burke Aaron Hinsdale*, ed. Mary L. Hinsdale, (Ann Arbor, Mich., 1949), 309. Republican Henry Pierce of Massachusetts thought the force bill "worse than useless" and "working solely for the continuation of party supremacy," while Luke Poland of Vermont, G. F. Hoar, and H. B. Smith of New York all thought it grossly unconstitutional. *Cong. Record*, 43 Cong., 2 sess., 1885-86; appendix, 142 (Feb. 27, 1875). More than fifty Republicans voted with the Democrats in late February to keep the Texas Pacific bill off the House calendar. *Ibid.*, 1600-1601 (Feb. 22, 1875).
[107] The *Nation* asserted that the force bill would convert the President into a "sort of tawdry Caesar." XX (Feb. 18, 1875), 108. Charles Eldredge of Wisconsin called it "a most infamous measure"; Samuel S. Cox of New York thought it the culmination of "ten years of mockery" of liberty; James B. Beck of Kentucky condemned the bill as "revolutionary." *Cong. Record*, 43 Cong., 2 sess., 1886, 1915, appendix, 142 (Feb. 27, 1875). Of course, the President's military intervention in Louisiana merely increased moderate Republican and Democratic disgust with the Radical program. Allan Nevins, *Hamilton Fish: The Inner History of the Grant Administration* (2d. ed., New York, 1957), II, 748-61.
[108] New York *Tribune*, Feb. 18, 1875.
[109] For Blaine's exposition of the rule see *Cong. Record*, 43 Cong., 2 sess., 786 ff. (Jan. 27, 1875).

Butler accordingly decided to make his civil rights bill the spearhead of a House fight for a rules change.[110] Thereby the bill suddenly assumed a political significance entirely out of proportion to its original importance in the Radical program. Why Butler decided to use his civil rights bill for this purpose is not entirely clear. The measure was anathema to the Democratic minority, while many Radicals were expressing open skepticism as to the wisdom, in terms of party strategy, of enacting the bill at all.[111] But Butler's own prestige was to some extent bound up with the measure, while not a few Republicans thought it morally desirable and politically sound.[112]

Before the bill could serve party purposes adequately in a rules fight, however, it was necessary to eliminate the mandatory mixed school clause. In mid-December, the House Judiciary Committee, after a sharp internal struggle, struck out the critical clause and replaced it with one permitting "separate but equal" facilities in public schools.[113] This decision, which effectively emasculated the bill, was principally Butler's. Although he offered no public explanation for his action, the reasons for it were evident enough. The President's opposition to the clause had become well known, while the Peabody Fund had recently issued another strong denunciation of any federal mixed school law.[114] A number of state superintendents in the South lately had warned repeatedly that a civil rights bill would ruin both white and Negro education in the South for an indefinite period.[115] Numerous southern Republicans were warning that a mixed school law would badly damage the party in the South, and was not desired by either whites or Negroes.[116]

---

[110] New York *Tribune*, Jan. 27, 1875.
[111] The Washington *National Republican* thought Negroes little interested in the measure and that they preferred their own schools. Dec. 5, 1874.
[112] *Harper's Weekly* campaigned for the bill with the mixed school clause as an "act of justice and party necessity." XVIII (Nov. 14; Dec. 19, 1874), 930, 1038. Vice-President Wilson wrote that the civil rights bill would help remedy the party's defeat by helping to rally old Whigs and Negroes into the Republican party in the South. New York *Tribune*, Jan. 19, 1875.
[113] A subcommittee headed by Butler, Poland of Vermont, and Alexander White of Alabama first reported the modified Butler bill with a "separate but equal" clause. This action elicited bitter objection from John Cessna of Pennsylvania, Jeremiah M. Wilson of Indiana, William P. Frye of Maine, and Jasper D. Ward of Illinois. The full committee of eleven members then took more than twenty votes without coming to any agreement. But a motion to substitute the Senate bill and thereby restore a mandatory mixed school provision then failed, 7 to 4, and the committee voted to report out the bill with Butler's amendment. Washington *National Republican*, Dec. 17, 1874; New York *Tribune*, Dec. 16, 17, 1874.
[114] The trustees had adopted a resolution, the work of a subcommittee headed by the distinguished attorney, William R. Evarts, which asserted that "the prospects and hopes of the public system of education in the South will receive a serious, if not fatal, blow" from any mandatory mixed school law, "which would fall very heavily upon the colored people." *Peabody Fund Proceedings*, I, 409-12, 436-39.
[115] *Ibid.*, 420; *Cong. Record*, 43 Cong., 1 sess., 377 (Jan. 5, 1874).
[116] The Alabama Republican Convention of August, 1874, warned the party that "the Republican party in Alabama does not desire or seek mixed schools or accommodations for the colored people." *Nation*, XIX (Sept. 17, 1874), 180-81.

Congressional Controversy, School Segregation 559

Some evidence indicated that a few southern whites, including some of impeccable political antecedents, actually favored mixed schools as a means of quieting racial hostility, and ex-Confederate General P. T. Beauregard had been working to that end for some time.[117] But Butler must have realized that a mixed school clause would so weaken the bill's support among southern Republican Radicals and moderate Republicans generally that it could not possibly serve him as the "cutting edge" he desired it to be in the forthcoming rules fight. Accordingly, the mixed school clause was removed.

The rules fight began when Cessna of Pennsylvania, a Butler lieutenant, introduced a motion to forbid all dilatory motions "during the remainder of the present session."[118] This motion failed to muster the two-thirds majority required for its adoption. Eighteen Republicans, including such notables as Robert S. Hale of New York, Phelps of New Jersey, and John A. Kasson of Iowa, joined the solid Democratic phalanx in voting "nay," while Garfield of Ohio, Dawes of Massachusetts, and Kelley of Pennsylvania simply "dodged."[119] Not only was the proposal manifestly unfair; everyone also recognized that Butler's "real object" was passage of the enforcement bill and prospective army act.[120] Moreover, both Democrats and many Republicans feared that Butler's "hidden purpose" was enactment of the Texas Pacific bill[121] and perhaps, as Samuel J. Randall of Pennsylvania put it, "every conceivable scheme of public plunder."[122]

With the Cessna amendment hopelessly defeated, Butler moved to call up his civil rights bill and place it on the House calendar.[123] Since the bill had been recommitted the previous January, House rules also required a two-thirds vote on this procedure. The Democrats opening a major filibuster in response, forced seventy-five votes on dilatory motions within the next

[117] *Harper's Weekly,* XVIII (Nov. 14, 1874), 930; T. Harry Williams, "The Louisiana Unification Movement of 1873," *Journal of Southern History,* XI (Aug., 1945), 349–69.
[118] *Cong. Record,* 43 Cong., 2 sess., 700 (Jan. 25, 1875). A Republican caucus in the House had decided on the move. New York *Tribune,* Jan. 25, 1875.
[119] *Cong. Record,* 701 (Jan. 25, 1874). A few moments later, Butler's motion to take up the Senate civil rights bill, a momentary tactical move which had been agreed on in the caucus, failed, 147 to 93, to gain the required two-thirds majority. Significantly, numerous Republican moderates, including Garfield and Hale, now voted "yea." *Ibid.,* 704.
[120] The New York *Tribune* called the civil rights bill a "mere facade" for Cessna's motion. Jan. 26, 1875. The Washington *National Republican* warned that "there are matters of more importance than the civil rights bill that will find their final resting place unless the rule [requiring two-thirds vote for closure in the House] is suspended." Jan. 26, 1875.
[121] The New York *Tribune* reported that Texas Pacific lobbyists and proponents of the notorious "Chorpening claim" worked openly on the floor to obtain passage of the Cessna rule. Jan. 26, 1875.
[122] *Cong. Record,* 43 Cong., 2 sess., 700 (Jan. 25, 1874). The Washington *National Republican* admitted that the "real fear" of the Republican moderates was that the Cessna proposal "would open the treasury to all manner of plunder." Jan. 27, 1875.
[123] Technically, Butler moved to reconsider the vote whereby the bill had been recommitted the previous January. *Cong. Record,* 43 Cong., 2 sess., 785 (Jan. 27, 1875).

forty-eight hours, while the House remained in continuous session.[124] It was still quite generally recognized that the "real issue" was passage of the enforcement bill and the two-year army act.[125] At the end of two days Butler surrendered and permitted an adjournment. His leadership in the House was by this time badly damaged, but Garfield and other Republican moderates were disgusted with Democratic tactics, and they decided to intervene.[126]

Over the weekend, Speaker James G. Blaine called the House Rules Committee together. This body decided to submit to the House a proposed permanent rules change suggested by Garfield, whereby dilatory motions during debate would be virtually prohibited. But in return there could be no closure on the first day of debate without a three-fourths majority vote. Far more moderate than the defeated Cessna proposal, the Garfield proposal would probably insure the passage of the civil rights bill. At the same time, however, it promised to make virtually impossible the enactment of the remainder of the Radical program, simply because debate would be slowed down enough so that there would not be time.[127]

The Rules Committee attempted to present its proposal for a vote, and a new and incredibly complex parliamentary fight forthwith ensued. The Democrats fought desperately to block all rules change, but after a series of failures the Republicans finally mustered the two-thirds vote required on a motion to suspend the rules and allow the Committee to submit its proposal.[128] The House then adopted the Garfield rule, after first amending it to permit closure on the first day of debate by a two-thirds vote.[129] A final attempt by Butler to kill the one-day closure delay failed when Blaine him-

[124] *Ibid.*, 785–829 (Jan. 27, 1875).
[125] The "real issue," said the Washington *National Republican*, "is the loss or preservation to the Republican party of one hundred and thirty-eight electoral votes" in the southern states. Feb. 1, 1875. See also New York *Tribune*, Jan. 29, 1875; New York *World*, Jan. 26; Feb. 1, 1875; Chicago *Tribune*, Feb. 4, 1875.
[126] *Cong. Record*, 43 Cong., 2 sess., 829 (Jan. 27, 1875). Garfield wrote in indignation that Democratic tactics constituted "tyranny" and asserted that while he had opposed the Cessna amendment, "I am for making such changes in the rules as shall not make such obstruction possible." *Correspondence*, ed. Hinsdale, 316.
[127] The rule permitted one dilatory motion to adjourn and one motion to fix a day to adjourn in any debate. It prohibited "the previous question" on the first day of any debate, except by a three-fourths majority. But, significantly, it also provided that the new rule "shall not apply to any proposition to appropriate money or credit or property of the United States, except the regular annual appropriation bills." *Cong. Record*, 43 Cong., 2 sess., 880 (Feb. 1, 1875). Thus the rule obviously would permit unlimited debate on the Texas Pacific bill and similar subsidy measures. New York *Tribune*, Jan. 30, 1875; Washington *National Republican*, Feb. 1, 1875.
[128] *Cong. Record*, 43 Cong., 2 sess., 880–92 (Feb. 1, 1875). The vote, on a motion presented by Kasson of Iowa, was 181 to 90.
[129] *Ibid.*, 901–902 (Feb. 1, 1875). The amended rule passed 171 to 85, although with the rules suspended it required only a simple majority vote.

self took the floor to oppose the change.[130] The death of the enforcement, army, and subsidy bills was now virtually assured.[131]

Although Butler had failed in his apparent larger purpose, the way was now open for passage of his civil rights bill, and he accordingly called it up for debate. Immediately thereafter he yielded by arrangement for a new amendment to strike out entirely all reference to public schools. Of course, this was merely a somewhat less obvious way of accomplishing the same purpose as Butler's "separate but equal" clause; in either event the bill would not now carry any prohibition directed against school segregation.[132]

Although removal of the mandatory mixed school clause had cut the very heart out of the bill, there was no open dissent on the floor. On the contrary, debate elicited from the Republican Negro Richard Cain of South Carolina an expression of belief that southern Negroes did not particularly desire mixed schools. Questioned directly, he replied that "So far as my experience is concerned, I do not believe they do."[133] And when Phelps of New Jersey, a moderate Republican, added the warning that "If Congress sought thus to regulate the schools, the southern states will give you no schools to regulate," there was no disposition to disagree.[134]

The debate in the House was characterized by great bitterness, although it produced little that was new. Butler repeatedly taunted the southerners with charges of lawlessness and sexual promiscuity. John Y. Brown of Kentucky in turn made an unrestrained verbal attack on Butler, for which the House rebuked him with a formal resolution of censure.[135] An amusing and impish feature of the debate was the adoption by a large majority of the clause on civil rights from the Democratic party platform of 1872 as the preamble to the bill.[136]

[130] Butler charged that "with the country breaking into civil war," the Garfield rule was deliberately designed to allow one-day filibusters, and that there would now be no new way to get legislation before the House. *Ibid.*, 896–99 (Feb. 1, 1875). However, the Washington *National Republican* thought the rules change decisive enough to allow enactment of the bills for the South and so to "produce ultimate Republican victory" in 1876. Feb. 4, 1875. See also New York *Tribune*, Feb. 3, 1875, and New York *Times*, Feb. 3, 1875.

[131] The Texas Pacific bill died February 22 when a move to place it on the House calendar failed 117 to 126. *Cong. Record*, 43 Cong., 2 sess., 1600–1601 (Feb. 27, 1875). The enforcement bill passed the House 135 to 114, but the Senate failed to act. *Ibid.*, 1935, 2035 (Feb. 27; Mar. 1, 1875). Blaine, Garfield, and Poland all had opposed the bill in caucus, while Blaine's delaying tactics left no time for the Senate to act. Rhodes, *History of the United States*, VII, 89–90; Edward Stanwood, *James G. Blaine* (Boston, 1905), 117–18. The one-year army bill became law, but the two-year amendment failed of introduction in either house. Washington *National Republican*, Feb. 11, 17, 1875; New York *Evening Post*, Feb. 26, 1875.

[132] *Cong. Record*, 43 Cong., 2 sess., 938–39 (Feb. 3, 1875).

[133] *Ibid.*, 981–82 (Feb. 4, 1875).

[134] *Ibid.*, 1002 (Feb. 4, 1875).

[135] *Ibid.*, 991–92 (Feb. 4, 1875). See also Hans L. Trefousse, *Ben Butler: The South Called Him Beast!* (New York, 1957), 7–10, 230–31, and Cate, *Lucius Q. C. Lamar*, 187–91.

[136] *Cong. Record*, 43 Cong., 2 sess., 1011 (Feb. 4, 1875). The vote was 218 to 26. The

After two days of discussion the House passed the Kellogg amendment by a large majority. An attempt to restore the mixed school clause by striking out the entire text of the Butler bill and substituting that of the Senate bill failed, and the Butler bill then passed.[137] All affirmative votes were Republican; no Democrat voted for the measure. Significantly, fourteen Republicans voted against the bill, all but two of them from the South.

Mixed school legislation was altogether dead. When the Butler bill reached the Senate in late February, the Radicals made no attempt whatsoever to restore the school clause, nor did they attempt to take up once more the text of the Senate bill passed the previous May. After two days of sparse debate under closure rules, the Senate passed the House bill without amendment.[138] The Civil Rights Act of 1875 then became law on March 1, with President Grant's signature.[139]

The new law attracted no great attention and was generally regarded as little more than a tactical device in Radical party strategy. The Washington *National Republican* bluntly described it as "a mere piece of legislative sentimentality," while the *Nation* thought it "a harmless bill," the principal objection to it being its "entire unconstitutionality." Negro public opinion apparently showed little interest in the act once the school clause had been stricken out. *Harper's Weekly* asserted dourly that the act had been "emasculated." It bitterly condemned Butler, who "in striking the school section out of the bill struck at the principle of the whole Republican policy of Reconstruction."[140] In actual practice the new law proved to have little meaning. The Supreme Court was to declare it unconstitutional in entirety in 1883.[141]

---

purpose of the amendment was, of course, to embarrass the Democratic minority by compelling them either to accept the preamble or to vote against their own platform. New York *Times*, Feb. 6, 1875.

[137] *Cong. Record*, 43 Cong., 2 sess., 1010–11 (Feb. 4, 1875). The vote on the Kellogg amendment was 128 to 48; on the Butler bill, 162 to 99.

[138] *Ibid.*, 1870 (Feb. 27, 1875). The vote was 38 to 26. An attempted filibuster was soon abandoned. New York *Times*, Feb. 27, 1875.

[139] 18 *United States Statutes at Large*, 333. The law stipulated that "all persons within the jurisdiction of the United States shall be entitled to the full and equal enjoyment" in inns, public conveyances on land and water, theaters, and "other places of public amusement," subject only to provisions "applicable alike to citizens of every race and color, regardless of any previous condition of servitude." It made violation of the statute a misdemeanor subject to a fine of five hundred to one thousand dollars and imprisonment of thirty days to one year, and permitted civil suits for damages of five hundred dollars for each offense.

[140] Washington *National Republican*, Feb. 6, 1875; *Nation*, XX (Mar. 4, 1875), 141; New York *Tribune*, Mar. 3, 1875; *Harper's Weekly*, XVIII (Mar. 20, 1875), 231.

[141] *Civil Rights Cases*, 109 U. S. 2. Ironically, a mandatory school clause would have survived the Court's test of constitutionality. Justice Bradley rested his opinion on the fact that the Fourteenth Amendment prohibited only certain forms of state action, whereas the statute prohibited various acts by private persons, a distinction which would have left a prohibition on segregation in public schools intact.

Congressional Controversy, School Segregation 563

Thus by 1875 Congress had reached a kind of negative decision regarding a possible federal statute prohibiting segregated schools. After lengthy debate it had decided not to interfere. In effect, this left the issue of segregated schools up to the several states. By the 1880's most of the northern states prohibited segregated schools, either by constitutional provision, statute, or court decision.[142] At the same time, the southern and border states, as rapidly as they were able, either made segregated schools mandatory or struck all reference to mixed schools from their laws.[143]

Thus when the Supreme Court in *Plessy* vs. *Ferguson* (1896)[144] finally spoke in favor of the constitutionality of "separate but equal" facilities, it merely gave sanction to a long-established situation that had been generally accepted for a generation. The Court's opinion also undoubtedly reflected accurately the dominant American public opinion and social myths of the day. It was to stand for two generations as "the law of the land," until at length a new wave of "Radical" idealism on the Negro question, inspired by much the same spirit that had moved Charles Sumner, reached the Court and broke down the "separate but equal" dictum.

Wayne State University

[142] See, for example, *Michigan Session Laws*, 1867, I, 43; *Clark* vs. *Board of Directors*, 24 *Iowa* 266 (1868); *Illinois Laws*, 1874, p. 62; *Pennsylvania Laws*, 1881, p. 220; *New Jersey Pamph. Laws*, 1881, p. 196; 84 *Ohio Laws* (1887), 34; *Conn. School Laws of 1872*, chap. 3, sec. 23; *Minn. School Law*, 1873, title I, sec. 47; *R. I. Gen. Stat.* 1874, chap. 58; sec. 1. A few northern states maintained racial school segregation until after 1900. See *People ex rel. Gallagher*, 93 N. Y. 438 (1883); *People ex rel. Cisco* vs. *Board*, 161 N. Y. 598 (1900); 3 *Ind. Stat.* (1869) 472; *Cory* vs. *Carter*, 48 *Ind.* 327 (1874); *State* vs. *Duffy*, 7 *Nev.* 342 (1874).

[143] Georgia (1877), North Carolina (1876), and Tennessee (1870) adopted mandatory constitutional provisions. See Thorpe, *Federal and State Constitutions*, I, 868; V, 2838; VI, 3469. Louisiana in 1877 struck out its mandatory mixed school constitutional provision. *Ibid.*, III, 1508. See also *Virginia Laws*, 1869-70, p. 413; *Kentucky Gen. Stat.*, 1887, p. 1180 (for 1874 law); and West Virginia and Missouri constitutional provisions of 1872 and 1875 in Thorpe, *Federal and State Constitutions*, VII, 4061, and IV, 2263. C. Vann Woodward, *The Strange History of Jim Crow* (New York, 1955), points out how much more rapidly the South moved toward school segregation than it did toward other aspects of racial segregation.

[144] 163 U. S. 537.

Separate but *not* Equal: The Supreme Court's First Decision on Racial Discrimination in Schools

By J. Morgan Kousser

In 1899, three years after the "separate but equal" decision of *Plessy* v. *Ferguson,* the U. S. Supreme Court for the first time confronted the problem of racial discrimination in education. Writing for a unanimous court, Justice John Marshall Harlan, whose recently refurbished reputation rests chiefly on his liberal opinions in Negro rights cases, decided in effect that the judiciary would do no more to guarantee equality in public services than it had to stop legalized segregation. ". . . the education of the people in schools maintained by state taxation is a matter belonging to the respective States," the justice, who was rarely a protector of states' rights, concluded, "and any interference on the part of Federal authority with the management of such schools cannot be justified except in the case of a clear and unmistakable disregard of rights secured by the supreme law of the land. We have here no such case to be determined . . . ."[1] Attracting even less attention at the time than *Plessy* did, the case of *Joseph W. Cumming, James S. Harper, and John C. Ladeveze* v. *School Board of Richmond County, Ga.* has never received the attention *Plessy* gained in the wake of the outlawing of segregation in the 1954 *Brown* decision.[2] The leading

[1] 175 U.S. 528, 545. On Harlan's reputation and the reasons for changes in it see G. Edward White, *The American Judicial Tradition: Profiles of Leading American Judges* (New York, 1976), 129. Research for this paper was partially supported by the Arnold L. and Lois S. Graves Award and by research funds from the Division of Humanities and Social Sciences at California Institute of Technology. I owe a great deal of thanks to several people who provided me with information and leads to further information: Professor Edward J. Cashin of Augusta College, Mr. Joseph B. Cumming, Mrs. Virginia de Treville of the Augusta College Library, and especially Mrs. Mary Harper Ingram; and to colleagues who were kind enough to comment on an earlier version of the paper, Robert F. Engs, Clayton R. Koppes, and Stanley N. Kutler.

[2] According to Raymond P. Stone *Plessy* v. *Ferguson,* 163 U.S. 537 (1896) "went virtually unnoticed" in newspapers and legal journals at the time, attracting less attention in most of the newspapers which regularly covered the Court's decisions than an obscure civil case

Mr. Kousser is professor of history at the California Institute of Technology.

case on educational discrimination for four decades, *Cumming* has neither been specifically overruled by judges nor subjected to more than passing mention by legal scholars or historians.[3] A thorough analysis of the *Cumming* case will cast new light on the nature of race relations, racial politics, and the character of the black elite in the postbellum South; raise serious questions about Justice Harlan's devotion to civil rights; and contribute to the growing tendency to substitute a broader social history for the narrow study of abstract legalistic principles which has until recently constituted the history of law.[4]

Four factors shaped the course of black education in Augusta and the surrounding county of Richmond in the late nineteenth century: the black masses' strong desire for education, black political power, the activities of the black elite, and the attitudes of white leaders. Denied an education, at least in law, before 1865, the former slaves and free people of color developed "an almost limitless faith in the possibilities of advancement through schooling."[5] As early as June 1866 the blacks' push to learn led the local Inferior Court, which served at the time as Augusta's school board, to hold a public meeting to offer local financial support for a few schools for Negroes until the legislature could set up a formal state-funded system. At

---

decided the same day. The New York *Times* briefly summarized *Plessy* in a column headlined "Railway News," and the Washington *Post*, noting that carpetbagger-lawyer-novelist Albion Winegar Tourgée had represented Plessy, curtly dismissed the case as "another fool's errand," a reference to Tourgée's most famous novel. See Stone, " 'Separate But Equal': The Evolution and Demise of a Constitutional Doctrine" (unpublished Ph.D. dissertation, Princeton University, 1964), 263-64. There are brief newspaper reports on *Cumming* in Washington *Post*, December 19, 1899, p. 5; Cleveland *Gazette*, December 30, 1899; Philadelphia *Public Ledger*, December 19, 1899, p. 12; and, of course, longer treatments in the Georgia newspapers. The best of the numberless treatments of *Plessy* are C. Vann Woodward, *American Counterpoint: Slavery and Racism in the North-South Dialogue* (Boston and Toronto, 1971), 212-33; and Otto H. Olsen, ed., *The Thin Disguise: Turning Point in Negro History*, Plessy v. Ferguson . . . (New York, 1967). See pp. 25-27, 123-30, of Olsen's book for another treatment of the response to *Plessy*.

[3] The National Association for the Advancement of Colored People (NAACP) and the Court majority tiptoed around *Cumming*, much to the dissenters' disgust, in *Missouri ex. rel. Gaines v. Canada*, 305 U.S. 337, 340, 353 (1938), and lawyers for both sides in *Brown* handled the by then doddering *Cumming* precedent gingerly. See Leon Friedman, ed., *Argument: The Oral Argument Before the Supreme Court in Brown v. Board of Education* . . . (New York, 1969), 42n, 57, 231: *Brown v. Board of Education*, 347 U.S. 483, 491 (1954). Most of the treatments of the case devote only one or two paragraphs to it. For specific citations see below, notes 47-48, 53-56.

[4] For a variety of attempts to escape the coils of narrow constitutional doctrine as the exclusive focus of legal history see Wythe Holt, ed., *Essays in 19th Century American Legal History* (Westport, Conn., 1976); and Richard Kluger, *Simple Justice* (New York, 1975).

[5] John M. Matthews, "Studies in Race Relations in Georgia, 1890-1930," (unpublished Ph.D. dissertation, Duke University, 1970), 9. The 1829 law making it illegal to teach any black to read or write seems to have been widely ignored. See Edward F. Sweat, "The Free Negro in Ante-Bellum Georgia" (unpublished Ph.D. dissertation, Indiana University, 1957), 205-207.

the urging of spokesman Robert Augustus Harper, the blacks at the meeting agreed to accept the court's proposal as a gesture of good faith. Though it is unclear from surviving records whether the whites followed through completely on their promise, the fact that they gave it does indicate a desire on their part to conciliate the blacks or at least to keep control of the Negroes' education in the hands of the southern whites.[6] But since the 1866 Johnsonian legislature confined fiscal support to white schools and the turbulence of Congressional Reconstruction in Georgia prevented the establishment of a stable state educational system, schooling for Augusta blacks in the 1860s and early 1870s depended entirely on the efforts of the local community, the Freedmen's Bureau, and northern missionary societies.[7] Only after the Democrats regained control of Georgia in 1871 and 1872 was the biracial public school system put on a firm footing in Richmond County.

Black political power left its impress on the state legislature's 1872 passage of a bill, drawn up by a local committee of nineteen whites, which established a countywide system of education in Richmond County and granted its school board extraordinary powers.[8] Section 9 of the bill, though mandating segregation, specifically provided that the Richmond County School Board "shall provide the same facilities for both [white and Negro children], both as regards schoolhouses and fixtures, attainments and abilities of teachers, length of term time, and all other matters appertaining to education . . . ." Unlike most other school boards in Georgia, the Richmond County board could establish high schools (Section 10) and levy local taxes without a referendum, and no general law on education could supersede the 1872 special act. Furthermore, Richmond County was expressly excused from the 1877 state constitution's prohibition on public high schools.[9]

Their rights guaranteed in law, black leaders pressed for full im-

[6] Augusta *Chronicle,* July 1, 1866. The Augusta *Daily Press,* May 3, June 21, 1866, quoted in Alan Conway, *The Reconstruction of Georgia* (Minneapolis, 1966), 86, favored setting up schools for blacks by southern whites to preempt northerners from control.

[7] On the bureau schools see Conway, *Reconstruction,* 84-96. The local school board did partially subsidize the salaries of bureau teachers in Augusta. See Jacqueline Jones, "The 'Great Opportunity': Northern Teachers and the Georgia Freedman, 1865-1873" (unpublished Ph.D. dissertation, University of Wisconsin, 1976), 403.

[8] The fact that it was drafted locally implies that the law reflected the opinion of the Augusta white elite, at least, and not simply that of a legislative committee. On the writing of the bill see Augusta *Chronicle,* May 21, 24, 1872. For the act see Public Law 456, Georgia, *Public Laws Passed by the General Assembly . . . 1872* (Atlanta, 1872).

[9] See Article VIII, Section V, Paragraph I, of the 1877 constitution, Francis N. Thorpe, comp., *The Federal and State Constitutions . . .* (7 vols., Washington D. C., 1909), II, 868. The board was allowed, if it wished, to charge tuition in high schools by Section 10, Public Law 347 of 1877.

plementation by the board. Pointing out that the buildings allocated to blacks could not accommodate all those who sought admission during the 1872-1873 term, former Freedmen's Bureau agent William Jefferson White offered the Richmond County School Board three buildings which had been owned by the bureau and two rooms in the black Harmony Baptist Church, of which he was pastor.[10] Stressing both student demand and the need to train teachers for the elementary schools, White also petitioned for a black public high school. In response, the city's leading newspaper noted the provisions of the law and endorsed White's request as "just and fair." "If the whites have high schools, grammar, intermediate and primary schools," the *Chronicle*'s editorial continued, "let the colored children have them also. Let no children, white or colored, be turned away for want of teachers, or school room, or books, whose parents or guardians are desirous that they should receive an education. Give both races exactly the same opportunities and equal advantages."[11]

Described by the Negro Atlanta *Age* as "the father of [Negro] education" in Georgia, White had started Augusta Baptist Institute, which later became Morehouse College, in 1867. Originally devoted to upgrading the meager educational attainments of black Baptist ministers, the institute seems to have functioned primarily as a high school for the black community during the 1870s. When its trustees decided in 1879 that a move to Atlanta would put the school on a firmer financial footing, the long-delayed issue of a public high school for blacks came to a head.[12]

Richmond County in 1880 supported one semipublic and two public high schools for whites and from time to time had partially subsidized the venerable Academy of Richmond County for boys.[13] It was, therefore, obvious to county school commissioner William Henry Fleming that the 1872 law required the school board to take

[10] Augusta *Chronicle*, April 13, 1873.
[11] *Ibid.*, July 22, 1873.
[12] Atlanta *Age*, quoted in Savannah *Tribune*, April 30, 1898; John A. Dittmer, "The Black Man and White Supremacy in Georgia During the Progressive Era" (unpublished Ph.D. dissertation, Indiana University, 1971), 183; Mrs. Mary Blocker (daughter of William J. White) to Laura Harper, April 8, 1962, in a collection of papers now in possession of Mrs. Mary Harper Ingram of Atlanta, which will be referred to hereinafter as Harper Family Papers; Ridgely Torrence, *The Story of John Hope* (New York, 1948), 122; Willard Range, *The Rise and Progress of Negro Colleges in Georgia, 1865-1949* (Athens, Ga., 1951), 8, 16, 24-26, 53, 108; Benjamin G. Brawley, *History of Morehouse College* (Atlanta, Ga., 1917), 12-27.
[13] The mix of public and private funding and the charging of tuition in "public" high schools was quite typical of the pragmatic, unbureaucratized school systems of the South during this period. See John L. Maxwell, Pleasant A. Stovall, and T. R. Gibson, *The Handbook of Augusta* (Augusta, 1878), 63-66; Augusta *Chronicle*, June 18-21, September 18-20, 1895; February 12, 1900.

positive action on a July 1880 petition requesting a black public high school. Appointed at a mass meeting of the black population, the committee of five leading Negroes, which included William J. White, Robert Harper's son James S. Harper, and Colored Methodist bishop Lucius Henry Holsey, "respectfully but earnestly" called for compliance with the law. In response, Fleming, an outspoken racial moderate whose views did not prevent his later election as speaker of the state House of Representatives and as congressman from Augusta, reminded the board of Section 9 of the 1872 law and reiterated his previous recommendation in favor of a black high school. "To grant to-day the petition of the colored people," Fleming announced, "would be only an act of tardy justice."[14]

Asserting that the law compelled the establishment of a black high school eventually but not immediately, the lawyer for the board and chairman of its high school committee, Joseph Ganahl, moved successfully to "accept" rather than "adopt" Fleming's report, and it appeared that the board would bury the blacks' petition in committee. Between the July and October board meetings, however, the issue of black schools agitated both state and national elections. Reminding his audience at a political rally that black as well as white taxes supported the white high schools, 1880 Republican national convention delegate and former state legislator Edwin Belcher condemned the board: "The school law says equal facilities shall be given white and colored children. Now the white children have a high school and the colored have none. . . . That will not do."[15] The Eighth Congressional District Republican Convention, moreover, heard William J. White's denunciation of "the discrimination against colored children and colored teachers in many of the counties of the State." And in the hotly contested gubernational race between Alfred Holt Colquitt and Thomas Manson Norwood, the young Thomas Edward "Tom" Watson claimed in an

[14] On the black petition and meeting see "Minutes of the Richmond County School Board, 1876-1891," 132-33, bound manuscript, in the school board offices, Augusta, hereinafter referred to as "Minutes." On Fleming see Edward L. Cashin, "Thomas E. Watson and the Catholic Laymen's Association of Georgia" (unpublished Ph.D. dissertation, Fordham University, 1962), 13, 59-61, 91-92; Augusta *Chronicle,* July 11, 1880 (quotation); May 13, June 5, 6, 1902; June 20, 22, 1906; Fleming, *Slavery and the Race Problem in the South* (Boston, [1906]). For further information and more complete citations of sources of information on Fleming and other Augustans treated in this paper, see my "Separate but *Not* Equal: The Supreme Court's First Decision on Discrimination in Schools," unpublished California Institute of Technology Working Paper, No. 204 (March 1978).

[15] On the board meeting see Augusta *Chronicle,* July 11, October 10, 1880; Ganahl's motion is in "Minutes" (1876-91), 126-27. Belcher's speech is in Augusta *Chronicle,* July 28, 1880. On Belcher, a light-skinned Negro who was a forceful proponent of black political power, see Edward E. Young, "The Negro in Georgia Politics, 1867-1877" (unpublished M.A. thesis, Emory University, 1955), 35; Olive H. Shadgett, *The Republican Party in Georgia from Reconstruction Through 1900* (Athens, Ga., 1964), 78-79.

Augusta speech that blacks should support Norwood because he would give them "a fair share in education." Because there was no registration law and the poll-tax prerequisite was seldom strictly enforced (an 1881 grand jury investigation showed that only 30 percent of the voters in the 1880 municipal election had paid their taxes), the blacks voted freely in local as well as state and national elections, and, according to the *Chronicle,* "their votes were sought by all the candidates," Democrats as well as Republicans. Perhaps responding to the pressure of the black electorate, the school board at its October 1880 meeting voted to establish a black high school, overriding the objection of one board member that the shortage of places in black primary schools should be alleviated before allocating money to the higher branches.[16]

The black community demonstrated its control over its own schools immediately, as William J. White was allowed to recruit perhaps the best-qualified black teacher in the state as the high school's principal-teacher. Born a slave in 1855, the new principal, Atlanta University graduate Richard Robert Wright, quickly gained the respect of the local black leadership as well as the white school board.[17] As if to underline the independence of the high school from southern white control, Wright named it for his mentor, the Massachusetts-born white carpetbagger and Freedmen's Bureau officer who founded and served as president of the then highly controversial Atlanta University, Edmund Asa Ware.[18]

Ware High, which offered the same classical curriculum as the white schools, quickly became a "complete success" in the words of 1881 county school commissioner Benjamin Neely. It was the only public high school for Negroes in Georgia before 1915 and one of perhaps four in the eleven ex-Confederate states in 1880. Providing

[16] The quotations are taken, respectively, from the Augusta *Chronicle,* September 2, October 2, and July 22, 1880. The grand jury investigation was reported in Augusta *Chronicle,* October 30, 1881. Supported by other state black leaders, Colquitt carried the black vote in Augusta, 780 to 133. Augusta *Chronicle,* October 7, 1880. On black participation in Augusta politics during this period see William B. Hamilton, "Political Control in a Southern City: Augusta, Georgia, in the 1890s" (unpublished A.B. thesis, Harvard University, 1972), 34–54; Richard H. L. German, "The Queen City of the Savannah: Augusta, Georgia, During the Urban Progressive Era, 1890–1917" (unpublished Ph.D. dissertation, University of Florida, 1971), 46, 152. Until about 1900 black votes bought lenient enforcement of the law for Augusta Negroes according to A. G. Coombs and L. D. Davis, "Crime in Augusta," in W. E. Burghardt Du Bois, ed., *Some Notes on Negro Crime, Particularly in Georgia* (Atlanta, Ga., 1904), 52–53.

[17] Elizabeth R. Haynes, *The Black Boy of Atlanta* (Boston, 1952), 99–101, 120, and *passim*; and Clarence A. Bacote, "The Negro in Georgia Politics, 1880–1908" (unpublished Ph.D. dissertation, University of Chicago, 1955), 52–53, 236; Shadgett, *Republican Party,* 84–85; Augusta *Chronicle,* April 16, 1881; June 9, July 2, 8, 1897.

[18] On Ware see *National Cyclopedia of American Biography,* V (New York, 1907), 380. On integrationist Atlanta University see Range, *Rise and Progress of Negro Colleges,* 60–63.

comparatively well-trained teachers for Richmond and the surrounding counties, the school served as well as a source of pride and an avenue of mobility for Augusta's energetic, striving black community.[19] Although sectarian pride and the insatiable black demand for education led the Baptists, Methodists, and Presbyterians to open separate black high schools in Augusta over the next dozen years (at least one of which unsuccessfully petitioned for a subsidy from the school board) Ware remained, according to the *Chronicle*, "the leading high school among the colored people of this state."[20]

Ware High served political as well as educational purposes. Straining for every vote in his three congressional contests with the Populist Tom Watson, Democrat James Conquest Cross Black appealed for Negro votes in Augusta on the ground that in Richmond County, "the colored girls and colored boys are educated at the expense of the whites and given the benefits not only of a common school, but a high school education." The $800 yearly net expense of Ware High was, so long as Negroes voted, a good investment for the Democrats. In response to Black, Watson claimed that Negroes paid approximately as much through direct and indirect taxes as they received for schools. The Populists, Watson asserted, would allocate to Negroes their "share of the public school fund" on grounds of simple justice, without the Democrats' "misleading" and specious pretensions to paternalism.[21]

In fact, the Democratic claims were exaggerated, for Augusta's black schools were by no means equal to those for whites. Housed in

[19] "Minutes" (1876-91), 153, for Neely's statement; *13th Annual Report of the Public Schools of Richmond County, 1885* (Augusta, 1886), 15-16; German, "Queen City," 36-37; Matthews, "Race Relations in Georgia," 300, for facts on Ware and other schools in Georgia. *House Executive Documents*, 47 Cong., 1 Sess., No. 1: *Report of the Secretary of the Interior* (4 vols., Serials 2017-20, Washington, 1881-1883), IV, 4-307, gives statistics of secondary schools. On the place of Ware and other public schools in the life of the Augusta black community see Augusta *Chronicle*, July 2, 22, August 31, September 24, 1880; June 10, 24, July 17, August 5, September 16, December 31, 1894; March 3, 12, April 13, 14, June 14, August 18, 1895; August 25, October 14, 22, 1897; September 29, 1898; January 11, 13, November 16, 29, December 24, 1899; February 11, 18, March 7, 1900; Washington *Bee*, April 30, 1898; Savannah *Tribune*, April 23, 1898; Augusta *Union*, January 27, 1900; Haynes, *Black Boy of Atlanta*, 99-112; J. L. Nichols and William H. Crogman, *Progress of a Race, or the Remarkable Advancement of the American Negro* (Napierville, Ill., 1929), 373; German, "Queen City," 135-37. For the changing attitude of School Superintendent Lawton Bryan Evans toward the propriety of providing public high school education for blacks, compare pp. 309-11 with p. 403 of "Minutes" (1876-91).

[20] Matthews, "Race Relations in Georgia," 297-98; George E. Clary, Jr., "The Founding of Paine College—A Unique Venture in Interracial Cooperation in the New South, 1882-1903" (unpublished Ed.D. dissertation, University of Georgia, 1965), 24. The quotation is from the Augusta *Chronicle*, June 9, 1897.

[21] Both quotations are from the Atlanta *People's Party Paper*, November 2, 1894; for a similar appeal by Black in 1895 see Augusta *Chronicle*, September 26, 1895. Naturally, Black also sought Negro votes on the more conventional grounds of patronage and of putting Negroes on juries.

the 1880s in four "disreputable structures" which had been used for hospitals during the Civil War, the black schools, despite some upgrading during the 1890s, could not hold all the children who wished to attend. In 1897 the board owned or rented forty-one schools with an average value of $4,622 for whites, but only twenty-two worth about $1,100 each for blacks. As Commissioner Lawton Bryan Evans noted repeatedly in his annual reports, the primary schools each year had to turn away three hundred to a thousand Negro children for lack of seats, and more probably would have attempted to register if the board had overridden efforts, led by Joseph Ganahl, to keep tax rates low.[22] Enrollment figures support Evans's statements. Although the percentage of Richmond County's six-to-eighteen-year-old blacks enrolled rose from 18 percent in 1881 to 34 percent in 1897, the whites retained a comfortable lead, enrolling 47 percent in 1881 and 59 percent in 1897. Moreover, black children, who composed a slight majority of Richmond's school-age population, had half as many teachers as the whites: in 1881 there were 212 blacks age six to eighteen for every black teacher, and only 97 whites; in 1897, 151 and 76; in 1900, 171 and 71; and in 1910, 173 and 66. And the black teachers were less well paid. In 1877 the white teachers received an average of $40 per month to the blacks' $25; in 1888 the range for whites was $35 to $50 a month, while the blacks got $20 to $40; in 1897 the whites averaged $43 compared to $30 for the Negroes; and in 1907 the figures were $50 and $25, respectively.[23]

When the fragmentary figures on the salaries paid to the teachers of each race are divided by the numbers of each race within the school ages, the degree of discrimination becomes clearer. As Table 1 shows, Richmond County spent three or four times as much on

[22] Ware High in 1895 was taught in a building described by the *Chronicle* of June 9 as "a relic of past days." The quotation in the text is from Helen Chapman, "The Contributions to Education of Lawton B. Evans" (unpublished M.A. thesis, University of Georgia, 1949), 20. See also Augusta *Chronicle,* June 17, September 15, 18, October 14, 1894; January 20, September 22, 1895; Evans, *Thirteenth Annual Report of the Public Schools of Richmond County, 1885* (Augusta, 1886), 16; and Evans, *Fifteenth Annual Report of the Public Schools of Richmond County, 1887* (Augusta, 1888). In addition, see "Minutes" (1876-91), 235-36, 384; and "Minutes" (1900), 53-57.

[23] The statistics for teachers' salaries for 1897 are incomplete, since the totals for salaries in the printed state report for 1897 do not match those computed by adding up the average salaries multiplied by the number of teachers of each "grade" by race. Apparently, the salaries of principals (who also taught) were left out of the average salary figures, for their salaries were high enough to have raised the averages above the stated 1897 figures. Since the racial differential in the principals' salaries was higher than that for other teachers, exclusion of them reduces the measured racial disparity for 1897. It also understates the level of support per student for white schools in 1897 by perhaps $1 to $1.50. Figures for Table 1 come from the published reports of the Augusta school board, as well as the unpublished "Minutes" for the relevant years.

TABLE 1
Expenditures on Teachers' Salaries per
School-Age Child, Richmond County, Georgia

Year	White	Black	Ratio of White to Black
1877	$6.48	$1.66	3.90
1895	6.69	1.46	4.58
1897	5.14	1.80	2.86
1899	6.34	2.04	3.11
1900	6.30	1.84	3.42
1901	6.89	1.61	4.28
1907	7.72	1.69	4.57

each white as each black pupil, and if the figures on expenses for buildings and maintenance were available by race, the measured degree of discrimination would no doubt rise. In 1907 and 1908, for instance, the board made no physical improvements on its black schools, but completed two new white schools valued at $85,000 and $100,000, respectively. Finally, despite giant strides in imparting bare literacy to Augusta teenagers, discrimination in the outputs of the school system paralleled discrimination in service levels: in 1894, 5 percent of the white and 13 percent of the black youths over ten in Richmond County could not read and write; in 1898 the figures were 4 percent and 12 percent; in 1908, 0.2 percent and 2 percent.[24]

And though whites appear to have partially subsidized black schools in Augusta, James C. C. Black greatly exaggerated when he claimed that Negroes were educated "at the expense of the whites." Assuming that Negroes paid indirect taxes, which were levied chiefly on liquor, in proportion to their numbers, rather than their wealth, it is possible to compute the blacks' share of total taxes and fees. Column 1 of Table 2 gives the figures for the years around the turn of the century for which both tax and expenditure statistics are available. Column 2 of the table shows the proportion of teachers' salaries which went to Negroes, column 3 the resultant white "subsidy" in dollars, and column 4 the increase in the tax rate, in mills, which whites in the county had to pay because of their subsidy to black schools. It cost the average white male adult in Richmond County, who owned $3,018.89 worth of property, only $1.42 per year to subsidize the black schools at the height of the subsidy in

[24] The reports on the cost of building the white schools come from the Georgia, Department of Education, *Thirty-sixth Annual Report* (Atlanta, 1907), 382; and *Thirty-seventh Annual Report* (Atlanta, 1908), 482; other statistics from the printed annual reports of the Richmond County Board of Education as well as the state school reports for the appropriate years.

TABLE 2

PROPORTION OF TAXES PAID, EXPENDITURES ON BLACKS IN RICHMOND COUNTY, AMOUNT OF WHITE SUBSIDY, AND INCREASE IN TAX RATE FOR WHITES DUE TO BLACK SUBSIDY

Year	Percent Taxes Paid by Blacks	Percent Expenditures on Blacks	White Subsidy	Change in White Tax Rate (in mills)
1895	15.2	19.7	$ 3,351	0.15
1897	14.8	28.0	10,152	0.47
1900	10.9	24.2	10,668	0.47
1901	11.4	20.3	7,407	0.33

1900, and if statistics for buildings and maintenance existed, even this subsidy would probably disappear.

To show how the figures for column 1, Table 2, were calculated, 1895 can be used as an example. The state appropriation to Richmond County in that year was $31,880. This derived from indirect taxes, the lease on the state-owned railroad, and property taxes, amounting to $146,828, $210,006, and $600,000, respectively, at the state level. It was assumed that blacks were "due" income from the lease and indirect taxes in proportion to the percentage of black adult males to all adult males (proxies for households) in the state. Blacks made up about 44.7 percent of the adult males. Thus, the blacks in Richmond County were "due" 44.7 percent of that part of the state appropriation which was made up of indirect taxes (37.3 percent), or $5,315 from indirect taxes.

Blacks owned 3.5 percent of the taxable property in Richmond County in 1895. Thus, they were "due" 3.5 percent of that part of the state appropriation which came from property taxes (62.7 percent) or $700.

Poll taxes all went to schools in the county where they were collected. Richmond County blacks paid $4,121 in poll taxes in 1895. After the institution of the white primary in 1898 and 1899 the number of blacks who paid their poll taxes dropped off drastically, which accounts for the decline in the percentages in column 1 from 1897 to 1900 and 1901.

Finally, blacks paid about 3.5 percent of the $45,000 local property tax for schools, or $1,575.

Thus, the total estimated taxes paid by blacks for schools was $11,711, or 15.2 percent of the $31,880 state and $45,000 local taxes.

Black schools in 1895 actually received in salaries $12,955, which would make the subsidy $1,244, but, under the assumption that the expenses for building and maintenance were distributed proportionately to salaries—an assumption which no doubt overestimates the white subsidy—the total subsidy from whites amounted to $3,351. The relatively small funds which the school board received from private sources and tuition have been disregarded in these calculations because of insufficient evidence about their origins.

In 1897 seventeen-year-old Ware High was thriving, having doubled the number of students and added an assistant teacher over its life span. Its principal since 1891, Henry L. Walker, had organized the Negro State Teachers' Association and served as its president for a decade and was highly regarded by both the Augusta black community and the school board. Since Ware, like the white public high schools, charged tuition, the black high school's net cost to the board in 1897 came to only $842.50, which amounted to less than 1 percent of the board's total expenditures or approximately 5 percent of the money spent on black schools. Yet on July 10, 1897, the board, pointing to the need for more black primary schools and claiming that the schools were financially hard pressed, voted to terminate Ware and use the $842.50 to hire four elementary teachers to teach fifty students for $25 a month.[25] Though the evidence is fragmentary, it appears likely that the initial impetus to end Ware came from Lucy Laney, the (black) principal of one of the competing private black high schools.[26]

Announced without previous public discussion, the board's decision aroused a storm of protest in the black community. Within five days 155 Augusta blacks signed a petition, which cited the egalitarian requirement of Section 9 of the 1872 Public Law 346 and quietly punctured the board's declaration of poverty by pointing out that the increase in funds for 1898 recently voted by the state legislature would allow the board easily to satisfy the needs for both primary and secondary schools for the blacks.[27] Considerably wealthier than the average Augusta Negro, the petitioners were mostly professionals or skilled craftsmen who, despite their economic dependence on white customers or employers, were not afraid to assert their rights.[28]

[25] Augusta *Chronicle,* June 17, 1897; "Minutes" (1891-99), 370-72.

[26] For evidence of Laney's role in this affair, which may have been motivated by a desire to expand black primary education or may simply represent an effort to kill off the chief competitor of her private high school see the working-paper version of this paper, note 38.

[27] Since the legislature had increased its general school appropriation, Richmond County would receive 41 percent more from the state in 1898 than in 1897. Thus, the projected total 1898 budget for Richmond County's schools would rise by $13,000 or approximately 23 percent over the 1897 level.

[28] The multiplicity of often obscure sources for my information on individual Augustans prevents their extensive citation here. I instead refer interested scholars to my previously cited working paper, which I shall be happy to supply upon request.

The chief organizers of the protest, who also directed and largely financed the subsequent court case, were first cousins whose families' intertwined personal, business, and church relationships predated the Civil War. Virtually indistinguishable in surviving photographs from men classed as Caucasians, John C. Ladeveze and James S. Harper employed the wealth, education, and resultant social position which constituted the legacy of their white ancestors to become pillars of black society, and, in this case, to fight against racial discrimination. Grandsons of a white Frenchman who had lived openly with a mulatto woman in antebellum Augusta, Harper and Ladeveze were playmates in childhood and business associates as adults, as their fathers had been. Their lieutenants in the Ware movement, Joseph W. Cumming and William J. White were, like Harper and Ladeveze, very light-skinned, comparatively wealthy, and quite active in all aspects of the life of the black community. A Republican, Populist, and later Socialist, White was the single most influential figure in nineteenth-century black education in Augusta as well as editor of the most important local black newspaper. Like Cumming, whose name seems to have been listed first in the eventual court case for purely alphabetic reasons, White had a Caucasian father and appears, from his role in this and other black protest movements, to have been particularly sensitive to racial slights which came from men barely lighter in skin tone than himself.

Although agreeing to meet in special session to consider the black petition, the school board on August 28, 1897, rejected the arguments of the written document and oral presentations by Ladeveze and White and reaffirmed its decision by a vote of 23 to 3, with two abstentions. It is significant that all three of the school board's dissenters represented the Fifth Ward, a lower-class factory area which was the strongest Populist ward in the city, that at least one of the pro-Ware board members, a former grand master workman of the Knights of Labor, Milledge M. Connor, was an active member of the People's party, and that another, Dr. James P. Smith, was widely "recognized as a true & stanch [sic] friend of the mill people," most of whom were of the white working class.[19] Although a compromise had been rumored before the meeting, the board merely offered to restore Ware when economic conditions permitted. Recognizing the hollowness of this promise, the blacks immediately brought two suits in the local Superior Court.

The Negroes chose as their lawyers three whites who had never before publicly exhibited any special sympathy for the race, but

[19] German, "Queen City," 92; Augusta *Chronicle*, July 27, 1894; May 14, 1895; July 11, 16, August 26, 29, September 23, 1897; February 19, 1900. The description of Smith is in Augusta *Tribune*, January 10, 1899.

who were each, in some respect, rebels against the close-knit Augusta establishment. Born in New York, the chief counsel, Salem Dutcher, Jr., was an intellectual and a fellow-traveler with the Populists and had led an abortive crusade in 1894 against Augusta's most powerful politician. One of Dutcher's cocounsels, Hamilton Phinizy, though born to affluence and social status, was a public agnostic. The other, Joseph S. Reynolds, was a self-made man who worked as a drugstore clerk and traveling salesman to support himself while he read law. Neither Dutcher, Phinizy, nor Reynolds was then among the recognized leaders of the Augusta bar.

The briefs which these lawyers filed in the Superior Court in *Cumming* and a companion case, *Albert S. Blodgett and Jerry M. Griffin* v. *School Board,* focused directly on the equal-protection clause of the Fourteenth Amendment to the United States Constitution. For the board to continue to support the Tubman and Hephzibah high schools for whites while eliminating Ware, they contended, was simply an unconstitutional denial of equal protection. If, as the school board alleged, it lacked the means to extend black primary schools to all who desired to enroll, that condition arose from "the illegal action of said Board in appropriating to the white school population of said City largely more of the public school fund than it is legally entitled to." Their clients having exhausted the available nonjudicial remedies, counsel asked in the *Blodgett* case for a mandamus directing the board to reinstate Ware and in *Cumming* for injunctions to prevent the county tax collector from gathering that part of the school tax which went to high schools and to bar the board from spending any money on white high schools unless they also continued Ware.[30]

The lawyers filed two separate cases because they disagreed about the appropriate mode of action in the complicated area of the nineteenth-century "extraordinary remedies," such as writs of mandamus and injunction. Originally instituted in the English courts of equity and common law because general laws failed to do justice in particular cases, the writs circumvented the harsh principles and ponderous usages of the common-law courts. Although the prac-

[30] The quotation is from George F. Edmunds's printed brief in "File Copies of Briefs, 1899," Vol. 14, Case No. 164, p. 21, in U. S. Supreme Court Library, hereinafter referred to as Supreme Court File. Other information on the local briefs is in Augusta *Chronicle,* September 22, 1897; and Transcript of Record No. 621, October Term, 1898, Appellate Case File No. 17206, in National Archives, Washington, D. C., referred to hereinafter as National Archives File. Since *Blodgett* was never considered as important a case by counsel and since the plaintiffs in that case apparently took no part in raising money or propagandizing for the cases, I have devoted less attention to them. Blodgett, a mulatto who may have been the son of white Reconstructionist Foster Blodgett, Jr., was a grocer whose son married one of John Ladeveze's sisters. Griffin was a brown-skinned barber and president of one of the town's largest benevolent societies, whose son later married one of James Harper's daughters.

tices and procedures of law and equity courts had been gradually merged in the United States and although the "extraordinary" remedies were fast becoming more ordinary in the late nineteenth century, the writs retained something of their special character. Neither writ would be issued until the petitioners had exhausted all other possible courses of legal action, and neither would be granted in "doubtful" cases. Moreover, an injunction was purely negative, an order by a court of equity designed to prevent someone from acting. By contrast, the common-law writ of mandamus was an order to a public official to carry out some positive act, usually to do something he had refused to do, more rarely to rescind or reverse an action already taken. Of equal importance in these cases, the circumstances in which courts would issue writs of mandamus were changing in the late nineteenth century. Thus, a leading legal text of the era repeated the traditional view that "mandamus will lie to compel the performance of duties purely ministerial in their nature, when they are so clear and specific that no element of discretion is left in their performance," but it also stated that "where a discretion is abused, and made to work injustice, it may be controlled by mandamus."[31]

Largely ignoring the equal-protection clause argument, school board counsel Joseph Ganahl, who had been chairman of the board's high school committee since 1876, and Frank H. Miller, a respected legal craftsman in whose offices Dutcher, Phinizy, and Reynolds had all studied law, concentrated on the question of how much discretion the board had.[32] It was clear that under Section 10 of the 1872 act setting up the Richmond County schools the board could establish, maintain, or close any number of high schools, set tuition fees at any sum, hire and fire high school personnel, erect or demolish high school buildings. And in fact, in 1878 the board had dropped its subsidies to two previously semipublic high schools for

---

[31] On the development of equity law, see John N. Pomeroy, *A Treatise on Equity Jurisprudence* . . . (San Francisco, 1907), 5-20; Owen W. Fiss, *Injunctions* (Mineola, N. Y., 1972), 9-11, 75-76. The quotations are from Thomas C. Spelling, *A Treatise on Injunctions and Other Extraordinary Remedies* (2d ed., Boston, 1901), 250, 1255. For similar treatments of mandamus see Thomas M. Cooley, *A Treatise on the Constitutional Limitations* . . . (6th ed., Boston, 1890), 136-37; and Forrest G. Ferris and Forrest G. Ferris, Jr., *The Law of Extraordinary Remedies* (St. Louis, Mo., 1926), Sections 206 and 209. Only Dutcher signed the later brief appealing *Blodgett* to the Georgia Supreme Court. For the disagreement on strategy between counsel see Augusta *Chronicle,* March 25, 1898.

[32] For biographical details on Miller see William J. Northen, *Men of Mark in Georgia* (7 vols., Spartanburg, S. C., 1974), IV, 33-38; Lucian L. Knight, *A Standard History of Georgia and Georgians* (6 vols., Chicago and New York, 1917), V, 2777-78. The ironic fact that all three lawyers for the blacks were Miller's pupils I learned from *Scholes' Directory of the City of Augusta* (Augusta, 1886), 311; Augusta *Chronicle,* December 24, 1917; and a private letter from Mary R. Powell to author.

whites, the Richmond and Summerville academies. The question was whether Section 9 of the 1872 act or the equal-protection clause limited the board's discretion in governing high schools. Arguing that Section 9 applied only to the previous sections of the act, which required the board to establish a system of primary schools, and that Section 10 on high schools granted the board absolute discretion, Ganahl and Miller contended that the board was within its rights in "temporarily" suspending Ware because of a lack of funds. Since it would have been "unwise and unconscionable to keep up a high school for sixty pupils and turn away three hundred little negroes who were asking to be taught their alphabet and to read and write," the board's actions were also equitable. Therefore, the plaintiffs' contentions had no basis in either law or equity.[33]

In a decision which the *Chronicle* termed "what most of those familiar with the law thought it must be," Superior Court judge Enoch H. Calloway, a plantation-born former state senator whose reputation as a racial moderate did not prevent his later becoming chairman of the State Democratic Executive Committee, enjoined the board but denied other relief.[34] Granting the contention of Ganahl and Miller that the board had discretion to abolish all the high schools or tailor them to fit the needs of students of different races and geographical areas, Calloway contended that once the board did decide to open public high school facilities for whites, it had to offer them to blacks as well. Properly declining to rest his decision on a constitutional provision if a statutory basis was possible, Calloway argued that unless Section 9 was read as limiting the board's discretion under Section 10 the whole scheme would contravene the equal-protection clause. Therefore, solely on the basis of the statute, he enjoined the board from spending any money on white high schools without reopening Ware. Yet, since he admitted that the board could at its discretion abolish the high schools entirely and since there was some doubt whether it had sufficient funds to run the high schools, Calloway declined to issue the mandamus called for in *Blodgett*. And because the tax levy for high schools was not separable from that for elementary schools, it would have been "unwise," according to the judge, for the court to engender confusion by enjoining the tax collector.

Raising no new arguments in their beliefs, counsel for both the

[33] See Ganahl and Miller, "Return to Rule," 16, National Archives File.
[34] The quotation is from the Augusta *Chronicle*, December 24, 1897. For biographical details on Calloway see the *Chronicle*, November 11, 1894; September 29, November 3, 5, 15, 1898; Augusta *Herald*, October 30, 1898; Allen D. Candler and Clement A. Evans, eds., *Georgia* (3 vols., Atlanta, Ga., 1906), I, 295-99, for more biographical details. For his opinions in *Cumming* and *Blodgett* see Augusta *Chronicle*, December 23, 24, 1897.

board and the blacks appealed the decisions to the Georgia Supreme Court. Speaking for a unanimous court, Chief Justice Thomas Jefferson Simmons, a former Confederate colonel and president of the state Senate, and a leading delegate to the 1877 state constitutional convention, ruled in favor of the board. In an opinion studded with factual inaccuracies and petty technicalities, Simmons, who had gone far out of his way in an earlier case to declare constitutional the practice of refusing to spend on black schools in the town of Eatonton any money derived from local taxes on whites, overruled Calloway's construction of the 1872 act and blithely dismissed, without giving any reasons or citing any precedents, the equal-protection argument. Section 9, in Simmons's view had no effect on Section 10, which granted the board entirely unlimited discretion over high schools. Moreover, the black taxpayers had no more right to complain that they were taxed to support high schools without receiving any benefits from them than did white taxpayers who had no children currently enrolled in the public high schools. Finally, the same arguments which he cited to dissolve the injunction dictated denial of the petition for mandamus against the board.[35] Although it had expected the state Supreme Court to uphold Calloway, the *Chronicle* of March 25, 1898, greeted Simmons's decision as providing "the greatest good for the greatest number." "While the movers in the opposition . . . were, no doubt, impelled by a desire to maintain the interests of their race as they saw them, they will in the end see that the board has acted wisely in the matter . . . ." It was better to give the black masses the "bread and meat" of primary schools, the paper had stated in December 1897 than to provide the "pati de foie gras [sic]" of high schools for the Negro elite.[36]

Ladeveze, Harper, and their compatriots did not despair. Rather, they enlarged the scope of their fund-raising and propaganda efforts (garnering, for example, the munificent sums of $5.06 from two churches in Savannah and $5.00 from Booker T. Washington) and recruited as their counsel for the appeal to the United States Supreme Court one of the country's outstanding constitutional and

---

[35] 29 S.E. 488 (1898). For biographical facts about Simmons see Augusta *Chronicle*, October 29, 1894. The briefs are in the Supreme Court File. Simmons's earlier dictum came in *Reid v. Town of Eatonton*, 80 Ga. 755, 758 (1888). In an attempt to strengthen his case against allegations of racial discrimination by the board, Simmons denied, contrary to facts stipulated by both sides, that the board had ever supported a boys' high school for whites. To buttress his contention that Section 10 was completely separate from the foregoing regulations of the free common schools, he patently misread the 1877 amendments as requiring tuition at high schools, instead of merely allowing the board discretion on whether or not to charge tuition.

[36] Augusta *Chronicle*, January 28, March 25, 1898 (first quotation); December 24, 1897 (other quotations).

corporation lawyers, George Franklin Edmunds.[37]

A United States senator from Vermont from 1866 to 1891, Edmunds was an unreconstructed Radical Republican who, along with many other Republicans of the late nineteenth century, believed that the Fourteenth Amendment was meant to protect human rights as well as those of corporations. One of the leading lawyers for the Southern Pacific Railroad in the important *San Mateo* and *Santa Clara* cases, which established the proposition that corporations were meant to be included as "persons" under the Fourteenth Amendment, and for the challengers of the federal income tax in *Pollock* v. *Farmers' Loan and Trust,* Edmunds had been one of the principal framers of the 1890 Sherman Antitrust Law as well as the 1871 Ku Klux Klan bill and the 1875 Civil Rights Act. Indeed, it was to Edmunds that Justice John Marshall Harlan had turned for consultation when he drafted his famous dissent in the 1883 *Civil Rights Cases,* and Harlan's opinion in that case closely followed the arguments and even some of the phraseology of Edmunds's earlier Senate speeches in defense of the Civil Rights Act. A close adviser to Presidents Ulysses Simpson Grant and Rutherford Birchard Hayes and a serious candidate for the Republican nomination for President in 1884, Edmunds had turned down two offers of appointment to the Supreme Court. Recruited by Harper while wintering at the resort town of Aiken, South Carolina, which was only fifteen miles from Augusta, Edmunds was so touched by the blacks' plight that he took the case without fee.[38] Thus, even before the founding of the National Association for the Advancement of Colored People (NAACP) in 1909, black litigants in civil rights cases were repre-

[37] For the fund raising see Savannah *Tribune,* November 5, 12, 1898; Ladeveze to Washington, June 1898; November 11, 17, 1898, in Container 142, Booker T. Washington Papers (Manuscript Division, Library of Congress, Washington, D. C.). Despite the appeal to Washington to help in the fund raising, the Augustans were forced to rely almost entirely on their own resources. For earlier fund-raising activities see Augusta *Chronicle,* January 14, 1898. In contrast, the NAACP received a $100,000 grant from the liberal Garland Fund in 1929 to fight for equalization of school facilities among other things. See Kluger, *Simple Justice,* 132-33.

[38] The fact that Edmunds burned all his papers before he died probably accounts for the lack of a published biography. Selig Adler's "The Senatorial Career of George Franklin Edmunds, 1866-1891" (unpublished Ph.D. dissertation, University of Illinois, 1934) provided most of the scanty biographical details. Other information derives from *Santa Clara County* v. *Southern Pacific Railroad Co.* 118 U.S. 394 (1886); Howard J. Graham, *Everyman's Constitution: Historical Essays on the Fourteenth Amendment, the "Conspiracy Theory," and American Constitutionalism* (Madison, Wis., 1968), 88n; Alan F. Westin, "John Marshall Harlan and the Constitutional Rights of Negroes: The Transformation of a Southerner," *Yale Law Journal,* LXVI (April 1957), 240n, and an undated note by Laura Harper in the Harper Family Papers. It is interesting to compare the devotion of Edmunds to the rights of the downtrodden with the scorn shown by a leading twentieth-century corporation lawyer, John W. Davis, on whom see William H. Harbaugh's *Lawyer's Lawyer: The Life of John W. Davis* (New York, 1973).

sented by well-qualified—in this case, superlative—counsel. The Supreme Court's repeated rulings against Negroes in this period did not, with one exception, result from inadequate lawyers.[39]

In what may have been a tactical error, Edmunds decided to appeal only *Cumming,* on which there was a full record of depositions, briefs, and decisions, but to let *Blodgett* go. Since Chief Justice Simmons had not bothered to file a full opinion in *Blodgett,* it was unclear on the face of the decision whether a "substantial federal question" was involved. Probably more important, the Georgia Supreme Court had ruled that the 1872 statute granted the board complete discretion in governing high schools, and a mandamus, at least according to the traditional view, could not control a discretionary act. Since the federal courts would not overturn the highest state court's construction of its state's laws, the question of discretion must have seemed muddled, at the very least. Confident that he had a winnable case, Edmunds may have thought that the *Cumming* case raised the issues sufficiently that the question of the form of remedy made little difference.[40] And there was good reason for that confidence.

Though the Supreme Court had never before ruled on racial discrimination in education *per se,* its previous Fourteenth Amendment decisions seemed to support the position of Edmunds's clients. The Court had been willing to intervene to protect railroads and Chinese laundrymen from "arbitrary classifications" or discriminatory actions of legislative, executive, or judicial officers of the states and to launch independent investigations to determine whether in fact the discretion allowed by various statutes had been employed in an "unjust" or "unethical" manner. Despite its negative phraseology, the equal-protection clause had been held to provide blacks with a "positive immunity" against legal discrimina-

[39] The attorney general or solicitor general appeared for the blacks in *U.S.* v. *Reese* et al. (92 U.S. 214); *U.S.* v. *Cruikshank* (92 U.S. 542); *Strauder* v. *West Virginia* (100 U.S. 303); *Ex parte Virginia* (100 U.S. 339); *Ex parte Siebold* (100 U.S. 371); *U.S.* v. *Harris* (106 U.S. 629); *Ex parte Yarbrough* (110 U.S. 651); *The Civil Rights Cases* (109 U.S. 3); and *James* v. *Bowman* (190 U.S. 127). In *Plessy* the chief lawyer was the respected "Judge" Albion Tourgée; in the 1903 Alabama disfranchisement cases, *Giles* v. *Harris* (189 U.S. 475) and *Giles* v. *Teasley* (193 U.S. 146), black lawyer Wilford H. Smith filed competent briefs; and in the 1904 Virginia disfranchisement cases of *Jones* v. *Montague* (194 U.S. 147) and *Selden* v. *Montague* (194 U.S. 153) the blacks were represented by John Sergeant Wise, an excellent lawyer who practiced on Wall Street as well as in Virginia. The exception referred to was Cornelius J. Jones, a blustering black Vicksburg attorney, whose failure to present the disfranchisement case of *Williams* v. *Mississippi* (170 U.S. 213) correctly allowed the Court easily to sidestep the crucial precedent. For his bluster see the file on *Williams* v. *Mississippi* in the National Archives.

[40] Edmunds's confidence is reflected in his correspondence with the Supreme Court (National Archives File) and in a letter from Ladeveze to Booker T. Washington, November 11, 1898, in Container 142, Washington Papers.

tions which "lessen[ed] the security of their rights which others enjoy." Moreover, the *Plessy* case, on which Ganahl and Miller put so much emphasis, actually allowed racial distinctions only if the accommodations on segregated railway cars were equal. Even if the segregation of school children was constitutional—and Edmunds did not challenge it directly in his brief—the opportunities offered students of each race had to be substantially the same, if the court followed the "equal, but separate" rule of *Plessy*. Abolishing Ware was, Edmunds charged, an "arbitrary denial of the equal protection of the law," not an action which the Fourteenth Amendment left to the discretion of the school board.[41]

While Edmunds did not examine state and federal district court opinions on school discrimination, the vast majority of previous decisions in both southern and northern courts favored his views, and his failure to discuss them was probably a mistake. The leading federal cases were *U. S.* v. *Buntin* and *Claybrook* v. *Owensboro*. In *Buntin* Judge John Baxter instructed a federal jury that it did not have to grant the petition of a black child who wished to enter a white school as long as the segregated school provided by the states offered "substantially the same facilities and educational advantages that were offered in the school established for the white children . . . ." In *Claybrook* Judge John Watson Barr, a friend of Justice Harlan's, declared unconstitutional a Kentucky statute which set up a racially segregated local taxation and expenditure system for schools in Owensboro, Kentucky. The equal-protection clause, Barr asserted, "can only mean that the laws of the states must be equal in their benefit, as well as equal in their burdens . . . ," and while absolute equality was "impracticable," the distribution had to be made "upon some fair and equal classification or basis."[42] State court decisions from Arkansas, California, Kentucky, New York, and North Carolina all upheld the view that the equal-protection clause guaranteed "equal benefits" or "equal advantages."[43] Summarizing state and federal cases on the subject

[41] Quotations are from Edmunds's printed brief, 12-15, in Supreme Court File, citing *Chicago, Burlington and Quincy Railroad Co.* v. *Chicago*, (166 U.S. 226); *Gulf, Colorado, and Santa Fe Railroad Company* v. *Ellis* (165 U.S. 150); *Yick Wo* v. *Hopkins* (118 U.S. 356); *Strauder* v. *West Virginia* (100 U.S. 303); and *Plessy* v. *Ferguson* (163 U.S. 537). In his opinion in *Cumming* Harlan implied that at the oral argument Edmunds had challenged school segregation *per se*. The Court, however, declined to rule on that question on the stated grounds that the legality of segregation had been conceded in the lower courts and in the briefs.

[42] *U. S.* v. *Buntin*, 10 F. 730, 735 (1882); *Claybrook* v. *Owensboro*, 16 F. 297, 302 (1883).

[43] *Maddox* v. *Neal*, 45 Ark. 121 (1885); *Ward* v. *Flood*, 48 Cal. 36 (1874); *Dawson* v. *Lee*, 83 Ky. 49 (1885); *People ex. rel. King* v. *Gallagher*, 93 N.Y. 438 (1883); *Puitt* v. *Gaston County Commissioners*, 94 N.C. 709 (1885). For discussions of these and similar cases see Gilbert T. Stephenson, *Race Distinctions in American Law* (New York, 1910), 196-99;

in the 1891 edition of his *General Principles of Constitutional Law,* Judge Thomas McIntyre Cooley, the leading legal commentator of the day, declared school segregation constitutional only if "the schools are equal in advantages, and the same measure of privilege and opportunity is afforded in each."[44] To rule against the black appellants in *Cumming,* therefore, the Supreme Court would have to set its face against a line of precedent firmly established in the lower courts.

Yet in a deeper, less strictly logical sense the trend of Supreme Court decisions was unfavorable to the blacks' cause. The overwhelming fact was that the Court had rarely been willing to act or even to allow Congress to act to protect blacks against the assaults of the states or individuals. *The Slaughter-House Cases* had narrowed the scope of the privileges and immunities of U. S. citizens so much that the clause of the Fourteenth Amendment became nearly meaningless; *Reese, Cruikshank, Harris,* and *Williams* had undermined federal protection of voting rights; the *Civil Rights Cases* had outlawed federal power to prohibit racial discrimination in most commercial transactions by a very strict definition of "state action"; *Plessy* had ruled segregation constitutional.[45] Moreover, at the same time that it stripped Negro rights of the Fourteenth Amendment's protections the Court had increasingly employed it to restrict congressional and state legislative efforts to control the economy. Committed to the difficult and controversial task of judicial oversight of the regulation of businesses, the Court must have hesitated to get involved in reviewing decisions of school boards, too. Suppose the Supreme Court granted the injunction and the school board complied by erecting a new building in which to house the black high school. Then, Ganahl suggested in his brief, could not the Negroes demand that the local court ensure that the black and white schools were entirely equal in facilities brick by brick, in staff salary by salary, and in other respects? Would not such a situation inextricably intertwine the courts in matters better left to "political" bodies such as the school board, whose actions could be

---

Charles S. Mangum, Jr., *The Legal Status of the Negro* (Chapel Hill, N. C., 1940), 89-91, 126-31; Maurice L. Risen, *Legal Aspects of Separation of Races in the Public Schools* (Philadelphia, 1935), 48-51, 70-84.

[44] Cooley, *The General Principles of Constitutional Law in United States of America* (2d ed., Boston, 1891), 242; and similarly, Cooley's *A Treatise on the Law of Torts, or the Wrongs Which Arise Independent of Contract* (2d ed., Chicago, 1888), 338-39, which was still the current edition of this book in 1899.

[45] *The Slaughter-House Cases,* 83 U.S. (16 Wall.) 36 (1873). For citations to the other cases, see note 39 above. There are good discussions of these cases (but a misleading treatment of *Cumming*) in Robert J. Harris, *The Quest for Equality: The Constitution, Congress and the Supreme Court* (Baton Rouge, La., 1960), 57-109.

reviewed directly by the voters? Should the courts intervene in a case where it was doubtful whether a high school for sixty pupils served the interests of blacks better than elementary classes for two hundred? Even granting all these points, Miller and Ganahl continued, wasn't it necessary for the appellants to show bad faith on the part of the board to be able to claim a remedy at equity? Since "no evil eye or combination is averred or shown against the Board of Education," should the courts step in to reverse what was at most "an error of judgment," not an act directed at the blacks "on account of" their race?[46]

The indifference to Negro rights of most of the justices who faced these questions on the United States Supreme Court is too well known to require comment. But what of John Marshall Harlan, whose caustic, lonely dissents in *Civil Rights, Plessy,* and other cases have led prominent scholars to describe him as a man with "a messianic commitment to Negro rights," who gave "undeviating support to Negro civil rights" on the bench?[47] That a former slaveholder and staunch antebellum defender of the *Dred Scott* decision, who before 1868 bitterly denounced the Thirteenth and Fourteenth Amendments and Negro suffrage should become a more faithful defender of black rights than any of his northern colleagues on the Court has lent a certain air of romance to his career and intrigued historians attracted by paradoxes and Pauline ideological conversions.[48] And in addition to his generally pro-Negro judicial stance, Harlan had a special reason to look favorably on the appellants'

[46] Ganahl brief, 8, 12, 17, Supreme Court File; Miller brief, 14, 20, *ibid.*

[47] The quotations are, respectively, from White, *American Judicial Tradition,* 133; and Westin, "John Marshall Harlan and the Constitutional Rights of Negroes," 697; Similarly, see Lewis I. Maddocks, "Justice John Marshall Harlan: Defender of Individual Rights" (unpublished Ph.D. dissertation, Ohio State University, 1959), 108; Westin, *An Autobiography of the Supreme Court* (New York and London, 1963), 118; Florian Bartosic, "The Constitution, Civil Liberties, and John Marshall Harlan," *Kentucky Law Journal,* XLVI (Spring 1958), 446. For a more careful and qualified opinion see Louis Filler, "John M. Harlan," in Leon Friedman and Fred L. Israel, eds., *The Justices of the United States Supreme Court 1789-1969: Their Lives and Major Opinions* (4 vols., New York and London, 1969), II, 1281-95.

[48] Maddocks, "Justice John Marshall Harlan," 1-47; David G. Farrelly, "Harlan's Formative Period: The Years Before the War," *Kentucky Law Journal,* XLVI (Spring 1958), 367-406; Ellwood W. Lewis, "Document: The Appointment of Mr. Justice Harlan," *Indiana Law Review,* XXIX (Fall 1953), 46-74; Westin, "John Marshall Harlan and the Constitutional Rights of Negroes" 658-69; E. Bruce Thompson, "The Bristow Presidential Boom of 1876," *Mississippi Valley Historical Review,* XXXII (June 1945), 3-30. The only published biographies of Harlan, those of Floyd B. Clark, *The Constitutional Doctrines of Justice Harlan* (Baltimore, 1915), and Frank B. Latham, *The Great Dissenter: John Marshall Harlan, 1833-1911* (New York, 1970), add no important details. Woodward, *American Counterpoint,* 224; White, *American Judicial Tradition,* 131-33, 138-43; and Westin, "John Marshall Harlan and the Constitutional Rights of Negroes," 698, are attracted by the paradoxes of Harlan. Westin particularly emphasizes his alleged "conversion" on black-rights issues in 1868.

case in *Cumming*. As Republican gubernatorial candidate in Kentucky in 1871 Harlan had made equal education for all whites one of his main themes. Nominated again in 1875, Harlan extended his call for equality across racial lines, announcing at every speech in his extensive canvass his belief in equalizing state school expenditures for blacks and whites. "The education of the colored children of the Commonwealth is a matter of the profoundest concern to every right-hearted, liberal-minded citizen," candidate Harlan announced in one typical debate with his 1875 Democratic opponent. "There is no question of graver moment presented for our consideration." Approvingly, he quoted the 1875 state Republican platform's statement on the issue: ". . . as a measure of justice, no less than wise statesmanship, we hold that the provision now made for the education of colored children shall be increased until they are afforded, in their separate schools, facilities for obtaining instruction in every respect equal to those provided for white children."[49] Thus, the issues raised by *Cumming* were hardly new to Harlan. Fully aware of the importance of public education in providing equal opportunities to poor whites and blacks, Harlan had twenty-four years earlier committed himself wholeheartedly to equal expenditure regardless of race or the amount of taxes paid.

Yet in his opinion for the Court Harlan almost casually accepted the arguments and statements of fact of Miller and Ganahl. Citing no previous cases from either state or federal courts, the justice circumvented the question of whether *Plessy* required equal privileges by simply not discussing it. Predicting ingenuously that the school board would respond to an injunction by closing the white high schools instead of by reopening Ware, Harlan concluded that the proposed injunctive remedy would damage white children without assisting blacks.[50] Ignoring the fact that mandamus had rarely been held to control discretionary acts and seemingly unaware of the existence of the *Blodgett* case, Harlan suggested that if the blacks had sought an order compelling the board to reopen Ware, "different questions might have arisen in the state court."[51]

[49] The Democratic platform was silent on the issue, and gubernatorial candidate James B. McCreary opposed taxing whites to pay for black schools. For the speech see Louisville *Courier-Journal*, July 5, 1875. During the campaign Harlan did constantly condemn "mixed schools" and the public-accommodations sections of the 1875 Civil Rights Act, which he later defended in his *Civil Rights Cases* dissent.

[50] Everyone appears to have assumed from the first that the board, if enjoined, would reestablish Ware, and Ganahl's brief, 15-16, Supreme Court File, conceded as much.

[51] Although the printed record of *Cumming*, 46, Supreme Court File, did refer to "the mandamus case," *Blodgett* was nowhere stressed. If such considerations had occurred to Harlan early enough, of course, he might have satisfied them at the oral argument, but since no record of that argument survives, we cannot determine whether Harlan misstated the facts

But Harlan went beyond all previous cases in acceding to the argument of the board lawyers that the blacks to sustain an equal-protection claim had to demonstrate "that the Board proceeded in bad faith . . . ," that the allegedly discriminatory action was motivated by "hostility to the colored population because of their race." And he qualified his acknowledgment that "all admit that the benefits and burdens of public taxation must be shared by citizens without discrimination against any class" by adding the words "on account of their race," and implicitly transferred the burden of proof on the question of motivation from the board to the blacks.

Unlike the Fifteenth Amendment, which prohibited denial of the suffrage "on account of race" (and therefore seemingly not on account of property, literacy, or other correlates of race), the Fourteenth Amendment stated its guarantee of nondiscrimination without qualification. "No State shall," the Fourteenth Amendment commanded, ". . . deny to any person within its jurisdiction the equal protection of the laws." The wording implies that not only could there be no discrimination because of race but also that the denial of equal treatment for any reason was unlawful, that no subterfuge for racial discrimination would pass constitutional muster. Harlan's judicial amendment of the Constitution, interpreted in light of the circumstances in *Cumming,* meant that it would not be possible for a Negro to prove discrimination by demonstrating that whites got a disproportionate share of public benefits. Instead, states could blatantly deny blacks equal protection so long as there was no direct evidence that they did so because of race. Yet, what other rationale could have underlain the board's decisions (detailed in Edmund's brief) to provide sufficient elementary schools for whites but not blacks, to pay substantially higher salaries to white than black teachers, to close Ware while continuing two white high schools? If, as Harlan's statement implied, a public body could evade the Fourteenth Amendment's requirements by dissimulating about its reasons for acting sufficiently to demonstrate to a southern state court that there was some other rational basis for its behavior, and if, to overcome this defense, the blacks had to show positively that it was race and race alone which led to the public body's move, then the promise of equal protection became only a derisive taunt.[52]

---

of the state court case—the blacks had, indeed, asked for a mandamus—deliberately or by mistake.

[52] All quotations are from 175 U.S. 544-45; on the "racial hostility" test, see E.J.R. "Legality of Race Segregation in Educational Institutions," *University of Pennsylvania Law Review,* LXXXII (December 1933), 157-64.

What accounts for Harlan's opinion? Why did he not dissent in *Cumming* as he had so sharply and memorably in *Civil Rights* and *Plessy*, thereby laying the groundwork for some future court to reverse its racist direction? Though his voluminous papers at the Library of Congress and the University of Louisville Law School contain no information on *Cumming* and shed little light on Harlan's attitude toward Negro rights, scholars have offered several explanations for his decision. Some, focusing on his unwillingness to rule on the segregation question, merely note his strict construction of the judicial practice of refusing to decide matters which have not been fully argued and ignore or minimize the overall inconsistency of *Cumming* with Harlan's opinions in other cases on black equality.[53] Concentrating too narrowly on segregation, which is merely one form of racial discrimination, they appear to underestimate how much difference it might have made in the lives of black people in America if the court had enforced equal benefits even if the services were segregated.

A second group has tried to explain the inconsistency by suggesting, without bothering to examine the full record of the case, that the lawyers for the blacks had not placed sufficient emphasis on the equal-protection clause or "clumsily presented" the issues.[54] While Edmunds did make the tactical mistakes of not appealing *Blodgett* and not discussing lower court decisions, it seems very unlikely that these errors determined the result, for his brief presented the essential inequity and unconstitutionality of the situation clearly and in sufficient detail for the Court, acting within the relatively loose constraints of equity principles, to have decided in his clients' favor had it so desired.

A third attempt to explain Harlan's stance suggests that the justice was moved by the facts that closing Ware allowed the board to increase the opportunities for black elementary students and that former Ware students could attend private high schools with no increase in tuition. But, as Edmunds's brief pointed out, the board could have met the demand for more places in the black elementary

---

[53] Albert P. Blaustein and Clarence C. Ferguson, Jr., *Desegregation and the Law: The Meaning and Effect of the School Segregation Cases* (New Brunswick, N. J., 1957), 100; Loren Miller, *The Petitioners: The Story of the Supreme Court of the United States and the Negro* (New York, 1966), 213-14; Westin, "John Marshall Harlan and the Constitutional Rights of Negroes," 689.

[54] Derrick A. Bell, Jr., *Race, Racism, and American Law* (Boston and Toronto, 1973), 449-51; Clark Spurlock, *Education and the Supreme Court* (Urbana, Ill., 1955), 181-84 (quotation on p. 183); Monte Canfield, Jr., " 'Our Constitution Is Color-Blind': Mr. Justice Harlan and Modern Problems of Civil Rights," *University of Missouri at Kansas City Law Review*, XXXII (Summer 1964), 311-12; Maddocks, "Justice John Marshall Harlan," 98; Kluger, *Simple Justice*, 121.

schools by the constitutionally preferable means of raising the tax rate or diverting funds from the comparatively affluent white schools. The presence of private high schools, as Edmunds also noted, was irrelevant to the constitutional question of equality in public services.[55]

A fourth view is that in *Cumming* "Harlan was probably continuing a subtle war against segregation legislation . . . ," undermining the "separate but equal" standard by denying the Court's right to look into most exercises of state "police power," thereby showing that the Court could never guarantee equality in racially separate institutions and implying that the only way to fulfill the goal of the equal-protection clause was to end segregation. This overrefined apologetic ignores Harlan's stout defense of segregated schools in Kentucky during the 1870s. Since the Court took no cases from 1877 to 1911 in which the issue of public school integration could not be sidestepped and since his private papers contain nothing bearing directly on the problem, there is simply no evidence that Harlan changed his mind on school integration after he went on the Court.[56]

A fifth line of argument would simply downplay the importance of the case. Perhaps Harlan just did not spend very much time thinking about it, did not realize how much more important it was to the vast majority of Negroes that they have adequate educational opportunities than that they ride in a "first-class" car on a railroad. Perhaps he was ignorant of the rapidly growing gulf between expenditures for black and white schools in the South. But Harlan had certainly long been aware of the problem of racial discrimination in education and believed in the centrality of equalizing educational opportunities during his gubernatorial campaigns of 1871 and 1875. And, as chief judge on the Sixth Circuit Court after February 1896 he must have known of the continuing efforts by his home state to deny blacks equal schools.[57] Even if he had forgotten what he had said two decades earlier and failed to observe widely known facts, why would he have bothered to erect such a high barrier to further

---

[55] Loren P. Beth, "Justice Harlan and the Uses of Dissent," *American Political Science Review*, XLIX (December 1955), 1091-92; Edmunds's brief, 11-12, Supreme Court File.

[56] Edward H. Hobbs, "Negro Education and the Equal Protection for the Laws," *Journal of Politics*, XIV (August 1952), 495-97 (quotation on p. 496). Harlan could have dealt with public school segregation in *Plessy* or in the 1908 case of *Berea College* v. *Commonwealth of Kentucky*, 211 U.S. 45, but chose not to do so.

[57] On the extensive litigation of such questions in Kentucky see Stephenson, *Race Distinctions*, 196-98; Mangum, *Legal Status of the Negro*, 120-25. The 1896 case of *Davenport* v. *Cloverport*, 72 F. 689, decided by Harlan's friend Judge John W. Barr, raised issues very similar to *Cumming*. In the 1898 case of *Henderson Bridge Co.* v. *Henderson City*, 173 U.S. 592, Harlan's opinion for the Court cited an earlier state court case dealing with the same issues, *Marshall* v. *Donovan*, 73 Ky. 681 (1874).

challenges to discrimination if he merely thought this a minor case rather than a crucial precedent in a key area of the law?

Nor will an explanation drawing on Harlan's judicial habits or general philosophy shed much light on *Cumming*. Customarily straightforward in logic, he was impatient with legal casuistry, accusing the majority in the *Civil Rights Cases,* for instance, of undermining the Fourteenth Amendment through "a subtle and ingenious verbal criticism." Yet his assumption that the board would close the white schools rather than reopen Ware was casuistical in the extreme, and his "racial hostility" test for equal protection was just the sort of outright judicial amending of the Constitution for which Harlan often berated his colleagues on the bench.[58] An ardent nationalist who generally opposed state economic regulation as well as state infringements on noneconomic rights, Harlan in this case exalted states' rights at the expense of enforcement by the federal courts of constitutional guarantees.[59] Unconstrained by such sophisticated theories as legal realism, which might have led him to defer to legislatures or cautioned him against projecting his own policy predilections into the Constitution, Harlan loosely followed a model of judging which, in G. Edward White's words, "was primarily designed to implement his individual convictions. It placed a premium on arriving at desirable results, not on internal consistency."[60]

But these observations merely complicate the *Cumming* puzzle, for if "intuition" was Harlan's chief guide, and satisfaction of his policy ends his only thread of consistency, one is left with the view that Harlan simply desired the result in *Cumming,* that while he was eager to defend the largely symbolic exercises of their rights by the few turn-of-the-century blacks who could afford to attend integrated colleges, to patronize integrated theaters or hotels, or to buy first-class railway tickets, he was either blind to the much more practical problem, which directly affected much larger numbers of Negroes, of obtaining a decent education, or he opposed, at this time in his career at least, granting equal public services to blacks.

Whatever Harlan's motives, the results of *Cumming* were very clear. The case gave the southern and other states a green light to heighten discrimination in publicly funded activities and dis-

---

[58] *Civil Rights Cases,* 109 U.S. 3, 26 (1883); Henry J. Abraham, "John Marshall Harlan: The Justice and the Man," *Kentucky Law Journal,* XLVI (Spring 1958), 450. For an example of Harlan's criticism of his colleagues' amendment of the Constitution by judicial decree see his bitter dissent in *Pollock* v. *Farmers' Loan and Trust Company,* 158 U.S. 601 (1895).

[59] For Harlan's nationalistic views on economic matters see Mary Porter, "John Marshall Harlan and the Laissez-Faire Court (1877-1910)" (unpublished Ph.D. dissertation, University of Chicago, 1971).

[60] White, *American Judicial Tradition,* 130.

couraged black litigants from seeking redress in the federal courts. After all, if the court would not overturn a system which flatly denied to blacks a service which it offered to whites, it surely would not intervene to adjust mere discrepancies in teachers' salaries, school and other facilities, and the like. In addition, the burgeoning disfranchisement movement and the refusal of the courts to block that practical nullification of the Fifteenth Amendment meant that blacks would be unable to employ the ballot box to put pressure on white officials for equal treatment.

The consequences of *Cumming* were nowhere more apparent than in Augusta, where to accommodate a continuing stream of students cheaply, the black elementary schools were put on double sessions in 1898, despite which a thousand black children were still unable to obtain seats in schools as late as 1910; and where the "temporary" suspension of the public high school for blacks was continued until 1937.[61] Augusta also witnessed a dramatic collapse of the limited political power blacks had enjoyed since Reconstruction. A white primary eliminated blacks from municipal politics in 1899; a murder and lynching led to the absolute segregation of streetcars in 1900. The blacks' optimism was gone. As one previously hopeful black spokesman, Silas Xavier Floyd, commented, "Many say that the relations between the two races, hitherto so pleasant in Augusta, are now strained forever and that the breach can never be healed."[62] Their rights no longer protected, the four light-skinned Negroes who had initiated the case responded variously. William J. White never quit protesting but was nearly lynched for his part in organizing a statewide movement against a disfranchisement law and for his denunciation of the infamous 1906 Atlanta race riots. James Harper remained in Augusta, continuing his business and religious activities and apparently refraining from more active dissent, but one of his sons moved to Chicago where he later became a militant editor of the influential black newspaper, the *Daily Defender*. John Ladeveze, who according to family tradition was despondent over the outcome of the case, moved to Los

---

[61] "Minutes" (1891-99), 435; "Minutes" (1900), 61; W. E. Burghardt Du Bois and Augustus G. Dill, eds., *The Common School and the Negro American* (Atlanta, 1911), 63; Range, *Rise and Progress of Negro Colleges*, 181. It was 1945 before a full four-year public high school, which was what Ware had been, was reestablished, according to the annual reports of the Georgia State Department of Education.

[62] Augusta *Chronicle*, November 13, 17, December 7, 1899; May 15-17, 20-21, 25, 1900. The Floyd quotation appears in the May 21, 1900, issue. The lynching was in stark contrast to a similar experience in 1895, when the local militia had been called out to maintain law and order, and Joseph Rucker Lamar, a leading local lawyer who later became justice on both the Supreme Court of Georgia and of the United States, was appointed special counsel for the black accused of murder and defended his penniless client with considerable vigor.

Angeles in 1900, passed over the racial barrier, and became a well-to-do real estate and insurance broker. Joseph W. Cumming stayed in Augusta until 1913 or 1914, when he migrated to Philadelphia, passed for white, and also sold real estate.[63] When even Justice Harlan reneged on the Reconstruction Amendments' promise of federal guarantees of black rights, the only safe way to obtain those rights was to cease to be a southern Negro.

[63] Harper Family Papers; correspondence between Mrs. Emile Veze of Arcadia, California, and author; city directories of Los Angeles, 1900 to 1930, and Philadelphia, 1915 to 1930.

CHIEF JUSTICE VINSON AND THE POLITICS OF DESEGREGATION*

by Irving F. Lefberg**

The year 1974 marked the twentieth anniversary of the historic decision of the United States Supreme Court in Brown v. Board of Education *that overturned the long upheld policy of "separate but equal" facilities in elementary education as being violative of the United States constitutional guarantee to equal protection of the law. While the American society continues to struggle with the meaningful implementation of integration in the schools, scholars have begun to debate over the antecedent bases of the decision in* Brown—*whether that decision represented the first great civil rights victory for the Supreme Court under Chief Justice Earl Warren or whether the decision in* Brown *was an inevitable consequence of earlier decisions of the Court in the areas of graduate education and housing racial discrimination under Chief Justice Fred M. Vinson. Mr. Lefberg offers a behavioral analysis of Chief Justice Vinson that suggests that the former conclusion is correct, and that the decision in* Brown *would likely have been decided differently or at best in the same way with a divided Court had Chief Justice Vinson still been on the Court. Mr. Lefberg first analyzes Chief Justice Vinson's other racial discrimination opinions in relation to his generally anti-civil libertarian reputation and then suggests two behavioral explanations for these otherwise anomalous decisions. Mr. Lefberg concludes by discussing the implications of these behavioral variables for the analysis of appellate decision-making in general and for racial discrimination cases in particular.*

I. INTRODUCTION

The Paucity of Literature on Vinson

Twenty years have elapsed since the Supreme Court's momentous decision in *Brown v. Board of Education*[1] and more than twenty-five since civil rights forces achieved their first major judicial victory in *Shelley v. Kraemer*.[2] Both scholarly and popular literature have

---

*I am grateful to Jeffrey B. Morris of Columbia University for inspiring an interest in the Vinson Court and in its fascinating role in the early phases of the civil rights struggle in America.

At various stages of completion the manuscript was read and commented upon incisively by Jeffrey B. Morris, Walter Dean Burnham, Roy Feldman, Jeffrey Pressman, Lucian Pye, Martin Shapiro, William K. Muir, Louis Menand and William C. Bowers. Some of those who read the manuscript do not concur entirely with its major conclusions; all, however, were generous with comments, criticisms and support.

Final revisions of the manuscript were completed under a grant from the National Science Foundation.

**National Science Foundation Fellow, Department of Political Science, Massachusetts Institute of Technology. B.A., The City College of the City University of New York, 1972.

[1] 347 U.S. 483 (1954).
[2] 334 U.S. 1 (1948).

chronicled contributions by personalities on both sides of those great issues; but, except for a handful of scattered, impressionistic observations, the part played by Chief Justice Frederick Moore Vinson in the restrictive covenant and school desegregation cases[3] has been painfully overlooked in the literature. Though Fred Vinson, Earl Warren's immediate predecessor as Chief Justice, authored the Court's unanimous decision in *Shelley* as well as the decisions in *Sweatt v. Painter*[4] and *McLaurin v. Oklahoma*[5]—which for some foreshadowed the Court's invalidation of grade school segregation in *Brown*—Vinson's part in these judicial victories has not been granted the scholarly attention it deserves.[6] The oversight is magnified when one considers that it was the Vinson and not the Warren Court which first noted probable jurisdiction in *Brown v. Board of Education*.[7]

Indeed, Fred M. Vinson is probably the most unwritten-about Chief Justice in the history of the Court;[8] the essential "literature" on the Chief Justice consists of a memorial issue of one law review and an end-of-term article in another—both published shortly after his death in 1953.[9] Yet his tenure on the Court merits scholarly attention not merely because he is one of only fifteen men to have occupied the highest judicial office in the land but principally because his part in the constitutional assault on racial segregation must be acknowledged in the ongoing exegesis of that most critical period in the Court's history. At a time when numerous retrospectives will appear on the *Brown* decision, an explanation and appraisal of Fred Vinson's part in the desegregation cases constitutes a necessary contribution to the literature.

The problem of Chief Justice Vinson and desegregation will be

---

[3] The phrase "school desegregation cases" is employed throughout to connote *Sweatt v. Painter*, 339 U.S. 629 (1950); *McLaurin v. Oklahoma*, 339 U.S. 637 (1950); *Brown v. Board of Education* and the companion cases to *Brown*.
[4] 339 U.S. 629 (1950).
[5] 339 U.S. 637 (1950).
[6] *See* Morris, Book Review, 20 U.C.L.A. L. Rev. 1430 (1973).
[7] 343 U.S. 989 (1952).
[8] Compare the bibliography on Chief Justice Vinson with those of other Justices in W. SWINDLER, COURT AND CONSTITUTION IN THE TWENTIETH CENTURY 525-28 (1970).
[9] Frank, *Fred Vinson and the Chief Justiceship*, 21 U. CHI. L. REV. 212 (1954) [hereinafter cited as Frank]; 49 NW. U.L. REV. (1954), which is dedicated to Chief Justice Vinson.

attacked from several perspectives. The approach will in part be behavioral: it assumes that judicial decisions can, in some measure, be attributed to the backgrounds, experiences and life styles of individual justices; that certain persistent doctrinal tendencies may be explained in the light of personal psychological histories and that short term political and social forces—situational variables—condition the behavior of actors in the judicial process. Chief Justice Vinson's part in the desegregation cases may well be explainable in these terms. But while the behavioral perspective dominates, there is also considerable reliance on more traditional doctrinal and historical analyses of judicial behavior and judicial process. A major portion of this study is in fact devoted to a reappraisal of the legal doctrine set forth in *Shelley, Sweatt* and *McLaurin* and to an assessment of the impact of these decisions in an historical and developmental perspective.

Anomalies in Vinson's Behavior

Interest in Chief Justice Vinson began with a perfunctory analysis of Vinson's behavior in the aforementioned racial civil rights cases: *Shelley, Sweatt* and *McLaurin*. In *Shelley*, the Chief Justice, speaking for a unanimous Court, held that judicial enforcement of private, racially restrictive covenants is "state action" in violation of the Equal Protection Clause of the Fourteenth Amendment. In *Sweatt*, speaking again for a unanimous Court, Chief Justice Vinson found the Negro law school of the University of Texas to be an unequal facility in violation of the Fourteenth Amendment. And finally in *McLaurin*, the Chief Justice, once again with assent of the full Court, found that a Negro student already attending a white graduate institution was denied equal protection when he was required to sit in segregated sections of the classroom, library and dining hall.

Commenting shortly after those decisions, John Frank observed that Vinson "will be remembered as a Judge who, in two great opinions [*Shelley* and *Sweatt*], did much to break the grasp of racial prejudice in the land;"[10] and one of Chief Justice Vinson's former law clerks, later a professor of law, suggested that Vinson's decisions in the race discrimination cases "require a substantial

---

[10] Frank, *supra* note 9, at 246.

modification" of the Chief Justice's anti-civil libertarian reputation.[11] It is now the conventional wisdom, not necessarily concurred in by the present author, that these decisions were unequivocally libertarian in outlook and perhaps even revolutionary in implication or impact.[12]

These apparently libertarian decisions were, in a sense, a behavioral anomaly; for the truth was that all available data on the Chief Justice pointed to an uncommonly conservative, even reactionary, attitude on questions of political freedom, political equality, the right to fair procedure and the right to individual privacy. To see why these apparently liberal decisions seem unusual in context it is necessary to consider some of the data on the Chief Justice's background and emotional characteristics, attitudinal predispositions and manifest behavior in public service.

As a Supreme Court Justice Fred M. Vinson generally cast his vote in favor of restricting freedom of speech and political dissent,[13]

---

[11] See Allen, *Chief Justice Vinson and the Theory of Constitutional Government: A Tentative Appraisal*, 49 Nw. U.L. REV. 3, 7 (1954) [hereinafter cited as Allen].

[12] See S. WASBY, THE IMPACT OF THE UNITED STATES SUPREME COURT: SOME PERSPECTIVES 7 (1970); F. LEVY, NORTHERN SCHOOLS AND CIVIL RIGHTS 109-10 (1971); L. PFEFFER, THIS HONORABLE COURT: A HISTORY OF THE UNITED STATES SUPREME COURT 409-10, for examples of this interpretation of the Vinson opinions and for the implication that the Vinson decisions somehow "led" to the decision in *Brown*.

[13] In *American Communications Ass'n v. Douds*, 339 U.S. 382 (1950), Vinson upheld provisions of the Taft-Hartley Act which conditioned access of unions to the N.L.R.B. upon the filing of oaths by union officers that they are not affiliated with the Communist Party and that they neither "believe in" nor are members of any organization "that believes in" the overthrow of government. In *Dennis v. United States*, 341 U.S. 494 (1951), Vinson upheld convictions under the Smith Act which forbade conspiracy to teach the "duty, necessity, desirability or propriety" of violent overthrow of government. In *Feiner v. New York*, 340 U.S. 315 (1951), Vinson affirmed a conviction for disturbing the peace of a young man who made a street corner speech which resulted in the audience getting out of hand. In *Kovacs v. Cooper*, 336 U.S. 77 (1949), Vinson voted to approve a soundtruck ordinance that banned soundtrucks emitting "loud and raucous" noises.

In *Terminiello v. Chicago*, 337 U.S. 1 (1949), Vinson dissented on procedural grounds from a decision reversing the conviction of an anti-Semitic rabble rouser whose fighting words allegedly incited a turbulent crowd outside the arena in which he was speaking. In *Rogers v. United States*, 340 U.S. 367 (1951), Vinson upheld a contempt conviction of a Communist Party member on the grounds that she failed specifically to claim the privilege against self-incrimination in time. Justices Black, Douglas, and Frankfurter dissented.

In *United States v. Bryan*, 339 U.S. 323 (1950) and *United States v. Fleischman*, 339 U.S. 349 (1950), Chief Justice Vinson upheld convictions growing out of H.U.A.C. subpoenas in which the defendants were required by the committee to produce certain records of the Joint Anti-Fascist Committee. In a dissent in *Joint Anti-Fascist Committee v. McGrath*, 341 U.S.

increasing the breadth of searches and seizures,[14] decreasing the

---

123 (1951), Vinson in effect voted to uphold the Administration's Loyalty-Security program and the Attorney General's power to list the names of subversive organizations. In *Adler v. Board of Education*, 342 U.S. 485 (1952), Vinson voted with the majority to uphold New York's Feinberg Law which gave the Board of Regents the duty of listing those organizations which it found were advocating violent overthrow and then dismissing, after a hearing, any teacher found to have been a member of the designated organizations.

In *In re Disbarment of Isserman*, 345 U.S. 286 (1953), Vinson barred attorney Isserman from practicing before the Supreme Court. Isserman had been one of the defense attorneys in the *Dennis* case and had previously been convicted of contempt in *Sacher v. United States*, 343 U.S. 1 (1952), in which Vinson voted with the majority. Isserman was also disbarred from practice by New Jersey.

In *Rosenberg v. United States*, 346 U.S. 271 (1953), Vinson convened the Court for a special term to quash a stay of execution granted by Justice Douglas for Julius and Ethel Rosenberg. In *Craig v. Harney*, 331 U.S. 367 (1947), Vinson dissented from a decision denying a Texas court the right to punish by contempt the publisher and certain employees of a newspaper for commenting critically and unfairly upon the judge's handling of the trial. In *Garner v. Board of Public Works*, 341 U.S. 716 (1951), a majority, including Vinson, upheld a Los Angeles loyalty oath under which individuals were not permitted to hold public office if in the past they had been affiliated with a subversive organization; no scienter was required. In *Beauharnais v. Illinois*, 343 U.S. 250 (1952), the Court, with Vinson in the majority, upheld the Illinois group libel law as applied to a person who was circulating a petition to the Chicago City Council to adopt an ordinance segregating the city along racial lines. The statute was upheld as a criminal libel law.

[14] See Harris v. United States, 331 U.S. 145 (1947), in which Vinson upheld a conviction based on evidence found by rummaging and ransacking the defendant's house for five hours without the benefit of a search warrant. Vinson dissented in two cases which seemed to undermine the anti-libertarian opinion in *Harris: Di Re v. United States*, 332 U.S. 581 (1948), and *Johnson v. United States*, 333 U.S. 10 (1948). In *Trupiano v. United States*, 334 U.S. 699 (1948), Vinson wrote his first dissent when the Court very narrowly limited the anti-libertarian opinion in *Harris*. In *McDonald v. United States*, 335 U.S. 451 (1948), Vinson dissented as the Court held illegal a search in which police peered through a window, saw a crime being committed, sneaked into the house without a warrant, and seized the evidence. In *United States v. Rabinowitz*, 339 U.S. 56 (1950), a majority including Vinson modified the *Trupiano* doctrine in a partial return to the conservative *Harris* opinion. In *Wolf v. Colorado*, 338 U.S. 25 (1949), with Vinson voting in the majority, the Court refused to apply the exclusionary rule of *Weeks v. United States*, 232 U.S. 383 (1914), to the use of illegally seized evidence in state trials. In *On Lee v. United States*, 343 U.S. 747 (1952), the government secured evidence against a man through a supposed friend who entered the defendant's laundry and engaged On Lee in conversation. The friend was wired for sound, and On Lee's statements were picked up by narcotics agents. Vinson, voting with the majority, upheld On Lee's conviction. The Court ignored the distinction in *Olmstead v. United States*, 277 U.S. 438 (1928), where the Court had allowed electronic eavesdropping on the ground that it did not involve entry. Other cases in which Vinson voted to reject claims based on the Fourth Amendment are: *Donaldson v. Read Magazine*, 333 U.S. 178 (1948); *United States v. Wallace & Tiernan Co.*, 336 U.S. 793 (1949); *Lustig v. United States*, 338 U.S. 74 (1949); *Brinegar v. United States*, 338 U.S. 160 (1949); *United States v. Morton Salt Co.*, 338 U.S. 632 (1950); *United States v. Jeffers*, 342 U.S. 48 (1951); *District of Columbia v. Little*, 339 U.S. 1 (1950); *Stefanelli v. Minard*, 342 U.S. 117 (1951); *Schwartz v. Texas*, 344 U.S. 199 (1952).

freedom from forced confessions,[15] maintaining the limits on the right to counsel[16] and restricting the rights of aliens.[17] Of course

---

[15] In *Haley v. Ohio*, 332 U.S. 596 (1948), Vinson dissented as the Court invalidated the murder conviction of a fifteen year-old Negro boy who had been arrested at midnight, questioned for five hours with no friend or counsel present, and held incommunicado for three days. In *Watts v. Indiana*, 338 U.S. 49 (1949); *Turner v. Pennsylvania*, 338 U.S. 62 (1949); and *Harris v. South Carolina*, 338 U.S. 68 (1949), a suspect was taken into custody by police and questioned intensively for long periods of time with confession as the final result. In each case the Court held the confessions to be illegally secured and reversed the convictions. In each case Vinson dissented. In *Stein v. New York*, 346 U.S. 156 (1953), two murder suspects were questioned intermittently for twelve hours of a thirty-two hour period. The defendants were incommunicado during the period. One defendant had a broken rib and bruises, the other had bruises. The two defendants gave confessions which were "self-confirming." The majority, including Vinson, upheld the convictions. In the case of *Upshaw v. United States*, 335 U.S. 410 (1948), a majority declared inadmissible a confession acquired after the defendant had been detained for thirty hours primarily because the police did not have sufficient evidence to present charges. Vinson dissented, refusing to apply the *McNabb* rule. *See* McNabb v. United States, 318 U.S. 332 (1943).

[16] In *Wade v. Mayo*, 334 U.S. 672 (1948), and *Townsend v. Burke*, 334 U.S. 736 (1948), Vinson dissented from the majority opinion which ruled that the defendants had been denied right to counsel in violation of the Sixth Amendment. In *Palmer v. Ashe*, 342 U.S. 134 (1951), the majority reversed a conviction of a twenty-one year-old with a record of confinement in a mental institution as well as a previous criminal record who had a one-minute trial at which he pleaded guilty to what he thought was a breaking-and-entering charge. He neither had nor was offered counsel. He later found out he had been convicted of robbery. Vinson dissented, voting to uphold the conviction. In *Bute v. Illinois*, 333 U.S. 640 (1948), a fifty-seven year-old man pleaded guilty to charges of taking indecent liberties with children. The Court held that, since these offenses were noncapital and "elementary," the special circumstances were not sufficient under the *Betts* rule to appoint counsel. Vinson also dissented in *Von Moltke v. Gillies*, 332 U.S. 708 (1948), as the Court reversed a conviction on the ground that the defendant had been denied the right to counsel. In *Foster v. Illinois*, 332 U.S. 134 (1947); *Gayes v. New York*, 332 U.S. 145 (1947); *Gryger v. Burke*, 334 U.S. 728 (1948); and *Quicksall v. Michigan*, 339 U.S. 660 (1950), Vinson voted with the majority as the Court sanctioned the absence of counsel in state court proceedings.

[17] In *Jordan v. De George*, 341 U.S. 223 (1951), Vinson, writing for the majority, upheld the Immigration Service's decision to deport an alien who had spent twenty-nine years in this country for bootlegging. In *Guessefeldt v. McGrath*, 342 U.S. 308 (1952), a German alien who had resided in Hawaii for forty years had his property seized while on vacation in Germany on the strength of a statute which permitted the government to seize all property owned by enemies of the U.S. The majority ruled the seizure illegal, holding that the defendant could not be considered an enemy. In a written opinion Vinson dissented. 342 U.S. 320-29. In *Ludecke v. Watkins*, 335 U.S. 160 (1948), the Court held that German citizens lawfully in the U.S. during wartime could be deported after the war under the Alien Enemy Act of 1789 without the right to judicial review. Vinson voted with the majority. In *United States ex rel. Knauff v. Shaughnessy*, 338 U.S. 537 (1950), Vinson voted to permit the Attorney General unlimited discretion in the exclusion of a German war bride. In *Harisiades v. Shaughnessy*, 342 U.S. 580 (1952), Vinson voted to deport an alien who had been a Communist as a young man more than a decade before the act making membership a ground for deportation was passed. In *Carlson v. Landon*, 342 U.S. 524 (1952), the majority, including Vinson, voted to

517

POLITICS OF DESEGREGATION   249

there were, aside from the apparently liberal decisions in the desegregation cases, some libertarian votes;[18] but, as Table 1 shows, his record is overwhelmingly conservative. According to Table 1, Chief Justice Vinson's libertarian support score is next to the lowest among the eleven Justices who served on the Court from 1946 to 1952. The percentages in support of libertarian claims in individual categories are also important. It should be noted that Chief Justice Vinson was the only Justice to vote against Negro claims in each of the four non-unanimous civil rights cases of the period.

Vinson's conservative orientation toward political liberalism is equally evident from his tenure as a judge of the Court of Appeals for the District of Columbia. In one decision while on the court of appeals, Judge Vinson held that a National Mediation Board sanctioned and conducted election in which Negro coach cleaners were denied the right of representation by members of their own race at the bargaining table was not a violation of due process.[19] He stated:

> . . . the Brotherhood, a private association, acting on its own initiative and expressing its own will may limit the rights of its colored members without thereby offending the guarantees of the Constitution.[20]

His position in this 1940 court of appeals decision is thus diametrically opposed to the broad interpretation of the "state action" doctrine announced eight years later in *Shelley*. In another court of appeals decision, Judge Vinson joined with Chief Judge Groner in holding that restrictive covenants "are valid and enforceable by way of injunction,"[21] a position, again, directly contrary to *Shelley*.

---

permit the Attorney General to hold aliens charged with Communism without bail until hearings and other proceedings could take place. Deportation proceedings often drag on for years. In *Shaughnessy v. United States* ex rel. *Mezei*, 345 U.S. 206 (1953), the Court with Vinson in the majority held that the Attorney General had the power to exclude a returning alien who had lived in America for twenty-five years on the basis of information "of a confidential nature." Mezei had been visiting his dying mother in Romania.

[18] *See* Burstyn v. Wilson, 343 U.S. 495 (1952); Rochin v. California, 342 U.S. 165 (1952); Breard v. City of Alexandria, 341 U.S. 622 (1951); Blau v. United States, 340 U.S. 332 (1951); Kunz v. New York, 340 U.S. 290 (1951); Niemotko v. Maryland, 340 U.S. 268 (1951); Uveges v. Pennsylvania, 335 U.S. 437 (1948); Saia v. New York, 334 U.S. 558 (1948).

[19] National Fed'n of Ry. Workers v. National Mediation Bd., 110 F.2d 529 (D.C. Cir.), cert. denied, 310 U.S. 628 (1940).

[20] 110 F.2d at 537.

[21] Hundley v. Gorewitz, 132 F.2d 23 (D.C. Cir. 1942).

Table 1: Voting Record of Supreme Court Justices
in Principal Non-Unanimous Civil Rights Cases,
1946-1952*
(In Percentages)

	for aliens claims	for Negro claims	for criminal defendant's claims state	for criminal defendant's claims federal	for free speech claims state	for free speech claims federal	total
No. cases	23	4	37	21	16	12	113
Murphy	100	100	100	100	100	100	100
Rutledge	100	100	100	85	100	100	96
Douglas	63	100	97	84	100	100	89
Black	100	100	86	62	94	100	87
Frankfurter	82	75	46	85	13	83	61
Court	39	75	35	43	25	17	35
Jackson	50	33	14	55	6	45	31
Clark	14	67	32	14	10	...	24
Burton	35	75	19	14	19	8	22
Minton	19	33	12	0	27	0	14
Vinson	30	0	16	0	19	0	14
Reed	9	33	14	10	31	0	13

*Source: C. PRITCHETT, CIVIL LIBERTIES AND THE VINSON COURT 190 (1954).

It should be emphasized that table 1 presents statistics only on non-unanimous civil liberties cases decided by the Vinson Court. Therefore, votes in *Shelley*, *Sweatt* and *McLaurin* are not included in these statistics.

Other opinions of Vinson while on the court of appeals reveal a conservative perspective on First Amendment rights. In at least two decisions Vinson denied that First Amendment freedoms occupy a "preferred position" in the hierarchy of freedoms the judiciary is assigned to protect.[22]

---

[22] See *Parmelee v. United States*, 113 F.2d 729 (D.C. Cir. 1940), in which Vinson dissented from an opinion by Judge Miller which held that several tiny 1½-by 3-inch photographs of nude humans which accompanied a scientific and educational study of nudism was permitted by "present day concepts of propriety," and *Viereck v. United States*, 130 F.2d 945 (D.C. Cir. 1942), where Vinson broadly construed the Propaganda Agency Act of 1938 to obtain the conviction of a German "author and journalist" for engaging in certain political propagandistic work which he "willfully omitted to disclose to the federal government." 130

While in the executive branch of the federal government, as Secretary of the Treasury, Vinson is alleged to have "played a major role in setting a 'trap' for Harry Dexter White, a prominent civil servant in the Truman administration who was suspected of being disloyal."[23] And as a young congressman, in one of his first speeches on the floor of the House, Vinson's intemperate utterances on the immigration question led one observer to remark that the congressman from Kentucky "voiced the sentiment normally associated only with Southern white supremacists, not with the typical border state politician."[24]

F.2d at 952. This decision, reversed by the Supreme Court, occasioned a strong rebuke of Vinson's holding by Chief Justice Stone. See Viereck v. United States, 318 U.S. 236 (1943).

[23] See J. Bolner, Mr. Chief Justice Vinson: His Politics and His Constitutional Law 236 (Ph.D. dissertation, University of Virginia, 1962) [hereinafter cited as Bolner].

[24] J. Hatcher, Fred Vinson: Congressman From Kentucky—A Political Biography: 1890-1938, 11, n.24 (Ph.D. dissertation, University of Cincinnati, 1967) [hereinafter cited as Hatcher].

At the high point of his speech in Congress, Vinson questioned the proposition that all men are created equal. Said Vinson:

> Oh, yes; spellbinders representing the foreign element can take the Declaration of Independence and plead its language that "all men are created equal" in their attempt to prove the case of unrestricted immigration. We submit that this utterance was and is an axiomatic truth; that equality does exist in the eyes of the benevolent Creator; but generalities such as the one quoted must be viewed with care as applied to the particular instance, because we know that in the natural course of our life there are racial distinctions that are recognized by everyone. God made the different races and instilled into their bosom race distinction. Created of God, I submit that it cannot be wrong to make distinction between races, and any person who states that he considers all other persons as his equal, when pinned down to the question of association and marriage undoubtedly gives the lie to such utterance.

CONG. REC. 6119 (April 11, 1924).

Vinson had opened this debate by proudly describing his congressional district as follows:

> The district which honors me is situate in old Kentucky and contains a minimum of foreign born; in fact, the ethnologists of our day assert that in that district can be found the purest strain of the Anglo-Saxon blood coursing the veins of Americans.

Id. at 6118. Vinson also gratuitously pointed out that:

> There need be no issue of superiorities of races injected into the discussion. It is sufficient to say that it was people of similar characteristics and blood [Anglo-Saxon] that has made America the great Nation that she is.

Id.

Vinson also asserted that the National Origins Act which was being debated at the time would have little effect on the "old" immigration from Western Europe, which included English, Irish, Scotch, and French. Said Vinson:

> It goes without argument that the traits and characteristics of the "old" immigration are of such nature as entails no danger to our country. . . . Were the immi-

What is known of Vinson's background, emotional characteristics and attitudinal predispositions offers little succor in the quest to understand and explain the apparently liberal decisions in *Shelley, Sweatt* and *McLaurin*. The Chief Justice was born and raised in one of the most provincial, nativist and isolated sections of the country—the blue grass region of eastern Kentucky:

> The natives of the Big Sandy Valley [where Vinson was born and raised] are proud and paradoxical people . . . [who] delight in tracing their ancestry to Stuart and Cromwellian England. . . . They are fiercely patriotic . . . with an abundance of hospitality, frankness, courage, suspicion of the outside world, longlasting and deep enmities and stern religious beliefs.[25]

Vinson was apparently raised in a strict, even authoritarian, atmosphere. His mother implanted in him "a deep regard for religion and respect for law,"[26] and he himself acknowledged that he had been "'reared in a disciplinarian household—justice, but discipline. . . .' being its chief characteristic."[27] And that Vinson's father "was anything but the stern, forbidding father-image seems very well established by Vinson's own admission."[28]

Vinson's basic attitudes remained essentially unchanged from those he brought with him to Washington in 1924. They were the attitudes of one who had achieved success in the American system and who wanted that system preserved and perpetuated.[29] Others, particularly former law clerks, have pointed to Vinson's essential skepticism and anti-intellectualism. The Chief Justice frequently protested the tyranny of words and dismissed neat academic generalizations as sophistry.[30] Fred M. Vinson was not, however, a moral relativist; his thinking was firmly anchored to certain basic truths,

---

grants now flooding our shores possessed of the same traits, characteristics, and blood of our forefathers I would have no concern upon this problem confronting us, because, in the main, they belonged to the same branch of the Aryan race.
Id.
[25] Hatcher, *supra* note 24, at 10.
[26] *Id.* at 102.
[27] *Id.* at 101.
[28] *Id.*
[29] *Id.* at 504.
[30] Allen, *supra* note 11, at 5; Lester, *Fred Vinson in the Executive Branch*, 49 Nw. U.L. Rev. 36 (1954).

certain eternal verities, or as Vinson called them: ". . . foundation rocks . . . of civilization which are essential and timeless."[31] That Vinson believed these eternal verities to be imminent in American society is clear from his militant patriotism and "unaffected devotion to his country."[32]

The Chief Justice believed that these fundamental values upon which our society is built were under severe attack by totalitarian ideologies—particularly communism—both at home and abroad.[33] It may not be exaggeration to suggest that Vinson was obsessed with a sense of urgency and crisis which pervaded his thinking during his seven year tenure on the high court. John J. Parker, former Chief Judge of the United States Court of Appeals for the Fourth Circuit,

---

[31] Vinson, *Age of Great Challenge*, 1947 ABA Rep. 335.
[32] Allen, *supra* note 11, at 5.
[33] A speech given by Chief Justice Vinson before the American Bar Association in 1947 is replete with references to the "crises of the times." Much concern is also evidenced for critical dangers posed by totalitarian communism. It is worth quoting from the speech at length.

> There can hardly be a thinking person in our country today who has not experienced the sense of urgency and crisis which our age envisions. The challenges cannot be ignored. They confront us in every aspect of human activity—in the political and economic, in the social and intellectual, and in the moral and spiritual realms. Fundamental values upon which we have erected the edifice of our civilization are under attack. . . .
>
> The symptoms of this age of crisis are many and familiar. Perhaps the most striking evidence of the confusion of our time is the conception of the nature of man which forms a part of many widely-held ideologies. Under this view, man is a mere automaton incapable of sharing in the determination of his own destiny, bereft of dignity, capable of responding only to the grosser of materialistic motivations and irrational passions. That such a creature is incapable of exercising the high privilege of self-government is obvious. Essentially this conception of the nature of man underlies all of the totalitarian doctrines of our day, and unfortunately it underlies the thinking of some in our midst who shrink from its inevitable and logical conclusion. This conception contains the seeds of destruction. We must resist it and prove it fallacious. . . .
>
> But we see the evidence of crisis elsewhere. We are confronted with the challenge of the weakening of the family and the loss of the spiritual values growing out of the strong family bond. As lawyers we have been made disturbingly aware of a growing lack of faith in the respect for law and the legal process. After the first world war, the ideal of the supremacy of law was subjected to successful attack in many countries with the result that the legal systems of those nations abdicated their high functions and in cynical subservience served the demands of all powerful States. But the challenge to the supremacy of law has not been confined to the totalitarian regimes. In our own country we have seen evidences that there are those who have failed to realize that the only alternative to the supremacy of law is anarchistic chaos or the reign of the impersonal dictator. 1947 ABA Rep. 334.

approvingly observed that the key words in Vinson's constitutional lexicon were not "individual liberty" but "an ordered society" and a "strong America."[34] An obsession with "keeping America strong" was intrinsic to the Chief Justice's psychology. Frank has noted that Vinson had "a low threshhold of crisis surprising in so generally affable and unexcitable a man. He saw full blown emergencies where someone else might have thought there were only shadows . . . ."[35]

Vinson possessed a not quite Hobbesian view of man. He believed in original sin. He believed in the essential selfishness and acquisitiveness of man. He believed that conflicts of interest were inevitable and that therefore the good society is one that can reconcile opposing interests.[36] "Stability" thus becomes a primary and even transcendent good; "law and order" was indeed a fundamental element of Vinson's psychology.

There was a strong populist component to Vinson's ideology. He characteristically proclaimed support for the "little man" and loyalty to the "folks back home," but these "little people" Vinson championed were those he viewed as underdogs to the "big eastern moneyed interests." There was no place in the Chief Justice's heart for "left-wingers, aliens, suspected criminals, all who do not conform to the conformist picture of a one-hundred per cent Amurrican [sic]."[37]

Finally, Chief Justice Vinson held a profound respect for authority. Throughout his years in public service he was a team-player and was, almost without exception, deferential, respectful, and even obedient to persons in positions of authority; from Sam Rayburn and John Nance Garner in the House[38] and Chief Judge Groner of the court of appeals, to Presidents Roosevelt and Truman.[39]

A perusal of the outstanding features of Vinson's psycho-social background and attitudinal predispositions fails to explain the anomaly of three apparently libertarian racial civil rights opinions

---

[34] Bolner, *supra* note 23, at 358-59.
[35] Frank, *supra* note 9, at 226.
[36] Allen, *supra* note 11, at 6.
[37] F. RODELL, NINE MEN 311 (1955) [hereinafter cited as RODELL].
[38] Hatcher, *supra* note 24, at 148.
[39] See text accompanying notes 141-65 *infra*.

within the context of an uncommonly conservative behavioral pattern in thirty years of public service. If the Chief Justice's anti-civil libertarian reputation merits modification due to the race discrimination cases, then some theory or set of explanations consistent with data on Vinson's psycho-social characteristics, manifest attitudes and behavior is required to achieve the reassessment. If that is not forthcoming, then a sober reevaluation and reconstruction of Vinson's behavior in the race discrimination cases is called for. It may be that *Shelley, Sweatt* and *McLaurin* are less libertarian in orientation than perfunctory analyses have revealed.

The remainder of this study undertakes the following: first, ε careful and perhaps controversial reconsideration of Vinson's part in the judicial invalidation of restrictive covenants, focusing on the *Shelley* decision and on the less well known case of *Barrows v. Jackson*;[40] second, an analysis of Vinson's behavior in the school desegregation cases, focusing on *Sweatt, McLaurin* and the early proceedings in the *Brown* case. The study will conclude with a modestly proposed hypothesis which endeavors to explain and to account for Chief Justice Vinson's behavior in the race discrimination cases, as reconstructed in the previous pages.

Though the emphasis is on a single case, the imaginative reconstruction of the behavior of an individual Justice may represent some tentative, but important, steps toward a more general explanation of Supreme Court decision-making in the sensitive arena of racial civil rights.

II. CHIEF JUSTICE VINSON AND HOUSING DISCRIMINATION:
THE PROBLEM OF RESTRICTIVE COVENANTS

Vinson and the Opinion in Shelley

In the much celebrated decision of *Shelley v. Kraemer*,[41] the Supreme Court was faced with the question of whether the judicial enforcement of racially restrictive covenants by injunction[42]

---

[40] 346 U.S. 249 (1953).
[41] 334 U.S. 1 (1948).
[42] The racially restrictive covenant was an agreement among white property owners not to sell, rent, or lease their property to Negroes. Violators, *i.e.*, whites who sold, rented, or leased property to Negroes, were subject to sanctions specified in the covenant. Before the *Shelley* decision these sanctions could be enforced by the courts.

constituted discriminatory state action prohibited by the Fourteenth Amendment. Chief Justice Vinson, writing for a unanimous Court, had little difficulty demonstrating that a judicial decree was no less "state action" than was an executive order or a legislative command. He cited numerous precedents expressly designating the judicial act as an act of the state, stating:

> That the action of state courts and judicial officers in their official capacities is to be regarded as action of the State within the meaning of the Fourteenth Amendment, is a proposition which has long been established by decisions of this Court.[43]

The theoretical significance of the *Shelley* decision should not be understated, for Vinson upset a long held judicial attitude that had clearly favored the interests of the white property owners. In none of the precedents listed by Vinson as designating the judicial decree an act of the state did the court's action involve anything so passive as the enforcement of a voluntary agreement between private parties. In most of the precedents he cited, the judicial proceedings themselves were in some manner violative of due process or equal protection. In other precedents cited, the courts involved had enforced a common-law rule *formulated by those courts*.[44] In *Shelley*, however, the action being enjoined—the selling of a house by a white property owner to a Negro buyer—did not violate any common-law rule laid down by any court; nor had any court conducted a judicial proceeding which in any manner violated due process or equal protection. It is equally vital that the inspiration and impetus for the discrimination in *Shelley* was initially provided by private individuals; thus, to many the decision seemed to obliterate the distinction between private and state action.

The *Shelley* decision has excited, fascinated and disturbed legal scholars for years. Louis Henkin observed that *Shelley* "suggested a new and far-reaching domain of federal jurisdiction, a new and far-reaching readjustment of relationships between government and

---

[43] 334 U.S. at 14.
In his concluding remarks Vinson held "that in granting judicial enforcement of restrictive agreements in these cases, the states have denied petitioners the equal protection of the laws and that therefore the action of the state courts cannot stand." 334 U.S. at 20.

[44] A common-law rule, as an act of judicial law-making, is no less a violation of the Fourteenth Amendment, if discriminatory, than if formulated by a legislative body.

the individual."[45] *Shelley v. Kraemer* was also, in the words of Henkin, "hailed as the promise of another new deal for the individual—particularly the Negro individual."[46]

When one considers the actual impact of *Shelley*, as opposed to its significance as abstract legal doctrine, however, the Henkin view requires modification. Especially in the area of housing discrimination *Shelley*, it seems, was never adapted toward instigating genuine social reform. In spite of the revolutionary implications of *Shelley*, the Court was compelled to pay at least nominal tribute to legal precedent and to the distinction between private and state action. Chief Justice Vinson therefore had to reconcile the decision in *Shelley* with *Corrigan v. Buckley*,[47] where the Court upheld the validity of the restrictive covenants themselves. In *Shelley*, though Vinson prohibited *judicial enforcement* of the covenants, in deference to *Corrigan* he permitted the *covenants themselves* to stand. The Chief Justice observed that:

> . . . the restrictive agreements standing alone cannot be regarded as violative of any rights guaranteed to petitioners by the Fourteenth Amendment. So long as the purposes of those agreements are effectuated by voluntary adherence to their terms it would appear clear that there has been no action by the State and the provisions of the Amendment have not been violated.[48]

In preserving the concept of state action Chief Justice Vinson expressly and enthusiastically reaffirmed the *Civil Rights Cases*.[49] Frank has observed that Vinson went "almost gratuitously out of his way to reaffirm cases [on the subject of state action] not immediately in issue."[50] And Frank has noted elsewhere:

> [The reaffirmation of the *Civil Rights Cases*] is the most seriously disappointing aspect of [*Shelley*] for it was wholly unnecessary to reaffirm the *Civil Rights* cases [sic] and the issues presented in them deserve reconsideration upon argument

---

[45] Henkin, *Shelley v. Kraemer: Notes for a Revised Opinion*, 110 U. Pa. L. Rev. 473 (1962).
[46] *Id.*
[47] 271 U.S. 323 (1926).
[48] 334 U.S. at 13.
[49] 109 U.S. 3 (1883).
[50] Frank, *supra* note 9, at 237.

which is directed squarely to the issue. The dissenting opinion of Justice Harlan in the *Civil Rights* cases [sic] has never been satisfactorily answered, and the current decision buries it even deeper in oblivion.[51]

The reaffirmation of the *Civil Rights Cases* forced the federal government to take a "back-stairs" approach to civil rights legislation. The notion that it is acceptable to deny Negroes fundamental rights so long as it is done "privately" required Congress to pass the 1964 Civil Rights Act[52] under the Commerce,[53] rather than the Equal Protection Clause.[54] Scrupulous preservation of "state action" also diminished the likelihood that *Shelley* could be applied to discrimination in public accommodations.

It can also be shown that of all situations in which a state is called upon to aid and abet private discrimination, the case of racial restrictive covenants is perhaps the only one in which Negroes stood to gain little from prohibitions upon state action. Suppose a Negro wishes to patronize a "white only" theater. He is refused entrance —perhaps even threatened physically—but persists. He then lays down the price of the ticket and proceeds, by force if necessary, to enter the theater. The outraged proprietor notifies the police that a trespass has occurred. The police arrive and the Negro is promptly arrested on criminal trespass charges. If, in this very typical scenario, the state were prohibited from intervening in aid of the proprietor, the discrimination would be effectively subverted. If the police could then be prohibited in the general case from enforcing such trespass laws, Negroes would be enabled, *on their own initiative and at their own discretion*, to force an end to "white only" restrictions in any number of public accommodations, theaters being only one example.

Such gratifying possibilities, however, are not attendant to judicial invalidation of state participation in the enforcement of restrictive covenants. *For so long as the restrictive covenants themselves remain legal and so long as two or more Caucasian parties fulfill*

---

[51] Frank, *The United States Supreme Court, 1947-48*, 16 U. CHI. L. REV. 1, 24 (1948) [hereinafter cited as Frank II].
[52] 42 U.S.C. §§ 1981 *et seq.* (1964).
[53] U.S. CONST. art. I, § 8, cl. 2.
[54] U.S. CONST. amend. XIV, § 1.

their obligations under the covenant, there is nothing a Black can do, on his own initiative and under the law announced in Shelley *to subvert the noxious discrimination.*

In short, under the law announced in *Shelley*, a Black cannot force his way into a community in which white residents have agreed to abide by the requirements of the restrictive covenant. It takes the not very likely event of a white real estate owner in such a community reneging on his contract and exposing himself to the opprobrium of the community, for a Black even to raise the issue of illegal discrimination. For *Shelley* to have achieved a palpable impact on housing discrimination or to have *crystallized* the issue of racial segregation, Blacks must have been afforded real opportunities to litigate; but for this the "state action" concept needed to be repudiated or at least modified[55]—a step that Chief Justice Vinson and the Vinson Court were unwilling to take.

Regrettably, "impact studies" were not in fashion during the period *Shelley* was decided and no rigorous analysis of *Shelley*'s impact is available. Frank does, however, provide the results of an informal inquiry into the impact of a companion case to *Shelley* on the Indianapolis community:

> An examination of the situation in Indianapolis illustrates that in many cities the restrictive covenants are so firmly supported by extra-legal sanctions that the covenants themselves are of no significance.[56]

It is true, of course, that the Chief Justice's decision in *Shelley* was a notable psychological and symbolic victory for the fledgling civil rights forces of the period. *Shelley* indeed struck a philosophic blow for political equality and racial justice in America, but the tangible impact of the *Shelley* doctrine on housing discrimination was meager. And though the theoretical implications of the decision

---

[55] The failure to modify or reject the state action concept has meant that Congress had to rely on its power to control those who receive its financial help (see the Fair Housing Section of the Civil Rights Act of 1968) and its power to regulate commerce among the states (see the Federally Protected Activities Section of the Civil Rights Act of 1968) to pass open housing legislation. In *Jones v. Mayer*, 392 U.S. 409 (1968), however, the Court avoided the state action concept by holding that Congress had the power under the anti-slavery Thirteenth Amendment to prevent discrimination by both government and private individuals in the sale and rental of housing.

[56] Frank II, *supra* note 51, at 24.

seemed tremendous the scrupulous preservation of the *Civil Rights Cases* and the "state action" concept meant that *Shelley* was an obstacle, rather than a spur, to future efforts at open housing legislation.[57]

Shelley appears to be the opinion of a Justice prepared to place the moral and symbolic weight of Court and Government behind the cause for racial equality, but whose disposition to effect tangible progress toward equality of the races—to strike at the jugular vein of race discrimination—remains in doubt. It is the decision of a cautious judicial mind reluctant to upset the delicate sensibilities of a nation habituated to racial apartheid. This, provisionally, may be said of all who participated in the disposition of *Shelley*, and particularly of Chief Justice Vinson, as the author of the opinion.

To be sure, *Shelley* was a philosophical victory for the American Negro and no doubt enhanced America's image before the eyes of the world, but at no time was the decision likely to upset customary patterns of racial segregation nor elicit widespread political opposition. A careful reconsideration of *Shelley* therefore suggests, as a preliminary conclusion, that Chief Justice Vinson's behavior in the restrictive covenant cases is not so strikingly out-of-character as one might suppose from a more cursory examination of the decision. *Shelley*, however, was decided unanimously, and for that reason may be a poor indicator of Vinson's personal contributions to the restrictive covenant cases. A more conclusive analysis of the Chief Justice's behavior in those cases may be gleaned from a careful reading of his lone dissent in the important but somewhat obscure case of *Barrows v. Jackson*.[58]

---

[57] See note 55 *supra* and note 58 *infra*.

In *Reitman v. Mulkey*, 387 U.S. 369 (1967), however, the Court did in effect rule that a state may not, in its constitution, protect the right of an owner to sell real estate to whomever he chooses. *Reitman v. Mulkey* appears to be the only major extension of *Shelley* in the area of housing discrimination. On the other hand, *Reitman* did not require the state of California to pass positive legislation protecting the right of Negroes to purchase, lease, or rent real estate. In states where no such open housing legislation existed, private discrimination could continue unabated. The "state action" concept affirmed enthusiastically in *Shelley* remained the major obstacle to genuine reform in the area of housing discrimination until the Congress successfully sidestepped *Shelley* and the *Civil Rights Cases* by passing the 1968 Civil Rights Act.

[58] 346 U.S. 249, 260-69 (1953) (Vinson, C.J., dissenting).

Although the case of *Hurd v. Hodge*, 334 U.S. 24(1948), has not been discussed in the

The Lone Dissent in Barrows

Shelley could work to the benefit of Blacks only if white property owners breached their contracts. Given the intensity of white attitudes in both the North and the South toward racial integration, it was improbable that a white covenanter would violate an oath to keep his community segregated. In the case where *Shelley* was not subverted by unanimous observance of the contract, what recourse was left to ardent segregationists bent on thwarting further integration of a white community? Leo Pfeffer has described the strategy of real estate lawyers in neighborhoods where it seemed *Shelley* might achieve some impact:

> If the real estate lawyer could not call upon the courts to enforce racial restrictive covenants by enjoining whites from selling to Negroes and Negroes from purchasing from whites, they could make it unprofitable to do so, or at least make the white rebels pay for their ungentlemenly conduct. Accordingly, instead of suing for injunctions, they began to bring action for

---

text, it deserves some mention. Vinson's decision in *Hurd* is particularly interesting in light of the Court's more recent decision in *Jones v. Mayer*, 392 U.S. 409 (1968). The *Hurd* case arose in the District of Columbia where the Equal Protection Clause does not apply. The Court was urged to base its decision on the Due Process Clause of the Fifth Amendment. Vinson, however, was apparently fearful of the consequences of deciding that racial discrimination by the government is inherently violative of due process. Instead of the Due Process Clause, the Chief Justice based his decision on Section One of the Civil Rights Act of 1866, which provides that "All citizens of the United States shall have the same right in every state and territory as is enjoyed by white citizens thereof to inherit, purchase, lease, sell, hold and convey real and personal property," 42 U.S.C. § 1982 (1964).

Vinson contended that this statute was passed in connection with the Fourteenth Amendment and was not meant to "invalidate private restrictive agreements so long as the purposes of those agreements are achieved by the parties through voluntary adherence to the terms. The action toward which the statute under consideration is directed is governmental action." 334 U.S. at 31.

In *Jones v. Mayer*, Justice Stewart, no judicial radical, contradicted Chief Justice Vinson, ably demonstrating that the Civil Rights Act of 1866 was "meant to prohibit all racially motivated deprivations of the rights enumerated in the statute. . ." and that the Act was in fact passed in connection with the Thirteenth Amendment, which does apply to private action. 392 U.S. at 426. It is probable, then, that given the chance, Vinson would have dissented, along with Harlan and White, from the majority opinion in *Jones v. Mayer*. Justice Harlan in the dissenting opinion in *Jones* in fact cites Chief Justice Vinson's opinion in *Hurd* as evidence that the 1866 Civil Rights Act was meant to apply only to state action. 392 U.S. at 452 (Harlan, J., dissenting).

Vinson's decision in *Hurd* thus lends support to the provisional statement that the Chief Justice's decisions in the restrictive covenant cases were never meant to achieve major revisions in constitutional doctrine pertaining to racial civil rights.

damages for breach of contract, claiming that the breach of covenant depreciated the value of the nearby previously white property. In addition, they inserted in racial restrictive covenants provisions for payment of large sums to neighboring owners as liquidated damages should any signer breach the contract.[39]

If the courts could enforce damage claims by white covenanters against other whites for selling to Blacks, then what little hope *Shelley* held out to Blacks would be scandalously impaired. Knowing they could be successfully sued for breach of contract, white owners with an inclination to sell to Blacks would think twice—and refuse to sell. The question whether the Court would enforce damage claims for breach of contract against white covenanters for selling property to Negroes arose in *Barrows v. Jackson*.[40]

In *Barrows* a white property owner who violated the conditions of a restrictive covenant was sued by three co-covenanters on the ground that their property values had fallen after Negroes moved into the neighborhood. Justice Sherman Minton, who along with Chief Justice Vinson and Justice Reed possessed the poorest civil liberties record on the Vinson Court,[41] wrote a compassionate and sensitive opinion in *Barrows*. The most difficult problem for the Court was the question of standing: Did the white covenanter have standing to raise the constitutional issue? The right of no *specific* Negro was before the Court; the white covenanter could not claim violation of his Fourteenth Amendment rights—only that the rights of *unspecified* Negroes were threatened. In a *Shelley*-like case, judicial enforcement of a restrictive covenant caused the displacement of a Negro resident occupying property purchased from a white covenanter. In *Barrows*, however, no specific non-Caucasian was injured by the judicial enforcement of the damage claim. Even though the white seller was sued for damages, the Negro buyer was safely ensconced in the new property—his status wholly unaffected by the proceedings in *Barrows*.

Regardless of whose rights were immediately threatened, the cru-

---

[39] L. Pfeffer, The Liberties of an American 258 (1963).
[40] 346 U.S. 249 (1953).
[41] *See* Rodell, *supra* note 37, at 312-14; Table 1, p. 250 *supra*; Schubert, The Judicial Mind 125 (1965).

cial point was that enforcement of damage claims in *Barrows* would ultimately touch untold numbers of Blacks who might attempt in the future to purchase property from white real estate owners. Judicial enforcement of damage claims in any specific case would in the general case discourage whites from selling to Blacks in violation of the covenant. In his majority opinion Justice Minton appreciated the consequences of judicial enforcement of damage claims:

> To compel respondent to respond in damages would be for the State to punish her for her failure to perform her covenant to continue to discriminate against non-Caucasians in the use of her property. The result of that sanction by the State would be to encourage the use of restrictive covenants. To that extent, the State would act to put its sanction behind the covenants.[42]

The Court has generally adhered to the rule that one who attacks a statute as unconstitutional must show that he is injured by its operation and that *as applied to him* the statute is invalid.[43] When the Court has been faced with a tough constitutional issue, however, begging for judicial resolution, it has often managed to relax "standing" requirements.[44] *Barrows* presented circumstances which anticipated *Flast v. Cohen*[45] and Justice Minton took note of them saying that

> . . . in the instant case, we are faced with a unique situation . . . in which it would be difficult if not impossible for the

---

[42] 346 U.S. at 254.

[43] *See, e.g.*, Tileston v. Ullman, 318 U.S. 44 (1943), where the Supreme Court dismissed an appeal by a physician from a state court ruling which sustained the validity of a Connecticut statute prohibiting the use of contraceptives (or advice in their use) on the grounds that the physician had not shown that *as applied to him* the statute was unconstitutional, or that he personally was injured by its application.

[44] *See* Buchanan v. Warley, 245 U.S. 60 (1917), where the white appellant contracted to sell his property to the appellee, a Negro, assuming that the latter would have a right to occupy it. In a suit for specific performance the Court permitted the appellants to challenge, under the Equal Protection Clause, a city ordinance making it illegal for Negroes to reside on a block inhabited predominantly by whites. In *Pierce v. Society of Sisters*, 268 U.S. 510 (1925), the Court upheld a suit by a parochial school to enjoin the enforcement of a statute making it illegal for parents to fail to send their children to a public school. And in *Flast v. Cohen*, 392 U.S. 83 (1968), the Court permitted a taxpayer to challenge expenditures which were allegedly in support of religious activity. The Court permitted the challenge in *Flast* essentially because no one else could have raised the constitutional issue.

[45] 392 U.S. 83 (1968).

person whose rights are asserted to present their grievance before any court.[66]

Justice Minton was obviously determined to slice through jurisdictional technicalities to achieve a desired libertarian result. He was troubled more by the evils attendant to judicial enforcement of damage claims than by court-imposed jurisdictional limitations; he was prepared, therefore, to depart somewhat from settled constitutional doctrine to move toward the more liberal stance of *Flast*.[67] In his words:

> There is such a close relationship between the restrictive covenant here and the sanction of a state court which would punish respondents for not going forward with her covenant, and the purpose of the covenant itself, that relaxation of the rule is called for here. . . . The relation between the coercion exerted on respondent and her possible pecuniary loss thereby is so close to the purpose of the restrictive covenant, to violate the constitutional rights of those discriminated against, that respondent is the only effective adversary of the unworthy covenant in its last stand.[68]

Thus, six Justices[69] struck down the one effective legal method of discouraging even those few whites who were willing to sell property to Negroes; *the lone dissenter was Chief Justice Vinson.* Doctrinal conservatives like Justices Minton and Burton as well as institutional conservatives like Justices Jackson and Frankfurter overcame various obstacles to condemn state support of restrictive covenants in any manner whatsoever. Only Chief Justice Vinson was unable to avoid the technical barriers to a libertarian outcome.

In a dissenting opinion written in bitter tones, Vinson could not agree that the circumstances in *Barrows* were so unique as to warrant abandoning "normal" jurisdictional rules to allow the defendant "to avail herself of the Fourteenth Amendment rights of total strangers." Apparently unbothered by the obvious consequences of enforcing damage claims in *Barrows*-like cases, Chief Justice Vinson stoically argued:

---

[66] 346 U.S. at 257.
[67] See note 64 *supra*.
[68] 346 U.S. at 258-59.
[69] The five Justices who voted with Justice Minton were Justices Clark, Frankfurter, Black, Douglas and Burton. Justices Jackson and Reed did not participate in the case.

> The plain admitted fact that there is no identifiable non-Caucasian before this Court who will be denied any right to buy, occupy or otherwise enjoy the properties involved in this lawsuit, or any other particular properties, is decisive to me. It means that the constitutional defect, present in the *Shelley* case, is removed from this case. It means that this Court has no power to deal with the constitutional issue which respondent seeks to inject in this litigation as a defense to her breach of contract. It means that the covenant, valid on its face, can be enforced between the parties . . . without running afoul of any doctrine ever promulgated by this Court, without any interference from this Court.[70]

Continuing in the same vein, Vinson was unmoved by the argument that rights of unspecified Negroes would be jeopardized unless the Court sidestepped a self-imposed jurisdictional limitation:

> If it should be, as the majority assumes, that there is no other way that the rights of unidentified non-Caucasians can be vindicated in court, that is only an admission that there is no way in which a substantial case or controversy can be predicated upon the right which the majority is so anxious to pass upon. I cannot assent to a manner of vindicating the constitutional rights of persons unknown which puts personal predispositions in a paramount position over well-established proscriptions on power.[71]

In a number of interesting ways, the dissent in *Barrows* was uncharacteristic of the Chief Justice, suggesting that he went out of his way to register a tough anti-libertarian vote.[72] His self-righteous defense

---

[70] 346 U.S. 262.

[71] *Id.* at 267.

[72] Vinson's dissent in *Barrows* was unusual in several respects. First, although Vinson was not ordinarily given to sharp language, his dissent in *Barrows* was bitter, caustic, and angry. *See* C. VOSE, CAUCASIANS ONLY 237 (1959). Second, after nearly seven years on the Court, Vinson had never dissented alone. In *Barrows* the Chief Justice "dissented by himself, for the first and last time on the Court." C. PRITCHETT, CIVIL LIBERTIES AND THE VINSON COURT 143 (1954) [hereinafter cited as PRITCHETT]. Third, Chief Justice Vinson and Justice Minton were in agreement more often in nonunanimous opinions between 1949 and 1952 than any pair of Justices except Vinson and Clark. PRITCHETT at 184. Minton was also in agreement more often with Vinson in dissenting opinions than with any other Justice. Fourth, Vinson was ordinarily highly flexible and pragmatic. He adhered to precedent when it suited his purposes and ignored precedent when it did not. *See* Harris v. United States, 331 U.S. 145 (1947), where Vinson skimmed by precedent to arrive at an anti-civil-libertarian result; United Mine Workers v. United States, 330 U.S. 258 (1947), where Vinson, ignoring prece-

of a thrice violated jurisdictional rule in the face of a serious attack on *Shelley* is even more significant. The dissent in *Barrows* led one observer to comment, "The strain of treating a morally disapproved, 'unworthy' device as legal was too great for all the Vinson Court except Vinson."[73]

Vinson and the Restrictive Covenant Cases in Perspective

Chief Justice Vinson's dissent in *Barrows*, viewed in retrospect, is the product of a conservative judicial mind. It is the decision of a Justice for whom "racial equality" occupied a lower position on the hierarchy of values than "judicial self-restraint." Even the most conservative of Vinson's associates could attach a higher valence to the libertarian values present in *Barrows*. The perspective of *Barrows* shows that it is highly questionable whether Vinson's anti-civil libertarian reputation merits reformation in light of his celebrated decision in *Shelley*. His *Barrows* dissent suggests, first of all, that Vinson's decision in *Shelley* was hardly the classic posture of a crusading Chief Justice leading his Court in a spirited attack on political inequality and social injustice. Quite to the contrary: *Barrows* lends support to the belief that Vinson in fact occupied the most conservative position on the Court among those deciding *Shelley*, and was perhaps the least willing of the Justices to cross the libertarian Rubicon in the restrictive covenant cases.

The literal application by Vinson of *Shelley* to the extenuating circumstances in *Barrows* suggests just how seriously he took his own scrupulous preservation of the *Civil Rights Cases*; to him, the

---

dent, held that John L. Lewis was obligated to obey a temporary injunction even though the court which issued it had no jurisdiction. 330 U.S. at 307. Vinson's objections to the majority's departure from jurisdictional precedent in *Barrows* is therefore a bit disingenuous. In discussing the jurisdictional precedent "violated" by Vinson's brethren, the Chief Justice showed a respect for hard, fast formulas which is certainly at odds with his own remarks in the *Dennis* case where he said: "Nothing is more certain in modern society than the principle that there are no absolutes, that a name, a phrase, a standard has meaning only when associated with the considerations which gave birth to the nomenclature . . ." 341 U.S. 508. And in a case decided by Vinson on the United States Court of Appeals for the District of Columbia, the Chief Justice observed that ". . . history is replete with instances of hasty overgeneralizations thought to be fundamental truths, drawn from the solution to a particular problem." Nueslein v. District of Columbia, 115 F.2d 690, 692-93 (D.C. Cir. 1940). It is thus clear that Vinson's dissent in *Barrows* was in numerous ways uncharacteristic of the Chief Justice, suggesting very strongly that he went out of his way to register an anti-libertarian vote.

[73] PRITCHETT, *supra* note 72, at 143.

reaffirmation of those cases was more than just ritualistic recitation of precedent. Thus, it is possible that in the conference stages of the decision it was Vinson, perhaps with Justices Burton and Frankfurter, who took the most pains to limit the scope and impact of *Shelley*.[74] Quite plausibly, Justices Douglas and Murphy argued for reconsideration of the *Civil Rights Cases*; presumably, Chief Justice Vinson resisted. The result was a unanimous decision which placed Court and government symbolically and moralistically behind the cause for racial equality; yet at the same time it was a decision never likely to produce changes in customary patterns of racial segregation nor to inflict the widespread dislocation which accompanies genuine efforts at racial reform. In Edelman's terms *Shelley* may exemplify, even more than the typical exercise of judicial power, the "symbolic use of politics."[75] On the basis of the *Barrows* dissent one

---

[74] Justices Reed, Jackson, and Rutledge took no part in the *Shelley* decision.

[75] *See* M. EDELMAN, THE SYMBOLIC USES OF POLITICS *passim* (1964).

It is not taken for granted that the decisions of subsequent Courts in the racial civil rights area, beginning with the Warren Court's decision in *Brown*, produced unmitigated *tangible* benefits for Black Americans. The situation is surely more complex and ambiguous than that. In retrospect, however, it is possible to distinguish the primarily *symbolic* effects of *Shelley* from the more *tangible* ones of *Brown* and other Warren Court decisions in the area of racial civil rights.

At the time it was decided it seems that the *Brown* decision produced two situations which in retrospect appear to have contributed positively to the *material* progress that has been made in the area of racial civil rights. Because *Brown* struck at the jugular vein of racial apartheid—the separation of Black and white individuals during the impressionable and formative years of childhood—and because it broached the issue of racial segregation in such pointed terms, making it "less feasible than formerly to isolate. . . attitudes of democratic fair play [and equality] from engagement," Smith, *A Map for the Analysis of Personality and Politics*, 24 J. SOCIAL ISSUES 21 (1968), the *Brown* decision, more so than *Shelley*, could place certain strategic political actors in positions where it was socially unprofitable and morally indefensible to persist in the obstruction of genuine efforts toward racial reform. And because it posed the question so dramatically, *Brown*, more so than *Shelley*, could crystallize the issue of racial equality, arousing potent forces on both sides, and activating a great many Blacks and sympathetic whites to carry forward the cause for racial justice. This, it is suggested, the *Shelley* decision was ill-equipped to do.

Thus, on its own, *Brown* may be considered to have produced symbolic benefits of very great magnitude, but to have additionally, and separately, inspired the allocation of more tangible and material benefits in the area of racial civil rights. The primarily symbolic impacts of *Shelley*, on the other hand, seem not only to have been of less magnitude than *Brown*'s but seem as well to have been *confined to the symbolic level*. In sum, *Brown* may be considered to have produced a *mixture* of symbolic and tangible benefits, and ones not limited merely to numerical integration of public schools, while the impact of *Shelley* seems to have been narrower in scope and almost exclusively symbolic.

Many of these points seem to apply with equal force to the *Sweatt* and *McLaurin* deci-

may also conclude that the Chief Justice contributed marginally, if at all, to whatever libertarian features one finds in *Shelley*. Indeed, *Barrows* suggests that Vinson may have advocated, in conference, circumscriptions and limitations on the scope and potential impact of *Shelley*.

Vinson's dissent in *Barrows* and hypothesized foot-dragging in *Shelley* are predictable and explainable in terms of the Chief Justice's emotional and background characteristics, and also consistent with attitudes and behavior manifest in over thirty years of public service.[76] That *Shelley* was more symbolic than instrumental in character is also understandable in terms of Vinson's general conservatism. But the Chief Justice, no matter how begrudgingly, did make some uncharacteristic concessions to libertarian values in *Shelley*. That Vinson could vote for Shelley *at all* is significant and will require behavioral explanation. Yet several other Justices—notably Justices Minton, Reed, Burton and Clark—made even more striking concessions to racial equality. An understanding of Chief Justice Vinson's behavior in these and other race discrimination cases may therefore lead to a more general understanding of Supreme Court decision-making in the field of racial civil rights. In that respect, as well as to obtain a more complete understanding of his position, it is pertinent to consider Chief Justice Vinson's role in the early school desegregation cases.

III. Chief Justice Vinson and School Desegregation: the Cases of *Sweatt*, *McLaurin* and *Brown*

The Opinions in Sweatt *and* McLaurin

Before considering *Sweatt* and *McLaurin*, the opening skirmishes in the school desegregation cases deserve mention. In two related

---

sions. *See* note 135 *infra*. For a brief discussion of the behavior of Warren and Burger Court Justices in terms of their symbolic versus tangible commitments to racial equality, see note 215 *infra*.

For a more comprehensive analysis of the possible effects of racial desegregation decisions, see J. Eisenstein, Politics and the Legal Process (1973), especially chapter 12; Levine, *Methodological Concerns in Studying Supreme Court Efficacy*, in Compliance and the Law 106 (Krislov ed. 1966); H. Rodgers, Jr. & C. Bullock, III, Law and Social Change ch. 4 (1972); S. Wasby, The Impact of the United States Supreme Court 169-85 (1970).

[76] See text accompanying notes 13-39 *supra*, and notes 13-17, 22, 24, 33 *supra*.

cases, *Sipuel v. Board of Regents*[77] and *Fisher v. Hurst*,[78] Chief Justice Vinson joined in per curiam opinions which effectively reaffirmed the "separate but equal doctrine" set forth in *Plessy v. Ferguson*[79] and updated in *Missouri* ex rel. *Gaines v. Canada*.[80] What is of particular interest about *Fisher* are the dissenting opinions by Justices Murphy and Rutledge. Justice Rutledge voiced the opinion that, at least in the circumstances pertaining to the *Fisher* case, a separate law school for Negroes would not meet the constitutional mandate of "substantial equality."[81]

Justices Murphy's and Rutledge's uneasiness with the reasoning

---

[77] 332 U.S. 631 (1948).
[78] 333 U.S. 147 (1948).
[79] 163 U.S. 537 (1896).
[80] 305 U.S. 337 (1938). In the *Gaines* case Justice Hughes in effect sanctioned the "separate but equal" doctrine. In requiring the state of Missouri to provide law school facilities for a Negro student within the state rather than in an adjacent state, Chief Justice Hughes said: "The admissibility of laws separating the races in the enjoyment of privileges afforded by the state rests wholly upon the equality of the privileges which the laws give to the separated groups within the state." The facilities afforded the Negro plaintiff in *Gaines*, must, according to Justice Hughes, be "substantially equal to those which the state there afforded for persons of the white race." *Id.* at 349. In the *Sipuel* case Miss Ada Sipuel was denied admission to the only facility for legal education in the state of Oklahoma, solely because she was Negro. In a per curiam opinion in which the Chief Justice joined, the Court held that "the petitioner is entitled to secure legal education afforded by a state institution. To this time it has been denied her although during the same period many white applicants have been afforded legal education by the state. The state must provide it for her in conformity with the equal protection clause of the Fourteenth Amendment and provide it as soon as it does for applicants of any other group." 332 U.S. at 632-33. The principle of the *Gaines* case was expressly reaffirmed in *Sipuel*. Oklahoma was required to provide facilities for Miss Sipuel that were "substantially equal" to those afforded whites. Under the circumstances this meant that Oklahoma had at its disposal one of three alternatives. It could admit Miss Sipuel to the white law school; it could admit Miss Sipuel to a Negro law school, provided it was completed in time for the new semester; or it could eliminate the entire freshman class at the white law school. *Sipuel* was remanded to the state court for action consistent with the Court's per curiam opinion. The state court issued precisely those three alternatives listed above. By this time Miss Sipuel had married and her name had changed to Fisher. In the *Fisher* case Mrs. Fisher contended that the alternatives offered by the state were not in compliance with the Court's mandate in *Sipuel*. Mrs. Fisher argued that the state court, in permitting Oklahoma the alternative of establishing a separate law school for Negroes, had violated the Supreme Court's order in *Sipuel*. In another per curiam opinion, this time without even hearing argument on the case, the Court found nothing in the state court opinion that conflicted with the decision in *Sipuel*. *Sipuel* had not dealt with the question whether "a state might not satisfy the equal protection clause by establishing a separate school for Negroes." 333 U.S. at 150. In other words, the Court in *Fisher* was interpreting its opinion in *Sipuel* to allow separate but equal facilities in legal education.

[81] See PRITCHETT, *supra* note 72, at 133.

in *Sipuel* and *Fisher* implies that at least two Justices—neither of them Vinson—may have been prepared to undertake a revolutionary construction of the Equal Protection Clause a full two years prior to Vinson's decisions in *Sweatt* and *McLaurin*. There is at least the strong presumption that Vinson was not a factor behind any sympathies on the early Vinson Court for the invalidation of *Plessy*.

While the *Sipuel* and *Fisher* cases invite interesting speculation, the substance of Chief Justice Vinson's record on school desegregation is found in *Sweatt* and *McLaurin*. In *Sweatt v. Painter*,[82] plaintiff Sweatt had applied for admission to the University of Texas Law School and was rejected solely because he was a Negro. The trial court acknowledged his right to a legal education, but continued the case while the University of Texas hurriedly put together a Negro law school which, it claimed, was "substantially equal" in facilities to its white counterpart.[83] Sweatt, refusing a tendered admission to the hastily constructed school, contended that the Negro law school was factually unequal to its white counterpart. When the Texas appellate courts ruled otherwise,[84] Sweatt appealed the Texas decision to the Supreme Court.

Chief Justice Vinson wrote the opinion in *Sweatt* for a unanimous Court.[85] Though "the NAACP attempted to precipitate the issue of the validity of segregation as such,"[86] Vinson asserted emphatically that the Court was not prepared to decide the validity of "separate but equal." He explained:

> Broader issues have been urged for consideration, but we adhere to the principle of deciding constitutional questions only in the context of the particular case before the Court. . . . Because of this traditional reluctance to extend constitutional interpretation to situations of facts which are not before the Court, much of the excellent research and detailed argument presented in these cases is unnecessary to their disposition.[87]

---

[82] 339 U.S. 629 (1950).
[83] *Id.* at 631-32.
[84] 210 S.W.2d 442 (Tex. Civ. App. 1948).
[85] 339 U.S. 629 (1950).
[86] Frank II, *supra* note 51, at 34.
[87] 339 U.S. 629, 631 (1950). The argument by counsel for petitioners cited various social scientific authorities on the harmful effects of segregation as such. These were substantially

Having at the outset narrowed the scope of the Court's inquiry, the Chief Justice proceeded to a systematic comparison of the Negro and white law schools. After citing impressive data, Vinson concluded that there was not in fact

> substantial equality in the educational opportunities offered white and Negro law students by the State. In terms of the number of faculty, variety of courses and opportunity for specialization, size of the student body, scope of the library, availability of the law review and similar activities, the [white] University of Texas Law School is superior.[88]

In view of his findings, Vinson was apparently pursuing the doctrine laid down by Chief Justice Hughes in the *Gaines* case, affirmed in *Sipuel* and *Fisher*, that the Equal Protection Clause only requires the state to provide educational facilities for Negro students "substantially equal" to those afforded whites; only if such facilities are not available in separate schools may Negroes enroll in previously all white facilities. Vinson was not challenging segregation as such. Any such challenge of *Plessy* would preclude the need to draw careful comparisons between tangible facilities of Negro and white schools; the mere existence of separate schools—one for whites, the other for Negroes—would be *prima facie* illegal.

Had Vinson concluded his inquiry with the discussion of tangible facilities, the decision in *Sweatt* would have done little more than reiterate *Gaines*, *Sipuel* and *Fisher*. But the Chief Justice continued his inquiry and, in what seemed almost an afterthought, issued the most important words of the decision:

> Moreover, although the law is a highly learned profession we are well aware that it is an intensely practical one. The law school, the proving ground for legal learning and practice cannot be effective in isolation from the individuals and institutions with which the law interacts.

> The law school to which Texas is willing to admit petitioner excludes from its student body members of the racial groups which number 85% of the population of the State and include

---

the same arguments as those used in the 1954 cases. In the present case, however, Vinson skirted, if not avoided altogether, the very issues that were central to the disposition of the 1954 cases.

[88] *Id.* at 633-34.

> most of the lawyers, witnesses, jurors, judges and other officials with whom petitioner will be dealing inevitably when he becomes a member of the Texas Bar. With such a substantial and significant segment of society excluded, we cannot conclude that the education offered petitioner is substantially equal to that which he would receive if admitted to the University of Texas Law School.[89]

Vinson seemed to be saying that segregated law school facilities could not, under any circumstances, meet the standard of "substantial equality." The result it would seem is the invalidation, *sub silentio*, of "separate but equal" as applied to legal education. Vinson appeared to have taken a critical step beyond *Gaines, Sipuel* and *Fisher*; but the hope that "separate but equal" had sustained a critical blow was doused in the last few words of the opinion. After delineating the Court's decisions in *Gaines, Sipuel* and *Fisher* the Chief Justice said:

> In accordance with these cases [*Gaines, Sipuel, Fisher*], petitioner may claim his full constitutional right: legal education equivalent to that offered by the State to students of other races. Such education is not available to him in a separate law school as offered by the State. We cannot, therefore, agree with respondents that the doctrine of *Plessy v. Ferguson* requires affirmance of the judgment below. Nor need we reach petitioner's contention that *Plessy v. Ferguson* should be reexamined in the light of contemporary knowledge respecting the purposes of the Fourteenth Amendment and the effects of racial segregation.[90]

Though it could be interpreted as merely ritualistic reiteration of legal precedent, Chief Justice Vinson had expressly reaffirmed the *Gaines, Sipuel* and *Fisher* decisions; at the least, there was an explicit disinclination to review the *Plessy* doctrine.

What is most important about *Sweatt*, however, is the ambiguity of the Chief Justice's words,[91] particularly in the paragraph just quoted. When the Chief Justice held that equal education "is not

---

[89] *Id.* at 634.
[90] *Id.* at 635-36 (1950).
[91] The clarity or ambiguity of a decision is one of the factors conditioning its impact. As will be shortly demonstrated, Vinson's ambiguous language enabled lower court judges to project their private views upon Vinson's decision.

available [to petitioner] in a separate law school as offered by the state," did he mean that an equivalent legal education was not available because separate law school facilities were presumptively unequal, or that an equivalent legal education was not available in *the particular* Negro law school because its tangible facilities were factually inferior to its white counterpart's? The latter would merely reaffirm *Gaines*; the former would seriously weaken the *Plessy* doctrine. In more general terms, the *Sweatt* decision is ambiguous because it declares the Negro law school unequal on the basis of *both* tangible and intangible factors. It explicitly reaffirms *Gaines, Sipuel* and *Fisher*, but gives the appearance of weakening *Plessy*.

Since Vinson was not characteristically obscure, the ambiguity might be attributable to dissension on the Court. There were undoubtedly two blocs of Justices: one endeavored to weaken *Plessy* by declaring separate law school facilities presumptively unequal, the other wished to reaffirm *Gaines* by declaring *the particular* Negro law school inferior on the basis of tangible inequalities. A major purpose of this inquiry will be to determine which of the two blocs enjoyed the support of Chief Justice Vinson.

The case of *McLaurin v. Oklahoma State Regents*,[12] decided the same day as *Sweatt*, is equally obscure in intent and purpose. McLaurin, the petitioner, had been admitted to the University of Oklahoma to pursue graduate studies in education. Once admitted, McLaurin was segregated from his fellow students by being required to sit apart from his white classmates in an anteroom adjacent to the classroom, to sit at a separate table in the cafeteria, to eat at a different time, and to sit at a separate table in the library.

Having failed to rectify the situation in the district court,[13] McLaurin petitioned the Supreme Court. Just prior to the hearing, however, the University of Oklahoma modified the conditions of McLaurin's segregation. He was assigned a seat in the same classroom, though in a separate row for Negroes; he was given a table on the main floor of the library, though still separated from other tables and was permitted to eat at the same time with other students in the cafeteria, though still at a designated table.

---

[12] 339 U.S. 637 (1950).
[13] 87 F. Supp. 528 (W.D. Okla. 1949).

The Chief Justice opened his opinion in *McLaurin*, as he did in *Sweatt*, with a disclaimer, carefully limiting the scope of the opinion with the following words:

> In this case we are faced with the question whether a state may, after admitting a student to graduate instruction in its state University, afford him different treatment from other students solely because of his race. We decide only this issue.[14]

In *McLaurin*, as in *Sweatt*, the Chief Justice refused to reconsider the *Plessy* doctrine, but seemed to hold that segregated graduate instruction in education was inherently unequal:

> The result is that appellant [McLaurin] is handicapped in his pursuit of effective graduate instruction. Such restrictions impair and inhibit his ability to study, to engage in discussions and exchange views with other students, and, in general, to learn his profession.[15]

Chief Justice Vinson was suggesting that education, like law, is a profession involving close contact and communication with the general community. Preparation for such service must involve exposure of the student to a wide range of persons and experiences:

> Our society grows increasingly complex, and our need for trained leaders increases correspondingly. Appellant's case represents, perhaps, the epitome of that need, for he is attempting to obtain an advanced degree in education, to become, by definition, a leader and trainer of others. Those who will come under his guidance and influence must be directly affected by the education he receives. Their own education and development will necessarily suffer to the extent that his training is unequal to that of his classmates.[16]

Vinson's opinion in *McLaurin* adds little in terms of clarity to *Sweatt*. What is clear, however, is that *McLaurin* could be interpreted even more narrowly than its companion case: The State of Oklahoma, having refused to supply a graduate school with separate and equal facilities for McLaurin, and having already admitted McLaurin to its white graduate school, is obligated to grant him full

---

[14] 339 U.S. at 638.
[15] *Id.* at 641.
[16] *Id.*

equality within the white institution—in effect an amplification and application of the *Gaines* doctrine.[17]

Sweatt *and* McLaurin: *Interpretation and Impact*

The ambiguity of *Sweatt* and *McLaurin* was a precursor of their impact. John P. Roche, writing shortly after those decisions observed that:

> . . . the Court left several avenues of precedent open for lower courts to follow. In analyzing a segregated situation a judge may:
>
> 1. Cite the *Sweatt* and *McLaurin* cases as precedents for ruling that "separate but equal" facilities do not violate the equal protection clause of the Fourteenth Amendment—"*Plessy* was not overruled."
> 2. Cite the *McLaurin* case as precedent for ruling that where the state has combined Negroes and whites in the same facilities it may not enforce segregation.
> 3. Cite the *Sweatt* case as precedent for ruling that where unequal separate facilities have been established the Fourteenth Amendment has been violated.
> 4. Cite the *Sweatt* and *McLaurin* cases as precedents for ruling that in certain situations the very fact of segregation engenders inequality, violating the Fourteenth Amendment.[18]

That *Sweatt* and *McLaurin* were never adapted toward achieving judicial reassessment of *Plessy* and *Gaines* is apparent from the immediate responses of lower courts, state courts and the Supreme Court itself in cases following *Sweatt* and *McLaurin*. In two cases the Supreme Court took action on the basis of *Sweatt* and *McLaurin*; first by a per curiam opinion and then by a denial of certiorari from which Justices Black and Douglas dissented, the Supreme Court upheld lower court decisions in which *Sweatt* and *McLaurin* were interpreted as mere elaborations of *Gaines*.[19] Three

---

[17] Roche, *Education, Segregation and the Supreme Court*, 99 U. PA. L. REV. 949, 952 (1951) [hereinafter cited as Roche].

[18] Roche, *supra* note 97, at 953.

[19] In *Rice v. Arnold*, 340 U.S. 848 (1950), the Supreme Court vacated the judgment of a Florida court which upheld an arrangement whereby Negroes were permitted to use a municipal golf course one day per week on the ground that they constituted only one-seventh of those wishing to use the course. Upon remand the Florida court reaffirmed its original judgment holding that the segregated arrangement did not violate *Sweatt* and *McLaurin* because the

segregation cases concerning recreational facilities, military education and legal education were decided on the court of appeals level. In the first two decisions,[100] the Courts of Appeals for the Fourth and Eighth Circuits respectively upheld segregated recreational facilities and segregated educational facilities, basing their decisions squarely on the *Plessy* rule. Both courts assumed that *Sweatt* and *McLaurin* had merely confirmed and upheld *Plessy*. In the third decision,[101] the Court of Appeals for the Fourth Circuit ordered the University of North Carolina Law School integrated on the basis of the "substantially equal" doctrine of *Gaines*.

Eight cases were decided in the state courts on the basis of *Sweatt* and *McLaurin*. In the first decision,[102] a state court held that a white teachers college in St. Louis need not be integrated, the Negro teachers college being, according to the Court, "substantially equivalent" in facilities to its white counterpart. In five additional cases[103] the Florida Supreme Court upheld the right of the University of Florida to establish "separate but equal" facilities for Negro students wishing to study law, engineering, pharmacy and agriculture. The Florida court "entirely ignored the implication [of *Sweatt*] that separate legal training could not be equal."[104]

In two more decisions, in Delaware[105] and Missouri,[106] involving

---

facilities offered Negro golfers were identical to those enjoyed by whites. When the Negro petitioners appealed again the Supreme Court denied certiorari on a nonfederal ground. Rice v. Arnold, 342 U.S. 946 (1952) (Black, J. and Douglas, J., dissenting).

In *Louisiana State University v. Wilson*, 340 U.S. 909 (1950), the district court ordered a white law school integrated on the basis of the "substantially equal" doctrine of *Gaines*. In a per curiam opinion the Supreme Court upheld the lower court without discussion.

[100] Boyer v. Garrett, 183 F.2d 582 (4th Cir. 1950); Brown v. Ramsey, 185 F.2d 225 (8th Cir. 1950).
[101] Roche, *supra* note 97, at 955.
[102] State v. Bd. of Educ., 230 S.W.2d 724 (Mo. 1950).
[103] The lead case was *Florida ex rel. Hawkins v. Board of Control*, 47 So.2d 608 (Fla. 1950).
[104] Roche, *supra* note 97, at 957, *citing* State *ex rel.* Hawkins v. Board of Control, 47 So.2d 608, 614 (Fla. 1950). The specific words of the Florida court were as follows:
No court in the land has ever required of a sovereign state any more than is encompassed within the plan proposed by the Board of Control in its answers [The establishment of separate equal law schools.] Every individual political right and privilege guaranteed the citizen by the provisions of the Federal Constitution is maintained under the program, while at the same time the right of the State to adopt such method as it finds best designed to afford substantially equal educational opportunities to Florida citizens of different race groups has been preserved.
[105] Parker v. University of Delaware, 31 Del. Ch. 381, 75 A.2d 225 (1950).
[106] State *ex rel.* Brewton v. Bd. of Educ., 233 S.W.2d 697 (Mo. 1950).

segregated education in a state college and vocational high school respectively, the state courts employed "separate but equal" as if it were still good law. The Delaware court held:

> As recently as June of this year the United States Supreme Court applied the separate but equal test in two cases involving graduate and professional schools.[107]

The court was of course referring to *Sweatt* and *McLaurin*.

This summation of lower court responses to *Sweatt* and *McLaurin* "demonstrates the degree to which the Supreme Court's decision [in those cases] can be interpreted as merely a refinement of the *Plessy v. Ferguson* doctrine."[108] In none of the instances cited were *Sweatt* and *McLaurin* interpreted or applied as if to foreshadow the landmark decision in *Brown*. In no decision were the two Vinson opinions afforded a construction even remotely anticipating the Court's revolutionary invalidation of elementary and secondary school segregation.

Such limited constructions of *Sweatt* and *McLaurin* appeared right up to the moment of the *Brown* decision itself. Judge Parker in the district court opinion in *Briggs v. Elliott*,[109] the companion case to *Brown*, said the following about *Sweatt* and *McLaurin*:

> Plaintiffs rely upon expressions contained in opinions relating to professional education such as Sweatt v. Painter . . . where equality of opportunity was not afforded. Sweatt v. Painter, however, instead of helping them, emphasizes that the separate but equal doctrine of Plessy v. Ferguson has not been overruled, since the Supreme Court, although urged to overrule it, expressly refused to do so and based its decision on the ground that the education facilities offered Negro law students in that case were not equal to those offered white students. . . . The case of McLaurin v. Oklahoma State Regents, involved humiliating and embarrassing treatment of a Negro graduate student to which no one should have been required to submit. Nothing of the sort is involved here.
> The problem of segregation as applied to graduate and pro-

---

[107] 75 A.2d at 230.
[108] Roche, *supra* note 97, at 957.
[109] 98 F. Supp. 529 (E.D.S.C. 1951).

fessional education is essentially different from that involved in segregation at lower levels.[110]

References to *Sweatt* and *McLaurin* in the *Brown* decision itself support these conclusions. Though Chief Justice Warren cited *Sweatt* and *McLaurin* in partial support of his own use of "intangible inequalities" in *Brown*, he specifically pointed out that in neither *Sweatt* nor *McLaurin* was it necessary for the Court to reexamine *Plessy*, and that in *Sweatt* "the Court expressly reserved decision on the question whether *Plessy v. Ferguson* should be held inapplicable to public education."[111] Chief Justice Warren further distinguished *Sweatt* from *Brown*:

> Here, unlike *Sweatt v. Painter*, there are findings below that the Negro and white schools have been equalized, or are being equalized, with respect to buildings, curricula, qualifications and salaries of teachers and other "tangible" factors. Our decision therefore cannot turn on merely a comparison of those tangible factors in the Negro and white schools involved in each of the cases. We must look instead to the effect of segregation itself on public education.[112]

Chief Justice Warren's language reveals that the paternity of *Brown* cannot be easily traced to the two Vinson opinions. Edmund Cahn's argument, for example, that *Sweatt* and *McLaurin* "supplied the intellectual and emotive conditions for the School Desegregation Cases of 1954"[113] must be regarded a considerable exaggeration. Had the 1954 Court held that since Negro children in the lower grades are not being trained for professions involving community service or leadership it is quite unnecessary for them, at this point in their education, to attend integrated schools—a perfectly reasonable deduction based on the two Vinson opinions—Cahn might have instead lashed out angrily at *Sweatt* and *McLaurin* for having supplied the doctrinal basis for the *segregation* cases of 1954. It seems only in retrospect that one finds strong relational ties between *Sweatt/McLaurin* and *Brown*. Had the Warren Court decided

---
[110] *Id.* at 535.
[111] Brown v. Board of Educ., 347 U.S. 483, 492 (1954).
[112] *Id.* at 492.
[113] E. Cahn, *Quoted in* ARGUMENT xvi (L. Friedman ed. 1969) [hereinafter cited as Friedman].

Brown differently, history may have regarded the two Vinson opinions in an entirely different light.

The broader historical view of one scholar supports this conclusion. The perspective is that of Alfred Kelly, one of two historians commissioned by Thurgood Marshall to prepare a research paper on "the passage and ratification of the Fourteenth Amendment by Congress and the states."[114] Kelly reported that

> It was obvious to Marshall and his lieutenants that the Sweatt and McLaurin cases were of great significance, for they could be used to destroy racial segregation in graduate education virtually everywhere in the South. *On the other hand, technically the Court had done nothing whatever to undermine the old Plessy "separate but equal rule." On the contrary, in one sense, at least, it had strengthened it, since in both cases it had held that the facilities in question were inadequate solely because they failed to meet the standard that the "separate but equal" rule had required.* Although equality in segregated facilities might well be impossible to achieve at the graduate level, there seemed to be no reason why the South at large, given a little time and the willingness to spend a goodly amount of money, might not achieve such equality for its Negro primary and secondary schools. Indeed, all over the South white boards of education, reading this implication into the Sweatt and McLaurin decisions, began crash programs of Negro school building, calculated, as Governor Byrnes of South Carolina presently frankly confessed, "to remedy a hundred years of neglect" of Negro education, lest the Supreme Court "take matters out of the state's hands."
>
> Marshall later admitted that the NAACP was at this point at a kind of crossroads. The legal gap between the Sweatt and McLaurin cases on the one hand and an outright destruction of the Plessy precedent appeared to be appallingly wide, and he and his colleagues were not at all sure they could cross it.[115]

In sum, the legal gap between the holdings of *Sweatt* and *McLaurin* and of *Brown* was wide and the momentum from the two Vinson opinions hardly sufficient to cause reluctant judges to reexamine the

---

[114] Kelly, *The School Desegregation Case*, in QUARRELS THAT HAVE SHAPED THE CONSTITUTION, 243, 260 (J. Garraty ed. 1966) [hereinafter cited as Kelly].

[115] Kelly, *supra* note 114, at 256-57 (emphasis added).

Plessy doctrine. Indeed, the effect of *Sweatt* and *McLaurin* could well have been the opposite.

There may be two fundamental objections to the present characterization of the Vinson opinions. First, it may be plausibly argued that even if *Sweatt* and *McLaurin* contributed only marginally to the eventual abandonment of *Plessy*, their contribution to integration and equalization of facilities in graduate and professional education was a major achievement. Second, it may also be contended that, while *Sweatt* and *McLaurin* failed to supply clear doctrinal and intellectual precedent for *Brown*, to the extent they supported the claims of Negro petitioners and mandated even token integration, they contributed to an atmosphere which made *Brown* more socially palatable and politically feasible.

These objections may be answered in part by noting, as Frank has, that there was not much opposition in the South to integration on the graduate and professional level.[116] He noted "that many Southerners [did] not feel nearly as strongly about maintaining segregated education at the graduate level as they [did] about maintaining it in the [lower] grades."[117] And Leo Pfeffer has also pointed out, "The . . . *Sweatt* and *McLaurin* decisions raised little more than a ripple of discontent in the South."[118] These observations suggest that token integration and equalization of graduate and professional schools was, given the relative acquiesence of the South, something less than a major achievement. Further, if resistance to integration in the lower grades was infinitely more widespread and intense than it was to integration in the graduate and professional schools, it is difficult to imagine how *Sweatt* and *McLaurin* could make *Brown* more politically and socially acceptable.

Like the opinion in *Shelley*, the decisions in *Sweatt* and *McLaurin* seem to be less revolutionary in outlook and impact than more perfunctory analyses have revealed; like *Shelley*, *Sweatt* and *McLaurin* held out the prospect of tangible progress to just a few Negroes, similarly failing to strike at the jugular vein of racial

---

[116] Frank, *supra* note 51, at 36-37.
[117] *Id.* at 37.
[118] PFEFFER, *supra* note 12, at 264.

apartheid. And even though the Chief Justice succeeded, as he did in *Shelley*, in fostering a symbolic alliance between "government" and the "cause for racial equality," again, as in *Shelley*, the cautious perspective of the two opinions enabled these symbolic victories to occur in the absence of widespread political and social dislocation and to fall short of inducing genuine racial reform.

It may be objected that because *Sweatt* and *McLaurin* were decided unanimously they are poor reflections of Vinson's personal perspectives on school desegregation. Whether the views expressed in the two desegregation cases were shared by Vinson or not, however, a reevaluation of the two opinions seems to discredit the notion that the Chief Justice's anti-civil libertarian reputation merits revision in light of *Sweatt* and *McLaurin*. Given their conservative outlook and orientation, *Sweatt* and *McLaurin* do seem, upon reconsideration, largely explainable in terms of Vinson's conservative behavioral characteristics.[119] A more precise characterization of the Chief Justice's position, however, will be forthcoming from an analysis of the early stages of the *Brown* decision; it is in these proceedings that the Chief Justice's position may be viewed in isolation.

Vinson's Views in Isolation

It is the ambiguity of *Sweatt* and *McLaurin* which ultimately belies their insincerity. Ambiguity is often the defining characteristic of a governmental output which is more symbolic than instrumental. The more conservative of the two blocs on the Vinson Court is undoubtedly responsible for the symbolic rather than instrumental character of the two Vinson opinions. It is therefore of particular importance to isolate the Chief Justice's views—to determine which of the blocs enjoyed Vinson's membership and support. In the restrictive covenant cases, the Chief Justice's dissent in *Barrows* isolated his personal perspectives on desegregation. In the school desegregation cases an analysis of the Vinson Court's role in the early stages of *Brown* can perform a similar function.

The judicial struggle which ended in the *Brown* decision began with the filing of an appeal in the case of *Briggs v. Elliot*.[120] *Briggs* arose in Clarendon County, South Carolina, and represented the

---

[119] See text accompanying notes 13-39, *supra*, and notes 13-17, 22, 24, 33, *supra*.
[120] 98 F. Supp. 529 (E.D.S.C. 1951).

first all out attack on segregation in grade school education. The plaintiffs in *Briggs* sought to enjoin enforcement of certain provisions of the South Carolina constitution which required the segregation of Negroes and whites in public schools. The three-judge panel, carefully upholding the "separate but equal" doctrine, ordered the defendants to equalize facilities for Negro grade school children in Clarendon. The majority opinion by Judge Parker also called for a report in six months on the "progress toward equalization."

The plaintiffs were not interested in mere equalization, however, and appealed the decision directly to the Supreme Court. In January, 1952, a full six months after *Briggs* came to the Court, the Justices handed down a per curiam opinion remanding the case for purposes of obtaining the district court's views on the equalization report. Justices Black and Douglas issued a strong dissent:

> Mr. Justice Black and Mr. Justice Douglas dissent to vacation of the District Court on the grounds stated. They believe that the additional facts contained in the report to the District Court are wholly irrelevant to the constitutional questions presented by the appeal to this Court and that we should note jurisdiction and set the case down for argument.[121]

For Justices Black and Douglas the real issue was segregation *per se*; whether facilities of the Negro and white schools had been equalized was of no consequence. Chief Justice Vinson's and his associates' concern with "equalization" suggests a further application of the "substantially equal" test and therefore a lingering respect for *Gaines* and *Plessy*. The first Court action in *Briggs* thus implies that the Chief Justice had supported the more conservative of the judicial blocs apparently present in *Sweatt* and *McLaurin*.

On June 9, 1952 the Supreme Court noted probable jurisdiction in two cases involving grade school education; both placed the question of the constitutionality of "separate but equal" before the Court.[122] One case was the appeal by Negro petitioners from the second trial of *Briggs*.[123] The other was *Brown v. Board of Education*

551

---

[121] 342 U.S. 350, 352 (1952).
[122] 343 U.S. 959 (1952).
[123] 103 F. Supp. 920 (E.D.S.C. 1952). Judge Parker, writing for a unanimous three-judge panel on remand, found that substantial equality had been achieved and that inequalities remaining were in the process of being rectified.

of Topeka.[124]

The minutes of the conferences in which the Court noted probable jurisdiction in *Briggs* and *Brown* would undoubtedly say much about the Chief Justice's personal perspectives on the desgregation question. While minutes of those conferences are, of course, unobtainable, the recent opening of the Harold H. Burton papers and Sidney Ulmer's use of them in a study of "Earl Warren and the *Brown* Decision,"[125] enables an unobscured view of Vinson's role in the judicial activities leading up to *Brown*. In his analysis Ulmer quotes Justice Burton to the effect that the Justices voted to "note jurisdiction" in *Briggs* in conference on June 7, 1952. Burton recorded the vote as seven to "note" and one (Justice Jackson) to "hold" but *"No vote [was] recorded for Chief Justice Vinson."*[126] (Emphasis added.)

The absence of a recorded vote for Vinson is mysterious. It is doubtful that Burton's omission was accidental. It is more likely that Vinson either abstained, or voted negatively on the jurisdictional question—the latter, an event which Burton may have found too sensitive to record.[127] In either case the implication is that Vinson played no part in bringing the *Brown* case to the high court. Though highly speculative, this conclusion will be supported by additional evidence from the Burton papers.

---

[124] 98 F. Supp. 797 (D. Kan. 1951).

[125] Ulmer, *Earl Warren and the* Brown *Decision*, 33 J. POLITICS 689 (1971).

[126] Ulmer, *supra* note 125, at 690 n. 6 (emphasis added).

[127] Two observers, Fred Rodell and Daniel Berman, have independently noted that a bare minimum of four votes brought the *Brown* case to the Court. D. BERMAN, IT IS SO ORDERED 47 (1966); F. RODELL, *It is the Earl Warren Court*, N.Y. Times, March 16, 1966, (Magazine) at 93. Rodell cited former Supreme Court law clerks as his sources. Now, Justice Burton, as noted above, recorded seven Justices in favor of noting jurisdiction. If the Rodell-Berman, rather than the Burton view, is correct, it is even less likely that the Chief Justice voted to bring the *Brown* case to the high Court. It is a virtual certainty that Black and Douglas noted jurisdiction in *Brown* and if Rodell and Berman are correct that only four votes brought the case to the Court, only two additional Justices from among Vinson, Minton, Reed, Burton, Jackson, Frankfurter, and Clark noted jurisdiction. Had the third Justice noting jurisdiction been Vinson, it seems unlikely that the Chief Justice, employing his famed powers of persuasion and applying sufficient pressure, would have brought just *one* additional Justice along. At least three more Justices (Minton, Clark, and Burton) might have voted to note jurisdiction if Vinson had insisted. Minton and Clark were both "satellites" of the Chief Justice, and Burton was generally considered favorable to Negro civil rights and receptive to persuasion on the desegregation issue. So that even from the Rodell-Berman perspective it is unlikely that Vinson voted to note jurisdiction in *Brown*.

284   EMORY LAW JOURNAL

The Court subsequently noted jurisdiction in three additional desegregation cases, and the five cases, including *Brown* and *Briggs*, were finally heard on December 9, 10, and 11, 1952. Chief Justice Vinson's performance during the oral argument of these cases has been summarized by Leon Friedman who observed that

> even allowing that Vinson's statements were merely to elicit information his few questions in the oral arguments indicated a lack of sympathy with the plaintiffs position.[128]

At one point during oral argument, counsel for Brown admitted that while physical facilities in the white and Negro schools of Topeka were substantially equivalent, the heart of the case concerned *intangible inequalities inherent in segregation itself*. Responding to this argument the Chief Justice remarked: "That is all you really have here to base your segregation issue upon."[129] If Vinson could so casually dismiss the doctrinal basis of the final *Brown* decision, his commitment to the libertarian position in the school desegregation cases is called seriously into question.

At various other times during oral argument Vinson, in obvious sympathy for the "substantially equal" test, displayed great concern for the equality of physical facilities between Negro and white schools.[130] In other places Vinson endeavored to show that while Congress was mindful of segregated schools in Washington, D.C., it had never undertaken to remedy the situation.[131] At another point, Vinson suggested that the Fourteenth Amendment was never meant to prohibit segregation.[132]

Several days after oral argument, on December 13, 1952, the Court held a conference on the cases. Ulmer, relying again on the Burton papers, described the highlights of the meeting as follows:

> Speaking first in the conference, Vinson observed that public schools in the District of Columbia were segregated in 1868 when the Fourteenth Amendment was adopted. Moreover, the Congress sitting at that time declined to pass a statute barring

---

[128] Friedman, *supra* note 113, at vii.
[129] *Id.* at 18-19.
[130] *Id.* at 41, 18-19, 84, 169-70.
[131] *Id.* at 110-11.
[132] *Id.* at 114-15, 124-25.

racial segregation in District schools. Though he voiced no disagreement with Harlan's dissent in *Plessy v. Ferguson*, he argued that Harlan was careful to avoid a reference to public schools. This he thought was highly significant since the opinion otherwise bore down so heavily on racial segregation. With regard to the role of the Court, Vinson expressed the view that if Congress failed to act, the Court would have to confront the problem and would need wisdom to deal with it. *He is recorded by Burton as probably upholding the validity of segregation at that time.*[133]

Six months after the first oral argument, in June, 1953, the Court set the whole group of cases for reargument with specific questions addressed to attorneys on both sides. It may be inferred from the postponement that the Vinson Court could not have achieved unanimity in *Brown* during the spring of 1953. Indeed, as Ulmer notes, "Harold Burton [recorded in his diary] the view that in May 1953 six members of the Court were in favor of and three opposed to outlawing segregation—*with Chief Justice Vinson in dissent.*"[134]

Based primarily on evidence highlighted in the Burton papers, it appears that Chief Justice Vinson had supported the most conservative of the judicial blocs in *Sweatt* and *McLaurin*. The ambiguity of the two Vinson opinions, which cushioned their impact on prevailing patterns of racial segregation, was clearly due to conflict among liberal and conservative elements on the Court. And the Chief Justice's apparent support of the conservative faction undoubtedly guaranteed the symbolic, rather than instrumental character of the two Vinson opinions.

Just eight months after Vinson's untimely death, Earl Warren achieved unanimity in *Brown* with the identical eight Justices who had served Vinson. It would appear that the best a Vinson led Court could have accomplished in 1954 is a six-three desegregation opinion with the Chief Justice in dissent—a highly undesirable outcome inviting political risks for the court. It is more probable then that a Vinson led Court, in search of unanimity, would have assembled an ambiguous compromise, after *Sweatt* and *McLaurin*, in which *Plessy* emerged barely scathed.

---

[133] Ulmer, *supra* note 125, at 691 (emphasis added).
[134] *Id.* at 697 (emphasis added).

Vinson and the Race Discrimination Cases in Perspective

A careful reconsideration of *Shelley, Sweatt* and *McLaurin* from a doctrinal, historical and developmental perspective has revealed that the three Vinson opinions were less liberal in orientation, implication, and impact than more perfunctory analyses have disclosed. The three Vinson decisions were more symbolic and cathartic than instrumental or substantial, and in general, exemplified a cautious, incrementalist approach to the desegregation question which was soon rejected by the Warren Court.[135]

An analysis of Vinson's dissent in *Barrows* and his performance in judicial activities leading up to *Brown* has served to isolate the Chief Justice's views on the desegregation question and has illuminated, retrospectively, his personal contributions to *Shelley, Sweatt* and *McLaurin*. These efforts suggest that Vinson not only supported the multifaceted opinions in *Shelley, Sweatt* and *McLaurin*, but was partially responsible for the ambiguity and incrementalist bias which nullified their practical effects. The conservative elements of the three opinions bear heavily the imprint of Chief Justice Vinson.

These conservative features and Vinson's hypothesized contributions to them are very largely explainable in terms of known background and emotional characteristics of the Chief Justice and com-

---

[135] The distinction between the primarily symbolic effects of *Shelley* and the more tangible ones of *Brown* seems to define the difference between *Sweatt/McLaurin* and *Brown* equally well. See note 75, *supra*.

The proximal impacts of *Brown*, which were admittedly more symbolic than tangible, could nevertheless ignite a chain of complex political and social forces which in the longer run resulted in *material* progress in the area of racial civil rights. *Brown* joined the issue of racial equality far more emphatically than either *Sweatt* or *McLaurin* (or *Shelley*). While it is true that numerous judges and politicians could successfully, and with impunity, avoid the dictates and implications of *Brown*, other strategic actors, such as the "58 Lonely Men" of the South whose story was told by Jack Peltason, could find no way around the *relatively* clear and emphatic language of *Brown*. It being a much simpler matter for reluctant judges and politicians to misperceive the "enormous implications" which some found in *Sweatt* and *McLaurin*, the latter produced no similar profiles in political or judicial courage.

In improving upon the Vinson Court's ambiguous treatment of "racial equality" as a value, and in coming down squarely on the side of racial justice, the Warren Court increased the probability that the proximal symbolic effects of civil rights decisions could, in the longer run, be transformed into more tangible and material ones which were not limited merely to the numerical integration of public schools. This factor more than any other distinguishes the bolder synoptic approach of the Warren Court from the more cautious, incremental approach of its immediate predecessor. For a brief discussion of the performance of Warren and Burger Court Justices in the racial civil rights area, see note 215 *infra*.

pletely consistent with attitudes and behavior manifest in over thirty years of public service.[136] Thus, to the extent that *Shelley, Sweatt,* and *McLaurin* are cathartic rather than instrumental, and gradualist rather than revolutionary, one is not inclined, as Francis Allen is, to modify the Chief Justice's anti-civil libertarian reputation.[137]

At the same time, however, the Chief Justice, no matter how reluctantly, did join in three opinions which made *some* concessions to libertarian values—whose symbolic character was, after all, a psychological lift to the embryonic civil rights movement—in spite of a more general disposition, revealed in *Barrows, Brown,* and elsewhere, to vote negatively on matters of racial civil rights. The fact that these concessions were little more than symbolic and gradualist is understandable in terms of Vinson's general conservatism; but that these concessions were made at all is of considerable significance and begs for behavioral explanation. The remainder of this study undertakes an explanation of what is, in effect, the "unexplained variance" in Chief Justice Vinson's behavior in the race discrimination cases in order to understand why the Chief Justice could support even the minimalist positions of *Shelley, Sweatt,* and *McLaurin.*

IV. A Theory of Chief Justice Vinson's Behavior in The Race Discrimination Cases[138]

Problems of Validation

The intensive analysis of judicial behavior—what may otherwise be termed "judicial biography"—involves the explanation of judicial events (decisions) in terms of both distal and situational factors (social, political, historical, normative) as well as factors peculiar to the judicial actor under study: his role perceptions, personality pro-

---

[136] See text accompanying notes 13-39, *supra,* and notes 13-17, 22, 24 and 32, *supra.*
[137] Allen, *supra* note 11, at 7.
[138] It must be reiterated that the Chief Justice's general conservatism is presumed to explain most of the variance in Vinson's behavior in the race discrimination cases, i.e., Vinson's behavior in *Shelley, Sweatt,* and *McLaurin* is understandable largely in terms of his conservative predispositions. The theory of Vinson's behavior in the race discrimination cases presented in this section undertakes to explain that which is left unexplained by Vinson's general conservatism: the fact that Vinson could vote for *Shelley, Sweatt,* and *McLaurin* at all, the fact that he could make even symbolic concessions to libertarian values.

cesses and attitudinal dispositions. Most traditional judicial biography admittedly accomplishes its objective without benefit of the conceptual armamentaria of contemporary behavioral science. Nevertheless, endemic to any intensive analysis of judicial behavior are serious, sometimes insuperable, problems of validation: how does one know that some rival set of variables—and not those chosen by the judicial biographer—are not responsible for the judicial behavior under scrutiny? How is one to have confidence in the explanation proferred by the judicial biographer? How is one to judge the correctness or plausibility of the explanation advanced by the theorist?

To remedy these problems of validation, "A Theory of Chief Justice Vinson's Behavior in the Race Discrimination Cases" will be presented in the context of certain methodological constraints which underlie most social science theorizing about "political behavior."[139] Explanations of political behavior—including judicial behavior—are most often stated in terms of "values" assumed to be held by the political actor(s) in question: Actor A behaved as he did because he possessed values x, y and z. The x which is valued is an *event*, an *object*, or a *relationship* that is desired by the actor; it is desired because it is felt, by the actor, to "maximize indulgences and minimize deprivations."[140] The theory of Chief Justice Vinson's behavior will likewise be stated in terms of certain values assumed to be held by the Chief Justice: Chief Justice Vinson behaved as he did in the race discrimination cases because he possessed values x, y and z; that is, because he desired a specific event, object or relationship which maximized indulgences and minimized deprivations.

Most accounts or explanations of judicial behavior—whether

---

[139] This is not to suggest of course that judicial biographies which pay no explicit tribute to "scientific rigor" are of necessity less valid than ones that do. It is only to suggest that conscious endeavor to mitigate these problems of validation is likely to provide more "scientifically defensible" and more plausible explanations of judicial behavior than ones that do not.

[140] *See* H. LASSWELL & A. KAPLAN, POWER AND SOCIETY 61-62 (1950). In the words of Lasswell and Kaplan:

Indulgences and deprivations are general terms for any improvement or deterioration in value position or potential. The concepts have nothing to do with the pleasure-pain ratio of the utilitarians; no useful purpose is served by describing all the various values in hedonic terms.

Id. at 61.

written in the literary idiom of a Beveridge or Mason or in the behavioral science idiom of a Lasswell—take the form of such value-based explanation. One apparent danger of value-based explanation is that the values selected in explanation (the "explanatory values") by the theorist may be chosen capriciously; the "explanation" may assume the character of an arbitrary, *post hoc* reconstruction (or empathetic rationalization) of political behavior.

To avoid this danger, some conditions or constraints must be placed upon the selection and identification of those values upon which a theory of judicial behavior may be based (the explanatory values). In the case of Chief Justice Vinson, to mitigate the possibility of arbitrariness and to enhance plausibility, the theory proposed to explain why the Chief Justice could vote for *Shelley, Sweatt,* and *McLaurin* at all—why he could make even symbolic, begrudging concessions to libertarian values in those opinions—must meet the following conditions:

(1) The values upon which the theory is based must be functionally interdependent with values manifest in Vinson's behavior as a public servant. They must be particularly consistent with values manifest in Vinson's principal decisions as a Supreme Court Justice.

(2) The values upon which the theory is based must be inferrable from emotional and background characteristics of the Chief Justice.

(3) Situational or contextual variables must be identified which could have plausibly provided stimuli for the engagement or activation of the values referred to in (1) and (2).

The precise nature and importance of these limiting conditions will become clearer as the discussion proceeds; but, provisionally, it should be understandable how these constraints guard against the arbitrary selection of explanatory values and enhance the plausibility of a value-based explanation. The valuations upon which the theory of Chief Justice Vinson's behavior in the race discrimination cases is based, and which seem to satisfy the foregoing conditions, may be stated, at first, very briefly:

(1) The valuation by Vinson that in the case where President Truman and the Democratic administration

support a strong civil rights program, it is *indulgent* for Vinson to support, even if superficially, similar libertarian measures in spite of the value *deprivations* more generally attendant to voting positively on matters of civil rights and civil liberties. This may be termed the *Pro-Truman Valuation*.

(2) The valuation by Vinson that in the case where communists are using the alleged oppression of Negroes in America as grist for their propoganda mill, it is *indulgent* to support, even if symbolically, civil rights measures that mitigate the effects of communist propagandizing and strengthen America's reputation before the eyes of the world; this, in spite of the value *deprivations* more generally attendant to voting positively on matters of civil rights and civil liberties. This may be termed the *Anti-Communist Valuation*.

The theory of Chief Justice Vinson's behavior in the race discrimination cases thus consists of two major explanatory factors, each corresponding to one of the two principal valuations just articulated. The Chief Justice's behavior is hypothesized to be a resultant of these two principal factors. The Pro-Truman Valuation and the Anti-Communist Valuation will now be considered as explanations of the Chief Justice's behavior in the race discrimination cases.

The Pro-Truman Valuation as an Explanatory Factor

Vinson's tendency to defer to authority and leadership, particularly party and presidential leadership, may offer an explanation of the Chief Justice's behavior in the race discrimination cases. This characteristic, alluded to previously,[141] will be elaborated upon here.

Throughout his career in public service, Vinson was a party regular—an uncompromising loyalist-Democrat. In the 1928 election, for example, Vinson assumed the unpopular responsibility of managing Alfred E. Smith's campaign in Kentucky.[142] As a result he lost his congressional seat—a dear price to pay for party loyalty. After his return to Congress in 1930, Vinson became one of the most loyal of the New Deal Democrats. Congressman Vinson supported the entire

---

[141] See text accompanying notes 38-39, *supra*.
[142] Hatcher, *supra* note 24, chapter 4 *passim*.

New Deal program and was largely responsible for guiding several pieces of important legislation through the House.[143] Vinson was in fact the Congressman who introduced the Court packing bill in the House[144] and was indispensible to the drafting of the Social Security Act.[145] Congressman Vinson was clearly an "administration man" during the Roosevelt presidency. He was admitted to the inner circle of White House advisers[146] and in House politics was recognized as the right hand aide and lieutenant of House majority leader Sam Rayburn.[147]

Vinson's ties with the Truman administration and with Truman personally were even closer. By June 1946, just prior to his nomination to the Court, Vinson had become one of the President's most trusted advisers.[148] The *Truman Memoirs* reveal the close relationship between Vinson and Truman. Truman discussed his desire to take Vinson with him to Potsdam in 1945[149] and the President considered Vinson several times for Secretary of State.[150]

Truman spoke favorably of Vinson as an administrator and adviser:

> I knew Vinson socially, but after I went down to the White House and became acquainted with him I became highly appreciative of his capacity as an administrator and of his ability to see clearly through a situation as it arose. I valued his judgment and advice very highly, and until he was appointed to the Supreme Court he was in on nearly every conference on every subject.[151]

Truman also revealed that Vinson was his personal choice to succeed him as President:

> [After I decided not to seek reelection in 1952] [t]he most logical and qualified candidate, it appeared to me, was the Chief Justice of the United States, Fred M. Vinson.[152]

---

[143] *Id.* at chapters 5-6 *passim*.
[144] *Id.* at 361.
[145] *Id.* at 349-50.
[146] *Id.* at 269.
[147] *Id.* at 495-96.
[148] Bolner, *supra* note 23, at 59.
[149] 1 H. TRUMAN, MEMOIRS 332 (1955-56) [hereinafter cited as TRUMAN].
[150] Bolner, *supra* note 23, at 78.
[151] TRUMAN, *supra* note 149, at 327-38.
[152] 2 TRUMAN, *supra* note 149, at 489.

And, testifying to Vinson's loyalty, Truman observed:

> Vinson was gifted with a sense of personal and political loyalty seldom found among the top men in Washington. . . . He was a devoted and undemonstrative patriot who could also consistently practice personal and party loyalty.[153]

The Truman-Vinson friendship continued through Vinson's tenure on the high Court. Democratic Party politics as well as the personal political embroilments of Truman undoubtedly remained salient for Vinson even in the depoliticized atmosphere of the Supreme Court. As one Washington columnist observed:

> [Truman and Vinson] are warm friends. When they are together, as they often are . . . their talk is not all trivial. Nor is it about the business of the Supreme Court. It's about some of Mr. Truman's problems as President and Democratic Party leader—subjects on which he values the Chief Justice's counsel.[154]

Indeed, while on the Court the Chief Justice was asked by Truman to go on a special mission to Moscow for an informal exchange of views with Stalin. Vinson, after initial reluctance, complied.[155]

Another columnist of the period[156] said the following of the Truman-Vinson friendship:

> The relationship between the Chief Justice and the Chief Executive is as unusual as it is informal. It is the mutual affection, respect and confidence of two men who have come through a lot together. . . .
>
> . . . .
>
> . . . Both men keep telephones handy at their bedsides and many are the problems that are hammered out between them in the late hours with the aid of that convenient gadget. It was not without experience that the President recently said of Judge Vinson that "he's one in a million."[157]

There is crucial and compelling evidence that while he was on the

---
[153] *Id.* at 489-90.
[154] Lindley, *Truman and Vinson*, NEWSWEEK 29 (Dec. 3, 1951).
[155] 2 TRUMAN, *supra* note 149, at 213-14.
[156] F. Blair, *Mr. Truman's Friend—and His Nominee?*, N.Y. Times, Dec. 16, 1951 (Magazine) at 13.
[157] *Id.*

Court Vinson's propensity for supporting "the administration" and his intimate association with Truman were reflected in his voting record. Vinson's support of the Truman administration was never more evident than in the *John L. Lewis* case[158] and the *Steel Seizure* case.[159]

In the *Lewis* case, Chief Justice Vinson, speaking for the majority, ignored the clear language of the Norris-Laguardia Act to uphold both a district court's order restraining John L. Lewis and his union from striking and a contempt punishment for ignoring the injunction; this, in spite of the Norris-Laguardia Act's denial of jurisdiction to federal courts to enjoin parties involved in labor disputes. John L. Lewis had been a nemesis to Truman and the Democratic administration and it was clear that the Chief Justice was out to "get Lewis." Indeed, Frank has observed that "when Truman broke the post-World War II coal strike by seizing the coal mines, Chief Justice Vinson may have been so determined to uphold the President that, so far as he was personally concerned, the argument might as well not have been made."[160]

In the *Steel Seizure* case Chief Justice Vinson issued a strong dissent from a majority opinion by Justice Black which, in essence, held that the President did not, even in the absence of a specific constitutional prohibition, possess inherent power to act in what he conceived to be the national interest. In arguing that President Truman possessed the power to seize the steel mills, Vinson largely ignored the legislative history of the Taft-Hartley Act and brushed aside the lack of precedent for peacetime seizure of private property by the President. Vinson had once again swept aside history and precedent to achieve a desired result.

Vinson's general disposition as Chief Justice to support the administration has been discussed by Clement Vose:

> One thing stands out about Fred Vinson's work as chief justice of the United States from 1946 to 1953—his consistent support of the Democratic Administration.
> . . . .

---
[158] United States v. United Mine Workers, 330 U.S. 258 (1947).
[159] Youngstown Sheet & Tube Co. v. Sawyer, 343 U.S. 579 (1952).
[160] J. FRANK, MARBLE PALACE: THE SUPREME COURT IN AMERICAN LIFE 97 (1958).

Vinson had thus [from his years in the executive branch] gained the outlook of the administration as he took his seat at the center of the Supreme Court.

. . . .

In 1947 when the United States enjoined John L. Lewis, Vinson infuriated his colleague Murphy by asking for help "to get the Administration out of this jam."[161]

The nexus between Vinson's support of the Truman administration and his behavior in the race discrimination cases becomes clearer once the Truman administration's commitment to racial civil rights is documented. In 1946 President Truman, by Executive Order, established the President's Committee on Civil Rights.[162] The ensuing report of the Committee supplied the raw materials for the invalidation of judicial enforcement of restricted covenants and the undermining of segregated education. The Committee's report, *To Secure These Rights*,[163] called for the elimination of prejudice and discrimination from the operation of our public and private schools and colleges and emphasized that "[o]pportunities for Negroes in public institutions of higher education in the South—particularly at the professional graduate school level—are severely limited."[164]

With regard to housing discrimination the President's Committee made recommendations which foreshadowed the Court's decision in *Shelley*:

> The effectiveness of restrictive covenants depends in the last analysis on court orders enforcing the private agreement. The power of the state is thus utilized to bolster discriminatory practices. The Committee believes that every effort must be made to prevent this abuse. We would hold this belief under any circumstances; under present conditions when severe housing shortages are already causing hardship for many people of the country, we are especially emphatic in recommending measures to alleviate the situation.[165]

---

[161] C. VOSE, CAUCASIANS ONLY 183 (1959).
[162] Exec. Order 9808, 11 Fed. Reg. 14153 (1946).
[163] PRESIDENT'S COMM. ON CIVIL RIGHTS, TO SECURE THESE RIGHTS (1947).
[164] *Id.*, quoted in THE STRUGGLE FOR RACIAL EQUALITY 37 (Commager ed. 1967).
[165] Ming, *Racial Restrictions and the Fourteenth Amendment: The Restrictive Covenant Cases*, 16 U. CHI. L. REV. 203, 204 n.2 (1949).

Shortly before the *Shelley* decision, in an historic message to Congress of February 2, 1948, President Truman proposed a comprehensive civil rights program which included the establishment of a permanent Commission on Civil Rights and a Civil Rights Division of the Justice Department. The message also urged the passage of a Fair Employment Practices Law, laws outlawing the poll-tax, and anti-lynching laws.[166] And, on July 26, 1948, the President, by Executive Order, required "that there shall be equality of treatment and opportunity for all persons in the armed forces without regard to race, color, religion or national origin."[167]

Even more importantly, the government was *directly* involved in the *Shelley* case. In *Shelley* the Department of Justice filed an *amicus curiae* brief on the side of the Negro claimants, and in the person of Solicitor-General Phillip Perlman presented an oral argument before the Court in which the findings of the President's Committee on Civil Rights were reiterated.[168] Included in the *Shelley* brief were letters from various members of the Truman administration denouncing restrictive covenants.[169] The Justice Department also filed briefs in *Sweatt* and *McLaurin* which cited the recommendations of President Truman's Committee on Higher Education.[170]

In sum, the Truman administration's advocacy of civil rights was both comprehensive and demonstrable, extending to the direct support of Negro petitioners in *Shelley*, *Sweatt* and *McLaurin*. When these cases were introduced as stimuli, Truman's support of Negro civil rights and Vinson's strong feelings for the President must have produced serious conflict for the Chief Justice, whose general approach to such matters was cautious, conservative, and incrementalist. One resolution of the cognitive imbalance and value conflicts produced by the introduction of the race discrimination cases was to lend symbolic support to the value of racial equality through decisions of a limited, non-instrumental character, never intended, nor ever likely, to upset delicate patterns of racial segregation in the land.

---

[166] H.R. Doc. No. 516, 80th Cong., 2d Sess. (1948).
[167] Exec. Order No. 9981, 13 Fed. Reg. 4313 (1948).
[168] See Vose, *NAACP Strategy in the Covenant Cases* in THE COURTS: A READER IN THE JUDICIAL PROCESS 196-97 (R. Scigliano ed. 1962).
[169] *Id.*
[170] 18 U.S.L.W. 3227 (1949).

By behaving as he did in the race discrimination cases, Vinson could act on a predisposition to support Truman and the Democratic Party while satisfying a contrary disposition to move conservatively and cautiously on matters of civil rights and civil liberties. Vinson's behavior in the race discrimination cases represents an *optimum reconciliation of conflicting values*—in Lasswellian terms, maximization of the ratio of indulgences to deprivations. Lending even token support to racial civil rights was indulgent in terms of Truman's valued friendship, but insuring that these concessions to libertarian values were more cathartic than substantial could minimize deprivations associated with enthusiastic support of instrumental civil rights measures.

This explanation of Chief Justice Vinson's behavior in the race discrimination cases has been touched on by several scholars but never carefully developed. Vose, for example, has observed, "Throughout his tenure as chief justice, Vinson's associations with President Truman were exceedingly close. Vinson's position [in *Shelley*] might then be determined in part by his view of the president's civil rights program."[171]

The Pro-Truman factor would appear to explain an additional amount of the "unexplained variance" in Chief Justice Vinson's behavior in the race discrimination cases. It is appealing as an explanatory factor for three reasons:

> (1) It is based upon valuations which are interdependent with values manifest in Vinson's behavior in over thirty years of public service—particularly values evident from Vinson's principal decisions as a Supreme Court Justice. Vinson's pro-administration, pro-Truman propensities, as a congressman, executive official, and Supreme Court Justice, have already been demonstrated.
>
> (2) It is based upon valuations which are inferable from emotional and background characteristics of the Chief Justice. Vinson's pro-leadership propensities and attachment to the Democratic Party through years of socialization into Democratic Party politics have been considered.

---

[171] Vose, *supra* note 161, at 183.

(3) It is based upon valuations which could have clearly been engaged or activated by specific situational or contextual variables. The Truman civil rights program and the Democratic Party's sudden interest in racial justice and equality surely qualify as appropriate situational variables.

In short, the explanation based upon the Pro-Truman Valuation is plausible because it fulfills those very conditions and constraints imposed upon the selection of "explanatory values" stipulated earlier.

The Anti-Communist Valuation as an Explanatory Factor

The postwar anti-communist hysteria and the communist campaign to exploit the oppression of Negroes in America may offer an added explanatory dimension to Vinson's behavior in the race discrimination cases. The Chief Justice's staunch opposition to communism at home and abroad, his militant patriotism and unaffected devotion to country have already been discussed at considerable length.[172] The Chief Justice's strong sense of urgency and crisis during the postwar period, his obsession with keeping America strong and his preoccupation with stability and order have also been accorded treatment.[173]

Vinson's absorption, as a Supreme Court Justice, with communism and subversive activity was apparent in the *Dennis, Douds, Feiner, Fleischman, Adler, Isserman, Sacher, Rosenberg,* and *Joint Anti—Fascist* decisions.[174] His opinion in *Douds,* for example, upheld the non-communist oath requirement of the Taft-Hartley Act, while his opinion in *Dennis* upheld the validity of the Smith Act.[175] In general, Vinson was much caught up in the anti-communist hysteria of the late forties and early fifties, believing

---

[172] See text accompanying notes 25-39 *supra.*
[173] *Id.*
[174] See note 13, *supra.*
[175] In both *Douds* and *Dennis,* particularly *Dennis,* the Chief Justice emasculated the "clear and present danger" test so that if the substantive evil legislated against was serious enough, advocacy of it need not be accompanied by a "clear and present danger" of success for it to be punishable. "The government's success against communist party leaders in *Dennis* was immediately followed by similar Smith Act prosecutions of second- and third-string communists throughout the country." PRITCHETT, *supra* note 72, at 77.

profoundly that the United States was in a *de facto* state of war with the Soviet Union.[176] The threat of communism and its challenge to the American way of life was highly salient for the Chief Justice. The connection between these valuations and Vinson's decisions in *Shelley*, *Sweatt*, and *McLaurin* is apparent when pertinent features of the cold war struggle are considered.

The cold war was fought on many fronts. In the desperate struggle neither side failed to exploit even the slightest weakness in the other's ideological armor. The race problem has, and always will, make America vulnerable to its ideological adversaries. Consequently, in the cold war between East and West "[n]o component of American society. . . received more continuous attention from the Communist Party than the Negro minority comprising some 10% of the total population."[177]

Communists in America set up an organization for Negro veterans, published a special Harlem edition of the Daily Worker with a Negro editor and made gains in trade unions with predominantly Negro membership.[178] An organization called the National Negro Congress insisted "that the realization of Negro rights in the U.S. was inseparable from the forward march of the 'People's Democracies' and that American Negroes had a responsibility to support these countries, thereby opposing American foreign policy."[179] In speeches, Paul Robeson pledged that American Negroes would refuse to fight the Soviet Union[180] and would resist the "imperialist foreign policy being pursued by America in Africa and Asia."[181] Efforts were also made to dissuade Negroes from fighting in Korea.[182]

Another organization, the Southern Negro Youth Congress, endorsed the Progressive Party and its candidate Henry Wallace for the Presidency.[183] In 1948, "the Wallace movement reached its peak

---

[176] Bolner, *supra* note 23, at 360.
[177] W. RECORD, RACE AND RADICALISM 1 (1964) [hereinafter cited as RECORD].
[178] *Id.* at 168-71.
[179] *Id.* at 147.
[180] W. NOLAN, COMMUNISM VS. THE NEGRO 1, 192 (1951) [hereinafter cited as NOLAN].
[181] *Id.* at 173.
[182] *Id.* at 201-02.
[183] RECORD, *supra* note 177, at 150.

of influence with Negroes."[184] In his study of communism and Negroes, Nolan alleges that "the Communist Party set itself two main goals with regard to its post war campaign among Negroes: (1) Capture the NAACP and (2) Get Negroes into the Progressive Party."[185] The purpose in pursuing the latter, according to Nolan, was to sabotage the Truman civil rights program and elect an anti-civil rights President and Congress.[186]

The major objective of American communists in the post war period was to embarrass American democracy before the African, Asian and Latin American nations. Every manifestation of discrimination and oppression was exposed and magnified. The Negro's plight in America was clearly an important aspect of the East-West ideological struggle during the post war period. In the competition for the hearts and minds of third world peoples, communist ideologists skillfully exploited the very real plight of Negroes in America.

There is also little doubt that international politics was a factor in the gains achieved by Negroes during the cold war period. The Truman civil rights program, which included desegregation of the armed forces and the appointment of a Negro to the United Nations delegation, was promulgated partly for international consumption. Nolan observed, for example, that "while considerable progress had been made against discrimination in the armed forces prior to the outbreak of hostilities—nevertheless the immediate need for creating a favorable impression on the colored masses of Asia greatly intensified the trend toward full integration."[187]

Judges, like other political actors, are not insensitive to the salient political and social struggles of their time. Blaustein has very aptly observed:

> It is inconceivable that the international discord between East and West had no effect upon the nine men who were to determine a national discord between North and South . . . [T]he men in the high tribunal know very well the problems of coexistence and the search for allies.[188]

---

[184] NOLAN, *supra* note 180, at 205.
[185] *Id.* at 178.
[186] *Id.* at 182.
[187] *Id.* at 203.
[188] A. BLAUSTEIN & C. FERGUSON, DESEGREGATION AND THE LAW 12 (1957) [hereinafter cited as BLAUSTEIN].

The "cold-war" argument was invoked very strongly in legal briefs and in oral arguments before the Court. In *Henderson v. United States*,[189] Attorney General McGrath issued the warning that "[u]nless segregation is ended, a serious blow will be struck at our democracy before the world."[190] In the *Briggs* and *Brown* cases, the lawyers for the NAACP in briefs submitted to the Court wrote, "Survival of our country in the present international situation is inevitably tied to resolution of this domestic issue."[191] And the brief submitted by the United States in the same case as *amicus curiae* contained the following passage:

> It is in the context of the present world struggle between freedom and tyranny that the problem of racial discrimination must be viewed . . . for discrimination against minority groups in the U.S. has an adverse effect upon our relations with other countries. Racial discrimination furnishes grist for the communist propaganda mills and it raises doubts even among friendly nations as to the intensity of our devotion to the democratic faith.[192]

The very same argument was tendered by the President's Committee on Civil Rights and by the government in its *amicus curiae* brief in the *Shelley* case.[193]

---

[189] 339 U.S. 816 (1950).
[190] 18 U.S.L.W. 3227 (1950).
[191] BLAUSTEIN, *supra* note 188, at 11.
[192] *Id.* at 12.
[193] CIVIL RIGHTS AND THE AMERICAN NEGRO (Blaustein, Zangrando eds. 1968). It is worth quoting from the report of the President's Committee at length:

> Our position in the postwar is so vital to the future that our smallest actions have far reaching effects. We have come to know that our own security in a highly interdependent world is inextricably tied to the security and well-being of all people and all countries. Our foreign policy is being designed to make the United States an enormous, positive influence for peace and progress throughout the world. We have tried to let nothing, not even extreme political differences between ourselves and foreign nations, stand in the way of this goal. But our domestic civil rights shortcomings are a serious obstacle.
>
> . . . .
>
> We cannot escape the fact that our civil rights record has been an issue in world politics. The world's press and radio are full of it. This Committee has seen a multitude of samples. We and our friends have been, and are, stressing our achievements. Those with competing philosophies have stressed—and are shamelessly distorting—our shortcomings. They have not only tried to create hostility toward us among specific nations, races, and religious groups. They have tried to prove our democracy an empty fraud, and our nation a consistent oppressor of under-

The communist-Negro perspective on the discrimination cases must have been salient for many including the nine Justices who sat on the high Court during the post war period. This aspect of the race issue was particularly salient for Americans keenly sensitive to the ideological struggle between East and West, to those fiercely patriotic and vigilant and to those who believed America must emerge victorious in the "contest for the friendship of the world's great colored races."[184] Chief Justice Vinson was, of course, such a man.

The Chief Justice surely appreciated the shame to America if the Supreme Court failed to express even symbolic support for racial equality. Conversely, by requiring the University of Texas to integrate its law school and the University of Oklahoma its graduate school and by striking at the judicial enforcement of restrictive covenants, America could demonstrate to the black and brown races of the world its commitment to racial justice. In spite of a more general disposition to move conservatively on questions of civil rights and civil liberties, Vinson could find it indulgent to support a libertarian program in *Shelley, Sweatt* and *McLaurin* which might mitigate the effects of communist propagandizing and strengthen America's reputation before the eyes of the world. And, by insuring that these measures were cautious and gradualist, deprivations associated with support of progressive civil rights measures could be minimized.

Rodell, in an equally cynical interpretation of judicial motivations has embraced the Anti-Communist explanation and extended it to the entire Court:

> privileged people. This may seem ludicrous to Americans, but it is sufficiently important to worry our friends.
>
> . . . .
>
> Our achievements in building and maintaining a state dedicated to the fundamentals of freedom have already served as a guide for those seeking the best road from chaos to liberty and prosperity. But is is not indelibly written that democracy will encompass the world. We are convinced that our way of life—the free way of life—holds a promise of hope for all people. We have what is perhaps the greatest responsibility ever placed upon a people to keep this promise alive. Only still greater achievements will do it. *The United States is not so strong, the final triumph of democratic ideal is not so inevitable that we can ignore what the world thinks of us or our record.*

Id. at 378-79.
[184] Y. Kamisar in Friedman, *supra* note 113, at xiv.

> ... [T]here is no doubt that the pro-Negro pronouncements ... were pushed to such unprecedented lengths to help counter communist propaganda in Asia and Africa about American maltreatment of people whose skins are not white.[103]

The Anti-Communist explanation of Chief Justice Vinson's behavior in the race discrimination cases is appealing for several reasons:

> (1) The valuation upon which it is based proves functionally interdependent with Vinson's anti-communist, patriotic impulses apparent in over thiry years of public service. Moreover, by reconceptualizing *Shelley*, *Sweatt* and *McLaurin* as anti-communist rather than pro-civil rights decisions, the attitudes manifest in these cases now appear quite consistent with Vinson's notable anti-communist decisions of the period.
>
> (2) The valuations upon which it is based are inferable from emotional and background characteristics of the Chief Justice. Vinson was reared by, and for many years resided among, a fiercely patriotic, militantly anti-communist people. Later in life the Chief Justice exhibited a characteristic preoccupation with national security and the threat of communist subversion.
>
> (3) It is based upon valuations which could have plausibly been activated by specific situational or contextual variables. The communist hysteria of the period is clearly such a variable.

The Anti-Communist Valuation, like the Pro-Truman Valuation, thus satisfies the conditions laid down earlier for the selection of "explanatory values." It is hoped that by placing these constraints on the selection of explanatory values the plausibility of certain *rival theories* is precluded, or at least brought seriously into question.[104]

---

[103] RODELL, *supra* note 37, at 303.

[104] Two rival theories of Vinson's behavior in the race discrimination cases may be briefly considered:

One plausible rival explanation is that Chief Justice Vinson voted with the majority in *Shelley*, *Sweatt*, and *McLaurin* merely to gain an opportunity to assign the opinion, write the opinion himself or influence the final outcome. This may be termed the "strategic" explanation of Vinson's behavior. The strategic explanation assumes that Vinson was privately inclined to vote negatively in the three opinions, but seeing that majorities already existed in support of a libertarian result, decided he could minimize the effects of the three decisions by voting with, rather than against, the majority. Two observations must be made regarding the strategic explanation. First, the strategic explanation in part presupposes the validity of the principal hypotheses of this study. It presupposes at least some degree of ambivalence on the part of Vinson toward the libertarian values that were present in *Shelley*, *Sweatt*, and *McLaurin*. But secondly, and more importantly, the strategic explanation, while consistent with Vinson's general conservatism on matters of civil rights and civil liberties, is inconsistent with at least two major judicial events in Vinson's career on the high Court. In the *Barrows* case, detailed earlier, the Chief Justice issued a lone dissent from a libertarian decision—a decision which he might have influenced had he chosen to vote with the majority. And in the *Steel Seizure* case Vinson again passed up an opportunity to cushion the effects of the Court's strong rebuke of Truman's seizure of the steel mills by issuing a strong dissent from the majority opinion. (Actually Justice Black spoke for less than a majority in the *Steel Seizure* case.)

Barrows and the *Steel Seizure* cases suggest that where Vinson could find no positive indulgences in voting for a decision with which he disagreed privately, he would express outright dissent. Voting with the majority in *Barrows* could offer no indulgences for the Chief Justice. The case was decided in 1953 after Truman had left office and after the peak years of the Truman civil rights program. *Barrows* also received little publicity and attention in either the domestic or foreign press and did not involve the rights of any specific Negro. A positive vote by Vinson would therefore carry little weight in terms of America's reputation before the eyes of the world. In the *Steel Seizure* case, because the fortunes of the President were so directly involved and because the steel strike so obviously threatened the security of the nation, Vinson could derive no indulgences from voting with the majority for purposes of influencing the final outcome. Vinson therefore dissented outright. The "strategic" explanations of Vinson's behavior in the race discrimination cases is therefore much too simplistic. For Vinson to have taken the step of voting for an opinion with which he disagreed privately for purposes of influencing the final outcome, there must have been some indulgences involved other than the indulgences derived from minimizing the scope and impact of an undesired outcome. At best the strategic explanation is of secondary importance to the Pro-Truman and Communist-Negro explanations in accounting for Vinson's behavior in the race discrimination cases.

Another plausible rival explanation is that Vinson voted for *Shelley*, *Sweatt*, and *McLaurin* merely to preserve unanimity in cases where important political and social values were being affected by the Court. This explanation assumes that Vinson, in his role as Chief Justice, felt an obligation to preserve the power and legitimacy of the Court in the face of "court-curbing" efforts by affected individuals. This may be termed the "role theory" explanation of Vinson's behavior in the race discrimination cases. The problem with this explanation is that it conflicts seriously with Vinson's behavior in the *Steel Seizure* case. Vinson's dissent in that case clearly jeopardized the Court and placed it in an extremely vulnerable position. Vinson apparently felt no responsibility as Chief Justice to vote with the majority for the sake of unanimity. There being no indulgences for the Chief Justice in voting for an undesired decision, he could dissent outright from the majority opinion in the *Steel Seizure* case. Just as Vinson considered his role as Chief Justice secondary to his valued relationship with Truman and to his preoccupation with national security in the *Steel Seizure* case, so too, Vinson's concern for his role responsibilities as Chief Justice in the desegregation cases must have paled in significance next to the anti-communist and pro-Truman concerns. It should also be pointed out that, like the strategic explanation, the role theory explanation presupposes to some extent the validity of the principal hypotheses of this study. It presupposes that Vinson was at least ambivalent toward the libertarian values that were present in

To summarize, Chief Justice Vinson could vote for *Shelley*, *Sweatt*, and *McLaurin* at all only because (1) his votes fulfilled a need to maintain an "identifying" relationship with the President and (2) they satisfied a need to reiterate, in the face of the communist challenge, America's philosophic commitment to racial equality. And, by seeing to it that these decisions fell short of instigating genuine social reform (and its concomitant—social dislocation), deprivations associated with support of libertarian social measures could be minimized.

V. Conclusions and Implications

Summary and Recapitulation

In the first section of this article, it was proposed that Chief Justice Vinson's behavior in the race discrimination cases was anomalous. A perusal of the Chief Justice's emotional and background characteristics, a consideration of relevant personality variables, and an analysis of Vinson's manifest behavior in over thirty years of public service failed to account for the apparently liberal decisions in *Shelley*, *Sweatt*, and *McLaurin*. Vinson's behavior in the race discrimination cases was an apparent curiosity which demanded behavioral explanation. Before Vinson's anti-civil libertarian reputation could undergo revision based on those decisions, however, and before his apparently anomalous behavior could be properly explained, *Shelley*, *Sweatt*, and *McLaurin* had to be subjected to closer analysis.

The careful analysis of the restrictive covenant and school desegregation cases undertaken in Sections II and III endeavored to test the hypothesis that Chief Justice Vinson's anti-civil libertarian and conservative reputation required modification in light of the three apparently liberal opinions in *Shelley*, *Sweatt*, and *McLaurin*. The doctrinal, historical, and impact analyses performed on those three decisions suggested, however, that they were less revolutionary in orientation and impact than more perfunctory analyses have revealed. *Shelley*, for example, was never adapted toward instigating more than token desegregation of housing in America (even if the economic barriers to housing integration were not a factor). And

---

the three decisions (but refrained from dissenting because of his concern for the Court's prestige and legitimacy).

even the enormous theoretical implications of *Shelley* (for housing discrimination and beyond) were dampened by the scrupulous preservation of the *Civil Rights Cases*. *Shelley* was also ill-equipped to crystallize the issue of racial equality.

The reconsideration of *Sweatt* and *McLaurin* revealed that these cases, like *Shelley*, were more symbolic and cathartic in character than instrumental. *Sweatt* and *McLaurin* moved cautiously and incrementally on the desegregation question and in their aftermath were interpreted by most observers as reiterating *Gaines*, *Sipuel*, and *Fisher*, inflicting barely a dent in the armor of *Plessy*.

The reevaluation of the three Vinson opinions led to the tentative hypothesis that the Chief Justice's performance in the race discrimination cases was not nearly as inconsistent with his general conservatism on matters of civil rights and civil liberties as some have supposed. But, because *Shelley*, *Sweatt*, and *McLaurin* were decided unanimously this provisional conclusion required an isolation of the Chief Justice's views on the desegregation question. This was especially important in light of the ambiguous nature of the Vinson opinions—an ambiguity which guaranteed their symbolic rather than instrumental character and which indicated the presence on the Court of a conservative faction wishing to limit the scope and impact of the three decisions. Isolating the Chief Justice's views could specify the judicial bloc which enjoyed Vinson's support and could determine retrospectively his personal contributions to the final outcome of *Shelley*, *Sweatt*, and *McLaurin*.

The *Barrows* dissent enabled the isolation of the Chief Justice's views on housing discrimination. *Barrows* revealed that Vinson occupied the most conservative position on the Court in the restrictive covenant cases and that more than likely it was the Chief Justice who led a conservative faction in insisting that the *Civil Rights Cases* be enthusiastically reaffirmed.

An analysis of the oral arguments in *Brown* and *Briggs*, as well as evidence from the Burton papers, enabled the isolation of the Chief Justice's personal perspectives on school desegregation. The transcript of the oral arguments pointed to Vinson's hostility toward the plaintiffs' position in *Brown*; while the Burton papers revealed that Vinson was one of two or three Justices who resisted the arguments which enabled the Warren Court, just eight months later, to announce the historic verdict in *Brown*.

The tentative conclusion that Vinson's behavior in the race discrimination cases did not require a modification of his anti-civil libertarian reputation was thus confirmed by the *Barrows* dissent, the oral arguments in *Briggs* and *Brown*, and the recorded observations of Justice Burton. Yet, Vinson's general conservatism did not explain *all* of the variance in Vinson's behavior in the race discrimination cases. The question of why the Chief Justice could vote for *Shelley*, *Sweatt*, and *McLaurin* at all—why he could make even begrudging, symbolic concessions to libertarian values—begged for behavioral explanation.

Section IV undertook a theory of Chief Justice Vinson's behavior in the race discrimination cases. By carefully selecting—according to specific methodological constraints—certain "valuations" of the Chief Justice upon which to base our theory, it was concluded that Vinson could vote for *Shelley*, *Sweatt*, and *McLaurin* at all because (1) it fulfilled a need to maintain an "identifying" relationship with the President and (2) it satisfied a need to reiterate, in the face of the communist challenge, America's philosophic commitment to racial equality. And, by seeing to it that these decisions fell short of instigating genuine social reform (and its concomitant—social dislocation), deprivations associated with support of libertarian social measures could be minimized.

Implications I: Linkages Between the Supreme Court and the Rest of the Political System

The foregoing theory of Chief Justice Vinson's behavior in the desegregation cases stimulates speculation with regard to linkages between the Supreme Court and the rest of the political system and invites conjecture with respect to collective and macro-political responses to the race problem in America. In his seminal article on the "Supreme Court as a National Policy-Maker"[197] Robert Dahl proffers a simple, though compelling, explanation which accounts for the Supreme Court's interconnectedness with the political branches of government. "[I]t would appear," Dahl argues, ". . . somewhat unrealistic to suppose that a Court whose members are recruited in the fashion of Supreme Court Justices would long hold

---

[197] Dahl, *Decision-Making in a Democracy: The Supreme Court as a National Policy-Maker*, 6 J. PUB. L. 279 (1957).

to norms of Right or Justice substantially at odds with the rest of the political elite."[198] Put another way, the President with the consent of the Senate appoints an average of four Justices during an eight year presidential incumbency. It is thus understandable that the Supreme Court parallels, or does not stray very far from, presidential-legislative policies.[199]

A second look at the Pro-Truman explanation of Vinson's behavior in the race discrimination cases suggests that it is just one example of a more general parallelism between presidential and judicial policy-making. The intensive analysis of Vinson's behavior in the race discrimination cases merely enabled us to observe the Dahlian dynamic at work, exposing and reifying the mechanics of judicial-executive interdependency.

The Communist-Negro explanation also has implications that go beyond the specific case of Chief Justice Vinson. Vinson's symbolic concessions to racial equality in the context of invariant resistance to *genuine* racial reform is merely a special instance of a general ambivalence toward racial equality which is typically American. It is the dualism spoken of by Hartz[200] and alluded to by Dahl[201] in their analyses of American democratic traditions. To carry the Hartzian scenario forward one need only point out that it was the challenge of the communist ideology—in Hartzian language, "the past catching up with us"[202]—which precipitated even the symbolic tribute to racial equality on the part of Chief Justice Vinson. The Communist-Negro explanation, moreover, points to the general vulnerability of segregationist philosophy to the challenge of egalitarian ideologies, whether communistic or liberal-democratic.

Because several members of the Vinson Court, besides the Chief Justice, had been closely associated with the President and had been equally sensitive to the challenge of foreign ideologies, it is not unlikely that the factors motivating Chief Justice Vinson's behavior in the race discrimination cases were also instrumental in shaping

---

[198] *Id.* at 291.
[199] *Id.* at 284-85.
[200] L. Hartz, The Liberal Tradition in America 167-72 (1955); L. Hartz, The Founding of New Societies 16-20 (1964).
[201] R. Dahl, Pluralist Democracy in the United States 65-67 (1967).
[202] L. Hartz, The Founding of New Societies 44 (1964).

the response of the Vinson Court to the issue of race discrimination. Justices Burton, Minton, and Clark, for example, enjoyed close associations with President Truman,[203] and these Justices, together with Justices Jackson and Reed, displayed considerable concern for the challenges posed by foreign and domestic communism and by other subversive elements.[204]

---

[203] While Senate colleagues, Harry Truman asked Harold Burton to join him as an opposition member of the famous "Truman Committee" to investigate national defense contracts. Senators Truman and Burton cemented a close friendship while serving together on the Committee. The association of Truman and Tom Clark apparently goes back to Clark's tenure as Assistant Attorney General, when Clark is reputed to have performed political favors for several friends of the then Vice-President Truman. Truman later promoted Clark to the Attorney Generalship. As a Senate Whip during the New Deal, Sherman Minton forcefully backed the Administration program and during that period became a personal friend of Harry Truman. All three Justices—Burton, Clark, and Minton—were of course appointed to the high Court by President Truman. For a discussion of the association between these three Justices and President Truman see RODELL, *supra* note 37, at 309-13; PRITCHETT, *supra* note 72, at 19-20.

[204] The table immediately following records votes by Justices Minton, Reed, Burton, Clark, and Jackson in major cases involving the threat of communism and other "subversive" activity.

JUSTICES	Minton	Reed	Burton	Clark	Jackson
CASES					
Dennis	+	+	+	0	+
Douds	0	+	+	0	-
Feiner	-	+	+	+	+
Fleischman	+	+	+	0	+
Isserman	+	+	+	0	-
Sacher	+	+	+	0	+
Rosenberg	+	+	+	+	+
Joint Anti-Fascist	+	+	-	0	-

See note 13, *supra*, for a brief discussion of the cases listed in the table.
A plus (+) vote indicates a sensitivity to the threat of subversion. A minus (-) vote indicates a greater concern for other values present in the cases such as freedom of speech, due process, fair procedure. A zero (0) vote indicates non-participation in the case.

Because he had participated in their preparation as Attorney General, Justice Clark disqualified himself from hearing several of the major prosecutions against communists and other alleged subversives which came before the high Court. Nevertheless, Tom Clark's sensitivity to "communist subversion" is well established from the vigorous manner in which he administered the Truman Loyalty Program as Attorney General. In that regard Fred Rodell has observed that Clark's "running of the loyalty program took scant heed of civil liberties." RODELL, *supra* note 37, at 311.

Implications II: The Supreme Court and Political Liberalism: The Special Case of Racial Equality

This single case study of Chief Justice Vinson and desegregation may partially answer some of the questions about Supreme Court decision making in the field of Political Equality raised by Glendon Schubert.[295] In his *Judicial Mind* Schubert is interested in clarifying the nature of judicial liberalism. To align the Justices ordinally on a scale of Political Liberalism, and to compute "scale scores" for the performance of each Justice, Schubert analyzes their votes in relation to five major issue categories: (1) Political Equality, (2) Political Freedom, (3) Religious Freedom, (4) the Right to Fair Procedure, and (5) the Right to Individual Privacy.[296] These categories are termed by Schubert "the subcomponents of political liberalism."[297]

The Political Equality subcomponent is of special interest to Schubert. This component is defined to include "such legal issues as the white primary, public school and other forms of racial integration, legislative reapportionment and citizenship status."[298] *A major portion of the Political Equality component thus consists of racial equality cases.* The problem encountered by Schubert is that the performance of Justices on the Political Equality component of Political Liberalism correlates with their performance on Political Liberalism generally (i.e., all the five components taken together) at a level of only +.76, whereas their performance on the Political Freedom and Right to Fair Procedure components correlate with Political Liberalism generally at levels of +.97 and +.99 respectively. Schubert admits that Political Equality may therefore "represent attitudes that differ for many of the [Justices] from what they associate with the [entire political liberalism] scale."[299]

---

[295] G. SCHUBERT, THE JUDICIAL MIND (1965).

[296] Political Equality includes such legal issues as the white primary, public school and other forms of racial integration, legislative reapportionment, and citizenship status. Political Freedom includes freedom of speech, association, and press and loyalty dismissals. Religious Freedom includes free exercise and separation of church and state issues. The Right to Fair Procedure relates to claims based upon most of the Fifth, Sixth, and Eighth Amendments or to analogous claims based upon the Fourteenth Amendment. The Right to Individual Privacy includes claims that one's person has been violated either physically or psychologically by the government. It thus refers to both Fourth Amendment issues and such Fifth Amendment issues as coerced confessions and other forms of self-incrimination. See SCHUBERT, *supra* note 205, at 159.

[297] *Id.* at 158.
[298] *Id.* at 159.
[299] *Id.* at 173.

Chief Justice Vinson is of course one example of a Justice whose nominal support for Political Equality (based on his opinions in *Shelley, Sweatt,* and *McLaurin*) appears stronger than for other components of Political Liberalism. Intensive analysis of the Chief Justice, however, revealed that his nominal support for racial equality was largely explainable in terms of the very same factors which produced anti-liberalism votes on the other components of the Political Liberalism scale; anti-communism, that is, is a "conservative" explanation for apparently liberal behavior in *Shelley, Sweatt,* and *McLaurin.* The same Anti-Communist Valuation which appears to have stimulated the Chief Justice to pay nominal tribute to Political Equality in three race discrimination cases, may have at the same time motivated him to vote conservatively in Political Freedom, Right to Privacy and Fair Procedure cases involving "subversives," "radicals," and other "political undesirables." Moreover, on matters of *racial equality,* unlike other components of Political Liberalism, Chief Justice Vinson was subject to cross-pressures emanating from the White House and from other sources of partisan politics which doubtlessly contributed to his "inconsistent" behavior in these Political Equality cases.

While it is not possible to explain the low correlation between Political Equality and Political Liberalism in *precisely* the terms which account for Chief Justice Vinson's behavior in the race discrimination cases, the Pro-Truman and Anti-Communist factors are suggestive of plausible explanations for the behavioral anomalies reported by Schubert.[210] Factors related to the general dependence of judicial actors on the dominant political elite and to the extreme vulnerability of segregationist dogma to the challenge of egalitarian ideologies—including America's own traditions of democratic egalitarianism—may explain the special treatment accorded by judicial actors to the Political Equality component of Political Liberalism. It is important to note in that regard that the Justice whose "anom-

---

[210] The data on which Schubert's findings are based were collected after three of the four Truman Justices had left the Court and after the Court's sensitivity to the communist challenge had apparently peaked. Nevertheless, the *general class of explanatory factors*, of which the Pro-Truman and the Anti-Communist are special cases, would seem to be suggestive of explanations. See the discussion relating to Dahl, Hartz, and the more general factors which may underlie the Pro-Truman and Anti-Communist explanatory factors at text accompanying notes 197-204, *supra.*

alous" performance contributed the most, by far, to the low correlation between Political Equality and Political Liberalism was Justice Tom Clark,[211] the lone remaining Truman appointee. Since he was quite susceptible to precisely the Pro-Truman and Anti-Communist Valuations,[212] these factors may have shaped Justice Clark's early responses to the race issue, and having done so, may have established a pattern of behavior toward racial equality which was strikingly at odds with his performance on other components of the Political Liberalism scale.[213]

On these other components of Political Liberalism, such as Political Freedom and Fair Procedure, the predilections of conservative Justices were not in conflict with cues from the dominant political elite, nor with the blandishments of powerful opinion leaders and interest groups; neither were conservative dispositions on these matters so starkly at cross purposes with America's own liberal, egalitarian traditions. On matters of racial equality,[214] however, unique political pressures, stimulated by the migration of Negroes to the urban North, channelled through partisan politics, and coupled with the challenge of egalitarian ideologies, moved Chief Justice Vinson and conceivably other Justices to make at least symbolic concessions[215] to the cause for racial equality. For a number of judi-

---

[211] SCHUBERT, note 205 *supra*, tables 25 and 26 at 171-72.

[212] See notes 203 and 204 *supra*.

[213] On a scale of +1 (most liberal) to -1 (most conservative), the scale scores for Justice Clark were as follows:

Political Equality	+.53
Political Freedom	-.94
Right to Fair Procedure	-.94
Right to Individual Privacy	-.33

SCHUBERT, note 205 *supra*, table 25 at 171.

[214] It is important to reiterate that a major portion of the Political Equality scale contains *racial equality* cases.

[215] The intensive analysis of Chief Justice Vinson's behavior in the race discrimination cases, particularly in *Barrows* and in the early stages of *Brown*, enabled us to conclude with some confidence that his support of racial equality was more symbolic than tangible and that the gradualist perspective of the *Shelley*, *Sweatt* and *McLaurin* decisions were both intended and supported by the Chief Justice. It was also asserted that, having rejected its predecessor's cautious approach, the Warren Court in *Brown* produced a decision which ultimately resulted in the allocation of tangible benefits for Black Americans. See notes 75 and 135 *supra*. In order, however, to characterize *reliably* the performance of individual Justices in the *Brown* decision in terms of their tangible or symbolic concessions to racial equality, it would be

cial actors, like Chief Justice Vinson, concessions to racial equality would appear at least nominally inconsistent with normally conservative behavioral tendencies and would pose challenging problems for the analysis of judicial behavior.

---

necessary to view their attitudes in isolation, as was done for Chief Justice Vinson in the analysis of the *Barrows* dissent and the preliminary proceedings in *Brown*. In the case of Chief Justice Earl Warren there is considerable evidence that he personally intended and supported the tangible benefits that eventually resulted from *Brown*, and that therefore his concessions to racial equality were quite sincere and genuine. BERMAN, note 127 *supra*, and Ulmer, note 125 *supra*, recount Earl Warren's personal role in the disposition of *Brown*. One could also reliably conclude that the pro-civil rights decisions of other Justices such as Black, Douglas, Brennan, and Marshall, were not meant merely as symbolic gestures to racial equality or as *purely pragmatic* responses to external political pressure or to the challenges of egalitarian ideologies.

The Supreme Court's recent decision in the case of *Milliken v. Bradley*, 418 U.S. 717 (1974), however, suggests that some Justices are still making symbolic gestures toward racial integration. Though Chief Justice Burger's previous decision in *Swann v. Charlotte-Mecklenberg Bd. of Educ.*, 402 U.S. 1 (1971), supported busing as a permissible remedy to achieve integration, he carefully limited the decision to the circumstances of the case. The Court's decision in *Milliken* (or the "Detroit Busing Case") confirmed the worst fears of some integrationists that the commitment of several Justices to "desegregation *now*" was less than complete. In the Detroit Busing Case, Justices Burger, Powell, Rehnquist, Blackmun, and Stewart (in a concurring opinion) held that a district court had exceeded its equity powers in ordering the city of Detroit and its outlying suburbs to bus black and white pupils across district lines as the only feasible means of achieving integration. In refusing to uphold the district court's remedy, Justice Burger asserted explicitly what was implicit in *Swann*, "that desegregation in the sense of dismantling a dual school system does not require any particular racial balance. . . ," 418 U.S. at 740. Justice Stewart's concurring opinion, which was quite explicit as to the kinds of factual situations which would enable him to uphold inter-district busing, held out more hope for integrationists. See 418 U.S. at 753 (Stewart, J., concurring).

The Detroit Busing Case, therefore, brings into serious doubt the commitment of the Nixon Justices, and possibly Justice Stewart as well, to the specific goal of racial integration in the nation's inner-city public schools. The difference, however, between the Burger and the Vinson Courts' hesitancy to further the cause of racial integration is that the Burger Court's decision in *Milliken* takes place at a time when there are potent forces in other sectors of the political and social system actively promoting racial equality. During the period of the Vinson Court, however, the Supreme Court was one of the few institutions in American life to which the Negro could conceivably have looked for help.

... ... *Notes and Suggestions* ... ...

The *Roberts* Case: Source of the "Separate but Equal" Doctrine

LEONARD W. LEVY AND HARLAN B. PHILLIPS

IN mid-nineteenth century Massachusetts the prejudice of color sought its last legal refuge in Boston's system of public schools. But no institution was safe from the pitiless criticism of conscience, for it was an age, presided over by the universal reformers, which pulsated with the spirit of social justice. Only the intoxicated visions of a perfect society delimited their imagination. Quite proper then that in William Lloyd Garrison's state the reformers should devote some measure of their energies toward improving the status of the colored American. The law prohibiting intermarriage had been rescinded in 1843, and railroads had been forced to abandon Jim Crow cars.[1] Separate schools for Negroes had been abolished, where they had existed, in Salem, Lowell, New Bedford, Nantucket, and in the smaller towns.[2] In the Supreme Judicial Court, in 1849, Charles Sumner, arguing the cause of Sarah Roberts before the great Chief Justice Shaw, eloquently coupled the "civilization of the age" to an appeal for the abolition of segregated education in Boston.[3]

For half a century schools for the exclusive use of colored children had been maintained in Boston. It was agreed by both parties to the *Roberts* case that the first school was originally established, in 1798, at the request of Negro citizens "whose children could not attend the public schools on account of the prejudice then existing against them."[4] Boston refused to incur the expense of the colored school which was made possible by the benefactions of white philanthropists, including John Lowell, Jedidiah Morse, and John T. Kirk-

[1] *St.* 1843, ch. 5; *Twelfth Annual Report, Presented to the Massachusetts Anti-Slavery Society, by its Board of Managers, January, 1844*, pp. 5, 7; *Argument of Charles Sumner, Esq. against the Constitutionality of Separate Colored Schools, in the Case of Sarah C. Roberts vs. The City of Boston. Before the Supreme Court of Mass., Dec. 4, 1849* (Boston, 1849), p. 32. (Hereafter cited as *Sumner's Argument*.)
[2] See letters to Edmund Jackson from school committees of various towns on the results of abolishing separate schools, in *Report of the Minority of the Committee of the Primary School Board, on the Caste Schools of the City of Boston with some remarks* [by Wendell Phillips] *on the City Solicitor's Opinion* (Boston, 1846), Appendix, pp. 21–27.
[3] *Sumner's Argument*, p. 31.
[4] *Roberts v. City of Boston*, 59 Mass. 198, 200 (1849). See also *Sumner's Argument*, pp. 27-28.

510

land. The school met in a private home until the contributions of Abiel Smith, Chief Justice Parsons, and others, in 1806, secured the basement of the newly erected African Baptist Church in Belknap Street as a permanent site. In 1815 Abiel Smith, "the merchant prince," died and left an endowment of $4,000 for the school, which took his name. Not until 1812 had Boston assisted the school; the town's grant of $200 was continued yearly till 1815, when the board of selectmen assumed control. Five years later, after the primary school for children of four to seven had become a part of the public school system, Boston legally fixed the pattern of segregation by establishing a separate primary for Negroes.[5]

For more than twenty years thereafter, the Smith Grammar School and its primary appendages continued undisturbed. Meanwhile, the Boston Negro had been growing in the political maturity which comes of being a free American. When the battle against the Jim Crow car had been won, colored militants, urged on by the Massachusetts Anti-Slavery Society, turned their forces against the Jim Crow school, once a blessing, now a discriminatory abomination. In 1846 they petitioned the primary school committee for the abolition of exclusive schools. Despite the protests of its two abolitionist members, Edmund Jackson and Henry I. Bowditch, the committee decided against the petition. The majority report stated candidly: "The distinction is one which the Almighty has seen fit to establish, and it is founded deep in the physical, mental, and moral natures of the two races. No legislation, no social customs, can efface this distinction."[6] To them, therefore, the segregated education of Negroes was "not only legal and just, but is best adapted to promote the education of that class of our population."[7] That very year, the white master of Smith School officially reported that the institution was shamefully neglected, desperately in need of repairs.[8] For over four years the issue was the occasion of discord among public officials and among the Negroes themselves, who were bitterly divided. In the press, and at public

---

[5] *Report of a Special Committee of the Grammar School Board, presented August 29, 1849, on the petition of sundry colored persons praying for the abolition of the Smith School* (Boston, 1849), pp. 18-21, 68-69.
[6] "Extracts from the Majority Report on the Caste School," in the *Liberator*, Boston, Aug. 21, 1846. To the abolitionists, such remarks were "flimsy yet venomous sophistries." *Ibid.*, editorial.
[7] Quoted in *Roberts v. City of Boston*, 59 Mass. 198, 201 (1849).
[8] "The school rooms are too small, the paint is much defaced, and every part gives evidence of the most shameful negligence and abuse. There are no recitation rooms, or proper places for overclothes, caps, bonnets, etc. The yards, for each division, are but about fifteen feet square, and only accessible through a dark, damp cellar. The apparatus has been so shattered and neglected that it cannot be used until it has been thoroughly repaired." Remarks of Ambrose Wellington, Master of Smith School, quoted in *City Document No. 28: Reports of the Annual Visiting Committees of the Public Schools of the City of Boston* (Boston, 1846), p. 151.

meetings, the issue was long debated, and no less than two majority and two minority school committee reports were published. Without action by the legislature, which alone could end the controversy, all the circumstances were at hand for a court case.[9]

Benjamin Roberts was one of the Negro leaders in the fight against segregation. Four times he tried to enter his five-year-old daughter, Sarah, in one of the white primary schools of the district in which he resided, and as many times she was rejected by authority of the school committee, solely on ground of color. On the direct route from her home to the primary school in Belknap Street connected with the Smith School, Sarah passed no less than five other primaries. Roberts was informed that his child might be admitted at any time to the colored school, but he refused to have her attend there.[10] Determined to test the constitutionality of the school committee's power to enforce segregation, Roberts brought suit in Sarah's name under a statute[11] which provided that any child, illegally excluded from the public schools, might recover damages against the city.

To argue Sarah's cause, Roberts retained Charles Sumner, a man of cultivated erudition, oratorical eloquence, and exalted moral fervor. Soon he was to become New England's greatest senator and slavery's most implacable foe. The city of Boston was represented by its solicitor, Peleg W. Chandler, Massachusetts' foremost expert on municipal law and founder of one of the earliest legal journals, the *Law Reporter*.[12] On the bench sat Chief Justice Shaw, whose probity, legal learning, and exceptional ability to penetrate to the basic issues of a case, combined to make him the pre-eminent state jurist of his day. For two decades—another was yet to come—he had gained imperishable fame for his profound influence on the development of American law. Historians best remember him for his decision that a labor union, organized on the basis of maintaining a closed shop, is not a criminal conspiracy; for his part in the celebrated Webster-Parkman murder case; and for his rigorous enforcement of the fugitive slave law.[13]

Sumner's argument before Shaw deserves to be included in a volume of

---

[9] *Sumner's Argument*, p. 4; *Report of a Special Committee of the Grammar School Board . . . August 29, 1849*, pp. 1–10, passim; *Liberator*, Aug. 10, Sept. 7, Dec. 7, 14, 21, 1849, Jan. 4, Feb. 8, 15, 1850.
[10] *Roberts v. City of Boston*, 59 Mass. 198, 200–201.
[11] *St.* 1845, ch. 214.
[12] Chandler's argument in the *Roberts* case is not reported by Cushing, the court reporter. But see the *Liberator*, Aug. 28, 1846, for the full text of his opinion given as city solicitor three years earlier to the school committee. Much of what Chandler said on the constitutionality of segregated education was adopted by the court.
[13] *Commonwealth v. Hunt*, 45 Mass. 111 (1842); *Commonwealth v. Webster*, 59 Mass. 295 (1850); *Thomas Sims's Case*, 61 Mass. 285 (1851). For an appreciative biography, see Frederic H. Chase, *Lemuel Shaw* (Boston, 1918).

The Roberts Case

great documents on American democracy, for its nobility of sentiment, literary excellence, and grasp of principles which have been validated by modern sociology. "Which way soever we turn," he told the court, "we are brought back to one single proposition—*the equality of men before the law.*"[14] Quoting the paragraphs of the Massachusetts constitution[15] which courts of a later day were to construe as meaning the same as the "equal protection" clause of the Fourteenth Amendment,[16] Sumner observed that every form of inequality and discrimination in civil and political institutions was thereby condemned. "These are not vain words," he remarked. Within their sphere of influence, no person could be created or born with privileges not enjoyed equally by all, nor could any institution be established which recognized distinction of birth.

Sumner's second point was that the state legislature, in harmony with the constitution, had made no discrimination whatever in providing for an educational system.[17] Proceeding from constitution and legislation to judicial decisions, he showed that the Supreme Judicial Court had never countenanced any discrimination in the administration of the public schools. On the contrary, the court had declared: "The schools required by the statute are to be maintained for the benefit of the whole town, as it is the wise policy of the law to give all the inhabitants equal privileges for the education of their children in the public schools. Nor is it in the power of the majority to deprive the minority of this privilege."[18]

Sumner further alleged the unconstitutionality of the segregated school on ground of its "caste" nature, and he proved that the school committee had admittedly acted out of racial discrimination. The power of the committee was merely to superintend the public schools and to determine "the number and qualifications of the scholars."[19] A power to segregate could not be implied, argued Sumner, for the committee "cannot brand a whole race with the stigma of inferiority and degradation." To imply the existence of that power "would place the Committee above the Constitution. It would

---

[14] *Sumner's Argument*, p. 31.
[15] Declaration of Rights, Art. I: "All men are born free and equal, and have certain natural, essential and unalienable rights, among which may be reckoned the right of enjoying and defending their lives and liberties . . ." Art. VI: "No man, nor corporation, or association of men, have any other title to obtain advantages, or particular and exclusive privileges, distinct from those of the community, than what arises from the consideration of services rendered to the public . . ."
[16] See *Lehew v. Brummell*, 103 Mo. 546, 553 (1890); *Gong Lum v. Rice*, 275 U.S. 78, 86–87 (1927).
[17] See *Rev. Sts.*, ch. 23.
[18] *Commonwealth v. Dedham*, 16 Mass. 141, 146 (1819). See also *Withington v. Eveleth*, 24 Mass. 106 (1928); *Perry v. Dover*, 29 Mass. 206, 213 (1831).
[19] *Rev. Sts.*, ch. 23, secs. 10, 15.

enable them, in the exercise of a brief and local authority, to draw a fatal circle, within which the Constitution cannot enter; nay, where the very Bill of Rights shall become a dead letter."[20] Only factors of age, sex, and moral and intellectual fitness might be considered by the committee as qualifications, not complexion. Just as the law required the regulations and by-laws of municipal corporations to be reasonable, Sumner asserted, so must the acts of the school committee be reasonable.[21] But an *a priori* assumption by the committee that an entire race possesses certain qualities which make necessary a separate classification of that race, was an unreasonable exercise of the committee's discretion, and therefore an illegal one.

Anticipating the "separate but equal" doctrine, Sumner argued that the segregated school could not be an "equivalent" because of the inconveniences and the stigma of caste which it imposed, and because a public school, by definition, was for the benefit of all classes meeting together on terms of equality. On such reasoning, he found that the school in question was not a public school, and as such, had no legal existence. It could not, then, be considered a legal equivalent. Yet if there could be an equivalent at law, "still the colored children cannot be compelled to take it." They could not be required to renounce one jot of their rights to "precise Equality."[22]

Before closing Sumner discussed certain matters "not strictly belonging to the juridical aspect of the case," yet necessary for understanding it. What he said with nineteenth century elegance has been validated by twentieth century scholarship, but not nationally acted upon. His remarks, which deserve to be remembered, were, in part, as follows:

The whites themselves are injured by the separation. . . . With the law as their monitor . . . they are taught practically to deny that grand revelation of Christianity—the Brotherhood of Mankind. Their hearts, while yet tender with childhood, are necessarily hardened by this conduct, and their subsequent lives, perhaps, bear enduring testimony to this legalized uncharitableness. Nursed in the sentiment of Caste, receiving it with the earliest food of knowledge, they are unable to eradicate it from their natures. . . . The school is the little world in which the child is trained for the larger world of life. It must, therefore, cherish and develop the virtues and the sympathies which are employed in the larger world . . . beginning there those relations of equality which our Constitution and laws promise to all. . . . Prejudice is the child of ignorance. It is sure to prevail where people do not know each other. Society and intercourse are means established by Providence for human improvement. They remove antipathies, promote mutual adaptation and conciliation, and establish relations of reciprocal regard.[23]

[20] *Sumner's Argument*, p. 21.
[21] See *Commonwealth v. Worcester*, 20 Mass. 462 (1826); *Vandine's Case*, 23 Mass. 187 (1826); *City of Boston v. Shaw*, 42 Mass. 130 (1840). In the last-named case, as Sumner pointed out, the court had voided a city by-law as unequal and unreasonable.
[22] *Sumner's Argument*, pp. 24-25.   [23] *Ibid.*, pp. 28-30, *passim*.

Chief Justice Shaw, delivering the unanimous opinion of the court, upheld to the fullest extent the power of the school committee to enforce segregation.[24] The case required for its disposition no fine analysis of difficult legal points, and Shaw confined himself, as did counsel before him, primarily to general principles—and to predilections as well. That his opinion has had an enduring influence may be attributed, in part, to the fact that these principles were announced with sweep and force, and those predilections articulated.

Pointing out that plaintiff had access to a school for colored children as well fitted and conducted in all respects as other primaries,[25] the court rejected the contention that she had been unlawfully excluded from public school instruction. The issue, rather, was one of power, "because, if they [the committee] have the legal authority," said Shaw, "the expediency of exercising it in any particular way is exclusively with them."[26] The latter half of this unqualified proposition, which invested the school committee with discretionary powers to classify pupils by race, religion, economic status, or national origin, was stated as a fixed legal fact in support of which the court risked no reasons. Similarly, other conclusions which were adopted regarding the points at issue were characterized by a singular absence of considered judgment.

For example, Shaw proceeded directly from *carte blanche* approval of the committee's discretionary powers, to an unwarranted assumption—in itself sufficient to decide the case—that all individuals did not possess the same legal rights. And whom else could he have had in mind but Negroes? What the chief justice said was so exceptional that his own words are given here in full:

> The great principle, advanced by the learned and eloquent advocate of the plaintiff, is, that by the constitution and laws of Massachusetts, all persons without distinction of age or sex, birth or color, origin or condition, are equal before the law. This, as a broad general principle, such as ought to appear in a declaration of rights, is perfectly sound; it is not only expressed in terms, but pervades and animates the whole spirit of our constitution of free government. But, when this great principle comes to be applied to the actual and various conditions of persons in society, it will not warrant the assertion, that men and women are legally clothed with the same civil and political powers, and that children and adults are

---

[24] Associated with Shaw were Justices Samuel S. Wilde, Charles A. Dewey, and Theron Metcalf. Justice Richard Fletcher, who had given an opinion at the bar on the unconstitutionality of segregated schools, unexplainedly did not sit in the *Roberts* case. *Ibid.*, p. 24.

[25] The fact that the segregated schools provided equal facilities was not challenged by plaintiff. Expensive but timely improvements were completed in September of 1849. The case was argued less than three months later. *Report of a Special Committee of the Grammar School Board . . . August 29, 1849*, pp. 13, 70.

[26] 59 Mass. 198, 206.

legally to have the same functions and be subject to the same treatment; but only that the rights of all, as they are settled and regulated by law, are equally entitled to the paternal consideration and protection of the law, for their maintenance and security. What these rights are, to which individuals, in the infinite variety of circumstances by which they are surrounded in society, are entitled, must depend on laws adapted to their respective relations and conditions.[27]

Stripped of its rhetoric, this paragraph set forth two contradictory propositions which were more succinctly expressed by that favored class, the pigs of George Orwell's satirical novel, *Animal Farm:*[28]

ALL ANIMALS ARE EQUAL
BUT SOME ANIMALS ARE MORE EQUAL THAN OTHERS

Having by now virtually decided the case, by asserting unreasoned grounds for decision, the chief justice defined the question before the court—an inversion of the order of logic. He stated the question in such a way as to make possible by his answer the "separate but equal" doctrine:

Conceding, therefore, in the fullest manner, that colored persons, the descendants of Africans, are entitled by law, in this commonwealth, to equal rights, constitutional and political, civil and social, the question then arises, whether the regulation in question, which provides separate schools for colored children, is a violation of any of these rights.[29]

By way of answer, Shaw established in detail the undisputed facts that legal rights depend upon provisions of law; that the state constitution declared broad principles intended to direct the activities of the legislature; that the legislature, in turn, had defined only the general outlines and objects of an educational system; and that the school committee had been vested with a plenary power to make all reasonable rules for the classification of pupils.[30] Shaw was impressed with the fact that the committee, after long deliberation, believed that the good of both races was best promoted by the separate education of their children. The court, he said, perceived no ground to doubt that the committee formed its belief "on just grounds of reason and experience, and in the results of a discriminating and honest judgment."[31]

In introducing into the jurisprudence of Massachusetts the power of a governmental body to arrange the legal rights of citizens on the basis of race, the chief justice was bound to show for the court not only that the discrimination, in the face of an equality of rights clause, was not forbidden; he should have shown that such discrimination was reasonable. Instead, he contented

[27] Ibid. [28] (New York, 1946), p. 112. [29] 59 Mass. 198, 206.
[30] Ibid., 206–209. [31] Ibid., 209–10.

himself with the thought that the prejudice which existed "is not created by law, and probably cannot be changed by law." He added, moreover, that it would likely be fostered "by compelling colored and white children to associate together in the same schools."[32] This was the court's answer to Sumner's contention that the maintenance of separate schools tended to perpetuate and deepen prejudice. It did not occur to Shaw to appraise the experience of the remainder of Massachusetts, where children, without regard to race, attended the same schools, with the most successful results.[33] Thus the doctrine of "separate but equal" as a constitutional justification of racial segregation in public schools first entered American jurisprudence.

By 1855 the unceasing efforts of the abolitionists and Negroes proved to be of greater weight in Massachusetts than the opinion of its distinguished chief justice. A new statute was enacted which rooted out the last legal refuge of discrimination.[34] Nevertheless, courts throughout the nation continued to play the Shaw record of "separate but equal" long after it had worn out its validity as law in the state of its origin.

In constitutional history, however, Shaw's opinion has had a continuing vitality. It was initially cited with approval by the high court of the Territory of Nevada in 1872.[35] Two years later the California Supreme Court endorsed the doctrine by quoting most of Shaw's opinion, and concluded: "We concur in these views and they are decisive. . . ."[36] The courts of New York, Arkansas, Missouri, Louisiana, West Virginia, Kansas, Oklahoma, South Carolina, and Oregon have also relied upon the *Roberts* case as a precedent for upholding segregated education.[37] It has been mentioned by lower federal courts twice in recent years, as well as on earlier occasions.[38] In the United States Supreme Court, the *Roberts* case was first discussed by Justice Clifford in *Hall v. De Cuir* as an authority for the rule that "equality

---

[32] *Ibid.*, 209.   [33] See above, note 2.
[34] *St.* 1855, ch. 256, sec. 1: "In determining the qualifications of scholars to be admitted into any public school or any district school in the Commonwealth, no distinction shall be made on account of the race, color or religious opinions, of the applicant or scholar."
[35] *State ex rel. Stoutmeyer v. Duffy*, 7 Nev. 342, 386; 395–96 (1872).
[36] *Ward v. Flood*, 48 Cal. 36, 41, 52–56 (1874).
[37] *People ex rel. King v. Gallagher*, 93 N. Y. 438, 441, 448, 453 (1883); *Maddox v. Neal*, 45 Ark. 121, 125 (1885); *Lehew v. Brummell*, 103 Mo. 546, 547, 553 (1890); *Ex parte Plessy*, 45 La. Ann. 80, 85, 87–88 (1893); *Martin v. Board of Education*, 42 W. Va. 514, 516 (1896); *Reynolds v. Board of Education of the City of Topeka*, 66 Kan. 672, 684–86 (1903); *Board of Education of the City of Kingfisher v. Board of County Commissioners*, 14 Okla. 322, 332 (1904); *Tucker v. Blease*, 97 S. Car. 303, 330 (1913); *Crawford v. School District No. 7*, 68 Ore. 388, 396 (1913).
[38] *Claybrook v. City of Owensboro*, 16 Fed. 297, 302 (1883); *Wong Him v. Callahan*, 119 Fed. 381, 382 (1902); *Westminster School District of Orange County v. Mendez*, 161 Fed. 2d. 774, 779 (1947); *Corbin v. County School Board of Pulaski County, Va.*, 84 Fed. Supp. 253, 254–55 (1949).

does not mean identity."[39] In *Plessy* v. *Ferguson,* the court turned to Shaw's opinion as a leading precedent for the validity of state legislation which required segregation of the white and colored races "in places where they are liable to be brought into contact. . . ."[40] When it is considered that the *Plessy* case itself is deemed the leading authority on the constitutionality of the "separate but equal" doctrine, and is universally cited in all segregation cases, the influence of the *Roberts* case has been immeasurable. In *Gong Lum* v. *Rice,* it was referred to by a unanimous bench to support the proposition that segregation in education "has been many times decided" to be constitutional.[41] Chief Justice Taft, the spokesman in *Gong Lum,* also added that the Massachusetts court had upheld "the separation of colored and white schools under a state constitutional injunction of equal protection, the same as the Fourteenth Amendment. . . ."[42] Currently a subject of controversy in the public forums and courts, Shaw's doctrine in the *Roberts* case is still the law of the land.[43] Its uncritical acceptance by the highest courts of so many jurisdictions, in a nation whose Constitution is color-blind—or should be, warrants its re-examination.

New York, N. Y.

[39] While his concurring opinion was directed at the unconstitutionality of *La. Rev. St.* sec. 1, 1870, which barred separate accommodations for Negroes on common carriers, Clifford addressed himself to the subject of education to show that, "Questions of a kindred character have arisen in several of the States, which support these views in a course of reasoning entirely satisfactory and conclusive." *Hall v. De Cuir,* 95 U. S. 485, 503, 504, 505 (1877).

[40] 163 U. S. 537, 544–45 (1896). "Plessy v. Ferguson was upon the right of the state to require segregation of colored and white persons in public conveyances, and the act so providing was sustained . . . upon the principles expressed by Chief Justice Shaw." *Westminster School District of Orange County v. Mendez,* 161 Fed. 2d. 774, 779 (1947).

[41] 275 U. S. 78, 86 (1927). As a matter of fact, the United States Supreme Court has always assumed, but has never actually decided, the constitutionality of "separate but equal" as regards public schools. See *New York University Law Quarterly Review,* XXIII (1948), 298–303, note.

[42] 275 U. S. 78, 86–87. For the provisions of the Massachusetts "injunction of equal protection," see above, note 15.

[43] *Sweatt v. Painter,* 70 S. Ct. 848 (decided June 5, 1950). "Nor need we reach petitioner's contention that Plessy vs Ferguson should be reexamined . . ." *Ibid.,* at 851.

Black Enfranchisement in Mississippi: Federal Enforcement and Black Protest in the 1960s

By NEIL R. MCMILLEN

MISSISSIPPI, AS ONE OF ITS MORE MODERATE RECENT GOVERNORS acknowledged, has often been the "architect" of its own "doghouse."[1] Applicable, perhaps, to much of the state's history, this observation bears particular relevance to the Voting Rights Act of 1965. For that measure, so remarkably effective and so clearly needed throughout much of the South, was dire necessity itself in Mississippi. Indeed, in no other southern state, not even in unyielding Alabama, was official behavior better calculated to provoke the sweeping federal intervention permitted by this statute.

Gradually, grudgingly, each of the other southern states made modest concessions to the Fifteenth Amendment. In regional terms black voter registration rose sharply between 1940 and 1960 and even more sharply between 1960 and 1964. Within each state progress was spotty, and in each there were hard-core counties, pockets of extreme resistance where Negro registration was negligible. Yet by 1964 Tennessee had enfranchised 69 percent of its adult blacks to become the region's leader; Florida and Texas followed with 64 and 58 percent respectively. Even the traditionally recalcitrant Deep South states of Georgia (44 percent), South Carolina (39 percent), Louisiana (32 percent), and Alabama (23 percent) had registered significant, if still appallingly low, percentages of their voting-age black populations. Mississippi, however, lagged far behind even the most dilatory of its southern sisters. Elsewhere a quarter of a century of social ferment and rising black aspirations had appreciably broadened the region's attenuated electorate. But Mississippi, apparently unmoved by either the democratic ideology

[1] Paul B. Johnson, quoted in New Orleans *Times-Picayune*, March 7, 1965.

MR. MCMILLEN is associate professor of history at the University of Southern Mississippi. He wishes to acknowledge gratefully the financial assistance of the National Endowment for the Humanities and the University of Southern Mississippi.

of World War II or the moral imperatives of the cold war, or even by increasingly equalitarian federal policies, permitted fewer blacks to vote for Lyndon Baines Johnson in 1964 than had been eligible to vote for William McKinley in 1896. In a population of more than 422,000 eligible black citizens, only 28,500 (6.7 percent) were registered voters; many, perhaps most of these, voted only in general or federal elections, prudently avoiding the all-important Democratic primaries in a one-party state.[2]

In part, Mississippi's dismal registration record was a product of the Negro's traditionally low social status, his poor income, and limited education, factors which adversely affect voting behavior in any population. Devoid of all but a skeletal middle class, lacking a sense of identity with the larger community in either state or nation, plagued by the nation's highest illiteracy rate, Mississippi blacks were unlikely electoral participants. Although well schooled in Deep South racial etiquette, they had little training in civic rights and responsibilities. Indeed, as the case of Fannie Lou Hamer suggests, democracy was not even an abstraction in the lives of many of the state's rural Negroes. Recalling her own remarkable journey from Sunflower County field hand to SNCC field worker, this middle-aged Ruleville woman remarked: "I had never heard until 1962 that black people could register to vote.... I didn't know we had that right." She did not even know that there were state and federal constitutions until Student Nonviolent Coordinating Committee (SNCC) workers began their registration campaign in Sunflower County.[3]

Yet even with more favorable demographic characteristics blacks could not have registered to vote in significantly greater numbers; for Mississippi, the pioneer state in the southern disfranchisement movement, had no peer in the denial of black rights. Whether by force or fraud or by such legal sophistries as the all-white primary and stringent literacy, poll-tax, and residency requirements Mississippi for three quarters of a century provided the standard by which all southern states could measure their devotion to white supremacy. In 1965, on the eve of the enactment of the Voting Rights Act, even as in 1890 when white rule was formalized, the state's black citizens found the obstacles to suffrage insurmountable. Before casting a ballot a Negro had first to demonstrate to the satisfaction of a skeptical white registrar that he could read,

[2] Mississippi has no state registrar of voters. All registration figures in this paper are estimates, made (unless otherwise stated) by the Voter Education Project of the Southern Regional Council. *V.E.P. News,* April 1968; January–February 1970.

[3] Interview with Fannie Lou Hamer, April 14, 1972, Mississippi Oral History Program (University of Southern Mississippi, Hattiesburg, Miss.).

write, and interpret the state constitution. He was required to possess "good moral character," a "reasonable understanding" of his civic obligations, and the ability to execute, unassisted and letter-perfect, a long and complicated application form. To be qualified he could not have committed any of a list of crimes presumed peculiar to his race: bigamy, adultery, theft, perjury, child abandonment, nonsupport, or fornication. To discourage federal investigations on his behalf county officials were permitted by law to destroy voting records; to invite reprisals and challenges to his qualifications registrars were required to publish his name and address in local newspapers. When he failed to qualify, as he nearly always did, he could not be informed of the reason for his failure lest it constitute "unlawful assistance."[4]

Constitutional proscription, however, was less an obstacle to black enfranchisement than informal or extralegal sanctions. Except in a few comparatively enlightened counties, where registration tests were often administered fairly, formal suffrage requirements even in the 1960s had little bearing on voter registration. Registrars, often of questionable literacy themselves, exercised broad powers of discretion in determining literacy and other voter qualifications.[5] In some counties poll-tax payments from Negroes were simply refused. In others the levy was cheerfully collected, but the registration process itself was arbitrarily denied. Many registrars refused outright to permit blacks to make application for the ballot; but even when Negroes were permitted to complete the registration form, their circumstances were not greatly improved. Some were rebuffed when they could not recite the state constitution from memory; others were refused for their inability to identify by name every officeholder and committeeman in their counties; still others were disqualified for minor omissions and errors. But the white registrar's most common complaint was the Negro's uncertain grasp of the state constitution—a document, according to Theodore G. Bilbo, "that damn few white men and no niggers at all

[4] Convenient summaries of Mississippi's voting restrictions include *Voting in Mississippi: A Report of the United States Commission on Civil Rights, 1965* ([Washington], 1966), 2-10; Frederick M. Wirt, *Politics of Southern Equality: Law and Social Change in a Mississippi County* (Chicago, 1971), 97-98.

[5] For example, whites were frequently asked to interpret Article 3, Section 30 ("There shall be no imprisonment for debt.") and Article 12, Section 240 ("All elections by the people shall be by ballot.") of the state constitution. Negroes were more likely to be assigned Article 3, Sections 21 (habeas corpus) and 22 (double jeopardy). Irregularities in the registration of white Mississippi voters were the subject of many Department of Justice investigations, and, hence, interoffice memoranda. See for example John Doar to Burke Marshall, November 11, 1962; Marshall to J. Edgar Hoover, September 4, 1963; December 8, 1964; Frank E. Schwelb to Harold H. Greene, February 26, 1964; Marshall to Solicitor General, April 17, 1964, Civil Rights Division Files (Department of Justice, Washington, D. C.); cited hereinafter as CRD.

can explain ...."[6] Whether field hand or college professor, domestic servant or physician, a black Mississippian could rarely meet the exacting standards of the county courthouse.[7]

A more effective deterrent, however, than even the rankest official discrimination was the Negro's peculiar vulnerability. A dependent people in a land of unremitting white supremacy, blacks in some quarters of Mississippi lived under what James W. Prothro chose to call "a totalitarian local system." "... it is very difficult," this political scientist observed, "to imagine some of these counties existing in the United States."[8] Fannie Hamer, from the perspective of her own eminently practical experience, agreed. Calling the roll of the state's martyrs to suffrage, she could find no more telling commentary on the perils of democracy in "the land of the tree and the home of the grave" than the names of James Chaney, Vernon Dahmer, Medgar Evers, and the other black casualties of the voter-registration drives of the 1960s.[9]

Thus confronted by white hostility at every turn, the Negro could look only to Washington, where he found little help before 1965. For not until passage of the Voting Rights Act did the effectiveness of federal safeguards of Negro rights approach even those of the post–Civil War period. As guarantors of black suffrage the Civil Rights Acts of 1957, 1960, and 1964 proved, if anything, less availing than the ineffectual Enforcement Acts of 1870 and 1871. Unquestionably, the impotence of federal enforcement was rooted in the inadequacy of the laws themselves. But virtually all civil rights workers and many constitutional lawyers believed that the potential of federal civil rights legislation was never fully exercised.[10]

[6] Quoted in *Voting in Mississippi*, 5.
[7] See for example the following letters and interoffice memoranda: Marshall to Joe T. Patterson, May 13, 1961; Gordon A. Martin, Jr. to Doar, August 27, 1962; Doar to Marshall, November 7, 1962; Marshall to Hoover, September 4, 1963; Marshall to R. E. Griffin, November 7, 1963; Doar to Marshall, December 5, 1963; Schwelb to Greene, February 26, 1964; Marshall to Solicitor General, April 17, 1964, CRD.
[8] U. S. Commission on Civil Rights, *Hearings Held in Jackson, Miss., February 16–20, 1965* (2 vols., Washington, [1965]), I, 212; cited hereinafter as USCCR, *Hearings*. On matters of officially sanctioned or condoned coercion see CRD files generally, as well as Southern Regional Council, *Special Report: Law Enforcement in Mississippi* (Atlanta, 1964); Student Nonviolent Coordinating Committee, *A Chronology of Violence and Intimidation in Mississippi Since 1961* ([Atlanta, 1964]); and Council of Federated Organizations, *Case Studies in Intimidation* (Jackson, Miss., [1964]).
[9] Hamer interview; see also Jerry DeMuth, " 'Tired of Being Sick and Tired'," *Nation*, CXCVIII (June 1, 1964), 548–51.
[10] Ira M. Heyman, "Federal Remedies for Voteless Negroes," *California Law Review*, XLVIII (May 1960), 190–215; Donald P. Kommers, "The Right to Vote and Its Implementation," *Notre Dame Lawyer*, XXXIX (June 1964), 365–410; L. Thorne McCarty and Russel B. Stevenson, "The Voting Rights Act of 1965: An Evaluation," *Harvard Civil Rights Law Review*, III (Spring 1968), 358–63.

Enforcement during the Eisenhower Administration was especially languid. The ambivalence toward civil rights exhibited by both President Dwight David Eisenhower and Attorney General William Pierce Rogers found reflection in the diffident leadership of William Wilson White (December 1957–September 1959), the first assistant attorney general in charge of civil rights. Preferring conciliation to litigation, White ordered no Civil Rights Division (CRD) investigations of voter discrimination in the South and encouraged probes by an unenthusiastic Federal Bureau of Investigation (FBI) only upon receipt of sworn letters of complaint. Although the United States Commission on Civil Rights in its first report to the President found overwhelming evidence of a region-wide pattern of suffrage denial, the CRD during White's tenure filed only three voter-discrimination suits, none of them in Mississippi. Even during the brief but vigorous leadership of White's successor, Harold Russell Tyler, Jr., from January 1960 to January 1961 the Eisenhower Justice Department found no occasion to enforce federal voting statutes in Mississippi. Reflecting on the Republican record, one veteran black Justice Department official observed that "it could hardly have been worse had [James Oliver] Eastland himself been in charge."[11] Indeed, many observers, including some inside the Department of Justice, traced the administration's apparent reluctance to file complaints in the senator's home state to an arrangement with the powerful chairman of the Committee on the Judiciary. An explicit compact with Senator Eastland probably did not exist, but it seems likely that the Eisenhower policies, no less than those of his Democratic successors, were tempered by the recognition that Eastland's committee ruled on important legislation and appointments.[12]

The enforcement record of the Department of Justice under John Fitzgerald Kennedy seems bold and forceful only by contrast. Although many essential documents are still restricted, materials now available at the Kennedy Library suggest an administration whose caution and circumspection in civil rights matters belied its

[11] Interview with Maceo W. Hubbard, June 3, 1972. The Eisenhower enforcement policies and practices are fully documented by the early Mississippi voting files (1957–1961) of CRD. See especially the following documents related to voter registration in Forrest County: affidavits of Clyde Kennard, November 15, 1957, and January 28, 1958; Kennard to William P. Rogers, undated (received November 18, 1957); Rufus D. McLean to Kennard, November 26, 1957; Clarence Mitchell to W. Wilson White, February 7, 1958; William J. Holloran to Henry Putzel, Jr., March 9, 1960; Putzel to Harold Tyler, Jr., May 24, 1960.

[12] The possibility of an Eastland-Eisenhower arrangement as an explanation for Mississippi's apparent immunity from federal action is considered and dismissed in Allan Lichtman, "The Federal Assault Against Voting Discrimination in the Deep South, 1957–1967," *Journal of Negro History*, LIV (October 1969), 353–54.

popular reputation for passionate commitment.[13] To be sure, civil rights was initially not a high-priority item in Kennedy's New Frontier program; and not until Teamster boss Jimmy (James Riddle) Hoffa was safely behind bars in 1963 did the focus of Attorney General Robert Francis Kennedy's considerable energies shift from organized crime and labor corruption to racial injustice.[14] Yet the brothers Kennedy managed from the outset to project a mood of executive engagement in civil rights not apparent during the Eisenhower years. Initially chary of close identification with the broader struggle, they nevertheless readily embraced the franchise as an instrument of social change. Voting, President Kennedy affirmed, was the "master right" through which came all other civil rights. Indeed, the President claimed for his office clear responsibility for the protection of suffrage: "... this administration," he vowed soon after his inauguration, "will pursue ... that protection with all vigor."[15]

Regrettably, New Frontier deeds often did not match New Frontier rhetoric, and its unfulfilled promises would leave a bitter legacy of black resentment. Yet, however ineffectual its action, the Kennedy Justice Department, unlike its predecessors, took seriously its responsibility to investigate and litigate matters of voting denial. Under the able direction of Assistant Attorney General Burke Marshall from February 1961 to December 1964 Division lawyers scoured the South in search of registration bias. In July 1961 they filed the first federal voting suits in Mississippi. By election eve 1964 twenty-four additional suits were initiated, twenty-three of which alleged either discriminatory registration procedures or the intimidation of registrants, and one, *United States* v. *Mississippi* which charged that Mississippi laws were in themselves discriminatory. By August 1965, as President Lyndon Johnson signed the voting rights bill into law, federal proceedings were pending against sixty of the state's eighty-two county registrars.[16]

[13] Useful collections now available at the John F. Kennedy Library (Waltham, Mass.) include the White House Files of Harris L. Wofford, Jr., and Lee C. White; the Central Subject and Office Files of the President; the Civil Rights File of Robert F. Kennedy; and the Burke Marshall Papers. The Attorney General's File is, as yet, disappointingly thin; Box B, Mississippi File, Marshall Papers, is closed, as are portions of several important recorded interviews.

[14] Victor S. Navasky, *Kennedy Justice* (New York, 1971), 97, 99, 440–41.

[15] Harold C. Fleming, "The Federal Executive and Civil Rights: 1961–1965," *Daedalus*, XCIV (Fall 1965), 938; see also news conference, January 25, 1961, *Public Papers of the Presidents of the United States: John F. Kennedy ... 1961* (Washington, 1961), 10.

[16] *United States* v. *Mississippi*, 380 U.S. 128 (1964); see also *Voting in Mississippi*, 52–55; and Hugh S. Whitaker, "A New Day: The Effects of Negro Enfranchisement in Selected Mississippi Counties" (unpublished Ph.D. dissertation, Florida State University, 1965), 37–38.

In every case, litigation was begun only after painstaking investigation and negotiation. Under standard Civil Rights Division procedures, Marshall, or his top aide and successor John Doar, first called voting irregularities to the attention of local and state officials and then sought "specified assurances," under terms of a "freezing agreement," that Negroes would be registered thereafter on the same basis and by the same standards as whites already enrolled on registration books. Simply to end discrimination and apply equally to both races a new and higher standard than had been applied to whites already registered, the government argued, was in itself discriminatory since it would "freeze" into the voting rolls the effects of past prejudicial procedures. Invariably, those federal allegations brought letters of denial and refusal of voluntary compliance from state officials. State Attorney General Joe T. Patterson was capable even of advising Marshall that "The laws of Mississippi, as I am sure you are well aware, prohibit discrimination."[17] Thus, with no other recourse, federal negotiation gave way to litigation.

Adjudication, however, proved to be a slow and unsatisfactory remedy. The average time elapsed from first filing to final judgment in all southern voting cases was nearly thirty months. In Mississippi the first case to reach final decision required thirty-two months; the first case filed in the state required forty-seven months.[18] In most instances this leaden pace was attributable to the state's federal district courts, the most immediate interpreters and enforcers of federal law in Mississippi. Whether for reasons of personal preference or public pressure, Mississippi judges, like southern judges generally, were slow to enforce black voting rights. But Judge William Harold Cox of Mississippi's southern district proved the most dilatory by far. A former college roommate and close friend of Senator Eastland's, Cox was Kennedy's first appointment to the bench and doubtless his worst.[19] A master of obstruction and delay, he may well have been the greatest single obstacle to equal justice in the South. Not above mocking "our colored gentry" from the bench, Cox openly referred to black litigants before him as "nig-

[17] See for example an exchange of letters regarding discrimination in George County: Marshall to Patterson, September 1, 1961; Patterson to Marshall, October 6, 1961, CRD.

[18] *United States v. Duke*, 332 F.2d 759 (1964), at 761; *United States v. Lynd*, 349 F.2d 785 (1965), at 786. On lengthy litigation procedures see "Prepared Statement of Mr. Burke Marshall . . . February 18, 1965," reprinted in USCCR, *Hearings*, 257–59.

[19] Materials now open at the Kennedy Library reveal little about this appointment. But in an unrestricted passage of one interview, Burke Marshall concedes that Cox's racial views were known to the Department of Justice before his appointment, but that Kennedy "did it anyway because of the system." Marshall, fourth recorded interview, June 14, 1964, John F. Kennedy Library Oral History Project.

gers" and "chimpanzees" and filled court transcripts with some of the most remarkable obiter dicta in modern judicial history. At first reluctant even to permit routine government inspection of courthouse records, he regularly resisted federal appeals for temporary restraining orders and virtually always issued verdicts in direct conflict with even his own findings of fact. In the face of the most egregious evidence of prejudicial registration procedures he could find no pattern or practice of discrimination and invariably denied the government's pleas for freezing relief. His judicial antics brought sharp rebuke from the attorney general and reprimand from the American Bar Association, and his decisions were overturned by the Fifth Circuit Court of Appeals with a regularity and a reproach uncommon in the federal judiciary. His counterpart in the state's northern district, Judge Claude Feemster Clayton, who had himself been pointedly overturned by the Fifth Circuit, eventually won respect for his impartial rulings. But Judge Cox remained obdurate. Not until late in the 1960s were his decisions generally in line with those of other occupants of the federal bench.[20]

As a matter of policy both the Kennedy and Johnson administrations construed their prosecutorial powers narrowly. Adhering to a strict theory of federalism that valued state autonomy above federal legal supremacy, the Justice Department rarely interfered with local police prerogatives. "Under our federal system," Marshall often observed, "the primary responsibility for maintaining law and order rests with state and local authorities." Pleas for a vigorous show of federal force as a deterrent to voter intimidation invariably brought reminders that the United States maintained no national police, its marshals were mere "process servers," and its FBI an investigative, not a protective, agency.[21]

However questionable its theoretical basis, this conservative construction of federal police powers had great practical value. Short of martial law, effective enforcement of the Fifteenth Amendment would have been difficult at best in Mississippi. State officials and law-enforcement agents were in fact the principal violators of fed-

[20] See especially William Harold Cox folder, Special Correspondence, Marshall Papers. Illuminating assessments of Cox's judicial behavior include Marshall to Solicitor General, March 21, 1963, CRD; Gerald M. Stern, "Judge William Harold Cox and the Right to Vote in Clarke County, Mississippi," in Leon Friedman, ed., Southern Justice (New York, 1965), 165-86; Alexander M. Bickel, "Impeach Judge Cox," New Republic, CLIII (September 4, 1965), 13; and Charles V. Hamilton, "Southern Judges and Negro Voting Rights: The Judicial Approach to the Solution of Controversial Social Problems," Wisconsin Law Review, LXV (Winter 1965), 84-86; "Judicial Performance in the Fifth Circuit," Yale Law Journal, LXXIII (November 1963), 101-102n, 107.

[21] For an example of the CRD's standard reply to appeals for a "federal presence" see Marshall to Lynda Erinoff, November 23, 1964, CRD. The fullest statement of the "theory of federalism" is Burke Marshall, Federalism and Civil Rights (New York and London, 1964).

eral civil rights law, and local police, as Burke Marshall observed, were "widely believed to be linked to extremist anti-Negro activity."[22] Federal marshals were neither well trained nor suited to combat officially sanctioned lawlessness, and J. Edgar Hoover's FBI, never more independent of the attorney general than in matters of civil rights, was of uncertain dependability in this context. And there were vexing legal considerations as well. Criminal intent in voting cases was hard to prove, and all-white Mississippi juries were loath to convict. Thus it seemed, to Marshall and Kennedy at least, sound policy to avoid criminal sanctions whenever possible and to use federal injunctive powers sparingly. In so doing, they reasoned, the Department of Justice could focus its limited resources more constructively on broad county-by-county proceedings designed to free the way to black registration en masse. Whatever its other limitations, this cautious policy with its scrupulous attention to procedural due process minimized unseemly and embarrassing state and national confrontations.[23]

This prudence in suffrage matters found reflection in the administration's distaste for executive action in the broader struggle for black equality. Unquestionably, its emphasis on the right to vote owed much to its desire to steer civil rights activism down the ordered avenues of due process. Following the clamorous and violence-plagued Freedom Rides of 1961 Robert Kennedy urged movement activists to honor a "cooling-off" period, and Burke Marshall of the CRD and Harris L. Wofford of the White House staff joined officials of private philanthropic foundations in meetings with James Farmer, Martin Luther King, Jr., Roy Wilkins, and other representatives of the major Negro rights organizations to bargain for a shift from campaigns of direct action to voter registration. In return the foundations offered badly needed money to finance the campaigns, and the administration—or so black activists believed—offered assurances of federal protection for black voting aspirants and voter-registration workers. Although militant elements had misgivings, an informal agreement was reached, financial assistance materialized as promised, and even SNCC and the Congress of Racial Equality (CORE) were diverted from preferred tactics of nonviolent direct action to voter registration. The effort was coordinated by a Voter Education Project organized by the Southern Regional Council to administer funds from the Ta-

---

[22] Marshall to Robert Kennedy, June 5, 1964, Alphabetical File-RFK, Marshall Papers.
[23] For the Kennedy-Johnson position on the use of criminal statutes see Marshall to Thomas H. Kuchel, January 8, 1965, CRD; and Marshall, *Federalism, passim*. The political implications of federal policy are argued in Navasky, *Kennedy Justice*, 159–242.

conic and Field foundations and the Edgar Stern Family Fund.[24]

Federal protection, however, was not forthcoming. Before leading a small band of SNCC field workers into the southwestern Mississippi counties of Amite, Pike, and Walthall to launch the state's first organized registration campaign in July 1961 Robert G. Moses, a black Harlemite with a Harvard master's degree in mathematical logic, made written inquiry about federal intentions should lawlessness occur. The Justice Department's response was rapid and emphatic: the government would "vigorously enforce" federal statutes forbidding the use of intimidation, threats, and coercion against voter aspirants.[25] In fact, the statutes were not enforced. The first trickle of black applicants unleashed a torrent of unpunished white violence ranging from assault to murder. By mid-autumn, only months after it was begun, the campaign in the southwest was abandoned as local Negroes withdrew behind a wall of fear. The percentages of eligible Negroes registered to vote in Amite, Pike, and Walthall counties remained almost unchanged: 0.03, 2.2, and 0.1 respectively.[26]

In the summer of 1962 a second registration campaign was begun in the northwestern plantation counties of the Delta—primarily Bolivar, Coahoma, Holmes, Leflore, Marshall, Sunflower, and Washington. Again SNCC provided much of the enthusiasm and most of the personnel. But theoretically at least the Delta campaign was the work of the Council of Federated Organizations (COFO), an uneasy coalition of the Student Nonviolent Coordinating Committee, the Congress of Racial Equality, the Southern Christian Leadership Conference (SCLC), and the National Association for the Advancement of Colored People (NAACP). Formed in 1961 during the Freedom Rides crisis and revived in early 1962 to prevent duplication of effort, COFO was largely a paper organization through which Voter Education Project funds were channeled. Torn from the outset by intergroup rivalries, COFO failed to provide a truly united front, and its work was seldom smoothly coordi-

[24] Interview with Aaron Henry, May 1, 1972, Mississippi Oral History Program; memoranda, Marshall to Voter Registration files, July 31, September 1, 1961, Subject File, Marshall Papers; Fleming, "The Federal Executive and Civil Rights," 938; Marshall, *Federalism*, 10; Navasky, *Kennedy Justice*, 21, 118-19; Pat Watters and Reese Cleghorn, *Climbing Jacob's Ladder: The Arrival of Negroes in Southern Politics* (New York, 1967), 47.

[25] Moses to John Doar, July 11, 1961; Doar to Moses, July 17, August 14, 1961, CRD.

[26] The 1955 percentages for Amite, Pike, and Walthall counties were 0.03, 1.3, and 0.0 respectively. U. S. Commission on Civil Rights, *Civil Rights '63* (Washington, [1963]), 34. For more detailed coverage of the campaigns in the southwestern counties see Moses's testimony, U. S. House of Representatives, Committee on the Judiciary, 88 Cong., 1 Sess., *Civil Rights: Hearings Before Subcommittee No. 5* . . . [May 8-August 2, 1963] (Washington, 1963; cited hereinafter as *Civil Rights Hearings*), 1249-51; and Howard Zinn, *SNCC: The New Abolitionists* (Boston, 1964), 62-78.

nated. Each group in its own way contributed materially to the effort. But except in Coahoma County, where Aaron Henry, president of the state NAACP, conducted an active registration drive, most COFO endeavors were in fact the work of SNCC.[27]

The Delta campaign triggered another round of unpunished lawlessness. As in the southwest, frivolous arrests and police harassment, shootings from ambush, fire bombings, and unprovoked assaults were the expected, almost daily, risks of voter registration.[28] In addition, the white community employed economic coercion and intimidation—weapons of devastating effect in plantation counties where the head of virtually every black family was either a tenant or sharecropper. Always dependent on the beneficence of white landowners, these Delta Negroes were made doubly vulnerable by the encroachments of such labor-displacing developments as chemical herbicides and mechanical harvesters. Well before rural sociologists explained the phenomenon, black field hands and white planters encountered the revolutionary implications of post–World War II science and technology. Unquestionably, the attitudes of both races toward COFO's presence were conditioned by a mutual recognition that abundant labor was no longer a requirement of cotton culture. Both races clearly understood that the threat of losing even uncertain employment was the most effective restraint on black political ambitions.[29]

Whites also controlled county welfare programs, and these too were manipulated to deter black political activity. For example, in Leflore County, scene of the most concentrated COFO activity, public authorities terminated in December 1962 a program for the

[27] Henry interview; Council of Federated Organizations, *Mississippi: Structure of the Movement, Present Operations and Prospectus for the Summer*, No. 6 (Jackson, Miss., [1964]), 1. The best account of VEP-sponsored activity is Watters and Cleghorn, *Climbing Jacob's Ladder*, passim; but see also Leslie W. Dunbar and Wiley A. Branton, *First Annual Report of the Voter Education Project of the Southern Regional Council, Inc., April 1, 1962–March 31, 1963* (Atlanta, n.d.); SNCC, *Survey: Current Field Work, Spring, 1963* (Atlanta, [1963]).

[28] "Break-Through in Mississippi," *Southern Patriot*, XXI (April 1963), 1, 4; John Fischer, "A Small Band of Practical Heroes," *Harper's Magazine*, CCXXVII (October 1963), 20–25; Jack Minnis, "Courage and Terror in Mississippi," *Dissent*, X (Summer 1963), 228–31; Jackson *Mississippi Free Press*, March 9, 23, April 6, 20, May 11, 1963; Student Nonviolent Coordinating Committee, "Fact Sheet—Greenwood–Leflore County Mississippi [August 1962–March 1964]," mimeograph, CRD; NAACP press release, March 8, 1963, CRD; Howard Zinn, "The Battle-Scarred Youngsters," *Nation*, CXCVII (October 5, 1963), 193–97.

[29] The intimidating effects of economic reprisals are described in a letter from Charles R. McLaurin, a SNCC worker, to John F. Kennedy, September 21, 1962, Central Subject File of the President, Kennedy Papers. See also Harry C. Dillingham and David F. Sly, "The Mechanical Cotton-Picker, Negro Migration, and the Integration Movement," *Human Organization*, XXV (Winter 1966), 344–51; Anthony Dunbar, *The Will to Survive: A Study of a Mississippi Plantation Community Based on the Words of Its Citizens* (Atlanta, 1969), 1–10.

distribution of surplus federal commodities to all but the physically handicapped and the aged without Social Security. The action, county officials maintained, was an economy measure in no way related to voter registration. But the county's seasonally employed black poor (whose annual family income averaged only $1,185) believed otherwise. Not until the U. S. Department of Agriculture threatened direct federal assumption of commodity distribution was the program resumed in the spring of 1963. By then, however, more than 20,000 persons had been deprived of the basic food items that in other winters were the staples of their diet, and much of COFO's energies had thereby been diverted from voter registration to relief operations. With similar effect, authorities in neighboring Sunflower County withheld federal commodities from all save those endorsed by "responsible citizens."[30] When civil rights groups organized their own relief programs, whites countered—sometimes under color of law. In Coahoma County, for example, police intercepted a truck load of used clothing, basic foods, and household medicines bound for distribution in Clarksdale. COFO workers aboard were charged with "illegal possession of narcotics."[31]

In the face of this white war of attrition the Delta campaign collapsed in the spring of 1963. Soon thereafter the Voter Education Project withdrew its financial support from Mississippi. Having registered fewer than four thousand new voters in nearly two years of concentrated effort at a cost of over $50,000, project leaders concluded that without massive federal intervention further extension of the black franchise in Mississippi was unlikely. State voter registration figures bore out this judgment. Although Leflore County was the scene of the movement's most determined efforts, its black voting population increased almost imperceptibly. In June 1962, on the eve of COFO's arrival, 268 (1.97 percent) of Leflore's 13,567 adult Negroes were registered to vote. By January 1964 the county's black electorate had grown by only 13 (281 or 2.07 percent.)[32] Yet, though it left no appreciable increment of black voters,

[30] "[Staff] Report to Assistant Attorney General Burke Marshall on Surplus Food Distribution Question in Leflore County, Mississippi," 1963, CRD; Bobby Talbert, " 'The Plantation Families Have Nothing'," *Southern Patriot*, XXI (April 1963), 4; Jackson *Mississippi Free Press*, December 8, 22, 1962; March 30, 1963; Watters and Cleghorn, *Climbing Jacob's Ladder*, 132.

[31] Jackson *Mississippi Free Press*, December 12, 1962; January 5, March 9, 1963; "Operation Freedom," *Southern Patriot*, XXI (February 1963), supplement, 1-2; CORE and NAACP press releases, December 26, 1962, March 15, 1963, Southern Education Reporting Service Files, microfilm series (Fisk University Library, Nashville, Tenn.; hereinafter cited as SERS).

[32] By contrast, 7,168 (69.8 percent) of the county's 10,274 adult whites were registered by June 1962. By January 1964 white registrants totaled 7,348 (71.5 percent). See Appendixes B and C, *Voting in Mississippi*, 70-71; Leslie W. Dunbar and Wiley A. Branton, *Second Annual Report of the Voter Education Project of the Southern Regional Council, April 1, 1963-March 31, 1964* (Atlanta, n.d.), 9-10.

the Delta campaign did rouse the somnolent political consciousness of black-belt Negroes. Until COFO's arrival Leflore County blacks exhibited little overt interest in voting. In the seven years preceding the Delta campaign only 40 Negroes (but 1,664 whites) had attempted to register. But in the seven months that Leflore served as COFO's "testing ground for democracy," at least 167 blacks made formal application, while many more stood in courthouse lines waiting in vain to be given voter-registration tests.[33]

Unremarkably, many black activists emerged from these early voter-registration experiences in Mississippi with a sense of bitterness and betrayal. Encouraged by the government they put on the armor of federal law and assailed the ramparts of lily-white democracy. During the struggle the Justice Department, to be sure, had not remained neutral;[34] but neither had it provided the active support they believed it had promised. While it had supplied doughty lip service and brandished unfailingly its policy of litigation, it had done little either to prevent or punish even the most flagrant acts of violence and coercion. Indeed, so derelict did SNCC regard Attorney General Kennedy and FBI Director Hoover that in the early spring of 1963 Robert Moses and six other Mississippi SNCC workers filed suit in federal court "to compel the defendants . . . to perform [their] duties . . . ." The SNCC workers charged that "the Federal Government has only weakly asserted its existing powers . . . in our defense."[35] SNCC's critical assessment, widely accepted throughout the movement, was echoed by the federal Commission on Civil Rights, its Mississippi advisory committee, and a host of distinguished jurists.[36] Clearly, to many interested observers the lofty expressions of the Kennedy administration

[33] See text of federal complaint and related documents in *United States* v. *City of Greenwood*, CRD. During the period from June 1, 1964, to June 1, 1965, over 2,700 Leflore County blacks took the registration test; only 6 passed. Whitaker, "A New Day," 44-45.

[34] Under Title 18, Section 594, and Title 42, Section 1971 (b), of the *United States Code* the Justice Department had authority to prosecute those who used violence and intimidation against voters or would-be voters. These criminal statutes were invoked seven times in Mississippi. See *Voting in Mississippi*, 55-56; "Prepared Statement of Mr. Burke Marshall," USCCR, *Hearings*, 260-61; Kommers, "The Right to Vote," 390-91; Burke Marshall, "Federal Protection of Negro Voting Rights," *Law and Contemporary Problems*, XXVII (Summer 1962), 455-67.

[35] An eighth litigant was William Higgs, a liberal, white Jackson attorney; the complaint was dismissed by the United States District Court, District of Columbia. See *Moses* et al. v. *Kennedy and Hoover*, 219 F. Supp. 762 (1963), at 764 (first quotation); *Civil Rights Hearings*, 1247 (second quotation).

[36] See Haywood Burns, "The Federal Government and Civil Rights," in Friedman, ed., *Southern Justice*, 228-54; Pauli Murray, "Protest Against the Legal Status of the Negro," American Academy of Political and Social Science, *Annals*, CCCLVII (January 1965), 63-64; "Notre Dame Conference on Congressional Civil Rights Legislation," *Notre Dame Lawyer*, XXXVIII (June 1963), 430-46; "Theories of Federalism and Civil Rights," *Yale Law Journal*, LXXV (May 1966), 1007-52; Michael E. Tigar and Madeleine R. Levy, "Reconsidering RFK," *New York Review of Books*, XVIII (June 29, 1972), 25-27; William W. Van Alstyne, book review, *Villanova Law Review*, X (Fall 1964), 203-207.

could not obscure its failures to act decisively in Mississippi. Not a few could join SNCC chairman John Lewis in the query: "... which side is the Federal Government on?"[37]

The collapse of the Delta campaign marked the close of the first phase of the struggle for Negro suffrage in Mississippi. In the phase that followed—a phase perhaps best described metaphorically—COFO's battle-scarred veterans shifted to more favorable ground, adopted tactics better suited to their circumstances, and engaged the foe on a dramatically different plane. Abandoning for the most part bruising frontal assaults, they slashed deftly at the enemy's most vulnerable flank, public opinion. Frequently, their maneuvers more nearly resembled guerrilla theater than guerrilla warfare. Actual voter registration generally became secondary to the exposure of the hazards of voter registration. And in a very real sense the movement came to assume the characteristics of a live production. The whole of Mississippi became the stage, its public officials and law-enforcement personnel unwitting, but perfectly cast, villains, its 400,000 disfranchised adult Negroes the principal players, and the nation at large the audience to which "live" television presentations were offered each evening with the news. Without benefit of either playwright or script, the cast worked extemporaneously; and its directors, the ever-quarreling elements of COFO, offered frequently conflicting advice. Inevitably, distracting playlets in the wings competed occasionally with developments center stage. Nevertheless, the guerrilla-theater phase of voter registration in Mississippi proved to be theater of compelling realism. The audience was swayed as it had rarely been before.

This analogy does not suggest, of course, that voteless black and student volunteers were cynically manipulated. Most emphatically it does not imply, as white extremists often did, that the bombed-out black churches and burned-out black homes—even the Philadelphia murders of 1964—were "staged" by civil rights groups to "win sympathy" for their cause. What is contended here, however, is that the idealistic crusaders for black suffrage emerged from two years of utter defeat with a healthy sense of realism. If the early voter-registration experiences had demonstrated anything, COFO leaders realistically concluded, it had been that Negro suffrage could be realized in Mississippi only through sweeping federal intervention and that such intervention was unlikely without broad public support. "The struggle for freedom in Mississippi," coalition spokesmen believed, "... cannot be won without the massive aid

[37] The "scorched-earth" passages deleted from Lewis's March on Washington address of 1963 perhaps best express militant disillusionment with the administration. See Watters and Cleghorn, *Climbing Jacob's Ladder*, xiv–xv.

of the country as a whole, backed by the power and authority of the federal government," and that " ... Negro efforts to win the right to vote cannot succeed against the extensive legal weapons and police powers of local and state officials without a nationwide mobilization of support."[38] Thus, in effect, the allied Negro rights movement took the case of Mississippi's disfranchised Negroes to the American people. It subordinated, but did not altogether abandon, its localized and comparatively quiet registration drives to highly publicized statewide campaigns. By exposing the gap between American principles and Mississippi practices COFO could hope to prick the national conscience and thereby prod federal officials into enforcing federal civil rights guarantees.[39]

The first manifestation of this strategy was the "Freedom Election," an event staged to coincide with the regular gubernatorial election of 1963. Open to all adult citizens, registered or otherwise, this underground canvass offered a slate of "Freedom Candidates" led by Aaron Henry, COFO's state chairman. It was a symbolic gesture, Henry's campaign manager Robert Moses confided to a friend—one perfectly suited to COFO's purposes. "The Freedom Ballot will show," he wrote, "that if Negroes had the right to vote without fear of physical violence and other reprisals, they would do so." More particularly, one youthful campaign worker informed a northern senator, the canvass would demonstrate to "people all over the nation ... the extent to which freedom of suffrage is denied the Negroes of Mississippi."[40] The balloting succeeded on both counts. Norman M. Thomas, who joined student volunteers from Yale and Stanford in an effort to get out the vote, declared in an open letter to President Kennedy that whites employed "every conceivable device" to frustrate the effort. The campaign, Thomas observed, was shrouded by an "atmosphere of fear" without "parallel or precedent" in all his years of electioneering. Similarly, Allard Kenneth Lowenstein, a trusted Henry adviser and future congressman from New York, found conditions in Mississippi "as-

---

[38] Council of Federated Organizations, *Prospectus for the Mississippi Freedom Summer*, No. 10 (Jackson, Miss., [1964]), 1. Issued March 18, 1964, as a report to the Mississippi Advisory Committee to the United States Commission on Civil Rights, *Prospectus* represents COFO's most important published statement of policy. Most COFO documents contained similarly realistic appraisals of the situation in Mississippi. See for example, undated, unaddressed COFO form letter, [Summer 1964], SERS.

[39] Credit for the interpretation presented in the two paragraphs immediately above is due, in part, to George S. Burson, Jr., whose research and writing on the Summer Project influenced the author's views on COFO strategy. See Burson, "The 1964 Mississippi Freedom Summer Project" (unpublished M.A. thesis, University of Southern Mississippi, 1972), *passim*.

[40] Moses to Allard Lowenstein, October 18, 1963; Kenneth Klotz to Birch Bayh, October 28, 1963, CRD.

tonishing to an American citizen not experienced in the ways of this state." In a formal statement to the Department of Justice he likened electoral conditions in Mississippi to those in "the Soviet Union or Cuba under communism."[41] On election day, some 80,000 "votes" were cast for Henry, some of them by mail from areas too remote or dangerous to be reached by COFO's roving "votemobiles." Although the ballots fell short of the 200,000 predicted by Moses, the mock election was a remarkable demonstration of the possibilities of registering black political protest outside regular political channels. It served also to remind the nation, whose moral indignation throughout much of the spring and summer of 1963 was focused on Eugene "Bull" Connor's brutal confrontations with Martin Luther King's youthful demonstrators in Birmingham, Alabama, that the racial climate in Mississippi remained unchanged.[42]

The Summer Project of 1964, which featured some seven hundred student volunteers, was much the same kind of enterprise, although on a grander scale. COFO's more militant elements resented the intrusion of these advantaged white, collegiate, "summer soldiers,"[43] but the movement's leadership recognized that by engaging the children of the middle class "Freedom Summer" would be assured maximum news coverage. "Previous projects have gotten no national publicity on the crucial issue of voting rights," a COFO publication observed in March 1964, "and hence, have little national support either from public opinion or from the federal government." But an influx of northern students "making the necessary sacrifices to go South" would focus national concern on Mississippi.[44] Similarly, Moses declared soon after the volunteers

[41] Thomas to Kennedy, November 1, 1963; "Statement from Allard Lowenstein, Chairman, Advisory Committee, Henry for Governor of Mississippi," October 1963, CRD.

[42] CRD documents detailing the atmosphere of officially sanctioned repression and white violence include Nicholas Katzenbach to Thomas H. Kuchel, December 5, 1963; "Statement by Yale Junior," October 24, 1963; Henry et al. to Robert F. Kennedy, November 4, 1963; press release by Henry, October 29, 1963. Published accounts by campaign workers include that of four Yale Divinity School students, "A Week in Mississippi," *Presbyterian Life*, XVI (December 15, 1963), 26–29; Anne Moody, *Coming of Age in Mississippi* (New York, 1968), 297–98, 307–309; *Stanford Daily*, October 28, 1963; "Notes from Southern Diaries: Ivanhoe Donaldson, SNCC Field Worker," *Freedomways*, IV (Winter 1964), 139–42. See also "The Mississippi Freedom Vote," *New South*, XVIII (December 1963), 10–13; Jeannine Herron, "Mississippi: Underground Election," *Nation*, CXCVII (December 7, 1963), 387–89; Jackson *Daily News* and Greenville *Delta Democrat-Times*, October 30, 1964.

[43] Pat Watters, *Down to Now: Reflections on the Southern Civil Rights Movement* (New York and Toronto, 1971), 297–301; Pat Watters, *Encounter with the Future* (Atlanta, 1965), 31–32. On black-white tensions during the summer, see Elizabeth Sutherland, ed., *Letters from Mississippi* (New York, 1965), 2–7; and Tracy Sugarman, *Stranger at the Gates: A Summer in Mississippi* (New York, 1966), passim.

[44] COFO, *Prospectus*, 1; see also, Burson, "Freedom Summer," 86; and Watters, *Encounter with the Future*, 11–12.

arrived: "These students bring the rest of the country with them. They're from good schools and their parents are influential. The interest of the country is awakened, and when that happens, the Government responds to that interest."[45] There was also a growing conviction among civil rights activists that public opinion, so apparently indulgent of terrorism against blacks, would more likely be outraged when whites themselves were the victims of Mississippi lawlessness.[46] It is too cynical to assume, as some Justice Department officials did, that it was COFO's ulterior purpose to "get some white kids hurt and the country would be up in arms."[47] But Mississippi's seasoned black tacticians surely knew that violence was the most likely reaction to what most of the state's newspapers and virtually all of its public officials called an "invasion" by "unwashed beatniks" and "communist agitators."[48] While COFO exercised every reasonable precaution to minimize the dangers inherent in its Summer Project, it expected casualties, and it advised the volunteers accordingly.[49] Clearly, the organization hoped to use national concern for its youthful white cohorts to force a change in federal civil rights enforcement policies.

As events would prove, Freedom Summer fully justified its sponsors' expectations. Volunteers and COFO regulars working in twenty-five communities in twenty counties brought perhaps as many as 17,000 black applicants to courthouses across the state. To be sure, only about 1,600 were able to register, and most of these did so in the single county of Panola under a federal court order.[50] But the project's success was to be found in media impact not registration figures. Quite literally, its triumph may be measured in column inches of newsprint and running feet of video tape. Easily the most spectacular and sustained single event in recent civil rights history, it provided summer-long, nationwide exposure of the iniquities of white supremacy in the deepest of the Deep South states.

[45] Quoted in James Atwater, "'If We Can Crack Mississippi,'" *Saturday Evening Post*, CCXXXVII (July 25–August 1, 1964), 16. CRD files abound with wires and letters from anxious parents (and their congressmen) inquiring about the welfare of sons and daughters in Mississippi and demanding more rigorous federal enforcement of civil rights laws.

[46] This conviction was reinforced by the government's response to the Philadelphia, Mississippi, slayings. During the manhunt for the three victims, Rita Schwerner, widow of one of the slain activists, remarked: "We all know that this search with hundreds of sailors is because Andrew Goodman and my husband are white. If only Chaney was involved, nothing would've been done." Quoted in Len Holt, *The Summer that Didn't End* (New York, 1965), 30.

[47] John Doar, quoted in Navasky, *Kennedy Justice*, 125.

[48] In July 1964 a special six-member state legislative committee began "a full-scale investigation" into alleged communist influences in the Summer Project. *Meridian Star*, July 23, 31, 1964; Jackson *Daily News*, July 23, 25, 1964; *Washington Post*, August 17, 1964.

[49] Burson, "Freedom Summer," 41; Sugarman, *Stranger at the Gates*, 9–10.

[50] USCCR, *Hearings*, I, 156–57; Wirt, *Politics of Southern Equality*, 139

The Mississippi Freedom Democratic Party had a similar effect. The most remarkable development in Mississippi politics since 1948, the MFDP was formed in the early spring of 1964 in an audacious move to wrest national party recognition from the state's lily-white Democratic organization. Toward that end, it established a duplicate party structure, opened its precinct, county, and state caucuses to all voting-age citizens, and sent a nearly all-black delegation to the national Democratic convention in Atlantic City. This extraordinary challenge to political orthodoxy, was, of course, denied. Forced to choose between what the New York *Times* aptly called "political tradition and political morality,"[51] the party offered the black challengers only a pair of at-large seats and a promise to bar Jim Crow delegations from future conventions. Although this token recognition was bitterly refused, the FDP, nevertheless, scored a telling victory. Not only had it carried its case to the high council of the Democratic party, but it had told its moving story to the nation during nationally televised credentials hearings.[52]

In January 1965 the FDP found yet another national forum. When Congress convened the party challenged the electoral legitimacy of the state's five congressmen and urged the seating of three black winners of its second Freedom Election.[53] Again there was victory in defeat. This unprecedented challenge was denied, but not before the FDP presented to the House of Representatives 10,000 pages of testimony from some 600 witnesses on voter discrimination in Mississippi. During the months ahead, as Congress debated the revolutionary implications of the Voting Rights bill of 1965, this body of material proved valuable to the friends of civil rights on Capitol Hill.[54]

It is both unsatisfying and unsatisfactory to treat so complex and

---

[51] Quoted in Watters and Cleghorn, *Climbing Jacob's Ladder*, 290.

[52] Several Mississippi blacks testified, but none with such telling effect as Fannie Lou Hamer. For the substance, though not the transcript, of her testimony, see Hamer interview; De Muth, " 'Tired of Being Sick and Tired'," 548-51; and Watters and Cleghorn, *Climbing Jacob's Ladder*, Appendix 1. Other useful statements by participants include: MFDP, *Mississippi Freedom Democratic Party* (n.p., [1966]); MFDP, *A Primer for Delegates to the Democratic Convention* (n.p., [1964]); MFDP, *The Convention of the MFDP* (n.p., n.d.); and the 1965-1966 issues of the quarterly *Freedomways*.

[53] In the straw canvass of 1964 four Freedom Democratic Party candidates were "elected" to the U. S. House of Representatives and Lyndon Johnson "defeated" Barry Goldwater by a landslide of 63,000 to 17. In the regular election, however, Johnson carried only 13 percent of the Mississippi vote. See "Memo from MFDP to Summer Volunteers," undated, and COFO, "Running Summary of Incidents During the 'Freedom Vote' Campaign," November 1964, SERS; and COFO, *Freedom Candidates* (n.p., [1967]).

[54] New York *Times*, December 5, 1964, p. 19; January 5, 1965, p. 17; Columbia (S. C.) *State*, January 11, 1965; New Orleans *Times-Picayune*, January 31, 1965; Memphis *Commercial Appeal*, February 2, 1965; St. Louis *Post-Dispatch*, March 28, 1965.

momentous a phenomenon as this one merely as theater staged for national consumption. Clearly, it was much more. The mock elections, Freedom Summer, and the MFDP heralded the birth in Mississippi of a proud new black psyche, a new sense of militancy and racial solidarity. Indeed, not since the first Reconstruction had events done so much to politicize the state's black masses, to develop its indigenous black leadership, and to school the descendants of its former slaves in the rights and responsibilities of full citizenship. Yet, however welcome, these were only the concomitants of COFO strategy; in themselves, without a massive breakthrough in voter-registration procedures, they could have meant little.

The breakthrough, of course, came in the form of the Voting Rights Act of 1965, which bypassed the laborious processes of litigation and permitted federal examiners to register voters in the hard-core areas of the old Confederacy. The enactment was not COFO's victory alone. Unquestionably, Martin Luther King's bold undertaking in Selma, Alabama, in March 1965 was its immediate catalyst. But the need for this revolutionary measure was nowhere more compellingly demonstrated than by the civil rights alliance in Mississippi. Ironically, however, COFO did not survive to see its greatest triumph. Never a harmonious coalition, the organization dissolved soon after the NAACP withdrew in January 1965 to steer an independent course. Superficially, the breakup could be traced to the natural antagonism between what some local Negroes called "come-here" and "been-here" black activists. But a more fundamental cause was the recurring conflict between NAACP moderates and the militant elements of SNCC and CORE.[55]

In its implementation of the voting statute the government was as circumspect as ever. Paced by state NAACP officials, Mississippi Negroes inundated the Department of Justice with appeals for intervention in each of Mississippi's eighty-two counties. There was no need to await formal complaints, state NAACP spokesman Charles Evers wired acting Attorney General Nicholas de Belleville Katzenbach; a statewide "pattern of denial" had already been "clearly and consistently demonstrated."[56] But the Justice Department met all demands for broad federal action with a reaffirmation

---

[55] SNCC's grievances against COFO's other elements are detailed in Holt, *Summer That Didn't End*, 32–33 and *passim*. The NAACP's position is set forth in Mrs. Medgar Evers and William Peters, *For Us, the Living* (Garden City, N. Y., 1967), 251–54; Charles Evers, with Grace Halsell, *Evers* (n.p., 1971), 116–17, 140–53; and "Mississippi and the NAACP," *Crisis*, LXXIII (June-July 1966), 315–18.

[56] Evers to Katzenbach, August 10, 1965, CRD; see also Evers to Lyndon Baines Johnson, August 10, 1965; Aaron Henry to Katzenbach, September 24, 1965, CRD.

of its preference for voluntary compliance to federal constraint. The law's intent, Washington argued, was not the "deployment of an army of Federal examiners" but the insurance of "normal and fair local procedures." Initially, then, although it vowed that "noncompliance will not be tolerated," the government assigned registrars to only Leflore and Madison counties.[57] Mounting evidence of persistent discrimination soon made it apparent, however, that additional federal examiners were needed. Encouraged by the state attorney general, who unsuccessfully sought judicial relief from the new federal law, registrars in many counties with traditions of universal white suffrage denied registration to black illiterates. In others, county officials waged rearguard holding actions through frequent absences, limited and inconvenient office hours, and petty discourtesies to black applicants. Still others refused compliance altogether and permitted no Negro registration at all.[58] The registrar of Sunflower County remained so implacable that in March 1966 the Fifth Circuit Court voided a municipal election there on the ground that blacks had been systematically excluded from the voting lists. Confronted by an avalanche of local complaints and the organization of a "National Committee for Free Elections in Sunflower County," the Department of Justice at last overcame its customary reluctance to intervene in Senator Eastland's home county. By March 1967 registrars had been assigned to Sunflower and twenty-seven other Mississippi counties.[59]

The result of this growing federal presence was a much broadened electorate. Although Governor Paul Burney Johnson warned that the dispatch of federal registrars to Mississippi "could almost bring civil war,"[60] the state adjusted to the new era with remarkable ease. The very presence of federal registrars, white officials often conceded, was enough to stimulate local compliance.[61] In Coahoma, Humphreys, Neshoba, and nine other hard-core counties, for example, where no blacks had been registered in 1964, a total of 16,482 Negroes were enfranchised during the first year of the new

[57] The government's cautious procedures are described in Doar to John Conyers, Jr., September 1, 1965, CRD; and McCarty and Stevenson, "Voting Rights Act," 375–84. For an especially critical assessment see Washington Research Project, *The Shameful Blight: The Survival of Racial Discrimination in Voting in the South* (Washington, 1972), 51–60.

[58] See especially the following CRD interoffice memoranda: Terry Lenzner to Robert Owen, August 4, 1965; J. Harold Flannery to file, August 18, 1965; Robert Crossman to file, February 28, 1966; James P. Turner to Doar, March 14, 1967.

[59] Letters in CRD files to the President, congressmen, and the attorney general demanding federal intervention in Sunflower County number in the hundreds. See also McCarty and Stevenson, "Voting Rights Act," 383–84; New York *Times*, March 26, 1967, p. 14.

[60] Quoted in Washington *Post*, February 22, 1965.

[61] United States Commission on Civil Rights, *The Voting Rights Act: Ten Years After* ([Washington], 1975), 34; cited hereinafter as *Ten Years After*.

federal policy. Altogether the twenty-four "noncompliance" counties to which United States examiners had then been assigned, accounted for more than 70,000 of the nearly 140,000 Mississippi Negroes registered by September 1966.[62] Nevertheless, the Justice Department continued to minimize the importance of federal action, and the attorney general even asserted that the rapid expansion of the South's nonwhite electorate owed more to local black initiative than to examiners sent by Washington.[63] But figures released by a second Voter Education Project in July 1966 suggested otherwise. In Mississippi and Alabama, VEP concluded, results were best in counties which had both federal examiners and organized voter-registration campaigns. Counties with federal examiners but no local campaigns fared somewhat less well, although substantially better than counties with campaigns alone. Counties with neither were, of course, found to fare worst of all.[64]

Until the end of the decade black registration figures continued to rise. By 1970, according to one (perhaps overly optimistic) estimate, the percentage of the state's eligible blacks registered to vote (67.7) exceeded the regional average (66.9) for the first time in this century. Only Arkansas (79.4), Tennessee (77.1), and Texas (84.7) could claim higher percentages. The absolute increase in black registered voters in Mississippi from 1964 to 1972 was exceeded by no other southern state except Georgia.[65] At this writing, some ten years after the first federal examiners entered the state, blacks make up some 22.3 percent of all Mississippi voters. While this figure is substantially below the Negro's share of the total voting age population (31.5),[66] it reflects nevertheless a changing sociopolitical order in this Deep South state. Symptomatically, white candidates for public office now openly solicit black support, and in statewide political campaigns, and most local ones as well, the rhetoric of white supremacy is conspicuous by its absence. Like the segregated lunch counter and the "colored" drinking fountain, the lily-white voting list has disappeared.

[62] Nearly 48,000 of these were registered directly by federal registrars. As of June 30, 1974, a total of 62,273 Negroes had been so registered in thirty-four counties. Since that date there has been virtually no federal activity. Watters and Cleghorn, *Climbing Jacob's Ladder*, 246; *Ten Years After*, 33–34.
[63] Watters and Cleghorn, *Climbing Jacob's Ladder*, 266–67.
[64] Southern Regional Council, *Special Report: The Effects of Federal Examiners and Organized Registration Campaigns on Negro Voter Registration* (Atlanta, 1966), 2–3.
[65] Voter Education Project, *Voter Registration in the South, Autumn, 1970* (Atlanta, 1970); *Ten Years After*, 41, 43.
[66] The authoritative Institute of Politics, Millsaps College, Jackson, Mississippi, which since March 1971 has provided the most accurate and detailed registration and election statistics for Mississippi, estimates that by November 1975 blacks numbered 250,131 in a total electorate of 1,120,000 voters. The 1970 voting-age population figures for the state are: blacks, 429,051; whites, 934,846. *In the Public Interest*, IV (February 1976).

Yet it is well to remember that voter registration is not voter participation. A decade of consistently low black-voter turnout and the defeat of all but a token few black candidates for office suggest that barriers to full black political participation in Mississippi still survive. Overt violence and blatant official discrimination are still occasional facts of life in some counties, as are efforts to dilute black voting strength through such relatively subtle devices as the racial gerrymander, the at-large election law, and countywide reregistration.[67] Moreover, during the decade after 1965 the Justice Department, in a continuing campaign against election fraud, has found it necessary to dispatch nearly as many federal election observers to Mississippi as to all other southern states combined.[68] Clearly, evidence abounds to challenge the optimism embodied in the Voting Rights Act. The elimination of formal, legal obstacles to black voting has not significantly altered the complexion of the state legislature nor the distribution of power in most counties and municipalities. Until and unless that happens, a democratic nation can ill afford to forget the tragically checkered career of the Fifteenth Amendment. Nor should it doubt that Jim Crow, that veritable phoenix, justly deserves his reputation as the most pertinacious bird in the southern skies.

[67] *Ten Years After*, 174–82, 268–87; *Shameful Blight, passim*. Turnout in Mississippi's twenty-nine black majority counties is analyzed in Lester M. Salamon and Stephen Van Evera, "Fear, Apathy, and Discrimination: A Test of Three Explanations of Political Participation," *American Political Science Review*, LXVII (December 1973), 1288–1306. See also the comment by Sam Kernell and a rejoinder by Salamon and Van Evera in the same issue, 1307–26.

[68] *Ten Years After*, 35.

THE INDIAN BILL OF RIGHTS AND THE CONSTITUTIONAL STATUS OF TRIBAL GOVERNMENTS

INTRODUCTION

A large proportion of the approximately 280,000 American Indians living on reservations in the United States [1] are subject to the jurisdiction of their tribal governments [2] and are not subject to the jurisdiction of the state in which the reservation is located.[3] The tribal government and individual Indians are not

---

[1] COMMISSION ON THE RIGHTS, LIBERTIES, & RESPONSIBILITIES OF THE AMERICAN INDIAN, THE INDIAN: AMERICA'S UNFINISHED BUSINESS 218 (W.A. Brophy & S. Aberle eds. 1966) [hereinafter cited as BROPHY] (1960 reservation population).

[2] The following states have been given jurisdiction by federal statute over the reservations within their borders: Alaska, California, Minnesota, Nebraska, Oregon, and Wisconsin. 18 U.S.C. § 1162 (1964); 28 U.S.C. § 1360 (1964). The tribes within these states no longer exercise governmental functions independent of the state. Moreover, Congress has authorized all states to extend jurisdiction over tribes within their borders by official act. Act of Aug. 15, 1953, §§ 6-7, 67 Stat. 588, 590, as amended, 25 U.S.C.A. §§ 1321-22 (Supp. 1969) (now requiring tribal consent). Nevada, North Dakota, and South Dakota have moved toward assumption of jurisdiction, see BROPHY 185. This Note is concerned only with those tribes which continue to exercise self-government. For the geographical location of Indian reservations in the United States, see BROPHY 14-15.

[3] The classic rule is that states have no jurisdiction over Indians on the reservation in the absence of an explicit grant by Congress because federal power is exclusive. See U.S. SOLICITOR FOR THE DEPARTMENT OF INTERIOR, FEDERAL INDIAN LAW 501 (1958) [hereinafter cited as FEDERAL INDIAN LAW]. Several cases in the last 25 years have seemed to cast doubt on this proposition either by upholding states' exertions of authority over reservation Indians, e.g., Oklahoma Tax Comm'n v. United States, 319 U.S. 598 (1943) (state estate tax of reservation Indian's personalty valid); Kake Village v. Egan, 369 U.S. 60 (1962) (Alaskan regulation of Indian village's fishing practices upheld), or by voiding state actions only on finding contravening federal statutes rather than because of the exclusiveness of federal power, e.g., Kirkwood v. Arenas, 243 F.2d 863 (9th Cir. 1957) (California inheritance tax on Indian trust allotment voided because prohibited by federal statute). But a close reading reveals that these cases say nothing to support state authority except where states have been recognized as acquiring general jurisdiction over tribes. In *Oklahoma Tax Commission* the Court determined that the Oklahoma tribes were then amenable to state jurisdiction as the state had in fact been exercising general jurisdiction over the reservation due to the breakdown of tribal government. *Cf.* FEDERAL INDIAN LAW 985-99 (Oklahoma Indians' status unique). In *Kake*, Alaska had been given jurisdiction by Congress over Indians except where fishing rights were protected by federal law. The Court held that federal law regulating fishing extended only to reservation Indians and that this nonreservation tribe was completely amenable to state jurisdiction. In *Kirkwood*, California had been given general jurisdiction by a federal statute; another federal statute exempted the trust allotment from state tax. For a reaffirmation of the

completely free of outside control: they are subject to the plenary authority of Congress to legislate for them.[4] This power has been exercised only to a limited extent, leaving much of tribal government unregulated by the federal government. Thus the tribal governments exercise the most important governmental power for most reservation Indians. Although tribal governments possess less powerful criminal sanctions than states do, they traditionally have had greater power over their constituencies in at least two important respects. First, most of the wealth is communally owned or controlled, and tribal governments determine its allocation.[5] Second — and more important for purposes of this Note — a federal judicial doctrine has exempted the tribal governments from any constitutional restraints in their exercise of power over tribal members.[6]

Tribal governmental actions have sometimes exceeded constitutional limits imposed on state and federal governments. Some of these departures can be attributed to the lack of finances and education that would be necessary to meet constitutional standards.[7] For instance, criminal defendants in tribal courts have not been allowed professional attorneys as counsel because resources are unavailable to train the prosecutors and judges. Other departures from constitutional standards are rooted in the concept of a separated ethnic community which has as an important goal the retention of a culture developed in a context entirely different from that of Anglo-American constitutional history. Thus tribal membership is ethnically restricted and non-Indians have on some occasions been ejected from the reservation by tribal councils for engaging in activities believed to threaten the tribe's cultural practices. Additionally, some tribes support an established religion. The federal government's Indian policy has recognized as legitimate the preservation of tribes as self-governing, culturally autonomous units.[8] In the instances mentioned above,

---

classic rule that federal authority is exclusive, see Williams v. Lee, 358 U.S. 217 (1959); Littell v. Nakai, 344 F.2d 486 (9th Cir. 1965). *See also* note 11 *infra*.

[4] *See* pp. 1346-48 *infra*.

[5] BROPHY 34. *See generally id.* at 73-79; FEDERAL INDIAN LAW 583-840.

[6] *See, e.g.,* Talton v. Mayes, 163 U.S. 376 (1896); Native American Church v. Navajo Tribal Council, 272 F.2d 131 (10th Cir. 1959). *But see* Colliflower v. Garland, 342 F.2d 369 (9th Cir. 1965).

[7] *See* BROPHY 37; STAFF OF SUBCOMM. ON CONSTITUTIONAL RIGHTS OF SENATE COMM. ON THE JUDICIARY, 88TH CONG., 2D SESS., CONSTITUTIONAL RIGHTS OF THE AMERICAN INDIAN 20-22 (Comm. Print 1964); Note, *The Constitutional Rights of the American Tribal Indian*, 51 VA. L. REV. 121, 138 (1965).

[8] *See, e.g.,* Wheeler-Howard (Indian Reorganization) Act, 48 Stat. 984 (1934) (strengthening tribal governments); Williams v. Lee, 358 U.S. 217 (1959); 25 U.S.C.A. §§ 1321-22 (Supp. 1969) (requiring tribal consent for state assumption of jurisdiction). Historically the federal government's Indian policy has fluctuated

plus others, the imposition of traditional constitutional restraints on the exercise of tribal governing power would seriously threaten these values, perhaps in turn undermining the tribes as functioning units. If the constitutional immunity doctrine were to be overruled by the federal courts they would face the problem of the relevance of a different culture in determining constitutional standards limiting tribal governmental activity.

In 1968 Congress, exercising its plenary authority over the self-governing tribes, enacted the Indian Bill of Rights as part of the Civil Rights Act.[9] Where the courts had been unwilling to find tribal power restricted by the Constitution, Congress statutorily imposed on tribal governments a list of specific restraints consisting almost entirely of language copied verbatim from the Constitution, mainly from the Bill of Rights. This statute poses for the federal courts a problem similar to what they would face if the constitutional immunity doctrine were overruled: whether

---

radically between protection of tribal existence and assimilation. See BROPHY 17-23. The requirement of tribal consent for state assumption of jurisdiction, passed with the Indian Bill of Rights, 25 U.S.C.A. §§ 1321-22 (Supp. 1969), and actions of the committee investigating the bill, see pp. 1359-60 infra, show the present policy to be favorable to the preservation of tribal communities as self-governing, culturally autonomous entities.

[9] Act of April 11, 1968, Pub. L. No. 90-284, tit. II, 82 Stat. 77 (codified at 25 U.S.C.A. §§ 1302-03 (Supp. 1969)), the text of which is as follows:

§ 1302. Constitutional rights
No Indian tribe in exercising powers of self-government shall—
(1) make or enforce any law prohibiting the free exercise of religion, or abridging the freedom of speech, or of the press, or the right of the people peaceably to assemble and to petition for a redress of grievances;
(2) violate the right of the people to be secure in their persons, houses, papers, and effects against unreasonable search and seizures, nor issue warrants, but upon probable cause, supported by oath or affirmation, and particularly describing the place to be searched and the person or thing to be seized;
(3) subject any person for the same offense to be twice put in jeopardy;
(4) compel any person in any criminal case to be a witness against himself;
(5) take any private property for a public use without just compensation;
(6) deny to any person in a criminal proceeding the right to a speedy and public trial, to be informed of the nature and cause of the accusation, to be confronted with the witnesses against him, to have compulsory process for obtaining witnesses in his favor, and at his own expense to have the assistance of counsel for his defense;
(7) require excessive bail, impose excessive fines, inflict cruel and unusual punishments, and in no event impose for conviction of any one offense any penalty or punishment greater than imprisonment for a term of six months or a fine of $500, or both;
(8) deny to any person within its jurisdiction the equal protection of its laws or deprive any person of liberty or property without due process of law;
(9) pass any bill of attainder or ex post facto law; or
(10) deny to any person accused of an offense punishable by imprisonment the right, upon request, to a trial by jury of not less than six persons.

§ 1303. Habeas corpus
The privilege of the writ of habeas corpus shall be available to any person, in a court of the United States, to test the legality of his detention by order of an Indian tribe.

Congress' use of constitutional language is to be taken as requiring modification of tribal governmental procedures and laws to fully comply with the same constitutional standards imposed on state and federal governments, whatever the disruption to the tribe's culture and ability to function, or whether Congress' use of constitutional language mandates the court to evolve constitutional standards appropriate to the concept of Indian tribes as ethnically and culturally autonomous. The Indian Bill of Rights, however, enumerates only some of the governmental restraints that are included in the Constitution. The federal judiciary [10] must therefore also ascertain the present validity of constitutional immunity in light of Congress' action.

Section I of this Note will examine the constitutional immunity doctrine. Section II will analyze the Indian Bill of Rights with a view toward developing a theory of the statute's interpretation. Section III will then suggest a reconciliation of the statute with the Constitution if the latter should be made applicable by the overruling of the immunity doctrine. Finally, the last section will examine the question of remedies to enforce the statute.

I. THE CONSTITUTIONAL IMMUNITY DOCTRINE

The doctrine that the Constitution does not restrict the actions of tribal governments grew out of the tribes' historically anomalous position in our governmental structure. Therefore the tribes' historical position among governmental units should be analyzed before the constitutional immunity doctrine is discussed in detail.

The Supreme Court held in 1832, in *Worcester v. Georgia*,[11] that an Indian tribe was not subject to the jurisdiction of the state within which it was located.[12] The holding was based on two fac-

---

[10] Federal courts would have jurisdiction to determine tribal governments' amenability to the Constitution, see Bell v. Hood, 327 U.S. 678 (1946), based on the following statutes: 28 U.S.C. § 1331 (1964) (civil claim exceeding $10,000); 28 U.S.C. § 2241(c)(3) (1964) (habeas corpus); 42 U.S.C. § 1983 (1964) and 28 U.S.C. § 1343(3) (1964). See generally pp. 1348-53 *infra*. The question might arise whether state courts would have jurisdiction to hold the Constitution applicable to self-governing tribes. Although state courts may adjudicate a federal claim in a case over which they have jurisdiction, see Claflin v. Houseman, 93 U.S. 130, 136-38 (1876), they have no jurisdiction over tribal governmental activity because federal authority is exclusive, see Williams v. Lee, 358 U.S. 217, 220 (1959) (state court jurisdiction prohibited where it would "infring[e] on the right of reservation Indians to make their own laws and be ruled by them").

[11] 31 U.S. (6 Pet.) 536 (1832) (Marshall, C.J.).

[12] *Id.* at 561. Later state enabling acts and constitutions incorporated disclaimers of state jurisdiction. See FEDERAL INDIAN LAW 503 & n.17. *Worcester's* concept of the tribe's exclusive authority over its territory has been modified so

tors: the tribal Indians retained their character as a "distinct political communit[y]"; and state jurisdiction over this entity was preempted by Congress' exclusive authority based on its power to declare war, make treaties, and regulate commerce with the Indian tribes.[13] The Court in *Worcester* characterized the tribes as "distinct political communities" having "national character,"[14] and it emphasized the use of treaties to determine United States-tribal relations.[15] These factors might suggest that tribes were considered sovereign nations at this time. Although the tribes' status was anomalous, they would seem at least not to have been sovereign nations in the sense of being completely free of outside legal authority.[16]

Whatever the tribes' theoretical status in the 1830's, they were in fact not sovereign by the end of the 19th century, as shown by congressional legislative authority over them. Although *Worcester* had determined that Congress had the exclusive right to deal with the tribes, Congress did not test the limits of its authority until late in the century. In 1871 Congress unilaterally changed its method of dealing with the tribes from treaty to statute.[17] In 1885 it passed the Major Crimes Act,[18] making

---

that states can exercise jurisdiction over non-Indian affairs within the reservation, for instance, over the murder of one non-Indian by another, *see* United States v. McBratney, 104 U.S. 621 (1881); New York *ex rel.* Ray v. Martin, 326 U.S. 496 (1946), and taxation of personalty of a non-Indian within the reservation, *see* Thomas v. Gay, 169 U.S. 264 (1898). Also, states have been given jurisdiction over certain welfare and educational activities on the reservation. Act of Feb. 15, 1929, ch. 216, 45 Stat. 1185 (codified at 25 U.S.C. § 231 (1964)). Some states have acquired under congressional acts complete jurisdiction over the tribes within their borders. *See* note 2 *supra*.

[13] 31 U.S. (6 Pet.) at 557, 559. The Court found these powers to "comprehend all that is required for the regulation of our intercourse with the Indians." *Id.* at 559.

[14] *Id.* at 556–57.

[15] *Id.* at 559.

[16] The Supreme Court had held that, for purposes of its constitutionally-determined original jurisdiction, tribes were not foreign nations. Cherokee Nation v. Georgia, 30 U.S. (5 Pet.) 1 (1831) (Marshall, C.J.). The holding was based on treaty recognition of Congress' authority to manage Indian affairs, the assertion by the people of the United States of ultimate title to Indian lands, and the commerce clause's separate listing of foreign nations and Indian tribes. *Id.* at 17–18. The first two of these factors militate against the concept of the tribes as independent; it is questionable whether the use of treaties would in itself confer the status of a sovereign entity. *See generally* FEDERAL INDIAN LAW 149; Higgins, *International Law Consideration of the American Indian Nations by the United States*, 3 ARIZ. L. REV. 74 (1961).

[17] Act of March 3, 1871, ch. 120, § 1, 16 Stat. 566 (codified at 25 U.S.C. § 71 (1964)).

[18] Act of March 3, 1885, ch. 341, § 9, 23 Stat. 362 (codified, *as amended*, at 18 U.S.C. § 1153 (1964)).

enumerated serious offenses among reservation Indians into crimes punishable in federal courts. The constitutionality of the statute was challenged, not on the grounds of any concept of tribal sovereignty, but rather on the ground that punishing such crimes was properly a state function rather than a federal one.[19] The Supreme Court validated the statute on the grounds that the tribes were separate entities with no allegiance to states but with a special relation to the national government stemming from their dependent status and location within the national borders.[20] Therefore congressional authority to legislate for Indian tribes was not limited as was its authority to legislate for states.

The Indian tribes, then, were seen as self-governing units within the United States, free from state control and subject to federal control when exercised. There is no general legal category in which the tribes can be classified which determines a well-defined set of governmental relations and an appropriate allocation of power among state, federal, and tribal authorities. The early cases seem to warrant only the conclusion that the tribes are not to be classified as sovereign nations, states, or federal territories.[21]

The question whether the Constitution limited the exercise of tribal governmental power arose in *Talton v. Mayes.*[22] Talton, a Cherokee convicted of murder by a Cherokee court, sought a writ of habeas corpus against Mayes, high sheriff of the Cherokee nation, in a United States district court; he claimed that his indictment by a grand jury consisting of only five members offended both the fifth and fourteenth amendments of the Constitution. The Court first dealt with the fifth amendment contention. It held that the Cherokee nation had existed as a self-governing unit, with the right to punish offenses, prior to the Constitution, that federal treaties and statutes merely recognized the continuation of these rights, and that therefore the tribe in punishing offenders was not exercising powers derived from the federal government. Since the fifth amendment was applicable only to federal governmental actions, the tribal action in punishing Talton was not restricted by it. On the fourteenth amendment contention the Court, relying on *Hurtado v. California,*[23] held that the due process clause did not preclude indictment by a grand jury of five. Thus the *Talton* court did not base the separate status of the tribe on

---

[19] United States v. Kagama, 118 U.S. 375 (1886).

[20] *See id.* at 379, 383-84.

[21] *See id.* at 381-82. *But cf.* p. 1352 *infra.*

[22] 163 U.S. 376 (1896).

[23] 110 U.S. 516 (1884) (California's prosecution of defendant for murder on bill of information rather than indictment by grand jury not violation of due process).

sovereignty, but rather on the ground that its powers were not federal powers; and the question of the tribe's amenability to the fourteenth amendment was left open.

Later federal courts have followed *Talton's* reasoning on non-applicability of the Bill of Rights.[24] Additionally, the substantive development of the fourteenth amendment has had no significance for tribal governments because it has generally been held that tribes "are not states within the meaning of the Fourteenth Amendment."[25] Thus constitutional protection of free exercise of religion was held not to limit tribal governments[26] although the fourteenth amendment had already been construed to extend this limitation to the states.[27]

However, increasing contact between the federal and tribal governments and the judicial tendency to expand constitutional protection of individual rights against governmental abuses casts doubt on the twin tenets of the constitutional immunity doctrine. The non-federal-government characterization of tribal governments was rejected in 1965 for one tribal court in *Colliflower v. Garland*.[28] Mrs. Colliflower was sentenced by a Gros Ventre tribal court to five days in jail for failing to remove her cattle from land leased by another person. In the federal district court she sought a writ of habeas corpus against the county sheriff,[29] claiming denial of rights to counsel and confrontation of witnesses. The district court decided it had no jurisdiction to issue the writ. Reversing, the Ninth Circuit held that the tribal court was partly a federal agency since the Department of Interior had organized, funded, appointed judges for, and provided jail space for it and that therefore federal courts had jurisdiction to grant the writ under the federal habeas corpus statute,[30] which allows the writ for anyone in custody under the authority of the federal government or in violation of the Constitution.[31] Characterization as a

---

[24] *See, e.g.,* Native American Church v. Navajo Tribal Council, 272 F.2d 131 (10th Cir. 1959).

[25] Glover v. United States, 219 F. Supp. 19, 21 (D. Mont. 1963). *See, e.g.,* Barta v. Oglala Sioux Tribe, 259 F.2d 553, 556 (8th Cir. 1958), *cert. denied,* 358 U.S. 932 (1959); *cf.* Toledo v. Pueblo de Jemez, 119 F. Supp. 429 (D.N. Mex. 1954) (tribe not state or territory under 28 U.S.C. § 1343(3) (1964)).

[26] Native American Church v. Navajo Tribal Council, 272 F.2d 131 (10th Cir. 1959).

[27] *See, e.g.,* Cantwell v. Connecticut, 310 U.S. 296, 303–04 (1940).

[28] 342 F.2d 369 (9th Cir. 1965).

[29] The county jailed those sentenced by the tribal court under a contract with the federal government. 342 F.2d at 374.

[30] 28 U.S.C. § 2241 (1964).

[31] As a basis for jurisdiction to issue the writ, the court held only that Mrs. Colliflower was being held under authority of the federal government. 342 F.2d at 379. On remand, the district court held that Mrs. Colliflower's detention vio-

federal agency might be limited to Courts of Indian Offenses,[32] as dealt with in *Colliflower*, since only with respect to those courts is the federal government in substantial control. Other federal involvement is limited to authority to review many tribal government actions [33] and the provision of financial aid. Federal involvement in an activity challenged may alone lead to application of constitutional restrictions.[34] Yet federal involvement in Indian matters preexisted *Talton* [35] and was not even suggested as a determining factor in that case. Because of the historically unique status of the tribes, federal involvement is not conclusive on the applicability of constitutional restrictions.

Another approach to extending constitutional restrictions would be to reexamine the applicability of the fourteenth amendment in light of *Marsh v. Alabama*.[36] There the Court held the fourteenth amendment invalidated a company town's prohibition of distribution of religious literature. In finding state action on the *Marsh* facts the Court appears to have relied on the government-like nature of the town's activities and the company's infringement of the residents' constitutional interests.[37] The activity of tribal governments, considered in relation to the interests of Indian citizens, seems to be a clear case of "governmental activity" in the *Marsh* sense. However, *Marsh* alone cannot dispose of the constitutional immunity doctrine; here, as with federal involvement, labelling tribal activities "governmental" does not answer the question whether the tribes' unique status exempts this kind of governmental activity from constitutional restrictions.

---

lated the Constitution. Colliflower v. Garland, Civil No. 2414 (D. Mont., Aug. 19, 1965), *noted in* 79 HARV. L. REV. 436, 438 (1965).

[32] For different types of reservation courts, see note 64 *infra*.

[33] Although in theory the Indian Reorganization Act, 48 Stat. 984 (1934), provided for independently drawn up corporate charters and constitutions for tribal governments, in fact these documents were uniformly prepared by the Bureau of Indian Affairs. *See Hearings on Constitutional Rights of the American Indian Before the Subcomm. on Constitutional Rights of the Senate Comm. on the Judiciary*, 87th Cong., 1st Sess., pt. 1, at 165 (1962). The BIA inserted in all of these basic documents requirements that the Secretary of Interior approve such tribal actions as the enactment of ordinances and expenditure of money. *See* BROPHY 35; STAFF OF SUBCOMM. ON CONSTITUTIONAL RIGHTS OF SENATE COMM. ON THE JUDICIARY, 88TH CONG., 2D SESS., CONSTITUTIONAL RIGHTS OF THE AMERICAN INDIAN 3 (Comm. Print 1964).

[34] *See* Public Utilities Comm'n v. Pollack, 343 U.S. 451 (1952) (District of Columbia transit system). *But see* Oliver v. Udall, 306 F.2d 819 (D.C. Cir. 1962), *cert. denied*, 372 U.S. 908 (1963) (federal approval of tribal action is mere recognition of tribal self-government).

[35] *See* FEDERAL INDIAN LAW 188–99, 222–51.

[36] 326 U.S. 501 (1946).

[37] In *Marsh* the state enforced the company town's rules, but the Court's emphasis on the interests of the residents and the activities of the town would seem to make the lack of state enforcement in the tribe not a crucial distinction.

Ultimately, then, the question of constitutional immunity requires an assessment of the present relevance of the tribes' historically unique status. It might be suggested that *Talton* places the tribes altogether beyond constitutional restraints. But as a matter of constitutional philosophy, it seems fundamental that a group of people brought permanently within the ambit of federal authority and made United States citizens [38] should not be excluded completely from the protection of the Constitution. If *Talton* stands for the contrary it should be rejected. Allowing that the tribes should stand within the constitutional system of restraints on governmental power, an appropriate theory of the tribes' constitutional status must be articulated. Although the cases following *Talton* reason mechanistically that the tribes are not restrained by the Constitution, these cases do implicitly recognize an important fact: Indian tribes — brought into our system by force and continuing geographically apart from other citizens — are culturally much more different from mainstream America than any other group within our system. As a matter of policy, Indians should be recognized as having a legitimate interest in maintaining traditional practices that conflict with constitutional concepts of personal freedom developed in a different social context. The question arises whether, given the tribes' anomalous status, this interest is constitutionally cognizable.

There are two appropriate constitutional categories that would impose restraints on the tribes and also permit the development of constitutional standards which recognize tribal culture as a proper value to be weighed against Anglo-American concepts of personal freedoms. One approach, consistent with *Talton*, would conceive the tribes as exercising the governmental powers which, under *Marsh v. Alabama*,[39] are subject to constitutional control under the due process clause of the fourteenth amendment. Due process need not mean the same for tribes as for non-Indian America. American courts, in defining due process by incorporating specific substantive rights, have reflected Anglo-American legal values. A more appropriate definition of due process for the tribes would require fairness as defined in their different culture. Standards of due process should be evolved which synthesize tribal culture and Anglo-American personal freedoms.

An alternate approach — which sees federal involvement in tribal activities as relevant in assessing the tribes' constitutional

---

[38] All tribal Indians were assured United States citizenship by the Act of June 2, 1924, ch. 233, 43 Stat. 253 (codified, *as amended*, at 8 U.S.C. § 1401(a)(2) (1964)). For the status of Indian citizenship prior to 1924, see FEDERAL INDIAN LAW 517-20. The granting of citizenship to Indians has been held not inconsistent with continued jurisdiction of tribal courts. Iron Crow v. Oglala Sioux Tribe, 231 F.2d 89, 96-98 (8th Cir. 1956).

[39] 326 U.S. 501 (1946).

status and to that extent is inconsistent with *Talton* — is to hold that tribes are within the constitutional category of unincorporated territories of the United States.[40] In the case of such entities, the activities of the federal government itself and those of the territorial government are not restricted by the full Bill of Rights, but only by basic constitutional guarantees, such as that of due process.[41] This limitation of guarantees arose as a result of the cultural differentness of the areas, the need for congressional discretion in determining what restrictions should apply to the local governments, and the authority conferred upon Congress by the Constitution to make rules for the territories.[42] Thus heavy federal involvement in tribal government would not result in the full application of the Bill of Rights to tribal governmental activity.

Under either theory the use of the requirement of due process would serve the need for flexible application of standards to tribal governments. While due process has come to have very definite meanings in the context of Anglo-American development of legal protections, application of these substantive standards, as such, to the tribal governments would infringe on what is asserted to be the tribal Indians' right to differentness. Therefore

---

[40] Although the early territories — which were populated by Americans from the existing states and which were themselves slated for statehood — were controlled by the Bill of Rights as federal entities, the acquisition by the United States of areas populated by peoples of different cultures led to the development of the category of unincorporated territory to which the full Bill of Rights did not apply and for which Congress had discretion in applying the nonfundamental rights; bulking large in the Court's mind was the prohibitive problem of applying constitutional standards to culturally different peoples. *See* Hawaii v. Mankichi, 190 U.S. 197, 217 (1903); Dorr v. United States, 195 U.S. 138, 145-48 (1904); Coudert, *The Evolution of the Doctrine of Territorial Incorporation*, 26 COLUM. L. REV. 823, 827, 832 (1926). It was for Congress to determine whether a territory was to be incorporated or not. *See* Dorr v. United States, *supra*, at 143; Balzac v. Porto Rico, 258 U.S. 298, 305 (1922). Citizenship is not inconsistent with unincorporated territory status. *See* Balzac v. Porto Rico, *supra*, at 307. Although the tribes have not been categorized as unincorporated territories for purposes of determining constitutional rights, they have been classified as territories for purposes of a federal statute granting standing to sue in federal courts. *See* Mackey v. Cox, 59 U.S. (18 How.) 100, 103 (1856). Congress has shown its intent not to "incorporate" the tribes by passing a statute which clearly omits some of the restraints of the Bill of Rights. *Cf.* Balzac v. Porto Rico, *supra*, at 306. When the tribes' cultural differentness is seen as a crucial factor with respect to their place in the constitutional system, treatment of the tribes as unincorporated territories would be consistent with the impulse that led the Court to create the category.

[41] *See, e.g.,* Balzac v. Porto Rico, 258 U.S. 298, 312-13 (1922); Fournier v. Gonzales, 269 F.2d 26 (1st Cir. 1959); Arroyo v. Puerto Rican Transp. Authority, 164 F.2d 748 (1st Cir. 1947).

[42] *See* Virgin Islands v. Rijos, 285 F. Supp. 126, 129 (D.V.I. 1968); note 40 *supra*.

the courts should resort to a more universal definition of due process, that of fundamental fairness.[43] In applying this standard under the fifth or fourteenth amendment, the courts' function would be to reject, for the tribes, the definition of due process developed for the states by incorporation of the Bill of Rights, and to evolve a set of standards of fairness in the tribal context [44] — standards that would accommodate Anglo-American ideas of due process on the one hand with tribal Indians' values on the other.

The passage of the Indian Bill of Rights changes, though it does not necessarily moot, the question of the validity of the doctrine of constitutional immunity. Before courts consider the impact of the statute on the constitutional question, the scope of the congressional enactment must be determined by statutory interpretation.

II. STATUTORY INTERPRETATION OF THE INDIAN BILL OF RIGHTS

A. An Approach to Interpretation

The 1968 Indian Bill of Rights,[45] in language copied from the Constitution, enumerates specific rights that are not to be abridged by Indian tribal governments. The bulk of the statute incorporates amendments one and four through eight of the Bill of Rights, with the following variations: establishment of religion is not prohibited; the right to counsel is guaranteed only at the defendant's own expense; and, complementing the statute's limitation of Indian courts to criminal penalties of six months and $500 for one offense, there is no right to indictment by a grand jury and the petit jury right assures a jury of six members in all cases involving the possibility of imprisonment. In addition to language from the Bill of Rights, two other constitutional word formulas are included: the requirement that the tribe not "deny to any person within its jurisdiction the equal protection of the laws" [46]

---

[43] As both the fifth and fourteenth amendments' due process requirements seem to allow the development of the same standards, it would not be crucial to determine which applied. See Figueroa Ruiz v. Delgado, 359 F.2d 718, 723 (1st Cir. 1966).

[44] See id. (implication that due process standards might be formulated in light of experience of territory); Fretz, *The Bill of Rights and American Indian Tribal Governments*, 6 NAT. RES. J. 581, 600–16 (1966) (characterizing due process as requiring fairness as defined within cultural context and developing particular standards for tribal governments).

[45] See text of statute at note 9 *supra*.

[46] U.S. CONST. amend. XIV, § 1.

and the prohibition against bills of attainder and ex post facto laws.[47]

The extensive verbatim copying of constitutional language could be interpreted as manifesting, by use of terms of art, congressional intent to apply to the tribal governments the same substantive standards that the federal courts have evolved in applying the language to state and federal governments. This view is strengthened by statements in the legislative history to the effect that tribal governments were to respect the "same constitutional rights" as state and federal governments.[48]

But these factors are not dispositive of the meaning of the statute.[49] Courts' enforcement of statutes inherently involves interpretive problems: statutes are general rules covering many situations, all of which cannot be foreseen and accounted for in the process of legislation. To find the purpose of the legislature in concrete situations, courts rely on expressions of intent in the legislative record; they also make use of the assumption of rationality and consistency in the law by interpreting statutes to mesh with existing legal policies, absent an expression by the legislature of an intention to change these policies. Usually interpretation poses no great problems for the courts. But when, in the factual context in which the statute will operate, the most obvious interpretation of its language would have results that impinge on valid interests and that controvert the past policy of the legislature, courts must determine whether the legislature really meant to nullify its past policies. Courts must first be aware of the factual context and the existing policies of the law to see the conflict.[50] Having seen that a likely interpretation will interfere with a strong preexisting legislative policy, a court should examine the legislative record specifically to determine whether the legislature intended the result. In inspecting the record for purpose, courts will have to be wary of taking general

---

[47] *Id.* art. I, §§ 9, 10.

[48] *See, e.g.,* S. REP. No. 841, 90th Cong., 1st Sess. 6, 10–11 (1967).

[49] The theory of statutory interpretation presented herein is based generally on H.M. HART & A. SACKS, THE LEGAL PROCESS: BASIC PROBLEMS IN THE MAKING AND APPLICATION OF LAW 1144–1417 (tent. ed. 1958).

[50] To realize the importance of going to the legislative record for illumination, courts must inform themselves of the broad outlines of tribal life. In other areas of the law, the court is often sufficiently familiar with possible results of different interpretations of a statute so that it realizes whether there are interpretive problems without specially having to inform itself of the factual context. In matters of Indian cultural autonomy, however, the court's frame of reference may not be adequately informed by general experience; thus a threshold inquiry into the factual situation and the statute's possible impact would be required in determining whether interpretive problems require seeking congressional purpose in the legislative record. For organizational purposes of this Note, the order of presentation is factual picture, legislative purpose, and possible interpretations.

language to be conclusive, as the gist of the problem of interpretation may be that the legislature did not realize, either in formulating the statute or in creating its record, that the effect of the language chosen might be to destroy other proper legislative objectives. Therefore the court must look for expressions of purpose that take into account the issues which make interpretation problematical.

In interpreting the Indian Bill of Rights a court should thus realize that a literal reading of some of the provisions to mean "the same standards as applied to state and federal governments" would result in seriously undermining the tribes' cultural autonomy, in some cases threatening the tribes' capacity for survival in the long run. For instance, the prohibition against racial discrimination carried over to Indian tribes might require equal access to reservation resources for cultural foreigners, substantially undercutting the tribe as an ethnic unit.[51] In construing the statute, courts should remember that Congress has strongly supported the policy of allowing Indian tribes to maintain their governmental and cultural identity.[52] Such a strong legislative policy should not be seen to be reversed by the legislature unless explicitly done. Unless the record shows a willingness to modify tribal life wherever necessary to impose ordinary constitutional standards, courts should take this legislation as a mandate to interpret statutory standards within the framework of tribal life.

The balance of this section will develop the bases of a rational interpretation of the statute in the following ways: the legislative record will be examined for the light it throws on legislative intent; the possible interpretations of illustrative sections of the Act will be considered, showing the likely impact of an interpretation that carries over judicial definitions and standards developed in the context of constitutional adjudication and indicating what an alternative standard of interpretation might look like; then a particular mode of purposive interpretation will be proposed.

B. Tribal Self-Government: The Legislative Record

Congressional attention to the problems of the rights of tribal Indians spanned seven years and resulted in a legislative record of hearings and reports [53] that provides both a factual picture of

---

[51] See pp. 1358, 1361–63 infra.
[52] See note 8 supra.
[53] Hearings in the Senate during 1961–63 resulted in *Hearings on Constitutional Rights of the American Indian Before the Subcomm. on Constitutional Rights of the Senate Comm. on the Judiciary*, 87th Cong., 1st Sess., pt. 1 (1962), 87th Cong., 1st Sess., pt. 2 (1963), 87th Cong., 2d Sess., pt. 3 (1963), and 88th Cong.,

tribal governmental activity and insight into the concerns of Congress. First a description of tribal governmental activity will be presented to show the context in which the statute will apply. The description will be based on the information presented in committee hearings, which comprises the factual understanding with reference to which legislative intent should be conceived.

An Indian reservation must be seen as an ethnic community banded together under the pressure of being surrounded by an alien society, given ownership of compact geographical areas, and allowed a great measure of self-government. Separation has been fostered by the desire to retain — and has in turn fostered the retention of — a traditional culture. Poverty due to the loss of ancient means of livelihood and the inability of the Indians to participate productively in the American economy has reinforced separation and affected tribal life.

Much of the focus of congressional attention was on procedural rights of those charged with offenses before tribal courts. The criminal justice systems of the tribes, for the most part, are crude copies of state and municipal systems in the rest of the country. The tribes have their own police forces and jails; they are often provided through federal aid.[54] The courts resemble justice of the peace courts. They exercise very limited jurisdiction, having authority over only Indians on the reservation

---

1st Sess., pt. 4 (1964) [hereinafter cited as *1961–63 Senate Hearings*]. The committee issued an investigative report, STAFF OF SUBCOMM. ON CONSTITUTIONAL RIGHTS OF SENATE COMM. ON THE JUDICIARY, 88TH CONG., 2D SESS., CONSTITUTIONAL RIGHTS OF THE AMERICAN INDIAN (Comm. Print 1964) [hereinafter cited as 1964 SENATE COMM. PRINT]. Additional committee hearings in 1965 resulted in *Hearings on Constitutional Rights of the American Indian, S. 961–68 & S.J. Res. 40, Before the Subcomm. on Constitutional Rights of the Senate Comm. on the Judiciary,* 89th Cong., 1st Sess. (1965) [hereinafter cited as *1965 Senate Hearings*]. Another investigative report followed: STAFF OF SUBCOMM. ON CONSTITUTIONAL RIGHTS OF SENATE COMM. ON THE JUDICIARY, 89TH CONG., 2D SESS., CONSTITUTIONAL RIGHTS OF THE AMERICAN INDIAN (Comm. Print 1966) [hereinafter cited as 1966 SENATE COMM. PRINT]. The committee reported the bill, as later passed, to the Senate in S. REP. No. 841, 90th Cong., 1st Sess. (1967) [hereinafter cited as 1967 S. REP.]; it passed after only perfunctory discussion, 113 CONG. REC. 35,471–77 (1967). Hearings on the bill were then held in the House, *Hearings on Rights of Members of Indian Tribes Before the Subcomm. on Indian Affairs of the House Comm. on Interior & Insular Affairs,* 90th Cong., 2d Sess. (1968) [hereinafter cited as *1968 House Hearings*]. As the House was not moving fast enough on the bill to please Senator Ervin, he amended S. 1843 onto the House Civil Rights Bill under consideration in the Senate in order to force consideration of the Indian Bill of Rights in the full House, 114 CONG. REC. S2459–62 (daily ed. March 8, 1968). The House accepted the amendment, with some discussion on the floor concerning the lack of substantive consideration in the House, 114 CONG. REC. H2757, H2819–20, H2825–26 (daily ed. April 10, 1968).

[54] See *1961–63 Senate Hearings* 138, 147, 152, 154.

and no jurisdiction over non-Indians.[55] Jail sentences usually are no longer than six months.[56] The judges seldom have any legal training, and there are no professional prosecutors. To retain equality of parties, the tribes have allowed defendants to have only non-attorney representatives as counsel,[57] and this privilege is seldom exercised.[58] Few written records are kept, due to lack of finances and education.[59] Although some tribes have accorded the right to a jury trial,[60] defendants seldom exercise this right.[61] There was some evidence in the hearings that the defendant is expected to tell the truth when questioned by the judge. If he confesses, this is the basis of conviction; if he refuses to talk, a tribal judge testified, this is seen as evidence of guilt; it was contended that if the defendant says the charge is not true he is believed and released.[62] There is no appeal outside the tribe, and although many of the tribes in theory provide for appeals to the council or to an enlarged panel of judges, the right to appeal is seldom exercised.[63] Thus the legislative record reveals a system in which defendants often confess with little pressure, aid of counsel is of a limited type and is seldom requested, juries are seldom asked for, and appeals are seldom prosecuted.

A separate tribal court does not exist in all the tribes.[64] In some of the small Pueblo tribes in New Mexico the punishment of tribal members is determined by the governor of the tribe with the assistance of the council, a legislative body which varies in size from eight to thirty members. There is no jury option and sometimes no right to any counsel. The governing body of

---

[55] *See id.* at 383, 679. The tribal courts claim no criminal jurisdiction over non-Indians; they exercise civil jurisdiction where the defendant is a member of the tribe within their jurisdiction and in all other cases between members and non-members of the tribe which are brought before them by stipulation of both parties. *See* FEDERAL INDIAN LAW 323-25, 369-71, 451.

[56] *See 1961-63 Senate Hearings* 67, 384, 872; 1966 SENATE COMM. PRINT 3.

[57] *See 1961-63 Senate Hearings* 13, 54, 73, 427, 605, 825; *1965 Senate Hearings* 138. *But see 1961-63 Senate Hearings* 606, 679.

[58] For information on the number of cases in which defendant has non-attorney counsel and in which juries are used, see *1961-63 Senate Hearings* 247-50.

[59] *Id.* at 103, 135, 151.

[60] *See 1961-63 Senate Hearings* 445, 872. *But see id.* at 436.

[61] *See* note 58 *supra.*

[62] *See 1961-63 Senate Hearings* 366; *1968 House Hearings* 127.

[63] *See 1961-63 Senate Hearings* 390, 436, 446.

[64] The types of courts on reservations are as follows: 12 Courts of Indian Offenses (established by Department of Interior); 53 "tribal" courts (organized by tribal members under Bureau of Indian Affairs guidance, along justice-of-the-peace pattern); approximately 19 traditional courts (not copied from Anglo-American model, sometimes same institution as tribal council). *See* 1964 SENATE COMM. PRINT 15; Fretz, *supra* note 44, at 583.

law sometimes is entirely customary with no written code of ordinances.[65]

The legislative hearings also developed some information about governmental institutions other than courts. All of the tribes seem to have a governor and council. The general practice is to elect the governor by a vote of the entire tribe — though in some tribes he is elected by the council — and to choose council members by an election also.[66] Some of the small, theocratic Pueblo tribes exhibit the greatest variation from this pattern, having a non-elected group of elders which selects the governor, who in turn becomes a councilman when his term is finished.[67]

The hearings elicited limited information about substantive practices of tribal governments. Some mention was made of the ethnic restrictions on tribal membership,[68] and the committee was informed of other ethnic-distinction practices. A minimum percentage of Indian blood has been made a prerequisite for inheriting rights in tribally controlled property within the reservation[69] and for voting in tribal elections.[70] The committee hearings also revealed a tribal practice of councils acting to exclude from the reservation, at will, racially-defined non-members of the tribe.[71] Reservation Indians have historically exercised this prerogative.[72] And tribal governments have used their con-

---

[65] See *1961–63 Senate Hearings* 430–31, 481–85; cf. *1968 House Hearings* 52. For instance, such a governor-council court exists in San Juan Pueblo, population 1,000. The court handles only about one case per month. *1961–63 Senate Hearings* 481–85. The maximum sentence imposed by this body is 90 days, and often it only admonishes offenders or prescribes community work or restitution. *Id.* at 484; *1968 House Hearings* 37–38, 51–52. Not all Pueblo courts exhibit such extensive unification with the council, but many are partially integrated with other governmental branches: in one, the governor is a judge, *1961–63 Senate Hearings* 142; in Zuni Pueblo, a council member is a judge, *id.* at 460; in Isleta Pueblo, appeal from the tribal court lies to the council, *id.* at 424.

[66] See *1961–63 Senate Hearings* 872; *1965 Senate Hearings* 256 (elections); *1968 House Hearings* 55 (governor appointed by council). But cf. note 67 *infra*.

[67] *1961–63 Senate Hearings* 481–83; *1968 House Hearings* 55. Not all Pueblo councils and governors are appointed: In Isleta Pueblo, for instance, the three top candidates in a tribewide election become executive officials and appoint the remainder of the council. *1961–63 Senate Hearings* 424; *1965 Senate Hearings* 263.

[68] *1965 Senate Hearings* 18.

[69] *Id.* at 65; *1961–63 Senate Hearings* 12; cf. FEDERAL INDIAN LAW 428–35.

[70] *1965 Senate Hearings* 18, 50, 221.

[71] *1961–63 Senate Hearings* 120–21, 149. For instance, in 1965 a religious — political dispute between a Catholic priest and the tribal government of Isleta Pueblo resulted in the priest's exclusion. Msgr. Stadtmueller was accused of attacking the tribal religion, refusing sacraments to those participating in traditional tribal customs, and advocating political reforms such as improved police and fire protection and changes in the governmental structure. *1965 Senate Hearings* 265; *1968 House Hearings* 94–99.

[72] See FEDERAL INDIAN LAW 438–39.

trol over communal property such as grazing lands to penalize tribal members. For instance, in one of the Pueblo tribes the governor suspended grazing rights on community land for members of the Native American Church, an Indian religion centered around the use of the drug peyote in ceremonies.[73]

An overview of the legislative record shows that the Senate committee was concerned primarily with criminal trial procedures.[74] Information concerning governmental structure and non-court practices received less attention. This predominant concern for procedural rights in criminal trials was reflected in the great care taken to assure that federal court review of procedural guarantees in tribal courts would not be nullified by lack of an extensive court record. This was attempted first through a federal court de novo trial[75] and then by authorizing federal habeas corpus review.[76]

Discussion of the Indian Bill of Rights showed no intent to use the statute as an instrument for modifying tribal cultural attitudes in order to facilitate assimilation of Indians into the non-Indian community. In fact, the committee showed a positive intent to avoid requirements injurious to the tribes' capacity to function as autonomous governmental units. It continually asked witnesses in the hearings whether the imposition of criminal procedural standards would be too heavy a burden on the tribal courts.[77] The first proposed statute would have imposed the substantive requirements of non-establishment of religion and the fifteenth amendment prohibition on racial classification in voting, and when the objection was raised that the first requirement would threaten the survival of the theocratic Pueblos while the second would be inconsistent with the cultural autonomy of all the tribes, the committee changed the bill to omit these requirements.[78] Arguably, the explicit deletion by the committee of these particular restrictions on governmental activity can be interpreted as manifesting legislative intent to force modifications of tribal ethnic and cultural autonomy where necessary for the application of those restrictions on governmental conduct which remain in the statute. This interpretation would make sense if the legislative record showed close attention to the possible conflicts between the values of racial and cultural autonomy and the language remaining in the statute, but the record does not show

---

[73] *1961–63 Senate Hearings* 98.
[74] *See* 1966 SENATE COMM. PRINT 24–26; *cf. 1965 Senate Hearings* 136, 206, 224.
[75] *See, e.g.,* 1966 SENATE COMM. PRINT 11–12.
[76] 25 U.S.C.A. § 1303 (Supp. 1969).
[77] *See, e.g., 1961–63 Senate Hearings* 99, 147, 873–75.
[78] *See 1965 Senate Hearings* 18, 21, 221; 1966 SENATE COMM. PRINT 9–11.

such attention. It is more plausible to view the modifications as manifesting a general purpose not to impose requirements that would cause serious disruption of tribal life.

Patently the Indian Bill of Rights has the effect of rejecting the *Talton* line of federal decisions refusing to give any review on the merits to controversies within the tribe. The focus of the legislative committee was upon accomplishing this result,[79] and much less attention was given to determining and evaluating standards of review. The committee's adoption of constitutional language was not the result of serious consideration of the problem of standards, but an easy way to avoid its difficulties. The record shows that Congress intended to establish new individual rights for the Indians in their relationships with their governments, but the committee's willingness to modify requirements in conflict with legitimate tribal interests indicates that the scope of these individual rights is to be determined by balancing them against the interests of the tribe in maintaining its cultural autonomy.

C. *The Statute's Impact on Tribal Government: Possible Interpretations*

This part will analyze the impact of selected sections of the statute on tribal life if the statute is interpreted to impose standards identical to those imposed on state and federal governments by the Constitution. Alternative interpretations designed to reconcile the statute's language with potentially conflicting tribal values will also be suggested and analyzed in light of the legislative record, as characterized above.

1. Equal Protection. — Statutory adoption of the language of the equal protection clause raises the problem whether the validity of a tribal legislative purpose is to be tested by Indian or non-Indian cultural standards. Two of the questions arising from this problem are the applicability of constitutional standards for state reapportionment to the various methods of selecting tribal governing authorities and the extent of the prohibition against racial classifications.

Application of constitutional reapportionment standards would not impinge greatly on tribal cultural autonomy where the tribe purports to have a council elected by the people from equal-population districts. On the other hand, there may be situations — for instance, where more than one tribe or ethnic group is covered by a council[80] — in which equal population has been

---

[79] 1964 SENATE COMM. PRINT 5-6; 1966 SENATE COMM. PRINT 3-4; 1967 S. REP. 8-10.

[80] *See* FEDERAL INDIAN LAW 454 (tribes of different ethnic backgrounds and

deliberately and significantly departed from as a standard for election districts. Since tribes are ethnically based communities, a court should avoid using a per se illegality rule in determining the fairness of council representation in such situations.

In other tribes, such as some of the Pueblos of New Mexico, the council and governor are not elected by the tribal membership but appointed by a nonelected group of elders. The reapportionment cases do not require that an executive be elected rather than appointed,[81] although if an election is used the votes of all participants must be weighed equally; [82] governing bodies with general legislative authority rather than a limited purpose must be elected, and by equal population districts.[83] But these constitutional cases have not covered any systems in which there was no popular election at all, even for the legislative body. An assumption in some of the legislative apportionment cases seems to be that the constitutional guarantee to the states of a republican form of government [84] requires an election. Since the statute contains no such requirement for the tribes, it seems that the tribe could continue its nonelective system. An equal protection problem might be seen in the difference of influence between the appointers and other tribal members. At least in the theocratic tribes, where the principle of classification between appointers and non-appointers is based on the theocratic status of the appointing group, the classification should be held non-invidious, since the legislative record recognizes theocracy as a legitimate tribal cultural value to be preserved.[85]

Tribal distinctions based on fractions of Indian parentage are rendered doubtful by the equal protection requirement, since racial classifications are generally presumed to be invidious.[86] A minimum percentage of Indian ancestry is often used to define the ethnic limit of the tribe, determining those eligible to be tribe members, vote in tribal elections, and inherit tribal property. A complete prohibition of racial distinctions in defining those eligible for various participating roles in the tribe would destroy the tribe as it has been known: it would have to accept

---

speaking different languages have been grouped together for political and administrative purposes).

[81] Fortson v. Morris, 385 U.S. 231, 233-35 (1966). The Court's willingness to allow the state governor to be appointed by the legislature may be based on the assumption that the legislature will be properly apportioned.

[82] Gray v. Sanders, 372 U.S. 368, 379-80 (1963).

[83] *Compare* Avery v. Midland County, 390 U.S. 474, 485-86 (1968), *with* Sailors v. Board of Educ., 387 U.S. 105 (1967).

[84] U.S. CONST. art IV, § 4.

[85] *See* p. 1359 *supra*.

[86] *See, e.g.*, McLaughlin v. Florida, 379 U.S. 184, 191-92 (1964).

any outsider who wanted membership. However, the legislative record suggests that racial definition of membership rights is proper.[87] Since the purpose of preserving the tribe is a legitimate one in the congressional scheme, and is objectively proper in light of tribal history, racial classifications carrying out the purpose ought to be upheld and the statute's equal protection prescription should not be read to prohibit them.

It would seem a different matter when membership restrictions and others — such as limiting enjoyment of communal resources on the basis of lineage [88] — are used to distinguish among those with a stake in the tribe. This might occur if the ancestry requirements for enjoyment of any aspects of community participation were higher than those for membership; there, individuals who had lived all their lives in the tribe and previously been recognized as full members would be treated differently from other members. Even if such lineage requirements are the same as the standard for tribal membership, ethnic distinctions may still work hardship upon individuals with a significant stake in the tribe: for instance, those offspring of unions between a tribal member and a non-member whose Indian ancestry may therefore fall below the required minimum. When a tribe has allowed a non-member on the reservation or has allowed a member to return with the "diluted" offspring, and such person has lived all or most of his life with the tribe, to allow the tribe to impose lineage distinctions is not justified by the need to preserve the tribe's ethnic base.[89] If the statute's guarantee of equal protection is intended to have any meaning outside the criminal context, it must bar such classifications. Thus, in the recognition

---

[87] *See* 1967 S. REP. 14 (analysis of equal protection section of proposed Indian Bill of Rights by committee: "Denying *to any individual Indian* within its jurisdiction equal protection of the laws or deprive [sic] *any person* or [sic] liberty or property without due process of law . . . ." [emphasis added]); *1965 Senate Hearings* 18 (Frank J. Barry, Solicitor, Department of Interior, suggesting some blood restrictions are legitimate).

[88] In the Oglala Sioux tribe, in which membership was open to all descendants of the people recognized as members at the original enrollment of the tribe, the council limited use of communal grazing areas to individuals with one quarter or more Indian ancestry despite the tribal constitution's prohibition of discrimination among tribal members. *See* Note, *The Indian: The Forgotten American*, 81 HARV. L. REV. 1818, 1827 & n.77 (1968).

[89] On the other hand, it might be valid for the tribe to maintain blood distinctions among those with a stake in the community in order to preserve the tribe's ethnic base if the individuals thus disadvantaged are adequately warned prior to their entrance into the community that their rights will be limited. Yet this might be held to be an infringement too great to be overcome by the merely rational, as opposed to compelling, relationship to the purpose of preserving ethnic identity. *Cf. Developments in the Law — Equal Protection*, 82 HARV. L. REV. 1065, 1131 (1969).

that some reliance on ethnic distinctions may be crucial to retaining the ethnic character of the tribe, a line must be drawn which will avoid total prohibition of all ethnic distinctions and yet preserve the spirit of equal protection. An approach taking into account the avowedly exclusive nature of the tribe is consistent with congressional purpose: outsiders have no recognized right to share in the community, and the tribe may apply its own cultural standards to determine who the outsiders are. But once the individual has been defined as being within the cultural group, or has been allowed to develop a substantial stake in it — especially insofar as he is ethnically related to the tribe — his official status ought not to be affected by blood distinctions.[90]

2. *Free Speech and Free Exercise of Religion.* — A major question in the free speech area is whether the statutory prescription of free speech should be read to embody the strict constitutional standards developed in such cases as *New York Times Co. v. Sullivan.*[91] It has been urged that, since Indian tribes are homogeneous communities which have traditionally suppressed open internal conflict or partisanship, full protection for free speech would undermine a cultural value.[92] Although free speech might cause some disruption in the tribe, it would seem that to protect the priority of interests thought important by Congress requires that tribal members be privileged in their political speech. Congressional respect for tribal culture must have been based on the assumption that tribal culture is accepted by the members, and that tribal practices would change if significant numbers of members were dissatisfied. Free speech is the engine by which change would be wrought by dissatisfied members, and is therefore important as an internal mechanism furthering effectuation of the views of tribal members. The disruption that might be caused to the tribe by free speech would be greatest when the dissatisfaction of members with tribal life was greatest, exactly the situation in which tribal culture should receive least protection. Additionally, protection of free speech is an apposite principle for courts to enforce because it tends to foster tribal practices consistent with members' desires and thus enables the

---

[90] Another ethnic distinction issue that outsiders might attack under the equal protection guarantee is the practice by tribal councils of levying a tax on non-member lessees of Indian property according to the acreage being used and the type of use. See *1961–63 Senate Hearings* 45. Yet where this tax has been used it is not discriminatory but simply a way of sharing the tax burden: tribal members in effect pay for governmental services through expenditure of communal resources, and taxing of non-members equalizes the burden. *Id.* at 220–21.
[91] 376 U.S. 254, 279–80 (1964).
[92] See Fretz, *supra* note 44, at 609–10.

court to give greater deference to the determinations of a tribal government when its actions are attacked as unfair.[93]

The statute's protections extend to all persons;[94] yet the question remains whether free speech guarantees should prohibit tribes from excluding non-members from the reservation because of political agitation.[95] The concept of autonomy for an internally-determined culture makes important the protection of a member's free speech; but the same concept militates against protection for the speech of the outsider. Cultural autonomy is antagonistic to political pressure from the outside. It might be argued that free speech for the outsider is necessary as an aid to the efforts of dissident tribal members, as outsiders often have greater education and legal training than members. But allowing the exclusion of an outsider for political speech would not prevent him from consulting off the reservation with dissident tribal members; this role allows aid to internal dissidence while making difficult outside creation of dissidence and is thus in greater harmony with cultural autonomy. There are no strong individual interests involved which outweigh the need to control speech by outsiders on the reservation. In the context of a consciously limited community, an outsider seems to have minimal acknowledged interests in participating in or determining the development of the tribe. Therefore the free speech protection should be interpreted, consistent with Congress' affirmation of cultural autonomy, not to protect the political speech of the outsider.

The free religious exercise prescription also raises questions for the courts. In most constitutional cases concerning religious rights, the federal courts have not had to distinguish between the requirements of non-establishment and free exercise because where they overlapped they were mutually reinforcing.[96] But Congress omitted the prohibition against establishment from the Indian Bill of Rights in response to testimony that such a bar

---

[93] It might be argued that the policies favoring strong protection of free political speech also militate for requiring even in theocratic Pueblos that the councils all be elected by tribal members rather than appointed on due process grounds, though not because of any requirement of a republican form of government. Whereas free speech protects the potentiality of dissent within the tribe and the impact of such dissent on the tribe is affected by the numbers dissenting, judicial imposition of democratic elections would unquestionably entail a significant impact on the tribe's theocratic value system without necessarily bearing any relationship to the wishes of the membership.

[94] The statutory language refers to tribal governmental action impinging on "any person." See statute at note 9 *supra*. But see note 87 *supra*.

[95] For two examples of exclusions, see note 71 *supra* and note 102 *infra*. Both of these exclusions by tribal governments involved aspects of censorship.

[96] See, e.g., Abington School Dist. v. Schempp, 374 U.S. 203, 222 (1963).

would distintegrate the theocratic tribes.[97] In cases involving these tribes, courts will therefore have to allow establishment while protecting free exercise. A specific divergence from first amendment standards will probably have to be the allowance of tribal government involvement in religious practices which result in psychological pressures on the individual to conform.[98] The practical effect of a free exercise clause in a theocratic context should be to proscribe only overtly coerced involvement in community practices or overt prohibition of divergent practices.[99] For instance, prohibiting members of the Native American Church from using communal grazing areas [100] should be an impermissible burden on free exercise.

3. Procedural Due Process. — The statute's due process requirement calls into doubt actions by tribal councils in several contexts. The statute's prohibition of bills of attainder helps focus a discussion of procedural due process problems in these situations. Constitutional litigation has defined bills of attainder as "legislative acts, no matter what their form, that apply either to named individuals or to easily ascertainable members of a group in such a way as to inflict punishment on them without a judicial trial." [101] While the force of the bill of attainder prohibition standing alone might be questioned, in conjunction with the due process requirement it raises doubts concerning certain council actions.

The first problematic situation is the exclusion of non-members from the reservation by tribal councils where there are functionally separate tribal courts.[102] On analysis these actions of

---

[97] See p. 1359 *supra*.
[98] For examples of pressures from tribal religious practices, see Fretz, *supra* note 44, at 612.
[99] For examples of restrictions that might be prohibited, see Native American Church v. Navajo Tribal Council, 272 F.2d 131 (10th Cir. 1959) (criminal ban on peyote traditionally used in religious ceremonies); Toledo v. Pueblo de Jemez, 119 F. Supp. 429 (D.N. Mex. 1954) (Pueblo officials penalizing Protestantism by denial of community rights).
[100] See *1961–63 Senate Hearings* 98.
[101] United States v. Lovett, 328 U.S. 303, 315–16 (1946).
[102] For instance, although the Navajo tribe has functionally separate tribal courts, it was a subcommittee of the tribal council that in 1968, objecting to activities of a federally-funded legal services agency, excluded its non-Indian director from the reservation. This action was challenged as contravening the statute. The federal district court issued a permanent injunction prohibiting the tribal government from excluding the director, Dodge v. Nakai, Civil No. 1209 (D. Ariz., Feb. 28, 1969), on the following grounds: first, although a tribe need not have a separate legislature and court, the statute's bill of attainder prohibition makes illegal trial by legislative act, and the subcommittee that expelled the director was legislating as the tribal code contained no general rule covering the offense; second, the statute's protection of free speech extends to non-members and also protects

legislative bodies would seem not to be prohibited by either the due process or the bill of attainder section of the statute. The councils' traditional exercise of the power of exclusion of non-members complements the tribal courts' jurisdictional limitation to tribal members,[103] and provides the only mechanism of tribal control over the behavior of non-members. In addition, where exclusion of non-members is related to the preservation of cultural autonomy, the decision to exclude is a discretionary, political decision that could be more flexibly handled by a council than a court. The seriousness of the impingement on the individual must be considered in determining whether a procedure comports with the standard of fairness required by due process.[104] The non-member should be seen to have less legitimate interest in the tribe than the member, and thus the impact of exclusion is less for him.[105] The non-member's interest is such that it seems not unfair to have his exclusion determined by the tribal council, but his interests would still seem to be sufficiently significant to warrant a minimum hearing requirement as a precondition to exclusion for political reasons. Where the person is excluded under criminal charges rather than under the tribe's discretionary power, thus working a harm to reputation, the council should be forced to extend greater procedural protections to the individual in the process of determining the truth of the charge.

A second problem arises when the council, in tribes where courts exist, imposes sanctions on *members* of the tribe: for instance, the deprivation of an individual's membership rights and his exclusion from the reservation.[106] The interests of the person so injured seem significantly greater because he is a member; and the tribal court is available as an alternative body

---

the right of members to have non-members as their spokesmen within the reservation; third, imposing exclusion because of political disfavor is barred by the due process requirement of reasonable means to achieve a legitimate end. The court adopted a flexible approach to the statute but it departed from this Note's analysis in not accepting the needs of cultural autonomy as validating the council's discretionary use of exclusion and as militating against outsiders' free speech. *See* p. 1364 *supra*.

[103] *See* note 55 *supra*.

[104] *See In re* Gault, 387 U.S. 1 (1967); Wolf v. Colorado, 338 U.S. 25 (1949).

[105] *Cf.* note 87 *supra* for support for treating non-Indians as having less claim to remain in the tribe.

[106] *See* Martinez v. Southern Ute Tribe, 249 F.2d 915 (10th Cir. 1957), *cert. denied*, 356 U.S. 960 (1958); *1968 House Hearings* 31. Deprivation of membership rights and exclusion from the reservation might also be voided under the statutory restrictions as to maximum penalties, as a member of the tribe has great financial and social stakes in the tribe; and exclusion, comparable to banishment from his country, might be seen as a cruel and unusual punishment, prohibited by the statute. *See* text of statute at note 9 *supra*.

to hear the case. Also, as cultural autonomy requires no exclusion of members, there is no need for a discretionary decision on this issue by the council in cases involving members. In terms of the interests thought important by Congress, requiring that actions penalizing members in these tribes be determined by tribal courts would significantly enhance individual rights without great disruption for the tribe.

A third situation is the imposition of sanctions on tribal members in the Pueblo tribes which function with no separate tribal courts. There the governor and council together handle all the obedience problems of the group.[107] The disruption of requiring trial by a separate institution would be great, as it would necessitate the creation of a separate tribal court, which might very well undercut the theocratic base of the tribe.[108] While theocracy must not be allowed to swallow up the protections of the statute wherever they impinge on established religion, recognition by Congress of established religion as a proper value of tribal life requires that it be considered in weighing opposing interests. The contrary interests here do not seem great, since the trial of individuals by the governor-council institution does not involve the serious problems of the historical bills of attainder in England.[109] The governor and council handle the routine cases, whereas trial by Parliament occurred only for serious political crimes attended by popular passion. Therefore Pueblo trials are not likely to be subjects of community emotion, and the governor-council institution might well be as independent of popular feeling as a judge. Also, the Indian defendant is present and speaks in his own defense rather than being absent and unrepresented as in the historical legislative "trials." Additionally, the sanctions imposed are much less severe than Parliament's, involving

[107] The question of the jury trial right arises here also, but the spirit of the requirement is met in the collegiality of the decision-making process. *See 1968 House Hearings* 52 (Representative Meeds, asserting compatibility of public trial by Pueblo governor-council with the statutory jury guarantee: "Since you have eight people, if there is a minimal requirement that six people sat, you would be well within that requirement . . .").

[108] The religious positions of the leaders may involve the conception of all authority and truth in the collective body of leaders; to require separate institutions raises questions about which is the repository of truth, especially to the extent that it leads to conflict between institutions. And a trial court with a jury of lay members of the tribe would undercut the idea of hierarchical religious authority. *Cf. 1965 Senate Hearings* 21 (statement of Frank J. Barry, Solicitor, Department of Interior: "[T]he Indian political system in many tribes is deeply rooted in their religious system and [a prohibition on establishment of religion] . . . would result in the probable destruction of tribal government in some cases"); FEDERAL INDIAN LAW 914–15.

[109] *See* United States v. Brown, 381 U.S. 437, 444 (1965) (description of historical use of bills of attainder); note 65 *supra*.

often only reprimands or community work requirements. Therefore the statute should not lead a court to void the imposition of penalties on a tribal member by the governor-council institution in the Pueblo tribes that have no separate tribal court.

D. Outline of a Purposive Interpretation

On the view of statutory interpretation developed previously, possible interpretations of the statute should be examined in relation to the factual situation in which operative language would be applied and in terms of existing policies of the law. An examination of some of the broader, more general sections of the statute leads to the conclusion that to interpret the statutory language in line with ordinary constitutional decisions would directly conflict with some cultural values central to tribal life and would therefore threaten the viability of the tribe. The legislative record manifests no intention to impair the tribe's capacity to function as an autonomous unit. To the contrary, it shows an affirmative desire to avoid imposing destructive requirements on the tribes — for instance, the Senate committee made particular changes in the statute to protect tribal theocracy and ethnic identity. The congressional committee was mainly concerned in its hearings to assure to defendants in criminal trials basic procedural rights, the impact of which it scrutinized extensively, and to assure to tribal members *some* federal court review of general governmental activities. It gave less attention to developing the standards to be applied to these activities and to determining the impact of the general statutory language on tribal life. It could be secure in the knowledge that a rational court would not read an unreasonable meaning into the statute. The statute should not, therefore, be read to require imposing judicial precedents from constitutional litigation which would significantly jeopardize essential aspects of tribal life.

An alternative to literal application of constitutional precedents is available. The statute can be construed as rejecting the *Talton* line of cases refusing review of tribal practices and as mandating courts to evolve standards that will reconcile protections of individual rights as defined by Anglo-American experience with essential tribal values. In the criminal procedure area, where tribal courts suffer from ignorance and poverty, these courts are most likely incapable of being sensitive to exacting, technical standards in the near future.[110] Although the problem of tribal courts' divergence from constitutional standards is not directly a result of opposing cultural values, it is important for

---

[110] See *1961–63 Senate Hearings* 59, 147, 213; Note, *The Constitutional Rights of the American Tribal Indian*, supra note 7, at 138.

tribal autonomy that tribal courts continue to function. As exacting standards could not be met by the tribal courts, federal courts should look for the essence of conformity with the standards rather than require technical adherence.[111] When dealing with the more general substantive provisions of the statute, the courts should be aware that Congress recognized the validity of important tribal values; it also wanted to assure greater protection of individual rights. Therefore courts must weigh individual rights and tribal values to determine operative standards for each situation. Where very important personal rights are at stake — for instance if a theocratic tribe's religion required that those speaking against governmental officials be punished — even important cultural values would have to give way. But in many situations divergence from constitutional precedents in order to protect cultural values of the tribes would not greatly impinge on individuals' interests. No general answer can therefore provide the standards to be enforced under the statute; the court must simply make judgments weighing the interests thought important by Congress. To do this, courts will have to receive evidence on the culture of the particular tribe. Full protection of free speech as an internal tribal decision mechanism will make the depth of the cultural evaluation less crucial, for the tribe can be expected to reach its own equilibrium.

III. THE STATUTE AND THE CONSTITUTION

The discussion in Section I concluded that the Indian tribes must be considered as being within the orbit of constitutional protection of rights. It was also concluded that the uniqueness of the tribes' status seemed to be best handled by means of categories that made the tribes subject to the general requirements of either the fifth or fourteenth amendments. Within these general constitutional requirements, it was suggested, the right of Indians to their different culture strongly argued for the development of new standards tailored to tribal life under the flexibility of the due process clause.

---

[111] Representative Meeds, in the House hearings, strongly expressed the opinion that the present practices of tribal courts would be sufficient to meet the statutory requirements though not technically conforming to standards required of state courts. He explicitly mentioned jury rights, see note 107 *supra*, and non-attorney representation as meeting the guarantee of counsel. *1968 House Hearings* 53, 69. He summarized his point, speaking to a representative of a Pueblo tribe: "I cannot understand any problem you have with the Indian bill of rights, because that is all it does — all those things we have just mentioned. And you are already doing them." *Id.* at 61; see *1961–63 Senate Hearings* 147 (Senate Subcommittee Chief Counsel and Staff Director suggesting flexible application of the procedural requirements).

Congress passed the Indian Bill of Rights because the constitutional immunity doctrine appeared vigorous. If the Constitution were held to apply to tribal governments, the relationship between the statute and the Constitution would have to be determined. The federal courts should conclude, under the rationale suggested above, that the operative constitutional standards are no more antagonistic to tribal culture than those which the statute is interpreted to require under the process suggested in this Note. Several factors support this conclusion that constitutional interests will adequately be protected by the statutory standards to be evolved. First, in applying the Constitution the courts should develop for the tribes standards which recognize the validity of tribal culture and therefore weigh it against Anglo-American ideas of individual rights to reach an accommodation. In evolving standards that take into account both developed ideas of individual rights and tribal values, courts might well give weight to, though not see as determinative, Congress' recognition that certain Anglo-American values are inconsistent with tribal culture and that individual rights do not always outweigh the tribal values. This should be done both because they are well-founded determinations based on reliable information and also because the federal courts have traditionally deferred to Congress to determine policies for Indians.[112] Also, the statute itself must undergo a process of interpretation to carry out the purpose of Congress, and the factors that would guide that interpretation should be the same factors considered in development of constitutional standards; therefore the statutory standards should match any constitutional standards. Together these factors make it unlikely that in applying the concept of due process a court would find that the constitutional standards applying to the tribe require more than the statute. For instance, the most obvious departure from traditional constitutional standards would be the allowance of establishment of religion. A court should not void a religious establishment as it involves an important cultural value, essential to the functioning of some tribes, and does not seem to greatly impinge on the interests of individuals. Congress made this determination in the statute, and it should be given weight by the courts.

Under this analysis of the relation between the Constitution and the statute, the determination that the Constitution does apply to the Indian tribes would not have great substantive impact on them. Perhaps a court might avoid the question of whether the Constitution applies by holding that even if it did apply it would require nothing more than the statute. Yet careful judicial

---

[112] *See, e.g.,* Williams v. Lee, 358 U.S. 217 (1959).

consideration of the minimal constitutional protections for individual Indians will only follow a clear decision that the Constitution applies to tribal governmental activity.

IV. REMEDIES AVAILABLE TO ENFORCE THE STATUTE

The Indian Bill of Rights contains the following provision: "The privilege of the writ of habeas corpus shall be available to any person, in a court of the United States, to test the legality of his detention by order of an Indian tribe." [113] No other remedy for enforcing the rights guaranteed by the statute is mentioned. The question arises whether this is the only remedy to enforce the statutory restrictions on tribal governments.

The Senate committee expressed no intention to limit remedies to habeas corpus. Rather, provision of the writ resulted from the special concern that there be means of assuring that the statute's procedural rights were effectively guaranteed to criminal defendants. The committee did not want to abolish tribal courts; a regular appeal would be ineffectual because there would not be an adequate trial record. The first proposal to deal with this problem, S. 962, guaranteed the right to appeal to the federal district courts for a de novo trial with the right to a jury.[114] This was changed into the habeas corpus guarantee, which accomplished effectively the same protection of procedural rights. Also the Senate committee, in its report listing habeas corpus amidst the other guarantees,[115] seems to have regarded habeas corpus not simply as a remedy but also as a right. For these two reasons, the provision for habeas corpus should not be taken as implying that other remedies were intended not to be available.

If no remedy other than habeas corpus were available, a large portion of the rights guaranteed by the statute — all those which might be infringed without "detention by order of an Indian tribe" — would be unprotected and therefore ineffectual. For instance, exclusion of members from the reservation or revocation of tribal membership rights, discriminatory allocation of communal resources, prevention of religious practices on the reservation and the taking of private property for public use without just compensation would be infringements of rights declared by the statute that would receive little or no protection from the habeas corpus provision. Lack of other remedies would clearly defeat congressional purpose. The federal courts, in situ-

---

[113] 25 U.S.C.A. § 1303 (Supp. 1969).
[114] 1966 SENATE COMM. PRINT 11-12.
[115] *Id.* at 10.

ations similar to this, have implied the appropriate remedies in order to effectuate the purposes of Congress.[116]

There is still a question of the jurisdiction of district courts to imply such remedies. The federal courts have no general statutory jurisdiction over Indian reservations. Yet there would necessarily be jurisdiction for the enforcement of this federal statute through implied remedies under 28 U.S.C. § 1331(a) when the jurisdictional minimum of $10,000 is met. It also seems that 28 U.S.C. § 1343(4), providing jurisdiction for "relief under any Act of Congress providing for the protection of civil rights" should allow jurisdiction in all cases involving the infringement of rights guaranteed by the statute.[117] Most of the small number of courts that have cited the subsection have done so for jurisdiction in voting rights cases [118] or have given it little attention separate from other subsections of section 1343.[119] In the latter use, courts have characterized section 1343 as giving jurisdiction only for statutes providing remedies under the fourteenth amendment, against activity under color of state law. But the language of subsection four is much broader and does not require state action except insofar as it is implicit that "civil rights" can be infringed only by state action. A tribe, engaged in governmental activity,[120] can deny civil rights. The reasons courts have limited section 1343 jurisdiction to statutes passed under the fourteenth amendment and to forms of state action might be twofold: this mechanism limits jurisdiction with no dollar minimum to situations of important individual rights; and the protection that Congress can provide for individuals' civil rights often can be based only on the fourteenth amendment, which had been thought to require state action. The Indian Bill of Rights protects the same types of important individual rights against infringement by governmental activity. It did not have to be passed under the fourteenth amendment as Congress had independent authority over the tribes because of their special

---

[116] "[I]t is the duty of the courts to be alert to provide such remedies as are necessary to make effective the congressional purpose." J.I. Case Co. v. Borak, 377 U.S. 426, 433 (1964); *see* Jones v. Alfred H. Mayer Co., 392 U.S. 409 414 n.13 (1968); Tunstall v. Brotherhood of Locomotive Firemen, 323 U.S. 210, 213 (1944). The district court in the Navajo exclusion case held it proper to imply a civil remedy under the statute. Dodge v. Nakai, Civil No. 1209 (D. Ariz., Dec. 16, 1968). It enjoined the tribe from excluding the agency director. Dodge v. Nakai, Civil No. 1209 (D. Ariz., Feb. 28, 1969); *see* note 102 *supra*.

[117] *Cf.* Cleary v. Bolger, 371 U.S. 392, 414 n.3 (1963) (Brennan, J., dissenting) (leaving open question of broad scope of § 1343(4)).

[118] *See* Baker v. Carr, 369 U.S. 186, 247 (1962) (Douglas, J., concurring).

[119] *See* CORE v. Clemmons, 323 F.2d 54 (5th Cir. 1963), *cert. denied*, 375 U.S. 992 (1964).

[120] *See* p. 1350 *supra*.

status. Since the statute provides for the protection of individual rights against governmental activity, it could have been passed under the authority of the fourteenth amendment. Additionally, the Supreme Court has upheld the use of section 1343(4) to give jurisdiction to enforce a statute that was not passed under the fourteenth amendment and does not require state action.[121] Considering the inclusive language of section 1343(4) and the statute's similarity to fourteenth amendment legislation, the implication of remedies to enforce the Indian Bill of Rights should be within the scope of jurisdiction granted by section 1343(4).[122] As section 1343(4) is inclusive as to types of remedies within their jurisdiction,[123] federal courts would be able to give the relief most appropriate to congressional purpose.

The question remains whether federal courts should imply a condition of exhaustion of tribal remedies before giving federal remedies to enforce the statute. This determination should be based on the statutory purposes. One purpose was to continue the policy of strengthening tribal courts;[124] this would support an exhaustion requirement. Yet the purpose of protecting individual rights might be defeated by such a condition in some cases, as where delay risks serious harm with little chance of a tribal remedy. Where the balancing of these purposes is not determinative of this and similar questions, courts should refer to federal judicial policies concerning relations with other decisionmaking bodies, and yet articulate these policies' import in light of the unique relations between federal courts and tribal institutions.[125]

---

[121] Jones v. Alfred H. Mayer Co., 392 U.S. 409, 412 n.1 (1968) (§1343(4) provides jurisdiction for implication of remedies to enforce statute passed under thirteenth amendment and prohibits private racial discrimination in sale of housing).

[122] Jurisdiction in the Navajo exclusion case, *supra* notes 102 and 116, was based on 28 U.S.C. §§ 1331, 1343(4) (1964). Dodge v. Nakai, Civil No. 1209 (D. Ariz., Dec. 16, 1968) (opinion and order on defendant's motion to dismiss).

[123] "To recover damages or to secure equitable or other relief. . . ." 28 U.S.C. § 1343(4) (1964).

[124] Compare *1965 Senate Hearings* 23 *and* 1966 SENATE COMM. PRINT 12, *with* Williams v. Lee, 358 U.S. 217 (1959).

[125] In the Navajo exclusion case, the district court suggested that an implied condition of exhaustion of tribal remedies should usually operate; this suggestion was based on congressional policy favoring Indian self-government, enhancement of the Indian judiciary through responsibility, and diminution of federal intervention. The court held, though, that no exhaustion was required in that case because, due to the presence in the case of defendants not amenable to tribal court jurisdiction, such a requirement would result in a multiplicity of lawsuits and a delay of any effective remedy. Dodge v. Nakai, Civil No. 1209 (D. Ariz., Dec. 16, 1968) (opinion and order on defendant's motion to dismiss).

Walter White and the Atlanta NAACP's Fight for Equal Schools, 1916-1917

EDGAR A. TOPPIN

IN 1917 A DELEGATION OF NEGROES went before the Board of Education in Atlanta, Georgia, to demand equal facilities for colored school children. (1) This marked the beginning of the work in Atlanta of the National Association for the Advancement of Colored People. The youthful branch secretary who sparked this drive, Walter Francis White, called this "our first fight and our first victory and . . . we have only begun to fight." (2) Despite his enthusiasm, Atlanta moved at a glacial pace toward parity in the dual school systems.

The separate but equal concept sanctioned by the Supreme Court in the Plessy case of 1896 was a sham from the start. Thirty percent of the school-age children in the southern states in 1900 were colored, yet they received only thirteen percent ($4,675,504) of the school funds, while $31,755,320 went to white schools. The disparities increased. In 1911, W. E. B. DuBois concluded "that the Negro common schools are worse off than they were twenty years ago. . . ." Disfranchisement of the Negro at the turn of the century had smoothed the path for greater discrimination, moving DuBois to complain "That the result and apparently one of the objects of disfranchisement has been to cut down the Negro school fund. . . ." (3) The impact of this in Georgia was seen in salaries, the largest item of educational expenditure. In 1905, three years before the state disfranchised the Negro, the average yearly salary for white teachers was $214.25, for Negro teachers $124.20. In 1911, three years after most Negroes lost

---

Mr. Toppin is Professor of History at Virginia State College.

the right to vote in Georgia, white teachers received $318.63, colored teachers $119.35. In 1917, white teachers averaged $69.78 a month and Negroes $32.42. (4)

From the start of public education in Atlanta there were inequalities. Prior to the Civil War, Georgia had made it a crime to teach a "slave, Negro, or free person of color to read or write. . . ." (5) Hence, Negroes were eager for, and badly in need of, education when emancipation came. White children in Atlanta had had only a few private schools and one free "pauper" school before the carpetbag era. With Negroes voting in favor of public education during Reconstruction, authorities set up a public school system in Atlanta. Though votes of Negroes helped to establish this system, it included only two elementary schools for Negroes when it opened in 1872, while whites had two high schools as well as five elementary schools. (6) In later years the city built other elementary schools for Negroes, including the Gray Street School in the Fifth Ward, which was secured by Negro leaders using black voting power as a bargaining lever in a close election for mayor in 1888. In the 1890's the superintendent of schools boasted that Atlanta had "four, full graded [colored] grammar schools . . . supplied with equal accommodations with the white schools. The same course of study, the same curriculum and same laws are given them as are given the white race. Atlanta has been liberal to her colored population. . . ." (7)

Atlanta's liberality did not include high schools for Negroes. As early as 1872, local Negroes petitioned the city council to provide a colored high school or else to make arrangements for their children to attend Atlanta University's high school department free of charge. (8) That year, the President of Atlanta University offered to provide high school training for the city's colored youth at a nominal fee. The Board of Education declined; admittedly, there was such strong opposition to any public secondary schooling that the white high schools were nearly abolished several times. (9) Hence, the city was content to let Negro parents pay for high school education out of their own pockets. DuBois commented that the Negro is "double taxed . . . since he pays his share of the public school tax and in addition is forced to pay tuition charges for his high school training in private institutions. . . ." (10) Because Atlanta and other Georgia communities neglected Negro public schooling, the private Negro institutions in Atlanta had to devote much of their effort to pre-college work. In the 1916-1917 school year, Spelman and Morehouse colleges and Atlanta University had a combined enrollment of only 130 college students but had 1,471 in their high school and elementary departments. In 1916 there were only sixty-four Negro high schools in all the South; the year before ten southern states reported a total of 147,163 whites in high school, but only 6,239 Negroes. (11)

Some Georgians defended such inequalities on grounds that Negroes did not need much education or that they received more than their share of school funds. Governor Hoke Smith asserted in 1909 that "Mere instruction from books will accomplish almost nothing for [the Negro].... He must lean upon the direction of the white man and grow by imitation." His predecessors, Governors Allen Candler and Joseph Terrell, also disparaged Negro education. (12) Walter White revealed that a member of the Atlanta school board objected "to giving one nickel more for the education of the Negro children as they were already getting more than they deserved." Another observer insisted that Negroes "paid but a small part of the state tax." (13)

Careful analysis explodes this myth of southern white taxpayers nobly sacrificing to furnish schools for Negroes. True, Southerners had burdens trying to operate a dual system of separate schools, while bearing more children and possessing only half the average wealth and income of the North. Although the average national expenditure per pupil was $20.29 in 1900, Massachusetts spent $37.36, while the southern seaboard states (including Georgia) ranged from Virginia's $9.70 to North Carolina's $4.34 per pupil. (14) Yet Negroes received far less than the inadequate sums the South spent on the average child. Disfranchisement left the Negro vulnerable to increasing deprivation. While South Carolina in 1900 spent one sixth as much for Negro schooling as for white, in 1915 the state spent only one twelfth as much, doubling the disparity. Separate schools provided for all the southern states, as Louis R. Harlan has shown, "a convenient means of economizing at the expense of Negro children." (15) Those who contended that the Negro paid little in taxes generally counted only the property tax and ignored the substantial indirect taxes paid by Negroes. DuBois reported the findings of two studies of Negro taxes and school costs. From 1870 to 1899 colored schools cost the southern states sixty-nine million dollars, but Negroes paid a total of seventy million dollars in taxes. In 1908, in each of three states studied—Virginia, North Carolina, and Georgia—Negroes paid more in taxes than the cost of their schools. For Georgia, the gap was widest with Negroes receiving from the Georgia school fund only $506,170, which was $140,000 less than the $647,852 in taxes they paid. (16) The Governor of Georgia, Hugh M. Dorsey, admitted in 1917, in a message to the General Assembly, that more needed to be done for Negro education. Although "negroes constitute about forty-five per cent of the population of the State," he pointed out, educational funds were "disbursed about ninety-six and one-half per cent to the whites and three and one-half per cent to the negroes." (17)

Inequalities were gravest in the rural, black belt counties where officials took the funds apportioned for Negroes and spent them on whites. In Georgia, where county school systems were financed by state funds distributed on the basis of school-age population, counties with few Negroes could not discriminate at the Negro's expense so easily. Hence, counties in which Negroes were less than 1 percent of the population spent $4.20 per white child and $2.39 per Negro child in 1910. This was discriminatory, but it was practically equality compared with what the black counties did. Counties in Georgia where Negroes constituted 75 percent or more of the population spent $19.23 per white child and only $1.61 per Negro child. Typical was Randolph County which received $12,000 in state funds because of its 2,680 school-age Negroes, yet it spent less than half of this on the Negro, using the rest for the 1,423 school-age whites, expending nearly twenty dollars per white and only two dollars per Negro child. (18)

Similarly, though to a less degree, Atlanta's schools were always separate but never equal. As an independent school district, Atlanta could levy taxes on the substantial property and business in the city to provide schools far superior to the county schools. Nonetheless, Atlanta made little effort, out of its abundance, to provide proper education for the Negroes, who were a third of the city's 1917 population of some 185,000. (19) DuBois charged that the city, in 1908, supported Negro schools out of the Negro's pro rata share of the $65,000 allotted by the state, while it used for the white schools alone the entire $330,000 raised for schools from local taxes—including taxes paid by Negroes of Atlanta on over one million dollars worth of property. (20) The famed muckraker journalist, Ray Stannard Baker, visited the city in 1906 and described the Negro schools:

> ... the Negro is neglected. Several new schools have been built for white children, but there has been no new school for coloured children in fifteen or twenty years.... The president of the board of education... calls attention to... "the ... Negro schools, ... their overcrowded condition. In every Negro school many teachers teach two sets of pupils, each set for one half of a school day."

DuBois observed that "The Negro school buildings are in bad condition and sorely in need of improvements. Some of them could be improved as they now stand. Others should be razed. ... All are in need of better equipment." (21)

Atlanta's Negro schools were declining at a time when the white schools were getting increasing support. The state constitution was amended in 1912 to permit aid to high schools; almost all of the seventy-eight high schools established in Georgia in the next few years were for whites. (22) President John Hope of Morehouse College testified in 1917 that since 1898 "Atlanta had gone backward in public school facilities for the Negro. There is no Negro high school in Atlanta ... and only about three in the State.... In the Atlanta colored schools there was no industrial training at all." Overcrowding in the city's eleven Negro schools had a silver lining revealed by DuBois:

> ... attendance is good, averaging about ninety-two per cent. This is accounted for in part by the fact that irregularity in attendance results in the loss of one's seat, for almost every one of these eleven schools has its waiting list of those who are desirous of attending but are unable to do so because of lack of school facilities.... At least 250 pupils who apply ... each year are turned away. Hundreds do not apply ... because of the crowded condition....

Despite teaching double sessions, Atlanta's Negro teachers received less pay than the white teachers, all of whom taught only one set of children in a single, school-day session. Salaries for colored teachers began at $310 a year and advanced in eleven steps to $439; white teachers started out at $475 and advanced to $738. (23) Such were the fruits of separate and equal.

Negroes resented the double sessions and lack of a high school, but Atlanta paid little heed until prodded by Walter White and the NAACP. The National Association for the Advancement of Colored People had been formed in 1910 by liberal whites and militant Negroes, alarmed at the steadily deteriorating status of the Negro. Booker T. Washington's conciliatory tactics seemed powerless to stem the tide of disfranchisement, discrimination, lynching, and racial rioting. The NAACP turned to protest, publicity, and legal action. Education was among its major concerns. One of the seven goals listed in the official literature of the national NAACP at the time of the Atlanta school fight was "To secure for colored children an equal opportunity to public school education through a fair apportionment of public education funds." (24) Any organization so dedicated was needed by Negroes in Atlanta.

Beginning in 1913, several unsuccessful efforts were made to organize a branch of the NAACP in Atlanta, including an attempt by Walter White as he entered his senior year at Atlanta University in the fall of 1915. A native of Atlanta, White had experienced the inequities of Atlanta's dual school system. (25) In December 1916, White initiated a new, and successful, move to form a branch. Despite national office suggestions to include workingmen as well as professional Negroes, the branch was overwhelmingly middle-class from the start. Its leadership was taken by businessmen, physicians, professors, and ministers. The President, Harry Pace, was an executive of Standard Life Insurance Company, one of Atlanta's leading Negro firms, and the Branch Secretary, Walter White, was the company's cashier. Standard Life's Founder-President, Heman Perry, was also a charter member of the branch. The newly-appointed Field Secretary for the national NAACP, James Weldon Johnson, was strongly impressed by White's work when he visited Atlanta to confer with the branch's founders. The cocky Branch Secretary was sure that other branches "are liable to be compelled to 'take our dust.' " (26)

Even before the branch received its charter, it had begun to fight against school inequality. White had described Atlanta as a "hot bed of discrimination" that had long needed a chapter of the NAACP. When he sent in the application for the branch's charter on February 3, 1917, he said:

There are so many things that need correction here in Atlanta that it is hard to decide just what to fight first, but this quandary was settled for us by word that has come to us that the city board of education is planning to take away the seventh grade from the colored public schools, they having taken away the eighth grade two years ago. If this is done, they will have to do so, figuratively speaking, "over the bodies of the Atlanta branch of the NAACP."

Although White asserted that the eighth grade was removed from the colored schools alone, it was actually abolished in all of the city schools in 1914, leaving an awkward 7-4 arrangement in place of the old 8-4 system. This 7-4 setup remained until the conversion to a city-wide K-6-3-3 plan in 1923. The move to drop the seventh grade was discriminatory, involving only the Negro schools. An emergency NAACP committee on the seventh grade in Negro schools was formed; three of its six members were businessmen; the others were an editor, a physician, and a college president. On the morning of Washington's birthday, February 22, 1917, the committee learned that the Board of Education was to meet at 3:00 that afternoon. The committee went before the Board to "present the views of the thinking Negro and the tax-paying Negro...." White, who was not on this committee, hoped that the protest would produce some good, but "If it doesn't then we will resort to other measures that the white people of this town evidently think we haven't sense enough to use or backbone enough to try to use." (27)

The Board of Education, however, backed down, giving the NAACP its "first victory" in Atlanta. The triumph vindicated the decision of Walter White and the NAACP to demand "as taxpayers and citizens...every...facility being given to white students." The older generation of Atlanta Negroes had counseled "submission to prevent angering the dominant whites," and even some of the NAACP group had suggested merely pleading for the seventh grade. (28) On the emergency committee's return from the meeting with the Board, White reported what took place in the meeting as told to him by the delegation. After the Negroes protested strongly against cutting off the seventh grade, one board member, James L. Key, who was Fourth Ward councilman, stated: " 'I want to go on record as being against every move that will take away any of the rights' " of Atlanta Negroes. Key also contended that "every word spoken by these men is true. We have not given them a square deal...." According to White, other board members spoke in the same vein and even the Mayor, Coca-Cola millionaire Asa G. Candler, said "what these dear colored brethren said is true." (29)

Ten days later, White gave a different version of the same encounter, revealing more opposition. The Board of Education pleaded lack of money, but the NAACP delegation pointed to the fifty fine schools built for the whites. The Board suggested that the Negro colleges in Atlanta could adjust their curricula to the dropping of the seventh grade, but the delegation reminded the Board that these were private institutions and that the Board should not push substitutes but should "grant what they as citizens and taxpayers were justly entitled" to. While Councilman Key asserted "I want to plead guilty . . . we would be derelict to our duty if we did not grant their demands," Mayor Candler argued "I do not agree.... I do not wish to plead guilty. Let us not give way to hysteria, but look at this matter in a sane manner." Key hit back, accusing Candler of being the root of all hysteria in Atlanta; Key pledged to do his utmost to get the Negroes their rights. (30)

The daily press acknowledged the Negro triumph. According to news accounts, the Board "went on record . . . as opposed to the elimination of the seventh grade or any other grammar school work, either in the negro or white schools...." Further, the Chairman of the Board of Education, R. J. Guinn, promised that the schools would be reorganized to give junior high school training, including industrial courses geared to the vocational needs of the great many pupils (95 percent of the whites and 99 percent of the Negroes) who would never go to college. "Whenever this was done, the negroes would receive consideration in the junior high schools as well as the whites." These concessions and promises came as a result, the papers reported, of "a committee of negro taxpayers protesting against the suggested abolition of the seventh grade in the negro grammar schools and urging the establishment of some kind of a high school for negroes." (31)

White was jubilant over the outcome, commenting that "if the N.A.A.C.P. does no more, it has earned its right for existence." Enough interest was generated to expand the Atlanta branch to 393 members (139 paid up) by the end of March 1917. In April the NAACP approved the Atlanta branch and granted it a charter, which was transmitted to the group in May. (32) Now the NAACP was officially in business in Atlanta.

The Atlanta branch did not rest on the laurels of its initial success. The emergency committee was slated to meet with the Board again on April 26, 1917. At Walter White's urging, the branch pushed a campaign to deluge the Board with letters beforehand. In mid-April, the branch sent out a printed letter urging the three hundred members to write to the Board. As White explained, "The psychological effect of three hundred letters... is planned to show that our protest was not a mere 'flash-in-the-pan' performance... of a few self-appointed men acting as a protest committee, but that they are the representatives of the thinking men and women of the race." (33) The printed letter, apparently drafted by White, reminded NAACP members of the "work accomplished by the [emergency] committee...." This resulted, the letter continued, in the Board of Education awakening from its "indifference toward... better facilities for Negro youth," and also in the board promising "to remedy conditions and provide better facilities for our children." Promises were not enough because "they are not going to do these things if our efforts are allowed to lag." Therefore, each member was urged to write to the Board at once demanding those things "which are rightfully ours." The printed letter then asked: "Are you willing to do this much to give your children and other people's children a fighting chance in life?" Each member was to write in his own words, but the four things each should stress were:

1. We want the absolute elimination of all double sessions in all the public schools.
2. We want better school buildings, the destruction of all the unsanitary fire traps called schools....
3. We want a Junior High School, commercial and industrial, for the training of those of our youth who cannot afford a college education....
4. We want high schools for our boys and girls. Atlanta is the only city of her size that has so great a Negro population that does not at least pretend to give high school facilities for Negroes. Colored people pay taxes on over a Million and a Half Dollars worth of property in Atlanta, and yet have a smaller pro rata share... expended on them in... schools ... than any city in the country.

The printed letter was signed "Yours for better schools," by the Atlanta branch of the NAACP. (34)

After this letter-writing campaign, the branch languished until September. The entry of America into World War I on April 6, 1917, diverted the attention of the Negroes of Atlanta. When the branch committee met with the Board of Education late in April, it found that the Board had stiffened and was less eager to provide better facilities for colored pupils. (35) But the branch took no action when the Board reneged on its promises.

Interest perked up in September when Clark Howell's Atlanta *Constitution* vigorously denounced a proposal by School Superintendent Wardlaw to run a temporary double session for one year in three grades of one of the white schools (the Tenth Street School) to relieve overcrowding until a new building was ready; there was a hint that other schools (white) might have to start double sessions also. The *Constitution* labelled the proposal "reversion to a policy that is inhumane, barbaric and wholly out of keeping with Atlanta's place and pride." A suggestion for double sessions had been killed a few years before when "the people of Atlanta ... rose up in opposition to the outrageous injustice ..., demanded ... that the order be revoked—and it was revoked!" The school board found a solution other than a double session, the editorial roared, "because another way had to be found!" Editor Howell called for a new campaign against the proposed double sessions because "It is a nefarious thing, and the parents of Atlanta's children will be derelict ... if they tolerate it for a day!" The editorial drew a pathetic picture of little ones toddling to class "at an unseemly hour in the morning" while the second set had to drag off to school in the afternoon, exhausted from a day of play, and return "at an hour of almost darkness." The paper thundered: "Such a system is unfair from any angle ... and an injustice.... There's nothing right about it, and there is no condition nor pretext that can justify it." The only solution was to rent room space in the neighborhood to seat every child "at reasonable school hours. ... That was done before ... and must ... be done again." Meanwhile, "let the city get busy—get the money, somehow, somewhere; but get it...." And, the editorial closed, "The proposal of the outrageous double-session system should be ended just where it is!" (36)

This editorial outraged the Negroes of Atlanta. All agreed with the harsh indictment of double sessions as barbaric, nefarious, and unjust. But, in all of Clark Howell's philippic against the idea of starting temporary double sessions in one white school, there was not the slightest hint that double sessions had always existed in all the colored schools. Negroes felt no better about Howell's stand when they recalled that he and Hoke Smith had engaged in an inflammatory campaign for governor in 1906 that sparked the bloody Atlanta race riots of that year. Double sessions might be out of keeping, as Howell insisted, with Atlanta's pride, and Atlanta's parents might not tolerate them, and they might have killed off similar proposals in years past, but Negroes for decades had had to endure the outrageous double-session system. Obviously, the Negro was the city's invisible man, and his schools did not count at all in Atlanta's way of thinking. When public pressure forced the Board of Education to rent extra space, Atlanta news articles appeared with the heading "Double sessions end today," thus giving, as Walter White pointed out, "the impression that the Negro Schools as well as the White did not have this barbaric handicap...." A committee of the Atlanta NAACP went to the Board of Education and argued futilely for two hours for better schools and more space for Negroes; one board member, W. H. Terrell, flatly opposed spending any more money on "the Negro children as they were already getting more than they deserved." So incensed were the Negroes of Atlanta, White revealed, that "We are now planning a monster silent parade similar to the one held in New York in order to make some tangible move toward abolishing... double sessions." The parade in New York had been held in July 1917 to protest the East St. Louis race riots of that month. (37)

Meanwhile, Walter White wrote a letter to the editor of the *Constitution*, a letter printed by the paper, prominently, on September 28, 1917. White agreed that the editor's "protest against the proposed double sessions in the white schools... is unanswerable." But, White pointed out, all fourteen of Atlanta's Negro schools had double sessions. "This is not a new condition in the colored schools, but has been that way ever since there were public schools for negroes; yet, not a single word of protest has been uttered against this condition." White contended that if Atlanta whites were sincere in their protestations of good will for Negroes they could show this tangibly by improving the colored schools. "In ... the negro public schools," he went on, "there are teachers who have sixty students from 8:30 to noon and sixty more from 12:30 to 4 p.m. ... and undergo such a strain in an ill-ventilated, poorly-lighted, crowded schoolroom." Negro children had to endure such conditions even though their parents were law-abiding taxpayers who paid their pro rata share of funds collected for the public good. White insisted that "The colored people of the city do not begrudge the white children any advantages that they have.... But at the same time the white children are being educated, we ask that the colored children be given the same opportunity." He concluded his letter by pointing out that his people only sought "those things which are rightfully theirs as taxpayers and law-abiding citizens." Instead of signing the letter as Branch Secretary of the NAACP, he signed as Cashier of Standard Life. In printing the letter, Howell left out some portions and also altered White's spelling of Negro to make it lower case. Omitted was a statement in which White said that he asked that since Southern whites believed "the Negro race was an inferior race, how could the White man give the Negro child half the education that he gives his own child and yet hope to make him a decent law-abiding citizen...." (38)

Clark Howell commented on the letter in an editorial in which he introduced White as a member of a firm directed by some of the best Negroes in the city, men "whose influence may always be counted upon the side of conservatism and good citizenship." Howell agreed that White "makes an appeal to the conscience and to the sense of justice of the city which cannot be disregarded...." The editor revealed that the double sessions in the Negro schools had been discussed when the issue came up regarding the white schools. According to Howell, the Chairman of the Board of Education, R. J. Guinn, properly admitted "that the city had not up to this time been just in its arrangements as regards the negro schools." And, said Howell, Guinn "stated he believed the time had now come when the double sessions in the negro schools should be abandoned, as they had been in the white schools." Significantly, Howell revealed that the school board "unanimously indorsed" the Chairman's position and set up a committee "to arrange a plan by which the negro schools might be freed from double sessions." Howell reported that the committee was at work on this. Furthermore, Howell pointed out, "Aside from the justice involved, the city loses nothing by being fair in its treatment of its negro citizens. . . ." And he concluded by confessing that "undoubtedly up to this time they [Negroes of Atlanta] have not had a fair showing in the matter of educational facilities provided for them." (39)

If Howell accurately reflected the sentiments of the Board, the protest made by the NAACP delegation in its meeting with the Board in September was not in vain. Certainly, Walter White's cogent arguments in his letter to the editor bore fruit when he got the editor of Atlanta's leading newspaper to admit in his editorial columns that the Negroes of the city were not getting fair treatment in the handling of school funds. (40)

The Atlanta NAACP continued the fight for equal schools, but without White. On James Weldon Johnson's recommendation, White was offered a job with the national office. In January 1918 he left his promising position with Standard Life to become Assistant Secretary of the NAACP. After thirteen years, Walter White became the Executive Secretary of the NAACP, a post he held for a quarter of a century. In the weeks before his departure from Atlanta, the activity of the branch slackened noticeably. The national office wanted a representative of the branch to appear at the Mid-Winter Conference in New York at Christmas to give "a direct narrative of just how the Branch went about its fight on the school question," but no one showed. By June 1918 the branch had only forty-nine paid memberships to send in and Harry Pace resigned as Branch President; James Weldon Johnson felt the Atlanta branch should have had a thousand members. (41)

Ultimate success in the school fight came long after White's departure from the branch. When the Board of Education slowed to a snail's pace in improving the colored schools, Negroes resorted to the ballot box. Ascertaining that bond issues needed approval by two thirds of all persons registered, the Atlanta branch pushed a drive "increasing the colored registration from 700 to 3,000 names," in 1919. Thusly armed, the Negroes were able to thwart bond issues for municipal improvements and to stymie proposals for increasing taxes for schools; this was done in elections in 1918 and 1919. (42) In one campaign, 13,845 persons were on the poll books, thus requiring 9,230 affirmative votes; but with registered Negroes boycotting the polls, only 8,757 votes were cast, thus defeating the bond issue automatically regardless of how voters lined upon it. Now resistance to improvements in Negro schools collapsed. Definite pledges were made for new grammar schools and for a high school for Negroes in return for guarantees that the colored voters would not block bond issues. (43)

At the next bond election, in March 1921, a bond issue of $8,850,000 was presented to the voters, covering $4,000,000 for new schools and the rest for sewers, viaducts, and waterworks. The issue passed this time. There was a record turnout; of the 27,145 persons registered (21,240 whites and 5,905 Negroes), 22,223 cast ballots. The school bonds passed by 21,710 to 513. Negroes voted overwhelmingly for the school bonds as seen in the returns from the predominantly Negro first and fourth wards. In the first ward, which had 1,587 Negroes registered to 390 whites, the school bonds passed by 1,598 to 19, and in the fourth ward the victory margin was 2,808 to 17. Of the twenty-four members of the committee of prominent Negroes appointed to push the 1921 bond campaign among colored voters, five had been charter members of the Atlanta branch of the NAACP. As a result of this election, Atlanta had eighteen new schools under construction in 1923, including five for Negroes—four grammar schools and a combined junior-senior high school. The high school, which opened in 1924, was the first public high school for Negroes in the history of Atlanta, coming more than a half century after the city established public high schools for Caucasians. Considering the role of the Atlanta NAACP in securing the school, it might come as a surprise to learn that the school was named for Booker T. Washington, an inveterate foe of the NAACP and its militant tactics. (44)

Even these improvements left the Negro schools far from equal. White schools were improved at a much faster rate, causing Negro schools to be increasingly unequal into the 1930's everywhere in the South. For the 1929-1930 school year, Georgia spent $35.42 per white child enrolled and $6.38 per Negro pupil. The Southern average was $44.31 per white and $12.57 per Negro student, but for the entire United States in 1928, the average expenditure was $87.22. Thus, southern white pupils received half the national average, but the share for colored pupils in the South was only one seventh the national average. (45) In some places, the grossest disparities began to be eliminated in the 1940's, but it was not until the imminent Supreme Court desegregation ruling in the 1950's that southern states launched a frantic, eleventh-hour campaign to make the separate schools equal in fact as well as in name. As DuBois commented in 1911, "Negro education has never been actually tried in the South." (46)

The school situation in Atlanta in 1917 demonstrated that separate but equal meant inferior facilities and lower teacher salaries for Negroes because school officials deliberately provided Negroes far less than their fair share of tax revenue; instead they poured as much as possible of the city's limited resources into improving the white schools. Although the Negro resented the wretched facilities furnished him, many whites—thinking of the Negro as an inferior being with little need for book learning—felt that the Negro should be grateful for any crumbs thrown his way. Submission to the status quo and self-improvement (tactics counseled by Booker T. Washington) simply encouraged whites to remain indifferent to the Negro's needs so that disparities grew worse, especially after disfranchisement. Protest by Walter White and the NAACP cut into this apathy, with city officials readily conceding their past neglect of the Negro's interest and promising to do better; this showed they were conscious of their wrongdoing but were content to continue inequities as long as Negroes put up with it. The NAACP effort unified the articulate Negroes of the city, but active participation seemed to come from a small coterie of professional and business men; with only 139 paid-up memberships in a city containing 60,000 Negroes, the masses evidently remained untouched, untapped, and unmoved.

In protesting, the Atlanta NAACP, under Walter White's direction, shied away from abstract concepts of human rights or equality; instead, the pitch was mainly along middle-class, moderate lines of the inequity of denying colored taxpayers their fair share of school funds. While useful in the short run, this was a dangerous tack in the long, because it slighted a democratic society's inherent obligation to educate all its members irrespective of their tax contributions as individuals or a class. Apparently, the appeal met a favorable response at the time not only because it was moderate rather than radical, but also because the movement was a homegrown effort by respected local Negroes. The affiliation with the national NAACP was played down. While protest touched the consciences of Atlanta officials, it was not enough; really effective action came only with the application of muscle in the form of a drive that qualified enough Negroes to vote to enable them to block bond issues. Then, and only then, did Atlanta make a real start toward providing decently for Negro education, though still on a grossly unequal basis.

In the climate of the 1960's—with boycotts, sit-ins, and freedom marches effecting major changes in the Negro's status—the tactics employed by Walter White and the Atlanta branch seem mild indeed, and the results of their efforts pathetically meager. More drastic techniques and revolutionary gains were hardly to be expected in the climate prevailing in the Deep South at the time of the school fight, but there were shortcomings in White's approach. While he showed himself to be a skillful promoter and publicist, he did not prove, in the Atlanta struggle, to have the charisma to attract a large and devoted following that would improve his chances of bringing about change. His frequent stress on the thinking, taxpaying, law-abiding, upstanding element in Atlanta's colored population exposed a class bias that blocked effective communication with the toiling masses. Nonetheless, the effort initiated by White and the NAACP in Atlanta was a start, however small, toward remedying educational inequality in the city. If the gains seem far less dramatic today than White depicted them in his enthusiasm, it was still no little matter to budge Atlanta Negroes from decades of apathy and to begin educating the white power structure to the prospect that Negroes would speak out, write letters, form committees, demand their rights, and would later use the ballot as a lever to force modification of intolerable conditions. In this lies the significance of the fight for equal schools in Atlanta.

Notes

1. Walter White to James Weldon Johnson, February 22, 1917, No. 2, NAACP Branch Files, Atlanta, 1913-1931, NAACP Archives, Library of Congress. White's two letters to Johnson that day (before 3:00 and after 5:00) are designated No. 1 and No. 2 herein. Unless otherwise noted, all materials cited from the NAACP Archives come from the Atlanta file box, 1913-1931.

2. Walter White, *A Man Called White* (New York: The Viking Press, Inc., 1948), p. 30; White to Roy Nash, March 3, 1917, NAACP Archives. Nash was the NAACP national secretary; James Weldon Johnson was the field secretary.
3. W. E. Burghardt DuBois (ed.), *The Negro Common School*, Atlanta University Publication No. 6 (Atlanta: Atlanta University Press, 1901), p. 87; DuBois and Augustus G. Dill (eds.), *The Common School and the Negro American*, Atlanta University Publication No. 16 (Atlanta: Atlanta University Press, 1911), pp. 7, 137.
4. Dorothy Orr, *A History of Education in Georgia* (Chapel Hill: University of North Carolina Press, 1950), p. 317; *Georgia School Reports, 1917*, p. 439; *Georgia School Reports, 1918*, p. 7.
5. DuBois, *Negro Common School*, p. 18.
6. Henry R. Hunter, "The Development of the Public Secondary Schools of Atlanta, Georgia" (unpublished Ph.D. dissertation, George Peabody College for Teachers, 1937), pp. 9, 12, 16, 19-23, 62-63; Asa H. Gordon, *The Georgia Negro, A History* (Ann Arbor, Michigan: Edwards Brothers, 1937), pp. 151-52; Walter G. Cooper, *Official History of Fulton County* (Atlanta: Walter W. Brown, 1934), pp. 33, 449-53. Atlanta is in Fulton County.
7. Gordon, *Georgia Negro*, pp. 152-53; Superintendent Slaton's report as quoted in Richard R. Wright, *A Brief Historical Sketch of Negro Education in Georgia* (Savannah: Robinson, 1894), pp. 34-35.
8. Hunter, "Development of Secondary Schools of Atlanta," p. 63.
9. *Ibid.*, pp. 23-27, 64; Cooper, *Official History of Fulton County*, pp. 451-53.
10. DuBois and Dill, *Common School and Negro*, pp. 127-28.
11. John F. Slater Fund, *Proceedings and Reports for the Year Ending September 30, 1917* (n.p., n.d.), p. 42; Horace Mann Bond, *The Education of the Negro in the American Social Order* (New York: Prentice-Hall, Inc., 1934), pp. 206, 296.
12. Louis R. Harlan, *Separate and Unequal* (Chapel Hill: University of North Carolina Press, 1958), pp. 216, 227; Amanda Johnson, *Georgia: As Colony and State* (Atlanta: Walter W. Brown, 1938), p. 925.
13. White to Johnson, September 27, 1917, NAACP Archives; Amanda Johnson, *Georgia*, p. 925.
14. Harlan, *Separate and Unequal*, pp. 10, 35-36.
15. *Ibid.*, pp. 14-15.
16. DuBois, *Negro Common School*, pp. 88-91; DuBois and Dill, *Common School and Negro*, pp. 120-26.
17. Georgia General Assembly, *House Journal, 1917*, p. 662. The governor's message was dated July 25, 1917.
18. Harlan, *Separate and Unequal*, pp. 210-12, 239-40, 245; Orr, *History of Education in Georgia*, p. 316.

19. Harlan, *Separate and Unequal*, pp. 211-12; United States Bureau of the Census, *Negro Population, 1790-1915* (Washington: Government Printing Office, 1918), pp. 388-89; United States Bureau of the Census, *Negroes in the United States, 1920-1932* (Washington: Government Printing Office, 1935), pp. 54-55.
20. DuBois and Dill, *Common School and Negro*, pp. 62-63.
21. Ray S. Baker, *Following the Color Line* (New York: Harper & Row, Publishers, 1964), pp. 52-53. Originally published in 1908. DuBois and Dill, *Common School and Negro*, p. 63.
22. Orr, *History of Education in Georgia*, p. 319.
23. Harlan, *Separate and Unequal*, p. 263; DuBois and Dill, *Common School and Negro*, pp. 61-63.
24. Mary White Ovington, *The Walls Came Tumbling Down* (New York: Harcourt, Brace, & World, Inc., 1947), pp. 100-8; James Weldon Johnson, *Along This Way* (New York: The Viking Press, Inc., 1933), p. 310; NAACP, *Eighth and Ninth Annual Reports for the Years 1917 and 1918* (New York: NAACP National Office, January 1919), inside back cover (p. 95).
25. W. R. Scott to DuBois, September 30, 1913; reply to Scott, October 8, 1913; John Hope to May Childs Nerney, January 27, 1915; Nerney to J. P. Barbour, January 30, February 24, 1915; White to DuBois, September 7, 1915; Nerney to White, September 13, 1915, NAACP Archives. W. E. B. DuBois was Director of Publicity and Research for the national NAACP; May Nerney worked in the national office.
26. Nerney to White, September 13, 1915; White to Nash, December 16, 1916; Nash to White, December 19, 1916; Johnson to White, December 21, 1916; White to Johnson, January 5, 1917 [mistakenly dated as 1916]; White to Nash, February 3, 1917, NAACP Archives; James Weldon Johnson, *Along This Way*, pp. 308-9, 314-16.
27. White to Nash, December 16, 1916, February 3, 1917; White to Johnson, February 22, 1917, No. 1, NAACP Archives; White, *A Man Called White*, pp. 29-30; Hunter, "Development of Secondary Schools of Atlanta," pp. 49-50, 61.
28. *Constitution* (Atlanta), February 23, 1917, p. 8; White, *A Man Called White*, pp. 30-31.
29. White to Johnson, February 22, 1917, No. 2, NAACP Archives; "Asa Griggs Candler" in *Dictionary of American Biography*, III, 470-71.
30. White to Nash, March 3, 1917, NAACP Archives; White, *A Man Called White*, pp. 31-32.
31. *Constitution* (Atlanta), February 23, 1917, p. 8; *Journal* (Atlanta), February 23, 1917, p. 4.
32. White to Johnson, February 22, 1917, No. 2; White to Johnson, March 3, 1917; White to Nash, March 28, 1917 (telegram); Pace to Nash, March 26, 1917; Nash to White, May 19, 1917, NAACP Archives;

Minutes, Board of Directors, January 2, February 13, March 12, April 9, 1917, NAACP Archives (in box labelled Board Minutes, National NAACP).
33. White to Nash, March 19, 1917; White to Nash, April 12, 1917; White to Johnson, April 19, 1917, NAACP Archives.
34. Printed Letter, from Atlanta branch to membership, n.d., NAACP Archives.
35. White to Nash, May 9, 1917; White to Johnson, September 27, 1917, NAACP Archives; White, *A Man Called White*, pp. 32-33.
36. *Constitution* (Atlanta), September 8, 1917, p. 6.
37. White to Johnson, September 27, 1917, NAACP Archives; James Weldon Johnson, *Along This Way*, pp. 319-20; *Who Was Who in America*, I, 1897-1942, p. 596.
38. *Constitution* (Atlanta), September 28, 1917, p. 8; White to Johnson, September 27, October 1, 1917, NAACP Archives.
39. *Constitution* (Atlanta), September 28, 1917, p. 8.
40. Johnson to White, October 4, 1917, NAACP Archives.
41. White, *A Man Called White*, pp. 34-37; Johnson, *Along This Way*, pp. 316-17, 329; Ovington, *Walls Came Tumbling*, p. 148; White to Johnson, December 5, 1917; Johnson to Pace, December 12, 1917; Pace to Johnson, January 4, 1918; Johnson to Pace, January 18, 1918; White to Pace, April 22, 1918; Pace to White, June 22, 1918; Johnson to Pace, June 29, 1918; White to John R. Shillady, July 19, 1918, NAACP Archives. Shillady succeeded Roy Nash as NAACP Secretary (1918-1920), to be succeeded in turn by Johnson (1920-1931), White (1931-1955), and Roy Wilkins (since 1955) as NAACP Executive Secretary.
42. NAACP, *Tenth Annual Report . . . for the Year 1919* (New York: NAACP National Office, 1920), p. 72; White, *A Man Called White*, p. 33; *Constitution* (Atlanta), March 5, 1918, p. 7; March 6, 1919, p. 1; March 7, 1919, pp. 1, 4; March 18, 1919, p. 1.
43. Franklin M. Garrett, *Atlanta and Environs*, (3 vols.; New York: Lewis Historical Publishing Company, 1954), II, 756; White, *A Man Called White*, p. 38; NAACP, *Tenth Annual Report*, p. 72.
44. *Constitution* (Atlanta), March 1, 1921, pp. 1, 10; March 6, 1921, p. 7A; March 9, 1921, pp. 1, 16; Garrett, *Atlanta*, II, 779, 795-96; Hunter, "Development of Secondary Schools of Atlanta," pp. 66-68, 70-72.
45. Fred McCuistion, "Financing Schools in the South" (Nashville, Tennessee: Directors of Educational Research for Southern States, 1930), p. 16.
46. Walter White, *How Far the Promised Land?* (New York: The Viking Press, Inc., 1955), pp. 47, 58-62; DuBois and Dill, *Common School and Negro*, p. 133.

Earl Warren
and
the Brown Decision*

S. SIDNEY ULMER

If asked to name the most important decision made by the Supreme Court during the Chief Justiceship of Earl Warren, the layman could be excused if he answered quickly: the decision about segregation in the *Brown* case. For it is that decision that marked the new Chief Justice in 1954 as a major force in the American constitutional system. It is that decision that gave the Court's work a tenor and a tone that was to characterize it throughout Warren's tenure. When Warren himself was asked the same question in 1968, he selected *Brown* v. *Board of Education*[1] as one of the two most important cases decided by his Court, placing it only behind

---

*The research on which this paper is based has been supported by the National Science Foundation.

[1] 347 U. S. 483; 74 S. Ct. 686 (1954).

Baker v. Carr[2] in significance. It seems unquestionable, however, that the personal influence of the Chief Justice was more readily felt in the *Brown* case, in which he wrote the "opinion of the Court," than in the reapportionment case, in which the opinion was written by Justice Brennan. For Warren's opinion in *Brown* received unanimous support, a feat that most students of the Court would have thought unlikely if not impossible at the time.

The phenomenon of unanimity in *Brown* has elicited considerable speculation. One observer has written:

> Conceivably, we will some day know how unanimity was reached. What was the role of the Chief Justice's predecessor? Was it necessary to woo and win those members of the Court with Southern backgrounds? How were the lines drawn in December of 1953, when the cases were argued for a second time? Are the speculations correct which credit the newly arrived Chief Justice with the unanimous statement? Was the opinion in the cases shaped by adamant refusals to concur unless this or that approach was utilized?[3]

Answers to such questions would, of course, go far in helping one to assess correctly the contribution of Earl Warren to the decision in the *Segregation Cases*. Until now, however, a lack of appropriate data has inhibited the investigation. The recent opening of the Harold H. Burton Papers presents an opportunity to attempt a fuller and more complete evaluation of Warren's role than has heretofore been possible.[4] That is the purpose of this short paper.[5]

I

The background for the decision in *Brown* was laid by the Vinson Court, probable jurisdiction being noted on June 9, 1952.[6] On

---

[2]369 U. S. 186; 82 S. Ct. 691 (1962).

[3]Ira Michael Heyman, "The Chief Justice, Racial Segregation, and the Friendly Critics," *California Law Review*, 49 (March 1961), 104-125, 104.

[4]This is the manuscript collection of the late Justice Burton now deposited in the Library of Congress.

[5]Consideration is limited to the first Brown case decided on May 17, 1954.

[6]343 U. S. 989, 72 S. Ct. 1070 (1952). The justices voted to "note jurisdiction" in Conference on June 7, 1952. As recorded by Justice Burton, the vote was 7 to "note" and 1 (Justice Jackson) to "hold." No vote is recorded for Chief Justice Vinson. Harold H. Burton Papers, Library of Congress.

October 8th, it was decided to continue the cases so that they could be heard with the developing District of Columbia case.[7] This could have been a play for time, for the distinction between the applicable Fourteenth and Fifth Amendments was such as to complicate the finding of common ground for the federal and state cases. Or strategical considerations may have been involved. Some justices may have reasoned that a decision to ban segregation in the "federal city" would increase the pressure to bar it in the states. In any event, by so structuring the situation, the Court underscored its concern with public-school segregation as a social rather than a legal problem. After initial arguments, the Court, on June 8, 1953, redocketed the cases and scheduled reargument for October 12th.

All the above decisions were made by the Vinson Court, and they suggest that, in this period, the justices were finding a solution difficult. Just how difficult is reflected in the report of the Conference held on December 13, 1952,[8] i.e., in the interim between oral argument and the redocketing of the cases. Speaking first in the Conference, Vinson observed that public schools in the District of Columbia were segregated in 1868 when the Fourteenth Amendment was adopted. Moreover, the Congress sitting at that time declined to pass a statute barring racial segregation in District schools. Though he voiced no disagreement with Harlan's dissent in *Plessy v. Ferguson*,[9] he argued that Harlan was careful to avoid a reference to public schools. This, he thought, was highly significant since the opinion otherwise bore down so heavily on racial segregation. With regard to the role of the Court, Vinson expressed the view that if Congress failed to act, the Court would have to confront the problem and would need wisdom to deal with it. He is recorded by Burton as probably upholding the validity of segregation at that time.

The views of the other justices at that point appear to have been as follows: favoring or leaning toward reversal—Black, Douglas,

665

[7]Bolling v. Sharpe, 347 U. S. 497; 74 S. Ct. 693 (1954).
[8]The following references to what was said in this Conference are taken from notes made by Justice Burton. Harold H. Burton Papers, Library of Congress.
[9]163 U. S. 537; 16 S. Ct. 1138 (1896).

Burton, and Minton; favoring or leaning toward affirmance—Vinson, Reed, Frankfurter, Jackson, and Clark. Had this situation been inherited by Warren in October 1953,[10] it seems quite unlikely that the Court could have reached a decision to reverse, much less a decision unanimously taken.

Although reargument was scheduled initially for October, it did not occur until two months later. A Conference was held on December 12th with Warren presiding and as Chief Justice required to speak first. Knowing, as he undoubtedly did, the disparate views prevailing on his Court, knowing the views of his predecessor, and lacking prior experience on the bench, Warren might have been expected to proceed with caution. His statement, however, did not reflect such constraints. Remarking on the high quality of the arguments presented several days earlier, he quickly stated that the Court could not evade the issue but must decide whether segregation was allowable in the public schools. While he was concerned about the possible necessity of overruling earlier cases and lines of reasoning, he concluded that such segregation must now be prohibited. For in his view, the only basis for segregation and separate but equal rights was the inherent inferiority of the colored race. This, he thought, was the theory of *Plessy* and would have to be the theory of the present Court if segregation was to be approved.

Warren could not understand how, in this day and age, one group could be set apart on the basis of race and denied rights given to others. To do so, he argued, violated the Thirteenth, Fourteenth, and Fifteenth Amendments—amendments clearly designed to make slaves equal with all others. On a personal level, he could not fathom how—"today"—segregation could be justified solely on the basis of race. In discussing a possible remedy, he thought it important to avoid precipitous acts that would inflame the situation more than necessary. Conditions in the different states would have to be recognized. Kansas and Delaware with their Negro populations he considered little different from California with its Mexican and Japanese populations. In the deep South,

---

[10]Chief Justice Vinson died September 8, 1953. He was replaced by Warren, who took office on October 5, 1953.

however, he believed it would require all the wisdom at the command of the Court to abolish segregation with minimal upheaval and strife. He particularly stressed that *how* segregation was abolished was important. In summing up he is recorded by Burton as stating that his " . . . instincts and feelings would lead [him] to say that in these cases [we] should abolish in a tolerant way the practices of segregation in public schools."

Upon reflection Warren's opening statement was a masterly one. It condemned no one; it was unemotional; it recognized differences among the states and in conditions relevant to the problem; it suggested tolerance in disposing of the matter; it referred humbly to the need for wisdom. Thus it projected a reasonable and concerned man with malice toward none—a judge faced with a case to decide whatever the impediments. At the same time one must be struck by the firmness with which Warren asserted at the outset that he was prepared and that the Court was obliged to bar consciously segregated public schools. Given the uncertainties with which some of the other justices were plagued at this time, strong leadership on the question was undoubtedly a key factor in the ultimate solution.

By taking the unambiguous position that segregation by race could only be justified by a belief in the inherent inferiority of the Negro, Warren forced those in opposition to subscribe to a questionable theory or show that such a theory was not a fundamental support for the practice.

Finally, it may be noted that Warren made no reference to the inconclusive history of or the intentions behind the Fourteenth or other Amendments. Indeed, he asserted that all three of the Civil War Amendments were violated. But beyond that legal reference, his opening comment was not laden with "law language" or frequent reference to "constitutional requirements." Instead he sought to deny the inferiority of Negroes, to suggest that such anachronistic practices as segregation had no place in the modern day, and to follow his instincts and feelings in banning it. Clearly, we see here a man who had enlarged his horizons from the day when, as Governor of California, he had been a leading proponent of Japanese exclusion from the West Coast.

The reactions of the other justices to Warren's views were

mixed. Three of them possessed southern backgrounds although only one, Black, came from a deep-South state. Reed, of Kentucky, indicated that he understood Warren's attitude and that he (Reed) recognized the dynamic character of the Constitution. He conceded that the Constitution of *Plessy* might not be the Constitution of today and that equal protection, as defined by *Plessy*, had resulted in neither equal facilities nor equal justice for Negroes. Responding directly to Warren, however, Reed observed that the argument was not made before the Court that the Negro was an inferior race, adding that of course there was no inferior race. Though Warren expressed no concern about the meaning of the Civil War Amendments, Reed reminded his colleague that segregated schools had not been barred by the Congress that framed the Amendments. With regard to the legality of segregation, Reed argued that it was not a denial of liberty to say that people must go to separate schools. It was merely the exercise of a police power.

A second southerner was absent from this Conference. Hugo Black, Burton recorded, had departed for Alabama and Florida on December 10th. Black's sister-in-law was near death in Birmingham.[11] Thus Black could not have been influenced one way or the other by Warren's opening efforts to eliminate public school segregation from the national scene.

The member from Texas, Tom Clark, was present and ready to grapple with the question. Pointing out that he was closer to the problem, having lived with it, than any other justice except Black, Clark stressed the seriousness of the issues involved. He acknowledged that in some Mississippi and Alabama counties, the Negro population was as much as sixty percent of the total. He noted South Carolina Governor Jimmy Byrnes's threat to abolish public schools. But while opposed to relief by fiat, Clark was willing to pursue a flexible approach. He was surprised at the legislative history of the Fourteenth Amendment. He had always thought the amendment banned segregation by race, but he saw now that Congress had not ignored the question, that it had recognized segregated schools, and that the legislative history could not be used. Nevertheless, he was willing to support Warren if relief were care-

[11]Burton Diary, Library of Congress.

fully worked out with variations to fit different situations. Thus, the two "southern" justices present at this Conference appear to have had opposite preferences at this stage of the proceedings.

The remaining justices on the Court also expressed divergent views. Minton and Douglas were clearly in agreement with Warren, thus maintaining the positions they had taken in the earlier Conference in the Vinson Court. Minton could simply imagine no valid distinction based on race or color. He was in favor of outlawing public-school segregation on both equal-protection and due-process grounds and was inclined to let the District Courts have their heads in the matter. Douglas shared Warren's views concerning the states, though he believed that the legislative history shed a mixed light on the intention of the "framers." His position was essentially that discrimination by race or color could no longer be sactioned. With regard to the District of Columbia case, he favored sending it back to the Court of Appeals to determine whether segregation in the District was mandatory or permissive.

The last two justices recorded by Burton, Frankfurter and Jackson, provided some contrast in their responses to the new Chief Justice. Quoting Cardozo to the effect that the Court's work is partly statutory interpretation and partly politics, Jackson asserted that the *Segregation Cases* required a political decision. This, he said, was no problem for him, but he did not know how to justify the abolition of segregation on judicial grounds. The problem for him was how to create a judicial basis for a political conclusion. He indicated that he could support a political decision, but he may have threatened to label the decision as such. Suggesting that he had no particular loyalty to southern schools, Jackson predicted that trouble would occur when white children were sent to colored schools and colored teachers.

Frankfurter's position at this point was typically philosophical. He began by deploring the fact that the Court was the guardian of the due-process clause. Other nations (India, Australia, Ireland), he observed, had not burdened their high courts with this function. Like Reed and others, Frankfurter doubted that the legislative history of the amendments suggested the unconstitutional status of school segregation. To eliminate it would, he thought, require some psychological adjustments. In any event, he advised against a self-righteous attitude on the part of the Court.

Regarding Burton's position, some initial ambiguity exists. Burton did not record his own remarks in the Conference dealing with segregation. His diary, likewise, reveals nothing of what he may have said in the Conferences. Yet, we know that he was heavily involved in the intra-Court interactions that preceded and followed the *Segregation Cases* and the decisions in them. Burton records that conversations on these cases with one or more justices occurred on a number of occasions between December 1952 and June 1955. The most frequently mentioned justices were Frankfurter and Warren. On April 20, 1954, for example, Burton wrote: "After lunch the Chief Justice and [I] took a walk around the Capitol, then went to his chambers where he [one word illegible] his preliminary thoughts as to [one word illegible] Segregation Cases."[12] Conversations with Warren were also recorded throughout May. In these conversations, Burton indicated a high level of agreement with the way in which Warren was handling the cases. It may be inferred that Burton's position was never far from that of Warren. Certainly Burton was not among those justices to whom Warren had to "sell a bill of goods."

II

When Warren opened the Conference reported above, he suggested that discussion be informal and that no vote be taken. Thus no formal vote was cast. Yet, if one had to speculate about the outcome of a vote at that time, it seems likely that Warren would have had a majority with him. Added to his vote would have been those of Minton, Douglas, and Black (consistent with their earlier positions). He could also have counted on Burton and Clark. On the other hand, Jackson and Reed appear to have been two "no" votes, while Frankfurter was negative at least regarding the state cases.[13] Thus it appears that Warren began his tenure on the Court

---

[12]*Ibid.*

[13]Frankfurter is on record elsewhere as being opposed to taking shortcuts to discriminate as partisans in favor of Negroes or of appearing to do so. Felix Frankfurter to Hugo Black, February 19, 1962, Frankfurter Papers, Library of Congress.

with a 6-3 majority in favor of barring public-school segregation in the states.

In his diary, Harold Burton records the view that in May 1953, six members of the Court were in favor of and three were opposed to outlawing segregation—with Chief Justice Vinson in dissent. According to Burton a major reason for postponing a decision was the hope of getting a better result later.[14] In any event, Burton's comment suggests that either Frankfurter, Reed, or Jackson was a member of the majority in May 1953 and implies that a 7-2 lineup existed in December 1953.[15]

It does not appear from the evidence available that Warren made any converts to his position between coming to the Court in October and the conclusion of the December 12th Conference. This inference is buttressed further by a Diary entry made by Burton on December 17, 1953: "After lunch the Chief Justice told me of his plan to try [and] direct discussion of segregation cases toward the decree—as probably was the best chance of unanimity in that phase."[16] This information serves two purposes. It tells us

[14]Burton Diary, Library of Congress.
[15]The role of Frankfurter in the *Segregation Cases* is somewhat mysterious. In the Vinson Court Conference of 1952, he stated a willingness to vote that day that segregation in the District of Columbia was a violation of the due-process clause. But he excepted the states, arguing that the legislative history of the Fourteenth Amendment did not establish an intention to abolish segregation. He also disagreed at that point with Hugo Black's view that the states were more limited than the federal government—arguing instead the exact opposite. On December 3, 1953, he wrote to his brethren: " . . . the legislative history of the Amendment [14th] is, in a word, inconclusive, in the sense that the 39th Congress as an enacting body neither manifested that the Amendment outlawed segregation in the public schools or authorized legislation to that end, nor that it manifested the opposite." Harold H. Burton Papers, Library of Congress. In the 1953 Conference he stated flatly that "as a pure matter of history—1867—XIV *did not* have as purpose to abolish segregation." As recorded by Burton, Harold H. Burton Papers, Library of Congress. On January 1, 1954, Frankfurter sent a memo to his colleagues suggesting that the Court appoint a Master and arguing that the inequalities deriving from segregated schools should be eliminated as soon as possible without disrupting school systems or substantially lowering standards for any sizeable group. Harold H. Burton Papers, Library of Congress.
[16]Burton Diary, Library of Congress. I have considered the possibility that

definitely that the Conference held on December 12th had failed to produce the unanimity that Warren clearly sought. Beyond that it reveals poor judgment on Warren's part since the subsequent processes by which a decree was produced proved to be much more complicated and difficult than the processes leading to the initial decision. That this mistake was soon recognized is reflected in the May 1954 decision, which was not a decree but a highly general opinion and decision which did, indeed, have unanimous support.[17]

Was Warren responsible for the unanimity that eventually prevailed in the *Segregation Cases*? Reaching complete agreement in the Court on so volatile a social issue, as opposed to a divided Court with the Chief Justice in dissent, seems to have been important to Warren. He not only worked to achieve unanimity on the vote but also wanted his opinion in the cases to have the support of all the justices. To obtain the latter, he offered an appealing format in a memorandum sent to his brethren on May 7, 1954. The opinion, he wrote, should be short, non-rhetorical, unemotional and, above all, non-accusatory.[18]

That the Court finally stood as one in the *Segregation Cases* is attributed by Burton to the Chief Justice. In his diary for May 8, 1954, Burton records: "In AM the Chief Justice brought his draft of his segregation cases memoranda. They were in accord with our conversations. In PM I read them and wrote him my enthusiastic approval—with a few minor suggestions. He has done, I believe, a magnificent job that may win a unanimous court. . . ."[19] And on May 12, he writes: "The Chief Justice also read to me his latest re-

---

Burton intended "opinion" for "decree" but have rejected it since "decree" has such a specific meaning in the law.

[17] On the day of Warren's first reported Conference on the *Segregation Cases*, he lunched with Burton, Reed, Douglas, Clark, and Minton (four of whom supported him that day). On May 14, 1954, the day before the Conference that approved the opinions in these cases, Warren had lunch with Burton, Reed, Clark, Douglas, and Minton—the same justices. Burton recorded that this luncheon group met frequently throughout the intervening period, that Frankfurter and Jackson never attended, and that Black joined the group only infrequently.

[18] Harold H. Burton Papers, Library of Congress.
[19] Burton Diary, Library of Congress.

vision (slight) of his drafts in the Segregation cases. It looks like a unanimous opinion. A major accomplishment for his leadership...."[29]

Producing a unanimous opinion was indeed a major accomplishment. For only five days before the opinion was to be handed down, Burton was still uncertain whether there would be unanimous backing for it. The holdouts or doubtful members appear to have been Frankfurter and Jackson, or one of them. It seems not to have been Justice Reed, who lunched with Warren and Burton on this very day. Reed is also recorded as having lunch with Burton and Warren at least 20 times between the initial Conference and May 8th, including several days in April and early May. While this group was frequently joined by Clark and Minton, and less frequently by Black and Douglas, it was never joined by Frankfurter and Jackson. The inference is that Burton was probably more familiar with Reed's thinking on the question at that time than with that of Frankfurter or Jackson. Comments made by these justices in Conference are also consistent with such an interpretation. Subsequent to the Brown decision, Frankfurter is on record as saying that "it is not fair to say that the South has always denied the Negroes this Constitutional right. It was not a constitutional right till May 17/54."[21] Taking together all the evidence on Frankfurter, it seems likely that he was in doubt on the state cases until the last possible moment.

After maximizing support for his opinion, Warren considered it necessary to engage in a kind of administrative management that is undoubtedly rare in the Court. It appears that he and other justices were concerned lest there be "leaks" about the upcoming decision. Thus steps were taken to assure that the matter would remain private until decision day. Warren *personally* circulated his final draft opinion among the justices.[22] Burton tells us that on May 15th, in Conference, the opinions were "finally approved."[23]

[20]*Ibid.*
[21]Harold H. Burton Papers, Library of Congress. This is an unsigned, undated note. After close comparison with known specimens of Frankfurter's handwriting, however, there is no doubt that it came from his pen.
[22]Burton Diary, Library of Congress.
[23]*Ibid.*

But, then, "... no previous notice was given to [the] office staff, etc. so as to avoid leaks."[24] To avoid suspicion of leaks by the justices themselves, Burton writes that "most of us—including me—handed back the circulated prints to the C.J. to avoid possible leaks."[25]

Managing the timing of news releases is nothing new in government, but the measures taken here were unusual. It seems that the Court placed great importance on being the first to announce its own judgment. These maneuvers also hint that leaks from the Court prior to a formal announcement of case results are more common than one might suspect. Since Burton's recording of these arrangements suggests that they were rare, we have evidence that the Court was particularly sensitive to the subject matter of the cases and the social implications of the decisions in them.[26]

III

What answers can now be given to the questions quoted at the beginning of this article? Clearly, when Warren came to the Court, a majority of the justices were already in favor of holding public-school segregation unconstitutional. Though we can credit him with refraining from action that might have lost him that majority, we cannot conclude that Warren was responsible for it. At the same time, there were strong views in the Court as to how the decision should be formulated and carried out. Warren's low-key approach emphasizing fairness, understanding, and tolerance, combined with a strong plea for justice, clearly contributed to keeping the question on a mature level of discussion and to muting the differences (minor and major) among the justices.

Wooing the southern justices does not appear to have been necessary, at least as regards Black and Clark. It probably did occur in Reed's case. The southern backgrounds of first Vinson and

[24]*Ibid.*
[25]*Ibid.*
[26]Cf. Alexander M. Bickel, "The Original Understanding and the Segregation Decision," *Harvard Law Review*, 69 (November 1955), 1-65; and Albert Sacks, "Foreword" to "The Supreme Court, 1953 Term," *Harvard Law Review*, 68 (November 1954), 96.

later Reed, Black, and Clark were not, however, immaterial for the decision in the *Segregation Cases* and were of particular importance in the formulation of the 1955 decrees. Each southern justice was not only aware of his southern background, but referred to it in Conference. Indeed, having a southern background provided a justice with the aura of an "expert" who had lived with the problem, knew its magnitude, and understood the attitudes and ingrained habits of southern whites—an expert who could foresee the consequences of proceeding in alternative ways.

Deference to the "southern justice" familiar with the "Negro problem" is reflected in Frankfurter's apologetic comment that he had never lived closely with Negroes but had gained some insight into the matter while serving as assistant counsel to the NAACP. He also thought it pertinent to remark that he was a member of the Jewish community.[27] Presumably this gave him some understanding of the treatment of minorities in the United States. In any event, it is clear that the background of a justice was not thought to be beyond the pale of judicial notice.

Robert H. Jackson admitted with embarrassment that he had never really been conscious of the racial issue until he came to Washington. There he discovered that white lawyers, Catholic and Jewish, discriminated against Negroes.[28] Even Reed, from Kentucky, was moved to state that he did not know the deep-South—thereby suggesting that a knowledge of the deep-South was relevant to a decision in the case and that Black and Clark (particularly Black) were better informed and qualified to speak than those without such a background.[29] Neither Black nor Clark hesitated to draw upon his background and familiarity with racial matters in Alabama and Texas. Thus, on balance, it seems likely that the treatment of segregated public schools would have been harsher, in the sense of more immediate and demanding remedies, had the Court been deprived of southern representation at this stage. Southern critics who have been upset with the southern justices for their roles in the *Segregation Cases* and the decrees that

[27]Harold H. Burton Papers, Library of Congress.
[28]*Ibid.*
[29]*Ibid.*

followed have not adequately appreciated the more subtle influences exerted by those justices on the actions taken.

The unanimous opinion in the case must, of course, be attributed to Warren. Though he was reported as saying in 1968, "Well, gee, the Chief Justice doesn't write all of the important decisions,"[30] he did assign the *Segregation Cases* to himself and worked for unanimity from the start. Since we know he did not inherit a unanimous Court, it is probably correct to credit him with achieving the full agreement that ultimately prevailed. There is no hard and fast rule by which we can evaluate the significance of unanimity in these cases, though one supposes that the unanimity of the Court enhanced the acceptability of the decision. Had there been dissents, it is possible that dissidents in the concerned publics might have rallied around the dissenters. But that is mere speculation, for no appropriate historical evidence is available from earlier cases, and certainly none is available from the present decision, for there were no dissents.

The influence of the other justices on the segregation decisions was substantial. Undoubtedly the views of the Court accounted for the gradualism of the social change required and served to temper any tendencies toward precipitous action that might have been present in the Court. All of the justices were aware of the limitations on their ability to effect major social change quickly, and they reflected that belief in their words and actions. It is in circumstances like these that the possible value of having former political leaders on the Court can be appreciated. For political experience tempers the impulse to choose extreme options.

[30]*New York Times*, July 6, 1968, 42.

Separate and Unequal: The Civil Rights Act of 1875 and Defeat of the School Integration Clause

WILLIAM P. VAUGHN

NORTH TEXAS STATE UNIVERSITY

ALMOST A CENTURY AGO, SENATOR CHARLES SUMNER OF MASSACHUSETTS, avowed champion of Negro rights, attempted for four years to have Congress pass a civil-rights bill which contained an explosive school-desegregation clause.[1] Sumner had been a champion of "mixed" (integrated) schools for twenty years before introducing his civil-rights bill. As early as 1850, in the celebrated Roberts Case, he condemned school segregation in Massachusetts as contrary to the spirit of the Declaration of Independence and the Massachusetts Constitution of 1780.[2] In 1867 he unsuccessfully attempted to amend two reconstruction bills with provisions to force the "rebel" states to establish and maintain public schools for all children without distinction of race or color.[3]

In his advocacy of mixed schools, Sumner could depend on a hard core of Senatorial support which included Henry Wilson of Massachusetts, Theodore Frelinghuysen of New Jersey, Richard Yates of Illinois, Samuel Pomeroy of Kansas, George Edmunds of Vermont, John Sherman of Ohio, and Levi P. Morton of Indiana. In the House of Representatives, George and E. Rockwood Hoar and Ben Butler of Massachusetts were loyal to the "cause." However, Sumner had great difficulty in getting substantial support from the majority of Republican members in Congress for civil-rights and school-integration proposals, and received such support only "when it happened to coincide with the momentary, tactical or strategic interests of the Republican party." With the exception of a few idealists, the Republican radicals used the mixed-school question as a "party stalking horse."[4]

One of the early pieces of federal reconstruction legislation had been the first civil-rights act, passed on April 9, 1866. This measure, considered ineffective by the early 1870's, bestowed citizenship upon the Negro and granted equal rights to all citizens (except Indians), including "full and equal benefit of all laws and proceedings for the security of person and property."[5]

---

[1] See also L. E. Murphy, "The Civil Rights Law of 1875," *Journal of Negro History*, XII (1927), 110–127; Alfred H. Kelly, "The Congressional Controversy over School Segregation, 1867–1875," *The American Historical Review*, LXIV (1959), 537–563; James M. McPherson, "Abolitionists and the Civil Rights Act of 1875," *The Journal of American History*, LII (1965), 493–510. The work on this manuscript has been facilitated by a faculty research grant from North Texas State University.

[2] Kelly, "The Congressional Controversy," p. 539.

[3] U.S., *Congressional Globe*, 40th Cong., 1st Sess., March 16, 1867, pp. 165–170; *Ibid.*, July 11, 1867, pp. 580–581.

[4] Kelly, "The Congressional Controversy," pp. 539–540.

[5] U.S., *Statutes at Large*, XIV, 27.

Although the bill of 1866 never included any reference to mixed schools, some Congressmen raised questions concerning this problem during debates over the measure and expressed fears of the bill being used to integrate public schools. These Congressmen were assured that the bill's sponsors had never contemplated mixed schools.[6] Four years later Charles Sumner attempted to correct this omission when he introduced a new and comprehensive supplementary civil-rights bill to the Senate on May 13, 1870, hoping it would be the "crowning work" of reconstruction. It proposed equal rights on railroad cars, steamboats, public conveyances, hotels, licensed theaters, place of public entertainment, church institutions, cemetery associations incorporated by national and state authority, and "common schools and institutions authorized by law."[7]

For the next year and a half Sumner unsuccessfully attempted to get the Senate to consider his measure, unable to overcome apathy and overt hostility. At the beginning of the second session of the Forty-Second Congress, he attached his civil-rights bill as a rider to an amnesty bill (pardoning former Confederates disqualified from holding office by the Fourteenth Amendment) then before the Senate, hoping that a desire to pass the amnesty bill would carry his unpopular measure to victory. Sumner's proposal now became popular with Republican Radicals who despised amnesty as a nefarious means of reviving the Democratic Party in the South by removing the disabilities of the Fourteenth Amendment. They now favored Sumner's civil-rights amendment as a means of making the amnesty bill distasteful to conservative Republicans and Democrats alike and thus preventing the two-thirds vote necessary for passage. At the same time, the civil-rights rider could be used as a "sop" to pacify Negro leaders who were now demanding a federal mixed-school law.[8]

After several heated weeks of debate in January and February, 1872, Sumner's rider passed the Senate on February 9, with Vice-President Colfax casting the deciding vote. Virtually all of the Radicals voted for it, and their strategy proved successful, for adoption of the rider doomed the entire amnesty bill, which was killed a few minutes later when it failed to receive the necessary two-thirds vote.[9] A few days later *The Atlanta Constitution* predicted that Sumner would continue to bring up his civil rights amendment whenever an amnesty bill came before the Senate, as he wished to retain his position as champion of the Negro race and defeat amnesty as a means of injuring President Grant, who had removed him as chairman of the foreign relations committee because of the Santo Domingo imbroglio.[10]

Although Sumner's dislike of amnesty proposals did not lessen, the attitude of the Republican power structure changed completely in the spring

---

[6] U.S., *Congressional Globe*, 39th Cong., 1st Sess., March 1, 1866, p. 1117; *Ibid.*, March 9, 1866, pp. 1294–1295.
[7] *Ibid.*, 41st Cong., 2d Sess., May 13, 1870, p. 3434.
[8] Kelly, "The Congressional Controversy," p. 547.
[9] U.S. *Congressional Globe*, 42d Cong., 2d Sess., Feb. 9, 1872, p. 919.
[10] *The Atlanta Constitution*, Feb. 13, 1872.

of 1872. Motivation for this shift was the adoption of a strong amnesty plank by the Liberal Republican Convention in May. The "regular" or Grant Republicans were afraid this pro-amnesty stand might win over many white Republicans to the liberal side, especially in the South. They now decided to promote amnesty in order to heal the party's schism and destroy Horace Greeley's candidacy in the South. Bellwethers of the Grant Administration, such as *The New York Times*, began to denounce Sumner's killing of the previous amnesty bill with his civil-rights amendment.[11] The result of this strategy was a carefully negotiated bargain in the Senate between the Radical Republican clique, led by Roscoe Conkling of New York, and the Democrats, led by Allen G. Thurman of Ohio. The Democrats agreed to allow voting without further debate on an emasculated civil-rights bill that would not contain the jury and school provisions. In return the Republicans promised that immediately after the civil-rights vote they would call up one of the pending amnesty bills enacted by the House and pass it at once.[12]

The plan was followed without deviation during a late evening session which Sumner had left briefly, feeling ill. The clause relating to schools, churches, cemeteries, and juries was deleted by an amendment of Senator Matthew Carpenter of Wisconsin, and the civil-rights bill, as amended, was approved by a vote of 28 to 14, with 32 Senators absent. This was the last ever heard of this particular measure, for it was never considered by the House. The amnesty bill then passed as previously arranged by a vote of 32 to 2, one of the negative votes being cast by a furious Charles Sumner.[13]

Sumner waited seventeen months (December, 1873) before reintroducing his bill to the Senate, and it was identical to one the House judiciary committee reported about three weeks later. Both bills contained the school-integration clause. The subject of civil rights and especially federally enforced integrated schools caused acrimonious debate in Congress and the whole issue now began to receive a great deal of attention from the Southern press, which hitherto had tended to ignore the far-reaching implications of Sumner's proposal. This press, including some Republican papers, together with Southern public-school officials and sympathetic Congressmen from all parts of the nation, cried that integration would destroy the struggling public school systems in the South: white tax-payers would refuse to support the schools financially and white parents would withdraw their children from integrated schools. Barnas Sears, general agent of the Peabody Fund, hurried to Washington in early January, 1874, to confer with leading Republicans and urged them to delete the school provision from the bill, warning that if it were passed with this feature, it would kill the public schools in the South.[14]

[11] *The New York Times*, May 9–11, 1872.
[12] U.S., *Congressional Globe*, 42d Cong., 2d Sess., May 21, 1872, pp. 3730–3736.
[13] *Ibid.*, pp. 3735–3736, 3738.
[14] The Curry Manuscripts, Letters from Barnas Sears to Robert C. Winthrop, 1867–

Interest in the progress of the civil-rights bill was momentarily transferred to its author in the spring of 1874, for Charles Sumner suddenly died on March 12. Before he died, Sumner extracted a death-bed promise from E. Rockwood Hoar (a close friend and the United States Representative from Massachusetts) that he would not let the civil-rights bill fail.[15] Hoar fulfilled his promise in the House, and Theodore Frelinghuysen of New Jersey continued to promote the bill in the Senate.

The civil-rights bill containing the school clause passed the Senate on May 22, 1874, by a vote of 29 to 16, with 28 Senators not present. Many voting for the bill did so out of respect to Sumner, viewing it as a memorial to him.[16] Passage of the bill was generally condemned by the Southern press, and *The New York Times*, still an administration paper, described the school clause as the most important part of Sumner's bill, but opposed passage because this provision would destroy the public schools in the South. It insisted the Negroes would be better off if Congress merely recommended school integration to the Southern people instead of legislating on the education question.[17]

In many Southern states, the fear that Sumner's bill might become law and create havoc in the public schools led to long delays in signing contracts for the construction of new schoolhouses; superintendents declined to hire new teachers, and several school officials resigned.[18] One notable exception to the wave of opposition to the "equality bill" emanating from the South was a resolution prepared by the predominantly Negro General Assembly of South Carolina and sent to the House of Representatives. It called for passage of the bill with the mixed-school clause, stating that attendance in the public schools came under the principle that every right or occupation dependent upon our public laws should be exercised for the benefit of all.[19]

Politics once again intervened in the civil-rights imbroglio following the Congressional elections of November, 1874. Economic depression, charges of political corruption, and reconstruction problems in the South helped bring about a disaster for the Republicans, who lost their majority in the House of Representatives. More than half of the Republican incumbents failed to achieve reelection and were lame ducks for the second session of the Forty-Third Congress. President Grant indicated his belief that popular

---

76. Manuscript Division, Library of Congress, Washington. Barnas Sears to Robert C. Winthrop, Jan. 8, 1874.

[15] *The New York Daily Tribune*, March 12, 1874.

[16] U.S. *Congressional Record*, 43d Cong., 1st Sess., May 22, 1874, pp. 4175–4176.

[17] *The New York Times*, May 23, May 29, 1874.

[18] Edgar W. Knight, *Public School Education in North Carolina* (Boston: Houghton Mifflin, 1916), p. 255.

[19] U.S., Congress, House, *Resolution of the Legislature of South Carolina*, 43d Cong., 1st Sess., (1873–74), House Misc. Doc. No. 111, 1–2. This assembly elected in November, 1872, was composed of 106 Negroes and 51 whites. The Republicans held 130 of the 157 seats. John S. Reynolds, *Reconstruction in South Carolina, 1865–1877* (Columbia, South Carolina: The State Co., 1905), p. 226.

opposition to the "social-equality features" of the civil-rights bill, especially in the Southern and border states, was partially responsible for the Republican debacle.[20]

In the brief time that remained for both houses of Congress to be under Republican control, the Radicals, led by Ben Butler and Levi P. Morton, developed a new program which they hoped could be put into law before the new Congress convened. This included a variety of subsidy bills for various railroad interests and several bills to strengthen the Republican Party in the South. Among the latter was a new enforcement bill (giving the President power to suspend the writ of *habeas corpus* in several Southern states), a two-year army-appropriations bill (to make possible the maintenance of troops in the South for two years without securing Congressional approval), and passage of Sumner's civil-rights bill, now under the guidance of Butler, who was chairman of the House judiciary committee. Although the Radicals argued that Republican success in 1876 depended upon enactment of these bills, many party moderates including Garfield and Blaine (Speaker of the House) were opposed to all or part of this program.[21]

This Radical program had little chance of passage without a change in House rules to prevent a Democratic filibuster. Such a change in House rules required a two-thirds vote. For reasons which are clouded in mystery, Butler decided to make the civil-rights bill the forerunner of a House battle to change the rules. Thus, as one historian has pointed out, the bill suddenly assumed a political significance out of all proportion to its initial place in the Radical spectrum.[22]

On December 16, 1874, Butler reported the bill (H.R. 796) with amendments from the judiciary committee, where it had been under consideration since January. It was read and referred back to the committee. The fight over changing the House rules occurred in late January, 1875. Out of a most intricate series of maneuvers and manipulations emerged the basic plot. On January 25, one of Butler's "lieutenants," Richard Cessna of Pennsylvania, introduced a motion to forbid all dilatory motions during the remainder of the current session. This proposal failed to muster the necessary two-thirds vote, everyone realizing that Butler's true object was passage of the enforcement and army-appropriations bills. Two days later, Butler moved to call up the civil-rights bill and place it on the House calendar. Technically, this was a motion to reconsider the vote whereby the bill had been recommitted to the judiciary committee in January, 1874.[23] Passage of this motion required a two-thirds vote, which the Democrats tried to prevent by a 48-hour filibuster that included 75 votes on dilatory motions. Finally, Butler permitted an adjournment.

[20] *The New York Tribune*, Nov. 7, 1874.
[21] Kelly, "The Congressional Controversy," pp. 556–557.
[22] *Ibid.*, p. 557.
[23] U.S., *Congressional Record*, 43d Cong., 2d Sess., Dec. 16, 1874, p. 116; *Ibid.*, Jan. 25, 1875, p. 700; *Ibid.*, Jan. 27, 1875, p. 785.

Over the weekend, Speaker Blaine called the House rules committee together, and that body proposed a permanent rules change whereby dilatory motions during debate would be prohibited. The House adopted it only after a bitter fight, the original proposal being amended to permit cloture on the first day of debate by a two-thirds vote.[24] This made possible the passage of the civil-rights bill but precluded enactment of the remainder of the Radical program because debate would be slowed down to the point where not enough time remained for consideration of the other measures.

Removal of most of the major obstacles to passage of Sumner's civil-rights bill permitted Butler to call it up for debate. On February 3, 1875, he declared that as instructed by the judiciary commiteee he would (1) agree to substitute the provision of the Senate for H.R. 796; (2) allow Representative White to make an amendment; and (3) "then yield to a motion to amend the bill by striking out all relating to schools. I do this in order that all shades of republican [sic] opinion may be voted upon." Alexander White, Republican from Alabama and the only Southern member of the judiciary committee, then introduced his amendment to the Senate's version of the bill. This differed from Sumner's original bill in that the cemetery provision was missing and it contained a new provision for separate but equal accommodations and school facilities.[25]

More important in terms of the final outcome was Stephen W. Kellogg's brief amendment. If passed, this amendment would have completely eliminated any reference to schools in the civil-rights bill.[26] The heated discussion which occurred over this did not take place immediately, for various other proposals were placed before the House which ranged all the way from the Senate's bill (including schools and cemeteries) to the White Amendment, which permitted separate but equal facilities. However, it was now obvious that Butler had decided to omit the school clause.

The advocates of mixed schools, including the aging abolitionist William Lloyd Garrison, comprehended the significance of the White and Kellogg amendments. On February 1, 1875 (two days before the proposals were presented), Garrison wrote that he would prefer to see the bill defeated than be adopted with the "sanction of separate schools on account of complexional distinction by Congress." He denied the constitutional right of that body or any state legislature to recognize such racial distinctions.[27]

The introduction of the Kellogg Amendment rekindled the flames of

---

[24] *Ibid.*, Feb. 1, 1875, pp. 901–902.

[25] *Ibid.*, 43d Cong., 2d Sess., Feb. 3, 1875, pp. 938–939.

[26] *Ibid.*, Kellogg was a Republican from Connecticut who had served in the House since the 41st Congress (1869) but was defeated for re-election in 1874 and thus had less than a month left in office at the time he introduced this amendment.—*Biographical Directory of the American Congress, 1774–1961* (Washington, D.C.: Government Printing Office, 1961), pp. 1150–1151. Although not a member of the Committee on the Judiciary, he was obviously on good terms with Chairman Butler who introduced him for the purpose of offering the crucial amendment.

[27] *The Washington Chronicle*, Feb. 5, 1875.

controversy in the House of Representatives over the school clause in Sumner's bill and the problem of integrated schools in general. John Lynch (a Negro Republican and former slave) of Mississippi declared that passage of the bill with the school provision would *not* break up the public-school systems in the South. He thought that if Congress passed and enforced the school clause, mixed schools would result only in those areas of the South where one of the two races was in a small minority. In his opinion such a provision was necessary to nullify the separate-school requirements in some Southern state laws and constitutions. Richard Cain, a Negro Representative from South Carolina, thought that Negroes would lose nothing if the school proviso were cut out, but stated that the party "could afford, for the sake of peace in the Republican ranks, if for nothing else—not as a matter of principle—to accept the school clause." Milton Southard of Ohio did not believe that integration of schools was within the scope of federal authority, for he considered schools to be a state and local prerogative.[28]

Kellogg defended his amendment by saying that it was made in the interest of education, especially the education of colored children in the Southern states. He believed that the civil-rights bill proposed to make a distinction of race in the area of education, and he did not wish to see this happen. He emphasized that if Congress passed the bill with the school clause, "You will destroy the work of the last ten years and leave them [the schools] to the mercy of the unfriendly legislation of the states where the party opposed to this bill is in power."[29]

The speeches against the Kellogg proposal were in the minority. Ben Butler tried to resolve the issue by saying that he favored equal privileges for both races in the schools, but that he also felt the prejudice against mixed schools was so great in the South that its weak public-school systems would be broken up if the school clause were incorporated into the civil rights bill. He concluded that he would rather have the entire section relating to schools struck out than see Congress approve his judiciary committee's provision for mixed schools.

Butler's pronouncement was an indication of how the power structure in the Republican Party, including President Grant, regarded this controversial matter. The party's representatives in the House reflected this attitude in the voting on the Kellogg amendment, February 4, 1875. The amendment was accepted by a vote of 128 to 48. The civil-rights bill, as amended, and therefore *without* the school clause, passed on the same day, by a vote of 162 to 99.[30] All the affirmative votes were Republican; not a Democrat voted for it. Fourteen Republicans voted against the bill, twelve of them being from the South.

[28] U.S., *Congressional Record*, 43d Cong., 2d Sess., Feb. 3, 1875, p. 945; *Ibid.*, Feb. 4, 1875, p. 996.
[29] *Ibid.*, p. 997.
[30] *Ibid.*, pp. 999–1006; *Ibid.*, pp. 1010–1011. There were 194 Republicans and 92 Democrats in the 43d Congress.

Most of the leading Southern newspapers seemed relieved that the school proviso was omitted from the bill, but did not comment on this matter extensively. The Charleston *News and Courier* said that since "mixing" in the schools was not to be compulsory, it saw no reason why whites and blacks, with a little tact and forebearance on each side, could not live harmoniously and prosperously under the protection of a just system of laws which gave the same public rights and privileges to all citizens.[31] *The Atlanta Consiitution* was pleased that the school provision had been deleted from the bill, but described other sections as "all that the most revolutionary white villain or the densest negro brain could desire . . .," and said that it meant malicious persecutions, unnumbered troubles, and even civil war in the South.[32] In North Carolina, two Republican members of the state assembly were so upset over House passage of the bill, even without the school clause, that they resigned from their party, one declaring that he was aligning himself with "the great party that is now building up in the South and North for the preservation of constitutional government and the purity and salvation of the Anglo-Saxon race of our great land."[33]

The Senate soon approved the House bill without a struggle. The Republicans generally felt that to amend the measure was to lose it and Senators who had previously favored mixed schools and declared them to be the foundation of racial equality now remained silent when the bill came up for a vote on February 27. Among the most prominent of these was Geroge Boutwell of Massachusetts who, a week before on February 18, had argued against removal of the vital school clause.[34]

The bill passed the Senate by a vote of 38 to 26.[35] President Grant quickly signed the measure and it became law on March 1, 1875. Many Southern newspapers looked upon the new law as a conglomeration of empty legal phrases which would never be enforced. The Charleston *News and Courier* was pleased that the law did not contain the school and cemetery provisions, and stated that "it is not likely to do anybody much good or much harm." These sentiments were echoed by *The Atlanta Constitution*, which referred to the law as "a bill as full of false promises to the negro as it is of imaginary terrors to the white." Another Georgia paper reminded its readers that the law in its final form was not the measure desired by Sumner, Congress having wiped out the "most objectionable features" (*i.e.*, the school and cemetery clauses).[36]

What many feared to be the greatest threat to the Southern public

---

[31] *The News and Courier* (Charleston, S.C.), Feb. 8, 1875.
[32] *The Atlanta Constitution*, Feb. 6, 1875.
[33] *The Daily Journal* (Wilmington, N.C.), Feb. 9, 1875.
[34] *The New York Daily Tribune*, March 1, 1875.
[35] U.S., *Congressional Record*, 43d Cong., 2d Sess., Feb. 27, 1875, p. 1870. The Senate contained 49 Republicans and 19 Democrats.
[36] *The News and Courier* (Charleston, S.C.), March 2, 1875; *The Atlanta Constitution*, March 2, 1875; *The Daily Constitutionalist* (Augusta, Ga.), March 3, 1875.

schools since their creation failed to materialize. Under the highly political motivation of forcing a rules change to prevent a Democratic filibuster (and thus ensure passage of their new program), Republicans of the Forty-Third Congress had agreed to delete the school provision from the civil-rights law, and insistence by the federal government upon integrated schools was not to come until seventy-nine years later, with the Supreme Court decision in 1954. Perhaps had Congress included the school clause in the law, it would have seriously affected, at least for a time, the meager appropriations provided by Southern state and local governments for maintaining the schools. The course of time and the Supreme Court's decision of 1883[37] made the law a dead letter, but this could not be foreseen by the reconstruction-weary superintendents, teachers, and advocates of public education during those difficult years of 1870–1875. Nevertheless, failure to provide for federally enforced school integration in the 1870's made acceptance of this social and legal necessity a far more difficult task ninety years later.

[37] The unconstitutionality of the 1875 civil-rights law was affirmed by the United States Supreme Court in 1883, when the court had to render a decision in five cases involving the civil-rights of Negroes in hotels, railroad cars, and theaters. Justice Bradley, delivering the opinion of the court, stated that the first and second sections (the second section made it a penal offense to deny to any citizen any of the accommodations or privileges mentioned in the first section) of the law were unconstitutional because they were not authorized by the Thirteenth Amendment, for the separation of the races in public places was not a symbol of servitude. Nor was the civil-rights law authorized by the Fourteenth Amendment, which referred to action by the states, whereas the law applied to individual discrimination. *Civil Rights Cases*, 109 U.S. 3 (1883), pp. 3–25.

THE JOURNAL OF NEGRO HISTORY

Vol. XXXII—April, 1947—No. 2

NEGRO SUFFRAGE IN THE PERIOD OF CONSTITUTION-MAKING 1787-1865

During the period of the making of the constitution for the federal government and the states, developed considerable discussion and action concerning the suffrage for Negroes. It is interesting to observe that when our democracy was writing its beliefs into law there was either direct opposition to or neglect of a definition of the voting status of Negro citizens. Many Negroes had exercised suffrage in the colonial period. They had served as soldiers in the colonial wars and in the war of the American Revolution. They had been property owners and tax payers, heads of households, and members of the churches, but they were kept from the ballot boxes even when most of the constitutions were made. With so little definition of the meaning of the term "citizen" in the thinking of the makers of the constitutions, it was inevitable that misunderstandings should arise throughout this period between the states and their citizens and the federal government and the states. The Federal Convention, the state conventions, the United States Congress, and the state legislatures all followed the course of inactivity, neglect and indifference in reference to their citizens of color and their status as voters. It is of value to note, however, the aggressive attitude of Negroes and the friends of democracy in this struggle to make democracy work in the Pre-Civil War Period.

The Federal Convention of 1787 which met in the city of Philadelphia created a government of limited powers, whose theoretically expressed purpose was the operation of the central government upon the individual citizen. The dignity and worth of the individual were an inheritance of the American Revolution and the beginning of the Age of the Rights of Man. The main problem which was left unsolved was whether this new government should operate through its own coercion and that of its own agents, or through the sovereign states. It seemed evident that the central government needed to be sovereign within its limited sphere, but it was also clear that the states intended to be sovereign within their spheres. The incidents of the Convention turned again and again upon a search for this balance. A weak central government, a Confederacy with equal sovereign states, had been found faulty by experience dating from 1777. The Annapolis Convention had recommended that a general convention be called, "to take into consideration the situation of the United States, to devise such further provisions as shall appear to them necessary to render the Constitution of the federal government adequate to the exigencies of the Union." Thereupon the Congress invited the states to send delegates to a convention, "for the sole and express purpose of revising the Articles of Confederation." It is well known that the Convention of 1787 went beyond the limits of this invitation.

With the assembly of the Constitutional Convention on May 25, 1787 in Philadelphia, division appeared among the delegates. Differences developed between the large and the small states, the Tidewater section and the Piedmont section, the states-rights supporters and the strong central government advocates, and finally, the slaveholding and the non-slaveholding representatives. When the question of representation and the apportionment among the states arose, slaves had to be considered. When the rendition of fugitives was discussed, fugitive slaves had to be considered. When direct taxation was under discussion, the question of slaves as property or persons was presented for discussion. When commerce was in debate, the slave trade could not be avoided.

A motion was made on July 11, for the consideration of Negroes and whites as equals in the apportionment of representatives. It was interesting to note that Butler of South Carolina supported this motion. He would count Negroes in representation but the state could still prohibit Negroes from voting for these representatives. Reply was given to this view by Gouverneur Morris of Pennsylvania when he asked, "Upon what principle is it that slaves shall be computed in the representation? Are they men? Then make them citizens and let them vote. Are they property? Why, then, is no other property included?" Patterson of New Jersey said that he regarded slaves as property and that he did not see why they should be considered for purposes of representation. Wilson of Pennsylvania said that he did not understand why other property should not be admitted into computation for taxation if slaves were to be admitted. A compromise on this issue resulted in which it was agreed that three-fifths of the slaves would be counted in apportioning representation and taxes.[1]

This brought up the question of whether slaves were property or persons. If they were persons, then why should they be considered on the three-fifth basis. If they were property, then they should not have been considered at all. As Wilson of Pennsylvania asked, "Are they (Negroes) admitted as citizens? Then, why are they not admitted on an equality with white citizens? Are they admitted as property? Then, why is not other property admitted into the computation?" James Madison in dis-

[1] Max Farrand, (Ed.), *Records of the Federal Convention of 1787*, vol. 1, pp. 579, 580, 581, 587.

cussing the question said, "But we must deny the fact that slaves are considered merely as property, and in no respect whatever as persons. The true state of the case is, that they partake of both these qualities, being considered by our laws, in some respects as persons, and in other respects as property. The Federal Constitution, therefore, decides with great propriety on the case of our slaves, when it views them in the mixed character of persons and of property." The failure to settle this issue laid the foundation for considerable confusion concerning the Negro's right to vote, for if they were property manifestly, there was no adequate argument for the right.

Moreover, the citizenship of free Negroes among other free citizens remained unsettled. The section of the Constitution which gave the citizens of one state "all the privileges and immunities of citizens in the several states" was regarded by some statesmen, particularly in Northern states, as including free Negroes, but this view was not generally accepted. These views clashed often in the discussion of the fugitive slave question.

The language of the Articles of Confederation seemed clearer in this matter and could be interpreted to include free Negroes among "the free inhabitants of each state." The apparent duality of citizenship under the Constitution induced men to speak of themselves as citizens of their states and also of the United States. The lack of definition of citizenship led to confusion about the status of free Negroes as well as others. It was not until the Constitution was amended by its Fourteenth Amendment that this problem began to reach a type of solution. In the meantime, the Constitution, through its sanction of slavery, the rendition of fugitive slaves, the grant of increased representative power to slaveholders and the denial of the prohibition of the slave trade for twenty years, had given little hope to free Negro inhabitants and citizens for an improved status, even in the light of the liberty for which the framers of the Constitution had based their revolution against tyranny.

The suffrage right was not given specific mention in the Constitution. The implication seems rather direct that this right was a function within the province of the states. Representatives were to be elected every second year by the "Electors" in each state who were to have "the qualifications requisite for Electors of the most numerous branch of the State Legislature." The qualified voters of the states were to participate in these elections. This idea was recognized when Ellsworth of Connecticut in opposing the limitation of the suffrage to freeholders stated that, "The right of suffrage was a tender point, and strongly guarded by most of the State Constitutions. The people will not readily subscribe to the Natl. Constitution if it should subject them to be disfranchised."[2] Nevertheless, the old ruling class was kept in control in most of the states, for freehold qualifications were required in four states and substantial personal property in others. More than two generations would pass before the equality of political privileges would be secured even for white men, and a still longer period would be required for others to acquire these privileges. This delay, however, did not mean that Negroes were satisfied with the status assigned to them in spite of the philosophy of the Revolution and the adoption of the Constitution. Thousands of free Negroes regarded themselves as Americans, although proscribed, and this belief gave them capacity for expression as well as for survival.

According to the first census of 1790, there were 757,181 Negroes in the United States. The number of slaves was 697,624. The free Negroes numbered 59,557 or 7.9 per cent of the total number. These persons were concentrated in some centers of population where they found no racial limitations upon their vote. In New York City, there were

[2] U. S. Library of Congress, *Documents Illustrative of the Formation of the Union of the American States*, Washington, 1927, p. 487.

1,078 in a total population of 32,305; in Philadelphia, there were 1,420 in a total population of 28,522; and in Boston, there were 761 in a total population of 18,038. The Negro population increased between 1790 and 1800. The free Negroes increased from 59,557 in 1790 to 108,435 in 1800. The slaves increased from 697,624 in 1790 to 893,602 in 1800.

The free Negroes were distributed in the 1790 census as follows: In the New England states, there were 13,059 and of these there were 5,369 in Massachusetts, 3,484 in Rhode Island, 2,771 in Connecticut, 630 in New Hampshire, 536 in Maine and 269 in Vermont; in the Middle states there were 13,975, and of these there were 6,531 in Pennsylvania, 4,682 in New York, 2,762 in New Jersey; in the Southern states, there were 12,866 in Virginia, 8,043 in Maryland, 5,041 in North Carolina, 3,899 in Delaware, 1,801 in South Carolina, 398 in Georgia, 361 in Tennessee, and 114 in Kentucky.[3]

The free Negro was known as "free," but in none of these states was he as free as the white man. He was, however, a part of the community. It was possible that there were those who exercised political rights but even in the free states the property and special qualifications were barriers to a general participation by free Negroes in the exercise of the suffrage. The records of popular voting in presidential elections were very indefinite until 1824, and they are equally uncertain about the voting of Negro citizens. In the first election of George Washington, most of the state legislatures appointed the presidential electors, and there were few direct votes for them and for the national executive office. It is clear that on both the national and the state levels there were limitations and prohibitions placed upon Negroes. It has been asserted that even in Connecticut, it was not expected that Negroes should vote any more than Indians, women or children in

[3] U. S. Bureau of the Census, *Negro Population, 1790-1915*, pp. 55, 77.

the freemen's meetings or the town meetings. As a rule they were taxed but they were excluded from most of the rights of citizenship. They were restricted in their personal movements and were not allowed to travel without passes. In most slave states they were subject to courts of special jurisdiction and were restricted in trials by jury and witnessing in the courts. They were free to own land and to work under limitations but they exercised few of the legal and political rights common to all of the white citizens. With limited citizenship privileges, they occupied a subordinate position between the whites and the slaves. They were between freedom and bondage.

Although most of the agricultural work on the plantations was performed by the slave population, free Negroes were employed by some planters for this type of labor. Some of these employers were opposed to the use of slave labor. In the western parts of Virginia and North Carolina, there were employers who preferred free labor of Negroes to slave labor. In the northern and middle state, it was not uncommon to see free Negroes at work in the fields. A small proportion of these were landowners and farmers who had come into possession of their lands either by bequest or purchase. There were free Negroes who were artisans. In the towns and cities, they were barbers, coopers, carpenters, cabinetmakers, wheelwrights, bricklayers, tanners, plasterers, painters, shoemakers, blacksmiths, millers, sawyers, wooddealers, draymen, hucksters, garden workers, and household workers. Some of the best mechanics were free Negroes and were rated as master workmen in both northern and southern cities. A few hired slaves and others owned slaves who worked for them as for others. Some were property owners and substantial citizens as a result of the savings from their wages and small businesses. They were workers in the iron foundries and in the factories as forgemen, firemen and helpers. Competition between the races for work on these levels was keen, and opposition developed among white workers to Negro workers. As early as 1721, a petition was presented to the assembly by Pennsylvania white workers stating that "the practice of the blacks being employed was a great disadvantage to them who had emigrated from Europe for the purpose of obtaining a livelihood." The state assembly declined to pass an act to this effect and expressed the opinion that such a principle was a dangerous one.[4]

A proportion of the free Negro people was without any settled employment. This condition was due to the attitude of white communities which declined to give Negroes equal employment opportunities and it was also due to the disinclination on the part of some to work unless it was necessary. Without opportunities to labor open to them, there were free Negroes who became vagabonds and loafers, just as there were similar types in the white population. Facing legal obstructions to their economic opportunities, there were free Negroes who were idle and vagrant, and who were burdens upon their communities. This group has been too often described by observers and occasional travelers, and the more substantial ones were either unseen or forgotten. A Hessian officer writing in 1777 saw these persons and stated, "Here, too, there are many families of free Negroes, who live in good houses, have property, and live just like the rest of the inhabitants."[5]

The appeals made by religious and philanthropic organizations and by individuals had encouraged not only the more humane treatment of some slaves but had led in other cases to their education as free men. In one of these actions by an abolition society, it was stated that the Negroes would be under prohibitions and penalties until a radical abolition of slavery had exploded "the general opinion that the colour of a man is evidence of his deprivation of the rights of man" and the hope was expressed that

[4] E. R. Turner, *The Negro in Pennsylvania*, p. 5.
[5] G. W. Williams, *History of the Negro Race in America*, vol. i, p. 343.

those who were emancipated "might participate in civil rights and privileges as rapidly as they were qualified by education."[6] On the contrary, there was also the prevalent opinion that it was impossible practically to have the full enjoyment of equal rights and liberties by Negroes and whites.[7] With the organization of churches by Richard Allen, James Varick and other Negro religious leaders, there was also undertaken as a parallel work the organization of day schools. The Society for the Propagation of the Gospel in Foreign Parts had begun educational work among Negroes in northern and southern communities. The advertisements of runaway slaves describe the attainments of some free Negroes. These advertisements show that the slaves and those who became free by their flight were not all an ignorant, vicious lot. They were described as speaking good English and some had acquired a knowledge of French, Spanish, and Dutch. Others were described as artful and skillful and were individuals of merit in the American population of this day. Nevertheless, these people in spite of their abilities and attainments were denied the ballot in most places, although in other places they were granted this opportunity.

When the first Congress met under the new Constitution and began its work, memorials and petitions for the abolition of the slave trade and slavery were presented. The general attitude of Congress as expressed through its committees was that Congress could tax the slaves imported, regulate domestic slave traffic, forbid the traffic to foreign nations but that the slave trade could not be abolished until 1808. This attitude continued in Congress for many years. The first memorial to Congress on this subject was presented in 1790 by Benjamin Franklin, president of the Abolition Society. Basing its appeal upon the preamble to the Constitution, the memorialists declared that

[6] American Convention for Promoting the Abolition of Slavery, *Minutes of Proceedings*, 1794, pp. 15-16; 1795, pp. 18, 21; 1796, p. 11.

[7] Hopkins, *Works*, vol. ii, pp. 610-611.

powers were vested in Congress for promoting the welfare and securing the blessings of liberty to the people of the United States. It was stated that these blessings ought to be administered "without distinction of color, to all descriptions of people, so they indulge themselves in the pleasing expectation, that nothing which can be done for the relief of the unhappy objects of their care will be either omitted or delayed.[8] Another petition was presented by free Negro citizens themselves, who lived in Philadelphia. They requested a revision of the laws respecting the slave trade and the slaves who had fled to the free states. They also urged the adoption of measures for gradual emancipation.[9] This petition was referred to a committee and the report was that Congress had no authority to interfere in the internal affairs of the states. Other petitions directed attention to the rights of man as advocated in the American Revolution and the contrary practice in slavery and as they related themselves to free Negro citizens. Efforts were expended looking towards the abolition of the slave trade, the gradual emancipation of slaves and the rendition of fugitive slaves. Congress took no action with reference to the suffrage in its first sessions.

The first Naturalization Law of the United States, which was approved by Congress on March 26, 1790, bestowed citizenship as a matter of right and established a uniform law. It granted this right to "free white" aliens who had resided within the jurisdiction of the United States for two years. This period of residence was lengthened to five years in 1795. The Militia Law of 1792 also contained the word "white." The act to incorporate the District of Columbia of May 5, 1802, confined the franchise to "free white male inhabitants."[10] These acts and others indicate that Congressional trends were towards the restriction of

[8] *Annals of Congress*, I, Cong., 2 sess., p. 1197.
[9] *Ibid.*, 6 Cong., 1 sess., pp. 230-245, 2 sess., 1414-1415, 1474.
[10] *Annals of Congress*, vol. ii, pp. 2264-2265; vol. iii, p. 1392; xi, p. 1377; U. S. Statutes-at-Large, vol. i, pp. 103, 271; vol. ii, p. 196.

citizenship to free white males. This explains in part also why no action is to be found providing for Negro suffrage. Nevertheless, the paradox of citizenship interpretation was still apparent, for a resolution of the House of Representatives on December 21, 1803, stated that the Committee to enquire and report on the effectual protection of American seamen, resolved also "to enquire into the expediency of granting protection to such American seamen citizens of the United States, as are free persons of color.[11] While giving on the one hand some credence to the concept of citizenship for some, there was still the negation of suffrage participation.

This attitude continued in Congress into the Nineteenth Century. When the section of the Ordinance of 1787 was enacted for the Territory of Mississippi and the Territory of Indiana in 1800, the clause on suffrage without distinction was also applied to them. This right in the Mississippi Territory was confined to whites in 1808, and this was the first territorial act restricting the franchise to whites. The law incorporating the District of Columbia in 1802 restricted the vote to free white male inhabitants. The Illinois Act in 1809 was the last time that a territorial act with a suffrage clause was enacted prior to the Civil War, which did not prohibit Negroes from voting. The Federal Government would not act again until the Fourteenth and Fifteenth Amendments were adopted. In 1804, the act for the establishment of territorial government for Louisiana and Arkansas provided that only free white persons could serve on juries. When the Mississippi Territory was organized in 1808, only white males were permitted to vote for representatives to the general assembly. This was the first territorial act to contain this provision.[12]

[11] *Journal of the House of Representatives*, 1st Sess., 8th Cong., p. 224.
[12] Benjamin P. Poore, *Federal and State Constitutions, Colonial Charters and Other Organic Laws of the United States*, vol. i, pp. 435, 982, vol. ii, pp. 1051, 1052; Emil Olbrich, *The Development of Sentiment on Negro Suffrage to 1860, Bulletin of the University of Wisconsin*, No. 477, 1912.

New states were admitted to the Union, as a result of migrations westward, and the provisions of the Ordinance of 1787. Vermont in 1790, Kentucky in 1792, and Tennessee in 1796 made no provision in their constitutions concerning the exclusion of Negroes in the exercise of the ballot. With Maine, they were the only states which entered the Union, prior to the admission of Nebraska in 1867, without a provision against the vote by Negroes or of a color distinction in their suffrage provisions. Of these four states, Vermont and Maine were the only two which continued to have no suffrage discrimination. Negroes voted in Tennessee under the constitution but in 1834 the suffrage was confined to white males. A similar participation took place in North Carolina under the Constitution of 1776 which did not expressly prohibit Negroes from voting, but this right was taken away in 1835. However, Kentucky by the Constitution of 1799 confined this right to free white male citizens. Delaware confined the vote by its Constitution of 1792 to free white males.[13] An act of Maryland in 1783, reenacted in 1801, prohibited Negroes from voting, holding office and giving testimony against white persons. Later the right to vote was specifically restricted to free whites in this state by a constitutional amendment of 1801 and by acts of 1802 and 1810.[14] There is evidence, nevertheless, that a free Negro voted at an election of 1810 in Baltimore County.[15]

There were two states which ranked as important ones in the matter of Negro suffrage, New York and Pennsylvania. The state of New York with its large free Negro population had early experiences with Negro voters. Un-

---

[13] Olbrich, pp. 10, 21; Poore, vol. i, pp. 651, 654, 658, 670.

[14] J. T. Scharf, *History of Maryland*, vol. ii, p. 611.

[15] J. R. Brackett, *The Negro in Maryland*, p. 186-187. It is reported that this voter was a cousin of Benjamin Banneker; John H. Latrobe, ''Memoirs of Benjamin Banneker,'' *Maryland Historical Society Publications*, 1845, p. 6.

der the laws of this state, free Negroes could become voters if they owned a freehold of twenty pounds value or if they rented a tenement of the annual fee of forty shillings. When in 1799, an act was passed for the gradual abolition of slavery, freeing males at the age of twenty-eight and females at twenty-five, the free Negro voters increased in number and in activity. Negro freeholders exercised their suffrage rights on an equal footing with white citizens. They were reported as allying themselves with the Federalists. It will be recalled that they were workers in the homes of the more wealthy Federalists and their attitudes were more liberal towards the Negro population in both New York City and in up-state New York.[16] The Federalists had been in control of the legislature and the freedom granted to the slaves in the enactment of emancipation found them not ungrateful for the boon. The Democratic-Republicans seeing this relationship endeavored to break it by opposing and restricting the exercise of the ballot by Negroes. This action was motivated further by the election victories which were gained by Federalists. In the election of 1800, it was extravagantly said that "the political character of the national government was changed by the vote of a single Negro ward in the city of New York."[17] The Democratic-Republicans ridiculed this alliance with a campaign song, "Federalists with Blacks Unite." Wherever possible they rejected the Negro voters when they could not present certificate of freedom.[18]

One Negro orator in 1809, after describing the value of the suffrage to Negroes, said that there devolved upon them "the indispensable duty of bestowing our votes on those, and on those only, whose talents and whose political,

---

[16] Dixon Ryan Fox, "The Negro Vote in Old New York;" *Political Science Quarterly*, vol. xxxii, pp. 252-256.

[17] *Ibid.*, p. 256.

[18] *New York Spectator*, April 29, 1809.

moral and religious principles will most effectively promote the best interest of America." He urged the Negro voters to unite with their "Federalist friends."[19] Another expression of the attitude of Negro voters of this state was made at a General Meeting of the Electors of Colour. A resolution was adopted declaring that they would be protected to prevent them from voting. They stated that they would vote the Federal-Republican ticket.[20] The Negroes in large numbers continued to respond to such appeals and declared their support of "the Old Party," as it was called.

The opposition to the Negro voters gathered strength and in 1811, an act "to prevent frauds at election" was passed. Section III of this act was, "that whenever any black person or person of color shall present himself to vote at any election in this state, he shall produce to the inspectors or persons conducting such election a certificate of his freedom under the hand and seal of one of the clerks of the counties of this state, or under the hand of a clerk of any town within this state."[21] The act was finally passed after considerable debate.

The Council of Revision sent to the Senate and assembly several objections to the bill. These were summarized as, (1) the bill was "dangerous in precedent and against the public good;" (2) the description of a person of color was too vague; (3) many Negroes were born free and would find it difficult to secure freedom certificates; (4) the right to vote was subjected to the pleasure of others who in many cases would be interested in withholding the vote; (5) many Negroes lived and were far removed from the place of their birth or manumission; (6) provisions necessary to qualify for the vote were impossible to secure before the

---

[19] Joseph Sidney, *An Oration, Commemorative of the Abolition of the Slave Trade in the United States, Delivered before the Wilberforce Philanthropic Association*, New York, 1809, p. 9.

[20] *A Broadside, A Meeting in Mechanics Hall*, New York, April 24, 1809.

[21] *Journal of the Senate of New York*, 1811, p. 143.

election date of April 30, 1811; (7) there was no justification for the passing of an act which disfranchised a portion of the electors, even for a year; (8) there was no precedent for such a radical change in the election laws so close to an election.[22]

In spite of these objections, the Senate passed the act on April 8. The assembly agreed to the same, and it was enacted into law on April 9, 1811. This legislature now controlled by Democratic-Republican votes thus passed the act requiring proof of freedom by Negro voters.[23] It was required that the certificate should be obtained by going before one of the Judges of the Supreme Court or County Court or before the Mayor or Recorder of a city, where the proof of freedom could be obtained in writing. The services of a lawyer who had to be paid were needed for this purpose. Twenty-five cents was to be paid by the Negro applicant to the court, and the Judge giving the certificate was to be paid a shilling. Another shilling was to be paid to the County Clerk for filing the certificate in his office and an additional payment judged by the Clerk, was to be made to him for the certificate to be used by the voter. Then, too, the Negro voter would take an oath that he was the person whose name was listed in the certificate. Having fulfilled these conditions, the Negro was permitted to cast his vote. Many Negroes were discouraged from voting by these apparent obstacles.

In 1813 the Council of Revision, when an effort was made to revise and extend the act, changed its earlier decision and declared the act was a proper one and "should become a law of this State."[24] Again in 1815, this act to regulate elections was read in the Senate and an amendment was passed making void all certificates of freedom secured under the Act of 1813. Those who were in New

---

[22] *Journal of the Assembly of New York*, 1811, p. 360.
[23] *Ibid.*, pp. 394-395.
[24] *Ibid.*, pp. 404-406; *New York Evening Post*, April 16, 1811.

York City and county who had obtained their certificates prior to this act were not required to produce a new certificate, but they were required to register five days before the election and to deliver their affidavits to the Mayor for inspection. These provisions seemed on the one hand to make easier the opportunity to vote but the opposite result developed and many Negroes gave up the right to vote because of the inconveniences required by the act.[25] A considerable number of Negroes were potential voters at this period. A census of the Negro electors of the state by counties on January 31, 1815, showed this situation. New York City and county had the largest number, 8,271; Queen's County was second with 2,321, and Duchess County was third with 1,409. There was a total of 26,294 free Negroes.[26] By 1820 the number of free Negroes had increased to 29,278 in a white population electorate of 1,332,744.[27]

This limitation of the Negro vote was carried further by the Constitutional Convention of 1821. The debates on Negro suffrage were long and intense. Some delegates voiced the opinion that equal suffrage should be open to all citizens. Others used various arguments for additional restrictions. One delegate stated that he knew "that a few hundred Negroes in the city of New York virtually gave law to the state and in a period of war and danger paralyzed the arm of government," and he declared that the Negroes were "an organized and disciplined corps that was powerful enough to defeat necessary measures." Another delegate asserted that five hundred Negroes had applied for the vote in the election of 1820 but that only one hundred and sixty-three had been allowed to vote. Various arguments based upon the Negro as an inferior were used to aid these views.[28]

[25] *Journal of the Assembly of the State of New York*, 1813, p. 479.
[26] *New York Spectator*, April 19, 1815.
[27] *Journal of the Senate of the State of New York*, 1815, p. 158.
[28] *New York Spectator*, April 19, 1822.

Negroes themselves were not silent. A memorial was received at the opening of the convention from the Negro citizens of New York City headed by Thomas Sipkins. The memorial requested that a provision be inserted in the Constitution to prevent the legislature from passing laws interfering with their political rights. The convention laid the memorial on the table.[29]

This point of view was advocated by men like Peter A. Jay, who said that some thirty thousand Negro voters had their rights at stake and as they constituted only one-fortieth of the total vote, there were no such dangers of control as others had pointed out. Jay asked, "Why are they, who were born as free as ourselves, natives of the same country, and deriving from nature and our political institutions the same rights and privileges which we have, now to be deprived of all these rights and doomed to remain forever aliens among us?" Chancellor Kent said that the word "white" was too indefinite for inclusion in the act. Said he, "The Hindoo and the Chinese are yellow—the Indian red! Shall these be excluded should they come to reside among us?" In reply to the charge that the rich would dominate the Negro vote, Jay said that the failure of the Negroes to act independently would be no greater than that of "many thousands of white fawning, cringing sycophants." Jay, Kent, Radcliffe, Clarke and others opposed the restriction of the suffrage to whites. Van Vechten said that Negroes were working beside whites and serving with them in the militia, and he asked, "How can distinctions justify us in taking from them any of the common rights which every other free citizen enjoys." The amendment to restrict the vote to whites was lost. The provision was adopted on October 8, 1821, which placed the qualification for whites at the forty pound freehold, but Negroes

---

[29] *A Report of the Debates and Proceedings of the Convention of the State of New York, held August 28, 1821*, pp. 92, 100, 104.

were required to have a two hundred and fifty dollar freehold. Negroes were also required to live in the state for three years and to have paid taxes. White men could vote after one year's residence and the payment of taxes or the rendering of highway or military service. Thus New York adopted an additional restriction upon the privilege which Negro citizens had exercised of voting in this state on the same basis as whites.

The state of Pennsylvania was the scene of uncertainty about the status of the Negro's political activity. It was asserted that the Negro could hold property and be taxed but was an alien in respect to the exercise of the suffrage.[30] The Constitution of 1790 had given the suffrage to "every freeman of the age of twenty-one years, and during the debates the word, "white" before this phrase was stricken out by motion of Albert Gallatin.[31] There is evidence that Negroes voted after this period. In 1796, the Senate of Pennsylvania was presented a petition from Huntington County seeking action which would require masters of Negro servants to educate them for it was found that "many were poorly fitted to exercise citizenship to which they had been admitted."[32] Again in 1807, when a bill was under debate for the regulation of Negroes, a motion was made to exclude from regulation the Negroes who were "legal voters."[33] The Negro voters in Pennsylvania were small in number and seem to have varied from district to district. As late as 1826, Governor Schulze raised the question, "Is the term freeman so construed in one district as totally to exclude, and in another freely to admit persons of colour to exercise the right of suffrage?"[34] This indefinite condi-

[30] John F. Denny, *An Inquiry into the Political Grade of the Free Coloured Population, under the Constitution of the United States and the Constitution of Pennsylvania*, pp. 21-23.
[31] *Proceedings and Debates of the Convention*, 1790, vol. i, p. 164; *Constitution of 1790*, Art. iii, sect. i.
[32] *Journal of the Senate*, 1795-1796, p. 43.
[33] *Journal of the Senate*, 1806-1807, pp. 296, 297.
[34] E. R. Turner, *The Negro in Pennsylvania*, p. 184.

tion continued for another decade.

Among other states facing this issue was the state of Ohio which adopted its constitution in 1802. It is stated that Negroes voted for delegates to the convention which framed this constitution.[35] Opposition to the grant of the ballot to Negroes developed in the convention of 1850 and a proposal to disfranchise them was carried by a vote of 66 to 12.[36] In 1842, Justice Read of the Supreme Court of Ohio stated in the case of Thacker v. Hawk that it was known to old inhabitants that "No Negro or person of any degree of black blood, was ever permitted to vote during the territorial period." The New Jersey Constitution of 1776 declared that all inhabitants of this colony of full age who were worth fifty pounds proclamation money and are residents were entitled to the ballot. No restrictions were given as to race or sex. Under the interpretations of this act, women as well as men and Negroes were among the voters. On February 22, 1807, an act was passed to the effect that, "Whereas doubts have been raised and great diversities in practice obtained throughout the state in regard to the admission of aliens, females and persons of color, or Negroes to vote in elections, as also in regard to the mode of ascertaining the qualifications of voters in respect to estate —and whereas, it is highly necessary to the safety, quiet, good order and dignity of the state, to clear up the said doubts by an act of the representatives of the people, declaratory of the true sense and meaning of the Constitution, and to ensure its just execution in these particulars, according to the intent of the framers thereof," it was stated that no one should vote "unless such person be a free, white male citizen." This action was reaffirmed in 1820.[37]

[35] W. H. Smith, *A Political History of Slavery*, vol. i, p. 13.
[36] Carl Wittke, ed., *The History of the State of Ohio*, vol. iv, p. 133.
[37] Poore, vol. ii, p. 1315; J. B. McMaster, *History of the People of the United States*, vol. iii, p. 147.

Connecticut was the only New England state to forbid suffrage to Negroes. This was accomplished when the Convention of 1818 adopted an article granting the privilege of voting to white male citizens only, but it was also provided that those who had been previously admitted as "freemen" should also be electors. While there is some doubt that Negroes were among this latter group, opinions vary that Negroes voted prior to this period. A proposal to permit Negroes to vote was disallowed in 1847.[38]

These discussions within the state legislature were paralleled by a single period of discussion in the Congress of the United States during the debates leading to the Missouri Compromise. When the amendment to the Missouri Bill was presented on February 28, 1820, John Randolph moved that the word "white" be inserted in reference to suffrage. The proposal to strike out the word failed to pass; when the Constitution of Missouri was presented to Congress, it was finally agreed that the state would be admitted to the Union, if it would provide that "it never would exclude any citizen of another state from the privileges and immunities to which he was entitled under the Constitution of the United States." This phrase would have to be interpreted and applied, but it was a sufficient compromise to defer the inevitable clash of the sections.

A famous controversy in the history of Negro suffrage took place in Pennsylvania in 1837-1838. Negro citizens of Philadelphia manifested unusual courage and initiative in protest at this period. A decision of the State Supreme Court declared that the Negro was not a freeman, and accordingly was not entitled to vote. In 1837, a candidate for office in Bucks County, who was defeated, claimed his opponent's seat because Negroes had been permitted to vote for him and that such an action was contrary to law. There

[38] B. C. Steiner, *History of Slavery in Connecticut*, pp. 34-35.

were wealthy Negroes in Bucks County. One of them was reputed to be worth one hundred thousand dollars. The Democrats of this county met in convention and decided that they would petition the legislature to oppose the voting of Negroes, that they would use the courts to prevent this activity by Negroes and that they would amend the constitution to this effect. In December the court decided that the election was legal and that the right of the Negro to vote in the state depended upon the interpretation of the constitution in its use of the word freeman. The interpretation turned upon whether the Negro was a free man, in the sense of being free from slavery or a free man in accordance with the common law. The first state constitution of 1776 had provided that elections should be held by the participation of "every freeman," but since no provision was made for free Negroes, it was assumed by many that their status was unchanged. A state constitutional convention assembled in 1837 and discussed the question of Negro suffrage and decided on January 27, 1838, by a vote of 77-45 that the suffrage should be limited to whites. The constitution with this provision was ratified in October.[39] It was during this period that an assembly of Negro citizens was held in the Presbyterian Church on Seventh Street below Shippen on March 14, 1838. John H. Burr presided. The vice-presidents were Thomas Butler and Stephen H. Gloucester. James Forten, Jr., and James Cornish were secretaries. The report of a committee which had been appointed to prepare a statement for the consideration of the meeting was read. The committee consisted of Robert Purvis, James Cornish, J. C. Bowers, Robert B. Forten, Jr., J. G. Bias, James Needham and John P. Burr. The report was adopted unanimously by the assembled audience. It is known as the *Appeal of Forty Thousand Citizens, Threatened with Disfranchisement, to the*

[39] E. R. Turner, *The Negro in Pennsylvania*, pp. 171, 173; William Yates, *Rights of Colored Men to Suffrage, Citizenship and Trial by Jury*, p. 11.

People of Pennsylvania.[40] The appeal expressed grateful appreciation to their defenders in the convention who had advocated their rights as citizens and had so strenuously objected to the insertion of the word "white." Thanks were also expressed to their "abolition friends for their active though unavailing exertions to prevent the unrighteous act."

Turning directly to the issue, the document made a direct appeal to the citizens of Pennsylvania from the decision of the convention which had taken from them "a right peaceably enjoyed during forty-seven years under the constitution of this commonwealth." The appeal stated, "We honor Pennsylvania and her noble institution too much to part with our birthright, as her free citizens, without a struggle. To all her citizens the right of suffrage is valuable in proportion as she is free; but surely there is none who can so ill afford to spare it as ourselves." They said that taxation and representation were parallel rights and taking away the right to vote was "a step towards making it a despotism to all." They recalled the history of the suffrage right, when on the vote of Albert Gallatin the restrictive word "white" was stricken out, in order that Negro citizens might be included. They referred to the property held by them and that they had paid $3,252.83 for taxes and $166,963.50 for house, water and ground rent. Their churches and schools as well as their homes were testimonies of their well-being. It was said that all whites who sell to Negroes the necessities or luxuries of life made profits from these transaction. They asked for the vote only for the "industrious, peaceable and useful part of the colored people," and they would have it "only as the reward of industry and worth." The momentous question was asked, "Is Pennsylvania, which abolished slavery in 1780 and enfranchised her tax-paying colored citizens in 1790,

[40] Robert Purvis, *Appeal of Forty Thousand Citizens, Threatened with Disfranchisement, to the People of Pennsylvania*, Philadelphia, 1838.

now in 1838, to get upon her knees and repent of her humanity to gratify those who desecrate the very name of American liberty, by holding our brethren as goods and chattels?"

This document was typical of the attitude of the liberal and courageous Negroes of the state of Pennsylvania. Although the convention had shut the door to the vote in their faces, they would protest and appeal to their fellow-citizens in the spirit of the American tradition. A long line of petitions, memorials and protests continued to pour into the state conventions from Negro citizens. They took this aggressive action, although it was known to many Negroes that their suffrage right was opposed by large numbers. *The Pennsylvania* stated, "We are at least tolerably sure that nine-tenths of the people of Pennsylvania are opposed to granting equal rights to the Negro race—such, we are positive is the case with that proportion of the people of the city and county of Philadelphia."[41]

There were in 1840 in Pennsylvania, 47,854 free Negroes and 64 slaves in a total population of 1,724,033, but the Negroes were not permitted to be citizen-voters after 1838. As William Wells Brown said in 1854, "Pennsylvania deprives the black man of the elective franchise, and so does New York except with a property qualification. In most of the Northern states, he is looked upon as something to be knocked and kicked about as they see fit."[42]

In 1841, there was assembled a state convention of Negroes to take under consideration the restrictions placed upon their citizenship privileges. They passed resolutions condemning those who were the leaders in this action. These conventions continued to meet at various periods prior to the Civil War. The Negro citizens formed in 1848

[41] *The Pennsylvanian*, January 20, 1838.
[42] *The Liberator*, November 10, 1854, vol. xxiv, No. 45. Speech of William Wells Brown at the 17th Anniversary of the Pennsylvania Anti-Slavery Society.

the "Citizens' Union of the Commonwealth of Pennsylvania." The objective of this organization was the formation of a permanent organization to wage a fight for full citizenship for the Negro inhabitants of the state.[43]

A similar development of attitude took place in such states as Ohio and Connecticut as well as Pennsylvania. In 1854, a state convention of which John M. Langston was chairman presented a memorial to the Ohio legislature declaring Negroes had the right to vote and that, "it is unjust, anti-democratic, impolite and ungenerous to withhold from us the right of suffrage." Langston had been elected an Ohio Township Clerk, and was the first elected Negro office holder in Ohio and in the United States.[44]

While such treatment was not general, or else there would have been a greater Negro rebellion, the facts show that between the period of the formation of the Federal Constitution and 1865 during which state constitutions were also formulated the vote was restricted to whites in Kentucky, 1792 and 1799; Ohio in 1803 and 1850; New Jersey in 1807; Maryland in 1810; Louisiana in 1812; Indiana in 1816 and 1850; Mississippi in 1817; Illinois in 1818; Connecticut in 1818; Alabama in 1819; Missouri in 1821; North Carolina in 1835; Arkansas in 1836; Michigan in 1835 and 1850; Pennsylvania in 1838; Florida in 1845; Texas in 1845; Iowa in 1846; Wisconsin in 1848; California in 1850; Minnesota in 1858; Oregon in 1859; Kansas in 1861; West Virginia in 1863; and Nevada in 1864. There were five states in which Negroes could vote without restriction, Maine, New Hampshire, Vermont, Massachusetts, and Rhode Island, and one, New York, in which the privilege was limited by a property qualification of two hundred and fifty dollars. However, in several places within some of these states, such as, Ohio, Michigan, and Wisconsin, there were Negroes who voted and participated in party conven-

[43] Turner, *Ibid.*, p. 139.
[44] W. C. Nell, *Colored Patriots of the American Revolution*, pp. 336-341.

tions, as revealed by another study published in the JOURNAL OF NEGRO HISTORY in 1944.[45]

The fact that restrictive laws were adopted is evidence that the attitudes and mores of these communities were not strong enough to prevent Negro citizens from voting. Laws were necessary. Prejudice alone does not explain their cause. The fear of the power of the Negro vote and its alliance with the votes of others, and particularly the poor whites, was an important factor. After the Civil War and Reconstruction when constitutions were again remade, this desire to restrict the vote of Negroes was again made manifest. With the rise of the Populist Party, there was the fear that the Bourbon South would be overwhelmed by an alliance between the Negro and the poor white voters. The Bourbon leaders of the South saw in this relationship the menace to their own power.[46] The continuance of this belief mingled with a basic color prejudice, which has become a highly volatile emotion among some leaders, has led to the poll-tax, the White Primary, second-class citizenship and to the domination of Congress by Southern reactionaries elected by a restricted suffrage. These men now sit at the head of the major committees of Congress. The termination of the poll-tax and the White Primary mean the extension of the suffrage to Negroes and to whites, and change in the course of national as well as sectional politics.

This recital of historical facts concerning the period of constitution-making shows that neither Negroes nor the friends of democracy abandoned the battle against the restriction of their vote. With these Negro citizens living in slave America and endeavoring to be citizens, struggling to present petitions and appeals against powerful overlords,

---

[45] Charles H. Wesley, "The Participation of Negroes in Anti-Slavery Political Parties." *The Journal of Negro History*, January, 1944, vol. xxix, No. 1, pp. 32-74.

[46] John D. Hicks, *The Populist Revolt*, pp. 410-11.

what should be the position and the attitude of Negro citizens in 1947? It is important for those of us who have the opportunity, to act like citizens and to make our ballots count. We should awaken those who do not vote from their lethargy with respect to citizenship. We may not know the value of this right until it is taken from us, or until it is shackled by false propaganda and the direction of the dictatorships of the modern world. The Negro citizen voter has an opportunity to make definite contributions to American political life, for he can be influential as never before in the congressional elections of 1946 and the presidential election of 1948. The Negro vote is most important if not dominant and nearly decisive in New York, New Jersey, Ohio, Pennsylvania, Illinois, Indiana, and Michigan, precisely in those areas in which the suffrage struggles took place during the period of constitution-making. Estimates of the possible Negro vote this year, as a result of the half victories over the poll tax, the White Primary, and the interest of Negro and liberal organizations, vary from 600,-000 to a million even in the South. It is clear that in the North we can break the alliance between some Northern Republicans and Southern Democrats by showing to them the power of our ballot in all the areas where we are permitted to exercise this right. It is also clear that we can be courageous as are many Negroes and insist upon voting. It may well be that out of an evident balance of power in some states—if we are as fearless in freedom, as some of our ancestors were in oppression—there will come an era of constitutional amendment in which men and women shall vote their citizen judgment "for a' that and a' that." Let us not fail in our modern duties, as they did not fail in their historic ones.

CHARLES H. WESLEY

Wilberforce University

PREFACE

Many times history serves as a mirror of the future. Past occurences are seemingly repeated by future generations. This theory seemingly has proven valid in the area of legal aid to the poor. This article is designed to take an in-depth look at a past series of events which remarkedly resemble events of today. It is hoped that the American people will not repeat in the future the tragic mistakes of the past.

Howard Law Journal
Editorial Staff

Getting Justice for the Freedman

HOWARD C. WESTWOOD[*]

WHEN a cannon's roar broke a tense silence at Fort Sumter a social revolution was set in train. But hardly anyone thought so. It

---

[*] Partner in the law firm of Covington and Burling, Washington, D. C.; law clerk to Mr. Justice Harlan F. Stone, Supreme Court of the United States, 1933-1934; LL.B. Columbia University Law School 1933.

Acknowledgement: The author is deeply indebted to Miss Blossom Athey, the extraordinary Miss Legal Aid of the author's law firm, for the research of the records of the Bureau of Refugees, Freedmen and Abandoned Lands, commonly referred to as the Freedmen's Bureau, at the National Archives. He is indebted also to Mr. Fred Cooke, of the Howard Law School class of 1972, and to Mr. Courtenay Ellis, of the author's law firm, for their assistance to Miss Athey. With the kind guidance of Mrs. Elaine Everly of the Archives staff, those three, amidst their other regular duties, generously have devoted many hours to tedious examination, analysis, and checking of hundreds of documents, written in handscript and not a few barely legible, for the evidence, indeed the hints, of an activity never before researched. In the time available the research could not be complete; but it has been more than ordinarily sophisticated and has clearly established the contours of a significant pre-historic legal aid program. We have deposited with the office of the Howard Law Journal a memorandum identifying the particular Bureau files that have been examined.

Citations: All Freedmen's Bureau material at the Archives is filed in Record Group 105. Our footnotes cite it merely as BRFAL. Certain of the Bureau files

seemed, on one side, simply a fight for the independence of the homeland—and, on the other, a struggle to maintain the Union in status quo.

Everyone realized, to be sure, that slavery had had a good deal to do with the coming of conflict. There were some, even, who could foresee that a Union triumph would spell slavery's eventual doom. But few had any idea that slavery would be ended abruptly, and no one was trying to think through the problem of dealing with slavery's end. In the North such thought as there was consisted of little more than the fond idea of inducing the blacks to agree to colonizing in a foreign land.[1] In the South such thought as there was consisted of hardly more than the hysterical fixation, widely suf-

---

are on microfilm. Since our footnotes frequently cite material from "Records Issued by Commissioner, BRFAL, Microcopy 742," that designation is omitted in such citation, though Roll and Frame numbers are cited. Because of their frequent citation, our footnotes refer to certain publications only by author and page number. They are:

Abbott, The Freedmen's Bureau in South Carolina
(U. of N.C. Press, 1967)

Bentley, A History of the Freedmen's Bureau
(U. of Penna. Press, 1955)

Eaton, Grant, Lincoln and the Freedmen (Negro
Universities Press, 1969 repub. of 1907 pub.)

Green, Washington: Village and Capital, 1800-1878
(Princeton U. Press, 1962)

II Oliver Otis Howard, Autobiography (Baker &
Taylor Co., 1907)

Low, The Freedmen's Bureau and Civil Rights in Maryland,
XXXVII The Journal of Negro History 221 (1952)

Peirce, The Freedmen's Bureau (St. U. of Iowa Studies
in Sociology, Economics, Politics and History,
Vol. III, No. 1, 1904)

VI Richardson, Messages and Papers of the Presidents
(Gov't Print. Office, 1897)

Robinson, Justice in Grey (Harvard U. Press, 1941)

White, The Freedmen's Bureau in Louisiana (La. St. U.
Press, 1970)

Whyte, The Uncivil War (Twayne Publishers, 1958)

[1] Lincoln, in his first annual message to Congress, December 3, 1861, recommended provision for foreign colonizing of the blacks. Richardson, p. 54. Even in his second annual message, December 1, 1862—two months after his preliminary Emancipation Proclamation—he continued advocacy of such colonizing, noting with regret that blacks "contemplating colonization" did not seem willing to go to the only foreign countries where they could be sure of being received as citizens, Liberia and Haiti. *Id.*, p. 128. And see Peirce, p. 11.

fered at least since the Nat Turner episode, that an end of slavery would mean wholesale slaughter of gentle whites by bestial blacks. Virtually no one, North or South, had begun seriously and realistically to consider how a free society could or should absorb millions of bondsmen were the peculiar institution to disappear.

At first, North and South were bemused with the illusion that things would be brought swiftly to conclusion, each dreaming of triumph and a return to settled ways. Bull Run and its aftermath shattered the illusion. For the North the road to Richmond suddenly appeared long, and in the next spring Old Jack's thrusts in the Valley of the Shenandoah stretched it longer still. For the South the flush of battle victory receded as grim fact emerged: the North did not fold; Southern chivalry did not march into the old Capital. Rather, in the winter following, on western rivers the fatal ineptness of Confederate military leadership was starkly revealed; the dreary story of Southern failure, save only in Virginia, was begun. But still neither North nor South faced up to what was really in prospect: not a mere military decision but a vast social upheaval.

Yet there were portents even very early in the war. Occasional steps by Northern commanders, in the spirit of the Fugitive Slave Law, to return runaway slaves to their owners were too anachronistic to become the fashion. As early as May 1861 Ben Butler, politician in uniform, commanding the isolated Union post at Fortress Monroe, and confronted with a demand for the return of three slaves runaway from work on Confederate fortifications, refused the demand on the ground that the blacks were "contraband of war." Butler's action found favor in high quarters. A politician's neat euphemism was applied more and more broadly. By fits and starts during the next couple of years the North came to face reality.[2]

The reality grew large as the war went on. The reality was thousands, ultimately hundreds of thousands, of foot-loose, homeless, helpless blacks. Wherever the Northern armies went, especially in the West, those blacks appeared, clinging to the camps and columns. Nor was it long before the loping Western armies penetrated

---

[2] In Bentley, pp. 1-6, there is a good summary account of General Butler's action and its spreading consequences. See also Howard, pp. 163-193; Peirce, pp. 5-10.

the Deep South, the very heartland of slavery, to strike finally from Atlanta to the Eastern Sea. Crowding upon them came the blacks, groping for freedom.

Never in human history had there been, nor has there been since, a social upheaval so abrupt and extensive. Most of those blacks had been stabled like domestic animals on plantations and farms. The law had forbade their schooling. Their congregating had been rigidly regulated. Even their visiting of neighbors had been severely restricted. But suddenly, as the bluecoats ranged far, multitudes of blacks were freed of the old bans.

The North was forced to think about what to do with them. Military necessity alone demanded thought. In the first place the blacks got in the way of the armies; to smooth operations some disposition of these human impedimenta had to be made. In the second place the conditions of life for fleeing slaves could not be allowed to be so revolting that flight would be discouraged; it was the very premise of the Emancipation Proclamation that slaves fugitive weakened the South's military power.[3] Even had no one in the North been moved by pure humanity, the Union government would have had to make provision for the Negroes. Nor were humanitarians silent; they became increasingly vocal as the number of refugee blacks multiplied. Moreover there was fear in the North that it would be deluged with blacks if they were not decently provided for in the South. Finally some Northern speculators saw opportunity to exploit captured plantations if measures could be taken to put the blacks to work in an orderly way.

So the North acted.

One thing done by 1863, after great hesitation, was of special significance. Blacks were taken into the army, by the war's end nearly 200,000 of them.[4] Curiously there had been no prejudice against blacks' serving in the navy; from earliest days there had been black sailors. But the color line had long been rigid in the army.[5] Now, however, with the increasing drain on the North's manpower, with many thousands of strong-bodied refugee slaves, and with

---

[3] Eaton, pp. 172-173.
[4] Bentley, pp. 18-20; Eaton, pp. 51-58; McPherson, The Negro's Civil War (Vintage Books, 1965), p. 237.
[5] McPherson, *op. cit.*, n.4, p. 158.

clamor by free Negroes in the North to take part in a conflict against the Slave Power, prejudice was overcome and blacks were mustered in. While at first they were used mainly to take over non-combat duties, releasing whites to fight, increasingly they were allowed to fight also and acquitted themselves well. By doing so they staked out a claim to be treated as full citizens in future years.[6]

But this measure hardly solved the problem. For the mass of blacks there was no coherent program. The need was met by improvisation. In various and sometimes conflicting ways the army and the Treasury Department put blacks to work. Individual military commanders devised their own local measures, and to some extent the army as a whole attacked the problem. So did the Treasury, involved because it had been given control over abandoned lands in the rebel States in 1863.[7] The army likewise shouldered the burden of providing direct relief—food and shelter and care for the sick—and even, to some extent, schooling.[8]

These efforts, however, were palliatives, based solely on wartime authority. Some in the army and in the Treasury were looking ahead to post-war years,[9] but they could build no foundation for the blacks' long future. That would have to be done, were it to be done at all, by Congress.

Congress worried, fussed, debated. But it was not until 1864 that it concentrated on a concrete measure, egged on by a combination of speculators and humanitarians. Even then it could not reach decision.[10] It was not until March 3, 1865, at the very close of the last Congress before the war's end, that it acted. Then it created the Freedmen's Bureau in the War Department.[11] General Oliver Otis Howard was made its head, with the title of Commissioner.

The original legislation was very vague, literally not much more than a mandate that the Bureau help freedmen.[12]

---

[6] McPherson, *op. cit.*, n.4, pp. 161-172, 183-192, 205-239.
[7] Bentley, p. 26; Peirce, p. 22; Eaton, p. 143.
[8] Bentley, pp. 6-29, 43-46; Peirce, pp. 11-25; Eaton, *passim*.
[9] Eaton, p. 34.
[10] Howard, pp. 199-200; Bentley, pp. 36-43; Peirce, pp. 34-40; Eaton, pp. 221-224.
[11] Howard, pp. 200-205; Bentley, pp. 46-49; Peirce, pp. 41-45; Eaton, pp. 224-228.
[12] 13 Stat. 507-509 (1865).

The statute provided that the Bureau would last only for a year beyond the end of the war.[13] In February 1866 Congress sought to extend the Bureau's life and make its powers more specific; President Johnson vetoed the measure and he was sustained. In July Congress again acted and this time overrode the President's veto, extending the Bureau to mid-1868.[14] Ultimately it was continued until the end of 1868, with some very limited functions carried on for a little longer.[15]

During this short time the Bureau tried hard. At its peak its total manpower, including clerks, was only about 900 and they had to operate throughout the old slave territory.[16] Though thus thinly spread, they provided care for the destitute, helped establish schools and hospitals, acted as a vast employment agency and sought to as-

---

[13] President Johnson proclaimed an end of the insurrection in Tennessee on June 13, 1865, and in the other Confederate States, except Texas, on April 2, 1866; for Texas the end was proclaimed on August 20, 1866. Robinson, p. 600, n.26.

[14] 14 Stat. 173-177; Bentley, pp. 121-135; Peirce, pp. 59-63, 66-68. For President Johnson's July veto message see Richardson, pp. 422-426. His February veto message states Johnson's position more fully. *Id.*, pp. 398-405. The full story of the February bill and its veto appears in McFeely, Yankee Stepfather (Yale U. Press, 1968), pp. 211-244. See also Howard, pp. 280-282.

[15] In June 1868 Congress adopted an act to continue the Bureau for one year beyond July 16, 1868, except that the "educational division" of the Bureau was to be continued thereafter in any State not making "suitable provision for the education of the children of freedmen . . ." This act became law on July 6 without the approval of the President. 15 Stat. 83-84. But within a few days Congress acted again, prompted by a rumor that the President intended to remove the head of the Bureau, General Howard, who was popular with Congressional Republicans. This time it adopted an act providing that General Howard should continue in office, but that he should wind up the Bureau on January 1, 1869, except that "the educational department of the said bureau and the collection and payment of moneys due the soldiers, sailors and marines, or their heirs, shall be continued as now provided by law until otherwise ordered by act of Congress." (The Bureau had been given the job of handling such payments in the case of blacks. *Infra,* n.50.) This enactment was vetoed on July 25. Richardson, p. 654. On the same day the veto was overridden. 15 Stat. 193-194; Howard, pp. 358-360; Bentley, pp. 201-202; Peirce, pp. 69-74. Legislation finally terminating the Bureau was contained in an appropriations act of June 10, 1872, providing for the Bureau's discontinuance on June 30, 1872. 17 Stat. 347, 366.

[16] There is some uncertainty as to the peak figure for the Bureau's personnel. Bentley, p. 136, states that, "By the end of 1868 the Bureau's personnel had increased to 901 men . . . this was the high point . . ." He cites the Washington Chronicle for April 7, 1874, "quoting Eliphalet Whittlesey." That paper, at p. 6, quotes testimony of General Whittlesey in current proceedings of a Court of Inquiry examining charges against General Howard growing out of his administration of the Bureau. (The story of that inquiry is recounted in Carpenter, Sword and Olive Branch (U. of Pitts. Press, 1964), pp. 220-235). General Whittlesey gives the Bureau personnel (including clerks) as 833 for 1866, 901 for 1868, 158 for 1869, and 87 for 1870. The 1868 figure of 901 appears also in General Howard's autobiography,

sure and to enforce fair employment contracts, tried to protect blacks from violence, did the little they could to aid their charges to acquire land, and cajoled, exhorted, and encouraged the former slaves to live responsible, moral lives according to the precepts of the white society.[17]

From the very outset of its work the Bureau recognized that its effort would come to naught unless the blacks could get equal justice. It was all very well for a black man to learn to read and write, to observe the marriage institution (largely unknown to slavery), to settle down to a steady job—but if white men could assault him and

---

where he quotes from his annual report of October 1869 that "one year ago" there were 901 Bureau personnel. Howard, p. 361. But it would seem likely that October 1868 would not have been quite the "high point" as Bentley says. For by then General Howard was reducing the personnel of the Bureau which, by the July 1868 amendment to the Bureau's Act, was to come to an end, save for limited functions, by January 1, 1869. Supra, n.15. But in view of the figures for 1866 referred to by General Whittlesey it is probable that, if 901 were not the "high point," it was reasonably near the high. However in General Howard's autobiography there is a statement that soon after he had set up his organization in 1865 "the whole Bureau force operating amounted to upward of 2,000 officers, agents, and other employees." Howard, p. 217. This statement (of course made in 1907 and without supporting citation) is puzzling. For Bentley says, also at his p. 136, that "Towards the end of 1865 there were 799 men in the organization . . ." He cites a speech by Representative Ritter of Kentucky opposing the originally proposed 1866 extension of the Bureau. Supra, n.14. In that speech, on February 3, 1866, the Congressman argued strongly against extension of the Bureau on the ground that it would be an expensive bureaucracy. Concluding his argument on this point he stated that in a recent report to Congress General Howard had advised that the Bureau had a total force of 799. Cong. Globe, 39 Cong., 1st Sess., p. 634. Certainly the Congressman would not have wanted to understate the number on the Bureau staff. The likelihood is that General Howard's statement in his 1907 autobiography that there had been "upward of 2,000" is a simple failure of memory. It is possible, of course, that at any given time there were more people working on affairs of the Bureau than were on the Bureau's own personnel roll. In General Whittlesey's testimony at the Court of Inquiry, as reported in the Washington Chronicle, he says that his figures do not include army staff officers and details who might have been assigned work on behalf of the Bureau "as the necessity seemed to require it." However, such special assignments hardly could account for the difference between General Howard's "upward of 2,000" figure in his autobiography and the figure of 799 referred to by Congressman Ritter taken from a recent report by General Howard.

The conclusion must be that, while 901 may not have been quite the "high point" as stated by Bentley, certainly the true peak figure could not greatly have exceeded it, and, in any case, that the Bureau's force was spread almost ridiculously thin over the huge area of the former slave territory.

[17] There are two comprehensive histories of the Bureau, Bentley and Peirce. Bentley had access to the Bureau's records; Peirce wrote long before they had been put into order in the National Archives. General Howard's autobiography also contains a history of the Bureau. Howard, pp. 206-455. See also Carpenter, op. cit., n.16, pp. 87-208, 220-235; McFeely, op. cit., n.14, passim; Bronson, The Freedmen's Bureau: A Public Policy Analysis (Dissertation, University Microfilms, Ann Arbor, Mich., 1971), passim.

cheat him with impunity and if he could be arrested and jailed without excuse and forced to abide by legal codes discriminating against him because of his race, the abolition of slavery would be a mockery. Worse, without the protection of equal justice, and stripped of the protection, such as it was, of the master's obligation to care for the slave, the freed black would be in a pariah caste lower than any known to civilization. He would have no abiding incentive to improve himself and attain a responsible position in the white man's world.

To its great credit, the Bureau saw at once and very clearly this elemental requirement in any program to make of slaves truly freed men. One of its earliest measures was the establishment of Bureau courts to function in much of the old slave domain. These courts were variously constituted and their jurisdiction was not defined with clarity. Generally they were to adjudicate disputes, including minor criminal matters, between blacks or between blacks and whites.[18]

At first these courts filled a void, for immediately after the war there were no civil governments functioning in the bulk of the former Confederacy.[19] But that void did not last long. Even before the end of 1865 civil governments had been restored everywhere but in Texas.[20] Yet the mere existence of civil authority did not guarantee justice to a freedman. Among the old slave States Negro testimony was incompetent, at least as against a white man, and often that testimonial disability continued to be adhered to in one way or another. That, if nothing else, made justice for the freedman impossible. Hence even after civil courts were re-established the Bureau courts continued for a time.

The very existence of these courts, however, was regarded by the whites in the South as an irritating affront,[21] and there was an extraordinarily prevalent desire, on the part of the North and its agencies at that time, to restore a feeling of harmony. Nor was the

---

[18] For the story of the Bureau courts see Bentley, pp. 152-168; see also Peirce, pp. 143-147; Howard, pp. 251-256. The basis for the Bureau courts' jurisdiction presumably was that they were an arm of military government. See *infra*, nn.28 and 31. The Bureau, it will be recalled, was within the War Department.

[19] There was a void even with respect to Federal courts in the South; in some Federal districts there was no judge in office until the spring of 1866. Robinson, pp. 595-600.

[20] McKitrick, Andrew Johnson and Reconstruction (U. of Chicago Press, 1960), p. 168.

[21] Bentley, pp. 154-156; Peirce, pp. 158-159.

Bureau equipped in talent, manpower, or facilities to administer a judicial system on more than the most informal, make-shift basis.[22] Accordingly the Bureau, and other Northern authorities, exerted considerable effort to persuade the Southern governments to legalize receipt of Negro testimony and otherwise to create the appearance, at least, of equal justice for blacks.[23] As that was done the Bureau courts often were discontinued.[24]

Hence anything approaching a universal system of Bureau courts lasted for but a short time. Thus in Mississippi the Bureau courts were ended by the first of November 1865.[25] And even where they were continued for a significant time after civil courts were re-established, the Bureau sometimes seemed over-eager to terminate them. For example, in Tennessee there occurred in Memphis at the beginning of May 1866 a shocking, wholesale slaughter of Negroes with never a hand lifted to punish the guilty; yet in that State the Bureau courts were abolished less than a month later when State law was amended to grant the black man, on the face of things, nearly full civil rights.[26]

There was another judicial system trying to assure justice for the freedmen, the army's system. For serious criminal problems there were the military commissions.[27] There were also the provost courts, less formal institutions created from place to place and time to time largely at the discretion of the area military commander who would establish their rules of procedure. They were intended to cope with minor criminal problems, but tended also to handle small civil disputes. Since criminal and civil disputes involving blacks on one or both sides were likely to be explosive it was natural that the provost courts would deal with them. Hence they could and did play a role very similar to that of the Bureau courts. Depending on the area commander they might function even while there were Bureau courts;

---

[22] Bentley, pp. 160-162. Revealing examples of loose informality in Louisiana are given in White, pp. 152-153.
[23] Bentley, pp. 64-68.
[24] Bentley, p. 156.
[25] Harris, Presidential Reconstruction in Mississippi (La. St. U. Press, 1967), p. 87.
[26] Report No. 101, July 25, 1866, U.S. House of Representatives Reports, Vol. 3, 39th Cong., 1st Sess. (1865-1866); McFeely, *op. cit.*, n.14, pp. 274-282; Sefton, The United States Army and Reconstruction (La. St. U. Press, 1967), pp. 73, 83-84; Coulter, Parson Brownlow (U. of N.C. Press, 1937), p. 292.
[27] Sefton, *op. cit.*, n.26, p. 31.

or they might operate in lieu of Bureau courts or continue after Bureau courts were abolished.[28]

Nor were Bureau courts uniformly abolished; and, once abolished in a given area, sometimes they were re-established for a time.[29] Indeed a report to General Howard from his Assistant Commissioner for South Carolina as late as April 1868 indicates that Bureau agents in that State even then were empowered to adjudicate minor cases, civil and criminal, "and it is often done."[30] Actually Congress had expressly authorized the Bureau, under War Department regulations, to exercise "military jurisdiction" over all cases concerning the free enjoyment of civil rights by the blacks in every former rebel State until its re-Union had been recognized by the seating of its representatives in Congress; this was provided in the July 1866 amend-

---

[28] Sefton, *op. cit.*, n.26, pp. 31-32; Howard, p. 253; Peirce, pp. 145-147; Abbott, pp. 100-104. Jurisdiction over non-military matters by a provost court (or, indeed, any other military tribunal) is an incident of military government as distinguished from martial law. Generally speaking, military government is government over inhabitants of enemy country in a foreign or civil war. Winthrop's Military Law and Precedents (vols. 1 and 2, 2d ed., Gov't Print. Office, 1920 reprint), pp. 799-801. It includes the power to create and administer judicial systems to deal with both criminal and civil problems of civilians. *Id.*, pp. 803-805. Thus during the war, when the Northern army was ruling New Orleans and its hinterland, provost courts adjudicated even divorce cases. Robinson, pp. 108, 110. Likewise for a few weeks after the close of hostilities provost courts in various localities in Georgia exercised a quite broad jurisdiction over the ordinary civil affairs of the whites. *Id.*, p. 608. The Supreme Court sustained such jurisdiction. Mechanics and Traders Bank v. Union Bank, 89 U.S. 276 (1874); *cf.* The Grapeshot, 76 U.S. 129 (1869). Such jurisdiction does not necessarily terminate with the close of hostilities; it can continue until "adequate provision has been made" for a new civil regime. Winthrop, *op. cit.*, p. 801; *cf.* Burke v. Miltenberger, 86 U.S. 519 (1873); Texas v. White, 74 U.S. 700 (1868). The Southern whites' irritation at the Bureau courts, which we have noted *supra* p. 499, probably was directed in scarcely less degree toward the provost courts also. There appears to have been a strong tradition among the people of the Confederacy against military jurisdiction over civil matters. In June 1862 the Confederacy's War Department prohibited provost marshals from "taking cognizance of civil cases." Robinson, p. 360. Even on military matters there was a Confederate proclivity for regular judicial process. In 1862 the Confederate Congress provided for a unique system of military courts, one with each army corps, which was manned by officers with distinguished judicial experience and functioned in a manner comparable to the civil courts. While creation of this system was recommended by General Lee in part at least because of the awkwardness of reliance on courts-martial, it doubtless reflected also antipathy toward traditional military courts. It may be noted that these courts when functioning in hostile occupied areas exercised jurisdiction over civil matters. *Id.*, pp. 366-371, 627.

[29] Howard, pp. 286, 287, 291; Bentley, pp. 158-159. A good summary of varying policy in Louisiana between 1865 and 1868 is to be found in White, pp. 136-140.

[30] Asst. Comm'r, S. C., to O. O. Howard, Apr. 24, 1868, Letters Sent by Asst. Comm'r, S.C., BFRAL, Vol. 13 (Jan. 1, 1868-Dec. 31, 1868), p. 183.

ment to the Bureau law.[31] Moreover, when in 1867 Congress imposed Military Reconstruction on all the former Confederate States except Tennessee, fresh impetus was given to some use of Bureau courts.[32]

Finally, throughout the Bureau's life, its agents exercised an informal judicial function, acting as arbitrators, mediators, or mere diplomats to dispose of disputes. It is sometimes difficult to distinguish between a Bureau agent's acting as a "court" and his acting as a kind of Big Brother.[33] Most often this informal intervention was exercised in disputes between blacks; but it was exercised considerably in disputes between blacks and whites as well. Not a few of the Bureau's agents were sorely burdened by the demands of that role.[34]

So there was no absence of machinery for securing justice for

---

[31] 14 Stat. 176-177 (1866). Prior to this legislation the Supreme Court had decided Ex parte Milligan, 71 U.S. 2 (1866). The decision invalidated a war-time conviction of a resident of Indiana by a military commission in Indiana for treasonable acts committed during the war. The Court's order was announced on April 3, 1866, but its opinion was not rendered until December 17. See the report of the case in 18 L. Ed. 281. Thus the basis for the Court's decision was not known at the time of the July amendment to the Bureau law. Five Justices placed decision on the ground that the military commission had been unconstitutional; one dictum denied military jurisdiction over civilians "where the courts are open and their process unobstructed" (71 U.S. at 121); a few pages later the dictum was restated to deny such jurisdiction "where the courts are open, and *in the proper and* unobstructed exercise of their jurisdiction" (71 U.S. at 127; emphasis supplied). Four Justices refused to join in placing decision on constitutional grounds, relying instead on a lack of authority, in the premises, under a controlling act of Congress. For a discussion of the case, and its political significance, see III Warren, The Supreme Court in United States History (Little, Brown, and Co., 1924), pp. 140-176; Gambone, Ex parte Milligan: The Restoration of Judicial Prestige? 16 Civil War History 246 (1970). President Johnson insisted that the decision applied wherever civil courts were functioning, even in the lately rebelled States, so invalidating military— and Bureau—courts' jurisdiction over civilians in the South. General Howard, emphasizing the second of the two dicta quoted above, hoped that such jurisdiction would not be barred if civil courts were not functioning fairly (*i.e.*, "properly"); he wanted a test case to determine the question. He never succeeded in bringing about a test. Bentley, pp. 163-165; Abbott, p. 103. In fact both Bureau and provost courts operated from time to time in cases involving civilians in many areas long after the Milligan decision. Probably, in view of the course of judicial decisions under the Military Reconstruction Acts, President Johnson's constitutional position would not have been sustained had General Howard succeeded in effecting a test case; most likely the issue as to legality of Bureau courts would have been deemed purely statutory. Winthrop, *op. cit.*, n.28, pp. 847-858; *cf.* Texas v. White, 74 U.S. 700 (1868).
[32] Bentley, pp. 165-166.
[33] White, pp. 152-153; Bentley, p. 160.
[34] See, *e.g.*, Abbott, p. 24.

the freedmen. It varied greatly from place to place and from time to time. But, in one way or another, it was fairly abundant.[35] Furthermore, the law in the statute books and ordinances of the old slave States soon tended to be stated with apparent fairness, color-neutral. It may be that, in some respects and on the face of things, there came to be a greater equality of justice for the black in parts of the Southland than was to be found in the North.

But the Bureau knew, from intimate experience, that the face of things was illusory. The law is not what appears in the books. The law is what happens in its administration. And no mere printed words could eradicate an ages old prejudice against the black man, especially in circumstances where many whites thought, rightly or wrongly, that their economic rehabilitation after war's destruction demanded a black labor pool at the barest minimum of cost.

Prejudice ran deep indeed. It was rooted no less deep in the North than in the South.[36] A number of the Northern military shared it.[37] Neither the provost courts nor the army's commanding officers were uniformly intent on securing justice for the blacks.[38] And there is evidence of the prejudice of some of the Bureau's own agents.[39] Finally, needless to say, the ordinary civil courts in the South, and their attendant police and administrative personnel, were generally strongly prejudiced.[40] Unquestionably, prior to the North's surrender to the South and its abandonment of Reconstruction, there were examples of genuine concern by some Southern judges to effect

---

[35] Additional machinery was provided in the Civil Rights Act of April 9, 1866. 14 Stat. 27-30. Bureau agents were admonished to resort to that Act where necessary. White, p. 138. The Act's first section provided that persons of every race should have the same civil rights as white persons—*i.e.*, to contract, sue, testify, inherit, purchase, lease, sell, hold, and convey property, and to have the full benefit of all laws and proceedings for the security of person and property. 14 Stat. 27. The third section included a provision that Federal courts should have jurisdiction "of all causes, civil and criminal, affecting persons who are denied or cannot enforce . . . any of the rights secured to them by the first section . . ." *Ibid.* The fourth section included Bureau agents among those officials having authority to arrest and institute proceedings against violators of the Act. *Id.* 28.

[36] Northern prejudice is compellingly detailed in Litwack, North of Slavery (U. of Chicago Press, 1961), and in Voegli, Free but not Equal (U. of Chicago Press, 1967). See also Bentley, pp. 17-18; Gara, The Liberty Line (U. of Kentucky Press, 1967), pp. 62-67.

[37] Abbott, pp. 13-14, 101.

[38] Howard, p. 253; Abbott, p. 102.

[39] Carpenter, *op. cit.*, n.16, pp. 98, 100-101; White, p .164.

[40] Howard, pp. 285-292, 300; Bentley, pp. 157-158, 166-168.

equal justice.⁴¹ But that concern did not prevail.

There was an additional complicating factor. Blacks were poor and uneducated, with few exceptions. It is difficult enough for a man of means and sophistication to cope with the law in his civil affairs, or with its criminal strictures, without a lawyer. But for the poor and uneducated to attempt it is all but hopeless.

To meet the problem the Bureau agents were widely instructed not only to advise the blacks of their rights as best they could but also to act as next friend to them in both civil and military courts. In addition, Bureau agents often were required to observe judicial proceedings either generally or in specific cases where there seemed reason to do so. They were to report to military authorities or their own superiors instances of irregularity or apparent injustice.⁴²

The Bureau's records contain much to show that this function, difficult as it was, was carried out with about as much diligence as one could expect of a relative handful of agents scattered throughout the old slave dominion and harassed with countless other jobs. But the effectiveness of Bureau agents rarely trained in the law was limited. Moreover, even when acting as a next friend of a black, and not as a mere observer, a Bureau agent was not the same as a lawyer acting for a client.

Within a few weeks after the Bureau was inaugurated some of its officials saw the need for having lawyers for the blacks if justice were to be done, and arranged for lawyers' service. This was well before the legal aid movement was born in our nation. It was not until a decade later that a society for helping German immigrants in New York City began to provide legal aid to its constituency; it was not until about 1890 that that project evolved into the New York Legal Aid Society, the near beginning of the legal aid movement.⁴³ And it was a full century before legal aid became sturdy, with financial support from the Federal Office of Economic Opportunity. But back in 1865 some officers of the Freedmen's Bureau realized that a

---

⁴¹ Abbott, pp. 104-105; White, p. 164, n.151.
⁴² Bentley, pp. 156-157; Peirce, pp. 145-146.
⁴³ Tweed, The Legal Aid Society, New York City (The Legal Aid Society, 1954), pp. 6-8. The Society now claims its date of birth to be 1876 when the German Society was formed. The Legal Aid Society of New York, Ninety-Fifth Annual Report, p. 2 (1970). But it was not until 1890 that the German Society served all indigents. Tweed, *op. cit.*, p. 7.

poor man, especially were he black, could not be assured of justice, however evenly the law might be stated in the books, unless he had access to a lawyer.

No scholar has systematically combed the Bureau's archives to determine the nature and extent of this first of all legal aid projects. There seems but the most passing reference in publications thus far.[44]

Difficulties faced now in recreating what happened are formidable. The Bureau records were not well kept at the time; the few agents in a vast territory had far too much to do, and their paper work often was neglected.[45] Nor was there tidy system; not only was General Howard a poor administrator, but in the very nature of things administrative controls were loose and methods varied greatly even within a single area.[46] And when the Bureau finally was closed down, its records were not collected in an orderly way but were dumped into a careless War Department storage, with important documents lost or destroyed.[47]

Furthermore, records do not always distinguish between the representation of a black as a next friend and representation as a lawyer. A number of documents may refer to the provision of lawyers' services, but the reader cannot be sure because wording is consistent with the widespread practice of a Bureau agent's attendance at court with a freedman to be of such help as the agent could provide. Moreover, though there are some records indicating a direction to Bureau agents to act as "attorneys" for the freedmen where necessary,[48] which doubtless they did on occasion, it is virtually certain that even then the non-lawyer agent, ordinarily at least, often was able to be nothing more than a next friend. One suspects that the role of a Bureau

---

[44] The only references we have found are McFeely, op. cit., n.14, p. 270; Abbott, p. 104; Peirce, p. 145; Wharton, The Negro in Mississippi, 1865-1890 (Harper Torchbooks 1965), p. 134. See also Bronson, op. cit., n.17, p. 136 n.25.
[45] Bentley, pp. 136-138.
[46] Peirce, pp. 51-52, 54; White, pp. 14-16, 32.
[47] Howard, pp. 448-449; Carpenter, op. cit., n.16, p. 225; Bentley, p. 212; Peirce, pp. 119-120. Abbott's bibliographical note on the Bureau's records in his study of the Bureau in South Carolina is illuminating. Now located in the War Records Office of the National Archives, assembled in reasonable order, and with a checklist finally compiled in 1946, they are nonetheless incomplete and spotty. Furthermore various collections of the private papers of officials of the Bureau and of others have to be examined for complete research. Abbott, pp. 145-147. See also the bibliographical note in Bentley, pp. 266-268.
[48] White, pp. 138, 139.

agent as a so-called "attorney" was best described by General Howard himself when, in his autobiography, he referred to "the counsel of a Bureau officer as a friend present in court."[49]

Nonetheless a search has turned up substantial evidence that, in some areas, the Bureau itself retained a lawyer on a salaried basis to handle freedmen's problems or paid fees to lawyers to handle selected cases.[50] It is very probable, also, that at least in criminal cases the Bureau sometimes succeeded in persuading judges to appoint lawyers to represent freedmen, although at that time court appointment of counsel was not the common practice that it later became.[51]

The most complete picture of the Bureau's legal aid program appears in the records for the District of Columbia and for Maryland.

The original Bureau law was limited, in its terms, to the slave States that had rebelled.[52] But slavery had existed also in the District of Columbia, and in the loyal States of West Virginia, Maryland, Missouri, Delaware and Kentucky.[53] No less than the rebel States

---

[49] Howard, p. 283.

[50] A special situation prevailed respecting the handling of claims by black soldiers and their families for bounties and other benefits provided for by Congress. In 1867 Congress enacted that only the Bureau could determine and pay such claims. Howard, pp. 353-355; Bentley, p. 87; Peirce, pp. 107-108. That Bureau function, indeed, was continued until 1872, after the remainder of the Bureau's activities had been terminated by 1869, except for its aid to education which had lasted in some measure until 1870. *Supra*, n.15; Bentley, pp. 209-212. Claims collections offered obvious opportunities for abuse by private attorneys and by so-called claims agents against which the Bureau diligently struggled. Howard, pp. 293, 353, 355-357; Bentley, p. 148. In at least one instance the Bureau hired an attorney as a Bureau agent to represent claimants without charge. White, pp. 160-162. Such a situation should be distinguished from provision of legal aid more generally.

[51] In the Bureau's records we have found a printed copy of a Mississippi statute of November 24, 1865, allowing assignment of counsel in criminal cases in county courts. An Act To Establish County Courts, Nov. 24, 1865, §§ 14, 32, pp. 8, 14, Synopsis of Bureau Records Relating to the Subject of Justice, Office of the Commissioner, BRFAL (1865-1870). And in Florida the Assistant Commissioner of the Bureau advised his agents of his belief that it was "the right and duty of . . . the Court to appoint . . . counsel" for freedmen. Asst. Comm'r to Stearns, Oct. 6, 1866, No. 468, Letters Sent by Asst. Comm'r, Florida, BRFAL, Vol. 5 (Sept. 24, 1866-Aug. 31, 1868), p. 13.

[52] 13 Stat. 507-508 (1865).

[53] Slavery was abolished in the District in 1862, with compensation to loyal slave-owners. An appropriation to aid in foreign colonizing of the blacks became a dead letter through non-use. Whyte, p. 31; Green, pp. 274-275. A measure of gradual emancipation was required of West Virginia as a condition of its admission into the Union in 1863. Conley, Beacon Lights of West Virginia History (W. Va.

this loyal territory had a problem of absorbing the blacks into a free society. General Howard was not one to read his statute with a grudging eye; he ignored its limitation to the rebel States and extended the Bureau's operations to the other slave territory from the beginning, though its activity in West Virginia and Delaware was only incidental.[54]

The District of Columbia presented a unique situation. The 1860 census disclosed a population of 75,000, of whom 14,300 were black. There were 11,100 free blacks; only 3,200 were slaves, many of them house servants. The census ten years later showed a total population of 131,700, a third, 43,400, black.[55] The blacks had multiplied more than three-fold, but the whites by less than half. The black influx had come largely during and immediately after the war,[56] changing significantly the make-up of the black population. On the eve of war, the District's blacks had been a stable and sophisticated group.[57] But after the abolition of slavery in the District

---

Pub. Co., 1939), pp. 233-235; Curry, Blueprint for Modern America (Vanderbilt U. Press, 1968), pp. 48-52. In Maryland slavery was abolished, without compensation, by the Constitution of 1864. The Constitution of the State of Maryland (John Murphy & Co., Baltimore, 1864), pp. 16, 40. In Missouri, on July 1, 1863, the State Convention adopted "An Ordinance to provide for Certain Amendments to the Constitution and for Emancipation of Slaves." Journal of the Missouri Convention, 1863, p. 3. This provided for emancipation by a gradual process, but was so hedged about with conditions restricting the freedom of slaves that pressure grew for unconditional abolition. On January 11, 1865, the reassembled State Convention adopted an ordinance abolishing slavery entirely without provision for compensation, followed the next day by another ordinance prohibiting apprenticeship except in pursuance of such laws as might be passed subsequently by the General Assembly. Constitution of the State of Missouri as Revised, Amended and Adopted in Convention begun and held at the City of St. Louis on the Sixth day of January, 1865, together with the Ordinances of the said Convention (Emory S. Foster, Public Printer, Jefferson City, 1865), pp. 31-32. On April 8 the Convention adopted a new Constitution incorporating the substance of these provisions. *Id.*, p. 3, Article I § 3, and p. 26, Article XI § 11. See also Trexler, Slavery in Missouri, 1804-1865 (Johns Hopkins Press, 1914), pp. 235-240. In Delaware President Lincoln had sought to initiate a plan of compensated emancipation early in the war. The prospect seemed likely for in 1847 a bill for gradual emancipation had been lost in the legislature by but one vote. However an informal poll of the legislature on the President's plan, in February 1862, fell one vote short of approval and the plan was abandoned. 7 Encyclopedia Britannica (1970), pp. 190-191. In both Delaware and Kentucky slavery was abolished only by the Thirteenth Amendment. U.S.C.A. (1961), Constitution Amendments 6-14, p. 269.

[54] Bentley, Appendix, pp. 215-216. The July 1866 amendment to the Bureau law (*supra*, n.14) eliminated the restriction of the Bureau to the rebel States, ratifying Howard's *de facto* operation.
[55] Green, p. 21.
[56] Green, pp. 295, 303, 306; Whyte, p. 31; Low, p. 225.
[57] Green, pp. 182-183; Whyte, pp. 28-30.

in 1862, it had attracted refugee slaves, fleeing from Maryland and pouring in from the war-torn South.

By the war's end blacks in the District suffered most acute overcrowding, with housing and sanitary conditions deplorable, and destitution extreme.[58] There was no substantial agriculture to provide hands with work, nor was there industry. The military demobilized rapidly. Thereafter, as largely since, the Capital had little business save government and, needless to say, slaves just freed had minimal skills to contribute to that business. At the same time, however, the judicial institutions were functioning smoothly. There was also local self-government, and Negroes were about to be enfranchised.[59] Hence much more in the District than elsewhere in the old slave territory there seemed the possibility that a black man could achieve real freedom.[60]

With the Bureau's headquarters located in Washington it is not surprising that the condition of the blacks in the District immediately enlisted the Bureau's interest. In his autobiography General Howard notes that during his very first week in office there had come to him "such an accumulation of subjects relating to the District of Columbia, to the freedmen's village near Arlington, and to the neighborhood of the District of Columbia in Maryland and Virginia" that he had to find a man "to take this care and worry" off his shoulders. On General Grant's recommendation the man he picked was Col. John Eaton; Howard made him an Assistant Commissioner of the Bureau for the District of Columbia district, which included Maryland (though in early 1866 only the neighboring counties of Maryland were included, with the rest of Maryland made a separate district).[61] Eaton had had a considerable experience with freedmen's affairs; in late 1862 Grant had put him in charge of contrabands gathering about his army in the West,[62] and eventually his jurisdiction had embraced the whole Mississippi Valley as far as southern Louisiana where many thousands of blacks were in his care.[63] Indeed he had

---

[58] Bentley, pp. 77-78; Green, pp. 272-284, 301-308; Whyte, pp. 31-33.
[59] Congress enacted Negro suffrage for the District of Columbia in January 1867. Green, pp. 297-301, 311; Whyte, pp. 49-58.
[60] In the immediate post-war years many blacks, especially those whose District residence ante-dated the war, achieved substantial success in a variety of enterprises and tended to keep aloof from the "refugee freedmen." Whyte, p. 250.
[61] Howard, pp. 224-225; Low, pp. 225-226.
[62] Bentley, pp. 21-22; Eaton, p. 5; Grant, Personal Memoirs (Chas. L. Webster & Co., 1885), pp. 424-426.
[63] Eaton, pp. 123-125, 133-134, 216.

been endorsed by Grant to head the Bureau before Howard was chosen.[64]

Eaton at once saw the need to provide the freedmen with a lawyer's service.[64a] The Bureau, however, had no appropriation at that time and resorted to numerous devices to finance itself.[65] In this instance Eaton entered into a verbal agreement with a lawyer in Washington, Mr. James C. Carlisle, who was felt to be trustworthy, that from August 1, 1865, his district of the Bureau would refer to Carlisle all freedmen needing legal help with the understanding that he could charge them "at a fair rate;" he was not expected to devote his full time to these matters. It was further agreed that when there was an appropriation for the Bureau he would receive a "written appointment of Solicitor, at a fair salary."[66] As of May 1, 1866, Carlisle got the formal appointment at a salary of $100 a month.[67] The July 1866 amendment to the Bureau law was to provide that, with certain exceptions, the maximum annual salary for Bureau agents was $1200; the pay category of $100 a month was common for Bureau agents, as it was for other government employees.[68]

No records have been found to show whether, before he was put on a salary, Carlisle was expected to serve freedmen who could not pay. However that must have occurred. During the spring of 1866 another lawyer, Mr. A. K. Browne, began angling for Carlisle's assignment. General Howard's brother, General Charles Howard, who had succeeded to the Assistant Commissionership for the District of Columbia district, wrote Browne that Carlisle "had always

---

[64] Bentley, pp. 50-51.

[64a] Eaton may have got the idea of providing for a lawyer's service from an 1863 special War Department commission's report on a program for the freedmen. It had recommended, *inter alia*, authority "in important cases, where necessary, to employ legal counsel" for freedmen. Preliminary Report of The American Freedmen's Inquiry Commission, Sen. Exec. Docs. No. 53, Ser. 1176, 38th Cong., 1st Sess., June 30, 1863, p. 19. See also Bronson, *op. cit.* n.17, pp. 75-77.

[65] Howard, pp. 263-268; Bentley, pp. 63-64, 72-75.

[66] The Bureau's version of this agreement appears as an endorsement to a voucher submitted by Carlisle on December 19, 1866, for payment of $900 "for Services as Solicitor, from August 1st, 1865, to April 31 [sic], 1866." Payment was disapproved. Clark to Headquarters, Asst. Comm'r, D.C. (Endorsement to Voucher), Dec. 21, 1866, No. 1386, Letters Received by Asst. Comm'r, D.C., BRFAL, Vol. 2 (1867). See also C. H. Howard to O. O. Howard, July 20, 1868, No. 801, Letters Sent by Asst. Comm'r, D.C., BRFAL, Vol. 4 (Nov. 18, 1867-Nov. 4, 1868), p. 325.

[67] Special Order No. 36, May 23, 1866, Special Orders & Circulars, Asst. Comm'r, D.C., BRFAL, Vol. 1 (June 22, 1865-Dec. 31, 1868).

[68] 14 Stat. 174; O. O. Howard to Husband, June 12, 1867, No. 578, Letters Sent, Vol. 3 (Jan. 2-Sept. 30, 1867), p. 274 (Roll 3, Frame 0191); Whyte, *op. cit.*, p. 16.

given satisfaction" and had "often undertaken these cases without prospect of adequate remuneration."[69] The fact that Carlisle finally was put on the payroll suggests that theretofore he must have performed much service either free or at a nominal fee. Yet he was jealous of his position. In September 1865 he wrote Assistant Commissioner Charles Howard asking that the people referred to him be given sealed envelopes addressed to him personally; he complained that they seemed to be going into offices of other lawyers in a neighboring building and that those lawyers copped their cases.[70]

The job apparently was attractive for Browne waged a persistent campaign to supersede Carlisle. He succeeded in August 1866.[71] There is some indication that Carlisle was reluctant to relinquish the job and may have continued to give the impression that he was a Bureau Solicitor. In December 1866, upon inquiry from Browne, Assistant Commissioner Charles Howard wrote that since July Carlisle had not been authorized to act for the Bureau,[72] and in January of the next year the Assistant Commissioner's office again wrote Browne requesting him to place a statement in the daily press that Browne's law firm was the only authorized Solicitor for the Bureau in the District of Columbia and that Carlisle had been relieved of the post.[73]

Carlisle's service for so long without salary may not have been as selfless as Assistant Commissioner Charles Howard had thought when Browne began bucking for the job. There are several documents reflecting charges that Carlisle kept for himself funds collected for others; complaints persisted for some time.[74] And at one point General Howard endorsed a claim made by Carlisle for "allowances"

---

[69] Howard, pp. 24, 285; Bentley, Appendix, p. 215; C. H. Howard to Browne, Mar. 15, 1866, No. 62, Letters Sent by Asst. Comm'r, D.C., BRFAL, Vol. 2 (Mar. 14, 1866-Mar. 11, 1867), p. 35.

[70] Carlisle to C. H. Howard, Sept. 7, 1865, Letters Received (Unentered) by Asst. Comm'r, D.C., BRFAL (1865-67).

[71] *Infra*, p. 513.

[72] C. H. Howard to Browne, Dec. 12, 1866, No. 561, Letters Sent by Asst. Comm'r, D.C., BRFAL, Vol. 2 (Mar. 14, 1866-Mar. 11, 1867), p. 297.

[73] Rogers to Browne, Jan. 31, 1867, No. 749, Letters Sent by Asst. Comm'r, D.C., BRFAL, Vol. 2 (Mar. 14, 1866-Mar. 11, 1867), p. 383.

[74] From Vandenburg [addressee not shown], June 21, 1867, No. 2210; Brewer to Paymaster General Brice, Jan. 21, 1867, No. 818; Farran to O. O. Howard, Jan. 25, 1867, No. 682, Register of Letters Received by Asst. Comm'r, D.C., BRFAL, Vol. 2 (Oct. 29, 1866-Aug. 17, 1867); Clark to Browne, Jan. 23, 1867, No. 704, Letters Sent by Asst. Comm'r, D.C., BRFAL, Vol. 2 (Mar. 14, 1866-Mar. 11, 1867), p. 362.

for the period from August 1865 to February 1866, approving payment if Carlisle had settled all claims filed against him with the Bureau.[75]

In Browne's campaign to get Carlisle's assignment he certainly was not reticent. He was in communication on the subject with Assistant Commissioner Charles Howard as early as March 1866, who, as we have noted, wrote him that Carlisle had been satisfactory, adding that "it does not seem right to displace Mr. Carlisle without a cause."[76] But by May 28 Browne was telling General Howard himself that he "would like a position."[77] He got results for on June 30 the Assistant Commissioner's office wrote Carlisle to forward to "these Head Quarters as early as practicable all papers in your hands relating to the affairs of freedmen . . ." This peremptory order was modified on July 2 to apply only to such papers "as you have concluded action upon," with instructions to complete pending business "as soon as practicable."[78]

Browne probably had planted the idea of letting Carlisle wind up pending business, but he was impatient. On the next day, July 3, he wrote Assistant Commissioner Charles Howard asking for "a sett [sic] of your orders, instructions," and other pertinent documents. He added,

> I am anxious to get to work as soon as possible, and while I admire your highly honorable views as well as kind disposition towards Mr. Carlisle which assures me of the same kindness and consideration when I shall be similarly associated with you yet I cannot on reflection see the objection to your appointing me now and at the same time continuing Mr. C. until the middle of the month or until he shall have finished the business he has on hand. Our duties certainly cannot conflict and I believe it is the usual way in such matters of law &c. and will be for the interest of the Bureau.
>
> If, however, you think differently, I, of course, submit as grace-

---

[75] O. O. Howard to Balloch, Mar. 25, 1867, Endorsements Sent, Vol. 3 (Mar. 18-Sept. 27, 1867), p. 21 (Roll 3, Frame 0398).
[76] C.H. Howard to Browne, Mar. 15, 1866, No. 62, Letters Sent by Asst. Comm'r, D.C., BRFAL, Vol. 2 (Mar. 14, 1866-Mar. 11, 1867), p. 35.
[77] Browne to O. O. Howard, May 28, 1866, No. 1514, Register of Letters Received by Asst. Comm'r, D.C., BRFAL, Vol. 1 (Sept. 1865-Oct. 27, 1866), p. 253.
[78] Rogers to Carlisle, June 30, 1866, No. 239; Rogers to Carlisle, July 2, 1866, No. 242, Letters Sent by Asst. Comm'r, D.C., BRFAL, Vol. 2 (Mar. 14, 1866-Mar. 11, 1867), pp. 161,162.

fully as my peculiar circumstances will admit, for the month, or half month (as the case may be), but at the expiration of *that* time, I cannot see without someone else to attend to the *new* business how Mr. C. will be any nearer to having his business closed than he is now. Hope to hear from you soon.[79]

Browne was on tenterhooks. Two days later, on July 5, he again wrote Assistant Commissioner Charles Howard acknowledging receipt of a "list of Circulars, etc.," but hastening to supplement what he had said in his July 3 letter. He said that "if the matter of salary during the time required for Mr. C_____ to close unfinished business makes any difference, you may make the condition that mine is not to commence until the 15th inst. or until his ceases." For, he added,

My anxious desire is, if it pleases you, that I may have my commission now, and be prepared to attend promptly to any business that may come up.

I have conversed with several members of the Bar and find there are cases occurring each day in the Criminal Court where Freedmen are convicted without anyone to defend them. At your suggestion, I have opened my office at 476 Seventh St. and if I have your authority shall be there henceforth or in the Courts constantly.[80]

Charles Howard replied on the same day that,

There are no good grounds of complaint that Mr. Carlisle has neglected any cases committed to him. I therefore am unwilling to take any action which might cast such imputation upon him. After the expiration of this month, if I then find it desirable to have a Solicitor, there will be no objection to your appointment.[81]

Apparently Charles Howard shortly left town. On July 27 Browne wrote General Howard stating that,

I suppose I am to enter upon my duties as solicitor for your Bureau for the District Aug. 1st. This was the assurance given me by your Brother, i.e.: "If he had any Solicitor at that time" upon which fact or necessity I apprehend there can be no doubt.

---

[79] Browne to C. H. Howard, July 3, 1866, No. 1734, Letters Received by Asst. Comm'r, D.C., BRFAL, Vol. 1 (1866).
[80] Browne to C. H. Howard, July 5, 1866, Letters Received (Unentered) by Asst. Comm'r, D.C., BRFAL (1865-1867).
[81] C. H. Howard to Browne, July 5, 1866, No. 108, Letters Sent by Asst. Comm'r, D.C., BRFAL, Vol. 2 (Mar. 14, 1866-Mar. 11, 1867), p. 62.

His letter continued,

> He instructed me to say the same to Judges Fisher & Carter and I have made my arrangements accordingly. I sincerely trust I may not again be disappointed by reason of your Brothter's absence.[82]

Finally on August 9 Browne got action. On that date, by order of General Thomas, Carlisle's appointment was revoked as of July 2 and Browne was appointed at the same salary—$100 a month—to date from August 1.[83] General Thomas undoubtedly was Samuel Thomas who as a Colonel previously had been Assistant Commissioner for Mississippi where, as we shall see, he had instituted a legal aid program in the fall of 1865.[84] He had been transferred to the Bureau's Washington headquarters in the spring of 1866 and was brevetted Brigadier General.[85] Probably he was filling in for Assistant Commissioner Charles Howard while the latter was out of town.

Two days after Browne's appointment Mr. E. J. Smithers also was appointed a Solicitor for the District of Columbia district at the same salary as that for Browne; this, too, was done by order of General Thomas.[86] Thereafter Browne and he functioned as the firm of Browne & Smithers. In his annual report of November 1, 1866, General Howard refers to "Browne and Smithers, the present solicitors," in describing their work.[87] On September 1 Assistant Commissioner Charles Howard had written the Justices of the Peace of the City of Washington,

> I send you card of Brown and Smithers who are the authorized solicitors for Freedmen for Dept. of Washington—including Dist. Col., six counties Md., viz Montgomery, Prince Georges, Charles, St. Mary, Calvert, and part of Ann Arundel, including

---

[82] Browne to O. O. Howard, July 27, 1866, No. 2008, Letters Received by Asst. Comm'r, D.C., BRFAL, Vol. 1 (1866).

[83] Special Order No. 58, Aug. 9, 1866, Special Orders & Circulars—Asst. Comm'r, D.C., BRFAL, Vol. I (June 22, 1865-Dec. 31, 1868).

[84] *Infra*, pp. 529-530.

[85] Special Order No. 53, Apr. 10, 1866 (Roll 7, Frame 0181); Special Order No. 74, May 23, 1866 (Roll 7, Frame 0188).

[86] Special Order No. 59, Aug. 11, 1866, Special Orders & Circulars—Asst. Comm'r, D.C., BRFAL, Vol. I (June 22, 1865-Dec. 31, 1868).

[87] Commissioner to Secretary of War, Nov. 1, 1866, p. 23, Reports of the Commissioner of the Bureau of Refugees, Freedmen and Abandoned Lands (1865-1870).

Annapolis, and would request that when parties are arraigned before you, without counsel, you would be kind enough to notify said Solicitors, when practicable. When parties are unable to pay their cases will be attended to without charge.

We find that many of the freedpeople are not aware of this arrangement, and will thank you to disseminate the information as you may have opportunity.[88]

In January 1867 Assistant Commissioner Charles Howard's office asked Browne, if he had not already done so, to publish "the card of Browne and Smithers as Solicitors of this Bureau in the Chronicle and other papers that you may select." At the same time Browne was requested to have the Daily Chronicle publish a statement drafted by the Assistant Commissioner's office warning against "the frequent impositions upon freed people in this District by persons pretending to be authorized Advocates in the Courts" and calling attention to the advertisement of "Browne & Smithers, the present Solicitors of Freedmens Bureau," and to the fact that they had been "the only Solicitors authorized by said Bureau, in the Dist. of Columbia, since August 9th, 1866."[89]

In the spring of 1867 Smithers resigned, breaking up the Browne & Smithers team. He had taken a post with the State Department before the end of a period for which he already had been paid by the Bureau, and found that it was illegal to receive pay for two positions at the same time. He therefore returned his Bureau pay check but asked that, since he had been doing Bureau business during that time, he be paid the same amount "as a special fee."[90] Smithers had submitted a somewhat ambiguous resignation theretofore.[91] Thereafter he was ordered to go to Warrenton, Va., to handle some cases for the Bureau.[92] This perhaps is what he thought warranted the "special fee" even though his salary from the Bureau had to be stopped. His partner, Browne, who tried to get Smithers's fee paid, was told that it was too large and, two days later, that

---

[88] C. H. Howard to Justices of the Peace, Sept. 1, 1866, No. 128, Letters Sent by Asst. Comm'r, D.C., BRFAL, Vol. 2 (Mar. 14, 1866-Mar. 11, 1867), p. 96.

[89] *Supra*, n.73.

[90] Smithers to Browne, Apr. 15, 1867, No. 1701, Letters Received by Asst. Comm'r, D.C., BRFAL, Vol. 2 (1867).

[91] O. O. Howard to Smithers, Apr. 1, 1867, No. 303, Letters Sent, Vol. 3 (Jan. 2-Sept. 30, 1867), p. 145 (Roll 3, Frame 0125).

[92] Special Order No. 54, April 10, 1867 (May 22, 1865-June 27, 1872), p. 187 (Roll 7, Frame 0228).

Smithers had not been employed by the District of Columbia office (presumably for the Warrenton mission) but should present his bill to the Bureau's general headquarters.[93] In the meantime his resignation had been accepted.[94]

Shortly before Smithers's resignation, Assistant Commissioner Charles Howard had made special provision for the handling of apprenticeship cases in the neighboring Maryland counties embraced in his district. On February 26, 1867, he appointed Mr. W. H. Owen as Solicitor to handle cases "of illegal and unjust apprenticeship of children of freed people and for such other cases as may be referred to him" for such counties.[95] Owen was a lawyer in Washington, D. C.[96] Then on April 3 General Howard appointed Owen as Solicitor of the Bureau at $120 a month.[97] Apparently this meant that Owen became Solicitor for the general headquarters of the Bureau, whereas Browne was Solicitor only for the District of Columbia district under Charles Howard.[98] We shall see that they worked together closely.

With Smithers gone and with Owen shifted, Browne hardly could meet the burden of all the cases in the neighboring Maryland counties, notably apprenticeship cases. So on June 15, 1867, in an order that also reaffirmed Browne's employment at $100 a month, Assistant Commissioner Charles Howard appointed Mr. Henry Stockbridge, likewise at $100 a month, to have the same duties as

---

[93] Rogers to Browne, Apr. 17, 1867, No. 107; Rogers to Browne, Apr. 19, 1867, No. 119, Letters Sent by Asst. Comm'r, D.C., BRFAL, Vol. 3 (Mar. 12, 1867-Nov. 20, 1867), pp. 56, 62.
[94] O. O. Howard to Smithers, Apr. 13, 1867, No. 344, Letters Sent, Vol. 3 (Jan. 2-Sept. 30, 1867), p. 166 (Roll 3, Frame 0137).
[95] Special Order No. 28, Feb. 26, 1867, Special Orders & Circulars—Asst. Comm'r, D.C., BRFAL, Vol. I (June 22, 1865-Dec. 31, 1868).
[96] Boyd's Washington and Georgetown Directory (1866), pp. 50, 197; Boyd's Directory of Washington and Georgetown (1867), p. 444.
[97] O. O. Howard to Owen, Apr. 3, 1867, No. 310, Letters Sent, Vol. 3 (Jan. 2-Sept. 30, 1867), p. 148 (Roll 3, Frame 0127). There is also a letter, by order of General Howard, to W. H. Owen dated the day before, April 2, appointing him an agent in Tennessee at a salary of $900. *Id.*, Apr. 2, 1867, No. 305, p. 146 (Roll 3, Frame 0126). On Sept. 19, 1867, there is a revocation of that appointment at the request of the Assistant Commissioner for Tennessee. *Id.*, Sept. 19, 1867, No. 1218 (Roll 3, Frame 0336). If this W. H. Owen was the same as the W. H. Owen who received the $120 a month appointment of April 3 he must have been something of an operator.
[98] See *infra*, n.117.

those specified in February for Owen.[99] Stockbridge was a Baltimore lawyer.[100] On April 2, 1867, Stockbridge had been appointed to handle apprenticeship cases for the Maryland district which did not include the counties neighboring the District of Columbia,[101] so his appointment by Charles Howard extended his role to reach all of Maryland.

Then in July General Howard received a recommendation from his Assistant Commissioner for Maryland, General Gregory, that Stockbridge be appointed Solicitor for that district—presumably meaning that his duties would be all-embracing instead of being limited to apprenticeship cases.[102] On January 2, 1868, General Howard did enlarge Stockbridge's duties to include the duties of Solicitor of the Bureau for Maryland and Delaware, reporting to General Gregory; curiously this enlarged scope of his work was noted as effective from June 17, 1867.[103] This must mean that Stockbridge had been discharging his enlarged function during the interim.

The delay in General Howard's formal action may have been due to a misunderstanding. During the summer Stockbridge had gone to Europe. On his return in September he found a letter from Assistant Commissioner Charles Howard which he construed as criticism for leaving his post. He explained, to Charles Howard, that when he had been persuaded to undertake his assignment he had made it clear that he would do so only on the understanding that he could deputize others to handle cases under his general direction, that during his absence matters were handled by a deputy entirely satisfactorily, and that he supposed his "position was fully understood." Somewhat testily he intimated that he was putting affairs in shape so that he could be relieved of his duties and wanted exoneration "from the imputation of abandonment or neglect of official du-

---

[99] Special Order No. 97, June 15, 1867, Special Orders & Circulars—Asst. Comm'r, D.C., BRFAL, Vol. I (June 22, 1865-Dec. 31, 1868).
[100] Wagandt, The Mighty Revolution (Johns Hopkins Press, 1964), p. 85; Low, p. 228.
[101] Commissioner to Secretary of War, Nov. 1, 1867, p. 41, Reports of the Commissioner of the Bureau of Refugees, Freedmen and Abandoned Lands (1865-1870); see also O. O. Howard to Gregory, Apr. 20, 1867, No. 368, Letters Sent, Vol. 3 (Jan. 2-Sept. 30, 1867), p. 177 (Roll 3, Frame 0142); Low, pp. 226, 228.
[102] O. O. Howard to Asst. Comm'r, D.C., July 11, 1867, Endorsements Sent, Vol. 3 (Mar. 18-Sept. 27, 1867), p. 345 (Roll 3, Frame 0560).
[103] O. O. Howard to Stockbridge, Jan. 2, 1868, Letters Sent, Vol. 4 (Oct. 1, 1867-Aug. 31, 1868), p. 222 (Roll 4, Frame 0160).

ties."[104] Charles Howard promptly replied, assuring Stockbridge that he had merely wanted to ascertain what provision had been made for the work during Stockbridge's absence, that he had had no doubt that the provision had been proper. This reply seemed to assume that Stockbridge was about to "close up" his "relations with the Bureau." Perhaps this meant only a termination of his work for the District of Columbia district. Actually virtually all of Stockbridge's work had been for General Gregory's Maryland district.[105] In any case General Howard's retroactive approval of Stockbridge's enlarged role for the Bureau's Maryland district suggests that any misunderstanding was straightened out. That is hardly surprising. Massachusetts born, Amherst educated, and former Whig, Stockbridge had been one of the most prominent Maryland Unionists and a strong anti-slavery man during the war.[106] Stockbridge's services did continue until the summer of 1868 when the Bureau began to curtail its activities; "high satisfaction" with his work was expressed.[107]

In at least one instance another lawyer was engaged by the Bureau in Maryland. In Calvert County there was a serious apprenticeship problem which the Bureau wanted to bring before the local court. It was thought that "the court would be more disposed" to give the problem "favorable consideration if the cases were presented by a lawyer of the county." Hence the Bureau appointed Mr. J. S. Dalrymple, a lawyer of that County, to present those cases.[108]

At some point Owen, as Solicitor for the general headquarters in Washington, was joined by a Mr. Wilson. In Browne's annual report to Assistant Commissioner Charles Howard dated October 10, 1868, he refers to Messrs. Owen and Wilson as the "Solicitor at

---

[104] Stockbridge to C. H. Howard, Sept. 25, 1867, No. 346, Letters Received by Asst. Comm'r, D.C., BRFAL, Vol. 3 (1867).
[105] C. H. Howard to Stockbridge, Sept. 30, 1867, No. 628, Letters Sent by Asst. Comm'r, D.C., BRFAL, Vol. 3 (Mar. 12, 1867-Nov. 20, 1867), pp. 322-324.
[106] Wagandt, *op. cit.*, n.100, pp. 85, 103, 146, 192, 194, 222, 261; Low, pp. 243-244.
[107] C. H. Howard to O. O. Howard, July 6, 1868, No. 722, Letters Sent by Asst. Comm'r, D.C., BRFAL, Vol. 4 (Nov. 18, 1867-Nov. 4, 1868), p. 292; C.H. Howard to Stockbridge, June [sic] 6, 1868, No. 723, Letters Sent by Asst. Comm'r, D.C., BRFAL, Vol. 4 (Nov. 18, 1867-Nov. 4, 1868), p. 292.
[108] Commissioner to Secretary of War, Nov. 1, 1867, p. 41, Reports of the Commissioner of the Bureau of Refugees, Freedmen and Abandoned Lands (1865-1870).

large."[109] When, in the summer of 1868, the Bureau put Browne on leave of absence he was directed to arrange for the handling of his business by "Mr. Owen or Mr. Wilson."[110] Wilson doubtless was Mr. Thomas Wilson. In 1866, 1867 and 1868 W. H. Owen and Thomas Wilson were listed as in the law practice together in Washington.[111]

The duties of Owen and Wilson as "Solicitor at large" and their differentiation from the duties of Browne are not clear. In Browne's annual report of October 10, 1868, it is stated that he and Owen and Wilson had "an office in common—a circumstance which has rendered it convenient, in practice for either one or the other of us to attend to any business appertaining to freedmen coming there just as the occasion might demand." He then mentions that "the business of the office has required the presence either of myself or of one of the gentlemen before referred to, at courts in Erie Co. Penna., Baltimore, Prince George's, St. Mary's Charles, Louden and Montgomery Counties Md. and at Culpepper and Warrenton Va."[112] It seems likely that there had been this "office in common" from the beginning of the "Solicitor at large" arrangement. For on April 6, 1867, three days after General Howard had enlarged Owen's duties, he was advised that Browne and Owen, "solicitors," had been compelled to move their office and approval was sought for their new location.[113] By the end of the year, on December 2, 1867, Browne was reporting again to Assistant Commissioner Charles Howard,

> We are compelled to remove from and quit our present offices this week. Forty—fifty and even as high as *sixty-three* freedmen pr. day is too much for our Landlady and her boarding house.
>
> We have, however, rented the offices corner 5th & D Streets

---

[109] Browne to C. H. Howard (Report of Operations Since July 1st, 1867), Oct. 10, 1868, B. 74, pp. 1, 2, Operations Reports—Asst. Comm'r, D.C., BRFAL, Vol. 5 (1868).

[110] Eldridge to Browne, July 15, 1868, No. 781, Letters Sent by Asst. Comm'r, D.C., BRFAL, Vol. 4 (Nov. 18, 1867-Nov. 4, 1868), p. 314.

[111] Boyd's Washington and Georgetown Directory (1866), pp. 50, 197; Boyd's Directory of Washington and Georgetown (1867), p. 444; *id.*, (1868), p. 365.

[112] *Supra*, n.109, pp. 1-3.

[113] Browne & Owen to O. O. Howard, Apr. 6, 1867, Registers and Letters Received by Comm'r, BRFAL (Jan.-May 1867) (Microcopy 752, Roll 6, Frame 101).

formerly occupied by Judge Day opposite City Hall where you will please address communications hereafter to us.[114]

This letter speaks in the plural, and in 1868 both Browne and the firm of Owen and Wilson were listed as attorneys at the same address—the 5th & D address referred to in Browne's December 1867 letter.[115]

The Bureau paid the rent for the office. It may be that during the Browne & Smithers regime they had to absorb the rent. In March 1867 Browne protested this burden; in view of the amount of work done and the small salary he felt that the Bureau should pay the rent. General Howard agreed.[116] That the Bureau assumed rent payment is confirmed by the fact that when, in 1868, Browne was advised that his services would be needed no longer the reason given was that only "one solicitor should do all necessary business for both Headquarters, renting but one office and employing but one assistant or clerk."[117] The Bureau also paid the rent for Stockbridge's Maryland office.[118]

Travel expense on Bureau business likewise was paid by the

---

[114] Browne to C. H. Howard, Dec. 2, 1867, No. 998, Letters Received by Asst. Comm'r, D.C., BRFAL, Vol. 3 (1867).

[115] Boyd's Directory of Washington and Georgetown (1868), pp. 173, 365. Interestingly Browne must have continued close association with Owen and Wilson after his Bureau duties ended. In 1869 also the three gentlemen were listed at a common address, though different from their 1868 Bureau address. Boyd's Directory of Washington and Georgetown (1869), p. 28.

[116] O. O. Howard to Browne, Apr. 2, 1867, Endorsements Sent, Vol. 3 (Mar. 18-Sept. 27, 1867), p. 49 (Roll 3, Frame 0412); Browne to O. O. Howard, Mar. 28, 1867, Registers and Letters Received by Comm'r, BRFAL (Jan.-May 1867) (Microcopy 752, Roll 6, Frame 100).

[117] Eldridge to Brown, July 9, 1868, No. 739, Letters Sent by Asst. Comm'r, D.C., BRFAL, Vol. 4 (Nov. 18, 1867-Nov. 4, 1868), p. 298. The reference to "both Headquarters" confirms our assumption that Owen and Wilson were Solicitors for the general headquarters of the Bureau and Browne for the District of Columbia district. *Supra*, p. 515.

[118] Assistant Commissioner Charles Howard assured Stockbridge that his rent would be paid. He suggested that it should be paid by the Maryland district office from the time Stockbridge "began to act for *Genl Gregory*" but that he would pay it if General Gregory refused to do so. C. H. Howard to Stockbridge, Sept. 30, 1867, No. 628, Letters Sent by Asst. Comm'r, D.C., BRFAL (Mar. 12, 1867-Nov. 20, 1867), Vol. 3, pp. 322-324. (This statement shows that Stockbridge was acting as the Solicitor for the Maryland district prior to General Howard's approval of that assignment; hence the retroactive approval. *Supra*, pp. 516-517. When Stockbridge's services were terminated in the summer of 1868 he was told that his rent would be paid until the end of the month of his discharge. C. H. Howard to Stockbridge, July 9, 1868, No. 748, Letters Sent by Asst. Comm'r, D.C., BRFAL, Vol. 4 (Nov. 18, 1867-Nov. 4, 1868), p. 302.

Bureau. Such expense was supposed to be handled in accordance with Army travel regulations, requiring a special order for each journey.[119]

The 1868 notice to Browne just quoted also shows that the Bureau was providing clerical help. This is further revealed in a notice, at about the same time, that the services of Browne's clerk had been terminated.[120]

In addition the Bureau furnished Browne (and presumably Owen and Wilson) with office supplies—stationery, pens, pencils, ink, etc.[121] There is the possibility that office furniture also was provided[122] and that the Bureau paid for newspaper advertising of Browne's services as Bureau Solicitor.[123]

One would surmise that Browne was permitted to engage in his own private practice during his work for the Bureau. In 1867 he published his card in Boyd's Directory, holding himself out as "Attorney and Counselor at Law," as well as "Solicitor for the Bureau of Freedmen and Abandoned Lands."[124] Unclear is whether he could charge fees to freedmen when they were able to pay. Carlisle of course could do so before he received a salaried appointment. But after receiving that appointment did he do so? And did Browne? There is no evidence that they did. Yet if Browne continued to engage in his own private practice, and if a black appeared in his office with means to pay some fee—and in Washington there were a good many blacks who could have done so—one cannot but guess that

---

[119] C. H. Howard to Stockbridge, Sept. 30, 1867, No. 628, Letters Sent by Asst. Comm'r, D.C., BRFAL, Vol. 3 (Mar. 12, 1867-Nov. 20, 1867), pp. 322-324.

[120] Eldridge to Maj. J. M. Brown, July 18, 1868, No. 795, Letters Sent by Asst. Comm'r, D.C., BRFAL, Vol. 4 (Nov. 18, 1867- Nov. 4, 1868), p. 323.

[121] Browne to C. H. Howard, Sept. 24, 1867, No. 279, Letters Received by Asst. Comm'r, D.C., BRFAL, Vol. 3 (1867).

[122] Browne & Owen to O. O. Howard, Apr. 6, 1867, Registers and Letters Received by Comm'r, BRFAL (Jan.-May 1867) (Microcopy 752, Roll 6, Frame 101).

[123] O. O. Howard to Browne, May 4, 1867, Endorsements Sent, Vol. 3 (Mar. 18-Sept. 27, 1867), p. 147 (Roll 3, Frame 0461); cf. Rogers to Browne, Jan. 31, 1867, No. 749, Letters Sent by Asst. Comm'r, D.C., BRFAL, Vol. 2 (Mar. 14, 1866-Mar. 11, 1867), p. 383.

[124] Boyd's Directory of Washington and Georgetown (1867), p. 165. A further shred of evidence that Browne could do business on his own account is found in a letter from Smithers to Browne, when Smithers was winding up their relationship, stating that if Browne succeeded in a pending collection matter there was the promise of a "liberal fee" by an attorney who had referred the business. Smithers to Browne, Apr. 15, 1867, No. 1701, Letters Received by Asst. Comm'r, D.C. BRFAL, Vol. 2 (1867).

Browne, and Carlisle before him, would take what they could get. That was a time of loose standards, and it would not have been difficult then to square with conscience the taking of a fee from a client "willing" to pay.

Browne was a very busy lawyer. In General Howard's annual report of November 1, 1866, it is stated that Browne and Smithers had reported for the months of August and September (their first two months of work): "Number of civil cases referred to them by the bureau, 115; persons charged with crime, for whom they are engaged to appear at the present term, 88."[125] A year later Assistant Commissioner Charles Howard's annual report for the year ending Sept. 30, 1867, states that Browne's report for the year shows:

Number of Civil cases attended to	230
" " " " tried before Magistrate	135
The remainder either settled or dismissed.	
Number of Criminal cases attended to in Courts	185
" " " " dismissed by order of the Court, the parties being either falsely accused or charged with frivolous offenses	44[126]

These statistics seem to cover a period of eleven months. Browne began his work on August 1, 1866. In a report to Assistant Commissioner Charles Howard on October 10, 1868, Browne gives the statistics on his work since July 1, 1867. Doubtless, therefore, the statistics we have just quoted cover the period August 1, 1866, to July 1, 1867.

In his report of October 1868, Browne tabulates his work since July 1, 1867, as follows:

---

[125] *Supra*, n.87. There is also a letter to Assistant Commissioner Charles Howard, signed "Browne & Smithers," dated October 31, 1866, stating that during those two months they had acted on "nearly two hundred complaints of the freedmen of this district, arising, principally, from the non-payment of wages and the non-fulfillment of contracts for the letting of lands." It was stated that in all such cases they had endeavored, without litigation, to obtain redress "where we had reason to suppose that injustice had been done" but that "not unfrequently" it had been necessary "to seek redress at the law." It was also stated that at the current session of the criminal court they had defended "over fifty freedmen" and that there then were in prison awaiting trial "more than this number for whom we are engaged as counsel." Browne & Smithers to C. H. Howard, Annual Report, Oct. 31, 1866, No. 71, Operations Reports—Asst. Comm'r, D.C., BRFAL, Vol. 2 (1866).

[126] C. H. Howard to O. O. Howard, Oct. 10, 1867, No. 758a, Letters Sent by Asst. Comm'r, D.C., BRFAL, Vol. 3 (Mar. 12, 1867-Nov. 20, 1867), p. 385.

Number of civil cases docketed since July 1st 1867					. .	592
"	"	"	"	tried in different courts	153	
"	"	"	"	otherwise settled	128	
"	"	"	"	dismissed	115	396
"	"	"	"	undisposed of		196
"	"	"	"	above enumerated outside this District		38
"	" criminal cases attended to					291
"	"	"	"	had dismissed as frivilous [sic] &c		101
"	" letters written in above cases					789
"	" calls at jail and on different parties in the city in above cases (besides many others not recorded)					683[127]

This total of 883 civil and criminal cases seems like a very large load for one man without typewriter, automobile, or telephone. On its face it appears to cover work for a year and a quarter. Yet it may not have been for much more than a year. In General Howard's own annual report of October 1868 (where he summarized Browne's statistics) he noted a large reduction in his personnel in the District of Columbia, West Virginia, Maryland, and Delaware, as a result of the Civil Rights Act and the ability of the freedmen to secure "their own rights in labor contracts and before the courts . . ."[128] And the fact is that on July 9, 1868, Browne had been notified that his services would not be required after August 1. This notice was superseded by a somewhat apologetic letter of July 15 saying that it had not been intended to notify him that he "would be discharged" but simply to say that "a reduction in force is contemplated" and that he was being granted a leave of absence for thirty days from July 21 "in compliance with your verbal application of today."[129] Three days later the revocation of Browne's appointment

---

[127] Browne to C. H. Howard (Report of Operations Since July 1st, 1867), Oct. 10, 1868, B. 74, p. 5, Operations Reports—Asst. Comm'r, D.C., BRFAL, Vol. 5 (1868).

[128] Commissioner to Secretary of War, Oct. 14, 1868, p. 19, Reports of the Commissioner of the Bureau of Refugees, Freedmen and Abandoned Lands (1865-1870).

[129] Eldridge to Browne, July 9, 1868, No. 739, Letters Sent by Asst. Comm'r, D.C., BRFAL, Vol. 4 (Nov. 18, 1867-Nov. 4, 1868), p. 298; Eldridge to Browne, July 15, 1868, No. 781, Letters Sent by Asst. Comm'r, D.C., BRFAL, Vol. 4 (Nov. 18, 1867-Nov. 4, 1868), p. 314.

was postponed "until further orders," although Browne's clerk was put on leave of absence with his employment to cease on August 15.[130] No other pertinent records have been found. It certainly is possible that Browne in fact continued to work after his thirty day leave. As his campaign to get the job in the first place indicated, he was not easily put off. And his report of October 1868 makes no reference to his having wound up his work, but speaks as though the work were continuing.

Whether the report covered work for a year or for a year and a quarter the work-load seems to the modern reader improbably large, particularly since it seems to refer to cases formally docketed in court. Surveys of the work-load of legal aid lawyers in recent years disclose staggering per-lawyer figures of total matters handled for clients, but even they suggest a doubt that one lawyer could handle so many court cases.[131] And these 1867-1868 figures are more than double the figures for the eleven months previous, when Smithers was with Browne for over half the time. One wonders whether Browne's 1868 report covers not only his work but also that of the "Solicitor at large" in the same office; close reading, though, does not suggest this. Whatever the precise fact, the Bureau's legal aid office in Washington in 1867 and 1868 was humming with activity.

Reports both by Carlisle and by Browne on the nature of the problems they dealt with are very revealing.

On March 27, 1866, Carlisle answered at length an inquiry put by Assistant Commissioner Charles Howard as to the "practical disabilities under which the Colored people of Maryland labor." Carlisle emphasized that the problem was not so much "actual statutory disabilities" as "a settled disposition to hinder and embarrass the operation of existing laws . . ." Whites refuse to act as guardian to black orphans "in the simplest matter or proceeding . . ." Nor would "the declarations" of a black be effective; "especially is this so when it operates against a white man." Moreover a white "who

---

[130] Eldridge to Maj. J. M. Brown, July 18, 1868, No. 795, Letters Sent by Asst. Comm'r, D.C., BRFAL, Vol. 4 (Nov. 18, 1867-Nov. 4, 1868), p. 323.
[131] The classic surveys of modern legal aid work-load per lawyer appear in Brownell, Legal Aid in the United States (The Lawyers Cooperative Pub. Co., 1951), pp. 219-226; Supplement (1961), pp. 49-53.

cherishes enmity" against a black can complain to a magistrate that he "fears bodily injury" and have the black arrested and imprisoned until "he finds bail for his good behavior which it is perhaps utterly impossible to find." Furthermore, white executors of wills containing provisions for the benefit of a black cheat, or connive to cheat, the black. While such abuses occur "occasionally" in cases involving only whites, they are rare, and whites "have no trouble in finding counsel to plead their cause and friends to aid them in putting the machinery of law in operation all of which are beyond the reach of the Colored man." Special complaint is made of Justices of the Peace—generally men "of but little principle and almost entirely under the control of their white neighbours . . ." The great problem arises "rather from the perversion of law by bad men and the want of active sympathy with the blacks by those who would not do them a positive wrong, than from the operation of positive law . . ." But the most "grievious [sic] inconveniences of all" are traceable to the State law discriminating against the testimony of blacks in court.[132]

The report of Browne & Smithers on their first two months of work—August and September 1866—significantly focused on what would be called, in modern legal aid parlance, "law reform." They pointed out that most of the crimes committed by blacks came "under the denomination of larceny." But the existing law gave a Judge no discretion to make punishment less than imprisonment for a year if the property stolen had a value of five dollars. "Both witnesses and jurors are often tempted to estimate at too high a value the property charged as having been stolen, in order that the accused may receive the severest penalty of the law." They urged that "the attention of congress should be called to this subject at an early day of the next session."[133] They also urged a change in the law which permitted no challenges of jurors on the ground of prejudice except in capital cases. Finally they urged that Congress consider

---

[132] Carlisle to C. H. Howard, Mar. 27, 1866, No. 1251, Letters Received by Asst. Comm'r, D.C., BRFAL, Vol. 2 (1867).
[133] Browne & Smithers to C. H. Howard, Annual Report, Oct. 31, 1866, No. 71, Operations Reports—Asst. Comm'r, D.C., BRFAL, Vol. 2 (1866). Their report refers to "imprisonment at Albany." At this time there apparently was no penitentiary in the District of Columbia; it had been taken over by the Ordnance Department of the Army during the war and prisoners were sent to the State penitentiary in Albany, N. Y. Green, p. 253. In those days there were no federal penitentiaries outside the District of Columbia. Robinson, p. 65, n.93.

amending the law regarding enforcement of money judgments rendered by Justices of the Peace. The existing law permitted a stay of execution of six months upon giving security for satisfaction of the judgment. That law, they said, should be modified or repealed where the plaintiff is a servant. For servants are imposed on by the delay in execution; they "need all they earn to procure the necessaries of life."[134]

A year later, in a supplement to Assistant Commissioner Charles Howard's annual report of October 1867, there is a summary of a complaint by the Bureau agent "who has acted as counsel for freedmen" in the District of Columbia district (i.e. Browne) concerning abuses in police court. The complaint cited a case where a black man and his wife had been charged with larceny; after full hearing, a magistrate had dismissed the charge. But the same charge was preferred against them before another magistrate who, without an opportunity for hearing by counsel, committed them to jail in default of $500 bail; later they were released "on reasonable bail." The agent also reported that magistrates made a practice of charging "colored plaintiffs" a dollar for issuance of "warrants" and then failing to execute them. He reported, further, that blacks often are arrested "on mere suspicion," hurried off to the station house, and, when brought before the magistrate, suffer summary disposition "usually on the testimony of the officer who arrested them, and without opportunity of being heard, either by themselves or by counsel," with a fine or committal to the workhouse or jail.[135]

Browne's report of October 1868, covering his work since July 1, 1867, is especially interesting. His civil business, he said, was mostly the prosecution of claims for money, ranging up to hundreds of dollars. There were also a few cases involving claims to realty. And there were fourteen paternity cases, involving illegitimate children of black women; in most such cases the putative father had been compelled to support the children. He added that much of the civil business could not be recorded "without the consumption of too much time," involving title searches and conveyancing, "answering ques-

---

[134] Browne & Smithers to C. H. Howard, Annual Report, Oct. 31, 1866, No. 71, Operations Report—Asst. Comm'r, D.C., BRFAL, Vol. 2 (1866).
[135] C.H. Howard to O. O. Howard, Oct. 22, 1867 (Suppl. to No. 758), Letters Sent by Asst. Comm'r, D.C., BRFAL, Vol. 3 (Mar. 12, 1867-Nov. 20, 1867), pp. 418-419.

tions, giving information and counsel, writing letters in cases not before the courts, and, also, furnishing written opinions upon points of law, when called for by different offices of the Bureau."

His criminal business consisted mainly of prosecuting people for outrages committed upon freedmen, and the defense of freedmen when indicted. There was no provision in the District of Columbia for assigning counsel, so he appeared for blacks when they or the Court requested. He also visited those in jail who were unable to employ counsel. Finally he sought pardons for freedmen believed to have been wrongfully convicted.

He estimated that parties coming to his office averaged 25 a day—noting that he had counted as many as 63 in one day.[136]

His experience led him to opine "that there is still a great indisposition on the part of the former Slave-owners and of others in sympathy with them, to accept the new condition of affairs . . . Deprived of their proprietary rights they still seem to regard the freedmen as their legitimate prey and therefore they do not scruple to defraud them as hirelings of their contract wages, to render them the butts of malice and persecution and to baffle as much as possible every effort made for a redress of their grievances before the Courts." Conditions were especially bad in Maryland. But he hoped that "with the continued diffusion of education and sound morals among the freedmen, ensuring their elevation in the scale of respectability there will be a complete reformation wrought . . ."

He then turned to the failure of District of Columbia law to punish a husband for failing to support his wife. " . . . a man's wife here is in a worse condition than his baker or grocer, for they can enforce the payment of the debts due them but She for the debts contracted at the Altar is without remedy until her recreant partner Sees fit to superadd physical abuse to moral brutality." He urged that the attention of Congress be called to this matter "to the end that Summary proceedings may be provided for redress in such cases."[137]

In his work Browne was able to make use of the Bureau's network of offices. For example, a client claimed an interest in an es-

---

[136] Note that he had had to move because of the number of callers. *Supra*, p. 518.

[137] Browne to C. H. Howard (Report of Operations since July 1st, 1867), Oct. 10, 1868, B. 74, pp. 6-9, Operations Reports—Asst. Comm'r, D.C., BRFAL, Vol. 5 (1868).

tate apparently being administered in Buckingham County, Virginia, and Browne secured an order from General Howard that a Bureau agent in that area "investigate the circumstances of the case" and seek "a fair adjustment," with the direction that if relief could not be secured through the courts there should be resort "to the military authorities who may be able under the new law to act . . ." The new law, of course, was the Civil Rights Act of 1866.[138]

In his report of October 1868 Browne referred to his furnishing of legal opinions to Bureau offices. Quite evidently he acted as a legal advisor to the Bureau as well as a legal aider. Again for example, when there was a request that the Bureau furnish transportation to persons who were to be witnesses at a trial in Ellicott City, Md., Browne's opinion was sought as to whether the court would pay such expense; he replied that the court would not do so until after the trial.[139]

In addition Browne apparently was something of a watch dog respecting possible faults in the community's institutions. In 1862 Congress had incorporated the Guardian Society to care for homeless children who had come under court supervision.[140] In 1867 Browne inquired into the Society and reported that a grand jury had found it to be a nuisance and that its secretary was an imposter. Upon reference of his report to the secretary of the Society that worthy replied that the court clerk advised that there had been no grand jury action; it was suggested that Browne had been misinformed.[141]

A final example of the scope of Browne's concerns strikes an amusing note. In February 1868 Browne wrote Assistant Commis-

---

[138] O. O. Howard to Harris, Apr. 11, 1867, Endorsements Sent, Vol. 3 (Mar. 18-Sept. 27, 1867), p. 83 (Roll 3, Frame 0429). Another example: Browne was able, through General Howard, to have the Bureau agent "at Culpepper Court House" in Virginia seek a settlement of an indebtedness of parties at that place on notes in favor of one of Browne's clients. O. O. Howard to Browne, July 2, 1867, Endorsements Sent, Vol. 3 (Mar. 18-Sept. 27, 1867), p. 325 (Roll 3, Frame 0550). See also O. O. Howard to Asst. Comm'r, D.C., Aug. 21, 1867, Endorsements Sent, Vol. 3 (Mar. 18-Sept. 27, 1867), p. 460 (Roll 3, Frame 0619).

[139] O. O. Howard to Browne, June 13, 1867, Endorsements Sent, Vol. 3 (Mar. 18-Sept. 27, 1867), p. 280 (Roll 3, Frame 0528); O. O. Howard to Asst. Comm'r, D.C., June 19, 1867, Endorsements Sent, Vol. 3 (Mar. 18-Sept. 27, 1867), p. 293 (Roll 3, Frame 0534).

[140] Green, p. 259.

[141] O. O. Howard to Browne, Apr. 5, 1867, Endorsements Sent, Vol. 3 (Mar. 18-Sept. 27, 1867), p. 61 (Roll 3, Frame 0418).

sioner Charles Howard about "a seeming evil which is increasing to an extent almost alarming," and asked for remedy. The evil was the "crowd of colored persons attending daily at the Criminal Court . . . They have no apparent business there but idly lounge there from day to day attracted only by the excitement of the trials, producing an atmosphere that is terrible. They have monopolized almost the entire space in the Court Room assigned to spectators and ousted the former squad of white spectators who have left them in undisputed possession. This crowd by actual count today numbered 186." The Chief Justice, he said, had requested the Bureau's intervention. "He is friendly to the Bureau, to the colored race and does not desire to make a public example of the matter . . . The legal remedy if it has to be resorted to, will be to arrest this army and if found idling about there without any business and without visible means of employment commit them *en masse* to prison or the workhouse." A postscript suggested that these people be referred to Delaware and the Eastern Shore where there was "a great scarcity of hands."[142] Quite obviously the blacks were abundantly enjoying one of the privileges of free men that has vexed judges from time immemorial. Entranced at the drama of court, they were displacing the white idlers!

It is not surprising that after his Bureau career Browne became a prominent community figure. In 1870 he was one of the members elected from the fourth ward of the City of Washington to the Board of Common Council. The City of Washington ceased to exist as a separate municipality on June 1, 1871, when Territorial government for the entire District of Columbia took effect. In that government, in addition to an elected House of Delegates, there was a Presidentially appointed Council as one of the two houses of the legislative body. Browne was a member of the Council both in 1872 and 1873. (In 1874 Congress abolished the Territorial government substituting the non-elective commission form.)[143] In 1873 Browne

---

[142] Browne to C. H. Howard, Feb. 21, 1868, No. C. 80, Letters Received by Asst. Comm'r, D.C., BRFAL, Vol. 4 (1868).

[143] In Boyd's Directory of Washington, Georgetown and Alexandria (1870), p. 479, Browne is listed under City Government as a member of the Board of Common Council. In Boyd's Directory of the District of Columbia (1872), p. 539, and (1873), p. 525, he is listed under Government of the District of Columbia as a member of the Council. For explanation of the governmental changes in the District of Columbia see Tindall, Standard History of the City of Washington (H. W. Crew and Co., Knoxville, 1914), pp. 225-226, 247-248.

introduced, and there was adopted, a bill denying theatres the right to reserve sections of seats not sold previous to the performance, a measure designed to prevent the circumventing of an anti-segregation law.[144]

It is apparent, then, that in the District of Columbia the Bureau had a vigorous and effective legal aid program for the freedmen. The program reached also into Maryland. In his annual report of November 1, 1866, General Howard referred to the program in the District and in Maryland in terms seeming to suggest that it was unique. He ascribed it to the fact that in that area there were no Bureau or provost courts.[145] In a later report, referring to the continuation of the program, General Howard stated that it was necessary because of "representations of judges and others of the injustice to freedmen" arising from their ignorance and "inability to employ suitable counsel."[146]

Doubtless the District of Columbia/Maryland program was unique in its extent and its consistent application. But even an incomplete survey of Bureau archives has turned up evidence strongly indicating that legal aid was provided to some extent in a number of the other districts, in some places even on a considerable scale.

In Mississippi the Assistant Commissioner for the Bureau at the outset was Col. (later General) Samuel Thomas. He had been appointed at the suggestion of Col. Eaton,[147] who had originated the legal aid program in the District of Columbia by his arrangement with Carlisle.[148] Thomas had been Eaton's assistant when Eaton was in charge of freedmen's affairs in the Mississippi Valley during the war.[149] As early as October 2, 1865, instructions in Mississippi called upon Bureau agents to "engage an attorney to defend the Freedmen before the civil authorities," and if a fair trial were denied

---

[144] Tested in court, the measure was invalidated as beyond the District's legislative police power. District of Columbia v. Saville, II Washington Law Reporter 2 (1875); Whyte, pp. 246-247.
[145] *Supra*, n.87.
[146] Commissioner to Secretary of War, Nov. 1, 1867, p. 40, Reports of the Commissioner of the Bureau of Refugees, Freedmen and Abandoned Lands (1865-1870); *cf*. District of Columbia Annual Report for Year Ending Sept. 30, 1867, Synopses of Reports, Asst. Adj. General, BRFAL, Vol. 136 (Jan. 6, 1867-Dec. 31, 1868), p. 185.
[147] Eaton, p. 237.
[148] *Supra*, p. 509.
[149] Eaton, p. 237.

to have the attorney forward a statement of the facts.[150] On November 24 Thomas appointed Mr. James W. Davis as "attorney for the Freedmen's Bureau to appear before the Courts of the State of Mississippi for the defense of Freedmen, where it may be necessary that this Bureau should furnish counsel. . . ."[151]

In writing General Howard on January 10, 1866, reviewing his work to that time, Col. Thomas described Davis as "a lawyer of ability from the North, thoroughly imbued with correct ideas on the subject of Freedmen . . ." Thomas referred to Davis's report to him which showed that Davis had defended 19 criminal cases, with seven acquittals and twelve convictions; Davis had expressed satisfaction with the integrity of the State judges, and asserted that juries would not knowingly convict an innocent black man, though in the case of a black's testimony "the color of his skin materially affects his evidence . . . and any slight discrepancies in his testimony would materially invalidate it." Also Thomas reported that, with Davis's advice, he had "sworn out" seventeen writs of habeas corpus for "Freedmen improperly imprisoned;" all were released after a hearing "before the proper judicial authority."[152]

Davis apparently was paid by the case for in March 1866 he received word that Bureau expenses had to be reduced "to the lowest possible figure" and that thereafter no bills "for defence of Freedmen" would be paid unless the case had been undertaken by special order from the Assistant Commissioner.[153] Indeed economy was enforced. The law firm of Simmons and Crump had submitted a bill in December 1865 for $400 for the defense of blacks in Panola County, Mississippi; eventually the firm was allowed $150 by the Bureau.[154]

---

[150] Eldridge to Donaldson, Oct. 2, 1865, Letters sent by Asst. Comm'r, Mississippi, BRFAL (June 22, 1865-Nov. 4, 1865), pp. 379-380.
[151] Special Orders No. 53, Nov. 24, 1865, Special Orders—Asst. Comm'r, Mississippi, BRFAL, Vol. 33 (June 21, 1865-Dec. 31, 1868), pp. 27-28.
[152] Sam'l Thomas to O. O. Howard, Jan. 10, 1866, Letters Sent by Asst. Comm'r, Mississippi, BRFAL (Nov. 4, 1865-May 29, 1866), pp. 196-197.
[153] Eldridge to Davis, Mar. 9, 1866, Letters Sent by Asst. Comm'r, Mississippi, BRFAL (Nov. 4, 1865-May 29, 1866), p. 387.
[154] From J. R. Simmons, Attorney [addressee not shown], Dec. 14, 1865, S-53, Register of Letters Received by Asst. Comm'r, Mississippi, BRFAL (June 16, 1865-Feb. 19, 1866); Capt. and A.D.C. [illegible] to Simmons, Mar. 27, 1866, and Eldridge to Simmons, May 16, 1866, Letters Sent by Asst. Comm'r, Mississippi, BRFAL (Nov. 4, 1865-May 29, 1866), pp. 475-658. At least one other lawyer

A revealing instance of the civil services of lawyer Davis is found in a letter from Col. Thomas to the army's department commander in March 1866. Davis had provided a statement "of the case of *Beach and Edwards* versus *Harris Boys* (colored) . . . supported by Judge Harris" and Thomas requested that an order be issued against certain parties who held funds of Beach and Edwards requiring that payment be made to the Harris boys.[155]

In Florida, too, there seems to have been employment of counsel for blacks on occasion. In June 1866 a local agent was instructed that "you are under the Civil Rights Bill authorized to employ competent counsel to defend the rights of injured parties . . ."[156] In October of the same year another Florida agent was authorized to employ counsel "at a moderate compensation" to defend six freedmen charged with murder in the event the court would not seasonably appoint counsel to defend them; the Assistant Commissioner for Florida noted that he would "endeavor to defray" the expense if counsel had to be employed.[157]

In both Louisiana and North Carolina it seems fairly clear that instructions to Bureau agents to act as next friend or attorney for the blacks included the duty to bring suits for black plaintiffs and to defend black defendants.[158]

In the case of South Carolina there was at least one instance, in 1867, when the Bureau's general headquarters authorized the Assist-

---

in Mississippi, Harper P. Hunt of Vicksburg, presented a bill to the Bureau in December 1865 for $175 for defending freedmen in a county criminal court. From Hunt [addressee not shown], Rec'd Dec. 11, 1865, H-63, Register of Letters Received by Asst. Comm'r, Mississippi, BRFAL (June 16, 1865-Feb. 19, 1866).

[155] Sam'l Thomas to Wood, Mar. 27, 1866, Letters Sent by Asst. Comm'r, Mississippi, BRFAL (Nov. 4, 1865-May 29, 1866), p. 481.
[156] Unspecified officer to Quentin, June 12, 1866, No. 339, Letters Sent by Asst. Comm'r, Florida, BRFAL, Vol. 4 (Sept. 15, 1865-Sept. 21, 1866), p. 406.
[157] Asst. Comm'r to Stearns, Oct. 6, 1866, No. 468, Letters Sent by Asst. Comm'r, Florida, BRFAL, Vol. 5 (Sept. 24, 1866-Aug. 31, 1868), p. 13.
[158] Circular No. 24, Oct. 30, 1865, Headquarters, Bureau of Refugees, Freedmen and Abandoned Lands, State of Louisiana, U. S. House of Representatives Executive Documents (39th Cong. 1st Sess., 1865-66), Vol. 8, No. 70, p. 27; Report of Asst. Comm'r for Louisiana, Dec. 2, 1865, U. S. House of Representatives Executive Documents (39th Cong. 1st Sess., 1865-66), Vol. 8, No. 70, p. 398; Commissioner to Secretary of War, Nov. 1, 1866, p. 38, Nov. 1, 1867, p. 49, Oct. 14, 1868, p. 25, Reports of the Commissioner of the Bureau of Refugees, Freedmen and Abandoned Lands (1865-1870); Report of Asst. Comm'r for N.C., Nov. 8, 1866, U.S. Senate Executive Documents (39th Cong. 2d Sess., 1866-67), Vol. 1, No. 6, p. 102; Circular No. 1, Feb. 1866, Asst. Comm'r for N.C., U.S. House of Representatives Executive Documents (39th Cong. 1st Sess., 1865-66), Vol. 12, No. 120, p. 11.

ant Commissioner for South Carolina to pay a fee of one hundred dollars to a lawyer for his services in representing one or more freedmen at their trial in Charleston on a criminal charge of rioting.[159]

A few weeks later, however, general headquarters may have had second thoughts about the Bureau's authority to pay lawyers' fees. In August 1867 a request came to headquarters to pay the fees of lawyers who had represented three freedmen in Georgia on a murder charge. The Assistant Commissioner for Georgia was notified that "there is no authority in law" for the employment of attorneys. A way around the difficulty was proposed. "Payment can only be made by taking the name on the payrolls as an Agent for a sufficient time to settle the claim for services." The Assistant Commissioner was told that he could do so if he deemed it "necessary."[160] It is possible, of course, that headquarters sought to curb only the retaining of an attorney by a local agent without specific authorization in advance by higher authority. Earlier in that year General Howard in response to an inquiry about a lawyer's service in Maryland, and prior to the arrangement with Stockbridge, had noted that he would not "pay for legal services already rendered the colored people by persons who expected their clients to remunerate them . . ." But he pointed out that, if General Gregory, his Assistant Commissioner for Maryland, deemed it "necessary in any particular case to engage the services of an attorney" for freedmen, he would "be ready to pay the gentlemen so employed for services actually rendered."[161]

* * *

In August 1965—exactly a century after Col. Eaton made his initial arrangement with Carlisle—Mr. Sargent Shriver, Director of the Office of Economic Opportunity, gave an historic address to the annual meeting of the American Bar Association on the proposed Legal Services program of the OEO.[162] The address marked an agree-

---

[159] O. O. Howard to Asst. Comm'r, S.C., May 3, 1867, Endorsements Sent (Mar. 18-Sept. 27, 1867), p. 147 (Roll 3, Frame 0461).

[160] O. O. Howard to Asst. Comm'r, Ga., Aug. 21, 1867, Endorsements Sent, Vol. 3 (Mar. 18-Sept. 27, 1867), p. 460 (Roll 3, Frame 0619).

[161] O. O. Howard to Bond, Mar. 11, 1867, No. 223, Letters Sent, Vol. 3 (Jan. 2-Sept. 30, 1867), p. 106 (Roll 3, Frame 106). See also McFeely, *op. cit.*, n.14 p. 270.

[162] Shriver, The OEO and Legal Services, 51 American Bar Association Journal 1064 (1965).

ment between Mr. Shriver and the leadership of the American Bar Association, joined enthusiastically by the leadership of the National Bar Association, upon a great common effort by OEO and the organized bar.[163] That was a program which has transformed the legal aid movement into a real instrument for dealing with the problems of the poor, mobilizing the skills and dedication of the bar in the service of people unable to meet the cost of retaining a lawyer.

The OEO program has not included criminal legal aid.[164] But by a happy circumstance the Ford Foundation, shortly before the appearance of OEO, had begun allotments, finally exceeding six million dollars, to the National Legal Aid and Defender Association for a program of grants to stimulate the organization or the enlargement of defender services in communities throughout the nation.[165] That program met with great success. It was continued through 1969.

A century before, the Freedmen's Bureau, with extraordinary prescience, had discerned how necessary it is that a poor man be provided with a lawyer if his legal rights are to be more than an empty form of words. Significantly, as General Howard said in one of his reports concerning the District of Columbia and Maryland, judges themselves had pointed out that need.[166] Yet our nation let the Bureau die away after but the briefest time, and an invaluable experience in the hard work of making legal rights real was forgotten, interred in dusty closets where the Bureau's records were dumped. Even General Howard, when he wrote his autobiography forty years later, seems to have forgotten that experience—for in his two hundred and fifty passionate pages on the Bureau[167] he never mentioned its legal aid program.

---

[163] Mr. Shriver's detailed account of the genesis of that common effort is given in an unpublished letter from Mr. Shriver to Mr. Bernard Segal, immediate past president of the American Bar Association, dated December 3, 1970.
[164] Originally the Economic Opportunity Act did not expressly prohibit financing of criminal legal aid, but OEO allowed only the most limited such financing. Then in 1967 the Act was amended expressly to exclude such financing except in narrowly defined circumstances. 42 U.S.C., sec. 2701, as amended by P.L. 90-222, 81 Stat. 672 (1967). For the legislative history and purpose of P.L. 90-222, see 1967 U.S. Code, Cong. and Adm. News, p. 2428.
[165] The Ford Foundation/NLADA program is described in Allison, National Defender Project—An Introduction, 26 Legal Aid Briefcase 97 (1968); Cleary, National Defender Project—A Progress Report, *id.*, 99.
[166] *Supra*, p. 529.
[167] Howard, pp. 206-455.

The legal aid movement did emerge some twenty years after the Bureau's program had been abandoned. As we have noted,[168] it was largely an outgrowth of an effort in New York City to provide the poor German immigrant, victimized by poverty, ignorance, and prejudice, with the lawyer's help that he had to have were the opportunity of America to be true. But from that time until the coming of the Ford Foundation and the OEO programs the movement had grown so slowly that in the last year before OEO—1964—the total amount spent on legal aid throughout the country (save for the then relatively few defender offices) was less than four and a half million dollars.[169] Starved for funds, barely kept alive by a small number of devoted lawyers, provided on any respectable scale in the merest handful of cities, the legal aid movement was the rejected, dwarfed offspring of a society preoccupied with the concerns of the great middle class majority.

The community of understanding and effort between the OEO, the Ford Foundation, and the organized bar wrought a great change. Legal aid began to grow and to expand. Though the pace has been far too slow in relation to the long neglected need, though the organized bar, the government, foundations and legal aiders themselves have been too timid still in the goals they have set, at least we have begun at last to realize what Col. Eaton saw in 1865. A poor man without a lawyer's advice and protection when need arises is helpless. He is not a free man.

Yet even as legal aid has finally achieved a measure of due recognition, there is curious misunderstanding. In 1969 there appeared among some Congressmen surprising support for the view that it is not proper for the OEO's legal aid projects to engage in efforts to improve the law as it bears on the poor man, that such projects should confine themselves to dealing with the legal problems of particular clients under the law as it appears to be at the moment. This view led to the near adoption of an amendment to the Economic Opportunity Act—known as the Murphy Amendment—designed to curtail or eliminate the vigorous effort of many OEO legal aid projects by test cases and advocacy of change in legal rules to create condi-

---

[168] *Supra*, p. 504.
[169] Summary of Proceedings of the 43rd Annual Conference of the National Legal Aid and Defender Association (1965), p. 85.

tions more conducive to the welfare of the nation's poor.[170]

The invalidity, indeed the futility, of such a view is well illustrated in the Bureau's experience. Hardly had Browne and Smithers begun their work than they saw the need for a number of changes in legal rules.[171] And General Howard's own annual report for 1867 elaborated at length on the grievous apprenticeship problem in Maryland. Mere case-by-case treatment would have been wholly inadequate. He described what today would be called "test cases" that the Bureau had brought about in an effort to reform the situation.[172] The notable test case, before Chief Justice Chase sitting in Circuit, was decided in October 1867 after argument by Stockbridge. It involved "all the important points in controversy under the Maryland apprentice law." The Chief Justice's decision invalidated the law, with its discrimination against blacks, under the Thirteenth Amendment and, alternatively, under the Civil Rights Act. Assistant Commissioner Charles Howard promptly circularized his agents with the text of the Chief Justice's decision, hoping that as a result of the decision "all the cases of unjust and illegal apprenticeship of colored people in Maryland may be remedied."[173]

The fact is, of course, that in legal aid there is no dichotomy as between "service" and "reform." To serve properly there must be

---

[170] See Senator Murphy's explanation of his proposed amendment. 115 Cong. Rec. 29890-29891 (1969).
[171] Supra, pp. 524-525.
[172] Commissioner to Secretary of War, Nov. 1, 1867, pp. 40-41, Reports of the Commissioner of the Bureau of Refugees, Freedmen and Abandoned Lands (1865-1870).
[173] C. H. Howard to O. O. Howard, Oct. 22, 1867 (Suppl. to No. 758), Letters Sent by Asst. Comm'r, D.C., BRFAL, Vol. 3 (Mar. 12, 1867-Nov. 20, 1867), pp. 415-417. The case is reported as In re Turner, 24 Fed. Cas. 337 (C. C. D. Md., 1867). It was a habeas corpus action, seeking the freedom of a black girl "apprenticed" to her former master two days after the effectiveness of Maryland's constitutional abolition of slavery in 1864. *Id.* 339. Stockbridge argued for the petitioner, the girl's mother. The respondent—the master—was not represented by counsel because, though "he wished to retain the girl," he did not have "sufficient interest in the case to spend money on it." *Id.* 338-339. The Chief Justice wanted argument on behalf of the respondent because of the importance of the case, and adjourned court "to give the claimant or any person interested in the decision of the case an opportunity to appear." None appeared and the next day he filed his opinion. *Id.* 339. In Low, pp. 229-247, there is an excellent discussion of the apprenticeship problem in Maryland and the Bureau's efforts to solve it, culminating in the Turner case. Low mistakenly says the decision was by the Supreme Court. *Id.* 245. The seriousness of the apprenticeship problem is indicated by the fact that, based on a Bureau survey in early 1867, there may have been as many as 10,000 black children "apprenticed" into practical slavery in Maryland. *Id.*, p. 233.

advocacy of reform in every lawyer-like way—in an isolated case, in the test case, in seeking administrative change, in urging statutory amendment. "Reform" is as much a part of legal aid's grist as it is of the grist of lawyering for consumers or labor unions or business enterprise. That was seen by the Bureau at the very beginning. It is passing strange that a century later there are some who still believe that there is a difference between "service" and "reform" in the legal aid movement.

In the Bureau's program for the achievement of equal justice for the freedman there was one fundamental aim. That was to assure that the former slave would become a truly independent man, able to make his own way.

In President Johnson's veto message, rejecting the original extension of the Bureau's law in 1866,[174] he sounded the note of rugged individualism. He viewed the Bureau as paternalistic, contrary to American tradition. He urged, instead, reliance on the "laws that regulate supply and demand" to assure the freedman fair wages, laws that the freedman could enforce by his "right to change his place of abode" to a place where his "labor is more esteemed and better rewarded." It was President Johnson's hope that the freedmen "will by their own efforts establish for themselves a condition of respectability and prosperity."[175]

That, too, was the hope of the Bureau. But it saw, as President Johnson and later a neglecting nation did not, that a man could get ahead by his own effort only if he were assured of equal justice. Assistant Commissioner Charles Howard reported to General Howard that the logic of "the condition of the freedmen" was that "whatever will tend most to secure and guarantee their independence will conduce most to their moral and intellectual improvement, as well as to their material prosperity and that of the community in which they live."[176] And conducing most to independence of a man is his right to justice.

But justice does not pervade our communities as does the air. It must be known to a man and he must have the means to invoke

---

[174] *Supra*, n.14.
[175] Richardson, pp. 402-403.
[176] C. H. Howard to O. O. Howard, Oct. 22, 1867 (Suppl. to No. 758), Letters Sent by Asst. Comm'r, D.C., BRFAL, Vol. 3 (Mar. 12, 1867-Nov. 20, 1867), p. 420.

it and if need be to fight for it. For that, if he is poor and ignorant, he must be provided with a lawyer. The Bureau saw that. It took a hundred years for the nation to glimpse it. The nation's vision is imperfect still.

The Great Writ and Reconstruction: The Habeas Corpus Act of 1867

By WILLIAM M. WIECEK

HISTORIANS LONG REGARDED THE RECONSTRUCTION PERIOD AS A time of decline in the prestige and power of the federal courts, particularly the United States Supreme Court. This opinion was derived from their belief that the Reconstruction Congresses were dominated by Radicals determined to sweep away all constitutional obstacles to military Reconstruction. According to this view, unscrupulous Radicals intimidated the Supreme Court and forced it to acquiesce in their program.[1] A fortiori, the historians assumed that there could have been no growth in judicial power in this period.[2] Perceptive scholars have recently noted how misleading these assumptions and conclusions can be.[3] A survey of the statutes and federal court decisions of the Reconstruction

[1] The myth of judicial intimidation is repeated in Bernard Schwartz, *The Reins of Power: A Constitutional History of the United States* (New York, 1963), 109–16; William R. Brock, *An American Crisis: Congress and Reconstruction, 1865–1867* (London and New York, 1963), 7, 262–64; Kenneth M. Stampp, *The Era of Reconstruction, 1865–1877* (New York, 1965), 146, n. 7; Avery Craven, *Reconstruction: The Ending of the Civil War* (New York, 1969), 72, 136, 209; and James G. Randall and David Donald, *The Civil War and Reconstruction* (2d ed., rev., Lexington, Mass., 1969), 643–45. This point of view currently flourishes in survey texts; see Samuel E. Morison, Henry S. Commager, and William E. Leuchtenburg, *The Growth of the American Republic* (2 vols., New York, London, and Toronto, 1969), I, 737, 754; Richard B. Morris and William Greenleaf, *USA: The History of a Nation* (2 vols., Chicago, 1969), I, 720; T. Harry Williams, Richard N. Current, and Frank Freidel, *A History of the United States to 1877* (3d ed., New York, 1969), 715–16.

[2] Judicial impotence is most strenuously asserted in Patricia C. Acheson, *The Supreme Court: America's Judicial Heritage* (New York, 1961), 127–39 (the Supreme Court suffered an "emasculation" of its powers, p. 127); Robert H. Jackson, *The Struggle for Judicial Supremacy: A Study of the Crisis in American Power Politics* (New York, 1941), 326–27 ("Judicial power was all but extinct," p. 326).

[3] Robert G. McCloskey, *The American Supreme Court* (Chicago, 1960), 101–11; Rembert W. Patrick, *The Reconstruction of the Nation* (New York, London, and Toronto, 1967), 117; Eric L. McKitrick, *Andrew Johnson and Reconstruction* (Chicago, 1960), 118. Stanley I. Kutler's *Judicial Power and Reconstruction Politics* (Chicago and London, 1968) is a major contribution toward correcting the cliché of a cowed judiciary submitting to a hostile Congress.

MR. WIECEK is assistant professor of history at the University of Missouri at Columbia.

years reveals a consistent determination by Congress and the courts to enhance the powers and role of the federal courts, not to emasculate them.

As a matter of fact, the business and the powers of the federal courts were expanded by Congress in the Reconstruction period to an extent that has no parallel before or since. Between 1863 and 1875 the United States judiciary was for the first time given jurisdiction fully commensurate with the broad grant of power in Article III of the Constitution. The federal courts shared fully in the increase of national power that was one of the greatest legacies of Reconstruction. They enjoyed an expansion of their role within the federal system and asserted their superiority over the state courts in all questions of national concern. It was in the Reconstruction era that Congress laid the foundations for the judicial dynamism of the late nineteenth and early twentieth centuries.

Congress enlarged federal jurisdiction in two principal ways: first, by increasing the number and nature of suits that could be removed from state courts to lower federal courts for trial, and second, by permitting a person imprisoned or detained under state authority to seek a writ of habeas corpus from the federal courts if he believed that his rights under the United States Constitution or statutes were violated by the state. The evolution of removal jurisdiction of the federal courts has been treated elsewhere;[4] this paper traces the origin and the later effects of federal habeas jurisdiction conferred by the Habeas Corpus Act of 1867.[5]

When Congress passed this act, it did more than merely increase the number of cases which might be brought into the federal courts by the writ of habeas corpus. It changed the nature of the writ itself, making it a means of obtaining review after trial and conviction. Previously the writ could be sought only before trial, and it could be used only to question the legality of detention by executive officials. It could not be used to challenge a conviction by a competent court. After 1867 habeas corpus emerged as a form of review *after trial* of federal and state convictions.[6]

[4] Kutler, *Judicial Power and Reconstruction Politics*, 143–60.
[5] Act of February 5, 1867, Ch. 28, *Statutes at Large of the United States*, XIV (1868), 385 (to be distinguished from the immediately preceding statute on the same page, Ch. 27, also a habeas statute).
[6] Dallin H. Oaks, "Legal History in the High Court—Habeas Corpus," *Michigan Law Review*, LXIV (January 1966), 451–72. The widely held belief that

More important, the Habeas Corpus Act of 1867 enabled the federal courts to supervise the administration of criminal justice in the state courts. Before 1867 a person convicted of a crime in a state court had no way outside the state judicial system of asserting that his conviction violated his federal constitutional rights. The act of 1867 and its judicial construction over the following century made it possible for anyone to get collateral review in the federal district courts as well as direct appellate review in the United States Supreme Court of all federal constitutional issues presented by his conviction, no matter how fully these might have been litigated and reconsidered in the state trial and appellate courts. In this way the 1867 Habeas Corpus Act enabled the federal courts to assert their primacy in deciding questions affecting individual liberty.[7]

Before 1867 habeas corpus had been of only limited importance in the federal courts for several reasons. For one thing, the final draft of Article I, Section 9, of the Constitution dealt only with the writ's suspension, not its scope.[8] Since there is no "common-law" federal jurisdiction to issue the writ, the power of the federal courts in habeas matters depends entirely on the grant of power in Article III, the judiciary article. Habeas corpus can be granted by a federal court only in cases falling in the classes enumerated in Section 2 of that article. The Constitution, besides being silent on the habeas corpus powers of the federal courts, also makes no provision for federal regulation of habeas corpus in the state courts. Hence, all persons in the United States depend exclusively on the state courts for protection of their right to the writ in all matters not involving the federal Constitution, laws, or treaties.[9]

habeas corpus was exclusively a pretrial remedy has been challenged by Professor Paul Freund of the Harvard Law School. He has suggested that habeas corpus may have been a postconviction remedy at common law. See Paul A. Freund, *United States of America, Petitioner, vs. Herman Hayman: Brief for the Respondent* (n.p., n.d.; filed in U. S. Supreme Court, October 11, 1951), 30–32.

[7] Paul M. Bator, "Finality in Criminal Law and Federal Habeas Corpus for State Prisoners," *Harvard Law Review*, LXXVI (January 1963), 441–528; Henry M. Hart, Jr., "The Supreme Court, 1958 Term—Forward: The Time Chart of the Justices," *ibid.*, LXXIII (November 1959), 84, 103; "The Freedom Writ: The Expanding Use of Federal Habeas Corpus," *ibid.*, LXI (April 1948), 657–75.

[8] "The Privilege of the Writ of Habeas Corpus shall not be suspended, unless when in Cases of Rebellion or Invasion the public Safety may require it" (Clause 2).

[9] The original phrasing of the habeas corpus clause was: "The privileges and benefit of the writ of habeas corpus shall be enjoyed in this government in the most expeditious and ample manner: and shall not be suspended by the Legislature except upon the most urgent and pressing occasions, and for a limited time not exceeding [blank] months." Max Farrand, ed., *The Records of the Federal*

One of the earliest accomplishments of the First Congress, and perhaps the greatest, was its provision for the organization and functioning of the federal courts in the Judiciary Act of 1789. Section 14 of this statute, regulating the use of habeas corpus, provided:

And be it further enacted, That all the before-mentioned courts of the United States, shall have power to issue writs of *scire facias, habeas corpus,* and all other writs not specially provided for by statute, which may be necessary for the exercise of their respective jurisdictions, and agreeable to the principles and usages of law. And that either of the justices of the supreme court, as well as judges of the district courts, shall have power to grant writs of *habeas corpus* for the purpose of an inquiry into the cause of commitment.—*Provided,* That writs of *habeas corpus* shall in no case extend to prisoners in gaol, un'ess where they are in custody, under or by colour of the authority of he United States, or are committed for trial before some court of the same, or are necessary to be brought into court to testify.

This was an extremely restrictive grant of habeas power, and (except for the Force Act of 1833 and the "*Caroline* Act" of 1842) it remained the only statutory authorization for federal habeas corpus until 1867.[10]

The first clause of Section 14 granted federal courts, as courts, the power to issue the writ only as it was "necessary for the exercise of their respective jurisdictions." The only explicit grant of substantive habeas power was in the next clause and was limited to the individual judges; it was not a grant of power to the courts themselves. Finally, the proviso prohibited federal courts from issuing the writ to persons held in custody under state authority, which effectively denied all state prisoners the benefit of federal

---

Convention of 1787 (4 vols., New Haven and London, 1911), II, 334 (Journal, August 20). Had this version been adopted, the Supreme Court might have taken a more expansive view of federal habeas powers. See Dallin H. Oaks, "The 'Original' Writ of Habeas Corpus in the Supreme Court," *Supreme Court Review* (1962), 154, 156–59; Milton Cantor, "The Writ of Habeas Corpus: Early American Origins and Development," in Harold M. Hyman and Leonard W. Levy, eds., *Freedom and Reform: Essays in Honor of Henry Steele Commager* (New York, Evanston, and London, 1967), 74–76; Rex A. Collings, Jr., "Habeas Corpus for Convicts—Constitutional Right or Legislative Grace?" *California Law Review,* XL (Fall 1952), 335–61.

[10] Judiciary Act of 1789, Ch. 20, Section 14, *Statutes at Large,* I (1845), 81–82. A clue as to why Congress should have been so niggardly in its grant of habeas power to the federal courts is found in Charles Warren, "New Light on the History of the Federal Judiciary Act of 1789," *Harvard Law Review,* XXXVII (November 1923), 49–132. His insistence (p. 53) that the act was a compromise, trimmed down to please the "Anti-Federalist" faction in the First Congress, has special pertinence to the restrictive Section 14.

habeas corpus, no matter how glaring the violation of their federal constitutional rights.

Federal judicial development of the writ before the Civil War was as restrictive as Section 14. Only once, in the celebrated *Bollman* case, did the Supreme Court give an expansive reading to Section 14, by holding that the first clause permitted it as a court to issue the writ of habeas corpus in aid of its jurisdiction.[11] Otherwise, the Court consistently avoided opportunities to construe Section 14 liberally. It refused to use its habeas powers to review civil arrests;[12] it declined to issue the writ to a person who had already been convicted (and thereby reaffirmed the pretrial nature of habeas appeals);[13] it refused the writ to a person held by a judge's order made in chambers;[14] and most important, it held that the proviso of Section 14 meant just what it said: federal habeas relief was not available to persons held under the authority of a state.[15] As a result of these pre–Civil War holdings, federal habeas relief was available only when the petitioner had been confined by an order of a federal court and only before trial.

In the period between the Judiciary Act of 1789 and the Habeas Corpus Act of 1867 Congress increased habeas jurisdiction of the federal courts twice, both times in response to crises which challenged federal control of the purse or the sword. The first such response was contained in two sections of the Force Act of 1833, passed after South Carolina adopted its ordinance of nullification and implemented it with laws making it a criminal offense for federal revenue officials to collect the tariff in the state. Section 3 made the writ of habeas corpus *cum causa* available to any federal official who was sued or prosecuted for acts done under the authority of federal revenue laws.[16] Section 7 made the Great

---

[11] *Ex parte Bollman* and *Ex parte Swartwout*, 4 Cranch 75 (1807).

[12] *Ex parte Wilson*, 6 Cranch 52 (1810).

[13] *Ex parte Kearney*, 7 Wheat. 38 (1822), and *Ex parte Watkins*, 3 Peters 193 (1830).

[14] *In re Metzger*, 5 Howard 176 (1847).

[15] *Ex parte Dorr*, 3 Howard 103 (1845).

[16] There are several writs of habeas corpus. The Great Writ is technically known as habeas corpus *ad subjiciendum;* the others, of which habeas corpus *cum causa* is one, are the "ancillary" writs, so called because they are merely procedural writs whose function is to bring a party, a witness, or a document before a court. *Cum causa*, for example, assured the physical removal of the official to the custody of the federal court so as to prevent bodily harm to him while he was in the state's custody. See generally Maxwell Cohen, "Habeas Corpus Cum Causa—The Emergence of the Modern Writ," *Canadian Bar Review*, XVIII (January 1940), 10–42.

Writ available to any person held in custody by the state "for any act done, or omitted to be done, in pursuance of a law of the United States . . . ." This was a major breach in the barrier between the state and federal judicial systems erected by the proviso in Section 14 of the Judiciary Act of 1789.[17]

The second pre–Civil War habeas corpus act was passed to prevent a recurrence of incidents like that arising from the "*Caroline* crisis" of 1837. The federal government's inability to persuade New York courts to release Alexander McLeod, a British subject who was charged with the killing of an American citizen during the burning of the *Caroline,* precipitated a diplomatic impasse between the British and American governments. To cope with similar events in the future, Congress passed the Habeas Corpus Act of 1842, which extended the benefit of federal habeas corpus to aliens committed by a state for acts done under the authority of a foreign nation.[18]

Two important developments in the use of habeas corpus in the state courts before the Civil War embroiled state-federal relations and contributed to the need for the assertion of federal supremacy embodied in the Habeas Corpus Act of 1867. The first was a curious throwback to an obsolete fourteenth-century predecessor of the habeas procedure, the writ *de homine replegiando*. This was a writ of replevin used to remove a human being rather than a chattel from the custody of a private person. Abolitionists found this antique writ useful in rescuing Negroes from slave catchers in the northern states. It was also technically available to slaveowners seeking to recapture their human chattels, but one procedural feature of the writ nullified its utility for southerners: issues raised by the writ were triable by jury, and few northern juries in the 1850s sympathized with slave catchers.[19]

---

[17] Act of March 2, 1833, Ch. 57, Sections 3, 7, *Statutes at Large*, IV (1846), 634. In the 1850s Section 7 was extensively used to protect federal officials who had been imprisoned by state court order for attempted enforcement of the Fugitive Slave Act of 1850. For an example of this use, see *Ex parte Robinson*, 20 Fed. Cases 965 (No. 11,934, Circuit Court, Southern District of Ohio, 1856).

[18] Act of August 29, 1842, Ch. 257, *Statutes at Large*, V (1846), 539–40. In its original form, the 1842 bill, S. 181, anticipated the 1867 act in providing habeas relief "on account of anything done" "Under or by virtue of the Constitution, or any law or treaty of the United States . . . or any alleged right, authority, title, privilege, protection, or exemption, set up or claimed under the same, or under color thereof . . . ." This broad language was stricken from the bill before passage. S. 181 can be found in Senate Bill File, 27 Cong., 2 Sess., Records of the U. S. Senate, Record Group 46 (National Archives, Washington, D. C.).

[19] See Dallin H. Oaks, "Habeas Corpus in the States—1776–1865," *University of Chicago Law Review*, XXXII (Winter 1965), 243–88.

The second development was the use of habeas corpus by abolitionists to impede the seizure of Negroes under the Fugitive Slave Act of 1850. This use of the writ was denounced in the case of *Ableman v. Booth* (1859), in which Chief Justice Roger B. Taney held that state habeas corpus could not be used to liberate persons held in custody under federal authority. It was ironic that the assertion of federal supremacy in *Ableman*, meant by Taney to preserve the legal bulwarks of slavery, should serve as a precedent for the Habeas Corpus Act of 1867, which was enacted in part to destroy the vestiges of slavery.[20]

Historians discussing the evolution of habeas corpus in the Civil War years have usually been concerned with the controversial and exciting issue of suspension of the privilege of the writ to the exclusion of everything else. Yet in terms of the altered state-federal balance and the ultimate guarantees of individual liberty, the suspension question was but a momentary diversion compared with the profound and lasting impact of the later Habeas Corpus Act of 1867.

Suspension of the habeas privilege by President Abraham Lincoln and Congress did not deprive the federal courts of their role as guardians of individual liberty during the Civil War. Justices of the Supreme Court twice rebuked Congress and the President for suspending the writ. Chief Justice Taney, in the well-known *Merryman* case, reminded Congress and the nation at large that suspension of the writ did not suspend the Bill of Rights. Even if the writ were suspended, Taney pointed out, a civilian could not be kept in prison without trial or be tried by a military court because the imperatives of the Sixth Amendment, guaranteeing jury trial and other safeguards of criminal justice, remained in full force. Taney's assertions notwithstanding, John Merryman remained in custody for a time. But the opinion gave notice that the nation's courts would continue to provide a forum to enforce the guarantees of the Bill of Rights. The principle of *inter arma silent leges* was emphatically rejected.[21]

Congress, moreover, was nearly as scrupulous of individual

[20] *Ableman v. Booth*, 21 Howard 506 (1859). Charles Warren, "Federal and State Court Interference," *Harvard Law Review*, XLIII (January 1930), 345–78; Maxwell Cohen, "Some Considerations on the Origins of Habeas Corpus," *Canadian Bar Review*, XVI (February 1938), 92–118.

[21] *Ex parte Merryman*, 17 Fed. Cases 144 (No. 9,487, Circuit Court, District of Md., 1861). Taney was not alone in his refusal to surrender judicial prerogatives in the face of suspension of habeas corpus. Justice Nathan Clifford, on circuit, in a case similar in its facts to *Merryman*, refused to admit defeat when a writ of habeas corpus was not honored by military officials. Observing that "the court has not the command of the physical force needful to effect a service of this writ at the present

liberty as the Court itself. In the very act that ratified President Lincoln's suspension of the writ, Congress erected additional safeguards to prevent abuses by military authority. Section 2 of the Habeas Corpus Suspension Act of 1863 provided that lists of all persons detained by military or civilian authority must be given to the federal courts in the districts where the detainees lived or were arrested. Those detained were to be discharged from confinement if a grand jury thereafter met and disbanded without returning an indictment against them. Thus, the federal courts during the Civil War were not thrust into the background and rendered unable to defend individual liberty; nor were they impotent and acquiescent in the face of a supposed congressional onslaught.[22]

Throughout the first half of the nineteenth century Congress had turned to the federal courts when it needed help in implementing federal policy or protecting federal officials, as it did in the habeas corpus acts of 1833 and 1842 and in a half-dozen removal statutes. This pattern of congressional-judicial partnership in the execution of national policy continued after the Civil War, but the expanded scope of federal activity during Reconstruction, together with the problems facing the freedmen, made it apparent that the objectives of the partnership would have to be expanded. By 1865 it had become obvious that the overriding result of the Civil War was the supremacy of the Union over the claims of state autonomy. Federal policy was to take precedence over state objectives in the event of a clash between the two, and the federal courts were to protect this precedence.[23]

---

time," Clifford entered this order: "Let the writ be placed on file, to be served when and where service may become practicable." *In re Winder,* 30 Fed. Cases 288, at 294 (No. 17,867, Circuit Court, District of Mass., 1862). See David M. Silver, *Lincoln's Supreme Court* (Urbana, 1956), 182–84; confidential memorandum of Attorney General Edward Bates, January 31, 1863, cited and discussed in James G. Randall, *Constitutional Problems Under Lincoln* (New York and London, 1926), 132; Bates's official opinion of July 5, 1861, *Opinions of the Attorneys General,* X (1868), 74. Sherrill Halbert, "The Suspension of the Writ of Habeas Corpus by President Lincoln," *American Journal of Legal History,* II (April 1958), 95–116.

[22] The Habeas Corpus Suspension Act was the act of March 3, 1863, Ch. 81, *Statutes at Large,* XII (1863), 755. Section 2 of the act further strengthened the powers of the federal judges, who were authorized to exact prospective loyalty oaths, sureties for good behavior, and periodic reexaminations of the persons thus set at liberty. Sections 5 and 6, providing for removal of suits by federal officials and appeals to the Supreme Court, were other notable increments to judicial power. The charge of impotence and restraint is made in an otherwise astute study of the Court; McCloskey, *American Supreme Court,* 98–99.

[23] Anthony G. Amsterdam, "Criminal Prosecutions Affecting Federally Guaranteed Civil Rights: Federal Removal and Habeas Corpus Jurisdiction to Abort

These objectives of the congressional-judicial partnership were realized in the Habeas Corpus Act of 1867. Most congressmen and senators, however, did not foresee the ultimate consequences of that act. Possibly no federal statute of equivalent importance had such an inconspicuous beginning; probably none was enacted so inadvertently. Early in the first session of the Thirty-ninth Congress, James F. Wilson (R., Iowa), chairman of the House Judiciary Committee, "introduced a bill to secure the writ of *habeas corpus* to persons held in slavery" as one means of enforcing the recently ratified Thirteenth Amendment. Wilson's bill was referred to his own committee, where it was replaced by what was to become Section 1 of the Habeas Corpus Act of 1867. The substitute was reported out on July 25, 1866.[24]

The debates on the bill are remarkable for their scantiness and opacity. Only two persons, Congressman William Lawrence (R., Ohio) of the House Judiciary Committee, who reported the bill out of committee, and Senator Lyman Trumbull (R., Ill.), who guided it through the Senate, commented on the bill's objectives, and they disagreed with each other. Lawrence's explanation of the committee's intent was ambiguous. He stated that the bill's genesis was a resolution for the protection of the wives and children of freedmen who had served in the Union military forces, but added that "the [bill's] effect . . . is to enlarge the privilege of the writ of *habeas corpus,* and make the jurisdiction of the courts and judges of the United States coextensive with all the powers that can be conferred upon them. It is a bill of the largest liberty . . . ." It passed the House without further exegesis.[25]

State Court Trial," *University of Pennsylvania Law Review,* CXIII (April 1965), 793–912. Several of the removal statutes referred to in the text are reviewed in Kutler, *Judicial Power and Reconstruction Politics,* 145–46. In general, they permitted a federal official who was sued or prosecuted in a state court for performance of his official duties to remove the suit or prosecution to a federal court. The underlying assumption of such statutes was that the trial of such an official would be fairer in a federal court than in a state court and that the mere possibility that such suits or prosecutions could be removed would discourage them.

[24] *Congressional Globe,* 39 Cong., 1 Sess., 135 (January 8, 1866). The text of the Wilson bill, which was not printed, may be found in Lewis Mayers, "The Habeas Corpus Act of 1867: The Supreme Court as Legal Historian," *University of Chicago Law Review,* XXXIII (Autumn 1965), 34. Section 2 of the act had no relation to habeas corpus; it enormously widened Supreme Court appellate review by writs of error under Section 25 of the Judiciary Act of 1789. This was another example of Congress' willingness to increase the power of the federal courts in the Reconstruction period.

[25] *Cong. Globe,* 39 Cong., 1 Sess., 4151 (July 25, 1866). Lawrence was one of the most competent legislators of his era. Highly respected by his colleagues, he accomplished many necessary and far-reaching reforms of the federal court sys-

In the Senate Trumbull reported the bill out of the Judiciary Committee, stating:

... the *habeas corpus* act of 1789 [Section 14 of the 1789 Judiciary Act], to which this bill is an amendment, confines the jurisdiction of the United States courts in issuing writs of *habeas corpus* to persons who are held under United States laws. Now, a person might be held under a State law in violation of the Constitution and laws of the United States, and he ought to have in such a case the benefit of the writ, and we agree he ought to have recourse to the United States courts to show that he was illegally imprisoned in violation of the Constitution or laws of the United States.

Trumbull's explanation of the bill's effects was more explicit and precise than Lawrence's, but the ensuing debate revealed that he had obviously not done his homework. He virtually admitted as much, after fumbling with answers for objections to the bill. Because of his embarrassing position, he suggested that the bill lie over. It carried over to the next session, when, with one minor amendment, it passed both houses.[26]

Section 1 of the 1867 act provided that all federal courts and judges could grant a writ of habeas corpus "in all cases where any person may be restrained of his or her liberty in violation of the constitution, or of any treaty or law of the United States . . . ." It was not limited to restraints by federal authority. The court or judge was permitted to make its own fact-finding anew. Extensive procedural liberalizations were made, and appeals were authorized to the federal circuit courts and the Supreme Court.

Congressional intent in passing the Habeas Corpus Act of 1867 is unusually murky, even for a piece of Reconstruction legislation. In debates on the bill in the House, Representative Edwin R. V. Wright, a New Jersey Democrat, protested: "I would ask whether anybody in this House, when he gives his vote on these amendments, knows what he is voting upon? [Laughter]." The act was therefore open to several interpretations. A narrow one would limit its benefits to the classes of former slaves mentioned in the original bill that was the forerunner of the act. Nevertheless, it is at least as plausible that Congress meant to protect all persons, and not just freedmen, in broadening habeas protection

---

tem. Neither a florid orator nor an egregious Radical, he has been overlooked by historians tracing the controversies of Reconstruction. See the biographical sketch of Lawrence by Reginald C. McGrane in *Dictionary of American Biography* (22 vols. and index, New York, 1928–1958), XI, 52–53.

[26] *Cong. Globe*, 39 Cong., 1 Sess., 4229 (July 27, 1866); *ibid.;* 2 Sess., 790, 903 (January 28, 31, 1867).

for all federal constitutional and statutory rights. Three reasons, any one of them almost conclusive, support this interpretation. First, the House Judiciary Committee rejected the narrower bill in favor of the more inclusive one. Second, the language of Section 1 itself contains no limitations on the scope of its beneficiaries. Third, both Lawrence and Trumbull, who furnished the only explanations of the bill's purpose, supported the broader interpretation.[27]

Later congressional interpretations of the act do little to clarify the intent of Congress in 1867. The 1868 debates on the McCardle repealer statute (discussed below) presented the anomalous spectacle of Republicans depreciating the scope of their 1867 habeas corpus measure, while the Democrats argued for a liberal reading of the act. Republicans like Wilson and Trumbull insisted in 1868 that they had intended to benefit only freedmen and southern Unionists. Democrats asserted that the act was intended for all persons. Democrat Reverdy Johnson, who seems to have taken charge of the bill in the Senate Judiciary Committee, argued against the narrow interpretation: "That, I know, Mr. President, was one of the objects; but it was necessary to make the law comprehensive, and it therefore covers all cases in which any man entitled to any right under the Constitution and laws of the United States, or who claimed to be entitled to any right under either, should have the decision of that question brought by appeal to the Supreme Court of the United States."[28]

Perhaps all that can be concluded about the intent of Congress in passing the Habeas Corpus Act of 1867 is that, in attempting to secure the narrow objective of protecting certain southern Negroes, Congress enacted a statute of comprehensive terminology, being vaguely aware of the possibilities inherent in the act and

[27] *Ibid.*, 899 (January 31, 1867). The argument in favor of the narrow interpretation has been made persuasively by Professor Lewis Mayers of the University of Chicago Law School in "The Habeas Corpus Act of 1867." See also federal district judge Charles Wyzanski's views in *Geagan* v. *Gavin*, 181 F. Supp. 466 (District of Mass., 1960). For a contrary view, based more on assumptions than on evidence, see "Federal Habeas Corpus Review of State Convictions: An Interplay of Appellate Ambiguity and District Court Discretion," *Yale Law Journal*, LXVIII (November 1958), 98–112.

[28] *Cong. Globe*, 40 Cong., 2 Sess., 2168 (March 27, 1868), 2120 (March 26, 1868), quote on page 2120. See Trumbull's argument as counsel for the United States in *Ex parte McCardle*, 7 Wall. 506 (1869). The Democratic position was put forward by Senator Thomas A. Hendricks of Indiana (*Cong. Globe*, 40 Cong., 2 Sess., 2115 [March 26, 1868]) and President Andrew Johnson in his veto message, in *A Compilation of the Messages and Papers of the Presidents* (20 vols., New York, [191?]), VIII, 3844–46.

willing to see how it would be nurtured and matured in the courts. Even this conservative conclusion indicates the extent to which Congress was ready to expand the powers of the federal courts, since it would be the courts that would, in effect, prescribe the limits of their own jurisdiction.

Scarcely was the ink dry on the act when it was used to thwart southern judicial enforcement of the Black Codes. Chief Justice Salmon P. Chase, on circuit, awarded a writ of habeas corpus under authority of the act to a young ex-slave who was bound over to her former master under a Maryland apprenticeship act. In this case, *In re Turner* (1867), Chase struck down the Maryland law on the ground that it imposed a state of involuntary servitude contrary to the provisions of the Thirteenth Amendment; he also upheld the constitutionality of the Civil Rights Act of 1866. Chase's use of the new habeas corpus provisions caused no comment. It was entirely within the scope of even the narrow interpretation soon to be advanced by the act's Republican sponsors, and the decision promoted ends which Congress sought to secure.[29]

But the Supreme Court soon learned that, however nebulous Congress might have been about the purposes of the act, congressional Republicans did not intend that it should become a means of judicial interference with Reconstruction. William H. McCardle, a Mississippi editor critical of Republican Reconstruction policy, after being remanded to military custody by a United States circuit court, appealed the lower court order to the Supreme Court. In *Ex parte McCardle* (1868), Chief Justice Chase chose to treat the appeal as being under Section 1 of the 1867 act, rather than the habeas corpus provisions (Section 14) of the Judiciary Act of 1789, and held that the act of 1867 authorized McCardle's appeal because he had been committed by order of a lower federal court. Chase's statement of the scope of the 1867 act was exuberant in its expansiveness: "This legislation is of the most comprehensive character. It brings within the *habeas corpus* jurisdiction of every court and of every judge every possible case of privation of liberty contrary to the National Constitution, treaties, or laws. It is impossible to widen this jurisdiction."[30]

[29] *In re Turner*, 24 Fed. Cases 337 (No. 14,247, Circuit Court, District of Md., 1867).
[30] *Ex parte McCardle*, 6 Wall. 318, at 325–26 (1868) (hearing on motion to dismiss). The significance of the *McCardle* decision has been thoughtfully examined by Professor Stanley I. Kutler in "*Ex parte McCardle*: Judicial Impotency? The Supreme Court and Reconstruction Reconsidered," *American Historical Re-*

Chase said little more about the act than either Lawrence or Trumbull had, and his remarks might have attracted little attention had congressional Democrats not misinterpreted and exploited them. Democrats inside Congress and out presumed that the Court's acceptance of jurisdiction under the 1867 act, considered in the light of its earlier *Milligan* decision, indicated that it would nullify the use of military commissions in the southern states. They gleefully nagged the Republicans about this possibility, because destruction of the commissions would have enervated military Reconstruction in the South.

Alarmed and unified, Republicans in the House tacked onto an innocuous writs-of-error bill the "McCardle repealer," which was by its terms applicable only to the 1867 act. This repealer prohibited Supreme Court review of the disposition of habeas cases by lower federal courts under Section 1 of the 1867 act. It passed the House easily but ran into violent Democratic opposition in the Senate. The Democrats became ardent defenders of the federal judiciary and taunted the Republicans with charges of cowardice and fear of the high court. In spite of this, Trumbull, defending the repealer bill, foreshadowed the dictum of the second *McCardle* case and the holding of *Ex parte Yerger* when he suggested that the "liberties of the people" protected by habeas corpus "are left just as they always have been." The Republicans seemed to wish to restrict their repealer to as narrow a scope as possible so long as it kept McCardle's case out of the Supreme Court. The bill passed easily. President Andrew Johnson's veto message, written in the midst of his impeachment trial, was an ironic and futile encomium to the high court. The veto was overridden easily in both houses.[31]

Faced with this *fait accompli*, the Court acceded and de-

---

view, LXXII (April 1967), 835–51; and in *Judicial Power and Reconstruction Politics*, 100–108.

[31] Act of March 27, 1868, Ch. 34, Section 2, *Statutes at Large*, XV (1869), 44; *Cong. Globe*, 40 Cong., 2 Sess., 2096 (March 25, 1868). The statute did not withdraw all appellate authority from the Supreme Court in all habeas corpus matters as some writers assert or imply; for example, Stampp, *Era of Reconstruction*, 146, n. 7; Brock, *American Crisis*, 264; Patrick, *Reconstruction of the Nation*, 116; Williams, Current, and Freidel, *History of the United States to 1877*, p. 716; Randall and Donald, *Civil War and Reconstruction*, 645; Howard J. Graham, "Justice Field and the Fourteenth Amendment," *Yale Law Journal*, LII (September 1943), 851–89, reprinted in Graham, *Everyman's Constitution: Historical Essays on the Fourteenth Amendment, the "Conspiracy Theory," and American Constitutionalism* (Madison, 1968), 110–50. It did nothing more than prohibit the Supreme Court from taking appeals in cases brought under the 1867 act alone. The Court's jurisdiction under other habeas statutes remained unaffected.

clared itself without jurisdiction to entertain McCardle's appeal. It could hardly have done otherwise in view of the "exceptions" clause of Article III, Section 2, of the Constitution. Nevertheless, Chief Justice Chase took the opportunity to emphasize the scope of the Court's power left unaffected by the McCardle repealer: "Counsel seem to have supposed, if effect be given to the repealing act in question, that the whole appellate power of the court, in cases of *habeas corpus*, is denied. But this is an error. The act of 1868 does not except from that jurisdiction any cases but appeals from Circuit Courts under the act of 1867. It does not affect the jurisdiction which was previously exercised."[32]

Within a year this dictum bore fruit in *Ex parte Yerger* (1869). Edward M. Yerger had appealed to the Supreme Court from a denial of habeas relief by a federal circuit court. The Supreme Court held that the 1868 repealer did not prohibit the appeal or limit the Supreme Court's general habeas corpus jurisdiction. In several remarkable passages, it scolded Congress for the 1868 act ("legislation of this character is unusual and hardly to be justified except upon some imperious public exigency") and asserted that its habeas corpus jurisdiction was "derived from the Constitution" and merely "defined by the Act of 1789." It concluded that "the general spirit and genius of our institutions has tended to the widening and enlarging of the *habeas corpus* jurisdiction of the courts and judges of the United States; and this tendency, except in one recent instance, has been constant and uniform...."[33]

The Court thus emerged from the McCardle affair slightly bloodied but emphatically unbowed. Judicial power had been preserved nearly unscathed except for the niche carved out by the McCardle repealer. It was therefore something of an anticlimax when Congress restored even this bit of appellate authority in 1885. The House Judiciary Committee, which drafted the act, stated that its purpose was to permit the Supreme Court to define the jurisdictional limits of the 1867 act, concluding with the pointed hint that "it can then be seen whether further legislation is necessary." The House committee was not raking over the ashes of the Reconstruction era in this report; it was addressing itself to a problem that had by then become most heatedly de-

[32] *Ex parte McCardle*, 7 Wall. 506, at 515 (1869). This holding has recently been questioned by Justices Douglas and Black, dissenting in *Glidden Co. v. Zdanok*, 370 U. S. 530, at 605 (1962).
[33] *Ex parte Yerger*, 8 Wall. 85, at 104 and 102 (1869).

bated: review of state court proceedings by lower federal courts.[34]

The Habeas Corpus Act of 1867 came to have two major effects on habeas practice in the United States. For the first time in its centuries-long evolution, habeas corpus was to be used as a postconviction mode of relief. In this aspect, the new powers of the federal courts did not excite much controversy, and habeas corpus as a form of postconviction relief was established by 1880. It was otherwise with the second principal change effected by the 1867 act, federal court review of state court decisions. This struck directly at traditional powers of the state courts, and the protests of the partisans of the state judiciaries still continue.

Criticism of the 1867 act on the ground that it subordinated the state benches to the federal courts was not long in coming. The first protest, ironically, came from a justice of the United States Supreme Court, Joseph P. Bradley. In a circuit court decision, *Ex parte Bridges* (1875), Bradley issued a writ of habeas corpus to a former slave convicted of a federal offense in a state court, but he recommended in a dictum that Congress repeal the act on which his decision was based. What troubled him, and later critics as well, was that the 1867 act permitted a lower federal court to reverse the conviction of a habeas petitioner even if the conviction had been affirmed by a state supreme court. This, Bradley thought, was degrading to the state appellate courts.[35]

Bradley's objection was taken up by lawyers, state officials, legal commentators, and congressmen. Complaints that the dignity of the state supreme courts was besmirched by habeas reversals in the United States district courts found their way into bar journals and received a sympathetic hearing in Congress. The House Judiciary Committee in 1884 insisted, without support, that it was not the intention of the Thirty-ninth Congress to confer such authority. The committee's solution for the problem, an odd one in view of its concern with the encroachments of the federal judiciary, was to restore the appellate jurisdiction of the Supreme Court taken away by the McCardle Act and let the high court pass on the question. Its conclusion that "it can then be seen whether further legislation is necessary" was not to be ignored.[36]

[34] Act of March 3, 1885, Ch. 353, *Statutes at Large*, XXIII (1885), 437; *House Reports*, 48 Cong., 1 Sess., No. 730 (Serial 2255), 6.
[35] *Ex parte Bridges*, 4 Fed. Cases 98 (No. 1,862, Circuit Court, Northern District of Ga., 1875).
[36] See Seymour D. Thompson, "Abuses of the Writ of Habeas Corpus," Ameri-

The Supreme Court took the hint. The period from 1885 to 1920 saw a steady attrition of the expansive possibilities contained in the 1867 act. The federal courts formulated doctrines which inhibited the opportunities of habeas petitioners seeking federal court vindication of federal constitutional and statutory rights. The retreat began in the 1886 case of *Ex parte Royall.* William L. Royall was originally prosecuted in a Virginia court for violation of a Virginia licensing statute for bondsellers. The United States Supreme Court's decision on his habeas petition held that a federal circuit court on a habeas petition from a person confined by state authority may, in its discretion, require (1) that the petitioner first be tried by the state court (if he petitioned before trial) so as to give the state court an opportunity to try the case on its merits and (2) that the petitioner first exhaust his appeals to the state supreme court (if he petitioned after conviction) to give that court a chance to deal with the merits of the appeal before it came to the lower federal courts on habeas.[37]

The Supreme Court retreated further in *In re Wood* (1891), holding that the 1867 act did not authorize lower federal courts to retry the merits of federal constitutional questions unless the state trial suffered from some jurisdictional defect. Supreme Court decisions often reflect a choice between conflicting values. In *Wood* the Court squarely faced the choice between (1) affirming the competence of state courts and emphasizing finality in litigation or (2) protecting the role of habeas corpus as a guarantee of individual liberty and as a means of protecting federal rights. The Court emphatically chose the former set of values.[38]

---

can Bar Association, *Reports,* VI (1883), 243–67; "Federal Abuses of the Writ of Habeas Corpus," *American Law Review,* XXV (January–February 1891), 149–53; Act of March 3, 1885, Ch. 353, *Statutes at Large,* XXIII, 437 (restored jurisdiction taken away by McCardle repealer). The views of the House Judiciary Committee were set forth in *House Reports,* 48 Cong., 1 Sess., No. 730, cited above. For a different interpretation of the motives of Congress in restoring the McCardle jurisdiction, see Graham, *Everyman's Constitution,* 141–43, n. 114.

[37] *Ex parte Royall,* 117 U. S. 241 (1886). The *Royall* rule came to be known as the "exhaustion" doctrine. Charles Warren aptly observed that passage of the 1867 act "caused great friction and intense opposition to the federal courts, particularly in the southern and western states. And the Supreme Court has been forced to allay the antagonism by so applying the *habeas corpus* statutes, in practice, as to discountenance the issue of the writ by a federal court until the resources of the state courts have been exhausted by the petitioner." Warren, "Federal and State Court Interference," *Harvard Law Review,* XLIII (January 1930), 345–78, quote on page 359.

[38] *In re Wood,* 140 U. S. 278 (1891).

Joseph Wood was a Negro who alleged that Negroes were excluded from the juries that indicted and convicted him. The Supreme Court's growing indifference toward the rights of southern Negroes and its willingness generally to contract the use of habeas corpus are parallel developments that are more than merely coincidental.

Judicial conservatism alone does not adequately explain the eclipse from 1880 to 1920 of federal habeas corpus review of state decisions. Other considerations, some more rationally supportable, contributed to the trend. The Court wished to relieve pressure on all federal dockets, particularly its own. Further, the Supreme Court was given power to review federal convictions by writ of error in 1889, and the need for habeas corpus as a form of review in federal criminal actions was removed. The Court was also motivated by a not unreasonable desire to strike some sort of balance in federal-state relations. In redressing what it thought to be the excesses of Reconstruction, the Supreme Court merely overcompensated and became acquiescent toward the pressures of the states.

The seeming victory for the finality of state court decisions was short-lived, however. A minority on the twentieth-century Court, led by Justice Oliver Wendell Holmes, Jr., chipped away at the artificial jurisdictional limitations on the use of the writ. The minority position finally prevailed in *Moore* v. *Dempsey* (1923), a prosecution arising out of the Elaine, Arkansas, race riots. Holmes, writing for the new majority, reversed and remanded a district court's refusal to try factual issues which, if proved, would have constituted a deprivation of the petitioner's federal constitutional rights.

The *Moore* case reversed both the progressive enfeeblement of habeas corpus and the Court's growing indifference to problems faced by Negroes in the South. The petitioners were all Negroes, convicted of murder by an Arkansas court, which, they alleged, was dominated by a lynch mob that intimidated all parties as well as counsel and tortured witnesses to persuade them to testify for the state. To have reaffirmed the values of finality and state court competence in this case would have been to deny a recourse to federal justice that, on the basis of facts uncontroverted by the state, was necessary if any semblance of justice was to be preserved.[39]

[39] *Moore* v. *Dempsey*, 261 U. S. 86 (1923). See "The Writ of Habeas Corpus in the Federal Courts," *Columbia Law Review*, XXXV (March 1935), 404–16.

Moore put the federal courts back where they were in 1885. The pre-1867 notion that federal courts should not receive a habeas petition from a person convicted by a jurisdictionally competent state tribunal was moribund after 1923 and was finally laid to rest in the 1942 case of *Waley* v. *Johnston.* The Supreme Court was then free to exploit fully the possibilities of the Habeas Corpus Act of 1867, and this it did after World War II. Habeas corpus emerged as a primary means of protecting federal constitutional rights specified in the first eight amendments to the Constitution, the most important of which were the procedural safeguards guaranteed in criminal trials.[40]

The chrysalis that had been spun in 1867 finally burst open. Habeas corpus became another mode of appellate review. This result in itself was not surprising, since federal courts had claimed this power in the nineteenth century. More controversial was the power of lower federal courts to review cases affirmed by state supreme courts on all questions of both fact and law affecting rights guaranteed by the federal Constitution.

The states' reaction, echoing the objections raised in the 1880s, was swift and radical. In 1954 a habeas appeal in the Third Circuit was chosen as the vehicle for an attack by forty state attorneys general on the constitutionality of the 1867 act itself. It was challenged on the grounds that (1) Congress could not constitutionally authorize review of facts in criminal trials except by a new trial, not an appeal, and (2) habeas review in the federal courts becomes a suit against the state itself within the meaning of the Eleventh Amendment. The seven-judge circuit court panel rejected both contentions out of hand.[41] Realizing that pursuit of the issue to the Supreme Court would be futile, state officials then turned to Congress, where a bill was introduced in 1955 which would have drastically curtailed the fact-reviewing powers of the federal district courts. This bill never got out of the House.[42]

The states' assault on the 1867 act in 1954 and 1955 was the

[40] *Waley* v. *Johnston*, 316 U. S. 101 (1942).
[41] *United States ex rel. Elliott* v. *Hendricks*, 213 F. 2d 922 (Court of Appeals, Third Circuit, 1954); certiorari denied, 348 U. S. 851 (1954).
[42] The bill is discussed at length in House Committee on the Judiciary, 84 Cong., 1 Sess., *Habeas Corpus: Hearings Before Subcommittee No. 3 on H.R. 5649 . . . June 7 and 24, 1955.* The only opposition in the hearings came from the American Civil Liberties Union and, significantly, the National Association for the Advancement of Colored People. Louis H. Pollak, "Proposals to Curtail Federal Habeas Corpus for State Prisoners: Collateral Attack on the Great Writ," *Yale Law Journal*, LXVI (November 1956), 50–66.

last serious challenge to the greatly expanded habeas powers of the federal courts. The failure of this attack left the federal courts free to supervise the entire state court administration of justice. This was made clear in a 1963 case, *Townsend* v. *Sain*, which held that the federal courts sometimes had the duty as well as the power to re-try factual issues fully litigated in the state courts. The *Townsend* decision indicated that for the protection of rights guaranteed by the federal Constitution the federal courts were supreme over the state courts. An individual no longer had recourse only to the states to protect his constitutional rights; he had the additional and supervening protection of the federal government acting through its courts. The 1867 act thus was, in retrospect, a decisive element in tipping the federal-state balance in favor of the national government.[43]

The development of habeas corpus in the federal courts is of course not yet ended. But whatever new directions habeas development may take as a means of reviewing convictions after trial in the state courts and of asserting federal supremacy in the protection of individual liberty, it will be on the basis of the reconstruction of federal judicial power that took place a century ago.

[43] *Townsend* v. *Sain*, 372 U. S. 293 (1963).

ON REVISING RECONSTRUCTION HISTORY: NEGRO SUFFRAGE, WHITE DISFRANCHISEMENT, AND COMMON SENSE

One of the most continuous and pertinacious themes of Reconstruction history is the notion that the Radical control of the South was based on a broad, ill-gotten electorate made up largely of Negroes. While scholars have made some inroads in challenging this interpretation,[1] a great deal of additional research needs to be done before any definitive revision can be made. Compounding the difficulty is the fact that many of the vital statistics are incomplete, thus the historical record may never be conclusive.

In the meantime, the traditional view—a view more compatible with sectional loyalties and romantic myths—lingers. Predicated on the assumption that vast numbers of Negroes were enfranchised while thousands of southern whites were being denied the ballot, it holds that a Radical Congress overthrew without cause the legitimate state governments established in the immediate post-war period. Negro suffrage and southern white disfranchisement, the tradition goes, were the twin keys to the success of the carpetbag governments. It was bellowed from both North and South during the Reconstruction; and historians of almost all persuasions have perpetuated it ever since. One student has asserted that "white majorities were cut down or wiped out entirely,'"[2] a view repeated so frequently that few have dared to question it. That such universal opinion could be based on such tenuous and fragmentary evidence is one of the enigmas of Reconstruction history.

According to the Eighth Census (1860), two southern states—South Carolina and Mississippi—had Negro majori-

---

[1] Of the several revisionist studies, two of the best are: John Hope Franklin, *Reconstruction: After the Civil War* (Chicago, 1961); and, Kenneth M. Stampp, *The Era of Reconstruction, 1865-1877* (New York, 1965). Both works, while pointing to the accomplishments and failures of these years, suggest that the South was more a victim of its own inertia than any Radical conspiracy.

[2] William A. Russ, Jr., "Registration and Disfranchisement under Radical Reconstruction," *Mississippi Valley Historical Review*, XXI, 2 (September, 1934), pp. 163-180. See also, Russ, "The Negro and White Disfranchisement during Radical Reconstruction," *Journal of Negro History*, XIX, 2 (April, 1934), pp. 171-192.

ties. By 1870, Louisiana probably became the third.³ The Negro percentages of the populations in the other southern states in 1870 ranged from 48.8 in Florida to 25.2 in Arkansas. Three of them—Alabama, Georgia, and Virginia—had, like Florida, populations that were over 40 per cent Negro.⁴ It was obvious from the outset that any plan to enfranchise the freedmen, unlike suffrage proposals in the North, would involve vast numbers of blacks. In giving the ballot to 800,000 ex-slaves, one northern critic lamented, "considerations of mere temporary expediency, of mere party advantage, fall paralyzed to the ground." We in the North, refusing to grant impartial suffrage in our own states, force it upon others "by the bushel." "A little retail negro suffrage here, where it can do little harm, is denied," Congressman Samuel Sullivan Cox observed; "wholesale negro suffrage there is enforced where it is supreme."⁵

According to most critics, the freedman's appalling ignorance would destroy the democratic process in' the South. Many ex-slaves, they complained, had never heard of the candidates they were asked to support. Others allegedly could not identify their home county or give their exact ages. A few critics went so far as to claim that some freedmen were of such low intelligence that they had trouble remembering their own names. After interviewing an illiterate field hand in Georgia, a northern traveler regretfully conceded that this man represented the lowest intelligence "among that class on whom it is proposed to confer the right of suffrage." As Tennessee's Governor Brownlow put it: impartial suffrage would "open the ballot-box to the uninformed and exceedingly stupid slaves of the Southern cotton, rice and sugar fields."⁶ While the governor was obviously referring to the

---

³ The Ninth Census (1870) showed a fractional Negro majority in Louisiana, but an admitted undercount for both races makes a precise determination impossible.

⁴ United States Bureau of the Census, Department of Commerce, *Negro Population, 1790-1915* (Washington, D. C., 1918), pp. 25-27.

⁵ Thomas W. Hartley, *Universal Suffrage-Female Suffrage* ([New York], 1867), pp. 26-28; Samuel Sullivan Cox, *Speeches of Hon. S. S. Cox, in Maine, Pennsylvania and New York, during the Campaign of 1868* (New York, 1868), p. 7.

⁶ Whitelaw Reid, *After the War: A Southern Tour, May 1, 1865 to May 1, 1866* (New York, 1866), p. 371; *The American Annual Cyclopedia and Register of Important Events* (84 vols., New York, 1870-1903), 1865, p. 781.

Negroes of the Black Belt, he was not overlooking the presumed dangers of impartial suffrage in his own state. There was no doubt, of course, that the ignorance of the vast majority of the freedmen was staggering; thus most whites, without considering the causes of or the remedies for that ignorance, concluded that Negro suffrage would lead to the absolute ruin of the South. As a northern poet put it:

> 'Cause now I'se got de franchise
> Dough I neber goed to school,
> And if Massah Bullock's 'lected,
> I gits forty acres and a mule![7]

For a variety of reasons, there was an almost ingenuous confidence among white Southerners that northern public opinion would not permit the Congress to force Negro suffrage on the South. The truculent words of northern racists were reassuring. "[J]udging by myself, and comparing the limited extent of my prejudice against the colored race with that of the generality of the Northern people," one writer sanctimoniously declared, "I do not believe that the people of the North will allow large armies to be raised for any such unfair and oppressive purpose."[8] More important, the returns from the state elections in the North seemed to justify this optimism. To be sure, the Democratic party's surprising show of strength in such Republican strongholds as Maine, New Hampshire, and Minnesota was especially encouraging. A month after the elections of 1867, white conservatives in Little Rock, Arkansas, pledged to "preserve the principles of the national Constitution by co-operating with the Democratic party of the Union." "In view of the astonishing results of the recent elections in different portions of the Union," they added, "the voices of the Democratic and Conservative masses of the North call upon us to assist in defeating the attempt of radicalism to destroy our old constitutional government and set up in its place one in which others than white men shall have the controlling influence." Democrats in Louisiana met in the following year and, on the

---

[7] La Crosse *Democrat*, May 12, 1868.

[8] William Archibald Dunning, *Essays on the Civil War and Reconstruction and Related Topics* (New York, 1898), pp. 189-190; Hartley, *Universal Suffrage-Female Suffrage*, p. 32.

basis of the same elections, expressed confidence that northern Democrats and conservatives would not let them down.⁹

Nevertheless, other southern whites, less optimistic than their neighbors and refusing to take heart from northern elections, displayed genuine fear over possible Negro enfranchisement. In fact, there were signs during the early months of Radical Reconstruction that some of them, sensing the inevitable, hoped to capitalize on the black vote and recruit it for their own purposes. While such moves never amounted to much, they did suggest an attempt to make the most of what seemed to be an intolerable but unavoidable development. In 1879, Wade Hampton, a former Confederate general and later governor of South Carolina and a United States Senator, boasted that he had been the first white man in the South to recommend Negro suffrage, and that many "intelligent and reflecting whites" had agreed with him.[10] Hampton was only guessing, of course. In February, 1866, a Texas conservative had offered his state a sweeping plan, including three alternatives, for extending the ballot to the Negro.[11] Seven months later, John H. Reagan, former Postmaster-General of the Confederacy, wrote to Governor Throckmorton of Texas and urged him to consider limited Negro suffrage in order to guarantee white supremacy. Otherwise, he insisted, the Radicals would force mass Negro suffrage on the state.[12] Nonetheless, Hampton's boast that other whites agreed with him, though misleading, was true.

Attempts by southern conservatives to exploit the Negro vote, of course, were examples of political expediency rather

[9] New York *Herald*, November 6, 9, 1867; *Ann. Cyc.*: 1867, p. 55; 1868, p. 432.

[10] Robert Selph Henry, *The Story of Reconstruction* (New York, 1938), p. 253; C. Vann Woodward, *The Strange Career of Jim Crow* (revised, New York, 1957), p. 34.

[11] E. Degener, *The Minority Report in Favor of Extending the Right of Suffrage, with Certain Limitations, to All Men without Distinction of Race or Color Made in the Texas Reconstruction Convention* (Austin, Tex., February 24, 1866). The three plans were: universal suffrage by the end of 1866; universal suffrage by the end of 1876; and universal suffrage to all "born free" by 1866. The convention refused to consider any of the plans.

[12] The letter set off a storm of controversy among several Democratic editors in the North. See especially Columbus *Crisis*, November 21, December 5, 1866; New York *World*, November 19, 20, 1866.

than a genuine concern for the freedman's civil rights. The idea of using the ex-slaves to check the economic encroachments of poor whites and the countermoves of political enemies must have appealed to more than a few former slaveowners. If Negroes are granted the ballot, a northern writer predicted, "I for one should not at all be surprised to see the great majority of them voting the ticket of their masters." Governor Brownlow recommended the forced removal of all the Negroes in his state to a separate territory because "the great majority of them would be influenced by leading secessionists to vote against the Government, as they would be largely under the influence of this class of men for years to come, having to reside on and cultivate their lands."[13]

Though not always including an endorsement of suffrage, white conservatives did occasionally express sympathy for the freedmen. In December, 1867, delegates to a meeting in Richmond, Virginia, resolved to do all that they could for the Negroes, insisting, however, that the ballot belonged in the hands of the whites only. Conservatives in South Carolina, where Negroes outnumbered whites by three to two, were much more generous and expressed a willingness, "when we have the power," to grant the Negroes, "under proper qualifications as to property and intelligence, the right of suffrage." Even with these ambiguous conditions, the statement was surprising. A short time later, Democrats in Texas announced a desire to see all the freedmen protected by the laws of the state. Pleading for the restoration of white rule, the Democratic State Central Committee of Louisiana even asked the Negro leaders of their state for support.[14]

While predictions of a Negro-supported white conservative oligarchy were certainly exaggerated, they were menacing enough to frighten northern Negro leaders who saw in them a Republican excuse for backing down. In July, 1865, delegates to a convention of colored men in Philadelphia insisted

[13] Hartley, *Universal Suffrage-Female Suffrage*, p. 35; New York *World*, April 3, 20, 1867; *Ann. Cyc.*, 1865, p. 781.

[14] *Ann. Cyc.*: 1867, p. 763; 1868, pp. 696, 731; 1870, p. 457. T. Harry Williams, "An Analysis of Some Reconstruction Attitudes.": *Journal of Southern History*, XII, 4 (November, 1946), pp. 474, 476-479, argues that this view has been exaggerated and that the planter class, as a whole, opposed Negro suffrage under any conditions.

that there was absolutely no basis for the suspicion that former slaveowners would control the southern Negro's vote. The Negro cannot be made to do, "now that he is free, what he could not be forced to do when a slave," the convention proclaimed. As to the charge that the Negro's gross ignorance would corrupt the ballot and make him the tool of a beguiling white Southerner, the delegates pointed to that class of poor whites exploited by the racists and resolved: "That the apparent anxiety to preserve the ballot-box from the influence of the ignorance of the colored man is proved, by the class of [white] men invited and urged to the polls at every election, to be but a hypocritical and malignant subterfuge." In short, those who most feared a white planter oligarchy based on a manipulated uneducated Negro electorate were themselves exploiters of hatred, prejudice, and ignorance.[15]

Since southern Negroes had majorities in at most three states, impartial suffrage in the South involved more than simply enfranchising the freedmen. According to the traditional interpretation of Reconstruction history, Radical Republicans hoped to disfranchise thousands of southern whites, a move that would easily create black majorities in Alabama, Florida, Georgia, and Virginia. Theoretically, this would add fourteen men to the United States Senate who, representing Negro majorities, could obstruct any legislation; or voting with the Radical senators from the northern states, pass any bill. To the white Southerner the outlook must have seemed, at best, grim, and, at worst, catastrophic.

Suggestions of mass disfranchisements had first appeared during the war when certain congressmen had proposed test oaths for southern whites as a condition for the reinstatement of civil rights.[16] After Appomattox, what began as a remote suspicion became a genuine fear, at least among the most fanatical opponents of the government. On Saturday morning, April 15, 1865, a few hours after Lincoln's death, a

[15] *Ann. Cyc.*, 1865, p. 694.
[16] One student, Harold M. Hyman, *Era of the Oath: Northern Loyalty Tests During the Civil War and Reconstruction* (Philadelphia, 1954), has concluded that the oaths generally were ineffective, thus further deflating the argument that vast numbers of ex-Confederates were excluded from government. Moreover, it must be remembered that it was Andrew Johnson's wholesale distribution of pardons to former rebel officials that triggered a great deal of the congressional resistance.

Copperhead extremist savagely denounced an alleged abolitionist plot to secure "Nigger Supremacy" by disfranchising southern whites. It is not just a matter of a few thousand, he complained. On the contrary, Frederick Douglass and Horace Greeley are determined to enfranchise *all* blacks and disfranchise *all* whites. After military reconstruction began in 1867, many whites were certain that their original fears had been justified. The venomous La Crosse *Democrat* attacked the "black niggers from the cotton fields and the white niggers from New England" for stealing the ballot from respectable white Southerners and giving it to illiterate blacks. In a separate pamphlet, *Democrat* editor Marcus Mills "Brick" Pomeroy accused the Radicals of encouraging multiple registration among the freedmen. "[T]he hideous villainy of the reconstruction infamy lies, not in giving the negroes suffrage," the Chicago *Times* lamented in the summer of 1868, "but in disfranchising white men and so legislating as to give the negro party ascendancy." In the South, of course, white conservatives were convinced that mass disfranchisement was an accomplished fact.[17] Thus did the extremist critics of the government propagate a notion that has lingered for a century.

In truth, the fear of white disfranchisements may have been the most exaggerated reaction of the entire Reconstruction era. Since the Radicals *did* overthrow the white conservative state governments that had been set up under the Johnson Reconstruction program, most alarmed observers carelessly concluded that there *must* have been mass disfranchisements. But their conclusions—as well as those of many since—simply

[17] New York *Weekly Day Book*, April 15, 1965; La Crosse *Democrat*, February 25, 1868; [Marcus Mills Pomeroy], *Condensed History of the War, Its Causes and Results: Plain Home-Told Facts for the Young Men and Working Men of the United States* (n.p., 1868), p. 11; Chicago *Times*, July 15, 1868; Edward A. Pollard, *The Lost Cause Regained* (New York, 1868), pp. 37-39. A few alarmists even predicted the disfranchisement of northern whites. On July 23, 1868, Congressman S. S. Cox asked a Brooklyn audience: "If Congress can overturn white suffrage South, can it not establish black suffrage North, and withhold it from the whites? If the States South have not the sovereignty power in this regard, have the States North?" A few days later, editor Wilbur Storey of the Chicago *Times* named one Anthony O. Hesing as the leader of a drive, already in progress, to disfranchise northern whites. See Cox, *Speeches of 1868*, p. 7; and, Chicago *Times*, July 29, 1868.

do not stand up after a careful examination of the evidence; and, where the evidence is scanty or nonexistent, they do not pass the test of common sense. Known disfranchisement statistics, pertaining only to the preliminary elections held under the Reconstruction Acts of 1867, are available for five states—Virginia, North Carolina, South Carolina, Georgia, and Florida—and in all five, white disfranchisements *did not* give Negro voters a majority![18] South Carolina and Florida were the only states with more registered Negroes than whites. In the former state the whites, with slightly over 40 per cent of the total population, were in the minority to begin with, thus the disfranchisements were hardly necessary to insure a "Negro ascendancy." While it was true that registered Negroes in Florida outnumbered registered whites by a substantial amount, the total number actually disfranchised was so small that, after Negro disfranchisements were subtracted, there was a net loss of only one hundred and fifty white registrations.[19]

In the other three states for which statistics are available, the registered whites retained their majorities in spite of the disfranchisements. Over 16,000 were disfranchised in Virginia, but the whites retained their majority by over 14,000. Registered whites in North Carolina outnumbered registered Negroes by a wide margin: 34,000 out of a total of 179,000 registrations. Oddly, Georgia provided what was probably the best rebuttal to the charge that the Radicals disfranchised whites for the sole purpose of guaranteeing a Negro majority. Though 10,500 were denied the ballot, whites nonetheless retained a narrow margin of slightly over 1,000 voters

[18] Russ, *MVHR*, pp. 178-179, cites *Letter Book*, First [Military] District, II, pp. 261-262, for the figures on Virginia, and *Senate Executive Document*, 40 Cong., 2 Sess., No. 53, for the statistics on North Carolina, South Carolina, Georgia, and Florida. These are the standard sources and are quoted in several works: see David G. Croly, *Seymour and Blair, Their Lives and Services: with an Appendix Containing a History of Reconstruction* (New York, 1868), p. 277 of appendices; and, Edward McPherson (ed.), *The Political History of the United States of America during the Period of Reconstruction, from April 15, 1865 to July 15, 1870* (Washington, D.C., 1880), p. 374.

[19] The exact figures are: South Carolina: white registrations, 46,882; Negro registrations, 80,550; white disfranchisements, 8,244; Negro disfranchisements, 625. Florida: white registrations, 11,914; Negro registrations, 16,089; white disfranchisements, 350; Negro disfranchisements, 200.

out of almost 200,000 registrations. If the Radicals had been determined to insure a Negro majority in this state, they could have done so easily by merely disfranchising 1,000 more whites—but they did no such thing. In addition, critics of the government almost always ignored the fact that Negroes were also disfranchised—1,118 in the Carolinas—usually for serious crimes. In short, in at least half of the ten reconstructed states, the disfranchisement of white voters did not create Negro majorities.[20]

The argument does not end here. In the five states where disfranchisements were not recorded, the registrations alone are revealing. Louisiana and Mississippi had registered Negro majorities, but since Mississippi and probably Louisiana had more Negroes than whites to begin with, this should not have been surprising. As in South Carolina, disfranchisements were not "necesssary." In Texas and Arkansas the situations were similar to those in Virginia, North Carolina, and Georgia; the white voters retained registered majorities in spite of alleged disfranchisements. Only in Alabama, where the freedmen constituted slightly less than half of the total population (47.7 per cent in 1870), did the figures suggest that disfranchisements could have created a black majority. Here, Negroes had a five to three margin in voter registrations. Yet to get such a result, the Radicals would have had to disfranchise over 60,000 whites. For them to have gone to such lengths is difficult to believe because they could have had the same result—a simple Negro majority—by merely disfranchising a few thousand whites. Thus the traditional complaint loses much of its force for the only state where it made any sense in the first place.[21]

An example of how much guess-work has been involved in

[20] The exact figures are: Virginia: white registrations, 120,101; Negro registrations, 105,832; white disfranchisements, 16,343; Negro disfranchisements, none recorded. North Carolina: white registrations, 106,721; Negro registrations, 72,932; white disfranchisements, 11,688; Negro disfranchisements, 493. Georgia: white registrations, 96,333; Negro registrations, 95,168;; white disfranchisements, 10,500; Negro disfranchisements, none recorded.

[21] The exact figures are: Alabama: white registrations, 61,295; Negro registrations, 104,418. Arkansas: white registrations, 43,470; Negro registrations, 23,261. Louisiana: white registrations, 45,218; Negro registrations, 84,436. Mississippi: white registrations, 59,330; Negro registrations, 80,360. Texas: white registrations, 59, 633; Negro registrations, 49,497.

the standard view of Reconstruction history can be seen by simply adding the known disfranchisements under the Reconstruction Acts. They total 47,125 for five states; yet many sources, estimating for all ten states, cite a number far higher —some as high as 200,000.[22] A look at the figures makes these guesses seem rather absurd. The five states with recorded disfranchisements accounted for 53 per cent of the total southern white population, including the three largest states. If one merely doubled the known disfranchisements to account for the other five states, the total is considerably less than 100,000. A computation based on the state with the most known disfranchisements would result in an overall estimate of 97,000. Or one based on the state with the highest percentage of known disfranchisements would be about 108,000. In short, no matter how the figures are juggled, they strongly suggest that both the contemporary estimates and the guesses that many have made since were gross exaggerations.

This is not to say that disfranchisements were not significant in the carpetbag control of the South. The difficulty lies in the fact that the statistics are very meager and apply only to the preliminary elections under the Reconstruction Acts. Moreover, there is no guarantee that the existing facts are accurate. After all, the military districts were instruments of the Congress; it may not have been politically expedient to advertise in the North the fact that large numbers of whites were being disfranchised in the South. The fact that five states failed to record any disfranchisements is itself enough to make one suspicious of the figures that do exist. In addition, the figures for Florida and Georgia, since they were so conveniently rounded off, are especially suspect. In other words, the test of "common sense" works both ways.

It also needs to be pointed out that subsequent state and local elections provided many additional opportunities for the Radicals to improve their political positions (or for the conservatives to undermine them); and Congress took it upon itself to deny the ballot to former rebel officials, though certainly not on a massive scale. In any case, the point is not that there were few disfranchisements, but that the critic

[22] For example, see: Michael Martin and Leonard Gelber (eds.), *Dictionary of American History* (Paterson, New Jersey, 1959), p. 518.

of the government had so little real evidence on which to base his complaints and thus that much of the contemporary and subsequent criticism of the Radicals is groundless. Indeed, it is far safer to say that there was no widespread, permanent disfranchisement in the South until late in the nineteenth century when white conservative state governments began the mass disfranchisement of Negroes.

A far more credible explanation of both the registration and disfranchisement figures and the subsequent course of southern politics is that the white people of the South lost control of their state governments by refusing to register; or, in some cases, after registering, refusing to vote.[23] They wallowed in self-pity and whined over the odious Radical grip from Congress when they should have been blaming themselves—a reaction that had plenty of eyewitnesses. As arrangements were being made for the various state constitutional conventions under the Reconstruction Acts, the editor of the Charlottesville (Virginia) *Chronicle* bitterly criticized those white Southerners who, "sullen and discontented," had declared they would refuse to register. Their announcement that they "would prefer military government to negro suffrage" was based on a delusion. The only way to guarantee white control, he insisted, was for all eligible white men to register and vote.[24]

The southern boycott was also obvious to Northerners, including some of the same Copperheads who complained of mass disfranchisements. The editor of the Columbus *Crisis*, an avowed opponent of Radical Reconstruction, denounced those Southerners who, "paralyzed by supineness," were just as responsible for the detestable carpetbag governments as the enfranchised blacks. By organizing on Democratic principles, he insisted, the southern whites could easily cast off the Radical-Negro yoke—but they refuse to do so. In Congress, Senator Aaron H. Cragin, Republican from New Hampshire, cited the results of the constitutional referendums in nine of

[23] This latter situation was motivated largely by the fact that, under the first Reconstruction Act, it was easier to defeat a proposed Radical state constituition by registering and not voting than by not registering or by registering and voting against it. A supplementary bill quickly changed this practice.
[24] Charlottesville *Chronicle*, June 18, 1867.

the ten reconstructed states to show that it was the white voters, and not the Negroes, who were responsible for the new state governments. While many southern whites apparently supported the Radical programs, most did nothing. Though it was within their power to control the elections, Cragin concluded, they nevertheless refused to register: "If a man sleep upon his rights shall he complain if he lose them?"[25] Indignation and apathy, not disfranchisements, were major deterrents to white voter registration in the South. Many whites were either defiant or they simply did not care. In either case, they forfeited their right to self-government by keeping their names off the registration rolls or refusing to vote.

There were several reasons for the political abdication of the southern white conservative, some so obvious that critics frequently overlooked them. For example, many whites simply could not accept the idea of standing alongside a Negro—perhaps one of their own former slaves—at the polls. "God save the people of the South," a northern congressman cried, "from the depredations by which they would be obliged to go to the polls and vote side by side with the negro." In addition, the continuous racist reference to the "savage African" certainly frightened many. One observer conceded that most "white voters deny themselves the franchise, rather than be brought in collision at the polls with a race whose savage fiendishness is well known, and whose weapon of defence is a 'razor.'" Some stayed away from the polls in order to avoid an implied recognition of racial equality; while the refusal to register was, for still others, simply an act of protest. To show their contempt for the Radicals, they decided to disassociate themesleves completely from all things related to Reconstruction.[26]

More generally, the feeling of humiliation and disillusionment shared by most white Southerners was extremely im-

---

[25] Columbus *Crisis*, April 1, 1868; Congressional *Globe*, 40 Cong., 2 Sess., January 30, 1868, pp. 849-850.

[26] Marion Mills Miller (ed.), *Great Debates in American History* (14 vols., New York, 1913), VII, p. 440, quoting Congressman Andrew Jackson Rogers, Democrat of New Jersey; J. R. Hayes, *Negrophobia "On the Brain,"* in *White Men, or an Essay upon the Origin and Progress, both Mental and Physical, of the Negro Race, and the Use to be Made of Him by Politicians in the United States*

portant. Surrounded by the ruins of war, disenchanted over the "Lost Cause," stunned by the presence of an army of occupation, and reluctant—after putting their faith in men who had led them into a disastrous war—to become involved in politics and government, many southern whites, like General Lee, decided to refrain from participation in political affairs. A defeated, war-weary population, faced with the monumental task of rebuilding a ravaged countryside, had no time for the luxury of partisan politics and, as Howard K. Beale has observed, "remained politically indifferent through the various turns of political fortune."[27] In short, the southern white man, while complaining of mass disfranchisements, surrendered the right to control his own affairs. It must have been quite obvious from the beginning that the Radicals were going to have things their way; and that the establishment of military districts indicated that they were going to depend on federal bayonets, not Negro voters. Had southern whites turned out in force, it is probable that the Radicals would have resorted to the most obvious expedient: simply secure the disfranchisement of more whites. This probability may have discouraged many from even bothering to make the trek to the registration office. But the existence of such an apprehension, however justified, while it served as a convenient excuse, cannot detract from the fact that many southern whites did not even try and thus were guilty of complicity in their own misery.

One of the reasons for the durability of the traditional version of Reconstruction history is the customary political habit of defining one's terms to suit one's purposes—and the post-war opponent of the government was no exception. Northern and southern critics, despite their obvious sincerity, based their complaints of Negro political domination on some rather illusory arguments. To begin with, they defined "majority" in a peculiar way. As they put it, the freedmen did not need a numerical majority in order to enjoy a political majority. Rather, if the total number of *eligible* Negro voters

---

(Washington, D. C., 1869), pp. 6-7. William A. Russ, Jr., *MVHR*, pp. 178-179, agrees that there were many who, after registering, refused to vote.

[27] Howard K. Beale, "On Rewriting Reconstruction History," *American Historical Review*, XLV, 4 (July, 1940), p. 814.

was greater than the difference in the number cast for each party, the Negroes had a "majority." By selling their votes to the candidate who promised them the most, and by voting as a bloc, the ex-slaves presumably would have the balance of power. Strangely, few defenders of the Radical program challenged this definition.

Though inherently false, such nebulous thinking appeared again and again in complaints against the government's reconstruction policies. Congressman Daniel Voorhees, a staunch Indiana racist, claimed that seventy electoral votes from the Negro-dominated South could decide a presidential election, regardless of the vote in the North. "The negroes of Georgia, in their dense barbarity, are to out vote the freemen of Indiana in the choice of a chief magistrate," he lamented. "The negro on the levees of the Mississippi is to drown the voice of the intelligent farmer of the North. ... [T]he negro shall make the next President." Speaking before the Jackson Central Association in New York City, Horatio Seymour, disregarding the fact that senators represented states rather than populations, declared that "you cannot give three millions of negroes more Senators than are allowed to fifteen millions of white men living in New York, Pennsylvania, Ohio, Illinois, Indiana, Wisconsin, Iowa, Kentucky, Missouri, and Michigan."[28] Since the ten southern states would have the *same* number of senators as any ten northern states, Seymour apparently ignored his listeners' ability to multiply ten times two. Speaking strictly in terms of proportion, Seymour was technically correct. But this basis of representation has been true of all senators since the adoption of the Constitution. The Governor's reference to it was obviously little more than a specious attempt to excite and distort.

To the really zealous critic, mathematical deception was an art. With a bewildering display of clamorous histrionics, Francis P. Blair, Jr., tried to show how a few million

[28] Columbus *Crisis*, October 29, 1868; Democratic Party, Indiana, *Proceedings of the Indiana Democratic State Convention, held in Indianpolis, Wednesday, January 8th, 1868* (Indianapolis, 1868), pp. 25-26; James D. McCabe, Jr., *The Life and Public Services of Horatio Seymour: Together with a Complete and Authentic Life of Francis P. Blair, Jr.* (New York, 1868), p. 222.

freedmen would have more congressmen than twenty million whites. On another occasion he attacked the Reconstruction Acts for allegedly making "three millions of ignorant negroes . . . supreme over six million of the white race in the South." The congressmen and electoral votes controlled by the Radical-led ex-slaves are "relied upon to overcome the majority against the Radicals in the North, and enable a minority to control a majority in both sections."[29] In short, Blair contended that two minorities, when added together, would outvote two majorities. Other critics, through speeches, editorials, pamphlets, and articles hammered away at this theme so relentlessly that few dared to challenge them.[30]

The Negroes of the South, of course, "dominated no state or national election, a fact that has been obvious to anyone who has looked beyond the façade of racist rhetoric. References, both graphic and verbal, to the legislatures of South Carolina and Louisiana have appeared with such regularity that one is left with the impression that all of the reconstructed states were so organized and that black legislators recently freed from slavery controlled them. Yet, even in the five states where Negroes had registered majorities, whites retained virtually all important positions of leadership and made almost all major decisions. Moreover, Negroes who held local or minor offices usually did so at the pleasure of a white official; while the handful who did hold important positions generally served with distinction. As a prominent southern editor admitted, "leaders of the Radical party, with professions of Negro suffrage hot in their mouths, have been sending advice to the Southern Conventions that Negroes should not run for Congress, or aspire to any conspicuous office; that they should be satisfied to fill the lowest seat in

[29] Chicago *Times*, August 8, 1868; McCabe, *Life and Public Services of Horatio Seymour*, pp. 460-461, 487-497.
[30] *Ann. Cyc.*, 1868, p. 495; Columbus *Crisis*, October 23, 1867; Philadelphia *Age:* April 2, May 17, 19, 25, June 13, 20, 1866; March 8, 1867; September 23, 1868; New York *Herald*, September 9, 1867, February 7, 1868; Detroit *Free Press*, August 11, 30, 1867; New York *World*, July 12, 1868; La Crosse *Democrat*, February 26, 1868; S. S. Cox, *Speeches of 1868*, p. 11; Horatio Seymour, *Public Record: Including Speeches, Messages, Proclamations, Official Correspondence, and Other Public Utterances of Horatio Seymour; from the Campaign of 1856 to the Present Time* (New York, 1868), p. 300; McCabe, *Life and Public Services of Horatio Seymour*, pp. 460-461.

political synagogues."[31] Carpetbaggers in South Carolina, a northern traveler observed, were beginning to fear the Negro's desire for public office. As the white supremacist La Crosse *Democrat's* "De Intelligent Woter" put it: "Dis ijee ob nigro suprimecy is gittin' intirely too much feared an' talked ob and even de Ripublicans was beginning to be scared on it, too."[32]

The critic's "balance of power" definition only made sense in a state where the parties were evenly divided and a substantial number of Negroes could be counted on to vote together—which was nowhere. A carpetbag congressman from Mississippi complained that the southern Negroes frequently were unpredictable as a political bloc. If the racist's specious definition of majority was valid, he argued, the Negroes of New York could have decided some presidential elections.[33]

In short, there was never any danger that the southern state governments would fall under the control of the Negroes, a fact strikingly underlined by the speed with which white conservatives regained control when they took the initiative. Tennessee, restored to the Union before military reconstruction had begun, became, in October, 1869, the first former Confederate state to return to the control of the white conservatives. Whites in Virginia regained control of their state government in the same month and engineered the state's restoration to the Union in January, 1870; thus the Old Dominion never fell into official carpetbag hands. In the next seven years, the other nine states followed the same course. "Bill Arp's" caustic observation that "slavery for the white foaks and freedom for the nigger runs mity well together now-a-days," was completely groundless; and the traditional interpretation of Negro suffrage and white disfranchisement under the Reconstruction Acts equally indefensible.[34]

FORREST G. WOOD

Fresno State College

[31] [Edward A. Pollard], "Universal Suffrage in a New Disguise," *The Political Pamphlet*, I, 2 (September 12, 1868), p. 40; Pollard, *Lost Cause Regained*, p. 100.

[32] James S. Pike, *The Prostrate State: South Carolina Under Negro Government* (New York, 1935 [1873]), p. 45; La Crosse *Democrat*, March 24, 1868.

[33] John R. Lynch, *The Facts of Reconstruction* (New York, 1914), pp. 94-99.

[34] [Charles Henry Smith], *Bill Arp's Peace Papers* (New York, 1873), p. 184.

NOV 7 1989

FEB 2 6 1990